## The Constitution of the Commonwealth of Australia
### History, principle and interpretation

This book examines the body of Australian constitutional jurisprudence in an original and rigorous yet accessible way. It begins by exploring the historical and intellectual context of ideas surrounding the Constitution's inception, and closely examines its text, structure, principles and purposes in that light. The book then unpacks and critically analyses the High Court's interpretation of the Constitution in a manner that follows the Constitution's own logic and method of organisation. Each topic is defined through detailed reference to the existing case law, which is set out historically to facilitate an appreciation of the progressive development of constitutional doctrine since the Constitution came into force in 1901.

*The Constitution of the Commonwealth of Australia* provides an engaging and distinctive treatment of this fundamental area of law. It is an excellent book for anyone seeking to understand the significance and interpretation of the Constitution.

**Nicholas Aroney** is Professor of Constitutional Law and an Australian Research Council Future Fellow at the TC Beirne School of Law at the University of Queensland.

**Peter Gerangelos** is Professor of Constitutional Law at Sydney Law School.

**Sarah Murray** is an Associate Professor at the University of Western Australia Law School.

**James Stellios** is an Associate Professor at the Australian National University College of Law.

# The Constitution of the Commonwealth of Australia

## History, principle and interpretation

Nicholas Aroney
Peter Gerangelos
Sarah Murray
James Stellios

CAMBRIDGE
UNIVERSITY PRESS

CAMBRIDGE
UNIVERSITY PRESS

477 Williamstown Road, Port Melbourne, VIC 3207, Australia

Cambridge University Press is part of the University of Cambridge.

It furthers the University's mission by disseminating knowledge in the pursuit of education, learning and research at the highest international levels of excellence.

www.cambridge.org
Information on this title: www.cambridge.org/9780521759182



First published 2015

Cover designed by Tanya De Silva-McKay
Typeset by Aptara Corp.
Printed in Singapore by C.O.S Printers Pte Ltd

*A catalogue record for this publication is available from the British Library*

*A Cataloguing-in-Publication entry is available from the catalogue of the National Library of Australia at* www.nla.gov.au

ISBN 978-0-521-75918-2 Paperback

# Foreword

*Chief Justice Robert French AC,*
*High Court of Australia*

This book, by four leading constitutional law academics, presents a critical perspective on the development of constitutional law in Australia as an historical and legal narrative. It is a well-known saying, sometimes attributed to Arnold Toynbee, that history is 'just one damned thing after another'. Inadequately presented, constitutional law can seem to the harried student to be just one damned case after another. In this text the authors give an account of Australian constitutional law informed by a large vision of their subject and accompanied by measured critical observations of its development, reflected in decisions of the High Court, over the 115 years since the Constitution came into force. Their presentation is more in the nature of a conversation with the reader, than legal analysis of a long stream of decisions.

The book demonstrates the dynamic character of constitutional law. The text of the Constitution is definitive but necessarily open textured as befits a document designed for an unknown future. Woven into any comprehensive treatment of constitutional law must be the strands of history and of political and social change and the interactions between major institutions that shape and are shaped by the Constitution over many decades. So much appears from the opening quotation from Andrew Inglis Clark:

> The constitutional law of a country may be defined as that portion of its fundamental law which prescribes or determines the structural character of the various governmental organs included in its total political organisation, their relations *inter se,* and the particular powers and functions of each of them.

The introductory chapter gives an account of the origins of the Constitution and the *Constitution Act* and the historical resonances of various elements of the Preamble, particularly the term 'agreement of the people'. It places the Constitution in the development of British constitutionalism, including the emergence of the idea of a 'parlement' in the thirteenth century, the relationship between Crown and parliament, the idea of the supremacy of parliament and the concept of 'parliamentary sovereignty'. The Constitution gives effect to the 'federal' idea in four senses, explained in the opening chapter. The first was derived from the Latin 'foedus', meaning a 'compact', and carried with it the idea of a union of states. The second was that of a new political community, a federal state which was itself to be a union of constituent states. The third was that of a dual system of government with two distinct sets of governing institutions. The fourth involved the notion of a federal government with general authority over the federation as a whole. Each of those ideas informed strands of constitutional interpretation particularly in relation to the legislative power and the demarcation and limits of that power.

The Commonwealth of Australia was formed by six self-governing Australian colonies of the United Kingdom each with its own constitution deriving authority from an imperial statute. The authors set out the colonial background and describe the emergence of self-government in the colonies. That history culminates with the observation that:

> This status of the six colonies as self-governing and self-constituting political communities was the fundamental presupposition upon which they agreed to federate in 1901, under a Constitution which they each played an equal part in debating, drafting, and approving.

There follows the story of the movement to federation, including the Conference of Colonial Premiers in 1883, the Australasian Federation Conference in 1890, the Drafting Conventions of 1891 and 1897–1898, the popular referenda, the enactment of the *Commonwealth of Australia Constitution Act* by the British Parliament in 1900, and the coming into force of the Constitution on 1 January 1901. The opening chapter also provides an overview of Commonwealth institutions, fundamental principles informing the Constitution and constitutionalism in practice. Under the latter heading the historical narrative post-federation is foreshadowed with the observation that the practical operation of Australia's constitutional system of government is primarily shaped by the interaction between its governing institutions, Commonwealth and State, influenced by the electoral process and popular elite opinion, the scrutiny of the media and many other public and private bodies and institutions. The initial approach to constitutional interpretation by the High Court giving effect to the Constitution as a federal compact between the States and the shift, after the *Engineers Case* in 1920, to treating the Constitution as a British statute conferring powers upon the Commonwealth, to be interpreted as widely as the language used could sustain, is outlined. The gradual cutting of legal and political ties to the United Kingdom and Australia's evolution to full nationhood is reflected in the evolution of its constitutional system of government. The interpretive methods of the High Court are set out and the various methodological 'isms' are mentioned, including originalism, literalism, textualism, structuralism, progressivism and intentionalism. The general perspective of the book is designated by the authors as 'documentarian'. That is to say their goal is to explain the law of the Constitution as interpreted by the High Court and to evaluate that interpretation in light of the Constitution considered as an authoritative document focusing upon its text and structure and understood in the light of its enactment history.

Each of the nine chapters that follows the introductory chapter is an essay on one of the themes opened in that chapter. The legislature and the legislative power of the Commonwealth, in their federal setting, are discussed in Chapters 2–5 inclusive entitled 'The Parliament', 'Legislative power', 'Demarcations of power' and 'Limits on power'. An historical grounding is maintained by reference back to the Convention Debates and early commentaries on the Constitution, particularly those of John Quick and Robert Garran. Those references help to remind the reader of the broad purposes of the founders, which are properly taken into account by those who have the task of interpreting and applying the Constitution in response to the concrete demands of a world which is very different from that of the late nineteenth century. The founders' vision was not a narrow one. There was much of statesmanship in the Convention Debates and the sense of an unimagined and unimaginable future into which the new nation would be projected. That awareness was well evidenced by Sir John Downer at the 1898 Convention when, speaking of the future judiciary of the Commonwealth, he said:

> With them rests the obligation of finding out principles which are in the minds of this Convention in framing this Bill and applying them to cases which had never occurred before, and which are very little thought of by any of us.

A similar perspective was famously reflected in the observation of another leading member of the Convention, Andrew Inglis Clark, who said of the Constitution:

> It must be read and construed, not as containing a declaration of the will and intentions of men long since dead, and who cannot have anticipated the problems that would arise for solution by future generations, but as declaring the will and intentions of the present inheritors and possessors of sovereign power, who maintain the Constitution and have the power to alter it, and who are in the immediate presence of the problems to be solved.

The historical purposes served by those who drafted the Constitution began to play an explicit part in interpretation after the High Court in *Cole v Whitfield* discarded its self-denying ordinance against consulting the Convention Debates. In that case in which the Court finally brought order to the jurisprudence of s 92, it said:

> Reference to the history of s 92 may be made, not for the purpose of substituting for the meaning of the words used the scope and effect – if such could be established – which the founding fathers subjectively intended the section to have, but for the purpose of identifying the contemporary meaning of language used, the subject to which that language was directed and the nature and objectives of the movement towards federation from which the compact of the Constitution finally emerged.

The self-denying ordinance had its origins in *Municipal Council of Sydney v Commonwealth* in which Griffith CJ described the Convention Debates as 'no higher than parliamentary debates' and 'not to be referred to except for the purpose of seeing what was the subject-matter of discussion, what was the evil to be remedied, and so forth.' The latter qualification, which on its face accepted purposive use of the Convention Debates, may not have been given sufficient weight in the decades that followed before *Cole v Whitfield* was decided.

In the chapter entitled 'Limits on power' there is discussion of the absence in the Australian Constitution of a bill of rights of the kind found in the United States Constitution. The prevailing view at the time of the Conventions was, as the authors put it, that 'appropriately operating systems of representative and responsible government at a Commonwealth and State level would, on the whole, provide adequate protection for civil and political rights'. The authors also point to the historical fact that the framers of the United States Constitution had taken a similar approach in 1787 but were forced by Antifederalists to agree to the insertion of the ten amendments known as the Bill of Rights in order to enable the Constitution to go forward. On the other hand, the nineteenth century perspectives of the Convention delegates were not necessarily directed to extensive legislative provisions, executive powers and regulatory activity associated with the rise of the bureaucratic State in the twentieth and twenty-first centuries. That phenomenon however might be thought to have had an influence on invocation of the implications from the Constitution imposing limits on legislative power, particularly the implied freedom of political communication and the line of cases concerned with the institutional integrity of the national judicial system.

The foundry of judicial review of legislative action and indeed of constitutional implication was the demarcation of power between Federal and State Parliaments and the constitutional guarantees and prohibitions supporting that demarcation. That feature of the Constitution is discussed in Chapter 4 entitled 'Demarcations of power'. The perennial question of inconsistency of State and Commonwealth laws under s 109, not without difficulty in its practical application, is comprehensively discussed, as is the recently revisited question of the limits of Commonwealth power to impair the capacity of the States to fulfil their constitutional functions. The issues raised by demarcation are perennial. The authors, in their conclusion to that chapter quote Sir Owen Dixon's observation that '[t]he foundation of the Constitution is the conception of a central government and a number of State governments separately organized'. As they then observe:

> Constructing such a system of partly independent, partly interdependent, self-governing political communities requires a complex set of rules demarcating their respective powers and ensuring their capacity to exercise them.

The Executive as an institution and the executive power conferred by s 61 of the Constitution warrant two separate chapters. There is an important discussion in that context about the relationship between responsible government and federalism. As the authors observe, '[r]esponsible government is fundamental to an understanding of the structure of the executive, as well as to an understanding of the "executive power of the Commonwealth" ...'. The tension between responsible government and a bicameral parliament with two Houses of equal standing was appreciated by the founders and their concerns are recounted in the chapter on the Executive. The authors quote Sir Richard Baker who observed:

> The essence of responsible government is the existence of one chamber of predominant power. Now, how are we to reconcile two irreconcilable propositions.

The executive power which has been the subject of close consideration in recent decisions of the High Court is comprehensively discussed in Chapter 7. The authors there observe presciently:

> At the time of writing, it is not possible to predict with any certainty how this particular issue will develop. It nevertheless will ensure that the issue of the ambit of the executive power of the Commonwealth will continue to constitute a major, if not the major, focus of attention in Australian constitutional law and policy.

As with the Executive and executive power, the authors devote two chapters respectively to the judicature and judicial power. The objectives of the creation of a federal judicature by Chapter III of the Constitution are put in historical perspective. They were the creation of a general court of appeal and of a judicial arm of government essential to an effective federal system.

Three core concepts are identified which are central to an understanding of the way in which the federal judicial system works. They are federal jurisdiction, Commonwealth judicial power and the concept of the 'matter' in respect of which federal jurisdiction is conferred. The heads of federal jurisdiction, the investing of federal jurisdiction in State courts and the expanding reach of federal jurisdiction, are covered in Chapter 8. The facilitation by decisions of the High Court of an understanding of the Australian judiciary as 'an integrated judicial system with the High Court at its apex' is acknowledged. Separation of judicial powers from other powers is discussed and its significance for federalism, rights-protection and the independence of the courts as providing a check on the other arms of government. The authors observe:

> Under each rationale, judicial independence and impartiality operate as the core functional attributes that are needed by the courts. Whether the courts are seen as protecting the federal compact, protecting liberty or operating as a check on the other arms of government, the judiciary is required to be independent and impartial, and independence and impartiality are said to be advanced by a separation of judicial power.

The defining distinction of judicial power as involving the determination of rights rather than their creation provides a conceptually neat framework for differentiating between judicial and non-judicial power. There is a cautionary observation in the judicial power chapter about an over rigid distinction constraining the federal parliament when designing government institutions and allocating decision-making authority, particularly in the modern regulatory State where non-judicial bodies are increasingly entering fields occupied previously by judicial decision-makers. The practical application of that caution may be debated. Separation of powers must operate in a practical environment, but within the framework of principle. The authors properly draw attention to the existence of historically based judicial functions which have not involved the determination of pre-existing rights. They are perhaps not so much an example of the difficult proposition that 'the exception proves the rule' as they are of the historical untidiness of the law.

The line of cases deriving from the decision of the High Court in *Kable v Director of Public Prosecutions (NSW)* is considered at some length with the conclusion offered that despite the inapplicability of the federal separation of power principles to State parliaments and the absence of an entrenched separation at the State level, the distinctiveness of State judicial systems has, in various ways, been eroded.

The last chapter concerns the States, their role in the federation and the functioning of State Constitutions, including manner and form provisions and their intersection with the Australia Acts. The authors refer to the late Professor George Winterton's description of State Constitutions as 'constitutional "Cinderellas"'. They rightly say, however, that a proper understanding of the Commonwealth Constitution and the basis on which it was formed requires a familiarity with the State constitutional landscape. The Commonwealth Constitution can only be properly comprehended alongside an appreciation of the Constitutions of the States.

This book is a valuable addition to the body of Australian constitutional scholarship. Not everybody will agree with every aspect of the analyses which it offers. It would be much less interesting if they did. What it offers is an invaluable and engaging conversation about Australia's Constitution, where it has come from, where it is today and where it is going.

# Contents

# About the authors

**Nicholas Aroney** is Professor of Constitutional Law and an Australian Research Council Future Fellow at the TC Beirne School of Law at the University of Queensland. His primary research interests are in constitutional law and comparative federalism. His publications include *The Constitution of a Federal Commonwealth: The Making and Meaning of the Australian Constitution* (Cambridge University Press, 2009), *The Future of Australian Federalism: Comparative and Interdisciplinary Perspectives* (co-editor, Cambridge University Press, 2012) and *Courts in Federal Countries: Federalists or Unitarists?* (co-editor, forthcoming 2016).

**Peter Gerangelos** is Professor of Constitutional Law at Sydney Law School where he teaches constitutional law at both undergraduate and advanced levels. A former Principal Solicitor in the Office of the Australian Government Solicitor, he is author of *The Separation of Powers and Legislative Interference in Judicial Process: Constitutional Principles and Limitations* (Hart Publishing, 2009) and lead author of *Winterton's Australian Federal Constitutional Law: Commentary and Materials* (3rd ed, Thomson Reuters, 2013). He continues to be a consultant to legal counsel in constitutional cases in Commonwealth jurisdictions.

**Sarah Murray** is an Associate Professor at the University of Western Australia Law School, where she teaches public law and researches in the areas of constitutional law and legal institutional change. Her publications include *Constitutional Perspectives on an Australian Republic: Essays in Honour of Professor George Winterton* (editor, Federation Press, 2010) and *The Remaking of the Courts: Less-Adversarial Practice and the Constitutional Role of the Judiciary in Australia* (Federation Press, 2014).

**James Stellios** is an Associate Professor at the Australian National University College of Law. His primary research interest is constitutional law and he has published widely in that field. His publications include *The Federal Judicature: Chapter III of the Constitution* (LexisNexis, 2010), and he is the author of the 6th edition of Professor Leslie Zines' classic work, *The High Court and the Constitution*. He is also a practising barrister at the NSW Bar and has appeared in a number of constitutional cases.

# Preface

This book is about the history, principles and interpretation of the Australian Constitution. It is based on the conviction that federalism is one of the Constitution's most important organising principles. The Constitution itself refers to the Australian polity as a 'federal commonwealth', by which was meant that the Commonwealth of Australia was to be federal in its foundations, its institutions and its powers, and that its development into the future would be dependent upon its federal character and design. As to its foundation in 1901, the Australian Constitution is based upon the consent of the people of the six colonies that would become the constituent States of the federation. As to its institutions, the Commonwealth of Australia consists of a Parliament that represents the people of the States (in the Senate) and the people of the Commonwealth as a whole (in the House of Representatives), an Executive Government that is responsible to that Parliament, and a federal supreme court, called the High Court of Australia, that is responsible to ensure that the Parliament and the Executive Government function within the bounds of the Constitution. As to its powers, the Commonwealth Parliament is limited to making laws with respect to a list of specified matters, the executive powers of the Commonwealth are said to extend only to the maintenance and execution of the Constitution and of laws enacted by the Commonwealth Parliament, and the judicial power of the Commonwealth is again limited to specified matters. At the same time, the Constitutions, institutions and powers of the States are preserved and continued, subject only to certain overriding provisions of the Commonwealth Constitution, validly enacted Commonwealth laws, certain activities of the federal Executive, and decisions of the High Court of Australia on appeals from State courts.

To construct such a federal system, many other constitutional principles were also recognised as essential to its fundamental design. These include the rule of law, representative democracy, responsible government, judicial review and the separation of powers. However, even these principles, important as they may be, are shaped by the federal structure and design of the whole. The rule of law, which requires that all government power must be authorised by law – principally the law of the Constitution – is shaped by the federal imperative of ensuring that both the Commonwealth and the States operate within their constitutionally-defined limits. Judicial review functions in tandem with the rule of law, for according to it the courts have the constitutional responsibility to adjudicate in cases where it is alleged that these constitutional limits have been trespassed. Representative democracy is also qualified by federalism. The democratic principle that the legislative and executive powers of government are exercised by persons who represent the people is qualified by the idea that there is more than one manifestation of 'the people' – the people of the constituent polities and the people of the federation as a whole – and that a federal democracy ensures that both are recognised as locations of authentic self-governance. The closely related principle of responsible government poses a potential challenge to the idea of federal democracy, however, to the extent that it is insisted that the Executive Government ought to be accountable only to the people of the Commonwealth as a whole (in the House of Representatives), and not the people of the States (in the Senate). But while the Constitution, in laying the foundations for the operation of responsible government, accords a certain priority to the House of Representatives in respect of proposed laws imposing taxation or appropriating moneys for expenditure, it affirms the general principle that apart from certain important exceptions, the powers of the Senate are equal to those of the House. The separation of powers also has a qualified operation under the Australian Constitution, partly because responsible government requires that the powers of the Executive Government are exercised on the advice of Ministers of State who are members of the Parliament and have the support, at least, of the House of Representatives. Yet even here, it is the very existence of the Senate as an essential component of the Parliament which ensures that the legislative will of the Parliament is not necessarily identical with that of Government Ministers. Moreover, the separation of the judicial from the political branches of government, although related closely to the principle of the rule of law generally, is considered vital in the federal system, for it ensures that disputes about whether the Commonwealth or the States have transgressed constitutional boundaries will be determined by courts that are independent of both parties to the dispute.

These are the leading principles, as we understand them, which animate the Australian Constitution. In this book, we seek to exposit the meaning of the Constitution by placing the document in its historical and intellectual context, explaining the concepts and principles that it embodies, and critically analysing the High Court's interpretation of the Constitution in a manner that follows the Constitution's own logic and method of organisation. We begin, in Chapter 1, with an introduction to the Constitution which explains the political development of the Australian colonies prior to federation, the historical origins of the Constitution itself, its fundamental principles and key institutions, and the vital role of the High Court in interpreting the Constitution to resolve disputes over its meaning and application. We then turn, in Chapters 2 and 3, to a detailed description of the Commonwealth Parliament and its powers, focusing on its component parts (the Queen, the Senate and the House of Representatives) and its internal procedures and privileges, and the nature and scope of its legislative powers. Throughout these and the following chapters, we explain, analyse and evaluate the High Court's interpretation of the Constitution in the many cases that have been decided since the Court was established in 1903. In Chapter 4 we turn to the demarcations of Commonwealth and State power, principally through the Constitution's provisions for the resolution of inconsistencies between Commonwealth and State laws and the rules that the High Court has developed for determining cases where it is alleged that the Commonwealth is unconstitutionally interfering with the due performance by the States of their constitutional functions, or the States are unconstitutionally interfering with the Commonwealth. In Chapter 5, likewise, we review the various 'limitations' on the powers of the Commonwealth and the States. (In the main, we deliberately do not refer to them as 'rights'). Chapters 6 and 7 turn to the Executive Government and the executive power of the Commonwealth. They explain the operation of the system of responsible government in the relationship between the Queen, the Governor-General, Ministers of State (including the Prime Minister and Cabinet) and the Parliament; they discuss the relationship of responsible government and federalism; and they critically assess the High Court's jurisprudence concerning the nature and scope of the executive power of the Commonwealth. Chapters 8 and 9 do much the same thing in relation to the courts and the judicial power of the Commonwealth. The federal court system, and its relationship to the State court systems, is explained; the principle of the separation of judicial power is expounded and its operation in relation to both federal and State courts is examined; the nature and scope of federal jurisdiction is explained; and specific principles, such as requirements of due process and jury trial, are elucidated. Finally, Chapter 10 turns to the constitutions, governing institutions and powers of the States. Their continuing status and role within the federation is explained; their histories, institutional structures, and legislative powers are examined; and the chapter concludes by elucidating the role of the people of the States and the Commonwealth in the ongoing amendment of the Constitution. The book thus seeks to follow, as closely as possible, the original design and structure of the Constitution itself, with its successive chapters on the Commonwealth Parliament, the Commonwealth Executive, the Commonwealth Judicature and the States.[1]

Through all these chapters, one basic theme emerges. It is that although the design of the Constitution is plainly to establish a political community that is 'federal' in its foundations, its institutions, its powers and its future development, many of the Commonwealth's activities and many of the High Court's decisions have contributed to a centralisation of power in the Commonwealth in a manner and to a degree that is in certain respects in tension with the Constitution's fundamental design as envisioned by its founders. We recognise that the task of constitutional interpretation is a vast and taxing undertaking, and we acknowledge the care and skill with which members of the High Court

1 That is, Chapters I, II, III and V of the Constitution. We found it convenient to deal with various matters of Finance and Trade (Chapter IV) where they were relevant to an exposition of the Executive Government and the powers of the Parliament. We have also touched on New States (Chapter VI) and Alteration of the Constitution (Chapter VIII) in our discussion of the States.

approach this very daunting responsibility. We aim in this book to expound the Court's varied reasoning in the cases in a manner that does justice to the gravity and complexity of the task. We seek to explain the historical development of the Court's jurisprudence from its very beginnings, and from its intellectual foundations, with careful regard to the many intriguing, and sometimes very significant, nuances in the various judgments. We note that some of the older and more neglected cases contain insights of great significance, and we observe many important conflicts in constitutional assumptions, interpretive methods and conceptions of the judicial role among the justices of the Court. Our task as legal academics is to critique the work of the Court; our obligation is to do so courteously, generously and in a manner that is well-informed. Whether we have succeeded in doing so is for others to judge.

This book is a collective effort. We divided the primary responsibility for particular chapters among ourselves, but also accepted as a mutual responsibility the task of reading and suggesting revisions for each other's chapters. Nicholas Aroney is primarily responsible for Chapters 1 to 5; Peter Gerangelos for Chapters 6 and 7; James Stellios for Chapters 8 and 9; and Sarah Murray for Chapter 10. As will be evident, much of what we have written draws on our prior work. The basic idea for this book derives from the thesis advanced in Aroney's *The Constitution of a Federal Commonwealth*,[2] and the corresponding analysis of the federal court system draws on Stellios's *The Federal Judicature*.[3] Several other prior works that we draw upon are cited in the footnotes, for which we beg the reader's indulgence. Nicholas Aroney gratefully acknowledges the support of the Australian Research Council's Future Fellowship funding scheme: FT100100469. James Stellios acknowledges the benefit he received from the Australian Research Council's Discovery Projects funding scheme: DP140101218.

While this is a long book, it cannot pretend to be an exhaustive treatise, but is rather a principled analysis of the most important themes and trends, although, we trust, a reasonably comprehensive one. The law as stated is current as at 1 November 2014.

There are many people to whom we are indebted in allowing this book to come together, particularly past and present staff at Cambridge University Press, including Zoe Hamilton, Bridget Ell, David Jackson, Martina Edwards, Antonietta Anello, Lucy Russell and Jane O'Regan. Nicholas thanks Lisa, Michelle, Samuel, Nathaniel and Josiah for their steadfast support. Peter acknowledges Nicholas Condylis for his excellent research assistance provided in the completion of Chapters 6 and 7 on executive power. Sarah thanks Jim Thomson and Ian Murray. James would like to thank Marita Rendina and Elesa Stellios.

**2** Nicholas Aroney, The Constitution of a Federal Commonwealth: The Making and Meaning of the Australian Constitution (Cambridge University Press, 2009)
**3** **James Stellios**, *The Federal Judicature: Chapter III of the Constitution* (LexisNexis Butterworths, 2010).

# Table of cases

# Table of statutes

## Australia

## Australian Capital Territory



## New South Wales

## Northern Territory



## Queensland



## South Australia



## Tasmania

## Victoria



## Western Australia



## United Kingdom

## United States of America



## Scotland



## Canada



## Ireland

## Germany



## South Africa



## Switzerland

# Table of statutory instruments

## Treaties

# 1

# The Constitution

> *The constitutional law of a country may be defined as that portion of its fundamental law which prescribes or determines the structural character of the various governmental organs included in its total political organisation, their relations inter se, and the particular powers and functions of each of them.*[1]

## I Introduction

So wrote Andrew Inglis Clark, one of the chief architects of the Australian Constitution. As he pointed out, constitutional law is only one part of the entire law of a country, but it is arguably the most fundamental. Constitutional law defines and regulates the institutions by which a country is governed. These governing institutions typically have the authority to make law, to enforce the law and to resolve disputes about the content and application of the law. Constitutional law is thus concerned with ultimate questions about *what* the law is, *how* the law can be changed and *who* has the authority to make law, interpret its meaning and enforce it.

Another highly influential framer of the Australian Constitution, Robert Garran, defined a constitution as follows:

> A Constitution is a general law for the government of a political community, unamendable and unrepealable, except in the manner and on compliance with the conditions prescribed by the authority which created it. It deals with the sovereign power of Government and the various forms, organs, and agencies through which that power is brought into action and the relations, interdependence, and co-operation of those forms, organs, and agencies, in the performance of the work of government.[2]

On Garran's view, a constitution is a special type of law which not only defines and regulates the government, but which exists by virtue of an authority that is distinct from the ordinary institutions of government and which can only be altered in accordance with conditions prescribed by that authority. When Garran

**1** Andrew Inglis Clark, *Studies in Australian Constitutional Law* (Charles F Maxwell, 1901) 2.
**2** John Quick and Robert Randolph Garran, *The Annotated Constitution of the Australian Commonwealth* (Angus and Robertson, 1901) 314.

said this, although he was speaking generally, he undoubtedly had the Australian Constitution specifically in mind. This leads to several questions. What, on his view, was the authority by which the Australian Constitution had come into being? By what authority or special procedures could it be amended? How does it define the sovereign power of government? What are the institutions that it recognises, establishes and regulates? What is the proper operation of those institutions, and how are they meant to relate to one another? It is with questions such as these that this book is chiefly concerned.

The Australian Constitution established the Commonwealth of Australia in 1901 as a federation of the six self-governing British colonies which then occupied the Australian continent. The Constitution contains the constitutional terms on which these colonies – the constituent States – agreed to federate. Prior to federation, each of the colonies had its own constitution under which it governed itself, independently of the others but ultimately subject to British authority. To understand Australian constitutional law properly, it is necessary to appreciate the history of the making of the Constitution and the motivating ideas lying behind it. There is no better way to begin to understand those ideas than to consider what the framers of the Constitution believed themselves to be establishing. They gave expression to this understanding in the preamble to the Australian Constitution.

## II Historical origins

### 1 Preamble to the Constitution

The Constitution of the Commonwealth of Australia is contained within a British statute entitled the *Commonwealth of Australia Constitution Act 1900*.[3] Although a British statute, the Constitution was drafted by elected Australian politicians and approved by Australian voters prior to its enactment into law. Because the Constitution created a federation of the Australian colonies it was also influenced by the leading model of federalism at the time, the United States of America. The Australian Constitution thus reflects a history and embodies values and ideas that are partly British and partly American, combined into a unique Australian synthesis. This history and those ideas are well summarised in the preamble to the *Constitution Act*. Several important propositions are contained within its succinct and eloquent statement of political history and constitutional principle:

> Whereas the people of New South Wales, Victoria, South Australia, Queensland, and Tasmania, humbly relying on the blessing of Almighty God, have agreed to unite in

**3** The *Commonwealth of Australia Constitution Act 1900* (UK) consists of nine sections (often called 'covering clauses'), the ninth of which contains the Constitution of the Commonwealth of Australia, which itself consists of a further 128 sections divided into eight chapters.

> one indissoluble Federal Commonwealth under the Crown of the United Kingdom of Great Britain and Ireland, and under the Constitution hereby established ...

Firstly, the preamble refers to an *agreement of the people*. The idea that constitutions are formed by an agreement of the people has a long and complex history. It owes much of its inspiration to the ideals of Athenian democracy and the Roman and Hebrew republics.[4] However, none of these ancient cultures had a conception of an authoritative written 'constitution' in quite the sense in which the framers of the Australian Constitution understood it.The modern notion of an 'agreement of the people' can be traced more directly to certain revolutionary political events in seventeenth-century England,[5] and to the constitutional ideas that developed around that time. Between 1647 and 1649, a series of manifestos were prepared, under the title of *An Agreement of the People*, by participants in Oliver Cromwell's New Model Army,[6] one of which read as follows:

> We the free People of England, to whom God hath given hearts, means and opportunity to effect the same, do with submission to his wisdom, in his name, and desiring the equity thereof may be to his praise and glory; Agree to ascertain our Government, to abolish all arbitrary Power, and to set bounds and limits both to our Supreme, and all Subordinate Authority, and remove all known Grievances.[7]

While these agreements never became law, an *Instrument of Government* (1653) was adopted as the written constitution of England during the rule of Oliver Cromwell, following the deposition and execution of Charles I in 1649. Around the same time, English colonists in North America had established self-governing political communities in which 'advanced ideas of colonial independence and autonomy' were developing.[8] Viewed from the perspective of British law, the constitutional foundations of these settlements derived from the authority of the Crown, but the practice of many of the colonies was to 'self-constitute' themselves into a body politic through a solemn pact or covenant. The framers of the Australian Constitution were well aware of this background.[9] James Bryce, whose book *The American Commonwealth* was cited by the Australian framers more frequently than any other, drew attention to many of these founding compacts and agreements.[10] One of the most famous was the Mayflower Compact of 1620, subscribed by the first inhabitants of the colony established at Plymouth in what is now the American State of Massachusetts. It declared the formation of the colony in the following terms:

**4** David Bederman, *The Classical Foundations of the American Constitution* (Cambridge University Press, 2008); Eric Nelson, *The Hebrew Republic* (Harvard University Press, 2010).

**5** Particularly during the period of the English Civil War (1642–51), Commonwealth or Interregnum (1649–60), Restoration (1660–88) and Glorious Revolution (1688–9). See Part II.2.

**6** See A S P Woodhouse (ed), *Puritanism and Liberty* (Dent, 1938); David Wootton (ed), *Divine Right and Democracy* (Penguin, 1986).

**7** John Lilburne, William Walwyn, Thomas Prince and Richard Overton, *An Agreement of the Free People of England* (1649).

**8** Quick and Garran, above n 2, 14.

**9** See, eg, ibid, 9–17, 282–310.

**10** James Bryce, *The American Commonwealth* (Macmillan, 2nd ed, 1889) vol 1, ch 37.

> In the name of God, Amen. We, whose names are underwritten, the loyal subjects of our dread Sovereign Lord King James, by the Grace of God, of Great Britain, France, and Ireland, King, defender of the Faith, etc.
>
> Having undertaken, for the Glory of God, and advancements of the Christian faith and honor of our King and Country, a voyage to plant the first colony in the Northern parts of Virginia, do by these presents, solemnly and mutually, in the presence of God, and one another, covenant and combine ourselves together into a civil body politic; for our better ordering, and preservation and furtherance of the ends aforesaid; and by virtue hereof to enact, constitute, and frame, such just and equal laws, ordinances, acts, constitutions, and offices, from time to time, as shall be thought most meet and convenient for the general good of the colony; unto which we promise all due submission and obedience.[11]

Another example given by Bryce was the original constitution of the American State of Connecticut, which was based upon a federating covenant between the people of three separate towns.[12] The *Fundamental Orders of Connecticut* declared as follows:

> [W]e the Inhabitants and Residents of Windsor, Hartford and Wethersfield ... do ... associate and conjoin ourselves to be as one Public State or Commonwealth; and do for ourselves and our successors and such as shall be adjoined to us at any time hereafter, enter into Combination and Confederation together ...[13]

Drawing inspiration from these kinds of documents, the highly influential English philosopher and publicist, John Locke (1632–1704), gave elegant and sophisticated expression in his *Second Treatise of Government* (1689) to the underlying idea of a 'social contract' by which the people constitute themselves into a political society and a 'contract of government' by which they establish a government that is accountable to them. But the basic idea of a founding covenant was much older than Locke. Johannes Althusius (*c* 1563–1638), a German jurist and early theorist of a kind of 'social federalism',[14] had more than half a century earlier set forth an account of society in which all groups – families and villages, towns and cities, guilds and religious associations, provinces and commonwealths – are formed and joined together by a series of federative compacts and agreements.[15]

Reflecting this general outlook, the Constitution of the United States recites the following:

> We the people of the United States, in order to form a more perfect union, establish justice, insure domestic tranquility, provide for the common defense, promote the general welfare, and secure the blessings of liberty to ourselves and our posterity, do ordain and establish this Constitution for the United States of America.

**11** This compact and numerous others are collected in Donald Lutz, *Colonial Origins of the American Constitution* (Liberty Fund, 1998). See also Stephen Schechter, Richard Bernstein and Donald Lutz (eds), *Roots of the Republic* (Madison House, 1990).

**12** Bryce, above n 10, vol 1, 415.

**13** Fundamental Orders of Connecticut (1639).

**14** Thomas Hueglin, *Early Modern Concepts for a Late Modern World* (Wilfrid Laurier University Press, 1999).

**15** Johannes Althusius, *Politica Methodice Digesta* (Frederick Carney trans, Liberty Fund, [3rd ed, 1614] 1995).

Notably, the preamble to the Australian Constitution does not quite say that it is ordained by the people or derives directly from their authority, for it was enacted by the British Parliament. The Australian Constitution is different from the republican constitutions of the United States, Switzerland, Germany and India, which appeal directly to the people as enacting or establishing the Constitution by their own authority. But the preamble to the Australian Constitution certainly gives emphasis to the agreement of the people to unite under it, and in so doing suggests that its political legitimacy flows, at least in part, from this fact.

The second thing that is noticeable about the preamble to the Australian Constitution is that it refers specifically to the people *of the constituent States*. This reflects the fact that the Constitution was the product of a long process of deliberation, drafting and ratification that involved the active participation of the governments, legislatures and citizens of each of the Australian colonies – a process that was unprecedentedly democratic by the standards of the time, although certainly less than fully inclusive.[16] The process of federating was determined by the legislatures of the Australian colonies. The process involved a federal convention composed of delegates for each of the colonies. The delegates were directly elected by the voters of the colonies, and each colony was equally represented. The convention prepared a draft constitution that was submitted to the legislatures for comment, revised by the convention and then submitted to the voters in each colony for approval at a referendum. Not until all these steps were taken was the proposed constitution then conveyed to the British authorities for enactment by the Imperial Parliament at Westminster, London, in 1900. Only five of the Australian colonies are mentioned in the preamble, however, because the people of Western Australia had not yet agreed to federate on the terms of the proposed constitution. Rather than an affront to Western Australia, its omission from the preamble is a mark of respect, for it was a fundamental principle of the federation that no colony would be forced to join against its will. Specific provision for its inclusion was made elsewhere in the *Constitution Act* so that when its people did at last give their consent in July 1900, it was possible for Western Australia to be included among the Original States.[17] The preamble to the Constitution thus articulates what is one of the most fundamental principles of Australian constitutional law when it recites that the federation rests on the agreement of the people of *each* of the constituent States.

Thirdly, the preamble states that the people of the colonies agreed to unite in a *federal commonwealth*. The Commonwealth of Australia is declared to be a federal commonwealth because the constituent States continue to operate as mutually independent, self-governing political communities, while at the same time they are collectively united into the larger self-governing community of

**16** Most women, along with most Indigenous, Chinese and South Pacific Islander people, were not counted as citizens in 1900, although women did secure the vote in South Australia and Western Australia prior to federation, and throughout all of Australia soon thereafter. Indigenous people did not secure voting rights in all Australian jurisdictions until the 1960s. See Helen Irving, *To Constitute a Nation* (Cambridge University Press, 1997) chs 6, 8–11.

**17** *Commonwealth of Australia Constitution Act 1900* (UK), cl 3.

the Commonwealth. As Quick and Garran explained in their important and influential *Annotated Constitution of the Australian Commonwealth*, the term 'federal' as used in the Constitution and as understood by the framers, had at least four distinguishable meanings.[18] The 'primary and fundamental' meaning, they pointed out, is associated with the term's etymological roots, derived from the Latin *foedus*, meaning a 'league', a 'treaty' or a 'covenant', and associated with the Latin *fides*, meaning 'faith'. This sense of the term 'federal' carried with it the idea of a *union of states* in the sense of the federating agreement between the Australian colonies which established the federal commonwealth – the point being that while the preamble certainly appeals to the *people*, it just as clearly appeals to the *peoples* of each colony as having agreed to federate. The second sense in which the term 'federal' is used in the Constitution concerns the nature of the new political community created by this federating agreement. The reference here is not to the bond of union between the federating States, but to the new political community created by that bond: a *federal state*, which is itself a *union of constituent states*.[19] According to Quick and Garran, it is in this particular sense that the expression 'federal commonwealth' is used in the Australian Constitution. The idea is of a composite entity: a polity in which the incorporation of a plurality of states into one state, while preserving the separate identities of the constituent states, is taken to be the very essence of the federal commonwealth. Thirdly, Quick and Garran pointed out that the term 'federal' is frequently used to refer to a *dual system of government* consisting of two separate sets of governing institutions: a federal government with authority over the whole political community, and several state governments with authority over their respective provinces or regions. On this understanding of federalism, the federal and state governments are considered to be largely independent of each other and to exercise governing authority over different types of matters as determined by the 'distribution of powers' set out in the Constitution. This notion is closely related to a final and fourth sense of the term 'federal' which is used to designate the *federal government* in particular, which has general authority over the federation as a whole.

The Australian Constitution gives effect to the 'federal' idea in all four of these senses. The term 'federal' is used explicitly in the sense of a federating agreement and a federal commonwealth in the preamble to the Constitution,[20] and the idea of a dual system of government consisting of two sets of governing institutions – federal and state – is alluded to throughout the Constitution. All of the main governing institutions of the Commonwealth – the Parliament, the

**18** Quick and Garran, above n 2, 292–4, 332–42.

**19** Accordingly, the *Commonwealth of Australia Constitution Act 1900*, cl 6 defines 'the States' as constituent 'parts of the Commonwealth'. Quick and Garran, above n 2, 336–7, pointed out that the States 'are welded into the very structure and essence of the Commonwealth'; 'they are inseparable from it and as enduring and indestructible as the Commonwealth itself'; and they form 'the buttress and support of the entire constitutional fabric'.

**20** The term 'federal commonwealth' also appears in the *Commonwealth of Australia Constitution Act 1900*, cl 3.

Executive Council and the High Court – are called 'Federal', as are the additional 'federal courts' that may be created and the 'federal jurisdiction' that is exercised by them.[21] As Quick and Garran observed, the federal idea 'pervades and largely dominates the structure of the newly-created community, its Parliamentary executive and judiciary departments'.[22]

A fourth thing to note about the preamble to the Australian Constitution is that it declares the federal commonwealth to be *indissoluble* – a quality that is clearly meant to attach to the federation itself, but arguably to the constituent States as well. Just as it was intended that the federation could not be dissolved by the unilateral action of any one or more of the States withdrawing or seceding,[23] it was similarly intended that the States would each continue to enjoy a constitutionally-guaranteed existence within the federation.[24] Accordingly, the Constitution effectively provides that no change to the fundamental character of the federation as a territorial composition of the Commonwealth and the States can lawfully be achieved without the consent of the Commonwealth and all of the States concerned.[25] As the Supreme Court of the United States has observed of the American federation, the Constitution establishes an 'indestructible Union, composed of indestructible States'.[26]

Fifthly, the preamble refers to the Australian people's *humble reliance on the blessing of Almighty God* – a religious reference which, in the view of its leading proponent, Patrick Glynn, served to acknowledge in a suitably non-sectarian way the important role played by religion in fortifying the kinds of social bonds which all political communities need in order to be held together.[27] Lest this acknowledgement of the divine be taken to imply anything more than a non-sectarian expression of solidarity, there was inserted in the main body of the Constitution a prohibition on the Commonwealth making any law that would establish a religion, impose a religious test for holding public office, impose a religious observance, or interfere with the free exercise of religion.[28] The Constitution is thus presented as establishing a 'secular' commonwealth which does not exclude public acknowledgment of religion and measures for its non-sectarian recognition and accommodation.[29]

Sixthly, the preamble declares that the Australian Commonwealth is to be established *under the Crown of the United Kingdom*. This statement reflects the fact that the framers of the Constitution certainly did not intend to establish a republic.[30] However, this did not mean that the recognised authority of the Crown

**21** Commonwealth Constitution, ss 1, 62, 63, 64, 71, 73(ii), 77(i)–(ii), 79.
**22** Quick and Garran, above n 2, 332.
**23** Gregory Craven, *Secession* (Melbourne University Press, 1986).
**24** Commonwealth Constitution, s 106.
**25** Commonwealth Constitution, s 128, para 5.
**26** *Texas v White* 74 US (7 Wall) 700 (1869), 725.
**27** *Official Record of the Debates of the Australasian Federal Convention, Melbourne* (1898) 1733.
**28** Commonwealth Constitution, s 116.
**29** See Chapter 5, Part IV.
**30** The most republican among them was Inglis Clark: John Williams, '"With Eyes Open": Andrew Inglis Clark and Our Republican Tradition' (1995) 23 *Federal Law Review* 149.

was in any way to be autocratic or unlimited. As early as the thirteenth century, Henry de Bracton, one of the councillors of King Henry III, had famously maintained that while the king might not be subject to any man, he is subject to God and the law, because the law makes the king, and there is no king where 'will' rules rather than 'law'.[31] This statement of Bracton's was cited by Chief Justice Coke in the case of *Prohibitions del Roy* (1607) to support the proposition that the king cannot personally act as a judge but must allow the ordinary courts to fulfil that function in accordance with the law of the land.[32] Through the tumultuous events of the seventeenth century, it eventually became firmly established in English law that not only is the Crown subject to the law and to the courts, but also to the Parliament. The supremacy of Parliament is a fundamental assumption of Australia's contemporary system of representative and responsible government.[33]

The doctrine of parliamentary sovereignty was influentially articulated by A V Dicey at the time that the Australian Constitution was being drafted, approved and enacted.[34] That doctrine maintained that the British Parliament had full authority to make laws on any topic that it wished and that British courts were under an obligation to give full effect to such statutes whatever their content might be.[35] On this view, the sovereignty of the Parliament extended to the making of laws binding in all of the Queen's overseas colonies and possessions, including those in Australia. As will be seen, it was pursuant to that authority that the Australian colonies were granted full power to make laws for their own self-government, including a capacity to alter their own colonial constitutions, subject only to any over-riding requirements that might otherwise be imposed.[36]

One of the most fundamental premises of the *Commonwealth of Australia Constitution Act* was the sovereign authority of the British Parliament to enact it. By reciting the authority of the British Crown, the preamble to the *Constitution Act* made clear that Australia's governing institutions, at both a Commonwealth and a State level, would continue to derive their legal validity from the British Crown and Parliament – unless and until Australia's constitutional links with Britain might lawfully be terminated. The Australian Constitution was not, in other words, premised on a revolutionary assertion of republican independence and constitutional autochthony.[37] And yet – despite this ultimate dependence upon British authority – the framers of the Australian Constitution insisted on

**31** Henry de Bracton, *On the Laws and Customs of England* (S E Thorne trans, Harvard University Press, [c 1235–60] 1968–77) vol II, 33.
**32** *Prohibitions del Roy* (1607) 12 Co Rep 63; 77 ER 1342.
**33** For more detail, see Part II.2 below.
**34** A V Dicey, *Introduction to the Study of the Law of the Constitution* (Macmillan, 5th ed, 1897). Dicey was Vinerian Professor of English Law at Oxford University.
**35** Jeffrey Goldsworthy, *The Sovereignty of Parliament* (Clarendon Press, 1999) ch 2.
**36** *Colonial Laws Validity Act 1865* (UK), discussed in Part III.1 below and Chapter 10, Parts IV.1–4.
**37** The term 'autochthony', when used in this context, means 'self-constituting' or 'constitutionally autonomous'. See Kenneth C Wheare, *The Constitutional Structure of the Commonwealth* (Clarendon Press, 1960) chs 3 and 4; Geoffrey Marshall, *Constitutional Theory* (Clarendon Press, 1980) 57–72; Michael J Detmold, *The Australian Commonwealth* (Law Book Company, 1985) ch 6.

the inclusion of a provision in the Constitution enabling it to be amended by a procedure that depends solely upon decisions taken by the Commonwealth Parliament and the Australian people, voting in a referendum;[38] and they also inserted a local capacity to exercise the powers of the British Parliament within Australia, provided the Parliaments of the Commonwealth and the States agree.[39] Changes to Australia's Constitution, as well as the gradual development of Australia's constitutional independence from the United Kingdom, have all been secured in conformity and continuity with these provisions and fundamental principles.[40]

Finally, the preamble to the *Constitution Act* refers to the Constitution itself. Just as the Commonwealth was established by the authority of the British Parliament, it was also established *subject to the Constitution*. The Constitution of the Commonwealth of Australia is the primary source of positive law under which the Commonwealth was established and continues to operate to this day. The principle of the rule of law ensures that all Australian institutions of government must operate in accordance with the law – ultimately, the law of the Constitution. The Australian Constitution is not, however, the only source of fundamental law which contributes to the establishment and regulation of the Commonwealth as a federation of six constituent States. Each of the States has its own constitution which continues to operate subject to the Commonwealth Constitution.[41] Indeed, Australian constitutional law consists not only of the Commonwealth and State constitutions, but also a whole range of fundamental British statutes, along with the entire body of constitutional rules and principles derived from the common law of England,[42] including those rules and principles which regulate the legal relationships between the United Kingdom and its former colonies and dominions, now together members of the British Commonwealth of Nations.[43] To understand Australian constitutional law properly and well, it is important to have an appreciation of this wider historical, political and legal background.

## 2 British constitutionalism

The British constitution is the result of a long evolution.[44] Its primary institutions, the Crown, the Parliament and the Courts, took centuries to develop into their recognisably modern forms. Relatively little is directly known of the legal

**38** Commonwealth Constitution, s 128.
**39** Commonwealth Constitution, s 51(xxxviii).
**40** See *Statute of Westminster 1931* (UK), *Statute of Westminster Adoption Act 1942* (Cth), *Australia Acts 1986* (UK) and (Cth).
**41** Commonwealth Constitution, s 106.
**42** Sir Owen Dixon, 'The Common Law as an Ultimate Constitutional Foundation' (1957) 31 *Australian Law Journal* 240.
**43** Bruce McPherson, *The Reception of English Law Abroad* (Supreme Court of Queensland Library, 2007).
**44** Michael Rush, *Parliament Today* (Manchester University Press, 2005), 26 remarks: 'Parliamentary government in Britain is the product of a long and complex historical process. It has no clearly defined origins and its development was not continuous, or regular, or inevitable'.

customs of the Brittonic peoples of early Britain, save that which can be inferred from archaeological evidence or derived from the written observations of the occupying Romans, such as Julius Caesar, who described the priestly-judicial functions of the druids.[45] Somewhat more is known of the legal practices of the invading Germanic tribes, especially as Anglo-Saxon kings began from the beginning of the seventh century to produce written laws, often under the guidance of Christian bishops.[46] Like most Celtic and Germanic rulers of the time, it was the practice of early British kings to issue laws and to govern their domains with the advice of a group of powerful councillors or *witan* ('the wise'), the meeting of which was called a *witenagemot*. This practice, though variable, continued after the several Anglo-Saxon kingdoms were consolidated into the one realm of England, particularly under Alfred the Great (871–99), Edward the Elder (899–924) and Æthelstan (924–39).

The written laws of the Danish king Cnut (1016–35) and of Edward the Confessor (1042–66) are prime sources for our knowledge about the customary laws and practices of the time. Like Alfred's earlier collection of 'dooms', they presupposed a rich and complex variety of local customs and practices which it was the purpose of the written laws to organise, consolidate and moderate, such as through the Christian preference for showing mercy and accepting monetary compensation instead of exacting personal vengeance for wrongs.[47] But the extent to which the laws and judgments of early English kings shaped and controlled local customs was limited, for communal justice or *folcriht* ('folk-right') remained the basic law for many centuries, administered on the scale of village assemblies, as well as among the progressively larger groupings of 'tithings', 'hundreds' and 'shires' (or 'counties').[48] The feudal system, particularly after the Norman Conquest (1066), introduced yet another set of courts, based on the idea that every 'lord' held court for his 'vassals', again extending from the smallest local manor through to the court of the king himself. In this context, the provision of justice through the king's courts – especially in matters of violent crime against the 'king's peace' and to remedy miscarriages of justice in local or feudal courts – was a primary means by which the authority of English kings penetrated more deeply into the society. Another important instrument of royal influence was the king's appointment of 'reeves' to act as his local officials in the various manors, boroughs, hundreds and shires of the country; the king's control of the shires became particularly strong, and the 'shire-reeves' (or 'sheriffs') became among the most important officers in the country.[49]

As one scholar has recently observed, the early Anglo-Saxon *witenagemot* 'were often large in size, geographically and socially diverse in composition, and

**45** Julius Caesar, *The Gallic Wars* (W A McDevitte and W S Bohn trans, Harper, 1869) bk 6, ch 13.
**46** See Benjamin Thorpe (ed), *Ancient Laws and Institutes of England* (Cambridge University Press [1840] 2012).
**47** J H Baker, *An Introduction to English Legal History* (Butterworths, 4th ed, 2002) 3.
**48** Ibid, 6–8.
**49** Ibid, 9.

frequent and regular in occurrence'.[50] The functions of these council-assemblies were also diverse: they included confirmation of the accession of a new king, appointments to various offices, resolution of disputes, promulgation of laws and, occasionally, the restraint of a tyrannical king based on the commitments he had made in his coronation oath.[51] As the 'virtual representative' of the people, the *witenagemot* often acted as a kind of intermediary between the king and his most powerful subjects, sometimes negotiating the terms of the appointment of a king and expressing the consent of 'the people' to his rule.[52] It was also the means by which political stability was maintained through the distribution of royal patronage and favour among the magnates of the realm.[53] After the Norman Conquest under William the Conqueror (1066–87), the Anglo-Saxon *witenagemot* was succeeded in name by the *curia regis* ('king's court') and later the *magnum concilium* ('great council'). These council-assemblies consisted largely of the king's tenants-in-chief in addition to the leading clergy and the king's personal courtiers. The traditional feudal obligation to provide *fidele consilium et auxilium* ('faithful council and aid') was overlaid on the older Anglo-Saxon relationship between the king and his magnates.[54]

John of Salisbury (*c* 1110–80) expressed a widely shared ideal to which the reality did not always conform when he said in his influential *Policraticus* that the king should rule by law, according to justice, and with the counsel of the wise.[55] The kings of England needed financial, military and spiritual support in order to govern, and especially to conduct armed campaigns, and meetings of the *magnum concilium* had to be convened to obtain this support. In exchange, the nobility and clergy were able to secure the acknowledgment of what they considered to be their rights and liberties through royal grants such as the *Charter of Liberties* of Henry I (1110) and *Magna Carta* of John (1215), which was reissued and confirmed by English kings on numerous occasions over the next three centuries.[56]

Over time, sharper institutional distinctions were drawn between the various institutions of the king's government. The most fundamental of such emerging distinctions was between the *magnum concilium* (or *concilium regis in parliamento*), which was the major assembly of nobles and bishops periodically convened to discuss the most important affairs of the kingdom, and the smaller *curia regis*, consisting of sworn ministers who advised and served the king on a more permanent basis.[57] Within the *curia regis* there also developed the

**50** J R Maddicott, *The Origins of the English Parliament, 924–1327* (Oxford University Press, 2010) 4.
**51** Ibid, ch 1.
**52** For example, the Oxford Agreement and Code of King Cnut (1018), composed by Archbishop Wulfstan, recorded the responsibility of the king and his judges to act with justice and mercy to both rich and poor: *Law Code of Cnut*, [3.1], [4.1].
**53** Maddicott, above n 50, 55.
**54** Ibid, 76–7.
**55** Cary Nederman (ed), *Policraticus* [1159] (Cambridge University Press, 1991) bk IV, ch 6, 41–6. This work was written while John of Salisbury was secretary to Theobald, Archbishop of Canterbury.
**56** Maddicott, above n 50, ch 3.
**57** Ibid, 188–9.

beginnings to two distinct departments of state, the Exchequer and the Chancery. The Court of Exchequer dealt with the collection of the king's revenue, and also dispensed justice, while the Chancery was responsible for drafting official documents and the safe-keeping of the Great Seal. The Chancellor himself was usually a member of the clergy and, as 'keeper of the king's conscience', also dispensed 'equitable' remedies in the king's name as a corrective supplement to those available at common law. There were also two important courts dispensing common law in the name of the king: the Court of Common Pleas, largely for actions between subject and subject, and the Court of King's Bench, for criminal matters and cases involving the king himself.[58] At first, the King's Bench went on circuit with the king himself (*coram rege*), but by 1318 it had become established in Westminster Hall in London.[59] In relation to the *magnum concilium* (called a *parlement* from around 1236),[60] there had also developed a distinct means of summoning the tenants of the king and the powerful men of the realm: by individual writs addressed to each of the archbishops, bishops, abbots, earls and greater barons, and by general summons issued through the sheriffs to the lesser tenants.[61] When, during the latter part of the thirteenth century, general summons were more frequently issued to the elected knights of the shires and the burgesses of the boroughs and cities,[62] this became the basis for the distinction between the two houses of Parliament: the lords spiritual and temporal, and the commons.[63]

The power relationship between the Crown and the Parliament has long been fundamental to the English constitution. When Sir John Fortescue insisted, in 1469, that English kings possess *dominium politicum et regale* ('political and regal lordship') rather than *dominium regale*, he meant that they could only rule through laws to which the people themselves had assented in Parliament.[64] Indeed, Parliaments had deposed or forced the abdication of kings twice in the fourteenth century (Edward II in 1327, Richard II in 1399), and would do so again twice in the seventeenth century (Charles I in 1649, James II in 1688); and since at least the fourteenth century they had confirmed the succession to the throne. Kings had also long been reliant on Parliaments for the approval of taxation, but powerful rulers, such as Tudor monarchs Henry VII (1485–1509), Henry VIII (1509–47) and Elizabeth I (1558–1603), were generally able to lead, control and manipulate their Parliaments through statecraft, patronage and

**58** Baker, above n 47, 12–20.
**59** Ibid, 39.
**60** The word 'parliament' is derived from the French word *parler*, which means 'to speak' or 'to talk'. The Old French sense of the word *parlement* carried the primary sense of a 'discussion', a 'conversation', and a 'meeting' at which 'negotiations' were held, and eventually came to mean a deliberative council or assembly which shared in the government of a political community. See *Oxford Dictionary of English* (2nd ed, Oxford University Press, 2003) at 'parliament'.
**61** *Magna Carta* (1215) cls 12, 14. See Maddicott, above n 50, 80, 198–9.
**62** Ibid, 198–206, 275–6, 288–97, 310–16. See also F W Maitland, *The Constitutional History of England* (Cambridge University Press, 1908) 172–7. On the famous parliaments summoned by Simon de Montfort in 1261, 1264 and 1265, see Maddicott, above n 50, 234–5, 257, 275–6, 411.
**63** Maddicott, above n 50, 335–64.
**64** Sir John Fortescue, *In Praise of the Laws of England* [c 1469]. See Maitland, above n 62, 198–9.

intimidation.[65] Henry VIII especially consolidated his power over both church and state through the parliamentary enactment of the *Ecclesiastical Appeals Act 1532* (which prohibited all appeals to the Pope), the *Act of Supremacy 1534* (which declared the king to be the supreme head of the Church of England), and the *Treasons Act 1534* (which made it high treason to refuse to take the Oath of Supremacy).[66] Stuart kings James I (1603–25) and Charles I (1625–49) sought to exercise similar control over their realms but, influenced by the 'divine right of kings doctrine',[67] they did so by seeking to rule without their Parliaments rather than through them.[68] Opposition to the Stuarts both within and outside Parliament led to the English Civil War (1642–6) and the establishment of the Commonwealth (1649–59), at first under the rule of the Parliament, and later under Oliver Cromwell, and his son, Richard, as Lord Protector.

Central to the constitutional resistance to Stuart rule was the view that Parliaments should be summoned regularly, that the privileges of Parliament (including freedom of speech) should be respected, that all laws and taxes should be approved by Parliament and that the king did not have any general right to 'suspend' the operation of duly enacted laws. It was also believed that the law must be applied by the ordinary courts of the land rather than by prerogative courts established by the king, such as the notorious Star Chamber and High Commission, which had been used by the Stuarts to govern by proclamation and to suppress political opposition and religious dissent.[69] Against these kinds of abuses, the so-called Long Parliament (1640–48) enacted the *Habeas Corpus Act 1640* (which abolished the Star Chamber and the High Commission), and the *Triennial Act 1641* (which required that Parliament be summoned at least once every three years). Following the forced removal of 41 members of Parliament by officers of Cromwell's Army in 1648, members of the House of Commons remaining in the so-called Rump Parliament (1648–53) established a High Court of Justice to try Charles I for treason. Following the execution of the king in 1649, the Commons also voted to abolish the monarchy and the House of Lords, approved the establishment of a Council of State, and declared England to be a Commonwealth.[70]

In ruling without the king during the Interregnum, in voting for the restoration of Charles II in 1660, and in inviting William and Mary of Orange to become joint sovereigns of England in 1688, the Parliament acted in a manner that was technically 'revolutionary' or 'self-constituting'. The *Bill of Rights* (1688)

**65** Maitland, above n 62, 251–5; G R Elton, *The Tudor Constitution* (Cambridge University Press, 2nd ed, 1982), 290–94, 307–12.

**66** Bishop of Rochester John Fisher and former Lord Chancellor Sir Thomas More were executed for refusing to acknowledge Henry VIII's supremacy over the church.

**67** See James I, *True Law of Free Monarchies* (1598) and *Basilikon Doron* (1599), written in response to such works as George Buchanan's *De Jure Regni apud Scotos* (1579), which had asserted the accountability of the king to his people through the Parliament.

**68** Charles I did not summon a Parliament between 1629 and 1640. See J P Kenyon, *The Stuart Constitution* (Cambridge University Press, 2nd ed, 1986) 30–31, 59.

**69** Maitland, above n 62, 256–75; Kenyon, above n 68, 119–20, 176–80.

**70** Blair Worden, *The Rump Parliament* (Cambridge University Press, 1974) 171–2.

confirmed the accession of William and Mary to the throne on condition that their prerogatives would be limited by law and that they would recognise the supremacy of Parliament, but the really revolutionary thing was that the Parliament which did these things had effectively summoned itself into existence.[71] In addition, the *Act of Settlement 1701* not only required a Protestant succession to the throne, but also supported the independence of the judiciary from government interference by providing that judges' commissions would remain valid *quamdiu se bene gesserint* (during good behaviour) and that they could only be removed on the basis of proved misbehaviour upon an address of both houses of Parliament. The supremacy of the Parliament and the independence of the courts were thenceforth firmly established as fundamental principles of English law.

While the Parliament had successfully asserted its relative supremacy through the so-called 'Glorious Revolution' of 1688–9, English monarchs continued in the next century to exercise direct powers of government, particularly through the appointment of ministers who were accountable to them and could be dismissed by them at will. Kings and their leading ministers were also able to exercise substantial influence within the Parliament through patronage and a corrupt electoral system.[72] Through the course of the 1700s, however, as one historian has put it:

> A firmer grip on finance gave parliament a surer hold on measures and men; and parliamentary influence over the executive was bound to grow as succeeding monarchs came to terms with this truth, as they gradually learned that a ministry and policy could founder on the rock of supply.[73]

One early device of independent parliamentary influence was the impeachment of ministers, on the basis that seriously mistaken ministerial advice was regarded as a kind of criminal treason rather than merely a failure of policy or administration.[74] During the eighteenth century, it gradually became accepted that the Parliament could force the resignation or dismissal of ministers of whom it disapproved,[75] a development which made the drastic expedient of impeachment eventually unnecessary. But it was not until the later emergence of disciplined parties in the nineteenth century that a majority in the Parliament could use their powers over taxation, expenditure and legislation consistently enough to force the king or queen into always appointing ministers in whom they had confidence.

Changes to the electoral system in the nineteenth and early twentieth centuries reinforced these developments by making the Parliament more democratic.

**71** The form of a summons was issued by William while he was still only Prince of Orange. See Maitland, above n 62, 283–5.
**72** The notorious 'rotten boroughs' were parliamentary constituencies or districts which had very small numbers of electors who could be personally bribed, while the 'pocket boroughs' were electorates that could be controlled by an individual who owned most of the land in the district.
**73** E N Williams, *The Eighteenth Century Constitution* (Cambridge University Press, 1965) 5.
**74** Ibid.
**75** Ibid, 68.

The *Reform Act* of 1832 eliminated 57 'rotten boroughs'[76] and redistributed House of Commons seats more equitably, while successive *Reform Acts* of 1867, 1884, 1918 and 1928 expanded the franchise to include, eventually, all adult males and females (ie, universal adult suffrage). The *Ballot Act* of 1872 also made electoral bribery more difficult by requiring secret ballots. The power balance between an elected House of Commons and an hereditary House of Lords was also an important part of the equation. At least by the mid nineteenth century, it had become widely accepted that the monarch must appoint as Prime Minister a person who had the confidence of the House of Commons and could guarantee financial supply. However, this did not mean that the House of Lords had to give its consent to all bills passed by the Commons. In 1893, the Lords rejected a Home Rule Bill for Ireland which had been a central aspect of the government's program; and between 1906 and 1909, ten bills introduced by the Liberal party and passed by the Commons were rejected or 'amended out of recognition' by the Lords, including, in 1909, the first financial bill to be rejected by the upper house for more than 150 years. This prolonged confrontation between the two houses culminated in the *Parliament Act 1911*, passed reluctantly by the Lords in the face of the threat by the Liberal government to 'pack' the upper house with their supporters. Among other things, the *Parliament Act* prevented the Lords from delaying a money bill for more than one month and a non-financial bill for more than two years. The 1911 procedure was used again in 1949, in the context of anticipated House of Lords resistance to the nationalisation program of the Labour government of Clement Attlee, to enact the *Parliament Act 1949*, which reduced the delaying period for non-financial bills to only one year.[77]

The convention that the monarch must appoint a Prime Minister who has the support of the House of Commons and act on the advice of the Prime Minister and other ministers is the most fundamental principle of what is today known as the Westminster system of parliamentary responsible government.[78] Essential to this system is the institution of the Cabinet, which evolved from the practice of English kings to summon a 'cabinet council' and, later, an even smaller 'efficient cabinet' to provide confidential advice in relation to the most important matters of state.[79] By 1865, as Walter Bagehot acutely observed,[80] the Cabinet had become the 'efficient secret' of the English Constitution, particularly because it provided a 'connecting link' between the Executive Government and the Parliament. However, it has been debated whether the 'nearly complete fusion' of executive and legislative power in the Prime Minister and Cabinet which has resulted is indeed a 'characteristic merit' of the Westminster

**76** See above n 72.
**77** On the political and constitutional background to the *Parliament Acts*, see *Jackson v Her Majesty's Attorney General* [2005] UKHL 56.
**78** See Chapter 6, Part V.
**79** Kenyon, above n 68, 478.
**80** Walter Bagehot, *The English Constitution* (Collins, 1963) 59, 65.

system, as Bagehot thought.[81] Writing in 1748, the French political thinker Baron de Montesquieu (1689–1755) famously claimed in his *The Spirit of Laws* that individual liberty was most effectively protected in England because the constitution distributed the legislative, executive and judicial powers of government into three distinct and separate institutions.[82] Writing about two decades later, Sir William Blackstone (1723–80) similarly observed in his highly influential *Commentaries on the Laws of England* that the English constitution established a 'balance' between the Crown and the two houses of the Parliament so that each performed a 'mutual check' upon the other.[83] Whether or not Montesquieu and Blackstone were entirely accurate in their descriptive claims about the English system, the idea that there should be an institutional separation of powers profoundly influenced the design of the United States Constitution, which separately vests legislative, executive and judicial power in the Congress, the President and the Judiciary.[84] However, as will be seen, the dominance of the House of Commons within the British Parliament does not cohere neatly with the principle that the upper house or second chamber within a federation, such as the United States Senate or the Swiss Council of States (*Ständerat*), is meant to represent the constituent states and should for this reason be no less powerful than the first chamber or lower house. The question of whether and, if so, how these two principles could be coordinated within one constitutional system was one of the most important issues that the framers of the Australian Constitution had to address.

## 3 Parliamentary sovereignty

Did the relative 'supremacy' of British Parliament over the king, clearly established by 1689, make it 'sovereign'? As Frederic Maitland observed, the modern idea of sovereignty certainly did not exist in medieval times. The king was himself 'under law', and this law was something that existed independently of the will of any ruler. Moreover, the authority of a king was always counter-balanced by the authority of the church and the general conviction was that church and state were independent of each other, for 'neither derive[d] its authority from the other'.[85] Medieval society was characterised by a multiplicity of institutions and authorities, none of which was able to claim unlimited jurisdiction

**81** A former Lord Chancellor once described the English parliamentary system as involving a kind of 'elective dictatorship': see Lord Hailsham, 'Elective Dictatorship' (1976) (21 October 1976) *The Listener* 496.

**82** Charles de Secondat Montesquieu, *The Spirit of Laws* (Thomas Nugent trans, Hafner, 1949) bk XI, ch 6.

**83** William Blackstone, *Commentaries on the Laws of England* (Clarendon Press, 1765–69) vol 1, 149–51. Blackstone was the first Vinerian Professor of English Law at Oxford University from 1758 to 1766.

**84** James Madison, *The Federalist No 51* (1788), in Clinton Rossiter (ed), *The Federalist Papers* (New American Library, 1961). The separation of powers is discussed further in Chapter 3, Part II.1, Chapter 6, Part II.3–4 and Chapter 9, Part II.1–3.

**85** Maitland, above n 62, 101–2, 250. As Maitland also observed, 'it is difficult to think of sovereignty being vested in so fleeting an affair as a medieval parliament, which exists for a month or two and disappears'.

and command unqualified obedience. While the exact boundaries of the many different authority structures were always shifting and contested, there was a widespread belief that these boundaries were defined, in principle, by a law which transcended any particular earthly authority.[86]

This theory of the sovereignty of the law derived from the general conviction that the authority of human laws depended on the extent to which they gave effect to the fundamental principles of the law of nature. According to St Thomas Aquinas (1225–74), there were four essential categories of law: the *eternal law* by which God rules the entire universe, the *divine law* revealed by God in the Bible, the *natural law* built into the creation and discovered by human reason, and *positive laws* enacted by human agents.[87] All law, he said, is necessarily a rule of reason directed to the common good; therefore, positive enactments, in order truly to be 'law', must be consistent with reason and contribute to the common good.[88] In accord with this general outlook, as Otto von Gierke pointed out, the medieval doctrine:

> never surrendered the thought that Law is by its origin of equal rank with the State and does not depend upon the State for its existence. To base the State upon some ground of Law, to make it the outcome of a legal act, the medieval Publicist felt himself absolutely bound. Also his doctrine was permeated by the conviction that the State stood charged with a mission to realize the idea of Law: an idea which was given to man before the establishment of any earthly Power, and which no such Power could destroy. It was never doubtful that the highest Might, were it spiritual or were it temporal, was confined by truly legal limitations. …
>
> The properly medieval and never completely obsolete theory declared that every act of the Sovereign which broke the bounds drawn by Natural Law was formally null and void. As null and void therefore every judge and every other magistrate who had to apply the law was to treat, not only every unlawful executive act, but every unlawful statute, even though it were published by Pope or Emperor.[89]

It is true that already by the end of the thirteenth century, writs for the summoning of Parliament had required that the representatives must have 'full power' (*plena potestas*) to give the consent of their communities to parliamentary decisions, especially the grant of taxes.[90] The idea was that the communities were thus bound by that consent and, as a consequence, the *acta* of Parliament were considered generally binding and the Parliament itself eventually came to be regarded as the highest authority in the land. However, this did not amount to the kind of legally unlimited power of command which Thomas Hobbes (1588–1679) later called 'Soveraigne Power'.[91] For the *plena potestas* originally

**86** Ibid, 506–7. See, further: Brian Tierney, *Religion, Law and the Growth of Constitutional Thought* (Cambridge University Press, 1982); Harold Berman, *Law and Revolution* (Harvard University Press, 1983).
**87** Thomas Aquinas, *Summa Theologica*, Part II-I, Question 91.
**88** Ibid, Part II-I, Question 90.
**89** Otto von Gierke, *Political Theories of the Middle Age* (Frederic Maitland trans, Cambridge University Press, [1900] 1922) 74, 84.
**90** Goldsworthy, above n 35. See also Maddicott, above n 50, 289–90.
**91** Thomas Hobbes, *Leviathan* (Cambridge University Press, 1991) ch 18.

carried with it only the quasi-'judicial' sense of enabling the representatives to make submissions to the king's court, and entailed the acceptance of the power of the ruler to summon, ask for information and demand consent to measures decided upon for the common good.[92] Parliamentary sovereignty in its modern Hobbesian sense could only be contemplated after Henry VIII successfully asserted through the Parliament his headship over the Church of England, and once sittings of Parliament had become a constitutionally regular occurrence.[93]

Indeed, even as late as 1610, in the celebrated *Dr Bonham's Case,*[94] Sir Edward Coke (1552–1634), then Chief Justice of the Court of Common Pleas, claimed that there had been many cases in which the common law had 'controlled' Acts of Parliament and sometimes 'judged them to be void', particularly when it was found that they were 'against Common right and reason, or repugnant, or impossible to be performed'. What did Coke mean? At the least, it seems likely that by referring to 'common right and reason' he had in mind the 'artificial reason' of the common law itself, rather than the innate capacity to reason with which all human beings are naturally endowed.[95] Some scholars, especially in the United States and also in Australia, have understood him to have been suggesting that unreasonable statutes would actually be declared entirely void and inoperative by the courts.[96] Others have argued that he did not mean that the courts would regard unreasonable statutes as simply void, but rather that they would be interpreted in accordance with reason.[97] Certainly, Coke himself later affirmed in his *Institutes of the Laws of England* that 'the power and jurisdiction of the Parliament for making of laws ... is so transcendent and absolute [that] it cannot be confined either for causes or persons within any bounds'.[98]

Henry VIII gave expression to a comparable view of the authority of the King in Parliament when he declared to the House of Commons in 1542: 'We be informed by our judges that we at no time stand so highly in our estate royal as in the time of Parliament, wherein we as head and you as members are conjoined and knit together into one body politic'.[99] In similar terms, Sir Thomas Smith (1513–57), Secretary of State to Elizabeth I, said in 1583 that '[t]he most high and absolute power of the realm of England consisteth in the Parliament'.[100] Blackstone, reflecting on the tremendous developments of the sixteenth and seventeenth centuries, went so far as to say that the Parliament has:

**92** Gaines Post, 'Plena Potestas and Consent in Medieval Assemblies' (1943) 1 *Traditio* 355.
**93** Goldsworthy, above n 35, 48–53.
**94** *Thomas Bonham v College of Physicians* (1610) 8 Co Rep 107; 77 ER 638.
**95** *Prohibitions del Roy* (1607) 12 Co Rep 64; 77 ER 1342.
**96** Edward Corwin, 'The "Higher Law" Background of American Constitutional Law' (1928) 42 *Harvard Law Review* 149, 365; Geoffrey de Q Walker, *The Rule of Law* (Melbourne University Press, 1988) 114–15. See the survey of the literature in Goldsworthy, above n 35, 111–24.
**97** Goldsworthy, above n 35, 109–24. See also J G A Pocock, *The Ancient Constitution and the Feudal Law* (Cambridge University Press, 1957) ch 11.
**98** Edward Coke, *The Fourth Part of the Institutes of the Laws of England* (1671) 36.
**99** *Ferrers' Case* (1542) in Elton, above n 65, 275–7.
**100** Sir Thomas Smith, *De Republica Anglorum; the Manner of Government or Policie of the Realme of England* (1583) Bk II, ch 1.

> sovereign and uncontrollable authority in the making, confirming, enlarging, restraining, abrogating, repealing, reviving, and expounding of laws, concerning matters of all possible denominations, ecclesiastical or temporal, civil, military, maritime, or criminal: this being the place where that absolute despotic power, which must in all governments reside somewhere, is entrusted by the constitution of these kingdoms.[101]

Nonetheless, there remained in his thought a tension between the sovereignty of the Parliament and the capacity of the courts to declare that parliamentary statutes are contrary to law. Blackstone also said that:

> This law of nature, being coeval with mankind, and dictated by God himself, is of course superior in obligation to any other. It is binding over all the globe in all countries, and at all times; no human laws are of any validity, if contrary to this: and such of them as are valid derive all their force, and all their authority, mediately or immediately, from this original.[102]

The sovereignty of the British Parliament is today challenged, or at least qualified, by the suggestion that there are some statutes, such as the *European Communities Act 1972* and the *Human Rights Act 1998*, which have a special kind of 'constitutional' status which binds later Parliaments. The claim is that if a later Parliament wishes to repeal or amend them it must purposefully and explicitly provide for this, rather than merely legislate in a manner that is inconsistent with them. Relatedly, it is also argued that parliamentary sovereignty must be understood in a 'self-embracing' rather than a 'continuing' sense, meaning that a Parliament can effectively redefine itself and its powers in a manner that will bind its successors.[103]

The jurisdiction of the Parliament is certainly territorially defined and limited in effect. English authority did not extend into Wales until its annexation between 1277 and 1283, and English law did not generally apply there until the *Law in Wales Act 1536*, which granted the Welsh the same legal rights as English subjects, including representation in Parliament.[104] Scotland and England were brought together under a 'personal union' when in 1603 James VI of Scotland also became James I of England, but the two countries were not united as one kingdom until the *Acts of Union 1706–7* merged the Parliaments of England and Scotland into one Parliament of the United Kingdom of England and Scotland.[105] In 1800, Ireland was also incorporated into the United Kingdom pursuant to *Acts of Union* enacted concurrently by the Irish and British Parliaments. However, since that time, the trend has generally been in the opposite direction. In particular, the Republic

**101** Blackstone, above n 83, vol 1, 156.
**102** Ibid, Introduction, sec II, 41. For a discussion of Blackstone's meaning, see Goldsworthy, above n 35, 181–3.
**103** Compare Paul Craig, 'Sovereignty of the United Kingdom Parliament after Factortame' (1991) 11 *Yearbook of European Law* 22; Sir William Wade, 'Sovereignty – Evolution or Revolution?' (1996) 112 *Law Quarterly Review* 574. For the distinction between 'self-embracing' and 'continuing' sovereignty, see H L A Hart, *The Concept of Law* (Clarendon Press, 1961) 149.
**104** 27 Hen VIII, c 26. The statute also abolished the semi-independent regions in Wales known as the Welsh Marches.
**105** Treaty of Union 1706; *Union with Scotland Act 1706* (Eng); *Union with England Act 1707* (Scot). See also *MacCormick v Lord Advocate* [1953] SC 396; *Gibson v Lord Advocate* [1975] SC 136.

of Ireland became independent of Britain in 1922 following a War of Independence,[106] and in the 1990s the British Government established 'devolved' legislatures in Scotland, Wales and Northern Ireland, as well as independent governments responsible to those Parliaments.[107] The people of Scotland voted against separation from the United Kingdom in a referendum held in 2014.

Similar principles apply to the overseas colonies and dependencies of the British Crown, including those of Australia. As will be explained, when the *Commonwealth of Australia Constitution Act* was enacted in 1900, the authority of the British Parliament to legislate for Australia was unquestioned. However, over the course of the twentieth century Australia's institutions of government have become increasingly independent, especially after the British Parliament abdicated its authority to legislate for Australia in 1986.[108] The legal foundation for these developments lies in the fact that British colonists in Australia brought with them this constitutional background as part of the common law, which was considered to be the 'birth-right' of all subjects of the British Crown.

## 4 Colonial background

William Blackstone influentially proposed that there were three ways in which English law might come to apply to distant lands external to the realm of England.[109] Such lands might become established as colonies, he said, by reason of occupation, conquest or cession. Occupation would occur when lands found to be 'desert and uncultivated' were settled by English colonists.[110] Conquest or cession would occur when lands that had already been 'cultivated' were gained from their former inhabitants by military conquest or by consensual treaty. These differences in the context and mode of colonisation, Blackstone reasoned, led to differences concerning the law that would apply in such lands. Because lands acquired by conquest or cession were already occupied by peoples governed under their own laws, Blackstone considered that those existing laws would continue to operate unless they were repugnant to morality or were deliberately altered by legislation. The common law would not apply automatically in such lands because they were 'distinct (though dependent) dominions', and statutes of Parliament would only apply in such dominions if they were 'particularly named' in the relevant enactment. If, on the other hand, a territory had not previously been occupied and governed by existing laws, as much of the

**106** Articles of Agreement for a Treaty Between Great Britain and Ireland 1921; *Irish Free State Constitution Act 1922* (UK). Compare *The State (Ryan) v Lennon* [1935] Irish Reports 170 and *Moore v Attorney-General of the Irish Free State* [1935] AC 484 (PC).

**107** *Scotland Act 1998*; *Government of Wales Act 1998*; *Northern Ireland Act 1998*. See, further, Vernon Bogdanor, *Devolution in the United Kingdom* (Oxford University Press, 2001).

**108** See Part V.1 below.

**109** Blackstone, above n 83, vol 1, Introduction, sec IV, 104–6. Blackstone's classification, which reflected international law on the point, has been affirmed by the High Court: *Mabo v Queensland (No 2)* (1992) 175 CLR 1, 33.

**110** On the common law's earlier resistance to the Roman Law category of 'occupation' of unoccupied lands (*terra nullius*), represented in *Calvin's Case* (1608) 7 Co Rep 2a; 77 ER 377; 2 St Tr 559, see Alex Castles, *An Australian Legal History* (Law Book Company, 1982) 7–9.

common law of England as was applicable to the circumstances of the country would automatically be in force in the new settlement, for this was the 'birthright' of every subject of the Crown.[111]

Around the time that Blackstone penned these words, Captain James Cook was sent on an expedition to the south pacific island of Tahiti to observe the transit of Venus across the sun, but with sealed instructions to see whether a 'Continent or Land of great extent' might also be discovered in the southern waters of the Pacific Ocean. His instructions stated that if he was to discover this mysterious continent *Terra Australis Incognita* he was 'with the Consent of the Natives to take Possession of Convenient Situations in the Country in the Name of the King of Great Britain', and if he found the country to be uninhabited, he was to 'take Possession for his Majesty by setting up Proper Marks and Inscriptions, as first discoverers and possessors'.[112] As it happened, although he was certainly not the first European to do so, Cook did discover such a continent and, despite encountering several groups of indigenous inhabitants, considered them to be existing in a 'pure state of nature', and so proceeded, on 22 August 1770 at Possession Island in the Torres Strait, to claim possession of the eastern coast of Australia on behalf of King George III.[113]

Blackstone had observed that the English possessions and colonies of North America, which had been first established in the early seventeenth century, were obtained principally by 'conquest and driving out the natives ... or by treaties'; and he added, somewhat wryly, that the 'natural justice' with which that dispossession had occurred was something into which he would not 'at present inquire'.[114] Despite the justifications relied upon by the European nation-states to support their colonising practices, concern about the justice of such dispossessions of peoples had indeed been expressed by several jurists, philosophers and theologians. Francisco de Vitoria, a leading theologian at the School of Salamanca in Spain, had argued in the early 1500s that European powers ought not to suppose that native peoples lack the reason or capacity to hold property over their lands under settled laws, and that it would be contrary to the law of nature to dispossess them without morally objective justification.[115] As Blackstone himself later remarked, again not without some irony and implied criticism:

> so long as it was confined to the stocking and cultivation of desert uninhabited countries, it kept strictly within the limits of the law of nature. But how far the seizing on countries already peopled, and driving out or massacring the innocent and defenceless natives, merely because they differed from their invaders in language, in religion, in customs, in government, or in colour; how far such a conduct was consonant to nature, to reason, or to Christianity, deserved well to be considered by those who have rendered their names immortal by thus civilizing mankind.[116]

**111** See, further, *Mabo v Queensland (No 2)* (1992) 175 CLR 1, 35.
**112** Instructions to Captain James Cook, 30 July 1768.
**113** *Kaurareg People v Queensland* [2001] FCA 657, [3].
**114** Blackstone, above n 83, vol 1, Introduction, sec IV, 105.
**115** Francisco de Vitoria, *De Indis Et De Jure Belli* (James Brown Scott trans, Oceana, [1557] 1964).
**116** Blackstone, above n 83, vol 1, bk II, ch 1, 7.

Prior to British settlement in the late eighteenth century, the continent of Australia was inhabited by numerous indigenous peoples, speaking their own languages and practising their own customs, laws and religions. The legality, if not the justice, with which Australia's indigenous peoples were subsequently dispossessed of their traditional lands has been the subject of discussion in several cases decided by Australian courts. As to its legality, the High Court has persistently held that the original acquisition of territory by Captain Cook on behalf of the British Crown is a sovereign 'act of state' the validity of which cannot be challenged by the courts of that state.[117] According to the Court, this requires the conclusion that there can be no continuing indigenous sovereignty, even in the North American sense of a 'domestic dependent nation',[118] nor any parallel indigenous law-making capacity apart from that which might be conferred by Parliament.[119] In *Mabo v Queensland (No 2)*, however, the High Court held, despite the acquisition of British sovereignty over the Australian continent, that the common law recognises the existence of pre-existing native title which, provided it has not been extinguished by some inconsistent grant of property, gives rise to legally-enforceable rights. As Brennan J declared in that case, upon settlement the common law 'became the law of the land, protecting and binding colonists and indigenous inhabitants alike and equally'.[120] In fact, the territorial sovereignty claimed by the British Crown remained incompletely realised for many years after it was first asserted, but it was increasingly exercised from the 1820s, as is illustrated in the conviction of European settlers for crimes perpetrated against Aboriginal people, and of Aborigines for crimes against Europeans, although there remained hesitancy about the application of settler law to crimes committed by Aborigines against other Aborigines as late as 1841.[121]

In addition to the common law, important constitutional enactments of the British Parliament also eventually became part of the law of the Australian colonies. As Bruce McPherson explained:

> Whether Parliamentary enactments like the Habeas Corpus Act 1679 or the Bill of Rights 1688 limited royal prerogatives in the overseas possession as they did in England was for some time a matter of contention between the crown and colonists. Probably the correct view is that, although at first not all of the rights guaranteed by Acts like those were immediately in force at the settlement of a colony, they or some of their provisions were attracted to and received as and when a colony attained the stage of constitutional development at which those Acts became reasonably capable of being applied as a part of the locally adopted English statute law.[122]

**117** *New South Wales v Commonwealth (Seas & Submerged Lands)* (1975) 135 CLR 337, 388; *Mabo v Queensland (No 2)* (1992) 175 CLR 1, 31.
**118** *Coe v Commonwealth (No 2)* (1993) 118 ALR 193, 199–200.
**119** *Yorta Yorta v Victoria* (2002) 214 CLR 422, 443–4.
**120** *Mabo v Queensland (No 2)* (1992) 175 CLR 1, 37.
**121** Bruce Kercher, 'R v Ballard, R v Murrell and R v Bonjon' (1998) 3 *Australian Indigenous Law Reporter* 410.
**122** McPherson, above n 43, 98–9, cited with approval in *Port of Portland v Victoria* (2010) 242 CLR 348, 359.

What principally delayed the practical reception of important statutory rights deriving from English laws such as *Magna Carta 1215*, the *Petition of Right 1627*, the *Habeas Corpus Acts 1640* and *1679*, the *Bill of Rights 1688* and the *Act of Settlement 1701* was that the early Australian settlements at Sydney Cove, Norfolk Island, Hobart, Port Phillip and Moreton Bay were initially established as penal colonies. As foreign penitentiaries, they were ruled by autocratic governors whose terms of appointment gave them wide powers of administration and coercive control. Nonetheless, it became recognised by the courts of New South Wales, and was confirmed by British legislation,[123] that both convicts, officials and free settlers carried with them as much of the statutory and common law of England as was applicable to the circumstances of the colony.[124] And with this came the fundamental principle of the rule of law.

As understood in the nineteenth century, the rule of law meant that the powers of government can only be exercised according to pre-existing law and that all persons, no matter what their rank and status, are subject to the same set of legal rules and principles. As Dicey put it, 'the rule of law is contrasted with every system of government based on the exercise by persons in authority of wide, arbitrary, or discretionary powers of constraint', for it involves the principle that 'every official, from the Prime Minister down to a constable or a collector of taxes, is under the same responsibility for every act done without legal justification as any other citizen'.[125] According to David Neal, in early New South Wales, the rule of law initially called for something even more basic, namely the capacity of convicts to commence proceedings in court for the vindication of their legal rights.[126] Emancipated former convicts soon agitated for the rights to trial by jury, to serve on juries and to practise as lawyers. Proceedings were successfully brought before the courts to require Governors and their administrations to exercise their powers within the limits of the law. And although it did not come without struggle, emancipists, the native born and increasing numbers of free settlers eventually secured the right to participate in their own local self-government through the development of representative legislatures, responsible governments and control over their own constitutions.

## III Political development

### 1 Local self-government

When Australia was first settled by the British, the powers of the Governor over the penal colony of New South Wales were largely autocratic. He had power to

**123** *Australian Courts Act 1828* (UK), 9 George IV, c 83. Contemporary State laws clarify which Imperial legislation continues to operate: see, eg, *Imperial Acts Application Act 1969* (NSW), *Imperial Acts Application Act 1980* (Vic), *Imperial Acts Application Act 1984* (Qld).
**124** *Quan Yick v Hinds* (1905) 2 CLR 345, 366. See Alex Castles, 'The Reception and Status of English Law in Australia' (1963) 2 *Adelaide Law Review* 1.
**125** Dicey, above n 34, 180, 185.
**126** David Neal, *The Rule of Law in a Penal Colony* (Cambridge University Press, 1991) ch 1.

make rules or orders that had binding force. He could declare martial law. He could make grants of land as he saw fit. He appointed his military officers to be judges of the early criminal and civil courts established in the colony. There was no formal executive council that provided him with advice, and certainly no representative assembly to give expression to the views of the general population.[127] Apart from the Governor's humanitarian self-restraint, the only substantial limitation on the 'discretionary gubernatorial rule' which he exercised consisted in his accountability to the British government and to the general principles of British law operating within the colony.[128] The territory over which the Governor's authority theoretically extended was also vast. At its height, the colony of New South Wales extended to approximately two-thirds of the Australian continent, including Van Diemen's Land (Tasmania) and, for a short period, New Zealand as well.[129] Although additional settlements were soon established across the far reaches of the continent, they were all originally ruled by the Governor and his provincial administration located in Sydney.

However, largely under pressure from emancipated convicts, free settlers and their native born children, this gradually changed. Under the leadership of figures like William Charles Wentworth, there were increasing demands for the recognition within the colony of traditional British rights and liberties, such as trial by jury and representative government.[130] As a result of a commissioned report made by John Bigge, former Chief Justice of Trinidad, a Legislative Council for New South Wales, appointed by the King, was instituted in 1823.[131] The legislature was reconstituted in an expanded form in 1828,[132] but did not include locally-elected representatives until 1842.[133] Through the same period, the settlements at Hobart (1803), Moreton Bay (1824), Swan River (1829), Port Phillip Bay (1835) and Holdfast Bay (1836) were established as independent colonies, some at the time of settlement, others some time later: Van Diemen's Land in 1825, Western Australia in 1829, South Australia in 1836, Victoria in 1851 and Queensland in 1859. The territories of all these colonies except Western Australia were at one time a part of New South Wales.

If there was a general motivating goal behind these constitutional developments, it was the growing aspiration for 'local self-government', a principle which suggested not only that the colonists should be granted the capacity to govern themselves through representative institutions, but that these governing institutions should be 'local' to each settlement.[134] Accordingly, when local

**127** Castles, above n 110, ch 3.
**128** R D Lumb, *Australian Constitutionalism* (Butterworths, 1983) 38–9.
**129** A C V Melbourne, *Early Constitutional Development in Australia* (University of Queensland Press, 1963) 107.
**130** Peter Cochrane, *Colonial Ambition* (Melbourne University Press, 2006).
**131** *New South Wales Act 1823* (UK).
**132** *Australian Courts Act 1828* (UK). Compare *Western Australia Act 1829* (UK), establishing a similar Council for Western Australia.
**133** *Australian Constitutions Act (No 1) 1842* (UK), under which 12 members of the Legislative Council were appointed by the Queen and 24 were elected by the inhabitants of the colony.
**134** Nicholas Aroney, *The Constitution of a Federal Commonwealth* (Cambridge University Press, 2009) ch 5.

self-government was ultimately secured mid-way through the nineteenth century, it involved at least four basic elements, namely the separate establishment of each colony, the institution of elected legislative assemblies, the conferral of parliamentary responsible government, and the grant to each colony of the capacity to amend its own constitution. Thus, the separate establishment of Victoria in 1851 and Queensland in 1859 came as result of a 'struggle for separation' from New South Wales, in which colonists in those districts sought the same degree of independence that was being enjoyed elsewhere.[135] By the 1850s each of the Australian colonies had its own a bicameral legislature, consisting of a Legislative Assembly or House of Assembly (lower house) elected on a limited franchise and a Legislative Council (upper house) which was either also elected or consisted of members nominated by the Governor. Also by that time, every colony except Western Australia was granted responsible government, which meant that the powers of the Governor henceforth would ordinarily have to be exercised on the advice of ministers who had the confidence or support of the lower house of the colonial legislature.[136] Most of the colonies also secured at this time the power to amend their own constitutions – a capacity that was later extended to all British colonies possessing representative legislatures by the *Colonial Laws Validity Act 1865* (UK).[137] Western Australia, although established as a separate colony in 1829, did not obtain a bicameral legislature and responsible government until 1889/90.[138]

As a consequence of these developments, by the end of the nineteenth century there were six mutually-independent, self-governing colonies established in Australia, each governed under local adaptations of the Westminster system of parliamentary responsible government, and each possessing the capacity to amend their own constitutions. It was in this context that the Australian colonies began seriously to consider the possibility of federation, particularly from 1890 onwards. This status of the six colonies as self-governing and self-constituting political communities was the fundamental presupposition upon which they agreed to federate in 1901, under a Constitution which they each played an equal part in debating, drafting and approving.

## 2 Federal conventions

Although British authorities, such as Earl Grey, Secretary of State for War and the Colonies (1846–52),[139] had urged the Australian colonies to federate as

**135** W G McMinn, *A Constitutional History of Australia* (Oxford University Press, 1979) 35.
**136** R D Lumb, *The Constitutions of the Australian States* (University of Queensland Press, 5th ed, 1991) chs 1, 2. The key legal documents included *Australian Constitutions Act (No 2) 1850* (UK), *New South Wales Constitution Act 1855* (UK), *New South Wales Constitution Statute 1855* (UK), *Victoria Constitution Act 1855* (UK), *Constitution Act 1855–56* (SA) and Order in Council, 6 June 1859 (Qld). See also *Constitution Act 1867* (Qld).
**137** On the extent of colonial legislative power, see Chapter 3, Part II.1–2 and Chapter 10, Parts I, III and IV.
**138** *Constitution Act 1889* (WA). See also *Constitution Act 1899* (WA).
**139** John Ward, *Earl Grey and the Australian Colonies* (Melbourne University Press, 1958).

early as 1847, the idea was long resisted by local political leaders who were more concerned to establish the rights of each colony to its own local and independent self-government. As Quick and Garran explained:

> Local politics, and the development of local institutions, engrossed the attention of the people; and probably no colony would have been prepared to accept the compromises and the partial sacrifice of local independence which a federal union would have involved.[140]

This did not mean that the Australians were necessarily opposed to federation. Indeed, colonial leaders like Henry Parkes, John Dunmore Lang and James Wiltshire formed the Australian League in 1850 to pursue as one of its objectives the union of the colonies in a federation.[141] But most Australian political leaders were insistent that federation, if it were to occur, would have to be a local initiative, without any 'meddlesome interference' from England, as a former Premier of Queensland put it in a letter to his later Victorian counterpart.[142] It would also need to be on the basis of inter-colonial equality. Thus, early proposals by New South Wales which claimed a certain pre-eminence for the 'mother colony' were rejected by the other colonies on the ground that each would have to join as an 'equal contracting partner'.[143] The path forward, it seemed, had to be initiated and agreed to by the political leaders of all of the colonies.

A potentially important step was taken in 1883 when a conference of colonial premiers approved a bill for the establishment of a Federal Council of Australasia which had been drafted by the Queensland Premier, Samuel Griffith. The bill was enacted into law by the British Parliament in 1885,[144] but New South Wales never attended meetings of the Council, and it fell into disuse. Rather, it was not until 1889, when the Premier of New South Wales, Henry Parkes, gave a stirring and now famous speech in favour of federation at the border town of Tenterfield in northern New South Wales that the cause of federation received the invigoration and support that it needed. Declaring that the time for a union of the colonies had come, Parkes proposed that the legislatures of each colony should appoint delegates to attend a convention to draft a constitution under which the colonies might federate.

The Australasian Federation Conference, which was accordingly held in Melbourne in 1890, was the first opportunity for colonial leaders to debate in some detail the kind of federation they thought best. Parkes argued that Canada presented the most appropriate model, but he was met by Inglis Clark, Griffith and several others who maintained that the United States presented a more

**140** Quick and Garran, above n 2, 99–100.
**141** See, eg, John Dunmore Lang, *The Coming Event, or Freedom and Independence for the Seven United Provinces of Australia* (Sherriff, 1870).
**142** Charles Lilley to Charles Gavan Duffy, 7 November 1870, *Papers of Sir Charles Gavan Duffy* (State Library of Victoria). Lilley was Premier of Queensland (1868–70) and Chief Justice of the Supreme Court of Queensland (1879–93); Duffy was Premier of Victoria (1871–2).
**143** Aroney, above n 134, 138–45.
**144** *Federal Council of Australasia Act 1885* (UK).

appropriate scheme of federation. The Canadian system was considered by them to be too imperialist, unitary and centralist. The Canadian provinces had formulated a series of general resolutions under which they had agreed to unite, but the exact terms of the union as stipulated in the *British North America Act 1867* (UK) had been drafted and enacted into law by the British authorities, and Canadians were not given a general power to make constitutional amendments to the arrangement. The powers of the central government in Canada were wider and more general than those of the constituent provinces, it was thought, and there were several respects in which the provinces were made subordinate to the central authority. Furthermore, the provinces were not all treated as equal partners in the federation. In comparison, the United States Constitution had been drafted and agreed to by representatives of each of the constituent States and therefore presupposed their equal status as independent, self-governing and self-constituting political communities. A true federation, Inglis Clark argued, would ensure that each local legislature remained sovereign within its own sphere, the federation would be granted only limited powers, and the federal legislature would necessarily consist of two houses, one of which represented the constituent states on an equal basis. Such a model, he and his colleagues generally agreed, was most appropriate for Australia. For, as Griffith put it, the Australians had been 'accustomed for so long to self-government' that they regarded themselves as having become 'practically almost sovereign states', indeed 'a great deal more sovereign states, though not in name, than the separate states of America'.[145]

The conference of 1890 agreed to a proposal of Alfred Deakin that the colonial legislatures should appoint delegates to a National Australasian Convention empowered to 'consider and report upon an adequate scheme for a Federal Constitution'.[146] This convention was duly held in 1891 in Sydney. It was composed of delegates nominated by the legislatures of the Australian colonies, as well as New Zealand. Each Australian colony was equally represented, and the representation was bipartisan: the delegates included both conservatives and liberals, protectionists and free traders. Only the emergent labour party was not directly represented, for it would be another decade before representatives of labour interests were routinely elected in substantial numbers to the Australian legislatures.

Unlike the famous convention that was held in Philadelphia in 1787 at which the US Constitution was drafted, delegates to the Australasian federal convention of 1891 agreed to admit the press to the proceedings and ensured that an official and complete record of their formal deliberations was made public.[147] The convention of 1891 began by debating a series of resolutions proposed by Henry Parkes, and then proceeded to draft a Constitution Bill for eventual consideration

**145** *Official Record of the Proceedings and Debates of the Australasian Federation Conference, Melbourne* (1890) 10.
**146** Ibid, 261.
**147** *Official Report of the National Australasian Convention Debates, Sydney* (1891) 9–10, 12–22, 937–8.

by the colonial legislatures.[148] Parkes' resolutions were concerned, among other things, to ensure that: (1) the powers, privileges and territorial rights of the colonies would remain intact except as was agreed to be necessary to form a federal government; (2) trade and intercourse between the federated colonies would be absolutely free; (3) the federal parliament would consist of a senate and a house of representatives, the former consisting of an equal number of members from each colony, and the latter to be elected by districts formed on a population basis; (4) a federal court would be established constituting a high court of appeal for the whole of Australia; and (5) the federal executive government would be responsible to the lower house of the federal parliament. There was general agreement about these resolutions, except on two points. On one hand, a large number of delegates questioned whether in a genuine federation the executive government should be responsible only to the lower house of the federal parliament, given that it is in the upper house that the states are particularly represented. On the other hand, a different group of delegates questioned whether the states should be equally represented in the Senate, arguing that this was inconsistent with the idea of a national democracy governed by elected representatives of the people of the federation as a whole. These two distinct visions of the kind of federation that Australia would become went to the heart of the debate over the design of the Australian Constitution. They were competing visions that had deep roots in Western political and constitutional thought.

Two delegates, Inglis Clark and Charles Kingston, came to the Convention of 1891 with draft constitutions. After debating Parkes's resolutions, a drafting committee consisting of Griffith, Inglis Clark, Kingston and later Edmund Barton, prepared a Constitution Bill which reflected many, but not all, of the structural ideas and fundamental principles contained in Inglis Clark's draft. These included: (a) distinct chapters separately establishing the legislative, executive and judicial branches of the federal government; (b) the principle that the states would continue to exercise general legislative and governing powers subject only to the specific responsibilities conferred upon the federation; and (c) the principle of equal representation of the states in the federal upper house. Ultimately, the federal convention approved a Constitution Bill that broadly gave effect to these principles.

The Constitution Bill of 1891 did not receive a warm reception in the colonial parliaments, and the momentum towards federation stalled until, at an informal 'People's Convention' held at Bathurst in 1895, John Quick proposed that a second convention be held, this time to be elected directly by the voters of each colony, on the understanding that each legislature would commit itself to submitting the resulting draft constitution to the voters in a referendum and, if so approved, present it to the British authorities for enactment into law. A federal convention on this basis was held between 1897 and 1898, with successive sittings in Adelaide, Sydney and Melbourne. As in 1891, the convention

**148** Ibid, 23.

began by debating a series of fundamental resolutions, this time prepared by Barton, the acknowledged leader of the convention. The convention ultimately produced a draft constitution the basic structure and principles of which were largely similar to those of the draft of 1891 except that the senate was to be directly elected by the voters of each state rather than chosen by the state legislatures, and the constitution itself could be amended by a referendum in which a majority of people of the entire federation and a majority of people in a majority of states approved the proposed change. This draft constitution was eventually approved by the voters in each Australian colony and duly enacted into law by the British Parliament in 1900. The Commonwealth of Australia came into being as a federation on 1 January 1901.

This formative process, and the constitutional principles and values that it presupposed, informed the deliberations and shaped the institutions created by the Constitution in several fundamental ways. Having come into being through a federal compact among pre-existing, self-governing colonies, the Constitution established a federal commonwealth consisting of co-existing federal and state institutions of government, the jurisdictions of which were carefully defined and limited. The Commonwealth's powers were confined to particular topics; the federal Parliament was designed to represent and be accountable to both the people of the States and the people of the federation as a whole; and the Constitution itself could only be altered with the consent of the people of the Commonwealth and the peoples of the States. The foundation, structure, intended operation and anticipated development of the Constitution was in these and many other ways shaped fundamentally by the principles and the aspirations which motivated the framers. Whether all of their hopes and expectations have been fulfilled is an important question, but the fact that they believed in such principles and endeavoured, despite their disagreements, to embody them in the Constitution, is undeniable. Much of this book will be concerned to describe and explain the practical working of Australia's constitutional system, and to assess exactly how far the practices of its parliaments, governments and courts have been faithful to that constitutional vision.

## IV Institutions and principles

### 1 Commonwealth institutions

The entire body of constitutional law operating in Australia identifies and defines the institutions of government of the Commonwealth and the States, confers powers on them and controls their exercise. Australia's governing institutions exercise various legal powers, principally the power to make law, the power to execute or administer law, and the power to resolve disputes over the meaning and application of law. The constitutional law of the Commonwealth, as well as the constitutional law of each of the States, vests these powers in separate institutions called the Parliament, the Executive Government and the Judicature or Courts.[149]

The legislative power of the Commonwealth is vested in the Commonwealth Parliament, which consists of the Queen, the Senate and the House of Representatives (s 1). The Senate is composed of senators chosen by the people of the States, each Original State being equally represented (s 7). It presently consists of 76 senators, 12 senators representing each of the six States and two senators representing each of the two self-governing mainland Territories. The House of Representatives is composed of members chosen by the people of the Commonwealth as a whole (s 24). It presently consists of 150 members, each representing a particular local electoral district.[150] The legislative powers of the Commonwealth Parliament are limited to a specific list of topics. Most of these legislative powers are concurrent with the States (s 51), while a smaller number are exclusive to the Commonwealth (s 52).[151] The general legislative powers of the States conferred by their respective Constitutions are declared to continue under the federation, subject to the Commonwealth Constitution (ss 106 and 107). The States accordingly are not able to legislate with respect to matters that fall within the exclusive jurisdiction of the Commonwealth or are expressly removed from them by prohibitions contained in the Constitution (ss 52, 90, 92). The Constitution also provides that if there is an inconsistency between a Commonwealth and a State law, the Commonwealth law prevails to the extent of the inconsistency (s 109).[152]

The executive power of the Commonwealth is formally vested in the Queen and is exercised by her representative in Australia, the Governor-General (s 61). The Constitution also provides for a Federal Executive Council to advise the Governor-General (s 62), and empowers the Governor-General to appoint ministers of State to administer such departments as the Governor-General may establish (s 64). Consistent with the principles of parliamentary responsible government, such ministers cannot hold office for more than three months unless they are elected as members of Parliament (s 64). This ensures that ministers, including the Prime Minister, have been elected by the people to hold seats in Parliament and can be held to account by the Parliament. In accordance with the practices of responsible government, the Governor-General ordinarily exercises the executive power of the Commonwealth on the advice of the Prime Minister and other ministers. The Prime Minister and a group of senior ministers responsible for the major government departments comprise the Cabinet, which meets regularly to determine the most important matters of government policy. A small number of the Governor-General's powers, commonly called 'reserve powers', are exercised apart from the advice of the ministers. These primarily involve decisions to appoint and dismiss the Prime Minister on the basis of whether that

**149** See Commonwealth Constitution, chs I, II and III.
**150** For more detail, see Chapter 2, Part II.
**151** See Chapter 3, Parts III–IV.
**152** See Chapter 4, Part II.

person has the support of the Parliament. The support of Parliament is ordinarily indicated by the passage of the annual financial appropriation bills which authorise government expenditure (commonly called the 'supply' bills) (ss 81 and 83). It can also be indicated by a vote of confidence in the House of Representatives. There is a tension in the Australian constitutional system insofar as the Senate also has the power to refuse to pass the appropriation bills, a possibility which actually occurred in 1975. The Prime Minister refused to resign and the Governor-General controversially exercised his 'reserve powers' to dismiss him.[153]

The judicial power of the Commonwealth is vested in the High Court of Australia, such other federal courts as may be created by the Commonwealth, and such State courts as the Commonwealth chooses to invest with federal jurisdiction (s 71). All federal judges hold office until the age of 70, and can only be removed for proved misbehaviour on an address from both houses of the Commonwealth Parliament (s 72). The High Court of Australia has constitutional jurisdiction to hear appeals from the supreme courts of the States (s 73). It also has original jurisdiction in matters concerning the interpretation of the Constitution, the interpretation of a federal law, and several other matters (s 76). As a result, the High Court has the authority to determine whether a Commonwealth or State law is consistent with the Constitution as well as whether action by the Commonwealth or State executive is lawful. This power of judicial review can result in a declaration by the Court that such laws or executive actions are constitutionally invalid or *ultra vires* (beyond power) and therefore void and of no legal effect.[154] Much of this book will be concerned with decisions of the Court in which it has been asked to exercise this power of judicial review. The Constitution also originally preserved the appellate jurisdiction of the Judicial Committee of the Privy Council, except that no such appeal would lie in cases involving a question as to the limits inter se of the constitutional powers of the Commonwealth and the States without the certification of the High Court (s 74).[155]

Similar legislative, executive and judicial institutions exist in each of the Australian States, as well as the two mainland self-governing Territories.[156] Queensland and the two Territories are partial exceptions, in that they each only have one house of Parliament, the Legislative Assembly, whereas the Parliaments of the other five States each have two houses, the Legislative Council and the Legislative Assembly or House of Assembly. The constitutional systems of the Commonwealth, the States and the Territories are also different in that while the Commonwealth Constitution can only be changed following approval at a referendum (s 128), the State Constitutions are ordinarily statutes of the State

**153** For more detail, see Chapter 6, Parts I and V.
**154** Because this function of judicial review has a significant influence on the development and functioning of the Australian federal system, the Attorneys-General of the States and the Commonwealth have standing to commence proceedings to challenge the constitutionality of statutes: see *Attorney-General (NSW) v Brewery Employees Union of New South Wales* (1908) 6 CLR 469, 499–500, 520, 552–3, 557–8; see also 597–9.
**155** The Australian jurisdiction of the Privy Council has since been abolished. See Part V.1 below and Chapter 8, Part II.
**156** The Australian Capital Territory and the Northern Territory.

Parliaments. As a consequence, the general principle is that the State Constitutions can be amended by ordinary State legislation. However, there are also certain 'manner and form' provisions in the State Constitutions that for some kinds of constitutional changes require special procedures to be followed, such as special majorities in the Parliament or approval at a referendum.[157]

## 2 Fundamental principles

As the historical context and political development of Australia suggests, there are at least five fundamental principles which underlie the Australian constitutional system. These are the rule of law, parliamentary sovereignty, judicial review, the separation of powers, representative and responsible government, and federalism. There are many other principles, practices, conceptions and values that are part of the general Western idea of law that Australia has inherited,[158] but these five principles are the most decisively important for understanding the Australian constitutional system.

As explained earlier, the rule of law essentially means that all government power is established and limited by pre-existing law. As a consequence, all of Australia's governing institutions, including the Executive Government, the Parliament and the High Court are deemed to be subject to the law, including and especially the law of the Constitution. Individuals who hold and exercise executive power, including the Queen, the Governor-General, the State Governors, the Prime Minister, the State Premiers and other Commonwealth and State ministers, are all bound by and accountable to the law. The Commonwealth and State Parliaments are not able to make laws that are contrary to the Commonwealth and State Constitutions. Federal and State courts, including the High Court of Australia, are responsible for applying the law in the cases that come before them.

Parliamentary sovereignty has a qualified meaning in Australia and must be understood together with the principle of judicial review. While in the United Kingdom, parliamentary sovereignty means that the courts must always, in the final analysis, apply the law enacted by the Parliament, in Australia the powers of the Commonwealth and State Parliaments are limited by the Constitution, and it is ultimately the responsibility of the courts to exercise judicial review by applying the Constitution in priority to ordinary statutes and government actions.[159] In Australia the principle of parliamentary sovereignty still has an application, however, for governments remain subject to any validly enacted parliamentary statute and, provided a statute is consistent with the Constitution, the courts are responsible to apply it to the case at hand.

**157** For more detail, see Chapter 10, Part IV.4.
**158** For an introduction to the Western legal tradition in relation to Australia, see Patrick Parkinson, *Tradition and Change in Australian Law* (Law Book Company, 1994) ch 2.
**159** This basic idea is traceable to Alexander Hamilton, *Federalist No* 78 (1788), in Rossiter, above n 84, and *Marbury v Madison* 5 US 137 (1803), which established the exercise of judicial review in the United States. On the framers' expectation that it would apply in Australia, see Brian Galligan, *Politics of the High Court* (University of Queensland Press, 1987) ch 2.

The separation of powers supports the operation of these principles in several ways. In particular, it ensures that the courts are independent of the Executive and are able to use their own unfettered judgement concerning the application of the law, including the Constitution, to alleged breaches of the law. The separation of powers thus supports the courts in their independent exercise of judicial review in relation to both executive action and legislation enacted by the Parliament. As such, it helps to ensure that the rule of law is maintained. The principles of representative and responsible government are also of major importance within the constitutional system. In short, they ensure that members of Parliament are elected by the people and that ministers of State are responsible to the Parliament for their administration of the government.

Finally, Australia is a federation, and the effective operation of the federation depends also on these principles. The rule of law, the separation of powers and judicial review help to ensure that the Commonwealth and the States only exercise those powers and responsibilities that are given to them under the Constitution. These principles, as well as those of representative and responsible government, necessarily apply to both the Commonwealth and the States.

The operation of these principles is not always complete or ideal, and there are important qualifications on their operation at a Commonwealth and State level. In particular, the separation of powers is not fully implemented because parliamentary responsible government effectively enables the political leaders of the political party or coalition of parties that holds a majority in the lower house of Parliament to exercise a great deal of control over the legislative agenda of the Parliament, as well as to control the exercise of executive power. It is the existence of an upper house at both a Commonwealth and State level that can help to ensure that the leaders of the governing party or parties will only be able to have their preferred laws enacted with the agreement of the party, parties or independent members which constitute a majority of the upper house.[160]

## V Constitutionalism in practice

### 1 Political change and constitutional evolution

The practical operation of Australia's constitutional system of government is primarily shaped by the interaction between Australia's governing institutions at a Commonwealth and State level, operating under the influence of the electoral process, popular and elite opinion, and the scrutiny of the media and many other public and private bodies and institutions. Over the course of time, the size of government has increased dramatically and the balance of power has

**160** See Samuel Charles Patterson and Anthony Mughan, *Senates* (Ohio State University Press, 1999); J Luther, P Passaglia and R Tarchi (eds), *A World of Second Chambers* (Giuffre Editore, 2006); Nicholas Aroney, Scott Prasser and John Nethercote (eds), *Restraining Elective Dictatorship* (University of Western Australia Press, 2008).

shifted increasingly towards the Commonwealth over the States. Party discipline has enabled Executive Governments to exercise greater control over their Parliaments than was possible around the time of federation. Federal and State courts have been vigilant to maintain the rule of law, and governments have generally been respectful of their constitutional role. The High Court has been less concerned to maintain an appropriate balance of power between the Commonwealth and the States; indeed, it has repeatedly denied that its role is to maintain such a 'balance'.[161]

Between 1903 and 1920, the High Court tended to interpret the Constitution in a manner that gave effect to it as a federal compact between the States. On this view, it was understood that the Commonwealth's powers over such matters as interstate trade and commerce, trading and financial corporations and external affairs[162] were deliberately limited so as to enable the States to continue to operate as autonomous governments exercising independent governing authority over many important matters, such as public education, hospitals, transport and crime. However, in 1920, the High Court rejected the idea that the Constitution should be interpreted as a federal compact, and regarded it rather as a British statute that confers powers upon the Commonwealth which should be interpreted as widely as the language used can possibly sustain, without any consideration of the 'residue' of responsibilities left to the States.[163] Over the course of time, this approach to constitutional interpretation has led the High Court to approve laws enacted by the Commonwealth which very substantially regulate matters such as education, hospitals and transport, despite the States' primary responsibility for these and other matters. The High Court has also approved the Commonwealth's monopolisation of the imposition and collection of income taxes,[164] in addition to its exclusive control over customs duties and excise duties (s 90),[165] and has affirmed the Commonwealth's capacity to make financial grants to the States on the conditions that it sees fit (s 96).[166] A great deal of Commonwealth regulation of matters originally understood to be reserved to the States is achieved through these mechanisms.

By contrast, the High Court has generally been more concerned to ensure that the separation of powers is maintained between the courts and the other two branches of government. In order to maintain the independence of the judiciary, the High Court has insisted that the independence of the judiciary must be maintained so that functions cannot be conferred upon federal courts that are inconsistent with the exercise of judicial power, and that functions cannot be conferred upon the political branches of government which are inconsistent

**161** Most recently in *New South Wales v Commonwealth* (2006) 229 CLR 1, discussed in Chapter 3, Part IV.1.
**162** See Commonwealth Constitution, s 51(i), (xx), (xxix).
**163** *Amalgamated Society of Engineers v Adelaide Steamship Co Ltd* (1920) 28 CLR 129. For more detail, see Chapter 3, Part III.2 and Chapter 4, Part III.2.
**164** *South Australia v Commonwealth* (1942) 65 CLR 373; *Victoria v Commonwealth* (1957) 99 CLR 575.
**165** See *Ha v New South Wales* (1997) 189 CLR 465.
**166** See *Victoria v Commonwealth* (1926) 38 CLR 399; *ICM Agriculture Pty Ltd v Commonwealth* (2009) 240 CLR 140.

with the judicial power that is exclusively vested in the courts.[167] Similarly, the High Court has held that the constitutional provision for a system of representative and responsible government implies that none of the Australian parliaments can make a law which unduly interferes with freedom of communication with respect to political matters.[168] Whether the framers of the Australian Constitution intended this to be the case and whether this is a valid inference to be drawn from the text and structure of the Constitution is widely debated.

According to some judges and commentators,[169] the High Court has through its interpretation helped to keep the Constitution 'up-to-date', even though the people have generally rejected proposals to amend the Constitution when these have been put to referendum. So far, of 44 constitutional amendment proposals, only eight have been successful. Most of the proposals have involved, in one way or another, an increase in the powers and responsibilities of the Commonwealth at the expense of the States. Most have failed simply because they did not secure majority support among the people of Australia as a whole, let alone support of the majority of people in a majority of States as is also required by s 128 of the Constitution.

Australia's constitutional system of government has also evolved through the gradual cutting of Australia's legal and political ties to the United Kingdom. At an Imperial Conference held in 1926, political leaders of countries within the British Empire unanimously agreed to a statement, commonly known as the Balfour Declaration,[170] which acknowledged and declared that such countries, including Australia:

> are autonomous Communities within the British Empire, equal in status, in no way subordinate one to another in any aspect of their domestic or external affairs, though united by a common allegiance to the Crown, and freely associated as members of the British Commonwealth of Nations.[171]

As a consequence of this statement, it was further acknowledged that the Governor-General of each such 'Dominion' was not a representative or agent of the British government but of the Crown, responsible to act on the advice of the ministers of State responsible to the Parliament of the Dominion. Soon thereafter, the British Parliament enacted the *Statute of Westminster 1931*, which affirmed, among other things, that no Act of the Parliament would henceforth apply to a Dominion unless it was expressly declared that the Dominion had requested and consented to its enactment, that no law of a Dominion would be

**167** *R v Kirby; Ex parte Boilermakers' Society of Australia* (1956) 94 CLR 254. For more detail, see Chapter 9, Parts II and III.

**168** *Australian Capital Television Pty Ltd v Commonwealth* (1992) 177 CLR 106; *Lange v Australian Broadcasting Corporation* (1997) 189 CLR 520, discussed in Chapter 5, Part V.

**169** Michael Kirby, 'Constitutional Interpretation and Original Intent' (2000) 24(1) *Melbourne University Law* Review 1.

**170** The declaration was drafted by the Inter-Imperial Relations Committee of the Imperial Conference under the Chairmanship of Lord Arthur Balfour (1848–1930), a former Prime Minister, Foreign Secretary and at the time Lord President of the Privy Council.

**171** Inter-Imperial Relations Committee, *Report, Proceedings and Memoranda* (Imperial Conference, 1926).

void or inoperative on the ground that it is repugnant to the law of England or to an Act of the British Parliament, and that each Dominion Parliament would in general have the capacity to repeal or amend any British statute which applied to the Dominion.[172] While the *Statute of Westminster* applied immediately to Canada, Ireland and South Africa, it did not apply to Australia, New Zealand or Newfoundland until adopted by them. The Australian Parliament enacted the *Statute of Westminster Adoption Act* in 1942, which gave the *Statute of Westminster* retrospective operation from 3 September 1939, to coincide with the beginning of the Second World War.

In 1968, the Commonwealth Parliament passed a law which significantly limited the range of cases that could be appealed to the Privy Council from decisions of the High Court, by requiring, in effect, that such appeals must not involve the interpretation of the Constitution or a law of the Parliament and must not arise from the decision of a State Supreme Court exercising federal jurisdiction.[173] In 1975, even this limited range of appeals from the High Court to the Privy Council was abolished.[174] Most recently, the British, Commonwealth and Australian State parliaments cooperated in the enactment of the *Australia Acts 1986* (UK and Cth).[175] By these statutes, the capacity of the British Parliament to legislate for Australia was abolished altogether, as were all remaining avenues of appeal to the Privy Council, such as directly from a decision of a State Supreme Court.[176]

Bearing in mind the fundamental role played by the British Parliament in the enactment of the Australian Constitution and in the establishment of the Australian States, the passage of the *Australia Acts* was a profoundly important milestone in Australia's constitutional development.[177] Indeed, it appears to have prompted members of the High Court to reconsider the fundamental nature of the Australian Constitution and the implications that this might have for its interpretation. Even though the Australian Constitution is still contained in a British statute, it has nonetheless been suggested by several High Court justices that its legitimacy, if not also its legal validity and bindingness, must now be understood to rest upon its acceptance by the Australian people.[178] This conception of the Constitution provided some members of the High Court with reason to conclude that the Constitution's provision for a system of representative democracy necessarily implies the existence of a constitutional freedom of political communication, and it has been suggested that other civil and political

**172** *Statute of Westminster 1931* (UK), ss 2, 4.
**173** *Privy Council (Limitation of Appeals) Act 1968* (Cth).
**174** *Privy Council (Appeals from the High Court) Act 1975* (Cth).
**175** See Peter Oliver, *The Constitution of Independence* (Oxford University Press, 2005) and Anne Twomey, *The Australia Acts 1986* (Federation Press, 2010).
**176** See, generally, *Sue v Hill* (1999) 199 CLR 462; *Fitzgibbon v HM Attorney-General* [2005] EWHC 114 (Ch). For more detail, see Chapter 8, Part II and Chapter 10, Part IV.1.
**177** Geoffrey Lindell, 'Why Is Australia's Constitution Binding?' (1986) 16 *Federal Law Review* 29.
**178** *Australian Capital Television Pty Ltd v Commonwealth* (1992) 177 CLR 106, 138; *Theophanous v Herald & Weekly Times Ltd* (1994) 182 CLR 104, 171, 173; *McGinty v Western Australia* (1996) 186 CLR 140, 230. See also *Joosse v Australian Securities and Investment Commission* (1998) 159 ALR 260, 264.

rights might also be implied.[179] In one such case, *McGinty v Western Australia*, it was argued that the democratic foundations of the Constitution necessarily imply that both Commonwealth and State electoral boundaries must be constructed so that each electorate contains an approximately equal number of voters in order to ensure that all voters have equal 'voting power'. In considering this argument, a majority of the High Court pointed out that the Constitution provides not only for a system of representative democracy, but for a federal democracy in which the people of each State are equally represented in the Senate notwithstanding the vastly different populations of the States. This 'adaptation' of the principles of democracy to federalism, it was pointed out, means that the Constitution cannot be conceived to rest upon an abstract principle of equality of voting power, for in relation to the Senate voters in Tasmania have substantially greater 'voting power' than those in New South Wales, and yet this is a legitimate and important feature of the federal system.[180] It was also pointed out, in response to the argument that the legitimacy of the Australian Constitution rests in its acceptance by the Australian people, that there are several features of the Australian Constitution and the *Australia Acts* which point to the role, not only of the people and governing institutions of the Commonwealth as a whole, but of the peoples and governing institutions of the constituent States. In particular, it was noted that, consistently with s 51(xxxviii) of the Constitution, the Commonwealth version of the *Australia Act* was itself enacted following the request and consent of the Parliaments of the Australian States. Moreover, the Australian Constitution can only be amended with the agreement of a majority of people in a majority of States, and changes to the boundaries of a State or of its representation in the Commonwealth Parliament can only be altered with the agreement of the people of that State.[181] It was pointed out that Australia's Constitution thus rests upon principles that are not only democratic, but also thoroughly federal in character.

## 2 Methods of interpretation

In its determination of constitutional issues, the High Court routinely uses several different techniques of legal reasoning and constitutional interpretation.[182] These may conveniently be classified into arguments based on text, structure, history, ethics, prudence and comparison.[183] Textual argument and interpretation focuses on the exact words, phrases and sentences used in the Constitution

**179** John Toohey, 'A Government of Laws and Not of Men?' (1993) 4 *Public Law Review* 158.
**180** *McGinty v Western Australia* (1996) 186 CLR 140, 236–40, 243–5, 266–7, 269–78, 291–2.
**181** Ibid, 274–5. For more detail, see Chapter 2, Part II.3.
**182** See the discussion, in Chapter 2, Part II.3, of *Attorney-General (Cth); Ex rel McKinlay v Commonwealth* (1975) 135 CLR 1 and *McGinty v Western Australia* (1996) 186 CLR 140.
**183** Philip Bobbitt, *Constitutional Fate* (Oxford University Press, 1982). Bobbitt does not refer to comparison, but adds 'doctrine', meaning the precedents and reasoning of the courts themselves, as another modality of constitutional reasoning. For more detail, see Peter Gerangelos et al, *Winterton's Australian Federal Constitutional Law* (Thomson Reuters, 3rd ed, 2013) ch 14.

and seeks to interpret them in accordance with their ordinary or natural meaning. Such an approach is sometimes called 'literalism'. One important reason why this approach is advocated is that a Constitution, like a statute or other written source of law, is typically drafted and approved by groups of elected representatives who, after due debate, determine by majority vote upon a specific form of words as the authoritative result of their deliberations.[184] Unlike structuralism, textualism is not so much concerned with understanding the Constitution's text within the context of the document as a whole, but rather with the words of the specific clause or section that is being interpreted and applied in a particular case. Unlike historical approaches to interpretation, textualism does not draw upon external evidence that might shed light on the intention or understanding of the text at the time that the Constitution was enacted, but focuses on the words themselves, understood in their ordinary or natural meaning. This does not mean that textualism necessarily leads to what is sometimes called 'progressivism', an approach that seeks to adapt the Constitution to contemporary understandings, expectations or values, but it can have this effect if the ordinary meaning of the Constitution is identified by reference to current understandings of that meaning. Similarly, textualism generally resists what is sometimes called ethical interpretation, except to the extent that the Constitution uses words that themselves are morally-laden, for the textual approach to interpretation generally does not seek to go beyond the words to underlying principles or moral purposes that the Constitution might be thought to presuppose or imply without saying so explicitly. Nor does textualism seek to interpret the Constitution in a manner that takes into consideration the practical effects of the law, or any other prudential considerations which might otherwise influence a pragmatic decision-maker. Purely conceived and applied, textualism focuses on the actual words used in the Constitution to the exclusion of all other considerations and potential sources of law, such as the constitutions of other countries and the constitutional decisions of their courts.

Structuralism is a method of interpretation that is especially concerned to understand specific constitutional texts in the context of the Constitution as a whole.[185] Such an approach to interpretation seeks to understand how each part of the Constitution makes sense in connection with the Constitution's other aspects. Because constitutions make provision for the governing institutions of a country, structuralism is usually oriented to the establishment and functioning of these institutions. A structuralist approach will often be concerned with the practical operation of the Constitution, and it can readily lead an interpreter to consider whether the Constitution's institutions are operating as originally intended or as they should operate as a matter of ethical principle or political morality.[186] However, considerations of practical effectiveness, original intention

**184** Jeremy Waldron, *Law and Disagreement* (Oxford University Press, 1999) ch 4.
**185** Charles Black, *Structure and Relationship in Constitutional Law* (Louisiana State University Press, 1969).
**186** John Hart Ely, *Democracy and Distrust* (Harvard University Press, 1980).

and political principle represent distinguishable approaches to constitutional interpretation which are not necessarily focused on the structural features of the Constitution considered as a document. Structuralism, when disciplined by the Constitution conceived as an authoritative document, is closer to textualism than these other methods of constitutional interpretation and argument.[187]

Historical methods of constitutional interpretation seek to understand the Constitution in the light of reliable external evidence of its intended or generally understood meaning at the time of its enactment.[188] Sometimes called 'intentionalism' or 'originalism', these approaches are similar to textualism and structuralism in their respect for the Constitution understood as an authoritative document, but they maintain that the meaning of the Constitution ought to be historically ascertained. Intentionalism, as distinct from originalism, seeks to identify the actual subjective intentions of the persons by whose authority the Constitution was enacted as law. Intentionalism is thus usually tied to a theory of law which sees it as the authoritative will of a legislator.[189] In the case of democratically enacted constitutions, this legislator is understood to be either the people or the democratically elected representatives of the people, meeting together in a constitutional assembly or convention. Originalism, by contrast, seeks to identify how the Constitution was understood at the time that it was enacted. Originalists often defend this approach as being required by the very nature of language and the necessary conditions of effective communication. On this view, when a speaker's words are ambiguous or vague (which is almost always the case in some respect), their meaning is conventionally and most reliably ascertained by reference to external evidence of what the speaker must have meant when the words were uttered.[190] Both intentionalists and originalists have to acknowledge that the necessary external evidence of intent or meaning is not always readily available, and that the intentions of a group of legislators or the understandings of the then contemporary community of language users can be difficult to ascertain. However, they are aware of these issues and offer well-reasoned defences of their approaches to interpretation.[191]

Historical methods of interpretation are not altogether unrelated to ethical, prudential and comparative methods of constitutional interpretation and argument. This is because historical enquiry can shed light on the ethical principles, prudential compromises and comparative models which demonstrably influenced the framers of a constitution. However, ethical, prudential and comparative arguments can also be understood and applied in a way that decouples

**187** Laurence Tribe, 'Taking Text and Structure Seriously' (1995) 108 *Harvard Law Review* 1221.
**188** Jeffrey Goldsworthy, 'Constitutional Interpretation: Originalism' (2009) 4(4) *Philosophy Compass* 682.
**189** Richard Kay, 'Adherence to the Original Intentions in Constitutional Adjudication' (1988) 82 *Northwestern University Law Review* 226.
**190** Jeffrey Goldsworthy, 'Implications in Language, Law and the Constitution' in Geoffrey Lindell (ed), *Future Directions in Australian Constitutional Law* (Federation Press, 1994) 150.
**191** Richard Ekins, *The Nature of Legislative Intent* (Oxford University Press, 2012).

them from strictly historical, textual and structural methods of interpretation.[192] Some forms of ethical constitutional reasoning claim that what is being discovered and applied is nothing more than the ethical principles and purposes that actually motivated the framers of the Constitution or are necessarily implied by its text, structure and institutional design.[193] However, these approaches to constitutional interpretation and reasoning usually articulate the requisite principles and purposes at a level which is much more abstract than the Constitution's text and structure necessarily implies. Ethical approaches to constitutional interpretation are often less concerned to show that such principles are necessarily implied by the Constitution than to demonstrate and rely upon the moral force of the principles themselves or their supposed consistency with contemporary or prevailing values and expectations.[194] Similar observations can be made about approaches to constitutional reasoning which emphasise the role of practical or economic consequences of the law or prudential considerations about the function of the courts in the context of the political system as a whole – consisting as it does of various forces, pressures and influences, which the court must consider, balance and negotiate.[195]

Comparative constitutional law can similarly be used to shed light on a constitution conceived as an authoritative document, or to enable the injection of ethical principles or apparently more universal values into the constitutional reasoning of a particular country. When the Australian Constitution was drafted, the framers drew critically on other constitutional models, such as those of the United Kingdom, the United States, Canada, Switzerland and Germany. In some respects, they deliberately sought to incorporate aspects of those models into their design of the Australian Constitution; in other respects, they deliberately rejected certain aspects of those models. Understanding the Australian Constitution in comparative perspective can thus shed light on its text, structure and historical meaning. However, when decoupled from the task of interpreting the Constitution as an authoritative document, comparative constitutional law can also be used as a means of drawing upon values or principles recognised in other countries in order to avoid aspects of the text, structure or original understanding of the Constitution. Foreign constitutional law is sometimes used by judges in this way, as are aspects of international law, especially international human rights law, but its undisciplined use remains controversial.[196]

**192** Thomas Grey, 'Do We Have an Unwritten Constitution?' (1975) 27 *Stanford Law Review* 703.

**193** Ronald Dworkin, *A Matter of Principle* (Clarendon Press, 1986).

**194** Sotirios Barber and James Fleming, *Constitutional Interpretation* (Oxford University Press, 2007).

**195** Anthony Kronman, 'Alexander Bickel's Philosophy of Prudence' (1985) 94 *Yale Law Journal* 1567; Richard Posner, 'The Constitution as an Economic Document' (1987) 56 *George Washington Law Review* 4.

**196** Cheryl Saunders, 'The Use and Misuse of Comparative Constitutional Law' (2006) 13 *Indiana Journal of Global Legal Studies* 37; Nicholas Aroney, 'Comparative Law in Australian Constitutional Jurisprudence' (2007) 26(2) *University of Queensland Law Journal* 317; Adrienne Stone, 'Comparativism in Constitutional Interpretation' [2009] *New Zealand Law Review* 45.

## 3 Explanation and evaluation

Books on constitutional law, including the present one, unavoidably adopt particular stances in relation to the appropriateness or desirability of each of these methods of constitutional interpretation. In this book, our general perspective is documentarian.[197] Our goal is to explain the law of the Australian Constitution as interpreted by the High Court, and to evaluate the High Court's interpretations in the light of the Constitution itself considered as an authoritative document, focusing upon its text and structure, understood in the light of its enactment history. Approached in this way, the Constitution undoubtedly presupposes certain ethical principles, seeks to establish certain political institutions and aims to give effect to certain moral purposes, but it is our conviction that these principles, institutions and purposes are most coherently understood by reference to the Constitution's text, structure and history, rather than in a manner that is ultimately indifferent to the status of the Constitution considered as an authoritative document.[198] Justices of the High Court of Australia undoubtedly undertake the task of interpreting the Constitution carefully and conscientiously, but this does not mean that there is no place for criticism of their interpretations. In this book, we seek to do that in a manner that is disciplined by the Constitution itself.

**197** See Akhil Reed Amar, 'The Document and the Doctrine' (2000) 114 *Harvard Law Review* 26.
**198** Nicholas Aroney, 'The Modalities of Constitutional Reasoning' (2013) 36 *University of New South Wales Law Journal* 863.

# 2

# The Parliament

> *The legislative power of the Commonwealth shall be vested in a Federal Parliament, which shall consist of the Queen, a Senate, and a House of Representatives, and which is hereinafter called 'The Parliament', or 'The Parliament of the Commonwealth'.*[1]

## I Introduction

The Commonwealth Parliament is the first of the three principal institutions of government established by the Australian Constitution. Its pre-eminence in the Constitution is not accidental. It is mentioned first not only due to its inherent importance as an institution, but also on account of the normative priority of legislative power over the other powers of government, associated with the principle of the rule of law. Quick and Garran put it this way:

> Legislation consists in the making of laws. It is contrasted with the Executive power, whose office is to enforce the law, and with the Judicial power which deals with the interpretation and application of the law in particular cases.[2]

On this view, there can be no executive or judicial power without a pre-existing law to enforce, interpret and apply, and the usual source of this law is an exercise of legislative power by the Parliament. The Parliament is thus conceived as having a temporally prior role in making the law which it is the function of the Executive and the courts to administer. If read literally, this would mean that unless the Parliament legislates, the Executive Government and the Judiciary will simply have nothing to do. While an important principle is at stake here, Quick and Garran's statement cannot be taken quite literally, because parliamentary statutes are not the only kind of law which has to be administered and applied. The relevant law is the whole body of constitutional, statutory and common law operating in Australia at a Commonwealth, State and Territory level. Thus, the executive power of the Commonwealth extends not only to the enforcement of

**1** Commonwealth Constitution, s 1.
**2** John Quick and Robert Randolph Garran, *The Annotated Constitution of the Australian Commonwealth* (Angus and Robertson, 1901) 385.

federal laws, but also to execution and maintenance of the Constitution itself (s 61), and includes the historic prerogatives of the Crown recognised by the common law.[3] While the principle of parliamentary supremacy, established in England since at least 1689, means that the prerogatives of the Crown are subject to any statute enacted by the Parliament, the Executive has certain constitutional powers and responsibilities that can only be altered by a formal constitutional amendment (eg, ss 5, 42, 56, 57, 58, 64 and 72). The High Court has also held that the Executive may exercise legislative power delegated to it by the Parliament, subject to the capacity of either of the two houses to disallow such delegated legislation.[4]

The Commonwealth Parliament is deliberately described as a 'Federal Parliament'. The federal nature of the Parliament is manifested in two important ways. First, the 'legislative power of the Commonwealth' is constitutionally limited. In principle, it extends only to the specific topics enumerated in the Constitution (ss 51 and 52),[5] in contrast to the broad legislative powers of the States, which 'continue' subject to the Constitution (ss 106 and 107).[6] Second, the Federal Parliament consists of the Queen, the Senate and the House of Representatives. This tripartite structure resembles the British Parliament, except that the two houses of the Australian Parliament are specifically designed to give effect to the federal character of the Constitution by providing, as in the United States of America, that the people of the States are represented in the Senate and the people of the Commonwealth are represented in the House of Representatives (ss 7 and 24).

It was recognised by the framers of the Constitution that the bicameral nature of the Parliament would contribute several advantages to the system of government as a whole.[7] It would increase the democratic representativeness of the Parliament through two different electoral systems, generating two politically different chambers.[8] This would improve parliamentary deliberation and the quality of legislation by subjecting any proposed law to two independent legislative processes.[9] The bicameral structure of the Parliament would also contribute to the separation of powers by countering the tendency of Westminster systems of responsible government to consolidate control over both executive and legislative power into the same political hands.[10] Although the leader of the party or coalition of parties which secures a majority in the House of Representatives will ordinarily be commissioned as Prime Minister and form a Government, the governing party or coalition will not necessarily control the Senate and will therefore

**3** Commonwealth Constitution, s 61. See Chapters 6 and 7.
**4** *Victorian Stevedoring & General Contracting Co Pty Ltd v Dignan* (1931) 46 CLR 73; *Legislative Instruments Act 2003* (Cth). See Chapter 3, Part II.1.
**5** See Chapter 3, Parts III and IV.
**6** See Chapter 10.
**7** Quick and Garran, above n 2, 385–7; Richard Baker, *A Manual of Reference to Authorities for the Use of the Members of the National Australasian Convention* (E A Petherick and Co, 1891) ch 6.
**8** *Official Record of the Debates of the National Australasian Convention, Second Session* (Sydney, 1897) 321.
**9** Ibid, 548.
**10** Quick and Garran, above n 2, 381–2.

often require the support of the Opposition, minor parties or independent members of the Senate to pass legislation.[11]

The design of the Parliament, as Quick and Garran observed, 'has its roots deep in the past' and was built 'on lines suggested by the best available models of its kind'.[12] Traditionally, the composition of the British Parliament was understood in terms of the theory of the mixed constitution, through which the respective advantages of monarchy, aristocracy and democracy were thought to be secured; namely, the unity of purpose and leadership provided by the rule of an individual, the virtue and wisdom provided by the rule of a select few, and the practical sense and good judgement provided by the rule of the many.[13] With the formation of the Constitution of the United States, the theory of the mixed constitution was largely substituted by the principle of the separation of powers, supplemented by the idea that the three institutions of government would be designed so as to place 'checks and balances' on each other.[14] The British and American models, including the ideas and principles according to which they were understood and justified, were the most influential sources upon which the framers of the Australian Constitution drew for inspiration and guidance. The Australians were also deeply influenced by the Swiss and Canadian systems, as well as by their own close experience of parliamentary government in each of the Australian colonies.

## II Composition of Parliament

### 1 The Queen and the Governor-General

The Queen is a constituent part of the Commonwealth Parliament (s 1).[15] In Australia, her Majesty's constitutional powers, including her particular functions in relation to the Parliament, are ordinarily exercised by the Governor-General, who is appointed by the Queen as her representative in the Commonwealth (s 2), just as the State Governors are the representatives of the Queen in each of the States.[16] The Letters Patent issued by the Queen, by which the office of Governor-General is established, require the appointee to take the Oath or Affirmation of Allegiance set out in the schedule to the Constitution and the Oath or Affirmation of Office provided for in the Letters Patent.[17] Each Governor-General is

**11** See, further, Nicholas Aroney, 'Four Reasons for an Upper House: Representative Democracy, Public Deliberation, Legislative Outputs and Executive Accountability' (2008) 29(2) *Adelaide Law Review* 205.
**12** Quick and Garran, above n 2, 383.
**13** Corinne Weston, *English Constitutional Theory and the House of Lords 1556–1832* (Routledge & Kegan Paul, 1965).
**14** Gordon Wood, *The Creation of the American Republic, 1776–1787* (University of North Carolina Press, 1969).
**15** See also *Constitution Act 1902* (NSW), s 3; *Constitution Act 1867* (Qld), s 2A; *Constitution Act 1934* (Tas), s 10; *Constitution Act 1975* (Vic), s 15; *Constitution Act 1889* (WA), s 2(2). In South Australia, royal assent is required for the enactment of laws, but the Queen is not formally included in the definition of Parliament: *Constitution Act 1934* (SA), s 4. See Chapter 10, Part IV.2.
**16** *Australia Acts 1986* (UK and Cth), s 7(1).
**17** Letters Patent Relating to the Office of Governor-General of the Commonwealth of Australia (21 August 2008), published in Commonwealth of Australia, *Special Gazette*, No S179, 9 September 2008.

appointed by a Commission personally signed by the Queen (her Majesty's Royal Sign Manual) to which an imprint of the Great Seal of Australia is affixed.[18]

Consistent with British tradition, the Governor-General and the State Governors are responsible for summoning their respective Parliaments into existence, determining when they will meet and giving the royal assent to proposed laws passed by the houses of Parliament. Because the framers of the Constitution wished to ensure that the Commonwealth Parliament would be regularly elected and would sit frequently, the Constitution provides that Parliament must be summoned within 30 days after the date set for the return of the writs for each general election (s 5),[19] elections for Parliament must occur at least every three years (ss 13, 28),[20] and there must be at least one session of Parliament every year (s 6). Furthermore, because the Senate represents the people of the States, it is the State Governors who issue writs for the election of senators in each State (s 12), whereas the Governor-General issues writs for elections of members of the House of Representatives because it represents the people of the Commonwealth as a whole (s 32).

In relation to the Governor-General's responsibility to give the royal assent to proposed laws passed by the two houses of Parliament (s 58), the Constitution says that the Governor-General may withhold assent or reserve a proposed law for the Queen's pleasure (s 60), and that the Queen may disallow a law within one year of the Governor-General's assent (s 59). In addition, the Constitution requires that a proposed law limiting the matters in respect of which special leave to appeal from the High Court to the Privy Council may be sought must be reserved by the Governor-General for the Queen's pleasure (s 74). These provisions are similar to sections in the colonial constitutions which enabled the British Government to intervene in colonial law-making, largely to protect Imperial interests.[21] This power of intervention was exercised on the advice of responsible ministers – originally those in Britain, but since the 1920s, those of the colony or dominion concerned.[22] While the Queen's power of disallowance has never been exercised, and is probably now a 'dead letter',[23] over the course of the twentieth century several bills were returned by the Governor-General with recommended amendments,[24] and several others were reserved for the Queen's pleasure, some on account of their subject matter and others because they dealt

**18** On the constitutional relationship between the Great Seals of Australia and the United Kingdom, see *Fitzgibbon v HM Attorney-General* [2005] EWHC 114 (Ch).

**19** Pursuant to the *Commonwealth Electoral Act 1918* (Cth), s 152, the timing and conduct of elections are regulated by the issue of writs which stipulate the date for the close of the rolls of registered electors, the nomination of candidates, the polling and the return of the writs. The results of the election are certified by the Australian Electoral Commission.

**20** During the First and Second World Wars, a limited extension to the life of the Parliament was considered. See B C Wright and P E Fowler, *House of Representatives Practice* (Department of the House of Representatives, 6th ed, 2012) 224–5.

**21** Alpheus Todd, *Parliamentary Government in the British Colonies* (Longmans, Green and Co, 1880) 41, 125–8.

**22** *Sue v Hill* (1999) 199 CLR 462, 495–6.

**23** Gabriel Moens and John Trone, *Lumb & Moens' The Constitution of the Commonwealth of Australia Annotated* (LexisNexis Butterworths, 7th ed, 2007) 241.

**24** Wright and Fowler, above n 20, 393–4, Appendix 19.

with appeals to the Privy Council.[25] Bills are now only likely to be reserved because the subject matter is of personal interest or relevance to the Sovereign.[26] At a State level, reservation for the Queen's pleasure has been terminated.[27]

Except in very extraordinary circumstances, all of the powers of the Governor-General and State Governors are exercised on the advice of the Prime Minister, State Premier or other relevant Government Minister in accordance with the conventions of parliamentary responsible government.[28] Nonetheless, as Walter Bagehot observed, the Queen and her Governors retain the constitutional right to be consulted, to encourage, and to warn,[29] and it has been argued that royal assent to bills passed by the two houses might legitimately be refused, provided that it occurs on the advice of responsible ministers,[30] and that a 'reserve power' to refuse assent might even be exercised independently to uphold fundamental constitutional principles where the matter cannot otherwise be addressed by the courts.[31] The exercise of such powers is unusual and highly controversial, however.[32]

Most bills are specified to become law on the day of assent, although some specify some other date or a day to be specified by the Governor-General by proclamation.[33] The date for commencement is usually prospective, but can be retrospective.[34]

## 2 The Senate

Quick and Garran considered the Senate to be 'one of the most conspicuous, and unquestionably the most important, of all the federal features of the Constitution', for it is the chamber in which the States are represented 'as separate entities', as 'co-equal political communities' and as 'corporate parts of the Commonwealth'.[35] The framers of the Constitution deliberately used the term 'Senate' rather than 'Legislative Council' or 'House of Lords'. The term was derived from the Constitutions of the United States and Canada, which had in turn been inspired by the ancient Roman Senate, which had once exercised supreme power within the Roman Republic.[36] The term used in Switzerland for the

**25** *Privy Council (Limitation of Appeals) Act 1968* (Cth); *Privy Council (Appeals from the High Court) Act 1975* (Cth).
**26** Wright and Fowler, above n 20, 394, offer the *Flags Act 1953* (Cth) and *Royal Style and Titles Act 1973* (Cth) as examples.
**27** *Australia Acts 1986* (UK and Cth), ss 8 and 9.
**28** A fuller list of the Governor-General's constitutional functions is given in Quick and Garran, above n 2, 404–6. The principles of parliamentary responsible government are discussed in more detail in Chapter 6, Part V.
**29** Walter Bagehot, *The English Constitution* (Collins, 1963) 111.
**30** Greg Taylor, 'Two Refusals of Royal Assent in Victoria' (2007) 29 *Sydney Law Review* 85, 108–10, 130.
**31** Anne Twomey, 'The Refusal or Deferral of Royal Assent' (2006) *Public Law* 580, 601–2, who considers such circumstances to be very limited.
**32** See Chapter 6, Parts I, II and V.
**33** Harry Evans and Rosemary Laing, *Odgers' Australian Senate Practice* (Department of the Senate, 13th ed, 2012) 340. Section 3A of the *Acts Interpretation Act 1901* (Cth) provides that a bill comes into operation as law on the 28th day after the Governor-General's assent, unless the bill specifies another day.
**34** On retrospective laws, see Chapter 3, Part II.1.
**35** Quick and Garran, above n 2, 414.
**36** The term is derived from the Latin word *senatus*, meaning a chamber or council of the older or senior members of the community. See Ibid 415.

corresponding institution is the *Conseil des Etats* (French) or *Ständerat* (German), which means 'Council of States', and this idea of a 'States' house' is essential to the American Senate as well. In both the United States and Switzerland, each constituent State or Canton is equally represented in the Senate or Council of States, whereas in Canada the 10 Provinces are divided into four divisions (Ontario, Quebec, the Maritime Provinces and the Western Provinces), with each division being represented by 24 senators appointed by the Governor-General on the advice of the Prime Minister. There was general agreement among the framers of the Australian Constitution that the Commonwealth Parliament should consist of two houses,[37] but one of the most sharply and extensively debated questions was whether or not the Australian States should be equally represented, as in America and Switzerland, notwithstanding their significant differences in population and resources. In the end, an overwhelming majority voted for equal representation of the States in the Senate, but only after very long and complex debate about the matter.

### Equal representation of the States

The representation of the people of the States in the Senate went to the very fundamentals of the federation. Henry Bournes Higgins put the argument against equality of representation of the States in its clearest and most logically consistent form. He believed that political communities ought to be formed on the basis of the consent of the people, by which he meant the people of the nation as a whole, and that accordingly, the Parliament should consist of representatives of the people, and not of the States.[38] Alfred Deakin, who held similar views, went so far as to question the very existence of the 'states' as entities distinct from their constituent people:

> I cannot conceive of an entity called the state apart from the people whose interests it embodies; nor can I conceive anything within the state which can claim an equal authority with the final verdict, after solemn consideration, of the majority of its citizens. If the hon. Gentleman [Griffith] has any metaphysical entity in his mind which can be placed above this, I shall be glad to learn its nature.[39]

However, he was met by the response of Samuel Griffith, who agreed that the States should be understood as 'aggregations of their own people', but pointed out that 'the majorities of the separate States might be of a different opinion from the majority of the people of Australia'.[40] Edmund Barton similarly argued that it would be 'possible for the representative principle to be preserved and instituted from its very foundation in two chambers just as well as in one': the Senate would represent the people collected together as States, while the House of Representatives would represent the people of the entire Commonwealth, organised in

**37** *Convention Debates, Sydney* (1891) 23, 500; *Convention Debates, Adelaide* (1897) 17, 395.
**38** *Convention Debates, Sydney* (1897) 259–60.
**39** *Convention Debates, Sydney* (1891), 74–5.
**40** Ibid, 78.

local electorates.[41] An overwhelming majority of the framers of the Constitution agreed with this latter view. Their fundamental reason, as Richard Baker put it, was that the federation was necessarily founded upon a 'compact ... between the constituent states',[42] and that an essential feature of a genuinely 'federal commonwealth' was that the States would continue to exist as self-governing political communities entitled to representation as such in the Parliament.

The Constitution accordingly provides that there shall be six senators for each Original State and that, while the Parliament may alter the number of senators, the 'equal representation' of the Original States must be maintained and no Original State can have less than six senators (s 7). The Parliament has indeed altered the number of senators on several occasions, most recently in 1984, at which time the number of senators for each State was increased to twelve.[43] However, the representation of a State cannot be diminished, even by formal constitutional amendment, without the consent of the people of that State (s 128, para 5). For, as the authors of *Australian Senate Practice* point out, the equal representation of the Original States in the Senate is 'vital to the architecture of Australian federalism':

> It was a necessary inclusion at the time of federation in order to secure popular support for the new Commonwealth in each state especially the smaller states. It ensures that a legislative majority in the Senate is geographically distributed across the Commonwealth and prevents a parliamentary majority being formed from the representatives of the three largest cities and their environs alone. In contemporary Australia it acknowledges that the states continue to be the basis of activity in the nation whether for political, commercial, cultural or sporting purposes. Many organisations in Australia, at the national level, are constituted on the basis of equal state representation or with some modification thereof; this includes the two nation-wide political parties. By contrast, very few nation-wide bodies are organised on the principle of the election and composition of the House of Representatives. Indeed, in Australia's national life, a body such as the House of Representatives is, if not an aberration, at least relatively unusual. This demonstrates that in Australia federalism is organic and not simply a nominal or contrived feature of government and politics.[44]

### Directly chosen by the people

Although the Australian Constitution followed the United States Constitution in providing for the equal representation of the States, it departed from the American model in several important respects. One of these is that, prior to an amendment introduced in 1913, American senators were chosen by the Legislature of each State, rather than directly by the people.[45] This reflected the view that the most important and effective means by which democratic decision-making would occur was through deliberative assemblies, which would gather regularly in the

**41** Ibid, 91.
**42** Ibid, 111.
**43** *Representation Act 1983* (Cth), s 3.
**44** Evans and Laing, above n 33, 112.
**45** United States Constitution, art I, s 3, cls 1 and 2, altered by Amendment XVII.

form of elected legislatures or specially elected conventions to debate issues and make determinations in an environment of rational discussion.[46] Much the same idea influenced the delegates to the first Australian Federal Convention in 1891. The delegates had themselves been appointed by the colonial legislatures, and they agreed to a draft constitution in which senators would be chosen by those legislatures. However, the Federal Convention of 1897–8 was itself directly elected by the voters in four of the five colonies represented, and the value of 'direct democracy' which this presupposed led a majority of the framers of the Constitution to settle upon a Senate that would be 'directly chosen' by the people of each State, just as the House of Representatives would be 'directly chosen' by the people of the Commonwealth as a whole.[47] The requirement of a direct choice by the people not only excluded the idea that Senators would be chosen by the State Parliaments, but also excluded the possibility of using some other indirect means of election, such as through an electoral college.[48] As a consequence, the Senate represents the people of the States rather than the political institution of the States. As explained below, this distinction has important implications for how the purposes and functions of the Senate should be understood. The requirement of a 'direct choice' has also given rise to certain wider implications in relation to the functioning of the democratic system as a whole.[49]

### Each State voting as one electorate

The Constitution provides that senators shall be chosen by the people of each State voting, until Parliament otherwise provides, 'as one electorate' (s 7). There is an exception, however, for the State of Queensland, the Parliament of which is authorised to make laws dividing the State into divisions and determining the number of senators to be chosen for each division. This special provision was included because at the time of federation many residents and political leaders from northern and central Queensland were expressing a desire to separate from Queensland and form into a separate colony or state. In response to this pressure, Griffith, when he was Premier of Queensland, had introduced a resolution into the Queensland Legislative Assembly which proposed the transformation of the colony into a kind of federation of 'United Provinces' consisting of the northern, central and southern districts, each possessing its own Legislature and Executive Government.[50] This proposal was rejected by the Legislative Council,

**46** Jack Rakove, *Original Meanings: Politics and Ideas in the Making of the Constitution* (Alfred A Knopf, 1996) 236; Melvin Bradford, *Original Intentions on the Making and Ratification of the United States Constitution* (University of Georgia Press, 1993) 9–10.
**47** Commonwealth Constitution, ss 7 and 24. For more detail, see Nicholas Aroney, *The Constitution of a Federal Commonwealth: The Making and Meaning of the Australian Constitution* (Cambridge University Press, 2009) 56–60, 164–7, 217.
**48** *Attorney-General (Cth); Ex rel McKinlay v Commonwealth* (1975) 135 CLR 1, 21, 44, 56, 61, 68; *Australian Capital Television Pty Ltd v Commonwealth* (1992) 177 CLR 106, 228; *McGinty v Western Australia* (1996) 186 CLR 140, 170, 180–81, 276; *Mulholland v Australian Electoral Commission* (2004) 220 CLR 181, 189, 250, 288.
**49** See Part II.3 below in relation to the franchise and electoral districting, and Chapter 5, Part V, in relation to the implied freedom of political communication.
**50** Queensland, *Legislative Assembly Debates* (1890) vol 62, 1330–31.

but the issue remained so divisive that the Queensland Parliament was not able to agree on the terms of an Enabling Act to authorise Queensland's participation at the Federal Convention of 1897–8. To meet the concerns of separatists in northern and central Queensland, and the possibility that the three regions of Queensland might one day develop into separate States,[51] the Parliament was empowered to divide the State into separate divisions for the election of senators – a power that has never been exercised, and has since been constitutionally overridden by Commonwealth legislation.[52]

Although the Parliament has power to provide otherwise, the electoral system adopted for the Senate has consistently been based on the principle that the people of each State vote as one electorate. A majority of the framers of the Constitution favoured this as the default rule because it emphasised the idea, as Barton put it, that the Senate would represent each State as a whole, just as the House of Representatives would represent the people of the Commonwealth organised into local electorates.[53] Consistent also with the federal foundations of the Constitution, the detailed rules regulating elections for both the Senate and the House of Representatives were initially to be determined by the State Parliaments, subject to the Commonwealth Parliament providing otherwise. During the debate over the design of the electoral system, the framers of the Constitution had to consider exactly which aspects of the system would be entrenched in the Constitution and what powers the State and Commonwealth Parliaments would have to shape its details. They decided to entrench those features they considered essential (such as the equality of the Original States), to maintain the initial responsibility to each State to determine the details that would apply to federal elections within the State, and to grant the Commonwealth Parliament a 'supervisory' power to 'correct' any resulting distortions and to establish a uniform electoral system if this was deemed necessary.[54] In practice, this has meant that the Commonwealth Parliament has power, subject to the Constitution, to determine such matters as the franchise, the qualifications of candidates, the number of members of Parliament, voting procedures, the size and location of electoral divisions and other related matters.[55] While the first federal election was conducted in 1901 on the basis of the State electoral systems, since 1902 the Commonwealth has legislated to impose a uniform regulatory system for federal elections.[56]

**51** Quick and Garran, above n 2, 421.

**52** *Commonwealth Electoral Act 1918* (Cth), s 39, enacted pursuant to s 51(xxxvi) of the Commonwealth Constitution, read with s 7 of the Constitution ('until the Parliament [of the Commonwealth] otherwise provides').

**53** *Convention Debates, Adelaide* (1897) 669; *Convention Debates, Sydney* (1897) 360–61, 377; *Convention Debates, Melbourne* (1898) 1923–5.

**54** *Convention Debates, Sydney* (1897) 454. See Aroney, above n 47, 234–5. This was similar to the reasoning of Harlan J in relation to the United States Constitution in *Wesberry v Sanders* 376 US 1 (1964), 30–40.

**55** Commonwealth Constitution, ss 7–10, 27, 29–31, 34 (but see s 44). See Part II.3 below.

**56** *Commonwealth Electoral Act 1902*, replaced by the *Commonwealth Electoral Act 1918*.

### Block voting and proportional voting

In relation to the Senate, the *Commonwealth Electoral Act 1902* originally provided for a multiple-member plurality 'block-vote' system in which voters were presented with a list of candidates and were required to cast a ballot for as many candidates as there were seats to be filled. The required number of candidates who obtained the most votes in each State were elected as senators. With the development of disciplined political parties early in the twentieth century, this method of election tended to encourage a two-party system which often produced landslide victories for one party or the other and frequently enabled one party to gain majorities in both houses of the Parliament, weakening the role of the Senate as an effective house of review.[57] This tendency became even more pronounced when preferential block voting was instituted for the Senate in 1919,[58] with one party sometimes securing virtually all of the Senate seats in one election, only to lose most of them in the next.[59]

As early as 1902, the government of Prime Minister Edmund Barton proposed the adoption of a proportional electoral system based on a 'single transferrable vote'.[60] Such a system had been advocated prior to federation by figures such as Catherine Helen Spence (1825–1910), Andrew Inglis Clark (1848–1907) and Edward Nanson (1850–1936), who drew on the earlier work of Thomas Hare (1806–91) and John Stuart Mill (1806–73). It was not until the 1949 election, however, that such a system was implemented for the Senate. The change in voting system has had a pronounced effect, with the number of seats won by each party much more closely reflecting the popular vote received by that party.[61] Given that each State is currently represented by 12 Senators, half of whom are re-elected every three years, a candidate for election must secure a quota of 14.3 per cent of the total number of valid votes made in a State, either through primary votes received or the distribution of preferences. This ensures that candidates from each political party and independents secure representation in the Senate at a level which is reasonably proportionate to their popular vote. In practice, neither of the two major political groupings, the Labor Party and the Liberal-National coalition, usually secure a majority in the Senate, leaving the so-called 'balance of power' to minor party and independent senators. With the introduction in 1983 of optional 'party-ticket' voting, electors are able to choose whether to vote 'below the line' by indicating their numbered preferences for every candidate in the State, or 'above the line' by voting for a particular party

**57** For example, in the 1910 election the Labor Party secured 43 of 75 House of Representatives seats and 22 of 36 Senate seats, and in the 1914 election the Labor Party secured 42 of 75 House of Representatives seats and 31 of 36 Senate seats.
**58** For example, in the 1919 election the Nationalist Party secured 37 of 75 House of Representatives seats and 35 of 36 Senate seats, and in the 1946 election the Labor Party secured 43 of 74 House of Representatives seats and 33 of 36 Senate seats.
**59** David Farrell and Ian McAllister, *The Australian Electoral System: Origins, Variations and Consequences* (University of New South Wales Press, 2006) 41.
**60** Ibid 29–36.
**61** For example, in the 1949 election the Labor Party secured 45.24 per cent of Senate seats (19 of 42) with 44.89 per cent of the first preference vote, while the Liberal and Country Parties secured 54.76 per cent of Senate seats (23 of 42) with 50.41 per cent of the first preference vote.

or independent candidate and accepting the preference flows that are publicly registered by that party or candidate with the Australian Electoral Commission.

### Term of office and casual vacancies

The function of the Senate as a mature house of review, intended to bring an additional layer of careful deliberation to the consideration of proposed legislation and the scrutiny of government policy and administration, is reinforced by the provision that senators ordinarily hold office for six years and that half of the senators must stand for re-election every three years (s 13). The Senate, unlike the House of Representatives, is thus a semi-continuous body that is dissolved only when there is a double dissolution, which is part of the intended solution to resolve deadlocks between the two houses over proposed legislation (s 57).[62] Following a double dissolution, the elected senators are divided into long-term and short-term senators, with terms of office of six and three years respectively. According to resolutions of the Senate, the first half of senators elected in each State are declared to be long-term senators, and the second half short-term.[63]

When a senator dies, is disqualified or resigns prior to the expiration of his or her term in office,[64] special provision must be made for that senator's replacement. To avoid the expense and inconvenience of holding a State-wide election to fill the vacancy, s 15 of the Constitution originally provided for a replacement to be determined by the two houses of the relevant State Parliament, sitting and voting together (or, where the Parliament was not in session, to be determined by the State Government).[65] This reflected the view that senators are representatives of their respective States and, where direct popular election is not feasible, it is appropriate that the replacement be determined by the State Parliament or State Government. Since the introduction of proportional representation in 1949, the general practice was for the replacement senator to belong to the same political party as the senator being replaced.[66] However, in 1975 two casual vacancies, one occurring in New South Wales and the other in Queensland, were filled in a manner that did not meet with these expectations: one replacement senator was not a member of the same party, the other belonged to the same party but was liable to expulsion from the party for standing as a candidate against another person nominated by the party. These two decisions by the respective States altered the balance of power in the Senate and contributed to the Senate's refusal to pass the annual supply bills in that same year – a series of events which culminated in the dismissal of the Prime

**62** See Part III.2 below.

**63** The resolutions now adopt *Commonwealth Electoral Act 1918* (Cth), s 282, which requires the Australian Electoral Officer after a double dissolution election to undertake a special count of the vote in each State to determine the order of election as if it had been a half-Senate election. See Evans and Laing, above n 33, 129–30.

**64** See Commonwealth Constitution, ss 19, 20, 45.

**65** This procedure does not apply where the place of a senator is declared vacant because of an irregularity in the election (*Vardon v O'Loughlin* (1907) 5 CLR 201) or where an elected candidate, due to disqualification, never validly began a term of service as senator, in which latter case the vacancy is to be filled by recounting ballots cast for candidates in the election (*Re Wood* (1988) 167 CLR 145).

**66** Geoffrey Sawer, *Federation under Strain* (Melbourne University Press, 1977) 129–35.

Minister by the Governor-General in highly controversial circumstances.[67] In 1977, s 15 of the Constitution was amended in an attempt to prevent this from occurring again. The section now provides that where a senator was publicly recognised by a particular political party as being an endorsed candidate of that party and publicly represented himself or herself as such, his or her replacement must be a member of that party, unless there is no member of that party available for appointment.[68] The amendment does not apply to independent senators, and it does not obligate a State Parliament to nominate a replacement, or to do so within any particular time.[69] However, while a State Parliament is not obliged to accept a person nominated by the relevant political party, but only to appoint a person belonging to that party, in practice the procedure is frequently used by political parties to nominate replacement senators of their choice, and a substantial proportion of sitting senators first enter the Parliament through this process rather than by popular election.[70]

**Representation of new States and Territories**

The Constitution provides for the addition of new States in three ways: through admission of a country external to Australia into the federation, separation of territory from an existing State, or union of two or more States (ss 121 and 124).[71] These last two procedures involve an existing State or States, and so they can only occur with the consent of the Parliament of the State or States concerned (s 124; see also s 123). Apart from this, the terms and conditions upon which a new State is established or admitted to the federation are determined by the Commonwealth Parliament, and these terms and conditions may include a grant of representation in either House of the Parliament as it thinks fit (s 121). As a consequence, equality of representation of the States in the Senate is not treated by the Constitution as a necessary principle applying to new States, but is left as a matter for political determination and negotiation. If a country external to Australia were to seek admission, or a State wished to divide itself into two States, the terms of admission, including representation in the Parliament, would be a matter to be agreed between the Commonwealth and the State or States concerned. This was a deliberate decision by the framers of the Constitution, a majority of whom appear to have considered that the most fundamental principle of the federation was its foundation in a negotiated agreement among the constituent States, which principle embraced the proposition that there would need to be a similar agreement formed between the Commonwealth and any State wishing to be admitted to the federation.[72] What was thought not

**67** See Chapters 6, Parts I and V.
**68** *Constitution Alteration (Senate Casual Vacancies) 1977* (Cth).
**69** The Tasmanian Parliament did not appoint a replacement for Labor Senator Don Grimes in 1987. See Evans and Laing, above n 33, 134–6.
**70** John Nethercote, 'Senate Vacancies: Casual or Contrived?' in *Upholding the Australian Constitution: Proceedings of the Seventeenth Conference of The Samuel Griffith Society* (2005) vol 17, ch 4.
**71** See also *Commonwealth of Australia Constitution Act 1900* (UK), cl 6 (definition of 'the States').
**72** Aroney, above n 47, 266–71.

negotiable was that if a new State were to be admitted or established, its constitution, powers and laws would, like the Original States, continue as at the date of its admission or establishment (ss 106 and 107).

Even though the framers of the Constitution looked forward to the possible emergence of 'embryo states' from existing Australian territories, and the admission of independent States external to Australia (as was once contemplated for Fiji and New Zealand),[73] no new States have in fact been added to the federation since its formation in 1901. What have been created are several new Commonwealth territories, some through surrender of territory by a State to the Commonwealth, others by external transfer or acquisition. The Commonwealth's external territories include Norfolk Island, Christmas Island, the Cocos (Keeling) Islands and the Australian Antarctic Territory,[74] and once included the territories of Papua, New Guinea and Nauru.[75] The Commonwealth's two mainland territories are the Australian Capital Territory, which was transferred by New South Wales to the Commonwealth, and the Northern Territory, which was transferred by South Australia, both effective from 1911.[76] The Australian Capital Territory is the location of the seat of government of the Commonwealth, which according to the Constitution must be in New South Wales and not less than 100 miles distant from Sydney (s 125). Both of the mainland territories are deemed to have been surrendered to the Commonwealth pursuant to s 111, and have been held not to have involved any diminution or alteration of the limits of a State so as to require approval at a referendum pursuant to s 123.[77]

The Constitution authorises the Commonwealth Parliament to make laws for the government of any Commonwealth Territory and to provide for the representation of such Territory in either House of Parliament to the extent and on terms which it thinks fit (s 122). Relying on this section, the Commonwealth enacted legislation in 1973 providing for the representation of the Australian Capital Territory (including the Jervis Bay Territory) and the Northern Territory in the Senate each by two senators. These senators are directly chosen by the people of each Territory voting as one electorate,[78] and have all of the

**73** *Capital Duplicators Pty Ltd v Australian Capital Territory* (1992) 177 CLR 248, 271. See also *Commonwealth of Australia Constitution Act 1900* (UK), preamble: 'it is expedient to provide for the admission into the Commonwealth of other Australasian colonies and possessions of the Queen'.

**74** *Re Governor, Goulburn Correctional Centre; Ex parte Eastman* (1999) 200 CLR 322, 331. On Norfolk Island, see *Berwick Ltd v Grey* (1976) 133 CLR 603 and *Bennett v Commonwealth* (2007) 231 CLR 91.

**75** See *Ffrost v Stevenson* (1937) 58 CLR 528; *Re Minister for Immigration, Multicultural and Indigenous Affairs; Ex parte Ame* (2005) 222 CLR 439; *Ruhani v Director of Police* (2005) 222 CLR 489; *Berwick Ltd v Grey* (1975–76) 133 CLR 603; and *Bennett v Commonwealth* (2007) 231 CLR 91. See also *Nauru Independence Act 1967* (Cth) and *Papua New Guinea Independence Act 1975* (Cth).

**76** *Seat of Government Surrender Act 1909* (NSW); *Seat of Government Acceptance Act 1909* (Cth); *Northern Territory Surrender Act 1908* (SA); *Northern Territory Acceptance Act 1910* (Cth). Compare *Lamshed v Lake* (1958) 99 CLR 132, 140–41; *Capital Duplicators Pty Ltd v Australian Capital Territory* (1992) 177 CLR 248, 285–7; *Re Governor, Goulburn Correctional Centre; Ex parte Eastman* (1999) 200 CLR 322, 331.

**77** *Paterson v O'Brien* (1978) 138 CLR 276, 280–81. According to the Court, the two provisions are 'quite disparate' and concern 'quite different matters and powers'. Section 111 involves a 'surrender' of 'territory', whereas s 123 involves alteration of the 'limits of a State'; s 111 involves acceptance by the Commonwealth Executive in response to the initiative of the State, whereas s 123 grants a power to the Commonwealth Parliament conditioned on the consent of the State Parliament and the electors of the State.

**78** *Senate (Representation of Territories) Act 1973* (Cth), s 4.

powers, immunities and privileges of a senator for a State, including the right to vote on all questions arising in the Senate.[79] This provision for Territory senators possessing the same rights as State senators gave rise to a tension with the principle that the Senate is the 'States' house'. In its early decisions, the High Court frequently drew attention to the 'fundamental' nature of the requirement that the Senate is to consist of senators for each State chosen by the people of the State. In *Vardon v O'Loughlin* it was called a 'dominant provision', to which other provisions, such as the mechanism for the filling of casual vacancies, were merely 'ancillary'.[80] It was thus possible to argue that the capacity of the Commonwealth to make laws for the representation of the Territories in the Senate must be subject to this more fundamental principle. However, it could also be argued that the Parliament had an unfettered discretion to determine the representation of the Territories 'to the extent and on the terms which it thinks fit' (s 122).

In two successive cases decided in 1975 and 1977, the High Court had to determine the constitutional validity of the territorial senators legislation.[81] In effect, the question concerned whether s 7 or s 122 would prevail in the determination of the composition of the Senate. Would the requirement that the Senate is to be composed of senators chosen by each State qualify the discretion of the Commonwealth to determine the representation of the Territories in the Parliament, or vice versa? In *Western Australia v Commonwealth*, a majority of 4:3 held that it was within the power of the Parliament to provide for representation of each of the two mainland Territories by two senators, each having full voting rights within the Senate but holding office for a maximum of only three years in order to coincide with elections for the House of Representatives. In his dissenting judgment, Barwick CJ considered that the 'central and dominating purpose' of the Constitution was to establish an 'indissoluble Federal Commonwealth' possessing an 'essentially bicameral' Parliament, including a Senate in which the people of the States are represented. His Honour noted that this particular feature of the Senate is not only constitutionally entrenched, but cannot be altered even by formal constitutional amendment pursuant to s 128 without the consent of the people of the State or States concerned.[82] Further, the Chief Justice pointed out that s 122 needs to be read with s 121. Section 121 enables the Parliament when admitting a new State to determine the *extent* of its representation in either House of Parliament, whereas s 122 allows the Parliament to determine *whether* a Territory will have any representation at all. The reason for the difference between these two provisions is that once a new State is admitted to the federation it will ordinarily be entitled to parliamentary representation pursuant to s 7, and the

**79** Ibid, s 5.
**80** *Vardon v O'Loughlin* (1907) 5 CLR 201, 206.
**81** *Western Australia v Commonwealth* (1975) 134 CLR 201; *Queensland v Commonwealth* (1977) 139 CLR 585.
**82** *Western Australia v Commonwealth* (1975) 134 CLR 201, 226–8; see also 246–8.

only salient question will be the extent of that representation. In this context, he reasoned, the capacity of the Parliament to provide for the representation of either a new State or a Territory in the Parliament must be read subject to the essential nature of each House. The House of Representatives consists of members chosen by the people of each State in proportion to their respective populations, just as the Senate consists of senators for each State. Neither of these essential characteristics can be overturned by providing for an inconsistent mode of representation of a new State or a Territory in either House. It thus followed, he reasoned, that provision for the representation of a Territory in the Senate cannot alter the fundamental characteristics of the Senate, such as its character as a 'States' house'.[83] Gibbs J, who agreed with this conclusion, also considered that the requirement that the Senate is to be 'composed' of senators for each State, according to its ordinary and natural meaning, requires that the Senate shall be 'constituted' by such senators, meaning that 'they, and they alone, make up the Senate'.[84] Drawing on the interpretive principle that the Constitution is to be construed 'as a whole so as to give its provisions, if possible, a meaning that will avoid any inconsistency and that will give effect to all of them', he observed that '[i]t may be necessary ... to restrict the literal meaning of one section' to render it 'harmonious' with another provision. Accordingly, he concluded, any 'representation' given to a Territory must be read down to mean 'representation by persons who do not become senators', that is, as agents or delegates of the Territory, who can speak on its behalf, but do not have the full voting rights of senators.[85]

However, a majority of the Court, led by Mason J, disagreed. They considered that although 'the conception of a senator as the representative of a State' pervades the Constitution, the 'wide and general' words used in s 122 to describe the capacity of the Parliament to provide for the representation of a Territory 'to the extent and on the terms which it thinks fit' suggest that it can confer upon a Territory representative 'privileges identical or inferior to those enjoyed by a member of either House'.[86] On this view, the idea of 'representation' referred to in both s 121 and s 122 is not to be read down by reference to the definition of the Senate in s 7 or the House of Representatives in s 24. Rather these provisions, though fundamental, are not to be read as 'necessarily speaking for all time', but only as fixing the character of the Parliament until such time as the Parliament might wish to confer representation rights on the

**83** Ibid, 228–32. See also *Queensland v Commonwealth* (1977) 139 CLR 585, 616–19.
**84** *Western Australia v Commonwealth* (1975) 134 CLR 201, 244; see also 260.
**85** Ibid, 246. Limited representation rights were granted by the *Northern Territory Representation Acts* of 1922, 1959 and 1968. Gibbs J pointed out (at 249) that limited representation of this kind had also been given to Territories of the United States in the House of Representatives: *Ex parte Lane* 135 US 443 (1890), 447. Stephen J noted (at 258–9) that this system had been described in James Bryce, *The American Commonwealth* (Macmillan, 2nd ed, 1889) vol I, 555 and vol II, 414, and in several other Supreme Court decisions. His Honour also drew attention (at 260) to the possibility that the rights of Territory representation could be restricted as to subject matter (eg, territorial affairs). See also *Re Governor, Goulburn Correctional Centre; Ex parte Eastman* (1999) 200 CLR 322, 367.
**86** *Western Australia v Commonwealth* (1975) 134 CLR 201, 268–70.

Territories.[87] Moreover, in relation to the 'grim spectre' of a Parliament swamping the Senate with senators from the Territories and thereby disproportionately reducing the representation of the States, Mason J pointed out that this assumed the 'willing participation' of the senators, 'notwithstanding that it would hasten their journey into political oblivion', and it also disregarded the framers' assumption that Parliament will act responsibly in the exercise of its powers.[88] Murphy J reasoned similarly, observing that the 'extremely wide' language used in s 122 should be interpreted in a manner 'applicable to changing conditions',[89] and that the desirability of interpreting the Constitution in a manner which accords with its 'democratic' purposes means that the Parliament should be able to provide for full and effective representation of the people of the Territories within the Senate.[90]

Soon after *Western Australia v Commonwealth* was decided, Barwick CJ observed in another case that the correctness of the decision had been questioned by two States, and he suggested that if the issue were to be revisited it should occur before 'a serious departure from the federal nature of the Constitution ... becomes entrenched'.[91] Emboldened by this, the State of Queensland commenced proceedings seeking declarations that the Territory representation laws were unconstitutional, essentially on the grounds raised in the earlier case. In *Queensland v Commonwealth*, a 5:2 majority declined to make such declarations, the significant difference being that although Gibbs and Stephen JJ continued to think that, properly construed, the Constitution did not authorise the election of Territory senators having full voting rights, and while they did not consider the High Court to be strictly bound by its previous decisions, they could not simply 'ignore' them. As Gibbs J put it, a 'justice, unlike a legislator, cannot introduce a programme of reform which sets at nought decisions formerly made and principles formerly established'.[92] It was also relevant for Gibbs and Stephen JJ that senators for the Territories had already been elected, and thus to reverse the earlier decision would be to 'defeat the expectations of the people of the Territories'.[93] However, Gibbs J warned that if the Parliament were to 'further distort the federal balance' by providing for the election of more senators for the Territories, this might well justify a reconsideration of the whole matter.[94] As it happens, no relevant change to the representation of the two mainland Territories in the Senate has been instituted. The voting rights of the residents of the other external Territories remains a matter of discretion for the Commonwealth.[95]

**87** Ibid, 270–71; see also 273, 282–3.
**88** Ibid, 271; see also 275.
**89** Ibid, 282.
**90** Ibid, 284, 286.
**91** *Attorney-General (NSW); Ex rel McKellar v Commonwealth* (1977) 139 CLR 527, 532.
**92** *Queensland v Commonwealth* (1977) 139 CLR 585, 599.
**93** Ibid, 600, 603–4; contrast 592–4, 620–31.
**94** Ibid, 600–1; see also 605.
**95** *Kruger v Commonwealth* (1997) 190 CLR 1, 69–70; *Bennett v Commonwealth* (2007) 231 CLR 91, 109–110.

### Effectiveness of the Senate

It is often observed that the Senate has failed to represent the interests of the States, largely because it is dominated by party politics.[96] It is argued that there are very few if any examples where the Senate has adopted a view different to the House of Representatives on a matter in which the interests of the States were opposed to the interests of the Commonwealth as a whole.[97] It is also argued that the Senate has failed to be a forum where the smaller States are protected from the larger ones, and some who draw attention to this consider the construction of the Senate as a 'States' house' to be a mistake.[98]

In assessing these criticisms, close attention needs to be given to the way in which the framers of the Constitution deliberated about the design of the Senate. One of the strongest proponents of the Senate, Charles Kingston, put it this way: 'under a system of two chambers, both voices ought to be heard – the voice of the nation and the voice of the states as different constituent entities'.[99] Clearly, Kingston was speaking metaphorically when he referred to these two 'voices'. However, his application of the metaphor to *both* the 'nation' and the 'states' suggests that we might just as much ask whether the House of Representatives has adequately represented the nation as whether the Senate has adequately represented the States. Identifying such a 'voice', 'will' or 'interest' – of either the Commonwealth or the States – is always going to be elusive, and politically contested. What Kingston and his colleagues hoped for when they insisted on the bicameral design of the Parliament was that it would recognise the two constituencies which they believed the two houses ought to represent. They were well aware that to speak of some ascertainable voice, will or interest was to speak metaphorically, and that deliberation within the Parliament would involve a contest of many different opinions.

It also needs to be recognised that when delegates at the Federal Conventions spoke about the Senate representing the interests of the States, the exact composition and design of the Senate and its relationship to parliamentary responsible government had not yet been settled. At the Federal Convention of 1891 it was expected that senators would be chosen by the State Parliaments, rather than directly elected by the people of each State. Given that each of the Australian colonies had fully functioning systems of responsible government, such a system would have given each State Government substantial influence, if not complete control, over the appointment of senators. Although James Bryce had drawn attention to the operation of the party system in the United States and had observed that the American Senate had not protected the smaller States,[100]

**96** Members of the first Australian Senate took the view that party divisions were not appropriate in the chamber: Geoffrey Sawer, *Australian Federal Politics and Law 1901–1929* (Melbourne University Press, 1956) 19. But since then, party politics has been a dominating force in the Senate as well as in the House of Representatives.
**97** Sawer, above n 96, 128–9.
**98** Leslie Finlay Crisp, *Australian National Government* (3rd ed, 1973) ch 11.
**99** *Convention Debates, Sydney* (1897) 285.
**100** Bryce, above n 85, vol II, pt III.

there was no system of parliamentary government in the American States and accordingly each State legislature tended to represent a much more diverse array of political interests than did the Governor of each State. An Australian system of nomination of senators by the State Parliaments would therefore have been likely to work in a manner more like that which today occurs in Germany, where members of the *Bundesrat* (Federal Council) are nominated by the *Länder* governments and undoubtedly represent the political interests of those governments.[101]

It is true that John Macrossan, Alfred Deakin and others, drawing on their experience of responsible government in the Australian colonies, were able to foresee, even as early as 1891, that party politics would increasingly shape the practical functioning of the Senate.[102] However, while responsible government in the Australian colonies was widely endorsed, many of the delegates in 1891 doubted whether such a system was appropriate at a federal level, and some, like Richard Baker, actively promoted adoption of a system modelled on Switzerland, where federal executive power is vested in a Federal Council elected by both houses of the Federal Assembly.[103] If such a system had been adopted in Australia, it would have encouraged the development of a multi-party system with weaker party discipline, making representatives in both houses more independent and therefore relatively more likely to represent the interests and expectations of their immediate constituents, at a State or local level. But by the time that the second Federal Convention was held in 1897–8, majority opinion had moved in favour of both responsible government and direct election of senators. Popular election removed any direct influence that could be exercised by State politicians over the appointment of senators, and responsible government would, in the long term, encourage the development of a system of strict party discipline applying not only in the House of Representatives, but also in the Senate. This meant that the rationale for the Senate had to change, albeit subtly. The Senate would now be representative of the people of the States, not the State legislatures or governments.[104] And given that party discipline would require senators to vote in accordance with party policy, their function as representatives of the peoples of their respective States would be channelled through their participation in decisions within the parliamentary caucus rather than on the floor of the house.[105] In such circumstances, it is significant that the Senate has been shown to ensure that, even when one of the major parties performs so poorly in the House of Representatives that

**101** Donald Kommers, *The Constitutional Jurisprudence of the Federal Republic of Germany* (Duke University Press, 2nd ed, 1997) 96.
**102** *Convention Debates, Sydney* (1891) 434; *Convention Debates, Sydney* (1897) 584.
**103** Richard Baker, *The Executive in a Federation* (C E Bristow, Government Printer, 1897).
**104** Evans and Laing, above n 33, 2–3. See the contrary opinion of Quick and Garran, above n 2, 414, asserting that the Senate is representative of the States, not the people, and arguing that its purpose is to 'advocat[e] their peculiar and special interests' as well as to 'ventilat[e] … their grievances'.
**105** Percy Joske, *Australian Federal Government* (Butterworths, 3rd ed, 1976) 75–7; Peter Howell, 'The Strongest Delegation: The South Australians at the Constitutional Convention of 1897–98' (1998) *The New Federalist* 44.

it has no or very few representatives from a particular State, it will secure at least some such representatives in the Senate.[106] Moreover, numerous independent members of the Senate have been well-known for negotiating strongly and effectively for the interests of their constituencies, at both a local and State level.[107]

Certainly, debate in the Senate tends to be shaped by party politics and conceptions of the 'national interest'. But this does not mean that the Senate is not effectively representative of the peoples of the States or is failing to fulfil its purposes. John Downer articulated it well when he pointed out that so long as the States were guaranteed equal representation in the Senate:

> state rights will come very little into these matters, and the results will be highly satisfactory, because we shall know that we really have become so much one people that these smaller considerations never occur to anybody at all.[108]

Downer seemed to suggest that a successful Senate would be marked by such a sense of unity and national purpose that senators would not often or even usually vote in defence of 'states' rights'. John Hackett's observation in 1891 had been to similar effect, when he argued that the 'main function of the Senate' would be:

> to cement these isolated communities together, to make a dismembered Australia into a single nation, ... to convert the popular will into the federal will ... to give full voice to the wishes of the populace, but, at the same time, to take care before that voice issues forth as the voice of Australia that it shall be clothed with all the rights and duties of the federal will.[109]

On this view, equality of representation in the Senate would ensure that the people of each State would be properly represented as 'a people', freeing them to engage in national debate in a non-parochial manner, knowing that they are entitled to that equal share of representation which befits an independent body politic, and could make use of this if their sectional interests were ever seriously in jeopardy.[110] In this sense, equal representation in the Senate would serve to unify rather than divide the nation, while at the same time recognising that, in essence, what was being created was a 'federal commonwealth' or a 'commonwealth of commonwealths'.[111]

**106** Campbell Sharman, 'The Australian Senate as a States House' (1977) 12(2) *Politics* 64, 68–9, shows that at the 1975 election, without the Senate, the Labor party would have had no member of Parliament from Tasmania and only one each from Western Australia and Queensland. The Senate increased these numbers to four, five and five respectively.

**107** Campbell Sharman, 'The Representation of Small Parties and Independents in the Senate' (1999) 34(3) *Australian Journal of Political Science* 353, 360; Brian Costar and Jennifer Curtin, *Rebels with a Cause: Independents in Australian Politics* (UNSW Press, 2004) ch 3.

**108** *Convention Debates, Sydney* (1897) 269; see also *Convention Debates, Adelaide* (1897) 539, 646, 665.

**109** *Convention Debates, Sydney* (1891) 280.

**110** As has happened very occasionally: see Sharman, above n 106, 70.

**111** Nicholas Aroney, 'A Commonwealth of Commonwealths: Late Nineteenth-Century Conceptions of Federalism and Their Impact on Australian Federation, 1890–1901' (2002) 23(3) *Journal of Legal History* 253.

## 3 The House of Representatives

The Australian House of Representatives is named after its American counterpart and, like it, is composed of members 'directly chosen by the people of the Commonwealth' (s 24).[112] The framers of the Constitution thus intended that the House of Representatives would represent the people of the Commonwealth as a whole. In theory, this could have been achieved by requiring that the House be elected by the entire people of the federation voting as one electorate. However, the framers also envisaged the House as the institution through which local communities across the entire federation would be represented, much like the system of counties, boroughs and cities that had been the basis of the traditional mode of representation within the House of Commons in the United Kingdom, and the similar systems that had been adapted to local conditions of each of the Australian colonies. This two-fold character of the House of Representatives posed an interesting set of questions about how the people of the Commonwealth as a whole might be represented through a system of local electorates.[113] The questions included:

- How much of the electoral system would be stipulated by the Constitution, and how much left to political determination? In relation to those matters to be determined politically, what would be the roles respectively of the State and Commonwealth Parliaments?
- To what extent and in what way would representation in the House be based on the principle of proportionality to population? In particular, would proportionality to population be constructed on the basis of the States or the localities as political units? Also, would there be any minimum representation for every State so as to protect the interests of the very smallest States?

These questions were in turn complicated by another set of issues arising out of the power relationship between the House of Representatives and the Senate. As explained in more detail below,[114] the framers arrived at the view that deadlocks between the two chambers should be resolved ultimately at a joint sitting in which the House of Representatives would have the preponderant influence by virtue of it having twice the number of members.

### Text, structure and history

All of these factors resulted in the complex set of requirements set out in Chapter I, Parts II–IV of the Constitution, of which s 24 is the leading provision. It requires that:

1. the House of Representatives shall be composed of members directly chosen by the people of the Commonwealth;

**112** The United States House of Representatives is 'composed of Members chosen … by the People of the several States': US Constitution, art I, s 2, cl 1.
**113** Aroney, above n 47, 224–7.
**114** See Part III.2 below.

2. the number of the members of the House chosen in the several States shall be in proportion to the respective numbers of their people;
3. the number of the members of the House shall be, as nearly as practicable, twice the number of the senators; and
4. five members at least shall be chosen in each Original State.

Section 24 also contains a preliminary formula to determine the number of members chosen in each State. This formula requires that:

(i) a quota shall be ascertained by dividing the number of the people of the Commonwealth, as shown by the latest statistics of the Commonwealth, by twice the number of the senators;

(ii) the number of members to be chosen in each State shall be determined by dividing the number of the people of the State, as shown by the latest statistics of the Commonwealth, by the quota; and if on such division there is a remainder greater than one-half of the quota, one more member shall be chosen in the State.

Subject to these important general requirements, the specifics of the electoral system were left to parliamentary determination, in the first place by the State Parliaments, and ultimately by the Commonwealth Parliament. The role of the States and the Commonwealth in the determination of these matters was partly a matter of practicalities, partly a matter of principle. Given that it was not appropriate to spell out all the details of the electoral system in the Constitution, the first Commonwealth election had to adopt the existing State laws regulating the mechanics of their respective electoral systems. The decision to do this coincided with the prevailing conception of the federation as resting upon the peoples of the States as pre-existing, self-governing political communities, each of which had agreed to the establishment of a federal commonwealth in which they would be the constituent members. However, there was concern that allowing the details of the federal electoral system to be determined separately by each State Parliament might lead to undesirable inconsistencies in approach, and so it was also decided that the Commonwealth would have ultimate authority to supervise and regulate the federal electoral system. This regulatory power of the Commonwealth would be subject only to certain fundamental principles which the framers considered ought to be laid down by the Constitution itself as binding upon both the Commonwealth and the States, particularly in the form of the requirements of s 24.[115] According to this scheme, the following matters are determined initially by the States, subject to ultimate supervision and control of the Commonwealth Parliament:

- the qualifications of electors (ie, the franchise) – subject to the requirement that each elector may vote only once (ss 8 and 30);
- the electoral divisions in each State and the number of members chosen for each division – subject to the requirement that a division must not be formed out of parts of different States (ss 7 and 29);

**115** Aroney, above n 47, 232–7.

- the organisation and conduct of federal elections (ss 7, 9 and 31).

In addition, the Commonwealth Parliament is authorised to determine:

- the number of members of both the House of Representatives and the Senate (ss 7 and 27);
- the number of members chosen in each State for the House of Representatives (s 24); and
- the qualifications of members of Parliament (ss 16, 34, 43, 44 and 45).

As noted, these powers of the Commonwealth to determine the number of members of the Parliament are subject to the mandatory requirements of s 24 that the House be, as nearly as practicable, twice the size of the Senate and that each State be equally represented in the Senate. The Constitution also sets out a list of overriding qualifications for election to the Parliament (s 44), and provides that any adult person who had the right to vote in State elections will also have the right to vote in Commonwealth elections (s 41).

This complex array of regulatory powers and overriding constitutional requirements was intended to provide the foundations for a federal democratic system through which the people of the Commonwealth and the States would be represented and governed. The specific combination of principles of representative government, responsible government and federalism embedded in these provisions has given rise to several important constitutional questions that have been addressed by the High Court. These questions have included:

- What is entailed in the primary requirement in s 24 of the Constitution that members of the House of Representatives are to be 'directly chosen by the people of the Commonwealth'? In particular, does this requirement give rise to:
  - democratic rights such as the right to vote, freedom of political communication, freedom of assembly and freedom of association;
  - a requirement that the number of electors in or the population of each electoral district must be as nearly as practicable the same?
- Who are 'the people of the Commonwealth'? In particular, do they include the people of the Territories? To what extent can the people of the Territories be represented in the Senate and the House of Representatives?
- How are the other three requirements of s 24 concerning the size of the House (ie, proportionality to State population, twice the number of the senators, and a minimum of five members for each Original State) most effectively achieved? What if all three requirements cannot be secured entirely and simultaneously?

Although these are distinct questions, they raise similar issues about the nature and scope of the federal democratic electoral system that is mandated by the Constitution. Each question depends on certain specific phrases and clauses in the Constitution, but the answer to each also turns on conceptions of the representative system as a whole. For this reason, the High Court's jurisprudence in this area is best understood as a complex set of interrelated interpretations of the relevant provisions. Central to the Court's reasoning has been the fundamental determinative role of the text and structure of the Constitution and the extent to which the text and structure need to be read in the light of the Constitution's historical context, underlying principles and intended purposes.

### The nexus between the Senate and the House

The nexus between the size of the two houses of Parliament was an important Australian innovation. Framed primarily to ensure that, in a joint sitting, votes cast in the House of Representatives would weigh more heavily than those in the Senate,[116] linking the size of the two houses contributed to the resolution of a design problem that had caused difficulties in the United States and elsewhere. This problem was one of ensuring that the size of the House of Representatives could be increased in order adequately to represent a growing national population while at the same time maintaining an appropriate balance between the sizes of the two houses. The draft Commonwealth Bill adopted by the Federal Convention of 1891 had proposed that the size of the House would be tied to the national population through the two-fold requirement that each State would be represented in proportion to its numbers and that, until the Parliament should otherwise provide, each State would have one representative for every 30 000 of its people.[117] Such a scheme, influenced by the corresponding provision of the United States Constitution,[118] raised two difficult issues, however. The first was that parliamentary intervention would be required to prevent the size of the House from increasing indefinitely.[119] The second was that the House might increase in size without any corresponding adjustment to the size of the Senate, with implications for the relative power and prestige of the two houses.[120] With these two problems in mind, as well as the proposition that deadlocks between the two houses should ultimately be resolved by a joint sitting, the framers of the Constitution eventually settled on the current formula in s 24.[121] As Barton explained, the primary purpose of the 2:1 nexus was to protect the integrity of the Senate and was, as such, an 'essential of Federation'.[122]

The qualification that the nexus need only be secured 'as nearly as practicable' was inserted due to the unlikelihood that a distribution of seats in the House would be able to satisfy simultaneously the three requirements of proportionality, minimum representation and the nexus. Indeed, this was plainly recognised by the framers in the distribution of seats that they prescribed for the first Commonwealth election, in s 26. On the assumption that Western Australia would agree in time to be an Original State, this section effectively provided that the

**116** See Part III.2 below.
**117** *Convention Debates, Sydney* (1891) 947.
**118** United States Constitution, art I, s 2, cl 3.
**119** *Convention Debates, Adelaide* (1897) 683–6.
**120** Ibid, 435–7.
**121** The 2:1 nexus was adopted notwithstanding the objection of Isaac Isaacs that Victoria would be disadvantaged because its representation in the House would drop as its population failed to grow as quickly as other States: ibid, 694–8.
**122** Ibid, 703–7. See Aroney, above n 47, 227–31.

total number of members of the House of Representatives to be chosen at the first election would be 75, which is more than twice the 36 senators originally required by s 7.

The *Commonwealth Electoral Act* requires that the Electoral Commissioner, usually during the life of each Parliament, is to determine the number of members of the House of Representatives to be chosen in each of the several States.[123] For several decades, this determination was made on the basis of a formula that closely followed the method set out in s 24 of the Constitution:

(a) A quota shall be ascertained by dividing the number of people of the Commonwealth, as shown by the certificate (for the time being in force) of the Chief Electoral Officer, by twice the number of Senators.

(b) The number of Members to be chosen in each State shall, subject to the Constitution, be determined by dividing the number of the people of the State, as shown by the certificate (for the time being in force) of the Chief Electoral Officer, by the quota; and if on such division there is a remainder greater than one-half of the quota, one more Member shall be chosen in the State.[124]

However, in 1964 the provision in the *Commonwealth Electoral Act* was amended to remove the words 'greater than one-half of the quota'.[125] The effect was that any remainder, no matter how small, would result in a State being allocated an additional member of the House of Representatives, making the formula less likely to produce the required nexus. Another set of amendments, introduced in 1973 in connection with the grant of Senate representation to the two mainland Territories,[126] provided that for the purposes of the Act 'the people of the Commonwealth' would not include the people of any Territory, and that the House of Representatives formula would be based only on the number of senators for the States, excluding any Territory senators from the calculation.[127]

The validity of these amendments was addressed in *McKellar's* case.[128] There the Court unanimously struck down the 1964 amendment on the ground that it made it demonstrably less likely that the 2:1 nexus would be produced. Even though the Parliament is at liberty to alter the formula, it was pointed out that this is subject to the overriding requirement that the required nexus be secured 'as nearly as practicable'. The original s 24 formula, reflected in the terms of the electoral law before the 1964 amendment, presented a practicable alternative that is more likely to secure the nexus, and this practicable alternative, it was held, meant that the 1964 amendment was constitutionally invalid.

On the question of the 1973 amendment the reasoning in *McKellar* varied. Stephen J, with whom Mason J agreed, pointed out that the *First Territory Senators*

**123** *Commonwealth Electoral Act 1918* (Cth), s 48(2); see also ss 50, 59.
**124** *Representation Act 1905* (Cth), s 10.
**125** *Representation Act 1964* (Cth), s 3.
**126** See Part II.2 above.
**127** *Representation Act 1973* (Cth), ss 3 and 5, inserting s 1A and amending s 10 of the *Representation Act 1905*.
**128** *Attorney-General (NSW); Ex rel McKellar v Commonwealth* (1977) 139 CLR 527.

case[129] treated the capacity of the Commonwealth to make provision for Territory representation as a proviso to the requirements of both s 7, in relation to the Senate, and s 24, in relation to the House, with the implication that Territory representation need not comply with the nexus requirement in s 24.[130] Moreover, Stephen J observed, if Territory seats and Territory populations are introduced into the quota calculation, the result will usually be distorted.[131] Gibbs J came to a similar conclusion, observing that if the nexus requirement did apply to Territory representation, then the addition of Territory representatives in one house would require adjustments to be made to the number of State representatives in the other house.[132] Aickin J, however, dissented on this point. He considered that the *First Territory Senators* case had treated Territory senators as 'senators in the full sense', with the implication that the s 24 nexus requirement must apply to them just as it applies to State senators. Accordingly, Aickin J seemed to suggest that an increase in Territory senators without a corresponding increase in Territory members of the House would, in order to comply with the nexus requirement, necessitate an *increase* in State members.[133] However, he denied that an increase in Territory members of the House without a corresponding addition of Territory senators would require a *reduction* in State members. Rather, he considered that the additional Territory members would simply have to be added to the total number of State members, notwithstanding the impact on the nexus.[134] As Colin Howard pointed out, this was to treat the nexus not so much as ensuring that the Senate will never be outnumbered by *more* than a ratio of 2:1, but rather that the House of Representatives will never outnumber the Senate by *less* than 2:1. It was, in other words, to accord a certain primacy to the House of Representatives over the Senate.[135] However, as noted, Aickin J was in dissent on this point.

Subsequent to the decision in *McKellar*, the *Commonwealth Electoral Act* was amended to reinstate the original remainder rule so as to make it more likely a nexus will be achieved. Territory representation continues to complicate matters, however, because presently the two Territories are entitled to two members of the House and two senators each, which is a proportion of 1:1, not 2:1.[136] Accordingly, at the 2013 election for example, the representation of the States and Territories in the House of Representatives was: New South Wales 48, Victoria 37, Queensland 30, Western Australia 15, South Australia 11, Tasmania 5, Australian Capital Territory 2, Northern Territory 2, resulting in a total of 150 members (146 State and 4 Territory members).[137] This compares to a

**129** *Western Australia v Commonwealth* (1975) 134 CLR 201.
**130** *Attorney-General (NSW); Ex rel McKellar v Commonwealth* (1977) 139 CLR 527, 561–2.
**131** Ibid, 554.
**132** Ibid, 543. While both Stephen J and Gibbs J had dissented in the *First Territory Senators* case, they accepted it as binding in *McKellar*.
**133** Ibid, 576–7.
**134** Ibid, 581.
**135** Colin Howard, 'Attorney-General for the New South Wales, Ex Rel McKellar v Commonwealth' (1977) 11 *Melbourne University Law Review* 128, 133.
**136** *Commonwealth Electoral Act 1918* (Cth), ss 40, 48.
**137** For a full list of the number of members since 1901 see Wright and Fowler, above n 20, Appendix 11.

total representation in the Senate of 76 (72 State and 4 Territory senators). The resulting proportion between the two houses for the States is 2.03 and for the States and Territories combined is 1.97.

### Electoral districts and equality of voting power

As noted, the draft Commonwealth Bill adopted by the Federal Convention of 1891 had proposed that each State would have one representative in the House of Representatives for every 30 000 of its people.[138] This reflected the resolution moved by Henry Parkes at the outset of the Convention, which stated that the House of Representatives ought to be 'elected by districts formed on a population basis'.[139] If terms such as these had been inserted into the text of the Constitution, they would have provided some ground for the proposition that the Constitution requires that each electoral district must, as nearly as practicable, have an equal population resident within it. However, the framers of the Constitution eventually settled on the language of s 24, including the 2:1 nexus and the requirement of proportionality to the population of each State, without any specific mention of the basis on which particular local electoral divisions would be formed. They also provided in s 24 that each State would be guaranteed a minimum of at least five members in the House of Representatives, which was an increase from the guarantee of four members required by the draft Constitution of 1891. All three of these features, and especially the last, impose significant qualifications on the 'national-democratic' character of the House. In addition, s 29 of the Constitution, like the corresponding provision of the United States Constitution,[140] explicitly confers power on the State and Commonwealth Parliaments to determine electoral divisions for the House of Representatives, with the Commonwealth given what was intended to be a supervisory role in order to check any abuses and ensure an appropriate degree of consistency.[141]

Despite these features of ss 24 and 29, s 24 also requires that the House is to be composed of members 'directly chosen by the people of the Commonwealth'. Does this provide a basis for concluding that the Constitution requires that federal electoral divisions must have, as nearly as practicable, the same number of residents or the same number of eligible voters? Certainly, when the framers of the Constitution discussed the question, they rejected the idea, and it seems that they framed ss 24 and 29 to avoid any such implication.[142] However, in two important cases considered by the High Court, it was argued that the requirement of a 'choice by the people' implies that electoral divisions, for both Commonwealth and State elections, must be approximately equal in size.[143] Before considering those cases, it is helpful to put the issue into its present context.

**138** *Convention Debates, Sydney* (1891) 947.
**139** Ibid, 23, 499–500; see also *Convention Debates, Adelaide* (1897) 17.
**140** United States Constitution, art I, s 4, cl 1.
**141** Aroney, above n 47, 231–5. In 1902 the Commonwealth enacted comprehensive legislation to regulate federal elections, and has covered the field ever since: see *Commonwealth Electoral Act 1902* (Cth); *Commonwealth Franchise Act 1902* (Cth).
**142** Aroney, above n 47, 235–7.
**143** *Attorney-General (Cth); Ex rel McKinlay v Commonwealth* (1975) 135 CLR 1; *McGinty v Western Australia* (1996) 186 CLR 140.

The *Commonwealth Electoral Act* currently requires that each State is to be distributed into electoral divisions and that one member of the House of Representatives is to be chosen for each division.[144] Periodical redistributions of electorates are determined by special committees of politically independent electoral officials, who are required to follow a complex set of procedures and instructions.[145] These are intended, among other things, to ensure that:

- the number of electors in each electoral division is preferably within a range of 96.5 to 103.5 per cent of the average number of electors projected for each division in the State, and that any deviation from the quota of electors is at most no more than one-tenth;[146]
- due consideration is given to 'community of interests', including economic, social and regional interests, means of communication and travel, physical features and boundaries of existing divisions;[147]
- there is opportunity for suggestions, comments and objections in relation to possible and proposed redistributions to be lodged and considered, and written reasons made available.[148]

These requirements point to two countervailing conceptions of representative democracy.[149] One view, premised on the idea that democracy ought to be based on the equal rights of individual citizens, maintains that electoral divisions ought as nearly as practicable to have equal numbers of voters. The other view considers that democracy properly involves the representation of communities of people, united by such things as locality, geography, culture and economics. The use of local electorates, rather than electing representatives at large for the entire State, comports with the communal conception of representation, as does the basic premise of the Senate conceived as a house in which each Original State is equally represented. However, the requirement that representation in the House of Representatives is distributed among each State in proportion to its population suggests a more individualist conception of democracy in which each citizen's vote counts equally in the election of representatives of each State.

In *McKinlay*,[150] the High Court had to consider an earlier version of the *Commonwealth Electoral Act 1918*, which similarly established a discretion to deviate from the quota for each electorate up to a maximum of 10 per cent, and which required consideration to be given to such factors as community of interests, means of communication and travel, physical features and existing boundaries.

**144** *Commonwealth Electoral Act 1918* (Cth), ss 56, 57.
**145** Ibid, ss 60, 70, 78.
**146** Ibid, ss 66, 73. An electorate that differs by more than one-tenth from the average number of electors per electorate within the relevant State or Territory is deemed to be 'malapportioned', triggering a redistribution: ibid, s 59(2), (10).
**147** Ibid, ss 66, 73.
**148** Ibid, ss 64, 69, 72–4.
**149** See Nicholas Aroney, 'Democracy, Community and Federalism in Electoral Apportionment Cases: The United States, Canada and Australia in Comparative Perspective' (2008) 58(4) *University of Toronto Law Journal* 421.
**150** *Attorney-General (Cth); Ex rel McKinlay v Commonwealth* (1975) 135 CLR 1.

The evidence suggested that, largely because several years had elapsed since the last redistribution, at the time the case was decided this produced a degree of inequality between electorates within particular States as high as 38.5 per cent, although on the whole the disparity was significantly less than this. In *McGinty v Western Australia*,[151] the Court had to consider the *Electoral Districts Act 1947* (WA) and the *Constitution Acts Amendment Act 1899* (WA), which allowed even more extensive differences in the size of electorates for the Western Australian Legislative Assembly and Legislative Council.[152] The first of these Acts divided the State into two areas, metropolitan and non-metropolitan, and stipulated that the first be divided into 34 districts and the second into 23 districts, with the requirement that within each area the number of enrolled voters in each district must not be more or less than 15 per cent of the average number for each district within that area. As a result the largest electorate had 26 580 voters, while the smallest had 9135, which amounted to a 291 per cent difference in size. The second Act divided the State into six regions, each varying significantly in population, but returning either seven or five members of the Legislative Council. This scheme resulted in effective quotients (reflecting the proportion of voting population to number of members elected) of 34 161 for the largest region and 9 097 for the smallest, amounting to a difference of 376 per cent.

The Western Australian *Constitution Act 1889*, like the Commonwealth Constitution, effectively requires that members of the State Parliament are to be 'chosen directly by the people'.[153] *McKinlay* involved the question whether the Commonwealth provision, and *McGinty* involved the question whether either the Commonwealth or the Western Australian provisions, necessarily imply a guarantee of electoral equality such that the electoral distributions in each case were constitutionally invalid. In both cases a majority of the High Court declined to find that the legislation was unconstitutional on this ground. In coming to these conclusions, the justices drew on several modalities of argument, reasoning from the relevant Constitution's text, structure and history, seeking to identify the fundamental principles and purposes that it was designed to secure, and giving extended consideration to decisions in the United States and Canada in relation to the same general issue.

Several of the majority justices in both cases emphasised the importance of judicial restraint and fidelity to the text of the Constitution over and against judicially-devised implications.[154] In *McKinlay*, Barwick CJ maintained that the Constitution is to be interpreted as a legal document – not by reference 'to slogans or to political catch-cries or to vague and imprecise expressions of political philosophy', but rather according to a methodology of 'strict and complete legalism',

**151** *McGinty v Western Australia* (1996) 186 CLR 140.
**152** See also *Attorney-General (WA) v Marquet* (2003) 217 CLR 545, 566, 576–8, 599–608, 628–9, discussed in Chapter 10, Part IV.4.
**153** The requirement is 'entrenched' in the State Constitution through a 'manner and form' provision which prevents the requirement from being altered without approval by the people at a referendum: *Constitution Act 1889* (WA), ss 73(2)(c).
**154** *McGinty* (1996) 186 CLR 140, 168–71.

a method which requires close attention to the text of the Constitution, read as an entire document and understood in light of the historical context in which it was enacted.[155] Brennan CJ put the matter similarly in *McGinty*, when he insisted that constitutional implications must be based on the text and structure of the Constitution, and that it is for the Court to 'reveal' or 'uncover' such implications by 'judicial exegesis', rather than to take the broad concept of 'representative democracy', attribute to it a meaning derived from 'sources extrinsic to the Constitution', and invalidate a law on that basis.[156] This approach focused attention on s 29 of the Commonwealth Constitution, which in unqualified terms explicitly affirms the power of the Commonwealth Parliament to determine electoral divisions. Such a provision, it was noted, reflects the confidence that the framers had in the capacity of traditional Westminster-style parliamentary processes to maintain the existence of fair and workable systems of representative government.[157] However, did this mean that the discretion of the relevant Parliament was entirely unfettered? All members of the Court in both cases had to acknowledge the constitutional requirement that the Parliament is to be 'chosen by the people', and most in one way or another recognised that the Commonwealth and State Constitutions make provision for an operating system of representative government. The question came down to whether and if so to what extent this required that electoral divisions must be, as close as practicable, equal in size.

In his dissenting judgment in *McKinlay*, Murphy J took the implication the furthest. Drawing on interpretations of the corresponding provisions of the United States Constitution, he concluded that the Australian Constitution requires that electoral divisions must contain, as nearly as practicable, an equal number of electors.[158] Writing soon after the enactment of the Commonwealth Constitution, Harrison Moore had said that the 'predominant feature' of the Constitution is the 'prevalence of the democratic principle', and that this principle involves the proposition that the 'rights of individuals' are best secured by ensuring to each person '*an equal share* ... in political power'.[159] Picking up on this observation, Murphy J claimed that there is a 'democratic theme of equal sharing of political power which pervades the Constitution'.[160] Stephen J, however, took a different view. He pointed out that while the Constitution was undoubtedly intended to establish a system of representative government, this concept covers 'a whole spectrum of political institutions, each differing in countless respects yet answering to that generic description'.[161] The framers of the Constitution were particular about which features of the system would be entrenched in the Constitution and which features would be left to parliamentary discretion.

**155** *McKinlay* (1975) 135 CLR 1, 17.
**156** *McGinty* (1996) 186 CLR 140, 168–9; see also 184–5, 230–36.
**157** *McKinlay* (1975) 135 CLR 1, 20, 24, 46, 57–9; *McGinty* (1996) 186 CLR 140, 183–6.
**158** *McKinlay* (1975) 135 CLR 1, 70, 79.
**159** Harrison Moore, *Constitution of the Commonwealth of Australia* (John Murray, 1st ed, 1902) 329.
**160** *McKinlay* (1975) 135 CLR 1, 69, 71.
**161** Ibid, 56–7. Likewise *McGinty* (1996) 186 CLR 140, 183–4.

Also writing at the time the Constitution was enacted, Quick and Garran had observed, somewhat contrary to Moore, that it is the federal idea which 'pervades and largely dominates the structure of the newly-created community, its Parliamentary executive and judiciary departments'.[162] The Constitution clearly makes provision for a system of representative government, but it is a form of democracy that has been adapted to federalism. This point was made by several of the justices in *McGinty*, most emphatically by Gummow J, who referred to 'the adaptation of representative democracy to federalism by the framers of the Constitution.'[163] As Gummow J observed, a specifically 'federal' conception of representation is apparent in several features of the Constitution, including:

- equal representation of the States in the Senate;
- minimum of representation of the States in the House of Representatives;
- amendment of the Constitution through a referendum in which both a majority of Australian voters and a majority of voters in a majority of States must agree (with the further requirement that changes to the representation of any State in the federal Parliament or to the boundaries of any State can only occur with the consent of a majority of voters of the relevant State); and
- enactment of the *Australia Acts 1986* predicated upon the agreement of the Commonwealth and all of the Australian States (noting that the *Australia Acts* can also only be amended with the unanimous agreement of the Commonwealth and the States).[164]

These features, Gummow J reasoned, show that the framers constructed a complex system of federal democracy which contradicts the idea of electoral equality in the sense of an individual right to equal voting power. As McHugh J put it, 'inequality of individual voting power is one of [the Constitution's] striking features'.[165]

Federalism was influential in the reasoning in *McGinty* in another way as well. Part of the plaintiff's argument was that the Commonwealth Constitution, quite apart from the Western Australian Constitution, restricts the capacity of the Western Australian Parliament to provide for a State electoral system that impermissibly departs from the principle of electoral equality. However, this argument encountered the problem that it is difficult to see how an implication of the Commonwealth Constitution relating specifically to the federal electoral system should have any legal bearing on the power of the State Parliaments to regulate their own State electoral systems. This consideration seems to have been decisive for several members of the Court in *McGinty*, including the two dissenting justices, Toohey and Gaudron JJ.[166]

**162** Quick and Garran, above n 2, 332.
**163** *McGinty* (1996) 186 CLR 140, 236–40, 243–5, 266–7, 269–78, 291–2.
**164** Australian Constitution, ss 7, 24, 128; *Australia Acts 1986* (UK and Cth), s 15. These provisions have their counterparts in the United States and Canada. See United States Constitution, art I, ss 2 and 3, and art V; Canadian Constitution, s 22 and pt V.
**165** *McGinty* (1996) 186 CLR 140, 236.
**166** Ibid, 176, 189, 210, 216.

Toohey and Gaudron JJ's dissent was based on the Western Australian Constitution itself, Gaudron J observing that the adaptation to federalism that existed at a Commonwealth level did not apply to the Western Australian Constitution.[167] However, both judges considered that the State Constitution entrenched a concept of representative democracy which ought to be interpreted according to 'current democratic standards', and that the extreme disparities in electoral size were therefore unconstitutional.[168] How were these standards to be identified? Toohey J seemed to be especially concerned lest they should rest on 'no more definite standard than the personal opinion of the judge who declares it'.[169] He therefore drew attention to the fact that the Commonwealth and other State electoral systems required a much greater level of electoral equality than Western Australia's, and he commented that this 'move towards equality of electorate size reflects a change in society's perception of the appropriate expression of the concept of representative democracy'.[170] However, this did not quite resolve the problem, as it could still be asked why standards adopted in other electoral systems should inform the meaning of the Western Australian Constitution. For the question that federalism always poses in such cases is: which society, and which people?

Do these cases mean that the Commonwealth Constitution imposes no restrictions at all on the discretion of the Parliaments when constructing the electoral system? In *McKinlay*, several justices seemed to acknowledge that the Court would intervene if what was enacted meant that one could no longer say that there would be 'choice by the people',[171] especially in a case of very gross disproportionality.[172] For example, McTiernan and Jacobs JJ thought that while no 'exact content' can be given to the idea of a popular choice, an inequality in the distribution of electorates was a factor that could lead to the conclusion that the electoral system was unconstitutional.[173] However, the outcome in *McKinlay* and *McGinty* suggests that the constitutional requirement is not very exacting, and that it is acceptable regarding electoral divisions for the House of Representatives to take into consideration demographic and geographic factors, just as the representation of the States, rather than population, is the fundamental factor underlying the design of the Senate.[174] Apart from this, all that s 24 relevantly requires is that the total number of members of the House of Representatives for each State must be proportionate to its population, and the Court was willing in *McKinlay* to insist that redistributions must be undertaken in time for each general election (ordinarily held every three years) to ensure that this

**167** Ibid, 222–3.
**168** Ibid, 201–2, 216, 221–3.
**169** See *Amalgamated Society of Engineers v Adelaide Steamship Co Ltd* (1920) 28 CLR 129, 142.
**170** *McGinty* (1996) 186 CLR 140, 202; see also 221.
**171** *McKinlay* (1975) 135 CLR 1, 57–9.
**172** Ibid, 61.
**173** Ibid, 35; see also 38.
**174** At a referendum held in 1988, voters rejected a proposal to amend the Constitution to require that electoral divisions must not deviate by more than 10 per cent: *Constitution Alteration (Fair Elections) 1988* (Cth).

is the case.[175] Beyond this, the integrity of Australia's electoral systems relies, very substantially, on the decision of the Parliament to establish independent electoral commissions in each jurisdiction, removing such decisions from direct political influence or manipulation.[176]

### The franchise and the right to vote

Sections 8 and 30 of the Constitution effectively provide that the qualifications of electors for Commonwealth elections are, until the Commonwealth Parliament otherwise provides, to be as prescribed in each State. Section 41 also provides:

> No adult person who has or acquires a right to vote at elections for the more numerous House of the Parliament of a State shall, while the right continues, be prevented by any law of the Commonwealth from voting at elections for either House of the Parliament of the Commonwealth.

The immediate purpose of s 41 was to preserve the voting rights of women, who had secured the right to vote in South Australia in 1894 and in Western Australia in 1899. It also operated to preserve the existing voting rights of Aboriginal people, who were entitled to vote in four States, although few knew they had this right or had the opportunity to exercise it.

The *Commonwealth Franchise Act 1902* granted women the right to vote and to stand for election at a Commonwealth level. A proposal to extend the right to all Aborigines was also passed in the Senate but was rejected in the House of Representatives. It was not until the 1949 election that the Commonwealth franchise was extended to Aboriginal people who were or had been members of the Defence Force, and at the 1963 election to all Aboriginal people.[177] At the 1974 election the voting age was also reduced from 21 to 18. Registration to vote became compulsory in 1911, and voting has been compulsory since the 1925 election.[178]

The scope of s 41 has been a matter of controversy. The provision clearly applies to voting rights that any person had at the establishment of the Commonwealth, but it also applies to rights subsequently 'acquired'. The difficulty lies in understanding the relationship between the general power of the Parliaments to determine the franchise (ss 8, 30 and 51(xxxvi)) and the requirements of s 41. The first set of provisions confers a general power on the Commonwealth, and it is to be expected that the Commonwealth will ordinarily enact laws which have a uniform operation in all of the States, prevailing over any inconsistent State laws (pursuant to s 109). With this in mind, and reflecting on the evidence of the Convention Debates of the 1890s, Quick and Garran considered that despite the lack of any explicit time limitation,

**175** *McKinlay* (1975) 135 CLR 1, 29–35, 40–41, 49–53, 60, 63, 78.
**176** Eg, *Commonwealth Electoral Act 1918*, s 6, establishing the Australian Electoral Commission as an independent statutory authority.
**177** *Commonwealth Electoral Act 1949* (Cth); *Commonwealth Electoral Act 1962* (Cth).
**178** Wright and Fowler, above n 20, 82.

s 41 was intended to operate only until the time that the Commonwealth enacted a uniform franchise.[179]

In *King v Jones*, the question came up in a different form. In the early 1970s, some of the States, including South Australia, lowered the voting age for State elections to 18, prior to the Commonwealth doing so. It was argued by an 18-year-old South Australian that by virtue of s 41 she was entitled to vote in Commonwealth elections.[180] The Court rejected her claim on the basis that s 41 on its terms applies only to 'adult persons' and that this must be understood by reference to its meaning in 1900, at which time the term referred to a person who had attained the age of 21. Interestingly, a majority of the Court accepted for the sake of argument (but without deciding) that s 41 could have an application after the Commonwealth had established a uniform franchise. Menzies J was quite emphatic. He considered that s 41 is a 'permanent constitutional provision' which applies to a person who at any time acquires a relevant voting right in a State.[181]

The question of the time horizon of s 41 was determined in *R v Pearson; Ex parte Sipka*.[182] The case was brought by four persons entitled to vote in New South Wales but excluded from voting in a forthcoming Commonwealth election because they had not lodged their application to be registered to vote in time. Murphy J, who dissented, argued that s 41 should be given a purposive interpretation as a rights-protecting clause, an interpretation which happened also to be in accord with its literal meaning as well as the historical evidence of the Convention Debates.[183] However, a majority of the Court understood the provision to be effectively transitional, noting that to read it otherwise would destroy the capacity of the Commonwealth to enact a uniform franchise.[184] In 1988 a referendum to replace s 41 with a provision guaranteeing the right to vote was defeated in every State.[185]

Section 41 is not the only possible source of a constitutional right to vote. In *McKinlay*, McTiernan and Jacobs JJ suggested that the meaning of a 'choice by the people' in s 24, although a question of degree, falls to be applied to 'different circumstances at different times', and that what s 24 requires 'depends in part upon the common understanding of the time'.[186] Noting that universal adult franchise had been long-established, they said that it was 'doubtful whether … anything less than this could now be described as a choice by the people'.[187]

**179** Quick and Garran, above n 2, 483–7.
**180** *King v Jones* (1972) 128 CLR 221.
**181** Ibid, 246.
**182** (1983) 152 CLR 254.
**183** *R v Pearson; Ex parte Sipka* (1983) 152 CLR 254, 268–72.
**184** Ibid, 260–64, 276–80. In order to preserve the equality of the voting power of the States in any referendum on a proposed alteration to the Constitution, s 128 provides that until a uniform franchise is established only half the votes of any State in which there is full adult suffrage will be counted. It was noted that if s 41 had a continuing operation, a State could subvert the policy of s 128 to maintain an effective equality among the States.
**185** *Constitution Alteration (Fair Elections) 1988* (Cth).
**186** *McKinlay* (1975) 135 CLR 1, 36.
**187** Ibid.

Whether they meant that this implies that a federal law which diverges from this would be unconstitutional is not entirely clear, for they also referred explicitly to the power of the Parliaments to determine the qualifications of electors pursuant to s 30. Murphy J went further, arguing that the idea of a choice by the people implies a choice by 'all the people capable of choosing, only excluding those incapable, such as minors and those of unsound mind'.[188] He considered that although women were deprived of the vote in some of the States at the time of federation, the 'silent operation of constitutional principles' meant that a contemporary law which purported to do so would be unconstitutional.[189] However, Gibbs, Mason and Stephen JJ flatly disagreed with the proposition that s 24 guarantees a universal franchise.[190]

In a line of important cases beginning with *Australian Capital Television Pty Ltd v Commonwealth*,[191] decided in 1992, the High Court found the Constitution's provisions for a system of representative government, and especially the requirement that members of Parliament are chosen by the people, necessarily implies the existence of a constitutional guarantee of freedom of communication about political matters.[192] In the reasoning of some of the judges in those cases there were suggestions that the Constitution, as Deane and Toohey JJ put it, guarantees that 'all citizens of the Commonwealth are entitled to share equally in the exercise of those ultimate powers of governmental control'.[193]

This idea of a constitutionally implied right to vote was affirmed in *Roach v Electoral Commissioner*.[194] The case involved amendments to the *Commonwealth Electoral Act* which disqualified from voting in federal elections any person serving a sentence of imprisonment for an offence against a Commonwealth, State or Territory law. At the time of federation, most State laws disqualified persons convicted of 'treason, felony or infamous offence', and New South Wales and Victoria had even stronger disqualifications.[195] Between 1902 and 1983, Commonwealth law disqualified persons serving prison sentences of one year or more, enabling otherwise qualified persons serving shorter sentences to vote in federal elections. In 1983 the disqualifying period was increased to five years; in 2004 it was reduced to three years; and in 2006 the minimum period was removed altogether, so that a term of imprisonment of any duration disqualified a person from being eligible to vote.[196] The plaintiff, who was serving an effective six year sentence for burglary, theft and other offences, argued that the 2006 and 2004 amendments were constitutionally invalid on several grounds,

**188** Ibid, 68–9.
**189** Ibid, 69.
**190** Ibid, 44, 62, 57–8.
**191** (1992) 177 CLR 106.
**192** *Lange v Australian Broadcasting Corporation* (1997) 189 CLR 520, discussed in Chapter 5, Part V.
**193** *Nationwide News Pty Ltd v Wills* (1992) 177 CLR 1, 72. See also *McGinty* (1996) 186 CLR 140, 166–7, 221–2, 201, but contrast 183.
**194** (2007) 233 CLR 162.
**195** *Roach v Electoral Commissioner* (2007) 233 CLR 162, 212–13.
**196** Ibid, 212–13, 183.

the most important being that they were contrary to the constitutionally mandated system of representative and responsible government and the requirement in ss 7 and 24 that members of Parliament are to be 'directly chosen by the people'.

A majority of the Court held that the 2006 amendments were unconstitutional, while the 2004 amendments were validly enacted. While the general line of the Court's reasoning is clear enough, its exact nature and scope is not entirely clear as to whether the conclusion rests on an implication of the general concept of representative and responsible government or the specific requirement of a 'choice by the people'.[197] For Gleeson CJ, the ground of the decision seems to have been the latter. Acknowledging that the requirement of a choice by the people did not mandate universal adult franchise in 1901, and accepting that the 'meaning' of the phrase had not changed, he nonetheless considered that the long established fact of universal adult franchise was 'an historical development of constitutional significance' which shaped its application to contemporary circumstances.[198] Noting that the franchise 'lies at the centre of our concept of participation in the life of the community, and of citizenship', he concluded that disenfranchisement of any group of adult citizens other than for a 'substantial reason' would not be consistent with the constitutional requirement of a choice by the people.[199] Gummow, Kirby and Crennan JJ pointed out that the question concerned the relationship between the 'scope for legislative evolution' allowed by ss 8, 30 and 51(xxxvi) and the 'constitutionally mandated fundamentals' prescribed by ss 7, 24 and related provisions.[200] These fundamentals require, they said, that 'the franchise is held generally by all adults or all adult citizens unless there be substantial reasons for excluding them'.[201] The question then became whether the disqualification of prisoners could be justified, and they concluded that the restrictions imposed in 2006 were not justified, principally because they had the effect of 'stigmatising' prisoners rather than laying down appropriate standards of 'fitness and probity of character', based on the degree of culpability of the prisoner, as conditions on the right to vote.[202]

This reasoning involved the Court in an ethical evaluation of the Commonwealth law by reference to considerations that are not explicitly found in the text of the Constitution. The dissenting judgment of Hayne J (with whom Heydon J substantially agreed) focused rather on the relevant provisions of the Constitution, understood in the context of their enactment history.[203] That history suggests that the framers of the Constitution intended ss 8, 30 and 51(xxxvi) to give the Commonwealth Parliament power not only to establish a uniform franchise,

**197** Nicholas Aroney, 'Towards the "Best Explanation" of the Constitution' (2011) 30 *University of Queensland Law Journal* 145.
**198** *Roach v Electoral Commissioner* (2007) 233 CLR 162, 173–4.
**199** Ibid, 174.
**200** Ibid, 187.
**201** Ibid, 198, citing *McGinty* (1996) 186 CLR 140, 170.
**202** *Roach v Electoral Commissioner* (2007) 233 CLR 162, 192, 200–02.
**203** Ibid, 205–6.

but also to exercise a supervisory role in relation to any undue restrictions on the franchise laid down in State laws, just as s 29 was intended to operate in relation to electoral apportionment.[204] Some specific requirements were prescribed in the Constitution (eg, s 30: 'each elector shall vote only once'),[205] but the rest was deliberately left to parliamentary determination. Section 30 also picked up the requirements of State laws, all of which disqualified some prisoners from voting; and s 128, in referring to States in which 'adult franchise prevails', suggests that the principle of adult franchise was understood to be consistent with the exclusion of some prisoners from the vote.[206] Much of Hayne J's reasoning was thus directed to an interpretation of the Constitution that made sense of as much of its textual details and structural relationships as possible and which avoided importing 'a democratic theory which exists and has its content independent of the constitutional text'.[207]

The scope and nature of the franchise was also considered in *Rowe v Electoral Commissioner*.[208] The case concerned provisions of the *Commonwealth Electoral Act* which determined the point in time at which an application for enrolment as a voter, or for a transfer of enrolment to a new electorate, must be lodged. Since 1983, the electoral roll had closed seven days after the issue of writs for the election; in 2006 the rule operating prior to 1983 was restored, pursuant to which the roll closed at 8 p.m. on the day of the issue of the writs, subject to the right to make enrolment changes up to three days later. The ostensible reasons for the change were to enable sufficient time to check the roll for fraudulent enrolments and to facilitate the proper distribution of electorates based on reliable electoral data.[209] But as a consequence numerous young people who had recently reached the age of 18, as well as people who had recently changed residence, were not entitled to vote in the 2010 election – albeit that for many this was as a result of their contravention of the legal obligation to enrol or to register a change of address.[210] A majority of the Court held that in light of this practical effect, the change to the cut-off dates was unconstitutional because it was not reasonably appropriate and adapted to serve a legitimate end compatible with maintenance of the system of representative government prescribed by the Constitution. In so reasoning, the majority engaged with, but rejected, the rationales offered in support of the new cut-off period.[211] This amounted to an assessment of whether the 2006 law could be justified, measured by the majority's assessment of whether there was a compelling problem or difficulty that needed to be addressed, and whether the measures recommended by the Joint

**204** Ibid, 208–9.
**205** As was acknowledged in the joint judgment: ibid, 187.
**206** Ibid, 206, 211.
**207** Ibid, 214–15.
**208** (2010) 243 CLR 1.
**209** Joint Standing Committee on Electoral Matters, *Report of the Inquiry into the Conduct of the 2004 Federal Election and Matters Related Thereto* (2005).
**210** *Commonwealth Electoral Act 1918* (Cth), s 101.
**211** *Rowe v Electoral Commissioner* (2010) 243 CLR 1, 34–9, 58–61, 117–20.

Parliamentary Committee on Electoral Matters were appropriate to addressing them.

In his dissenting judgment, Hayne J objected to this approach on the ground that it drew on contestable ideas external to the text and structure of the Constitution and because it begged the question by assuming that the law prior to the 2006 amendment effectively laid down a constitutional requirement.[212] Heydon J similarly thought that the plaintiff's argument was self-contradictory in treating legislative developments as standards of constitutional validity, and that it resulted in the extraordinary proposition that a law which imposes a duty to enrol to vote is constitutionally invalid if it defers the processing of a late enrolment application until after the next polling day.[213] Kiefel J, who also dissented, did so on the more limited ground that she considered the measures to be proportionate to the legitimate objective of encouraging compliance with citizens' electoral obligations.[214]

Both *Roach* and *Rowe* relied on earlier *dicta* concerning the franchise that had been expressed, by McTiernan and Jacobs JJ in *McKinlay* and by Brennan CJ in *McGinty*, to the effect that the Constitution ought to be interpreted in a manner that accords with contemporary standards and current beliefs.[215] But in the circumstances of *Roach* and *Rowe* it was not at all clear that general contemporary beliefs about prisoners' rights and electoral enrolment obligations coincided with the propositions for which the plaintiffs in each case were contending. A subtly different line of argument was therefore required, which involved the proposition that the content of the constitutionally prescribed system of representative government had evolved as a consequence of statutory changes over time, and that there was a 'ratchet' effect according to which the Parliament, having adopted a particular standard of electoral participation, could not subsequently diminish it.[216] However, it has been pointed out that the result of this reasoning is remarkable, because it turns the provisions of the Constitution which explicitly grant past and present Parliaments power to determine the franchise as they deem fit (ss 8, 30 and 51(xxxvi)) into means by which the power of future Parliaments is controlled, when read in the light of provisions that make no explicit mention of the franchise (ss 7 and 24).[217] At stake in these cases are very important questions about the approach that the High Court ought to take in interpreting the Constitution. Should it seek to interpret the Constitution so that it conforms with 'contemporary' expectations and beliefs? If so, how is the Court to identify what these expectations and beliefs are? Alternatively, does the legitimacy of the Court's decisions depend on the extent to which it engages in a disciplined manner with the text and

**212** Ibid, 66–7; see also 129.
**213** Ibid, 102–3.
**214** Ibid, 145–7.
**215** *McKinlay* (1975) 135 CLR 1, 36; *McGinty* (1996) 186 CLR 140, 170.
**216** This was especially clear in the judgments of Gleeson CJ and French CJ in the two cases: *Roach v Electoral Commissioner* (2007) 233 CLR 162, 173; *Rowe v Electoral Commissioner* (2010) 243 CLR 1, 18–19.
**217** Anne Twomey, 'Rowe v Electoral Commissioner – Evolution or Creationism?' (2012) 31 *University of Queensland Law Journal* 181.

structure of the Constitution itself? If so, can this be done effectively without taking into consideration the historical context in which the Constitution came into being, and the ideas and values which demonstrably influenced its framers? And is it legitimate for the Court to read the specific, unfettered powers given to the Parliaments, to regulate elections and determine the franchise, in a manner that subordinates them to inferences drawn from very general provisions describing the broad characteristics of those Parliaments as representative of 'the people'? [218]

## Qualifications of members of Parliament

As noted, the qualifications of candidates and members of the Commonwealth Parliament are determined partly by the Constitution and partly by Commonwealth legislation. The Constitution lays down the following requirements:

- before taking his or her seat, every member of Parliament must subscribe an oath or affirmation of allegiance in the prescribed form (s 42);
- a person cannot be chosen or sit as a member of both houses (s 43);
- a person cannot be chosen or sit as a member of Parliament if he or she:
  - is under allegiance to, or a subject or citizen of, a foreign power;
  - is attainted of treason or convicted and sentenced or liable to a sentence of imprisonment of one year or longer;
  - is an undischarged bankrupt or insolvent;
  - holds an office of profit under the Crown or a pension payable out of Commonwealth revenue;
  - has a pecuniary interest in any agreement with the Commonwealth other than a shareholder of a company together with at least 25 other shareholders (s 44).[219]

Some of these constitutional requirements and related procedures have been altered by the *Commonwealth Electoral Act 1918* (Cth). In particular, the Commonwealth has provided that:

- to be qualified for election as a member of Parliament a person must be 18 years of age, be an Australian citizen and be either an elector entitled to vote or a person qualified to become so entitled;[220]
- disputed elections may only be addressed by the Court of Disputed Returns, which is declared to be the High Court of Australia, which Court can refer the matter to the Federal Court of Australia;[221]

**218** For further discussion of these issues, see Chapter 5, Part V.

**219** Section 44 clarifies that the rule in relation to holding an office of profit or receiving a pension does not apply to members of Parliament who are appointed as the Queen's Ministers of State or persons who are partly in the pay of the military forces as officers or members thereof. Section 45 disqualifies persons who, when sitting members, become subject to the same general disabilities. Section 46 provides for the payment of a monetary penalty for breach of these requirements by a sitting member. Section 47 provides that until the Parliament otherwise provides, each house shall determine any dispute concerning member qualifications, vacancies and disputed elections pertaining to that house.

**220** *Commonwealth Electoral Act 1918* (Cth), s 163, altering the requirements contained in the Commonwealth Constitution, ss 16 and 34, which required a member of the Parliament to be at least 21 years of age, to have been resident for at least three years, and to be a subject of the Queen either natural born or at least five years naturalised.

**221** Ibid, ss 353 and 354.

- disputes concerning the qualifications of members or vacancies may be referred by either house to the Court of Disputed Returns.[222]

The qualifications for membership of the two houses of Parliament exist primarily to protect the integrity of the Parliament from improper external influences. This has led the High Court to adopt a generally purposive approach to their interpretation. In *Re Webster*, Barwick CJ held that the requirement that a member not have any direct or indirect pecuniary interest in any agreement with the Commonwealth public service was directed to executory contracts current for a sufficiently substantial period of time so as to be conceivably capable of influencing a member of Parliament in the performance of his or her parliamentary duties.[223]

Notably, the citizenship requirement in the *Commonwealth Electoral Act* qualifies the right both to be nominated for election and to be elected as a member of either house of Parliament.[224] For this reason, the High Court, acting as the Court of Disputed Returns, held in *Re Wood* that a candidate for the Senate had not been duly elected at the 1987 election because at the time of the election he was a British and not an Australian citizen.[225] It was too late that the candidate became a citizen after the election had been held. Moreover, the Court held that the fact that the candidate was unqualified did not vitiate other aspects of the election; it only meant that indications of voters' preferences for the particular candidate were ineffective.[226] Furthermore, as the candidate was never duly elected, the finding in the case did not result in a casual vacancy under s 15 of the Constitution. Rather, it meant that further counting of the relevant ballots was required to determine who would be elected instead of the candidate.[227] *Re Wood* left open the question, however, whether a person would be disqualified if they held dual citizenship in both Australia and the United Kingdom on the basis that they were therefore citizens of a foreign power, contrary to s 44(i) of the Constitution.[228]

In *Sykes v Cleary (No 2)*,[229] the High Court had to consider whether Phil Cleary, who at the time of his nomination and election was employed as a teacher by the Victorian Education Department, was thereby disqualified on the basis that he held an office of profit under the Crown for the purposes of s 44(iv). The general purpose of this particular ground of disqualification is to maintain a degree of separation between the Executive and the Parliament in order to safeguard the independent and proper operation of both. As Mason CJ, Toohey and McHugh JJ pointed out, the Australian provision was modelled on sections of the *Act of Settlement 1701* (UK) and the *Succession to the Crown Act*

**222** Ibid, s 376.
**223** *Re Webster* (1975) 132 CLR 270, 279–80.
**224** *Commonwealth Electoral Act 1918* (Cth), s 163.
**225** *Re Wood* (1988) 167 CLR 145, 162.
**226** Ibid, 165.
**227** Ibid, 167–8; see also 166. After the required recounting, another candidate from the same party was declared elected: ibid, 176.
**228** Ibid, 169.
**229** (1992) 176 CLR 77.

*1707* (UK) in order to encourage the development of a politically neutral public service and to limit the influence of the Executive Government over members of the House of Commons.[230] The disqualification undoubtedly applies to public servants who are permanent officers of the departments of government. However, bearing in mind that one purpose of the disqualification is to reduce the potential for Executive influence, their Honours considered that a restricted meaning should not be given to the idea of an 'office'. Even though Cleary had taken leave without pay, under the *Teaching Service Act 1981* (Vic) he was still deemed to be a 'permanent officer' of the government, and the Court considered that this was sufficient to disqualify him.[231] Moreover, attending closely to the text, structure and historical understanding of the constitutional provision, Mason CJ, Toohey and McHugh JJ noted that the disqualification applies to '*any* office ... under the Crown', and thus includes both State and Commonwealth level appointments.[232] Finally, noting that the disqualification applies to the act of 'being chosen' as a representative, it was observed that 'it is the polling day rather than the day on which the poll is declared that marks the time when a candidate is chosen by the people', and that if the disqualification did not apply to the entire process of nomination and polling, it would enable a candidate to avoid the requirement, with 'adverse consequences for the electoral process'.[233] It followed for a majority of the Court that Cleary was incapable of being chosen as a member of the House of Representatives.[234] Moreover, because voters' preferences in the election had been expressed within the framework of a larger field of candidates than ought to have been the case, there was a risk that a special recount of the ballots would result in a 'distortion' of the 'real intentions' of voters, and it was therefore also held that the election was void and that a fresh election would have to be held.[235] It was also necessary in *Cleary* to consider the status of two other candidates on the ballot who, although Australian citizens at the time of their nomination and election, were also citizens or nationals of another country. A majority noted that although the two candidates when becoming Australian citizens had renounced all other state allegiances, they had not taken reasonable steps to divest themselves of foreign citizenship, and for this reason they were disqualified under s 44(i) of the Constitution.[236]

The question whether the United Kingdom is to be regarded as a 'foreign power' for the purposes of the disqualification rule was addressed in *Sue v Hill*.[237]

**230** *Sykes v Cleary (No 2)* (1992) 176 CLR 77, 95–6.
**231** Ibid, 97–8.
**232** Ibid, 98 (emphasis in original). It was also noted that the special exemption for Ministers in s 44 of the Constitution includes State as well as Commonwealth Ministers, and that this was the opinion of learned contemporaries such as Quick and Garran, above n 2, 492–3 and W Harrison Moore, *The Constitution of the Commonwealth of Australia* (Maxwell, 2nd ed, 1910) 128.
**233** Ibid, 99–100.
**234** Ibid, 101, 108, 130, 132.
**235** Ibid, 102, 108, 130–31, 132.
**236** Ibid, 107–8, 113–14, 131–2.
**237** (1999) 199 CLR 462.

Heather Hill, who had become an Australian citizen prior to her nomination and election, did not take steps to renounce her British citizenship until after her election. Hill argued that so long as the United Kingdom retained any residual legal or constitutional ties to Australia it could not be regarded as a foreign power, and she was able to point to many features of the close, formative relationship between Australia's political institutions and those of the British Crown, the British Parliament and British courts.[238] While these notorious legal facts could not be denied,[239] a majority of the Court[240] considered that over time the wider constitutional context had changed considerably, including changes to the exact nature of the British Crown and the United Kingdom,[241] and the independence of Australia's legislative, judicial and executive institutions at both a State and Commonwealth level, particularly as a result of the *Australia Act 1986* (Cth).[242] Significantly, this meant that, in practice, the citizens of the United Kingdom and of Australia owe different allegiances and are called upon to obey different sets of laws and to be engaged in different armed conflicts, with the result that the United Kingdom is to be considered a 'foreign power' for the purposes of s 44(i) of the Constitution.[243]

## III Powers, functions and procedures

The design of the Parliament turns on two fundamental factors. The first concerns the composition of the two houses as the chambers in which the people of the Commonwealth and the States are distinctly represented. The second concerns the respective roles and powers of the two houses, especially in relation to the enactment of legislation and the responsibility of the Executive Government to the Parliament. Among the framers of the Constitution, those who wished to create a strong national government resisted the proposition that the Original States should be equally represented in the Senate, but when they lost on this issue, they turned their attention to limiting the powers of the Senate vis-à-vis the House of Representatives. However, they were not especially successful on this second issue either.

**238** See Chapter 1.
**239** *Sue v Hill* (1999) 199 CLR 462, 523–4.
**240** Gleeson CJ, Gaudron, Gummow and Hayne JJ. McHugh, Kirby and Callinan JJ did not decide the question as they considered that the Court lacked jurisdiction by virtue of s 47 of the Constitution and ss 353, 354 and 376 of the *Commonwealth Electoral Act 1918* (Cth).
**241** As referred to in the preamble and covering clause 2 of the *Commonwealth of Australia Constitution Act 1900* (UK). See *Sue v Hill* (1999) 199 CLR 462, 488–92.
**242** *Sue v Hill* (1999) 199 CLR 462, 490–503. Gleeson CJ, Gummow and Hayne JJ pointedly placed reliance on the Australian, and not the British, version of the *Australia Act 1986*; see also 526–8 (Gaudron J). Kirby J called for judicial 'restraint' when addressing parliamentary powers and privileges, including the capacity under s 47 to determine whether candidates are qualified to be elected, and he declined to comment specifically on whether the United Kingdom is a 'foreign power': at 558, 569–70. Callinan J, on the other hand, expressed concern about the legal uncertainty entailed in the 'evolutionary theory' of constitutional development expounded by the majority: at 571–3.
**243** Ibid, 503.

At stake was the relationship between federalism and parliamentary responsible government. Federalism, as it is understood and implemented in the United States and Switzerland, involves the proposition that the Senate or States' House should be no less powerful than the House of Representatives. However, parliamentary responsible government, as developed in Westminster-derived political communities, gives a predominant role to the lower house of the Parliament, whether it be the House of Commons in the United Kingdom or Canada, or the Legislative Assemblies of the Australian colonies.

The roles and powers of the two houses of the Australian Parliament cannot be understood properly or fully, therefore, without an appreciation of the system of parliamentary responsible government through which the Executive Government is made responsible to the Parliament, which is explained in detail in Chapter 6. In the remainder of this chapter, the focus will be on the particular powers and functions of the two houses of Parliament as they are regulated by the Constitution. Chapter 6 will explain how the system of responsible government operates as a means of regulating the exercise of the executive power of the Commonwealth, which is vested in the Queen and exercised by the Governor-General on the advice of Ministers of State who have the confidence and support of the Parliament. The control of the Parliament over government finance is the critical means by which the accountability of the Executive Government to the Parliament, and hence to the people, is secured. The House of Representatives and the Senate play distinct roles in this process.

## 1 Parliamentary control over government finance

The Commonwealth Executive Government needs money to operate. It obtains its necessary finance primarily through taxation and borrowing, as well as through fines, penalties, and fees for licences and services. In accordance with Westminster tradition, the Government may not impose taxes,[244] or even borrow money,[245] without the approval of Parliament. This approval is granted through legislation enacted by the Parliament. Section 51 of the Constitution, which contains most of the specific topics in respect of which the Commonwealth is empowered to make laws,[246] provides in paragraphs (ii) and (iv) that the Parliament may make laws with respect to 'taxation' and with respect to 'borrowing money on the public credit of the Commonwealth'. There are several controls and limitations on the power of the Commonwealth to impose taxation, such as the requirement in s 51(ii) that a taxation law must not 'discriminate between

**244** *Bill of Rights 1688* (UK): 'levying Money for or to the Use of the Crown by pretence of Prerogative without Grant of Parliament for longer time or in other manner than the same is or shall be granted is Illegal'. See *Commonwealth v Colonial Combing, Spinning & Weaving Co Ltd* (1922) 31 CLR 421, 433–4, 443–5, 459–60.
**245** *Public Governance, Performance and Accountability Act 2013* (Cth), s 56.
**246** See Chapter 3, Parts III and IV.

States or parts of States'.[247] The Constitution also provides a framework for the coordination of Commonwealth and State borrowing.[248] For the time being it is sufficient to note that the Commonwealth's power to legislate with respect to taxation is otherwise open-ended as to the extent and kinds of taxes that are imposed.[249] The Commonwealth has imposed numerous types of taxes pursuant to this power, including personal income tax, corporate income tax, goods and services tax, and customs duties on goods imported into Australia. Relatedly, s 90 of the Constitution provides that upon the imposition of uniform customs duties by the Commonwealth (which occurred in 1901), the power of the Commonwealth to impose customs duties and excise duties, and to grant bounties on the production or export of goods, became exclusive, thereby prohibiting the States from doing so.[250]

Once the Commonwealth has acquired revenues and moneys from various sources, s 81 of the Constitution requires that they form one Consolidated Revenue Fund to be appropriated for the purposes of the Commonwealth in the manner and subject to the charges and liabilities imposed by the Constitution. This happens automatically upon receipt of money by or on behalf of the Commonwealth, whether or not the Commonwealth has credited the money to a particular fund or account. Section 83 further requires that no money shall be drawn from the Treasury of the Commonwealth except under appropriation made by law. This in effect means that parliamentary approval is required, not only for taxation and borrowing, but also to earmark Commonwealth revenue to be applied for particular purposes or in relation to particular matters. The Commonwealth cannot spend or otherwise deal with its finances other than as appropriated by law or otherwise required by the Constitution.[251]

Moreover, there are two principal ways in which the Commonwealth can use its appropriated finances – either through spending undertaken by its own departments and officers, or by making grants to other bodies or institutions, including the States and local governments. In relation to Commonwealth spending, in addition to an appropriation earmarking moneys for expenditure, the High Court has recently held that the act of spending the money must itself be authorised by law. Some such categories of expenditure are specifically

**247** These controls and limitations include the requirement that the Commonwealth and the States must not tax the property of the other (s 114). The High Court has also developed a doctrine of implied intergovernmental immunities which prevents the Commonwealth and the States from certain forms of interference with each other's constitutional status and functions. See Chapter 4, Part III.

**248** Section 105 of the Constitution authorises the Commonwealth to take over State debts (alluded to in s 87), and s 105A authorises the Commonwealth and the States to make agreements with respect to the public debts of the States, and the Commonwealth to make laws for the validation and carrying out of such agreements.

**249** Section 51(ii) enables the Commonwealth to legislate for the administration of Australian taxation revenues principally through the Australian Tax Office.

**250** There is a long and complex case-law concerning the prohibition on the States of imposing excise duties. The case-law is summarised in Moens and Trone, above n 23, 338–50.

**251** *Attorney-General (Vic); Ex rel Dale v Commonwealth* (1945) 71 CLR 237, 271; *Brown v West* (1990) 169 CLR 195, 205. See also *Williams v Commonwealth (No 1)* (2012) 248 CLR 156, discussed in Chapter 7, Part IV.2.

authorised by the Constitution,[252] but in many other respects the expenditure must be authorised by statute.[253] Commonwealth grants are authorised by s 96 of the Constitution, which provides that 'until the Parliament otherwise provides, the Parliament may grant financial assistance to any State on such terms and conditions as the Parliament thinks fit'. The High Court has held that, although a State cannot be legally compelled to accept a grant, the Commonwealth can determine the purposes for which a grant will be made and the manner in which those purposes are effectuated,[254] going so far as to make the grant conditional on a State refraining from imposing income tax,[255] notwithstanding that s 96 was originally intended to be a transitional provision, confined to supplementing State finances in special circumstances and imposing terms and conditions relevant to those circumstances.[256] This interpretation of the grants power has effectively enabled the Commonwealth to regulate fields lying beyond its limited legislative powers.

Parliamentary supervision of government finance is facilitated by the Constitution through several specific requirements, namely:

- proposed laws appropriating revenue or moneys for the ordinary annual services of the Government must deal only with such appropriation (s 54);
- laws imposing taxation must deal only with the imposition of taxation, and any provision therein dealing with any other matter is of no effect (s 55);
- laws imposing taxation (except laws imposing customs or excise duties) must deal with one subject of taxation only (s 55);
- laws imposing customs duties must deal with customs duties only, and laws imposing excise duties must deal with excise duties only (s 55).

The broad purpose of these provisions is at least twofold. In the first place, they ensure that both houses of Parliament have the opportunity to scrutinise proposed taxation and expenditure without the matter being confused with other questions of legislative policy or regulation. Both houses are also able to assess particular subjects or forms of taxation, including proposed customs and excise duties.[257] Secondly, they ensure that the Senate will be able to exercise the same powers as the House in relation to any matter in a bill that does not concern such appropriations and taxation. This is necessary because, for reasons shortly to be explained, s 53 prevents the Senate from initiating and amending proposed laws imposing taxation or appropriating revenue or moneys for the ordinary annual services of the Government (generally called 'money bills'). If the Government

**252** Some expenditures are authorised or regulated directly by the Constitution. In *Attorney-General (Vic); Ex rel Dale v Commonwealth (Pharmaceutical Benefits)* (1945) 71 CLR 237, 251, Latham CJ referred, among other things, to the salary of the Governor-General (s 3) and salaries of justices (s 72). See also *Victoria v Commonwealth and Hayden (Australian Assistance Plan)* (1975) 134 CLR 338, 353.

**253** See *Pape v Commissioner of Taxation* (2009) 238 CLR 1 and *Williams v Commonwealth (No 1)* (2012) 248 CLR 156, discussed in more detail in Chapter 7, Part IV.2.

**254** *Victoria v Commonwealth (Federal Aid Roads)* (1926) 38 CLR 399.

**255** *South Australia v Commonwealth (First Uniform Tax)* (1942) 65 CLR 373.

**256** *Victoria and New South Wales v Commonwealth (Second Uniform Tax)* (1957) 99 CLR 575, 609.

**257** *State Chamber of Commerce and Industry v Commonwealth* (1987) 163 CLR 329, 342–3.

were able, through a proposed law initiated in the House, to include a provision imposing taxation or appropriating revenue alongside other matter, s 53 would operate to prevent the Senate from amending the bill. Sections 54 and 55, by preventing the 'tacking' of extraneous matter into taxation and appropriations bills, are meant to ensure that the Senate will be able to exercise its full legislative rights in relation to a bill dealing with those other matters.[258]

The rule in s 54 concerning appropriations refers to 'proposed laws', and therefore applies only as a matter of procedure between the houses, whereas s 55 concerning taxation refers to 'laws' and states that any provision dealing with 'any other matter' in a taxation statute will be 'of no effect', giving rise to the conclusion that it is justiciable before the courts. One of the practical effects of s 55 has been that laws which provide for the assessment and collection of taxation are conventionally enacted separately from laws which impose the obligation to pay the tax.[259] However, the Court has recently clarified that a law which imposes taxation may validly contain provisions 'fairly relevant or incidental to the imposition of a tax', such as provisions 'incidental and auxiliary to the assessment, collection and recovery of the tax', without contravening s 55.[260] On the Court's view, there is no constitutional requirement for taxation measures to be split into separate taxing and assessment Acts, but nor is the practice constitutionally prohibited.[261] The High Court has also affirmed that a law imposing taxation which, contrary to s 55, deals with more than one subject of taxation will ordinarily be entirely invalid, for there is no objective way of determining which of the two taxes is to be preserved.[262] However, where a law imposing customs duties or excise duties also deals with something else, the Court has held that it is the provisions dealing with those other matters that will be invalid, and the excise or customs duty may survive.[263] Some cases have concerned amending Acts which have inserted a provision imposing an obligation to pay a tax into principal Acts which may have operated for some time. In such circumstances, the Court has held that only the amending Act is invalid.[264]

As noted, s 53 of the Constitution prevents the Senate from initiating and amending certain categories of money bills, with the implication that such bills can only be initiated and amended in the House of Representatives. The primary purpose of s 53 is to facilitate the operation of a system of parliamentary responsible government in which the House of Representatives, as the chamber in which the people of the Commonwealth as a whole are represented, will

**258** Quick and Garran, above n 2, 674.
**259** See *Osborne v Commonwealth* (1911) 12 CLR 321, 349–50; *State Chamber of Commerce and Industry v Commonwealth* (1987) 163 CLR 329, 340–42.
**260** *Permanent Trustee Australia Limited v Commissioner of State Revenue (Victoria)* (2004) 220 CLR 388, 419, citing *Osborne v Commonwealth* (1911) 12 CLR 321, 373 and *Federal Commissioner of Taxation v Munro* (1926) 38 CLR 153, 215.
**261** *Permanent Trustee* (2004) 220 CLR 388, 419–20.
**262** *Osborne v Commonwealth* (1911) 12 CLR 321, 353.
**263** *Mutual Pools & Staff Pty Ltd v Federal Commissioner of Taxation* (1992) 173 CLR 450, 471, 453.
**264** *Air Calédonie International v Commonwealth* (1988) 165 CLR 462, 472; *Australian Tape Manufacturers Association Ltd v Commonwealth* (1993) 176 CLR 480, 507–8.

have a certain priority over the Senate. The exact terms of s 53 reflect a closely negotiated compromise between two groups among the framers of the Constitution.[265] One group, led by Richard Baker and Samuel Griffith, believed that the principle of federalism, best understood, requires that the people of each State should be equally represented in a Senate possessing powers of legislation equal to those of the House of Representatives. Another group, led by Alfred Deakin and Isaac Isaacs, held that the principle of parliamentary responsible government, as practised in the United Kingdom and in the Australian colonies, requires that the lower house of Parliament have effective control over enactment of money bills, for it is in relation to control over the supply of money to the Executive Government that the Government is made responsible to the Parliament. Against this view, Baker went so far as to propose that the Government should be chosen by and responsible to both houses of the Parliament, on the model of the Federal Executive Council in Switzerland. On balance, however, a majority of the framers favoured a system more in line with the traditional system of responsible government with which they were familiar, a view which is reflected in the prohibitions on the Senate in s 53. However, there remained a majority who were not prepared to deny the Senate power to reject money bills, even if this meant that the Senate would have the capacity to bring a Government to its knees by refusing to pass the annual appropriation bills, which are traditionally understood within Westminster systems to be the key marker of the Parliament's confidence in the Government and essential for the Government to function. Several features of s 53 reflect this side of the equation as well.

The basic principle of the bicameral Parliament established by s 1 of the Constitution is that proposed laws must be passed by both houses before they are presented to the Governor-General for the royal assent and become law. Section 53 affirms this by providing that, except as provided in that section, the Senate shall have equal power with the House of Representatives in respect of all proposed laws. However, this is subject to a range of specific limitations on the powers of the Senate in relation to money bills. Thus, the Senate cannot:

- originate proposed laws appropriating revenue or moneys or imposing taxation;[266]
- amend proposed laws imposing taxation or appropriating revenue or moneys for the ordinary services of the Government; or
- amend any proposed law so as to increase any proposed charge or burden on the people.

In the *Petroleum and Minerals Authority* case, a majority of the High Court affirmed that these specific qualifications of the powers of the Senate leave it free to reject

**265** Aroney, above n 47, 191–206, 210–14, 237–9, 359–62.
**266** Under s 53 the Senate can, however, originate proposed laws imposing fines, penalties or fees for licences or services. In *Air Calédonie International v Commonwealth* (1988) 165 CLR 462, 469–70, it was said that a fee for service is 'exacted for particular identified services provided or rendered individually to, or at the request or direction of, the particular person required to make the payment'.

such bills outright.[267] As Stephen J said in that case, such a power is unusual in a modern upper house, but it reflects the federal nature of the Australian polity.[268] The Senate may, in addition, return any such bill to the House of Representatives requesting some alteration to it, which request the House is then able to consider. Although the words 'at any stage' in s 53 might be taken to imply that the request can be made only at one of the 'stages' through which a bill ordinarily progresses (eg, second reading, committee stage, etc), the House of Representatives has on several occasions received and considered requests by the Senate for amendments to money bills which have been presented by the Senate a second time.[269]

The prohibition in relation to the initiation of money bills needs to be understood with s 56, which provides that a vote, resolution or proposed law for the appropriation of revenue or moneys must not be passed unless the purpose of the appropriation has in the same session been recommended by message of the Governor-General. This further assures to the Executive Government control over the passage of proposed appropriations in either house of Parliament, enabling the Government to take responsibility for the financial integrity of the Budget as a whole. However, because s 53 relates to 'proposed laws', and s 56 concerns the passage of any 'vote, resolution, or proposed law', failure to comply with their requirements cannot be enforced by the Courts. The application of the provisions depends on processes within the two houses themselves.[270] In current practice, two major Appropriation Bills are introduced during the Budget Session of Parliament (usually in May), one of which contains appropriations for the ordinary annual services of government (ie, for expenditure by government departments and agencies on services for existing policies) and one of which contains appropriations for other expenditures (ie, for capital expenditure relating to land, buildings, plant and equipment, grants to the States and new policies not authorised by special legislation). These are followed, usually sometime between October and February, by three further corresponding Appropriation Bills to supplement funds appropriated by the three Budget Bills that may have been exhausted.[271] It is also customary for the Treasurer to present with the Budget any related bills together with other documents, known as Budget Papers, dealing with the economic and financial outlook, more detailed information about budget expenditure, and financial relations with the States, Territories and local government.[272] In addition to the regular annual appropriation bills, there are also standing or special appropriations which continue for a period of years or until repealed.[273] Some appropriations can be for an indefinite amount of money, and many are defined in very abstract and general terms. While such practices are not

**267** *Victoria v Commonwealth (Petroleum and Minerals Authority)* (1975) 134 CLR 81, 121, 143, 168, 185.
**268** Ibid, 168.
**269** Evans and Laing, above n 33, Appendix 6.
**270** See Wright and Fowler, above n 20, ch 11; Evans and Laing, above n 33, ch 13.
**271** There is also an Appropriation (Parliamentary Departments) Bill to fund the parliamentary departments: Wright and Fowler, above n 20, 414–15.
**272** Ibid, 420.
**273** Evans and Laing, above n 33, 378–9.

conducive to parliamentary scrutiny of government expenditure,[274] there is no constitutional constraint on the practice except potentially through the requirement that an appropriation must be 'for the purposes of the Commonwealth' and the additional requirement, recently articulated by the High Court, that the act of spending money by the Commonwealth must be specifically authorised by law quite in addition to the necessity that the requisite funds are duly appropriated out of consolidated revenue. [275]

## 2 Deadlocks between the houses

The bicameral nature of the Parliament means that laws proposed in one house may not be passed by the other house, producing a deadlock between the two houses. In some federations, such as the United States and Switzerland, a deadlock can only be resolved if a compromise is reached or one of the houses eventually gives way. After considerable debate, the framers of the Australian Constitution designed a mechanism, in s 57 of the Constitution, by which deadlocks between the two houses might be resolved.[276] The mechanism involves a dissolution of both houses, a general election and, if the deadlock persists, a joint sitting of the two houses to vote on the proposed law. As noted, the 2:1 nexus in the size of the two houses exists to give the House a numerical advantage over the Senate at such joint sittings.

There are several conditions that must be satisfied before the s 57 mechanism can come into play. The prescribed conditions and process are as follows:

- a proposed law is passed by the House of Representatives;
- the Senate rejects or fails to pass the law, or passes it with amendments to which the House will not agree;
- there is an interval of three months;
- in the same or next session, the House of Representatives passes the proposed law with or without any amendments made, suggested or agreed to by the Senate;
- the Senate rejects or fails to pass the proposed law, or passes it with amendments to which the House will not agree;
- the Governor-General dissolves the Senate and the House of Representatives simultaneously, but not within six months before the expiry of the House by effluxion of time (ie, two-and-a-half years after the first sitting of the House);
- after the ensuing election and in the next Parliament, the House of Representatives passes the proposed law with or without any amendments made, suggested or agreed to by the Senate;
- the Senate rejects or fails to pass the proposed law, or passes it with amendments to which the House will not agree;

**274** Ibid, 379–81.
**275** *Attorney-General (Vic); Ex rel Dale v Commonwealth* (1945) 71 CLR 237; *Victoria v Commonwealth and Hayden* (1975) 134 CLR 338; *Pape v Commissioner of Taxation* (2009) 238 CLR 1; *Williams v Commonwealth (No 1)* (2012) 248 CLR 156, discussed in Chapter 7, Part IV.2 in relation to executive power generally.
**276** Aroney, above n 47, 240–44.

- the Governor-General convenes a joint sitting of both houses;
- the members of both houses at the joint sitting (may) deliberate and (shall) vote together on the proposed law as last proposed by the House of Representatives and on any amendments made by one house and not agreed to by the other;
- if the proposed law, with or without any such amendments, is affirmed by an absolute majority of the total number of members of the two houses it shall be taken to have been passed by both houses and shall be presented to the Governor-General for the Queen's assent.

The double dissolution procedure has been invoked on five occasions: in 1914, 1974, 1975, 1983 and 1987, but there has been only one joint sitting: in 1974. The interpretive questions that have arisen have included the following:

- Are the procedures of s 57 merely directory or are they mandatory conditions essential for the valid enactment of the law?
- Does the High Court have jurisdiction to:
  - intervene in the legislative process by issuing an injunction?
  - declare legislation to be invalid because the procedures of s 57 were not complied with?
- Can a joint sitting deal with more than one bill?
- Can the Governor-General's proclamation of a joint sitting determine the bills that can be considered at the joint sitting?
- Do the special procedures of s 57 apply to both money bills and ordinary bills?[277]
- At what point in time will the Senate be deemed to have failed to pass a proposed law?
- From the time of which event will the required period of three months commence:
  - when the House first passes the law?
  - when the Senate fails to pass a proposed law?
  - when the Senate amends a proposed law?
  - when the House rejects the Senate's amendment?

The general principle is that it is for the houses of Parliament to determine their own procedures and to resolve disputes concerning them. Thus, even though the procedures of s 57 have been held to be mandatory and not merely directive,[278] the High Court has been cautious about its jurisdiction to intervene by way of injunction or similar remedy to correct what it may consider to be a failure to follow the constitutionally prescribed process before a double dissolution or joint sitting is proclaimed.[279] What is clear is that if a statute purportedly enacted through the s 57 procedure fails to meet one of the prescribed requirements, the

**277** See the discussion in Chapter 3, Part II.1 of the possibility of manner and form procedures being adopted at a Commonwealth level.
**278** *Victoria v Commonwealth* (1975) 134 CLR 81, 119–20, 155–62, 182–3; see also 179–80 (Stephen J, considering that even if the procedures are directory, substantial compliance would be required).
**279** *Cormack v Cope* (1974) 131 CLR 432, 453–5, 461, 465–6, 466–7, 472, 474.

Court has jurisdiction to declare the statute invalid.[280] A proclamation by the Governor-General which purports to determine the bills to be considered at a joint sitting does not prevent the two houses of Parliament, at the joint sitting, from deliberating upon and effectively passing any number of bills which meet the requirements of s 57; a Government is indeed able to 'stockpile' such bills over the entire life of the Parliament as triggers for a double dissolution and candidates for passage at a joint sitting.[281] The required interval of three months runs not from the time that the House of Representatives passes the proposed law but from the time at which the Senate fails to pass it, and the Senate fails to pass such a law at the time at which, allowing for the full and proper deliberative processes of the Senate, it ought to answer the question whether or not to pass it.[282]

In addition, there are several unanswered questions about the meaning and application of s 57 that have emerged:[283]

- Through the various stages of the process, to what extent must the proposed law remain identical?[284] Although the language of s 57 itself suggests that it may include amendments made, suggested or agreed to by the Senate, can it include amendments made or proposed by the House, during either one of the preliminary stages, or during the joint sitting? Is there any substantive limit to the content of the amendments that may be proposed by the House of Representatives at the joint sitting itself? Do merely formal changes to a bill mean that it is no longer the same proposed law?
- Must the Governor-General accept the advice of the Prime Minister to dissolve both houses or to convene a joint sitting if the Governor-General considers that the relevant requirements of s 57 have not been met?

There is also the curiosity, if not the anomaly, that the Prime Minister who advises the Governor-General to declare a double dissolution need not be the same person, or indeed, a member of the same Government or political party, that initiated the bill over which the two houses disagreed. As will be seen in the discussion of the events of 1975 in Chapter 6, it is therefore possible that the new Prime Minister is actively opposed to the passage of the bill and has no interest in its passage after the election. This possibility underscores the fact that, although s 57 was designed to facilitate the resolution of deadlocks between the houses over the enactment of laws, the framers deliberately looked to the double dissolution as a means of encouraging or pressuring members of the two houses to find ways to resolve their differences. Because a double dissolution puts at risk the seats of all members of Parliament – both of the Government and the Opposition – its use (or the threat of its use) is frequently directed to wider

**280** Ibid, 460, 463–5, 466–7, 472, 473–4; *Victoria v Commonwealth* (1975) 134 CLR 81.
**281** *Cormack v Cope* (1974) 131 CLR 432, 455–6, 461, 462, 468, 469–70, 474; *Western Australia v Commonwealth* (1975) 134 CLR 201, 237–8, 251–2, 265–6, 276–8, 288–9.
**282** *Victoria v Commonwealth* (1975) 134 CLR 81, 122–6, 146–50, 154–5, 166–77, 184–8.
**283** Peter Hogg, *Constitutional Law of Canada* (Carswell, 5th ed, 2007); Moens and Trone, above n 23, 230–40.
**284** See *Western Australia v Commonwealth* (1975) 134 CLR 201, 237.

'political' purposes unrelated to the proposed law or laws over which there is disagreement.

## 3 Parliamentary procedure

Although the term 'Parliament' is frequently used as if the Parliament were a continuing institution, it is more precise to speak of a succession of Parliaments, each Parliament coinciding with the cyclical life of the House of Representatives, which begins when the House first meets in response to the summons of the Governor-General following a general election and ends when the House is either dissolved by the Governor-General or expires after three years (s 28). Each Parliament is identified by reference to the House of Representatives, and not the Senate, because the Senate has a continuing existence, with only half of the Senators being elected every three years (ss 7 and 13).[285] Each Parliament is convened for one or more sessions as determined by the Governor-General, each session coming to an end when the Parliament is prorogued or when the House is dissolved by the Governor-General (s 5). The particular sitting times of each house of Parliament are determined by each house. Customarily, the sittings are held in three distinct periods in each calendar year known as the Autumn, Budget and Spring sittings. The distinction between a session and a sitting is significant because most items of parliamentary business, including proposed laws in the form of bills, do not survive prorogation, but must be recommenced or reinstituted afresh in the new session.[286] Partly for this reason, while there are no constitutional requirements concerning the number or length of sessions, it is now usual for each Parliament to consist of only one session.[287]

When the Queen is personally present for ceremonial sittings of the Parliament, she presides over the Senate. Ordinarily, however, meetings of the two houses of Parliament are presided over by a President elected by the Senate and a speaker elected by the House of Representatives (ss 17 and 35). At the beginning of each newly-elected Parliament, the Governor-General personally presides as the Queen's representative at a meeting of both houses of Parliament held in the Senate chamber. The term 'Speaker' was used in the United Kingdom to designate the presiding officer of the House of Commons who would communicate the resolutions of the House of Commons to the King.[288] This function is continued in the practice of Australia's Parliaments. Thus, it is the special role of the Speaker of the House of Representatives and the President of the Senate to act as spokespersons and representatives of the two houses in their dealings with the Governor-General, the Government and each other.

**285** That is, unless the entire Senate is itself dissolved in a double dissolution pursuant to s 57.
**286** Wright and Fowler, above n 20, 227.
**287** Ibid, 226, 228. This is considered to be consistent with s 6 of the Constitution, which only requires that there shall not be an interval of 12 months between consecutive sittings: ibid, 223.
**288** Philip Laundy, *The Office of Speaker* (Cassell, 1964) 137.

The offices of President and Speaker are exceptionally important. It is their official duty to preside over meetings of their respective houses and to maintain order by ensuring that the Standing Orders, precedents and any constitutional or statutory provisions regulating parliamentary procedure are followed. It is therefore vital that the President and Speaker perform their functions with impartiality and efficiency, and that they defend the respective rights and privileges of their chambers effectively.[289] They are also ordinarily responsible, with the assistance of the Clerks and their staff, for the administration of each House, and for the precincts of each Chamber and the parliamentary building as a whole, including its security.[290] It is the usual responsibility of the Government to nominate a Speaker, conventionally from within its own party ranks, bearing in mind that a working majority in the House of Representatives must ordinarily be secured without the benefit of the Speaker's casting vote.[291] The case is different in the Senate, where the President is entitled to vote in all cases in order to ensure the equal representation of each State, and where an equality of votes results in the negation of the question (s 23).[292]

The practical operation of Parliament as a working institution is regulated by the general requirements of the Constitution supplemented by several important parliamentary Acts and a detailed set of Standing Orders promulgated by each house of Parliament. The Constitution itself provides that decisions are made in each house of Parliament by majority vote, each member voting individually.[293] This effectively prevents the Parliament, or a house of the Parliament, from prescribing any special procedure for the enactment of legislation which departs from the requirement that the decision be made by simple majority vote, but it does not prevent it from adopting other procedural requirements.[294] The Constitution also stipulates that, until the Parliament otherwise provides, at least one third of senators or members must be present to constitute a meeting of the Senate or House of Representatives (ss 22 and 39). The Parliament has subsequently reduced the required quorum for the Senate to one quarter of senators and the quorum for the House of Representatives to one fifth of its members.[295]

The power of the Parliament to regulate its own affairs is based on s 49 of the Constitution, which provides:

> The powers, privileges, and immunities of the Senate and of the House of Representatives, and of the members and the committees of each House, shall be such as are declared by the Parliament, and until declared shall be those of the Commons House

**289** Wright and Fowler, above n 20, 163–5, 170.
**290** Ibid, 177–9.
**291** Commonwealth Constitution, s 40. See ibid 165–6, 182–5.
**292** See Quick and Garran, above n 2, 444.
**293** This is an implication of Commonwealth Constitution, ss 23, 40. See ibid, 444.
**294** George Winterton, 'Can the Commonwealth Parliament Enact "Manner and Form" Legislation?' (1980) 11 *Federal Law Review* 167, 191. On special procedures known as 'manner and form' requirements, see Chapter 3, Part II.1 in relation to the Commonwealth, and Chapter 10, Part IV.4, in relation to the States.
**295** *Senate (Quorum) Act 1991* (Cth), s 3; *House of Representatives (Quorum) Act 1989* (Cth), s 3.

of Parliament of the United Kingdom, and of its members and committees, at the establishment of the Commonwealth.

The effect of this provision is to enable the Parliament by enactment to determine the powers, privileges and immunities enjoyed by the two houses and their respective committees and members. It is also provided in s 50 of the Constitution that each house of the Parliament may make rules and orders with respect to the mode in which its powers, privileges and immunities may be exercised and with respect to the order and conduct of its business and proceedings. The Standing Orders of each house make detailed provision for these matters.[296]

The Parliament has, through several enactments, most notably the *Parliamentary Privileges Act 1987* (Cth), modified certain aspects of the law and custom of the Parliament, while declaring that apart from specific statutory alteration, the powers, privileges and immunities of each house are to continue.[297] The vast bulk of the law and custom of the Parliament is therefore still based on the *lex et consuetudo* of the House of Commons as at 1 January 1901, when the Constitution came into force. Notably, in the first half of the nineteenth century the legislatures of British colonies were recognised as possessing only those privileges that were considered necessary for their existence and the performance of their functions, which privileges were accordingly held to be less extensive than those enjoyed by the houses of the British Parliament at Westminster.[298] However, it was also recognised that colonial legislatures could make laws conferring the privileges of the House of Commons on each house,[299] and the Parliaments of the Australian colonies eventually legislated to this effect, although the exact position in each State varies considerably.[300]

The business of each house of Parliament is extensive and varied. It includes Question Time, when Ministers are subjected to questioning by members of Parliament. Committee reports, ministerial statements and government documents of varying kinds are tendered in Parliament as a means of public disclosure of information and to enable debate on their contents. A variety of motions are also brought before the two houses, including motions of no confidence in the Ministry, which are a key device by which the Executive Government (the Prime Minister and other Ministers of the Crown) are made responsible to the Parliament. Legislation is enacted by the Parliament through the passage of bills (proposed laws) through to the two houses. While any member of either house may initiate a bill, in practice most bills are introduced by a Government Minister in the House of Representatives. The key steps by which a bill is enacted by the Parliament are:[301]

**296** Rosemary Laing, *Annotated Standing Orders of the Australian Senate* (Department of the Senate, 2009); House of Representatives, *Standing Orders* (Department of the House of Representatives, 2013); see also House of Representatives, *Guide to Procedures* (Department of the House of Representatives, 4th ed, 2010).
**297** *Parliamentary Privileges Act 1987* (Cth), s 5.
**298** *Kielley v Carson* (1842) 4 Moo PC 63, 88; 13 ER 225, 234.
**299** *Doyle v Falconer* (1866) LR 1 PC 328, 341; *Barnes v Purcell* (1946) St R Qd 87, 108–9.
**300** Gerard Carney, *Members of Parliament: Law and Ethics* (Prospect, 2000) 167–9.
**301** For a more detailed description, see: Wright and Fowler, above n 20, ch 10; Evans and Laing, above n 33, ch 12.

- Initiation: introduction of the bill in one of the houses;
- First reading: a formal stage at which the long title of the proposed law is read by the Clerk of the house;
- Second reading: substantive debate on the principle of the bill;
- Possible referral to a committee of the house for advisory report (can occur before or after the second reading);
- Consideration in detail/committee of the whole: specific provisions of the bill are considered and amendments may be proposed;
- Third reading: review of the bill in its final form (when a bill has been read the third time, it has passed the house);
- Transmission to the other house for concurrence;
- First, Second and Third readings and possible reference to a committee are repeated in the other house;
- Transmission or return of bill from the other house, with or without amendment;
- If the bill is amended by the other house, consideration of the proposed amendments, to which there can be agreement, disagreement or further amendments proposed, or the amended bill can be rejected;
- Presentation of an agreed bill to the Governor-General for royal assent.

Both houses of the Commonwealth Parliament have an array of standing committees to which bills may be referred. Such committees have general responsibility for particular subject matters, many broadly corresponding to particular ministerial portfolios and government departments. Each house is also able to establish select committees to address emergent matters. There are also joint committees of both houses, some established by statute. The committees are an important way in which the two houses are able to scrutinise proposed laws, deliberate about government policies, hold Ministers to account and consider other matters of public importance.[302] Presently the Senate refers more than half of all bills – most initiated by the Government in the House of Representatives – to a committee for close consideration.[303]

## 4 Parliamentary privilege

Parliamentary privilege refers to the special immunities and powers which inhere in the two houses of Parliament as distinct corporate bodies as well as those special rights that are enjoyed by individual members of Parliament. Such rights are considered 'essential for the support of [the] authority [of the two houses], and for the proper exercise of their functions'.[304] The corporate powers of each house include control over its internal proceedings, discipline of its members, regulation of its committees, publication of its debates and admission to its

**302** See: Wright and Fowler, above n 20, ch 18; Evans and Laing, above n 33, ch 16.
**303** Evans and Laing, above n 33, 309.
**304** Thomas Erskine May, *A Treatise Upon the Law, Privileges, Proceedings and Usage of Parliament* (Charles Knight & Co, 1st ed, 1844) 44.

chamber. They also include power to summon non-members to appear before the house, to answer questions and to produce documents, as well as the power to adjudge and punish a person for contempt of the house or breach of any of its privileges. The important individual rights enjoyed by members of Parliament include freedom of speech in Parliament and immunity from legal proceedings in relation thereto, a right which extends to the evidence of witnesses and documents tabled in Parliament. The two houses acting together also have important additional powers conferred by the Constitution, such as determining whether a federal judge should be removed from office on the ground of proved misbehaviour or incapacity (s 72(ii)).

Parliamentary privilege is a part of the law of the land and is therefore cognisable by the ordinary courts. At one time, the two houses of the British Parliament claimed to be the only courts which could interpret and apply the law and custom of Parliament.[305] As William Blackstone explained:

> The privileges of parliament are likewise very large and indefinite; which has occasioned an observation, that the principal privilege of parliament consisted in this, that its privileges were not certainly known to any but the parliament itself. ... Privilege of parliament was principally established, in order to protect its members not only from being molested by their fellow-subjects, but also more especially from being oppressed by the power of the crown. If therefore all the privileges of parliament were once to be set down and ascertained, and no privilege to be allowed but what was so defined and determined, it were easy for the executive power to devise some new case, not within the line of privilege, and under pretence thereof to harass any refractory member and violate the freedom of parliament. The dignity and independence of the two houses are therefore in great measure preserved by keeping their privileges indefinite.[306]

By the second half of the nineteenth century, however, the two houses effectively abandoned the claim to being the sole judges of their legal privileges, thereby tacitly acknowledging the jurisdiction of the ordinary courts, while at the same time, the courts accepted the law and customs of Parliament as these had been formulated and developed by the two houses.[307] As Dixon CJ put it in *R v Richards; Ex parte Fitzpatrick & Browne*:

> it is for the courts to judge of the existence in either House of Parliament of a privilege, but, given an undoubted privilege, it is for the House to judge of the occasion and of the manner of its exercise.[308]

The result has been a delicately drawn jurisdictional division of responsibilities, the exact boundaries of which are sometimes contested. For example, the exercise of its privileges can draw a house into dispute with the Executive Government, as when the Senate or a State Legislative Council requires a Minister

**305** *House of Commons Journals* (31 May 1837), Vol 97, 419. But see *Stockdale v Hansard* (1839) 9 Ad & E 1; 112 ER 1112; *Stockdale v Hansard* (1840) 11 Ad & E 253; 113 ER 411; *Case of the Sheriff of Middlesex* (1840) 11 Ad & E 273; 113 ER 419. See also Carney, above n 300, 163–4.
**306** William Blackstone, *Commentaries on the Laws of England* (Clarendon Press, 1765–69) vol I, ch 2, 159.
**307** Evans and Laing, above n 33, 42.
**308** (1955) 92 CLR 157, 162.

of the Crown to produce documents which the Minister claims are subject to 'Crown immunity' or 'public interest immunity'.[309] The ordinary courts are sometimes called upon to adjudicate in such matters, but their jurisdiction is limited to determining whether a particular privilege exists at law, and not the occasion and manner of its exercise, a question which remains a matter for the houses of Parliament themselves.[310]

The houses of Parliament have a general power to punish for contempt, as well as a specific power to punish for breach of a particular parliamentary privilege. A contempt of Parliament has been described as:

> any act or omission which obstructs or impedes either House of Parliament in the performance of its functions, or which obstructs or impedes any Member or officer of such House in the discharge of his duty, or which has a tendency, directly or indirectly, to produce such results may be treated as a contempt even though there is no precedent of the offence.[311]

In *R v Richards*,[312] applications for *habeas corpus* were considered by the High Court in relation to the imprisonment by the House of Representatives of two journalists for contempt of Parliament when they published an allegation that a member of Parliament had engaged in trafficking of entry permits for refugee migrants. The two men had been called to the bar of the house and found guilty of a breach of privilege, and the Speaker of the House of Representatives had accordingly issued general warrants for their imprisonment for a period of six months. The High Court held that if the warrants had specified the ground of the commitment into custody, the Court might have determined whether it was sufficient in law, but because the warrants were in general terms and not on their face inconsistent with the breach of an acknowledged privilege, the Court had to accept them as conclusive.[313]

The obstacle to judicial review encountered by the High Court in *R v Richards* has since been removed by the *Parliamentary Privileges Act*, s 9 of which provides that a resolution of a house imposing a penalty of imprisonment and a warrant committing the person to custody must set out particulars of the matters determined by the house to constitute the offence. Section 6 further provides that words or acts shall not be taken to be an offence against a house by reason only that those words or acts are defamatory or critical of the Parliament, a house, a committee or a member, provided that they are not spoken or done in the presence of a house or a committee.[314] The penalties that a house can impose are also controlled by the Act. The maximum penalty of imprisonment that can be imposed is now limited

**309** *Egan v Willis* (1996) 40 NSWLR 650; *Egan v Willis* (1998) 195 CLR 424.
**310** *Egan v Willis* (1998) 195 CLR 424, 446.
**311** William McKay, *Erskine May's Treatise Upon the Law, Privileges, Proceedings and Usage of Parliament* (LexisNexis, 23rd ed, 2004) 128. Every breach of parliamentary privilege is by definition a contempt of the house, but it is not necessary to show that a particular privilege has been breached for a contempt to have occurred: Wright and Fowler, above n 20, 707–8; Evans and Laing, above n 33, 41–2.
**312** *R v Richards; Ex parte Fitzpatrick & Browne* (1955) 92 CLR 157.
**313** Ibid, 162.
**314** *Parliamentary Privileges Act 1987* (Cth), s 6.

to a period of six months, the maximum fine is $5 000 for a natural person and $25 000 for a corporation, and the houses are prohibited from imposing both imprisonment and a fine.[315] While the houses can still discipline members by excluding them temporarily, they cannot expel them from membership.[316] Witnesses before the houses are also granted special protections from intimidation, and the immunities of members, officers and witnesses have been statutorily clarified.[317]

One of the most important privileges is freedom of speech in Parliament. Technically, it is an immunity enjoyed by members of Parliament from civil or criminal action and examination in legal proceedings which extends to witnesses and others taking part in parliamentary proceedings.[318] It has its origins deep in English history but was not definitively guaranteed until the *Bill of Rights (*1688–9), Article 9 of which provided that 'the freedom of speech and debates or proceedings in Parliament ought not to be impeached or questioned in any court or place out of Parliament'.[319] The Commonwealth has extended the immunity to the publication and broadcasting of parliamentary documents and proceedings.[320] It has also provided that it is a defence to an action for defamation that the defamatory matter was contained in a fair and accurate report of parliamentary proceedings and was published without any adoption by the defendant of the substance of the matter.[321] In *R v Murphy*, Hunt J held that Article 9 of the *Bill of Rights* did not prevent the cross-examination of witnesses in respect of statements they had made to Senate committees when investigating allegations that Justice Lionel Murphy, a justice of the High Court, had attempted to pervert the course of justice.[322] However, s 16 of the *Parliamentary Privileges Act*, which affirms the existence of the privilege, defines the immunity in terms much wider than those applied in the *Murphy* case, that is, whether the parliamentary material is being called into question or not. This has given rise to the question whether s 16 is consistent with the general freedom of political communication that the High Court has said is a necessary implication of the Constitution.[323]

The privilege of freedom of speech is a vital immunity which protects the ability of members of Parliament to address issues, publicise facts and criticise policies without fear of retribution by the Government or powerful interests outside of the Parliament.[324] The absolute nature of the immunity brings with it substantial responsibilities, however, as allegations or disclosures made in Parliament may cause serious damage to the reputation or welfare of persons who

**315** Ibid, s 7.
**316** Ibid, s 8.
**317** Ibid, ss 12, 14.
**318** Evans and Laing, above n 33, 43.
**319** *Parliamentary Privileges Act 1987* (Cth), s 16, confirms and extends the scope of the immunity. The operation of the *Bill of Rights* at a State level is confirmed by statute, eg *Imperial Acts Application Act 1969* (NSW), s 6, Sch 2.
**320** *Parliamentary Papers Act 1908* (Cth); *Parliamentary Proceedings Broadcasting Act 1946* (Cth).
**321** *Parliamentary Privileges Act 1987* (Cth), s 10.
**322** *R v Murphy* (1986) 5 NSWLR 18.
**323** *Laurence v Katter* [2000] 1 Qd R 147; *Rann v Olsen* (2000) 76 SASR 450. On the implied freedom of political communication, see Chapter 5, Part V.
**324** Carney, above n 300, ch 6.

may have only limited means of protecting themselves. Members of a house of Parliament who are found by the house to have abused the freedom may therefore be liable to discipline.[325] A person who is referred to in debate may also be given the opportunity to have a response incorporated into the parliamentary record.[326]

## IV Conclusions

The Commonwealth Parliament is one of the three principal governing institutions established by the Australian Constitution, and arguably pre-eminent among them. The fact that it is first-mentioned in the Constitution is no coincidence of drafting. Its place in the Constitution is a reflection of the fundamental importance that the framers accorded to the rule of law and the idea that the Parliament ordinarily enacts the laws that it is the responsibility of the Executive to administer and the Judiciary to enforce. Alone among the three branches of government, the Parliament is the one whose members are 'directly chosen' by the people. It is also the institution in which the federal character of the Commonwealth is most clearly reflected, particularly in the design of the Senate and the House of Representatives as representative respectively of 'the people of the Commonwealth' and 'the people of the States'. This principle of federal democracy, fundamental to the Constitution, is worked out in many of the specific features of the two houses of the Parliament discussed in this chapter, including their composition, their powers and the relationship between them.

The Parliament also reflects the influence of the Westminster model of government. This is seen in the role of the Queen and the Governor-General in the enactment of legislation. It is also seen in the relative priority given to the House of Representatives in relation to the initiation and amendment of money bills. Not only does parliamentary control over bills authorising taxation and the appropriation of money enable these vitally important functions of government to be controlled by representatives of the people, but it is also one of the most important ways in which the government is made responsible to the Parliament. By virtue of the conventions of parliamentary responsible government, the executive power of the Commonwealth is exercised by the Governor-General on the advice of a Prime Minister and Ministry that have the confidence of the House of Representatives. The Parliament is thus the key means by which the Executive is made ultimately accountable to the people of the Commonwealth. The ultimate control of the Parliament over government expenditure is therefore a crucial feature of the Constitution, as is the capacity of the two houses of Parliament to control their own procedures, to act as the guardians of the special privileges and immunities of their members, and to exercise powers of inquiry, even in

**325** Wright and Fowler, above n 20, 753–4. See *Arena v Nader* (1997) 42 NSWLR 427; (1997) 71 ALR 1604.
**326** Wright and Fowler, above n 20, 751–2; Evans and Laing, above n 33, 95–6.

relation to performance and conduct of Ministers in the formation of government policy and in the administration of their departments.

The Parliament thus exercises several vital roles in the system of government established by the Constitution. It is the primary means by which the executive power of the Commonwealth, vested in a hereditary monarch, is exercised in a way that is ultimately accountable to elected representatives of the people. It is the key institution through which the principle of representative democracy, adapted to federalism, is given effect. Finally, the Parliament is also the particular branch of government in which the legislative power of the Commonwealth is vested. As will be seen in the next chapter, the federal principle also requires that the legislative power of the Commonwealth is limited in order to leave adequate room for the exercise of the legislative powers of the States.

# 3

# Legislative power

*The Parliament shall, subject to this Constitution, have power to make laws for the peace, order, and good government of the Commonwealth with respect to: ... .*[1]

## I Introduction

The formation of the Australian federation in 1901 presupposed the prior existence of the six colonies as independent, self-governing political communities. The federal union of those colonies involved the establishment of a federal government, to which particular powers were granted; but apart from those specific surrenders, the general principle was that the existing powers, privileges and territorial rights of the colonies would remain as they were prior to federation.[2] As the Premier of New South Wales, Henry Parkes, put it in one of the principal resolutions adopted by the Federal Convention of 1891:

> the powers and privileges and territorial rights of the several existing colonies shall remain intact, except in respect to such surrenders as may be agreed upon as necessary and incidental to the power and authority of the National Federal Government.[3]

A year earlier, at the inter-colonial Conference held in Melbourne, it had similarly been resolved that any federation of the colonies would have to occur 'on principles just to the several colonies'.[4] Parkes's resolution made it clear that it would be for the colonies themselves to determine what those principles would be, in line with the proposition that the federation must rest upon the agreement and consent of its constituent States. Each colony could thus be assured that its

**1** Commonwealth Constitution, s 51; see also s 52.
**2** See, eg, *Convention Debates, Adelaide* (1897) 29, 41–2, 175, 245, 271, 318, 338, 377. See, further, Nicholas Aroney, *The Constitution of a Federal Commonwealth: The Making and Meaning of the Australian Constitution* (Cambridge University Press, 2009) chs 9 and 10.
**3** *Convention Debates, Sydney* (1891) 23. Edmund Barton's corresponding resolution in 1897–8 was in similar terms except that it referred to 'such surrenders as may be agreed upon to secure uniformity of law and administration in matters of common concern': *Convention Debates, Adelaide* (1897) 17, 395.
**4** *Conference Debates, Melbourne* (1890) 18; see also *Convention Debates, Sydney* (1891) 2.

territorial rights would be secured and its legislative powers preserved.[5] Charles Kingston, who would later become Premier of South Australia, put it this way:

> [W]e are dealing with autonomous States, who have long enjoyed the blessing of self-government, and who should not be asked – and who, if asked, would not be likely to accede to the request – to sacrifice any of their existing powers other than those which it is absolutely necessary should be surrendered in the national interest.[6]

What principle would guide the identification of the limited powers to be conferred upon the Commonwealth? Richard O'Connor suggested that the colonies should retain power over all matters they could suitably manage themselves and that only 'necessary' matters should come within the jurisdiction of the federal government.[7] Frederick Holder said that the colonies should retain control of every matter that was 'local' or concerned each state considered in isolation, whereas matters of 'national' or 'inter-state' character or importance should be conferred upon the federation – provided they could be exercised 'more wisely and well and effectively' in that way.[8] Henry Dobson put the matter clearly when he proposed that the Constitution should reserve to the States 'those powers which they can better carry out for themselves', while conferring upon the federal government 'those powers of common or general concern which a united Government can manage much better for the good of the people than the individual States'.[9] William McMillan added that sufficient power ought to be given to the federal government to enable it to be a 'strong, stable national government ... able to confront the whole outside world', while reserving to the States sufficient powers to manage their local affairs.[10]

After long debate, the framers eventually settled upon a long list of matters in respect of which the Commonwealth Parliament would be able to legislate. Most of the Commonwealth's resulting powers were made concurrent with the States (s 51), which meant that both the States and the Commonwealth would be able to legislate in those fields. A smaller number of topics were made exclusive to the Commonwealth (s 52).[11] At the same time, the general or plenary legislative powers of the States, as established by their respective State Constitutions, were declared to continue subject to the Constitution (ss 106 and 107). As a consequence, the States are not able to legislate with respect to matters that fall within the exclusive jurisdiction of the Commonwealth or are expressly removed from them by prohibitions contained in the Constitution.[12] In addition, where a State law is inconsistent with a Commonwealth law, the

**5** *Convention Debates, Sydney* (1891) 24.
**6** *Convention Debates, Sydney* (1891) 153.
**7** *Convention Debates, Adelaide* (1897) 50–51.
**8** Ibid, 144.
**9** Ibid, 191.
**10** Ibid, 223.
**11** These concerned the seat of government of the Commonwealth, places acquired by the Commonwealth, and the Commonwealth public service.
**12** See Commonwealth Constitution, ss 52, 90, 92.

Commonwealth law prevails to the extent of the inconsistency (s 109).[13] For, as much as the framers wished to preserve the capacity of the States to operate as independent self-governing communities, they also wished to ensure that the Commonwealth would be effectively equipped to regulate matters within its jurisdiction notwithstanding any State laws to the contrary. Moreover, subject to certain constitutional limits on legislative power that are imposed on both the Commonwealth and the States, there are no 'gaps' in the combined legislative competence of the Commonwealth and State Parliaments. They can, by the cooperative exercise of their legislative powers, make laws effectively on any topic.[14] The framers also deliberately chose to invest the High Court of Australia with jurisdiction to determine disputes about the constitutional validity of federal legislation.[15]

Section 51 of the Constitution confers legislative power on the Commonwealth in the following terms:

> The Parliament shall, subject to this Constitution, have power to make laws for the peace, order, and good government of the Commonwealth with respect to: …

Thereafter follows a list of 40 specific matters in respect of which the Parliament has power to make laws. Even though there is also a separate list of 'exclusive' powers in s 52, several of the topics in s 51 are by their nature exclusive to the Commonwealth, principally because they were not possessed by the colonies prior to federation.[16]

Several general issues arise in relation to the terms in which legislative power is conferred upon the Commonwealth Parliament in ss 51 and 52. These issues include:

- What do the words 'for the peace, order, and good government' mean? Do they imply any substantive limitations on the legislative power that are justiciable before the courts? Are they a term of art which implies a particular quality of legislative power?
- Does the investiture of legislative power in 'the Parliament' allow the Parliament to delegate its legislative power to other bodies, to enact retrospective laws, or to impose upon itself special procedural requirements for the enactment of certain kinds of laws?
- In what respects is the power to make laws 'subject to' the Constitution?
- Do the words 'of the Commonwealth' imply that a law must have a sufficient connection to the Commonwealth, or can its laws have an unlimited extra-territorial operation?

**13** See Chapter 4, Part II.
**14** *R v Duncan; Ex parte Australian Iron & Steel Pty Ltd* (1983) 158 CLR 535, 589–91. For an example of a constitutional limit on the capacities of the Commonwealth and the States to cooperate through the joint exercise of their powers, see *Re Wakim; Ex parte McNally* (1999) 198 CLR 511, discussed in Chapter 8, Part IV.6.
**15** See, eg, *Convention Debates, Sydney* (1891) 698; *Convention Debates, Adelaide* (1987) 24–5, 115, 129, 272, 336, 369, 937, 938, 940, 950–51, 952–3, 953, 956; *Convention Debates, Melbourne* (1898) 268, 271, 272, 275, 279, 286, 289, 291.
**16** See Chapter 4, Part II.2.

- What sort of a connection between a law and the specific topics listed in ss 51 and 52 is required by the words 'with respect to'?
- How is each head of power to be interpreted? Should each power be interpreted in isolation or in the context of the others? Should each power be interpreted as widely as the language used can reasonably sustain, or in a limited manner bearing in mind the need to maintain a 'balance' between the powers of the Commonwealth and the powers of the States?

This chapter addresses these questions. It begins by examining the nature of legislative power in general, comparing the 'plenary' character of legislative authority with several possible limitations on legislative power. These limitations concern the delegation of law-making power, the enactment of retrospective laws, the imposition of special procedural requirements for the enactment of laws, territorial limitations on the operation of laws, and other limitations on law-making power that are expressed in or may be inferred from the text and structure of the Constitution. The chapter then turns to the interpretation of the Commonwealth's legislative powers. It critically introduces the methods and techniques of interpretation that have been developed by the High Court, and shows how the Court has moved over time from a set of approaches that understood the constitutional distribution of powers to be grounded upon a 'compact' between the States to a set of approaches premised on a conception of the Constitution as an exercise of British parliamentary sovereignty. Under this last approach, it is shown, the Commonwealth's heads of power have come to be interpreted virtually as widely as the words used can possibly sustain. The chapter deliberately emphasises several important techniques of constitutional interpretation that underwrite this approach. In this extended discussion, particular heads of legislative power are used to illustrate wider points about interpretive method. The chapter then closes with a more detailed analysis of three very important heads of power, namely those concerning 'corporations' and 'external affairs', and the so-called 'implied nationhood' power.

# II The nature of legislative power

## 1 Plenary power: 'Peace, order, and good government'

The words 'peace, order, and good government' were terms of art used frequently by the British Parliament to confer legislative power on colonial legislatures,[17] including those of the six Australian colonies.[18] Do these words imply any substantive limitations on the powers conferred such that it is necessary to determine whether a law is indeed enacted for the peace, order and good

**17** John Quick and Robert Randolph Garran, *The Annotated Constitution of the Australian Commonwealth* (Angus and Robertson, 1901) 511–15.

**18** The phrase 'peace, welfare, and good government' is used in the *Constitution Act 1902* (NSW), s 5 and 'in and for Victoria in all cases whatsoever' is now used in the *Constitution Act 1975* (Vic), s 16. However, the *Australia Acts 1986* (UK and Cth), s 2(2), use the traditional formula: 'peace, order and good government'.

government of the community? Certainly, at the time of federation it was widely thought that the legislative powers granted to the Commonwealth were 'delegated' to them by the British Imperial Parliament. As Quick and Garran explained, this act of delegation meant that although the Commonwealth was 'substantially free and practically independent' as a political community, it remained 'subject' to the British Parliament. In other words, the 'sovereignty' of the British Parliament, 'though dormant', was not extinguished or abandoned, but was 'merely' limited by 'an implied compact not to interfere', so long as the Commonwealth governed itself in accordance with the Constitution.[19]

At the same time, as Quick and Garran acknowledged,[20] the Privy Council had decided in a line of cases that when the British Parliament conferred legislative powers on a self-governing colonial legislature it granted powers 'as large, and of the same nature, as those of the Parliament itself',[21] and 'as plenary and as ample within the limits prescribed ... as the Imperial Parliament in the plenitude of its power possessed and could bestow'.[22] The result was that although the powers of a colony might be 'restricted' as to the topics on which it might legislate, within those topics the powers of the colonies were 'unrestricted'.[23] In a case decided in 1986, some members of the Supreme Court of New South Wales entertained the idea that the words 'peace, order, and good government' might import restrictions on the scope of the power of a Parliament.[24] However, soon thereafter this idea was definitively rejected by the High Court on the ground that the traditional formula conveys 'in British constitutional language' the 'widest law-making powers appropriate to a Sovereign'.[25] Consistent with this line of reasoning, the legislative powers of the Commonwealth have long been considered to be 'plenary' within the scope of the particular subject matters specified in the Constitution.[26] Within those particular topics, as Griffith CJ once put it, 'the Commonwealth Parliament has ... authority to make any laws that it may think fit' and 'it is not for the judicial branch ... to review their actions, or to consider whether the means that they have adopted are wise or unwise'.[27] As Dixon J similarly explained, 'the words appear to have been understood as giving a plenary character, within their ambit, to the powers over the specific subject matters afterwards enumerated'.[28]

**19** Quick and Garran, above n 17, 327–8.
**20** Ibid, 509–10.
**21** *R v Burah* (1878) 3 App Cas 889, 904 (concerning India).
**22** *Hodge v The Queen* (1883) 9 App Cas 117, 132 (concerning the Canadian Province of Ontario).
**23** *Powell v Apollo Candle Co* (1885) 10 App Cas 282, 290 (concerning New South Wales).
**24** *Building Construction Employees and Builders Labourers' Federation (NSW) v Minister for Industrial Relations* (1986) 7 NSWLR 372, 383–7, but see 404–6.
**25** *Union Steamship Co of Australia Pty Ltd v King* (1988) 166 CLR 1, 9–10, citing *Ibralebbe v The Queen* [1964] AC 900, 923. The Court, however, did bracket out the possibility that the legislative power might be restrained by rights deeply rooted in the democratic system of government and the common law. See Chapter 5, Part I.
**26** *Robtelmes v Brenan* (1906) 4 CLR 395, 403–4, 415, 419–21.
**27** Ibid, 404.
**28** *R v Sharkey* (1949) 79 CLR 121, 152.

The grant of legislative power of the Commonwealth in terms comparable to the corresponding power of the British Parliament gives rise to several potential implications, some of which have been confirmed by the High Court, others of which remain matters of academic discussion. These implications concern the capacity of the Parliament to delegate law-making power, to enact retrospective laws and to impose upon itself special procedural requirements for the enactment of certain kinds of laws.

### Delegated legislation

The Privy Council decisions just mentioned held that the Parliaments of self-governing colonies are not to be regarded as mere 'delegates' of the British Parliament and that, accordingly, their powers are not to be regarded as subject to the maxim that 'a delegate may not itself delegate' (*delegatus non potest delegare*).[29] Applying the reasoning in these decisions to Australia, the High Court has held that the Commonwealth Parliament is able to delegate law-making power to the Executive, usually in the form of regulations made by the Governor-General acting on the advice of the Ministry of the day.[30] In the leading case on the topic, *Victorian Stevedoring and General Contracting Co Ltd v Dignan*,[31] the Court had to consider an Act in which the Parliament had delegated to the Governor-General a general power to make regulations concerning the employment of transport workers.[32] The grant of power was extensive and unusual. The statute did not establish a general legislative framework in relation to which the Governor General would supply the necessary administrative and practical details. Rather, it conferred a very general power to make regulations 'with respect to the employment of transport workers'. Moreover, the regulations were declared to have 'the force of law' 'notwithstanding anything in any other Act'.[33] The primary ground of challenge was that such delegation was inconsistent with the distribution of legislative, executive and judicial powers separately and distinctly to the Parliament, the Executive and the Judiciary. It was argued that conferring such broadly defined legislative power upon the Executive was inconsistent with the principle of the separation of powers.[34]

Delivering the leading judgment, Dixon J accepted that the American doctrine of the separation of powers was, in principle, applicable to Australia,[35] but he noted that American cases that had limited the scope of the Congress's power to confer regulation-making power also depended on the *delegatus non potest delegare* principle. Drawing on the Privy Council decisions noted above,

**29** *R v Burah* (1878) 3 App Cas 889, 904–6; *Hodge v The Queen* (1883) 9 App Cas 117, 132; *Powell v Apollo Candle Co* (1885) 10 App Cas 282, 290.
**30** *Baxter v Ah Way* (1909) 8 CLR 626, 632–4, 642–4, 646; *Roche v Kronheimer* (1921) 29 CLR 329, 337, 340; *Crowe v Commonwealth* (1935) 54 CLR 69, 94–5.
**31** (1931) 46 CLR 73.
**32** *Transport Workers Act 1928* (Cth), s 3.
**33** *Victorian Stevedoring and General Contracting Co Ltd v Dignan* (1931) 46 CLR 73, 100.
**34** Ibid, 89–94.
**35** Ibid, 96–8.

his Honour pointed out that this second principle simply had no relevant application in Australia,[36] and he held, with the other members of the Court, that the regulation-making power, despite its general and overriding nature, was constitutionally valid.[37] He was aware that the Court was thus taking an approach to legislative power that was different to its insistence on the separation of judicial power,[38] but he defended the 'asymmetry', partly on the ground that legislative power is essentially different in nature from judicial power and partly because the refinements of 'juristic analysis' developed in the United States must give way to the peculiar 'history and usages of British legislation and the theories of English law'.[39] Dixon J nonetheless indicated that there remained limits on the capacity of the Parliament to delegate its powers. These potential limits were that the regulation-making power must remain subordinate to the Parliament and that the terms of the grant must not be so wide or so uncertain as to subject matter that it cannot be said that the Act is law with respect to any particular head or heads of power.[40] He also suggested that the principle that the Parliament is the 'exclusive repository of the legislative power of the Commonwealth' would continue to supply what he called 'considerations of weight' that could be brought to bear when any particular delegation was being evaluated.[41] Exactly how these considerations of weight might be applied was not explained. Expressing himself tentatively, he pondered that:

> it may be right to treat subordinate legislation which remains under parliamentary control as lacking the independent and unqualified authority which is an attribute of true legislative power, at any rate when there has been an attempt to confer any very general legislative capacity.[42]

Whatever this may mean in practice, what clearly flows from *Dignan* is that the power to delegate law-making power is very extensive indeed, and that the ability of the Parliament to supervise and, if necessary, to reverse delegated legislation is of critical importance. It is significant that the *Legislative Instruments Act*[43] requires, among other things, that regulations must be entered in the Register of Legislative Instruments as soon as possible and laid before each house of Parliament within six sitting days of registration, and that they may be disallowed within a further 15 sittings days by either house by resolution of the house or in circumstances where a disallowance motion is not dealt with by the house.

**36** Ibid, 94–5, 98–9.
**37** Ibid, 84, 86–7, 100–1, 118–19.
**38** See *R v Kirby; Ex parte Boilermakers' Society of Australia* (1956) 94 CLR 254, discussed in Chapter 9, Part II.
**39** *Victorian Stevedoring and General Contracting Co Ltd v Dignan* (1931) 46 CLR 73, 101–2.
**40** Ibid, 99, 101–2; see also 120–21, suggesting that such a law might properly be characterised as a law 'with respect to the legislative power to deal with the subject' rather than a law with respect to the subject matter itself. See also *Giris Pty Ltd v Federal Commissioner of Taxation* (1969) 119 CLR 365, 373–4, 379, 381, 385; *Plaintiff S157/2002 v Commonwealth* (2003) 211 CLR 476, 512–13.
**41** *Victorian Stevedoring and General Contracting Co Ltd v Dignan* (1931) 46 CLR 73, 101.
**42** Ibid, 102.
**43** *Legislative Instruments Act 2003* (Cth).

Whether this procedural safeguard is a sufficient remedy for the resulting concentration of power in the federal government and its departments is an important question. Certainly, the delegation of law-making power enables the Executive to enact the rules that it then administers and enforces, contrary to the principle of the separation of powers. Montesquieu argued that:

> When the legislative and executive powers are united in the same person, or in the same body of magistrates, there can be no liberty; because apprehensions may arise, lest the same monarch or senate should enact tyrannical laws, to execute them in a tyrannical manner.[44]

James Madison agreed with this general principle, arguing that the problem existed whether or not the person or body exercising this combination of powers was popularly elected or accountable to the people.[45] Criticisms of the practice of delegated legislation, as well as defences of its necessity and suitability, turn largely on judgments about the role and proper functioning of the state and the nature and scope of individual liberty.[46]

### Retrospective laws

A second implication of the plenary nature of the legislative power of the Commonwealth is that the Parliament is generally able to enact laws having a retrospective operation. This is a proposition that has often been affirmed. For example, in *R v Kidman*, which involved a retrospectively operating criminal law, Higgins J observed that, despite the expediency and injustice that may often accompany a retrospective law, there was no doubt that the British Parliament had power to enact such laws and had conferred upon the colonial legislatures, within the limits prescribed, legislative authority comparable to the plenitude of its own power.[47] Isaacs J affirmed this in *Ex parte Walsh and Johnson*, when he said that Commonwealth laws may be retrospective precisely because the Commonwealth Parliament possesses the same sovereign capacity as the Imperial Parliament.[48] The same basic idea was expressed by Dawson J in *Polyukhovich v Commonwealth*, which again concerned a retrospective criminal law, when he described the ability to legislate retrospectively as a necessary incident of the 'sovereign legislative power' conferred upon the Parliament by virtue of the 'peace, order, and good government' formula.[49] In *University of Wollongong v Metwally*, a similar point was made by Mason J (dissenting) in relation to the capacity of the Parliament, by virtue of the plenary

**44** Charles de Secondat Montesquieu, *The Spirit of Laws* (Hafner, 1949) bk 11, ch 6.
**45** James Madison, 'Federalist No 47' in Clinton Rossiter (ed), *The Federalist Papers* (New American Library, 1961).
**46** Compare Ivor Jennings, *The Law and the Constitution* (University of London Press, 1st ed, 1933) 50–51; Suri Ratnapala, *Welfare State or Constitutional State?* (Centre for Independent Studies, 1990); N W Barber, 'Prelude to the Separation of Powers' (2001) 60(01) *Cambridge Law Journal* 59.
**47** *R v Kidman* (1915) 20 CLR 425, 451–2; see also 443, 455, 459–61.
**48** *Ex parte Walsh and Johnson; In re Yates* (1925) 37 CLR 36, 81, 89; see also 127.
**49** *Polyukhovich v Commonwealth* (1991) 172 CLR 501, 633–6, 643–4.

nature of its legislative powers, to enact a law that creates a 'statutory fiction' which operates retrospectively.[50]

Although there are important statements in *Polyukhovich* and *Metwally* which thus affirm the general capacity of the Commonwealth to enact retrospective laws, the cases identify two important qualifications. *Polyukhovich* involved a retrospective criminal law which, it was argued, usurped or interfered with the proper exercise of judicial power by the courts. As will be seen in Chapter 9, although the law was upheld, a majority of the Court affirmed that the legislative power of the Parliament does not extend to the enactment of 'legislative judgments' in the form of 'bills of attainder' or 'bills of pains and penalties' which declare, in effect, that a particular person has committed a criminal offence and is liable to punishment. A retrospective criminal law must leave it to the courts to determine whether a person has actually engaged in the proscribed conduct.[51] *Metwally* concerned a federal law that the High Court had previously held was inconsistent with a state law on the topic and which therefore prevailed over the state law pursuant to s 109 of the Constitution.[52] The Parliament attempted to reverse the effect of that decision by declaring that the law that it had previously enacted be deemed 'never to have intended' to exclude or limit the operation of the State law. As will be seen in Chapter 4, a majority of the Court held that, although the Commonwealth can legislate retrospectively, it cannot retrospectively reverse the effect of s 109 of the Constitution.

### Manner and form requirements

The third implication that potentially flows from the nature of the Commonwealth's legislative power concerns the capacity of the Parliament to establish special procedures, known as 'manner and form' requirements, for the enactment of particular types of legislation. Such procedures may include requirements that legislation be passed: (a) by a special majority; (b) at a joint sitting; (c) with the concurrence of only one house of Parliament; (d) after the elapse of a specified time period between readings; or (e) following voter approval at a referendum. Special procedures such as these are usually enacted to protect important constitutional provisions from amendment or repeal by ordinary legislative processes. Because the State Constitutions are in the form of ordinary statutes of the State Parliaments, manner and form requirements are used to 'entrench' aspects of the State Constitution Acts, protecting them from amendment or repeal by ordinary statute. The legal effectiveness of such provisions at a State level turns largely on s 6 of the *Australia Acts 1986*.[53] The situation at a Commonwealth level is different because the Constitution already operates by paramount force to define and limit the powers of the Parliament, and because the Constitution already imposes its own particular manner and form requirement by providing that the Constitution

**50** *University of Wollongong v Metwally* (1984) 158 CLR 447, 465; see also 484, 486. See Chapter 4, Part II.3.
**51** *Polyukhovich* is also an important case on the scope of the external affairs power: see Part III.2 below.
**52** *Viskauskas v Niland* (1983) 153 CLR 280.
**53** See Chapter 10, Part IV.4.

cannot be amended without approval at a referendum.[54] However, given what some have regarded as the 'difficulty' in securing formal amendment of the Constitution,[55] it has been suggested that the enactment of alternative manner and form requirements at a Commonwealth level may be an effective way of addressing some of the constitutional problems that have arisen over time.[56]

The legal effectiveness of any manner and form requirement adopted at a Commonwealth level turns on two fundamental issues. The first revolves around the two competing theories of the nature of parliamentary sovereignty discussed in Chapter 1.[57] One of these theories treats the sovereignty of the Parliament as something which is 'continuing' in nature, with the implication that a particular Parliament cannot pass a law that requires later Parliaments to follow special procedures to amend or repeal that law.[58] The other theory regards parliamentary sovereignty as something that is 'self-embracing', with the implication that a particular Parliament is able to redefine itself, or its legislative procedures, in a way that is binding on later Parliaments.[59] Only if the latter theory were to be accepted would it possible, in principle, for a particular Commonwealth Parliament to impose manner and form requirements upon its successor Parliaments.

The second issue concerns the fact that the Constitution itself lays down manner and form requirements for its own amendment, which are binding on the Parliament. These include not only the formal amendment process in s 128, but also the special legislative powers of the Parliament in relation to matters in respect of which the Constitution has made temporary provision (s 51(xxxvi)), matters referred to it by the States (s 51(xxxvii)) and matters falling within the original power of the British Parliament to legislate for Australia (s 51(xxxviii)). In the minds of its framers, the Constitution thus made extensive and sufficient provision for its own entrenchment and alteration.[60] The framers were also very careful to define the composition of the Parliament (ss 1, 7 and 24) and to prescribe the respective powers of the two houses (ss 53 and 57). The Constitution likewise requires that decisions in each house will ordinarily be made by simple majority (ss 23 and 40),[61] and it anticipates that proposed laws will be passed by both houses of Parliament (s 58).[62] Without an amendment to the Constitution, the Commonwealth Parliament is not able to adopt binding manner and form requirements that are in any respect inconsistent with these provisions.

**54** Commonwealth Constitution, s 128.
**55** See Chapter 1, Part V.
**56** George Winterton, 'Can the Commonwealth Parliament Enact "Manner and Form" Legislation?' (1980) 11 *Federal Law Review* 167.
**57** See Chapter 1, Part II.3.
**58** H W R Wade, 'The Basis of Legal Sovereignty' [1955] *Cambridge Law Journal* 172.
**59** Geoffrey Marshall, *Constitutional Theory* (Clarendon Press, 1980) 35–57.
**60** Aroney, above n 2, ch 11.
**61** Absolute majorities are required by the special procedures of ss 57 and 128.
**62** There is also the remote possibility that the Commonwealth and State Parliaments, acting unanimously, might attempt to impose manner and form requirements through an amendment to the *Australia Acts 1986*. See Christopher Gilbert, 'Section 15 of the Australia Acts: Constitutional Change by the Back Door' (1989) 5 *Queensland University of Technology Law Journal* 55; R D Lumb, 'The Bicentenary of Australian Constitutionalism: The Evolution of Rules of Constitutional Change' (1988) 15 *University of Queensland Law Journal* 1.

Thus, the constitutional requirement that decisions be made by majority vote in each house almost certainly prevents the imposition of a manner and form requirement that certain bills must be passed by a special majority.[63] Moreover, the principle that the Parliament is meant to be the 'exclusive repository of the legislative power of the Commonwealth'[64] would probably also carry with it the implication that no manner and form requirement could effectively substitute a new legislature for the present one, such as by adding an additional element to the present legislative process in the form of a referendum.[65] Also, a redefinition of the Parliament such that laws could be enacted with only the agreement and assent of the House of Representatives and the Governor-General,[66] despite ingenious argument to the contrary,[67] would seem to be quite inconsistent with the essential role of the Senate prescribed and anticipated by the text and structure of the Constitution.[68] Indeed, it is arguable that the imposition of any manner and form requirement whatsoever would be inconsistent with the fundamental principle that underlies the entire Constitution, namely that it is the Constitution alone which defines and limits the powers of the Parliament, and that changes to those powers and limitations can only be made through the means the Constitution itself prescribes, principally (but not exclusively) formal amendment by referendum pursuant to s 128.[69]

## 2 Extra-territorial laws: 'of the Commonwealth'

In several Privy Council cases decided in the nineteenth century it was held that the legislative powers of a colony are limited to the territory of the colony or to persons naturally born within it, largely because the legislative power conferred was expressed to be for the peace, order and good government *of the colony*.[70] Such a conclusion made good sense in the context of a worldwide empire consisting of numerous colonial settlements over which only the Imperial Parliament claimed to have overriding and comprehensive authority.[71] Consistent with this approach, the framers of the Constitution framed the legislative powers of the Commonwealth Parliament in similar terms, namely as a 'power to make laws

**63** Winterton, above n 56, 191.
**64** *Victorian Stevedoring and General Contracting Co Ltd v Dignan* (1931) 46 CLR 73, 101.
**65** Winterton, above n 56, 192.
**66** See *Parliament Acts 1911* and *1949* (UK) and *Jackson v Her Majesty's Attorney General* [2005] UKHL 56, discussed in Chapter 1, Part II.2. See also *Constitution Act 1902* (NSW), s 5A.
**67** Winterton, above n 56, 196–201.
**68** Commonwealth Constitution, ss 1, 7, 24, 53, 57, 58, 128, discussed in Chapter 2, Parts II and III. See *Victoria v Commonwealth (Petroleum and Minerals Authority)* (1975) 134 CLR 81, 121, 143, 168, 185; *Williams v Commonwealth (No 1)* (2012) 248 CLR 156, 205–6, 316–17, 350.
**69** Compare Michael Detmold, *The Australian Commonwealth: A Fundamental Analysis of Its Constitution* (Law Book Company, 1985) 207–8, 212–13, 214–16, 217–18; Jeffrey Goldsworthy, 'Manner and Form in the Australian States' (1987) 16 *Melbourne University Law Review* 403, 404, 421–2; Nicholas Aroney, 'A Public Choice?: Federalism and the Prospects of a Republican Preamble' (1999) 21 *University of Queensland Law Journal* 205, 290. See also the discussion of *Attorney-General (WA) v Marquet* (2003) 217 CLR 545 in Chapter 10, Part IV.4.
**70** *Jefferys v Boosey* (1854) 4 HLC 815, 926; 10 ER 681, 725; *Macleod v Attorney-General (NSW)* [1891] AC 455, 458 (emphasis added).
**71** *Union Steamship Co of Australia Pty Ltd v King* (1988) 166 CLR 1, 11.

for the peace, order, and good government *of the Commonwealth*'.[72] When the Constitution came into force in 1901, did this mean that the legislative powers of the Parliament were territorially limited? Quick and Garran considered that it did, although they noted provisions in the Constitution which suggested certain exceptions.[73] For example, covering clause 5 of the *Commonwealth of Australia Constitution Act 1900* states that Commonwealth laws:

> shall be binding on the ... people of every State and of every part of the Commonwealth, notwithstanding anything in the laws of any State; and the laws of the Commonwealth shall be in force on all British ships, the Queen's ships of war excepted, whose first port of clearance and whose port of destination are in the Commonwealth.

This clause plainly affirms the legislative jurisdiction of the Parliament over the people and every part of the Commonwealth, but it also extends that jurisdiction to British ships whose first port of clearance and whose port of destination are in the Commonwealth.[74] In addition, some of the heads of legislative power in s 51 refer to matters that involve extraterritorial things and relationships, such as the power to legislate with respect to 'fisheries in Australian waters beyond territorial limits' (s 51(x)), 'external affairs' (s 51(xxix)) and 'relations ... with the islands of the Pacific' (s 51(xxx)).

Whatever may have been the position at the time of federation, in 1926 the Balfour Declaration proclaimed that the overseas Dominions of the Crown, Australia included, were 'autonomous communities', each responsible for its own domestic and external affairs.[75] Moreover, in 1931 the *Statute of Westminster* addressed the issue directly by declaring and enacting that 'the Parliament of a Dominion has full power to make laws having extra-territorial operation'.[76] Soon thereafter, in *Croft v Dunphy*, the Privy Council held that, quite apart from the *Statute of Westminster*, the Dominion of Canada was to be regarded as a 'fully Sovereign State' whose Parliament is not limited by any doctrine of extraterritorial incompetence.[77] Whatever may have been the position in 1901, therefore, there is no doubt that the legislative competence of the Commonwealth Parliament is no longer territorially limited.[78]

## 3 Limited power: 'subject to this Constitution'

The legislative powers of the Commonwealth are also 'subject to' the Constitution. The Constitution contains several explicit prohibitions and restrictions

**72** Emphasis added.
**73** Quick and Garran, above n 17, 354–5, 569–72, 631–2. For other contemporary views, see *XYZ v Commonwealth* (2006) 227 CLR 532, 587–8.
**74** See *Clarke v Union Steamship Co of New Zealand Ltd* (1914) 18 CLR 142.
**75** Inter-Imperial Relations Committee, *Report, Proceedings and Memoranda* (Imperial Conference, 1926).
**76** *Statute of Westminster 1931* (UK), s 3. By the *Statute of Westminster Adoption Act 1942* (Cth), the *Statute* is declared to apply in Australia from 3 September 1939. See Chapter 1, Part V.1.
**77** *Croft v Dunphy* [1933] AC 156, 163. See Chapter 1, Part V.1.
**78** *Union Steamship Co of Australia Pty Ltd v King* (1988) 166 CLR 1, 12; *Polyukhovich v Commonwealth* (1991) 172 CLR 501, 529, 550, 633–4, 695, 716; *XYZ v Commonwealth* (2006) 227 CLR 532, 539, 595. For discussion of the extra-territorial competence of the States, see Chapter 10, Part IV.4.

on the legislative powers of the Commonwealth Parliament. They include the following requirements:

- jury trial for indictable offences (s 80);
- freedom of interstate trade, commerce and intercourse (s 92);
- no preferences to one State or part of a State by any law or regulation of trade, commerce, or revenue (s 99);
- the reasonable use of waters or rivers for conservation or irrigation (s 100);
- no taxation of the property of a State (s 114);
- freedom of religion and non-establishment of religion (s 116).

In addition, the High Court has held that there are limitations on the legislative power of the Commonwealth that are implied by the text and structure of the Constitution. These implied requirements prohibit laws which unduly:

- interfere with the capacity of a State to perform its constitutional functions as an independent government;
- confer non-judicial powers on any court able to exercise federal jurisdiction or confer judicial powers on non-courts;
- interfere with freedom of political communication.

These express and implied limitations on legislative power are discussed in detail in Chapters 4, 5, 8 and 9.

## III Interpreting legislative power

The legislative power of the Commonwealth is deliberately limited to the specific topics primarily listed in ss 51 and 52. Williams J put it this way in the *Pharmaceutical Benefits* case:

> [T]he object of the Constitution was to superimpose on the existing body politics consisting of the States a wider overriding body politic for certain specific purposes. It was for these particular purposes and these alone that the body politics consisting of the States agreed to create the body politic known as the Commonwealth of Australia. These purposes must all be found within the four corners of the Constitution.[79]

As a consequence, as Griffith CJ noted in *R v Kidman*, '[t]he legislative power of the Commonwealth Parliament is not plenary in the sense that its ambit includes any enactment on any subject whatever'.[80] Rather, as Lord Haldane put it in the *Colonial Sugar Refining* case, the 'scheme' of the Constitution is to establish a 'federal' system 'in the strict sense of the term', by which he meant that the States had agreed to delegate a limited 'measure' of powers to the Commonwealth while 'in the main' continuing to 'preserve their original Constitutions'.[81] As Griffith CJ commented in *Kidman*, the idea was:

**79** *Attorney-General (Vic); Ex rel Dale v Commonwealth* (1945) 71 CLR 237, 282.
**80** (1915) 20 CLR 425, 433.
**81** *Attorney-General (Cth) v Colonial Sugar Refining Co Ltd* (1913) 17 CLR 644, 651–2.

> to select certain subjects ... enumerated in sec. 51, and most of which were already within the ambit of the legislative power of the federating Colonies, and to confer upon the Federal Parliament power to legislate with respect to them.[82]

The principle that all laws enacted by the Parliament must be sufficiently connected or related to one or more of the enumerated heads of legislative power has been affirmed by the High Court ever since.[83]

In determining whether a particular law is validly enacted by the Commonwealth Parliament, it is necessary to ask whether the law can be characterised as a law that is 'with respect to' one of the Commonwealth's legislative heads of power. This process necessarily involves three analytically distinguishable steps, namely:

(i) characterisation of the enacted law;
(ii) interpretation of the relevant head (or heads) of power; and
(iii) determination whether the law (as characterised) has a sufficient connection to the relevant head (or heads) of power (as interpreted).

Although these particular inquiries are distinguishable, each analysis is necessarily undertaken in the context of the others. The question will always be whether a particular law can be characterised in a way that connects it with a particular head (or heads) of power, and the interpretation of a head of power will be undertaken in a way that focuses on whether it provides authority for the enactment of the law that is particularly under consideration. In some cases, the characterisation of the law is relatively straightforward while the interpretation of the head of power is more contentious. In others, it is the characterisation of the law that is primarily in question, the interpretation of the relevant head of power being relatively straightforward, at least in the particular circumstances of the case. In yet other cases, it is the requisite 'connection' between the law and the head of power that is especially in issue.

Different general approaches to these questions are possible, and over the course of its history, the High Court's prevailing techniques have undergone change and development. As a general proposition, the more narrowly each head of power is interpreted, the more substantively each law tends to be characterised; and the more tightly the required connection between the law and the head of power is understood, the more likely a particular law will be held to be unconstitutional. Conversely, the more widely each head of power is interpreted, the more formally each law tends to be characterised; and the more loosely the required connection between the law and the head of power is understood, the more likely a particular law will be upheld as constitutional. As will be seen, over time the High Court has generally moved from a set of techniques that tended to limit the scope of federal power to a set of techniques that enlarges it considerably.

The High Court's approach to the federal distribution of powers has been shaped by particular dispositions and convictions concerning nature of the

**82** *R v Kidman* (1915) 20 CLR 425, 433. See, likewise, *R v Barger* (1908) 6 CLR 41, 64.
**83** *Amalgamated Society of Engineers v Adelaide Steamship Co Ltd* (1920) 28 CLR 129, 154.

Australian Constitution and the kind of federation that it establishes. As noted in Chapter 1, it is possible to describe the development of the Court's federalism jurisprudence by reference to three broad phases.[84] From its establishment in 1903, the Court consisted of three of the leading framers of the Constitution: Samuel Griffith, Edmund Barton and Richard O'Connor. Griffith was a former Premier and Chief Justice of Queensland, and had been leader of the Federal Convention of 1891. Barton was the leader of the Federal Convention of 1897–8 and became the first Prime Minister. O'Connor was a former Minister of Justice and Solicitor-General of New South Wales, the first Leader of the Government in the Senate and a close associate of Barton's at the 1897–8 Convention. Much of the wording of the Constitution was personally drafted by Griffith and Barton as leaders of their respective drafting committees, and their constitutional views generally cohered with the outlook of the framers of the Constitution as a whole. On this prevailing view, the Constitution was essentially understood to be a federal compact between the people of the States, pursuant to which, following the models of the United States and Switzerland, the States granted numerous important, but specific and limited powers upon the Commonwealth, while reserving to themselves the vast bulk of their pre-existing powers of local self-government. As Griffith put it in 1891:

> [T]he separate states are to continue as autonomous bodies, surrendering only so much of their powers as is necessary to the establishment of a general government to do for them collectively what they cannot do individually for themselves, and which they cannot do as a collective body for themselves.[85]

This perspective underlay an approach to the interpretation of the Constitution which resulted in several characteristic doctrines of the Court during Griffith's chief justiceship. One of these, known as the 'State reserved powers' or 'implied prohibition' doctrine, interpreted each head of Commonwealth power in a manner that deliberately left room for the powers reserved to the States. This was accompanied by a 'substantive' approach to the characterisation of federal laws well suited to determining whether a law should be categorised as falling within Commonwealth power or within the powers reserved to the States. A third major doctrine, known as the 'immunity of instrumentalities', conceived the Commonwealth and the States as 'sovereign' governments each operating within their respective spheres, a conception which implied that the means or 'instrumentalities' through which they pursued their governmental objectives must enjoy a far-reaching immunity from external interference. The Griffith Court also adopted an approach to identifying 'inconsistencies' between State and Commonwealth laws which restricted them to cases where the inconsistency is 'direct'.[86]

**84** Chapter 1, Part V.1.
**85** *Convention Debates, Sydney* (1891) 31–2.
**86** The immunity of instrumentalities and inconsistency between State and Commonwealth laws are discussed in Chapter 4. The reserved powers doctrine is discussed immediately below.

In 1906, Isaac Isaacs and Henry Bournes Higgins were appointed to the Court. Both were learned and skilled lawyers who had been prominent and articulate members of the Conventions of the 1890s, but they had advocated a kind of federation that differed very substantially from the predominant view. Rather than conceive the federation to be predicated on the agreement of the peoples of the several States, Isaacs and Higgins believed that it should be based on the consent of the Australian people as a whole. This especially led Higgins to advocate that the ratification of the Constitution should occur through a national referendum and to reason about the federal features of the Constitution in a manner that was premised on the sovereignty of the people of the entire nation, without regard to the distinct State communities into which they were grouped politically.[87] In 1912, O'Connor J died and was replaced by Gavan Duffy J, and in 1913, two additional justices, Powers and Rich JJ were appointed. The views of Griffith CJ, Barton and O'Connor JJ generally prevailed on the Court until 1920, when the places of Griffith CJ and Barton J were filled by Knox CJ and Starke J. In the landmark *Engineers* case of that year,[88] under the intellectual leadership of Isaacs J, the High Court explicitly overruled the immunity of instrumentalities doctrine and by implication rejected the reserved powers doctrine as well. Soon thereafter, the Court also expanded the grounds upon which a State law might be found to be inconsistent with a Commonwealth law by embracing the idea of 'indirect' inconsistency and the notion that a Commonwealth law might evince an intention to 'cover the field', thereby displacing all State laws within that field.[89] Eventually, the Court also settled on an approach to the characterisation of Commonwealth laws which effectively limited the inquiry to one of determining whether there is a sufficient connection between the Commonwealth law and a head of power, without taking into consideration whether the law could in some relevant sense be characterised in a way that took it outside of the Commonwealth's legislative powers. The basis of this fundamental shift in approach, in the *Engineers* case, was a renewed emphasis on the fact that the Constitution is in the form of a statute of the British Parliament and that it should be interpreted according to the traditional canons of interpretation of British statutes. These canons of interpretation, it was said, dictated that the grants of power to the Commonwealth Parliament ought to be interpreted with as much breadth as the words used can possibly sustain, without consideration being given to the 'residue' of powers left over to the States.

The *Engineers* case is widely regarded as the most significant and influential decision ever brought down by the High Court. Although several of its specific elements have since been moderated or modified, the basic approach to interpreting heads of power and characterising federal laws which it heralded have become the orthodoxy of the Court. While there are some important

**87** Eg, H B Higgins, *Essays and Addresses on the Australian Commonwealth Bill* (Atlas Press, 1900) 11; *Convention Debates, Sydney* (1897) 259–60, discussed in Aroney, above n 2, 130–33, 211–12, 218–21.
**88** *Amalgamated Society of Engineers v Adelaide Steamship Co Ltd* (1920) 28 CLR 129.
**89** On inconsistency between State and Commonwealth laws, see Chapter 4, Part II.

qualifications even to this latter proposition, there can be no doubt that the general method of interpretation introduced by the *Engineers* case has led to a considerable expansion in the scope and reach of the Commonwealth's legislative powers.The most important qualification has been the modified intergovernmental immunities doctrine first articulated in the *Melbourne Corporation* case in 1947.[90] This doctrine protects the States from Commonwealth interference that would prevent them from functioning as independent governments exercising their constitutional powers.[91] The development of the doctrine was very largely a reflection of the views of Sir Owen Dixon, who had been appointed to the Court in 1929. Dixon J was also responsible for the modified Commonwealth immunity doctrine adopted by the Court in the *Cigamatic* case in 1962,[92] a decision that was premised on the 'supremacy' of the Commonwealth and the fact that prior to federation, the colonies could have had no power over the Commonwealth simply because it did not as yet exist.[93]

## 1 Rise and fall of the federal compact

The early High Court affirmed from the outset that the Constitution is to be interpreted in accordance with the ordinary principles applied to the construction of parliamentary statutes, with the general objective of ascertaining the intention of the enacting legislature as this could be discerned from the words used, interpreted in their natural and ordinary sense.[94] At the same time, it was recognised that the meaning of those words might not always be clear in their application to the facts of a particular case, and so the Court accepted that evidence relating to the legislative history of the Constitution might be admitted in order to resolve the ambiguity. This did not mean that reference could be made to opinions expressed by individual members of the Conventions, but only to successive drafts of the Constitution.[95] Nonetheless, the literal meaning of the text was to be followed unless to do so would be manifestly contrary to the evident meaning and purpose of the Constitution as a whole,[96] and it was believed that the text and structure of the Constitution made those purposes and intentions in general quite clear.[97] Moreover, the first three justices of the High Court (Griffith CJ, Barton and O'Connor JJ) had played pivotal roles in the design and drafting of the Constitution and could not help but interpret the Constitution in the light of the historical context in which it had come into being.[98] As a consequence, the early High Court tended to interpret the Constitution in a way that

**90** *Melbourne v Commonwealth (State Banking)* (1947) 74 CLR 31.
**91** This description of the immunity was adopted in *Austin v Commonwealth* (2003) 215 CLR 185.
**92** *Commonwealth v Cigamatic Pty Ltd (in liq)* (1962) 108 CLR 372, adopting the reasoning of Dixon J in *In re Foreman & Sons Pty Ltd; Uther v Federal Commissioner of Taxation* (1947) 74 CLR 508.
**93** For a detailed discussion, see Chapter 4, Part III.
**94** *Tasmania v Commonwealth* (1904) 1 CLR 329, 338–9, 346–7, 358.
**95** Ibid, 333, 350–55, 358.
**96** Ibid, 339, 346–7, 359.
**97** Ibid, 348, 360.
**98** Ibid, 350, 359.

largely reflected the prevailing assumptions, understandings and intentions of the founding generation.

### Reserved powers: Theory

The reserved powers doctrine rested on the view that the Constitution received its political legitimacy and essential federal character from a federating compact negotiated between elected representatives of the several constituent States and ratified by their respective voters.[99] The framers of the Constitution had derived this idea of a compact between the States from their reading of a range of contemporary writers on the subject of federalism, the most influential of whom were James Madison, James Bryce, Edward Freeman and Albert Venn Dicey. All of these writers characterised federal systems – that is, political systems that are originally, structurally and operationally federal in nature – as being authentically founded upon treaty-like agreements between the constituent states.[100] Madison, whose incisive analysis of the American Constitution played a strategically important role in the federation debate in Australia, pointed to a systemic relationship between the formative basis of federal systems and the representative structures, configurations of legislative and executive power and amendment processes adopted therein.[101] Partly because the Australians were influenced by Madison, and partly because Madison's analysis provided a general insight into the underlying dynamics of federal constitution-making, the text, structure and principles of the Australian Constitution reflected this relationship between formation, representation, configuration of power and amendment.[102]

This view of the fundamental premises of the federation led to a certain view about the configuration of legislative power between the Commonwealth and the States. The States were seen by the early High Court as possessing original powers of local self-government, which they insisted would continue under the Constitution (ss 106 and 107), subject only to the carefully defined and limited powers specifically conferred upon the Commonwealth (ss 51 and 52).[103] As such, each head of power served not only to describe the power that was positively conferred upon the Commonwealth, but also to mark out that which was not granted and was therefore reserved to the States.[104] The distribution of powers between the Commonwealth and the States was thus understood as an integrated, coordinated whole, and it was recognised that whenever the validity

**99** *Federated Amalgamated Governmental Railway and Tramway Service Association v New South Wales Railway Traffic Employees Association (Railway Servants)* (1906) 4 CLR 488, 534; *Baxter v Commissioners of Taxation (NSW)* (1907) 4 CLR 1087, 1104, 1121, 1126.

**100** See, eg, James Bryce, *The American Commonwealth* (Macmillan, 2nd ed, 1889) vol I, 12–15, 17–22, 332; A V Dicey, *Introduction to the Study of the Law of the Constitution* (Macmillan, 5th ed, 1897) 137–8, 139, note 1.

**101** James Madison, 'Federalist No 39', in Rossiter, above n 45.

**102** For a fuller discussion, see Aroney, above n 2, 73–7, 107.

**103** See *R v Barger* (1908) 6 CLR 41, 67.

**104** See, eg, *Convention Debates, Sydney* (1891) 699; *Convention Debates, Melbourne* (1898) 502–4, 596–7, 600, 1008–10, 504–5.

of a Commonwealth law was in question, the Court was faced with a choice as to how broadly or narrowly to interpret the relevant head of power.[105] When faced with this interpretive choice, the reserved powers doctrine gave the Court a reason to adopt an interpretation that, as far as possible, left the reserved powers of the States intact.

The reserved powers doctrine effectively required the Court to determine whether a particular Commonwealth law related to *either* Commonwealth *or* State power. An approach to characterisation that facilitated this approach was therefore needed, and here the method adopted by the Privy Council in relation to the Canadian Constitution offered a suitable technique. Under the Canadian federal system, the respective legislative powers of the Dominion of Canada as a whole and each of the Canadian Provinces are specifically and exclusively conferred in separate sections of the Constitution.[106] This means that for any particular law (whether enacted by the Dominion Parliament or a Provincial Parliament) the analytical task is one of determining whether the law is to be characterised so as to bring it under a head of power within the exclusive Dominion list *or* a head of power within the exclusive Provincial list. The prime difficulty in applying such a scheme of distribution is that a law may have one characteristic which connects it with a matter that appears in one list of powers and another characteristic which connects it with the other list. During the early years of the Canadian federation, this problem led the Privy Council to direct the task of characterisation to the identification of what it called the 'pith and substance', or 'the true nature and character' of the law, in order to ascertain the head of power to which the law 'really belongs'.[107] To do so required a distinction to be drawn between the 'essential' or 'dominant' character of the law and other characteristics of the law that were 'non-essential' or merely 'incidental'.[108] When the High Court of Australia first embarked on its task of characterising Commonwealth laws, the decisions of the Privy Council on the Canadian Constitution offered an authoritative and attractive model.[109] The technique of the Privy Council was especially attractive because it had the practical effect of maintaining a degree of 'balance' between the powers of the Dominion and the powers of the Provinces notwithstanding that the Canadian Constitution had been designed to favour the Dominion Parliament. The pith and substance approach had this effect in Canada because it ensured that when assessing whether a Dominion law fell within the Dominion's powers, the question was whether

**105** Eg, *Huddart, Parker & Co Pty Ltd v Moorehead* (1909) 8 CLR 330, 354, 363, 369.
**106** *British North America Act 1867* (UK), ss 91 and 92; see also ss 92A–95. The Act is now formally called the *Constitution Act 1867* (UK).
**107** *Russell v The Queen* (1882) 7 App Cas 829, 839–40. See also *Union Colliery Co of British Columbia Ltd v Bryden* [1899] AC 580, 587.
**108** Bruce Ryder, 'The Demise and Rise of the Classical Paradigm' (1991) 36 *McGill Law Journal* 309.
**109** The pith and substance approach has since been applied to the grants of legislative power under the *Government of Ireland Act 1920* (UK) (*Gallagher v Lynn* [1937] AC 863) and the *Government of India Act 1935* (UK) (*Prafulla Kumar Mukherjee v Bank of Commerce, Limited, Khulna* [1947] LR 74 Ind App 23, 42–3) and has influenced the interpretation of the *Scotland Act 1998* (UK) (*Martin v HM Advocate* [2010] UKSC 10, [11]; but see *Imperial Tobacco Ltd v Lord Advocate* [2012] UKSC 61, [13]–[15]).

the law 'really belonged' to *either* the Dominion *or* the Provinces. The process of characterisation was thus undertaken with the legislative powers of both the Dominion and the Provinces in mind. This was attractive to the early High Court because it suggested that laws enacted by the Commonwealth Parliament would similarly need to be assessed not only by reference to the powers conferred upon the Commonwealth, but also by reference to the matters reserved to the States. For, although the Australian Constitution does not specify particular topics as being 'reserved', the idea that all powers not conferred upon the Commonwealth were retained exclusively by the States certainly seems to have been the prevailing intention and expectation.[110] The pith and substance approach offered a technique well-adapted to securing this outcome.

The reserved powers doctrine and the pith and substance technique were applied in a series of decisions of the High Court under the chief justiceship of Samuel Griffith. In all of these decisions, the majority of the Court were guided by the idea that the Constitution is the result of a federal compact; that its provisions should be read as an integrated whole; that the limited powers conferred upon the Commonwealth serve to define not only the positive scope of its powers, but also the fields of legislative competence reserved to the States; and that in the characterisation of Commonwealth laws it is necessary to determine the category of powers to which the law properly belongs. However, with the appointment of Isaacs and Higgins JJ in 1906 there emerged an alternative general conception of the nature of the federal system and of the appropriate method of constitutional interpretation. On this view, the Constitution was regarded principally as a statute of the British Parliament, and each of the legislative heads of power conferred upon the Commonwealth was read as widely as the language used could reasonably sustain, without any substantial consideration of limitations placed on other heads of Commonwealth power or of the intention of the framers that these limitations were meant to secure to the States a distinct body of reserved powers.

## Reserved powers: Practice

Each case decided by the Griffith Court under the influence of the reserved powers doctrine presented its distinct issues. In the first of these cases, *Peterswald v Bartley*,[111] the Court had to consider a New South Wales law, enacted in 1898, which required any person engaged in the business of brewing certain alcoholic beverages or selling liquor to obtain a licence upon payment of a stipulated licence fee. The main question was whether this scheme was invalid because it imposed an excise duty contrary to s 90 of the Constitution, which provides that the power to impose excise duties and customs duties is exclusive to the Commonwealth. Broadly understood, customs duties are taxes imposed on goods at the point of importation into a country, while excise duties are taxes imposed on

**110** Aroney, above n 2, 260–62, 273–4, 362–8.
**111** (1904) 1 CLR 497.

goods produced or sold within a particular country. The fee in *Peterswald* was of a fixed amount. A licence holder would have to recover the cost of the fee in the prices charged for goods manufactured or sold under the licence, but not in a way that would relate directly to the value or quantity of the goods. Was this enough to make it an excise duty?

Griffith CJ, delivering the judgment of the Court, considered that it was necessary to ascertain from the general scheme of the Constitution what exactly was intended to be withdrawn from the States by s 90.[112] The Constitution, he reasoned, does not empower the Commonwealth to interfere with the power of the States to regulate their internal affairs, especially intra-state business and trade, because the power of the Commonwealth to legislate with respect to 'trade and commerce' in s 51(i) is limited to trade and commerce 'with other countries' or 'among the States'.[113] Noting that the Constitution 'was framed in Australia by Australians, and for the use of the Australian people', the Chief Justice said the term 'duty of excise' ought to be given the meaning it had in Australia, rather than the sense it had acquired in the United Kingdom.[114] Following a review of the relevant cases and statutes, he concluded that an excise duty within the meaning of s 90 was 'a duty analogous to a customs duty imposed upon goods whether in relation to quantity or value when produced or manufactured, and not in the sense of a direct tax or personal tax'.[115] This finding led to the conclusion that the NSW brewer's licence fee was not a duty of excise, and that the States retained a capacity to regulate internal trade and commerce through such licensing schemes.

The next important case was *R v Barger*.[116] In that case the High Court had to determine the validity of the *Excise Tariff 1906*, a Commonwealth law which imposed a tax in the form of an excise duty on agricultural implements of various sorts. The law provided for an exemption from the excise duty where the goods were manufactured under labour remuneration conditions that were determined to be 'fair and reasonable' by resolution of both houses of the Parliament or by an industrial judge, or were in accordance with an industrial award or industrial agreement under the *Commonwealth Conciliation and Arbitration Act 1904* (Cth).[117] The purpose of the law was thus to encourage relevant employers to offer terms of employment which accorded with these standards. Now, there was no question whether the Commonwealth had, in general, the power to make laws which impose taxes of various kinds, including duties of excise, pursuant to the taxation power in s 51(ii) of the Constitution. The doubt about the constitutionality of the tax arose because of the nature of the law itself. Given that its purpose was to influence conditions of employment, could it be properly characterised as a law with respect to

**112** *Peterswald v Bartley* (1904) 1 CLR 497, 507.
**113** Ibid.
**114** Ibid, 509.
**115** Ibid.
**116** (1908) 6 CLR 41.
**117** *Excise Tariff 1906* (Cth), s 2.

taxation?[118] Answering this question required the Court both to characterise the law and to consider the nature and scope of the taxation power, for the question was whether the taxation power authorised the enactment of a law having these characteristics.[119]

In the reasoning of Griffith CJ, Barton and O'Connor JJ, decisions of the Privy Council regarding the process of characterisation were thought to be immediately relevant. *Russell v The Queen*[120] was cited for the proposition that 'the true nature and character of the legislation in the particular instance under discussion must always be determined in order to ascertain the class of subject to which it really belongs'. *Attorney-General (Quebec) v Queen Insurance Co*[121] was said to provide an example of the application of this principle to a taxation law enacted by the Quebec Parliament which could be characterised as an attempt to exercise the power of indirect taxation – an exclusive power of the Dominion Parliament.[122] However, since in Australia only certain definite powers are conferred upon the Commonwealth, whereas all other powers are 'reserved' to the States, it was pointed out that the scheme of distribution of power in Australia is more like that of the United States.[123] But because the powers reserved to the States are not spelt out, the only way to identify them is to draw inferences from the limits on the scope of other federal powers, especially the interstate trade and commerce power.[124] This led to a comparison of the taxation power with the other powers granted to the Commonwealth. According to the Court, when the framers of the Constitution intended to allow the Commonwealth to regulate the 'domestic affairs of the States' this was done explicitly and specifically. The Commonwealth's powers to make laws with respect to currency, incorporation of banks, bills of exchange, bankruptcy, and trading corporations were cited as examples. However, the power of taxation, they said, is unlike these other powers, for if it is not read in a limited way it has the potential to operate as a kind of general 'overriding power' which effectively obliterates the careful distinctions between Commonwealth and State power made by other heads of power. This is because taxation can be used to impose rules of conduct on any topic whatsoever by simply making liability to a tax depend upon observance of those rules.[125] Given the federal nature of the Constitution, and the potentially wide effect that the taxation power could have, they considered that the 'true nature and character' of the *Excise Tariff* must be ascertained by reference to its substance, and not merely its form. Thus, even though in form the law imposed a tax, its substantial

**118** *R v Barger* (1908) 6 CLR 41, 64.
**119** Ibid, 66, 68.
**120** (1882) 7 App Cas 829.
**121** (1878) 3 App Cas 1090.
**122** *R v Barger* (1908) 6 CLR 41, 65, citing *Russell v The Queen* (1882) 7 App Cas 829, 839–40 and *Attorney-General (Quebec) v Queen Insurance Co* (1878) 3 App Cas 1090. *Guy v Baltimore* 100 US 434 (1879), a decision of the United States Supreme Court, was also offered as an illustration of the same principle.
**123** *R v Barger* (1908) 6 CLR 41, 67.
**124** Ibid, 69.
**125** Ibid, 64, 71, 77.

purpose was to regulate employment conditions, and this made the law unconstitutional.[126]

The dissenting judgments of Isaacs and Higgins JJ in *R v Barger* approached the tasks of interpretation and characterisation very differently. As far as interpretation was concerned, what mattered for them was the specific language in which the particular head of power is expressed. As Isaacs J pointed out, the only explicit qualification on the power to legislate with respect to taxation in s 51(ii) is the requirement that such a law must 'not ... discriminate between States or parts of States'.[127] There is no other limit on the scope of the power, he said, and so none should be inferred from the unexpressed.[128] Indeed, Isaacs and Higgins JJ went so far as to say that Commonwealth taxation powers are not only plenary and unlimited,[129] but may be exercised as if the Commonwealth were a unitary State.[130] Federal powers are not to be limited in scope by first assuming a body of reserved State powers, for State powers are merely those that remain after full effect is given to Commonwealth powers.[131] There would be no more logic in assuming an area of reserved State power, Isaacs J reasoned, than there would be in trying to find out the residue of a deceased estate before first finding out what specific gifts had been made.[132]

This way of framing the issue placed the respective powers of the Commonwealth and the States into the context of an alternative theory about the origin and nature of the Australian federation, consistent with the outlook that Isaacs and Higgins JJ had unsuccessfully advocated at the Federal Conventions of the 1890s.[133] The testamentary analogy suggested that the testator was the Imperial Parliament, the primary beneficiary was the Commonwealth, and the secondary beneficiaries were the States. On this analogy, the distribution of the estate (legislative power) was entirely determined by the testator (the Imperial Parliament), not the secondary beneficiaries (the States). The analogy thus ingeniously contradicted the prevailing understanding that it had been the peoples of the States, through their elected representatives, who had determined that only specific powers would be granted to the Commonwealth, while the original, plenary powers of the State Parliaments would in all other respects be reserved.[134] On the reinterpretation of Isaacs and Higgins JJ, the decision to

**126** Ibid, 73–7.
**127** Ibid, 82.
**128** Ibid, 83–4, citing *Gibbons v Ogden* 22 US 1 (1824), 187; see also 114.
**129** Ibid, 85, citing *R v Burah* (1878) 3 App Cas 889, 904 and *Hodge v The Queen* (1883) 9 App Cas 117, 132; see also 114.
**130** *R v Barger* (1908) 6 CLR 41, 85, 105, 117.
**131** Ibid, 83.
**132** Ibid, 84–5; see also 113. Although Griffith CJ had also used the term 'residue', this designated the powers deliberately *reserved* to the States rather than those merely *left over*: *Deakin v Webb* (1904) 1 CLR 585, 605. Sir Owen Dixon would similarly observe around 40 years later that 'the attempt to read s 107 as the equivalent of a specific grant or reservation of power lacked a foundation in logic': *Melbourne Corporation v Commonwealth* (1947) 74 CLR 31, 83.
**133** However, somewhat inconsistently, Isaacs had acknowledged during the Federal Conventions that the scheme of the Constitution was to give to the Commonwealth 'certain powers of legislation', while 'reserving all others to the states': *Convention Debates, Melbourne* (1898) 670.
**134** Compare Geoffrey Sawer, *Australian Federalism in the Courts* (Melbourne University Press, 1967) 199.

confer positive grants upon the Commonwealth was to accord primacy to federal power and to treat State powers as secondary, indefinite and merely residuary. A restrictive approach to the characterisation of the federal law was also implied. According to Isaacs and Higgins JJ, the formal character of the law (the imposition of an obligation to pay tax) was more important than the substantive purpose or effect of the law (the regulation of employment conditions).[135] If the law had imposed a direct obligation to offer particular employment conditions, then the matter would have been different;[136] however, the mere fact that the law provided an incentive to offer such conditions of employment could not be decisive, partly because all taxation laws influence behaviour by creating incentives to avoid paying the tax.[137]

Reserved powers reasoning was also applied in the *Union Label* case.[138] In that case, the Court had to consider whether provisions of the *Trade Marks Act 1905* (Cth), which enabled trade unions to register their own 'workers' trade marks', were validly enacted pursuant to the Commonwealth's power to make laws with respect to 'copyrights, patents of inventions and designs, and trade marks' (s 51(xviii)). All members of the Court acknowledged that the meaning of these words needed to be ascertained by reference to their signification when the Constitution was enacted in 1900.[139] It was also generally accepted that the broad language of the Constitution was intended to apply throughout the changing conditions of society.[140] The difficulty in applying these principles, however, was that the term 'trade mark' had the potential to have both a relatively narrow technical legal meaning and a wider popular colloquial meaning.[141] Moreover, the technical meanings given to the term in various jurisdictions were different, and there were some American States that had legislatively recognised workers' marks.[142]

In determining which of these possible interpretations ought to be adopted, the problem was, as Barton J put it, one of identifying the true 'genus' signified by the term 'trade marks' and whether 'workers' marks' should be considered a 'species' of that genus.[143] Griffith CJ and O'Connor J considered that the general scheme of the Constitution – in particular, the limited power given to the Commonwealth in relation to trade and commerce and the reservation of the regulation of internal trade to the States – suggested that a narrower interpretation of the trade marks power was to be preferred.[144] They observed that the reason the Commonwealth had been given power over various forms of intellectual property was that they had become the subject of international treaties.[145]

**135** *R v Barger* (1908) 6 CLR 41, 114, 119.
**136** Ibid, 99.
**137** Ibid, 97–8, 112–13, 115.
**138** *Attorney-General (NSW) v Brewery Employees Union of New South Wales* (1908) 6 CLR 469.
**139** Ibid, 501, 521, 535–6, 610.
**140** Ibid, 501, 521–2, 534; see also 600–03.
**141** Ibid, 504, 521–2, 525, 531; but see 604.
**142** Ibid, 514.
**143** Ibid, 521–2.
**144** Ibid, 502–3, 518, 532; see also 520.
**145** Ibid, 503, 531–2.

The power was therefore directed to the coordination of Australian regulation of intellectual property with other countries – an objective which made the technical legal meaning of 'trade marks' highly relevant. Following a survey of the legal regimes of several other countries, Griffith CJ, Barton and O'Connor JJ concluded that the term carried with it the idea of an exclusive right of a person to use a mark to identify trading goods over which that person has proprietary rights – a definition which excluded workers' marks.[146]

In their dissenting judgments, Isaacs and Higgins JJ emphasised that the Commonwealth's powers are in principle as great as those of the Imperial Parliament, and that their scope is to be determined on ordinary legal principles.[147] The power to legislate with respect to trade marks should be understood in 'the fullest sense' of the term and defined only by reference to the 'essential' elements of the idea, rather than the merely 'accidental' features of specific trade mark regimes in particular jurisdictions.[148] In this respect, they contended that there were instances where trade mark rights had been recognised in the absence of certain elements which the plaintiffs had claimed were essential to the concept, such as the ownership of the goods or commercial trading in the goods.[149] All that was essential to the idea, Higgins J insisted, was that the marks are used to identify commodities with some person or body of persons for the purposes of attracting trade.[150] As his Honour put it, the usage of the term 'trade mark' in 1900 presents the 'central type', but it does not prescribe the 'circumference' of the power.[151]

An important aspect of Higgins J's analysis of the Commonwealth's heads of power was a distinction between 'natural' and 'artificial' kinds. Some of the paragraphs in s 51 refer to classes of things whose characteristics, he said, are 'fixed by external nature', while others refer to classes of things that are the 'artificial products of society'.[152] According to Higgins J, just as the Commonwealth might, under the 'marriage' power, prescribe which unions are to be regarded as marriages, so it could prescribe what printed trade names and other 'get up' would be deemed to be trade marks.[153] Nonetheless, there were limits. It would be a very different matter, he said, if the Commonwealth was to enact a 'sham' law which deemed some other entirely different subject matter to be a 'trade mark' and attempted to regulate that other matter under the trademarks power.[154]

Many of the matters or topics referred to in s 51 of the Constitution are 'artificial' in the sense used by Higgins J. One important example is the power in

**146** Ibid, 512–3, 525, 540.
**147** Ibid, 559, 585, 613–14.
**148** Ibid, 560, 605–6.
**149** Ibid, 560–76, 607–8.
**150** Ibid, 608.
**151** Ibid, 610–11; see also 584.
**152** Ibid, 611.
**153** Ibid, 610. This reasoning was applied to the marriage power in *Commonwealth v Australian Capital Territory* (2013) 250 CLR 441, [21]. See Part III.2 below.
**154** *Attorney-General (NSW) v Brewery Employees Union of New South Wales* (1908) 6 CLR 469, 614.

s 51(xx) to legislate with respect to 'foreign corporations, and trading or financial corporations formed within the limits of the Commonwealth'. The scope of this head of power was considered for the first time in *Huddart, Parker & Co Ltd v Moorehead*.[155] The case concerned the *Australian Industries Preservation Act 1906* (Cth). Sections 4 and 5 of the Act prohibited the formation of 'combinations' which 'restrain trade or commerce within the Commonwealth to the detriment of the public' or 'destroy or injure by means of unfair competition any Australian industry the preservation of which is advantageous to the Commonwealth'. Sections 7 and 8 also prohibited activity which 'monopolizes ... any part of the trade or commerce within the Commonwealth, with intent to control, to the detriment of the public, the supply or price of any service, merchandise, or commodity'. The two sets of provisions each applied in two different contexts: one where the conduct occurred in respect of trade or commerce with other countries or among the States (ss 4 and 7), the second where the conduct was engaged in by a foreign, trading or financial corporation (ss 5 and 8). The construction of the legislation in this way was designed to bring the law within the Commonwealth's power to legislate pursuant to ss 51(i) and (xx) of the Constitution. Because the legislative power with respect to 'trade and commerce' in s 51(i) is limited to trade and commerce 'with other countries and among the states', the Commonwealth had to rely on s 51(xx) to extend the reach of the law so that it would apply to trade and commerce internal to each State, albeit only when engaged in by the kinds of corporations referred to in s 51(xx).[156] There was no constitutional challenge to ss 4 and 7 because they were limited to the regulation of trade and commerce with other countries and among the States, and therefore fell squarely within the commerce power.[157] However, a majority of Griffith CJ, Barton, O'Connor and Higgins JJ (Isaacs J dissenting) held that ss 5 and 8 of the Act were unconstitutional.

A prime concern of the majority was that if s 51(xx) were read literally and in isolation, it would allow the Commonwealth to impose any kind of obligation whatsoever upon a trading, financial or foreign corporation.[158] As Higgins J put it, the results would certainly be 'extraordinary, big with confusion'.[159] Among these undesirable consequences was the possibility that the power might be used to regulate such diverse matters as libel laws, liquor licensing, interest rates, religious practices, alcohol consumption and the regulation of employee wages and salaries.[160] However, such a result was considered entirely inconsistent with the structure and purposes of the Constitution as a whole, for none of these topics are mentioned in ss 51 or 52. As O'Connor J put it, where the Constitution:

**155** (1909) 8 CLR 330.
**156** Ibid, 360–61, 365, 409.
**157** Ibid, 347, 360, 381, 409.
**158** Ibid, 348.
**159** Ibid, 409.
**160** Ibid, 409–10. Higgins J's list of undesirable consequences was later likened to a parade of 'horribles': P H Lane, *The Australian Federal System* (Law Book Company, 1979) 160.

> confers a power in terms equally capable of a wide and of a restricted meaning, that meaning will be adopted which will best give effect to the system of distribution of powers between State and Commonwealth which the Constitution has adopted, and which is most in harmony with the general scheme of its structure.[161]

For Griffith CJ, Barton and O'Connor JJ, the literal words of s 51(xx) had to be read, therefore, in the light of the limited powers conferred upon the Commonwealth generally, and especially with the reservation of intrastate trade and commerce to States.[162] If an exception to this reservation were to be established, it would have to be clearly shown, they said, in the affirmative powers conferred upon the Commonwealth. However, the corporations power did not provide the necessary authorisation. In their view, this power is given to the Commonwealth only to enable it to determine the conditions upon which a corporation may be permitted to operate in Australia, and does not authorise the regulation of the operations of a corporation when it lawfully enters into a field of operation the regulation of which is reserved to the States.[163]

Although he joined with the majority in the conclusion, this exact line of reasoning was not open to Higgins J as it involved the idea that certain specific matters had been reserved to the States.[164] Rather, he adopted what amounted to a pith and substance approach to the characterisation of the federal law.[165] On this approach, the question was whether the law was, in substance, a law with respect to corporations *or* with respect to trade – it could not be both. After a review of the scope and nature of the law, Higgins J concluded that the law was, in substance, concerned with the subject of trade and commerce generally, and was therefore outside the Commonwealth's legislative powers.[166] A law enacted under the corporations power, he said, must be directly regulative of 'corporations as corporations', by which he seems to have meant the special regulatory issues to which corporations give rise, noting that corporations are legal entities that are distinct from their individual shareholders and directors. On his view, s 51(xx) was therefore especially concerned to enable the Commonwealth to determine the conditions upon which foreign, trading and financial corporations would be permitted to operate within and throughout Australia.[167] In coming to this conclusion, while Higgins J reiterated his support for the 'residuary' theory of State power, and that each head of Commonwealth power should be interpreted 'to its utmost limit', he also maintained that the Commonwealth's powers must be read together in a way that gives effect to them all, including the limited

**161** *Huddart, Parker & Co Pty Ltd v Moorehead* (1909) 8 CLR 330, 369.
**162** Ibid, 350–54, 361, 366, 368, 370–71, relying specially upon the judgment of Chase CJ in *United States v Dewitt* 76 US 9 Wall 41 (1869). Higgins J observed that 'State power is the rule, the Federal power is the exception', and that it is for the Commonwealth to show that power had been given to it to make the law in question: 408.
**163** *Huddart, Parker & Co Pty Ltd v Moorehead* (1909) 8 CLR 330, 353–4, 366, 371–4.
**164** Ibid, 415–16.
**165** Ibid, 410–11, citing *Russell v The Queen* (1882) 7 App Cas 829, 839.
**166** Ibid, 411.
**167** Ibid, 412–14.

terms in which the Commonwealth is given power to legislate with respect to interstate trade and commerce.[168]

In his dissenting judgment, Isaacs J reiterated several themes he had emphasised in previous decisions. Although the Constitution is to be interpreted as a whole, he said, the Court must adhere to the language actually used, and ensure that 'fair and full effect' is given to the Commonwealth's powers, 'construed according to the recognized British rules of interpretation'.[169] The Court must not 'wander at large upon a sea of speculation searching for a suitable intent by the misty and uncertain light of what is sometimes called the spirit of the document' based on the subjective 'preconceptions of the individual observer'.[170] The Commonwealth has, within its enumerated powers, he maintained, 'plenary powers of legislation, as large, and of the same nature, as those of Parliament itself'.[171] Against the reserved powers doctrine, therefore, '[i]t is always a question of *grant*, not of prohibition, unless that is express'.[172] Read in this way, Isaacs J considered that the corporations power extends to 'the regulation of the conduct of the corporations in their transactions with or as affecting the public' in any respect whatsoever,[173] a finding which meant that ss 5 and 8 of the Act were validly enacted by the Commonwealth.

Although Higgins J and especially Isaacs J were consistently in the minority in cases such as *Barger*, *Union Label* and *Huddart, Parker*, they persistently refused to accept the method of interpretation advocated by the majority of the High Court. However, when the Constitution came into force in 1901, the Privy Council also had jurisdiction to hear appeals from Australian courts – including in constitutional cases – except that no such appeal could lie in cases involving a question as to the limits inter se of the constitutional powers of the Commonwealth and the States without authorisation by the High Court.[174] Only one such authorisation has ever been given, in *Attorney-General (Cth) v Colonial Sugar Refining Co Ltd*,[175] which was an appeal from a split decision in the High Court.[176] The case provides an insight into the view that was taken by the Privy Council as to the distribution of legislative powers during the period when the reserved powers doctrine was still shaping the jurisprudence of the High Court. The case concerned the limits of the Commonwealth's legislative power to authorise the Executive to conduct royal commissions of inquiry. The Executive has an inherent capacity to undertake inquiries into various matters, but it cannot exercise

**168** Ibid, 415–16, citing *Citizens Insurance Co of Canada v Parsons* [1881] 7 App Cas 96.
**169** Ibid, 388.
**170** Ibid.
**171** Ibid, 389.
**172** Ibid, 391.
**173** Ibid, 395–6.
**174** Commonwealth Constitution, s 74. The appellate jurisdiction of the Privy Council has since been abolished. For more details, see Chapter 8, Part II.2. In *Nelungaloo Pty Ltd v Commonwealth* (1952) 85 CLR 545, 573, Dixon J observed that 'the basal purpose of s 74 and of the principles upon which this court has proceeded has been to confine the final decision of the characteristically federal questions described by s 74 to a jurisdiction exercised within the federal system by a court to which the problems and special conceptions of federalism must become very familiar'.
**175** (1913) 17 CLR 644; [1914] AC 237.
**176** *Colonial Sugar Refining Co Ltd v Attorney-General (Cth)* (1912) 15 CLR 182.

coercive powers such as to require persons to give evidence or provide documents without statutory authority.[177] There could be no doubt that the Commonwealth Parliament had the capacity to confer such authority on a Royal Commission concerning a matter falling within the Commonwealth's legislative powers. However, s 1A the *Royal Commissions Act 1902* (Cth) went further than this, for it purported to provide for the appointment of royal commissions of inquiry in relation to 'any matter ... which relates to or is connected with the peace, order, and good government of the Commonwealth, or any public purpose or any power of the Commonwealth'.[178] Was this constitutional?

The Privy Council agreed with the view taken by Griffith CJ and Barton J in the High Court that the *Royal Commissions Act* could not validly give generic statutory authorisation for the conduct of a royal commission exercising coercive powers in relation to topics lying outside the Commonwealth's specific legislative powers.[179] The *Royal Commissions Act* was therefore considered to be ultra vires and void to the extent that it purported to provide royal commissions with general authority to exercise coercive powers in the conduct of their inquiries. In order to have a constitutionally valid operation, the Act had to be interpreted so that it only authorised and empowered the conduct of inquiries within the legislative powers of the Commonwealth, and it was upheld specifically and narrowly on that basis.

In the High Court, Griffith CJ and Barton J had reasoned that the distribution of legislative powers between the Commonwealth and the States is fundamental to the federal compact on which the Australian Constitution is founded,[180] and that the Commonwealth cannot legislate in a manner which intrudes into what Griffith CJ called the 'large sphere of action reserved to the States by the Constitution'.[181] While they affirmed that the Commonwealth does have 'incidental' power – expressly in s 51(xxxix) and implicitly in each head of power under s 51 – to legislate to support the conduct of inquiries into matters in respect of which the Commonwealth has power to make laws, they considered that this does not extend to those matters that are reserved to the States.[182] As such, the reasoning of Griffith CJ and Barton J rested, in part, upon the State reserved powers doctrine, pursuant to which the powers of the Commonwealth are read subject to those reserved to the States.

By contrast, Isaacs and Higgins JJ considered that the Commonwealth's incidental power to legislate includes power to authorise compulsory inquiries into matters which might be the object of a constitutional amendment pursuant to s 128, and that the subject matter of any such constitutional amendment is in

**177** *Clough v Leahy* (1904) 2 CLR 139.
**178** Other sections of the Act conferred coercive powers to support the conduct of such inquiries: *Royal Commissions Act 1902* (Cth), ss 2–6.
**179** The cases are briefly discussed in *Williams v Commonwealth (No 1)* (2012) 248 CLR 156, 206–7.
**180** *Colonial Sugar Refining Co Ltd v Attorney-General (Cth)* (1912) 15 CLR 182, 194–5, 208.
**181** Ibid, 195.
**182** Ibid, 194, 197, 205–6, 208. See, similarly, *Huddart, Parker & Co Pty Ltd v Moorehead* (1909) 8 CLR 330, 377. On incidental powers, see Parts III.2 and IV.3 below.

principle unlimited.[183] Their reasoning was that the power to amend the Constitution is, in essence, a legislative power of the Commonwealth,[184] even though any proposed amendment must be first approved in a referendum pursuant to s 128 of the Constitution. It therefore followed that the Commonwealth has incidental legislative power to make provision for the establishment and conduct of compulsory inquiries into virtually any matter at all, whether or not it falls within the ordinary legislative powers of the Commonwealth.

These competing conclusions were based on different perspectives about the nature and grounds of the Constitution itself. In Isaacs and Higgins JJ's view, the Constitution is essentially a statute enacted by the British Parliament which provides for the exercise of legislative power by the Commonwealth Parliament, including the underlying power of the British Parliament to amend the Constitution.[185] On this approach, the power to amend the Constitution is treated as nothing more than a capacity to make a particular kind of law which happens to be subjected to a special procedural requirement (ie, approval at a referendum). In Griffith CJ and Barton J's view, the Constitution is in substance a federal compact by which the people of the several States agreed to confer certain powers on the Commonwealth while reserving to themselves ultimate control over any amendments to the Constitution that the Commonwealth might propose.[186] The power to amend is therefore an aspect of the constitutive power to establish the Constitution in the first place; it is a power that is therefore distinct from the ordinary power to legislate. Barton J accordingly pointed out that the Constitution's framers did not regard the power of constitutional amendment to be a legislative power in the ordinary sense of the term, but rather a special capacity to 'amend the fundamental law by popular vote'.[187] Such amendments, he further noted, might result in either an expansion or a contraction of the powers of the Commonwealth,[188] for it was the States – from whom the federal compact originally derived – who continued to possess the necessary plenary powers of inquiry into such matters.[189]

On appeal, the Privy Council endorsed the conclusions of Griffith CJ and Barton J. Their Lordships pointed out that the Australian Constitution is 'federal' in the 'strict sense of the term',[190] meaning one in which 'self-contained States' agree, not only to delegate some of their powers to a common government, but 'in the main continue to preserve their original Constitutions' and 'reserve' all powers not delegated to themselves.[191] Given that the scheme of the Constitution was thus to create a 'true' federation,[192] the Judicial Committee considered

**183** *Colonial Sugar Refining Co Ltd v Attorney-General (Cth)* (1912) 15 CLR 182, 211–12, 232–3.
**184** Ibid, 211, 215–17, 232–3.
**185** Ibid, 211.
**186** Ibid, 194.
**187** Ibid, 207.
**188** Ibid.
**189** Ibid, 208.
**190** *Attorney-General (Cth) v Colonial Sugar Refining Co Ltd* (1913) 17 CLR 644, 651.
**191** Ibid, 651–3.
**192** Ibid, 651, 652.

that the 'burden' lay upon the Commonwealth to show that the *Royal Commissions Act* was constitutionally valid.[193] Although the Constitution is clearly contained in an Imperial statute, they pointed out that it was the 'people of Australia' who chose to prevent the Commonwealth Parliament from making any changes to the compact without a referendum.[194]

The High Court's application of the reserved powers doctrine did not mean that Commonwealth power always had to give way to the reserved powers of the States. The approach to interpretation which the doctrine invoked, when understood in its most sophisticated and persuasive form, recognised that the Constitution is necessarily drafted in 'broad and general' language, which on occasion requires the Court to make choices between alternative interpretations.[195] As O'Connor J put it in the *Jumbunna Coal Mine* case:

> [W]here it becomes a question of construing words used in conferring a power of that kind on the Commonwealth Parliament, it must always be remembered that we are interpreting a Constitution broad and general in its terms, intended to apply to the varying conditions which the development of our community must involve.
>
> For that reason, where the question is whether the Constitution has used an expression in the wider or in the narrower sense, the Court should, in my opinion, always lean to the broader interpretation unless there is something in the context or in the rest of the Constitution to indicate that the narrower interpretation will best carry out its object and purpose.[196]

This statement has often been quoted in subsequent cases for the proposition that a broader interpretation is usually to be preferred. But for O'Connor J, there were many things about the Constitution that often served to indicate that a narrower interpretation was more appropriate. In the *Union Label* case, he observed:

> The Constitution ... is an instrument of government which from its nature must express its meaning in general terms. It is not only a law in itself, but an authority for making laws, and was intended by means of its broad general terms to adapt itself as far as possible to the changing conditions of trade and commerce, and to the new conceptions of legal rights and obligations which might in the ordinary course of things be expected to be evolved in the development of Australia. On the other hand ... the Constitution is something more than an instrument of government. It embodies the terms on which the people of the several States agreed for the sake of union to surrender their autonomy in certain respects. Keeping both these aspects of the Constitution in view, the true rule of interpretation would appear to be that there should be given to all legal and technical expressions the widest meaning that is consistent with the terms of the contract of union.[197]

In cases such as *Barger*, *Union Label* and *Huddart, Parker*, the Court found that features of the text and structure of the Constitution reflected the intention of

**193** Ibid, 653.
**194** Ibid, 655.
**195** For more detail, see Nicholas Aroney, 'Constitutional Choices in the Work Choices Case, or What Exactly Is Wrong with the Reserved Powers Doctrine?' (2008) 32(1) *Melbourne University Law Review* 1.
**196** *Jumbunna Coal Mine, No Liability v Victorian Coal Miners' Association* (1908) 6 CLR 309, 367–8.
**197** *Attorney-General (NSW) v Brewery Employees Union of New South Wales* (1908) 6 CLR 469, 533.

the framers that the relevant fields of legislative power be reserved to the States. However, in other cases, such as *Farey v Burvett*,[198] the nature and scope of the power conferred upon the Commonwealth necessarily trumped what would otherwise have been the reserved powers of the States. In that case, the Court had to consider provisions of the *War Precautions Act 1914* (Cth), which authorised the Governor-General to make regulations for securing public safety, defence of the Commonwealth and effectual prosecution of the First World War, including regulation of the disposal of goods. In exercise of these powers, the Governor-General, acting on the advice of the government of the day, made a regulation and orders which determined the maximum prices that could be charged for flour and bread within Australia's cities. The proposed basis of these provisions was the Commonwealth's power to legislate with respect to 'the naval and military defence of the Commonwealth and of the several States, and the control of the forces to execute and maintain the laws of the Commonwealth' (s 51(vi)).

The nature of the defence power, and the urgency and seriousness of the conduct of the war itself, made the case very different from the others discussed so far. During the war, the very existence of the Commonwealth and the States was imperilled,[199] and the defence power was in these circumstances treated by the Court as a kind of 'paramount power' such that if it were to come into conflict with any reserved States' rights 'the latter must give way'.[200] As Isaacs J pointed out, the defence power is an effectively exclusive power and extends to the protection of the States as well as of the Commonwealth.[201] In their dissenting judgment, Gavan Duffy and Rich JJ considered that the defence power was limited to maintenance and conduct of the armed forces.[202] However, according to the majority, as Griffith CJ put it, the Commonwealth has all powers as may reasonably be necessary for its defence, including preparation for war in time of peace and 'any such action in time of war as may conduce to the successful prosecution of the war and defeat of the enemy', such as control over resources and trade in goods.[203] Provided the law on its face evinces a rational connection between the measure and the defence of the Commonwealth, the Court will not question the political judgement as to the wisdom and expedience of the measure. [204] The law was upheld on this basis.

### Immunity of instrumentalities

The second important federalism doctrine developed at an early stage by the High Court was the immunity of instrumentalities. The grounds of this doctrine and its application are discussed in detail in Chapter 4. For present purposes it is sufficient to observe that it rested on the idea that the Constitution establishes

**198** *Farey v Burvett* (1916) 21 CLR 433.
**199** Ibid, 453–4, 457.
**200** Ibid, 441, 451; see also 449–50, 458.
**201** Ibid, 451–2; see also 456–7, citing ss 51(vi), (xxxix), 61, 68, 114 and 119 of the Constitution.
**202** Ibid, 465.
**203** Ibid, 440–41; see also 452–3, 455.
**204** Ibid, 443, 445–9, 455–6, 460–61.

a federation in which the Commonwealth and each of the States possess a kind of 'sovereignty' which implies a far-reaching immunity from external interference by the other. As will be seen in Chapter 4, this immunity protected the Commonwealth and the States from virtually any interference unless there was something specific in the Constitution to suggest otherwise, such as a particular head of power conferred upon the Commonwealth which must by its nature entail some degree of interference with the States. The aim of the doctrine was thus to safeguard the independent operation of the self-governing powers of the Commonwealth and the States as a fundamental principle of the federation.

### The *Engineers* case

The interpretation of the federal nature of the Constitution that had prevailed under the leadership of Griffith CJ from the time the Court was established in 1903, was brought to a sudden end by the landmark *Engineers* case.[205] This 1920 case was decided under a differently composed Court, now consisting of Knox CJ, Isaacs, Higgins, Gavan Duffy, Powers, Rich and Starke JJ.[206] The central issue in *Engineers* concerned the immunity of instrumentalities doctrine, but the case also involved the conceptual foundations of the reserved powers doctrine. The basic proposition of the case was that the powers granted to the Commonwealth are to be interpreted with as much breadth as the words used to describe each head of power can sustain, without consideration being given to the impact on the reserved or residual powers of the States. As might be expected, such an approach has led, over time, to a considerable expansion in the scope and reach of the legislative powers of the Commonwealth.

The case concerned s 8 of the *Conciliation and Arbitration Act 1904* (Cth), which gave the Commonwealth Arbitration Court jurisdiction 'to prevent and settle … all industrial disputes'. Section 4 of the Act defined 'industrial dispute' to include 'any dispute in relation to employment in an industry carried on by or under the control of the Commonwealth or a State, or any public authority constituted under the Commonwealth or a State'. The Amalgamated Society of Engineers (a trade union) served a log of claims on 844 employers throughout Australia, including three Western Australian State government agencies. When a dispute concerning the claims arose, the trade union commenced proceedings before the Commonwealth Arbitration Court. The central question that arose in the case was whether Commonwealth arbitration powers extended to engineers employed by State government instrumentalities. It was argued that the Act could not apply to the State instrumentalities due to the implied immunities doctrine. However, the High Court rejected the very existence of the doctrine as it has been articulated by the Griffith Court, and held that the Commonwealth law could apply to them. The opinion of the Court was expressed principally in the joint judgment, delivered and probably drafted by Isaacs J, and in which

**205** *Amalgamated Society of Engineers v Adelaide Steamship Co Ltd* (1920) 28 CLR 129.
**206** However, Powers J did not sit in the case.

Knox CJ, Rich and Starke JJ joined. Higgins J wrote a separate concurring judgment, and Gavan Duffy J dissented. Despite its seminal importance, the joint judgment is poorly organised and the reasoning is at times difficult to understand. The exposition that follows attempts to reconstruct the reasoning in a more logical form.

First of all, it was maintained that the immunity of instrumentalities doctrine had become incoherent[207] because the doctrine rested upon nothing more than 'the expectations and hopes of persons undefined'[208] and relied upon a principle of 'necessity' that was 'referable to no more definite standard than the personal opinion of the judge who declares it'.[209] Indeed, the principle of 'necessity', it was said, is incapable of consistent application as a legal standard because the 'political' sense in which it is used will vary according to the nature of the power and the ever-changing circumstances in which the power is exercised.[210] It therefore gives the Commonwealth and the States no certain basis of action.[211]

Secondly, it was considered that the implied immunities doctrine was 'based on distrust, lest powers, if once conceded to the least degree, might be abused to the point of destruction'. Against this, it was maintained that the 'possible abuse of powers is no reason in British law for limiting the natural force of the language creating them'.[212] Rather, the proper remedy for abuse of powers is for the people themselves 'to resent and reverse what may be done'.[213] After all, the Constitution itself had been enacted with the consent of 'the whole of the people of all the States of Australia'.[214] The Court must therefore limit itself solely to the text of the Constitution, finding the intention from the words themselves, and interpreting the document in accordance with the settled rules of construction and the natural meaning of the words used.[215] The Constitution is contained in an Imperial Act, and is to be interpreted as a British statute. The task of the Court, therefore, is to 'discover in the actual terms of the instrument their expressed or necessarily implied meaning'.[216]

In support of this approach, the joint judgment relied on decisions of the Privy Council which had suggested that the legislative powers of the Commonwealth are, in principle, 'as plenary and ample' as the powers of the British Parliament in its sovereignty.[217] Here it could be observed that s 51(xxxv) of the Constitution grants the Commonwealth legislative power in what may be described as general terms, with no exception for industrial disputes where States are parties, and with no other provisions cutting down the scope of the power.[218] The

**207** *Amalgamated Society of Engineers v Adelaide Steamship Co Ltd* (1920) 28 CLR 129, 141.
**208** Ibid, 145.
**209** Ibid, 142.
**210** Ibid, 150.
**211** Ibid, 145.
**212** Ibid, 151.
**213** Ibid, 151–2.
**214** Ibid, 153.
**215** Ibid, 142, 148–9, see also 162.
**216** Ibid, 155.
**217** Ibid, 153 citing *Hodge v The Queen* (1883) 9 App Cas 117, 132; see also 166.
**218** Ibid, 154; see also 161–2.

joint judgment concluded that it is the duty of the Court to give full effect to this grant of power, without considering any supposed sphere of powers reserved to the States under s 107. Whatever 'reserved' powers might be retained by the States, these are merely the 'residue' of power that remains after full effect is given to all of the powers positively conferred upon the Commonwealth. The States and their instrumentalities are therefore subject to Commonwealth legislation under s 51(xxxv).

This approach led to a reinterpretation of the past decisions of the Court concerning the immunity of instrumentalities doctrine, as explained in more detail in Chapter 4. It also entirely undermined the conceptual grounds of the reserved powers doctrine. As will be seen in Chapter 4, a modified intergovernmental immunities doctrine was revived in the 1940s, displacing the Court's comprehensive denunciation of the immunity doctrine in *Engineers*.[219] For this reason, it has been the Court's rejection of the foundations of the reserved powers doctrine that has had a more decisive influence over the long term. Indeed, it is largely on account of its effect on the interpretation of the Commonwealth's heads of legislative power that the *Engineers* case is widely regarded as the single most significant decision ever handed down by the High Court. And yet, explanations of why it has had this effect and significance have varied.

Windeyer J famously once said that he did not consider the case to have been a correction of 'antecedent errors' or the 'uprooting of heresy' but rather a recognition that Australia had 'become a nation', with the seemingly inevitable consequence that the Commonwealth has waxed while the States have waned.[220] However, the mechanism by which this has occurred is unusual in the sense that it has depended on a judicial method that is highly literalistic, both as to the task of interpretation of Commonwealth powers and the characterisation of Commonwealth laws.[221] Subsequently, the High Court abandoned the application of literalistic techniques to several aspects of the Constitution, allowing the development of a modified intergovernmental immunities doctrine and an implied freedom of political communication,[222] but this has not resulted in any change to the Court's basic approach to interpreting the Commonwealth's legislative powers.[223] When faced with a choice, a majority of the Court have usually adopted the widest possible interpretation of federal power consistent with the language used to define each head of power. They have also developed a corresponding approach to characterisation of federal laws which effectively

**219** *Melbourne Corporation v Commonwealth* (1947) 74 CLR 31.
**220** *Victoria v Commonwealth (Payroll Tax)* (1971) 122 CLR 353, 396. See also R T E Latham, 'The Law and the Commonwealth' in W K Hancock, *Survey of British Commonwealth Affairs, vol 1: Problems of Nationality 1918–1936* (Wiley, 1937) 563–4.
**221** See Greg Craven, 'Cracks in the Facade of Literalism: Is There an Engineer in the House?' (1992) 18 *Melbourne University Law Review* 540; James Allan and Nicholas Aroney, 'An Uncommon Court: How the High Court of Australia Has Undermined Australian Federalism' (2008) 30 *Sydney Law Review* 245.
**222** See Chapter 4, Part III and Chapter 5, Part V.
**223** See Leslie Zines, 'Engineers and the "Federal Balance"' in Michael Coper and George Williams (eds), *How Many Cheers for Engineers?* (Federation Press, 1997) 81.

enables the Commonwealth to regulate matters that do not fall squarely within its heads of power. Several specific interpretive principles and techniques have contributed to both of these developments.

## 2 Expansionist techniques of interpretation

### From 'singular' to 'multiple' characterisation

In *R v Barger* the High Court sought to identify the 'true nature and character' of the Commonwealth law by examining its substantive effect and not merely its form. Thus, although the law imposed a duty to pay tax, its substantial purpose was to regulate employment conditions.[224] The underlying concern was that taxation could be used by the Commonwealth to impose rules of conduct on any topic whatsoever, simply by making liability to a tax depend upon a failure to observe those rules.[225] This problem is especially acute in relation to taxation, but it arises in relation to other heads of power as well.[226] This is because the operation of a law will typically depend upon specific criteria such as the classes of persons to whom it is directed, the activities which it regulates and the objectives it seeks to achieve. If a law singles out a particular set of persons, activities *and* objectives, by reference to which of these is the law to be characterised? For example, if a law imposes an obligation upon all trading corporations to comply with certain requirements in the conditions of employment that they offer employees, is the law to be characterised as a law with respect to 'trading corporations' or 'conditions of employment'?

To put the question in this way is to assume, as the High Court did in *Barger*, that the task of characterisation is to identify the one 'true nature and character' of the law, on the view that while a law may have many characteristics, it is necessary to distinguish its 'essential' or 'dominant' character from those that are 'non-essential' or merely 'incidental'. But to do so is no easy task. Three years after the High Court decided *Barger*, it had to consider in *Osborne v Commonwealth*[227] whether the Commonwealth's *Land Tax Act 1910*, which imposed a land tax the rate of which increased as a person's land holdings increased, and therefore discouraged the ownership of numerous parcels of real estate, was properly to be characterised as a law with respect to taxation or a law with respect to land holdings. In *Osborne*, the Court distinguished the *Land Tax Act* from the *Excise Tariff Act* considered in *Barger* on the basis that the *Land Tax Act* was in both form and substance a taxation law, whereas the *Excise Tariff Act* was in substance directed to regulating employment conditions, the taxation power and the interstate trade and commerce powers being manipulated as the 'means' to achieve this objective.[228] As Barton J explained, it is not for the Court

**224** *R v Barger* (1908) 6 CLR 41, 73–7. See Part III.1 above.
**225** Ibid, 64, 71, 77.
**226** See *Bank of New South Wales v Commonwealth (Bank Nationalisation)* (1948) 76 CLR 1, 183–4.
**227** (1911) 12 CLR 321.
**228** *Osborne v Commonwealth* (1911) 12 CLR 321, 334–5, 343–4, 358, 360–62, 374.

to characterise a law by reference to predictions about the law's practical or indirect effects, or conjectures about the intentions of the Parliament, but only by reference to what appears from the terms in which the law is expressed.[229] Isaacs J went further when he observed that:

> [t]he lines of human affairs from their inherent complexity cross each other at innumerable points, and it is impossible to frame an arbitrary classification, such as that contained in sec. 51 of the Constitution, which will completely segregate the transactions of life.[230]

Thus, even before the *Engineers* case challenged the reserved powers doctrine, questions were being raised about the difficulty of determining the 'true nature and character' of a law, principally because a law may have more than one 'character'.[231] However, with the rejection of reserved powers reasoning in *Engineers* it was no longer even necessary to identify the true nature and character of a law in order to determine whether the law related to a head of power *or* a matter reserved to the States. The pith and substance approach to characterisation might certainly have continued, but it was no longer conceptually or logically necessary for it to do so. All that was strictly necessary was to determine whether a Commonwealth law possessed some characteristic – it need not be the law's leading or most dominant characteristic – that enabled it to be classified under one of the Commonwealth's heads of power. While the *Engineers* case did not require a shift in the Court's approach to characterisation, it made such a shift conceptually feasible.

The shift took some time to consolidate. The Court continued for several years to use the term 'pith and substance' to describe the process of characterisation of Commonwealth laws,[232] although the expression eventually fell out of favour.[233] The related term, 'true nature and character', proved more enduring. In *Bank of New South Wales v Commonwealth*, the Court was asked to consider the constitutionality of the *Banking Act 1947* (Cth). The purpose of the Act was the nationalisation of Australian's banking industry, which it sought to do by making it illegal for private banks to carry on the business of banking and by transferring the control, shares and assets of the private banks to the then government-owned Commonwealth Bank.[234] As will be seen in Chapter 5, the law was held unconstitutional on the ground that it failed to comply with the requirement of just terms in s 51(xxxi) and infringed s 92 of the Constitution as an interference with interstate trade and commerce. It was also argued,

**229** Ibid, 344, 346.
**230** Ibid, 361.
**231** In *Fairfax v Federal Commissioner of Taxation* (1965) 114 CLR 1, 14–15, Taylor J said he found it very difficult indeed to distinguish *Barger* and *Osborne* on this point.
**232** *Duncan v Queensland* (1916) 22 CLR 556, 580, 623–4; *Bank of New South Wales v Commonwealth (Bank Nationalisation)* (1948) 76 CLR 1, 253–4; *Melbourne v Commonwealth (State Banking)* (1947) 74 CLR 31, 67, 98–100; *Victoria v Commonwealth (Payroll Tax)* (1971) 122 CLR 353, 399–400.
**233** *Bank Nationalisation* (1948) 76 CLR 1, 182–7; *Commonwealth v Bank of New South Wales* [1950] AC 235, 312–3 (Privy Council).
**234** *Bank Nationalisation* (1948) 76 CLR 1.

however, that the law could not be characterised as a law with respect to 'banking' under s 51(xiii). One of the lines of argument was that, following the Privy Council's pith and substance approach, the law should be characterised by reference to its substantive effect. Rich and Williams JJ appeared to indicate agreement with this approach and found that several aspects of the law could not be authorised by the banking power.[235] While disagreeing with their conclusions on this point, Starke J also referred to the pith and substance test with apparent approval.[236] Similarly, although he questioned the usefulness of the term 'pith and substance', Latham CJ seemed to agree with the underlying idea that the task is one of identifying the 'true nature and character' of the law in order to determine whether it is 'in reality and substance' a law 'upon the subject matter'.[237] Dixon J framed the question quite differently, however. He rejected the argument that the *Banking Act* was not a law with respect to banking. Adopting previous statements of principle by O'Connor and Higgins JJ, he focused on the scope of the banking power itself and concluded that it should not receive a restricted interpretation, such as would limit it to the regulation of banking as a continuing activity or as one involving consensual transactions between private individuals.[238] Dixon J's approach would become the prevailing orthodoxy of the Court, but this was not yet apparent when the *Bank Nationalisation* case was decided in 1948.

The underlying concern that seems to have motivated Latham CJ in the *Bank Nationalisation* case is that if the requisite 'connection' between a law and a head of power is too easy to establish, the Commonwealth's powers might be used, as was feared in *R v Barger*, 'to pass laws upon any subject whatever by imposing a tax upon specified acts or omissions'.[239] Even Dixon J elsewhere expressed caution when he said that a law will not be constitutional if the connection to its head of power is 'tenuous, vague, fanciful or remote'.[240] And so it took a case squarely involving the taxation power for the characterisation question finally to be brought to a head. *Fairfax v Federal Commissioner of Taxation*,[241] decided in 1965, provided that opportunity. There the High Court had to consider the constitutionality of a Commonwealth tax imposed on the investment income of a superannuation fund unless a certain proportion of the funds were invested in 'public securities' of various kinds issued by or under the authority of the Commonwealth, a State or a Territory. The trustees of a superannuation fund argued that the law imposing the tax was

**235** Ibid, 253–5.
**236** Ibid, 303.
**237** Ibid, 182–7. See, similarly, *Commonwealth v Bank of New South Wales* [1950] AC 235, 212–3 (Privy Council).
**238** *Bank Nationalisation* (1948) 76 CLR 1, 332–4, citing *Jumbunna Coal Mine, No Liability v Victorian Coal Miners' Association* (1908) 6 CLR 309, 367–8 and *Attorney-General (NSW) v Brewery Employees Union of New South Wales (Union Label)* (1908) 6 CLR 469, 611–12.
**239** *Bank Nationalisation* (1948) 76 CLR 1, 183–4.
**240** *R v Sharkey* (1949) 79 CLR 121, 151; see also *Melbourne Corporation v Commonwealth* (1947) 74 CLR 31, 79.
**241** *Fairfax v Federal Commissioner of Taxation* (1965) 114 CLR 1.

unconstitutional because it was properly to be characterised as a law with respect to 'the investment of the moneys of superannuation funds' rather than a law with respect to taxation.[242]

The Court unanimously held that the law was validly enacted under the taxation power. Writing the leading judgment, Kitto J acknowledged that the characterisation of laws ought to be directed to the 'substance' and not just their 'form'. However, he also insisted that it would be incorrect to think that this requires 'a speculative inquiry as to which of the topics touched by the legislation seems most likely to have been the main preoccupation of those who enacted it'.[243] Rather, as he put it, the question:

> is always one of subject matter, to be determined by reference solely to the operation which the enactment has if it be valid, that is to say by reference to the nature of the rights, duties, powers and privileges which it changes, regulates or abolishes; it is a question as to the true nature and character of the legislation: is it in its real substance a law upon, 'with respect to', one or more of the enumerated subjects, or is there no more in it in relation to any of those subjects than an interference so incidental as not in truth to affect its character?[244]

In focusing attention on 'the operation which the enactment has if it be valid', this approach to characterisation deflects consideration of any characteristic or aspect of the law that would take it outside of power. It is therefore an approach that tends to cohere with the rejection of the reserved powers doctrine, for there is no need, after *Engineers*, to ask whether a Commonwealth law relates to matters reserved to the States; all that matters is the existence of a positive link to a head of power.[245] As Sir Owen Dixon stated in *Melbourne Corporation v Commonwealth*:

> [O]nce it appears that a federal law has an actual and immediate operation within a field assigned to the Commonwealth as a subject of legislative power, that is enough. It will be held to fall within the power unless some further reason appears for excluding it. That it discloses another purpose and that the purpose lies outside the area of federal power are considerations which will not in such a case suffice to invalidate the law.[246]

Kitto J's approach to characterisation directed attention to the 'rights, duties, powers and privileges' which the law 'changes, regulates or abolishes'. On this so-called 'criterion of operation' test, while the question remains one of 'substance', the character of the law is to be determined not by its indirect effects or intended results, but by the legal obligations that it directly imposes. In *Fairfax*,

**242** Ibid, 6.
**243** Ibid, 6–7.
**244** Ibid, 7.
**245** As Kitto J later observed, the majority in *R v Barger* had 'treated the task of choosing the correct inference as one to be performed against a background provided by the doctrine ... that the Constitution was to be interpreted as intending to reserve to the States all such powers as were not expressly conferred upon the Commonwealth': *Fairfax v Federal Commissioner of Taxation* (1965) 114 CLR 1, 11.
**246** *Melbourne Corporation v Commonwealth* (1947) 74 CLR 31, 79, cited in *Fairfax v Federal Commissioner of Taxation* (1965) 114 CLR 1, 13.

what was being imposed was a duty to pay tax in certain prescribed circumstances relating to the investment of superannuation funds. While the imposition of the tax was likely to influence investment decisions, the law did not impose a duty to invest the funds in a certain way. The law only imposed a duty to pay tax, and it was with respect to this obligation that the law was to be characterised.[247]

The status of *Barger* was left in serious doubt after *Fairfax*, especially given the critiques delivered by Kitto and Taylor JJ.[248] However, all of the justices still insisted that characterisation remained a matter of substance, not form. At the very least, this must mean that the Court is not bound by either the name the Parliament has chosen to give an Act or the name that it has given to the thing that it seeks to regulate; what matters is not the label, but the real nature of the subject matter of the law.[249] Whether the principle of substantive characterisation could mean more than this remains a somewhat open question.

In *Herald & Weekly Times Ltd v Commonwealth*,[250] the Court had to consider whether a law regulating the ownership and control of commercial television stations could be supported by the Commonwealth's power to legislate with respect to 'postal, telegraphic, telephonic, and other like services' (s 51(v)). As will be seen below, the High Court had previously held that this head of power authorises laws with respect to radio and television broadcasting.[251] The question in *Herald & Weekly Times* was whether the Commonwealth could control levels of ownership or control of television stations by imposing conditions on the holding of licences to engage in television broadcasting. The Court held that it could do so. As Kitto J put it, although it is a question of whether there is a 'substantial connexion' between the law and the head of power, it did not matter that the law in some of its applications might regulate individuals in situations where they would have no real prospect of exercising any relevant control over the operation of a television station, for it was sufficient that the provisions in question operated as part of a legislative plan to insulate the control and management of stations from the possibility of influence of persons who hold any of the proscribed positions of potential influence.[252]

Similarly in *Murphyores Inc Pty Ltd v Commonwealth*,[253] the Court upheld a Commonwealth law that prohibited the exportation of certain minerals except as approved by the relevant Minister. The Minister decided not to approve the exportation by the plaintiff companies of zircon and rutile extracted from sand mining operations on Fraser Island until an environmental impact assessment had been undertaken. Delivering one of the Court's leading judgments in the case, Mason J rejected the argument that, to be characterised as a law with

**247** *Fairfax v Federal Commissioner of Taxation* (1965) 114 CLR 1, 13, 16.
**248** Ibid, 10–13, 14–15.
**249** Ibid, 7, 19.
**250** (1966) 115 CLR 418.
**251** See the discussion of *R v Brislan; Ex parte Williams* (1935) 54 CLR 262, 273 and *Jones v Commonwealth (No 2)* (1965) 112 CLR 206 in Part III.2 below.
**252** *Herald & Weekly Times Ltd v Commonwealth* (1966) 115 CLR 418, 436–7.
**253** (1976) 136 CLR 1.

respect to 'trade and commerce with other countries' (pursuant to s 51(i)), the decision whether to give the approval would have to be based on considerations of 'trading policy'.[254] It was sufficient that the law operated squarely on the topic of trade and commerce with other countries. It was no objection that the approval was determined on the basis of criteria having little or no relevance to the topic of trade and commerce as such.[255]

In the course of his reasoning, Mason J went so far as to say that *R v Barger* could no longer be regarded has having authority, especially after the Court's decision in *Fairfax*.[256] Despite the Court's decisions in cases such as *Fairfax*, *Herald & Weekly Times* and *Murphyores*, however, it remained possible for certain individual justices to characterise laws by reference to their dominant character, particularly when a Commonwealth law was in some way directed to, or purported to bind, the States or their agencies. Thus, as will be seen in Chapter 4, in the *Melbourne Corporation* case, Latham CJ considered that legislation which singled out or discriminated against the States could not be characterised as falling within one of the heads of Commonwealth legislative power because it 'really' was a law with respect to 'a State or State functions'.[257] Adopting similar reasoning, in the *Payroll Tax* case, Barwick CJ observed that:

> when a law may possibly be regarded as having either of two subjects as its substance, one of which is within Commonwealth power and the other is not, a decision must be made as to that which is in truth the subject matter of the law.[258]

This approach adopted by Latham CJ and Barwick CJ to the problem of Commonwealth laws directed specifically at the States has not, however, been accepted by a majority of the Court. As will be seen in Chapter 4, the now prevailing method is to address the question, not through characterisation, but through what Dixon J in the *Melbourne Corporation* case referred to as a 'further reason' for limiting the operation of such a law, namely that the Commonwealth cannot enact laws which interfere with the capacity of the States to function as independent governments.[259]

The clearest statement of the approach to characterisation that now shapes the High Court's reasoning was articulated by Stephen J in the *Actors & Announcers Equity* case.[260] In that case, the Court had to determine whether s 45D(1)(b)(i) of the *Trade Practices Act 1974* (Cth) could be supported by the corporations power (s 51(xx)). Section 45D(1)(b)(i) protects trading and financial corporations from 'secondary boycotts', which are activities, often engaged in by trade unions, which prevent a supplier from providing goods or services to a corporation. Writing the leading judgment in the case, Stephen J observed that an accurate description of

**254** Ibid, 19.
**255** Ibid, 19–20.
**256** Ibid, 23.
**257** *Melbourne Corporation v Commonwealth* (1947) 74 CLR 31, 61.
**258** *Victoria v Commonwealth (Payroll Tax)* (1971) 122 CLR 353, 372–3.
**259** *Melbourne Corporation v Commonwealth* (1947) 74 CLR 31, 79, cited in *Fairfax v Federal Commissioner of Taxation* (1965) 114 CLR 1, 13.
**260** *Actors & Announcers Equity Association of Australia v Fontana Films Pty Ltd* (1982) 150 CLR 169.

any complex law must necessarily involve a detailed account of the several elements that constitute it.[261] Even a relatively simple law, he pointed out, will single out particular activities engaged in by particular classes of persons. Frequently, such laws will be accurately described by reference to both aspects – the regulated activities and the regulated class of persons. More complex laws will usually involve yet other elements which define the scope of the law. In such cases, it will often be difficult to identify which of this variety of elements determines the one true nature and character of the law. Indeed, trying to do so is likely to give rise to disagreement among reasonable minds, for each element is often 'reasonably capable of fairly describing the law as a whole'. However, such a 'subjective' process, Stephen J maintained, can largely be avoided if it is accepted that it is sufficient that the law 'fairly answers the description of a law "with respect to" one given subject matter appearing in s 51, regardless of whether it may equally be described as a law with respect to other subject matters' falling outside s 51.[262] As his Honour explained:

> Once it is recognized that a law may possess several distinct characters, it follows that the fact that only some elements in the description of a law fall within one or more of the grants of power in s 51 or elsewhere in the Constitution will be in no way fatal to its validity. So long as the remaining elements, which do not fall within any such grant of power, are not of such significance that the law cannot fairly be described as one with respect to one or more of such grants of power then, however else it may also be described, the law will be valid. If a law enacted by the federal legislature can be fairly described both as a law with respect to a grant of power to it and as a law with respect to a matter or matters left to the States, that will suffice to support its validity as a law of the Commonwealth.[263]

On this approach, the Court was able to conclude that s 45D(1)(b)(i) had a sufficient connection to the corporations power because it prohibited conduct that caused substantial loss or damage to trading and financial corporations.

The orthodox approach to characterisation that is now applied by the Court has been described in these terms:

> [A] single law can possess more than one character in the sense that it can properly be characterized as a law with respect to more than one subject-matter. It suffices for constitutional validity if any one or more of those characters is within a head of Commonwealth legislative power. In determining validity, it is not necessary to single out the paramount character. It is enough that the law 'fairly answers to the description of a law "with respect to" one given subject-matter appearing in s 51' regardless of whether it is, at the same time, more obviously or equally a law with respect to some other subject-matter … .[264]

Occasionally, protesting voices are heard, but the prevailing view seems well established. In the recent *Work Choices* case, for example, Kirby J adopted what

**261** Ibid, 190.
**262** Ibid, 192–4.
**263** Ibid, 192.
**264** *Re F; Ex parte F* (1986) 161 CLR 376, 387–8. See, similarly, *Fisher v Fisher* (1986) 161 CLR 438, 453; *Grain Pool of Western Australia v Commonwealth* (2000) 202 CLR 479, 492.

appears to have been a substantive approach to characterisation when he concluded that the corporations power 'does not extend to a power to make laws that, *in truth*, relate to industrial disputes'.[265] However, this proposition was squarely rejected by the majority in that case, who observed:

> To describe a law as 'really', 'truly' or 'properly' characterised as a law with respect to one subject-matter, rather than another, bespeaks fundamental constitutional error. That error is compounded if the conclusion which is reached about the one 'real' or 'true' or 'proper' character of a law proceeds from a premise which assumes, rather than demonstrates, a particular division of governmental or legislative power … .[266]

While, as a matter of logic, the Court's method of characterisation is distinct from its approach to the interpretation of the Commonwealth's heads of power, as this passage suggests, the two methodological issues are closely related in practice. Windeyer J put the point clearly when he observed in the *Payroll Tax* case:

> The question under s 51 is always whether a particular enactment is within Commonwealth power. It is never whether it invades a State's domain. The question is one of subsumption under a particular description. It is not one of classification into categories mutually exclusive; for a law may be quite properly described as with respect to more than one subject, one perhaps within and another without Commonwealth power.[267]

While such an approach to characterisation may avoid the problems of 'subjective' judgment to which Stephen J drew attention, it also has the effect of contributing very considerably to the expansion of the effective scope of the Commonwealth's power to make laws.

### Connotation and denotation: Original meaning and contemporary application

One of the most fundamental principles of interpretation of the Constitution is that its words are to be understood by reference to their meaning when the Constitution was enacted in 1900. This proposition was accepted by all members of the Court in the *Union Label* case,[268] and it has been endorsed on numerous occasions since.[269] Closely accompanying this principle, however, has been the idea that a distinction needs to be drawn between the meaning that the words had in 1900 and the application of those words to changing circumstances. The Court has used the philosophical terms 'connotation' and 'denotation' to draw this distinction. The connotation is the meaning of a word understood as the definition or essence of the concept referred to by the word, whereas the denotation is the

**265** *New South Wales v Commonwealth (Work Choices)* (2006) 229 CLR 1, 203, 226, 229.
**266** Ibid, 72.
**267** *Victoria v Commonwealth (Payroll Tax)* (1971) 122 CLR 353, 400.
**268** *Attorney-General (NSW) v Brewery Employees Union of New South Wales* (1908) 6 CLR 469, 501, 521, 535–6, 610.
**269** In this sense, the approach of the Court has been broadly 'originalist', but not 'intentionalist'. See Jeffrey Goldsworthy, 'Originalism in Constitutional Interpretation' (1997) 25 *Federal Law Review* 1.

class of objects or things which at any particular time are designated by that concept. Thus, for example, the connotation of the adjective 'blue' is the concept of 'blueness', whereas the denotation of the word refers to all things that happen to be coloured blue. While on this view the concept of blueness does not change, the particular things in the world that are coloured blue do change, and might well expand.

Windeyer J put it this way in the *Professional Engineers* case:

> We must not, in interpreting the Constitution, restrict the denotation of its terms to the things they denoted in 1900. The denotation of words becomes enlarged as new things falling within their connotations come into existence or become known. But in the interpretation of the Constitution the connotation or connotations of its words should remain constant. We are not to give words a meaning different from any meaning which they could have borne in 1900. Law is to be accommodated to changing facts. It is not to be changed as language changes.[270]

In that case, the question was whether an employment dispute to which an association of professional engineers was a party could be regarded as an 'industrial dispute' as that term is used in s 51(xxxv) of the Constitution.[271] To determine this question, the Court had to decide whether the engineers were employed in an 'industry'. Although, as Windeyer J observed, the word 'industry' had undergone dramatic changes in use and meaning, he considered that it was its meaning in 1900 that mattered as far as its connotation was concerned. In his opinion, the connotation that the word bore in 1900 was 'work directly concerned with the production, maintenance, repair, distribution or transport of tangible things and also with the provision of intangible things such as gas and electricity'.[272] The question then was whether the work of the professional engineers in 1965 fell within that definition. He considered that some of it certainly did, but not necessarily all, for some of the work of professional engineers could concern non-industrial matters, such as when they are employed by State agencies to engage in the development of government policy.[273] Addressing the issue in this way avoided the question whether in 1900 the work of professional engineers was in any respect industrial in nature. The constitutional connotation of the word was fixed in 1900, but its denotation in 1965 was not limited to its denotation in 1900.

The distinction between connotation and denotation has been criticised. The main point of the criticism is that the distinction does not of itself resolve difficult questions of constitutional interpretation because it still remains necessary to identify the meaning of the terms used by the Constitution, which is not

**270** *R v Commonwealth Conciliation and Arbitration Commission; Ex parte Association of Professional Engineers* (1959) 107 CLR 208, 267.
**271** Section 51(xxxv) grants the Commonwealth power to legislate with respect to 'conciliation and arbitration for the prevention and settlement of industrial disputes extending beyond the limits of any one State'.
**272** *R v Commonwealth Conciliation and Arbitration Commission; Ex parte Association of Professional Engineers* (1959) 107 CLR 208, 267.
**273** Ibid, 269.

a straight-forward task.[274] An often cited example is *R v Brislan; Ex parte Williams*.[275] In that case, the Court had to determine whether the Commonwealth's power to legislate with respect to 'postal, telegraphic, telephonic, and other like services' (s 51(v)) enabled it to regulate radio broadcasting under the *Wireless Telegraphy Act 1919* (Cth). The wording of s 51(v) suggests that 'like services' must have features in common with services designated as 'postal', 'telegraphic' and 'telephonic'. But what are those features? On one view, each of these services is a 'means of communication over distance' – a definition that would embrace radio broadcasting. However, on another view, the services referred to enable communication between two identifiable individuals – one the maker of the communication, the other the recipient. On such a definition, radio broadcasting would not be included because it facilitates one-way communication with an indefinite number of people. While the distinction between connotation and denotation certainly suggests that the 'other services' alluded to could embrace technological means of communication that had not been invented in 1900, this does not determine which of the two meanings should be ascribed to s 51(v). In *Brislan*, a majority adopted the wider view – that the power extends to all services that enable communication over distance, including radio broadcasting.[276] For Rich and Evatt JJ, it was significant that the power was 'intended to cover unknown and unforeseen developments'.[277] In his dissenting judgment, Dixon J agreed that the objective of s 51(v) was to include 'every present and future mode' of providing the kinds of services referred to, but he insisted that the feature those services have in common is enabling inter-personal communication that can be initiated by one individual to another, thus excluding generalised communication through broadcasting.[278]

In *Brislan*, Dixon J considered that the subject matter of s 51(v) must be defined on the basis of certain 'definite characteristics'.[279] How are the defining characteristics of the variety of topics referred to in s 51 to be identified? Much depends on the nature of the subject matter in question. It could be argued that none of the heads of power in s 51 refer to what might be called 'natural kinds', meaning those naturally occurring physical, chemical and biological things that are studied by the hard sciences. Rather, they refer to human activities and the products of human activity: constructed objects such as 'lighthouses' (s 51(vii)), cultural institutions such as 'marriage' (s 51(xxi)), economic activities such as 'trade and commerce' (s 51(i)), and legal concepts such as 'copyrights, patents of inventions and designs, and trade marks' (s 51(xviii)). In addition, at least

**274** Leslie Zines, *The High Court and the Constitution* (Federation Press, 5th ed, 2008) 19. For a defence of the concept, see Jeffrey Goldsworthy, 'Original Meanings and Contemporary Understandings in Constitutional Interpretation' in H P Lee and Peter Gerangelos (eds), *Constitutional Advancement in a Frozen Continent* (Federation Press, 2009) 245.
**275** (1935) 54 CLR 262.
**276** *R v Brislan; Ex parte Williams* (1935) 54 CLR 262, 273, 282; see also 287. See also *Jones v Commonwealth (No 2)* (1965) 112 CLR 206 in relation to television broadcasting.
**277** *R v Brislan; Ex parte Williams* (1935) 54 CLR 262, 283.
**278** Ibid, 292–3.
**279** Ibid, 294.

one of the heads of power is defined by reference to a particular purpose or goal, namely 'the naval and military defence of the Commonwealth and of the several States' (s 51(vi)).[280]

Things that are entirely legal in origin and nature, such as patents (as distinct from the inventions or works that are the subject of such patents), must derive their meaning from the laws that have brought such legal artefacts into being. This suggests two theoretical limits to the scope of the Commonwealth's power over such matters. On one hand, the meaning of the constitutional term 'patent' cannot simply be identical with the existing legal definitions of the concept, for otherwise the relevant head of power would not confer any real capacity to change the law on the topic.[281] On the other hand, the Parliament cannot declare simply anything to be a 'patent', a 'trade mark', an 'alien' or a 'marriage' as a means of regulating such a thing pursuant to the intellectual property, marriage or aliens powers (s 51(xviii), (xxi), (xix)).[282] Constitutional categories cannot be entirely malleable or else it would be possible to declare anything to fall within a constitutional category as a pretext for regulating it.

The problem is well illustrated by *Commonwealth v Australian Capital Territory*,[283] a case in which the Court had to consider whether the provision for same-sex marriage in the *Marriage Equality (Same Sex) Act 2013* (ACT) was inconsistent with the definition of 'marriage' in the *Marriage Act 1961* (Cth) and the *Family Law Act 1975* (Cth). The power of the Australian Capital Territory to make laws under the *Australian Capital Territory (Self-Government) Act 1988* (Cth) is limited by s 28(1) of that Act, which provides that a Territory enactment will have no effect to the extent that it is inconsistent with another law in force in the Territory. The point of potential inconsistency was that s 5(1) of the Commonwealth's *Marriage Act 1961* defined 'marriage' as 'the union of a man and a woman to the exclusion of all others, voluntarily entered into for life', whereas the Territory Act defined 'marriage' as 'the union of 2 people of the same sex to the exclusion of all others, voluntarily entered into for life', but excluded a marriage within the meaning of the *Marriage Act*. Crucially, the Court considered that the purpose of the Commonwealth law was to provide that the *only* kind of marriage that could be solemnised or recognised in Australia was a union between a man and a woman, while the Territory law attempted to create an alternative kind of marriage between people of the same sex, and not merely some other form of legally recognised relationship different from marriage.[284] In a rare unanimous judgment (from which Gageler J recused himself), the Court held that there was a relevant inconsistency between the two laws because the Commonwealth Act was intended to contain a 'complete statement of the law'

**280** *Stenhouse v Coleman* (1944) 69 CLR 457, 471.
**281** *Attorney-General (NSW) v Brewery Employees Union of New South Wales* (1908) 6 CLR 469, 611: 'Power to make laws as to any class of rights involves a power to alter those rights, to define those rights, to limit those rights, to extend those rights, and to extend the class of those who may enjoy those rights'.
**282** Ibid, 614; *Pochi v McPhee* (1982) 151 CLR 101, 109.
**283** (2013) 250 CLR 441.
**284** Ibid, [3]–[4], [56], [59]–[60].

concerning marriage, and the Territory law could not operate concurrently with such a law precisely because it attempted to provide for an alternative form of marriage.[285]

Intrinsic to the Court's reasoning was an assessment of the scope of the Commonwealth's power with respect to marriage (s 51(xxi)). On the Court's analysis, there were two stark alternatives. If the Commonwealth *did not* have power to legislate for same-sex marriage then there could be no inconsistency between the two laws, essentially because the Territory law dealt with a subject matter lying outside Commonwealth power. However, if the Commonwealth *did* have power to provide for same-sex marriage, but had provided that the *only* form of marriage should be between a man and woman, then the two laws would not be able to operate concurrently, because the Commonwealth law had 'covered the field'.[286] On this analysis, it was not possible that the marriage power might be limited to heterosexual marriage *and* that a Commonwealth law could prevent the recognition of same-sex marriage in State or Territory law.

In determining the scope of the marriage power, the Court acknowledged that at the time of federation the settled common law understanding of marriage was of a 'voluntary union for life of one man and woman to the exclusion of all others'.[287] However, it was considered that the marriage power is not to be construed by reference to the common law's particular legal conception of marriage in 1900, but as a generic 'topic of juristic classification' that is not tied to the peculiarities of any one particular legal regime.[288] In fact, it was claimed that the legal status of marriage, the social institution which that status reflects, and the rights and duties incident upon marriage, are not fixed or immutable, but rather have evolved over time and vary from one legal system to another.[289] Thus, marriages are today readily dissolved; polygamous marriages are in some respects recognised; and in some jurisdictions same-sex marriage is legally sanctioned. In support of this approach, the Court drew attention to the problem identified by Higgins J in the *Union Label* case that if a constitutional power were to be fixed by reference to the state of the law in 1900 then there would be no power to alter or repeal the law, contradicting the whole point of s 51, which is to confer power to 'make laws'.[290] What the Court did not also observe was that Higgins J had also identified the opposite problem of 'sham' laws which artificially identify something to be a 'trade mark', a 'lighthouse' or even a 'marriage' as a pretext to legislating with respect to that thing under the relevant head of power.[291] Without acknowledging this side of the problem, the Court recognised that it was necessary to ascribe some definite meaning to the juridical

**285** Ibid, [52], [57], [61]. See, further, Chapter 4, Part II.3.
**286** Ibid, [9].
**287** Ibid, [12], citing Quick and Garran, above n 17, 608.
**288** Ibid, [14], citing *Attorney-General (Vic) v Commonwealth* (1962) 107 CLR 529, 578.
**289** Ibid, [16]–[18], [22]–[23].
**290** Ibid, [19], citing *Attorney-General (NSW) v Brewery Employees Union of New South Wales* (1908) 6 CLR 469, 612.
**291** *Attorney-General (NSW) v Brewery Employees Union of New South Wales* (1908) 6 CLR 469, 614.

category of 'marriage'. According to the Court, marriage within the meaning of s 51(xxi) is to be understood as:

> a consensual union formed between natural persons in accordance with legally prescribed requirements which is not only a union the law recognises as intended to endure and be terminable only in accordance with law but also a union to which the law accords a status affecting and defining mutual rights and obligations.[292]

Several problems with this definition are immediately apparent. In some jurisdictions and at some points in history, non-consensual 'arranged' marriages have been recognised. The Court seems to be suggesting that legislation with respect to non-consensual marriages might lie outside the scope of the Commonwealth's legislative power. The Court was highly critical, in its reasoning, of any definition of marriage that might carry with it some 'preconceived notion of what marriage "should" be',[293] and yet is there not a tacit moral disapproval of non-consensual marriages in this definition? One also has to ask whether the definition is over-inclusive, for it seems to embrace any 'union' between persons intended to 'endure', and if read literally could include relationships that we might otherwise call commercial partnerships, professional associations, religious confraternities, trade unions and so on. Surely the marriage power does not really extend to the regulation of these kinds of relationships. But in distancing itself from the traditional classical and Christian definitions of marriage that have historically informed the common law,[294] the Court seems to have enacted an alternative definition which carries with it problems of over- and under-inclusion that do not seem to have been fully considered in the judgment. While it must be true that the constitutional power over marriage is not restricted to the content of the law in 1900, the content of the power cannot be entirely malleable either, and there are serious questions to be asked about how the Court is to define the relevant 'topic of juristic classification' when it reasons selectively in this way.

A comparable problem has arisen in relation to the defence power. As was seen in *Farey v Burvett*,[295] what is necessary for the defence of the Commonwealth will depend on the nature and extent of the threats to its security that Australia faces at any particular point in time. What can be legislated under the defence power during a time of imminent or declared war is much more extensive than during peacetime. As such, the scope of the defence power is contingent on certain constitutionally relevant facts, known as 'constitutional facts'. How are these facts to be established? This question came to the fore in the *Communist Party* case.[296] In that case the Court had to consider the constitutional validity of the *Communist Party Dissolution Act 1950* (Cth), which declared the Communist Party to be unlawful, dissolved it as an organisation and provided

**292** *Commonwealth v Australian Capital Territory* (2013) 250 CLR 441, [33].
**293** Ibid, [36].
**294** Ibid, [19]–[20], [29]–[31], [36].
**295** (1916) 21 CLR 433.
**296** *Australian Communist Party v Commonwealth* (1951) 83 CLR 1.

for the forfeiture of its property to a receiver designated by the Commonwealth government. The main question was whether the law was authorised by the defence power (s 51(vi)).[297] At the time, although Australian forces were engaged in hostilities in Korea, it was considered that Australia was not 'upon a war footing', and therefore the case had to be addressed on the basis that a state of peace existed.[298] In order to provide a connection between the measures being taken against the Communist Party and the defence of Australia, the recitals to the Act claimed that communists were engaged in activities including treason, sabotage and espionage intended to overthrow the established system of government in Australia, and that the dissolution of the Communist Party was necessary for Australia's defence. This recital of asserted facts raised the question whether it was for the Parliament or the High Court to determine the factual context in which the constitutionality of the Act would be determined. In a 6:1 decision, the Court held that the Parliament cannot recite itself into power by asserting in the preamble to an Act that a particular threat to the security of the Commonwealth exists and that certain government activities are necessary to protect Australia from that asserted threat.[299] As Fullagar J put it:

> The validity of a law or of an administrative act done under a law cannot be made to depend on the opinion of the law-maker, or the person who is to do the act, that the law or the consequence of the act is within the constitutional power upon which the law in question itself depends for its validity. A power to make laws with respect to lighthouses does not authorize the making of a law with respect to anything which is, in the opinion of the law-maker, a lighthouse. A power to make a proclamation carrying legal consequences with respect to a lighthouse is one thing: a power to make a similar proclamation with respect to anything which in the opinion of the Governor-General is a lighthouse is another thing.[300]

If Australia had been fully at war, or war had been imminent, such measures against communists might have been authorised by the defence power; indeed, it has been held that in time of war a law can be made to operate upon the opinion of a designated person, and that opinion may provide the only link between the law and the defence power.[301] However, in the circumstances of the *Communist Party Dissolution Act* such a state of affairs had not been established to the satisfaction of the Court. The relevant facts must be proved in evidence, agreed by the parties, or be so publicly evident and notorious that they are a matter of judicial notice. Although the Court will sometimes have to determine constitutional facts 'as best it can',[302] it follows that the means by which such facts are established need to be treated with caution.[303]

**297** On the incidental power and the implied nationhood power, see Part IV.3 below.
**298** *Australian Communist Party v Commonwealth* (1951) 83 CLR 1, 196, 207.
**299** Ibid, 205–6, 264.
**300** Ibid, 258.
**301** Ibid, 195, 208, 258, citing *Lloyd v Wallach* (1915) 20 CLR 299.
**302** *Commonwealth Freighters Pty Ltd v Sneddon* (1959) 102 CLR 280, 292.
**303** James Stellios, 'Choice of Law and the Australian Constitution: Locating the Debate' (2005) 33 *Federal Law Review* 7.

## Core powers, incidental powers and proportionality

It was noted in relation to the characterisation of Commonwealth laws that the Court has accepted that so long as there is a 'sufficient connection' between the law and a head of power, it will not matter that the law was intended to achieve some other purpose lying outside of power.[304] The Court has also said that both the 'practical' and the 'legal' operation of the law 'must be examined to determine if there is a sufficient connection between the law and the head of power'.[305] In the *Payroll Tax* case, Windeyer J considered that the connecting phrase 'with respect to' should be understood as a 'compound preposition' that does not substantially differ in meaning from other terms that may be used to describe the connection between a law and a topic of legislative power such as 'in relation to',[306] 'concerning', 'touching', 'about', 'of' or 'on'.[307] In *Mulholland v Australian Electoral Commission*, McHugh J observed that '[a] law of the Parliament is made "with respect to" the subject matter of a power when it relates to or affects that subject matter and the connection is not "so insubstantial, tenuous or distant" that it cannot properly be described as a law with respect to that subject matter'.[308] In the *Melbourne Corporation* case, Dixon J said that, '[s]peaking generally, once it appears that a federal law has an actual and immediate operation within a field assigned to the Commonwealth as a subject of legislative power, that is enough'.[309] As Dixon J emphasised, however, the nature of the requisite connection will depend on both the nature of the law and the nature of the head of power. In this respect, it is important to note that the Court has long recognised that each head of power includes matters falling within what has been called the 'core' of the power, as well as matters said to be 'incidental' to it. The core and incidental aspects of each head of power are still part of the one unified power, and the ultimate question in either case is whether there is a sufficient connection between the law and the power; but the kind of reasoning that gives rise to the required connection differs.[310]

The core of a head of power is the 'subject matter' of the power. However, it is not always easy to distinguish matters falling with the core from those that do not. For example, it has been said that the core of the industrial arbitration power (s 51(xxxv)) concerns 'the prevention and settlement of interstate industrial disputes by conciliation and arbitration', whereas a law that imposes 'penal sanctions on persons who stand outside that subject matter', such as a law that prohibits criticism of the Industrial Relations Commission, concerns matters

**304** See, eg, *State Chamber of Commerce and Industry v Commonwealth (Second Fringe Benefits)* (1987) 163 CLR 329, 354.
**305** *Grain Pool of Western Australia v Commonwealth* (2000) 202 CLR 479, 492.
**306** As used in the *British North America Act 1867* (UK), ss 91 and 92.
**307** *Victoria v Commonwealth (Payroll Tax)* (1971) 122 CLR 353, 399. The connecting term 'for' used in s 122 has been considered to be an equivalent expression: *Lamshed v Lake* (1958) 99 CLR 132, 141.
**308** *Mulholland v Australian Electoral Commission* (2004) 220 CLR 181, 203, citing *Melbourne Corporation v Commonwealth* (1947) 74 CLR 31, 79.
**309** *Melbourne Corporation* (1947) 74 CLR 31, 79.
**310** On the unity of each head of power, see *Gazzo v Comptroller of Stamps (Vic)* (1981) 149 CLR 227, 267; *Cunliffe v Commonwealth* (1994) 182 CLR 272, 318; *Leask v Commonwealth* (1996) 187 CLR 579, 602, 633.

lying outside the core of the power which can only be authorised as 'incidental' to the head of power.[311] On the other hand, a law that regulates the conduct of persons who provide immigration assistance to aliens, especially by representing them and giving them advice, has been said to fall within the core of the aliens power (s 51(xix)).[312] Overuse of the distinction between the core and incidental scope of a head of power has therefore been criticised as deflecting attention away from the fact that each head of power is a unity,[313] and that the question before the Court is always whether a specific law falls within the power and not the wider task of describing the 'metes and bounds' of the head of power in the abstract.[314]

In *Thomas v Mowbray*,[315] the High Court was asked to consider whether anti-terrorism provisions of the *Criminal Code* (Cth) authorising the issue of interim control orders to protect the public from the perpetration of terrorist acts was supported by the defence power. Interim control orders could only be issued if a federal magistrate was satisfied that the making of an order would substantially assist in preventing a terrorist act and that the obligations, prohibitions and restrictions imposed on the person were reasonably necessary and reasonably appropriate and adapted to protecting the public from a terrorist act. A terrorist act was defined as action or the threat of action done for the purpose of advancing a political, religious or ideological cause with the intention of coercing or intimidating government or intimidating the public or a section of the public. The case tested the scope of the defence power because the law was directed to the prevention of terrorist acts by non-government actors, rather than the engagement of Australia's military forces in a conventional war between nation-states. Nonetheless, a majority of the Court held that the legislation was authorised by the defence power. Gummow and Crennan JJ considered that protection from a terrorist act fell within 'the central conception of the defence power', for, unlike the *Communist Party Dissolution Act*, the interim control orders were specifically aimed at suppressing violence and disorder, and their issue depended upon the satisfaction of objective criteria that could be judicially assessed.[316] Hayne J similarly considered that although the defence power is centrally concerned with the protection of the Commonwealth from external enemies, it extends also to protection from terrorist acts, and he did not accept that a distinction could be drawn between the defence of the Commonwealth and the States as bodies politic and the defence of their citizens and inhabitants.[317] Hayne J and especially Callinan J also criticised the relatively sharp distinction drawn in the *Communist Party* case between the scope of the defence power in times of war and peace, noting the 'increasing capacity of small groups to carry out

**311** *Nationwide News Pty Ltd v Wills* (1992) 177 CLR 1, 27.
**312** *Cunliffe v Commonwealth* (1994) 182 CLR 272, 294–5.
**313** Ibid, 317–18.
**314** *Singh v Commonwealth* (2004) 222 CLR 322, 382–3.
**315** (2007) 233 CLR 307. See, further, Chapter 9, Part III.4.
**316** Ibid, 363–4.
**317** Ibid, 456–9.

threats of widespread harm to persons and property', bearing in mind 'the potential of weaponry for massive harm'.[318]

As *Thomas v Mowbray* illustrates, when a law falls within the 'central conception' of a head of power, there is little need for discussion of the distinction between the core and the incidental aspects of the power. It is usually only when the incidental scope of a power is at stake that explicit discussion of the distinction is necessary or relevant. Here it also needs to be noted that the incidental aspect of each head of power is distinct from, but in practice largely overlaps with, the explicit incidental power conferred by s 51(xxxix).[319] As Griffith CJ explained in *D'Emden v Pedder*:

> where any power or control is expressly granted, there is included in the grant, to the full extent of the capacity of the grantor, and without special mention, every power and every control the denial of which would render the grant itself ineffective. This is, in truth, not a doctrine of any special system of law, but a statement of a necessary rule of construction of all grants of power, whether by unwritten constitution, formal written instrument, or other delegation of authority, and applies from the necessity of the case, to all to whom is committed the exercise of powers of government.[320]

Four members of the Court put it similarly in *Grannall v Marrickville Margarine Pty Ltd* when they pointed out that:

> every legislative power carries with it authority to legislate in relation to acts, matters and things the control of which is found necessary to effectuate its main purpose, and thus carries with it power to make laws governing or affecting many matters that are incidental or ancillary to the subject matter.[321]

The incidental dimensions of legislative power have been held to support laws that authorise or require the imposition of penalties, forfeiture of property, reporting of transactions, issue of licences, establishment of agencies and incorporation of companies for purposes associated with a head of power. The Commonwealth has no explicit power to do these things, but they have been upheld as constitutional provided they are necessary to achieve objectives lying within the Commonwealth's legislative powers.

In a passage frequently cited in relation to the incidental scope of legislative power, Marshall CJ of the United States Supreme Court observed in *McCulloch v Maryland*:

> Let the end be legitimate, let it be within the scope of the constitution, and all means which are appropriate, which are plainly adapted to that end, which are not prohibited, but consist with the letter and spirit of the constitution, are constitutional.[322]

**318** Ibid, 458, 503–5.
**319** Note, however, that s 51(xxxix) confers legislative power with respect to matters incidental to the 'execution' of the powers of the Parliament, of the two houses of the Parliament, of the Executive and of the Judiciary. See *Le Mesurier v Connor* (1929) 42 CLR 481, 497–8; see also *Victoria v Commonwealth and Hayden* (1975) 134 CLR 338, 413–14. On the practical overlap as far as the legislative powers of the Parliament are concerned, see *Burton v Honan* (1952) 86 CLR 169, 177–8.
**320** *D'Emden v Pedder* (1904) 1 CLR 91, 110.
**321** *Grannall v Marrickville Margarine Pty Ltd* (1955) 93 CLR 55, 77.
**322** *McCulloch v Maryland* 17 US (4 Wheat) 316 (1819), 421.

The idea that the means adopted by a law must be both 'appropriate' and 'adapted' to achieving a constitutionally-authorised end or goal has given rise, more so in Australia than in the United States, to the idea that there must be a relationship of 'appropriateness' or 'proportionality' between the means and the end of the legislation. An inquiry into whether a law is proportional involves an identification of the goals or purposes of the law, and an assessment of whether the methods adopted by the law are appropriate for achieving those goals. It is therefore necessary, it is said, to assess the proportionality of a law whenever it is based on a source of power that is 'purposive' in nature. This is not normally the case when the core of a head of legislative power is invoked, because it has been considered that most heads of power are not purposive in character. However, when the incidental scope of a head of power is relied upon, the identification of the purpose of the law is essential to the inquiry. A similar inquiry is also necessary in relation to the defence power (s 51(vi)) because it, unlike the other heads of power, is considered to be purposive in its core nature. Proportionality analyses are likewise undertaken in relation to aspects of other heads of power that involve a purposive element. For example, under the external affairs power (s 51(xxix)), the Commonwealth can enact laws that implement Australia's international law obligations under treaties entered into with other countries.[323] It has been held that this aspect of the external affairs power is purposive, and therefore a law validly implementing an international treaty obligation must be reasonably capable of being considered appropriate and adapted to meeting that obligation.[324] As will be seen in Chapter 5, proportionality is also a very important ingredient in the Court's jurisprudence relating to the application of constitutional rights and freedoms, such as freedom of interstate trade and commerce (s 92) and the implied freedom of political communication.

The constitutional requirement of appropriateness or proportionality has been expressed in various ways: that the law must be 'necessary', 'proportionate', 'appropriate and adapted' or 'reasonably capable of being considered appropriate and adapted' to achieving a constitutionally legitimate objective. While these formulas are sometimes used interchangeably, and the idea that there is a material difference between them has been denied,[325] they do help to underscore that there are different degrees of scrutiny that can be applied to a law. One way of distinguishing them is by reference to the kind of connection between the 'means' and the 'end' that is required. Here, the weakest form of scrutiny simply asks whether a law is an *effective* means to achieve an objective. If a law cannot achieve, or is not likely to achieve, its legitimating objective, then the law cannot be validated by reference to that objective. A stricter form of scrutiny asks whether a law is an *appropriate* or *proportionate* means to achieve the objective, in the sense that any harmful effects of the law are weighed against its beneficial

**323** *Commonwealth v Tasmania* (1983) 158 CLR 1. See Part IV.2 below.
**324** *Richardson v Forestry Commission* (1988) 164 CLR 261.
**325** *Nationwide News Pty Ltd v Wills* (1992) 177 CLR 1, 30–31; *Cunliffe v Commonwealth* (1994) 182 CLR 272, 296; *Leask v Commonwealth* (1996) 187 CLR 579, 593, 635.

effects. Often, these negative aspects of the law concern its damaging effects on other interests, values or goods, such as the rights or liberties of those adversely affected by the law. Plainly, such a weighing of the good and bad effects of the law is likely to involve a moral evaluation of the law itself. Here, the 'balance' to be struck between the good and the bad effects of a law can be construed in different ways. Sometimes it is said that the weight of the values themselves, as well as the degree to which the law either supports or undermines them, ought to be taken into consideration. Thus, a far-reaching interference with a highly valued right or interest is not likely to be justified unless the intrinsic value of the objective – and the degree to which the objective is secured by the law – is considered to be of even greater weight. There are also differences in the degree to which a court may regard itself as authorised to substitute its own assessment of the constitutional legitimacy of the law for the assessment of the legislator. Here, a weak form of review asks only whether a law is *reasonably capable of being considered* an appropriate means to achieving the constitutionally legitimate objective. Here, the question is whether a legislator could have reasonable grounds for thinking that a law will achieve the objective – an approach to proportionality that may be said to accord a *margin of appreciation* in favour of the legislature. A stronger form of review asks whether the law is *narrowly tailored* to achieve its objective, by which is meant that the law will be considered disproportionate if there is another less-intrusive and yet effective means to achieve the objective that the legislator could have adopted.[326]

The High Court has often said that an inquiry into the proportionality of a law does not mean that the Court will engage in open-ended assessment of the justice, fairness, morality or propriety of the law. As Dixon CJ put it in *Burton v Honan*:

> [M]atters of incidental powers are largely questions of degree, but in considering them we must not lose sight of the fact that once the subject matter is fairly within the province of the Federal legislature the justice and wisdom of the provisions which it makes in the exercise of its powers over the subject matter are matters entirely for the Legislature and not for the Judiciary.
>
> In the administration of the judicial power in relation to the Constitution there are points at which matters of degree seem sometimes to bring forth arguments in relation to justice, fairness, morality and propriety, but those are not matters for the judiciary to decide upon. The reason why this appears to be so is simply because a reasonable connection between the law which is challenged and the subject of the power under which the legislature purported to enact it must be shown before the law can be sustained under the incidental power.[327]

It may be questioned whether in practice the High Court has entirely adhered to this approach. There has been a tendency in some cases to assess the

**326** For an insightful analysis, see Jeremy Kirk, 'Constitutional Guarantees, Characterisation and the Concept of Proportionality' (1997) 21 *Melbourne University Law Review* 1. For a range of perspectives, see Grant Huscroft, Bradley Miller and Grégoire Webber (eds), *Proportionality and the Rule of Law: Rights, Justification, Reasoning* (Cambridge University Press, 2014).

**327** *Burton v Honan* (1952) 86 CLR 169, 179. See, similarly, *Leask v Commonwealth* (1996) 187 CLR 579, 593.

proportionality of laws by reference not only to whether they are suitable means to achieve certain objectives, but also to whether their interference with other rights or freedoms is justified. This can be seen in *Polyukhovich v Commonwealth*, where Brennan J held that a law enacted in 1988 providing for the punishment of war crimes perpetrated during the Second World War was not authorised by the defence power because its abridgement of human rights (in this case, freedom from retrospective criminal laws) outweighed the benefits of a law that sought to ensure that certain wartime atrocities were effectively prosecuted.[328] It is also illustrated by *Davis v Commonwealth*,[329] where the Court struck down a law that prohibited the use of certain words associated with the commemoration of the Bicentenary of the British settlement of Australia because the law disproportionately interfered with freedom of speech. A similar line of reasoning was adopted by Mason CJ in *Nationwide News v Wills*, where his Honour held that a law prohibiting criticism of the Industrial Relations Commission was not authorised by the incidental scope of the industrial arbitration power (s 51(xxxv)) because the need to protect the reputation of the Commission was 'outweighed by the strength of the public interest in public scrutiny and freedom to criticise' the Commission.[330] As will be seen in Chapter 5, the tendency of proportionality tests to enable the Court to make far-reaching moral judgments about the appropriateness of a law is especially noticeable in relation to the implied freedom of political communication, although it also emerges in relation to the application of the guarantee of freedom of interstate trade and commerce in s 92 of the Constitution.

In *Nationwide News*, Dawson J expressed concern that the use of proportionality tests 'invites the Court to act upon its view of the desirability of impugned legislation rather than upon the connexion of the legislation with the subject-matter of the legislative power'.[331] This concern about the growing use and reach of proportionality came to a head in *Leask v Commonwealth*.[332] In that case, the Court had to consider whether the provisions of the *Financial Transaction Reports Act 1988* (Cth) could be supported by the taxation and currency powers (ss 51(ii) and (xii)). The purpose of the Act was to reduce the incidence of tax evasion and money laundering. Section 7 of the Act required cash dealers to report transactions to which they are parties where the transactions involve the transfer of not less than $10 000. Section 31(1) sought to prevent the avoidance of the reporting obligations under the Act, such as by splitting transactions into amounts less than $10 000. It provided that a person committed an offence in circumstances where it would be 'reasonable to conclude' that they had attempted to avoid the reporting requirements of the Act, bearing in mind such matters as the manner and form of the transactions and any explanation given

**328** *Polyukhovich v Commonwealth* (1991) 172 CLR 501, 592–3.
**329** (1988) 166 CLR 79.
**330** *Nationwide News v Wills* (1992) 177 CLR 1, 34.
**331** Ibid, 89.
**332** *Leask v Commonwealth* (1996) 187 CLR 579.

by the person. The plaintiffs argued that s 31(1) created a strict liability offence and that this was 'disproportionate' to the purposes of the Act. However, the whole Court upheld the legislation as being validly enacted under either the 'taxation' power or the 'currency' power.

In coming to this conclusion, there was general agreement among the justices that the fundamental question is always whether there is a 'sufficient connection' with the relevant head of power. As Brennan CJ put it, the character of an Act is always to be determined by reference to its 'operation and effect: its operation by reference to the rights, duties, powers or privileges that the Act creates or affects; its effect by reference to its operation in the circumstances to which it applies'.[333] Where a head of power is purposive (eg, the defence power), then the necessary connection may be determined more easily by reference to the law's purpose, but if the head of power is non-purposive (eg, taxation and currency) then the validity of the law is more likely to be determined by reference to its operation and effect.[334] According to the Chief Justice, it was not necessary to consider the proportionality of the law, because s 31 operated directly on the physical transfer of currency from one person to another and this was sufficient to characterise it as a law with respect to currency.[335] Dawson J, with whom Brennan CJ and Gummow J largely agreed,[336] strongly resisted the use of proportionality except in relation to purposive powers and constitutional limitations.[337] He considered that a Commonwealth law will be within power 'if the acts, facts, matters or things upon which it operates fall within the description of one or more heads of power'.[338] While ascertaining whether the necessary connection exists will often be a matter of degree, once a connection is established 'it does not matter that the legislature has chosen a means of achieving its aim which goes further than is necessary or desirable'.[339] It therefore followed that, even if the law created a strict liability offence which dispensed with the need for *mens rea*, the law would still be valid if it had a sufficient connection to a head of power, which it did.[340]

A somewhat less strict view was expressed by McHugh J. On one hand, he agreed that the sufficiency of the connection between the law and a head of power was the touchstone of validity, and that where such a connection exists it is irrelevant that the law is 'harsh, oppressive, or inappropriate'. However, he also maintained that where the dominant subject of a law is not itself a head of power, the 'sub-test of proportionality' may sometimes assist in determining whether there is a sufficient connection.[341] Gaudron J seemed to go even further, when she said that proportionality is one of several considerations that may be

**333** Ibid, 590–91 (references omitted).
**334** Ibid, 591. See, similarly, *Cunliffe v Commonwealth* (1994) 182 CLR 272, 317–19.
**335** *Leask v Commonwealth* (1996) 187 CLR 579, 595.
**336** See ibid, 624.
**337** Ibid, 605–6.
**338** Ibid, 601.
**339** Ibid, 602; see also 605.
**340** Ibid, 599, 606–7.
**341** Ibid, 616.

taken into account, not only when the purpose of a law is relevant to the assessment of its constitutionality, but also more generally when determining whether a law is relevantly connected to a head of power.[342] In this particular respect, she disagreed with Toohey J, who had restricted the use of proportionality to circumstances where there is a 'tension between two operative principles' – a situation most likely to arise when the Court is considering the application of a limitation on power, such as the implied freedom of political communication.[343] Kirby J also questioned whether proportionality could sensibly be used in relation to some heads of power but not others. Like McHugh J, he thought that proportionality 'may sometimes be helpful in the context of constitutional characterisation', although he insisted that it affords no 'authority for judging the desirability of the law or the means employed by the lawmaker'.[344]

### Clause-bound interpretation

The discussion so far has focused on the problem of interpreting specific words or phrases used in particular sections of the Constitution, understood more or less in isolation from other parts of the document. One of the important consequences of the *Engineers* case was to encourage exactly this kind of emphasis on the particular words used to describe each head of power in s 51. Indeed, this was the very point of the rejection in *Engineers* of the reserved powers and immunity of instrumentalities doctrines. As Evatt J later maintained, the 'true rule' established in *Engineers* was that 'each subject matter in sec. 51 must be regarded as a separate subject matter'.[345] Nonetheless, the reasoning in *Engineers* insisted that the Commonwealth is a government of strictly enumerated powers.[346] Accordingly, it is not doubted that words of qualification included in a particular head of power place limits on the scope of *that* power. The point is that, following *Engineers*, those limitations are of no relevance to the interpretation of *other* heads of power. Under s 51(i) of the Constitution, for instance, the Commonwealth does not have power to legislate with respect to 'trade and commerce' generally, but only in relation to trade and commerce 'with other countries, and among the States'. Compared especially with the interpretation given to the corresponding commerce power in the United States Constitution, the High Court has been relatively vigilant in ensuring that the distinction between intrastate and interstate commerce is not 'obliterated' by construction.[347]

Section 51(i) contains three elements: (a) 'trade and commerce', (b) 'with other countries' and (c) 'among the States'. Consistent with the tendency since *Engineers* to interpret each head of power as widely as the language used

**342** Ibid.
**343** Ibid, 614–16.
**344** Ibid, 635–6. For more on proportionality, see Part IV.2 below and Chapter 5, Parts III.4, IV.3 and V.3.
**345** *West v Commissioner of Taxation (NSW)* (1937) 56 CLR 657, 706.
**346** *Amalgamated Society of Engineers v Adelaide Steamship Co Ltd* (1920) 28 CLR 129, 150.
**347** *Wragg v New South Wales* (1953) 88 CLR 353, 385–6; *Swift Australian Co Ltd v Boyd-Parkinson* (1962) 108 CLR 189, 203; *Airlines of New South Wales Pty Ltd v New South Wales (No 2)* (1965) 113 CLR 54, 113–15. For a comparison, see Greg Taylor, 'The Commerce Clause – Commonwealth Comparisons' (2001) 24 *Boston College International & Comparative Law Review* 235.

permits, the Court has understood 'trade and commerce' to embrace not only the physical act of transportation of goods, but also all of the necessary commercial arrangements and accessory means by which such movement of goods is initiated and effectuated, including communications necessary for the negotiation and conclusion of contracts for supply of such goods, as well as their transportation and delivery.[348] Following the emphasis in *Engineers* on the literal text of the Constitution, the Court has further held that the trade and commerce power is not limited to authorising laws that *regulate* trade and commerce, but enables the Commonwealth to enter itself into the *conduct* of interstate or international trading and commercial activities, by enacting laws that establish government-owned enterprises, such as a national airline.[349] However, the two qualifications on the scope of the power – 'with other countries' and 'among the States' – are explicit requirements of the Constitution that must also be given effect. While the *Engineers* case determined that these qualifying words do not create a sphere of reserved powers for the States when the Commonwealth legislates under other heads of power, the Court has insisted that they do limit the scope of the trade and commerce power itself.[350] A Commonwealth law enacted under s 51(i) can only include some aspect of intrastate trade and commerce within its reach where this is necessary, in the sense that the law will only be effective in its regulation of interstate or international trade and commerce if it operates in a way that happens to include intrastate trade and commerce within its sweep. Dixon CJ put it this way in *Wragg v New South Wales*:

> The distinction which is drawn between inter-State trade and the domestic trade of a State for the purpose of the power conferred upon the Parliament by s 51 (i) to make laws with respect to trade and commerce with other countries and among the States may well be considered artificial and unsuitable to modern times. But it is a distinction adopted by the Constitution and it must be observed however much inter-dependence may now exist between the two divisions of trade and commerce which the Constitution thus distinguishes. A legislative power, however, with respect to any subject matter contains within itself authority over whatever is incidental to the subject matter of the power and enables the legislature to include within laws made in pursuance of the power provisions which can only be justified as ancillary or incidental. But even in the application of this principle to the grant of legislative power made by s 51 (i) the distinction which the Constitution makes between the two branches of trade and commerce must be maintained. Its existence makes impossible any operation of the incidental power which would obliterate the distinction.[351]

In *Airlines of New South Wales Pty Ltd v New South Wales (No 2)*,[352] the High Court had to consider whether 1964 amendments to the *Air Navigation*

**348** *W & A McArthur v Queensland* (1920) 28 CLR 530, 546–7, 549.
**349** *Australian National Airways Pty Ltd v Commonwealth* (1945) 71 CLR 29, 80–81.
**350** *R v Burgess; Ex parte Henry* (1936) 55 CLR 608, 628–9, 672; *Wragg v New South Wales* (1953) 88 CLR 353, 385–6; *Redfern v Dunlop Rubber Australia Ltd* (1964) 110 CLR 194, 220.
**351** *Wragg v New South Wales* (1953) 88 CLR 353, 386.
**352** (1965) 113 CLR 54.

*Regulations* made under the *Air Navigation Act 1920* (Cth) were authorised by the interstate trade and commerce power. The amendments extended the reach of the regulations in several respects. Regulation 198 prohibited the use of an aircraft to provide public transport without a licence, and reg 199 required the Director-General of Civil Aviation, when considering licence applications in relation to intrastate operations, only to consider matters relating to 'safety, regularity and efficiency of air navigation'. Regulation 200B provided that a licence authorised the conduct of airline operations generally, to the exclusion of any State laws regulating such matters. The Court upheld regs 198 and 199 under the trade and commerce power on the ground that it was not practically possible to maintain the safety, regularity and efficiency of interstate air navigation without also regulating intrastate air navigation. As Kitto J put it, air navigation in Australia is such a 'complex of activities ... that what happens at any given time and place in the course of an air operation may substantially, even dramatically, affect other air operations close or distant in time or space'.[353] On the other hand, reg 200B was struck down because it purported to authorise the conduct of intrastate air navigation without any necessary connection to the maintenance of a safe system of air navigation.

Delivering one of the leading judgments of the Court, Kitto J began by emphasising that neither 'intrastate air navigation' nor 'air navigation generally' is per se a subject of Commonwealth legislative power. The Commonwealth cannot legislate to affect such activities unless the law can fairly be characterised as a law with respect to some particular head of Commonwealth power. This, he said, followed not from any doctrine of reserved powers, but 'simply because of the limited nature of the positive grants of power made by the Constitution'.[354] Such an interpretation was necessary because the Constitution provides for a system of 'dual federalism', and 'until the Parliament and the people see fit to change it, a true federation it must remain'.[355] Unless and until the Constitution is relevantly amended, he insisted, the Court is responsible to preserve the constitutional distinction between intrastate and interstate commerce, notwithstanding arguments that the distinction might be unrealistic, impracticable or difficult to apply.[356]

Kitto J's reasoning in *Airlines of New South Wales (No 2)* turned on a fine distinction between a situation where a Commonwealth law regulates matters which, if not regulated, would have a prejudicial effect upon an activity which is itself within Commonwealth power (in which case the law would be valid) and a situation where the prejudicial effect concerns matters that are merely consequential to an activity within power, such as a reduction in the profitability of the activity (in which case the law would be invalid).[357] This, albeit very fine,

**353** *Airlines of New South Wales Pty Ltd v New South Wales (No 2)* (1965) 113 CLR 54, 116; see also 92–3, 116, 128, 155.
**354** Ibid, 112.
**355** Ibid, 115.
**356** Ibid.
**357** Ibid.

distinction indicates one of the important differences between the Australian and American jurisprudence in this area.[358] In the United States, the Supreme Court has upheld an exceptionally wide view of the commerce power, premised on a conception of trade and commerce as an economically integrated activity. Thus, it has been held to authorise federal laws regulating wholly intrastate economic activities, such as the production of wheat by a farmer solely for consumption on his farm, on the ground that, if also practised by other similarly situated farmers, it would have an effect on the market price of wheat in interstate trade.[359] Such a decision simply could not be made in Australia on the current state of the authorities.

This line of reasoning was further tested in the *Western Australian Airlines* case.[360] The case involved the *Australian National Airlines Act 1945* (Cth), which established the Australian National Airlines Commission. Relying on the Commonwealth's powers to legislate with respect to interstate trade and commerce (s 51(i)), incidental matters (s 51(xxxix)) and territories (s 122), the Act authorised the Commission to provide air transportation services between two States, between a Territory and a State, and within a Territory. Pressing the boundaries of the power, an amendment to the Act (s 19B) also authorised the Commission to provide transportation services within a particular State 'for the purposes of the efficient, competitive and profitable conduct of the business of the Commission' in respect of the provision of its interstate and territorial services and as otherwise incidental to the carrying on of that business. The case arose in connection with the Commission's proposal to establish a service between Perth and Darwin with an intermediate stop at Port Headland in Western Australia.

A majority of the Court (Stephen, Mason and Murphy JJ) upheld s 19B insofar as it applied in respect of the Commission's territorial services. However, a differently composed majority (Barwick CJ, Stephen and Gibbs JJ) considered that s 19B was not authorised insofar as it applied in respect of its interstate services. In coming to this latter conclusion, Barwick CJ, Stephen and Gibbs JJ affirmed suggestions in *Airlines of New South Wales (No 2)* that considerations of the economic efficiency, competitiveness and profitability of interstate trade would not be sufficient to bring a law within the commerce power.[361] However, Barwick CJ and Gibbs J went further. They considered that neither could s 19B be authorised by the territories power, for substantially the same reason as applied to the commerce power – namely that the economic considerations were insufficient to bring the law within power.[362]

**358** Ibid.
**359** *Wickard v Filburn* 317 US 111 (1942), 125: '[E]ven if [the] activity be local and though it may not be regarded as commerce, it may still, whatever its nature, be reached by Congress if it exerts a substantial economic effect on interstate commerce'. For a critical discussion, see Zines, above n 274, 4th ed, 68–72, 75–9.
**360** *Attorney-General (WA); Ex rel Ansett Transport Industries (Operations) Pty Ltd v Australian National Airlines Commission* (1976) 138 CLR 492.
**361** Ibid, 499, 502–3, 508–11.
**362** Ibid, 500–01, 503–5.

The reasoning of Barwick CJ and Gibbs J is liable to be criticised as incorporating into the interpretation of s 122 a limitation derived from s 51(i), after the fashion of the reserved powers doctrine. Thus, without adverting to the doctrine specifically, Stephen J responded that it was impermissible to incorporate restrictions derived from s 51(i) into the interpretation of s 122, and Mason J said that in the interpretation of s 122 it was improper to exclude economic considerations while admitting physical ones.[363] Objecting to the apparent 'persistence' of reserved powers reasoning, Murphy J went even further, rejecting the restrictive interpretation of the commerce power that the Court had affirmed. He denied that the scheme of the Constitution was to confer 'exclusive' power to the States over intrastate trade and commerce, and he insisted that it is permissible for the purposes of the commerce power to take 'commercial effects' into consideration.[364]

Any lingering role of reserved powers reasoning in these judgments needs to be assessed carefully. Although Barwick CJ and Gibbs J certainly applied to the territories power the same restrictive distinction the Court had developed in connection with the commerce power, this was based on the observation that the territories power 'does not confer on the Parliament a power to legislate for the government of Australia' and that, accordingly, the power must be limited to laws that are 'necessary to make effectual some valid exercise of the power'.[365] The necessity for the restriction, in other words, was based on the limited language of s 122, not on an inference derived from the limited language of s 51(i). Technically, therefore, their judgments did not rely on reserved powers reasoning in the classical sense in which it had been developed by the Griffith Court. The reasoning was more moderate – it was based on the proposition that, even when read in isolation, each head of power is limited, and that to apply such limitations, the Court has to draw distinctions between the permissible and the impermissible. Stephen J disagreed with Barwick CJ and Gibbs J about where the line was to be drawn in relation to the territories power, but he agreed that a line had to be drawn, and thus he joined with them in upholding the distinction between physical and economic effects in relation to the commerce power.

It has been suggested by Leslie Zines that even this latter argument smacks of reserved powers reasoning.[366] But, as Zines also observed, when working out the scope of the incidental aspects of various heads of power, 'it is hard to see how ... it is possible totally to ignore the effect of the law on areas of activity that are not subjects of Commonwealth power'.[367] How can one assess whether the impact of a law is 'slight', 'remote', 'tenuous' or 'indirect' in relation to a matter that falls within Commonwealth power, he suggested, without comparing its

**363** Ibid, 513–14, 523–4, 525–6.
**364** Ibid, 529–31. Mason J avoided addressing this specific issue, but in later extra-curial remarks he questioned the 'restrictive and formalistic reading' that the Court had given to the commerce power: eg, Anthony Mason, 'The Australian Constitution: 1901–1988' (1988) 62 *Australian Law Journal* 752, 755–6.
**365** *Western Australian Airlines* (1976) 138 CLR 492, 504, 505.
**366** Zines, above n 274, 4th ed, 77.
**367** Ibid, 78.

impact on some subject matter that prima facie falls outside Commonwealth power?[368]

Since *Engineers*, the Court has consistently denied that the commerce power implies a prohibition on the scope of *other* heads of legislative power. Nonetheless, it has been relatively vigilant to ensure that the limitations written into the commerce power are rigorously applied at least in relation to the commerce power itself. In both these respects, the Court's jurisprudence on the commerce power is an illustration of its essentially clause-bound approach to interpreting the Commonwealth's legislative powers. Nonetheless, as the discussion above suggests, it is difficult to apply the federal distribution of legislative power between the Commonwealth and the States without considering both what *is* granted to the Commonwealth and what is *not*.

### Exceptions to clause-bound interpretation

Despite the prevailing tendency of the Court to interpret each paragraph of s 51 in isolation, do any situations remain where limitations in one head of power are interpreted to imply limits on the scope of another? This question can be developed in at least three specific ways. Firstly, can the grant of one power in relatively specific terms have implications for the interpretation of another related power which is expressed in terms that are broader than and seem to overlap with the first-mentioned head of power?[369] For example, does the relatively narrow power with respect to 'the relations of the Commonwealth with the islands of the Pacific' (s 51(xxx)) have any implications for the meaning to be attributed to the apparently broader and more encompassing 'external affairs' power (s 51(xxix))? If 'external affairs' is interpreted to include everything referred to by 'relations of the Commonwealth with the islands of the Pacific', then what is the point of including s 51(xxx) in the Constitution? Or, to take another example, does the power to legislate with respect to 'divorce and matrimonial causes; and in relation thereto, parental rights, and the custody and guardianship of infants' (s 51(xxii)) imply that the power to legislate with respect to 'marriage' (s 51(xxi)) does not authorise laws that regulate the rights of marriage partners to the custody of infants in the absence of a matrimonial cause?[370] Put differently, the question here is whether the words 'external affairs' and 'marriage' are to be interpreted as widely as these words can reasonably sustain without regard to the more limited terms in which the powers to legislate with respect to 'islands of the Pacific' or 'divorce and matrimonial causes' are expressed? For, if this is so, the more narrowly-expressed heads of power might prove to be redundant or otiose.

Secondly, there are some heads of power or aspects of a single head of power that are defined by reference to a limited class expressed as a compound conception (eg, 'conciliation and arbitration for the prevention and settlement of

**368** Ibid.
**369** *New South Wales v Commonwealth (Seas & Submerged Lands)* (1975) 135 CLR 337, 471, 497.
**370** *Russell v Russell* (1976) 134 CLR 495.

industrial disputes extending beyond the limits of any one State' (s 51(xxxv))) while some are defined by reference to an unlimited class which is then qualified by a negative proviso (eg, 'banking, other than State banking' (s 51(xiii))). Even if it is considered that limitations on powers expressed in the first way do not limit the scope of other powers, does the use of negative language in the second example imply that it limits the scope of other heads of power as well? For instance, does the negative proviso 'other than State banking' limit the kinds of laws that can be authorised under the power to legislate with respect to 'financial corporations' (s 51(xx))?[371] Similarly, what if the qualification on a power, although not expressed as a negative proviso, imposes a condition that involves some kind of benefit or protection for those affected by a law (eg, 'acquisition of property … on just terms' (s 51(xxxi)))? Does such a qualification limit the scope of other heads of power to ensure that any head of power which might authorise the acquisition of property can only do so by providing just terms?[372]

Thirdly, given that the scheme of the Constitution is to confer only limited legislative powers on the Commonwealth (ss 51, 52) and to ensure that the existing plenary legislative powers of the States will largely continue (ss 106, 107), should the Commonwealth's powers nevertheless be interpreted so as to maintain: (a) that the Commonwealth does not, in effect, have power to legislate with respect to any topic;[373] (b) that there is a 'balance' between the powers of the Commonwealth and those of the States;[374] or (c) that there remains at least some 'sphere' of matters in respect of which the States can continue to legislate without the possibility of Commonwealth interference?[375]

The short answer to these questions seems to be that despite important dissentient views being expressed from time to time, only the second of these broad lines of argument has consistently found favour with a majority of the Court. A large part of the reason why the first line of argument has been rejected is that it would lead to a very strange result if the scope of each head of federal legislative power was limited by the scope of all the others. For, if this were so, the federal Parliament would only be competent to legislate in areas on which all heads of federal power happen to coincide – which is, of course, absurd. This is not to suggest that the reserved powers doctrine was ever formulated in such bizarre terms. As has been seen, it was just as often propounded in an 'interpretive' way, which recognised that issues of characterisation and interpretation are matters of degree involving choices between relatively narrow and wide constructions of the law. But the proposition that each head of power implies a prohibition, if generalised, would indeed have this result.

There are several cases in which it has been argued that the scope of one power should be read down so that another power is not rendered redundant or

**371** See *Bourke v State Bank of New South Wales* (1990) 170 CLR 276.
**372** See *Attorney-General (Cth) v Schmidt* (1961) 105 CLR 361, 370–73.
**373** *Commonwealth v Tasmania* (1983) 158 CLR 1.
**374** *Koowarta v Bjelke-Petersen* (1982) 153 CLR 168.
**375** *Huddart, Parker & Co Pty Ltd v Moorehead* (1909) 8 CLR 330.

otiose. In each instance, the argument has not secured the support of a majority of the Court, essentially on the ground that whether another head of power is made redundant is not a reason for reading down the natural language of the first-mentioned power. Thus, in the *Marriage Act* case,[376] the Court had to consider whether the Commonwealth's power with respect to 'marriage' authorised a law which, among other things, determined the legitimacy of children born to persons who later became married or whose marriages either occurred overseas or were later found to be void.[377] A majority of the Court upheld the relevant provisions of the law as validly enacted under the marriage power. One of the arguments against validity was that the marriage power (s 51(xxi)) should receive a relatively narrow interpretation in the light of the limited power with respect to 'parental rights, and the custody and guardianship of infants' (s 51(xxii)) because this latter power is specifically granted only in relation to 'divorce and matrimonial causes'. For, as Quick and Garran had observed, it was the deliberate intention of the framers of the Constitution to reserve to the States the 'control of children' except in relation to matrimonial proceedings for divorce and related remedies.[378] In his dissenting judgment, McTiernan J appeared to accept a version of this argument when he said that paragraphs (xxi) and (xxii) deal with different 'branches of family law' and that according to the common law, the marriage of two people does not ordinarily legitimise children born prior to the marriage.[379] However, directly rejecting this argument, in his majority judgment Taylor J observed that the power with respect to marriage is defined 'without limitation or qualification' and is therefore 'entitled to as wide an interpretation as it can reasonably bear'.[380] In his view, therefore, the marriage power is sufficient to authorise 'any law with respect to marriage considered as an institution', and therefore extends to the prescription not only of the form and requisites of valid marriages, but also to the rights, duties and incidents that arise out of the marriage relationship, including the status of children born to parents who are subsequently married.[381]

In *Russell v Russell*,[382] a majority of the Court similarly refused to interpret the scope of s 51(xxi) in light of the limited terms of s 51(xxii). At issue was whether the Commonwealth can invest courts with jurisdiction to make determinations concerning such things as spousal maintenance, distribution of property and custody of children in the absence of proceedings for divorce or some other matrimonial cause. It was argued, among other things, that because s 51(xxii) makes particular provision concerning parental rights and custody

**376** *Attorney-General (Vic) v Commonwealth* (1962) 107 CLR 529.
**377** *Marriage Act 1961* (Cth), ss 89–93.
**378** Quick and Garran, above n 17, 608–9.
**379** *Attorney-General (Vic) v Commonwealth* (1962) 107 CLR 529, 549–50. Dixon CJ's dissenting judgment was based the view that most of the challenged provisions were best characterised as concerning matters falling with the jurisdiction of the States: 544–6.
**380** Ibid, 560; see also 572, 602. Kitto J upheld the law on the basis that it had a sufficient connection to marriage: 554.
**381** Ibid, 560–61.
**382** (1976) 134 CLR 495.

arising only in relation to divorce and matrimonial causes, s 51(xxi) should not be interpreted to enable the Commonwealth to legislate in relation to parental rights and custody generally. In his dissenting judgment, Barwick CJ accepted this argument when he observed:

> Whilst each topic referred to in s 51 is an independent subject matter and some overlapping is possible, cognate topics and the terms in which they are expressed cannot be and never have been ignored in deciding the content and ambit of a topic described in s 51.

While the Chief Justice accepted that the marriage power extends to attaching legal consequences to the act of marriage, such as the creation of rights and duties of married persons and their children,[383] he considered that the particularity of the power concerning divorce and other matrimonial causes suggested that the marriage power does not extend to the enforcement of such rights and duties through judicial proceedings, for to conclude otherwise would render s 51(xxii) otiose and unnecessary.[384] Gibbs J generally agreed. He noted that paragraphs (xxi) and (xxii) not only appear together but deal with closely associated matters.[385] He also observed that if the limits placed by the second clause in paragraph (xxii) were not to apply to paragraph (xxi), they would be rendered quite ineffective.[386]

However, these lines of argument were not accepted by a majority of the Court. In his judgment, Jacobs J recognised the force of the argument that, in general, 'private and personal' matters are regulated by the States and that the Commonwealth's powers in relation to marriage and divorce are an exception to this general rule.[387] Indeed, prior to federation the social policies of the colonies had differed significantly, and although the framers were ultimately willing to grant the Commonwealth general power over marriage and divorce, they deliberately limited the scope of the Commonwealth's power in relation to parental rights, custody and guardianship.[388] However, Jacobs J considered that the concept of marriage needs to be understood as a social institution integral to the care and raising of children generally, and that the marriage power accordingly extends to regulation of the custody, guardianship and maintenance of children of a marriage or a dissolved marriage.[389] Mason J, with whom Stephen J agreed, rejected the argument based on s 51(xxii) even more forcefully, on the ground that:

> an individual grant of power should be ... accorded a full operation according to its terms, unrestricted by dubious implications drawn from the existence of another grant of legislative power touching an associated subject matter.[390]

**383** *Russell v Russell* (1976) 134 CLR 495, 509.
**384** Ibid, 510–12.
**385** Ibid, 526.
**386** Ibid, 527.
**387** Ibid, 546.
**388** *Convention Debates, Sydney* (1897) 1077–86.
**389** *Russell v Russell* (1976) 134 CLR 495, 547–50.
**390** Ibid, 539.

It followed for Mason J that the marriage power enables the Parliament to provide for the enforcement of such rights and duties as may be created in exercise of the marriage power.[391] This did not mean, however, that the Commonwealth has an unqualified capacity to legislate for the enforcement of rights with respect to custody, guardianship and maintenance. Such proceedings, he held, must have a sufficient connection to proceedings between the parties to a marriage, and the provisions of the *Family Law Act 1975* which exceeded this boundary were read down pursuant to s 15A of the *Acts Interpretation Act 1901* (Cth).[392]

Interestingly, one of the steps in Mason J's reasoning in *Russell* was that the words 'and in relation thereto, parental rights, and the custody and guardianship of infants' imply a limitation on the meaning that would otherwise be given to 'matrimonial causes'.[393] This reasoning does not seem to be quite consistent with what his Honour said about the relationship between paragraphs (xxi) and (xxii). This is because the reference to parental rights, custody and guardianship in paragraph (xxii) are words of positive extension, not negative limitation, yet Mason J regarded them as limiting the content that would otherwise be given to the meaning of the words 'matrimonial causes'. His reasoning was that these words of extension would not have been needed had the words 'matrimonial causes' already included them. As such, Mason J seemed to be placing reliance on the idea that the qualifying words should not be rendered otiose, but this is exactly the idea that underlies the argument concerning the relationship between paragraphs (xxi) and (xxii) that he rejected in *Russell*.

Nonetheless, the general tendency of the Court since the *Engineers* case has been to refuse to limit the scope of one grant of power by reference to the limited terms in which another grant of power is conferred. The only important exceptions to this general tendency have arisen where the limit imposed upon a head of power is expressed in the form of what might be called a 'negative proviso', or where the limitation is considered by the Court to establish a 'constitutional guarantee'. In *Attorney-General (Cth) v Schmidt*, Dixon CJ observed:

> [W]hen you have ... an express power, subject to a safeguard, restriction or qualification, to legislate on a particular subject or to a particular effect, it is in accordance with the soundest principles of interpretation to treat that as inconsistent with any construction of other powers conferred in the context which would mean that they included the same subject or produced the same effect and so authorized the same kind of legislation but without the safeguard, restriction or qualification.[394]

**391** Ibid, 539–40.
**392** Ibid, 540–42. On s 15A of the *Acts Interpretation Act 1901* (Cth), see the discussion of the *Industrial Relations Act* case in Chapter 4, Part III.3. The examples of this kind of reasoning can be multiplied. Thus, in *Pidoto v Victoria* (1943) 68 CLR 87 the High Court declined to read down the scope of the defence power (s 51(vi)) by reference to the industrial arbitration power (s 51(xxxv)) and in *New South Wales v Commonwealth (Work Choices)* (2006) 229 CLR 1, as will be seen, the Court refused to adopt a narrower interpretation of the corporations power (s 51(xx)) also in the light of the industrial arbitration power.
**393** *Russell v Russell* (1976) 134 CLR 495, 537–8.
**394** *Attorney-General (Cth) v Schmidt* (1961) 105 CLR 361, 371–2, as cited in *Nintendo Co Ltd v Centronics Systems Pty Ltd* (1994) 181 CLR 134, 160.

As will be seen in Chapter 5, in *Schmidt* the Court held that the 'just terms' requirement in s 51(xxxi) applies not only to laws enacted under that paragraph, but also generally in relation to laws involving the acquisition of property enacted under other heads of power. In *Bourke v State Bank of New South Wales*,[395] it was similarly held that the negative proviso in the banking power (s 51(xiii)) not only limits the scope of that power, but also limits the scope of the corporations power (s 51(xx)). In *Bourke*, the Court had to consider the constitutional validity of ss 52 and 52A of the *Trade Practices Act 1974* (Cth). Among other things, these sections made it an offence for a corporation to engage in 'misleading or deceptive' conduct in 'trade and commerce' (s 52) and to engage in 'unconscionable' conduct in connection with the supply of goods or services (s 52A). The application of these sections depended on the definition of 'corporation' in s 4(1), which was defined to include a 'financial corporation within the meaning of paragraph 51(xx) of the Constitution', a concept that was in turn defined to include 'a body corporate that carries on as its sole or principal business the business of banking (other than State banking not extending beyond the limits of the State concerned)'. The evident intention was to extend the application of the operative provisions of the Act as widely as constitutionally possible, by taking full advantage of the Commonwealth's powers over banking and financial corporations (ss 51(xiii) and (xx)).

In *Bourke*, it was alleged that the State Bank of New South Wales had been in breach of ss 52 and 52A. On the definition of 'State banking' that had previously been applied by the Court, it was confirmed that the bank engaged in State banking.[396] The question was whether ss 52 and 52A could validly apply to the bank's engagement in State banking. In approaching this question, the Court unanimously affirmed that the various paragraphs of s 51 'are not to be construed in a narrow or pedantic manner, but are plenary grants of legislative power to be construed with all the generality which the words used will admit'.[397] The Court also acknowledged that there is a general principle that 'a law with respect to a subject-matter within Commonwealth power does not cease to be valid because it affects a subject outside power or can be characterised as a law with respect to a subject-matter outside power'.[398] However, the Court considered that there is an exception to this general principle when this second subject matter is the subject of an explicit prohibition or restriction.[399] Concluding, for this reason, that the limitation in s 51(xiii) does indeed limit the scope of s 51(xx), the Court observed that it would be 'an extraordinary result' if State banks were 'subject to Commonwealth power'.[400]

**395** (1990) 170 CLR 276.
**396** *Bourke v State Bank of New South Wales* (1990) 170 CLR 276, 284, citing *Melbourne Corporation v Commonwealth* (1947) 74 CLR 31, defining 'State banking' as 'banking conducted by a bank owned or controlled by a State'.
**397** *Bourke v State Bank of New South Wales* (1990) 170 CLR 276, 284.
**398** Ibid, 285.
**399** Ibid, citing *Attorney-General (Cth) v Schmidt* (1961) 105 CLR 361, 371–2.
**400** *Bourke v State Bank of New South Wales* (1990) 170 CLR 276, 285. See also *Bank of New South Wales v Commonwealth* (1948) 76 CLR 1, 256.

The general mode of reasoning in *Schmidt* and *Bourke* has a potential application to several other heads of power where it can be said that there is an express power which is subjected to a safeguard, restriction or qualification.[401] These most clearly include the insurance power (s 51(xiv)), which is expressed in terms corresponding exactly to the banking power, but there are several other powers that potentially fall into this category as well.[402] Nonetheless, except in relation to the heads of power mentioned so far, such a line of argument has been steadfastly rejected by the Court as a form of reserved powers reasoning. In *Pidoto v Victoria*,[403] for example, the Court had to consider *National Security Regulations* made during the Second World War. The Regulations, enacted under the *National Security Act 1939* (Cth) in reliance on the defence power (s 51(vi)), extended the jurisdiction of the Commonwealth Court of Conciliation and Arbitration beyond that which could have been conferred by the industrial arbitration power (s 51(xxxv)). As Latham CJ (with whom Rich J agreed) pointed out, it had been held that under this power:

> the Commonwealth Parliament is limited to making laws for the prevention and settlement of industrial disputes (not for the direct regulation of industrial matters) and only of inter-State industrial disputes, and for the prevention and settlement of such disputes only by the methods of conciliation and arbitration.[404]

However, the Regulations in various ways dispensed with these elements and further provided that the jurisdiction of the Court included all cases considered by the Court 'desirable in the interests of industrial peace or national security'.[405] Nonetheless, the Regulations were upheld on the basis that they were related to the effectual prosecution of the war. As Latham CJ put it:

> In such a war as the present the authority responsible for defence must be able to organize and control the working capacity of the people and to assist the smooth working of the industrial system by preventing the friction and waste of time and energy which are inevitably involved in any industrial dispute.[406]

As such, the strict *ratio decidendi* of the case concerned the special nature of the defence power in time of war.[407] In the course of his reasoning, however, the Chief Justice also rejected the argument that the limited terms of the industrial arbitration power imply a negative limitation on the scope of other heads of power generally; and McTiernan and Williams JJ reasoned similarly.[408]

Although *Pidoto* concerned the defence power, it has subsequently been interpreted as authority for the wider proposition that there is no negative implication or prohibition that arises from the limited terms of the arbitration

**401** *Attorney-General (Cth) v Schmidt* (1961) 105 CLR 361, 371–2.
**402** It has been suggested that other possible examples are ss 51(ii), (iii), (xxiiiA), (xxxii), (xxxiii), (xxxiv): see *New South Wales v Commonwealth (Work Choices)* (2006) 229 CLR 1, 127, 208–9.
**403** (1943) 68 CLR 87.
**404** *Pidoto v Victoria* (1943) 68 CLR 87, 100.
**405** *National Security (Industrial Peace) Regulations 1940*, reg 11.
**406** *Pidoto v Victoria* (1943) 68 CLR 87, 102.
**407** See, similarly, ibid, 121–4, 127–8.
**408** Ibid, 101, 123, 127.

power.[409] One of the most significant cases in which this principle has been applied is the *Work Choices* case.[410] In that case, the High Court had to consider whether amendments to the *Workplace Relations Act 1996* (Cth) introduced by the *Workplace Relations Amendment (Work Choices) Act 2005* (Cth) were validly enacted under the corporations power (s 51(xx)). The Act effected a far-reaching transformation of Australian industrial relations law, displacing the previously existing federal system of compulsory conciliation and arbitration and purporting to apply to the exclusion of a range of State and Territory workplace regimes. The necessary connection to the corporations power was achieved in the Act through the definitions of 'employee', 'employer' and 'constitutional corporation'. An 'employee' was defined as an individual insofar as they are employed, or usually employed, by an employer under the Act; an 'employer' was defined as 'a constitutional corporation, so far as it employs, or usually employs, an individual'; and 'constitutional corporation' was defined as a corporation to which s 51(xx) of the Constitution applies. The substantive provisions of the Act conferred and imposed a range of powers, rights and duties upon employees and employers thus defined. In this way, the basic objective of the Act was to introduce a national workplace relations system that would apply to the majority of employer–employee relationships throughout Australia without the need for the restrictive elements contained in the industrial arbitration power (s 51(xxxv)) to be satisfied.

A majority of the Court upheld the entirety of the *Work Choices Act*, principally on the ground that the corporations power extends to any law that grants rights, confers powers or imposes duties upon a constitutional corporation, as well as to laws that have a less direct but nonetheless sufficiently substantial connection to constitutional corporations. Invoking the *Engineers* case on numerous occasions, the majority affirmed that the 'starting point' in interpretation must be the 'constitutional text', rather than a view 'formed independently of that text', such as the intentions of the framers or a view of the proper 'balance' to be maintained between the powers of the Commonwealth and the States.[411] Rather, they insisted that the Court should construe the corporations power 'with all the generality which the words used admit', without taking into consideration the limited terms in which the industrial arbitration power is defined.[412] Moreover, the majority rejected the argument – advanced by the plaintiffs and generally accepted by Kirby and Callinan JJ in their dissenting judgments – that the limited scope of the industrial relations power implies a limitation on the scope of the corporations power. In response to the argument that the principle in *Bourke* might apply, the Court distinguished the banking power from the industrial arbitration power on the basis that the former contains a 'positive prohibition or

**409** Eg, *Re Pacific Coal Pty Ltd; Ex parte Construction, Forestry, Mining and Energy Union* (2000) 203 CLR 346, 359–60.
**410** *New South Wales v Commonwealth* (2006) 229 CLR 1.
**411** Ibid, 71–3, 97, 103–4, 118–20.
**412** Ibid, 103–4, 117.

restriction', whereas the latter does not contain such a prohibition but rather 'is to be read as a whole'.[413]

It may be questioned whether to rely upon the difference between a limited class and an unlimited class qualified by a proviso is to depend upon what Julius Stone called a 'category of meaningless reference'.[414] Logically, when each head of power is considered in isolation, provided the qualifications are in substance the same, it makes no difference whether the power is defined as a 'limited class' or as an 'unlimited class qualified by a proviso'. Grammatically, the qualifying proviso in s 51(xiii) ('other than state banking') applies only to the word 'banking'. It was added to limit the scope of the Commonwealth's power so that the States could continue to legislate in that field. But the other limitations on Commonwealth power drafted in the form of 'limited classes' were included for the same basic reason. If there are good reasons to apply a negative proviso to other heads of power, the same kind of reasons can similarly apply to limited classes.[415] One reason why limited classes and negative provisos should have an effect on interpretation is that unless they do, the Commonwealth's powers can be interpreted in such a way that, in effect, there are very few topics that the Commonwealth cannot regulate. To interpret Commonwealth powers in such a way is arguably to undermine the careful demarcation of the Commonwealth's powers in ss 51 and 52, and to reverse the original conception of State power as original and plenary and Commonwealth power as derivative and limited.

### Effect on State power

However, only in some very isolated cases has the effect on State power been regarded by a majority of the Court as relevant to the characterisation of Commonwealth laws and the determination of the scope of Commonwealth power. An example is *Gazzo v Comptroller of Stamps (Vic)*.[416] The case concerned s 90 of the *Family Law Act 1975* (Cth), which provided that a maintenance agreement, or a deed or other instrument executed for the purposes of such an agreement or in accordance with an order under the Act, was not subject to any duty or charge under any law of a State or Territory. The question was whether this law, which purported to exempt such instruments from the application of State taxes, was validly enacted under either the marriage power, the divorce and matrimonial causes power or the express and implied incidental powers attaching to those powers. Gibbs CJ, Stephen and Aickin JJ (Mason and Murphy JJ dissenting) held that it was not.

Gibbs CJ began by drawing attention to the wide scope of s 90. It extended to agreements between two persons who were married, or were once married, concerning financial matters that might not be matrimonial property or arise out of the matrimonial relationship, and it might also involve some other person

**413** Ibid, 127.
**414** Julius Stone, *Human Law and Human Justice* (Maitland, 1965), 241–5.
**415** See Aroney, above n 2, 33–4.
**416** (1981) 149 CLR 227.

who had no connection to the marriage. It also applied not only to State and Territorial duties, but also to charges in the form of fees for the provision of services in relation to an agreement or instrument.[417] In previous cases, his Honour had insisted that to be valid under the marriage power a law must concern rights and duties that arise out of or have a close connection with the marriage relationship, and that it was not sufficient for a law simply to apply in relation to married persons.[418] It is not enough, he now said in *Gazzo*, that Parliament has 'seized on the fact of marriage as justification for the enactment of a law which really deals with some other topic'.[419] If s 90 is valid, he reasoned, it will have to be authorised by the Commonwealth's 'incidental' legislative powers, in particular the incidental power that attends the two primary heads of power in question, rather than the express incidental power in s 51(xxxix).[420] On this view, the question then became whether the law could be characterised as having the effect of enhancing the effectiveness of orders made by a court under the Act. However, the Chief Justice considered that such orders would remain just as effective whether or not State duties applied to instruments executed in accordance with them. Relinquishing someone from the liability to pay a tax would make compliance less onerous, but the duty to comply with the court order would remain undiminished even if the taxation liability remained.[421]

This was the primary basis of Gibbs CJ's reasoning. He added that the decisions in the *Royal Metals* case[422] and the *Second Uniform Tax* case[423] supported this conclusion. In the latter case, Dixon J had considered that a provision of the uniform tax scheme, that prohibited a taxpayer from paying State income tax until the Commonwealth tax had been paid, was not authorised by the incidental scope of the taxation power for it was an 'attempt to advance or extend the substantive power actually granted to the Commonwealth until it reaches into the exercise of the constitutional powers of the States'.[424] Gibbs CJ observed that this showed that 'in considering whether a law is incidental to the subject matter of a Commonwealth power it is not always irrelevant that the effect of the law is to invade State power'.[425]

In his dissenting judgment, Murphy J seized on what he regarded as elements of the 'reserved powers' doctrine that had invaded the reasoning of the Chief Justice. Citing Isaacs J in *Federal Commissioner of Taxation v Munro*, Murphy J urged that all Commonwealth laws must be presumed to be a valid and 'true expression of the national will' unless demonstrated otherwise, for such laws have been 'considered necessary or desirable for the public welfare' by no less than

**417** *Gazzo v Comptroller of Stamps (Vic)* (1981) 149 CLR 227, 232–3.
**418** Ibid, 234, citing *R v Lambert; Ex parte Plummer* (1980) 146 CLR 447, 456–7.
**419** *Gazzo v Comptroller of Stamps (Vic)* (1981) 149 CLR 227, 235.
**420** Ibid, 236.
**421** Ibid, 236–9.
**422** *Commonwealth v New South Wales* (1923) 33 CLR 1.
**423** *Victoria v Commonwealth* (1957) 99 CLR 575.
**424** Ibid, 614.
**425** *Gazzo v Comptroller of Stamps (Vic)* (1981) 149 CLR 227, 240. Stephen and Aickin JJ reasoned similarly at 241–4 and 264–6.

'the national Parliament, representing the whole people of Australia'.[426] According to Murphy J, this presumption of validity had recently been 'replaced ... by a presumption of invalidity' based, he argued, on nothing more than 'judicial hostility to remedial social legislation'.[427] Referring to Gibbs CJ's view that a 'close connection' must be shown between the law and the legislative head of power, Murphy J exclaimed that the 'once-discredited doctrine of reserved powers of the States' was 'having a triumphant, if unacknowledged, resurgence, at least in the areas of marriage and divorce'.[428] However, he believed that this would be only a 'transient' revival, and the doctrine would (soon) be 're-interred'.[429]

In subsequent cases, the reasoning of the majority in *Gazzo* was criticised. In *Fisher v Fisher*, Mason and Deane JJ rejected the suggestion that a 'close' connection must be established between a law and a head of power, especially when the law is within the 'central area' of the power and not something 'incidental' to it. They also said that while the decision in *Gazzo* must be 'respected' until it is overruled, they regarded its reasoning as 'fundamentally unsound'.[430] In response to this line of criticism, Gibbs CJ drew attention to the observation of Latham CJ in the *Bank Nationalisation* case that:

> [a] power to make laws with respect to a subject matter is a power to make laws which in reality and substance are laws upon the subject matter. It is not enough that a law should refer to the subject matter or apply to the subject matter ... .[431]

Pointing out that characterisation issues are always questions of degree, Gibbs CJ maintained that they depend on whether the connection between the law and the head of power is 'sufficiently close'.[432] In the *Bank Nationalisation* case, Latham CJ had considered that 'no single power should be construed in such a way as to give to the Commonwealth Parliament a universal power of legislation which would render absurd the assignment of particular carefully defined powers to that Parliament'.[433] Similar concerns have been expressed from time to time by other members of the Court. In *Koowarta v Bjelke-Petersen*, Gibbs CJ stated:

> Of course it has been established, since the *Engineers' Case* ... that it is an error to read s 107 of the Constitution, which continues the powers of the Parliaments of the States, 'as reserving any power from the Commonwealth that falls fairly within the explicit terms of an express grant in sec. 51, as that grant is reasonably construed, unless that

**426** Ibid, 252–3, citing *Federal Commissioner of Taxation v Munro* (1926) 38 CLR 153, 180.
**427** *Gazzo v Comptroller of Stamps (Vic)* (1981) 149 CLR 227, 253.
**428** Ibid, 255.
**429** Ibid, 261. Mason J agreed that the degree of connection between the law and the marriage power must be 'sufficient', rather than 'close', and affirmed that grants of Commonwealth power are to be interpreted as widely as the language used allows: 246, 248. But unlike Murphy J, his reasoning was closely tied to the previous decisions of the Court and to orthodox methods of constitutional interpretation, and he avoided any reference to the politics of the issue.
**430** *Fisher v Fisher* (1986) 161 CLR 438, 453.
**431** Ibid, 446–7, citing *Bank of New South Wales v Commonwealth* (1948) 76 CLR 1, 186.
**432** *Fisher v Fisher* (1986) 161 CLR 438, 447.
**433** *Bank of New South Wales v Commonwealth* (1948) 76 CLR 1, 184–5. See, likewise, *R v Foster* (1949) 79 CLR 43, 83.

> reservation is as explicitly stated' .... However, in determining the meaning and scope of a power conferred by s 51 it is necessary to have regard to the federal nature of the Constitution.[434]

Protests such as these have generally been to no avail, however. Although O'Connor J's statement in *Jumbunna Coal Mine* that the Court should usually lean to the 'broader interpretation' of Commonwealth power was subject to the proviso that a narrower interpretation should be preferred if the context and structure of the Constitution so required, subsequent citations and applications of his statement have often side-lined this important qualification.[435] This has been particularly apparent in the High Court's approach to the corporations and external affairs powers, discussed below.

## IV Particular legislative powers

Common law adjudication rests on the doctrine of precedent, pursuant to which judges regard themselves as bound by the *rationes decidendi* of prior decisions of superior courts. Constitutional cases in Australia usually proceed on this basis, except that the existence of the Constitution as supreme binding law leaves open the argument that a judge's highest allegiance must be to the Constitution itself. In the constitutional jurisprudence of the High Court, the doctrine of precedent has had the general effect of consolidating decisions applying expansionist techniques of interpretation to particular heads of power. This is best demonstrated by examining the evolution of the Court's interpretation of particular legislative powers. In this section, these propositions are illustrated by reference to the corporations and external affairs powers, as well as the so-called 'implied nationhood' power.

### 1 Corporations power

Section 51(xx) of the Constitution grants the Commonwealth power to make laws with respect to 'foreign corporations, and trading or financial corporations formed within the limits of the Commonwealth'. Prior to federation, each colony provided for the incorporation of joint stock companies and for the recognition of foreign corporations within its territory. While it appears that the framers of the Constitution did not consider that a general power to incorporate companies should be granted to the Commonwealth,[436] they did think that it should be

**434** *Koowarta v Bjelke-Petersen* (1982) 153 CLR 168, 199.
**435** Compare *Jumbunna Coal Mine, No Liability v Victorian Coal Miners' Association* (1908) 6 CLR 309, 367–8; *Bank of New South Wales v Commonwealth* (1948) 76 CLR 1, 332–3; *R v Public Vehicles Licensing Appeal Tribunal (Tas); Ex parte Australian National Airways Pty Ltd* (1964) 113 CLR 207, 225–6; *R v Coldham; Ex parte Australian Social Welfare Union* (1983) 153 CLR 297, 310, 314; *Grain Pool of Western Australia v Commonwealth* (2000) 202 CLR 479, 492, 521–2. An exception appears in Gibbs CJ and Dawson J's dissenting judgments in *Commonwealth v Tasmania* (1983) 158 CLR 1, 99–100, 302.
**436** *Convention Debates, Sydney* (1891) 685–6.

given power to provide for the recognition of such corporations throughout the Commonwealth and to prescribe uniform conditions upon which such corporations would be permitted to operate across State borders.[437] While the evidence from the Convention Debates is fairly meagre, the Commonwealth appears to have been given power to legislate with respect to trading, financial and foreign corporations on account of the unique regulatory issues to which such corporations characteristically give rise, particularly because corporations are artificial legal persons distinct from their directors and members, thus enabling shareholders to distance themselves from the corporation and, in the case of a limited liability company, to avoid personal responsibility for its debts and other obligations.[438] Despite the limited purposes for which s 51(xx) was included in the Constitution, in practice it has become a very significant head of power. The two most important issues to have arisen in its interpretation concern: (a) the kinds of corporations to which the power applies; and (b) the kinds of corporate activities that can be regulated. In connection with this second issue, a further important question has concerned the categories of persons other than corporations who can be regulated due to their relation to constitutional corporations. In all of these respects the Court has, over time, adopted increasingly wider views of the scope of the power.

### Types of corporations

In his dissenting judgment in *Huddart, Parker & Co Ltd v Moorehead*, Isaacs J observed that the corporations power extends only to corporations of a certain kind ('trading', 'financial' and 'foreign') and therefore 'leaves entirely outside the range of federal power' any 'domestic' corporation formed 'for municipal, mining, manufacturing, religious, scholastic, charitable, scientific, and literary purposes, and possibly others more nearly approximating a character of trading'.[439] This important observation, although it was cited recently in the *Work Choices* case,[440] has had little bearing on the Court's jurisprudence. Much of the reason for this lies in the methodology initiated by the *Engineers* case, which focuses attention not on whether the law addresses corporations that can be regarded as municipal, religious or charitable in character, but whether they can be deemed to be trading, financial or foreign corporations.

On this approach, the identification of foreign corporations has been regarded as relatively straight-forward – it depends upon the location of the jurisdiction in which the company has been incorporated.[441] However, in the case of trading

**437** *Convention Debates, Adelaide* (1897) 439.
**438** Ibid, 793–4.
**439** *Huddart, Parker & Co Pty Ltd v Moorehead* (1909) 8 CLR 330, 393–5.
**440** *New South Wales v Commonwealth* (2006) 229 CLR 1, 86. It was also cited by Menzies J in *R v Trade Practices Tribunal; Ex parte St George County Council* (1974) 130 CLR 533, 553.
**441** *New South Wales v Commonwealth* (1990) 169 CLR 482, 497–8; *Re Dingjan; Ex parte Wagner* (1995) 183 CLR 323, 365. Murphy J also expressed the idiosyncratic view that foreign corporations might include 'syndicates' and 'joint ventures' formed in overseas jurisdictions whose law of incorporation is different from Australia's: *R v Judges of the Federal Court of Australia; Ex parte WA National Football League* (1979) 143 CLR 190, 238.

and financial corporations, there are two basic alternative approaches. The first is to ascertain the character of the corporation by reference to its objectives and purposes as set out in its corporate constitution. The second is to attend to the actual activities of the corporation and to determine whether these are sufficiently 'trading' or 'financial' in character. Considered abstractly, either of these approaches might take in a large number of corporations and thus expose an array of corporations to the law-making power of the Commonwealth. However, in practice, this question of characterisation has usually arisen in cases in which the outer limits of the power are being tested, and has therefore often involved corporations formed chiefly for municipal, social or cultural purposes, and not primarily or solely to engage in profit-making trading or financial activities.

Adopting the view that the character of a corporation is to be ascertained by reference to its objectives as set out in its corporate constitution may often lead to the conclusion that a corporation is essentially municipal, social or cultural in character and is not a constitutional corporation. This was the approach adopted by a majority of the Court in the *St George County Council* case in 1974,[442] where the Court held that the Council, which had been established under the *Local Government Act 1919* (NSW), was not a 'trading corporation' within the meaning of the *Restrictive Trade Practices Act 1971* (Cth). However, if attention is focused on the practical activities in which the corporation engages, which was the approach taken by the Court in the *Western Australian Football League* case,[443] it becomes possible to conclude that a sufficiently significant proportion of a corporation's activities are trading or financial in character and that it therefore falls within the scope of the power. Indeed, this is especially the case if the Court decides, as some justices have suggested, that the trading or financial activities of the corporation need not be its 'predominant' undertaking, but merely a 'substantial' or at least a 'not insubstantial' proportion of its activities.[444] It is even more so if the Court allows the purposes and the activities tests to be used in the alternative, so that a corporation will be found to be a constitutional corporation so long as it meets the criteria either in terms of its purposes (prior to engaging in any activity) or its activities. This is the position at which the Court arrived in *Fencott v Muller* in 1983.[445]

### Types of corporate activities

As to the kinds of corporate activities that can be regulated, the text of the Constitution is again capable of several competing interpretations. One view, which was essentially that adopted in *Huddart, Parker*,[446] places emphasis upon the

**442** *R v Trade Practices Tribunal; Ex parte St George County Council* (1974) 130 CLR 533.
**443** *R v Judges of Federal Court of Australia; Ex parte Western Australian National Football League (Inc)* (1979) 143 CLR 190. See also *State Superannuation Board v Trade Practices Commission* (1982) 150 CLR 282 and *Commonwealth v Tasmania* (1983) 158 CLR 1.
**444** *R v Trade Practices Tribunal; Ex parte St George County Council* (1974) 130 CLR 533, 543; *R v Judges of Federal Court of Australia; Ex parte Western Australian National Football League (Inc)* (1979) 143 CLR 190, 234, 219, 239.
**445** *Fencott v Muller* (1983) 152 CLR 570.
**446** *Huddart, Parker & Co Pty Ltd v Moorehead* (1909) 8 CLR 330.

idea that the corporations power exists to enable the Commonwealth to address the special kinds of regulatory issues that corporations pose for government policy within a federation. Corporations are artificial legal persons, recognised by the law usually because a statute grants them legal status. Corporations are also distinct from their members or shareholders. Especially in the case of limited liability companies, the liability of the corporation to outsiders is limited to its paid-up share capital. Shareholders are able to pool their resources to achieve joint objectives, but they are also able to distance themselves from the corporation and avoid personal responsibility for its debts and other obligations. These characteristics of corporations raise distinct policy issues which give rise to special laws intended to ensure that corporations and their directors are appropriately accountable for their actions. In this context, in the case of both foreign companies and companies incorporated in a particular Australian State, there are questions about whether and, if so, on what terms and conditions their distinct legal personality and their capacity to engage in trade and commerce is to be recognised in other States.[447]

Considerations such as these led the majority of the Court in *Huddart, Parker* to settle broadly on the view that the corporations power is there to enable the Commonwealth to provide for the recognition and operation of corporations beyond their jurisdictions of origin and to place appropriate conditions upon this, such as making provision for the protection of creditors. Higgins J thus thought that legislation enacted on the basis of the corporations power would have to be directly regulative of 'corporations as corporations', with the implication that the power extends to the regulation of trading, financial and foreign corporations as to their status, the powers they may exercise, and the conditions under which they are permitted to carry on business.[448] O'Connor J similarly thought that the power might extend to prescribing the conditions under which corporations would be allowed to enter upon business within the Commonwealth.[449] Griffith CJ, with whom Barton J generally agreed, considered that the corporations power enables the Commonwealth to prohibit a trading or financial corporation from entering into a particular field of operation, and possibly also to deny such corporations capacity to engage in certain transactions.[450] In these judgments, the qualifying adjectives ('trading', 'financial' and 'foreign') were taken to indicate the types of corporations that can be the object of laws under the corporations power and to suggest reasons why they were singled out, but it was their nature as 'corporations' that carried most of the weight in the reasoning.[451]

In *Strickland v Rocla Concrete Pipes Ltd*, decided more than half a century later, this relatively narrow view of the scope of the power was rejected as

**447** See ibid, 371–3.
**448** Ibid, 412–14.
**449** Ibid, 369, 371, 373–4.
**450** Ibid, 353–4, 366.
**451** In the *Work Choices* case, much was made of differences in the precise formulations proposed by the individual justices in *Huddart, Parker*, as if this rendered the general approach somehow suspect: see *New South Wales v Commonwealth* (2006) 229 CLR 1, 79–89. Contrast, however, the observations of Rich and Williams JJ in *Bank of New South Wales v Commonwealth* (1948) 76 CLR 1, 255–6.

illegitimately founded upon the reserved powers doctrine.[452] Instead, a wider interpretation was adopted in which the reference to 'corporations' was given no real significance beyond identifying the kind of legal entity that is the object of the power, whereas the qualifying adjectives (especially 'trading' and 'financial') were given a special, additional significance.[453] In Barwick CJ's leading judgment, with whom several other justices agreed, these qualifying words were taken to indicate not only the particular kinds of corporation with which the power is concerned, but also the kinds of activities of those corporations that can be regulated under the power. Thus, it was held that the corporations power extends to the regulation of the *trading* activities of trading corporations and to the *financial* activities of financial corporations, and it does not matter if these activities are conducted on a wholly intrastate basis.[454]

*Strickland* involved the assessment of provisions of the *Trade Practices Act 1965* (Cth) which required companies to register trading agreements with the Commissioner of Trade Practices if those agreements contained terms or conditions that were restrictive of free trade. Such agreements were undoubtedly part of the trading activities of the companies.[455] However, the law was not limited in its operation to restrictive trade practices engaged in by foreign, trading and financial corporations but also applied to 'any persons carrying on businesses that are competitive with each other' (s 35). Because the law plainly applied beyond the scope of the corporations power, six members of the Court held that the law was invalid and five held, further, that the law could not be saved by the operation of s 15A of the *Acts Interpretation Act*.[456]

Although the Court thus considered that the corporations power extends, in principle, to the regulation of the trading activities of trading corporations, the justices were not willing to pronounce on what the 'outer limits' of the power might be, but rather restricted their observations to what was necessary to determine whether the particular law was constitutionally valid.[457] In subsequent cases this policy of deciding only so much as was necessary to determine the issues before the Court often meant that, while a determined minority sometimes wished to go further by way of *obiter dicta*,[458] they were often met by a countervailing majority of judges who either insisted on a narrower view or limited their decisions to the exact issues raised in each case.[459] Through the course of these

**452** *Strickland v Rocla Concrete Pipes Ltd* (1971) 124 CLR 468, 484–9, 509–11, 512, 515, 522.
**453** Ibid, 468.
**454** Ibid, 489, 499, 512, 531, 525.
**455** Ibid, 491, 512–13.
**456** Ibid, 492–9, 512–13, 515–22.
**457** Ibid, 489–91, 511, 515. See also *Actors & Announcers Equity Association of Australia v Fontana Films Pty Ltd* (1982) 150 CLR 169, 182; *Commonwealth v Tasmania* (1983) 158 CLR 1, 316.
**458** Eg, *Actors & Announcers Equity Association of Australia v Fontana Films Pty Ltd* (1982) 150 CLR 169, 207–8, 211; *Commonwealth v Tasmania* (1983) 158 CLR 1, 148–9; *Re Pacific Coal Pty Ltd; Ex parte Construction, Forestry, Mining and Energy Union* (2000) 203 CLR 346, 375.
**459** As examples of the latter, see *Actors & Announcers Equity Association of Australia v Fontana Films Pty Ltd* (1982) 150 CLR 169, 218–22; *Commonwealth v Tasmania* (1983) 158 CLR 1, 241.

decisions, three possible views emerged as to the scope of the power in relation to trading corporations: (a) it is limited to the regulation of trading activities of trading corporations; (b) it extends to activities of trading corporations engaged in for the purpose of trade; or (c) it can be used to regulate the activities of a trading corporation in any respect whatsoever.

The narrower of these views was based on the proposition, as Gibbs CJ put it in the *Actors & Announcers Equity* case, that 'the nature of the corporation to which the laws relate must be significant as an element in the nature or character of the laws'.[460] As Dawson J later explained in *Re Dingjan*: '[T]he way in which the law operates upon [a constitutional corporation] must be such that they impart their character to the law ... [T]he fact that it is a trading or financial corporation should be significant in the way in which the law relates to it'.[461] In the latter case, Gibbs CJ expressed concern that to conclude otherwise would produce the kinds of 'extraordinary consequences' that had troubled Higgins J in *Huddart, Parker*. Bearing in mind that the Constitution requires the maintenance of a 'federal balance' between the Commonwealth and the States, he maintained that the corporations power needs to be reconciled with the other limited powers conferred by s 51.[462] Nonetheless, Gibbs CJ was prepared in the *Tasmanian Dam* case to uphold a law which regulated activities undertaken by a trading corporation that were not of a trading character of themselves, but were engaged in for the purposes of engaging in trade, whereas Dawson J was not.[463]

The wider view, that the power extends to any activities of constitutional corporations, was explained by Mason J in *Actors & Announcers Equity* to rest upon the observation that s 51(xx) is a power with respect to corporations, not the activities of corporations, and that as a grant of legislative power it 'should be construed liberally and not in any narrow or pedantic fashion'.[464] Murphy J went even further, saying that the Commonwealth is empowered to make 'comprehensive laws covering all internal and external relations' of constitutional corporations, including the wages and conditions of employment of their employees, to legislate for the formation, operation and dissolution of such corporations, and to enact a comprehensive criminal and civil code dealing with the protection of such corporations, their property and their affairs, as well as protecting others in relation to them.[465]

As between these two broad views of the scope of the corporations power, the Court remained essentially divided for some time. In *Actors & Announcers*

**460** *Actors & Announcers Equity Association of Australia v Fontana Films Pty Ltd* (1982) 150 CLR 169, 182; *Commonwealth v Tasmania* (1983) 158 CLR 1, 117–19.
**461** *Re Dingjan; Ex parte Wagner* (1995) 183 CLR 323, 346. See also *Commonwealth v Tasmania* (1983) 158 CLR 1, 202.
**462** *Actors & Announcers Equity Association of Australia v Fontana Films Pty Ltd* (1982) 150 CLR 169, 182.
**463** *Commonwealth v Tasmania* (1983) 158 CLR 1, 119, 317–18; see also 202.
**464** *Actors & Announcers Equity Association of Australia v Fontana Films Pty Ltd* (1982) 150 CLR 169, 207–8; see also *Commonwealth v Tasmania* (1983) 158 CLR 1, 148–9.
**465** *Actors & Announcers Equity Association of Australia v Fontana Films Pty Ltd* (1982) 150 CLR 169, 211–12.

*Equity*, a majority upheld a provision of the *Trade Practices Act 1974* (Cth) that protected constitutional corporations from 'secondary boycotts' (action by trade unions which prevent a supplier from providing goods or services to a particular corporation). In the *Tasmanian Dam* case, a majority upheld s 10(4) of the *World Heritage Properties Conservation Act 1983* (Cth), which prohibited constitutional corporations from undertaking certain excavation or construction works within a declared 'world heritage' area, provided that the conduct was engaged in for the purposes of the corporation's trading activities.[466] In *Re Dingjan*, a narrow majority struck down s 127C(1)(b) of the *Industrial Relations Act 1988* (Cth), which effectively provided that the Industrial Relations Commission could examine an 'unfair contract' imposed upon an independent contractor in circumstances where the contract related only to the business of a constitutional corporation, and thus the connection between the law and the corporations power was too remote.[467]

The issue seems to have been resolved decisively in favour of the wider view in the *Work Choices* case in 2006. As has been seen,[468] in that case the High Court had to consider the validity of amendments to the *Workplace Relations Act 1996* (Cth) which conferred and imposed a range of powers, rights and duties upon constitutional corporations and their employees. In argument it was put to the Court that the question was whether the narrower 'distinctive character' or the wider 'object of command' test should be adopted in relation to the corporations power.[469] Appearing to accept the latter approach, a majority of the Court upheld the entirety of the *Work Choices Act*, with the result that there seems to be very little that the Commonwealth cannot do to regulate constitutional corporations, both as to their external relations and their internal affairs. Indeed, in the course of their reasoning, the majority adopted observations of Gaudron J in the *Re Pacific Coal* case where her Honour had said:

> I have no doubt that the power conferred by s 51(xx) of the Constitution extends to the regulation of the activities, functions, relationships and the business of a corporation described in that sub-section, the creation of rights, and privileges belonging to such a corporation, the imposition of obligations on it and, in respect of those matters, to the regulation of the conduct of those through whom it acts, its employees and shareholders and, also, the regulation of those whose conduct is or is capable of affecting its activities, functions, relationships or business.[470]

**466** *Commonwealth v Tasmania* (1983) 158 CLR 1. Mason, Murphy and Deane JJ were also prepared to uphold ss 10(2) and (3), which applied the prohibition without the proviso; Brennan J considered that it was unnecessary to determine the constitutionality of ss 10(2) and (3); Gibbs CJ, Wilson and Dawson JJ held that ss 10(2) and (3) were invalid.
**467** Ie, the corporation, although related in some way to the contract, was not a party to it: *Re Dingjan; Ex parte Wagner* (1995) 183 CLR 323.
**468** See Part III.2 above.
**469** *New South Wales v Commonwealth* (2006) 229 CLR 1, 103.
**470** *Re Pacific Coal Pty Ltd; Ex parte Construction, Forestry, Mining and Energy Union* (2000) 203 CLR 346, 375, cited in *New South Wales v Commonwealth* (2006) 229 CLR 1, 114–15.

## Interpretive choices

The reasoning in the majority joint judgment in *Work Choices* recapitulated several of the interpretive choices that the High Court has made in the many decided cases since *Engineers*. Thus, it was said that the Court must adhere to 'the accepted principles of constitutional interpretation established in the previous decisions of this Court'.[471] Frequently invoking the *Engineers* case,[472] the joint judgment added that the starting point in interpretation must be the 'constitutional text', rather than a view 'formed independently of that text'.[473] Criticising any attempt to divine the intentions of the framers of the Constitution as the pursuit of 'a mirage', it was observed that even if such a 'collective subjective intention' could be ascertained, it would divert attention from the real objective, which is to interpret the text 'in accordance with accepted principles'.[474] In particular, this meant that the Constitution is not to be interpreted by reference to preconceived ideas such as 'a view of the place to be accorded to the states formed independently of the text of the Constitution',[475] some 'particular division of governmental or legislative power'[476] or the proposition that the Constitution preserves some kind of 'static equilibrium' or 'federal balance'.[477] To reason in such a way, the joint judgment said, was to evoke '[m]ore than faint echoes' of reserved powers reasoning.[478] Rather, the Court should construe the text 'with all the generality which the words used admit'.[479]

In a long and erudite dissenting judgment, Callinan J cast doubt on the proposition, assumed by the majority, that there is any consistently applied method of constitutional interpretation evident in the judgments of the High Court through the course of its history.[480] In Callinan J's view, the importance of the *Engineers* case had to be acknowledged,[481] but he also pointed out that the case was 'an early instance of judicial activism' which 'does not deserve the reverence which has been accorded to it'.[482] Indeed, he pointed out that its reasoning is frequently said to be 'less than satisfactory': in certain respects it is simply 'not convincing' and in others it has been subjected to necessary 'revision' and certain 'qualifications'.[483] Noting that O'Connor J's dictum about leaning to the broader interpretation in *Jumbunna Coal Mine* was qualified by the context and purposes of the Constitution,[484] Callinan J urged that the Court should adopt an interpretation that is most in harmony with its federal origins, structure and purposes[485] – an approach which need not involve the

**471** *New South Wales v Commonwealth* (2006) 229 CLR 1, 71; see also 71–2, 97.
**472** Ibid, 71, 73, 118, 119.
**473** Ibid, 118–19; see also 89, 119, 121.
**474** Ibid, 97.
**475** Ibid, 119; see generally 118–20.
**476** Ibid, 72.
**477** Ibid, 73.
**478** Ibid, 85; see also 89, 97.
**479** Ibid, 103–4, 117.
**480** Ibid, 301–5.
**481** Ibid, 272, 350.
**482** Ibid, 308, 369.
**483** Ibid, 272, 305, 307–8.
**484** Ibid, 317, citing *Jumbunna* (1908) 6 CLR 309, 367–8.
**485** *New South Wales v Commonwealth* (2006) 229 CLR 1, 335.

assumption of some 'static equilibrium' but which is rather a result of the Court adopting an interpretation which in its judgment is most in harmony with, and will best give effect to, the Constitution's fundamental structures and underlying purposes.[486] Echoing the framers' views and the early position of the High Court, he concluded that the purpose of s 51(xx) was to 'ensure uniformity of status of corporations throughout Australia, rather than to appropriate State control over them'.[487]

For both dissenting judges, Callinan and Kirby JJ, the limits written into the industrial arbitration power (s 51(xxxv)) provided guidance for how widely the corporations power should be interpreted.[488] Kirby J especially placed emphasis on the proposition that the industrial arbitration power contains safeguards against the determination of industrial awards without there being an 'interstate' element and without the determination of an independent arbitrator.[489] To reason in this manner was to seize on what is perhaps the most important qualification on the clause-bound literalism that has generally dominated the High Court.[490] Notwithstanding these powerful counter-arguments, however, the majority of the Court decided to uphold the entirety of the *Work Choices* legislation, apparently on the ground that the Parliament can regulate constitutional corporations in any respect whatsoever, imposing duties upon them, granting rights to them and regulating the behaviour of third parties provided their actions have a sufficient connection to them.

### Incorporation of companies

The textual literalism that has so decisively shaped the High Court's approach to the Commonwealth's heads of power has in most cases advanced the cause of a broad interpretation of the Commonwealth's powers at the expense of the States. However, as has been seen,[491] where the terms of a head of power provide specific grounds for a limited interpretation, the Court has been prepared to give this effect. This is well illustrated by the Court's interpretation of the reference in s 51(xx) to trading and financial corporations that are 'formed within the limits of the Commonwealth'. Here, a clear majority of the Court has been led by the grammatical meaning of that phrase to hold that the Commonwealth does not have the capacity under the corporations power to provide generally for the legal creation of corporations. As six members of the Court observed in the *Incorporation* case, the word 'formed' is a past participle used adjectively, and is thus used to identify corporations that have been formed some time in the past. Accordingly, they held, the power with respect to corporations does not include the act of incorporation itself.[492] Indeed, drawing upon the enactment history of s 51(xx)

**486** Ibid, 317–18.
**487** Ibid, 353.
**488** Ibid, 344, 384.
**489** Ibid, 184–5, 190, 244.
**490** See Part III.2 above.
**491** See Part III.2 above.
**492** *New South Wales v Commonwealth* (1990) 169 CLR 482, 498.

as evidenced in the Convention Debates of the 1890s, the majority pointed out that the successive drafts of what became the corporations power consistently indicated an intention that the power was concerned with existing corporations, included in the Constitution to enable the Commonwealth to provide, as Samuel Griffith put it, for their 'recognition' throughout the Commonwealth.[493]

Apart from this insistence on the strict grammatical meaning of the past participle 'formed', the Court's interpretation of the corporations power has developed through successively wider approaches, taking in more and more corporations, and more and more kinds of activities and relationships within the purview of the corporations power. When the effect of these interpretations is combined, the Commonwealth is accorded a capacity to regulate vast areas of human activity, far beyond the expectations of those who framed and ratified the Constitution and, moreover, far beyond the scope of power that the voting public has been prepared to grant to the Commonwealth when proposals for the amendment of the Constitution have been submitted to referendum.[494] It is only in respect of the power to provide for the creation of corporations that a relatively narrow construction has been adopted (at least for the time being).[495] Yet even this particular limited interpretation functions to highlight the wide reading of the corporations power adopted in all other respects, for it underscores the idea that the Commonwealth's power with respect to constitutional corporations deals with them as *objects* of plenary legislative power.

## 2 External affairs power

Much the same thing has happened in relation to the external affairs power (s 51(xxix)). As conceived at the time of federation, this head of power was understood to be part of a series of provisions by which the Commonwealth was given control over external matters (eg, defence, aliens, immigration, naturalisation, customs, trade with other countries) while the States would retain substantial control over their own internal domestic affairs. Indeed, Samuel Griffith suggested that giving the Commonwealth responsibility for external affairs would free the States to focus on matters of greatest concern to their respective communities:

> The attention of the [State] Parliaments and Governments, no longer distracted by the necessity of dealing with external affairs, would be more freely directed to those matters which are of such a nature that legislation and administration with respect to them can exercise a direct influence, beneficial or injurious, upon the community. It

**493** Ibid, 501–3, citing *Convention Debates, Sydney* (1891) 686. This citation of Griffith's views recalls the original conception of the corporations power, to which the majority judges in *Huddart, Parker & Co Pty Ltd v Moorehead* (1909) 8 CLR 330 sought to give effect. For it was in *Huddart, Parker* that the Court first indicated, consistent with the framers' prevailing understanding of the matter, that the corporations power does not extend to the incorporation of companies: *Huddart, Parker*, 354, 362, 371, 393–4.
**494** Constitution Alteration (Legislative Powers) Bill 1910; Constitution Alteration (Industrial Matters) Bill 1912; Constitution Alteration (Industry and Commerce) Bill 1926, discussed in *New South Wales v Commonwealth* (2006) 229 CLR 1, 99–101, 187, 284–301.
**495** Note the dissenting judgment of Deane J in *New South Wales v Commonwealth* (1990) 169 CLR 482.

> has been said ... that the Colonies would be little better than glorified municipalities. This is not true ... . Indeed, a moment's consideration of the subjects reserved to the States affords a sufficient answer to the objection. ... There would still be a wide field for the exercise of political ability in State affairs ... .[496]

Quick and Garran said of the external affairs power that it 'may hereafter prove to be a great battleground', and Harrison Moore regarded the power to be a 'somewhat dark one'.[497] In making these statements, the question they had principally in mind was not about the balance between Commonwealth and State responsibilities, but how far the Commonwealth would have power to conduct a foreign policy and legislate with extra-territorial effect within the context of the British Empire. This reflected the general interest of the framers in securing the benefits and privileges of local self-government and constitutional self-determination – for the Commonwealth vis-à-vis the Empire and for the States vis-à-vis the Commonwealth.[498]

On Quick and Garran's view, the external affairs power was chiefly concerned with the representation of the Commonwealth in international affairs, the conduct of the business and promotion of the interests of the Commonwealth in outside countries, and the extradition of fugitive offenders from other countries.[499] Although at the time the British Government retained ultimate control over entry into international treaties on behalf of the Empire, self-governing colonies such as Canada were allowed to participate actively in the negotiation of treaties affecting their interests. Quick and Garran anticipated that Australia would enjoy the same privileges with respect to the formation of treaties and that the Parliament would have authority either to ratify or refuse to confirm them, such as by legislating to provide for the extradition of criminals in accordance with treaties entered into formally by the British Government. It thus seems that it was recognised that the external affairs power included a capacity to make laws giving effect to international treaties, the only qualification being that the Commonwealth would not have independent power to enter treaties itself.[500] However, as Harrison Moore also argued at the time, the power to implement treaties was 'limited to matters which *in se* concern external relations' because 'a matter in itself purely domestic and therefore within the exclusive power of the States, cannot be drawn within the range of federal power merely because some arrangement has been made for uniform national action'.[501]

**496** Samuel Griffith, *Notes on Australian Federation: Its Nature and Probable Effects* (Edmund Gregory, Government Printer, 1896) 30–31.
**497** Quick and Garran, above n 17, 631; W Harrison Moore, 'The Constitution of the Commonwealth of Australia' (1900) 16 *Law Quarterly Review* 35, 39.
**498** Eg, John Quick, *A Digest of Federal Constitutions* (J B Young, 1896) 10; Richard Baker, *Federation* (Scrymgour and Sons, 1897) 7–8; John Cockburn, *Australian Federation* (Horace Marshall and Son, 1901) 169. See, further, Aroney, above n 2, ch 11.
**499** Quick and Garran, above n 17, 632–7.
**500** This was reflected in the fact that an earlier version of the head of power referred to 'external affairs and treaties', but the latter term was apparently removed due to the inability of the Commonwealth to enter treaties: *Convention Debates, Sydney* (1897) 239–40; *Convention Debates, Melbourne* (1898) 30–31.
**501** W Harrison Moore, *The Constitution of the Commonwealth of Australia* (Maxwell, 2nd ed, 1910) 461–2.

The application of international law in Australia is dependent upon the rules of common law and statute.[502] In many countries today, as at an earlier time in England, international treaties apply directly as part of the domestic legal system.[503] However, the position in Australian law, at least since the time of federation, is that while the capacity to enter into international treaties is an aspect of the prerogatives of the Crown, such treaties have no domestic effect as law without the sanction of implementing legislation. Indeed, as will be seen in Chapter 4, the 'supremacy' clause in the *Commonwealth of Australia Constitution Act 1900* (UK) (cl 5) was amended to remove any suggestion that international treaties might be directly and automatically binding within Australia. In accordance with this general outlook, in *Brown v Lizars*,[504] an early case concerning the arrest of a person alleged to have committed a felony in another country, the High Court held that the only powers of arrest that can exist in Australia are those specifically conferred by statute. As Griffith CJ made clear, this rule protects the personal liberties of individuals from arrest and extradition except as authorised by municipal law, the substantive content of which prescribes certain 'precautions to be taken to prevent unwarrantable interference with individual liberty'.[505] This concern to maintain a proper separation of the power of the Executive to enter treaties and the power of the Parliament to legislate has fortified the High Court in insisting that the content of an international treaty, no matter how salutary, will not ordinarily enter Australian law directly, but only through legislative implementation.[506] Thus, although individual justices have referred to the role that international human rights law *ought* to play within the Australian legal system,[507] the Court as a whole has resisted the suggestion that Australian law, including the Constitution, should be interpreted in a manner consistent with international human rights law,[508] except in certain limited circumstances in relation to the exercise of the executive power.[509]

The capacity of the Australian Commonwealth Government to enter into treaties took some time to develop. On the eve of federation, it was acknowledged that the capacity to enter treaties was vested solely in the Imperial Government, although the practice of the Imperial authorities was to consult with self-governing colonies that would be affected by a proposed treaty and to include in such treaties a clause enabling them to adhere to them voluntarily.[510] Over time, Australia assumed international personality, evidenced by its being

**502** *Chow Hung Ching v R* (1948) 77 CLR 449, 478–9.
**503** Compare *Triquet v Bath* (1764) 3 Burr 1478; 97 ER 936 and *Walker v Baird* (1892) AC 491.
**504** (1905) 2 CLR 837.
**505** Ibid, 852.
**506** On the importance of legislative implementation, see Chapter 4, Part II.1.
**507** *Gerhardy v Brown* (1985) 159 CLR 70, 125.
**508** Compare *Chu Kheng Lim v Minister for Immigration, Local Government and Ethnic Affairs* (1992) 176 CLR 1, 38; *Kruger v Commonwealth* (1997) 190 CLR 1, 70–71; *Kartinyeri v Commonwealth* (1998) 195 CLR 337, 417–18, 386; *AMS v AIF* (1999) 199 CLR 160, 180; *Al-Kateb v Godwin* (2004) 219 CLR 562, 589–95, 622–9.
**509** *Minister for Immigration and Ethnic Affairs v Teoh* (1995) 183 CLR 273, 286–92; *Re Minister for Immigration and Multicultural Affairs; Ex parte Lam* (2003) 214 CLR 1, 27–34.
**510** *Victoria v Commonwealth (Industrial Relations Act)* (1996) 187 CLR 416, 476–7.

a signatory to the *Treaty of Versailles* in 1919, as well as developments noted in Chapter 1 such as the making of the Balfour Declaration in 1926 and the enactment of the *Statute of Westminster 1931* (UK). As Barwick CJ later pointed out:

> Whilst the new Commonwealth was upon its creation the Australian colony within the Empire, the grant of the power with respect to external affairs was a clear recognition, not merely that, by uniting, the people of Australia were moving towards nationhood, but that it was the Commonwealth which would in due course become the nation state, internationally recognized as such and independent. The progression from colony to independent nation was an inevitable progression, clearly adumbrated by the grant of such powers as the power with respect to defence and external affairs. Section 61, in enabling the Governor-General as in truth a Viceroy to exercise the executive power of the Commonwealth, underlines the prospect of independent nationhood which the enactment of the Constitution provided. That prospect in due course matured, aided in that behalf by the Balfour Declaration and the Statute of Westminster and its adoption.[511]

The content of the Commonwealth's undoubted legislative power to implement international treaties has inevitably grown as a consequence of these developments.[512] It is also often observed that the scope of the external affairs power with respect to the implementation of treaties has grown as the number and content of those treaties has expanded.[513] As Sir Robert Menzies once pointed out:

> When the draftsmen of the Constitution wrote down the magic words 'external affairs', there did not leap into their minds any vision of the complex and novel things that were to come many years later. Least of all could they have imagined a comprehensive world organisation of which Australia would be a member, that there would be an International Labour Organisation, or that the political stuff of 19th century treaties would largely have substituted for it the bargaining of merchants, of exporters and importers, agreements in the fields of health and science, the literally hundreds of matters engaging our attention and turning our eyes out to other lands and other peoples.[514]

But while the power of the Commonwealth to implement treaties under the external affairs power has never seriously been doubted,[515] it remained for some time a real question whether the legislative power of the Commonwealth to implement treaties could expand as indefinitely as the content of the treaties themselves.

In *R v Burgess*, the Court had to consider the constitutionality of regulations made under the *Air Navigation Act 1920* (Cth) which gave effect to the *Convention Relating to the Regulation of Aerial Navigation* (1919).[516] As such, the case

**511** *New South Wales v Commonwealth (Seas & Submerged Lands)* (1975) 135 CLR 337, 373.
**512** On the power, see *McKelvey v Meagher* (1906) 4 CLR 265, 286; *Roche v Kronheimer* (1921) 29 CLR 329, 338–9.
**513** Eg, *Koowarta v Bjelke-Petersen* (1982) 153 CLR 168, 227; *Victoria v Commonwealth (Industrial Relations Act)* (1996) 187 CLR 416, 478–80.
**514** Robert Menzies, *Central Power in the Australian Commonwealth: An Examination of the Growth of Commonwealth Power in the Australian Federation* (Cassell & Company Ltd, 1967) 116.
**515** On the power, see *McKelvey v Meagher* (1906) 4 CLR 265, 286; *Roche v Kronheimer* (1921) 29 CLR 329, 338–9.
**516** *R v Burgess; Ex parte Henry* (1936) 55 CLR 608.

concerned the domestic implementation of a treaty the subject matter of which was itself external in character, namely international air navigation. All members of the Court considered that a law that appropriately implements a treaty of this kind is in principle constitutional and that it was not for this reason strictly necessary in the case to determine the outer bounds of the power. Nonetheless, relying on the rejection of reserved powers reasoning in the *Engineers* case,[517] a majority of Latham CJ, Evatt and McTiernan JJ expressed the view that the external affairs power is not limited to the implementation of treaties dealing with external matters: it extends, they said, to the implementation of international treaties no matter what their subject matter.[518] Indeed, Evatt and McTiernan JJ said that it even included the implementation of recommendations and draft conventions made by international organisations such as the International Labour Organisation.[519] Starke and Dixon JJ, on the other hand, while they agreed that the Act itself, in authorising the making of regulations to implement the treaty, was validly enacted under the external affairs power, suggested there were limits on the scope of the implementing power. Starke J said that the treaty might have to concern matters of 'sufficient international significance to make it a legitimate subject of international co-operation and agreement', and Dixon J proposed that the subject matter would have to be 'indisputably international in character'.[520] As Dixon J put it:

> [I]t seems an extreme view that merely because the Executive Government undertakes with some other country that the conduct of persons in Australia shall be regulated in a particular way, the legislature thereby obtains a power to enact that regulation although it relates to a matter of internal concern which, apart from the obligation undertaken by the Executive, could not be considered as a matter of external affairs.[521]

Whatever view was taken of the scope of the power, all justices except Starke J held that the regulations were, in fact, beyond power because they were not 'in conformity' with the specific terms of the treaty.[522] As Dixon J put it, the regulations needed to be 'reasonably incidental to carrying out and giving effect to the convention'.[523] In effect this meant that the mere existence of a treaty on some topic does not give the Commonwealth general power to legislate with respect to that topic.

Although a majority in *Burgess* endorsed a wide view of the treaty aspect of the external affairs power, in the ensuing years members of the High Court expressed various degrees of hesitancy about the wider views expressed by Latham CJ, Evatt and McTiernan JJ.[524] It was not until two cases decided in 1982 and 1983 that the issue was squarely addressed and resolved. In the first

**517** Ibid, 680; see also 639.
**518** Ibid, 640–45, 687. The exact intent of Latham CJ's judgment is not entirely clear, however. See, eg, *Commonwealth v Tasmania* (1983) 158 CLR 1, 297.
**519** *R v Burgess; Ex parte Henry* (1936) 55 CLR 608, 687.
**520** Ibid, 658, 669.
**521** Ibid, 669.
**522** Ibid, 645–55, 673–5, 687–8.
**523** Ibid, 673. On the validity of the amended regulations, see *R v Poole; Ex parte Henry (No 2)* (1939) 61 CLR 634.
**524** Eg, *Airlines of New South Wales Pty Ltd v New South Wales (No 2)* (1965) 113 CLR 54, 85, 125–6, 152–3; *New South Wales v Commonwealth (Seas and Submerged Lands)* (1975) 135 CLR 337, 390, 450, 470.

of these, *Koowarta v Bjelke-Petersen*, the High Court had to consider the validity of the *Racial Discrimination Act 1975* (Cth). Section 9 of the Act prohibited any person from doing any act:

> involving a distinction, exclusion, restriction or preference based on race, colour, descent or national or ethnic origin which has the purpose or effect of nullifying or impairing the recognition, enjoyment or exercise, on an equal footing, of any human right or fundamental freedom in the political, economic, social, cultural or any other field of public life.

Section 12 of the Act, among other things, prohibited any person from 'refusing or failing to dispose of any estate or interest in land ... to a second person ... by reason of the race, colour or national or ethnic origin of that second person'. The Act was enacted to implement Australia's obligations under the *International Convention on the Elimination of All Forms of Racial Discrimination* (1966), Art 2 of which requires parties to the Convention to 'prohibit and bring to an end, by all appropriate means, including by legislation as required by circumstances, racial discrimination by any persons, group or organization'. The case arose when the Minister for Lands in Queensland refused to approve the transfer of a leasehold interest in Crown land to the Aboriginal Development Commission, a body established under Commonwealth legislation to assist communities of Aboriginal people to acquire land, engage in business enterprises and obtain finance for housing and other personal needs. The Minister refused approval on the ground of a State government policy opposed to the acquisition of 'large areas of additional freehold or leasehold land for development by Aborigines or Aboriginal groups in isolation'.

A majority of the Court upheld the *Racial Discrimination Act* on the ground that it was a valid implementation of Australia's obligations under the Convention. Mason, Murphy and Brennan JJ did so on the very wide view of the external affairs power that had been endorsed by the majority in *Burgess*, whereas Stephen J upheld the law on the somewhat narrower view that the subject matter of the treaty, racial discrimination, had become of sufficient international concern to make it a part of Australia's external affairs. Gibbs CJ, Aickin and Wilson JJ dissented on the ground that racial discrimination was not in itself a matter of international character and therefore not a topic in respect of which the Commonwealth has power to make laws under the external affairs power. Between these differing conclusions were divergent views about how the Commonwealth's legislative powers should be interpreted. Mason J emphasised that the external affairs power is comprehensive and plenary in nature and serves the important purpose of enabling the Commonwealth to implement its international obligations in a coherent way, avoiding the fragmentation, indecision and confusion that would occur if implementation were dependent upon State cooperation.[525] Drawing attention to the rejection of the reserved powers doctrine in *Engineers*, it would be a fallacy, he said, to interpret Commonwealth

**525** *Koowarta v Bjelke-Petersen* (1982) 153 CLR 168, 224–5, 229.

powers with a view to preserving State powers.[526] Murphy J put it even more bluntly when he said that the State's contentions in favour of the narrower view of the power were 'a hardly disguised representation of the State reserved powers doctrine'.[527] In his view, Australia would become an 'international cripple unable to participate fully in the emerging world order' if such submissions were to be accepted.[528] In considering the narrower tests that had been suggested in previous decisions, Mason J further considered that the very existence of international treaties, especially multilateral treaties brought into existence under the auspices of the United Nations, suggests that their subject matter is of international concern and therefore an external affair.[529] Brennan J, although in some respects more reserved, reasoned similarly when he said that the creation of an international obligation through a treaty 'stamps' the subject of the obligation 'with the character of an international affair', and that to try to identify some further 'international' or 'external' quality in an international treaty would be an act of 'supererogation'.[530]

In his dissenting judgment, Gibbs CJ (with whom Aickin and Wilson JJ agreed)[531] observed that the challenged provisions of the law operated entirely within Australia, indeed within one State, and concerned matters which in themselves involved no relationship with other countries or their inhabitants.[532] If the Commonwealth Parliament can make laws to carry into effect any treaty which the Executive might make, it would enable the Executive by its own act to 'determine the scope of Commonwealth power'.[533] Especially if the very wide view endorsed by Evatt and McTiernan JJ were to be adopted, it would be impossible, he added, 'to envisage any area of power which could not become the subject of Commonwealth legislation'. The Commonwealth would, in other words, acquire 'unlimited legislative power', the distribution of powers 'could in time be completely obliterated' and the 'federal balance … entirely destroyed'.[534] Reasoning in this way raised the question whether this was to invoke the reserved powers doctrine in disguise, as Murphy J had suggested. But although, as Gibbs CJ conceded, it was no longer legitimate to read s 107 as reserving particular powers to the States, it remained appropriate to have regard to the federal nature of the Constitution when interpreting the Commonwealth's legislative powers. Adopting an oft-cited dictum of Latham CJ, he observed that 'no single power should be construed in such a way as to give to the Commonwealth Parliament a universal power of legislation which would render absurd the assignment of particular carefully defined powers to that Parliament'.[535] For Gibbs CJ, a law giving effect

**526** Ibid, 227.
**527** Ibid, 241.
**528** Ibid.
**529** Ibid, 229–30.
**530** Ibid, 257–60.
**531** Ibid, 243, 244.
**532** Ibid, 192.
**533** Ibid, 198.
**534** Ibid.
**535** Ibid, 199, citing *Bank of New South Wales v Commonwealth* (1948) 76 CLR 1, 184–5.

to an international agreement will only be a valid exercise of the external affairs power if the subject matter of the agreement can be described as an external affair, such as by involving Australia's relationship with other countries or with persons or things outside Australia.[536]

In support of this general approach, Wilson J drew on an analysis undertaken by Stephen J in the *Seas and Submerged Lands Act* case of the distinction between Australia's external sovereignty vis-à-vis other countries and the division of sovereignty within Australia between the Commonwealth and the States.[537] On this analysis, while the Commonwealth is fully competent to engage in international relationships in exercise of its external sovereignty, the distribution of sovereign legislative power within Australia between the Commonwealth and the States may make the Commonwealth 'unable by its own laws to implement treaty obligations'.[538] This, Wilson J acknowledged, may make the conduct of foreign affairs more complex than in a unitary state, but such is the nature of federalism: it divides power; it does not consolidate sovereignty in one person or institution.[539]

In his decisive concurring judgment, Stephen J also acknowledged the important role that the federal division of power must play in the construction of the external affairs power. Adopting a position not unlike Starke J's in *Burgess*, his Honour recognised as legitimate the concern that the legislative powers of the Commonwealth be interpreted in the context of the federal nature of the Constitution, including the 'carefully limited' legislative powers that are conferred upon the Commonwealth Parliament and the risk that the capacity of the Executive to conclude treaties on any subject matter that it thinks fit could erode the residuary legislative powers of the States to the point of their 'extinction' altogether.[540] This gave the Court good reason to limit its reasoning in *Koowarta* to the 'highest common factor' evident in the decided cases,[541] while recognising that 'external affairs', like 'defence', is 'a fixed concept with a changing content', depending on what is generally regarded by the international community as a matter of international concern.[542] On Stephen J's analysis, however, racial discrimination *had* become a matter of international concern and was thus a proper subject for legislation under the external affairs power.[543] This led his Honour to uphold the legislation, albeit on a more limited basis than the other members of the majority. Significantly, the criterion of international concern as expounded by Stephen J was not necessarily limited to the content of formal international treaties – he also considered that some

**536** *Koowarta v Bjelke-Petersen* (1982) 153 CLR 168, 201–2.
**537** Ibid, 249, citing *New South Wales v Commonwealth (Seas & Submerged Lands)* (1975) 135 CLR 337, 451–5.
**538** *Koowarta v Bjelke-Petersen* (1982) 153 CLR 168, 249.
**539** Ibid, 249–51, drawing attention to *Attorney-General (Canada) v Attorney-General (Ontario)* [1937] AC 326, and the German *Concordat* case (1957) 6 BVerfGE 309.
**540** *Koowarta v Bjelke-Petersen* (1982) 153 CLR 168, 212–13.
**541** Ibid.
**542** Ibid, 218, citing *Australian Textiles Pty Ltd v Commonwealth* (1945) 71 CLR 161, 178.
**543** *Koowarta v Bjelke-Petersen* (1982) 153 CLR 168, 217–20.

issues, such as racial discrimination, slavery and genocide, have become part of customary international law and for that reason alone are topics upon which the Commonwealth may legislate, for failure by a nation to take action to suppress them will affect its relations with other countries.[544]

The strict *ratio decidendi* of *Koowarta* is difficult to identify. While a majority upheld the law, the reasons varied as between the wide view of Mason, Murphy and Brennan JJ and the middle view of Stephen J. Moreover, from the point of view of those disposed to regard the federal considerations adduced by the minority and Stephen J as compelling, it could be pointed out that a majority of the Court had actually rejected the wide view of the power. However, in the *Tasmanian Dam* case, decided in the very next year,[545] a decisive though close majority of four justices settled upon the wide view of the power. The case concerned provisions of the *World Heritage Properties Conservation Act 1983* (Cth) which purported to implement Australia's obligations under the *World Heritage Convention* (1972) to protect items and places of cultural and natural heritage. Notably, the Convention contained a 'federal' clause which provided that where the subject matter of the Convention falls within the jurisdiction of the constituent states of a federation, the obligation of the federal government is limited to informing and recommending to the states the adoption of the convention provisions.

In 1982, three national parks in Tasmania were upon nomination by the Commonwealth included in the World Heritage List, bringing them under the terms of the Convention. A year later, the Commonwealth enacted the *World Heritage Properties Conservation Act*. Section 6(2) of the Act authorised the Governor-General to make a proclamation for the protection of property to which one or more of the following applied: (a) the property was submitted for inclusion in the World Heritage list; (b) its protection or conservation was a matter of international obligation under the Convention or otherwise; (c) its protection or conservation was necessary or desirable to give effect to the Convention or for the purpose of Australia obtaining an advantage or benefit under the Convention; (d) its protection or conservation was a matter of international concern; or (e) its protection or conservation was a matter peculiarly appropriate to be safeguarded by the Commonwealth as the national parliament and government of Australia. Each of these grounds of proclamation was designed to pick up alternative bases upon which the Commonwealth might be able to legislate, several involving the external affairs power. In relation to any proclaimed property, s 9(1) of the Act made it unlawful, among other things, for a person to: (a) carry out excavation works; (c) erect a building or substantial structure; (e) kill, cut down or damage any tree; (f) construct any road or vehicular track; (g) use explosives on the property; or (h) do a proscribed act in relation to particular property. One of these specifically proscribed acts was to carry out works for the construction of a dam causing inundation of the protected property.

**544** Ibid, 220–21.
**545** *Commonwealth v Tasmania* (1983) 158 CLR 1.

The case arose when, in response to a decision taken by the Tasmanian Government to construct a dam on the Gordon-below-Franklin River within the World Heritage listed area, the Governor-General, acting on the advice of the Commonwealth Government, issued a proclamation that the Act applied to the area intended for the construction of the dam. In the result, Mason, Brennan and Deane JJ specifically held that s 6(2)(b), which authorised the proclamation of an area where its protection or conservation was a matter of international obligation under the Convention, was authorised by the external affairs power. They formed a majority on this point with Murphy J, who upheld all of s 6(2) except para (e).[546] Moreover, of these judges, only Mason and Murphy JJ upheld the entirety of s 9(1) as a valid implementation of the treaty, whereas Brennan and Deane JJ found that all of the provisions of s 9(1) except paragraph (h) were invalid because they were not proportionate implementations of Australia's obligations under the Convention. Further, for their part, Gibbs CJ, Wilson and Dawson JJ held that ss 6 and 9 were not authorised by the external affairs power in their entirety. As a consequence, only ss 6(2)(b) and 9(1)(h) were affirmatively upheld by a majority of the Court, but these, along with other provisions that were upheld,[547] were sufficient to prevent construction of the dam.

The reasoning on both sides of the issue was largely similar to that in *Koowarta*. Gibbs CJ, Wilson and Dawson JJ regarded themselves as bound by the authority of the earlier decision and considered that the judgment of Stephen J represented the authoritative statement of principle as far as the general scope of the treaty aspect of the power was concerned. As Gibbs CJ and Dawson J observed, a majority of four justices had in *Koowarta* considered that the federal nature of the Constitution required the wide view of the power to be rejected.[548] On the basis of Stephen J's test, Gibbs CJ, Wilson and Dawson JJ held that it had not been established that the protection of natural heritage areas was a matter of international concern, understood in the sense that it must be of such significance that it could affect Australia's relations with other countries,[549] especially when compared with the degree of evident concern about such matters as racial discrimination, slavery and genocide.[550]

Mason J also treated Stephen J's 'international concern' test as representing the binding content of the decision in *Koowarta*.[551] But he considered that if a topic is the subject of an international agreement, it necessarily is of international concern and international in character.[552] In his reasoning, the fact that there are virtually no limits to the topics that might be subjects of international co-operation and agreement suggested, not that the treaty implementation power

**546** In relation to the paragraphs that were not specifically upheld, individual justices either found them unconstitutional or considered it unnecessary to decide their constitutionality.
**547** These were s 69 of the *National Parks and Wildlife Conservation Act 1975* (Cth) and s 10(4) of the *World Heritage Properties Conservation Act 1983* (Cth): *Commonwealth v Tasmania* (1983) 158 CLR 1, 59.
**548** *Commonwealth v Tasmania* (1983) 158 CLR 1, 98–100, 301.
**549** Ibid, 100–01, 187, 305.
**550** Ibid, 101–2, 194, 310.
**551** Ibid, 122.
**552** Ibid, 125; see also 218–19.

must be limited, but that there is no stable criterion by which topics falling within and without the constitutional power can be distinguished.[553] He also rejected the 'federal balance' argument on the ground that it confused the constitutional distribution of powers with the content of the powers distributed as understood in 1900.[554] Rather, the power was to be interpreted with all the generality that the words used admit.[555] Brennan J agreed, observing that arguments from the 'federal balance' confused 'the political rhetoric of States' rights with the constitutional question of Commonwealth legislative powers the measure of which at any time is not referable to the powers previously exercised by the States'.[556] Murphy J was especially emphatic about his rejection of these kinds of arguments, which he again associated with the reserved powers doctrine.[557] Rather, a 'presumption of validity' should apply to Acts of Parliament, which he characterised as expressions of the 'authentic ... will of the people through their elected representatives'.[558] And in a revealing comment, Deane J dismissed the argument that a wide view of the power was not consonant with what the Constitution was intended to achieve on the basis that this was to take a position 'unduly harsh in its assessment of the foresight of the architects of our nation'.[559] Intended ironically, Deane J's remark reveals his own assessment that the framers would have been short-sighted if they had not given the Commonwealth sufficient power to participate fully in international affairs and to implement international treaties through legislation.

Given these strong views, did the majority consider that there are any limits to the treaty aspect of the power? Ignoring the view that the Court should avoid articulating unnecessarily broad statements of principle, Murphy J affirmed that the external affairs power not only extends to discharging the Commonwealth's treaty obligations and obtaining benefits under treaties, but also to responding to international recommendations or requests, and that expressions of international concern, although not always necessary, are sufficient to ground the power.[560] Even if there is no treaty, he said, the preservation of the world's heritage would still be a part of Australia's external affairs.[561] Deane J similarly considered the power embraced the 'assertion of rights and the discharge of obligations under both treaties and customary international law', and that 'responsible conduct of external affairs in today's world will ... require observance of the spirit as well as the letter of international agreements, compliance with recommendations of international agencies and pursuit of international objectives which cannot be measured in terms of binding obligation'.[562] The other

**553** Ibid, 124–5.
**554** Ibid, 126–7.
**555** Ibid, 127–8.
**556** Ibid, 222.
**557** Ibid, 168–70.
**558** Ibid, 161.
**559** Ibid, 255, citing *Convention Debates, Sydney* (1891) 14.
**560** *Commonwealth v Tasmania* (1983) 158 CLR 1, 170–72.
**561** Ibid, 174.
**562** Ibid, 258–9.

members of the majority were somewhat more circumspect, however. Mason J agreed that the treaty aspect of the power could embrace both the implementation of obligations and the securing of benefits.[563] However, both Mason and Brennan JJ limited their decisions to upholding s 6(2)(b) (relating to treaty obligations), considering it unnecessary to determine the constitutionality of the other paragraphs of s 6(2).[564]

All of the majority justices considered that the Commonwealth law in some sense had to conform to or implement the treaty.[565] Murphy J considered that there is no need for any rigid adherence to the terms of the treaty; the law need only be capable of being reasonably regarded as appropriate in the circumstances, and he upheld the entirety of the law without detailed explanation.[566] Mason J thought that it was sufficient that the law constituted a means to effectuate an end or purpose which is in power, even though its reach was 'wide' and its impact 'severe'.[567] However, Brennan J insisted that the power is to make laws which are really conducive to the purpose, not merely those thought by the Commonwealth to be so,[568] and Deane J similarly thought that there must be a 'reasonable proportionality' between the law and its purpose,[569] tests which they applied stringently to the legislation. As a consequence, in their view, only paragraph (h) of s 9(1) of the Act was sufficiently well proportioned to be valid.[570]

The *Tasmanian Dam* case represents one of the more remarkable examples of how the methods of interpretation settled upon by the Court have generally underwritten an ever-expanding scope of legislative power for the Commonwealth. In *Burgess*, Dixon J had remarked that 'the limits of the power can only be ascertained authoritatively by a course of decision in which the application of general statements is illustrated by example'.[571] However, Wilson J noted in the *Tasmanian Dam* case that there was so much open-ended *obiter dicta* in the cases that he felt constrained to make some general observations about the proper interpretation of the power.[572] Asking what significance would remain for the States if a great many of their traditional functions became the responsibility of the Commonwealth, he maintained that survival of the 'indissoluble federal Commonwealth' established by the Constitution was at stake.[573]

The wide view of the treaty aspect of the external affairs power endorsed in *Tasmanian Dam* has been accepted as authoritative ever since. In *Richardson v Forestry Commission*, while Dawson J adhered to the dissenting views he

**563** Ibid, 123–4, 129–30.
**564** Ibid, 143, 235–6.
**565** Ibid, 131–2, 138–9, 172, 259.
**566** Ibid, 172, 179.
**567** Ibid, 138–9.
**568** Ibid, 231.
**569** Ibid, 260.
**570** Ibid, 236–8, 265–8.
**571** *R v Burgess; Ex parte Henry* (1936) 55 CLR 608, 669.
**572** *Commonwealth v Tasmania* (1983) 158 CLR 1, 196–7; see also 306.
**573** Ibid, 197.

had articulated in *Tasmanian Dam*,[574] he recognised the important role of the doctrine of precedent in contributing to the consistency and coherence of the Court's judgments, as well as the rule that the Court had adopted that leave is required before the correctness of a previous decision can be re-argued. While the Court is not bound by its previous decisions, because the parties had not sought leave to question *Tasmanian Dam* he thought it proper to proceed on the assumption that the case was authoritative.[575] In the *Industrial Relations Act* case, five justices in a joint judgment likewise rejected the argument that the *ratio* of *Tasmanian Dam* could be restricted to Stephen J's narrower test.[576]

These more recent cases have generally turned, not on the scope of the treaty aspect of the external affairs power, but on the application of the proportionality requirement.[577] In these cases, as in *Tasmanian Dam*, the rigour with which the proportionality test is applied has generally been decisive. Thus, in *Richardson*, a majority of Mason CJ, Brennan, Wilson, Dawson and Toohey JJ were prepared to uphold a law which temporarily prohibited a range of works occurring in the Lemonthyme and Southern Forests of Tasmania, whereas Deane and Gaudron JJ, applying the proportionality test more stringently, considered the prohibitions to be disproportionate.[578] In the *Industrial Relations Act* case, the majority affirmed the possibility that an international treaty, though dealing with matters of international concern, may contain provisions that are so indefinite and aspirational that they lack the required specificity to enable an assessment to be made as to whether a Commonwealth law implements an international obligation. This, as Deane J had noted in *Tasmanian Dam*, is however a question of degree, and an absence of precision does not necessarily indicate an absence of obligation.[579] Nonetheless, the Court held in the *Industrial Relations Act* case that certain new provisions of the *Industrial Relations Act 1988* (Cth) were not proportional. The relevant international treaty required that the employment of a worker must not be terminated unless there is a 'valid reason' for such termination 'connected with the capacity or conduct of the worker or based on the operational requirements' of the business. However, the relevant provision of the Act not only prohibited termination of a person's employment without a 'valid reason', but added that this would occur where, having regard to the employee's 'capacity and conduct', the termination was 'harsh, unjust or unreasonable'. Here the disproportionality arose because the 'harsh, unjust or unreasonable' requirement was considered to impose an additional element that went beyond the terms of the treaty.[580]

**574** *Victoria v Commonwealth* (1996) 187 CLR 416, 564–9.
**575** *Richardson v Forestry Commission* (1988) 164 CLR 261, 320–2, citing *Queensland v Commonwealth* (1977) 139 CLR 585 and *Evda Nominees Pty Ltd v Victoria* (1984) 154 CLR 311.
**576** *Victoria v Commonwealth* (1996) 187 CLR 416, 484–5. The argument was based on the assumption that the protection of the world's natural heritage had in fact become a matter of international concern. The case is further discussed in Chapter 4, Part III.3.
**577** See Part III.2 above.
**578** See, eg, *Richardson v Forestry Commission* (1988) 164 CLR 261, 347.
**579** *Victoria v Commonwealth* (1996) 187 CLR 416, 486–7, citing *Commonwealth v Tasmania* (1983) 158 CLR 1, 260–61.
**580** *Victoria v Commonwealth* (1996) 187 CLR 416, 517–8. See also *R v Tang* (2008) 237 CLR 1, upholding provisions of the *Criminal Code Act 1995* (Cth) prohibiting slavery.

The wide view of the treaty aspect of the external affairs power needs to be understood in the context of two other important aspects. The external affairs power has been held to support laws enacted to preserve Australia's relations with other countries, such as laws prohibiting within Australia seditious activity and terrorist activity against other countries.[581] The power has also been held to extend to 'matters, things or persons' physically external to Australia without, a majority has held, any need for a connection or relationship to Australia to be demonstrated, even though the power refers to 'external affairs', not 'external matters'.[582] The Court has upheld laws dealing with Australia's territorial sea,[583] shipwrecks,[584] regions of the continental shelf between Australia and other countries,[585] and crimes perpetrated overseas.[586]

## 3 Implied nationhood power

As a result of the application of expansionist techniques of interpretation to the heads of power referred to in ss 51 and 52 of the Constitution, the Commonwealth has gradually acquired, directly or indirectly, a capacity to regulate or affect the regulation of almost anything that any government in Australia might wish to address. The corporations and external affairs powers, considered alongside the grants power in s 96, illustrate this capacity very clearly, as the number and reach of Commonwealth laws and grants made in reliance on these powers amply show. On the whole, it is only considerations of policy and expediency which dissuade or prevent Commonwealth governments from successfully proposing the enactment of many more laws reaching into all manner of fields not mentioned explicitly in ss 51 or 52 of the Constitution, such as transportation, education, hospitals and policing; and even in these areas the Commonwealth regularly finds ways of influencing and shaping the regulatory terrain when considered politically desirable and achievable. Individual judges of the Court on occasion protest against these developments, such as the dissenting judgments of Dawson J in the *Industrial Relations Act* case and Callinan J in the *Work Choices* case, but the Court as a whole has for the most part upheld and supported the gradual expansion of Commonwealth power and influence.

**581** *R v Sharkey* (1949) 79 CLR 121, 136–7, 149, 157, 163, discussed further below. See also *Kirmani v Captain Cook Cruises Pty Ltd (No 1)* (1985) 159 CLR 351, 439, in relation to the repeal of provisions of the *Merchant Shipping Act 1894* (UK) in their application with respect to Australia; and *Thomas v Mowbray* (2007) 233 CLR 307, 364, in relation to interim control orders over persons engaged in certain terrorist activities.
**582** See the dissenting judgments in *Polyukhovich v Commonwealth* (1991) 172 CLR 501, 552, 653–5, and in *XYZ v Commonwealth* (2006) 227 CLR 532, 591–4.
**583** *New South Wales v Commonwealth (Seas & Submerged Lands)* (1975) 135 CLR 337, 360, 470–71, 497–8, 502–4.
**584** *Robinson v Western Australian Museum* (1977) 138 CLR 283, 294–5, 335, 342, 343.
**585** *Horta v Commonwealth* (1994) 181 CLR 183.
**586** *Polyukhovich v Commonwealth* (1991) 172 CLR 501, 530–31, 602, 634, 696, 714. See also *R v Hughes* (2000) 202 CLR 535, 556, upholding a law extending to offences in respect of acts perpetrated overseas; and *XYZ v Commonwealth* (2006) 227 CLR 532, 538–9, 546, 575, upholding a law prohibiting Australian citizens or residents from engaging in sexual intercourse or acts of indecency with persons under the age of 16.

As argued in this chapter, much of the basis for these developments in the jurisprudence of the High Court is its application of a special kind of clause-bound textualism to the interpretation of most of the heads of power in s 51 of the Constitution. But that is not all. The apotheosis of Commonwealth power is the suggestion, now sanctioned by the Court, that the Commonwealth also possesses legislative and executive powers that are said to be implied by its status as the 'national government' of the country. On this basis, it is has been held that the Commonwealth may legislate for the celebration of nationally significant events such as the bicentenary of British settlement in 1988,[587] and in order to respond to national and international emergencies, such as the global financial crisis of 2007–8.[588] There has also been the suggestion that it includes an inherent power to protect and control the marginal seas, seabed, airspace and continental shelf and incline.[589]

A version of the so-called 'implied nationhood' power was first articulated in apparently benign form in *R v Kidman* in 1915. In upholding a law that retrospectively made it an offence to defraud the Commonwealth, Isaacs J considered that the express power to make laws with respect to 'matters incidental to the execution of any power vested by the Constitution … in the Government of the Commonwealth … or in any department or officer of the Commonwealth' (s 51(xxxix)) needed to be understood on the basis that when such power is granted it by implication includes 'every ancillary power that is necessary to the existence of the Government, and the proper exercise of the direct power it is intended to execute'.[590] Noting, however, that such ancillary powers must be 'truly "incident"', he adopted the view that the implied powers possessed by the Government and its departments and officers are 'protective and self-defensive powers only' and do not include any power to impose punishments.[591] If criminal sanctions were to be imposed for interference or attempted interference with the active operation of some Commonwealth function or activity, the Commonwealth would have to rely on its express incidental legislative power in s 51(xxxix)), he maintained.[592]

This view was generally followed and somewhat extended in *Burns v Ransley* and *R v Sharkey*.[593] In the first of these cases it was held that the Parliament may make laws under the express incidental power 'to protect and maintain' the Government and its departments and officers 'in the execution of their powers', not only through laws responding to threats of physical attack and interference, but also the utterance of words intended to excite disaffection against Australia's governing institutions or to prevent or impede the operation of government

**587** *Davis v Commonwealth* (1988) 166 CLR 79.
**588** *Pape v Commissioner of Taxation* (2009) 238 CLR 1.
**589** *New South Wales v Commonwealth (Seas & Submerged Lands)* (1975) 135 CLR 337, 373–5.
**590** *R v Kidman* (1915) 20 CLR 425, 440. See also *Ex parte Walsh and Johnson; In re Yates* (1925) 37 CLR 36, 94; *R v Hush; Ex parte Devanny* (1932) 48 CLR 487, 506.
**591** *R v Kidman* (1915) 20 CLR 425, 440, citing *Barton v Taylor* (1886) 11 App Cas 197, 203.
**592** *R v Kidman* (1915) 20 CLR 425, 441–2.
**593** *Burns v Ransley* (1949) 79 CLR 101; *R v Sharkey* (1949) 79 CLR 121.

agencies.[594] In the course of his reasoning in *Burns v Ransley*, Dixon J suggested that because the Constitution anticipates its amendment only 'by laws adopted peaceably by the appropriate legislative authority', a power to preserve the institutions established by the Constitution from violent subversion 'follows almost necessarily'.[595] In *Sharkey*, it was clarified that this legislative power extends to the protection and maintenance of the entire 'legal and political organization of the Commonwealth', including not only Australia's institutions of government, but also the person of the Sovereign, and the Government, Constitution and Houses of Parliament of the United Kingdom.[596] In his concurring judgment in that case, Dixon J further suggested that the Commonwealth possesses an implied legislative power to prohibit any utterance or publication that arouses resistance, excites insurrection or is reasonably likely to cause discontent with and opposition to the enforcement of federal law and the operation of the federal government. This, he said, 'arises out of the very nature and existence of the Commonwealth as a political institution'.[597] As significant as this power was, however, it was not unlimited. Thus, his Honour considered that the power did not extend to prohibiting utterances intended to promote 'feelings of ill-will and hostility' among individuals within the Commonwealth largely because none of the express legislative powers of the Commonwealth concern such matters as freedom of expression, public order and control over the liberty of the subject.[598] Nor, he said, could the express incidental power support a law dealing with matters 'prima facie within the province of the States' in circumstances where the connection with Commonwealth power is 'only tenuous, vague, fanciful or remote'.[599]

Illustrating the limits of the implied power, in the *Communist Party* case a majority considered that there was an insufficient connection between the Commonwealth's express incidental and implied powers to protect and maintain the Commonwealth and the *Communist Party Dissolution Act 1950* (Cth), largely because the Act, unlike the legislation in *Burns v Ransley* and *Sharkey*, did not prohibit specific conduct found to be prejudicial to the existence of the Commonwealth.[600] Significantly, Dixon J pointed out that the Australian system of government may need protection not only from external threats but also from dangers 'likely to arise' from within the institutions of government themselves, and that the Commonwealth's implied powers of self-protection should not therefore extend to empowering the Executive Government itself to exercise an

**594** *Burns v Ransley* (1949) 79 CLR 101, 109–10, 111, 116. Dixon J (at 115) explained that 'disaffection' means 'an estrangement upon the part of the subject in his allegiance which has not necessarily gone as far as an overt act of a treasonable nature or an overt breach of duty. It supposes that the loyalty and attachment to Authority, upon which obedience may be considered to depend, is replaced by an antagonism, enmity and disloyalty tending to make government insecure'.
**595** Ibid, 116.
**596** *R v Sharkey* (1949) 79 CLR 121, 135–6, 148–9, 163.
**597** Ibid, 148.
**598** *R v Sharkey* (1949) 79 CLR 121, 150–51, citing the limited terms of ss 51(vi) (defence) and 119 (protection of the States from invasion and domestic violence upon request by a State).
**599** Ibid, 151; contra 135–6, 157–8, 163, 259–61, 266.
**600** *Australian Communist Party v Commonwealth* (1951) 83 CLR 1, 192–4, 211–12, 231.

'unexaminable' power on the basis of some 'vague formula' of liability contained within legislation.[601]

In other more recent cases, the High Court has expanded the idea of an inherent power of self-protection and preservation into the notion that the Commonwealth has implied power to engage in undertakings appropriate to its character as a 'national government'. As explained in Chapter 7, these developments initially occurred in the context of Commonwealth laws authorising the appropriation of moneys from consolidated revenue to particular purposes as required by ss 81 and 83 of the Constitution. In the earliest of these, the *Pharmaceutical Benefits* case, Starke J seemed to refer relatively restrictively to a power arising by implication of the establishment of the Commonwealth as a 'Federal Government', while Dixon J described it more generally as a power that is 'incidental to existence of the Commonwealth as a state and to the exercise of the functions of a national government'.[602] In the *Australian Assistance Plan* case, Mason J suggested that the existence of the Commonwealth as a national government, considered with ss 51(xxxix) and 61, implied a capacity to engage in 'enterprises and activities peculiarly adapted to the government of the nation and which cannot otherwise be carried on for the benefit of the nation'.[603] But while Mason J also cautioned against too wide a view of the implied executive power,[604] Jacobs J went so far as to suggest that 'the complexity and values of a modern national society result in a need for co-ordination and integration of ways and means of planning for that complexity and reflecting those values'.[605] On the basis of these views, Barwick CJ, Jacobs and Mason JJ considered that among the powers inherent in the 'fact of nationhood' was the power to engage in what were described as 'exploratory' tasks, understood both as physical exploration of the wider world and more metaphorically in the form of scientific investigation through organisations such as the CSIRO.[606]

These ideas came to even fuller fruition in *Davis v Commonwealth*[607] and *Pape v Commissioner of Taxation*.[608] The first of these cases upheld in principle the capacity of the Commonwealth to legislate for the commemoration of the Bicentenary in 1988 even though, remarkably, it was the bicentenary of the settlement of the colony of New South Wales, not the establishment of the Commonwealth, that was being celebrated. In *Pape*, the implied nationhood principle was used (although not altogether in name) to support the making of fiscal stimulus payments to taxpayers as a response, it was said, to the global financial crisis. While the implied nationhood power was not held to support aspects

**601** Ibid, 187–8.
**602** *Attorney-General (Vic); Ex rel Dale v Commonwealth* (1945) 71 CLR 237, 266, 269–70.
**603** *Victoria v Commonwealth and Hayden* (1975) 134 CLR 338, 397; see also 405–6: 'all matters which are the concern of Australia as a nation'.
**604** Ibid, 398.
**605** Ibid, 412.
**606** Ibid, 361–2. The Commonwealth Scientific and Industrial Research Organisation (CSIRO) is established under the *Science and Industry Research Act 1949* (Cth).
**607** (1988) 166 CLR 79.
**608** *Pape v Commissioner of Taxation* (2009) 238 CLR 1, discussed further in Chapter 7, Part IV.1.

of the environmental legislation in the *Tasmanian Dam* case, Deane J went so far as to suggest that not only would the implied power almost certainly apply in areas where 'there is no real competition with the States'; it could even apply within fields 'under active State legislative and executive control', at least where they 'involve no competition with State authority'.[609] However, Wilson J sounded a strong note of caution in relation to the power, when he pointed out that the enactment of a coercive law on the basis of the implied nationhood power would be 'wholly subversive of the Constitution' and flatly contrary to the principle that the Commonwealth Parliament is meant to be a legislature of strictly 'specific' powers precisely because the Constitution provides for a federal commonwealth, not a unitary nation-state.[610]

## V Conclusions

When the people of the Australian colonies agreed in the late 1890s to unite in a federal commonwealth, they agreed to the establishment of a federal government of limited powers. The early High Court, under the leadership of Sir Samuel Griffith, interpreted the Constitution in a way that gave effect to this idea of a federal commonwealth formed on the basis of the consent of the people of the constituent States, principally through the doctrines of reserved powers, pith and substance, and immunity of instrumentalities. However, under the intellectual leadership of Sir Isaac Isaacs, in the *Engineers* case of 1920 the Court departed from this federal vision in favour of a more nationalistic conception which understood the Constitution fundamentally as a statute of the British Parliament.[611] Since then, several techniques of constitutional interpretation have contributed to an inexorable expansion in the scope of Commonwealth power as exercised by the Parliament and approved by the High Court. These techniques have included a flexible approach to the characterisation of federal laws, a clause-bound approach to the interpretation of most federal heads of legislative power, and the rejection of the proposition that consideration should be given to the extent of the powers retained by the States or the maintenance of a 'federal balance' between the Commonwealth and the States.[612] When particular heads of power are examined, a ratchet effect is also often in play, as relatively expansionist interpretations become accepted by a majority of the Court and become locked in as the established jurisprudence of the Court as a result of the doctrine of precedent.[613]

Some exceptions to these trends do exist in the case-law, but they are few and far between. One such exception is the willingness of the Court occasionally

**609** *Commonwealth v Tasmania* (1983) 158 CLR 1, 252–3.
**610** Ibid, 203–4.
**611** See Part III.1 above.
**612** See Part III.2 above.
**613** See Part IV above.

to attend to limits written explicitly into the terms of a particular head of power, such as the limitation of the 'trade and commerce' power to its 'interstate' aspects, and the limitation of the corporations power to corporations already 'formed' within the Commonwealth. Another exception occurs when a head of power is defined by reference to an unlimited class which is then qualified by a negative proviso (eg, 'banking, other than State banking'), or when a head of power is qualified by a condition that involves a benefit or a protection for those affected by the law (eg, 'acquisition of property … on just terms').[614] In these types of cases, the Court has been willing to find that the limitations written into these heads of power place limits on the scope of other heads of power. Apart from these exceptions, however, the High Court has generally interpreted the Commonwealth's legislative powers as widely as the language used can possibly sustain, without limiting this by reference to the evident intent of the framers that the Commonwealth was to be a government of enumerated and limited powers, in order to leave room for the States to continue to operate as self-governing political communities, each possessing a substantial and independent capacity to regulate its own affairs.

But this need not be so. Indeed, some very recent developments, in particular the Court's decisions in the two *Williams* cases,[615] suggest the possibility that the Court may be willing to reconsider its approach to the Constitution, at least to some extent. The first *Williams* case was concerned primarily with the scope of the executive power of the Commonwealth.[616] In deciding that the Commonwealth's executive power did not include an inherent general capacity to contract and spend money, the Court drew attention to the federal character of the Constitution as an important reason for reading the executive power as limited. French CJ went so far as to begin his judgment with a quotation from Andrew Inglis Clark to the effect that the whole purpose of the Constitution was to establish 'a truly federal government', the 'essential and distinctive feature' of which would be 'the preservation of the separate existence and corporate life of each of the component States of the Commonwealth' while at the same time securing the capacity of the Commonwealth to operate as a real 'government', whose laws would be enforced directly and effectively in each State.[617] Moreover, his Honour went on to cite an observation of Alfred Deakin that '[a]s a general rule, wherever the executive power of the Commonwealth extends, that of the States is correspondingly reduced'.[618]

**614** See Part III.2 above.
**615** *Williams v Commonwealth (No 1)* (2012) 248 CLR 156; *Williams v Commonwealth (No 2)* (2014) 309 ALR 41; 88 ALJR 701.
**616** See the discussion of the case in Chapter 7, Part IV.2.
**617** *Williams v Commonwealth (No 1)* (2012) 248 CLR 156, 178, citing Andrew Inglis Clark, *Studies in Australian Constitutional Law* (Charles F Maxwell, 1901) 12–13.
**618** *Williams v Commonwealth (No 1)* (2012) 248 CLR 156, 178, citing Alfred Deakin, 'Channel of Communication with Imperial Government: Position of Consuls: Executive Power of Commonwealth', in Patrick Brazil and Bevan Mitchell (eds), *Opinions of Attorneys-General of the Commonwealth of Australia, Volume 1: 1901–14* (Australian Government Publishing Service, 1981) 129, 132.

Whether this apparent solicitude for the position States might have wider consequences remains to be seen, but it is remarkable that in the second *Williams* case a large majority of the Court struck down a critical aspect of the legislation hurriedly enacted by the Commonwealth to provide legal authority for the funding of its very numerous spending projects, including the National School Chaplaincy program that had been challenged in the first *Williams* case.[619] The Commonwealth argued that the remedial legislation, in its application to the Chaplaincy program, was authorised by s 51(xxiiiA) of the Constitution, which confers power to make laws with respect to the 'provision' of a range of social security benefits, including 'sickness and hospital benefits' and 'benefits to students'. In previous cases, the Court had held that s 51(xxiiiA) authorised legislation for the provision of payments to alleviate the 'human wants' of persons that arise from the specific circumstances or condition in which they find themselves, such as the provision of specifically identifiable sickness and hospital benefits given to particular patients.[620] Remarkably, in *Williams (No 2)* the majority treated the criteria set down in these cases as definitive of the scope of the 'benefits' power, notwithstanding the fact that the term 'benefits' could have been interpreted more widely, in accordance with its 'natural meaning', to encompass the provision of some 'advantage or good' generally.[621] This relatively restrictive interpretation, based on the limited reasoning of the previous cases, proved decisive in the case because the 'benefits' provided to students through the Chaplaincy program did not provide 'material aid' for the 'human wants' of students; it did not provide such aid for 'any identified or identifiable student'; and it was not directed to the 'consequences of being a student'.[622]

The *Williams* cases show that it remains open to the Court to adopt an approach to the interpretation of Commonwealth powers that pays attention to the federal context and nature of the Constitution. How significant these cases will prove to be in the long run remains an open question.

**619** *Financial Framework Legislation Amendment Act (No 3) 2012* (Cth), s 32B.
**620** *Williams v Commonwealth (No 2)* (2014) 309 ALR 41; 88 ALJR 701, citing *British Medical Association v Commonwealth* (1949) 79 CLR 201 and *Alexandra Private Geriatric Hospital Pty Ltd v Commonwealth* (1987) 162 CLR 271.
**621** *Williams v Commonwealth (No 2)* (2014) 309 ALR 41; 88 ALJR 701.
**622** Ibid, [47]. The Court also placed limits on the scope of the 'implied nationhood' power that were advanced by the Commonwealth in the case, and affirmed the importance of recognising 'federal' limits on the scope of the Commonwealth's executive power. See *Williams v Commonwealth (No 2)* (2014) 309 ALR 41; 88 ALJR 701, 715–16.

# 4

# Demarcations of power

*When a law of a State is inconsistent with a law of the Commonwealth, the latter shall prevail, and the former shall, to the extent of the inconsistency, be invalid.*[1]

*The foundation of the Constitution is the conception of a central government and a number of State governments separately organized. The Constitution predicates their continued existence as independent entities.*[2]

## I Introduction

The Australian Constitution is primarily concerned with establishing the political institutions necessary for the founding of a federation of six constituent States. Many of the provisions of the Constitution are therefore directed to defining the nature and composition of those institutions and conferring positive powers and functions upon them. As seen in Chapters 2 and 3, the two essential means by which this was achieved were: the construction of a Parliament consisting of two houses representing the people of the Commonwealth and the people of the States (ss 7 and 24); and the conferral of specific legislative powers on the Commonwealth with a guarantee that the Constitutions and general powers of the States would continue subject to the Constitution (ss 51, 52, 106 and 107). The establishment of a federation on this basis meant the Commonwealth and the States would operate as partly independent, partly interdependent, self-governing political communities.

To facilitate the consistent and coherent operation of the federal system as a whole, the jurisdiction of the Commonwealth and the States had to be constitutionally regulated. This required not only the conferral and maintenance of positive powers of legislation, administration and adjudication upon the Commonwealth (ss 1, 61 and 71), but also the imposition of various constraints and limits on those powers, as well as on the powers of the States. On the whole, these constraints were shaped by federal considerations of one kind or another. Considerations of the rights of citizens were not primarily in view, largely

**1** Commonwealth Constitution, s 109.
**2** *Melbourne Corporation v Commonwealth* (1947) 74 CLR 31, 82.

because it was thought that appropriately operating systems of representative and responsible government at a Commonwealth and State level would, on the whole, provide adequate protection.[3]

The most fundamental limitation of power imposed by the Constitution concerns the demarcation of the legislative powers of the Commonwealth and the States. Here the basic principle is that the concurrent powers of the Commonwealth Parliament are limited to particular topics (s 51), but within those fields the laws of the Commonwealth prevail over any inconsistent laws of the States (s 109). As seen in Chapter 3, the limited nature of the Commonwealth's legislative powers is a very important principle of Australian constitutional law, although the High Court has found ways to interpret the Constitution to enable the Commonwealth to legislate over a very wide range of matters. One of the central objectives of this chapter is to show how the High Court has similarly interpreted s 109 in a way that enables the Commonwealth to displace State laws to a very considerable extent.[4]

Even if the Commonwealth and the States operate within their respective jurisdictions, there is potential for their laws to interfere with each other. In order to limit the extent to which this can occur, the Constitution contains several more specific limitations on the legislative powers of the Commonwealth and the States.[5] Some of these provisions protect the Commonwealth and the States from mutual interference, while others concern relationships between the States themselves. Only a relatively small number safeguard the rights of individuals, and even those rights that are constitutionally protected usually have some sort of federalism rationale underlying or shaping them. The particular limits on power and rights that are protected in the Constitution unavoidably deal with issues and concerns that were current when the Constitution was being debated and drafted. Not all are as pressing today as they were then, but they were the necessary conditions of a freely-negotiated federal compact.

As will be seen in this and the next chapter, the application of the various explicit provisions limiting governmental power often turns on questions of interpretation and characterisation similar to those that arise in relation to the Commonwealth's legislative powers discussed in Chapter 3. In addition to these explicit limitations on power, the High Court has held there are other limitations that are implications of the Constitution's text and structure, understood in the light of its underlying principles and overarching purposes. These implied limitations raise questions about how they are properly derived from the Constitution and what specific guidance its text and structure can provide for their application to particular cases.

This chapter focuses on the two most important forms of demarcation of power between the Commonwealth and the States: first, the resolution of

**3** For more detail, see Chapter 5, Part I.

**4** See Part II below.

**5** The legislative power of the Commonwealth is 'subject to' the Constitution (s 51), as is the continuing operation of the State constitutions (s 106).

inconsistent Commonwealth and State laws (s 109) and, second, the implied principle that the Commonwealth and the States cannot interfere with performance of each other's essential constitutional functions. Before undertaking a close examination of these matters, it is helpful, however, to have a more detailed appreciation of the many specific demarcations and limitations on Commonwealth and State power to which reference has been made.

## 1 Commonwealth and State protections

Several of the limiting provisions contained in the Constitution protect the States from discrimination by the Commonwealth. Thus, as was noted in Chapter 3, the power of the Commonwealth Parliament to make laws with respect to 'taxation' cannot be exercised so as 'to discriminate between States or parts of States' (s 51(ii)). Similarly, the Commonwealth cannot, by any law or regulation of trade, commerce or revenue, give preference to one State or any part of a State over another State or part thereof (s 99).[6] In addition, some heads of Commonwealth legislative power cannot be exercised without the consent of the State or States concerned. These requirements enable each State to be the guardian of its own interests. Examples of this kind of restriction can be found in the Commonwealth's legislative powers with respect to the acquisition of the railways of a State (s 51(xxxiii)), railway construction and extension in a State (s 51(xxxiv)),[7] matters referred to the Commonwealth Parliament by a State or States (s 51(xxxvii))[8] and the exercise in Australia of powers which at the establishment of the Constitution could only be exercised by the British Parliament or the Federal Council of Australasia (s 51(xxxviii)).[9]

Several related provisions are directed to the protection of the property and territory of the States. Thus, while the Commonwealth is empowered to make laws with respect to the acquisition of the property of a State, it can only do so on just terms (s 51(xxxi)).[10] The Parliament of a State may also voluntarily surrender territory to the Commonwealth, which upon acceptance by the Commonwealth has the effect that the territory becomes subject to the exclusive jurisdiction of the Commonwealth (s 111). The Commonwealth may also make laws for the government of any territory surrendered by any State, and may allow the representation of such territories in either house of the Commonwealth Parliament to the extent and on the terms which it thinks fit (s 122).[11] Again, the limits or boundaries of a State can be altered by the Commonwealth

**6** See *Elliott v Commonwealth* (1936) 54 CLR 657; *Federal Commissioner of Taxation v Clyne* (1958) 100 CLR 246; *Fortescue Metals Group Ltd v Commonwealth* (2013) 300 ALR 26.
**7** *Australian National Airways Pty Ltd v Commonwealth* (1945) 71 CLR 29, 59.
**8** *Graham v Paterson* (1950) 81 CLR 1; *R v Public Vehicles Licensing Appeal Tribunal (Tas); Ex parte Australian National Airways Pty Ltd* (1964) 113 CLR 207; *Thomas v Mowbray* (2007) 233 CLR 307.
**9** *Port Macdonnell Professional Fishermen's Association Inc v South Australia* (1989) 168 CLR 340; *Sue v Hill* (1999) 199 CLR 462; *Attorney-General (WA) v Marquet* (2003) 217 CLR 545.
**10** See Chapter 5, Part II.
**11** See Chapter 2, Part II.2.

Parliament, but only with the consent of the Parliament of the State concerned (s 123). Similarly, a new State may be formed by separation of territory from a State, but only with the consent of the Parliament thereof; and a new State may be formed by the union of two or more States or parts of States, but again only with the consent of the Parliaments of the States involved (s 124). Consistent with these provisions, in relation to the establishment of the Australian Capital Territory, although the Constitution stipulated the general location and size of the seat of government of the Commonwealth, it affirmed that the territory for the seat of government would have to be duly granted to or acquired by the Commonwealth from New South Wales (s 125).[12] Yet because the Constitution is primarily concerned with setting out the terms of union between the constituent States, once such territories are acquired by the Commonwealth they come under its direct jurisdiction and do not enjoy the same level of protection as the States.[13] The Constitution also contains provisions dealing with the transfer of officers and property of each State in connection with the departments of the public service of each State that were to be transferred to the Commonwealth (ss 84 and 85). The property of both the Commonwealth and the States is also protected from the imposition of taxes by the other (s 114) – a provision that has received a moderately narrow interpretation.[14]

Two provisions of the Constitution provide for the regulation of legal relations among the States themselves. One highly complex section empowers the Commonwealth to forbid certain forms of preference or discrimination by any State in relation to railways (s 102).[15] Another practically more significant section requires full faith and credit to be given throughout the Commonwealth to the laws, public acts and records, and judicial proceedings of every State (s 118).[16] There are also several provisions directed to protecting the people of each State from action by the Commonwealth or by another State. The Commonwealth is prohibited from using any law or regulation of trade or commerce to abridge the rights of any State or the residents of a State to the reasonable use of waters of rivers for conservation or irrigation (s 100).[17] Also relevant here is the prohibition on the Commonwealth from making any law for establishing any religion, imposing any religious observance or prohibiting the free exercise of any religion, and the stipulation that no religious test can be required as a

**12** On ss 111, 122–5, see *Paterson v O'Brien* (1978) 138 CLR 276; *Capital Duplicators Pty Ltd v Australian Capital Territory* (1992) 177 CLR 248; *Re Governor, Goulburn Correctional Centre; Ex parte Eastman* (1999) 200 CLR 322, discussed in Chapter 2, Part II.2.

**13** Nonetheless, the High Court has found that some of the general constitutional limits on the powers of the Commonwealth apply to its legislative powers with respect to Territories: see *Lamshed v Lake* (1958) 99 CLR 132; *Spratt v Hermes* (1965) 114 CLR 226; *Wurridjal v Commonwealth* (2009) 237 CLR 309, discussed in Chapter 5, Parts II.1–2 and IV.2.

**14** *Queensland v Commonwealth (First Fringe Benefits)* (1987) 162 CLR 74; *Deputy Commissioner of Taxation v State Bank of New South Wales* (1992) 174 CLR 219; *South Australia v Commonwealth* (1992) 174 CLR 235.

**15** See *Riverina Transport Pty Limited v Victoria* (1937) 57 CLR 327, 354–5.

**16** *John Pfeiffer Pty Ltd v Rogerson* (2000) 203 CLR 503. See, further, James Stellios, 'Choice of Law and the Australian Constitution: Locating the Debate' (2005) 33 *Federal Law Review* 7.

**17** *Commonwealth v Tasmania* (1983) 158 CLR 1. See, further, Paul Kildea and George Williams, 'The Constitution and the Management of Water in Australia's Rivers' (2010) 32 *Sydney Law Review* 595.

qualification for any office or public trust under the Commonwealth (s 116).[18] A further provision protects the residents of one State from discriminatory action taken by another State: a subject of the Queen resident in one State cannot be subject in any other State to any disability or discrimination which would not be equally applicable to him if he were a subject of the Queen resident in such other State (s 117).[19]

## 2 Protection of an integrated economy

Several other generally protective provisions, limiting both the Commonwealth and the States, are directed to the creation within Australia of an integrated economy. Indeed, the establishment of a free trade zone uniting all of the States was one of the primary goals of federation.[20] The central provision is s 92, which provides that 'trade, commerce and intercourse' among the States must be 'absolutely free'. This section has functioned as a very significant limitation on the powers of the Commonwealth and the States.[21] Section 92 did not come into operation, however, until after the imposition of uniform duties of customs by the Commonwealth, which occurred on 8 October 1901 in accordance with s 88. The guarantee of freedom of interstate trade, commerce and intercourse was thus integrated with the intention that the Commonwealth would have exclusive power over the imposition of customs duties and excise duties, and over the granting of bounties on the production or export of goods (s 90),[22] which was also a fundamental goal of federation.[23] However, bearing in mind that customs and excise duties were very significant sources of revenue for the Australian colonies, jurisdiction over them was only gradually transferred to the Commonwealth over a ten-year period and was subject to the States retaining certain rights to such revenue during that interim period (ss 86–89, 92–94).[24] Indeed, reflecting the origin of the Constitution in a negotiated bargain between the States, special provision was made allowing Western Australia to impose customs duties for a period of five years after the imposition of uniform customs duties by the Commonwealth (s 95). The Constitution also guarantees the States a continuing right to grant aid to or provide bounties on mining for gold, silver or other metals and, with the consent of the Commonwealth Parliament, to grant aid to or provide bounties on the production or export of goods (s 91).[25] The States are entitled to impose charges for the inspection of goods passing

**18** See Chapter 5, Part IV.
**19** *Street v Queensland Bar Association* (1989) 168 CLR 461; *Goryl v Greyhound Australia Pty Ltd* (1994) 179 CLR 463; *Sweedman v Transport Accident Commission* (2006) 226 CLR 362.
**20** *Federal Convention, Sydney* (1891) 23.
**21** Section 92 is discussed in detail in Chapter 5, Part III.
**22** See *Ha v New South Wales* (1997) 189 CLR 465.
**23** *Federal Convention, Sydney* (1891) 23.
**24** See Cheryl Saunders, 'The Hardest Nut to Crack' in Greg Craven (ed), *The Convention Debates 1891–1898* (Legal Books, 1987) vol VI, 149.
**25** *Seamen's Union of Australia v Utah Development Co* (1978) 144 CLR 120; *Fortescue Metals Group Ltd v Commonwealth* (2013) 300 ALR 26.

into or out of each State, albeit that the net produce of all such charges must be for the use of the Commonwealth and any such inspection laws can be annulled by the Commonwealth (s 112). Also, to meet the concern that these arrangements might detrimentally affect the financial capacities of the States, there is provision for the Commonwealth Parliament to grant financial assistance to any State on such terms and conditions as the Parliament thinks fit (s 96), as well as to take over the public debts of the States (s 105; see also s 105A). It is an indication of the extent to which a constitutional provision can be interpreted to have an effect that departs markedly from the expectations of its framers, that s 96 has been used by the Commonwealth not only to make grants to the States but to impose terms and conditions on such grants so as to gain effective policy-making influence over virtually any subject matter that it wishes, including such fundamentally State functions as taxation, education, health, transport and environment.[26]

Finally, several provisions in the Constitution are in the form of duties cast upon the Commonwealth or the States to perform cooperative functions. It was noted in Chapter 3 that the Commonwealth's legislative power with respect to 'defence' is directed to the military and naval defence not only of the Commonwealth but also of the several States (s 51(vi)). In addition, the Commonwealth is obliged to protect every State against invasion and, on the application of the Executive Government of a State, against domestic violence (s 119). In turn, each State is required to make provision for the detention in its prisons of persons accused or convicted of offences against the laws of the Commonwealth, and for the punishment of persons convicted of such offences, and the Commonwealth is empowered to make laws to give effect to this (s 120).[27] In addition, there is a complex body of law dealing with the extent of the capacity of the Commonwealth and the States to pool their constitutional powers in order to establish cooperative regimes or enterprises.[28]

## 3 Limits on legislative, executive and judicial power

Notwithstanding the fact that several of these provisions have proven to be practically unimportant as the circumstances and conditions of Australian government and society have developed over time, their combined effect has been far-reaching. In combination with the principle of the supremacy of validly enacted Commonwealth law over State law and the implied intergovernmental immunities doctrine, they collectively demarcate the jurisdictional limits of the

**26** *Victoria v Commonwealth* (1926) 38 CLR 399; *Deputy Federal Commissioner of Taxation v W R Moran Pty Ltd* (1939) 61 CLR 735; *South Australia v Commonwealth* (1942) 65 CLR 373; *Victoria and New South Wales v Commonwealth* (1957) 99 CLR 575. See, further, Cheryl Saunders, 'Towards a Theory for Section 96 – Parts I and II' (1988) 16 *Melbourne University Law Review* 1 and 699.
**27** *R v Turnbull; Ex parte Taylor* (1968) 123 CLR 28, 37; *Leeth v Commonwealth* (1992) 174 CLR 455, 479.
**28** See *R v Duncan; Ex parte Australian Iron and Steel Pty Ltd* (1983) 158 CLR 535; *Re Wakim; Ex parte McNally* (1999) 198 CLR 511; *R v Hughes* (2000) 202 CLR 535. See Chapter 8, Part IV.6.

Commonwealth and the States in a manner that enables both to function as partly independent, partly interdependent self-governing bodies politic. While many are principally directed to placing constraints on the exercise of legislative power, some are expressed in a way that suggests that they apply (directly or indirectly) to any exercise of governmental power, whether legislative, executive or judicial. For this reason, an understanding of the demarcations and limitations of power discussed in this and the next chapter requires a working understanding of the nature of executive and judicial power under the Australian Constitution. For that working knowledge, the reader is referred to the introductory explanations of legislative, executive or judicial contained in Chapter 1 and the detailed accounts in Chapters 6, 7, 8 and 9. Limitations and demarcations of power are discussed at this point in the book due to their special relationship to legislative power and the important role that they play, together with the distribution of legislative power discussed in Chapter 3, in contributing to the effective operation of the federation as a system of demarcated powers and responsibilities.

The remainder of this chapter accordingly focuses upon two of the most important demarcating constitutional principles, namely:

- inconsistency between Commonwealth and State laws (s 109); and
- intergovernmental immunities (implied).

In turn, Chapter 5 discusses the following important constitutional limitations and freedoms:

- acquisition of property on just terms (s 51(xxxi));
- freedom of interstate trade, commerce and intercourse (s 92);
- religious freedom and non-establishment of religion (s 116); and
- freedom of political communication (implied).

## II Inconsistency between Commonwealth and State laws

### 1 Constitutional supremacy

Section 109 is the primary provision of the Constitution which deals with inconsistency between Commonwealth and State laws. It provides:

> When a law of a State is inconsistent with a law of the Commonwealth, the latter shall prevail, and the former shall, to the extent of the inconsistency, be invalid.

The authority and bindingness of Commonwealth laws is also addressed in covering clause 5 of the *Commonwealth of Australia Constitution Act 1900* (Cth). It provides:

> This Act, and all laws made by the Parliament of the Commonwealth under the Constitution, shall be binding on the courts, judges, and people of every State and of every part of the Commonwealth, notwithstanding anything in the laws of any State; and the laws of the Commonwealth shall be in force on all British ships, the Queen's ships

of war excepted, whose first port of clearance and whose port of destination are in the Commonwealth.

Notably, cl 5 is much wider in scope than s 109. Its first function is to establish the supremacy of the *Constitution Act* itself and all that it contains, including the Constitution of the Commonwealth as set out in cl 9. The point of cl 5 is to make clear that the *Constitution Act* and the Constitution are binding on the courts, judges and people of every State and every part of the Commonwealth, including all of the territories of the Commonwealth. Although the supremacy of the Constitution might be regarded as a necessary presupposition of the entire constitutional system, when this principle has been challenged, the importance of cl 5 in making this clear has been emphasised.[29]

The language of cl 5 was influenced by Art VI, s 2 of the United States Constitution, which provides:

> This Constitution, and the Laws of the United States which shall be made in pursuance thereof; and all treaties made, or which shall be made, under the authority of the United States, shall be the supreme law of the land; and the judges in every state shall be bound thereby, anything in the constitution or laws of any state to the contrary notwithstanding.

There are two notable differences between the two clauses, however. The first is that the American provision refers to the 'supremacy' of the Constitution and laws of the United States, whereas the Australian provision says only that they are 'binding'. The second difference is that the American provision refers to the supremacy of all treaties made under the authority of the United States. In an early draft of the Australian provision, treaties entered into by the Commonwealth were similarly expressed to be binding. However, this was later removed, not merely because it was expected that the Commonwealth would not have an independent capacity to enter into treaties within the British Empire, but to ensure that a treaty would not have the force of law in Australia unless its terms were enacted into binding law by the Parliament.[30] In the United States, treaties first have to be confirmed by the Senate before they can be ratified by the President and become binding both as a matter of international and domestic law. There is no similar constitutional requirement of parliamentary confirmation of treaties in British or Australian law, and so it was important to ensure that the operation of the law within Australia would depend on the enactment of a statute to implement the terms of any treaty.[31]

Clause 5 and s 109 are directed to the bindingness and priority of particular categories of laws: the *Constitution Act*, the Constitution, and Commonwealth laws. Quick and Garran suggested that the reference to the 'laws of any State'

**29** *Joosse v Australian Securities and Investment Commission* (1998) 159 ALR 260, 264.
**30** See *Convention Debates, Sydney* (1897) 239–40.
**31** On the legislative implementation of treaties under the external affairs power, see Chapter 3, Part IV.2.

would include not only the statutes enacted by a State Parliament, but also Imperial Acts relating to the constitution and government of a State, Imperial Acts operating within a State, and the common law of such a State. Quick and Garran also pointed out that the reference to the 'laws of the Commonwealth' would have to include not only the Constitution and statutes enacted by the Commonwealth, but also amendments to the Constitution under s 128.[32]

While laws of the Commonwealth are made binding on the courts and judges of the States, cl 5 and s 109 make no explicit reference to acts of the Executive Government or to judgments of the courts. The superior authority of the High Court is, however, indicated in several ways in the Constitution. As is explained in more detail in Chapter 8, the High Court is referred to as a 'Federal Supreme Court' (s 71) and is invested with 'final and conclusive' jurisdiction to hear appeals from the 'judgments, decrees, orders and sentences' of the Supreme Courts and other courts of the States (s 73). This general appellate jurisdiction of the High Court underwrites the proposition that in Australia there is only one common law determined by the High Court of Australia, and not, as in the United States, distinct bodies of common law in each State as determined by the Supreme Court of each State.[33] The High Court is also given control over appeals to the Privy Council upon any question as to the limits inter se of the constitutional powers of the Commonwealth and the States (s 74). As noted in Chapter 1, it has also been argued that the Court's jurisdiction in relation to matters arising under the Constitution or under any laws of the Commonwealth Parliament (s 76) implies, as intended by the framers, that the Court has an ultimate power of judicial review.

The authority of the Executive Government of the Commonwealth stands upon a somewhat different basis. In some vital matters, such as the defence of the Commonwealth and the States (ss 51(vi) and 119), the Commonwealth is clearly in full command of the terrain, not least because the States are prohibited from raising or maintaining any naval or military force without the consent of the Commonwealth Parliament (s 114) whereas the command in chief of the naval and military forces of the Commonwealth is vested in the Governor-General (s 68). More generally, the supremacy of acts of the Commonwealth Executive vis-à-vis the States depends on the supremacy accorded by cl 5 and s 109 to any Commonwealth law authorising Commonwealth executive action or, in the absence of authorising legislation, on an implication of the Constitution as a whole. While in most cases disputes about the relative authority of the Executive Governments of the Commonwealth and the States can therefore be determined by the construction of the relevant Commonwealth law, the High Court has held that there are definite limits on the capacity of the States to interfere with the

**32** John Quick and Robert Garran, *The Annotated Constitution of the Australian Commonwealth* (Angus and Robertson, 1901) 356–7.

**33** *Kable v Director of Public Prosecutions (NSW)* (1996) 189 CLR 51, 102–3, 111–15, 137–9; *Re Wakim; Ex parte McNally* (1999) 198 CLR 511, 535, 574.

operations of the Commonwealth, as well as on the capacity of the Commonwealth to interfere with the States.[34]

## 2 Commonwealth exclusivity

Despite the importance of cl 5 in establishing the authority of the Constitution and the governing institutions which it creates, the High Court has dealt with cases of inconsistency between Commonwealth and State laws on the basis of s 109. Although s 109 is expressed to apply to all Commonwealth laws, in practice it usually applies only to laws enacted by the Commonwealth within its concurrent heads of power in s 51. This is largely because the exclusivity of the Commonwealth's legislative powers in s 52 means that the States are prohibited from legislating on those topics. However, the matter is not quite as simple as that, for two reasons.

### Types of exclusive powers

The first reason derives from the fact that there are different kinds of exclusive Commonwealth power. The point in time at which an exclusive power vests in the Commonwealth and thereby displaces State power depends on the basis and nature of the exclusive power in question. Section 52 grants the Commonwealth exclusive legislative power with respect to:

(i) the seat of government of the Commonwealth, and all places acquired by the Commonwealth for public purposes;

(ii) matters relating to any department of the public service the control of which is by this Constitution transferred to the Executive Government of the Commonwealth;

(iii) other matters declared by this Constitution to be within the exclusive power of the Parliament.

As Quick and Garran pointed out, the exclusive powers referred to in paras (i) and (ii) do not vest in the Commonwealth until the occurrence of certain prescribed events. Thus, until a relevant acquisition or transfer occurs in relation to a particular place or department, the States retain their general powers of legislation in relation to that place or department.[35] In addition, para (iii) refers to matters declared by the Constitution to be within the exclusive powers of the Commonwealth. The Commonwealth's exclusive power with respect to excise and customs duties (s 90) did not vest in the Commonwealth until uniform customs duties were imposed pursuant to s 88. Most of the other exclusive matters referred to in para (iii) arise from prohibitions directed against the States which seem to have applied from the time that the Commonwealth Constitution came into force. These include the prohibitions upon the States from coining money or from maintaining any naval or military force without the consent of the

**34** See Part III below.
**35** Quick and Garran, above n 32, 656–7. See also *R v Phillips* (1970) 125 CLR 93, 102.

Commonwealth Parliament (ss 114 and 115).[36] Notably, the Commonwealth's legislative powers in respect of many of these matters are in fact conferred by s 51, such as the powers to make laws with respect to taxation, bounties, defence and coinage (ss 51(ii), (iii), (vi) and (xii)).

Several other of the Commonwealth's powers in s 51 are exclusive for a different reason, namely because the powers in question were never vested in the colonies in the first place.[37] For example, the Commonwealth's powers with respect to 'borrowing money on the credit of the Commonwealth' and 'service and execution throughout the Commonwealth of the civil and criminal process and the judgments of the courts of the States' (ss 51(iv), (xxiv)) presuppose the existence of the Commonwealth, and could not have been part of the powers of the colonies prior to federation. Similarly, the Commonwealth's extraordinary capacity to exercise the powers of the United Kingdom Parliament throughout Australia (s 51(xxviii)), even though it can only be exercised with the consent of the States, was a power that was not possessed by the individual colonies prior to federation.[38] In addition, there is the general power of the Commonwealth to legislate for the government of any Commonwealth territory (s 122).

### Continuity of State laws

The second complicating factor concerning the Commonwealth's exclusive powers arises from the peculiar operation of s 108.[39] That section provides:

> Every law in force in a Colony which has become or becomes a State, and relating to any matter within the powers of the Parliament of the Commonwealth, shall, subject to this Constitution, continue in force in the State; and, until provision is made in that behalf by the Parliament of the Commonwealth, the Parliament of the State shall have such powers of alteration and of repeal in respect of any such law as the Parliament of the Colony had until the Colony became a State.

In *Commonwealth v New South Wales*, Isaacs J suggested that the main purpose of s 108 was to ensure that a 'state of anarchy' would not exist in places acquired by the Commonwealth prior to the Commonwealth making laws for them.[40] Plainly the section provides for the continuing operation of colonial laws in such cases, but its application seems to extend beyond that. Firstly, as Owen J pointed out in *R v Bamford*,[41] no distinction is drawn in s 108 between the concurrent

**36** The Court has held, however, that the entirety of the defence power (s 51(vi)) itself is not exclusive; s 109 therefore applies to laws enacted under it: *Carter v Egg & Egg Pulp Marketing Board (Vic)* (1942) 66 CLR 557.

**37** See Quick and Garran, above n 32, 656, 934.

**38** Quick and Garran drew attention to several other such powers, including the external affairs power (s 51(xxix)): ibid 934.

**39** See also *Commonwealth of Australia Constitution Act 1900 (UK)*, cl 4, confirming that the colonial Parliaments would continue to have power to make laws after the commencement of the *Constitution Act* but before commencement of the Constitution itself.

**40** *Commonwealth v New South Wales* (1923) 33 CLR 1, 43. Similar concerns were influentially discussed by Zelman Cowen, 'Alsatias for Jack Sheppards? The Law in Federal Enclaves in Australia' (1960) 2 *Melbourne University Law Review* 454.

**41** (1901) 1 SR (NSW) 337, 351.

and exclusive powers of the Commonwealth: on its face, it seems to apply to both without qualification. Section 108 is therefore open to the interpretation that it preserves the operation of colonial laws even within the exclusive powers of the Commonwealth. Moreover, the second limb of s 108 seems to preserve the competence of the States to alter or repeal such laws until the Commonwealth relevantly legislates. It is therefore possible to interpret the provision as preserving the power of the States to legislate within both the concurrent and exclusive jurisdiction of the Commonwealth – that is, until the Commonwealth legislates on the topic.[42] On this view, the exclusivity of the Commonwealth's legislative powers under s 52 does not, in principle, prohibit the States from making laws in those fields altogether, although it certainly has this effect once the Commonwealth relevantly legislates.

The difficulty with this conclusion is that it seems to contradict the apparent meaning of s 107, which provides:

> Every power of the Parliament of a Colony which has become or becomes a State, shall, unless it is by this Constitution exclusively vested in the Parliament of the Commonwealth or withdrawn from the Parliament of the State, continue as at the establishment of the Commonwealth, or as at the admission or establishment of the State, as the case may be.

While s 107 does not explicitly deprive the States of legislative power over matters exclusively vested in the Commonwealth Parliament, it certainly seems to presuppose that this is the case. How then are ss 107 and 108, together with s 52, to be understood? Quick and Garran observed that s 107 is concerned with the *powers* of the State Parliaments, whereas s 108 is concerned with the operation of colonial *laws* once the Constitution comes into force. This observation would suggest that, at the least, the first limb of s 108 can operate quite consistently with s 107 provided it is understood that the exclusion of State legislative *power* occurs as soon as a relevant exclusive power is vested in the Commonwealth, whereas a colonial *law* enacted prior to federation, operating upon a matter within the exclusive powers of the Commonwealth, will continue to be in force until the Commonwealth enacts a law upon that subject matter. However, Quick and Garran went further than this. They also considered that, although the second limb of s 108 is not expressly drafted in this way, it must be interpreted to apply only to concurrent powers because it would contradict the very nature of exclusivity to allow the States to alter or repeal their laws in relation to topics that fall within the exclusive powers of the Commonwealth.[43]

**42** See *R v Bamford* (1901) 1 SR (NSW) 337, 352.

**43** Quick and Garran, above n 32, 657–8, 937–8. See, likewise, W Harrison Moore, *The Constitution of the Commonwealth of Australia* (2nd ed, 1910) 411–12; Andrew Inglis Clark, *Studies in Australian Constitutional Law* (Charles F Maxwell, 1901) 93–5. Quick and Garran also drew a distinction between the effect of the first limb of s 108 in relation to powers that are exclusive by virtue of s 52 and powers that are exclusive because the States are expressly or by necessary implication prohibited from exercising them. In respect of the latter, they said, the relevant colonial laws were 'dislodged and displaced once and for all', whereas in respect of the former, the colonial laws would continue to operate until displaced by Commonwealth law.

Although Quick and Garran claimed that this interpretation was consistent with the view entertained by the framers of the Constitution,[44] this is not exactly the case. Rather, there was considerable confusion among the framers concerning the point in time at which the exclusivity of the Commonwealth powers would come into operation. Some thought that the States would not be prohibited from legislating within a field of exclusive Commonwealth power until the Commonwealth first legislated on the topic, while others thought that exclusivity would be triggered immediately the Constitution came into force. Sometimes they seemed to suggest that s 108 would preserve the capacity of the States to alter or repeal colonial legislation even within the exclusive powers of the Commonwealth, until the Commonwealth had actually legislated in the relevant field; while at other times they seemed to indicate that exclusivity would remove the State power automatically and entirely. And in advancing these views, they were not always clear about the kinds of distinctions that Quick and Garran proposed in their interpretation of Commonwealth exclusivity.[45]

The question of the precise operation of s 108 is a mostly theoretical one because the Commonwealth has legislated to apply most State laws to places acquired by the Commonwealth.[46] However, the cases on the question remain important and interesting because approaches to the interpretation of s 108 adopted by justices of the High Court reflect divergent views of the fundamental constitutional relationship between the Commonwealth and the States within the federal system. In two important cases, a majority of the Court have held that the exclusive power conferred by s 52 excludes any State law from operating with respect to the relevant subject matter, whether the State law is enacted before or after the event that brought the matter within the exclusive power of the Commonwealth.[47] Underlying this conclusion was the proposition, strongly advocated by Barwick CJ, that the Court should ordinarily 'lean to the broader interpretation' of the powers of the Commonwealth[48] – a maxim that was said to follow from the proposition that the Australian Constitution is not to be regarded as a 'compact between independent and sovereign states', but rather as an Imperial statute.[49] This conclusion has meant that upon the acquisition of places by the Commonwealth, it is necessary for the Commonwealth to legislate to fill the void created by the exclusion of general State laws that would otherwise have operated in such places.[50]

**44** Quick and Garran, above n 32, 657–8.
**45** Nicholas Aroney, *The Constitution of a Federal Commonwealth: The Making and Meaning of the Australian Constitution* (Cambridge University Press, 2009) 283–91.
**46** *Commonwealth Places (Application of Laws) Act 1970* (Cth), enacted in response to the cases discussed in this section. The Act is retrospective and ambulatory in operation: any relevant State law, whenever enacted, is made applicable: *R v Holmes* (1988) 93 FLR 405. See also *Commonwealth Places (Mirror Taxes) Act 1998 (Cth)*.
**47** *Worthing v Rowell and Muston Pty Limited* (1970) 123 CLR 89; *R v Phillips* (1970) 125 CLR 93; see also *Allders International Pty Ltd v Commissioner of State Revenue (Vic)* (1996) 186 CLR 630.
**48** *Worthing v Rowell and Muston Pty Limited* (1970) 123 CLR 89, 96.
**49** Ibid, 97; see also 125; *R v Phillips* (1970) 125 CLR 93, 101.
**50** *Worthing v Rowell and Muston Pty Limited* (1970) 123 CLR 89, 103; see, similarly, 132. See, further, Colin Howard, 'Federal Places and Exclusive Legislative Powers' (1970) 9 *University of Western Australia Law Review* 360.

## 3 Varieties of inconsistency

The establishment of a federal Commonwealth consisting of several constituent political communities gives rise to potential conflicts of jurisdiction between each set of governing institutions. The conflicts of jurisdiction that arise can be of various kinds. They may involve clashes between the laws of two States – a situation that can arise because the States are able to legislate with extra-territorial effect.[51] The resolution of such conflicts has proven especially difficult and has given rise to an exceptionally complex body of law that is far from coherent,[52] not least because there is nothing explicit in the Constitution that decisively indicates which law is to be applied. Some provisions of the Constitution, such as ss 117 and 118, limit the permissible scope and reach of State laws, thereby preventing a conflict arising in some circumstances. However, the resolution of conflicts between State laws depends largely on conflict of laws rules that have been developed by the common law, as well as an inference drawn from the nature of the federation as a whole that States are predominantly concerned with what occurs within their territories.[53]

Inconsistencies between State and Territory laws also raise unique problems.[54] Whether a law is enacted by the Commonwealth Parliament for the government of a Territory under s 122 of the Constitution, or by a legislative assembly created by the Commonwealth for a Territory, the Territory law may have extra-territorial effect. Consequently, conflicts can arise between Territory laws and State laws in the same way as conflicts arise between the laws of different States. If the Territory law is enacted by the Commonwealth Parliament, the law is 'a law of the Commonwealth' for the purposes of s 109 of the Constitution, and that provision will operate to resolve any conflict between the Territory law and State laws.[55] The rules to be applied to a conflict between a State law and a law of a Territory legislative assembly have not been fully established. Certainly, common law choice of law rules play an important role in resolving these conflicts.[56] To the extent these rules do not assist, it is likely that the Commonwealth Parliament, when creating the legislative assembly for the Territory, intended to place the Territory law in the same position as a State law for the purposes of resolving conflicts with a law of a State.[57]

**51** See Chapter 10.
**52** See, eg, *Breavington v Godleman* (1988) 169 CLR 41; *McKain v R W Miller & Co (SA) Pty Ltd* (1991) 174 CLR 1; *Stevens v Head* (1993) 176 CLR 433; *John Pfeiffer Pty Ltd v Rogerson* (2000) 203 CLR 503.
**53** See Stellios, above n 16, discussing the relevant cases and literature.
**54** *Kruger v Commonwealth* (1997) 190 CLR 1, 58; *Newcrest Mining (WA) v Commonwealth* (1997) 190 CLR 513, 557.
**55** *Lamshed v Lake* (1958) 99 CLR 132.
**56** See *John Pfeiffer Pty Ltd v Rogerson* (2000) 203 CLR 503.
**57** For more detail, see Mark Leeming, *Resolving Conflicts of Laws* (Federation Press, 2011) 242–6.

When there is a clash between a Commonwealth law and a law enacted by a legislative assembly of a Territory, the Commonwealth law will operate in the Territory as 'part of the Commonwealth',[58] and will prevail over inconsistent Territory law because a Territory cannot legislate in a manner that is repugnant to Commonwealth law, and because it is constrained by the terms of its grant of legislative power pursuant to s 122 of the Constitution.[59]

Conflicts between a Commonwealth law and a State law are resolved by reference to s 109. It will be recalled that s 109 provides:

> When a law of a State is inconsistent with a law of the Commonwealth, the latter shall prevail, and the former shall, to the extent of the inconsistency, be invalid.

Three concepts are crucial in s 109: 'law', 'inconsistency', and 'invalidity'.

## 4 Inconsistency between Commonwealth and State laws

### 'Law'

The term 'law' in s 109 can be dealt with briefly. It plainly includes statutes enacted by the Commonwealth and the States,[60] as well as delegated legislation in the form of Regulations made by the Governor-General or a State Governor.[61] Industrial awards, such as those made by the former Australian Industrial Relations Commission, are not of themselves 'law' but merely a 'factum' upon which the law may operate and give binding legal effect. The High Court has held that when industrial awards are given effect by a Commonwealth statute, however, they become part of the 'law of the Commonwealth' and can therefore be the basis of an inconsistency with a State law, at least where the Commonwealth law evinces an intention that the award is to operate to the exclusion of any State law.[62] Some Commonwealth laws have purported to declare that State laws and awards inconsistent with a Commonwealth award are invalid to the extent of the inconsistency, echoing the language of s 109 and appearing of their own authority to declare that such State laws are invalid. However, the High Court has interpreted such provisions as exhibiting an intention that the Commonwealth law is to operate to the exclusion of State law, not that the State law is invalid simply by force of the Commonwealth law.[63] Section 109 does not apply, moreover, to merely administrative orders or directions, even though

**58** *Capital Duplicators Pty Ltd v Australian Capital Territory* (1992) 177 CLR 248, 274, 285.

**59** The exact position is different in each of the Territories. See *Australian Capital Territory (Self-Government) Act 1988* (Cth), s 28; *Northern Territory (Self-Government) Act 1978 (Cth)*, Pt VI and s 57; *Norfolk Island Act 1979* (Cth), s 29; *Federal Capital Commission v Laristan Building and Investment Co Pty Ltd* (1929) 42 CLR 582, 588; *Northern Territory v GPAO* (1999) 196 CLR 553, 578–83, 636; *Commonwealth v Australian Capital Territory* (2013) 250 CLR 441, [48]–[54].

**60** Such Commonwealth laws may be enacted pursuant to s 51 or s 122: *Lamshed v Lake* (1958) 99 CLR 132.

**61** *O'Sullivan v Noarlunga Meat Ltd* (1954) 92 CLR 565; (1956) 95 CLR 177.

**62** *Ex parte McLean* (1930) 43 CLR 472, 479, 485; *T A Robinson & Sons Pty Ltd v Haylor* (1957) 97 CLR 177, 182–3.

**63** *Metal Trades Industry Association v Amalgamated Metal Workers' and Shipwrights' Union* (1983) 152 CLR 632, 648–9.

non-compliance with them might constitute an offence under a law of the Commonwealth.[64] Furthermore, although the term 'law of the Commonwealth' is wider than 'laws made by the Parliament of the Commonwealth', s 109 cannot apply to inconsistencies between the common law of the Commonwealth and of the States because there is only one common law in Australia,[65] so no inconsistency can arise.[66]Additionally, all Australian legislatures have power to displace the common law and, thus, legislative rules, irrespective of their source within the federation, will prevail over common law rules. Disputes over the application of Commonwealth and State laws in relation to the common law prerogatives and other rights and powers of the Crown are determined by reference to other principles, discussed in connection with the topic of intergovernmental immunities in Part III below.[67]

### 'Inconsistency'

Although the category of 'law' in s 109 has raised issues of some complexity, and at times obscurity, the concept of 'inconsistency' has proven to be even more elusive. Law is a form of practical reason: it is about 'what is practically to be done', not simply 'what is in fact the case'. Accordingly, the kind of inconsistency in view is not simply one of logical contradiction of propositions, but of inconsistency in the practical meaning and application of rules. The application of the idea of inconsistency in s 109 is thus complicated by the fact that laws can impose duties, grant liberties, confer powers and bestow immunities.[68] As a consequence, there are a variety of ways in which laws can potentially be inconsistent. One such way is when two laws impose incompatible duties in the sense that it is impossible for a person to obey both laws. Another occurs when one law grants a liberty to do something but another law imposes a duty not to do that thing. In such instances, it remains possible to comply with both laws by not performing the act in question, except that this seems to nullify the liberty. A third possible inconsistency arises when two laws grant liberties or confer powers upon two different persons or institutions in circumstances where it is not possible, in practice, for both liberties or powers to be exercised fully at the same time or in the same respect, giving rise to a kind of 'operational inconsistency'. Fourthly, each individual rule of law is usually part of a larger group of laws, usually in the form of an entire Act of Parliament, which is intended to operate as a

**64** *Airlines of New South Wales Pty Ltd v New South Wales (No 1)* (1964) 113 CLR 1, 31, 46.

**65** *Lange v Australian Broadcasting Corporation* (1997) 189 CLR 520; *Lipohar v The Queen* (1999) 200 CLR 485.

**66** *Kable v Director of Public Prosecutions (NSW)* (1996) 189 CLR 51, 102–3, 111–15, 137–9; *Re Wakim; Ex parte McNally* (1999) 198 CLR 511, 535, 574. Contrast *University of Wollongong v Metwally* (1984) 158 CLR 447, 468 and P H Lane, *The Australian Federal System* (Law Book Company, 1979) 866, but see (2nd ed, 1997) 768–9.

**67** *Commonwealth v Cigamatic Pty Ltd (in liq)* (1962) 108 CLR 372, 378.

**68** A duty may require a person to do or to refrain from doing something. A liberty is the freedom to do or not to do something (ie, to choose whether or not to do it). A power is the capacity to make a law (which may in turn impose duties, grant liberties, confer powers and bestow immunities). An immunity is the right that a law of a particular description cannot be made (ie, that there is 'no power' to do so). See John Finnis, 'Some Professorial Fallacies About Rights' (1972) 4(2) *Adelaide Law Review* 377.

coordinated whole. In such circumstances it is possible that those who drafted the statute expected that it would operate as a complete and exhaustive code of law, to the exclusion of all other rules of law operating within the same field or on the same topic.

In these many and various circumstances, it is not necessarily clear whether there can be just one test or standard according to which the existence of an inconsistency between a Commonwealth and a State law can be determined. It has also been controversial whether all of these possible kinds of conflict between laws should be regarded as forms of 'inconsistency' for the purposes of s 109 of the Constitution. Certainly, the legal effect of s 109 is that no State law which is inconsistent with a Commonwealth law can have a constitutionally valid operation. Thus, the larger the number of ways in which laws can be found to be inconsistent, the greater the capacity of the Commonwealth to regulate matters to the exclusion of the States. Over time, the High Court has found an increasing number of such grounds of inconsistency, thereby augmenting the regulatory powers of the Commonwealth and weakening the corresponding capacities of the States.

### Conflict of duties

The first two important cases on inconsistency that had to be considered by the High Court turned on the existence of a relevant conflict of duties. In *Australian Boot Trade Employees Federation v Whybrow & Co* the Court had to consider an industrial award made by the Commonwealth Court of Conciliation and Arbitration which required, among other things, that employees in the boot trade industry be paid a minimum wage of 1 shilling, 1½ pence per hour, and the *Factories and Shops Act 1909* (Vic) which required a minimum wage of only 1 shilling per hour.[69] The first question was whether the industrial award, made pursuant to the *Commonwealth Conciliation and Arbitration Act 1904* (Cth), itself enacted under the industrial arbitration power (s 51(xxxv)), could constitutionally prescribe minimum wage rules which displaced State laws regulating the field. Interpreting the power in the light of the reserved powers doctrine, Griffith CJ, Barton and O'Connor JJ pointed out that, as generally conceived, the concept of arbitration involves adjudication of disputes according to existing law, and does not usually include a power to make or abrogate State law on the subject. As the Chief Justice put it, an industrial dispute is not constituted by disagreement with the content of the law, and the power to make arbitral awards to settle industrial disputes is not a kind of legislative power to make new law.[70] This approach to the first question supported the majority's approach to the second question, whether there was an inconsistency between

**69** *Australian Boot Trade Employees Federation v Whybrow & Co* (1910) 10 CLR 266; see also *Federated Saw Mill, Timber Yard, and General Woodworkers Employés Association of Australasia v James Moore & Sons Pty Ltd* (1909) 8 CLR 465.

**70** *Australian Boot Trade Employees Federation v Whybrow & Co* (1910) 10 CLR 266, 279–85; see also 294–7, and compare 301–4.

the Commonwealth award and the State law. Griffith CJ affirmed that the test to be applied was whether obedience to both laws was possible. Because State law did not forbid employers to pay more than the minimum wage of 1 shilling per hour, he concluded that it remained possible for employers to comply with both requirements – that is, by paying the higher minimum wage under the industrial award.[71] Barton J agreed, observing that:

> It is impossible to say that the employer cannot obey the one without disobeying the other. Therefore, the former and the latter may stand together. Therefore, according to the proper test, they are not inconsistent.[72]

Also agreeing on this point, Higgins J observed that no conflict of duties arose: there was 'merely an additional duty, not an inconsistent duty'.[73] Isaacs J similarly concluded there was no inconsistency, but for a fundamentally different reason. He considered that inconsistency should be understood as arising from a conflict of legislative will as between the Commonwealth and a State. If the Commonwealth were to lay down an exhaustive code of regulation over a particular field, so as to take 'complete occupation of the field', there would be an inconsistency, he said, if a State 'appropriates that ground, and expressly or impliedly declares it to be its sovereign will that on that area it desires only the specific rules it thinks fit to make'.[74] On the facts of the case, however, Isaacs J did not consider that such an intention existed in the State law.

The conflict of duties test applied in *Whybrow* could therefore lead to an inconsistency, but only if it was impossible to obey both laws. This was illustrated in *R v Licensing Court of Brisbane; Ex parte Daniell*,[75] in which the Court had to consider a Commonwealth law and a State law, both of which imposed inconsistent duties in relation to the holding of votes or referendums. Section 166 of the *Liquor Act 1912* (Qld) authorised and required a 'local option vote' on liquor trading licences to be held on the polling day for a forthcoming Senate election held in 1917. However, s 14 of the *Commonwealth Electoral (War-time) Act 1917* (Cth) imposed a negative duty in the following terms:

> On the day appointed as polling day for an election of the Senate or a general election of the House of Representatives, no referendum or vote of the electors of any State or part of a State shall be taken under the law of a State.

The Court held there was an inconsistency between the two laws, that this meant the vote held under the State law was invalid and that this nullified all of the consequences the State law attached to the holding of the vote.[76] As Higgins J explained, the Commonwealth law imposed a binding duty which must prevail over the requirement of the State law that the local option vote was to be taken

**71** Ibid, 286–7.
**72** Ibid, 299.
**73** Ibid, 339.
**74** Ibid, 330.
**75** (1920) 28 CLR 23.
**76** *R v Licensing Court of Brisbane; Ex parte Daniell* (1920) 28 CLR 23, 29–30.

on that date.[77] However, expressing doubt about the wider conclusions of the majority in the case, Higgins J also noted that while the State law provided for a whole series of consequences concerning the holding of liquor licences, the Commonwealth law did not specifically require that a State referendum or vote held on a federal election day could not have the consequential effects prescribed by the State law. There was no 'direct inconsistency' between the two laws in this particular respect, he thought, and so the State law to this extent ought to survive.[78] For, as his Honour explained, the State law operates 'not *through* the Federal Act or the Constitution, but by virtue of the State Constitution; and it is valid in all respects except so far as the Federal Act and Constitution obstruct it'.[79]

### Modification of liberties

*Whybrow* and *Daniell* illustrate the potential reach, and also the limits, of the conflict of duties test. On this test, the critical question is whether it is possible to obey both laws. In *Clyde Engineering Co Ltd v Cowburn*,[80] however, a close majority of the Court held that there was at least one other way in which there could be an inconsistency between a Commonwealth and a State law. The case involved a clash between a Commonwealth industrial award and the *Forty-four Hour Week Act 1925* (NSW). The Commonwealth award fixed rates of pay and overtime on the basis of a 48-hour working week, and provided that a worker doing less than 48 hours work 'should lose his pay for the actual time of non-attendance'. The State Act provided that ordinary working hours for those employed under such an award should not exceed 44 hours, and required employers to pay full award wages for working a 44-hour week. The case arose when two employees worked a 44-hour week and invoked the State law as entitling them to full wages. However, pursuant to the Commonwealth Act, their employer deducted pay from their wages.

Basing their decision on the conflict of duties test, Higgins and Powers JJ held in their dissenting judgments that it was possible for an employer to obey both laws, by paying the full award wage for 44 hours work. As Higgins J explained, it was not enough to show that there might be some:

> inconsistency in policy or scheme or dominant intention of the award, or anything else so elusive and conjectural, or that the powers of State and Commonwealth, in their exercise, may possibly conflict.[81]

The reason for this was that State power, although restrained in its 'operations', is not restrained in its 'nature', for both the Commonwealth and the States derive their legislative powers directly from the Imperial Parliament.[82] As a consequence, as his Honour colourfully put it:

**77** Ibid, 32.
**78** Ibid, 33.
**79** Ibid, 35.
**80** (1926) 37 CLR 466.
**81** *Clyde Engineering Co Ltd v Cowburn* (1926) 37 CLR 466, 500.
**82** Ibid, 500–01.

> The State law is like the Nile River, which covers the whole area with its flood, except that part of the area which is appropriated to the villages. The State law fills, as it were, all the sponge except the fibre.[83]

Moreover, even though the case was decided some six years after the *Engineers* case, Higgins J further observed that to suggest that the State was 'invading the domain of the Commonwealth' was quite inappropriate because the subject of labour conditions was 'primarily and directly within the reserved powers of the State'.[84] He evidently considered that the conflict of duties test, which had been developed in *Whybrow* in the context of the reserved powers doctrine, ought to survive the Court's decision in *Engineers*.[85]

However, a majority of the Court held that the two laws were inconsistent. Knox CJ and Gavan Duffy J considered that the rule in *Whybrow* was neither sufficient nor appropriate in every case, for:

> [t]wo enactments may be inconsistent although obedience to each of them may be possible without disobeying the other. Statutes do more than impose duties: they may, for instance, confer rights; and one statute is inconsistent with another when it takes away a right conferred by that other even though the right be one which might be waived or abandoned without disobeying the statute which conferred it.[86]

On their analysis, the Commonwealth award effectively gave employers the right (in the sense of a liberty) to pay employees on the basis of the 48-hour working week, whereas the State law purported to take away this right by imposing an inconsistent duty to pay employees on the basis of a 44-hour week. This conflict of a liberty and a duty was enough to constitute an inconsistency under s 109.

Isaacs J came to the same conclusion. For him, the case concerned 'the power of the Australian nation as one component organism' to make laws regulating the subject matter of s 51(xxxv) of the Constitution. The Commonwealth's power, he said, ought to be exercised:

> on a broad national basis, and therefore with due regard to the general welfare of its people as a whole, free from disturbing and, in all probability, mutually opposing elements which particular States may for their own separate objects desire to introduce into the practical working of the national scheme.[87]

Plainly, the same kind of nationalist instincts that motivated Isaacs J when delivering the joint judgment in the *Engineers* case were again at play. After discussing the legislation in some detail, he analysed the possible tests of inconsistency in the following terms:

> The infallible test of whether … there is inconsistency is said for the respondent to be whether the two provisions of deduction on the one hand and extra payment on the

**83** Ibid, 500.
**84** Ibid, 501.
**85** Ibid, 503–4 (he also acknowledged, however, that in principle there might be inconsistency 'of powers, rights, and so forth'); see also 516.
**86** Ibid, 478.
**87** Ibid, 478–9.

> other could both be obeyed. No doubt the employer *could* obey both, that is physically. … But surely the vital question would be: Was the second Act on its true construction intended to cover the whole ground and, therefore, to supersede the first? … If … a competent legislature expressly or impliedly evinces its intention to cover the whole field, that is a conclusive test of inconsistency where another legislature assumes to enter to any extent upon the same field … . Where wholesale inconsistency does not occur, but the field is partly open, then it is necessary to inquire further and possibly to examine and contrast particular provisions. If one enactment makes or acts upon as lawful that which the other makes unlawful, or if one enactment makes unlawful that which the other makes or acts upon as lawful, the two are to that extent inconsistent. … In this case there is inconsistency in both of the senses I have described.[88]

Embedded in this passage are three distinct tests: conflict of duties, modification of liberties, and covering the field. On Isaacs J's analysis, all three tests are potentially applicable, but the covering the field test is the primary one, or at least this was so in the circumstances of *Cowburn's* case. The covering the field test depends, he explained, on the intention of the legislature. The primary question is whether the Commonwealth law evinces an intention to cover the whole field, in the sense of displacing State law within that field. This intention can be express or implied. There will be an inconsistency if such an intention is established and a State law enters to any extent into the same field. As a consequence, while the conflict of duties and modification of liberties tests require the Court to examine particular provisions in order to look for what Barwick CJ later called 'textual collision[s]',[89] the covering the field test depends upon the intention of the legislature ascertained by reference to the statute as a whole. On the basis of this test, Isaacs J joined with Knox CJ and Gavin Duffy J in finding that there was an inconsistency.

### Covering the field

Although *Cowburn* marked a departure from the narrow view articulated and applied in *Whybrow* and *Daniell*, only Isaacs J advanced in explicit terms a defence of the much wider covering the field test. However, very soon thereafter, in *Hume v Palmer* and in *Ex parte McLean*, clear statements endorsing and applying Isaacs J's approach were made.[90] *McLean* involved provisions of a Commonwealth award and a State law which laid down essentially the same basic obligation upon employees, namely to fulfil the terms and conditions of their contracts of employment. The *Masters and Servants Act 1902* (NSW) made employees liable to a fine not exceeding £10 for failing to do so, whereas the Commonwealth award, which was given force of law by the *Commonwealth Conciliation and*

**88** Ibid, 489–90.
**89** *Miller v Miller* (1978) 141 CLR 269, 275. These two tests of 'direct inconsistency' have been applied by judges in numerous cases, including: *Colvin v Bradley Bros Pty Ltd* (1943) 68 CLR 151; *Blackley v Devondale Cream (Vic) Pty Ltd* (1968) 117 CLR 253; *R v L* (1991) 174 CLR 379; *Mabo v Queensland (No 1)* (1988) 166 CLR 186; *Western Australia v Commonwealth* (1995) 183 CLR 373.
**90** *Ex parte McLean* (1930) 43 CLR 472, 479, 483; *Hume v Palmer* (1926) 38 CLR 441, 448, 450–51, 461–2; but see 455–8. See also *Union Steamship Co of New Zealand v Commonwealth* (1925) 36 CLR 130.

*Arbitration Act 1904* (Cth), could be enforced by a penalty not exceeding a maximum to be fixed by the Commonwealth Court of Conciliation. As a consequence, the two regimes required performance of essentially the same obligations, but imposed 'somewhat different penal sanctions' for failure to do so.[91]

The Court held that there was a relevant inconsistency in the different penalties, notwithstanding that the 'rule of conduct' was identical. Dixon J observed:

> When the Parliament of the Commonwealth and the Parliament of a State each legislate upon the same subject and prescribe what the rule of conduct shall be, they make laws which are inconsistent, notwithstanding that the rule of conduct is identical which each prescribes, and sec 109 applies. ... [T]he reason is that, by prescribing the rule to be observed, the Federal statute shows an intention to cover the subject matter and provide what the law upon it shall be. If it appeared that the Federal law was intended to be supplementary to or cumulative upon State law, then no inconsistency would be exhibited in imposing the same duties or in inflicting different penalties. The inconsistency does not lie in the mere coexistence of two laws which are susceptible of simultaneous obedience. It depends upon the intention of the paramount Legislature to express by its enactment, completely, exhaustively, or exclusively, what shall be the law governing the particular conduct or matter to which its attention is directed.[92]

Applying this test to the circumstances of the case, Dixon J considered that the Commonwealth award was materially inconsistent with the State law because the two dealt with the same subject matter (the industrial relationship between employer and employed) but imposed somewhat different punishments.[93]

The significance of the Court's decision in *McLean* is that because the duties imposed upon the employees were identical, it was not possible to find that there was any direct inconsistency between the two laws, either in terms of a conflict of duties or a conflict of a liberty and a duty. In finding that there was nonetheless an inconsistency, the Court's reasoning had to rely solely upon the covering the field test. The practical consequences of this finding are far-reaching. The capacity of the Commonwealth to displace State laws from an entire field, together with the Court's broad approach to the Commonwealth's power to legislate under its various heads of power (Chapter 3), means that if the Commonwealth considers it politically and practically advisable it can nullify the operation of State laws on a very wide range of topics, with significant implications for the effective autonomy of the States. On such an approach it is not necessary to show that there is a specific conflict of duties, or of duties and liberties. It is sufficient that the Commonwealth has evinced an intention to cover an entire field or topic with its own laws, excluding from operation any State laws within that field.

**91** *Ex Parte McLean* (1930) 43 CLR 472, 483; see also 479.
**92** Ibid, 483.
**93** Ibid, 484–6.

**Operational inconsistency**

Before discussing the application of the covering the field test in more detail, it is important to bear in mind that a potential conflict between Commonwealth and State laws can occur not only in relation to conflicts of duties and liberties, but also in relation to the exercise of liberties and powers granted by both Commonwealth and State laws. This possibility was first clearly seen in the *Kakariki* case.[94] There, the High Court had to consider s 13 of the *Marine Act 1928* (Vic), which provided for the removal by State authorities of any ship sunk in a port within Victoria which had not been removed by the owner, and s 329 of the *Navigation Act 1912* (Cth), which made similar provision for the removal by Commonwealth authorities of any ship sunk 'on or near the coast of Australia'. The Court held that there was no inconsistency on the facts of the case, because neither the Commonwealth nor the State authority had yet attempted to exercise its powers over the wreck of *The Kakariki*, which had sunk in Port Phillip Bay. As Latham CJ observed, there was no inconsistency 'in express terms' between the two provisions because each 'simply purports to confer power upon an authority to do an act', and there was no inconsistency by way of covering the field because the Commonwealth law could not be construed as prohibiting anyone other than a Commonwealth authority from removing the wreck.[95] However, the Chief Justice also observed that further questions about the inconsistency of the two laws could arise if both the Commonwealth and State authorities endeavoured to act simultaneously in relation to the same wreck.[96] As Starke J explained, no inconsistency would arise unless one or other authority interfered with or obstructed the other from performing acts authorised by the legislation, and such an event was unlikely given that the Commonwealth and State governments could be expected to act responsibly in such situations.[97]

The case had been brought because the advisers of the Commonwealth and State governments apprehended a potential problem if the State authority removed the wreck. The concern was that if the State law was found to be invalid under s 109, the State would not be authorised to recover its costs from the owner of the wrecked ship.[98] In Dixon J's view (with whom Rich J agreed), the whole question of inconsistency depended on whether the Commonwealth law evinced an intention to confer exclusive power upon Commonwealth authority.[99] He therefore reasoned as if the case turned on whether the Commonwealth law was intended to cover the field, but he also importantly seemed to suggest, like the other judges, that an inconsistency might alternatively arise if the Commonwealth authorities were to exert the powers given to them under the Commonwealth Act.[100] In his view, the law did not evince an intention to lay

**94** *Victoria v Commonwealth* (1937) 58 CLR 618. See also *Carter v Egg & Egg Pulp Marketing Board (Vic)* (1942) 66 CLR 557.
**95** *Victoria v Commonwealth* (1937) 58 CLR 618, 626.
**96** Ibid; see also 639.
**97** Ibid, 628.
**98** Ibid, 629, 633.
**99** Ibid, 629–30.
**100** Ibid, 630.

down an exhaustive statement of the law concerning the removal of wrecks, but it could certainly be interpreted as intending that the exercise by Commonwealth authorities of the power to remove wrecks was to be exclusive.[101] On this view, there was no inconsistency unless and until the statutory powers were actually exercised by the Commonwealth and State authorities; in other words, what was later called an 'operative inconsistency' could arise in these circumstances.

In the course of his reasoning, Dixon J restated the test of inconsistency that he had laid down in *Ex parte McLean* in the following terms:

> When a State law, if valid, would alter, impair or detract from the operation of a law of the Commonwealth Parliament, then to that extent it is invalid. Moreover, if it appears from the terms, the nature or the subject matter of a Federal enactment that it was intended as a complete statement of the law governing a particular matter or set of rights and duties, then for a State law to regulate or apply to the same matter or relation is regarded as a detraction from the full operation of the Commonwealth law and so as inconsistent.[102]

He then referred to what he had previously said in *Stock Motor Ploughs Ltd v Forsyth*:

> A provision which prevents or suspends the enforcement of an accrued right cannot do otherwise than impair the enjoyment of that right. In this Court an interpretation of sec 109 of the Constitution has been adopted which invalidates a law of a State in so far as it would vary, detract from, or impair the operation of a law of the Commonwealth. Further, when the Parliament appears to have intended that the Federal law shall be a complete statement of the law governing a particular relation or thing, it is considered that the operation of the Federal law would be impaired if the State law were allowed to affect the matter at all. Such an interpretation requires the consequence that, except in so far as the law of the Commonwealth appears otherwise to intend, enjoyment of a right arising under it may not be directly impaired by State law.[103]

In *Forsyth*, a majority of the Court had held that there was no inconsistency between the *Bills of Exchange Act 1909* (Cth) and the *Moratorium Act 1930* (NSW) even though the State Act, in providing that a person could not commence proceedings for recovery of an instalment under a hire purchase agreement without leave of the Court, placed an impediment upon the holder of a promissory note given as collateral security on a hire purchase agreement from taking action pursuant to common law rights conferred and confirmed by the Commonwealth Act.

### Commonwealth and State power

Although Dixon J dissented in *Stock Motor Ploughs Ltd v Forsyth*, the passages from his judgment in that case and in *Kakariki* have often been referred to in

**101** Ibid, 630–31.
**102** Ibid, 630.
**103** *Stock Motor Ploughs Ltd v Forsyth* (1932) 48 CLR 128, 136–7.

subsequent decisions as authoritative statements of general principle. There is some ambiguity, however, in both passages. One possible view is that Dixon J treated the so-called 'covering the field' test as distinct from the 'alter, impair or detract' formula. Another view is that the formula should be understood as embracing the covering the field test, for it represents the fundamental question that always has to be addressed.[104] These matters are not only of theoretical interest, for they can shape how the Court will respond to novel cases, and how far s 109 will be applied to displace State laws. Part of the reason for this is that where a direct inconsistency incontrovertibly exists, this cannot be avoided by the Commonwealth expressing an intention that the State law should continue to operate, for s 109 necessarily operates on the direct inconsistency.[105] And yet, according to orthodox methods of statutory interpretation, the construction of the Commonwealth law is a matter of ascertaining the intention of the Parliament. As a result very difficult questions of interpretation can arise where there is an expression of 'intention' by the Commonwealth which is capable of being understood in different ways.[106]

While he agreed with the result in *Kakariki*,[107] Evatt J expressed doubt about whether there was any 'rule of universal application' which could determine cases of inconsistency.[108] He drew attention to each of the conflict of duties, modification of rights and covering the field tests; he questioned the helpfulness of reducing the 'infinite complexities' involved in comparing legislation to the neat 'picture of a two-dimensional field'; and he suggested that, at least in the instant case, 'illustration' might be 'perhaps more helpful than general reasoning'.[109] Wishing to limit s 109 to dealing with real conflicts and not merely instances of 'administrative overlapping', he indicated a wish to resist the construction of some 'rule of general Commonwealth suzerainty' which would prevent a State from acting in the interests of its people 'merely because of Commonwealth inaction'.[110] Similarly, in *Stock Motor Ploughs*, Evatt J pointed out that 'covering the field' is both a 'very ambiguous phrase' and 'no more than a *cliché*'.[111] With these concerns in mind, he argued that while Commonwealth laws under some heads of power might certainly have the practical effect, through s 109, of terminating State power to legislate on the topic, other heads of power do not enable the Commonwealth to legislate with such an effect. In particular, he suggested that the taxation power could not, for example, be used to prevent or

**104** *Telstra Corporation Ltd v Worthing* (1997) 197 CLR 63, 76; *APLA Ltd v Legal Services Commissioner (NSW)* (2005) 224 CLR 322, 425; *Dickson v The Queen* (2010) 241 CLR 491, 502; *Jemena Asset Management (3) Pty Ltd v Coinvest Ltd* (2011) 244 CLR 508, 524–5; *Momcilovic v The Queen* (2011) 245 CLR 1, 111–12, 140–41, 233–4.
**105** *R v Loewenthal; Ex parte Blacklock* (1974) 131 CLR 338, 346–7; *R v Credit Tribunal; Ex parte General Motors Acceptance Corp* (1977) 137 CLR 545, 563–4.
**106** Compare *Momcilovic v The Queen* (2011) 245 CLR 1, 119–22, 123–49.
**107** *Victoria v Commonwealth* (1937) 58 CLR 618, 635–6, 638.
**108** Ibid, 633. See, similarly, *APLA Ltd v Legal Services Commissioner (NSW)* (2005) 224 CLR 322, 425.
**109** *Victoria v Commonwealth* (1937) 58 CLR 618, 634–6.
**110** Ibid, 636–8.
**111** *Stock Motor Ploughs Ltd v Forsyth* (1932) 48 CLR 128, 147.

interfere with the States imposing their own taxes, for the power only authorises the Commonwealth to require the payment of taxes to itself.[112]

Later, in *West v Commissioner of Taxation (NSW)*, Evatt J explained that the Commonwealth could not 'manufacture' inconsistency in such cases without going beyond the scope of its legislative powers.[113] To reason in this way comes close to suggesting that the question will be whether the Commonwealth law can be characterised as a law with respect to a topic within power *or* as a law that is actually concerned with State power – something very similar to the 'pith and substance' approach to characterisation discussed in Chapter 3. Indeed, Evatt J seemed to suggest exactly this in *Kakariki*, when he maintained that the Commonwealth does not have power to enact a provision which expressly excludes State laws from operating, precisely because the Commonwealth's legislative powers do not include 'power to define or limit the legislative or executive powers of a State'.[114] Interestingly, the Court has generally accepted that a limit of this kind does exist. As Brennan J later put it, the Commonwealth cannot legislate in a manner contrary to the continuance of State legislative power pursuant to ss 106 and 107 of the Constitution, such as by purporting to 'prohibit' a State from enacting a law.[115] Nonetheless, the High Court has also often upheld the capacity of the Commonwealth to express an intention to cover a particular field by stating explicitly that the Commonwealth law is to operate to the exclusion of State laws.

In *Wenn v Attorney-General (Vic)*,[116] for example, the High Court upheld a Commonwealth law enacted soon after World War II which dealt with the preferential employment of ex-service personnel, even though it was expressed to apply 'to the exclusion of any provisions ... of any law of a State'. The effect of the Commonwealth law, if valid, was to deny the operation of a State law which gave ex-service personnel a right to preference in promotion decisions, thus leaving employers at liberty to make such decisions without regard to that factor. Latham CJ rejected the suggestion that such a law was 'really an attempt to prevent State Parliaments legislating upon the subject'. Rather, the area within which the Commonwealth law was to apply to the exclusion of State law concerned, he said, 'a subject as to which the Commonwealth has full legislative power'.[117] While recognising Evatt J's 'powerful attack' on

**112** Ibid, 148, citing *Federalist No 33* (where it was stated by Alexander Hamilton that a federal law 'for abrogating or preventing the collection of a tax laid by the authority of the State' would be 'a usurpation of power not granted by the Constitution'). See, similarly, *Victoria v Commonwealth* (1957) 99 CLR 575, 614, where it was said that the 'federal character of the Constitution' suggests that Commonwealth legislation cannot cover the field of taxation so as to prevent the States legislating to raise their own revenues.

**113** *West v Commissioner of Taxation (NSW)* (1937) 56 CLR 657, 686, 707. As will be seen in Part III below, attempts by the Commonwealth and the States to impose taxes on each other, or in a manner which interferes with the taxation powers of the other, have been at the core of several important intergovernmental immunities cases.

**114** *Victoria v Commonwealth* (1937) 58 CLR 618, 638; *West v Commissioner of Taxation* (1937) 56 CLR 657, 707.

**115** See *Gerhardy v Brown* (1985) 159 CLR 70, 121.

**116** *Wenn v Attorney-General (Vic)* (1948) 77 CLR 84.

**117** Ibid, 111.

Commonwealth legislation that went beyond power, Dixon J drew a fine distinction between legislating 'exhaustively to the intent that the areas of liberty designedly left should not be closed up' and 'a bare attempt to exclude State concurrent power from a subject the Federal legislature has not effectively dealt with by regulation, control or otherwise'.[118] A Commonwealth law may overstep the mark, in other words, if it aims at 'preventing State legislative action' rather than 'dealing with a subject matter' with power; but within these limits, the Commonwealth law will survive scrutiny.[119]

A potential illustration of this latter principle is provided by *Airlines of New South Wales Pty Ltd v New South Wales (No 2)*,[120] where the Court struck down reg 200B of the Commonwealth Air Navigation Regulations because of its application to wholly intrastate air navigation. In that case, Kitto J suggested that the problem with reg 200B was that it was best characterised as a law 'with respect to the application of State laws', rather than a topic within power.[121] However, his was an isolated view. Provided a Commonwealth law can be characterised as falling within power, it seems the Commonwealth can indicate a whole list of particular State laws that are specifically overridden,[122] and in what respects they are overridden or not.[123] In the *Native Title* case, Mason CJ, Brennan, Deane, Toohey, Gaudron and McHugh JJ explained:

> Where it is within the legislative competence of the Commonwealth Parliament to prescribe an exclusive statutory regime, a Commonwealth law which merely expresses an exclusion of the operation of a State law is not construed as an attempt to invalidate the State law directly. It is construed as an expression of intention that the Commonwealth law should have exclusive operation. Being construed as a declaration of intention that the Commonwealth law should operate exclusively of State law on the topic, the Commonwealth law is within power. Unless the Commonwealth law were expressed in terms which precluded that construction, the form of expression does not take the law outside Commonwealth power.[124]

## Implied intention to cover the field

Despite the attempts of Evatt J to limit the operation of the covering the field test, there is no doubt that it has become a settled and important aspect of the law relating to s 109. Under the test, there appear to be three questions, namely: (1) What field is addressed by the Commonwealth law? (2) Did the Commonwealth intend to cover that field? (3) Did the State enter that field? As Evatt J pointed out, identifying the field and determining whether the Commonwealth has intended to cover it is a difficult, complex and often contested undertaking. The difficulties are

**118** Ibid, 120.
**119** Ibid.
**120** *Airlines of New South Wales Pty Ltd v New South Wales (No 2)* (1965) 113 CLR 54, discussed in Chapter 3, Part III.2.
**121** Ibid, 119; compare 84–8, 106–7, 125–8, 143–6, 148–9, 155, 165–8.
**122** Eg, *Botany Municipal Council v Federal Airports Corporation* (1992) 175 CLR 453.
**123** *Bayside City Council v Telstra Corporation Ltd* (2004) 216 CLR 595, 628–9; *New South Wales v Commonwealth* (2006) 229 CLR 1, 164–8.
**124** *Western Australia v Commonwealth* (1995) 183 CLR 373, 467–8.

especially keen in cases where the intention of the Parliament is not expressly stated but has to be inferred from the statute as a whole.

This latter point is well illustrated by *O'Sullivan v Noarlunga Meat Ltd*.[125] There the Court had to consider whether there was an inconsistency between the *Metropolitan and Export Abattoirs Act 1936* (SA) and the Commerce (Meat Export) Regulations made under the *Customs Act 1901* (Cth). The Commonwealth law, premised on the Commonwealth's legislative power with respect to trade and commerce with other countries (s 51(i)), prohibited the exportation of meat slaughtered in non-registered premises, whereas the State law prohibited the use of premises for slaughtering stock without a licence. A statutory majority of three justices (Dixon CJ, Fullagar and Kitto JJ) held that the two laws were inconsistent, while three other justices (McTiernan, Webb and Taylor JJ) considered they were not.[126] The difference of opinion turned on the characterisation of the Commonwealth Act. After recounting the requirements of the Commonwealth Regulations in some detail, Fullagar J observed that the Regulations prescribed 'an extremely elaborate and detailed set of requirements' as to the 'site, materials of construction, arrangement, dimensions and many other matters', and that this evinced an intention to 'express completely and exhaustively the requirements of the law with respect to the use of premises for the slaughter of stock for export', with the result that there was an inconsistency.[127] In his dissenting judgment, Taylor J considered that the Regulations 'present themselves not as rules of conduct with which the regulations imperatively require compliance, but as the antecedent specification of conditions the fulfilment of which will entitle an applicant to the issue of an export permit at the appropriate time'.[128] Plainly, both views of the Commonwealth Regulations were open: the first emphasised the exhaustive nature of the requirements laid down; the second emphasised the way in which the Regulations and the enabling legislation had to be framed so as to fall within the commerce power.

Another complex example is *Ansett Transport Industries (Operations) Pty Ltd v Wardley*.[129] In that case the Court had to consider whether the *Equal Opportunity Act 1977* (Vic) was inconsistent with an Airline Pilots Agreement registered under and given force of law by the *Conciliation and Arbitration Act 1904* (Cth). The Victorian Equal Opportunity Board found that Ansett had refused to employ Ms Wardley as a pilot because of her gender, in breach of the State Act, and ordered Ansett to employ her. Ansett commenced proceedings in the Supreme Court of Victoria for declarations that the relevant provisions of the State Act did not apply

**125** (1954) 92 CLR 565.
**126** The decision of the statutory majority prevailed pursuant to s 23 of the *Judiciary Act 1903*, which provides that in the case of a divided Court, the decision being appealed from will (in most instances) be affirmed, and in any other case, the opinion of the Chief Justice, or the senior justice, shall prevail. On further appeal, the Privy Council affirmed the decision of the High Court: *O'Sullivan v Noarlunga Meat Ltd* (1956) 95 CLR 177.
**127** *O'Sullivan v Noarlunga Meat Ltd* (1954) 92 CLR 565, 591–2.
**128** Ibid, 602–3.
**129** (1980) 142 CLR 237.

to it, which proceedings were removed into the High Court pursuant to s 40 of the *Judiciary Act 1903* (Cth). Ansett argued two grounds of inconsistency: the Agreement granted it a right to dismiss pilots which the State law could not constitutionally impair, and the Agreement was intended to cover the field, thus displacing the State law within that field. A majority of the Court held, however, that there was no inconsistency.

The reasoning of the Court was not entirely clear and tended to merge consideration of the two distinct lines of argument. Broadly considered, Mason, Murphy and Wilson JJ placed some emphasis on the proposition that, properly construed, the Agreement was not intended to cover the field of the employment and dismissal of airline pilots, but rather to leave room for the background operation of State laws, including anti-discrimination laws. Mason J said the Agreement 'should not be viewed as a general industry award which seeks to determine exhaustively the respective rights of employer and employee', but rather 'its emphasis is on setting out in exact detail the manner and procedure governing the advancement of a pilot in terms of seniority'.[130] Stephen J, although he also thought that there was no inconsistency, seemed to do so on the basis that the two laws were 'concerned with different subjects' which were 'essentially disparate in character': the State Act was concerned 'generally with the social problem of discrimination based upon sex or marital status', whereas the Agreement dealt with the settlement of 'an entirely orthodox industrial dispute'.[131] Such an analysis supported the conclusion that there was no inconsistency quite apart from any intention of the Commonwealth to cover the field.

In the apparently similar case of *Australian Mutual Provident Society v Goulden*,[132] the Court held that there was an inconsistency between a State anti-discrimination law and a Commonwealth Act. The federal law provided that a company shall not issue any insurance policy unless the premium payable had been approved by an actuary as suitable for its particular class of policy. Goulden, who was blind, argued that an insurance company had discriminated against him on the basis of his disability in refusing to vary one of the terms of his insurance policy. However, the Court considered that the Commonwealth Act was directed towards ensuring, among other things, the financial soundness of insurance companies. It was held that the State law purported to 'alter, impair or detract from' the policy of the Commonwealth law to enable insurers to determine the terms and conditions of their policies in a prudent manner bearing in mind the anticipated costs associated with insuring particular classes of risks.[133] In exercise of this power, a Commonwealth law may not only 'cover' the field; it seems that it can also 'clear'

**130** *Ansett Transport Industries (Operations) Pty Ltd v Wardley* (1980) 142 CLR 237, 262.
**131** Ibid, 250–51.
**132** (1986) 160 CLR 330.
**133** *Australian Mutual Provident Society v Goulden* (1986) 160 CLR 330, 336–7.

the field of all regulation except for any residual common law left to operate within it.

**Explicit intention not to cover the field**

The Commonwealth may also express an intention that its law does not cover the field but rather leaves room for State laws to operate. An example is s 6A(1) of the *Racial Discrimination Act 1975* (Cth), which provides:

> This Act is not intended, and shall be deemed never to have been intended, to exclude or limit the operation of a law of a State or Territory that furthers the objects of the [*International Convention on the Elimination of All Forms of Racial Discrimination*] and is capable of operating concurrently with this Act.

Section 6A(1) was enacted in response to the High Court's decision in *Viskauskas v Niland*.[134] In that case the Court had to determine whether there was an inconsistency between the *Anti-Discrimination Act 1977* (NSW) and the *Racial Discrimination Act 1975* (Cth). Both Acts prohibited discrimination on the basis of race in a variety of situations. The Commonwealth law was enacted under the Commonwealth's external affairs power (s 51(xxix)) to fulfil Australia's obligations under the *International Convention on the Elimination of All Forms of Racial Discrimination* (1966). In assessing whether the law was intended to cover the field, the Court observed that these obligations required Australia to eliminate racial discrimination 'in all its forms', and to 'assure to everyone' within Australia the benefit of 'effective protection and remedies'. To fulfil these obligations, the Commonwealth could not, it was reasoned, 'admit the possibility that a State law might allow exceptions' or 'detract from the efficacy' of the federal scheme. As such, the very subject matter suggested that the law was intended to be 'exhaustive and exclusive', an observation supported by the 'complete generality' of its provisions, leading to the conclusion that it was intended to be 'a complete statement of the law for Australia relating to racial discrimination'.[135] It was thus held that the Commonwealth law covered the field and that the State law was inconsistent and therefore inoperative.

Whatever may have been the intention of the Parliament when the *Racial Discrimination Act* was enacted in 1975,[136] it seems that at least by 1983 the Parliament did not wish it to be understood to exclude the operation of State anti-discrimination laws which were capable of operating concurrently with it. The insertion of the new s 6A into the Act was directed, however, not only to expressing the Parliament's intention prospectively, but also retrospectively. While it had been established that the expression of an intention not to cover the field could be effected prospectively, the question that arose in *University of Wollongong v Metwally*[137] was whether it could be done retrospectively as well.

**134** (1983) 153 CLR 280.
**135** *Viskauskas v Niland* (1983) 153 CLR 280, 292.
**136** Michael Coper, *Encounters with the Australian Constitution* (CCH, 1988) 21–2.
**137** (1984) 158 CLR 447.

For, on one hand, it is well-established that the Parliament can in most circumstances legislate retrospectively. But, on the other hand, it is s 109, not the Commonwealth Act, which operates to make an inconsistent State law invalid, and prior to the enactment of s 6A, it could be said that s 109 had operated to this effect. In such circumstances, could the Commonwealth effectively undo the past effect of s 109?

A majority of the Court held that it could not do this, for s 109 operates with the paramount force of the Constitution.[138] As Gibbs CJ put it, the invalidity of a State law under s 109 'cannot later be excluded by retrospectively declaring that the truth was other than it was', for this would 'retrospectively deprive s 109 of the Constitution of its operation', and 'Commonwealth statutes cannot prevail over the Constitution'.[139] He added that s 109 is 'of great importance for the ordinary citizen, who is entitled to know which of two inconsistent laws he is required to observe'.[140] Deane J reasoned similarly. He emphasised that the Constitution 'lies above the law which ... the parliament may make', that the Constitution operates 'upon the reality', rather than upon 'retrospective fictions' or 'falsehoods', and that s 109 is 'unqualified and self-executing' upon 'the reality of contemporaneous inconsistency'.[141] Going somewhat further than the Chief Justice, he said that the Australian federation is to be understood as 'a union of people', and that the Constitution is 'ultimately concerned with the governance and protection of the people from whom the artificial entities called the Commonwealth and States derive their authority'. For this reason, s 109 'serves the equally important function of protecting the individual from the injustice of being subjected to the requirements of valid and inconsistent laws of the Commonwealth and State Parliaments on the same subject'. Consequently, the individual has 'the constitutional right to ignore' a State law imposing duties inconsistent with those imposed by Commonwealth law.[142]

For Murphy and Deane JJ, this conclusion did not necessarily mean that the State could not seek to remedy the situation by now enacting a new law which retrospectively reproduced the provisions of its earlier Act. In such a circumstance, as Deane J explained, the question of the new State law's consistency would be determined by reference to the Commonwealth law after the enactment of s 6A, which in its prospective operation would prevent any relevant inconsistency from arising.[143] In this way, the Commonwealth law could 'clear the way for the State Parliament to make a fresh State Act to apply retrospectively in the same terms'.[144]

**138** *University of Wollongong v Metwally* (1984) 158 CLR 447, 457, 469, 474–5, 479.
**139** Ibid, 457.
**140** Ibid, 458.
**141** Ibid, 478.
**142** Ibid, 476–7.
**143** Ibid, 480–81.
**144** Ibid, 469.

In his dissenting judgment, Mason J noted the undoubted general principle that the Commonwealth has power to make retrospective laws, and that when the Commonwealth does so it can remove the inconsistency which attracts the operation of s 109. This does not nullify the effect of s 109, however, it only eliminates the basis on which it can operate.[145] To conclude otherwise, he maintained, is to attribute to s 109 'the character of a constitutional fetter on Commonwealth legislative power'.[146] Rather, when a State law is inconsistent with a Commonwealth law, it is not rendered 'void' but only 'inoperative', so that when the Commonwealth law is relevantly repealed, even if retrospectively, the State law becomes operative again.[147] On his view, s 109 does 'no more and no less' than establish the supremacy of Commonwealth law; it is not a source of individual rights and immunities.[148] Because the Commonwealth Parliament is 'sovereign' and its powers are 'plenary', there can be no objection to the enactment of statutes that retrospectively alter the law, whether they do so through a 'statutory fiction' which 'deems' the law to have had a certain operation in the past, or through a more direct statement as to the past intention of the Parliament.[149]

In order effectively to cover a particular field the Commonwealth must have power to legislate over the entire field. As seen in Chapter 3, in *Commonwealth v Australian Capital Territory*,[150] the High Court held that the provision for same-sex marriage in the *Marriage Equality (Same Sex) Act 2013* (ACT) was inconsistent with the definition of 'marriage' in the *Marriage Act 1961* (Cth) and the *Family Law Act 1975* (Cth). The Court considered that an inconsistency within the meaning of s 28(1) of the *Australian Capital Territory (Self-Government) Act 1988* (Cth) may arise where a Commonwealth law evinces an intention to provide a complete statement of the law concerning a particular relation or thing and a Territory law seeks to govern some aspect of that relation or thing.[151] It held that the provision in the ACT law for same-sex marriage was not capable of operating concurrently with the Commonwealth law within the meaning of s 28(1), because the Commonwealth law upon its proper construction provided that the only form of marriage permitted was marriage between a man and a woman as defined in the Act.[152] In so deciding, the Court considered that it was necessary to show that the Commonwealth's power extended over the entire topic of 'marriage' considered as a 'topic of juristic classification' – a topic which includes provision for same-sex marriage.[153] If the Commonwealth did not have power to legislate for same-sex marriage, the Court reasoned, then there could

**145** Ibid, 460.
**146** Ibid, 461.
**147** Ibid, 462. See Part II.5 below.
**148** Ibid, 462–3.
**149** Ibid, 465.
**150** (2013) 250 CLR 441.
**151** Ibid, [52].
**152** Ibid, [55]–[61].
**153** Ibid, [9].

be no inconsistency between the two laws, essentially because the Territory law would deal with a subject matter lying outside Commonwealth power. However, if the Commonwealth does have power to provide for same-sex marriage, and provides that the only form of marriage in Australia is to be between a man and a woman, then the two laws will not be able to operate concurrently, essentially because the Commonwealth law has 'covered the field'.[154] In formulating the issue in this way, it became necessary for the Court to pronounce upon the abstract scope of the marriage power and to articulate a general definition of the juristic topic of 'marriage'. The Court held that the Commonwealth did have the requisite power to legislate for same-sex marriage. However, as noted in Chapter 3, whether it was necessary for the Court to do so may be questioned. Certainly, submissions of the Commonwealth Solicitor-General that the Court could avoid going so far were rejected by the Court.[155]

### 5 Consequences of inconsistency

When a State law is inconsistent with a Commonwealth law, s 109 provides that the State law is, to the extent of the inconsistency, 'invalid'. However, bearing in mind that s 107 preserves the legislative powers of the States, the term 'invalid' has been understood by the Court to mean that the State law is 'suspended, inoperative and ineffective' rather than absolutely void.[156] This has several implications. First, the State law is only inoperative to the extent of the inconsistency, so that any aspect of the State law which can be severed from the inconsistent parts will continue to operate.[157] Second, once the inconsistency ceases to exist, the operation of the State law will be re-enlivened.[158] This latter possibility can clearly occur when a Commonwealth law is subsequently repealed or amended in some relevant respect. But it can also occur when it is subsequently held that the constitutional support for a Commonwealth law no longer exists, such as when a law enacted under the defence power can no longer be supported because the circumstances under which the law was enacted have relevantly changed.[159]

## III Intergovernmental immunities

The consensus of opinion in the 1890s was that the Australian colonies came into the federation as equal contracting parties possessing mutually independent

**154** Ibid.
**155** Patrick Parkinson and Nicholas Aroney, 'The Territory of Marriage: Constitutional Law, Marriage Law and Family Policy in the Same Sex Marriage Act Case' (2014) 28 *Australian Journal of Family Law* 1.
**156** *Butler v Attorney-General (Vic)* (1961) 106 CLR 268, 286; *University of Wollongong v Metwally* (1984) 158 CLR 447, 462.
**157** *Wenn v Attorney-General (Vic)* (1948) 77 CLR 84, 122.
**158** *Carter v Egg & Egg Pulp Marketing Board (Vic)* (1942) 66 CLR 557, 573.
**159** *Illawarra District County Council v Wickham* (1959) 101 CLR 467; *Butler v Attorney-General (Vic)* (1961) 106 CLR 268.

self-governing powers, including a capacity to determine their own constitutional destinies substantially free from Imperial interference.[160] The main way in which this was secured was through the institution of locally-elected Parliaments possessing virtually plenary legislative powers, and the establishment of local systems of parliamentary responsible government.[161] Federation did not entail the eradication of these independent legislative, executive and judicial powers of local self-government. Their continuance, subject to the Commonwealth Constitution (ss 106 and 107), was one of the fundamental presuppositions of the federal compact. However, federation also involved the establishment of the Commonwealth itself as a genuinely 'federal government' possessing similarly independent powers of self-government (ss 1, 61 and 71).

This assumption of the mutual independence of the Commonwealth and the States, qualified in specific ways by provision for mutual interdependence and cooperation, and with Commonwealth supremacy in certain respects (s 109), is fundamental to the design and structure of the Constitution. The governing institutions of the Commonwealth and the States are established separately and independently, and are directly elected by their respective peoples. There is no provision, as in the Federal Republic of Germany, for the appointment of members of the Senate by the State Governments;[162] nor, as was the case in the United States, for their appointment by the State Parliaments.[163] Nor is there any provision for the appointment of State Governors or judges by the Federal Government, as in Canada.[164] Full legislative, executive and judicial powers were given to the Commonwealth to enable it to govern without having to rely upon the intermediate action of the States, as had been the case with Federal Council of Australasia.[165] In addition, the colonies were called 'States' and not merely 'provinces' to convey the fundamental independence that they would continue to enjoy within the federation. As the Premier of New South Wales, George Dibbs, put it:

> I object, in connection with the independent state of New South Wales – a state as independent as any in the world, even England itself, so far as the freedom of our position is concerned – to the word 'province'. There may be something more dignified in the use of the word 'state'. We are not going to become provinces. I do not think we are going to give up the individual rights and liberties which we possess, and which those who have gone before us have fought for, to become mere provinces under a federal form of government.[166]

It is in the context of this fundamental assumption of mutual independence and limited interdependence that the specific provisions in the Constitution which either qualify the principle of independence or provide for additional

**160** *Convention Debates, Sydney* (1890) 10.
**161** For more on responsible government, see Chapter 6, Part V.
**162** Constitution of the German Reich (1871), Art 6; German Basic Law (1949), Art 51(1).
**163** United States Constitution (1787), Art I, sec 3 (altered by the 17th Amendment).
**164** *Constitution Act 1867* (UK), ss 58 and 96.
**165** *Federal Council of Australasia Act 1885* (UK).
**166** *Convention Debates, Sydney* (1891) 183.

guarantees thereof should be understood. Some of these provisions expressly prohibit the enactment of legislation that would bind the States or the Commonwealth. For example, Commonwealth legislation cannot apply to 'State banking' or 'State insurance' except State banking or insurance that extends beyond the State (ss 51(xiii) and (xiv)). Similarly, the Commonwealth cannot impose a tax on State property, and a State cannot impose a tax on Commonwealth property (s 114). Other provisions expressly grant the Commonwealth Parliament power to make laws binding the States. For example, the Constitution authorises Commonwealth legislation which acquires property from States (s 51(xxxi)), invests State courts with federal jurisdiction (s 77(iii)), confers rights to proceed against States (s 78), prescribes the number of State judges to exercise federal jurisdiction (s 79), deals with State railways (s 98), prohibits State preferences (s 102) and regulates the States' compliance with State debt agreements (s 105A).

Considered without reference to the federal origins and intent of the Constitution, it is conceivably possible to argue in two different directions on the basis of these provisions. The first line of argument is that the provisions which specifically protect the States or the Commonwealth from interference rest upon the assumption that in all other respects Commonwealth laws and State laws can interfere with the operations of the other. The second line of argument is that the provisions that authorise the enactment of Commonwealth laws which bind or affect the operations of the States imply that, apart from these specific instances, the general rule is that Commonwealth legislation cannot bind the States.

These lines of essentially textualist argument can, in turn, be complicated by arguments connected with other provisions of the Constitution that might be thought to bear on the issue. Arguments from s 109 of the Constitution can, for example, also cut both ways. On one hand, it might be seen as a provision which articulates a general principle of the relative supremacy of the Commonwealth over the States, which supremacy might be said to imply a general immunity from interference enjoyed by the Commonwealth. On the other hand, it may be argued that s 109 enables the Commonwealth to legislate to exclude the operation of any State law which interferes with it, making an implied immunity unnecessary.[167] Similarly, s 106, which preserves the State Constitutions 'subject to' the Commonwealth Constitution, might be interpreted to mean that State institutions of government are, in principle, subject to Commonwealth laws enacted pursuant to powers conferred by the Commonwealth Constitution. Alternatively, however, it might mean that at least some aspects of the State Constitutions, such as the States' governing institutions, are immune from Commonwealth interference.

Background conceptions of the constitutional relationship between the legislative, executive and judicial branches of government within each polity are also potentially relevant.[168] The doctrine of parliamentary sovereignty is a

**167** One possible difficulty with this argument is that the powers and capacities of the Crown in right of the Commonwealth may extend to matters outside the legislative powers of the Commonwealth.
**168** See Chapter 1, Part II.2–3.

well-established principle of English and British law which entails, among other things, that the various prerogatives, executive powers and privileges of the Crown and the Executive Government are subject to parliamentary enactment. However, this principle developed in England and later in the United Kingdom in the context of that polity's unitary system of government. While the principle undoubtedly applies to the relationship between the Parliament and the Crown within the Commonwealth and within each State, it does not necessarily follow that it can or should apply within Australia's federal system as between the Commonwealth Parliament and a State Government or a State Parliament and the Commonwealth Government. Relatedly, there is the doctrine of the indivisibility of the Crown, a principle which underlay prevailing nineteenth- and early twentieth-century conceptions of the role of the Crown as the unifying element of the British Empire.[169] As will be explained in more detail below, this doctrine was deployed in the *Engineers* case to combat the proposition that the States enjoy an immunity from Commonwealth legislation that would interfere with any of the agencies and other instrumentalities through which they pursue their governmental objectives. And yet, as H V Evatt pointed out, it can cogently be argued that it was the unity and ubiquity of the Crown that had facilitated the emergence of the Australian colonies as politically independent bodies politic possessing full powers of local self-governance in the form of the prerogatives of the Crown.[170]

These principles, although certainly important parts of the common law inherited by the Australian colonies and presupposed by the framers of the Constitution, do not shed decisive light on questions about the extent to which the legislation of the Commonwealth or the States can constitutionally interfere with or regulate the operations of the other. Nor do they explain why some powers to interfere, and some immunities from interference, were specifically included in the Constitution. These limited powers and immunities are better explained, it can be argued, by reference to the general underlying presuppositions and values which led the framers of the Constitution to define the powers and the immunities of the Commonwealth and the States in the ways that they did. Foremost among these was the general presupposition of the mutual independence of each of the Australian colonies and their collective determination to secure, preserve and extend their capacities of local self-government and constitutional self-determination through the act of federation. Their reasoning was that federation would entail the formation of a federal commonwealth having full and independent powers of local self-governance for the people of Australia as a whole, exercised without dependence upon the intermediate action of the States to enforce its measures or supply its necessary funds; and that the States would retain the independent powers of local self-governance with which they entered the federation, and would not become in any sense dependent or

**169** *R v Bank of Nova Scotia* (1885) 11 SCR 1, 19–20. See also *Calvin's* case [1572] 7 Co Rep 1a; 77 ER 377.
**170** H V Evatt, *The Royal Prerogative* (Law Book Company, 1987) 55–6.

subordinate to the Commonwealth in the exercise of their retained powers. This general perspective was made quite clear in the first of the resolutions that were carried at the Federal Conventions of 1891 and 1897–8. At the Second Convention, the relevant resolution stated:

> That, in order to enlarge the powers of self-government of the people of Australia, it is desirable to create a Federal Government which shall exercise authority throughout the Federated Colonies, subject to the following principal conditions:–
>
> I. That the powers, privileges, and territories of the several existing colonies shall remain intact, except in respect of such surrenders as may be agreed upon to secure uniformity of law and administration in matters of common concern.[171]

The delegates to the Convention plainly envisaged the creation of a 'national federal government' possessing a full array of legislative, executive and judicial powers that could be exercised independently of the States, but they also just as clearly envisaged the preservation and continuance of all of the existing self-governing powers, privileges and territorial rights of the colonies, subject only to such surrenders as might be agreed upon as necessary to the creation of the federal government. As Quick and Garran later observed:

> [T]he people of the Commonwealth, in the majority of States, will not feel inclined to interfere with the principles of local liberty, local self-government, State autonomy, and State individuality which pervade the Constitution. They will recoil from an Imperial policy of consolidation and centralization, which would swallow up, absorb, and obliterate the States.[172]

Understood against these background assumptions, it is not to be supposed that the Commonwealth or the States will ordinarily be able to legislate in a way that interferes with the operation of the governing institutions of the other, except as clearly required by the Constitution. A principle of mutual independence, with limited interdependence, was the underlying assumption of the framers of the Constitution, and they negotiated and drafted the terms and structure of the Constitution with this assumption constantly in mind. That it was a principle that went to the constitutional foundations of the Commonwealth and the States is seen most clearly in the debate over the extent to which the State Constitutions could legitimately be the subject of regulation in the Commonwealth Constitution. As will be seen in Chapter 10, an overwhelming majority of the framers rejected the proposition that it would be appropriate for the Commonwealth Constitution to contain any substantive or direct provision concerning the State Constitutions, save that they would 'continue' and that they would be 'subject to' the necessary limitation of their legislative powers in the terms of ss 107, 108 and 109, and other specific limitations (eg, ss 51(xxxi), 77(iii), 78, 79, 98 and 102). Apart from these qualifications, the framers resolutely resisted

**171** *Convention Debates, Adelaide* (1897) 17, 395; see also *Convention Debates, Sydney* (1891) 23, 499–500.
**172** Quick and Garran, above n 32, 992.

any suggestion that the Commonwealth Constitution, or the Commonwealth itself, should 'interfere' with the independent powers of local self-governance possessed by the colonies, soon to become States. So many important provisions of the Commonwealth and State Constitutions are directed to the establishment of their independent governing capacities that it would be tedious to recount them. As far as the Commonwealth is concerned, virtually the entire content of Chapters I, II and III is directed to establishing the Commonwealth as an independent government, while the corresponding provisions of each of the State Constitutions are plainly directed to the establishment and maintenance of similarly independent systems of local self-governance. Only a relatively small proportion of the provisions of the Commonwealth Constitution, most of them in Chapters IV and V, deal with the interrelationship and, in some respects, interdependence of the Commonwealth and the States.

The High Court of Australia, as first composed, consisted of three judges who interpreted the powers and immunities of the Commonwealth and the States largely in line with this general outlook. As will be seen, they understood the relationship between the Commonwealth and the States in terms of a conception of sovereignty which permitted absolutely no intergovernmental interference, no matter how slight, unless it could be justified by something specific in the Constitution. This approach was rejected by a differently composed Court in the *Engineers* case in 1920,[173] but the idea that the federal nature of the Constitution carries implications which limit the capacity of the Commonwealth to interfere with the States was reasserted, especially by Dixon and Evatt JJ, in a series of judgments from the 1930s, culminating in the *Melbourne Corporation* case of 1947.[174] Dixon J was also responsible for a very different doctrine of Commonwealth immunity from State laws, adopted by the Court in *Commonwealth v Cigamatic Pty Ltd* in 1962,[175] this time premised on a conception of the Commonwealth as relatively supreme and especially immune from State interference and regulation. As the foregoing discussion suggests, how much the *Cigamatic* doctrine, as distinct from the principle in *Melbourne Corporation*, is consistent with and justifiable by reference to the text, structure and manifest purposes of the Constitution may be doubted.

## 1 Independent sovereignty: Immunity of instrumentalities (1903–20)

### Commonwealth immunity

*D'Emden v Pedder*[176] was the first case in which the Griffith Court had the occasion to consider the distinctly federal nature of the Australian Constitution.

**173** *Amalgamated Society of Engineers v Adelaide Steamship Co Ltd* (1920) 28 CLR 129.
**174** *Melbourne Corporation v Commonwealth* (1947) 74 CLR 31.
**175** (1962) 108 CLR 372.
**176** (1904) 1 CLR 91.

The question before the Court was whether a Tasmanian statute which required the payment of 2d stamp duty on, among other things, any receipt issued for the payment of a sum between £5 and £50 could constitutionally apply to a receipt issued for the salary of a Commonwealth employee, in this case the Deputy Postmaster-General for Tasmania. Delivering the judgment of the Court, Griffith CJ began with the proposition that the Commonwealth and each of the States is 'sovereign' within the 'ambit of its authority':

> In considering the respective powers of the Commonwealth and of the States it is essential to bear in mind that each is, within the ambit of its authority, a sovereign State, subject only to the restrictions imposed by the Imperial connection and to the provisions of the Constitution, either expressed or necessarily implied.[177]

In support of this conclusion, Griffith CJ appealed to *Powell v Apollo Candle Co*,[178] in which the Privy Council had affirmed that the grant of legislative power to the Parliament of New South Wales effectively conferred 'sovereign authority, absolute and uncontrolled'.[179] Applying this to both the Commonwealth and the States, Griffith CJ drew attention to the direct Imperial source of State and Commonwealth legislative power, entailing as it did a conferral of sovereign power, within jurisdictional limits.

The next step in Griffith CJ's reasoning was to maintain that sovereign authority implies freedom from extrinsic control or interference:

> But a right of sovereignty subject to extrinsic control is a contradiction in terms. It must, therefore, be taken to be of the essence of the Constitution that the Commonwealth is entitled, within the ambit of its authority, to exercise its legislative and executive powers in absolute freedom, and without any interference or control whatever except that prescribed by the Constitution itself.[180]

This was a proposition that could apply equally to the protection of both State and Commonwealth authority, but in *D'Emden* it was applied specifically to State interference with the Commonwealth. The Chief Justice concluded:

> when a State attempts to give to its legislative or executive authority an operation which, if valid, would fetter, control, or interfere with, the free exercise of the legislative or executive power of the Commonwealth, the attempt, unless expressly authorised by the Constitution, is to that extent invalid and inoperative.[181]

Thus, subject to any specific provision in the Constitution to the contrary, the 'sovereignty' of the Commonwealth within its sphere of operation implied a complete immunity from any fetter, interference or control. Griffith CJ explained that this would include 'attaching … any condition to the discharge of a federal duty'.[182] A State tax on federal salaries would constitute such an

**177** *D'Emden v Pedder* (1904) 1 CLR 91, 109.
**178** (1885) 10 App Cas 282.
**179** *D'Emden v Pedder* (1904) 1 CLR 91, 110.
**180** Ibid, 110–11.
**181** Ibid, 111.
**182** Ibid, 119.

interference, because it would 'exercise control upon the action of a federal officer in the discharge of this duty to the Commonwealth'.[183] However, the Chief Justice considered that the Tasmanian Act could be construed so as not to apply to the Deputy Postmaster-General, and could be upheld on the basis of that narrow construction.[184]

Although none of the prevailing theories of legal and political sovereignty circulating at the time were directly cited in the judgment, Griffith CJ's reasoning asserted a conception of sovereignty very similar to that which had been proposed by British legal philosopher, John Austin. According to Austin, there must be a singular locus of sovereignty in every political society; such sovereignty entails complete independence from any external authority; and therefore in federal systems, sovereignty must be located in *either* the institutions of the federal state as a whole *or* in the governing institutions of the constituent states.[185] Austin's theory was highly influential, but it did not quite capture the way in which federal systems resist the identification of sovereignty with one or other order of government. A V Dicey therefore proposed an alternative theory, in which federations are marked by a 'division of sovereignty' between the national and state governments, the terms of which are contained in a constitution which is 'supreme' over both sets of governments and which is conclusively interpreted by an independent and tenured judiciary.[186] This more closely reflected the way in which modern federations are constitutionally constructed. However, even Dicey's attempt to reconcile the concept of sovereignty with federalism did not quite do justice to the origins and structure of integrative federations such as Australia's. This is because the idea of 'division' of sovereignty could not explain the fact the constituent colonies came into the federation with generally plenary powers of legislation and that they agreed to the conferral of only limited powers on the Commonwealth while retaining most of their original powers to themselves. Closer to the design and structure of the Constitution was James Bryce's conception of a 'Commonwealth' constructed out of 'commonwealths', in which the constituent states are understood to be 'more essential' to the existence of the federation than it is to theirs, thus creating a system in which two apparently contradictory propositions can be 'represented as both true, namely national and state sovereignty'.[187] Such a paradox could be reconciled, Edward Freeman had explained, provided it is understood that each order of government is 'wholly independent' or 'sovereign' in its particular 'sphere' of operation, albeit that

**183** Ibid, 118.
**184** Ibid, 119–20.
**185** John Austin, *The Province of Jurisprudence Determined* (Weidenfeld and Nicolson, [1832] 1954) 193–5, 245–6.
**186** A V Dicey, *Introduction to the Study of the Law of the Constitution* (Macmillan, 5th ed, 1897) 130–55, 410–13.
**187** James Bryce, *The American Commonwealth* (Macmillan, 3rd ed, 1893) vol I, 12–15, 306, 311–12, 332, 409.

the laws of the federation must be supreme over State laws in the case of any inconsistency.[188]

In the context of these background theories of federalism, *D'Emden v Pedder* is usually seen as giving effect to a 'coordinate' theory of Australian federalism in which sovereignty is 'distributed' into distinct spheres of operation. It is significant to note, however, that in support of his general conclusions, Griffith CJ extracted a very lengthy passage from the judgment of Marshall CJ of the US Supreme Court in *McCulloch v Maryland* in which the sovereign immunity of the United States from State taxation was supported on the basis of the federal government's supremacy over the States, rather than on the coordinate relationship between them. As Marshall CJ put it, 'though limited in its powers', the federal government 'is supreme within its sphere of action'.[189] He stated:

> [T]he people of all the States have created the General Government, and have conferred upon it the general power of taxation. The people of all the States, and the States themselves, are represented in Congress, and, by their representatives, exercise this power. When they tax the chartered institutions of the States, they tax their constituents, and these taxes must be uniform. But when a State taxes the operations of the Government of the United States, it acts upon institutions created not by their own constituents, but by people over whom they claim no control. ... The difference is ... between the action of the whole on a part, and the action of a part on the whole – between the laws of a Government declared to be supreme, and those of a Government which, when in opposition to those laws, is not supreme.[190]

There is a subtle sleight of hand in this reasoning, particularly in the reference to 'the people of all the States'. Although Marshall CJ acknowledged elsewhere in the judgment that the Constitution had been ratified separately by the distinct peoples of the several American States, he proposed that a unitary American 'people' had ratified the Constitution.[191] Such an approach cohered with 'national sovereignty' conceptions of federalism in which ultimate sovereignty is understood to reside in the people of the entire nation, understood in unitary terms. By citing Marshall CJ's judgment, Griffith CJ opened the way to an interpretation of *D'Emden v Pedder* based on this national sovereignty premise, rather than the theory of dual sovereignty which he seems to have preferred. As will be seen, this was precisely the point that would be taken by up Isaacs J in *Engineers*, and it bears a deep affinity with the approach that would be adopted by Dixon CJ when reconstructing a special and extensive immunity enjoyed by the Commonwealth in *Cigamatic*.

The principle in *D'Emden v Pedder* was applied to protect the Commonwealth from State interference in several subsequent cases which involved the

**188** Edward Freeman, *History of Federal Government in Greece and Italy* (Macmillan, 2nd ed, 1893) 1–3, 7–8.
**189** *McCulloch v Maryland* 17 US (4 Wheat) 316 (1819), 405.
**190** Ibid, 435; cf at 426, 429, 432–3.
**191** Ibid, 402–5.

imposition of municipal rates, State income taxes and stamp duty on transfers of property.[192] In these cases, the implied immunity was regarded as being so well established that counsel directed their arguments, not to foundational questions about the basis and justification of the doctrine, but to its application in the circumstances.[193] In *Commonwealth v New South Wales*, for example, O'Connor J could affirm that:

> it is impossible to hold that a State can legally impose such a tax under such circumstances. Those principles are now so well known and recognized in the interpretation of our Constitution that it is no longer necessary to state the arguments by which they are to be supported.[194]

Nonetheless, differences of opinion existed. In *Deakin v Webb*,[195] the Court had to consider the imposition of State income tax on two Commonwealth cabinet ministers, Alfred Deakin and William Lyne. Two of the opposing counsel were H B Higgins and Isaac Isaacs, both of whom would soon be appointed to the High Court. In his submissions to the Court, Isaacs KC, appearing for the Commissioner of Taxes, Thomas Webb, seemed especially concerned to distinguish the Australian Constitution from its American counterpart. He did so by underscoring, in terms that recalled the theories of Dicey and especially Austin, the overarching sovereignty of the Imperial Parliament:

> The United States Constitution is a grant by the people of the States. There is no power above them. The Australian Constitution is a grant and distribution of powers by the Imperial Parliament. The Constitutions of the States now depend on the Constitution of the Commonwealth. *Marshall*, CJ, said that the powers of a State legislature, which are conferred by a single State, cannot over-ride the powers of the United States, which are given by the people of all the States. That cannot be said of the Australian States and the Commonwealth. The powers of the Australian States and of the Commonwealth come from the same source. All that this Court can look at in construing the Constitution is its legal aspect.[196]

In response to this submission, Griffith CJ (with whom Barton and O'Connor JJ agreed) pointed to the structural similarities between the United States and Australian Constitutions. He said that it makes no difference that the source of legislative power in Australia is the Imperial Parliament whereas in the United States it might be 'the people'. The framers of the Australian Constitution adopted the American scheme of conferring 'definite and specified powers upon the Commonwealth' and of leaving 'the residue of power in the hands of the States'. More particularly, and unlike the situation in Canada, there is in Australia no

**192** *Sydney Municipal Council v Commonwealth* (1904) 1 CLR 208; *Deakin v Webb; Lyne v Webb* (1904) 1 CLR 585; *Commonwealth v New South Wales* (1906) 3 CLR 807.
**193** Eg, *Commonwealth v New South Wales* (1906) 3 CLR 807, 810.
**194** Ibid, 824.
**195** *Deakin v Webb; Lyne v Webb* (1904) 1 CLR 585.
**196** Ibid, 596–7.

'exclusive distribution of powers, except as to a limited class of cases', and no 'new' powers are conferred upon the States.[197]

**State immunity**

It was not until the *Railway Servants* case,[198] decided in 1906, that the federal principle established in *D'Emden* was applied reciprocally to protect the States from federal interference. The case concerned the *Commonwealth Conciliation and Arbitration Act 1904*, which provided for an arbitration system under which industrial organisations could be registered. The terms of the Act were wide enough to include unions consisting of employees of State instrumentalities such as the State Railways of New South Wales. Once again, Griffith CJ delivered the decision of the Court. He considered that if State railway authorities could be subject to the jurisdiction of the Commonwealth industrial court, 'the effective control of the State Railways may to a great extent be taken out of their hands'.[199] In determining whether the industrial arbitration power (s 51(xxxv)) extended to the State Railways, Griffith CJ observed that:

> The Constitution Act is not only an Act of the Imperial legislature, but it embodies a compact entered into between the six Australian Colonies which formed the Commonwealth. This is recited in the preamble to the Act itself.[200]

Since the States and Commonwealth are each 'within the ambit of its authority, a sovereign State', he continued, it follows that the States are likewise immune from 'any fetter, control or interference' by the Commonwealth.[201] In coming to this conclusion, Griffith CJ adopted the reasoning of the US Supreme Court in *Collector v Day*,[202] where it had been said by Nelson J that 'in respect of the reserved powers, the State is as sovereign and independent as the general government'.

Sir Samuel Griffith's doctrine of the reciprocal immunity of instrumentalities of both the Commonwealth and the States thus seems to have been influenced, directly or indirectly, by the theories of Freeman, Bryce, Dicey and Austin. At the foundation of Griffith's approach was Bryce's and Freeman's conception of a federative compact among autonomous states. However, Griffith also conceived of a Diceyan division of sovereignty among coordinate state and federal governments, in which each enjoyed a qualified Austinian sovereignty which admitted of no 'extrinsic interference or control'. It will shortly be seen that, while Griffith's Austinian idea of a 'complete' immunity from all interference has not survived, the more Brycean idea of governmental 'autonomy' has endured.

**197** Ibid, 605–6.
**198** *Federated Amalgamated Governmental Railway and Tramway Service Association v New South Wales Railway Traffic Employees Association* (1906) 4 CLR 488.
**199** Ibid, 532.
**200** Ibid, 534.
**201** Ibid, 537.
**202** 78 US (11 Wall) 113 (1871), 127, cited in *Federated Amalgamated Governmental Railway and Tramway Service Association v New South Wales Railway Traffic Employees Association* (1906) 4 CLR 488, 537.

Despite its ascendancy in Australia, the immunity of instrumentalities doctrine was directly contradicted by a decision of the Judicial Committee of the Privy Council in *Webb v Outtrim*,[203] an appeal from a judgment of the Supreme Court of Victoria in which the Privy Council held that a State could tax the income of a Commonwealth officer, the Deputy Postmaster-General for Victoria. Against the view that had been maintained by the Griffith Court, the Judicial Committee, much like Isaacs KC had urged in *Deakin v Webb,* approached the Australian Constitution primarily in its nature as a statute of the Imperial Parliament – an approach which prevented any relevant analogy being made between the Australian and American Constitutions. In the view of the Privy Council, when proposed laws of the Commonwealth or the States receive the royal assent, they acquire the sovereign authority of an Imperial Act and are subject only to overriding Imperial legislation. Indeed, the Judicial Committee went so far as to maintain that, in line with orthodox British understandings, there can be no such thing as 'judicial review' under the Australian Constitution – unlike the position in the United States, where there the courts have jurisdiction to declare statutes unconstitutional. Noting that the Constitution contains no explicit prohibition on State interference with the Commonwealth other than limited provisions such as s 114, the Privy Council concluded that the existence of an 'implied prohibition' would have to be rejected.[204]

In the course of its reasoning, the Privy Council quoted passages from judgments of Griffith CJ in which he had referred to matters of 'common knowledge', such as that the framers of the Australian Constitution had deliberately adopted the American, rather than the Canadian, approach to constructing the federal distribution of powers.[205] However, their Lordships observed that the Chief Justice had not specified the exact provisions of the three Constitutions that he was comparing, which made it difficult for their Lordships to understand, assess or accept his reasoning.[206] In *Baxter v Commissioners of Taxation (NSW)*,[207] Griffith CJ responded emphatically. In a majority judgment in which Barton and O'Connor JJ again concurred, he maintained that the High Court was not bound by the Privy Council in inter se matters (see s 74), and he reasserted that the States could not tax the income of Commonwealth customs officials.[208] In so concluding, he reaffirmed the reasoning in *D'Emden v Pedder* – particularly that the Commonwealth and the States were within their respective jurisdictions

**203** [1907] AC 81; (1906) 4 CLR 356.
**204** *Webb v Outtrim* (1906) 4 CLR 356, 358–61.
**205** Ibid, 359–60, citing *D'Emden v Pedder* (1904) 1 CLR 91, 110, 113 and *Deakin v Webb* (1904) 1 CLR 585, 606–7.
**206** *Webb v Outtrim* (1906) 4 CLR 356, 360.
**207** *Baxter v Commissioners of Taxation (NSW)* (1907) 4 CLR 1087.
**208** Higgins J dissented on the ground that the Privy Council decision in *Webb v Outrim* was binding; Isaacs J on the ground that while *D'Emden* stood, the State tax did not interfere with the Commonwealth. This particular issue was later resolved by the *Commonwealth Salaries Act 1907,* which subjected Commonwealth salaries to State income taxes. See Part III.2 below. For more on the role of the High Court and Privy Council in inter se matters, see Chapter 8, Part II.

sovereign, and that sovereignty admits no interference.[209] He acknowledged that the Constitution was in the form of an Act of the Imperial Parliament, but insisted that its underlying nature and purpose was to give effect to an 'international agreement' between the peoples of the several Australian colonies, and between the Australian people collectively and the United Kingdom.[210] This idea of an 'agreement' or compact underscored the 'local origin' of the Australian Constitution and the need to interpret it in the light of local aspirations. Indeed, while no 'disrespect' was of course implied, Griffith CJ obliquely likened the approach of the Privy Council to an interpretation of the Constitution by an 'astral intelligence ... merely by the aid of a dictionary'![211] Privy Councillors, he pointed out, would not necessarily be 'familiar with the history or conditions of the remoter portions of the Empire', nor have 'any sympathetic understanding of the aspirations of the younger communities which had long enjoyed the privilege of self-government'.[212] By comparison, the High Court was fully cognisant of the 'local history' that lay behind the Constitution,[213] and of how the provisions of the Constitution gave effect to those aspirations.[214] Accordingly, the High Court, not the Privy Council, must be the final authority to determine questions of 'purely Australian domestic concern', such as the limits inter se of the powers of the Commonwealth and the States.[215]

### Exceptions to immunity

The immunities enjoyed by the Commonwealth and the States were always stated to be subject to any specific exceptions established by the Constitution. These especially concerned several of the legislative powers of the Commonwealth which due to their nature and scope must necessarily authorise some form of interference with the States. In the *Steel Rails* case,[216] for example, the High Court held that the Commonwealth could levy customs duty on steel railway line imported by New South Wales, despite the implied immunities doctrine. It was held that the doctrine has no operation where an express power conferred on the Commonwealth by its very nature must involve the control of some operation of a State Government. The Constitution, it was reasoned, gives the Commonwealth power to control 'in every respect Australia's relations with the outside world', especially international trade, customs duties, immigration, quarantine and external affairs, and effective federal control over these matters requires that the States are not immune from federal customs duties.[217]

**209** *Baxter v Commissioners of Taxation (NSW)* (1907) 4 CLR 1087, 1120–21.
**210** Ibid, 1104, 1121.
**211** Ibid, 1106, 1109, 1111.
**212** Ibid, 1111–12.
**213** Ibid, 1109.
**214** Ibid, 1112–17, 1122–4, 1126–8. Indeed, he claimed (at 1124) that the Privy Council did not appear to have read the entirety of the High Court's decision in *Deakin v Webb* (1904) 1 CLR 585, 605, in which an analysis of the relevant provisions was set out.
**215** *Baxter v Commissioners of Taxation (NSW)* (1907) 4 CLR 1087, 1117–20.
**216** *Attorney-General (NSW) v Collector of Customs (NSW)* (1908) 5 CLR 818.
**217** Ibid, 833, 836, 842, 850, 853.

Similarly, in the *Engine-Drivers* case,[218] the Court held that the immunity did not protect State government instrumentalities, such as municipal corporations, insofar as they engage in trading operations and thereby bring themselves within the jurisdiction of the Commonwealth in relation to arbitration and conciliation of industrial disputes.[219] Furthermore, in the *Municipalities* case,[220] a new majority of Isaacs, Higgins, Gavan Duffy, Powers and Rich JJ (Griffith CJ and Barton J dissenting) held that local government bodies do not function as instrumentalities of a State insofar as they engage in 'the making, maintenance, control and lighting of public streets', and are not, therefore, immune from Commonwealth industrial arbitration legislation in that respect. Through the course of these decisions, Isaacs and Higgins JJ persistently indicated their preference for the Privy Council's approach to the question of intergovernmental immunities, but until the *Engineers* case in 1920 they had to accept the Griffith doctrine as orthodoxy and be content with crafting limitations on the doctrine.[221]

## 2 Parliamentary supremacy: *Engineers* (1920–47)

The facts, legislation and general reasoning in the *Engineers* case,[222] as well as its profoundly influential rejection of the reserved powers doctrine, have been explained in Chapter 3. The case concerned the *Conciliation and Arbitration Act 1904* (Cth), which gave the Commonwealth Arbitration Court jurisdiction extending to the resolution of 'any dispute in relation to employment in an industry carried on by or under the control of the Commonwealth or a State, or any public authority constituted under the Commonwealth or a State'.[223] The question was whether the Act validly authorised the Arbitration Court to arbitrate in such cases involving employees of a State or of a public authority or other instrumentality established by a State.

As such, the *Engineers* case mirrored the facts in the *Railway Servants* case. For a Court now minded to refashion the relevant law in a fundamental way, there were several possible lines of argument. The most conservative path would have been to decide the case in favour of the Commonwealth by concluding that the functions of the employee engineers were non-governmental and therefore were not protected by the immunity. More radically, the Court could have attacked the implied immunity itself. However, the immunity applied to protect both the States and the Commonwealth, and in *D'Emden v Pedder* two separate strands of reasoning had been relied upon to support the Commonwealth's

**218** *Federated Engine-drivers and Firemen's Association of Australasia v Broken Hill Pty Co Ltd* (1911) 12 CLR 398 and (1913) 16 CLR 245.
**219** *Federated Engine-drivers and Firemen's Association of Australasia v Broken Hill Pty Co Ltd* (1913) 16 CLR 245, 261–2, 271, 279, 284, adopting (1911) 12 CLR 398, 414–15, 425–8, 451–3.
**220** *Federated Municipal and Shire Council Employees' Union of Australia v Melbourne Corporation* (1919) 26 CLR 508.
**221** See, eg, *Attorney-General (NSW) v Collector of Customs (NSW)* (1908) 5 CLR 818, 852.
**222** *Amalgamated Society of Engineers v Adelaide Steamship Co Ltd* (1920) 28 CLR 129.
**223** *Conciliation and Arbitration Act 1904* (Cth), s 8, read with s 4 (definition of 'industrial dispute').

immunity in particular. One strand of reasoning, based on the idea that both the Commonwealth and the States are sovereign within their respective spheres, led to the conclusion that the implied immunity reciprocally protects both the Commonwealth and the States, as had been decided in the *Railway Servants* case. The second strand was that the Commonwealth was in a relevantly different situation to the States in that while the people of a State could, through the Parliament (and especially through the Senate), protect themselves from interference by the Commonwealth, the people of the Commonwealth as a whole could not directly influence or control what a particular State Parliament might decide to enact, even if that enactment interfered quite directly with the performance by the Commonwealth of its functions under the Constitution. In the *Engineers* case, a majority of the High Court adopted the latter line of reasoning. The *Railway Servants* case was overturned and the only form of intergovernmental immunity that potentially survived was the Commonwealth's.

### Reasoning in *Engineers*

As noted in Chapter 3, the majority joint judgment delivered by Isaacs J asserted that the case law applying the immunity of instrumentalities doctrine had become incoherent on account of the many 'qualifications' that had been placed on the doctrine.[224] Overlooking that the qualifications had been developed by the Griffith Court in consideration of the nature and scope of particular heads of Commonwealth legislative power which authorised some degree of interference, the joint judgment maintained that the incoherence arose from the use of a highly political, subjective and ambiguous principle of 'necessity', understood as the criterion according to which the applicability of the immunity was to be determined.[225] Rather, it was said, the Constitution must be interpreted as an Imperial statute, in accordance with British constitutional principles and canons of construction. According to these canons, the task of the Court is to 'discover in the actual terms of the instrument their expressed or necessarily implied meaning'.[226] For the possibility of an abuse of power, it was maintained, is 'no reason in British law for limiting the natural force of the language creating them'.[227] If there was a political principle that 'pervaded' the Constitution and provided the key to its interpretation, it was not federalism, but rather the indivisible sovereignty of the Crown and the institution of parliamentary responsible government.[228] Basic to responsible government is the subjection of the executive powers of the Crown to parliamentary legislation. If the Crown 'is one and indivisible throughout the Empire', then it seems to follow that the Crown will always be bound by a law enacted under the authority of the Constitution, even if the law

**224** *Amalgamated Society of Engineers v Adelaide Steamship Co Ltd* (1920) 28 CLR 129, 141.
**225** Ibid, 142, 145, 150. 'Necessity' was especially referred to in *Federated Engine-Drivers and Firemen's Association of Australasia v Broken Hill Pty Co Ltd* (1911) 12 CLR 398, 425–8.
**226** *Amalgamated Society of Engineers v Adelaide Steamship Co Ltd* (1920) 28 CLR 129, 148–9, 155.
**227** Ibid, 151.
**228** Ibid, 146.

is enacted by the Commonwealth and purports to bind the Crown in right of the States. The federal interrelationship between the Commonwealth and the States does not matter on this approach. All that matters is that the Constitution was passed 'for the express purpose of regulating the royal exercise of legislative, executive and judicial power throughout Australia' and is therefore 'by its own inherent force binding on the Crown to the extent of its operation'.[229]

On this reasoning, it was clear that the *Railway Servants* case could not stand. It had asserted the existence of a reciprocal immunity that protected the States from Commonwealth interference – a doctrine which had to be overturned entirely.[230] *D'Emden v Pedder*, however, involved the immunity of the Commonwealth from State interference. Here the Court proposed that the case could be reinterpreted as turning on a conflict between the State law which imposed the tax and provisions of the *Audit Act 1901* (Cth) which required that written vouchers must accompany payment of public moneys. Interpreting the latter Act to require that the vouchers must be under the sole control of the Commonwealth, it was held that the State law was 'manifestly inconsistent' with the Commonwealth law and therefore invalid to the extent of the inconsistency, pursuant to s 109. As the joint judgment concluded: 'The decision rests on the supremacy created by sec. 109, and is sound'.[231] Indeed, in his concurring judgment Higgins J went so far as to say that such a conclusion was consistent with the reasoning of Marshall CJ in *McCulloch v Maryland* concerning the relative supremacy of the federal government (and not just the legislature) – even though in *Baxter* Higgins J had expressed his personal disagreement with this reasoning.[232]

### Application of *Engineers*

Despite what the Court said in *Engineers* about *D'Emden*, its exact implications for the capacity of State laws to bind the Commonwealth were not entirely clear, not least because there were other cases that had partially relied on the implied immunity which the Court 'hesitated' to address.[233] This question was soon tested in *Pirrie v McFarlane*.[234] In that case the Court had to consider whether the requirement to hold a driver's licence under the *Motor Traffic Act 1915* (Vic) applied to a Commonwealth officer who had driven a vehicle on a public highway in obedience to orders he had received from a superior officer within the Royal Australian Air Force. Given the decision in *Engineers*, the only ground upon which the defendant might be successful seemed to be that the

**229** Ibid, 152–3.
**230** Ibid, 157–60; see also 168–71.
**231** Ibid, 156; see also 167–8. Other cases, such as *Deakin v Webb* and *Baxter*, were also said to rely partly on a conflict between Commonwealth and State laws and were also affirmed on this basis: ibid, 156–7. That the earlier cases did not really rely on s 109 inconsistency was noted in *West v Commissioner of Taxation (NSW)* (1937) 56 CLR 657, 665, 689–90, 692–4, 696, 699, 701.
**232** *Amalgamated Society of Engineers v Adelaide Steamship Co Ltd* (1920) 28 CLR 129, 168–9; *Baxter v Commissioners of Taxation (NSW)* (1907) 4 CLR 1087, 1164–5.
**233** *Amalgamated Society of Engineers v Adelaide Steamship Co Ltd* (1920) 28 CLR 129, 159–60.
**234** (1925) 36 CLR 170.

State Act was somehow inconsistent with the *Air Force Act 1923* (Cth), the *Defence Act 1903* (Cth) and related regulations concerning the discipline of the armed forces. These included provisions which made it an offence unlawfully to obstruct or interfere with the performance of military service or duty, and which required members of the forces to obey all lawful commands given by superior officers. Knox CJ, Higgins and Starke JJ found that there was no such inconsistency because the relevant provisions related only to the carrying out of lawful commands, and thus on their proper construction applied in a manner that did not contradict ordinary State laws such as the *Motor Traffic Act*. On their view, *D'Emden v Pedder* remained good law only insofar as it was based on an inconsistency between the Commonwealth and State law.[235]

Isaacs J (with whom Rich J agreed) dissented on two apparent grounds: first, that there was an inconsistency between the two laws; and second, that military order and discipline falls within the exclusive powers of the Commonwealth, and therefore lies entirely outside State regulation. This latter ground was curiously formulated, however. Drawing a distinction between a law which binds private individuals and one which purports to bind the Crown in right of another political community,[236] Isaacs J declared that there is a 'natural and fundamental principle' that:

> where by the one Constitution separate and exclusive governmental powers have been allotted to two distinct organisms, neither is intended, in the absence of distinct provision to the contrary, to destroy or weaken the *capacity* or *functions* expressly conferred on the other.[237]

The restriction of this principle to the protection of 'exclusive' powers was important, for it distinguished it from the finding in *Engineers*, where the legislative power exercised by the Commonwealth was concurrent, not exclusive. Isaacs J maintained that the Commonwealth's defence power, although it appears in s 51, not s 52, is effectively exclusive, principally because the colonies' former defence departments had been transferred to the Commonwealth (s 69) and therefore came under the exclusive jurisdiction of the Commonwealth (s 51(ii)). These considerations issued in the basic proposition that:

> the State Parliament cannot legislate at all so as to bind the Crown in right of the Commonwealth in the exercise of the very governmental functions *expressly taken from the States and exclusively vested in the Commonwealth* ... .[238]

As Isaacs J later put it, the States are not constitutionally able to enact a law which 'expressly or by necessary implication' purports to bind the Commonwealth in respect of the 'primary and inalienable functions' of 'constitutional government' that had been exclusively vested in it.[239] It followed from this

**235** *Pirrie v McFarlane* (1925) 36 CLR 170, 180–84, 212–15, 219, 225–9.
**236** Ibid, 190–91, citing *Macleod v Attorney-General (NSW)* [1891] AC 455.
**237** *Pirrie v McFarlane* (1925) 36 CLR 170, 191.
**238** Ibid, 192.
**239** Ibid, 199.

principle that the provision of the *Motor Car Act 1915* purporting to bind the Crown without qualification must be read down as binding the Crown in right of the State, and not the Commonwealth.[240]

Although Isaacs J's dissenting reasoning was limited to the exclusive powers of the Commonwealth, his invocation of the notion that the federal system necessarily protects certain governing 'capacities' and constitutional 'functions' introduced ideas that were absent from the reasoning in *Engineers*. In his majority judgment, Knox CJ also intriguingly observed that, as an additional consideration, there was nothing in the State Act which was 'specially aimed at, or in any way discriminated against' Commonwealth service personnel.[241] These ideas of governmental capacities, constitutional functions and discriminating laws would prove to be of great importance in the later emergence of a modified intergovernmental immunities doctrine in the hands especially of Dixon and Evatt JJ. In addition, as has been seen, some of the argument and reasoning in *Pirrie v McFarlane* was directed to the anterior question of whether the State law evinced an intention to bind the Crown in right of the Commonwealth. Here, the traditional common law presumption that no statute binds the Crown unless that intention is made unavoidably clear had a potentially important role to play, although Higgins J said that it could have no application in a federal system in relation to the law of a State binding the Crown in right of the Commonwealth.[242] In his dissenting judgment in *Engineers*, Gavan Duffy J had reasoned similarly: he maintained that the legislative power of each colony only binds the Crown within the colony itself; the Crown in right of other colonies is not bound.[243] In more recent cases, the High Court has softened the meaning and application of the general presumption that a statute does not bind the Crown (including its agencies and officers) unless the intention is made clear.[244] However, in the cases that came immediately after *Engineers* and *Pirrie v McFarlane*, the question whether the laws of the Commonwealth and the States *could* bind each other was tied up with the anterior question about whether the law *intended* to bind the Crown.

## Qualifications on *Engineers*

In the *Australian Railways Union* case, in the course of restating the general effect of *Engineers*, Dixon J suggested that the existence of 'discrimination' could be an important factor in these types of cases. He stated:

**240** Ibid, 198–9.
**241** Ibid, 184; see also 229.
**242** Ibid, 218, but see 226.
**243** *Amalgamated Society of Engineers v Adelaide Steamship Co Ltd* (1920) 28 CLR 129, 175–6, citing *Macleod v Attorney-General (NSW)* [1891] AC 455, 458.
**244** Compare *Bradken Consolidated Ltd v Broken Hill Proprietary Co Ltd* (1979) 145 CLR 107, 116 with *Bropho v Western Australia* (1990) 171 CLR 1, 15–24. See also *Jacobsen v Rogers* (1995) 182 CLR 572; *Re Residential Tenancies Tribunal (NSW) and Henderson; Ex parte Defence Housing Authority* (1997) 190 CLR 410 and *State Authorities Superannuation Board v Commissioner of State Taxation (WA)* (1996) 189 CLR 253.

> [U]nless, and save insofar as, the contrary appears from some other provision of the Constitution or from the nature or the subject matter of the power or from the terms in which it is conferred, every grant of power to the Commonwealth should be interpreted as authorizing the [Commonwealth] Parliament to make laws affecting the operations of the States and their agencies, at any rate ... if the Parliament confines itself to laws which do not discriminate against the States or their agencies.[245]

This general statement of principle was given during a discussion of the proposition, affirmed by other justices in the case, that while a Commonwealth law might bind a State, it remained entirely a matter for the Parliament of the State to authorise any necessary appropriation of funds from the State treasury.[246] The practical effect of the latter proposition was diminished, however, in the *Garnishee* case,[247] in which the High Court upheld a Commonwealth law which garnisheed taxes and moneys otherwise owing to the States as a means of enforcing the payment of interest due to it by the States under the Commonwealth–State Financial Agreement. The constitutional basis for the Commonwealth law was a combination of the incidental power (s 51(xxxix)), the jurisdiction of the High Court in matters in which the Commonwealth is a party (s 75(iii)), the power to make laws conferring rights to proceed against the Commonwealth or a State (s 78) and the special provision for the formation and enforcement of Commonwealth–State agreements with respect to State debts (ss 105 and 105A). Evatt J dissented, partly on the basis that the enforcement provisions of the Commonwealth law were only for the benefit of the Commonwealth, and in that sense discriminated against the States in not providing means for them to enforce the agreement against the Commonwealth; and that the Commonwealth's legislative power cannot extend to seizing revenue due to a State without parliamentary appropriation by the State Parliament, for such would be an 'invasion' of the revenues of the State.[248] However, Rich and Dixon JJ considered that s 105A(5) of the Constitution, in providing that such agreements shall be 'binding' on the Commonwealth and the States notwithstanding anything contained in the Commonwealth and State Constitutions, nullified any requirement of parliamentary appropriation of funds before any such liability could be incurred by a State.[249]

Despite the special result in the *Garnishee* case, Dixon J repeated and developed several of the themes he had articulated in *Australian Railways Union* in *West v Commissioner of Taxation (NSW)*.[250] In *West*, the Court had to consider whether the *Special Income and Wages Tax (Management) Act 1933* (NSW) could constitutionally authorise the taxation of the pensions paid to retired Commonwealth employees under the *Superannuation Act 1922* (Cth). Section 5 of the Commonwealth law stated that the income of the superannuation fund from

**245** *Australian Railways Union v Victorian Railways Commissioners* (1930) 44 CLR 319, 390.
**246** Ibid, 352–3, 388–90, but see 389–93.
**247** *New South Wales v Commonwealth* (1932) 46 CLR 155.
**248** Ibid, 195–201.
**249** Ibid, 175–7.
**250** (1937) 56 CLR 657, 686, 707. See Part II.4, above.

which West received his pension would not be subject to either Commonwealth or State taxation. Another Commonwealth law provided that the Governor-General could prescribe the maximum amount of State tax to which Commonwealth salaries and pensions could be subject.[251]

A majority of the Court decided the case on the basis of s 109. They considered that while the Commonwealth did have the constitutional power to do so, it had not effectively legislated to exclude the operation of the State taxation law with respect to the pensions of its retired officers because the necessary regulations had not been made.[252] The judgments of Latham CJ, Dixon and Evatt JJ went further. Latham CJ reasoned that there might be two grounds upon which such a law could be constitutionally invalid. Both involved a discriminatory law which 'singled out' another polity within the federation. The first ground, in terms similar to Isaacs J's dissenting judgment in *Pirrie v McFarlane*, prevented a State law from imposing a discriminatory tax on the salary or pension of a Commonwealth officer because such salaries and pensions would fall within the exclusive powers of the Commonwealth (s 52(ii)). The second ground was that such a law could not be characterised as a law for the peace, order and good government of the State, but was rather a law with respect to Commonwealth government salaries and pensions. This latter ground, he noted, would apply reciprocally to prevent the Commonwealth from legislating similarly with respect to State salaries and pensions.[253] Both propositions rested upon the characterisation of the law, and therefore entailed an approach that identifies the 'one true nature and character' of the law, rather than acknowledging that a law may have more than one feature or aspect which fairly characterises the law as a whole. As noted in Chapter 3, such an approach to characterisation would not be rejected decisively by the Court until the *Actors & Announcers Equity* case in 1982.[254]

In *West*, Dixon J considered that an additional ground of invalidity existed. Noting that the Commonwealth often exercises powers and makes payments of money pursuant to powers conferred upon the Executive directly by the Constitution (ss 61, 67, 69, 70, 81, 82 and 83), he suggested that it was surely 'implicit' in these powers that the 'incidents and consequences of its exercise shall not be made the subject of special liabilities or burdens under State law'.[255] In a frequently cited passage, he continued:

> Since the *Engineers Case* a notion seems to have gained currency that in interpreting the Constitution no implications can be made. Such a method of construction would defeat the intention of any instrument, but of all instruments a written constitution seems the last to which it should be applied. I do not think that the judgment of the

**251** Previously, the *Commonwealth Salaries Act 1907* (Cth) had authorised State taxation of Commonwealth salaries so as to avoid the result in *Deakin v Webb* and *Baxter*. See *Deputy Commissioner of Taxation (NSW) v Baxter & Flint* [1908] AC 214; 5 CLR 395, 399; *Chaplin v Commissioner of Taxes for South Australia* (1911) 12 CLR 375, 380–81; *West v Commissioner of Taxation (NSW)* (1937) 56 CLR 657, 695–6.
**252** *West v Commissioner of Taxation (NSW)* (1937) 56 CLR 657, 670–73, 674–6, 677–81, 683, 714.
**253** Ibid, 668–9.
**254** *Actors & Announcers Equity Association of Australia v Fontana Films Pty Ltd* (1982) 150 CLR 169.
**255** *West v Commissioner of Taxation (NSW)* (1937) 56 CLR 657, 681.

> majority of the court in the *Engineers Case* meant to propound such a doctrine. It is inconsistent with many of the reasons afterwards advanced by Isaacs J himself for his dissent in *Pirrie v McFarlane* … . The principle [adopted in *Engineers*] is that whenever the Constitution confers a power to make laws in respect of a specific subject matter, prima facie it is to be understood as enabling the [Commonwealth] Parliament to make laws affecting the operations of the States and their agencies. The prima facie meaning may be displaced by considerations based on the nature or subject matter of the power or the language in which it is conferred or on some other provision in the Constitution … . The first reservation is that in the *Engineers' Case* the question was left open whether the principle would warrant legislation affecting the exercise of a prerogative of the Crown in right of the States. The second is that the decision does not appear to deal with or affect the question whether the [Commonwealth] Parliament is authorized to enact legislation discriminating against States or their agencies.[256]

Dixon J also noted that the legislative powers of the Commonwealth are expressed to be 'subject to' the Constitution and he suggested that these words, read with s 106 and perhaps s 107, may be of importance in determining how far a Commonwealth law may affect the States.[257]

Evatt J based his reasoning on two related propositions. The first was that neither the Commonwealth nor the States could make laws which would grant a general immunity from non-discriminatory taxation imposed by the other.[258] The second was that neither could impose a discriminatory tax on the other.[259] He suggested two possible grounds for these propositions. One, resembling Latham CJ's position, was that the element of discrimination in the law would help to characterise it as unconstitutional. The other, resembling Dixon J's approach, was that, as a general implication of the federal nature of the Constitution, neither the Commonwealth nor a State may 'direct its legislation toward the destruction of the normal activities' of the other.[260] Moreover, Evatt J also observed that, even without discrimination, the quantum of a tax might impose such an 'onerous burden' and 'serious impediment' that it would be invalid.[261] His Honour's fundamental concern, it seems, was the Court's responsibility to protect the Commonwealth and the States from 'hostile' attacks by the other.[262]

### Commonwealth priority

Dixon J returned to some of these themes in *Federal Commissioner of Taxation v Official Liquidator of E O Farley Ltd*.[263] The case involved an insolvent company which owed debts to the Commonwealth, the States and other creditors. The High Court affirmed that in the absence of relevant legislation, the Crown enjoys a prerogative right to priority over other creditors to the payment of debts, and

**256** Ibid, 681–2.
**257** Ibid, 683.
**258** Ibid, 684–5.
**259** Ibid, 687.
**260** Ibid.
**261** Ibid, 690.
**262** Ibid, 698–9.
**263** (1940) 63 CLR 278.

that the Commonwealth and State governments have equal rights to such payment and will therefore share the money available in proportion to the amounts respectively owing to them. Beyond these points, Dixon J further considered the extent of the power of the Commonwealth and the States to make laws binding on each other. Importantly, in Dixon J's view, a State simply does not have power to postpone the rights of the Commonwealth to those of the State, as this would be to 'destroy or impair a governmental or fiscal right of the Commonwealth' which inheres in 'the Federal executive as such'.[264] Further, while he considered that the Commonwealth and the States stand on an equal footing within the federal system as independently established governments, he also affirmed the principle in *Engineers* that the legislative powers of the Commonwealth will ordinarily authorise laws that are binding on the States unless there is some specific constitutional reason against this.[265] The Commonwealth's powers with respect to bankruptcy and insolvency (s 51(xvii)) and corporations (s 51(xx)) thus might have provided the requisite power, except that the particular Commonwealth law could not be characterised as falling within either of these two powers; and nor could the incidental scope of the taxation power (s 51(ii)) support a law which would defeat the claim of a State to an equal right to payment of a debt due.[266]

Despite these cautions and qualifications, the practical capacity of the Commonwealth to control, limit and exclude the States from the exercise of the power to impose taxes was tested and emphatically affirmed in the two *Uniform Tax* cases, decided in 1942 and 1957. In the first of these, in the absence of Dixon J, the High Court upheld four separate Commonwealth laws the combined effect of which was: (a) to impose a very high graduated tax on personal income (up to 90% of income); (b) to provide a grant to each State on condition that it did not levy income tax, the quantum of the grant being roughly equivalent to the amount that it would have collected under its existing income tax laws; (c) to make it an offence for a person to pay any State income tax before paying the Commonwealth tax; and (d) to transfer State taxation officials temporarily to the Commonwealth public service in order to administer the scheme. The legislation was enacted during the Second World War, and was said to derive its constitutionality from a combination of the taxation, defence and incidental powers (ss 51(ii), (vi), (xxxix)), read with the grants power (s 96). In upholding the laws, the Court insisted that each Act had to be considered separately, and that it was not appropriate to question the constitutionality of the four Acts as an entire scheme directed to some unconstitutional objective.[267] The Court also rejected the argument that the Commonwealth laws – the Grants Act in particular – were unconstitutionally directed to 'destroying or weakening the constitutional functions or capacities of a State'. Latham CJ, for example, noted that the Commonwealth laws did not

**264** Ibid, 307–9, 312.
**265** Ibid, 312–13.
**266** Ibid, 313–17; contrast 324–6.
**267** *South Australia v Commonwealth* (1942) 65 CLR 373, 411.

purport to (i) repeal any State taxation statutes, (ii) require a State Parliament to abdicate its power to impose taxes, or (iii) directly deprive a State Parliament of the power to do so. Rather, they only provided the States with an inducement to abstain from exercising such power, and it did not matter if the inducement was something which the States could not really refuse.[268] On Latham CJ's approach, the only relevant limitation on the Commonwealth's powers with respect to the States derives simply from the absence of any power to legislate with respect to State powers or functions. However, he considered that the Commonwealth laws could not be characterised as laws with respect to the States in this way, for the true character of a law must be ascertained only by reference to the duties, rights and powers which it creates, abolishes or regulates, and not by reference to its motives, objectives or indirect effects, no matter what the practical consequences might be for the States.[269]

On this last point, Starke J dissented. He pointed out that Australia has a 'dual system' based upon a 'separation of organs and of powers', that the Constitution is as concerned with the maintenance of the States and their powers as it is with the Commonwealth and its powers, and that the Commonwealth therefore cannot exercise its powers to achieve ends or purposes inconsistent with the 'separate existence and self-government of the States'.[270] He considered that the legislative scheme had the objective of making the Commonwealth the sole taxing power in relation to incomes, and that the suggestion that the States had a choice in the matter was both 'specious' and 'unreal'.[271] Such an imposition on the States was neither contemplated nor sanctioned by the Constitution, he concluded, and therefore the *State Grant Act* in particular was invalid.

Although Starke J was alone on this point in the *First Uniform Tax* case,[272] the idea that the powers of the Commonwealth might be limited would be taken up and applied by a large majority of the Court in one of the most important decisions brought down by the Court when it considered yet another scheme that had been adopted during the Second World War but which the Commonwealth sought to implement on a broader and permanent basis. This case was *Melbourne Corporation v Commonwealth*.

## 3 Moderate State immunity: *Melbourne Corporation* (1947)

### Reasoning in *Melbourne Corporation*

*Melbourne Corporation v Commonwealth*[273] concerned a challenge by the Municipality of the City of Melbourne to the constitutionality of s 48 of the *Banking*

**268** Ibid, 415–17.
**269** Ibid, 423–7, 429.
**270** Ibid, 442.
**271** Ibid, 443.
**272** In the *Second Uniform Tax* case, the same legislative scheme was again challenged and largely upheld. As noted in Chapter 3, however, Dixon CJ convinced a majority of the Court to strike down the provision requiring taxpayers to pay the Commonwealth tax in priority to any State tax. See *Second Uniform Tax* (1957) 99 CLR 575, 614–15.
**273** (1947) 74 CLR 31.

*Act 1945* (Cth), which provided that '[e]xcept with the consent in writing of the Treasurer, a bank shall not conduct any banking business for a State or for any authority of a State, including a local government authority'. The effect of the law was that without such consent a State or local government authority would be forced to use either a State Bank or the Commonwealth Bank, which at the time was a government owned and controlled bank that was required to give effect to the Commonwealth's monetary and banking policies. The Commonwealth relied upon the banking power (s 51(xiii)) to support the law. This raised several questions about the nature of the banking power.

One argument, put by Barwick KC on behalf of the City of Melbourne, focused on the words 'other than State banking' in s 51(xiii). He argued that this qualification of the scope of the power should be read widely, to include the entire activity of 'State banking' – understood as embracing both parties to a banking transaction, namely the banker and the customer of the bank. On this view, the Commonwealth cannot legislate under the banking power to prohibit a State or a State authority (such as a local government body) from engaging in a banking transaction with a bank. The Court rejected this argument. The expression 'State banking', it held, refers only to banks established and conducted by or under the authority of a State.[274]

Rather, the case turned on the proposition that the legislation was unconstitutional because it was aimed at one of the essential governmental functions of the States, namely the 'custody, management and disposition' of public moneys.[275] However, as the various opinions in the cases that had followed *Engineers* suggested, the nature of the constitutional problem with such a law was not entirely clear. One view, adopted by Latham CJ, was that the fatal defect in s 48 was that, in singling out or discriminating against the States, the law was properly characterised as a law with respect to 'a State or State functions' and did not for this reason fall within one of the Commonwealth's heads of legislative power.[276] To strike down the law on the basis that it 'unduly' interfered with State governmental functions was to rely, the Chief Justice said, on a 'rather vague conception' in the application of which differences of opinion would be likely.[277] The other justices, however, were prepared to find that the law fell within the prima facie scope of the banking power. As Dixon J put it, a law may have two 'aspects': one which connects the law to a purpose which is to restrict State action, and a second which relates the law to a subject matter within Commonwealth power.[278] For Dixon J and the other majority justices, the validity of the law turned on a 'further reason' for limiting the operation of such a law, namely an implied intergovernmental immunity derived from the federal

**274** *Melbourne Corporation v Commonwealth* (1947) 74 CLR 31, 52, 64–5, 69–70, 78, 85–6, 96–8.
**275** Ibid, 52–3, 98.
**276** Ibid, 61.
**277** Ibid, 61–2.
**278** Ibid, 79.

nature of the Constitution.[279] However, they each formulated the test to be derived from this principle somewhat differently.

For Starke J, the 'dual system' of governments established by the Constitution implies that neither the Commonwealth nor the States may 'destroy the other' or 'curtail in any substantial manner' the exercise of their respective powers, and nor may either of them 'obviously interfere with' the 'governmental' or 'primary and inalienable functions' exercised by the other pursuant to the Constitution.[280] Thus, on his view, the existence of discrimination was not decisive. The ultimate question was whether, as a practical matter, legislation (or executive action thereunder) had the necessary curtailing or interfering effect. The existence of discrimination was something to be considered, but the crucial issue concerned the character and operation of the law and the nature and extent of the activity that was affected.[281]

Dixon J similarly thought that the 'dual system' of 'separate governments ... exercising independent functions' established by the Constitution necessarily implies certain limits on the powers of both the Commonwealth and the States to interfere with each other. In a frequently cited passage, he observed:

> The foundation of the Constitution is the conception of a central government and a number of State governments separately organized. The Constitution predicates their continued existence as independent entities. Among them it distributes powers of governing the country. The framers of the Constitution do not appear to have considered that power itself forms part of the conception of a government. They appear rather to have conceived the States as bodies politic whose existence and nature are independent of the powers allocated to them.[282]

However, unlike Starke J, he regarded the element of discrimination in a Commonwealth law as vital. Why he did so is not entirely clear, but it is possible that he considered it necessary in order to distinguish the modified immunity theory that he was expounding from the discredited immunity of instrumentalities doctrine. While discrimination was on his view necessary, he also linked it to a description of a Commonwealth law that interferes with a State's essential functions. In so doing, he offered several slightly different descriptions of the kind of law that would be unconstitutional, including a law which:

- 'discriminates against States';
- 'places a particular disability or burden upon an operation or activity of a State, and more especially upon the execution of its constitutional powers';
- 'discloses an immediate object of controlling the State';
- has the 'purpose of restricting or burdening the State in the exercise of its constitutional powers';

**279** Ibid.
**280** Ibid, 70, 74, citing *Graves v New York; Ex rel O'Keefe* 306 US 466 (1939) and several other United States cases.
**281** *Melbourne Corporation v Commonwealth* (1947) 74 CLR 31, 74–5.
**282** Ibid, 82.

- 'brings into question the independence from federal control of the State in the discharge of its functions';
- 'attempt[s] to burden the exercise of State functions';
- 'places a special burden upon the States';
- 'single[s] out States and place[s] upon them special burdens or disabilities';
- 'directly deprive[s] another government of powers or authority committed to it or restrict[s] that government in their exercise';
- 'single[s] out governments and plac[es] special burdens upon the exercise of powers or the fulfilment of functions constitutionally belonging to them'.[283]

Despite the clear message that the States are constitutionally protected from discriminatory federal laws, Dixon J qualified this by noting that some heads of Commonwealth power might, on account of their 'content, context or subject matter', authorise laws that would otherwise be unconstitutional because they are 'aimed at the restriction or control of a State in the exercise of its executive authority'.[284] He also noted that there was some danger in relying upon abstract formulas, and that the binding content of his decision ought to be limited to 'the constituent factors contained in s 48'.[285] Although the prohibition in s 48 was directed to the banks themselves, its effective operation was to 'deny to the States banking facilities open to others', and so to 'discriminate against them or impose a disability upon them'. This, he thought, rendered it a law 'directed to control or restrict the Executive Government of the States in the use of banks for the conduct of their banking business'.[286] The element of discrimination or singling out was thus critical, in his reasoning. While he acknowledged that if a State wished to avail itself of any service provided generally to the Australian community it must 'take it as it finds it' (including any constitutionally legitimate Commonwealth regulation of that service), the Commonwealth cannot 'isolate' a State and impose on it a 'particular disability' that is not imposed on others.[287]

In his concurring judgment, Williams J appeared to combine the considerations advanced by Latham CJ, Starke and Dixon JJ. Like Starke and Dixon JJ he referred to a 'necessary implication' which arises from 'the very nature of the federal compact' and the idea that the Constitution contemplates two 'independent political organisms' existing 'side by side'.[288] He also described the intergovernmental immunity, like Starke J, as requiring that neither the Commonwealth nor the States may exercise their powers 'for the purpose of affecting the capacity of the other to perform its essential governmental functions'.[289]

**283** Ibid, 79–82.
**284** Ibid, 83.
**285** Ibid.
**286** Ibid, 84–5.
**287** Ibid, 84.
**288** Ibid, 99.
**289** Ibid.

Like Latham CJ, he also said that it followed that a federal law must be examined to see whether it 'is really a law ... with respect to one of the enumerated subjects' or 'really a law the purpose of which is to interfere with such functions'.[290] And noting Dixon J's suggestion in *West* that one of the 'reservations' on the *Engineers* principle concerned discriminating laws, he concluded that the discriminatory character of s 48 marked it out as a law 'aimed at the States' and one which 'in pith and substance' seeks to 'give directions to the States as to the manner in which they shall exercise their executive, legislative or judicial governmental functions' or 'sovereign powers', making it not a law for the peace, order and good government of the Commonwealth, but rather 'an unlawful intervention in the constitutional affairs of the States'.[291]

In his dissenting judgment, McTiernan J rejected the conclusions of the majority on *Engineers* grounds. The proposed implied immunity is based, he said, on a 'vague, individual conception of the spirit of the compact' and is not the result of an interpretation of the 'specific language' of the Constitution.[292] In accordance with this approach, he pointed out, the Court had upheld several other far-reaching interferences with the States, and there was no reason in the language of the banking power to suggest that it must be specially limited when other heads of power are not.[293] Moreover, he considered that it would be illusory to protect the States from discriminatory burdens while allowing the same controls to be placed upon them by generally applicable laws.[294] He also relied upon the opinions of public finance experts who considered that the banking business of government is best provided by the central bank of the country. This, he suggested, supported the conclusion that s 48 was a law for regulating the conduct of particular banking transactions falling with the banking power.[295]

Apparently sensitive to this line of criticism, in his concurring judgment Rich J emphasised that the Constitution 'expressly provides for the continued existence of the States' and that a Commonwealth law which would 'prevent a State from continuing to exist and function as such is necessarily invalid because inconsistent with the express provisions of the Constitution'.[296] In a formulation which seemed to synthesise the approaches of Starke and Dixon JJ, he considered that there are two classes of case in which a Commonwealth law might thus be invalid: (i) a discriminatory law which 'prevents' or 'impedes' the States or their agencies from performing 'the normal and essential functions of government'; and (ii) a general law which, in its application to the States or their agencies, prevents or impedes them from performing those functions.[297] Although this twofold formula combines both approaches, the common and essential element

**290** Ibid.
**291** Ibid, 99–101.
**292** Ibid, 88, citing *Amalgamated Society of Engineers v Adelaide Steamship Co Ltd* (1920) 28 CLR 129, 145.
**293** *Melbourne Corporation v Commonwealth* (1947) 74 CLR 31, 86–8.
**294** Ibid, 89.
**295** Ibid, 91–4.
**296** Ibid, 66.
**297** Ibid.

seems to be that of preventing or impeding the States or their agencies from performing the normal and essential functions of government – a position most like that of Starke J, but without the qualification that the interference must, by virtue of its 'nature and extent' be sufficiently 'substantial'. As Rich J observed, what made s 48 unconstitutional was that it impaired a particular function of government that is 'essential to the efficient working of the business of government', namely 'the power freely to use the facilities provided by banks'.[298] In so concluding, Rich J seemed to adopt, like Williams J, the view that in its 'pith and substance', s 48 could not be characterised as a law with respect to banking because it was directed to 'an object which is beyond its powers'.[299]

**Three rationales, two limbs**

In *Melbourne Corporation* a majority of the Court thus clearly decided that s 48 was unconstitutional. However, there were at least three broad rationales for why this was the case: (1) because the law could not be *characterised* as a law with respect to banking; (2) due to an implied immunity against Commonwealth laws which *unduly interfere* with the constitutional functions of the States; or (3) due to an implied immunity against Commonwealth laws which *discriminate* against the States in the exercise of those functions. In the *Payroll Tax* case, decided more than twenty years later, these differences of opinion as to the basis and nature of the implied immunity were replicated, albeit in a unanimous decision which upheld provisions of the *Payroll Tax Act 1941* (Cth) which imposed a 2.5 per cent payroll tax on all wages paid by an 'employer'.[300] The tax applied to all employers, both private and public, including the Crown in right of a State, municipal corporations, local governing bodies and any other public authorities constituted under State law. Thus, although the tax extended to the States, the absence of discrimination against the States distinguished the case from the facts in *Melbourne Corporation*, and this lack of discrimination was decisive.

For Barwick CJ (with whom Owen J agreed) and McTiernan J, the non-discriminatory, general nature of the law meant that the Act could be characterised as a law with respect to taxation under s 51(ii) and not as a law with respect to the States or State functions or powers, as Latham CJ had put it in *Melbourne Corporation*.[301] Windeyer J, on the other hand, seemed to endorse something resembling Starke J's approach when he maintained that a Commonwealth law which would 'destroy' the States or 'impair' their 'essential functions in a substantial degree' would be unconstitutional. However, he too upheld the law, on the basis that the payment of a moderate payroll tax by the States would not have such an effect.[302] While he expressed caution against substituting 'words

**298** Ibid, 67.
**299** Ibid.
**300** *Victoria v Commonwealth* (1971) 122 CLR 353.
**301** Ibid, 369–73, 375, 381–3, 385–6.
**302** Ibid, 398.

of judicial exposition' for the language of the Constitution itself,[303] he thus affirmed the existence of an implied limitation on Commonwealth power, derived from the existence of the States as constituents of the federation, which required that no Commonwealth power could be used to prevent the States from carrying out their constitutional functions. He also questioned the appropriateness of the phrase 'discrimination against', but he concluded that as the law was not aimed at the States it could have a valid operation in relation to them.[304] Menzies, Walsh and Gibbs JJ delivered judgments broadly endorsing the approaches of Dixon, Rich and Starke JJ in *Melbourne Corporation*, while also expressing concern about the workability of the distinction between governmental functions that are 'essential' and those which are not, as well as the category of 'undue' interference.[305] But despite these misgivings, Gibbs J in particular affirmed that there are two categories of law which would be contrary to the federal nature, scheme and purposes of the Constitution, namely: (a) a law which 'discriminates against States, in the sense that it imposes some special burden or disability upon them, so that it may be described as a law aimed at their restriction or control'; and (b) a 'general law of the Commonwealth which would prevent a State from continuing to exist and function as such'.[306]

While the 'characterisation' approach that had been favoured by Latham CJ and Barwick CJ would be rejected, the idea of an implied immunity consisting of two distinct limbs came to be generally accepted by members of the Court in several cases which followed. In many, the validity of the law was upheld, but the suggestion that there are two distinct limbs or tests was often quite emphatic.[307] Even Dixon J himself, who had clearly affirmed the discrimination test in *Melbourne Corporation*, considered in *Bank of New South Wales v Commonwealth* that a non-discriminatory law might operate against the States in such a way as to be *ultra vires*.[308] In the *Tasmanian Dam* case, Mason J observed:

> [I]t is not necessary to show that the law discriminates against a State, though discrimination in itself will attract the principle. It is enough that the Commonwealth law inhibits or impairs the continued existence of a State or its capacity to function … as a government.[309]

This tendency to conceive of two distinct tests was also illustrated in a small number of cases in which Commonwealth laws were struck down on the basis of the *Melbourne Corporation* principle.

**303** Ibid, 403.
**304** Ibid, 403–4.
**305** Ibid, 391–2, 410–11, 423–4.
**306** Ibid, 424.
**307** See *Victoria v Australian Building and Construction Employees' and Builders Labourers' Federation* (1982) 152 CLR 25, 93; *Koowarta v Bjelke-Petersen* (1982) 153 CLR 168, 191–2, 225–6; *Commonwealth v Tasmania* (1983) 158 CLR 1, 139–40, 214, 281; *Australian Capital Television Pty Ltd v Commonwealth* (1992) 177 CLR 106, 163, 199–202, 241–5.
**308** *Bank of New South Wales v Commonwealth* (1948) 76 CLR 1, 338.
**309** *Commonwealth v Tasmania* (1983) 158 CLR 1, 139.

In *Queensland Electricity Commission v Commonwealth*,[310] the High Court considered provisions of the *Conciliation and Arbitration (Electricity Industry) Act 1985* (Cth) which applied an accelerated and streamlined Commonwealth arbitration process to a particular industrial dispute between the Electrical Trades Union of Australia, the Queensland Electricity Commission and several Queensland Electricity Boards. The law was undoubtedly directed to the particular dispute between these parties. It was also intended to apply in substitution for State-based arbitration or resolution of the dispute, for it included a provision which removed the ordinary discretion in the Commonwealth Commission to dismiss or refrain from hearing a matter where the dispute could be dealt with by a State industrial authority. In striking down the law, a majority of the Court accepted the argument that the law unconstitutionally singled out the agencies of the State and subjected them to special disabilities to which other employers were not subjected.[311] In so concluding, they affirmed that the *Melbourne Corporation* principle consists of two distinct limbs, and that the discrimination limb embraces laws that are aimed at either the States or a particular State.[312] They also considered that the principle protects any agency of a State, whether or not the agency formally represents the Crown in right of the State and, on one view, whether or not it is under State government control, provided it is brought into existence by a State for a public purpose.[313] It was also observed that the protection extends not only to the executive government of a State, but also its legislative and judicial institutions.[314] It was acknowledged that a Commonwealth head of power might, by virtue of its 'content, context or subject-matter', authorise the enactment of laws directed at the States, but it was considered that the industrial arbitration power was not one of these.[315] Mason J in particular pointed out that a Commonwealth law which merely places a State on an equal footing with others does not isolate the State from the general law and may not amount to unconstitutional discrimination.[316] Likewise, he thought that a Commonwealth law might impose requirements that are so minimal that they involve no real discrimination,[317] for there must be a real 'burden or disadvantage'.[318] However, in the view of Gibbs CJ, 'the integrity of a State' might be 'destroyed as effectively by a succession of minor infringements as by one gross violation of the principle'.[319] The Court would therefore have to be vigilant about even relatively minor interferences.

**310** (1985) 159 CLR 192.
**311** *Queensland Electricity Commission v Commonwealth* (1985) 159 CLR 192, 207, 209, 221, 229–30, 262; compare 243–4, 252–4.
**312** Ibid, 206–7, 215–18, 225–6, 231; compare 247–50, 260–62.
**313** Ibid, 207, 217–18, 225, 235–8, 247–8, 254–5, 262.
**314** Ibid, 207, 217, 232, 258; see also 226. On the protection of State courts from Commonwealth interference, see *Re Tracey; Ex parte Ryan* (1989) 166 CLR 518, 547, 574, 592, discussed in Chapter 8, Part IV.3. On the protection of the electoral processes of the States, see *Australian Capital Television Pty Ltd v Commonwealth* (1992) 177 CLR 106, discussed in Chapter 5, Part V.
**315** Ibid, 208, 219–20, 258; compare 233–43, 250–52, 260.
**316** Ibid, 217–18.
**317** Ibid, 208, 220.
**318** Ibid, 226–7; compare 262.
**319** Ibid, 208–9.

In several cases that immediately followed, much turned on the nature and degree of the necessary discrimination, and the possibility that the very nature of a Commonwealth head of legislative power might authorise interference with State functions. In *Re Lee; Ex parte Harper,*[320] certain unqualified remarks of Mason CJ, Deane and Gaudron JJ seemed to suggest that the first inquiry would be to ascertain the scope of the head of power such that if the power was found to authorise legislation interfering with the States' powers then that would be the end of the matter. However, in *Re State Public Services Federation,*[321] the justices maintained that this statement should not be understood to eliminate the implied immunity from consideration in the process of ascertaining the scope of the head of power. Rather, the scope of the power is to be determined by reference to its text, its subject matter and the entire context of the Constitution, including implications derived from its general structure.[322]

In *Re State Public Services Federation,*[323] as well as in *Richardson v Forestry Commission*[324] and the *Native Title Act* case,[325] the Court rejected arguments that Commonwealth laws that happened only to affect one State, or had a disproportionate effect upon it, unconstitutionally discriminated against that State. In *Richardson*, the Court considered that a law that implemented Australia's international obligation to protect a 'world heritage area' that happened to be located in Tasmania was valid because the law necessarily had to apply to particular properties, and the location of those properties in a particular State did not constitute unconstitutional discrimination against that State.[326] In the *Native Title Act* case, a Commonwealth law that curtailed the capacity of all States from legislating to extinguish or impair native title was upheld under the 'races' power (s 51(xxvi)) despite Western Australia's argument that the law had a differential, disproportionate and debilitating effect on its capacity to regulate and administer Crown lands within the State.[327] The discrimination argument was rejected for reasons similar to those in *Richardson*. It was also argued in the *Native Title Act* case that the law interfered with the State's capacity to function as a government. This argument was rejected on the ground that the effect of the law was confined to the scope of State power and the effectiveness of its exercise, and did not extend to the 'machinery of the government of the State' itself. Drawing upon Dixon J's suggestion in *Melbourne Corporation* that the 'existence and nature' of the States as self-governing bodies politic is distinct from the 'powers' allocated to them,[328] the Court held that the Commonwealth

**320** (1986) 160 CLR 430, 453.
**321** *Re State Public Services Federation; Ex parte Attorney-General (WA)* (1993) 178 CLR 249.
**322** Ibid, 271–2; see also 274–5.
**323** See ibid, 295–9.
**324** *Richardson v Forestry Commission* (1988) 164 CLR 261.
**325** *Western Australia v Commonwealth* (1995) 183 CLR 373.
**326** *Richardson v Forestry Commission* (1988) 164 CLR 261, 293–4, 304–5, 337.
**327** *Western Australia v Commonwealth* (1995) 183 CLR 373, 476–82.
**328** *Melbourne Corporation v Commonwealth* (1947) 74 CLR 31, 82.

law did not detrimentally affect the 'existence and nature' of the State as a body politic.[329] The Court observed:

> A Commonwealth law cannot deprive the State of the personnel, property, goods and services which the State requires to exercise its powers and cannot impede or burden the State in the acquisition of what it so requires.[330]

Notwithstanding the affirmation in the *Engineers* case that Commonwealth industrial arbitration laws can apply to State government employees, the employment relations between State governments and their public servants continued, as a matter of practice, to be regulated under State laws and awards. Part of the reason was that, until the *Australian Social Welfare Union* case reversed the situation,[331] the High Court had maintained that an 'industrial dispute' within the meaning of s 51(xxxv) only related to productive industries or businesses carried on for profit-making purposes. In the early 1990s, the Victorian Government determined to reduce the size of the State public sector and to replace the State industrial arbitration system with a system of individual employer–employee agreements. In response, the relevant employees' union sought coverage under Commonwealth awards pursuant to the *Industrial Relations Act 1988* (Cth).

The *Australian Education Union* case[332] concerned the question of the extent to which the Commonwealth Industrial Relations Commission could make awards applying to State government employees. It was argued by Victoria that the jurisdiction of the Commission was limited in respect of industrial disputes between a State government and its employees in the exercise of the State's governmental functions. The basis of this limitation, it was argued, was the limb of the *Melbourne Corporation* principle which protects the continued existence of States and their capacity to function as governments. Mason CJ, Brennan, Deane, Toohey, Gaudron and McHugh JJ (Dawson J dissenting) held that the federal Commission was not constitutionally precluded from making awards binding States and their employees in relation to minimum wages and general conditions of employment, provided such awards took into consideration any special functions and responsibilities of such employees. However, they also held that the Commission could not interfere with the State's ability to make employment-related decisions that were 'critical' to the State's capacity to function as a government. On the Court's assessment, these protected matters included:

- 'the number and identity of the persons whom a State wishes to employ' (including the 'qualifications and eligibility for employment' of such persons);
- 'the term of appointment of such persons';

**329** See, similarly, *Fortescue Metals Group Ltd v Commonwealth* (2013) 300 ALR 26, 66–7, upholding the Minerals Resource Rent Tax imposed by the Commonwealth despite its alleged interference with existing State mining royalties. Note also arguments concerning the application of the *Melbourne Corporation* principle to the idea of a 'federal balance' in the distribution of legislative powers in *New South Wales v Commonwealth* (2006) 229 CLR 1, 171–4, 320–33.

**330** *Western Australia v Commonwealth* (1995) 183 CLR 373, 480.

**331** *R v Coldham; Ex parte Australian Social Welfare Union* (1983) 153 CLR 297.

**332** *Re Australian Education Union; Ex parte Victoria* (1995) 184 CLR 188.

- 'the number and identity of the persons whom [the State] wishes to dismiss with or without notice from its employment on redundancy grounds'; and
- 'the number and identity of those whom [the State] wishes to engage at the higher levels of government' and 'the terms and conditions on which those persons shall be engaged'.[333]

Such 'higher level' officials and employees, the majority explained, would clearly include 'Ministers, ministerial assistants and advisers, heads of departments and high level statutory office holders, parliamentary officers and judges', and might possibly include others as well. Moreover, the majority further suggested that there might be a question, in some areas of employment, whether the 'promotion and transfer' of State employees would also be protected from interference.[334]

What was the Court's reasoning? The first thing to be observed is that while the majority proceeded on the assumption that the *Melbourne Corporation* principle consists of two distinct elements, they explicitly avoided deciding definitively whether it was better to regard the case law as having established 'two implied limitations, two elements or branches of one limitation, or simply one limitation'. It was sufficient to rely on the proposition that the legislative powers of the Commonwealth cannot be exercised to destroy or curtail the existence of the States or their continuing to function as governments, conceived as 'independent' entities, whose 'integrity' and 'autonomy' is to be protected.[335] This was to articulate a relatively high threshold for protection of the States from interference. The majority were clear that not just 'any impairment of capacity to exercise government functions' would suffice, for the scope of the protection of the States recognised by s 106 of the Constitution had to be considered together with the subordination of the powers of the States to Commonwealth laws by operation of s 109.[336] Determining the threshold in this way meant the operation of Commonwealth awards in relation to State government school teachers, health workers and similar categories of employees would not destroy or curtail the capacity of a State to function as a government.[337] However, it was considered that the determination of the number and identity of persons employed at any one time, as well as the terms and conditions of employees at the 'higher levels', were matters 'critical' to a State's capacity to function as a government. In effect, the Court affirmed the constitutional right of the Victorian Government to retrench a large number of its employees as a matter of government policy.

There is a tension in the reasoning in *Australian Education Union* between the abstract principles of 'integrity' and 'autonomy' and the very specific categories of State government employment decisions that were said to be protected from

**333** Ibid, 232–3.
**334** Ibid, 233–4.
**335** Ibid, 227–9, 231–3.
**336** Ibid, 228–30.
**337** Ibid, 230.

Commonwealth interference. Indeed, soon thereafter, in the *Industrial Relations Act* case,[338] the Court simply and directly applied the categories adopted in *Australian Education Union* to provisions introduced by the *Industrial Relations Reform Act 1993* (Cth). As seen in Chapter 3, the *Industrial Relations Reform Act* was enacted in reliance upon the corporations and external affairs powers of the Commonwealth (ss 51(xx) and (xxix)). The Act conferred rights upon employees in relation to such matters as minimum wages, equal pay, unfair dismissal, discrimination in employment, family leave, collective bargaining and the right to strike. These provisions were challenged on the basis that, among other things, they purported to apply to the conditions of those employed at the higher levels of government. A majority of the Court held that s 6 of the Act, which made the Act binding on the Crown in right of each State, would have to be read down pursuant to s 15A of the *Acts Interpretation Act 1901* (Cth) so that it did not bind the States in this respect.[339] Section 15A provides:

> Every Act shall be read and construed subject to the Constitution and so as not to exceed the legislative power of the Commonwealth, to the intent that where any enactment thereof would but for this section have been construed as in excess of that power, it shall nevertheless be a valid enactment to the extent to which it is not in excess of that power.

As the justices explained, s 15A may be applied to discrete clauses or provisions, as well as to general words or expressions found within an Act. However, the unconstitutional aspects of an Act cannot be severed from the valid aspects 'unless the operation of the remaining parts of the law remains unchanged', and a general term or expression cannot be read down if 'the law was intended to operate fully and completely according to its terms'. Moreover, if a general expression might be reduced by any one or more of several possible limitations, the choice of limitation must be based upon the law itself, as appears in its terms or arises from its subject matter.[340] In the present case, the Court reasoned, s 6 of the Act purported to bind the States to a regime specifying certain terms and conditions of employment, a subject matter which is itself limited by the rule in *Re Australian Education Union*, and thus the rule provided a basis for reading down the application of s 6 so that it did not bind the States in a manner that contravened the rule.[341]

### One principle and a single test

In the *Industrial Relations Act* case, the majority judgment continued to accept the two-element description of the *Melbourne Corporation* principle.[342] However, in *Austin v Commonwealth*, a majority of the Court rejected the proposition that

**338** *Victoria v Commonwealth* (1996) 187 CLR 416.
**339** Ibid, 501–3.
**340** Ibid, 502.
**341** Ibid, 503.
**342** Ibid, 498.

there are two distinct elements or tests, insisting rather that 'the essential question in all cases' is 'whether the law restricts or burdens one or more of the States in the exercise of their constitutional powers'.[343] *Austin* involved a complex legislative package directed to imposing a 15 per cent surcharge on financial contributions to superannuation retirement funds made by 'high income earners'. For administrative convenience, the tax liability was generally imposed on employers, although the burden of the tax was typically passed on to the employee beneficiaries of the superannuation funds in the form of reductions in their entitlements. The general law did not apply to State judicial officers because their retirement benefits were provided directly out of State consolidated revenue and the Commonwealth assumed (perhaps erroneously)[344] that it lacked constitutional power to tax the State Governments directly. In order to impose the surcharge upon all high income earners, the Commonwealth enacted a special Act which imposed a separate surcharge on the pension funds established by each State for its judges and other judicial officers. The amount of the annual surcharge was calculated by reference to the value of the benefits accruing to the judges, and the liability to pay the surcharge was imposed directly on the judges themselves. Because the surcharge accumulated over time, its total amount increased dramatically the longer the judges continued to hold office beyond their earliest retirement age. The surcharge debt amounted to a very substantial capital sum which placed them under a special practical financial disadvantage which was not experienced by federal judges and other high income earners. To ameliorate the effect on State judges, New South Wales found it necessary to make significant changes to its judicial pension scheme.[345]

A majority of the Court (Kirby J dissenting), held that the special superannuation surcharge on State judicial officers was unconstitutional. In coming to this conclusion, Gleeson CJ, Gaudron, Gummow and Hayne JJ (Kirby J agreeing and McHugh J disagreeing on this point) considered that the rule in *Melbourne Corporation* must be understood as involving a single principle, concerned ultimately with the preservation of the States as continuing, separately organised, independent governments. For Gleeson CJ, although the element of discrimination was a recurring feature in the previous cases and their reasoning, the requirement of discrimination ought to be considered an aspect of a 'wider principle' which determines 'what constitutes relevant and impermissible discrimination'. The foundation of the implication, he said, is the constitutional conception of the Commonwealth and States as 'constituent entities' and 'separately organised' governments. This foundational conception provides the reason why a Commonwealth law aimed at the destruction of the States or State agencies or their governmental attributes or their capacity to function as independent units will be unconstitutional. It is also the reason why a law of general application 'may so

**343** *Austin v Commonwealth* (2003) 215 CLR 185, 258.
**344** See ibid, 220.
**345** Ibid, 210.

interfere with or impede State activity as to impose an impermissible burden on the exercise of its functions'. Both the concepts of 'discrimination' and 'burden' need to be understood, he explained, in the light of the same general principle, which is concerned with the maintenance of the 'constitutional status' of the States and of their 'capacity to function as … government[s]'.[346]

Gaudron, Gummow and Hayne JJ broadly agreed. They were concerned to articulate what they regarded as the proper basis upon which the implied immunity is to be derived from the 'text and structure' of the Constitution, which they said was the continued existence and operation of the States as separately organised governments.[347] After surveying the way in which the element of discrimination had featured in the previous cases, they concluded that there was 'but one limitation', although the expression of it varied in each case. They acknowledged that the Court will always have to assess 'the impact of particular laws' by reference to a range of matters, such as whether such laws impose a 'special burden' or 'curtail' the 'capacity' of the States 'to function as governments',[348] but the 'essential question' will always be whether the law 'restricts or burdens one or more of the States in the exercise of their constitutional powers'.[349]

In their separate judgments, Gleeson CJ and Gaudron, Gummow and Hayne JJ considered that the Commonwealth law imposed an impermissible interference with arrangements made by the State for the remuneration of its judges. Gleeson CJ observed that this was especially manifest in the law's effect on a State's capacity to recruit judges and retain their services, reflected in the fact that New South Wales had to alter its arrangements in order to ameliorate the effect of the law.[350] Gaudron, Gummow and Hayne JJ similarly insisted that it is for the State to determine the terms and conditions upon which its judges are appointed and remunerated, and that the law imposed a 'sufficiently significant impairment' of the State's freedom to determine the 'manner and method' by which it would discharge its 'constitutional function' of determining the remuneration of its judges.[351]

In his concurring judgment, McHugh J rejected the proposition that there is only one limitation. His basic reason was that the idea of two distinct rules or elements had become the settled doctrine of the Court, having been confirmed by majorities of the Court in several decisions since *Queensland Electricity Commission*.[352] However, for essentially the same concrete reasons, he concluded that

**346** Ibid, 217.
**347** Ibid, 245–6, 258. Their concern was that judicial *dicta* can have a tendency to 'take on, by further judicial exigesis [sic], a life of their own which is removed from the constitutional fundamentals which must sustain them': at 258–9. On this concern, see the discussion of the implied freedom of political communication, in Chapter 5, Part V.
**348** Ibid, 249.
**349** Ibid, 258.
**350** Ibid, 219–20.
**351** Ibid, 261, 264–5.
**352** Ibid, 280–82.

the law was unconstitutional: it singled out State judicial officers, it imposed a special financial burden on them, and it thereby interfered significantly with the State's relationships with its judicial officers, hampering its capacity to obtain and retain their services.[353] Such a line of reasoning seemed to merge considerations of discrimination and interference, suggesting that the two-limbed approach to the *Melbourne Corporation* principle might not make a significant difference in practice.[354]

In his dissenting judgment, Kirby J considered that the two aspects of the implied limitation were 'essentially manifestations of the one constitutional implication', both 'referable to the underlying conception concerning the nature of the Australian federation'.[355] However, he insisted that the implied limitation should not be informed by an absolute conception of 'autonomy' that would deny the 'integrated character of the Australian federation'.[356] Australian federalism, he maintained, is characterised by a 'high degree of co-operation and of federal leadership', and he denied that there was a sufficient degree of interference with the States, noting that while the law might affect the decisions of some judges and prospective judges, it had not been demonstrated that this would amount to a 'significant and detrimental' effect on the capacity of the States to determine the remuneration of their judges.[357]

In *Clarke v Commissioner of Taxation*,[358] the Court also struck down the special superannuation surcharge in its application to the superannuation of a retired member of the South Australian Parliament. Applying largely the same reasoning as in *Austin*, Gummow, Heydon, Kiefel and Bell JJ affirmed that the element of discrimination is 'but an illustration of a law which impairs the capacity of the State to function in accordance with the constitutional conception of the Commonwealth and States as constituent entities of the federal structure'.[359] French CJ went further, proposing that an assessment of whether a Commonwealth law 'significantly' impairs, curtails or weakens the capacity of the States to exercise their constitutional powers and functions will require an evaluative judgment, and that in making such an assessment a 'multifactorial' approach would be necessary.[360] He suggested the relevant factors would include an assessment of:

1. Whether the law in question singles out one or more of the States and imposes a special burden or disability on them which is not imposed on persons generally.
2. Whether the operation of a law of general application imposes a particular burden or disability on the States.

**353** Ibid, 283–5.
**354** Ibid, 282.
**355** Ibid, 301. As a consequence, 'mere discrimination' would not of itself be necessarily sufficient: at 306.
**356** Ibid, 298.
**357** Ibid, 301–8.
**358** (2009) 240 CLR 272.
**359** *Clarke v Commissioner of Taxation* (2009) 240 CLR 272, 306.
**360** Ibid, 298–9.

3. The effect of the law upon the capacity of the States to exercise their constitutional powers.
4. The effect of the law upon the exercise of their functions by the States.
5. The nature of the capacity or functions affected.
6. The subject matter of the law affecting the State or States and in particular the extent to which the constitutional head of power under which the law is made authorises its discriminatory application.[361]

The Chief Justice considered that several features of the law significantly interfered with the remuneration arrangements that the State established for its parliamentarians and, in so doing, 'significantly burdened the exercise by the State' of its relevant powers and functions.[362]

By drawing attention to the evaluative nature of the assessment that has to be made under the *Melbourne Corporation* principle, French CJ's judgment serves to underscore what is at stake when the High Court develops doctrines that are based on inferences from the text and structure of the Constitution. It is clear that the Constitution was intended to establish a genuine federation in which the States would continue to operate as distinct, self-governing political communities. It seems contrary to this conception to suggest that the Commonwealth should be able to interfere with the States' capacity to exercise their constitutional powers.[363] However, the States and the Commonwealth each operate through human agents, and it is a fundamental principle that these agents are subject to the law – not only constitutional law, but also common law and statutory law. Constitutional lines therefore have to be drawn between the independence of the States from Commonwealth interference and the necessary subjection of the agencies of the States to law, including in some instances, Commonwealth statutes and regulations. The difficulty lies in determining exactly where the line is to be drawn, particularly because the Constitution provides little specific guidance. The reformulation of the relevant principles in *Austin* were intended, it seems, to ensure that the content and application of the immunity would be properly related to the rationale for its existence, grounded in the text and structure of the Constitution.[364] But the text and structure of the Constitution provide only so much guidance. Beyond this, the Court has to grapple with the fundamental question of the nature of the bodies politic whose continued existence is presupposed by the Constitution.[365]

**361** Ibid, 299.
**362** Ibid.
**363** See *Melbourne Corporation v Commonwealth* (1947) 74 CLR 31, 75, 79; *Koowarta v Bjelke-Petersen* (1982) 153 CLR 168, 216; *Queensland Electricity Commission v Commonwealth* (1985) 159 CLR 192, 207, 217, 232; *Austin v Commonwealth* (2003) 215 CLR 185, 258, 260 (see also 281, 301); *Clarke v Commissioner of Taxation* (2009) 240 CLR 272, 286, 298.
**364** *Austin v Commonwealth* (2003) 215 CLR 185, 258.
**365** Transcript of Proceedings, *Clarke v Commissioner of Taxation* [2009] HCA Trans 42 (11 March 2009). For a discussion, see Leslie Zines, *The High Court and the Constitution* (Federation Press, 5th ed, 2008) 440–66; Anne Twomey, 'Federal Limitations on the Legislative Power of the States and the Commonwealth to Bind One Another' (2003) 31 *Federal Law Review* 507; Sarah Murray, 'Constitutional Musings on *Clarke* and *Austin*' (2011) 6(1/2) *Public Policy* 121.

## 4 Strong Commonwealth immunity: *Cigamatic* (1962–)

In the *Engineers* case, the High Court established the general principle that not only the States, but also the Commonwealth would ordinarily be subject to each other's laws. Thus, in *Pirrie v McFarlane*,[366] the Court held that a Commonwealth officer was subject to the ordinary traffic rules and driver's licence requirements of the State of Victoria, even when performing his official duties for the Commonwealth. However, in a series of decisions from the 1930s, Dixon J proposed a range of qualifications to this fundamental idea culminating, as has been seen, in the principle that the Commonwealth is constitutionally prohibited from making a law which singles out the States and places special burdens upon the exercise of their constitutional powers and functions.[367] While at times expressing this principle in reciprocal terms, so that it would protect not only the States but also the Commonwealth, in *Melbourne Corporation v Commonwealth* Dixon J further maintained that the position of the Commonwealth is necessarily different to and stronger than the States.[368] The primary reasons for this, he suggested, were that the Commonwealth's enumerated powers are 'affirmatively granted', which grant carries with it all that is 'proper' for its 'full effectuation', and that in case of a conflict between the Commonwealth and the States, 'supremacy' is given to the Commonwealth's laws. These considerations, he concluded, both strengthened the implication protecting the Commonwealth from State laws and amplified the scope of its protection.[369]

### Commonwealth immunity denied

In *Uther's* case,[370] decided in the same year as *Melbourne Corporation*, the Court had to consider a State law, ss 282 and 297 of the *Companies Act 1936* (NSW), which expressly bound the Crown and was clearly intended to postpone the rights of the Crown in right of the Commonwealth to payment of debts owed to it.[371] The right of the Crown to be paid in priority to other creditors is a special privilege enjoyed by the Crown as part of its prerogatives recognised historically by the common law, and enjoyed by the Commonwealth upon its creation.[372] There is no doubt that the prerogative can be limited by a statute passed by a competent Parliament, and that a State Parliament could therefore legislate to postpone the rights of the Crown in right of that State. However, in a federation, the question arises whether a State Parliament is competent to interfere with the prerogatives vested in the Crown in right of the Commonwealth. It had been decided by the Court in the *First Uniform Tax* case that the Commonwealth could

**366** (1925) 36 CLR 170.
**367** *Melbourne Corporation v Commonwealth* (1947) 74 CLR 31, 81–2.
**368** Ibid.
**369** Ibid, 82–3. See also Dixon J's remarks in *Federal Commissioner of Taxation v Official Liquidator of E O Farley Ltd* (1940) 63 CLR 278, discussed in Part III.2 above.
**370** *In re Foreman & Sons Pty Ltd; Uther v Federal Commissioner of Taxation* (1947) 74 CLR 508.
**371** Ibid, 515.
**372** *R v Kidman* (1915) 20 CLR 425, 435–6.

make a law under the taxation power (s 51(ii)) giving it priority to payment of taxation debts notwithstanding anything contained in a State law.[373] However, the Commonwealth had not passed any such law in the circumstances of *Uther's* case. The question was simply whether the State law bound the Crown in right of the Commonwealth.

Delivering the leading judgment of the Court, Latham CJ reasoned that just as the State Parliament had power to determine the payment priorities that would apply in relation to company liquidations within the State, as well as in relation to the Crown in right of other States and other parts of the British Commonwealth (including the Crown in right of the United Kingdom), it had to follow that it had the same capacity as regards the Crown in right of the Commonwealth of Australia.[374] He also considered that the principle in *Melbourne Corporation* could not apply to protect the Commonwealth in the same way that it applies to the States, because the Commonwealth, unlike the States, is able to enact a protective law which will prevail over any inconsistent State law pursuant to s 109.[375] There are some Commonwealth matters, he noted, such as the prerogative of the Governor-General to summon and dissolve the Commonwealth Parliament, with which the States could not interfere.[376] However, he pointed out that the Commonwealth 'lives and moves and has its being within a system of law' consisting of both common law and statutory law, to which it is generally subject, including the general rules of property, contract and tort, and the ordinary rules of the road (as in *McFarlane*). In his view, other more specialised statutory rules, such as those concerning the ranking of creditors under the State's company law, bound the Commonwealth in the same way.[377]

Rich, Starke and Williams JJ delivered judgments in which they broadly agreed with this conclusion. In his dissenting judgment, however, Dixon J rejected the proposition that a State could legislate to affect the prerogative, fiscal or governmental rights of the Commonwealth in this way.[378] His reasons were several. Adopting language similar to that which he used in *Melbourne Corporation*, Dixon J pointed out that in a federal or dual system government 'you do not expect to find either government legislating for the other'.[379] In addition, however, he also maintained that under the Constitution, 'supremacy, where it exists, belongs to the Commonwealth'. This supremacy, he explained, consists in the fact that the Commonwealth has an affirmative grant of particular powers, some of which, such as the bankruptcy and taxation powers, may

**373** *South Australia v Commonwealth* (1942) 65 CLR 373, cited in *In re Foreman & Sons Pty Ltd; Uther v Federal Commissioner of Taxation* (1947) 74 CLR 508, 516, 524, 529, 540. The *Second Uniform Tax* case (1957) 99 CLR 575 had not yet been decided.
**374** *In re Foreman & Sons Pty Ltd; Uther v Federal Commissioner of Taxation* (1947) 74 CLR 508, 518–19; see also 523 ('there is but one Crown for the whole Empire').
**375** Ibid, 520–21.
**376** Ibid, 521.
**377** Ibid, 521–2.
**378** Ibid, 529–32. McTiernan J also dissented, but on the basis that there was a relevant inconsistency between the State and Commonwealth laws on the topic.
**379** Ibid, 529.

specifically authorise Commonwealth interference with the rights of the States, and that when the Commonwealth exercises these powers they operate with paramount force. This sets the powers of the Commonwealth in sharp contrast with the legislative powers of the States, which are only the 'undefined residue' which remains after 'full effect' is given to the exercise of Commonwealth legislative power.[380] Secondly, Dixon J argued, 'the Commonwealth' as such did not fall within State power. As he colourfully put it:

> Like the goddess of wisdom the Commonwealth *uno ictu* [with one blow] sprang from the brain of its begetters armed and of full stature. At the same instant the Colonies became States; but whence did the States obtain the power to regulate the legal relations of this new polity with its subjects? It formed no part of the old colonial power. The Federal constitution does not give it. Surely it is for the peace, order and good government of the Commonwealth, not for the peace, welfare and good government of New South Wales, to say what shall be the relative situation of private rights and of the public rights of the Crown representing the Commonwealth, where they come into conflict. It is a question of the fiscal and governmental rights of the Commonwealth and, as such, is one over which the State has no power.[381]

All of this did not mean that the Commonwealth could not be affected by State laws. Dixon J affirmed that if the Commonwealth enters a transaction regulated by State law, it may be bound by the legal consequences that the State law affixes to those given descriptions of transaction. But the effect on the Commonwealth in such instances is always dependent upon the Commonwealth entering into the transaction.[382] Apart from that, the general principle is that a State cannot interfere in any way with the prerogative, fiscal or governmental rights of the Commonwealth.

### Commonwealth immunity affirmed

On the majority view expressed in *Uther*, the relative positions of the Commonwealth and the States are asymmetrical: while the States enjoy an immunity in the terms established in *Melbourne Corporation*, the Commonwealth stands in a different position, essentially because it is able to protect itself from State interference through its own legislation, which prevails over inconsistent State law (s 109).[383] One alternative to this might have been to hold that the *Melbourne Corporation* principle applies equally to the Commonwealth and the States. However, this was not the path that the Court would eventually adopt. Rather, some fifteen years later, when in the *Cigamatic* case the same legislation again came before the High Court, Sir Owen Dixon, who was now Chief Justice, was able to convince a majority of the Court that they should adopt the position that he had articulated in *Uther*, producing an asymmetry in the implied

**380** Ibid, 529–30.
**381** Ibid, 530.
**382** Ibid, 528.
**383** Ibid, 519–21; compare 539.

constitutional protections accorded to the Commonwealth and the States, this time in favour of the Commonwealth.[384]

The foundations for this shift in opinion had been laid not only in *Uther*, but in two other cases. In *Essendon Corporation v Criterion Theatres Ltd*,[385] Dixon J had maintained that the States simply have no capacity to tax the Commonwealth when it is exercising its constitutional powers or functions, such as when the military forces of the Commonwealth occupy premises for wartime purposes. As he put it:

> To my mind the incapacity of the States directly to tax the Commonwealth in respect of something done in the exercise of its powers or functions is a necessary consequence of the system of government established by the Constitution. It is hardly necessary at this stage of our constitutional development to go over the considerations which make it impossible to suppose that the Constitution intended that the States should levy taxes upon the Commonwealth – the nature of the Federal Government, its supremacy, the exclusiveness or paramountcy of its legislative powers, the independence of its fiscal system and the elaborate provisions of the Constitution governing the financial relations of the central government to the constituent States. To describe the establishment of the Commonwealth as the birth of a nation has been a commonplace. It was anything but the birth of a taxpayer.[386]

In *Commonwealth v Bogle*,[387] decided six years later, Fullagar J put the position even more forcefully when, in a judgment with which Dixon CJ and Kitto J agreed and Webb J substantially agreed, he stated:

> To say that a State can enact legislation which is binding upon the Commonwealth in the same sense in which it is binding upon a subject of the State appears to me to give effect to a fundamental misconception. ... [If a State] statute ... purport[s] to bind the Crown in right of the Commonwealth, then a constitutional question arises. The Crown in right of the State has assented to the statute, but the Crown in right of the Commonwealth has not, and the constitutional question, to my mind, is susceptible of only one answer, and that is that the State Parliament has no power over the Commonwealth. The Commonwealth – or the Crown in right of the Commonwealth, or whatever you choose to call it – is, to all intents and purposes, a juristic person, but it is not a juristic person which is subjected either by any State Constitution or by the Commonwealth Constitution to the legislative power of any State Parliament.[388]

With this background in mind, in his leading judgment in *Cigamatic*, Dixon CJ found it necessary only to repeat in summary form some of the arguments that he had presented in *Uther*.[389] In his view, the whole question went 'deep in the nature and operation of the federal system'.[390] What was at stake was the

**384** *Commonwealth v Cigamatic Pty Ltd (in liq)* (1962) 108 CLR 372 (Dixon CJ, Kitto, Menzies, Windeyer and Owen JJ; McTiernan and Taylor JJ dissenting).
**385** (1947) 74 CLR 1.
**386** *Essendon Corporation v Criterion Theatres Ltd* (1947) 74 CLR 1, 22.
**387** (1953) 89 CLR 229.
**388** *Commonwealth v Bogle* (1953) 89 CLR 229, 259
**389** *Commonwealth v Cigamatic Pty Ltd (in liq)* (1962) 108 CLR 372, 378. Kitto, Menzies, Windeyer and Owen JJ wrote very brief concurring judgments.
**390** Ibid, 377.

capacity of the States to interfere with the legal rights and duties of the Commonwealth in relation to its people, especially in relation to the fiscal rights of the Commonwealth, such as the right of the Commonwealth to priority in the repayment of debts owed to it.[391] It was not a question of 'making some implication in favour of the Commonwealth', but rather concerned the capacity of the States to interfere with the rights of the Commonwealth.[392] Because the issue was so fundamental to the Constitution, Dixon CJ concluded, *Uther* should be overruled.

The reasoning expressed in *Uther* and *Cigamatic* has been the subject of much criticism. In an important essay, two lawyers who would become distinguished judges of the NSW Court of Appeal and High Court respectively, Roderick Meagher and William Gummow, trenchantly argued that Dixon J had offered 'no logical basis' for the *Cigamatic* doctrine.[393] It made no sense, they maintained, to suggest that the States could have no legislative power over persons or things that did not exist when they were first granted their self-governing powers as colonies; indeed, on the contrary, they pointed out that it is an undoubted proposition that the States have plenary powers to legislate in respect of any subject matter that might, from time to time, fall within their territorial jurisdiction.[394] In addition, they pointed out that Dixon J's emphasis on the legal relationship between the Commonwealth and its people obscured the real issue, which concerned the proper 'adjustment of concurrent claims' made over the people, considered as citizens of both the Commonwealth and the States.[395] Furthermore, the attempt to suggest that the Commonwealth might 'enter' a field and thereby 'submit' to the jurisdiction of the States in some respect, failed to grapple with the proposition that a State law is either valid or invalid under the Constitution. While the Commonwealth can by its legislation submit itself and its agencies to State legislation,[396] the capacity of State law to bind the Commonwealth cannot turn on choices or decisions made by the Commonwealth executive to enter into a particular kind of transaction.[397]

The climate of criticism surrounding the reasoning in *Cigamatic* gave rise to an expectation that the next time the High Court was squarely faced with the question of Commonwealth immunity it might take the opportunity to clarify and perhaps reform its doctrinal position. This opportunity seemed to arise in the *Residential Tenancies* case (also known as *Henderson's* case), decided in 1997.[398]

**391** Ibid, 377–8.
**392** Ibid.
**393** R P Meagher and W M C Gummow, 'Sir Owen Dixon's Heresy' (1980) 54 *Australian Law Journal* 25.
**394** Ibid, 28.
**395** Ibid, 29.
**396** Eg, *Salaries Act 1907* (Cth), *Taxation Debts (Abolition of Crown Priority) Act 1980* (Cth); *Crown Debts (Priority) Act 1981* (Cth); *Judiciary Act 1903* (Cth), ss 64, 79 and 80. See *Chaplin v Commissioner of Taxes for South Australia* (1911) 12 CLR 375; *Maguire v Simpson* (1977) 139 CLR 362; *Commonwealth v Evans Deakin Industries Ltd* (1986) 161 CLR 254; *Deputy Commissioner of Taxation v Moorebank Pty Ltd* (1988) 165 CLR 55; *Allders International Pty Ltd v Commissioner of State Revenue (Vic)* (1996) 186 CLR 630.
**397** Meagher and Gummow, above n 393, 29.
**398** *Re Residential Tenancies Tribunal (NSW) and Henderson; Ex parte Defence Housing Authority* (1997) 190 CLR 410.

The case involved s 24 of the *Residential Tenancies Act 1987* (NSW), which authorised landlords to enter and inspect rented properties. The Defence Housing Authority, an agency established by the Commonwealth under the *Defence Housing Authority Act 1987* (Cth), held a lease of a home unit which it sublet to defence service personnel. The unit was subsequently sold to Mr Henderson, who as head lessor tried to exercise his right to enter and inspect the unit under the NSW Act. When the Commonwealth Authority refused to allow him to do so, Henderson sought orders from the State Residential Tenancies Tribunal ordering it to comply. The Authority denied that the Tribunal had jurisdiction, and commenced proceedings in the High Court seeking prohibition against the Tribunal to prevent it from proceeding.

A majority of the Court rejected arguments that the matter fell within the exclusive power of the Commonwealth under s 52(ii) of the Constitution, and that there was an inconsistency between the Commonwealth and State Acts pursuant to s 109.[399] All members of the Court also rejected the proposition that the State Act could not apply to the Commonwealth Authority by virtue of the principle in *Cigamatic*. Kirby J came to this conclusion by rejecting the very principle laid down in *Cigamatic*, whereas the other members of the Court found that the principle did not apply in the circumstances.

The reasoning of Brennan CJ, Dawson, Toohey and Gaudron JJ turned on a somewhat elusive distinction between the capacities of the Crown in right of the Commonwealth (meaning its 'rights, powers, privileges and immunities') and the exercise by the Commonwealth of those capacities. As Dawson, Toohey and Gaudron JJ put it, a State law may regulate activities in which the Commonwealth chooses to engage in the exercise of its capacities, but it cannot impair the capacities themselves.[400] In this way, they sought to maintain the distinction Sir Owen Dixon had drawn in *Uther*, *Farley* and *Cigamatic* between the governmental rights and powers of the Commonwealth, which cannot be interfered with, and cases where the Commonwealth chooses to enter into a transaction to which the general laws of a State apply.[401] They also sought to integrate the reasoning in *Cigamatic* with the reasoning in *Melbourne Corporation* by maintaining that both were based on the same fundamental principle, 'namely, that the Constitution is predicated upon the continued separate existence of the Commonwealth and the States ... as bodies politic', but that in application of this principle, the constitutional situation of two are relevantly different.[402] Essentially repeating the main lines of Sir Owen Dixon's reasoning, they observed that the Commonwealth has specifically enumerated legislative powers 'which by

**399** Section 64 of the *Judiciary Act 1903* (Cth) was also considered not to apply, as the Tribunal was not a court exercising federal jurisdiction.

**400** *Re Residential Tenancies Tribunal (NSW) and Henderson; Ex parte Defence Housing Authority* (1997) 190 CLR 410, 438–9; see also 424.

**401** Ibid, 439, citing *Federal Commissioner of Taxation v Official Liquidator of E O Farley Ltd* (1940) 63 CLR 278, 308.

**402** *Re Residential Tenancies Tribunal (NSW) and Henderson; Ex parte Defence Housing Authority* (1997) 190 CLR 410, 440.

reason of their content, context or subject matter may authorise it to affect the executive capacities of a State' and in the exercise of which the Commonwealth is 'supreme'. By contrast, the States have only an 'undefined residue' of powers which do not authorise them to 'restrict or modify' the 'executive capacities' of the Commonwealth. The 'character of the Commonwealth as a body politic, armed with executive capacities by the Constitution, by its very nature places those capacities outside the legislative power' of the States, they concluded.[403]

To implement the distinction, Dawson, Toohey and Gaudron JJ further considered that the Commonwealth's relationship with its subjects may fall into one of two categories: the relationship may be one of equality, where the Commonwealth and the subject have the same capacities, such as the capacity to enter into a contract; or the relationship may be one of inequality, where the Commonwealth enjoys some special privilege or immunity, such as the common law right of the Crown to be paid in priority to other creditors. They considered that where the relationship is one of inequality, then any diminution of the rights of the Commonwealth by a State will alter the relationship; whereas if the relationship is one of equality, then a State law which singles out the Commonwealth and treats it differently will alter the relationship, but a law which treats the Commonwealth and the subject the same will not do so. They considered that where a State law thus alters the relationship, either by any change to a relationship of inequality, or a discriminatory law specifically altering the rights of the Commonwealth, it will be unconstitutional; but a general State law which subjects the Commonwealth and its subjects to the same rules in the context of a relationship of equality will not be unconstitutional.[404] While this line of reasoning was generally consistent with the reasoning in *Cigamatic*, it involved a repudiation of the unqualified dictum of Fullagar J in *Bogle* that the State cannot enact a law that is binding on the Commonwealth.[405] In application to the facts in the case, it followed that because the relationship between the Commonwealth Authority as tenant and Henderson as landlord under the State law was one of equality, and the law did not single out the Commonwealth for special treatment, the law did constitutionally bind the Commonwealth.

While McHugh and Gummow JJ agreed with this conclusion, they rejected the distinction upon which the reasoning of the other members of the majority had relied. McHugh J in particular doubted whether it was a distinction that would be easy to apply. What would be the result, he asked, if a State law purported to prevent the Commonwealth from using its contractual right to forfeit a lease or terminate someone's employment – would such a law fetter the Commonwealth's capacity or the exercise of this capacity?[406] Instead, McHugh J seemed to suggest that the distinction needs to be understood temporally, in

**403** Ibid, 440–41.
**404** Ibid, 442–3.
**405** Ibid, 445.
**406** Ibid, 455.

the sense that if the Commonwealth enters a particular legal relationship creating rights and duties, it may be bound by State laws ordinarily regulating such relationships, but it is not competent for a State subsequently to alter the legal consequences of the relationship.[407] He also proposed that the broad dictum of Fullagar J in *Bogle* be understood as a correct statement of the law concerning the exercise by the Commonwealth, not of all of its capacities, but only of the 'extraordinary executive powers and capacities' which it possesses as a 'political sovereign in the federation'.[408] On this approach, whether a State law could validly apply to the Commonwealth or its agents would depend on several factors the most important of which would be: the nature of the activity being performed; whether it was the Commonwealth directly, or its agent, that was being regulated; and whether the law directly discriminated against Commonwealth executive activity or was a general law which merely regulated the manner or mode of performing an activity by a servant or agent of the Commonwealth.[409]

Kirby J, although he agreed with the general result, considered that *Cigamatic* had been wrongly decided and should 'be reverently laid to rest'.[410] In his view, the Constitution constructed an 'integrated federal polity' in which the Commonwealth and the States are intended to operate 'together, and in relation to each other', allowing the laws of each to apply to the other, except that there should be a reciprocal application of the *Melbourne Corporation* principle to protect the Commonwealth as well as the States from any law which would 'impair the integrity or autonomy' of either government.[411]

## IV Conclusions

Sir Owen Dixon once said that '[t]he foundation of the Constitution is the conception of a central government and a number of State governments separately organized'.[412] Constructing such a system of partly independent, partly interdependent, self-governing political communities requires a complex set of rules demarcating their respective powers and ensuring their capacity to exercise them. The central means by which this is achieved in the Constitution is through the conferral of limited exclusive and concurrent legislative powers on the Commonwealth, the continuance of the originally plenary legislative powers of the States, and the rule that in areas of concurrent jurisdiction Commonwealth laws will prevail over inconsistent State laws. As has been seen, the High Court has discerned several ways in which a Commonwealth and a State law may be inconsistent, both directly and indirectly, and so doing has interpreted s 109 in a

**407** Ibid, 454–5
**408** Ibid, 456.
**409** Ibid, 457–8.
**410** Ibid, 509.
**411** Ibid, 504, 507–8.
**412** *Melbourne Corporation v Commonwealth* (1947) 74 CLR 31, 82.

way that enables the Commonwealth to displace State laws to a very considerable extent, especially through the 'covering the field' doctrine.

In addition, as has been seen, even when the Commonwealth or the States operate within these limits, it is possible for their laws to interfere with each other in various ways. Numerous specific provisions of the Constitution are directed to this problem. In addition, the High Court has developed a doctrine of implied intergovernmental immunities that protect both the Commonwealth and the States from interference. During its early years, the Court enforced a very strict rule, called the 'immunity of instrumentalities', which rendered any intergovernmental interference unconstitutional unless it could be justified as specifically required or authorised by the Constitution. In the *Engineers* case this doctrine was overturned and the view gained currency that no such implications were to be inferred from the federal nature of the Constitution. However, some years later, in *Melbourne Corporation* and *Cigamatic*, the High Court affirmed that a modified set of intergovernmental immunities was indeed implied by the text and structure of the Constitution.

One of the most noticeable features of the modern doctrine of implied immunities is the asymmetrical character of the protections accorded to the Commonwealth and the States. The immunity enjoyed by the States protects their capacity to function as constitutionally independent governments, whereas the immunity enjoyed by the Commonwealth is based on an expanded conception of the 'supremacy' of the Commonwealth and a diminutive view of the legislative powers of the States as merely derivative and residual in nature. Such asymmetry between the Commonwealth and the States seems rather inconsistent with the constitutional relationship between the States and the Commonwealth that was conceived by the framers and embedded in the text and structure of the Constitution as a whole. According to the framers, the powers of the States were not specified in the Constitution, not because they were in some general sense inferior to those of the Commonwealth, but because it was thought inappropriate to dictate to the States the content of those powers, let alone to purport to establish them in the federal Constitution. The powers and constitutions of the States were deliberately said to 'continue' under the Constitution (ss 106 and 107) to make clear that the underlying presupposition of the federation was one of respect for and recognition of their prior existence and continued operation as self-governing bodies politic. It makes little sense of the text, structure, history and manifest purposes of the Constitution to attribute to the Commonwealth the kind of privileged status accorded to it by a majority of the Court in *Cigamatic* and *Residential Tenancies*.

Sir Owen Dixon was surely correct to say that the Constitution provides for, and is predicated upon, the continued operation of both the Commonwealth and the States as independent, self-governing bodies politic.[413] This necessarily

**413** Ibid.

implies that no law or government action can constitutionally prevent this from continuing to be the case. Certainly, the application of such a principle of reciprocal intergovernmental immunities gives rise to difficult problems of application in relation to identifying the exact extent of the constitutional capacities and functions that must be preserved, and the degrees of permissible regulation that the Constitution must be interpreted to allow. But it is difficult to see how this task can be avoided if the Constitution is to be given effect as its text, structure, history and purposes, coherently understood, seem to suggest.

# 5

# Limits on power

*The Parliament shall, subject to this Constitution, have power to make laws for the peace, order, and good government of the Commonwealth with respect to:... (xxxi) the acquisition of property on just terms from any State or person for any purpose in respect of which the Parliament has power to make laws.*[1]

*On the imposition of uniform duties of customs, trade, commerce, and intercourse among the States, whether by means of internal carriage or ocean navigation, shall be absolutely free.*[2]

*The Commonwealth shall not make any law for establishing any religion, or for imposing any religious observance, or for prohibiting the free exercise of any religion, and no religious test shall be required as a qualification for any office or public trust under the Commonwealth.*[3]

## I Introduction

As noted in Chapter 4, the Australian Constitution is primarily concerned with establishing the institutional foundations of a federal commonwealth. The demarcations and limitations on power imposed by the Constitution are therefore chiefly directed to federal considerations of one kind or another. The Constitution does not contain a general bill of rights because the prevailing view, at the time it was drafted, was that appropriately operating systems of representative and responsible government at a Commonwealth and State level would, on the whole, provide adequate protection for civil and political rights.[4] This reflected the general view that had motivated the framers of the United States Constitution in 1787; that is, before pressure from Antifederalists compelled Federalist leaders such as James Madison to agree to the insertion of ten amendments to the Constitution which have since come to be known as the Bill of Rights. As Denis Galligan has explained:

**1** Commonwealth Constitution, s 51(xxxi).
**2** Commonwealth Constitution, s 92.
**3** Commonwealth Constitution, s 116.
**4** For a range of views on whether national constitutions such as Australia's should contain a comprehensive bill of rights, see Tom Campbell, Jeffrey Goldsworthy and Adrienne Stone (eds), *Protecting Human Rights: Instruments and Institutions* (Oxford University Press, 2003).

> On the [American] Federalists' view, Constitutions provide the means to good government; they are not concerned to dictate the substantive ends that good government should achieve. This approach has significant implications for the Bill of Rights issue. It is important to remember that the Federalists did not originally intend to include a Bill of Rights in the American Constitution; indeed they argued vehemently against it.[5]

Sir Owen Dixon put it this way in relation to Australia:

> The framers of the Australian Constitution were not prepared to place fetters upon legislative action, except and in so far as it might be necessary for the purpose of distributing between the States and the central government the full content of legislative power. The history of their country had not taught them the need of provisions directed to the control of the legislature itself.[6]

At the time that the Australian Constitution was being drafted, the general climate of opinion, as Jeffrey Goldsworthy has observed, had come to regard parliamentary democracy as the key to a more just and prosperous future.[7] There was not the same concern to limit the powers of government to protect rights that had motivated the American Antifederalists to insist upon a bill of rights. Dawson J put it this way:

> [T]hose responsible for the drafting of the Constitution saw constitutional guarantees of freedoms as exhibiting a distrust of the democratic process. They preferred to place their trust in Parliament to preserve the nature of our society and regarded as undemocratic guarantees which fettered its powers. Their model in this respect was, not the United States Constitution, but the British Parliament, the supremacy of which was by then settled constitutional doctrine.[8]

Accordingly, not only is there no bill of rights in the Australian Constitution, but the term 'right' appears nowhere in the document. Rather, following the grammar of the US Constitution, even when it was sought to protect rights or freedoms of one kind or other through constitutional provisions, these were expressed in the language of prohibitions on the exercise of legislative and other forms of governmental power rather than in the language of positive assertions of personal rights or freedoms. They were also usually shaped, in one way or another, by federal considerations. Section 116 is an example. It provides:

> The Commonwealth shall not make any law for establishing any religion, or for imposing any religious observance, or for prohibiting the free exercise of any religion, and no religious test shall be required as a qualification for any office or public trust under the Commonwealth.

Section 116 thus applies only to the Commonwealth, leaving the States free to exercise the powers they possessed, as colonies, prior to federation. It also

**5** D J Galligan, 'Judicial Review and Democratic Principles: Two Theories' (1983) 57 *Australian Law Journal* 69, 72.
**6** Owen Dixon, *Jesting Pilate* (Law Book, 1965) 102.
**7** Jeffrey Goldsworthy, 'The Constitutional Protection of Rights in Australia' in Gregory Craven (ed), *Australian Federation: Towards the Second Century* (Melbourne University Press, 1992) 151, 151–8.
**8** *Australian Capital Television Pty Ltd v Commonwealth* (1992) 177 CLR 106, 186; see also 135–6.

operates as a fetter on legislative power, rather than a positive affirmation of the right to freedom of religion. As such, s 116 presupposes a background legislative power vested in the Commonwealth, even though the topic of 'religion' does not appear in s 51. Section 116 was included in response to the decision to acknowledge God in the preamble to the Constitution and the apprehension that the Commonwealth would be able to legislate in ways that relate to religion through its various heads of power in s 51.[9] Section 51(xxxi) is similar to s 116 in this respect. It provides that the Parliament shall have power to make laws with respect to:

> the acquisition of property on just terms from any State or person for any purpose in respect of which the Parliament has power to make laws.

Section 51(xxxi) thus confers legislative power on the Commonwealth, but it also restricts it through the stipulation that any relevant Commonwealth law must provide for the acquisition of property 'on just terms'. It thus operates as a limitation on Commonwealth power, but like s 116 has no application to the States.

Two other important limiting provisions in the Constitution are ss 80 and 92. Section 80 requires that 'trial on indictment of any offence against any law of the Commonwealth shall be by jury' and s 92 stipulates that 'trade, commerce, and intercourse among the States... shall be absolutely free'. Both sections operate in the context of legislative powers of the Commonwealth to regulate the relevant subject matter. In the case of s 80, several of the Commonwealth's specific powers in s 51, together with its power in s 51(xxxix) to make laws with respect to 'matters incidental to the execution of any power vested by this Constitution... in the Federal Judicature', enable the Parliament to create criminal offences, confer jurisdiction on federal and State courts, and provide for criminal process in such matters generally. In the case of s 92, the Commonwealth has explicit power in s 51(i) to legislate with respect to 'trade and commerce... among the States'. Section 92 appears as a separate provision expressed in general and even hyperbolic terms ('*absolutely* free') largely in recognition, as will be seen, of the importance of interstate free trade as one of the prime reasons for the federation of the colonies.

It was the federal character of the Australian Constitution that laid the foundation for these and other qualifications that were placed upon the British principle of parliamentary sovereignty. As such, even the apparently 'rights-protective' limitations on power that do exist are best understood as aspects of the federal architecture of the Constitution.[10] Most of the protections are deliberately addressed only to the Commonwealth on the assumption that, unless some 'federating' imperative makes it necessary, any controls on the powers of the State governments are matters for the peoples of the States to address

**9** See Part IV.1 below.
**10** See W Harrison Moore, 'The Commonwealth of Australia Bill' (1900) 16 *Law Quarterly Review* 35, 40–43.

through their respective State Constitutions. Those rights-protective limitations that have a wider application to both Commonwealth and State power, such as s 92, have an obvious federal rationale.

The working drafts of the Constitution framed during the Federal Conventions of 1891 and 1897–8 originally contained a provision partially modelled on Article IV and the Fourteenth Amendment of the US Constitution. The Fourteenth Amendment had been inserted to protect the rights of emancipated slaves following the American Civil War (1861–5). The proposed Australian provision prohibited any State from making or enforcing any law 'abridging any privilege or immunity of the citizens of other States' or denying to any person 'the equal protection of the laws'.[11]

However, the framers of the Constitution ultimately decided not to include such a provision, opting instead for the more narrowly-worded s 117, which provides:

> A subject of the Queen, resident in any State, shall not be subject in any other State to any disability or discrimination which would not be equally applicable to him if he were a subject of the Queen resident in such other State.[12]

The framers' reasons for rejecting the wider language of the original proposal were several.[13] One was that such a rule would prevent the States from continuing to enact laws specifically directed at Chinese and South Pacific immigrants and indentured labourers. This anxiety was often connected with a more general desire not to multiply the points at which the Constitution would interfere with the independent legislative powers of the States. A second reason was that there was no pressing need for such a provision because the special circumstances that the United States faced following the Civil War did not exist in Australia, and it would be imprudent to include a provision of such generality into the Constitution without specific reason for it. A third was that, despite the discriminatory laws that had been enacted by the colonies, the framers did not believe that a comprehensive constitutional provision of such nature was needed. The fourth reason concerned disagreement about the nature of citizenship within a federation. Some of the framers wanted a kind of national citizenship to be established, but others insisted that in a federation there must be a 'dual' citizenship of both the Commonwealth and the States. The result was that the Constitution remained silent on 'citizenship', and left the decision as to whether the States would continue to enact racially discriminatory laws in the hands of their elected Parliaments. The States and the Commonwealth would indeed continue to enact such laws for several decades, but these were progressively repealed as community attitudes to such laws changed in the 1960s and 1970s.

**11** *Convention Debates, Sydney* (1891) 962; *Convention Debates, Adelaide* (1897) 1241.

**12** On the interpretation of s 117, see *Street v Queensland Bar Association* (1989) 168 CLR 461; *Goryl v Greyhound Australia Pty Ltd* (1994) 179 CLR 463; *Sweedman v Transport Accident Commission* (2006) 226 CLR 362.

**13** *Convention Debates, Melbourne* (1898) 246–8, 664–91, 1780–802, 2397.

Moreover, although Australians would also continue formally to be 'subjects of the Crown' until the *Australian Citizenship Act 1948* (Cth) came into force in 1949, an underlying idea of multiple citizenship existed from the time of federation.[14]

There have been several attempts since federation to insert rights-protective provisions into the Constitution. None have been successful. In 1944 a proposal to insert guarantees of freedom of expression and to extend the freedom of religion provision to the States was rejected by a majority of voters nationally and in all but two States. In 1988 a proposal to insert guarantees of the right to vote, and to extend to the States the existing protections in relation to acquisition of property on just terms, jury trial and freedom of religion, failed by very substantial margins to secure a majority in any State. Attempts to introduce statutory human rights laws at a Commonwealth level in the 1970s and 1980s were also unsuccessful.[15] Since then, Charters of Rights that provide for a 'weak' form of judicial review have been adopted in two Australian jurisdictions,[16] but not elsewhere. In 2009, a National Human Rights Consultation recommended a range of reforms, including a Human Rights Act,[17] but the Commonwealth decided only to implement the educative, administrative and procedural aspects of the recommendations, including provision for greater parliamentary scrutiny of legislation.[18] The debate over a bill of rights in Australia continues, shaped by evaluations of Australia's human rights record, which is generally very good when measured objectively against world standards.[19]

Despite the framers' reticence in relation to rights, and the unwillingness of the Australian people to approve the insertion of additional rights-protective provisions into the Constitution, the High Court has found that the Constitution contains certain implied limitations on power said to be derived by inference from the text, structure, principles and purposes of the Constitution. These include the intergovernmental immunities associated with the federal nature of the Constitution discussed in Chapter 4 and the several implied prohibitions derived from the separation of judicial power discussed in Chapter 9. It was also seen in Chapter 2 that the High Court has had to address the question whether the system of representative democracy established by the Constitution implies that electoral divisions for the House of Representatives must be equal in population so that individual voters are accorded an equality of voting power. Relatedly, the Court has affirmed that the democratic features of the Constitution have implications for the right to vote and the scope of the franchise. As will be seen in this chapter, the High Court has determined that the system of

**14** Brian Galligan and Winsome Roberts, *Australian Citizenship* (Melbourne University Press, 2004).
**15** George Williams, *A Charter of Rights for Australia* (University of New South Wales Press, 2007) 57–62.
**16** *Human Rights Act 2004* (ACT); *Charter of Human Rights and Responsibilities Act 2006* (Vic).
**17** *National Human Rights Consultation: Report* (Commonwealth of Australia, 2009).
**18** *Human Rights (Parliamentary Scrutiny) Act 2011* (Cth).
**19** Tom Campbell, Jeffrey Goldsworthy and Adrienne Stone, *Protecting Rights without a Bill of Rights* (Ashgate, 2006). See aso David Cingranelli and David Richards, 'The Cingranelli and Richards (CIRI) Human Rights Data Project' *Human Rights Quarterly* (2010) 32.2, 401–24.

representative and responsible government necessarily implies that the Commonwealth and the States cannot unjustifiably interfere with freedom of communication concerning political matters. Moreover, members of the Court have at times suggested that other civic freedoms, such as freedom of association and freedom of assembly, might also be protected.[20] These implications from the system of representative democracy, like the other prohibitions contained in the Constitution, work in conjunction with positive powers that the Australian Parliaments have to regulate the Commonwealth, State and Territory electoral systems.

As noted in Chapter 3, what the High Court has not done is to approve the suggestion of Sir Robin Cooke, then of the New Zealand Court of Appeal, that the legislative powers of Parliaments within the Westminster tradition might be restrained by judicially-enforceable rights deeply rooted in the common law.[21] In *Durham Holdings Pty Ltd v NSW*, the High Court rejected the argument that the common law gives rise to a limitation on the capacity of the Parliament of New South Wales to deprive a person of his or her property without just, or any properly adequate, compensation.[22] As the Court pointed out in that case, the existence of limitations on the powers of Australian Parliaments have to be found, rather, in the text and structure of the Constitution itself.[23]

The prohibitions contained in the Constitution, whether express or implied, need to be understood in the context of the background legislative and other powers of the Commonwealth and the States, both operating under systems of representative and responsible government. The development of the High Court's jurisprudence in relation to each constitutional prohibition can be examined separately, but it is also helpful to understand the development of doctrine across all of the constitutional limitations considered collectively. This chapter focuses upon the following provisions and doctrines:

- acquisition of property on just terms (s 51(xxxi));
- freedom of interstate trade, commerce and intercourse (s 92);
- religious freedom and non-establishment of religion (s 116); and
- freedom of political communication and associated democratic rights (implied).[24]

## II Acquisition of property on just terms

Property rights run deep in the common law. As Frederic Maitland pointed out in his *Constitutional History of England*, it is impossible to understand the evolution of modern public law without an appreciation of the integral role of

**20** See Part V below.
**21** Eg, *Taylor v New Zealand Poultry Board* [1984] 1 NZLR 394, 398; *Fraser v State Services Commission* [1984] 1 NZLR 116, 121.
**22** *Durham Holdings Pty Ltd v New South Wales* (2001) 205 CLR 399, 408–10, 418–23, 433.
**23** Ibid, 410, 431–2.
**24** Section 80 is discussed in Chapter 8, Part VII.

property law in that development. Rights to land were especially associated with the constitutional law of England through the institution of feudalism, which Maitland defined as 'a state of society in which all or a great part of the public rights and duties are inextricably interwoven with the tenure of land, in which the whole governmental system... is part of the law of private property'.[25] All lands were held of the king and, as the institutions of the central government developed, the House of Lords came to consist of many of the largest and most powerful landholders of the realm. *Magna Carta* (1215) reflected the importance of property as a constitutional principle, especially in the guarantee in clause 29 that 'no free man shall be... disseised of his free holds or liberties or free customs... but... by the law of the land'. As Sir William Blackstone understood it, the right to property is an inherent and natural right, consisting in 'the free use, enjoyment, and disposal' of one's land and possessions 'without any control or diminution, save only by the laws of the land'. 'So great', he continued, is the 'regard of the law for private property, that it will not authorize the least violation of it; no, not even for the general good of the whole community'. For Blackstone, the rule of law prevented the government from imposing taxes or taking property without the consent of the people expressed through the Parliament, but even when a duly enacted law might authorise a compulsory acquisition of property, he insisted that it does not do this by 'stripping the subject of his property in an arbitrary manner; but by giving him a full indemnification and equivalent for the injury thereby sustained'.[26]

The common law and the local statutory law which developed in the Australian colonies recognised the right to property and broadly adhered to the principles that Blackstone had articulated.[27] To this day, each of the States has a special enactment which authorises the compulsory acquisition of property for public purposes, such as for the construction of roads, but which also provides for the payment of compensation to owners for the value of the property that is acquired.[28] When the Commonwealth Constitution was being drafted, the principle that there should be no acquisition of property without compensation was therefore widely assumed and practised. The proposal that the Constitution include an explicit provision was to ensure that, being a government of only enumerated powers, the power of compulsory acquisition would be undoubted.[29] Given the underlying practices and principles of the common law, it seems to have gone virtually without saying that any such power would be subject to the duty to

**25** F W Maitland, *The Constitutional History of England* (Cambridge University Press, 1908) 23–4.
**26** William Blackstone, *Commentaries on the Laws of England* (Clarendon Press, 1765–69) vol I, 135.
**27** Douglas Brown, *Land Acquisition* (Butterworths, 1st ed, 1972) 8–16.
**28** Douglas Brown, *Land Acquisition* (LexisNexis Butterworths, 6th ed, 2009) 1–2, 102–4.
**29** John Quick and Robert Garran, *The Annotated Constitution of the Australian Commonwealth* (Angus and Robertson, 1901) 640; *Convention Debates, Melbourne* (1898) 151. Several other provisions were included in the Constitution to confirm, but also regulate, the powers of the Commonwealth with respect to the compulsory acquisition of property. These principally include: s 85, which deals with the transfer of State government departments and their property to the Commonwealth; s 114, concerning the taxation of Commonwealth and State property; and ss 52, 111, 122 and 125, which deal with the rights and powers of the Commonwealth over territories and property acquired by it. See Simon Evans, 'Property and the Drafting of the Australian Constitution' (2001) 29 *Federal Law Review* 121.

provide just terms. There were some who objected to its insertion on the ground that 'just terms' were not 'proper words to put into the Constitution'. Indeed, such a provision would be unnecessary, it was said, for it was to be 'assume[d] that the Federal Parliament will act strictly on the lines of justice'.[30] However, this objection did not prevail, and the proposed clause was later adopted with very little further discussion.[31]

During the Convention Debates, there seems to have been no explicit reference to the corresponding provision of the US Constitution, which stipulates that 'private property' shall not 'be taken . . . without just compensation'.[32] The two provisions were nonetheless understood to embody the same broad principle. Quick and Garran pointed out the similarity of the two provisions and argued that the purpose of s 51(xxxi) was 'to recognize the principle of the immunity of private and provincial property from interference by the Federal authority, except on fair and equitable terms, and this principle is thus constitutionally established and placed beyond legislative control', so that any Commonwealth law on the topic of acquisition that 'appeared to be unjust' would be 'liable to be declared unconstitutional and void'.[33] Nonetheless, there are important differences between the Australian and American provisions. The American provision leaves the positive power of acquisition to implication through the doctrine of 'eminent domain',[34] whereas the Australian provision positively authorises the enactment by the Commonwealth of laws providing for the acquisition of property from 'any State or person'; the American provision uses the term 'taken', rather than 'acquired'; and the American provision is limited to takings 'for public use', not 'any purpose in respect of which the Parliament has power to make laws'. These differences have proven significant.

## 1 Legislative power and constitutional right

Section 51(xxxi), Sir Owen Dixon once pointed out, is a 'dual' provision: it confers power to legislate for the acquisition of property and it provides a right against acquisition of property other than on just terms.[35] The provision itself is, however, primarily in the form of a head of power, expressed as a 'compound conception', namely, the 'acquisition of property on just terms'.[36] This gives rise to an important question at the outset: does the guarantee of just terms restrict only the enactment of laws specifically under s 51(xxxi), or does it apply more generally, that is, to restrict the enactment of laws under other heads of power?

**30** *Convention Debates, Melbourne* (1898) 153.
**31** Ibid, 1874.
**32** United States Constitution, Fifth Amendment.
**33** Quick and Garran, above n 29, 641.
**34** *Kohl v United States*, 91 US 367 (1875).
**35** *Bank of NSW v Commonwealth* (1948) 76 CLR 1, 349.
**36** *Grace Brothers Pty Ltd v Commonwealth* (1946) 72 CLR 269, 290.

As seen in Chapter 3, the approach to interpreting the Commonwealth's legislative powers derived from the *Engineers* case usually dictates that each head of power is read on its own, so that limitations written into one head of power do not ordinarily give rise to an implied limitation or prohibition which cuts down the scope of other powers. However, as was also seen, there are exceptions to this principle at least where the limitations or qualifications on the scope of a head of power are expressed in explicitly negative terms. Thus, the limitations written into the banking and insurance powers (ss 51(xiii) and (xiv)), stipulating that they do not extend to 'State banking' or 'State insurance', have been held to imply a prohibition of the use of other heads of power to make laws with respect to those restricted topics of State banking and State insurance.[37] Much the same logic has been held to apply to the acquisition of property under s 51(xxxi). The High Court has held that the requirement of just terms applies not only to the exercise of legislative power under s 51(xxxi) but also to any acquisition that might otherwise be authorised under another head of power, unless the subject matter of the power is of such a kind as to make the application of just terms requirement inapposite. Other heads of power cannot ordinarily be used to avoid the just terms requirement because, as Dixon J explained in *Attorney-General (Cth) v Schmidt*, the express grant of a power of acquisition subject to the just terms requirement precludes the implication of an acquisition power which might dispense with the requirement for just terms.[38]

As a consequence, the High Court has tended to treat s 51(xxxi) as having 'assumed the status of a constitutional guarantee of just terms' which is therefore 'to be given the liberal construction appropriate to such a constitutional provision'.[39] However, it has also been acknowledged that s 51(xxxi) will not invalidate Commonwealth legislation which is 'clearly within the intended scope of another legislative power' or is enacted under a head of power which authorises a 'law of a kind that does not permit of just terms'. Rather, s 51(xxxi) only applies to legislation which 'can properly be characterized as law with respect to the acquisition of property for a purpose for which the Parliament has power to make laws'.[40] Accordingly, it has been held that some heads of power can authorise 'acquisitions' that are not subject to the just terms requirement because the subject matter of the legislation is not appropriate. These include taxation under the taxation power (s 51(ii));[41] confiscation of prohibited imports under the trade and commerce power (s 51(i));[42] confiscation of enemy property under the defence power (s 51(vi));[43] confiscation of illegal fishing vessels under

**37** See, further, Chapter 3, Part III.2.
**38** *Attorney-General (Cth) v Schmidt* (1961) 105 CLR 361, 371–2.
**39** *Clunies-Ross v Commonwealth* (1984) 155 CLR 193, 202.
**40** *Mutual Pools & Staff Pty Ltd v Commonwealth* (1994) 179 CLR 155, 188.
**41** *Federal Commissioner of Taxation v Clyne* (1958) 100 CLR 246.
**42** *Burton v Honan* (1952) 86 CLR 169; *Commissioner of Australian Federal Police v Cox* (1986) 14 FCR 279; *Re Director of Public Prosecutions; Ex parte Lawler* (1994) 179 CLR 270. See also *Theophanous v Commonwealth* (2006) 225 CLR 101.
**43** *Attorney-General (Cth) v Schmidt* (1961) 105 CLR 361.

the fisheries power (s 51(x));[44] extinguishment of rights attached to ownership of copyright under the copyright power (s 51(xviii));[45] sequestration of property of a bankrupt under the bankruptcy power (s 51(xvii));[46] and imposition of pecuniary penalties as punishment for breach of some general rule of conduct prescribed by a valid law of the Commonwealth.[47] At one time it was also considered that laws enacted under the Territories power (s 122) were not controlled by the just terms requirement because it was considered that the provisions of s 51, including paragraph (xxxi), are concerned only with 'what may be called federal legislative powers as part of the distribution of legislative power between the Commonwealth and the constituent States'.[48] However, it has since been held that the just terms requirement does apply to the Territories power – a decision that is consistent with the developing tendency of the Court to adopt 'an integral approach to the place of the Territories power' within the Constitution as a whole which is therefore subject to generally applicable constitutional limitations.[49]

There are three further important limits on the application of s 51(xxxi). First, the provision is not concerned with acquisition of property by agreement with the owner. The idea of an 'acquisition of property on just terms' is understood to be one of compulsory exaction, not voluntary sale or transfer. If, as Stephen J maintained, under a challenged law an owner of property still has the right to determine the price at which the property will be sold, then the acquirer lacks a compulsive power and any transfer of property that occurs is effectively by agreement, not requisition.[50] Secondly, it is not necessary that the Commonwealth or a Commonwealth agency is the acquirer: s 51(xxxi) refers simply to an 'acquisition'.[51] Thirdly, the provision applies only to the enactment of legislation by the Commonwealth, not the States.[52] These last two points were relevant in *Magennis v Commonwealth* and *Pye v Renshaw*. In *Magennis* it was held that if the Commonwealth enacts a law that can be characterised as a law that is 'with respect to the acquisition of property', it does not matter that the entity compelling the acquisition or actually acquiring the property is not the Commonwealth but rather a State; the just terms requirement will still apply to the Commonwealth law.[53] In *Pye v Renshaw*, the Court seemed to suggest the Commonwealth can avoid this in practice by refraining from legislating, and instead entering an agreement with a State to acquire property on other than what would be 'just

**44** *Re Director of Public Prosecutions; Ex parte Lawler* (1994) 179 CLR 270.
**45** *Australian Tape Manufacturers Association Ltd v Commonwealth* (1993) 176 CLR 480.
**46** *Attorney General (Cth) v Schmidt* (1961) 105 CLR 361, 371.
**47** *Mutual Pools & Staff Pty Ltd v Commonwealth* (1994) 179 CLR 155, 186.
**48** *Teori Tau v Commonwealth* (1969) 119 CLR 564, 570.
**49** *Wurridjal v Commonwealth* (2009) 237 CLR 309, 356. See also *Lamshed v Lake* (1958) 99 CLR 132, 141–4.
**50** *Trade Practices Commission v Tooth & Co Ltd* (1979) 142 CLR 397, 417. See also *John Cooke & Co Pty Ltd v Commonwealth* (1924) 34 CLR 269, 282; *Poulton v Commonwealth* (1953) 89 CLR 540, 573; *British Medical Association v Commonwealth* (1949) 79 CLR 201, 270–71.
**51** *McClintock v Commonwealth* (1947) 75 CLR 1.
**52** *New South Wales v Commonwealth* (1915) 20 CLR 54, 77.
**53** *Magennis v Commonwealth* (1949) 80 CLR 47, 401, 423–4; *Pye v Renshaw* (1951) 84 CLR 58, 83.

terms', on the condition that the Commonwealth will grant the State money to provide some measure of compensation.[54] However, in *ICM Agriculture Pty Ltd v Commonwealth*, the Court appeared to narrow the scope of *Pye v Renshaw* by affirming that the power of the Commonwealth under s 96 of the Constitution does not extend to the grant of financial assistance to a State on terms and conditions requiring the State to acquire property on other than just terms.[55]

## 2 Acquisition of property

It was clear from the outset that the acquisition power contemplated the taking of property not only from private individuals, but also from the States. In this respect, s 51(xxxi) needs to be contrasted with s 51(xxxiii), which empowers the Parliament to legislate with respect to 'the acquisition, with the consent of a State, of any railways of the State on terms arranged between the Commonwealth and the State'. Early on, the Court held that the power to acquire property from the States even extended to the acquisition of the so-called 'royal metals' (gold and silver) which, on ordinary principles of common law and by virtue of the original grants of land by the Crown, remain vested in the Crown in right of the States as part of their prerogative rights.[56]

### Property as a 'bundle of rights'

In most of the decided cases the critical question for the application of s 51(xxxi) has been whether there is an 'acquisition of property' contemplated by the Commonwealth law. The first case to address this question squarely was *Minister of State for the Army v Dalziel*.[57] During the Second World War, the Commonwealth enacted the *National Security Act 1939*. Section 5 of the Act authorised the Governor-General to make regulations for securing 'public safety and defence', including the taking 'possession or control' of 'any property or undertaking', while s 19 limited the Commonwealth's possession of the property to no longer than six months after the end of the war. Regulation 54 of the National Security (General) Regulations in turn authorised the Minister of State for the Army to take possession of any land if to do so appeared necessary or expedient 'in the interests of public safety, the defence of the Commonwealth or the efficient prosecution of the war or for maintaining supplies and services essential to the life of the community'. The Regulations also created a Compensation Board. Clause (iii) of reg 60H provided: 'in assessing compensation, loss of occupation or profits shall not be taken into account'. Under reg 60H, the Minister for the Army passed a Basis of Compensation Order which required the Board not to take loss of profits into account when assessing compensation. Acting pursuant to reg 54, the Minister took possession of vacant land in Sydney owned by the

**54** *Pye v Renshaw* (1951) 84 CLR 58, 79–80.
**55** *ICM Agriculture Pty Ltd v Commonwealth* (2009) 240 CLR 140, 170.
**56** *New South Wales v Commonwealth* (1923) 33 CLR 1.
**57** (1944) 68 CLR 261.

Bank of New South Wales which was let on a weekly tenancy to Dalziel, who had used the land to operate a commercial car park. The Compensation Board assessed compensation to Dalziel for his weekly rental payment of £8, but did not compensate him for the loss of the net profits he gained from his business of about £15 per week.

A majority of the Court held that the Commonwealth's exclusive possession of the land for an indefinite period terminating no more than six months after the cessation of the war constituted an acquisition of property within the meaning of s 51(xxxi), and that there was a failure to provide 'just terms' because the Executive Government was accorded an 'arbitrary discretion as to the compensation, if any, to be paid'.[58] In his dissenting judgment, Latham CJ considered that the Commonwealth 'cannot be said to have acquired land unless it has become the owner of land or of some interest in land', and that the mere right to exclusive possession, without such a title or interest, did not amount to an acquisition of property.[59] However, delivering the leading judgment of the Court, Rich J responded to this line of argument by denying that the constitutional idea of property should be limited to the artificial refinements of any particular legal system. He stated:

> One of the characteristic features of a fully sovereign power is its legal right to deal as it thinks fit with anything and everything within its territory. This includes what is described in the United States as eminent domain (*dominium eminems*), the right to take to itself any property within its territory, or any interest therein, on such terms and for such purposes as it thinks proper, eminent domain being thus the proprietary aspect of sovereignty. The Commonwealth of Australia is not, however, a fully sovereign power.... What we are concerned with is... a Constitution containing a provision of a fundamental character designed to protect citizens from being deprived of their property by the Sovereign State except upon just terms. The meaning of property in such a connection must be determined upon general principles of jurisprudence, not by the artificial refinements of any particular legal system.... Property, in relation to land, is a bundle of rights exercisable with respect to the land. The tenant of an unencumbered estate in fee simple in possession has the largest possible bundle. But there is nothing in the placitum to suggest that the legislature was intended to be at liberty to free itself from the restrictive provisions of the placitum by taking care to seize something short of the whole bundle owned by the person whom it was expropriating.... It would, in my opinion, be wholly inconsistent with the language of the placitum to hold that, whilst preventing the legislature from authorizing the acquisition of a citizen's full title except upon just terms, it leaves it open to the legislature to seize possession and enjoy the full fruits of possession, indefinitely, on any terms it chooses, or upon no terms at all.[60]

Implicit in this reasoning was a wider conception of both 'acquisition' and 'property'. In relation to the constitutional concept of property, Starke J observed:

**58** Ibid, 289.
**59** Ibid, 276.
**60** Ibid, 284–6.

> Property, it has been said, is *nomen generalissimum* and extends to every species of valuable rights and interest including real and personal property, incorporeal hereditaments such as rents and services, rights of way, rights of profit or use in land of another, and choses in action. And to acquire any such right is rightly described as an 'acquisition of property'. On the other hand a mere personal licence such as is not assignable would not be rightly described as property. . . .[61]

Justice McTiernan similarly observed that 'property' is a 'general term' which signifies 'any tangible or intangible thing which the law protects under the name of property', and considered that 'the acquisition of the possession of land is an instance of the acquisition of property'.[62]

### Circuitous devices

This broad view of the nature of an acquisition of property was applied in the *Bank Nationalisation* case, discussed in Chapter 3. In that case the High Court had to consider a challenge to the *Banking Act 1947* (Cth), which sought to nationalise Australia's banks, in part, by transferring the control, shares and assets of the banks to the Commonwealth Bank.[63] The scheme was complex and multifaceted. Section 12 authorised the Commonwealth Bank to purchase shares in private banks. Section 13 authorised the federal Treasurer to issue a Gazettal notice whereby the Australian shares in any Australian bank became vested in the Commonwealth Bank of Australia. Section 15 directed the Commonwealth Bank to pay fair and reasonable compensation for any shares thus acquired. Section 17 provided that on the date of Gazettal, the existing directors of the banks would cease to hold office. Section 18 empowered the Governor of the Commonwealth Bank, with the approval of the Treasurer, to appoint directors to the bank. Section 19 gave the new directors full power to manage, direct and control the business of the bank, including a power to dispose of the business of the bank to the Commonwealth Bank. Section 24 authorised the compulsory takeover of the bank's business in Australia, including its Australian assets and liabilities. Section 46 empowered the Treasurer to require private banks to cease carrying on their banking businesses. Other parts of the Act created a Court of Claims, which was a superior court of record invested with the judicial power of the Commonwealth under s 71 of the Constitution and invested with exclusive jurisdiction to hear applications for compensation arising out of acquisitions under s 13 (shares) and s 24 (assets).

The Court found that, in substance, the Act provided for an acquisition of property without providing just terms. Delivering the leading judgment in the case, Dixon J observed that he understood *Dalziel's* case to have held that s 51(xxxi):

> is not to be confined pedantically to the taking of title by the Commonwealth to some specific estate or interest in land recognized at law or in equity and to some specific

**61** Ibid, 290.
**62** Ibid, 295.
**63** *Bank of New South Wales v Commonwealth* (1948) 76 CLR 1.

> form of property in a chattel or chose in action similarly recognized, but that it extends to innominate and anomalous interests and includes the assumption and indefinite continuance of exclusive possession and control for the purposes of the Commonwealth of any subject of property.[64]

Noting that s 51(xxxi) was included in the Constitution to protect individuals and States from the acquisition of property other than on just terms, Dixon J considered that it was a provision that 'should be given as full and flexible an operation as will cover the objects it was designed to effect'.[65] On his analysis, the provisions of the Act, understood collectively, were nothing but 'a circuitous device to acquire indirectly the substance of a proprietary interest'.[66] As he explained:

> The company and its shareholders are in a real sense, although not formally, stripped of the possession and control of the entire undertaking. The profits which may arise from it in the hands of the Commonwealth's agents are still to be accounted for and in some form they will be represented in what the shareholders receive. But the effective deprivation of the company and its shareholders of the reality of the proprietorship is the same. It must be remembered that complete dispositive power accompanies the control of the assets which passes to the nominees. It is as if an intending purchaser were enabled to put a receiver in possession of an estate and also to take a power of sale in the receiver's name, remaining however accountable, until he pays the purchase money, for the rents and profits, which nevertheless he may apply towards the upkeep of the property and, subject thereto, accumulate.[67]

Given that the law authorised an acquisition of property, the absence of provision for 'just terms' was fatal to the constitutionality of the Act. Although the Act gave the Court of Claims jurisdiction over claims for compensation, this jurisdiction purported to be exclusive, and was therefore held to be unconstitutional because it would have had the effect of ousting the original jurisdiction of the High Court to hear matters in which the Commonwealth is a party – a jurisdiction guaranteed by s 75(iii) of the Constitution. The absence of any constitutionally valid provision in the Act for compensating those deprived of property meant that the Act failed to provide the just terms required by the Constitution, rendering its provisions for the acquisition of property invalid.[68]

### Regulatory takings

Justice Rich's observation in *Dalziel* that property is a 'bundle of rights' and that the Commonwealth cannot avoid the just terms requirement 'by taking care to seize something short of the whole bundle' is potentially very far-reaching. Any regulation of the use of property has the effect of depriving the owner of certain rights previously enjoyed in respect of that property. At what point does

**64** Ibid, 349.
**65** Ibid, 350.
**66** Ibid, 349.
**67** Ibid.
**68** Ibid, 368.

'regulation' become a kind of regulatory 'taking' or 'acquisition'?[69] The Fifth Amendment to the US Constitution focuses on the concept of a 'taking' of property from the owner, rather than the 'acquisition' of property by someone else. The US Supreme Court has held that land use regulation can in some circumstances constitute a 'taking', but it has struggled to articulate a coherent set of principles to determine when this will be the case. In *Pennsylvania Coal Co v Mahon*, for instance, Holmes J stated that 'while property may be regulated to a certain extent, if the regulation goes too far it will be recognised as a taking'.[70] Similarly, in *Central Transportation Co v New York City*, it was observed that the Court had been unable to 'develop any "set formula" for determining when "justice and fairness" require that economic injuries caused by public action be compensated by the government, rather than remain disproportionately concentrated on a few persons'.[71] In Australia, however, the line has been drawn by emphasising that there must be an 'acquisition', and that the interest that is acquired must be 'proprietary' in nature.[72]

In *Trade Practices Commission v Tooth & Co Ltd*,[73] the Court had to consider whether s 47(1) of the *Trade Practices Act 1974* (Cth), which prohibited 'exclusive dealing' by a corporation, involved an acquisition of property without providing just terms. Exclusive dealing was defined by s 49(9)(a) of the Act as occurring when a corporation, among other things, refuses to grant or renew, or exercises a power to terminate, a lease of property for the reason that another party of the lease or licence has acquired goods or services from a competitor of the corporation. The point of the legislation was thus to prohibit anti-competitive behaviour by corporations. A majority held that there was no acquisition of property within the meaning of s 51(xxxi). Gibbs J, with whom Murphy J agreed, considered that the provision was of the same nature as a penalty or a forfeiture of property for a breach of the law or as a consequence of bankruptcy. It was not, therefore, in the nature of a law with respect to the acquisition of property on other than just terms, for it did not oblige a corporation to grant or renew a lease other than on fair commercial terms.[74] Stephen J thought that the provision, even though it obliged a corporation to grant or renew a lease against its will without expectation of compensation, did so only as incidental to the goal of supressing an undesirable trade practice.[75] Mason J similarly considered

**69** Compare, for example, Richard Epstein, 'Takings, Exclusivity and Speech' (1997) 64 *University of Chicago Law Review* 21 and Frank Michelman, 'The Common Law Baseline and Restitution for the Lost Commons' (1997) 64 *University of Chicago Law Review* 57.

**70** *Pennsylvania Coal Co v Mahon*, 260 US 393, 415 (1922). For a more recent statement, see *Lingle v Chevron*, 544 US 528 (2005).

**71** *Central Transportation Co v New York City*, 438 US 104, 124 (1978).

**72** Despite the relatively wide view of 'property' advanced in *Dalziel* and the *Bank Nationalisation* case, in *Australasian United Steam Navigation Co Ltd v Shipping Control Board* (1945) 71 CLR 508, the Court held that requisitioning a ship for use by the Commonwealth did not amount to an acquisition of property within the meaning of s 51(xxxi) principally because it did not deprive the ship owner of the possession, management, navigation and handling of the ship.

**73** *Trade Practices Commission v Tooth & Co Ltd* (1979) 142 CLR 397.

**74** Ibid, 408–9, 434.

**75** Ibid, 412, 425.

that although the law could result in a compulsory acquisition of property, it had not been established that in the circumstances the acquisition would be otherwise than on just terms.[76]

In the course of his reasoning in *Tooth*, after discussing the American approach to the takings clause, Stephen J observed that while a mere impairment of the exercise of a proprietary rights will often not trigger the application of s 51(xxxi), 'far-reaching restrictions upon the use of property may in appropriate circumstances be seen to involve such an acquisition', depending upon 'the particular circumstances' of the case.[77] The possibility that an acquisition of property might arise in this way was further tested in the *Tasmanian Dam* case.[78] It was argued by Tasmania in that case that the Commonwealth law which prohibited such activities as cutting down trees, establishing tracks or roads and erecting buildings on State Crown land, as a means of preventing the construction of the hydro-electric dam, amounted to an acquisition of property within the meaning of s 51(xxxi). While Gibbs CJ, Wilson and Dawson JJ did not need to address this argument because they held that the Commonwealth law was not authorised by either the external affairs or the corporations powers, the other members of the Court found it necessary to consider it. Mason, Murphy and Brennan JJ rejected the argument, principally on the ground that the law did not provide for the acquisition by any particular person or agency of a proprietary or possessory interest in the land;[79] at most it only provided for the extinction or limitation of property rights.[80] In his dissenting judgment on this point, Deane J held that there was an acquisition of property other than on just terms. He acknowledged that laws which merely prohibit or control a particular use of property will not constitute an acquisition of property.[81] However, a prohibition or regulation may sometimes result in the conferral of a benefit on someone else. In such cases, if this benefit represents nothing more than 'the adjustment of competing claims between citizens in a field which needs to be regulated in the common interest', s 51(xxxi) will not be activated; but if the effect of the law is to confer 'an identifiable and measurable advantage' or to apply the property to 'a purpose of the Commonwealth', then an acquisition of property may be involved.[82] In his view, while much of the legislation did not contravene s 51(xxxi), aspects of the *World Heritage Properties Conservation Act 1983* and Regulations made under the *National Parks and Wildlife Conservation Act 1975* (Cth) had the effect of preventing the Tasmanian Hydro-Electric Commission, without the Commonwealth's consent, 'from putting the land to any active use at all'. In effect, this gave the Commonwealth the benefit of a prohibition analogous to the rights which a landholder will have as a result of

**76** Ibid, 433.
**77** Ibid, 414–15.
**78** *Commonwealth v Tasmania* (1983) 158 CLR 1. For the facts of the case, see Chapter 3, Part IV.2.
**79** Ibid, 145–6, 246–8.
**80** Ibid, 181–2.
**81** Ibid, 283.
**82** Ibid.

the entry by another landholder into a restrictive covenant controlling the use and development of particular land.[83]

### Identifiable and measurable benefits

Deane J's suggestion in the *Tasmania Dam* case that the conferral of an identifiable and measurable advantage or benefit might constitute an acquisition of property bore fruit in *Georgiadis v Australian and Overseas Telecommunications Corporation*.[84] In that case, the Court had to consider whether a law extinguishing a chose in action would amount to an acquisition of property other than on just terms. Georgiadis sought to sue Telecom and the Commonwealth at common law for back injuries sustained in 1985 and 1986. The *Compensation (Commonwealth Employees) Act 1971* (Cth) had given employees injured in connection with their work the option of claiming worker's compensation or pursuing a common law action for damages. However, s 44 of the *Commonwealth Employees' Rehabilitation and Compensation Act 1988* (Cth) extinguished the cause of action.

Noting that s 51(xxxi) operates as a 'constitutional guarantee' which is to be construed 'liberally',[85] a majority of Mason CJ, Brennan, Deane and Gaudron JJ concluded that the concept of 'acquisition' in s 51(xxxi):

> extends to the extinguishment of a vested cause of action, at least where the extinguishment results in a direct benefit or financial gain (which, of course, includes liability being brought to an end without payment or other satisfaction) and the cause of action is one that arises under the general law. The position may be different in a case involving the extinguishment or modification of a right that has no existence apart from statute. That is because, prima facie at least and in the absence of a recognised legal relationship giving rise to some right, a right which has no existence apart from statute is one that, of its nature, is susceptible of modification or extinguishment. There is no acquisition of property involved in the modification or extinguishment of a right which has no basis in the general law and which, of its nature, is susceptible to that course.[86]

Even though the right to proceed against the Commonwealth was granted by statute, they held that s 44 extinguished a vested cause of action that arose under general law, and that this extinguishment had the effect of conferring on the Commonwealth a distinct financial benefit in respect of its pre-existing liability. As a consequence, they concluded, s 44 was a law for the acquisition of property, without providing the just terms required under s 51(xxxi) of the Constitution.

In his dissenting judgment, McHugh J agreed with the majority that Georgiadis had been 'deprived' of 'property' and that Telecom had 'acquired' a 'corresponding benefit of commensurate value', but he considered that Georgiadis's

**83** Ibid, 285–8.
**84** (1994) 179 CLR 297.
**85** *Georgiadis v Australian and Overseas Telecommunications Corporation* (1994) 179 CLR 297, 303.
**86** Ibid, 305.

right was dependent on federal law and could therefore validly be extinguished under a valid federal law enacted under a head of power other than s 51(xxxi).[87] Adhering to views they had expressed previously,[88] Dawson and Toohey JJ dissented on the ground that there had not been any constitutional acquisition of property: Toohey J partly because the right had been conferred and could be taken away by statute and partly because there had been no acquisition of a proprietary interest, and Dawson J because a mere 'financial benefit' or money claim is not 'property' and a release from such a claim cannot be an 'acquisition'.[89]

The decision in *Georgiadis* needs to be understood in the context of four other cases decided at the same time, each of which held that there was no relevant acquisition of property. In perhaps the most straightforward of these cases, *Re Director of Public Prosecutions; Ex parte Lawler*,[90] the High Court held that the forfeiture of a commercial fishing boat found to be fishing without licence in Australian waters did not fall within s 51(xxxi) because it imposed a penalty, by way of forfeiture, for the contravention of a law constitutionally enacted pursuant to the fisheries power (s 51(x)). Another seemingly straightforward acquisition issue arose in *Nintendo Co Ltd v Centronics Systems Pty Ltd*.[91] The case involved the *Circuit Layouts Act 1989* (Cth), which gave the designer of a circuit layout (silicon chip) intellectual property rights including the right to prevent others from using the circuit design. Centronics had imported and sold within Australia video games which used a circuit design over which Nintendo held the rights under the Act. Centronics argued, among other things, that the Act effected an acquisition of its property in the circuit layouts used in its video games. However, the Court promptly rejected this argument on two grounds. The first was that the grant of legislative power with respect to 'copyrights, patents of inventions and designs, and trade marks' (s 51(xviii)) necessarily entails the power not only to make laws which create intellectual property rights but also to 'limit and detract from the proprietary rights' of the owners of affected property. 'Inevitably', it was observed, 'such laws may, at their commencement, impact upon existing proprietary rights'. The second reason was that a law which is 'concerned with the adjustment of the competing rights, claims or obligations of persons in a particular relationship or area of activity is unlikely to be susceptible of legitimate characterisation as a law with respect to the acquisition of property'. The *Circuit Layouts Act 1989* was such an Act because it adjusted the competing claims of 'designers or first makers of original circuit layouts and those who take advantage of, or benefit from, their work'.[92]

**87** Ibid, 325.
**88** *Australian Tape Manufacturers Association Ltd v Commonwealth* (1993) 176 CLR 480, 528; *Mutual Pools & Staff Pty Ltd v Commonwealth* (1994) 179 CLR 155, 155.
**89** *Georgiadis v Australian and Overseas Telecommunications Corporation* (1994) 179 CLR 297, 314–16, 321.
**90** (1994) 179 CLR 270. See also *Theophanous v Commonwealth* (2006) 225 CLR 101.
**91** (1994) 181 CLR 134.
**92** Ibid, 160–61.

### Adjustment of competing interests

The idea that some heads of power authorise laws which are directed to the adjustment of competing claims and interests was also applied in the two *Mutual Pools* cases. A Commonwealth law which levied a tax on the construction of swimming pools was challenged on the ground that the law was contrary to s 55 of the Constitution.[93] Before that case was heard and determined by the High Court, the Swimming Pool and Spa Association of Australia agreed with the Commissioner of Taxation that its members would continue to pay the levy, but that if the constitutional challenge was successful each supplier would receive a refund of the amounts paid with interest. After the High Court upheld the challenge,[94] the Commonwealth enacted a law which provided, among other things, that the refund would not be paid to a pool supplier if the supplier had passed the cost of the levy to the purchaser, in which case the purchaser could claim the refund from the government.

In the second *Mutual Pools* case,[95] the Court had to consider whether the extinguishment of the contractual right of the pool suppliers to the refund constituted an acquisition of property other than on just terms contrary to s 51(xxxi). However, all members of the Court found a reason to uphold the law. Mason CJ drew attention to the character of the law as one which involved 'the adjustment of competing claims and obligations'.[96] Brennan J considered that although the law provided for an acquisition of property, the law adopted means which were 'appropriate and adapted' to secure an objective falling within its constitutional powers, namely that the refund should be given to those who actually bore the expense of the levy.[97] Deane and Gaudron JJ held that the law could not fairly be characterised as a law with respect to 'the acquisition of property on just terms' for reasons similar to those articulated by Mason CJ and Brennan J.[98] McHugh J similarly maintained that the law was properly characterised as a law with respect to taxation, and that the acquisition of property that it entailed was merely incidental to the objective of repaying invalid taxes to those who had borne the burden of paying them.[99] Somewhat differently, Dawson and Toohey JJ considered that an entitlement to be paid money in the form of a contractual debt simply does not constitute 'property' for the purposes of s 51(xxxi) because money only represents the 'value' of property, not property itself.[100]

Similarly, in *Australian Tape Manufacturers Association Ltd v Commonwealth*,[101] the Court had to consider whether amendments to the *Copyright Act 1968* (Cth) intended to address the problem of widespread taping of sound recordings in breach of copyright involved an acquisition of property. The

**93** On s 55, see Chapter 2, Part III.1.
**94** *Mutual Pools & Staff Pty Ltd v Federal Commissioner of Taxation* (1992) 173 CLR 450.
**95** *Mutual Pools & Staff Pty Ltd v Commonwealth* (1994) 179 CLR 155.
**96** Ibid, 171–2, 175.
**97** Ibid, 179–81.
**98** Ibid, 188–91.
**99** Ibid, 224.
**100** Ibid, 195–7, 201–2.
**101** (1993) 176 CLR 480.

amendments provided that there would no longer be an infringement of copyright if the recording was made for private and personal use only. They also introduced a royalty system whereby the proceeds of a levy imposed on the sale of blank tapes was distributed among copyright holders to reimburse them for their notional losses. The Court held that there was no acquisition of property within the meaning of s 51(xxxi) because the right to make the copies did not itself amount to a proprietary right, and the exclusive right to make copies of sound recordings which had been one of the rights afforded to copyright holders was extinguished altogether, rather than acquired by someone else.[102]

The *Mutual Pools*, *Nintendo* and *Tape Manufacturers* cases can be understood to have involved laws which sought to adjust the competing claims of particular persons or groups in the community.[103] The legislation in *Nintendo* was especially concerned to recognise the claims of designers or first makers of original circuit layouts vis-à-vis those who might benefit by manufacturing or selling goods which utilise those designs. The legislation in *Tape Manufacturers* adjusted the rights of manufacturers of blank tapes, copyright holders and the many individuals who were making illegal copies of sound recordings. The legislation in *Mutual Pools* regulated the competing interests of pool suppliers and their customers in the receipt of a refund for the unconstitutional levy, but was also concerned to do so in a way that husbanded the limited financial resources of the Commonwealth by restricting the payment of the refund to either the pool supplier or the customer, depending on which of them bore the ultimate cost. *Mutual Pools* thus involved both an issue of commutative or corrective justice insofar as the law provided for the refunding of an unconstitutional levy, but it also involved an issue of distributive justice in balancing the interests of the pool suppliers and their customers against the interests of the whole community in the careful management of the government's finances.

A similar problem of distributive justice arose in *Health Insurance Commission v Peverill*.[104] In that case, the Court had to consider whether social security entitlements under the Medicare scheme constituted 'property' and whether the extinguishment of those benefits would constitute a relevant 'acquisition' for the purposes of s 51(xxxi). Under the Medicare scheme, patient benefits are ordinarily assigned to medical practitioners to enable them to be paid by the government for the provision of medical services. The *Health Insurance (Pathology Services) Amendment Act 1991* (Cth) had the effect of retrospectively reducing the benefits that were payable for the provision of certain pathology services. The question was whether this amending law involved an acquisition of property on other than just terms.

**102** *Australian Tape Manufacturers Association Ltd v Commonwealth* (1993) 176 CLR 480, 499–500.
**103** In the *Australian Capital Television* case, discussed in Parts III.5 and V.2 below, a law which required holders of radio and television broadcasting licences to transmit certain amounts of 'free' political advertising during election periods did not amount to an acquisition of property because no proprietary rights had been thereby acquired: *Australian Capital Television Pty Ltd v Commonwealth* (1992) 177 CLR 106, 165–7, 197–9, 245. See, similarly, *Waterhouse v Minister for the Arts and Territories* (1993) 119 ALR 89.
**104** (1994) 179 CLR 226.

In finding that there was no relevant acquisition of property, Mason CJ, Deane and Gaudron JJ considered it crucial that the rights in question were statutory in origin, and that they were therefore 'inherently susceptible of variation', a quality that is especially the case with welfare benefits because such entitlements must periodically be assessed by reference to considerations such as the community's need for assistance and the capacity of the government to pay.[105] It followed, they decided, that any 'incidental diminution' of an individual's entitlements does not render a law adjusting those rights into a law with respect to the acquisition of property for the purposes of s 51(xxxi).[106] Brennan J agreed that there was no acquisition, on the ground that the Act did not create a debt enforceable by action in favour of the medical practitioner but only a right to be paid Medicare benefits in accordance with the Act.[107] Such a right, he continued, is not property, most fundamentally because it is 'not susceptible of any form of repetitive or continuing enjoyment and cannot be exchanged for or converted into any kind of property'.[108] Toohey and McHugh JJ reasoned similarly, emphasising that the Parliament is free both to create and to alter such rights in pursuit of its constitutional powers, and that the only rights possessed by individuals under the Medicare scheme are those which exist from time to time.[109] Indeed, McHugh J went so far as to characterise the benefit as a 'gratuitous statutory entitlement' which lies within the power of the Parliament both to give and to take away under the social security power (s 51(xxiiiA)).[110]

### Baseline property rights

The distinction drawn in these cases, especially in *Georgiadis* and *Peverill*, between rights that have their origin in the general law and those that have no existence apart from statute, highlights a fundamental question raised by the entrenchment of rights in a constitution. The question concerns the problem of identifying a criterion or standard according to which the exact content of a particular right can authoritatively be determined and applied by the courts. Constitutionally entrenched rights have a two-fold character. On one hand, they draw on a long-standing tradition in Western legal theory and political philosophy that human beings possess certain natural rights that antedate the state.[111] On this view, the existence, nature and meaning of such rights is ultimately to be determined philosophically. On the other hand, the very act of entrenching rights in a constitution can be understood as a recognition that philosophical advocacy may not be sufficiently effective, and that positive entrenchment of rights in a constitution is necessary to ensure that they will be recognised and respected by government. As such, constitutional rights declarations

**105** *Health Insurance Commission v Peverill* (1994) 179 CLR 226, 237.
**106** Ibid.
**107** Ibid, 242–3.
**108** Ibid, 243–4.
**109** Ibid, 256, 260, 262.
**110** Ibid, 260, 262; see similarly 244.
**111** Brian Tierney, *The Idea of Natural Rights* (Wm B Eerdmans Publishing, 1997).

simultaneously appeal to the existence of certain pre-political natural rights inhering in every human being as well as to the necessity of formulating such rights in a binding legal document. But merely to state in a constitution that a particular right exists does not determine the exact content or meaning of that right.

To stipulate in the Australian Constitution that the Commonwealth cannot legislate with respect to the 'acquisition of property' without providing 'just terms' does not tell us what 'property' precisely means and what 'rights' necessarily attach to it. Interpretation is necessary. By distinguishing in *Georgiadis* and *Peverill* between general law rights and statutory rights, the Court proposed that the baseline for the identification of the particular proprietary interests protected by s 51(xxxi) depends upon their prior recognition by the common law. The identity, nature and scope of the protected property rights therefore relies, not solely or directly upon philosophical propositions about natural rights, but upon the rights historically recognised by the common law. The common law was thus seen as offering a pre-statutory baseline definition of the proprietary rights protected by s 51(xxxi).

The reasoning and result in *Georgiadis* has been affirmed and applied in several cases, some of which have tested this distinction between common law and statutory rights as well as the proposition that laws that merely adjust competing interests will not infringe s 51(xxxi).[112] In the *Newcrest Mining* case, the Court applied the reasoning in *Georgiadis* to a decision of the Commonwealth to extend the boundaries of Kakadu National Park under the *National Parks and Wildlife Conservation Act 1975* (Cth).[113] This decision had the effect of prohibiting Newcrest from continuing its mining operations under mining leases held by the company under Territory law. The case tested the distinction between common law and statutory rights articulated in *Georgiadis* because Newcrest's mining rights did not arise at general law, but were statutory in origin and nature. A majority considered that there was nonetheless an acquisition of property.[114] Gummow J, with whom Gaudron and Toohey JJ agreed, accepted the argument of Newcrest that in substance the Commonwealth had acquired an identifiable and measurable advantage or benefit. He observed that the rights in question were not derived 'purely from statute' and were not of their 'very nature inherently susceptible to ... variation or extinguishment'; nor were they merely 'statutory privilege[s]'.[115] Kirby J agreed, observing:

**112** *Commonwealth v Mewett* (1997) 191 CLR 471; *Smith v ANL Ltd* (2000) 204 CLR 493; *Attorney-General (NT) v Chaffey* (2007) 231 CLR 651.
**113** *Newcrest Mining (WA) v Commonwealth* (1997) 190 CLR 513.
**114** At the threshold of the case was the question whether the just terms requirement applied to a Commonwealth law applying within a Territory. In *Teori Tau v Commonwealth* (1969) 119 CLR 564 the Court had held that laws passed under s 122 are not subject to s 51(xxxi). In *Newcrest Mining*, a majority found that s 51(xxxi) did apply in the circumstances: Toohey J on the ground that the law could be characterised as implementing an international treaty under the external affairs power (s 51(xxix)); Gaudron, Gummow and Kirby JJ also on the wider ground that s 51(xxxi) applies to laws passed under s 122: ibid 560–61, 561–9, 614, 640, 661–2. In *Wurridjal v Commonwealth* (2009) 237 CLR 309 a majority adopted this wider view.
**115** *Newcrest Mining (WA) v Commonwealth* (1997) 190 CLR 513, 634–5.

> It is one thing to expand a National Park for the benefit of everyone who will enjoy its facility. It is another to do so at an economic cost to the owners of valuable property interests in sections of the Park whose rights are effectively confiscated to achieve that end. Ordinarily, at least under federal law, the expansion of areas for public use is carried out at the price of compensating justly those private individuals who lose their property interests in order to contribute to the greater public good.[116]

Brennan CJ, who ultimately upheld the Commonwealth law on the basis that s 51(xxxi) did not apply, considered that apart from this, the law effected an acquisition of property within the meaning of s 51(xxxi). On his view, the law 'enhanced' the Commonwealth's reversionary proprietary interest in the land because it released it from the burden of Newcrest's right to conduct mining operations.[117]

One year later, the *WMC Resources* case tested the application of this reasoning to a Commonwealth law which extinguished an exploration permit over an area known as the Timor Gap, which is part of the continental shelf between Australia and East Timor.[118] A majority held that there was no acquisition of property within the meaning of s 51(xxxi). For Brennan CJ and Gaudron J, while there is a 'prima facie' rule that a statutory right is inherently susceptible of statutory modification, there may nonetheless be an acquisition of property when the modification or extinguishment of a purely statutory right results in some other person obtaining a consequential advantage or benefit in relation to property, as occurred in both *Georgiadis* and *Newcrest*. But what distinguished *WMC Resources* from those cases was that although the Commonwealth had the sovereign right to create proprietary interests in the continental shelf, it had not done so, and sovereignty is not of itself a proprietary interest.[119] In coming to the same ultimate conclusion, Gummow J considered that the exploration permit was not only statutory in nature, but also suffered from the 'congenital infirmity' that its content was inherently susceptible of variation.[120] McHugh J went further. He said that the suggestion that s 51(xxxi) is a guarantee of property 'rights' is misleading, for it is really only a 'power hedged with a qualification'.[121] For him, the focus must always be on whether the relevant head of power authorises the creation of a proprietary right in circumstances where no specific property right previously existed.[122] He considered that the distinction drawn by the joint judgment in *Georgiadis* between statutory rights and rights arising under the general law supported his view even though he had dissented in that case.[123]

**116** Ibid, 639.
**117** Ibid, 530–31.
**118** *Commonwealth v WMC Resources Ltd* (1998) 194 CLR 1. See also *Wurridjal v Commonwealth* (2009) 237 CLR 309, discussed in Part II.3 below.
**119** *Commonwealth v WMC Resources Ltd* (1998) 194 CLR 1, 16–20, 35–8.
**120** Ibid, 73–5.
**121** Ibid, 48.
**122** Ibid, 51.
**123** Ibid, 53–4.

### Public interests and private rights

The idea that a law might avoid s 51(xxxi) if directed to the adjustment of competing rights and interests was applied in the *Airservices* case.[124] The Court had to consider whether the imposition of a statutory lien under the *Civil Aviation Act 1988* (Cth) constituted an acquisition of property. The lien came into operation when an airline operating at Australian airports failed to pay fees for the provision of air traffic control and other services provided by the Civil Aviation Authority. The lien enabled the Authority to seize and sell aircraft and use the proceeds to recoup the unpaid fees. When aircraft belonging to the ill-fated Compass Airlines were seized under the Act, the company that leased the aircraft to Compass complained that its property in the aircraft had been acquired, without any wrongdoing on its part.

A majority of the Court rejected the argument of the lessor company. Gleeson CJ and Kirby J considered the scheme of the Act to be reasonable in the circumstances, especially in the light of the need for a safe and effective system of air traffic services and the ability of the lessor to know about the statutory lien and take measures to protect itself.[125] Gummow J, with whom Hayne J agreed, similarly observed that the purpose of the Act was, in the light of the 'competing public policy interests', to adjust the various rights of those who own, lease and operate aircraft, together with those of the public provider of air services to those companies.[126] Gaudron and Callinan JJ dissented. Gaudron J noted that the lien did not adjust the competing interests of related persons but rather simply appropriated an interest in the property owned by the lessor company in circumstances where that company had no relationship with, and did not owe any fees to, the service provider in whose favour the lien was created.[127] Callinan J similarly observed that the lien effected an 'extinction of all proprietary rights of innocent as opposed to complicit third parties'.[128]

Justice Callinan's objections to the narrow application of s 51(xxxi) in *Airservices* were repeated the next year in *Smith v ANL Ltd*.[129] The case arose in circumstances similar to *Georgiadis*, this time involving the purported extinguishment by the *Seafarers Rehabilitation and Compensation Act 1992* (Cth) of an employee's right to sue his employer for negligence and breach of contract. A majority of the Court held that the relevant provision effected an acquisition of property without providing just terms. In his concurring judgment, Callinan J subjected the idea that a law might avoid s 51(xxxi) if it involves an 'adjustment of competing claims' to extended criticism. His fundamental point was that, given the vagueness of the idea, all legislation can in some way be characterised as adjusting competing interests, rights and obligations, and that the mere fact

**124** *Airservices Australia v Canadian Airlines International Ltd* (1999) 202 CLR 133.
**125** Ibid, 179–81.
**126** Ibid, 265, 298–300, 304–5.
**127** Ibid, 196–7.
**128** Ibid, 309.
**129** (2000) 204 CLR 493.

that a law might be characterised as being directed towards this end should not enable the Commonwealth to avoid the requirement of providing just terms for any acquisition of property that might be involved.[130]

This question as to whether a Commonwealth law can or should be justified if it seeks to make some rational adjustment of competing rights or interests arose again in *ICM Agriculture Pty Ltd v Commonwealth*.[131] The case involved provisions of the *National Water Commission Act 2004* (Cth) which, pursuant to an intergovernmental agreement, effectively reduced the entitlements of farmers to the use of groundwater for irrigation by up to 70 per cent. The plaintiffs argued that the substitution of new 'aquifer access licences' for their pre-existing 'bore licences' under State law amounted to an acquisition of property without providing just terms. The plaintiffs argued that the bore licences regulated their pre-existing rights at common law to take possession and make use of subterranean water, such as by pumping the water to the surface.[132]

A majority of the Court rejected the plaintiffs' argument, observing that water is a finite and fluctuating resource that needs to be managed in a sustainable and efficient manner. For the majority, it was significant that the common law had treated water, like light and air, as 'common property' that is 'not especially amenable to private ownership and best vested in a sovereign state'.[133] According to Hayne, Kiefel and Bell JJ, there was no acquisition of property within the meaning of s 51(xxxi) essentially because, even though the bore licences were a species of property, there had been no acquisition of an identifiable and measurable benefit by the state in a sense analogous to the acquisition that occurred in *Newcrest*. Rights to water could be distinguished from rights to minerals, they maintained, due to such considerations as the 'replaceable and fugitive' nature of water, the longstanding hesitancy of the law to treat groundwater as an object of property rights, and the need to control access to it as a vital but limited public resource.[134]

Heydon J dissented, arguing that s 51(xxxi) should be understood in the light of the fact that the framers of the Constitution, in providing for the just terms requirement, were giving effect to a generally shared liberal commitment to the institution of private property. He appealed to the view, expressed by Nobel-prize-winning economist F A Hayek, that just terms requirements serve to ensure that private property will only be interfered with in circumstances where the public benefit is clearly greater than the cost borne by the individual owner.[135] He observed that the bore licences were proprietary interests of substantial value, that they were not inherently susceptible of variation, that their appropriation to the benefit of the state could not be justified on the ground that

**130** *Smith v ANL Ltd* (2000) 204 CLR 493, 550–52; see also 514.
**131** (2009) 240 CLR 140.
**132** *ICM Agriculture Pty Ltd v Commonwealth* (2009) 240 CLR 140, 144.
**133** Ibid, 171, 173; see also 188–90, 217–18, 223–4.
**134** Ibid, 201–3.
**135** Ibid, 208, citing F A Hayek, *The Constitution of Liberty* (University of Chicago Press, 1960) 217–18.

the law was merely adjusting competing rights and interests, and that an identifiable benefit or advantage had indeed accrued to the state.[136]

Similar issues arose in *JT International SA v Commonwealth*.[137] The case concerned Commonwealth legislation which prevented cigarette manufacturers from applying their registered trademarks and designs to the packets in which cigarettes are sold to the public, and which required them to use plain packaging with stipulated health warnings and other information displayed. The plaintiffs argued that the prohibition on the use of trademarks constituted, in substance, an acquisition of property without just terms. A majority of the Court held, however, that there was no acquisition of property because, even though rights had been 'taken', no proprietary interest had been acquired.[138] Hayne and Bell JJ, with whom French CJ and Gummow J agreed, considered that the Commonwealth could not be said to have gained 'control' over the packaging, in the sense in which Dixon J had used the term in the *Bank Nationalisation* case; all that had occurred was that certain packaging and labelling requirements had been stipulated by the law.[139]

Hayne and Bell JJ refrained from commenting on the Commonwealth's additional submission that there is a general exception to the application of s 51(xxxi) where legislation undertakes 'reasonable regulation of some activity for the greater good of society'.[140] In a strongly-worded dissent, Heydon J directly rejected this latter submission. On the contrary, he considered that an acquisition can be established even if the 'benefit' acquired is not of itself proprietary in nature, provided it relates to the ownership or use of property, and he concluded that such an acquisition had been established through the rights of control exercised by the Commonwealth through the legislation.[141] Furthermore, he expressed sympathy for earlier suggestions of Callinan J that the old distinction between laws that 'acquire' and laws that 'take' should not be regarded as decisive.[142] In his view, the injustice caused to the property owner lies in the uncompensated taking, not in the acquisition, and it is the injustice of the infringement of the property owner's rights that should be regarded as crucial. In other words, the concept of an 'acquisition of property' in s 51(xxxi) needs to be understood as being inextricably linked to the 'just terms' requirement.

## 3 Just terms

When the Court identifies that there is an 'acquisition of property' for the purposes of s 51(xxxi), the next step is to determine whether the legislation

**136** Ibid, 217–28, 231–5.
**137** (2012) 250 CLR 1.
**138** *JT International (Tobacco Advertising)* (2012) 250 CLR 1, 33, 60, 61–4, 67, 69, 70–73.
**139** Ibid, 70–73, 63.
**140** Ibid, 73.
**141** Ibid, 73, 77–8, 82–3.
**142** Ibid, 75–6, citing *Smith v ANL Ltd* (2000) 204 CLR 493, 546; *Commonwealth v Western Australia* (1999) 196 CLR 392, 488.

provides for 'just terms'. As interpreted by the Court, the concept of 'just terms' has a twofold connotation: firstly, the provision of appropriate monetary compensation and, secondly, a requirement of natural justice or procedural fairness in the way that the amount of the compensation is determined. In accordance with these general requirements, the *Lands Acquisition Act 1989* (Cth) lays down prescribed procedures for the acquisition of property designed to ensure, among other things, that acquisitions occur for a public purpose, and that land owners are given due notice and are given an opportunity to object to a proposed acquisition, to negotiate a sale price, to make claims for compensation and to have acquisition decisions and compensation assessments judicially reviewed.[143]

The use in s 51(xxxi) of the expression 'just terms', rather than 'just compensation', has given the High Court reason to consider that while an assessment of compensation must take into consideration the interests of the person from whom the property is acquired, all of the relevant interests are to be taken into account, including those of the community as a whole. As Dixon J once put it, whereas 'compensation' connotes 'full money equivalence', 'just terms' implies a standard of 'fairness'.[144] A general acquisition law may therefore set down reasonable rules for the fair and just assessment of compensation generally, even if in some cases something less than 'perfect' fairness is achieved.[145] This requirement would be satisfied, for example, by a provision that 'reasonable compensation' is to be paid, including interest, as determined by a court of competent jurisdiction.[146] It has been said that where there is a market for the property, market value is usually the appropriate measure,[147] but this may be supplemented by special considerations, such as the unique nature of the property,[148] and can include loss of profits associated with the acquisition.[149] The market value of the property may need to be adjusted or abandoned in unusual circumstances, such as where conditions of war create artificial inflation in the value of the property. Where no relevant market exists due to war time conditions, the valuation should be made by reference to the price that would be arrived at between a willing, but not anxious, buyer and seller.[150]

The Court has affirmed that procedural fairness requires that compensation assessments are undertaken by, or are subject to review by, an impartial tribunal. The compensation cannot be determined conclusively by a minister, a board or non-judicial tribunal.[151] Moreover, the process must accord the property owner an opportunity to be heard and afford him or her knowledge of the

**143** Brown, above n 28, ch 2.
**144** *Nelungaloo Pty Ltd v Commonwealth* (1948) 75 CLR 495, 569.
**145** *Grace Bros Pty Ltd v Commonwealth* (1946) 72 CLR 269, 290.
**146** *Wurridjal v Commonwealth* (2009) 237 CLR 309, 389–90, 429.
**147** *Nelungaloo v Commonwealth* (1948) 75 CLR 495, 506, 547.
**148** *Johnston Fear & Kingham & Offset Printing Co Pty Ltd v Commonwealth* (1943) 67 CLR 314; *Minister of State for the Army v Parbury Henty & Co Pty Ltd* (1945) 70 CLR 459.
**149** *Minister of State for the Army v Dalziel* (1944) 68 CLR 261.
**150** *Nelungaloo Pty Ltd v Commonwealth* (1948) 75 CLR 495, 507.
**151** *Australian Apple and Pear Marketing Board v Tonking* (1942) 66 CLR 77, 84, 89; see also *Bank of New South Wales v Commonwealth* (1948) 76 CLR 1, 351.

evidence or information on which an assessment has been made.[152] Compensation may be assessed by an agency of the government, provided that the agency is administratively separate from the agency that acquires the property.[153] In addition, there must not be an undue delay in the assessment or payment of compensation.[154]

The complications of applying these ideas of fair monetary compensation and procedural fairness to acquisitions of non-Western forms of proprietary 'interest', such as the connections that Australia's Indigenous and Torres Strait Islander people have with their traditional lands and waters, was illustrated in *Wurridjal v Commonwealth*.[155] The case concerned Commonwealth legislation associated with the 'Northern Territory Intervention' initiated by the Commonwealth government in an effort to address allegations of widespread child abuse and neglect in the Territory. As relevant to the acquisition issue, the *Northern Territory National Emergency Response Act 2007* (Cth) included provisions which created a five-year statutory lease over land held by the Arnhem Land Aboriginal Land Trust in the town of Maningrida, on the far northern coast of the Northern Territory. A majority of the Court held that the creation of the lease constituted an acquisition of property, notwithstanding the fact that the fee simple title held by the Land Trust was subject to numerous statutory controls and was argued to be 'inherently defeasible' for this reason.[156]

Section 60(2) of the Commonwealth Act provided that in the event of 'an acquisition of property to which paragraph 51(xxxi) of the Constitution applies... otherwise than on just terms, the Commonwealth is liable to pay a reasonable amount of compensation'. Members of the Court described this provision as a 'fail-safe' and 'sensible' statutory precaution needed to prevent the law from being found unconstitutional.[157] The plaintiffs submitted, however, that monetary compensation alone would not be sufficient to provide 'just terms' for the acquisition of their traditional use of the land. Kirby and Heydon JJ considered that this line of argument had merit, observing that Aboriginal rights and interests in land are uniquely tied to Aboriginal 'identity, culture and spirituality', and that such interests may not be readily replaced or compensated by the mere payment of money.[158] Kirby J suggested that just terms in such a context might include such things as special forms of consultation and participation of Indigenous people in the administration of the relevant laws.[159] Kiefel J, however, maintained that the suggestion that it may not be possible to attribute a market value to sacred sites should not be accepted.[160]

**152** *Australian Apple and Pear Marketing Board v Tonking* (1942) 66 CLR 77, 109, 99.
**153** *Andrews v Howell* (1941) 65 CLR 255, 282–4.
**154** *Commonwealth v Tasmania* (1983) 158 CLR 1, 290–91.
**155** (2009) 237 CLR 309.
**156** *Wurridjal v Commonwealth* (2009) 237 CLR 309, 364, 370–71, 420, 467. Other claims of effective acquisitions of property, such as through the ending of the 'permit system' through which access to Aboriginal land had formerly been controlled, were rejected by the Court: 365–6, 463, 468.
**157** See ibid, 389, 424, 470.
**158** Ibid, 425, 426.
**159** Ibid, 425–6.
**160** Ibid, 471.

### 4 Commonwealth purposes

It is finally necessary under s 51(xxxi) that the acquisition be for a purpose for which the Parliament has power to make laws. Thus every acquisition law needs to be supported by another head of power in addition to the acquisition power. In *Andrews v Howell*, Dixon J expressed doubt that a requisite purpose could be found merely in the objective of establishing a 'marketing pool' as a means of effectual sale and distribution of a marketable commodity by private producers.[161] However, in *Tonking*,[162] the Court approved the establishment of marketing pools as a legitimate means of coping with the conditions of war; and it seems other heads of power, such as the trade and commerce power (s 51(i)), may provide a constitutional basis for marketing pools more generally. In *Clunies-Ross v Commonwealth*,[163] an acquisition of land in the Cocos Islands was made simply to deprive the owner of the use of the land. It was held that this was not a purpose in respect of which the Parliament has power to make laws. In *WH Blakeley & Co Pty Ltd v Commonwealth*,[164] the Governor-General, under the *Lands Acquisition Act*, purported to declare conclusively that certain acquisitions were for the public purposes of accommodation for departments of the Commonwealth and for postal services. Despite objections, it was held that the Governor-General could conclusively declare the intended purpose of the acquisition, and no evidence would be received to show that this was not the true purpose. It was also considered that the declared purposes were in fact purposes in respect of which the Parliament had power to make laws.

## III Freedom of trade

When the Australian Constitution was being drafted, one of the most important issues dividing political opinion concerned the question of 'free trade' and 'protection'. Several colonies had adopted policies aimed at protecting local producers and manufacturers from external market competition; whereas New South Wales, in particular, had tended towards a free trade policy. A central problem of federation, therefore, was to find a way in which these two different policy outlooks might be conciliated. Much of the popular impetus for federation came from those who objected to the high tariff barriers that several of the colonies had administered through customs houses situated in many of the colonial border towns. In this context, many believed that free trade among the constituent States was essential to the formation of a federal commonwealth. William Russell, a delegate from New Zealand and a strong free trader, went so far as to suggest that free trade was not only important economically but was also essential

**161** *Andrews v Howell* (1941) 65 CLR 255, 281–2.
**162** *Australian Apple and Pear Marketing Board v Tonking* (1942) 66 CLR 77.
**163** *Clunies-Ross v Commonwealth* (1984) 155 CLR 193.
**164** *WH Blakeley & Co Pty Ltd v Commonwealth* (1953) 87 CLR 501.

to the task of binding the peoples of the colonies into one people. 'The true basis of federation', he said, 'is that interchange of products which leads to the expansion of trade, and a consequent rapprochement between the peoples of different communities'.[165] This was a proposition that even protectionists could accept, provided that it would remain constitutionally possible for the Commonwealth to establish customs duties and similar measures aimed at protecting all Australian producers and manufacturers generally, albeit without discrimination between the States: 'intercolonial free trade and protection against the outside world', as John Macrossan put it.[166] Understood in this way, freedom of interstate trade became one of the most generally supported principles of federation.

A shared commitment to freedom of interstate trade was evident throughout the debate that led to the drafting, ratification and enactment of the Constitution. In the original draft resolutions prepared by the Premier of New South Wales, Sir Henry Parkes, for consideration at the Federal Convention of 1891, the very first resolution declared that:

> trade and intercourse between the Federated Colonies, whether by means of land carriage or coastal navigation, shall be free from the payment of Customs duties, and from all restrictions whatsoever, except such regulations as may be necessary for the conduct of business.[167]

At the Convention itself the resolution that was actually proposed and adopted was expressed in even wider, less qualified terms, namely that 'trade and intercourse between the federated colonies' was to be 'absolutely free'.[168] The key provision of the Constitution that ultimately gave effect to this objective was s 92, the operative aspect of which repeated, almost verbatim, the terms of these resolutions. Section 92 provides:

> On the imposition of uniform duties of customs, trade, commerce, and intercourse among the States, whether by means of internal carriage or ocean navigation, shall be absolutely free.

Notably, the free trade requirement did not come into operation until the imposition of uniform customs duties by the Commonwealth, which was an exclusive preserve of the Commonwealth (s 90) and was required to occur within two years of federation (s 88). Together with the Commonwealth's concurrent power to legislate with respect to interstate and foreign trade (s 51(i)), these provisions meant the Commonwealth would be able to determine whether to adopt protectionist or free trade policies for the country as a whole, but always subject to the principle of interstate free trade.

**165** *Conference Debates, Melbourne* (1890) 123. He was echoing a widely shared view. See, eg, G R Parkin, 'Federation, Commercial' in Robert Palgrave (ed), *Dictionary of Political Economy* (Macmillan, 1896) II, 45–6: '[a]ll known precedents lead us to associate the idea of commercial federation with that of political federation'.
**166** *Conference Debates, Melbourne* (1890) 193.
**167** Henry Parkes, *Fifty Years in the Making of Australian History* (Longmans, 1892) vol II, 359.
**168** *Convention Debates, Sydney* (1891) 23, 499–500. The resolution at the second convention was in similar terms: *Convention Debates, Adelaide* (1897) 17, 395.

The simplicity, scope and unconditional nature of s 92 sets it apart from the relatively more precise and measured provisions of the rest of the Constitution. Although 'free trade' represented one of the cardinal principles of federation, occasional attempts were made during the conventions to qualify the language of s 92 and to limit its operation. With one important exception, however, all of these proposals were rejected. During the Adelaide sitting of the second Convention, Alfred Deakin worried that the broad language being proposed might prevent the States from prohibiting the introduction and sale of 'injurious' articles, such as opium or alcohol, and he proposed a specific clause making clear that this power would remain.[169] Isaac Isaacs went even further, expressing concern that the words 'throughout the Commonwealth' would extend to 'internal trade and commerce', and that the words 'absolutely free' could mean 'free of everything'. 'Taken literally', he suggested, these words would prevent the States from imposing licence fees to engage in certain forms of trade and commerce. Insisting that the Constitution should only prohibit the levying of customs duties on goods imported into a State, he proposed that instead of '*throughout* the Commonwealth' the words '*among* the States' should be used.[170] Richard O'Connor doubted, however, whether Isaacs's concerns were well founded. While the intention was that 'every part of the Commonwealth' should be open to the trade of 'every member of the Commonwealth' and that every member should be 'absolutely free from trade restrictions of every kind', he argued that the context in which the clause was situated in the Constitution implied that it was directed to the prohibition of border taxes and that the mere 'regulation' of trade or the institution of trading licences would not be prevented.[171] In the event, Deakin's proposed clause was narrowly rejected,[172] but Isaacs's criticisms of the wide language of the draft clause would be discussed again at the Melbourne sitting.[173]

At Melbourne, John Quick expressed concern that the words 'throughout the Commonwealth' were apt to include 'every locality' within the Commonwealth, whereas he believed the focus of the provision ought to be one of establishing 'absolute freedom of trade at the *frontiers* between the colonies'. To this end, he suggested that the words '*between* the States' should be adopted.[174] Quick's argument was met by John Downer, who argued forcefully for the retention of the original wording, containing as it did a 'cardinal principle' of the federation.[175] At this point, the Convention appeared to resolve the matter by voting in favour of the words 'between the States'.[176] However, the matter was not quite determined: Edmund Barton and George Reid continued to use the phrase 'among

**169** *Convention Debates, Adelaide* (1897) 830, 875–7, 1140–42.
**170** Ibid, 1141–2 (emphasis added).
**171** Ibid, 1144–6.
**172** Ibid, 1148.
**173** *Convention Debates, Melbourne* (1898), 1014–15.
**174** Ibid, 1016–17 (emphasis added).
**175** Ibid, 1018–19.
**176** Ibid, 1020.

the states', while Deakin insisted on 'between'.[177] In the event, Barton's preference prevailed when the clause was reintroduced for final consideration.[178] During this final debate, Isaacs expressed no concern about the use of the term 'among', but rather sought to have the words 'absolutely free' qualified by the insertion of the words 'from taxation or restriction'.[179] His objective was to make clear, as Samuel Griffith had recommended,[180] that the clause was not intended to prevent the ordinary internal regulation of persons engaged in trade, such as through licensing requirements, or the imposition of reasonable charges for the carriage of goods over State boundaries, but only to ensure that interstate trade was not to be 'restricted or interfered with by any taxes, charges, or imposts'.[181] However, Reid, an arch supporter of free trade, was concerned that a qualification of the words 'absolutely free' might leave too much room for development of 'legal technicalities' by which the scope of the interstate freedom might be restricted. He put it this way:

> This clause touches the vital point for which we are federating, and although the words of the clause are certainly not the words that you meet with in Acts of Parliaments as a general rule, they have this recommendation, that they strike exactly the notes which we want to strike in this Constitution. And they have also the further recommendation that no legal technicalities can be built up upon them in order to restrict their operation. It is a little bit of laymen's language which comes in here very well.[182]

Barton, who declared himself a protectionist, also supported the provision's unqualified words, maintaining that an absolute guarantee of interstate free trade was essential to the project of federation.[183] Isaacs' proposed amendment was rejected and the clause was approved by the Convention in its current form.

While the words '*among* the States' represented a narrower formulation than the original '*throughout* the Commonwealth', they were wider than '*between* the States'. While Isaacs preferred to place some qualification on the words '*absolutely* free', his proposal was resisted lest the free trade principle be restricted through legal technicalities. At the least, as J A La Nauze pointed out, it is highly arguable the phrase 'absolutely free' was understood to connote freedom not only from customs duties that were protectionist, but also those that were non-protectionist.[184]

**177** Ibid, 1319, 1384–5.
**178** Ibid, 2365.
**179** Ibid, 2365–6.
**180** Samuel Griffith, *Notes on the Draft Federal Constitution Framed by the Adelaide Convention of 1897, Australian Federal Convention Papers* (1897–1898), reprinted in *Queensland Legislative Council, Journal* (1897) vol 47, pt 1, 12.
**181** *Convention Debates, Melbourne* (1898), 2365.
**182** Ibid, 2367.
**183** Ibid, 2369–70.
**184** J A La Nauze, 'A Little Bit of Lawyers' Language: The History of "Absolutely Free" 1890–1990' in A W Martin (ed), *Essays in Australian Federation* (Melbourne University Press, 1969) 57, 76–7, arguing that Griffith understood 'free trade' to mean the absence of protectionist tariffs, whereas 'absolute free trade' meant freedom from all tariffs whether protectionist or not.

## 1 Preliminary analysis

Although s 92 represented one of the most widely acknowledged principles of federation, its broad language has given rise to more litigation than any other provision in the Constitution. Many of the interpretive difficulties have revolved around the issues raised during the federal convention debates. Section 92 appears in Chapter IV of the Constitution, and is surrounded by provisions dealing with customs, excise duties and bounties on the production or export of goods (ss 86–96).[185] Given its history and its location among these provisions, it seems clearly to be directed at least to the prohibition of the imposition of border taxes on goods. But the language of the section is not limited to taxes or goods; it refers simply to 'trade, commerce and intercourse among the States' and it requires that this must be 'absolutely free' without qualification.

Section 92 also necessarily operates in the context of the Commonwealth's power to legislate with respect to 'trade and commerce... among the States' (s 51(i)). It thus goes some way towards making explicit what the Supreme Court had held was implicit in the corresponding 'commerce clause' of the US Constitution, namely that the States are excluded from regulating the topic of interstate trade and commerce altogether and that the commerce power of the American Congress is effectively exclusive.[186] However, the two schemes remain different in important respects. The dormant commerce clause theory treats the field of 'interstate trade and commerce' as more or less co-extensive for purposes of both federal power and state disability, so that as widely as the commerce power is interpreted to extend, so too the prohibition, subject perhaps to certain limited qualifications. In Australia, however, s 92 is not, on its terms, limited in its application to the States: read literally, it seems to bind the Commonwealth as well. If this is so, it gives reason to adopt an interpretation that does not treat 'interstate trade and commerce' as co-extensive for the purposes of both legislative power under s 51(i) and prohibition under s 92, for otherwise the power to legislate might be completely nullified. As a consequence, on this line of reasoning, 'absolutely free' must leave room for Commonwealth regulation under s 51(i); and if it does, then it leaves room for State regulation as well. The problem is then one of identifying the line between allowable regulation and prohibited interference.

In working through this fundamental problem of interpretation, members of the High Court have proposed various solutions, some of which have been more influential than others, but none of which have, possibly until recently, commanded universal assent. The most restricted view is to regard s 92 as addressed only to the States and as limited to prohibiting laws which impose tariff barriers at State borders in the form of taxes on the importation of goods and

**185** It was also intended that the execution and maintenance of provisions of the Constitution and laws dealing with trade and commerce were to be administered by an Inter-State Commission (s 101); however, the Commission only operated for a short period of time in the 1910s and again in the 1980–90s.
**186** Quick and Garran, above n 29, 845.

perhaps services into the home State. One difficulty with such an interpretation is that s 90 already prevents the States from imposing customs or excise duties, which would leave s 92 with little to do. Certainly, s 92 also protects freedom of 'intercourse', but this raises another fundamental problem with such a narrow interpretation, namely that it is difficult to square with the 'intercourse' aspect of the provision. Noting that s 92 is not limited in its terms to taxes and similar imposts, the idea that trade, commerce and intercourse must be absolutely free seems to suggest that something more than merely taxes in the form of border customs duties are prohibited.

A slightly wider interpretation is that s 92 is directed to the prohibition of laws enacted by a State to protect its own producers, manufacturers or service providers from out-of-State competition. Such a view of s 92, like the 'customs duty' interpretation, suggests that s 92 is directed to a policy of interstate 'free trade' in contrast to a policy of 'protection'. The virtue of this view is its consistency with the prevailing preoccupation in the 1890s with the debate between these two contrasting approaches to political economy. However, such an approach involves the imposition of a very profound qualification on the literal words of s 92. Perhaps the shift in the drafting from 'throughout the Commonwealth' to 'among the States' suggests a narrowing of meaning, but not so far as the words 'between the States' would have implied; and, in any case, it is the conception of trade, commerce and intercourse 'among the States' that is the authoritative constitutional formula, not an interference with trade and commerce that is 'protective' in purpose or effect.

A still wider interpretation, is one that focuses on the constitutional language itself, and asks directly whether a law is contrary to freedom of 'trade, commerce and intercourse among the States' as such. Such an approach can be applied to the formal legal effect of the law in terms of creating, altering or eliminating legal rights, duties, liberties, immunities or powers, and asking whether the law adopts as its 'criterion of operation' some element or aspect of interstate trade, commerce or intercourse. Alternatively, it may focus on the substantial effect of the law, asking whether the law has the effect in practice of inhibiting freedom of interstate trade, whether or not its criterion of operation refers explicitly to that kind of trade. On either approach, the question is whether the law singles out some aspect of interstate trade, and imposes some special burden upon it.

In relation to these possible interpretive approaches, some members of the Court have treated the freedom protected by s 92 as an 'individual right', in the sense that a law will contravene s 92 if it in some way interferes with a particular individual's or corporation's freedom to engage in interstate trade. Such an approach tends to be associated with an interpretation that focuses on the relatively expansive language of s 92 itself. Others have understood the object of the freedom to be interstate trade itself, conceived as a collective phenomenon consisting of all of the many individual transactions entered into by multitudes of persons and enterprises engaged in interstate trading activities. On this approach, a law may prohibit an individual from engaging in a particular interstate commercial transaction, but it will only contravene s 92 if the law interferes with the cumulative flow of all such transactions over State borders. Such an approach tends to be associated with an interpretation of s 92 that reduces its application to the prohibition of protectionist laws.[187]

## 2 Early approaches

In the High Court's jurisprudence on s 92 there have been many more complications than this brief analysis of possible approaches suggests, but the most important and influential interpretations have generally been along these lines. An interpretation that focused on the existence of *discrimination* against goods manufactured in a different State was applied in the first case on s 92 decided by the High Court. In *Fox v Robbins*,[188] the Court had to consider a Western Australian law which imposed substantially different licence fees for the sale of wines, depending whether the wine was the product of fruit from within the State or from another State. Although the law did not impose a tariff or similar tax on the importation of goods into the State, the law discriminated against trade in goods produced outside the State.

The Court held unanimously that this was contrary to s 92. Griffith CJ considered that s 92 gave rise to a prohibition similar to that which had been found to arise by way of negative implication from the 'commerce' clause in the United States. This prohibition prevented a State from imposing a 'greater burden or restriction' upon the sale of wine produced in another State than is imposed on wine produced in the home State.[189] Barton J further pointed out that the US Supreme Court had held that 'no State has power to make any law or regulation which will affect the free and unrestrained intercourse and trade between the States ... or will impose any discriminating burden or tax upon the citizens or products of other States, coming or brought within its jurisdiction'.[190] He observed that the practical effect of the law on interstate trade was no different than if a duty on importation of the wine had been imposed at the border.[191] In short, the Act provided for 'inter-state protection, not inter-state free trade'.[192] For him, the critical question was whether there was discrimination: a State may tax goods of a particular description within the State, but all goods of that description must be 'taxed alike'.[193] O'Connor J reasoned similarly, observing that 'the Constitution does not permit a State by such discriminating charges to place at a disadvantage the goods of other States passing into it for sale'.[194] Isaacs and

**187** See Michael Coper, *Freedom of Interstate Trade Under the Australian Constitution* (Butterworths, 1983) 297–307.
**188** (1908) 8 CLR 115.
**189** *Fox v Robbins* (1908) 8 CLR 115, 120.
**190** Ibid, 122–3, citing *Brown v Houston* 114 US 622 (1885), 630.
**191** *Fox v Robbins* (1908) 8 CLR 115, 123.
**192** Ibid.
**193** Ibid, 124.
**194** Ibid, 126.

Higgins JJ agreed, emphasising the 'absolute' nature of s 92, but basing their decision on the discriminatory nature of the law.[195]

The next important case on s 92, *R v Smithers; Ex parte Benson*,[196] raised a further question that had concerned the framers: would a State be able to enact a law controlling the entry of persons convicted of crimes into the State, or would this be contrary to the guarantee of freedom of interstate 'intercourse'? Although this potentially raised a question about the meaning and application of s 92, Griffith CJ and Barton J avoided this specific question by relying on the proposition, derived from a decision of the US Supreme Court,[197] that the original 'police power' of the States to control immigration is cut down by the 'mere fact of federation'. This act of federation, it was said, involves the formation of a new federal polity the 'elementary notion' of which implies that every citizen has the right to travel across the territory of each State in order to approach the seat of government, including the administrative offices of the federal government and its courts of justice, and that the only ground upon which a State might restrict this right is for the purpose of promoting 'public order, safety, or morals'.[198]

As it happened, the particular law in question purported to prohibit a resident of Victoria from entering New South Wales on the ground that he had been sentenced to prison for at least 12 months for having 'insufficient lawful means of support'. It was held by Griffith CJ and Barton J that this was not a sufficient ground, although Barton J emphasised that the States would still retain a qualified capacity to protect themselves in such circumstances. Although Isaacs J agreed on the result, his point of departure was to rely, rather, on the British principle of statutory interpretation which first directs courts to the literal text of the Constitution. Here, the exact language of s 92 was significant, which Isaacs J pointed out provides that 'intercourse among the States shall be absolutely free'.[199] The natural meaning of the term 'intercourse', he considered, includes a personal right to travel over a State boundary, a right that must necessarily qualify the continuing powers of the States under their respective constitutions.[200] Affirming that s 92 contains an 'absolute guarantee of freedom', he concluded that:

> the guarantee of inter-State freedom of transit and access for persons and property under sec 92 is absolute – that is, it is an absolute prohibition on the Commonwealth and States alike to regard State borders as in themselves possible barriers to intercourse between Australians.[201]

Such a line of reasoning was, of course, remarkable. Having warned in 1897 that '[t]aken literally', the provision meant, 'free of everything',[202] Isaacs J now

**195** Ibid, 130–31, 131.
**196** (1912) 16 CLR 99.
**197** *Crandall v Nevada*, 73 US 35 (1868).
**198** *R v Smithers; Ex parte Benson* (1912) 16 CLR 99, 108–9, 109–111.
**199** Ibid, 111–12.
**200** Ibid, 113–14.
**201** Ibid, 117.
**202** *Convention Debates, Adelaide* (1897) 1141–2.

seemed to be exegeting s 92 very literally, consistent with his commitment to textual interpretation, but also in tune with his underlying nationalism. Higgins J thought likewise: he regarded the 'intercourse' aspect of s 92 as protecting 'all migration or movement of persons from one State to another'.[203]

The differences in judicial approach that emerged in *Smithers* tracked differences that had been surfacing in the interpretation of the distribution of powers between the Commonwealth and the States generally.[204] Isaacs J, although a prominent critic of the unqualified language of s 92 during the federal conventions, was apparently led by his textualism to become one of the High Court's strongest advocates of the 'absoluteness' of the free trade requirement. In his dissenting judgment in *Ex parte Nelson (No 1)*, for example, he insisted on the literal meaning of the words in s 92: 'absolutely', he said, means *absolutely* and 'free' means *free* – they do not mean 'conditionally', 'provisionally', 'partially', or 'subject to exceptions'.[205] Behind this literal reading of s 92 was also the incipient nationalism that had shaped Isaacs J's views about the relationship between the Commonwealth and the States generally, expressed, not the least, in the *Engineers* case.[206] In *Nelson*, he observed that s 92 came into operation only after 'the Commonwealth assumed legislative control on a national basis of the customs', and that this reflected a policy that in relation to trade and commerce, 'Australia should be one country'.[207] Consistent with this view, Isaacs J convinced several other members of the Court in *W & A McArthur v Queensland* to conclude that s 92 binds only the States, leaving the Commonwealth free to regulate interstate trade and commerce pursuant to s 51(i).[208] While the view that s 92 did not bind the Commonwealth did not last,[209] what remained was Isaacs J's insistence that, in effect, s 92 conferred a 'personal right attaching to the individual'.[210] This 'individual right' approach would shape the High Court's interpretation of the freedom conferred by s 92 for several decades thereafter.

## 3 Individual rights theory

The point of the individual rights theory of s 92 is not simply that an individual citizen or a private corporation may rely on the free trade guarantee. For on any view of s 92, if a law is constitutionally invalid for contravention of s 92, then any individual to whom the law purports to apply can rely on s 92 to provide constitutional protection. Rather, the point of the theory is that s 92 protects not just the overall flow of interstate trade conceived in collective or

**203** *R v Smithers; Ex parte Benson* (1912) 16 CLR 99, 118.
**204** See Chapters 3 and 4.
**205** *Ex parte Nelson (No 1)* (1928) 42 CLR 209, 225.
**206** *Amalgamated Society of Engineers v Adelaide Steamship Co Ltd* (1920) 28 CLR 129.
**207** *Ex parte Nelson (No 1)* (1928) 42 CLR 209, 227.
**208** *W & A McArthur v Queensland* (1920) 28 CLR 530, 556–8, 562–3, 569–70; but see 567.
**209** See *James v Commonwealth* (1935) 52 CLR 570, 593, 594, 602–3; contra 586; *James v Commonwealth* [1936] AC 578, 631.
**210** *James v Cowan* (1930) 43 CLR 386, 418.

cumulative terms, but every particular act of interstate trade engaged in by an individual.

### Isaacs: Literalism and nationalism

The roots of the individual rights theory lie, in part, in Isaacs J's commitment to interpreting s 92 literally. In the *Wheat* case,[211] the Court had to consider whether a State law which provided for the compulsory acquisition of wheat was contrary to s 92 because of its effect on interstate trade in wheat. In the course of finding that s 92 did not apply to the acquisition, Isaacs J observed that trade and commerce 'consists of acts not things', and that while the activities that constitute interstate trade are protected, ownership of the goods that are the subject of interstate trade is not.[212] This line of distinction was applied in *W & A McArthur v Queensland* to a State law which set a maximum price for the sale of certain commodities. Knox CJ, Isaacs and Starke JJ reasoned that while s 92 does not prevent the regulation of goods or persons, it does protect the acts which constitute trade, commerce and intercourse, and that the State law could not, therefore, have a constitutionally valid application to the interstate sale of those commodities.[213] In his dissenting judgment in *James v Cowan*, Isaacs J pushed this reasoning a step further, finding that a State law for the acquisition of dried fruit contravened s 92 because the law attempted to do indirectly what it is prohibited by s 92 from doing directly.[214] In his view, the problem was that the State law singled out for acquisition the particular dried fruit that would be used in interstate trade, leaving untouched fruit that was expected to be used in local consumption or exported overseas.[215] To this end, drawing on the proposition that s 92 protects the acts which constitute interstate trade, he proposed that s 92 therefore gives rise to 'a personal right attaching to the individual',[216] which cannot be avoided by indirect means.[217]

### Dixon: Criterion of operation

Dixon J developed a sophisticated and highly influential approach to s 92 which drew significantly upon Isaacs J's emphasis on the literal meaning of the section and the conception of freedom of interstate trade as a personal right. In a dissenting judgment in *O Gilpin Ltd v Commissioner for Road Transport and Tramways (NSW)*, Dixon J seemed to suggest three basic criteria:

1. The act or transaction to be protected must *form part of* trade, commerce or intercourse among the States.

**211** *New South Wales v Commonwealth* (1915) 20 CLR 54.
**212** Ibid, 100.
**213** *W & A McArthur v Queensland* (1920) 28 CLR 530, 550.
**214** *James v Cowan* (1930) 43 CLR 386, 421.
**215** Ibid, 415.
**216** Ibid, 418.
**217** On appeal to the Privy Council, Isaacs J's dissenting judgment was affirmed on the basis that the objective of the State law was to interfere with interstate trade: *James v Cowan* [1932] AC 542; (1932) 47 CLR 386, 397.

2. The interference, restriction or burden placed on such acts or transactions must be *on account of* the act or transaction's character as being a part of interstate trade, commerce or intercourse.
3. The interference, restriction or burden must be of a kind which constitutes an impairment of the *conception of freedom* protected by s 92.[218]

In explanation of the first criterion, Dixon J proposed that an act or transaction will form part of interstate trade, commerce or intercourse if it is something done as preparatory to, in the course of, or as a result of the interstate movement of things, persons or communications. In his view, the use of vehicles to transport goods from one State to another for commercial purposes clearly met this criterion. In relation to the second, Dixon J explained that some acts or transactions which form part of interstate trade, commerce or intercourse may nonetheless be regulated 'for causes which have no relation or relevance' to interstate trade. However, if a restriction is conditioned on '*any one* of the characteristics' connoted by the concept of 'trade commerce and intercourse among the States', then the criterion will be satisfied. In other words, the criterion is satisfied if a restriction is placed upon interstate trade and commerce even if it applies to other kinds of trade and commerce as well. Accordingly, it is sufficient that the law places a restriction on an act because it is trade, or commerce, or intercourse, or because it involves movement of things or persons into or out of a State. Finally, in explanation of the third criterion, Dixon J pointed out that not every regulation of interstate trade will involve an impairment of the freedom protected by s 92. He gave traffic regulations, road tolls, safety requirements and laws against fraudulent trading as examples.[219]

Applying this approach to the facts of the case, Dixon J observed that the State law authorised the imposition of a charge on the use of unlicensed vehicles to carry goods for purposes of sale. The law plainly applied to an activity that formed part of interstate trade. Further, the law used, as its criterion of operation, the commercial or trading purpose for which the carriage of the goods was being undertaken. Adopting, without quoting, Isaacs J's view of the matter, Dixon J went on to maintain that the trade, commerce and intercourse protected by s 92 describes 'the activities of individuals', and that the purpose of s 92 is to 'enable individuals' to engage in commercial dealings and personal intercourse 'independently of State boundaries'. The interstate trade that it protects is therefore to be regarded distributively, not as a consolidated whole, and it protects against both direct and indirect interferences.[220] For Dixon J, it was accordingly significant that the State law was imposed directly on the trader in respect of the transportation of his own goods intended for the interstate market. These

**218** This is an interpretive simplification. For Dixon J's own exposition, see *O Gilpin Ltd v Commissioner for Road Transport & Tramways (NSW)* (1935) 52 CLR 189, 204–6.
**219** Ibid, 204–6 (emphasis added). See also *Hospital Provident Fund Pty Ltd v Victoria* (1953) 87 CLR 1, 17; *Samuels v Readers' Digest Association Pty Ltd* (1969) 120 CLR 1, 30.
**220** *O Gilpin Ltd v Commissioner for Road Transport and Tramways (NSW)* (1935) 52 CLR 189, 211.

factors distinguished the case from previous ones and led him to the conclusion that the law contravened s 92.

Although his particular view was initially a dissentient one, in time Dixon J's approach to s 92 came to dominate the Court. The most striking application of the individual rights approach came in the *Australian National Airways* and *Bank Nationalisation* cases, both of which involved attempts by the Commonwealth to confer exclusive rights to provide certain kinds of commercial services by a government owned and controlled corporation.[221] In both cases, the attempt to grant the monopoly was struck down as contrary to s 92. As Williams J put it in *Australian National Airways*, because s 92 protects the personal right of the individual to engage in interstate trade and commerce, the attempt by the Commonwealth to prohibit an individual from engaging in the business of interstate air carriage was a 'direct negation of that right' and therefore unconstitutional.[222] Rich and Williams JJ reasoned similarly in *Bank Nationalisation*: the personal right to engage in interstate trade is contravened by a law that prevents a banker from carrying on business in more than one State.[223] In *Australian National Airways* the law was directed only to interstate trade, whereas in *Bank Nationalisation* the law was directed to both interstate and intrastate trade; but it was held in the latter case that this was not material – what mattered was that interstate trade was prohibited.[224]

There remained, however, limits. In its judgment largely endorsing the decision and approach of the High Court in *Bank Nationalisation*,[225] the Privy Council observed that certain reservations and qualifications concerning the 'absoluteness' of s 92 remained necessary. As members of the High Court had frequently observed, the kind of 'freedom' established by s 92 is freedom 'in a community regulated by law'. Thus, although s 92 protects the freedom of individuals, the Privy Council acknowledged that certain restrictions on individual action can be justified through the application of a series of distinctions,[226] such as those between 'prohibition' and 'regulation' of interstate trade,[227] between the 'essence' and 'incidents' of interstate trade,[228] between 'direct and immediate' and 'indirect and remote' interference,[229] and between matters 'antecedent', 'incidental', 'ancilliary' or 'subsequent' to the activity of interstate trade.[230]

**221** *Australian National Airways Pty Ltd v Commonwealth* (1945) 71 CLR 29; *Bank of New South Wales v Commonwealth* (1948) 76 CLR 1; *Commonwealth v Bank of New South Wales* [1950] AC 235.
**222** *Australian National Airways Pty Ltd v Commonwealth* (1945) 71 CLR 29, 110.
**223** *Bank of New South Wales v Commonwealth* (1948) 76 CLR 1, 283–4, 287, 291.
**224** Ibid, 290–91; *Commonwealth v Bank of New South Wales* [1950] AC 235, 311.
**225** Strictly speaking, the Privy Council found that it did not have jurisdiction as the matter involved 'inter se' questions in respect of which the High Court had not given its certificate (see s 73). Its observations were therefore highly authoritative *obiter dicta*.
**226** *Commonwealth v Bank of New South Wales* [1950] AC 235, 309–13.
**227** *Milk Board (NSW) v Metropolitan Cream Pty Ltd* (1939) 62 CLR 116, 127.
**228** *Hospital Provident Fund Pty Ltd v Victoria* (1953) 87 CLR 1, 17–18.
**229** *Commonwealth v Bank of New South Wales* [1950] AC 235, 312.
**230** *Wragg v New South Wales* (1953) 88 CLR 353, 386, 397; *Grannall v Marrickville Margarine Pty Ltd* (1955) 93 CLR 55, 79.

### Barwick: Practical economic consequences

Sir Garfield Barwick was also a strong supporter of the individual rights theory of s 92. However, he was inclined to press its effective reach beyond cases where the legal effect of a law was to interfere with an element of interstate trade to cases where the interference was constituted by the practical commercial or economic consequences of the law. He also endeavoured to limit the scope of the various qualifying doctrines that had been developed by the Court. He supported the application of s 92 to acts that were either 'preparatory' or 'antecedent' to interstate trade, and he sought to narrow the scope of permissible 'regulation'. While he was not successful in convincing the Court in relation to the protection of antecedent activities, such as the production of goods prior to their use in interstate trade,[231] he was able to convince a majority that 'the first sale across the border' either formed a part of interstate trade or was 'an inseparable concomitant consequence' of that trade.[232]

Significantly, Barwick CJ supported an extended reach for s 92 by appealing to the 'national' character of the free trade guarantee. In his dissenting judgment in the *Readers' Digest* case, he argued that it was in recognition of the vital importance of interstate free trade that the framers used such 'sweeping and absolute language' in s 92.[233] Repeating a familiar theme in his jurisprudence, he insisted that Australia is not a 'federation of separate and distinct peoples', and thus s 92 is directed to securing what he called 'freedom of national trade', understood as a 'peculiar advantage' enjoyed by 'all Australians' wherever they may happen to reside. This did not mean that the freedom is without legal regulation. As he put it, s 92 does not create a freedom *from* something, but is rather a freedom *of* trade, and therefore a freedom *to* trade. Moreover, it is freedom in a 'civilized society', rather than an 'unbridled licence in a lawless state'. Accordingly, the limitations on s 92 are to be found, not external to the concept, but in the concept of freedom itself. Furthermore, the Court is to apply 'the constitutional provision' itself, and not allow 'tests or formulae' to 'rise above' or 'qualify' the text.[234]

### Dissenting and divergent voices

Despite its strong support from leading judges such as Isaacs, Dixon and Barwick, the individual rights theory never quite commanded the support of all members of the Court. Evatt J maintained that the purpose of s 92 is to protect 'the free flow of goods inter-State' understood as a whole, rather than 'each and every one' of the 'infinite number of acts, transactions and operations' which occur in the course of interstate trade, commerce and intercourse.[235]

**231** *Damjanovic & Sons Pty Ltd v Commonwealth* (1968) 117 CLR 390, 398, 405, following *Grannall v Marrickville Margarine Pty Ltd* (1955) 93 CLR 55.
**232** *SOS (Mowbray) Pty Ltd v Mead* (1972) 124 CLR 529, 543–4; *North Eastern Dairy Co Ltd v Dairy Industry Authority of NSW* (1975) 134 CLR 559, 582, 599–600, 605–6, 629.
**233** *Samuels v Readers' Digest Association Pty Ltd* (1969) 120 CLR 1, 14.
**234** Ibid, 14–15.
**235** *R v Vizzard; Ex parte Hill* (1933) 50 CLR 30, 86–7.

Murphy J insisted that s 92 applied only to 'discriminatory fiscal burdens' and ought not to be understood as guaranteeing a philosophy of economic laissez-faire or what he called 'economic anarchy'.[236]

In *Clark King & Co v Australian Wheat Board*,[237] a majority upheld legislation enabling the Australian Wheat Board to compulsorily acquire all wheat and to exercise a monopoly over the marketing of wheat throughout Australia and overseas. The scenario was thus comparable to the *Bank Nationalisation* and *Australian National Airways* cases, but Mason and Jacobs JJ found that the scheme was the only practical and reasonable means by which the wheat trade could be regulated, drawing on qualifications the Privy Council had proposed in the *Bank Nationalisation* case.[238] They were joined by Murphy J on the basis of his much narrower reading of s 92, whereas Barwick CJ and Stephen J dissented. This meant there was no clear ratio in the case. When the same issues arose again in *Uebergang v Australian Wheat Board*, an even greater variety of approaches emerged, with Barwick CJ and Aickin J saying that the scheme was clearly invalid, Murphy J saying it was clearly valid, and Gibbs and Wilson JJ and Stephen and Mason JJ proposing different tests to be applied in determining whether the legislation could be justified.[239] These differences of opinion continued to be manifest in *Miller v TCN Channel Nine Pty Ltd*,[240] a case which involved a Commonwealth law that prohibited the unauthorised establishment, erection, maintenance and use of a television transmitter. While a clear majority of six judges held that s 92 did not apply to the *establishment* and *erection* of such a transmitting station because these were acts antecedent to interstate trade and commerce, a different and smaller majority of four judges held that s 92 did protect its *use*, while a yet different, but still close majority of four judges considered that it did not protect its *maintenance*.

Thus, as more and more cases were decided, the divergent opinions and approaches of the justices became increasingly apparent. As early as 1930, Rich J described the vexing task of the Court as having to 'explain the elliptical and expound the unexpressed', an undertaking which he described as 'the impossible task of supplying an exclusive and inclusive definition of a conception to be discovered only in the silences of the Constitution'.[241] At his retirement, Sir John Latham called for a rethinking of the Court's approach to s 92, famously exclaiming: 'When I die, section 92 will be found written on my heart'.[242] Sir Robert Garran wrote that he could well imagine 'a law student approaching the study of [s 92] for the first time... the student closes his notebook, sells all his

**236** *Buck v Bavone* (1976) 135 CLR 110, 132, 136; *Finemores Transport v New South Wales* (1978) 139 CLR 338, 356–7.
**237** *Clark King & Co v Australian Wheat Board* (1978) 140 CLR 120.
**238** Ibid, 186, citing *Commonwealth v Bank of New South Wales* [1950] AC 235, 311; (1949) 79 CLR 497, 640–41.
**239** *Uebergang v Australian Wheat Board* (1982) 145 CLR 266, 295, 300–01, 306, 307–9, 312, 326.
**240** (1986) 161 CLR 556.
**241** *James v Cowan* (1930) 43 CLR 386, 422–4.
**242** (1952) 85 CLR xii, ix.

law books, and resolves to take up some easy study, like nuclear physics or higher mathematics'.[243] By the time of *Miller*, Deane J exclaimed:

> [I]t is as if many voices of authority have been speaking differently at the same time with the result that, putting to one side some basic propositions, it is all but impossible to comprehend precisely what it is that authority has said.[244]

In the view of Mason J, the individual rights theory drew 'too heavily on the laissez-faire notions of political economy prevailing in 1900'. In such a state of confusion it was time to undertake 'a fundamental re-examination'.[245]

## 4 Free trade theory

It was in this context that the High Court decided *Cole v Whitfield*,[246] an extraordinary unanimous decision in which the Court abandoned the individual rights approach. Instead the Court adopted a 'free trade' theory of s 92 in which its purpose is understood to be to prevent the States from implementing protectionist policies. The case involved s 9 of the *Fisheries Act 1959* (Tas), which empowered the State Governor to make regulations prohibiting possession or control of undersized fish. Under the *Sea Fisheries Regulations 1962* (Tas), reg 31(1)(d) prohibited any person from taking, buying, selling, offering or exposing for sale or having possession or control of crayfish below a minimum carapace length of 105 mm for females and 110 mm for males. The intention of the law was to maintain a sufficient breeding stock of crayfish in Tasmanian waters. Whitfield was charged with possessing undersized crayfish which he had imported from South Australia and intended to sell throughout Australia and overseas. The legal size of crayfish under South Australian law was 98.55 mm, because its warmer waters enabled them to reproduce at a younger age.

### Historical basis for the theory

The Court began its reasoning by observing that no other provision of the Constitution had been 'the source of greater judicial concern or the subject of greater judicial effort', and yet 'judicial exegesis of the section has yielded neither clarity of meaning nor certainty of operation'.[247] While Dixon J's criterion of operation test did for some time command wide acceptance, it no longer did so, not least because it attended only to the formal legal character of a law and not its substantive or practical effect.[248] A re-examination of the provision was therefore thought necessary, and to do so, the Court took the remarkable step, contrary to

**243** Robert Garran, *Prosper the Commonwealth* (Angus and Robertson, 1958), 413–15.
**244** *Miller v TCN Channel Nine Pty Ltd* (1986) 161 CLR 556, 616.
**245** Ibid, 571.
**246** *Cole v Whitfield* (1988) 165 CLR 360.
**247** Ibid, 383–4.
**248** Ibid, 384.

its past practice,[249] of deliberately consulting the history of the making of s 92. As the Court explained, it did this:

> not for the purpose of substituting for the meaning of the words used the scope and effect – if such could be established – which the founding fathers subjectively intended the section to have, but for the purpose of identifying the contemporary meaning of language used, the subject to which that language was directed and the nature and objectives of the movement towards federation from which the compact of the Constitution finally emerged.[250]

For the Court, this allowed an examination of various primary sources, such as the convention debates and contemporary legislation, cases, reports and accounts of events, as well as secondary materials, such as the writings of professional historians.

From these historical sources, the Court derived several important propositions. One was that a central problem of federation had been to formulate a basis upon which 'intercolonial free trade within a uniform external tariff' might be established, and to do so in a way that would conciliate the divided supporters of protection and free trade.[251] Another conclusion was that the 'intercourse' aspect of the freedom had been conceived, from the outset, as something distinct from 'trade and commerce', making it possible to adopt different conceptions of the content of the 'freedom' guaranteed to each.[252]

At a critical point in the historical survey, the Court also noted the decision of the Convention of 1897–8 to substitute 'between the States' for 'throughout the Commonwealth'. From this it drew the conclusion that the intention was to 'ensure that the guarantee to be given by s 92 did not extend beyond interstate free trade' and thus to allow the States and the Commonwealth, as John Cockburn put it, to 'impose such restrictions and regulations of trade throughout the Commonwealth as may, from time to time, in the interests of the people, appear to be necessary'.[253] Given, as the Court recognised, that proposals of O'Connor, Barton and Isaacs to qualify the scope of the freedom were rejected by the Convention,[254] this shift in the language of s 92 provided the only textual basis for inferring a narrower interpretation. However, as noted earlier, the language adopted by the Convention later reverted to 'among the States', implying a wider meaning than 'between', and suggesting that the provision was understood to guarantee something more than just 'freedom at the frontier'.[255]

Nonetheless, according to the Court, the 'clear' purpose of s 92 was to ensure the 'free movement of people, goods and communications across State

**249** The past practice had restricted the Court to examining the successive drafts of the Constitution: see *Tasmania v Commonwealth* (1904) 1 CLR 329.
**250** *Cole v Whitfield* (1988) 165 CLR 360, 385. However, for references to what appear to be actual historical 'intentions' as to the intended 'purpose' and 'effect' of s 92, see: 389, 391, 403.
**251** Ibid, 386–7.
**252** Ibid, 387–8; see also 393–4.
**253** Ibid, 390, citing *Convention Debates, Melbourne* (1898) 1020.
**254** Ibid, 389–91, citing *Convention Debates, Adelaide* (1897) 1141; *Convention Debates, Sydney* (1897) 1064, 1041); *Convention Debates, Melbourne* (1898) 1017, 1020, 2373.
**255** See *Cole v Whitfield* (1988) 165 CLR 360, 374, 390, 397, 409.

boundaries'.[256] The prevailing concept of 'free trade', it was argued, was understood at the time to mean the absence of border taxes, discriminatory transportation charges (such as railway freight rates) and preferences.[257] The problem was that s 92 operated also 'as a rallying call for federationists', so that, although the goal was 'to be rid of discriminatory burdens and benefits in trade', there was resistance to any suggestion that this 'be muffled by nice qualifications'. Thus the unenviable task of construing the unexpressed fell to the courts, resulting in a great variety of approaches and many differences of opinion.[258] In this context, what mattered was how free trade was commonly understood in the nineteenth century. In the Court's view, it meant the absence of 'protection of domestic industries against foreign competition', whether by tariffs, non-tariff barriers such as quotas, differential railway rates, subsidies on goods or discriminatory burdens on dealings with imports. The Court therefore concluded: s 92 protects trade and commerce from 'discriminatory burdens of a protectionist kind', meaning burdens that have 'a protectionist purpose or effect'.[259]

The idea of a 'discriminatory burden of a protectionist kind' was presented by the Court as a compound conception, although it also suggested a threefold analysis: (a) is there a burden; (b) is it discriminatory; and (c) does it have an protectionist effect?[260] The concept of discrimination, the Court explained, necessarily embraces both the legal operation of the law considered on its face and the factual effect of the law in its practical operation.[261] To confer a protectionist effect, the Court explained, is to give domestic products a competitive or market advantage over other products of the same kind.[262] Applied to the facts in the case, the law plainly imposed a burden on interstate trade in crayfish, but it just as plainly did not do so in a way that was relevantly discriminatory *on its face*, because the law applied to Tasmanian and South Australian crayfish without distinction. (To use the old terminology, its criterion of operation did not single out crayfish from other States.) However, this left open the possibility that the law was discriminatory and protectionist *in effect*. Here the Court acknowledged that questions of fact and degree were raised, upon which minds might reasonably differ. And on this point, the Court seemed to equivocate, maintaining that the legislation did not confer a competitive or market advantage on the Tasmanian industry, but that even if it did, the prohibition on the sale and possession of undersized crayfish was a 'necessary means' of securing the legitimate objective of preventing them from being caught in Tasmanian waters, in order to maintain sufficient breeding stock. For there was no way of distinguishing between Tasmanian and South Australian crayfish by merely inspecting them.[263] For these reasons, the law was therefore upheld.

**256** Ibid, 391.
**257** Ibid.
**258** Ibid, 392.
**259** Ibid, 393–5, 404.
**260** Ibid, 399, 407–8.
**261** Ibid, 399–400.
**262** Ibid, 394, 407, 409.
**263** Ibid, 408–9. But see *Castlemaine Tooheys Ltd v South Australia* (1990) 169 CLR 436, 467–8, 471.

### Differences in application

*Cole v Whitfield* is one of the most significant decisions ever brought down by the High Court. However, as the Court acknowledged, the new method would inevitably bring 'a new array of questions in its wake'.[264] The promise of the new approach was that it would avoid the problems of uncertainty and confusion that had previously existed. But has the case actually had this effect? Even within the decision itself there was, as noted, a certain reticence in the conclusion that the law did not have a protectionist effect. There was good reason for this hesitation, because it was possible to argue that the Tasmanian law had the protectionist effect of nullifying the natural competitive advantage that South Australian crayfisheries enjoyed by reason of their warmer waters and more effective breeding stocks – conditions which enabled smaller crayfish to be caught in a sustainable way. To the extent that such arguments were available in a case such as this, it may be asked whether the protectionist test will prove, over the long run, to be quite as conclusive as its proponents might have hoped.

Certainly, *Bath v Alston Holdings*,[265] decided in the very same year, revealed a Court closely divided over the application of the *Cole* test. The case involved a Victorian law that imposed a differential fee for the issue of a licence to sell tobacco at a retail level, depending on whether the tobacco had been purchased from a Victorian wholesaler or not. The law plainly discriminated on its face, because the retail licence fee was calculated as the sum of a flat fee ($10 per month or $50 for an indefinite period) plus an *ad valorem* fee of 25 per cent of the value of tobacco products sold in the relevant period, unless the tobacco was purchased from the holder of a Victorian wholesaler's licence. However, the law also imposed a similar licence fee for Victorian wholesalers, calculated at the same *ad valorem* rate. The general policy of the law was thus to impose a licence fee, having an effect similar to a 25 per cent indirect tax,[266] on the sale of tobacco products in Victoria, which for ease of administration was imposed primarily at a wholesale level, but at a retail level where the tobacco was sourced from out of State. Did such a scheme impose a discriminatory burden of a protectionist kind?

A majority of Mason CJ, Brennan, Deane and Gaudron JJ held that the law contravened s 92. Focusing first on the retail licence fee, they considered that it was not only facially discriminatory, but that it also had a practical effect that was protectionist because it sheltered local tobacco wholesalers and their products from the competition of out-of-State wholesalers, whose products might well be cheaper in another Australian market because they were not subject to wholesale licence fees at all, or were but at a lower rate.[267] Secondly, even

**264** *Cole v Whitfield* (1988) 165 CLR 360, 408.
**265** (1988) 165 CLR 411.
**266** The fees avoided invalidity as 'excise duties' pursuant to s 90 of the Constitution by reason of their character as licence fees rather than taxes on goods. *Bath* was decided before *Ha v New South Wales* (1997) 189 CLR 465, which significantly reduced the capacity of the States to raise revenue in a manner that avoids the prohibition in s 90.
**267** *Bath v Alston Holdings Pty Ltd* (1988) 165 CLR 411, 425.

taking into account the Victorian wholesale licence fee, the majority still considered the retail licence fee to be discriminatory and protectionist. Their reasoning was as follows. If out-of-State wholesalers pay a licence fee equal to or higher than the Victorian wholesale fee, then the out-of-State wholesalers will be placed at a competitive disadvantage that will probably exclude them from the Victorian market, for their tobacco products will bear the burden of both the out-of-State and the Victorian wholesale licence fee. If, on the other hand, out-of-State wholesalers pay lower taxes or fees than Victorian wholesalers, the Victorian law will still protect the Victorian wholesalers from the competition of out-of-State wholesalers operating with a lower cost structure. On either analysis, there will be a protectionist effect.[268]

In their dissenting judgment, Wilson, Dawson and Toohey JJ considered the approach adopted by the majority to depend on an incomplete picture which overlooked the fact that interstate wholesalers were not subject to fees under the Victorian Act and could sell products to Victorian retailers at prices which reflected the absence of the Victorian fee. The law did not seek to give an advantage or a disadvantage to the retailer according to whether tobacco was obtained inside or outside the State. On their view, the rationale for the scheme of the Victorian Act was to impose the fee on all tobacco sold in Victoria, but to do so in a way that directed the tax to wholesalers wherever possible in order to make the administration of the scheme easier.[269]

On reflection, it is difficult to avoid the conclusion that the minority disagreed with the majority because they regarded the scheme of the Act as a whole to be a reasonable means of achieving a legitimate objective. But if so, what distinguished the two points of view? In *Castlemaine Tooheys v South Australia*, the next case to consider s 92 under the *Cole v Whitfield* test, it was suggested that the difference 'flowed more from disagreement about the appropriate perspective from which the particular legislative provisions should be viewed than from any disagreement about principle'.[270]

*Castlemaine Tooheys* involved provisions of the *Beverage Container Act 1975* (SA) which established a deposit and return system for beverage containers within the State. As enacted in 1975, the Act imposed a 5 cent deposit per bottle that was refundable upon return, except that Regulations made under the Act created an exemption from the deposit requirement for refillable bottles. Glass bottles could be returned for refund to a retailer who sold beverages in containers of that type, and other kinds of containers could be returned to a collection depot. Brewing companies manufacturing or selling their products in South Australia had to adjust their practices to these rules. Thus, South Australian and Victorian companies adopted the practice of selling most of their beer in refillable containers. However, the Bond group of companies, operating out

**268** Ibid, 426.
**269** Ibid, 432.
**270** (1990) 169 CLR 436, 468. See also *Sportsbet Pty Ltd v New South Wales* (2012) 249 CLR 298, 319.

of Western Australia, Queensland and New South Wales, continued to supply their beer in non-refillable bottles. Under the original regime this did not make a practical difference, for the evidence was that the original deposit and return requirement did not place the Bond companies at a competitive disadvantage compared to South Australian breweries.

In January 1986, the Bond group began a vigorous marketing campaign in South Australia and increased its market share from less than 0.1 per cent to 4 per cent at the expense of the leading South Australian brewer. Whether or not deliberately in response to this development, later that year substantial amendments were made to the Act and new Regulations came into force. The new scheme increased the refundable deposits to 15 cents per non-refillable beer and low-alcohol wine container while imposing only a 4 cent deposit for refillable beer containers. Significantly, it was acknowledged that an initial deposit of 6 cents for non-refillable bottles for twelve months, and 4 cents thereafter, would have been sufficient to ensure return of non-refillable bottles at the same rate as refillable bottles.[271] The collection and refund regime was also changed so that retailers were required to collect and pay the required refund on returns of non-refillable containers, while only refillable containers could be returned at public collection depots. This gave a retailer an incentive not to stock beers sold in non-refillable containers, especially if sales were low, for the retailer was required to accept the return of, and pay a refund for, any non-refillable bottles even if they were purchased from another retailer.

The Bond group argued that the new scheme imposed a discriminatory burden that had a protectionist effect by making it uneconomical for it to continue to compete in the South Australian market. The new 15 cent deposit raised Bond's effective 'bottle cost' from 16 cents to 26 cents per bottle, compared with South Australian Brewing's bottle cost of 16.65 cents. It was also uneconomic for the Bond group to convert its interstate plants to use refillable bottles. South Australia's main line of response to this argument was that the amendments pursued the legitimate objectives of litter control and conservation of energy and resources by encouraging return of non-glass and non-refillable containers, and by discouraging use of non-refillable containers through the higher deposits and the retail collection requirement.

The Court unanimously held that the law contravened s 92. In their joint judgment, Mason CJ, Brennan, Deane, Dawson and Toohey JJ recognised that while the law did not discriminate on its face, and while it appeared to be directed to securing legitimate objectives, its practical effect was to prevent the Bond group of companies from achieving a larger share of the beer market in South Australia, which was a protectionist effect.[272] As such, they characterised the case as involving a law that, on its face, was apt to secure a legitimate objective but the effect of which was to impose a discriminatory burden on interstate

**271** *Castlemaine Tooheys Ltd v South Australia* (1990) 169 CLR 436, 462.
**272** Ibid, 464.

trade. In such a case, they considered it relevant to consider whether there was an alternative non-discriminatory means of securing the objective and whether the burden placed on interstate trade was proportionate (ie, whether the burden was merely 'incidental' to achieving the legitimate objective).[273] In this respect, their underlying concern seems to have been to affirm the power of the States to enact legislation for the 'well-being' of their people in conformity with s 92, without undue intrusion by the courts into legislative decisions that have to be made in the context of a whole array of political considerations. In order to ensure that the immunity conferred by s 92 is not extended 'beyond all reason', the justices therefore affirmed that State laws may regulate interstate trade to the extent 'necessary or appropriate and adapted' to securing a legitimate objective.[274]

However, for a range of reasons, the various features of the law could not be justified on these grounds. For example, the admitted fact that a much smaller deposit would have been sufficient to ensure an adequate rate of return suggested that an alternative, non-protectionist means was available to achieve the objective. Moreover, the requirement that retailers would have to administer the return of the beverage containers seemed to have no rational connection with the objective of securing an adequate rate of returns. Further, there could be no way that the measures would help to preserve the State's finite energy resources because the Bond brewing companies used bottles manufactured outside the State. In sum, neither aspect of the scheme was merely incidental to the achievement of a legitimate objective, but rather the scheme imposed a disproportionate burden on interstate trade.[275] In addition, their Honours considered it did not matter whether the discrimination was 'directed at, or sustained by, all, some or only one of the relevant interstate traders'; all that mattered was that the Bond group were placed under a competitive disadvantage in comparison with their South Australian counterparts.[276]

### Balancing free trade and regulatory goals

The approach adopted by the majority in *Castlemaine Tooheys* required the Court to engage in a 'balancing' exercise in which the burden placed on interstate trade was weighed against the positive benefits of the law. In their separate concurring judgment, Gaudron and McHugh JJ proposed a slightly different and more stringent approach. They seemed to suggest that if a law is protectionist then it will be contrary to s 92, even if the law can be said to be appropriate and adapted to a legitimate objective, provided that there is no relevant difference between the subject matter of the interstate trade and the intrastate trade which justifies the differential treatment that creates the protectionist effect.[277]

**273** Ibid, 472.
**274** Ibid, 472–3.
**275** Ibid, 474–7.
**276** Ibid, 475.
**277** Ibid, 480.

In *Barley Marketing Board v Norman*,[278] the Court had to consider a marketing scheme established in New South Wales for the sale of barley produced in that State. Pursuant to a proclamation made under the relevant Act, the entire State crop was vested in the Barley Marketing Board, freed from prior proprietary and contractual interests in the barley, but with the rights and interests of every person in the commodity converted into a claim for payment out of the proceeds when the barley was sold. In a unanimous judgment, the Court held that there was no contravention of s 92. Although the marketing scheme benefitted State producers by enabling them to sell their barley at higher prices, this was not secured at the disadvantage of their interstate competitors. Likewise, although out-of-State purchasers had to pay higher prices for barley, the same applied to in-State purchasers, so there was no relevant discrimination.[279]

In this last respect, the Court found itself having to consider whether there was a protectionist effect not only for the producers of barley, but also for those who purchased it for the production or manufacture of other goods, such as maltsters who convert barley into malt for use in brewing and distilling. In *Cole v Whitfield*, the Court had indicated that the protectionist effect must concern products of the same kind.[280] In *Barley Marketing Board*, therefore, the Court found it necessary to make clear that relevant protection could occur through a State law that places a burden on the export of a necessary ingredient used by out-of-State manufacturers as a means of protecting manufacturers of the products of the same kind within the State. On this analysis, it would not matter that the necessary ingredient in the manufacturing process might not be of the same kind as the manufactured good itself.[281]

### Assessments of economic effect

The protectionist interpretation of s 92 requires the Court to engage in assessments of the economic effect of an impugned law. The proposition that protection must be directed to goods of the same kind seems to require the Court to consider the question of what economists call 'substitutability' or 'cross-elasticity' of demand, a concept that measures the effect of a change in the price or availability of a particular good on the demand for another good. To take a simple example: imagine a State law that restricts the importation of margarine as a means of protecting its butter industry. Whether this confers a competitive or market advantage seems to depend on the extent to which margarine and butter are 'goods of the same kind'. But how is the Court to apply the test in more complex scenarios, especially since the 'protectionist' approach to s 92 seems to call for an economically rigorous analysis of the facts in any particular case? In a series of recent cases concerning the regulation of online betting exchanges, several of these kinds of issues have been raised.

**278** (1990) 171 CLR 182.
**279** *Barley Marketing Board (NSW) v Norman* (1990) 171 CLR 182, 201–3.
**280** *Cole v Whitfield* (1988) 165 CLR 360, 394, 407, 409.
**281** *Barley Marketing Board (NSW) v Norman* (1990) 171 CLR 182, 204.

A betting exchange provides a means by which persons can bet against each other concerning the outcome of a sporting or other event. The betting exchange operator, unlike a bookmaker, does not personally incur a risk but rather facilitates the making of wagers between its customers, charging an administration fee for the service. State regulated Totalizator Agency Boards (TABs) also provide betting services, but through a system by which moneys are 'invested' into a pool on the basis of predictions of specified outcomes, with the money remaining after deduction of fees being distributed among those 'investors' whose predictions were correct. Betting exchanges are generally able to offer better odds than bookmakers and TABs and, especially in their online form, have successfully secured a very large part of the market for wagering in Australia. The first *Betfair* case,[282] decided in 2008, concerned a Western Australian law which made it an offence for a person to lay a bet through a betting exchange. The law also prohibited the publication of the details of a Western Australian race field without ministerial approval, this information being necessary to enable a betting exchange to offer the opportunity for wagers to be placed on horse races within the State. Betfair operated a betting exchange business under a licence granted under Tasmanian law. It successfully argued that both aspects of the Western Australian law were contrary to s 92.

In a joint judgment delivered by Gleeson CJ, Gummow, Kirby, Hayne, Crennan and Kiefel JJ,[283] their Honours began by affirming that, although it was accepted that *Cole v Whitfield* represented the authoritative source of present doctrine on s 92, it would be an 'error' to understand that case to have represented a 'complete break' with the past, for it had long been recognised that the economic consequences of a law, especially one that was protectionist, were relevant to an assessment of its constitutionality.[284] Highlighting themes that had influenced Isaacs J in the early formulation of the individual rights theory, the joint judgment drew attention to the role of s 92 in the 'creation and fostering of national markets' as a means by which a 'new federal nation' would be created and 'national unity' would be fostered.[285] The judgment also drew attention to the capacity of the internet to enable businesses to provide services to customers 'without regard to geographic boundaries', a development which made it conceptually difficult to focus attention upon the existence of protection and anti-competitive policies within a market defined by State boundaries.[286] Together with the emergence of a National Competition Policy, these developments posed difficulties for the notion that the capacity of the States to enact legislation for the 'well-being' of their people must be maintained. No longer, it seems, are 'the people' to be understood as members of distinct State communities, but rather as mobile individuals engaged from time to time in either 'the

**282** *Betfair Pty Ltd v Western Australia* (2008) 234 CLR 418.
**283** Justice Heydon delivered a separate concurring judgment.
**284** Ibid, 451.
**285** Ibid, 452.
**286** Ibid.

supply side or the demand side of commerce'.[287] Even though *Cole* promoted a return to the history of the Constitution and intentions of the framers, the Court thus now emphasised a conception of the Constitution adapted to new economic conditions.[288] Moreover, according to the joint judgment, although a return to the 'discredited' individual rights theory might be beyond the pale, the meaning of s 92 remained fundamentally 'debatable'.[289] Indeed, the schematic juxtaposition of 'free trade' versus 'protectionism' in *Cole v Whitfield* was said to oversimplify the complexity of the debate at the time that s 92 was drafted.[290]

On grounds such as these, the joint judgment developed an approach to the free trade theory of s 92 which brought it significantly closer, in effect, to the individual rights theory. Invoking without referring to the *Engineers* case, and emphasising the 'peremptory' language of the actual text of s 92, the Court questioned the suggestion in *Castlemaine Tooheys* that the scope and application of s 92 should be influenced by a concern to preserve the power of the States to enact legislation for the well-being of their people.[291] Against the apparent willingness in *Castlemaine Tooheys* to defer to the legislative judgment of the State, the joint judgment proposed and applied a more demanding test of 'reasonable necessity'.[292] Western Australia argued that it had prohibited betting exchanges for three reasons: (a) they do not contribute financially to the racing industry; (b) they allow punters to back a contestant to lose, threatening the integrity of the industry; and (c) their operation entails a loss of revenue to the State. Applying this test to these arguments, it was held that the prohibition was not reasonably necessary to secure these objectives because: (a) Betfair had contributed to racing in Victoria and was willing to do so in Western Australia; (b) a more proportionate means of protecting the integrity of the industry would be to license and regulate betting exchanges, as Tasmania had done; and (c) a loss of State revenue cannot justify protectionism.[293]

One of the recurrent observations in the joint judgment concerned the need to consider both the 'supply' and the 'demand' side of the relevant economic transactions, and the substitutability of goods and services.[294] Such cross-elasticity of demand clearly existed. Betting exchanges, with their lower commission rates, were evidently taking market share from the State TABs and licensed bookmakers. Clearly, the trade was of the 'same kind'.[295] The joint judgment showed that the prohibition on the publishing of the race field information placed Betfair under a competitive disadvantage and gave its competitors a corresponding advantage, while the prohibition on placing bets through a cross-border betting

**287** Ibid, 453.
**288** Ibid, 453–4.
**289** Ibid, 454, 456.
**290** Ibid, 455–6.
**291** Ibid, 473–6.
**292** Ibid, 476–7, citing *North Eastern Dairy Co Ltd v Dairy Industry Authority of NSW* (1975) 134 CLR 559, 608.
**293** *Betfair Pty Ltd v Western Australia* (2008) 234 CLR 418, 478–80.
**294** Ibid, 449, 453, 456, 461, 464, 477.
**295** Ibid, 480–81.

exchange had the same effect even though it applied, on its face, to both out-of-State and in-State wagering operators.[296]

In the second *Betfair* case,[297] the Court was asked to determine whether a NSW law which allowed Betfair access to race field information upon the payment of a fee calculated by reference to the appellant's 'wagering turnover' was contrary to s 92. Because Betfair's betting exchange business model, compared with other forms of betting, involved proportionately higher levels of turnover, Betfair argued that the fee imposed a discriminatory burden of a protectionist kind. The Court unanimously rejected this argument and upheld the NSW law.[298] French CJ, Gummow, Hayne, Crennan and Bell JJ in a joint judgment considered that it was necessary for Betfair to demonstrate that the law imposed a protectionist burden on interstate trade, rather than merely imposed a disproportionate burden on itself in particular. What was necessary was to demonstrate the existence of protection, not just discrimination; but by focusing only on the impact of the fee on its particular business model, Betfair's submissions were tacitly proceeding on the basis of an individual rights conception of s 92.[299] As they explained, the trading activities of a single trader may be representative of a class of activity, but Betfair was, at the time, the only betting exchange provider operating in Australia. As was said in *Castlemaine Tooheys*, s 92 may be contravened when all, some or only one of the relevant traders is affected, but in *Betfair II* the majority maintained that a contravention does not necessarily follow from the effect of a law on the business model adopted by a particular trader.[300] Despite all that was said in *Betfair I*, therefore, it was affirmed that s 92 does not confer an individual right to trade in this sense. The subject matter of s 92 is interstate trade, not traders.[301]

The joint judgment nonetheless considered whether Betfair could show that, in connection with its business model, the law imposed a discriminatory burden that was protectionist in effect. After all, in *Castlemaine Tooheys* the Court had regard to the particular way in which the Bond brewing group of companies had structured their plant operations. In *Castlemaine Tooheys* that analysis showed that it was uneconomical for Bond to adjust in a way that would enable it to secure more than 1 per cent of the market share. All Betfair could show was that the fees would absorb a higher proportion of its turnover than was the case for the TAB, its principal competitor in NSW. But this did not mean that it would suffer a loss of market share.[302]

In separate concurring judgments, Heydon and Kiefel JJ also emphasised the proposition that s 92 protects interstate trade, not persons engaged in trade.[303]

**296** Ibid, 481–2.
**297** *Betfair Pty Ltd v New South Wales* (2012) 249 CLR 217.
**298** A similar conclusion was arrived at in *Sportsbet Pty Ltd v New South Wales* (2012) 249 CLR 298 in relation to the effect of the NSW law on a bookmaker operating in the Northern Territory.
**299** *Betfair Pty Ltd v New South Wales* (2012) 249 CLR 217, [36], [42].
**300** Ibid, [43]–[50].
**301** Ibid, [50].
**302** Ibid, [53]–[56].
**303** Ibid, [60], [68]–[69], [110], [114]–[115].

Where they differed concerned the use of economic evidence and concepts of market competition developed in other areas of law.[304] Heydon J emphasised that while the Constitution has to be applied to new circumstances not anticipated by the framers, the meaning of the text remains stable, and cannot be affected by developments in economics, legislation or judicial doctrine.[305] On the other hand, Kiefel J repeated the point that *Cole v Whitfield* did not constitute a complete break with the past and noted the acknowledgment in that case that the words 'absolutely free' and 'intercourse' in s 92 arguably give the section a wider operation than merely prohibiting protectionist burdens.[306] Although the facts of the case did not raise the issue for decision, she drew attention to a question that might one day confront the Court, namely whether a lessening of competition within a market that operates without any reference to State borders might contravene s 92.[307]

## 5 Personal intercourse

The interpretation of the 'trade and commerce' aspect of s 92, after a period of stability following *Cole v Whitfield*, now seems with the *Betfair* cases to have entered a new stage of development, even if only in the form of a necessary adjustment of the free trade theory to the new circumstances of an electronic economy operating not only nationally, but also globally. Compared to 'trade and commerce', the 'intercourse' aspect of s 92 has received much less consideration, and the interpretation that it has received as been relatively more stable. What has changed, rather, is the way in which members of the Court have understood the relationship between the two aspects. In *Smithers*, as has been seen, Isaacs J considered that while the intercourse limb must add something to the meaning of trade and commerce, all of the aspects of s 92 convey a 'personal right' that is 'absolute', including 'freedom of transit and access for persons and property' across State borders.[308] Consistently with this, in *Gratwick v Johnson* the Court struck down an order purportedly issued under the defence power (s 51(vi)) which prohibited any person other than on military service from travelling interstate without a permit.[309] Intrinsic to the reasoning of all members of the Court was the view that the basal consideration, when determining whether s 92 is contravened, is the same whether interstate trade and commerce or intercourse is involved.[310]

In *Cole v Whitfield* the Court broke this connection between the two aspects of s 92. Part of the reason was that the 'free trade' theory on which *Cole v Whitfield* rested could have no operation in relation to the intercourse limb unless

**304** Ibid, [63], [65], [116]–[118], [120], [123].
**305** Ibid, [64].
**306** Ibid, [105], [125].
**307** Ibid, [127]; see also the joint judgment at [57].
**308** *R v Smithers; Ex parte Benson* (1912) 16 CLR 99, 113–14, 117.
**309** *Gratwick v Johnson* (1945) 70 CLR 1.
**310** Ibid, 13–15, 16, 17–19, 19–20, 21–2.

its scope were to be confined to the movement of persons in connection with trade and commerce, but authority and common sense suggested that intercourse must mean at least something independent of trade and commerce.[311] Of course, many interstate trading activities do involve the transportation of both goods and persons, and can therefore be characterised as concerning both trade and intercourse. Moreover, restraints on the movement of individuals can have very significant economic effects in themselves; indeed, such restraints may even have a protectionist effect where they hinder the availability of the labour needed for some productive enterprise across a State border. However, the case law after *Cole v Whitfield* has persisted with the notion that the intercourse aspect of s 92 must be interpreted separately from trade and commerce, at least to the extent necessary to protect the integrity of the free trade interpretation. As Kiefel J indicated in *Betfair II*, the two main textual challenges to the free trade interpretation are the inclusion of the intercourse limb and the 'absoluteness' of the freedoms protected by s 92. For, on its face, s 92 applies the *same* standard to trade, commerce and intercourse among the States: all three must be 'absolutely free'.[312]

Most of the recent cases that have dealt with interstate intercourse have involved the implied freedom of political communication said to be necessarily implied by the constitutional system of representative government.[313] This is because interstate intercourse has long been understood to include not only the movement of persons, but also communication between persons across state boundaries.[314] Thus, the *Miller* case, in addition to the s 92 issue, also involved the question whether the regulation of the use of transmitting stations to broadcast television programs was protected by a guarantee of freedom of political communication.[315] In that case, all members of the Court except Murphy J rejected this argument. Dawson J observed that although some support for the argument could be derived from statements of Griffith CJ and Barton J in *Smithers*, Isaacs and Higgins JJ had concluded that the intercourse aspect of s 92 expressly covered the issue raised in that case.[316] Six years after *Miller* was decided, however, the implied freedom of political communication was again put in argument and was accepted by a majority of the Court. In those cases, and several that followed them, arguments were advanced based on both the intercourse limb of s 92 and the implied freedom of political communication.

The general position articulated in the recent cases is that if a law is enacted for the primary purpose of burdening interstate intercourse (as in *Gratwick v Johnson*), then it will almost certainly be invalid; whereas if it is directed to some other legitimate objective, and adopts means that are appropriate and

**311** Compare *Cole v Whitfield* (1988) 165 CLR 360, 387–8, 393–4.
**312** *Betfair Pty Ltd v New South Wales* (2012) 249 CLR 217, [105], [125].
**313** See Part V below.
**314** See, eg, *Bank of New South Wales v Commonwealth (Bank Nationalisation)* (1948) 76 CLR 1, 381.
**315** *Miller v TCN Channel Nine Pty Ltd* (1986) 161 CLR 556, 579, 592, 615, 636–7; but see 583–4.
**316** Ibid, 636–7. The other members of the majority reasoned similarly in this respect: 569, 579, 592, 615, 625–6.

adapted to achieving that purpose, thus only incidentally burdening interstate intercourse, then it will be valid.[317] Such legitimate objectives appear to include such things as the maintenance of road safety, the apprehension of fugitives, and the control of the distribution of dangerous, infectious or noxious goods.[318] In developing these principles and approaches, some justices, like Brennan and McHugh JJ, have related their interpretation of the intercourse limb to the reasoning that had been adopted prior to *Cole v Whitfield* in relation to the idea of the 'permissible regulation of trade'.[319] Indeed, Dawson J went so far as to say that while the trade and commerce aspect might be informed by the history and context of the provision, the intercourse limb is best informed by the language of s 92 itself.[320] Others, like Mason CJ, Deane and Toohey JJ, related their interpretation of the intercourse limb primarily to specific observations about it in *Cole v Whitfield*,[321] albeit observing that the Court had there affirmed that the intercourse limb extends to a 'guarantee of personal freedom'.[322] Moreover, among the justices there are some who have limited the scope of the intercourse limb to only certain kinds of burdens on interstate intercourse, such as those imposed by laws that treat the crossing of a State border as the criterion of operation for the law (ie, laws that treat State borders themselves as barriers to movement);[323] whereas others appear to have assumed that a burden on interstate intercourse will be caught by s 92 unless it can be justified as proportionate to some other legitimate objective.[324] Lying behind these differences is a tension between treating the intercourse limb as guaranteeing an individual right and interpreting it in fundamentally federal terms as being about equality of treatment of interstate and intrastate intercourse and communication.[325]

In *AMS v AIF*,[326] the Court had to consider the application of the intercourse limb to a court order made under the *Family Court Act 1975* (WA) which granted a father an injunction restraining the mother from moving with their child from Perth to Darwin without 'compelling reasons' to do so. Movement between a State and a Territory is protected by s 49 of the *Northern Territory (Self-Government) Act 1978* (Cth), which provides that trade, commerce and intercourse between the Territory and the States shall be absolutely free. A majority of the High Court considered that the injunction was not authorised by the

**317** *Nationwide News Pty Ltd v Wills* (1992) 177 CLR 1, 53–60, 81–3; *Australian Capital Television Pty Ltd v Commonwealth* (1992) 177 CLR 106, 194–6; *Cunliffe v Commonwealth* (1994) 182 CLR 272, 307–8, 333, 346–7, 366–7, 384, 392, 395–7.
**318** *Australian Capital Television Pty Ltd v Commonwealth* (1992) 177 CLR 106, 193–4.
**319** *Nationwide News* (1992) 177 CLR 1, 53–60; *Cunliffe* (1994) 182 CLR 272, 395–7.
**320** *Australian Capital Television Pty Ltd v Commonwealth* (1992) 177 CLR 106, 194.
**321** *Nationwide News Pty Ltd v Wills* (1992) 177 CLR 1, 81–4; *Cunliffe v Commonwealth* (1994) 182 CLR 272, 307–8, 346–7, 384.
**322** *Cole v Whitfield* (1988) 165 CLR 360, 393, cited in *Nationwide News Pty Ltd v Wills* (1992) 177 CLR 1, 83.
**323** *Australian Capital Television* (1992) 177 CLR 106, 194; *Nationwide News* (1992) 177 CLR 1, 58–9; *Cunliffe v Commonwealth* (1994) 182 CLR 272, 333, 384; *AMS v AIF* (1999) 199 CLR 160, 192–3, 215.
**324** *Cunliffe v Commonwealth* (1994) 182 CLR 272 (1994) 182 CLR 272, 308, 346, 396.
**325** James Stellios, 'The Intercourse Limb of Section 92 and the High Court's Decision in APLA Ltd v Legal Services Commissioner (NSW)' (2006) 17 *Public Law Review* 10, 12.
**326** (1999) 199 CLR 160.

Act. Gleeson CJ, McHugh and Gummow JJ, with whom Hayne J agreed, made two points about the intercourse limb. The first was that the formulations of principle adopted in the previous cases had, despite their differences, reflected reasoning very similar to that adopted by the Privy Council in the *Bank Nationalisation* case with respect to the idea of 'reasonable regulation'.[327] Secondly, when it came to applying the intercourse limb to the court order, they asked whether the impediment that it imposed was 'greater than that reasonably required to achieve the objects' of the enabling legislation.[328] In the *APLA* case, Gleeson CJ and Heydon J applied this latter test to New South Wales regulations which prohibited certain forms of advertising for the provision of legal services, finding that although they applied to interstate communications, the impediment was not directed at interstate communications and was no greater than reasonably necessary to achieve the goal of regulating the advertising of legal services within the State.[329]

The Court's bifurcated approach to s 92 raises the question of which test is to be applied when a law presents aspects of trade, commerce *and* intercourse. In *Nationwide News*, Deane and Toohey JJ considered that such a conflict could be avoided as a matter of characterisation, by deciding whether the law is properly characterised as a law with respect to interstate trade and commerce *or* interstate intercourse (including communication).[330] In *APLA*, while Gleeson CJ and Heydon J found it unnecessary to resolve the issue, Gummow and Hayne JJ considered that where a law presents the characteristics of both limbs of s 92, then its character as 'trade and commerce' should prevail, and the question will be whether the law imposes a discriminatory burden of a protectionist kind.[331]

## IV Freedom of religion

### 1 The history

The preamble to the *Commonwealth of Australia Constitution Act 1900* (UK) records that the people of the Australian colonies agreed to unite in a federal commonwealth 'humbly relying on the blessing of Almighty God'.[332] When the Constitution was being drafted, several religious groups and denominations had advocated for the recognition of God in the Constitution.[333] Patrick Glynn, an

**327** *AMS v AIF* (1999) 199 CLR 160, 178.
**328** Ibid, 179.
**329** *APLA Ltd v Legal Services Commissioner (NSW)* (2005) 224 CLR 322, 353; see also 394, 461–2.
**330** *Nationwide News Pty Ltd v Wills* (1992) 177 CLR 1, 83–4.
**331** *APLA Ltd v Legal Services Commissioner (NSW)* (2005) 224 CLR 322, 390–92, 458.
**332** The recognition of God and the invocation of divine blessing is not uncommon in modern constitutions. Similar invocations appear in the Irish Constitution (1937), the German Basic Law (1949), the Canadian Charter of Rights and Freedoms (1982), the Constitution of South Africa (1996), and the revised Swiss Constitution (1999).
**333** Richard Ely, *Unto God and Caesar* (Melbourne University Press, 1976) ch 3.

Irish-Catholic delegate from South Australia, was its most articulate supporter. He put the case for a 'simple and unsectarian' acknowledgement of God on the basis that religion is an important source of social cohesion. He said:

> The stamp of religion is fixed upon the front of our institutions, its letter is impressed upon the book of our lives, and... its spirit, weakened though it may be by the opposing forces of the world, still lifts the pulse of the social organism. It is this, not the iron hand of the law, that is the bond of society; it is this that gives unity and tone to the texture of the whole; it is this, that by subduing the domineering impulses and the reckless passions of the heart, turns discord to harmony, and evolves the law of moral progress out of the clashing purposes of life ... .'[334]

Although many of the framers of the Constitution were not as devout as Glynn, a majority eventually supported the recognition of God in the preamble. Some, however, were concerned that this might imply that the Commonwealth had the authority to enact religious laws. If God were to be recognised in the Constitution, H B Higgins argued, 'a large number of good people' would need to be reassured that 'their rights with respect to religion will not be interfered with'.[335] This concern about the effect of the preamble was probably exaggerated, as Edmund Barton and John Quick pointed out,[336] for the preamble could not be used to confer positive legislative power on the Commonwealth. However, the possibility that the Commonwealth's explicit legislative powers might authorise laws that could interfere with religious faith and practice was a real one. While not as secularist as Higgins, Josiah Symon considered it important to 'protect every citizen in the absolute and free exercise of his own faith' and 'to take care that his religious belief shall in no way be interfered with'.[337] Similarly, Bernhard Wise thought that each person should be free to 'follow his own religious observances' and not be permitted to 'impose his will on anybody else'.[338] The prevailing concern was thus threefold: that there be some recognition of God in the Constitution; that the Commonwealth be prevented from imposing religious observances; and that it be prevented from interfering with the free exercise of religion.

Higgins in particular drew attention to the impact that Sunday observance laws might have on minority religious groups such as the Seventh-day Adventists, a protestant Christian denomination which observes a religious day of rest on Saturday rather than Sunday. The right to religious freedom was of particular importance to this group because an English law from 1677,[339] which prohibited Sunday 'desecration', remained in force in the Australian colonies and had been used to convict some members of the denomination.[340] The

**334** *Convention Debates, Melbourne* (1898) 1732–3.
**335** Ibid, 654.
**336** Ibid, 660–61, 1736. See also Quick and Garran, above n 29, 952.
**337** *Convention Debates, Melbourne* (1898) 659.
**338** Ibid, 1774.
**339** 29 Charles II, c 7 (1677).
**340** Milton Hook, *The Avondale School and the Adventist Educational Goals, 1894–1900* (Andrews University, Michigan, 1978) 25.

Adventists themselves had been campaigning vigorously against the recognition of God in the preamble and advocated for a constitutional prohibition on religious laws.[341] Higgins, who became their 'agent and ally in the Convention', argued that a clause that would give adequate protection to the Seventh-day Adventists was necessary.[342]

The religious freedom of the Seventh-day Adventists is emblematic of what s 116 seems to have been intended to secure on behalf of the people of all religions. Sabbath observance is an essential element of the beliefs and practices of Seventh-day Adventists as a religious group. They believe that Saturday is to be set aside as a shared day of rest and worship, not only for individual believers, but also for Adventist families, congregations, schools and businesses. The exercise of their religious freedom is thus intrinsically communal in character, for it is together that they, like people of most religions, engage in corporate worship and other religiously-inspired practices, including the provision of welfare, education and, in the case of the Adventist Sanitarium group of companies, the provision of goods and services. It was to protect religious freedom in all of these dimensions that s 116 seems to have been directed. As Higgins' use of the Adventist example suggests, s 116 was intended to prevent the Commonwealth from laying down a uniform Sunday observance law – not to prevent people of religious conviction from observing their particular holy days, but to enable them to do so freely, as communities of believers, while ensuring that those who do not share those beliefs could not be forced into such observances by the Commonwealth.[343]

Higgins' proposed clause, which went through several iterations, was eventually approved in the current terms of s 116.[344] At the Convention of 1891, Andrew Inglis Clark had proposed two clauses: one which bound only the States and protected only the free exercise of religion, and another which bound the Commonwealth and prohibited 'any law for the establishment or support of any religion, or for the purpose of giving any preferential recognition to any religion, or for prohibiting the free exercise of any religion'.[345] Only the first of these two clauses was adopted at the Convention, the second one being rejected because it was thought unnecessary as the Commonwealth would have no primary power to legislate with respect to religion.[346] The clause restricting the States appeared again in the draft Constitution prepared at the Adelaide sitting of the second Convention in 1897. When it was considered again at the

**341** Ibid, 24–5; Ely, above n 333, chs 3 and 6.

**342** *Federal Convention, Melbourne* (1898) 656, 1734–5, citing *Church of the Holy Trinity v United States* 143 US 457 (1892). On Higgins' misunderstanding of the case, see C L Pannam, 'Travelling Section 116 with a US Road Map' (1963) 4 *Melbourne University Law Review* 41, 53–4.

**343** Indeed, the Federal Convention, partly due to the religious convictions of some of its members, determined ordinarily not to meet on either Saturdays or Sundays: *Convention Debates, Adelaide* (1897) 6, 467–9, 638–41.

**344** *Convention Debates, Melbourne* (1898) 1779, 2463.

**345** R G Ely, 'Andrew Inglis Clark and Church-State Separation' (1975) 8(3) *Journal of Religious History* 271, 285.

**346** *Convention Debates, Sydney* (1891) 962.

Melbourne sitting in 1898, Higgins proposed an extension to the clause so that it would bind both the Commonwealth and the States and would prohibit the enactment of any law 'prohibiting the free exercise of any religion, or for the establishment of any religion, or imposing any religious observance'.[347] However, the entire clause, including this extension to it, was resisted by several delegates on various grounds. The most decisive of these objections was that it would be inconsistent with one of the fundamental principles of the federation, namely that the States were to 'retain all such powers as they do not hand over to the Commonwealth'.[348] Higgins saw the point, and focused his energies on convincing the Convention to adopt a clause that would bind only the Commonwealth, and in this he was ultimately successful.

## 2 The text

Section 116 provides:

> The Commonwealth shall not make any law for establishing any religion, or for imposing any religious observance, or for prohibiting the free exercise of any religion, and no religious test shall be required as a qualification for any office or public trust under the Commonwealth.

The language of the provision is largely borrowed from two provisions of the US Constitution, Art VI, cl 3 and the First Amendment. These provide:

> The Senators and Representatives before mentioned, and the members of the several state legislatures, and all executive and judicial officers, both of the United States and of the several states, shall be bound by oath or affirmation, to support this Constitution; but no religious test shall ever be required as a qualification to any office or public trust under the United States.

> Congress shall make no law respecting an establishment of religion, or prohibiting the free exercise thereof; or abridging the freedom of speech, or of the press; or the right of the people peaceably to assemble, and to petition the government for the redress of grievances.

Several observations can be made about both sets of provisions. The first is that, as originally enacted, both the Australian and the American provisions applied only at a federal level. In the United States, it has since been held that the First Amendment binds the States as a consequence of the incorporation by the Fourteenth Amendment of many of the freedoms protected by the Bill of Rights.[349] However, as no similar extension of s 116 has occurred in Australia, nothing in s 116 prevents a State from making a law that establishes a religion, imposes a religious observance, prohibits the free exercise of religion, or imposes a

**347** *Convention Debates, Melbourne* (1898) 658, 664.
**348** Ibid 662.
**349** *Cantwell v Connecticut* 310 US 296 (1940); *Everson v Board of Education* 330 US 1 (1947).

religious test as a qualification for public office.[350] As such, the federal context and orientation of s 116 has largely been preserved. Notably, it appears in Chapter V of the Constitution, dealing with 'The States'. Its location in this chapter is probably because the original clause had bound only the States and there is no alternative chapter in the Constitution dealing with 'rights' or 'freedoms' generally. As Dawson J observed in *Kruger v Commonwealth*, its appearance in Chapter V can be understood to indicate that s 116 is part of the division of legislative power between the Commonwealth and the States, and therefore places no restriction on the power of the Commonwealth with respect to its Territories pursuant to s 122 of the Constitution.[351] However, several members of the Court have considered that s 116 does apply to Territory legislation, although whether this would include laws enacted only by the Commonwealth or also by a Territory legislature remains unclear.[352]

A second important preliminary observation is that s 116 only prohibits the 'making of laws'. Thus, it directly restricts the exercise of only legislative power, including laws which appropriate moneys under s 81 or provide for State grants under s 96.[353] For this reason its impact on the exercise of executive or judicial power is indirect, by controlling the content of laws that confer functions, powers or jurisdiction upon executive agencies and the courts.[354] Thirdly, the specific prohibitions in s 116 appear to be 'purposive' in the sense that a law will only be found unconstitutional if it was enacted 'for' one of the prohibited purposes in s 116. As will be seen, this leaves open the argument that laws that are enacted for a constitutionally legitimate purpose might not be struck down, even if in practical effect they establish a religion or prohibit the free exercise thereof. Fourthly, s 116 refers to 'religion', rather than 'belief', or 'conscience', or 'religious conviction'. While the term 'religion' includes matters of personal belief and conviction, the meaning of the term naturally extends to the idea of religion as a 'body of doctrines', a 'set of rituals', and a 'code of conduct', all of which are participated in by a 'community of people' united around those doctrines, rituals and conduct. The ordinary meaning of the term 'religion' thus suggests a communal meaning which would not be so directly present if the more individualistic terms 'belief', 'conscience' or 'conviction' had been used.[355]

**350** *Grace Bible Church v Reedman* (1984) 36 SASR 376; *Durham Holdings Pty Ltd v New South Wales* (2001) 205 CLR 399. Proposals to amend s 116 to make it applicable to the States were rejected at referendums held in 1944 and 1988.

**351** *Kruger v Commonwealth* (1997) 190 CLR 1, 60. See, to similar effect, *Attorney-General (Vic); Ex rel Black v Commonwealth* (1981) 146 CLR 559, 593–4, and compare *Spratt v Hermes* (1965) 114 CLR 226, 250.

**352** *Lamshed v Lake* (1958) 99 CLR 132, 143; *Kruger v Commonwealth* (1997) 190 CLR 1, 121–3, 162, 166–7.

**353** *Attorney-General (Vic); Ex rel Black v Commonwealth* (1981) 146 CLR 559, 576, 593, 618, 621 and 651.

**354** Ibid, 580–81; *Minister for Immigration and Ethnic Affairs v Lebanese Moslem Association* (1987) 17 FCR 373, 378–9. There is, however, some doubt about its application to judicial orders: *New v New*, Unreported Special Leave Application, 5 March 1982, High Court of Australia.

**355** Compare *International Covenant on Civil and Political Rights* (1966), Art 1: 'Everyone shall have the right to freedom of thought, conscience and religion', including 'freedom, individually or in community with others and in public or private, to manifest his religion or belief in worship, observance, practice and teaching'.

Section 116 provides that the Commonwealth has 'no power' to make a law prohibiting the free exercise of any religion, which logically entails a correlative 'immunity' against any such law being enacted.[356] Who or what is protected by s 116? The freedoms protected by s 116 are often regarded by commentators as 'rights' enjoyed by individuals; but on logical analysis, the protection is enjoyed by any juridical entity, whether a natural person or an incorporated association, which might otherwise be the subject of the imposition of legal rights or duties. The prohibition in s 116 seems therefore to protect both individuals and religious groups insofar as they have legal personality. If a spiritual community does not have corporate legal personality, it will only be the individual members and office holders of the unincorporated association who can be the subject of legal duties imposed by law,[357] and these individuals will be entitled to the protection of s 116. The same also applies, in principle, to trusts formed for religious or charitable purposes: the settlors and trustees of such trusts must necessarily enjoy the benefit of s 116 directly, and those who are otherwise involved in their administration or enjoy the benefit of them are indirectly protected by s 116 as a result. Moreover, many religious organisations are 'federal' in structure: they consist of local, regional or state-based organisations which have agreed to become part of a larger 'national' or 'federal' association, with the result that the 'members' of the federal organisation may, strictly speaking, themselves be regionally-located corporations, and not merely or only individuals.[358] The immunities established by s 116 appear to operate in principle to protect all of these kinds of associations and corporations, as well as their individual members, at every level of organisation.

## 3 The cases

Section 116 has only been argued in a handful of cases before the High Court, and in none of those cases has a law been struck down as inconsistent with s 116. Nonetheless, the case-law unambiguously confirms that Commonwealth laws must comply with s 116. The decided cases have given rise to several questions. The most important of these have concerned:

- the meaning of the 'free exercise of any religion' and how much it protects 'actions' rather than merely 'beliefs';
- the meaning of 'religion' for general purposes in the law, including its meaning in s 116;
- the meaning of 'establishing any religion' and whether s 116 prevents financial aid to religious institutions, such as religious schools; and

**356** On logical correlatives generally, see W N Hohfeld, *Fundamental Legal Conceptions as Applied in Judicial Reasoning* (Yale University Press, 1946); Glanville Williams, 'The Concept of Legal Liberty' (1956) 56(8) *Columbia Law Review* 1129; John Finnis, 'Some Professorial Fallacies About Rights' (1972) 4(2) *Adelaide Law Review* 377.
**357** See *Scandrett v Dowling* [1992] 27 NSWLR 483.
**358** See, eg, *Scheme of Union of the Presbyterian Church of Australia* (1900).

- the meaning of 'religious tests' and whether s 116 prohibits federal financial aid to support chaplains in public schools.

**Free exercise of religion**

The first case in which the High Court was asked to consider the application of s 116 was *Krygger v Williams*.[359] In that case, Mr Krygger appealed to the High Court against a conviction for refusing on conscientious grounds to comply with provisions of the *Defence Act 1903* (Cth) which required him to participate in compulsory military training. His argument was that the law was contrary to s 116 because it prohibited the free exercise of his religion.[360] He was unsuccessful. The exact grounds of his failure are not entirely clear. On one hand, Griffith CJ said that the *Defence Act* required the appellant to do something which had 'nothing at all to do with religion'. As the Chief Justice put it, a law which requires a person to do something which his or her religion forbids may be morally objectionable, but this does not of itself bring it within the meaning of s 116.[361] The Act made allowance for persons who had conscientious objections to military service to be given non-combatant duties, and Griffith CJ considered that the appellant's real objection had to be against being trained to serve in a life-supporting role, such as within the ambulance corps, so that 'in time of war he may be competent to assist in saving life'. For the plaintiff to claim that he had a conscientious objection against undertaking such service, he concluded, was simply 'absurd'.[362] Barton J reasoned similarly: he too considered the appellant's argument 'absurd', indeed 'as thin as anything of the kind that has come before us'.[363]

*Krygger* concerned the religious convictions of an individual. In the *Jehovah's Witnesses* case, the Court had to consider the application of s 116 to a law which applied to a corporation formed for religious purposes.[364] The case arose when the Commonwealth purported to dissolve and take possession of the assets of the Adelaide Company of Jehovah's Witnesses, a body incorporated under the *Associations Incorporation Act 1929* (SA). The Commonwealth considered that the Jehovah's Witnesses were promulgating doctrines that were prejudicial to the defence of the Commonwealth and the efficient prosecution of the Second World War. It took action against the Adelaide Company under the *National Security (Subversive Associations) Regulations*, which had been made pursuant to the *National Security Act 1939* (Cth). Aspects of the Regulations were very far-reaching. They provided for the dissolution and forfeiture of the assets of any body the existence of which was declared to be prejudicial to the defence of

**359** (1912) 15 CLR 366.
**360** *Krygger v Williams* (1912) 15 CLR 366, 369.
**361** Ibid.
**362** Ibid, 370–71.
**363** Ibid, 371–3. A different view was indicated by Higgins J in *Judd v McKeon* (1926) 38 CLR 380, 387, where he suggested that an objection to voting on religious grounds would be a valid and sufficient reason for failing to vote, on the basis of s 116.
**364** *Adelaide Company of Jehovah's Witnesses Inc v Commonwealth* (1943) 67 CLR 116.

the Commonwealth or the efficient prosecution of the war, and they imposed a blanket prohibition on the dissemination of any doctrines or principles advocated by such a body. As Latham CJ and Williams J pointed out, this last prohibition applied to any person or body, whether declared under the Regulations or not, provided some of the doctrines or principles that they promulgated happened to coincide with some of the doctrines or principles promulgated by a declared body, whether or not the particular doctrines or principles were inimical to the war effort.[365]

Several questions were set out in the case stated formulated by Starke J, turning substantially on whether the Act, the Regulations and the action taken by the Executive in relation to the Jehovah's Witnesses: (a) were contrary to s 116; (b) were authorised by the defence power (s 51(vi)); or (c) unconstitutionally conferred judicial power contrary to s 71. All the members of the Court held that in various respects important aspects of the Regulations – particularly the most far-reaching – were not authorised by either the defence power or the enabling Act.[366] However, a majority of the Court declined to find that the Regulations were contrary to s 116, on the basis that freedom of religion is not an absolute right, and that the free exercise clause does not prevent the Commonwealth from prohibiting the activities of bodies which engage in activities that are prejudicial to the very existence of the Commonwealth. Only one judge, Williams J, held that the Regulation which made it illegal to print, publish or promote 'unlawful doctrines' was contrary to s 116, for it could apply to what he called 'perfectly innocent' beliefs and principles.[367]

The first question put to the Court was whether the Adelaide Company was a party competent to maintain in an action before the High Court that the Regulations and Executive acts contravened s 116. On this preliminary but fundamental question, a majority of Rich, Starke and Williams JJ held that the Company had the requisite competence to maintain the action, while Latham CJ (with whom McTiernan J agreed) thought not, but on the limited ground that the Company had been validly dissolved and was therefore no longer a competent plaintiff.[368] Significantly, Latham CJ also flatly said that '[i]t is obvious that a company cannot exercise a religion'.[369] Rich J seemed to reason similarly when he said that he did not consider that the 'suppression of the plaintiff corporation prohibits the free exercise of any part of the religious faith ascribed... to the individual corporators'.[370] On the other hand, the case stated by Starke J drew attention to both the Adelaide Company as an 'incorporated association' and the 'association of persons' commonly known as Jehovah's Witnesses.[371] Williams J, who noted

**365** Ibid, 143–4, 165.
**366** Ibid, 150, 154, 167.
**367** Ibid, 165.
**368** Ibid, 136–9, 147, 156–7.
**369** Ibid, 147.
**370** Ibid, 149.
**371** Ibid, 119.

this,[372] repeatedly referred in his judgment to the rights and freedoms of 'individuals', 'bodies of individuals' and 'corporations' as if the distinction between these did not make a difference.[373]

The leading judgment on the central question of whether there had been a contravention of s 116 was delivered by the Chief Justice. His interpretation of s 116 was based on the fundamental principle that 'religion should, for political purposes, be regarded as irrelevant'.[374] He said that s 116 operates as an 'overriding provision' that prohibits the enactment of any law which 'favours any religion' or which 'interferes with any religion'.[375] He observed that the section is directed to 'any' religion or religious observance, and therefore extends to 'all religions' and not just one religion in particular.[376] Moreover, it embraces all aspects of religion, whether conceived as a 'system of beliefs', a 'code of conduct' or a particular 'ritual or religious observance', notwithstanding differing views about the truthfulness, goodness or propriety of such beliefs, conduct or observances, even if those of an unpopular religious minority.[377] Indeed, s 116 not only protects 'freedom of religion', but also 'the right of a man to have no religion'.[378] As such, noting that s 116 is directed to the protection of the '*exercise* of religion', Latham CJ insisted that s 116 not only protects 'beliefs' or 'opinions', but also 'acts' or 'activities' undertaken for religious reasons.[379] Importantly, he also observed that many religious beliefs and practices concern not only theological matters but also many matters relating to civil government, such as whether to take an oath, to appear before civil courts, to bear arms or to take part in civil religious ceremonies. All of these kinds of matters, although 'political', also raise issues of religious conviction, and are therefore protected by s 116. 'Religious practice', he pointed out, 'cannot be absolutely separated from politics or from ethics'.[380]

Nevertheless, Latham CJ also pointed out that there are necessary limits to the scope of the freedom. Some religions have called for human sacrifice; others have regarded it a religious duty to rob and to kill, or to engage in other practices that are today prohibited by the general law, such as the practice of polygamy. Indeed, some religious beliefs and practices may be inimical to the very existence of organised society and civil government. Such practices give rise to challenging difficulties for the application of s 116.[381] Moreover, like s 92, s 116 uses the 'vague and ambiguous' term 'free', but it is a term which in the context of the Constitution implies a conception of freedom regulated by general law. It therefore presupposes the ability of the state to 'employ the sovereign power' to

**372** Ibid, 159.
**373** Ibid, 161–3.
**374** Ibid, 126.
**375** Ibid, 122–3.
**376** Ibid, 123.
**377** Ibid, 123–4.
**378** Ibid, 123.
**379** Ibid, 124 (emphasis in original).
**380** Ibid, 125–6.
**381** Ibid.

maintain that social order without which the guarantee of freedom of religion would be meaningless.[382]

Following a critical review of decisions of the US Supreme Court delivered prior to 1900, Latham CJ considered that 'full legal justification' existed for adopting a pragmatic approach to s 116 in which the balance to be struck between religious freedom and societal order is determined by the courts on the basis of an assessment of whether s 116 is '*unduly* infringed' in any particular case.[383] However, noting that such an approach could be criticised for not according sufficient weight to religious freedom, he settled upon a 'narrower' basis of decision, namely that the liberty that s 116 protects necessarily presupposes the continued existence of a civil society, and therefore allows the enactment of laws which restrain activities that are inconsistent with the civil government established by the Constitution. On this approach, the question is whether the law can 'fairly be regarded' as directed to the protection of the existence of the community or, alternatively, is better characterised as having been enacted 'for' the purpose of prohibiting the free exercise of religion.[384] Applying this test to the Regulations, Latham CJ concluded that none contravened s 116, and that most of them were authorised by the defence power, except for their more far-reaching aspects, such as the prohibition on the promulgation of 'unlawful doctrines'.[385]

The other judges delivered shorter judgments in which they generally agreed that the Regulations did not contravene s 116, although several could not be authorised by the defence power.[386] Rich J shortly stated that the Commonwealth has the power to protect itself from activities prejudicial to its defence and the efficient prosecution of the war.[387] Starke J similarly maintained that s 116 protects 'liberty and freedom . . . in a community organized under the Constitution', a conception which allows the Commonwealth to make laws controlling activities that are 'seditious, subversive or prejudicial' to the defence of the Commonwealth.[388] McTiernan J likewise affirmed that s 116 protects 'faith and worship', 'teaching and propagation' and 'the practices and observances' of religion, but agreed that the Regulations did not contravene s 116 in particular.[389] While canvassing many of the same considerations, Williams J drew attention to the 'easy toleration' practised in 'British communit[ies]' – a toleration which freely permits bodies having all kinds of beliefs to flourish, especially in times of peace.[390] In his view, while subversive activities could be prohibited, aspects of the

**382** Ibid, 126–7.
**383** Ibid, 127–31 (emphasis in original).
**384** Ibid, 131–2.
**385** Ibid, 147–8.
**386** Starke J criticised the Regulations as 'arbitrary, capricious and oppressive'; Williams J said that they were so 'drastic and permanent' in their effects that they could not be authorised by the defence power: ibid, 154, 166.
**387** Ibid, 149.
**388** Ibid, 155.
**389** Ibid, 156–7.
**390** Ibid, 160.

Regulations both exceeded the defence power and were contrary to s 116, especially to the extent that they made it illegal to advocate what might be quite 'innocent' doctrines; and they could have the effect of turning an ordinary 'church service' into an 'unlawful assembly'.[391]

It was some time before the High Court was again asked to consider the application of s 116. In the unreported decision of *Crittenden v Anderson*, decided in 1977,[392] a petitioner challenged the election of a candidate to the House of Representatives on the ground that, contrary to s 44(i) of the Constitution, the candidate, because he was a Roman Catholic, owed allegiance to a foreign power, namely the Pope and the Vatican State in Rome. Fullagar J dismissed the petition on the ground that effect could not be given to the petitioner's contention without the imposition of a 'religious test' contrary to s 116.[393] On his Honour's reasoning, the candidate's membership of the Catholic Church and his resulting 'allegiance' to the Pope and the Vatican State constituted a legitimate expression of religious freedom protected by s 116. The religious test clause was thus interpreted to protect one's membership of a religious organisation, even one that is recognised as having international personality as an independent state.

### Definition of religion

What, then, is 'religion' for the purposes of s 116? In the *Scientology* case,[394] the Court had to determine whether the Church of the New Faith (the Church of Scientology), incorporated under the *Associations Incorporation Act 1956* (SA) and registered as a 'foreign company' in Victoria, was a 'religious institution' and therefore entitled to an exemption from payroll tax under the *Pay-roll Tax Act 1971* (Vic). While this was the specific question before the Court, the parties approached the case by arguing whether Scientology was a 'religion', rather than whether the corporation was itself a 'religious institution'. While the Court largely accepted the parties' construction of the issues, Mason ACJ and Brennan J pointed out that these were distinguishable questions, for the religion of a particular 'group' does not stamp an institution 'founded, maintained or staffed' by members of that group as necessarily religious.[395] For Mason ACJ and Brennan J, the question at issue concerned the purposes and activities of the corporation itself, rather than the religious convictions of its members.

Further, although the case was technically concerned with the meaning and application of the *Pay-roll Tax Act*, it raised the wider and more significant question of the legal definition of religion generally. As Mason ACJ and Brennan J pointed out, this was an especially important question. As they put it:

**391** Ibid, 165.
**392** *Crittenden v Anderson* (1977) 51 ALJ 167, 171 (unreported judgment delivered on 23 August 1950).
**393** Ibid, 171.
**394** *Church of the New Faith v Commissioner of Pay-Roll Tax (Vic)* (1983) 154 CLR 120.
**395** Ibid, 128–9.

> Freedom of religion, the paradigm freedom of conscience, is of the essence of a free society. The chief function in the law of a definition of religion is to mark out an area within which a person subject to the law is free to believe and to act in accordance with his belief without legal restraint. Such a definition affects the scope and operation of s 116 of the Constitution and identifies the subject matters which other laws are presumed not to intend to affect.[396]

It was thus understood that the definition of religion adopted by the Court would have wider implications for Australian law generally, including the meaning of s 116. With this in mind, Mason ACJ and Brennan J defined 'religion' in the following manner:

> [T]he criteria of religion are twofold: first, belief in a supernatural Being, Thing or Principle; and second, the acceptance of canons of conduct in order to give effect to that belief, though canons of conduct which offend against the ordinary laws are outside the area of any immunity, privilege or right conferred on the grounds of religion. Those criteria may vary in their comparative importance, and there may be a different intensity of belief or of acceptance of canons of conduct among religions or among the adherents to a religion. The tenets of a religion may give primacy to one particular belief or to one particular canon of conduct. Variations in emphasis may distinguish one religion from other religions, but they are irrelevant to the determination of an individual's or a group's freedom to profess and exercise the religion of his, or their, choice.[397]

Mason ACJ and Brennan J very plainly here affirmed the freedom of both individuals and groups to profess and exercise the religion of their choice. They defined religion broadly, so that it would embrace non-theistic religions, but they also framed it in quite formal terms, as involving both beliefs and canons of conduct related to those beliefs.

Somewhat differently, Wilson and Deane JJ thought that there can be no 'formularized legal criterion' for determining what constitutes a religion. Rather, they considered that the answer lies in 'empirical observation of accepted religions' and the identification of indicia that emerge from such observation. They put it this way:

> One of the most important indicia of 'a religion' is that the particular collection of ideas and/or practices involves belief in the supernatural, that is to say, belief that reality extends beyond that which is capable of perception by the senses. If that be absent, it is unlikely that one has 'a religion'. Another is that the ideas relate to man's nature and place in the universe and his relation to things supernatural. A third is that the ideas are accepted by adherents as requiring or encouraging them to observe particular standards or codes of conduct or to participate in specific practices having supernatural significance. A fourth is that, however loosely knit and varying in beliefs and practices adherents may be, they constitute an identifiable group or identifiable groups. A fifth, and perhaps more controversial, indicium . . . is that the adherents themselves see the collection of ideas and/or practices as constituting a religion.[398]

**396** Ibid, 130.
**397** Ibid, 136.
**398** Ibid, 173–4.

Although the factors to be considered were largely the same, by framing the conception of religion in terms of empirical 'indicia', Wilson and Deane JJ's approach was considerably more flexible than Mason ACJ and Brennan J's. Thus, Wilson and Deane JJ went so far as to say that the existence of an identifiable group or groups is in itself an important indication of a religion's very existence, even if the adherents are only very 'loosely knit' and even if they adhere to 'varying... beliefs and practices', so long as there is a 'group' or set of 'groups' that can be identified.

Murphy J's definition took this idea further still. After adopting Latham CJ's dictum that 'each person chooses the content of his own religion',[399] Murphy J observed:

> [A]ny body which claims to be religious, whose beliefs or practices are a revival of, or resemble, earlier cults, is religious. Any body which claims to be religious and to believe in a supernatural Being or Beings, whether physical and visible, such as the sun or the stars, or a physical invisible God or spirit, or an abstract God or entity, is religious. For example, if a few followers of astrology were to found an institution based on the belief that their destinies were influenced or controlled by the stars, and that astrologers can, by reading the stars, divine those destinies, and if it claimed to be religious, it would be a religious institution. Any body which claims to be religious, and offers a way to find meaning and purpose in life, is religious. The Aboriginal religion of Australia and of other countries must be included. The list is not exhaustive; the categories of religion are not closed.[400]

On Murphy J's definition, it seems that literally *any* body that claims to be religious will be regarded as religious in the eyes of the law. Such a conclusion seems to have been driven by his Honour's adoption of the strict separationist view 'that it is not within the judicial sphere to determine matters of religious doctrine and practice' in any respect whatsoever.[401]

### Non-establishment of religion

In the *State Aid* case,[402] the Court had to determine whether government funding of religious schools breached the non-establishment clause in s 116. In addressing this question, the Court considered, among other things, how the term 'establishing a religion' was understood at the time the Constitution was enacted. Barwick CJ said it involves the 'identification of the religion with the civil authority' in a way that involves 'the citizen in a duty to maintain it' and an obligation on the civil government 'to patronize, protect and promote the established religion'.[403] Gibbs J similarly considered that in 1900 the term 'establishing any religion' meant 'to constitute a particular religion or religious body as a

**399** *Adelaide Company of Jehovah's Witnesses Incorporated v Commonwealth* (1943) 67 CLR 116, 124.
**400** *Church of the New Faith v Commissioner of Pay-Roll Tax (Vic)* (1983) 154 CLR 120, 151.
**401** Ibid 150, citing *Attorney-General (NSW) v Grant* (1976) 135 CLR 587 and *Attorney-General (Qld); Ex rel Nye v Cathedral Church of Brisbane* (1977) 136 CLR 353, 377.
**402** *Attorney-General (Vic); Ex rel Black v Commonwealth* (1981) 146 CLR 559.
**403** Ibid, 582.

state religion or state church'.[404] Wilson J, with whom Mason J agreed, likewise thought that the establishment of religion required 'statutory recognition of a religion as a national institution'.[405] Similarly, Stephen J held that an established religion meant the establishment of a 'state church', such as the special status that had been afforded to the Church of England in England.[406] On the basis of these views, a majority of the Court (Murphy J dissenting) held that the Commonwealth can fund religious schools, at least on a non-discriminatory basis, as this does not of itself amount to a law which has as its purpose the establishment of a state church or a state religion.

Notably, on the approach of the majority the core meaning of an 'establishment' is institutional, not philosophical or personal. Religion is something that can be established in institutional terms: in the form, for example, of a state church or other religious body that is given special privileges which associate it closely with the state itself. Consistent with this conception, there was discussion in the case about whether s 116, especially the non-establishment clause, should be understood as protecting 'individual rights'. Stephen J observed that s 116 is 'not, in form, a constitutional guarantee of the rights of individuals', but rather 'an express restriction upon the exercise of Commonwealth legislative power'.[407] Wilson J similarly said that s 116 'is a denial of legislative power... and no more'; it does not form part of a 'bill of rights' and does not constitute a 'personal guarantee of religious freedom'.[408] While Barwick CJ did not go quite so far, he also sharply distinguished s 116 from the US First Amendment, thus implying a similar view.[409] Gibbs J, having also distinguished s 116 from the First Amendment, commented that the non-establishment clause was only a 'fetter on legislative power' and, unlike the free exercise clause, does not exist to protect 'a fundamental human right'.[410] Somewhat in contrast, Mason J cited with approval the observation of Latham CJ in the *Jehovah's Witnesses* case that s 116 protects 'the right of a man to have no religion', and added that the section is directed to 'the preservation of religious equality' and 'freedom of religion'.[411] Murphy J, who dissented, took it even further, referring to s 116 as a 'great constitutional guarantee of freedom of and from religion', which specifically contains 'guarantees of personal freedom against the imposition of any religious observance and the prohibition of free exercise of any religion and the requirement of any religious test'.[412] He considered, on the basis of a strict 'separation' interpretation of the non-establishment clause, that all 'recognition and assistance to religion' is prohibited.[413]

**404** Ibid, 597.
**405** Ibid, 653.
**406** Ibid, 606–9.
**407** Ibid, 605.
**408** Ibid, 652.
**409** Ibid, 578–9.
**410** Ibid, 583, 598, 603.
**411** Ibid, 616.
**412** Ibid, 623.
**413** Ibid, 625, 628.

How are these varying statements to be understood? Certainly, s 116 does not refer explicitly to personal rights but operates as a restriction on legislative power, as Stephen and Wilson JJ pointed out. However, as has been noted, a restriction on power necessarily implies a corresponding immunity. The benefit of the immunity differs in relation to the various clauses in s 116: the non-establishment clause provides a very diffuse benefit enjoyed by all citizens, especially those who are opposed to an establishment of religion, whereas the benefit of the free exercise clause is more specific to particular persons who would otherwise be liable to the enactment of laws that prohibit the free exercise of any religion. In these two senses it is accurate enough to say, with Mason and Murphy JJ, that s 116 confers certain rights, in the nature of immunities, to the benefit of individual citizens. However, the bare existence of such immunity rights does not of itself necessarily imply the existence of additional personal capacities or powers, such as standing to bring an action seeking a declaration of the invalidity of a law said to be contrary to s 116, or an entitlement to damages for injury sustained as a result of the implementation of the law. These additional rights must rest on additional premises, for which independent legal grounds are necessary. For example, standing may properly exist because a person's interests are directly affected by an enacted law, and an action for damages may be available because the Executive has acted in a manner that, in the absence of legal warrant, would constitute a trespass or a breach of duty arising at common law. But these additional rights, both to bring an action and to obtain a remedy, depend on premises of the law that are separate from and independent of the immunity-rights conferred by s 116. And yet, they are rights which all legal persons – both natural and artificial – can possess and enforce.

### Review of administrative decisions

The *Lebanese Moslem Association* case[414] illustrates another way in which a religious group may have standing to invoke s 116. The case involved an application before the Federal Court of Australia to review a decision of the Minister for Immigration to deport a particular individual who had been invited to Australia by the Australian Federation of Islamic Councils and had been appointed Imam of the Lakemba Mosque by the Lebanese Moslem Association. The evidence before the Court suggested that, at the least, opinions within the Australian Lebanese community about the suitability of the Imam to hold office differed considerably. At first instance, Pincus J considered that the Minister was relevantly bound by s 116 in the exercise of his powers under the *Migration Act 1958* (Cth), that it was inconsistent with freedom of religion for the government to determine the suitability of an individual as a religious leader, and that the

**414** *Lebanese Moslem Association v Minister for Immigration and Ethnic Affairs* (1986) 11 FCR 543; 67 ALR 195; *Minister for Immigration and Ethnic Affairs v Lebanese Moslem Association* (1987) 17 FCR 373; 71 ALR 578.

Minister had failed to take into consideration the constitutional rights of the members of the Lebanese Moslem Association under s 116 to determine their own leadership.[415] On appeal, the Full Court reversed Pincus J's decision. Fox and Jackson JJ held that there had not been any prohibition of the free exercise of religion, either in the intention, purpose or effect of the Minister's decision.[416] Burchett J similarly considered that it was open to the Minister to deport the Imam on the ground that his presence in Australia was a 'catalyst for conflict in a divided community', and that this did not involve any clash with s 116.[417] In coming to this conclusion, Jackson J emphasised that s 116 operates as a limitation on legislative power, and that its application to executive acts is on the basis that the relevant authorising legislation cannot constitutionally permit an executive decision which amounts to a prohibition upon the free exercise of any religion.[418] In none of the reasoning, however, was there any challenge to the standing of the Lebanese Moslem Association to bring the action in the first place, or to the proposition that s 116 operates to protect its rights, as an association, to make decisions about the appointment of its religious leaders. All of this was taken for granted.

### Purpose and proportionality

The scope of the free exercise clause was again considered in *Kruger v Commonwealth.*[419] In that case, the Court had to consider, among other things, whether the *Aboriginal Ordinance 1918* (NT), which provided for the removal of Aboriginal children from their families and their communities, contravened the plaintiffs' freedom of religion. The argument ultimately failed: for some judges on the ground that s 116 is simply inapplicable to Territory legislation;[420] for others on the ground that the Ordinance could not be characterised as a law enacted 'for' the purpose of prohibiting the free exercise of their religion.[421] But while the argument was ultimately unsuccessful, there was no suggestion that there was any problem with the proposition that the plaintiffs' freedom of religion might be constituted in and through their families and communities. Indeed, the judges very clearly accepted the 'group' orientation of Aboriginal religion. Gummow J stated that the kinds of religion protected by s 116 plainly include 'the systems of faith and worship of Aboriginal people', and he seemed to acknowledge that one important aspect of this would be the rearing and instruction of Aboriginal children in the 'religious beliefs of their community'.[422] Toohey J similarly framed the

**415** *Lebanese Moslem Association* (1986) 11 FCR 543, 559–61. His Honour cited *Kedroff v Saint Nicholas Cathedral* 344 US 94 (1952) and *Serbian Eastern Orthodox Diocese v Milivojevich* 426 US 696 (1975) in support of the principle that freedom of religion 'inhibit[s] the right of legislatures to intervene in questions of control of churches' (at 559).

**416** *Minister for Immigration and Ethnic Affairs v Lebanese Moslem Association* (1987) 17 FCR 373, 374, 379, 388–9.

**417** Ibid, 374–5.

**418** Ibid, 378–9.

**419** *Kruger v Commonwealth* (1997) 190 CLR 1.

**420** Ibid, 60.

**421** Ibid, 40, 86, 160–61.

**422** Ibid, 160–61.

question as being whether one of the purposes of the Ordinance was to 'impair [or] prohibit the spiritual beliefs and practices of the aboriginal people'.[423]

Gaudron J discussed the application of s 116 at length. On her view, the free exercise clause is not limited to prohibiting laws that impose an outright 'ban' on the free exercise of religion, but extends to laws that 'prevent' the free exercise of religion or which authorise acts having that effect.[424] She stated:

> [I]f Aboriginal people had practices and beliefs which are properly characterised as a religion for the purposes of s 116, and if, as would seem likely, those practices were carried out in association with other members of the Aboriginal community to which they belonged or at sacred sites or other places on their traditional lands, removal from their communities and their traditional lands would, necessarily, have prevented the free exercise of their religion.[425]

Further, she pointed out that although s 116 is directed to laws that have the purpose of prohibiting the free exercise of religion, it is possible that a law may have several purposes, and that a particular purpose (eg, to prohibit the free exercise of religion by Aboriginal children removed from their families and tribal culture) may be subsumed within a larger or more general purpose (eg, to remove Aboriginal children from their families, ostensibly for their own good).[426] As her Honour further observed:

> [I]t might well be concluded that one purpose of the... Ordinance was to remove Aboriginal and half-caste children from their communities and, thus, prevent their participation in community practices. And if those practices included religious practices, that purpose necessarily extended to prohibiting the free exercise of religion.[427]

This raised the possibility that if the defendant were to plead (as had not been done) that the law had been enacted for a purpose entirely unconnected to the prohibition of the free exercise of religion, but rather for some other legitimate purpose, then it would be necessary for the Court to assess whether the interference with religious freedom (this being an incidental side-effect of the law) could be justified because the law was nonetheless appropriate and adapted (or reasonably proportionate) to achieving that legitimate objective.[428] In the circumstances of the case, these were questions that could not be answered by the Court, but could well arise in appropriate proceedings.[429]

### Religious tests

The most recent High Court decision to consider s 116 was *Williams v Commonwealth (No 1)*.[430] As explained in Chapter 7, the case involved a challenge to the

**423** Ibid, 86.
**424** Ibid, 130–32.
**425** Ibid, 132.
**426** Ibid, 132–3.
**427** Ibid, 133.
**428** Ibid, 134.
**429** See, similarly, ibid, 86–7.
**430** *Williams v Commonwealth (No 1)* (2012) 248 CLR 156.

Commonwealth's National School Chaplaincy Program. One of the constitutional questions was whether the arrangements made with Scripture Union to provide chaplaincy services to schools was contrary to the requirement in s 116 that 'no religious test shall be required as a qualification for any office or public trust under the Commonwealth'. This argument was disposed of shortly by the Court on the ground that the Chaplaincy Program did not involve the establishment of a 'public office'.[431] As Heydon J pointed out, an 'office' is a position under constituted authority to which duties are attached, and an 'officer' is a person who 'holds an office which is in direct relationship with the Commonwealth'.[432] For his Honour, it was significant that under the Chaplaincy Program the Commonwealth had no direct legal relationship with the chaplains: it could not 'appoint, select, approve or dismiss them' and it could not 'direct them'.[433] As Gummow and Bell JJ put it, it was necessary for there to be closer connection between the Commonwealth and the Chaplains for there to be a requisite 'office'.[434]

While the Court's reasoning in *Williams* plainly turned on the meaning of an office under the Commonwealth, it showed how religion, in the form of religious tests, might be established as a condition for appointment to public office. Section 116 plainly prohibits this, but the Court's reasoning suggests how both sides of s 116 – the 'free exercise' and the 'non-establishment' limbs – each imply a conception of religion that has an ineradicable personal and organisational dimension. The prohibitions on the 'imposition' of religion serve to prevent the institutional or organisational establishment of religion, while the free exercise clause protects the practice of religion in its many dimensions: personal, associational, communal, organisational and institutional.

While there have been no cases in which it has been held that a law contravened s 116, the provision is not, for these reasons, without its importance.[435]

# V Freedom of political communication

## 1 Introduction

It has been observed that the Australian Constitution is primarily concerned with creating the institutional architecture necessary for the establishment of a federal commonwealth. The framers of the Constitution generally believed that the institutions of representative and responsible government, federally organised, would provide adequate protection for civil and political rights without the

**431** Ibid, 223, 334–5.
**432** Ibid, 334–5.
**433** Ibid, 335.
**434** Ibid, 223.
**435** The foregoing draws on Nicholas Aroney, 'Freedom of Religion as an Associational Right' (2014) 33 *University of Queensland Law Journal* 153.

need for a judicially-enforced bill of rights.[436] Sir Robert Menzies, Australia's longest serving Prime Minister, put it this way:

> [T]he best guarantee of human rights in the future is to be found in our system of responsible government, where Ministers sit in Parliament, can be questioned, and give answers, and the government itself may be turned out if parliament feels that it is doing things which violate the proper rights of individuals.[437]

Menzies maintained that the framers of the Constitution had deliberately refrained from adopting a bill of rights because they understood that:

> to define human rights is either to limit them – for in the long run words must be given some meaning – or to express them so broadly that the discipline which is inherent in all government and ordered society becomes impossible.[438]

When the Australians did incorporate limits on governmental power in the Constitution, they did so selectively. Section 116 is one of the clearest examples: the framers drew upon the religion clauses of the First Amendment to the US Constitution, but deliberately refrained from adopting the First Amendment rights to freedom of speech, freedom of the press and freedom of assembly.[439]

It has been seen, however, that the High Court has held that the Constitution contains certain limitations on power considered to be implied by the text, structure, principles and purposes of the Constitution. These include the intergovernmental immunities associated with the federal nature of the Constitution discussed in Chapter 4, and several protective principles derived from the separation of judicial power explained in Chapter 9. It was also seen in Chapter 2 that the High Court has addressed the question whether the Constitution implies that voters are entitled to 'equality of voting power' and whether there is a 'right to vote'.[440] The arguments made in these latter cases were premised on the broad idea that the Constitution provides for a system of representative democracy the proper operation of which depends on the existence of a range of civil and political rights, such as the freedoms of speech, assembly and association. Murphy J had claimed that such implied rights existed, but his views were consistently rejected by other members of the Court until 1992.[441] In that year, in *Nationwide News v Wills*[442] and *Australian Capital Television v Commonwealth*,[443] a majority of the High Court accepted the argument that because the Constitution provides for a system of representative government, and since democracy requires freedom of speech in order to function effectively, the

**436** *Australian Capital Television Pty Ltd v Commonwealth* (1992) 177 CLR 106, 186.
**437** Robert Menzies, 'Common Law protects the individual', *The Sydney Morning Herald*, 12 March 1974, 6.
**438** Robert Menzies, *Central Power in the Australian Commonwealth* (Cassell & Company, 1967) 52.
**439** Harrison Moore, *The Constitution of the Commonwealth of Australia*, (Maxwell, 2nd ed, 1910) 614–15; and J A La Nauze, *The Making of the Australian Constitution* (Melbourne University Press, 1972) 227.
**440** *Attorney-General (Cth); Ex rel McKinlay v Commonwealth* (1975) 135 CLR 1; *McGinty v Western Australia* (1996) 186 CLR 140; *Roach v Electoral Commissioner* (2007) 233 CLR 162; *Rowe v Electoral Commissioner* (2010) 243 CLR 1.
**441** Eg, *Miller v TCN Channel Nine Pty Ltd* (1986) 161 CLR 556, 569, 579, 592, 615, 625–6, 636–7.
**442** (1992) 177 CLR 1.
**443** (1992) 177 CLR 106.

Constitution necessarily contains an implied protection of freedom of communication about political and governmental matters in order to ensure that the system operates effectively.

## 2 Freedom of speech in the Constitution

*Australian Capital Television* concerned a constitutional challenge to the *Political Broadcasts and Political Disclosures Act 1991* (Cth), which inserted a new Part IIID into the *Broadcasting Act 1942* (Cth). Part IIID imposed new conditions on holders of radio and television broadcasting licences under the Act. These conditions prohibited the broadcasting of political advertisements during election periods and provided for the allocation of mandatory free time political advertising in lieu of the prohibition. The changes were introduced in response to a parliamentary committee report that had expressed concern about the corruption made possible by the dependence of political parties upon financial donations needed to pay for political broadcast advertising.[444] Several broadcasters and the State of New South Wales commenced proceedings in the High Court seeking a declaration that the legislation was unconstitutional because it contravened 'an implied guarantee of freedom of access to, participation in, and criticism of, federal and State institutions amounting to a freedom of communication in relation to the political and electoral processes'.[445]

*Nationwide News v Wills* concerned a prosecution of the publisher of a newspaper article that was strongly critical of the Australian Industrial Relations Commission. The article claimed that Australian employees are:

> regulated by a mass of official controls, imposed by a vast bureaucracy in the ministry of labour and enforced by a corrupt and compliant 'judiciary' in the official Soviet-style Arbitration Commission.

It was alleged that the publication offended against s 299(1)(d)(ii) of the *Industrial Relations Act 1988* (Cth), which provided that 'a person shall not . . . by writing or speech use words calculated . . . to bring a member of the Commission or the Commission into disrepute'. Although the idea of an implied freedom of political communication was not initially raised, during oral submissions Deane J invited counsel to argue that s 92 of the Constitution protects freedom of speech. Counsel for the publisher returned with an argument based on s 92 together with a further argument that there exists a constitutionally implied freedom of political communication.

Because both cases raised the same question about the implied freedom of political communication, the Court considered them together. Four judges in *Nationwide News* and six in *Australian Capital Television* affirmed that the

**444** Joint Standing Committee on Electoral Matters of the Commonwealth Parliament, *Who pays the piper calls the tune: Minimising the risks of funding political campaigns* (Australian Government Publishing Service, 1989).
**445** *Australian Capital Television v Commonwealth* (1992) 177 CLR 106, 109.

Constitution's provision for a system of representative democracy gives rise to an implied freedom of communication in relation to government and political matters. One of the six judges in *Australian Capital Television*, McHugh J, restricted the operation of the freedom to election periods. Dawson J, who dissented, rejected the implication altogether, although he affirmed that the requirement in ss 7 and 24 of the Constitution that members of Parliament are to be 'chosen by the people' means that electors must have access to the necessary information to make a genuine choice of representatives.[446]

The entire Court in *Nationwide News* held that s 299(1)(d)(ii) was invalid. Mason CJ, McHugh and Dawson JJ considered that the law was not authorised by the incidental scope of the industrial arbitration power (s 51(xxxv)): Mason CJ and McHugh J because it was not 'reasonably proportionate' or 'appropriate and adapted' to the legitimate objective of protecting the reputation of and public confidence in the Industrial Relations Commission, and Dawson J because there was not a 'sufficient connexion' between the law and the subject matter of the power.[447] Brennan, Deane, Toohey and Gaudron JJ found that s 299(1)(d)(ii) was contrary to what Brennan J identified as an implied 'freedom to discuss governments and governmental institutions and political matters'.[448]

The complexity of the legislation in *Australian Capital Television* meant that the judges had to consider separately the prohibitions on broadcast advertising in respect of Commonwealth, State and Territory elections, the various exceptions to the prohibitions, and the allocation of free time advertising. In the result, Mason CJ, Deane, Toohey and Gaudron JJ held that the entirety of Part IIID contravened the implied freedom. McHugh J found that all of it was invalid except for the provision concerning Territory elections. Brennan J, who agreed with the implied freedom in principle, considered that Part IIID was justifiable as a reasonable restriction on the freedom in order to prevent corruption of the political process. Dawson J also upheld Part IIID, on the ground that it was authorised by the Commonwealth's power to regulate elections and did not prevent voters from making genuine electoral choices.

Despite subtle differences between them, the main line of reasoning of the majority in both cases proceeded in several broad steps. First, the judges placed emphasis on the popular foundations of the Constitution: that it was based upon the consent of the people of the Australian colonies to be united in a federal commonwealth, and that the system of government was designed to protect and enhance their powers of self-government.[449] Second, it was observed that, notwithstanding the *Engineers* case, it had been accepted that necessary implications have a legitimate role to play in the interpretation of the Constitution.[450]

**446** *Australian Capital Television v Commonwealth* (1992) 177 CLR 106, 187–9, 227, 230–33.
**447** Ibid, 29–34, 85–91, 93–5, 100–05, discussing *Davis v Commonwealth* (1988) 166 CLR 79.
**448** *Nationwide News v Wills* (1992) 177 CLR 1, 51; see also 76, 94–5.
**449** *Australian Capital Television v Commonwealth* (1992) 177 CLR 106, 136, 210–11, 228; *Nationwide News Pty Ltd v Wills* (1992) 177 CLR 1, 70.
**450** *Australian Capital Television* (1992) 177 CLR 106, 133–5, 209–10; *Nationwide News* (1992) 177 CLR 1, 41–5, 69.

Third, it was pointed out that the Constitution makes provision through several interconnected provisions (especially ss 7, 24, 64 and 128) for a system of representative government, responsible government and representative democracy.[451] Fourth, the judges attributed a particular substantive meaning to these ideas: namely that representative government signifies a system where the 'sovereign power' of government, residing in the people, is exercised through representatives chosen by the people in a 'free and democratic society'.[452] Fifth, the majority considered that freedom of political communication is necessary, fundamental and essential for the effective and efficacious operation of the system of representative government.[453] Sixth, it was noted that because the legislative powers of the Commonwealth in s 51 are expressed to be 'subject to' the Constitution, it followed that those powers do not authorise any law which is inconsistent with the constitutional implication.[454] However, seventh, it was also pointed out that freedom of political communication, like all freedoms, cannot be absolute; it is subject to limitations that are consistent with 'an ordered and democratic society' or a society 'organised under and controlled by law', and that these limitations are to be discerned and applied through a process of balancing the considerations for and against the restriction on freedom of political communication in the particular circumstances.[455]

In relation to this latter task, a variety of approaches were adopted. Deane and Toohey JJ proposed that the question is whether the restriction is reasonably necessary for the 'protection or vindication of the legitimate claims of individuals to live peacefully and with dignity' in an 'ordered and democratic society'.[456] Gaudron J considered that the principles by which the general law regulates free speech offer appropriate guidance.[457] In his dissenting judgment on this point, Brennan J maintained that the Court must accord the Parliament a 'margin of appreciation' in choosing what might be an appropriate legislative means to achieve its objectives, and he upheld the legislation in *Australian Capital Television* on this basis.[458] Mason CJ and Deane and Toohey JJ proposed a more exacting degree of scrutiny. Where a law targets the content of ideas or information, Mason CJ proposed, only a compelling justification will be sufficient and the restriction must be no more than is reasonably necessary to achieve the

**451** *Australian Capital Television* (1992) 177 CLR 106, 137–8, 210, 230; *Nationwide News Pty Ltd v Wills* (1992) 177 CLR 1, 47, 70–72.
**452** *Australian Capital Television* (1992) 177 CLR 106, 137–8, 215, 228, 234; *Nationwide News* (1992) 177 CLR 1, 72. The Chief Justice proposed that the enactment of the *Australia Act 1986* (UK) 'marked the end of the legal sovereignty of the Imperial Parliament and recognized that ultimate sovereignty resided in the Australian people'.
**453** *Australian Capital Television* (1992) 177 CLR 106, 139–40; *Nationwide News* (1992) 177 CLR 1, 47–8, 74–5.
**454** *Australian Capital Television* (1992) 177 CLR 106, 168, 215, 217, 219–20, 227, 233; *Nationwide News* (1992) 177 CLR 1, 40, 69, 94.
**455** *Australian Capital Television* (1992) 177 CLR 106, 142–4, 150–51, 169; *Nationwide News Pty Ltd v Wills* (1992) 177 CLR 1, 50–51, 76–7.
**456** *Australian Capital Television* (1992) 177 CLR 106, 169.
**457** Ibid, 217–21; *Nationwide News* (1992) 177 CLR 1, 93–5.
**458** Ibid, 159, citing the decision of the European Court of Human Rights in *Observer and Guardian v United Kingdom* (1991) 14 EHRR 153.

legitimate goal of the legislation; whereas if the law only restricts 'an activity or mode of communication' it will be more easily justified, for in such cases the relevant considerations are simply to be weighed against each other.[459] Deane and Toohey JJ similarly proposed a distinction between laws that prohibit or control communications relating to government and laws that are concerned with some other matter and whose effect on political communication is not determined by their political character.[460]

In three further cases decided in 1994, the Court went further. *Theophanous*[461] and *Stephens*[462] concerned defamation proceedings commenced by members respectively of the Commonwealth House of Representatives and the Western Australian Legislative Council. Both cases involved allegedly defamatory imputations against the character and integrity of the plaintiffs in connection with their activities as elected representatives. In each case it was argued that the common law principles governing the law of defamation should be reformulated in light of the implied freedom of political communication. Moreover, the *Stephens* case concerned the activities of members of a State Parliament, raising the question whether the State Constitution itself, or the Commonwealth Constitution indirectly, might carry the implication that communications about State, Territory and even local political matters are also protected. In *Australian Capital Television* and *Nationwide News*, Mason CJ, Deane, Toohey and Gaudron JJ had indicated that the implied freedom applied to communications and discussion relating to State political matters and not only Commonwealth ones.[463]

*Theophanous* and *Stephens* were accompanied by a third case, *Cunliffe v Commonwealth*,[464] in which there was a constitutional challenge to amendments to the *Migration Act 1958* (Cth). The new Part 2A of the Act prescribed a system for the registration of migration agents and placed restrictions, subject to certain exceptions, on the provision of immigration assistance and the making of representations on behalf of a migration applicant by an unregistered person. It was argued that the new provisions were beyond the Commonwealth's power to legislate with respect to 'aliens' and 'immigration' (s 51(xix) and (xxvii)), and that they were contrary to the implied freedom of political communication and freedom of intercourse guaranteed by s 92.

In *Theophanous*, a close majority of Mason CJ, Deane, Toohey and Gaudron JJ (Brennan, Dawson and McHugh JJ dissenting) held that the law of defamation must be adjusted so that it 'conforms' to the implied freedom of political communication. For Mason CJ, Toohey and Gaudron JJ, this meant that when a defendant publishes false and defamatory material relating to the suitability

**459** Ibid, 143–4.
**460** *Nationwide News* (1992) 177 CLR 1, 76–7.
**461** *Theophanous v Herald & Weekly Times Ltd* (1994) 182 CLR 104.
**462** *Stephens v West Australian Newspapers Ltd* (1994) 182 CLR 211.
**463** *Australian Capital Television* (1992) 177 CLR 106, 142, 168–9, 215–17; *Nationwide News* (1992) 177 CLR 1, 75.
**464** *Cunliffe v Commonwealth* (1994) 182 CLR 272.

of persons for public office or the discussion of government and political matters, there ought to be a defence available where the defendant establishes that it was unaware of the falsity of the publication, did not publish the material recklessly (ie, not caring whether the material was true or false) and acted reasonably in publishing the claims, such as by taking adequate steps to check their accuracy (or because it was justified in not doing so in the circumstances).[465] Deane J was prepared to go further: he considered that in relation to publications about the performance of parliamentarians and other holders of high public office, the publisher should not even be required to prove reasonableness or the absence of recklessness.[466] In *Stephens*, the same majority held that the Western Australian Constitution, which entrenches the requirement that the State Parliament is to be popularly elected, implies the existence of a similar freedom of political communication, and that this freedom gives rise to the same defence to the publication of defamatory imputations against members of the State Parliament.[467]

The Court's decisions in these cases generated considerable discussion and debate, and continue to do so.[468] Much of the early controversy concerned the legitimacy of the Court determining that an implied freedom of political communication existed when the framers of the Constitution had deliberately chosen not to include rights to freedom of speech, assembly or association. Some argued that political rights like freedom of speech fall into a special category because they are essential to the democratic nature of the Parliament.[469] Others questioned whether such an implication could be legitimate when all of the evidence suggested that no such intention or understanding existed when the Constitution was drafted, popularly approved and enacted into law.[470] Considered in isolation, each step in the reasoning seemed plausible, but when its cumulative effect was considered, the result was not only far-removed from the text of the Constitution, but involved a significant transfer of power to the courts to make determinations about the proper political balance to be struck in relation to the legal regulation of elections and political speech. While the Constitution was intended to establish a system of representative and responsible government, this did not necessarily imply all of the characteristics that some might think desirable in a democracy, such as a set of political constitutional rights enforceable by unelected judges against the determinations of a democratically elected the Parliament.[471]

**465** *Theophanous v Herald & Weekly Times Ltd* (1994) 182 CLR 104, 121, 136–7, citing *New York Times Co v Sullivan* 376 US 254 (1963).
**466** *Theophanous* (1994) 182 CLR 104, 188.
**467** *Stephens v West Australian Newspapers Ltd* (1994) 182 CLR 211, 232–4, 257.
**468** See, eg, the articles in the special edition of (1994) 16 *Sydney Law Review* and (2011) 30 *University of Queensland Law Journal*.
**469** Stephen Donaghue, 'The Clamour of Silent Constitutional Principles' (1996) 24 *Federal Law Review* 133.
**470** See Jeffrey Goldsworthy, 'Constitutional Implications and Freedom of Political Speech: A Reply to Stephen Donaghue' (1997) 32 *Monash University Law Review* 362.
**471** George Winterton, 'Popular Sovereignty and Constitutional Continuity' (1998) 26 *Federal Law Review* 1; Nicholas Aroney, *Freedom of Speech in the Constitution* (Centre for Independent Studies, 1998).

Concerns and misgivings were also expressed by members of the Court. In *Cunliffe*, Brennan, Toohey and McHugh JJ held that Part 2A of the *Migration Act* was supported by the aliens power and was not contrary to the implied freedom. They formed a close majority with Dawson J, who continued to express doubt about the implied freedom.[472] There was a significantly restrained note, however, in the judgments of Brennan and McHugh JJ in *Cunliffe* as well as in *Theophanous*. The common concern was that such implications must be securely based in the text of the Constitution. In *Cunliffe*, Brennan J emphasised, as he had done in *Australian Capital Television*,[473] that the implied freedom is not a personal right conferred on individuals; rather, it is a freedom that arises as a consequence of the implied constitutional prohibition on any law that is prejudicial to the system of representative democracy mandated by the Constitution.[474] In *Theophanous*, the point was made even more fundamentally. Dawson J reiterated his view that what the text of the Constitution requires is that members of Parliament are 'chosen' by the people, and that this choice must be 'genuine' and 'informed'.[475] McHugh J insisted that representative government is mandated by the Constitution only to the extent that the text and structure of the Constitution actually prescribes it, and that its meaning should not be extended by reference to value-laden conceptions conceived 'independently' of the Constitution.[476] Brennan J added that while 'judicial policy' may have a role in the development of the common law, it has no role in the interpretation of the Constitution. While he continued to maintain that the implied freedom arises from the structure of the Constitution and not from any 'particular word or phrase' in its text, he insisted that nothing in the Constitution requires that the common law must conform to the implied freedom.[477] Similar views were forcefully expressed a year later in *McGinty v Western Australia* when a majority rejected the proposition that State electoral divisions were contrary to a constitutionally implied right to equality of voting power: partly on the ground that the text and structure of the Constitution does not give rise to such an implication, and partly on the ground that the principle of federalism supports the separate representation and independent self-governance of local communities irrespective of disparities in population.[478]

**472** *Cunliffe v Commonwealth* (1994) 182 CLR 272, 360–66.
**473** *Australian Capital Television Pty Ltd v Commonwealth* (1992) 177 CLR 106, 150.
**474** As a consequence, he reasoned, the implied immunity is enjoyed by those entitled to vote in Australian elections, and therefore is not something enjoyed by non-citizens. See *Cunliffe v Commonwealth* (1994) 182 CLR 272, 326–9.
**475** *Theophanous v Herald & Weekly Times Ltd* (1994) 182 CLR 104, 189–90.
**476** Ibid, 195–205.
**477** Ibid, 143–4, 149–50, 153.
**478** *McGinty v Western Australia* (1996) 186 CLR 140, 168–9, 184–5, 230–36, discussed in Chapter 2, Part II.3. Also decided around this time were *Langer v Commonwealth* (1996) 186 CLR 302 and *Muldowney v South Australia* (1996) 186 CLR 352.

## 3 Text, structure and proportionality

### An agreed test, diverse value judgments

The misgivings expressed by Brennan, McHugh and Dawson JJ bore fruit in the *Lange* case,[479] a rare unanimous judgment in which the Court affirmed the existence of the implied freedom but insisted that it was based only on the 'text and structure' of the Constitution. The case involved defamation proceedings initiated by the former Prime Minister of New Zealand in relation to allegedly defamatory imputations made during an Australian television broadcast. The defendant argued, among other things, that the publication was in exercise of the constitutional freedom of political communication and therefore protected on the basis of the Court's decision in *Theophanous*.

The Court took the opportunity to clarify the constitutional basis and nature of the implied freedom. Disclaiming reliance on any 'free-standing' conception of representative democracy or a personal right to communicate, the Court insisted that the question is not 'what is required by representative and responsible government?', but rather 'what do the terms and structure of the Constitution prohibit, authorize or require?'[480] The implied freedom extends 'only so far as is necessary' to give effect to the Constitution understood in this way.[481] As a consequence, the test to be applied had to be tied to the text and structure of the Constitution, rather than derived from value judgments based on principles and ideas external to the Constitution. To this end, the Court proposed two conditions of validity:

> The first condition is that the object of the law is compatible with the maintenance of the constitutionally prescribed system of representative and responsible government or the procedure for submitting a proposed amendment to the Constitution to the informed decision of the people which the Constitution prescribes. The second is that the law is reasonably appropriate and adapted to achieving that legitimate object or end.[482]

Building on this, the Court proposed a two-stage inquiry:

> First, does the law effectively burden freedom of communication about government or political matters either in its terms, operation or effect? Second, if the law effectively burdens that freedom, is the law reasonably appropriate and adapted to serve a legitimate end the fulfilment of which is compatible with the maintenance of the constitutionally prescribed system of representative and responsible government and the procedure prescribed by s 128 for submitting a proposed amendment of the Constitution to the informed decision of the people?[483]

**479** *Lange v Australian Broadcasting Corporation* (1997) 189 CLR 520.
**480** Ibid, 567. The Court undertook a close textual examination of the provisions of the Constitution relevant to the establishment of the systems of representative government (ss 1, 7, 8, 13, 24, 28, 30, 128) and responsible government (ss 6, 62, 64, 49 and 83): ibid, 557–9.
**481** Ibid, 567.
**482** Ibid, 561–2.
**483** Ibid, 567–8.

This more cautious approach led the Court to reject the suggestion of a general constitutional defence to defamation that had been articulated in *Theophanous*. Instead, a narrower revised understanding of the defence of qualified privilege was adopted, based on the proposition that in a representative democracy members of the public share a general, reciprocal interest in the dissemination and receipt of information and views about political matters.[484]

Despite the unanimity in *Lange*, differences remained and individual members of the Court soon interpreted and applied the *Lange* test in divergent ways. In *Levy v Victoria*,[485] decided just weeks later, the Court had to consider Victorian regulations which made it an offence to enter a prescribed hunting area during the hunting season without a valid game licence. Lawrence Levy entered such an area in order to protest against the practice of duck shooting. His protest activities, while arguably communicative, were not in the form of speech or writing. On this point, a majority of the Court affirmed that the implied freedom extends, in principle, to conduct that communicates a political message.[486] Nonetheless, the Court was unanimous in rejecting Levy's argument. The regulations had been introduced following reports of dangerous confrontations between armed shooters and protestors, and the prohibition of entry into duck shooting areas could be justified in order to prevent potentially lethal encounters.

Although the result in *Levy* was unanimous, the Court split over the way in which a law that places a burden on political communication should be assessed. While he had joined in the unanimous decision of the Court in *Lange*, Dawson J interpreted the *Lange* test as not requiring the Court to 'balance' the various considerations for and against the law, but rather only to ask whether the impugned law precludes the holding of the free elections required by the Constitution.[487] Brennan CJ denied that the courts should 'assume the power to determine that some more limited restriction than that imposed by an impugned law could suffice'.[488] Gaudron J considered that the more stringent test favoured by the majority in *Australian Capital Television* should apply where the purpose of a law is to restrict the relevant freedom.[489] And while Kirby, Toohey and Gummow JJ referred to and applied the *Lange* test without adding any limiting qualifications,[490] Toohey and Gummow JJ noted the existence of a variety of tests applicable to various categories of interference with political communication,[491] and Kirby J suggested that 'a universally accepted criterion is elusive'.[492]

**484** Ibid, 568–75.
**485** (1997) 189 CLR 579.
**486** Ibid, 594–5, 613, 622–3, 641.
**487** Ibid, 608–9.
**488** Ibid, 598.
**489** Ibid, 620.
**490** Ibid, 610–11, 622, 624.
**491** Ibid, 614.
**492** Ibid, 643, 647.

**The elimination of balancing?**

These differences in approach underscored the variability in judgment that is invited whenever the Court is required to weigh up whether a law pursues a legitimate objective in a proportionate manner. Some critics accordingly argued that the Constitution's text and structure alone cannot provide the guidance needed to assess whether a law is justified as pursuing a legitimate objective in a proportionate manner, for judges will inevitably have to draw on substantive principles and values that are extraneous to the Constitution.[493] This line of criticism prompted a response by McHugh J in the next important case on the implied freedom, *Coleman v Power*.[494] The case involved protest activities being undertaken by a university student in a Townsville street mall during which he publicly accused a particular police officer of being corrupt. Coleman was convicted under several charges, including that he had used 'threatening, abusive, or insulting words' in or near a public place contrary to s 7A(1)(d) of the *Vagrants, Gaming and Other Offences Act 1931* (Qld). Coleman successfully appealed against the charge, ultimately to the High Court. Gummow, Hayne and Kirby JJ interpreted s 7A(1)(d) as applying only to words used to harm someone in a way that is provocative in the sense that they are intended or reasonably likely to provoke a violent reaction. They considered that interpreted in this way the section could not apply to Coleman's use of insulting words to a police officer because the police are trained and expected to respond in a lawfully appropriate way when insulted.[495] McHugh J considered that the section could not be interpreted in this way and that the implied freedom had to be applied to the facts in the case. He held that the law could not be justified as imposing a burden that was reasonably appropriate and adapted to achieving an appropriate objective in a manner compatible with the maintenance of the constitutionally prescribed system of representative government.[496]

In the course of his judgment, McHugh J responded to the criticism that the implied freedom necessarily requires the Court to engage in value judgments for which the bare text and structure of the Constitution does not provide any substantial guidance. His main point was to reject the proposition that in determining whether a law contravenes the freedom it is necessary to engage in a weighing or balancing of one social objective against another in a way that would require the Court to take into consideration 'political or other theories external to the Constitution'.[497] Because the implied freedom rests solely on the Constitution's text and structure, its scope is limited to what is strictly necessary to protect the constitutionally mandated system of representative and responsible government.[498] There is no question, therefore, of balancing; rather, it is a

**493** Adrienne Stone, 'The Limits of Constitutional Text and Structure' (1999) 23 *Melbourne University Law Review* 668.
**494** (2004) 220 CLR 1.
**495** *Coleman v Power* (2004) 220 CLR 1, 74, 79.
**496** Ibid, 53–4.
**497** Ibid, 48.
**498** Ibid, 49.

question of compatibility. Accordingly, even though the *Lange* formula asks whether the law is 'reasonably appropriate and adapted to serve a legitimate end', he maintained that this ought to be understood to be qualified by the requirement that both the end itself, and the means adopted to achieve the end, must be compatible with the constitutionally prescribed system.[499] To make this clear, he proposed that the formula should be reframed so that it expressly states that the law must serve the legitimate end 'in a manner' which is compatible with the constitutionally mandated system.[500] There is, he acknowledged, always a need for a value judgment to be made whether a law unreasonably burdens political communication; but by limiting the question in this way, he proposed that the Court would be able to avoid 'nice judgments as to whether one course is slightly preferable to another'.[501]

### Varying levels of scrutiny

Significantly, although they did not necessarily agree with McHugh J's particular line of reasoning, Gummow, Hayne and Kirby JJ expressed agreement with his reformulation of the *Lange* test.[502] Yet in the cases since *Coleman*, the judges have continued to interpret and apply the test differently. In *Coleman* itself, Gleeson CJ, Callinan and Heydon JJ dissented on the ground that the law could not be read down as Gummow, Hayne and Kirby JJ had proposed and that, contrary to McHugh J, it pursued a legitimate goal in an appropriate manner, namely to prohibit threatening, abusive or insulting speech in public places. For Gleeson CJ, the test to be applied was whether the law is 'reasonably appropriate and adapted', rather than 'proportional' in the broader sense, and that it is not proper for the courts to strike down legislation simply on the ground that some less restrictive legislative means would have achieved the objective.[503] Heydon J insisted that it is quite legitimate for the legislature to seek to maintain standards of civility in public places, and he agreed that the *Lange* test should not be understood as requiring the Court to determine whether the law is the 'sole or best means' of achieving such an objective. Reasonable minds may differ about what the best means might be, but it is not the role of judges to substitute their views of the matter for those of the democratically accountable Parliament and Executive.[504] On the other hand, defending a much more active role for the courts, Kirby J responded by characterising Heydon J's preference for civilised debate and discussion as a description of a kind of 'intellectual salon' where the insults, calumny and invective typical of Australian politics were somehow absent.[505] For Kirby J, 'the Constitution addresses the nation's representative government as it is practised'.[506]

**499** Ibid, 50.
**500** Ibid, 50.
**501** Ibid, 53.
**502** Ibid, 78, 82.
**503** Ibid, 31–2.
**504** Ibid, 123–4.
**505** Ibid, 91.
**506** Ibid. See also *Roberts v Bass* (2002) 212 CLR 1, 62–3, 78.

In several subsequent cases, the Court was asked to extend the application of the implied freedom to new situations. In *Australian Capital Television*, McHugh J had affirmed that the Constitution implies rights to political participation and association in addition to communication.[507] Similarly, in *Kruger v Commonwealth*, several judges, especially Gaudron and Toohey JJ, considered the possible application of an implied freedom of association and movement to the forced removal of Aboriginal children from their families;[508] and in *Mulholland v Australian Electoral Commission*,[509] McHugh and Kirby JJ affirmed the existence of an implied freedom of political association, while Gummow and Hayne JJ accepted that such a freedom might exist as a corollary to the implied freedom of communication. *Mulholland* involved challenges by the Democratic Labor Party (DLP) to provisions of the *Electoral Act 1918* (Cth) which required that a political party that did not hold seats in Parliament could only be registered if it could demonstrate that it had at least 500 members who were not members of other political parties. The DLP was unsuccessful in convincing the Court that the law contravened the implied freedom of political communication, for several reasons, including most importantly that the constitutional protection operates as a 'shield' to protect existing rights and not as a 'sword' to generate new rights or freedoms.[510] In *Wainohu v New South Wales* and *Tajjour v New South Wales* the proposition that a 'free-standing' freedom of political association might be derived independently from the Constitution, rather than as a corollary to the freedom of political communication, was rejected.[511] *Tajjour* involved a challenge to s 93X of the *Crimes Act 1900* (NSW), which provides that a person who 'habitually consorts' with two or more 'convicted offender[s]', and does so after receiving an 'official warning' from a police officer, is guilty of an offence. A majority held that s 93X did not contravene the implied freedom of political communication.

In *Nationwide News*, Deane and Toohey JJ had described the implied freedom as extending to discussion of the exercise of not only legislative and executive power but also judicial power.[512] In several State Supreme Court decisions, it has been held that the implied freedom does not extend to communications which discuss or are critical of judicial decisions as such, because these are not manifestations of the system of representative and responsible government itself.[513] In *APLA Ltd v Legal Services Commissioner (NSW)*[514] the Court similarly rejected the argument that provisions of a State law preventing legal practitioners from advertising their services in the field of personal injuries

**507** *Australian Capital Television Pty Ltd v Commonwealth* (1992) 177 CLR 106, 227, 232; see also 212.
**508** *Kruger v Commonwealth* (1997) 190 CLR 1, 91, 115–16.
**509** *Mulholland v Australian Electoral Commission* (2004) 220 CLR 181, 219–20, 229, 234, 271.
**510** Ibid, 233, 298, 303–4; but see 267–8, 276; and see also *Rowe v Electoral Commissioner* (2010) 243 CLR 1.
**511** *Wainohu v New South Wales* (2011) 243 CLR 181, 230–31, 251–2; *Tajjour v New South Wales* (2014) 88 ALJR 860, [4], [46], [95], [136], [242]–[244].
**512** *Nationwide News Pty Ltd v Wills* (1992) 177 CLR 1, 74.
**513** *John Fairfax Publications Pty Ltd v Attorney-General (NSW)* (2000) 181 ALR 694; *Herald & Weekly Times Ltd v Popovic* (2003) 9 VR 1; *Conservation Council of SA Inc v Chapman* (2003) 87 SASR 62.
**514** (2005) 224 CLR 322.

contravened the implied freedom of political communication on the ground that the communications did not concern the operation of the system of representative government. The Court also by majority rejected the proposition that a parallel implication could be derived from Chapter III of the Constitution.[515] In these cases, a majority of the Court reiterated the need to contain the implied freedom to its constitutional foundations, and only countenanced the application of the implied freedom to the administration of justice where the relevant communications involved the operation of the legislative and executive branches of government. In *Hogan v Hinch*[516] this approach was confirmed when the Court upheld a law prohibiting the publication of the identity of an alleged offender or a person giving evidence in the course of a prosecution. It was considered that the law did place a burden on political communication as the defendant in the case was advocating the repeal of the provision that prevented disclosure of the identity of the accused, but it was held that the law was nonetheless reasonably appropriate and adapted to the protection of the community, the rehabilitation of offenders and the protection of the court process.

In *Wotton v Queensland*,[517] the Court had to consider a challenge to parole conditions imposed on an Aboriginal elder and former local councillor convicted of participating in a riot following the death in custody of Mulrunji Doomadgee on Palm Island. Wotton was sentenced to six years imprisonment but was granted parole on conditions which required him, among other things, not to attend public meetings on Palm Island without the prior approval of his corrective services officer, not to receive any payment or benefit in connection with any dealings with the media, and not to speak to or have any interaction whatsoever with the media, although this latter condition was later revoked. Under the relevant Queensland Act, a parole order can include conditions which the parole board 'reasonably considers necessary . . . to stop the prisoner committing an offence', and a separate section makes it an offence for a person to interview or obtain a written or recorded statement from a prisoner, including a person who is released on parole, without written approval. It was argued that the Act contravened the implied freedom of political communication.

It was conceded by the Commonwealth – and a majority of the Court said that it was correctly conceded – that the case was appropriately dealt with on the assumption that the law placed a requisite burden on freedom of political communication in terms of the first limb of the *Lange* test.[518] The Court unanimously held, however, that the relevant sections of the Act were a reasonably appropriate and adapted means of securing the legitimate goal of maintaining community safety and crime prevention through the humane containment, supervision and rehabilitation of convicted offenders.[519] In a joint judgment,

**515** On implications from Chapter III of the Constitution, see Chapter 9.
**516** (2011) 243 CLR 506.
**517** (2012) 246 CLR 1.
**518** Ibid, 15.
**519** Ibid, 16.

Gleeson CJ, Gummow, Hayne, Crennan and Bell JJ considered that, notwithstanding the way in which the second limb of the *Lange* test is described, there is a distinction between laws which directly restrict communications that are inherently political and laws which only incidentally restrict political communication, and that the former category will be more difficult to justify.[520] They considered that the provisions of the Act were reasonably appropriate measures directed to such goals as the protection of the community, crime prevention and good conduct by parolees, and they intimated that the applicant should instead have commenced different proceedings in which he questioned whether the parole conditions had been imposed in accordance with the Act.[521]

### Individual right or structural implication?

In a forceful dissenting judgment in *Wotton*, Heydon J drew attention to the tendency of defendants to concede the satisfaction of the first limb of the *Lange* test and the tendency of the Court too readily to agree.[522] As his Honour put it, the common practice of conceding the first limb 'tends to generate an insidious belief that it will always be met'.[523] In Heydon J's view, because Queensland, the first defendant in the case, had not conceded the point, it remained necessary for the Court to determine it.[524] Adopting an approach that had been proposed by Callinan J, Heydon J asked whether the law imposed an effective burden or realistic threat to freedom of political communication,[525] and he concluded that it did not. This practice of so readily acknowledging the existence of a burden on political communication contrasts with the Court's approach to whether a law imposes a substantial burden on interstate trade and commerce for the purposes of s 92. However, on the Court's current interpretation, neither the implied freedom nor the trade and commerce aspect of s 92 give rise to an 'individual right'. The fundamental jurisprudence of both provisions is in this respect similar. Just as the free trade theory of s 92 looks to the systemic effect of the law on interstate trade, so the implied freedom exists to protect that degree of freedom of communication necessary to maintain an effective system of representative government. Neither gives rise to an individual right, and therefore the specific effect of a law on the conduct of an individual should not be regarded as decisive. However, too ready a concession that freedom of political communication has been burdened when a law restricts the speech rights of an individual will have the practical effect of treating the implied freedom as an individual right in this respect.

In *Monis v The Queen*,[526] the Court had to consider provisions of the *Criminal Code* (Cth) which made it an offence to use the postal service in a way that a

**520** Ibid, citing *Hogan v Hinch* (2011) 243 CLR 506.
**521** Ibid, 16.
**522** Ibid, 19.
**523** Ibid.
**524** Ibid.
**525** Ibid, 23, citing *Lange v Australian Broadcasting Corporation* (1997) 189 CLR 520, 567 and *Coleman v Power* (2004) 220 CLR 1, 112.
**526** (2013) 249 CLR 92.

reasonable person would regard as being, in all the circumstances, harassing or offensive. The case arose when letters were sent to parents and relatives of soldiers killed in Afganistan which criticised Australia's involvement in the war and accused the soldiers of being murderers of innocent civilians and children. An appeal to the High Court from the NSW Court of Criminal Appeal, which had rejected the argument that the law contravened the implied freedom, was narrowly unsuccessful, the High Court splitting 3:3, and the decision of the lower court being upheld pursuant to s 23(2)(a) of the *Judiciary Act 1903* (Cth). The case turned on whether the law pursued a legitimate objective and, more widely, on the kinds of communications which the implied freedom protects. In a joint judgment, Crennan, Kiefel and Bell JJ explained that they understood the second limb of the *Lange* test to involve three distinct inquiries: first, whether the law is reasonably appropriate and adapted, or proportionate, to a legitimate end; second, whether both the end and the means of the law are compatible with the constitutionally prescribed system; and, third, whether the law is itself a proportionate means of maintaining the system of representative government.[527] Finding, among other things, that the law sought to protect people from the intrusion of unsolicited material into their 'personal domain', they concluded that the law was proportionate in all these senses.[528] French CJ, Hayne and Heydon JJ, on the contrary, found that the law contravened the implied freedom. French CJ agreed that there were separate questions concerning whether the law pursued a legitimate object and whether the law was compatible with the constitutionally prescribed system, but considered that on the facts of the case the two limbs collapsed: in his view, the end of the law, which was the prohibition of the use of the postal services in a reasonably offensive manner, was neither legitimate nor compatible and indeed that its incompatibility made it illegitimate.[529] Hayne J, who reasoned similarly, added that, in his view, the law regulated the civility of discourse, and that *Coleman* had decided that this was not a constitutionally legitimate objective.[530] Heydon J agreed in the conclusion that the law contravened the implied freedom, understood according to the present state of the High Court's jurisprudence.[531] However, he took the opportunity to subject the prevailing doctrine to an extended critique.[532] On his view, the basis, nature and extent of the doctrine had never been clear. The 'reasonably appropriate and adapted test', he pointed out, does not mean what it says. Individual judges have disagreed over its meaning and application since the implied freedom was first articulated. The present state of the authorities required him to find that the law was constitutionally invalid, and yet this meant the Parliament was unable to protect the human rights of grieving parents from

**527** Ibid, 191–5.
**528** Ibid, 205–7, 212–16.
**529** Ibid, 134.
**530** Ibid, 172.
**531** Ibid, 184.
**532** Ibid, 181, citing *Australian Capital Television* (1992) 177 CLR 106, 177–91; *Australian Broadcasting Corporation v Lenah Game Meats Pty Ltd* (2001) 208 CLR 199, 298–309, 330–39.

suffering the indignity and anguish of having their deceased children reviled. In his view, the implied freedom was a 'noble and idealistic enterprise which has failed, is failing and will go on failing'.[533]

Finally, in *Unions NSW v New South Wales*,[534] the Court had to consider provisions of the *Election Funding, Expenditure and Disclosures Act 1981* (NSW) which sought to regulate the making of political donations and the expenditure of money on political advertising in relation to State elections. Like the legislation considered and struck down in *Australian Capital Television*, the professed objective of the law was to maintain the integrity of the political and electoral system. The Act required public disclosure of all political donations received and all electoral expenditure incurred by or on behalf of a political party, an elected member, a group or a candidate of the NSW Parliament. Third-party campaigners were required to disclose political donations received and expenditure on political advertising, and major political donors had to disclose political donations of $1000 or more. Caps for political donations were established at $5000 per year for political donations to registered parties and $2000 per year for donations to unregistered parties, elected members, candidates and third-party campaigners. Caps for electoral advertising for State election campaigns were also imposed. The Act provided for public funding of election campaigns for parties and candidates. Reportable donations and other relevant information were to be disclosed on a website.

Two additional sections were inserted into the Act in 2012. Section 96D made it unlawful for political donations to be made by persons other than enrolled voters, such as corporations and trade unions. In addition, for the purposes of the capping provisions, s 95G(6) aggregated the amount spent in electoral advertising and communications by a party and affiliated organisations, meaning any body that is authorised by the rules of a political party to appoint delegates to the governing body of the party or to participate in preselection of candidates. These provisions were expressed to apply only to State and local elections, and other sections of the Act provided for specific exceptions in relation to donations directed to federal election campaigns. A collection of trade unions affected by these provisions in relation to their practice of making donations to the Australian Labor Party and campaigning on its behalf challenged their constitutionality on the ground that they were contrary to the implied freedom of political communication, as well as a similarly implied freedom of political association and a corresponding implied freedom arising from the State Constitution.

In a joint judgment, French CJ, Hayne, Crennan, Kiefel and Bell JJ upheld the challenge on the basis of the implied freedom. They began their judgment with a statement which appeared to reconcile the tension in the Court's previous decisions between free-standing conceptions of popular sovereignty and

**533** *Monis v The Queen* (2013) 249 CLR 92, 181–3.
**534** [2013] HCA 58; 304 ALR 266.

representative democracy on one hand, and the proposition that the freedom is limited to what is necessarily implied by the text and structure of the Constitution.[535] However, they affirmed that despite the insistence in *Lange* on the system of representative and responsible government specifically provided for by the Constitution, the inseparability of political issues arising at a State and Commonwealth level meant that, in practice, the implied freedom arising out of the Constitution must apply to the discussion of State as well as federal political issues.[536]

In previous cases, Callinan and Heydon JJ had expressed concern that the first limb of the *Lange* test – the requirement that a burden be imposed on political communication – had too often been taken for granted. The implied freedom is not a personal right but is rather a prohibition on legislative power deemed necessary to protect the operation of the democratic system as a whole. The liberal approach to finding such burdens in political communication cases thus seemed inconsistent with the much more restrictive approach to finding burdens on interstate trade in s 92 cases. In *Unions NSW*, the joint judgment appeared to acknowledge the force of this point, but considered that the restriction on the making of donations constituted an indirect burden on freedom of political communication that was sufficiently consequential, and that it was not necessary to assess the extent of the burden to come to that conclusion.[537] Rather, the extent of the burden was said to be relevant to the second limb assessment of whether the law is a proportionate means of achieving its objectives.[538] Indeed, the Court must assess not merely whether the law is a suitable means to secure its objectives, but whether there might be 'alternative, reasonably practicable and less restrictive means of doing so'.[539] The majority thus directly rejected the proposition that legislatures are to be accorded a 'margin of choice' in devising means to secure their objectives, underscoring the willingness of members of the Court to substitute their own views as to the most appropriate means of securing the legislative objective.[540]

However, even this remained a moot point. While it was accepted that the maintenance of the integrity of the political process was a legitimate objective, it was held that neither s 96D nor s 95G(6) did anything to achieve that objective and that, indeed, they lacked any coherent legitimating purpose whatsoever.[541] Unlike the other prohibitions in the Act targeting large donations, it was observed that s 96D imposed a 'wide-ranging' but 'incomplete' prohibition on all donations from persons who were not electors and from corporations and other entities. Even though all laws regulating the making of political donations place burdens which fall on the corrupt and the non-corrupt alike, and are thus

**535** *Unions NSW v New South Wales* (2013) 304 ALR 266, 272.
**536** Ibid, 272–4.
**537** Ibid, 276–7.
**538** Ibid, 277.
**539** Ibid 278.
**540** Ibid.
**541** Ibid, 279–81, 281–2.

over-inclusive in this sense, s 96D was so over-inclusive that it was considered not only disproportionate, but entirely lacking in any rational connection with the goal of minimising political corruption.

In a separate judgment, Keane J also held that the provisions impermissibly burdened the implied freedom of political communication. However, he came to this conclusion on the basis that the two provisions were disproportionate. In his Honour's view, the basis of the implied freedom is the 'constitutionally protected interest... of the people of the Commonwealth in the free and informed exercise of the political choices required of them by ss 7, 24 and 128 of the Constitution', and he considered that the relevant question is whether the law prevents the constitutionally required free flow of politically salient information.[542] Observing that the second limb of the *Lange* test might be understood to require the Court to engage in decision-making that is more 'legislative' than 'judicial' in character,[543] he seemed to cast doubt on the proposition that the Court should assess whether a less intrusive means could have been adopted to achieve the objective of the law.[544] What matters is whether the law inhibits the flow of political communication necessary to preserve 'the political sovereignty of the people of the Commonwealth'.[545] Rather than maintain 'a level electoral playing field' in an appropriately 'calibrated' way, he considered that the two provisions discriminated against certain sources of political funding in a way that distorted the flow of political communication.[546]

*Unions NSW* forcefully affirms the power of the Court to undertake assessments of the proportionality of laws which place burdens on virtually any form of political communication, widely conceived. The fact that the joint judgment denied that the law lacked any rational connection to the objective of preventing political corruption emphasises the exacting scrutiny that members of the Court are prepared to apply in such cases. While the Court's decisions in *Lange* and *Unions NSW* were unanimous, in many freedom of political communication cases, such as *Theophanous*, *Coleman* and *Monis*, the Court has been closely divided – a fact that underscores the degree to which such cases give rise to questions about which reasonable minds are likely to differ. While this might suggest that a generous margin of choice should be accorded to the Commonwealth and State Parliaments, it seems clear from recent cases that the Court is going to scrutinise such laws closely, especially when they are directed at forms of communication as such.[547]

**542** Ibid, 290, 301.
**543** Ibid, 293.
**544** Ibid, 294.
**545** Ibid, 295.
**546** Ibid, 295, 296, 301–2.
**547** In *Tajjour v New South Wales* (2014) 88 ALJR 860, the law prohibiting consorting with convicted offenders was upheld on the ground that it did not impose an undue burden on the implied freedom. Part of the reason was that it was not directed at political communication, but rather limited the occasions on which such communications can occur (Hayne J at 885), and that the burden was not substantial (Crennan, Kiefel and Bell JJ at 891). Keane J found that the law did not burden the implied freedom because on its proper construction it did not proscribe political communication as such (at 900, 907).

## VI Conclusions

The framers did not include a bill of rights in the Constitution largely because they had confidence in the institutions of representative and responsible government that they had experienced in their respective colonies and expected to see established for the federation as a whole. Unlike many modern constitutions, the Australian document contains an apparently 'scattered' array of provisions which place limits on legislative power and protect certain freedoms. The reason they appear scattered, however, is because the purpose of the Constitution was not to protect individual rights through constitutional guarantees but rather to form the Australian colonies into a federation. The primary objective of the framers was to establish a federal system of government in which the functions and responsibilities of the Commonwealth and the States would be adequately defined and integrated into a coherent plan. For this reason, there was more concern to protect the rights of the States to operate as self-governing political communities than to protect the rights of individuals through judicially-enforceable constitutional guarantees. The limitations on governmental power that do exist in the Constitution were accordingly shaped more by the imperatives of federation than by an abstract concern to protect the rights and freedoms of individual citizens.

As the earlier chapters of this book have shown, the structure of the Commonwealth Parliament and the scope and demarcation of its legislative powers vis-à-vis the States are shaped profoundly by federal imperatives. As the chapters that follow will also demonstrate, the same is true of the provisions of the Constitution concerning the Executive and the Judiciary. This chapter has shown that much the same can be said for the various limitations that are imposed on the legislative powers of the Commonwealth and the States. Thus, the protections of property rights (s 51(xxxi)) and freedom of religion (s 116) are framed as limitations on the legislative powers of the Commonwealth, not the States; and the guarantees of freedom of trade, commerce and intercourse (s 92), trial by jury (s 80), and non-discrimination (ss 51(ii), 99, 102, 117) are federally defined and limited.

In addition to these explicit limitations on power, the High Court has constructed an implied constitutional guarantee of freedom of political communication that binds both the Commonwealth and the States and applies to the discussion of political matters at both levels of government. The extension of the implied freedom to the States is based on the proposition that although the Constitution establishes a system of representative democracy only for the Commonwealth, Australian politics is so integrated that a distinction cannot be drawn between discussions of politics at the two levels of government. Although this appears to adapt the implied freedom to the federal nature of the system, it has a nationalising effect. This is because the implied freedom is conceptually grounded upon an essentially unitary conception of the Australian democratic system, predicated upon a direct relationship between 'the people' and 'the government', and therefore requires the same uniform standard, derived from the Commonwealth Constitution, to be applied to both the Commonwealth and the States. However, this conclusion sits somewhat uneasily with the system of 'federal democracy' that the Constitution establishes, involving a complex set of interlocking but distinct relationships between the people of each State, the people of the Commonwealth, and their respective constitutions and governments at a Commonwealth and State level. As was seen in Chapter 2, the Constitution provides for an 'adaptation of representative democracy to federalism' which militates against the proposition that the rights of individual citizens must be absolutely uniform across the entire federation.[548]

For this reason it may be better to conceive the foundation of the implied freedom of political communication as based rather in a set of implied intergovernmental constraints, as the High Court seemed to envisage in its early decision in *Smithers*.[549] Here the idea would be that, building on the doctrine of intergovernmental immunities,[550] it lies beyond the power of the Commonwealth and the States to interfere with the independent functioning of the democratic systems of each other. On this view, it might also lie beyond the competence of the Commonwealth to interfere with the proper functioning of the democratic system operating at a federal level because the Commonwealth is itself constitutively federal, incorporating the component democratic bodies politic of the States into its own body politic in a way that maintains the integrity of each State as a self-governing body politic. If the implied freedom were to be reconceived in this way, there would be less warrant for an implied limitation on the capacity of the States to interfere with their own democratic systems, except that the integrity of the federal system is dependent on the integrity of the State systems as well. The High Court is of course far from reconceptualising the implied freedom in this way, but such an approach would at least cohere better, it is submitted, with the federal nature of the Constitution than the existing rationale.[551]

In its interpretation and applications of the 'limiting' provisions and doctrines discussed in this chapter, the Court has at times taken a relatively liberal approach and struck down legislation forthrightly and sometimes courageously. Its decisions in the *Bank Nationalisation* case and *Australian Capital Television* are prominent examples. At other times, the Court has been more guarded and has declined to find controversial legislation unconstitutional, at least on the basis of the express limits on power discussed in this chapter. Its decisions in the *Jehovah's Witnesses* and *Tobacco Advertising* cases are examples. Occasionally, the Court has delivered unanimous judgments which promise to provide certainty and stability in areas of law previously fraught with disagreement. Its decisions in *Cole v Whitfield* and *Lange* are obvious examples of this. But much more often

**548** Chapter 2, Part II.3.
**549** See the discussion of *R v Smithers; Ex parte Benson* (1912) 16 CLR 99 in Part III.2 above.
**550** See Chapter 4, Part III.
**551** See James Stellios, 'Using Federalism to Protect Political Communication: Implications from Fedreal Representative Government' (2007) 31 *Melboume University Law Review* 239.

the Court has been closely divided, reflecting the difficult judgments that have to be made in the application of constitutional guarantees that involve questions of value and 'balancing' of competing concerns and interests. Sometimes these differences of opinion seem to be shaped by varying views about the proper role of courts in assessing the constitutionality of legislation enacted by democratically elected parliaments. The way in which individual judges approach the application of the implied freedom of political communication seems to be especially influenced by these concerns. At other times, the differences seem to be shaped by varying views about the proper relationship between private rights and public values. Disagreements over the application of the just terms and free trade requirements seem often to be driven by underlying views of this nature.

The existence of explicit provisions in the Constitution that place limitations on the powers of the Commonwealth and the States require the High Court to undertake the task of interpreting and applying them. An assessment of whether the Constitution provides an adequate framework for the good governance of the federation and the well-being of its citizens without a comprehensive charter of rights needs to be undertaken not only in the light of a charter's glowing promises, but also in light of the practical operation of judicial review with respect to the limitations on power that do exist in the Constitution. Our judges approach the task of exercising judicial review very seriously and conscientiously, but they disagree about the results in particular cases as often as our elected representatives disagree about the policies contained in particular bills before our parliaments. Significant powers are given to judges to exercise judicial review, and we entrust these responsibilities upon them not because they are democratically accountable but due to their demonstrated knowledge and understanding of the law, and their accumulated wisdom in the task of applying the law to complex disputes. In such tasks, we expect our judges not only to do justice, but to do justice according to law. In constitutional cases this must mean, primarily, the law established by the Constitution and, only secondarily, the law laid down in doctrines and precedents of the Court.

# 6

# The Executive

*The executive power of the Commonwealth is vested in the Queen and is exercisable by the Governor-General as the Queen's representative ....*[1]

*A Governor-General appointed by the Queen shall be Her Majesty's representative in the Commonwealth ....*[2]

*The Governor-General may appoint offices to administer such departments of State of the Commonwealth as the Governor-General in Council may establish. Such officers shall hold office during the pleasure of the Governor-General. They shall be members of the Federal Executive Council and shall be the Queen's Ministers of State for the Commonwealth.*[3]

## I Introduction

Section 61 of the Constitution proclaims that the executive power of the Commonwealth is 'vested in the Queen'. Australia is a constitutional monarchy, and 'the Crown' is therefore at the apex of the Executive Government of the nation. As the preamble to the Constitution records, the people of the Australian colonies agreed to unite 'under the Crown of the United Kingdom'.[4] Provision was also made in the *Constitution Act* that references to the Queen would 'extend to Her Majesty's heirs and successors in the sovereignty of the United Kingdom'.[5] The current reference to the Queen in the Constitution indicates that the present ruling monarch presides over the government of the Commonwealth in her capacity as Queen of Australia. The Queen's 'Royal style and title' in Australia is 'Elizabeth the Second, by the Grace of God Queen of Australia and Her other Realms and Territories, Head of the Commonwealth'.[6] At her Coronation on 2 June 1953, the Queen swore an oath to govern the peoples of Australia and

**1** Commonwealth Constitution, s 61.
**2** Commonwealth Constitution, s 2.
**3** Commonwealth Constitution, s 64.
**4** See also *Commonwealth of Australia Constitution Act 1900* (UK), covering clause 3, which authorised the Queen, with the advice of the Privy Council, to declare by proclamation that the people of the Australian colonies would be united in a Federal Commonwealth.
**5** *Commonwealth of Australia Constitution Act 1900* (UK), covering clause 2.
**6** *Royal Style and Titles Act 1973* (Cth), s 2, schedule.

her other realms 'according to their respective laws and customs'.[7] This reference is significant, for it is apt to include the conventions of parliamentary responsible government as they operate in Australia.

Section 61 also refers to 'the executive power of the Commonwealth', not simply to 'executive power'. It is therefore to be understood as a separate construct to the executive power of the other constituent polities in the federation, the States. Two important questions therefore arise: first, what is 'executive power' and, second, what in particular is the 'executive power *of the Commonwealth*'? Part of the answer to these questions lies in s 61's affirmation that the executive power of the Commonwealth 'extends to the execution and maintenance of this Constitution, and of the laws of the Commonwealth'. No mention is made of the execution of the laws of the States, for it was plainly the intention of the framers of the Constitution that the colonies would continue to exercise their own capacities of local self-government through their independent exercise of legislative, executive and judicial power under their respective constitutions.[8] The executive power of the Commonwealth is thus limited in its 'breadth', to allow room for the exercise of the independent executive authority of the States.

The executive power of the Commonwealth is not only confined, however, to the execution and maintenance of the Constitution and laws of the Commonwealth. Important sources of executive power derive also from the fact that the government of the Commonwealth is vested in the Queen. As noted in Chapter 1, the institution of the Crown pre-existed the Constitution, and there were certain powers, privileges and capacities – commonly referred to as 'the prerogative', to adopt the usage of Dicey[9] – recognised by the common law and which included both powers unique to the Crown and those, otherwise referred to as 'capacities', which it shared with other legal persons by virtue of its juristic personality. While these are powers of the Crown which exist independently of s 61, they are nevertheless regarded as being incorporated therein.[10] In addition, as was noted in Chapter 3, the High Court has also given recognition to an 'implied national power'[11], derived from the status of the Commonwealth as a federal national polity. This power, generally speaking, includes a power to take action which is peculiarly adapted to the government of a nation and which cannot otherwise be carried out for the nation's benefit.[12] These latter aspects of executive power concern what has been called the 'depth' of the power. As will be seen, the nature and ambit of the executive power of the Commonwealth – in

**7** Edward Ratcliff, *The Coronation Service of Her Majesty Queen Elizabeth II* (Cambridge University Press, 1953) 3.

**8** Commonwealth Constitution, ss 106 and 107. See, further, Chapter 10.

**9** The older view of Blackstone was that 'prerogative' was reserved to those powers which uniquely belonged to the Crown and hence did not include those 'capacities' of the Crown which it enjoyed in common with other legal persons by virtue of legal personality. See Chapter 7, n 89.

**10** George Winterton, *Parliament, the Executive and the Governor-General* (Melbourne University Press, 1983) 48–51 and the case referred to therein.

**11** *Pape v Commissioner of Taxation* (2009) 238 CLR 1.

**12** As expressed in the influential statement of Mason J in *Victoria v Commonwealth and Hayden* ('the *AAP* case') (1975) 134 CLR 338, 397.

both its 'breadth' and 'depth' dimensions[13] – is an issue of great importance, and yet one which remains enveloped by a high degree of uncertainty. These questions will be dealt with in detail in Chapter 7.

Furthermore, s 61 declares that the executive power of the Commonwealth, while vested in the Queen, 'is exercisable by the Governor-General as the Queen's representative'. Section 2 provides that a 'Governor-General appointed by the Queen shall be Her Majesty's representative in the Commonwealth'. The government of the Commonwealth is thus carried on in the name of the Queen by the Crown's representative, the Governor-General in the Commonwealth; and analogously by the Governors in the respective States. However, within the system of representative and responsible government which has been constitutionally established in Australia,[14] these are but the formal repositories of the Commonwealth's executive power. According to the conventions of responsible government, they must act on the advice of Ministers of the Crown 'responsible' to Parliament. Section 64 facilitates this by providing:

> The Governor-General may appoint officers to administer such departments of State of the Commonwealth as the Governor-General in Council may establish.
>
> Such officers shall hold office during the pleasure of the Governor-General. They shall be members of the Federal Executive Council, and shall be the Queen's Ministers of State for the Commonwealth.
>
> **Ministers to sit in Parliament**
> After the first general election no Minister of State shall hold office for a longer period than three months unless he is or becomes a senator or a member of the House of Representatives.

Ministers of State for the Commonwealth are thus appointed by, and hold office 'during the pleasure' of, the Governor-General. Together they constitute, pursuant to s 62, the Federal Executive Council which is formed 'to advise the Governor-General in the government of the Commonwealth'. However, by providing that no Minister of State can hold office for a longer period than three months unless he or she becomes a member of Parliament, s 64 ensures that Ministers can be made accountable to the Parliament, such as through the exercise of the Parliament's powers to question Ministers and to require the production of documents.[15] As explained in Chapter 2, the two houses of Parliament are able to exercise substantial influence over the Government through control over taxation and appropriation bills.[16] Section 81 requires all revenues and moneys raised or received by the Commonwealth to form 'one Consolidated Revenue Fund to be appropriated for the purposes of the Commonwealth', and s 83 provides that no

**13** Winterton, above n 10, 70, chs 2 and 3.
**14** See especially *Lange v Australian Broadcasting Corporation* (1997) 189 CLR 520, 557–9; *Sue v Hill* (1999) 199 CLR 462, 499; *Re Patterson; Ex parte Taylor* (2001) 207 CLR 391, 416, 462–6. At a State level, see *New South Wales v Bardolph* (1934) 52 CLR 455 and *Egan v Willis* (1998) 195 CLR 424.
**15** See Chapter 2, Part III.3–4.
**16** Chapter 2, Part III.1.

money can be 'drawn from the Treasury of the Commonwealth except under appropriation made by law'. As also explained in Chapter 2, the relative powers of the House of Representatives and the Senate over money bills are calibrated by s 53 to ensure that the House has control over the initiation and amendment of such bills, while the Senate retains only the power to reject them outright. This reflects a conscious decision of the framers, even though they knew that it would enable the Senate, if it ultimately so wished, to bring down a government.[17] This capacity of the Senate was understood to be exceptional, however.

Nevertheless, this is precisely what occurred in 1975.[18] While the Whitlam Labor Government enjoyed a majority in the House of Representatives, having being in government since 1972, the Opposition Coalition parties gained control of the Senate in 1975. The entry into certain unorthodox financial arrangements and irregularities relating to the funding of proposed major government projects, referred to as 'The Loans Affair', climaxed in the resignation of senior Minister Rex Connor for misleading Parliament. The Opposition Leader, Malcolm Fraser, thereupon led the Shadow Ministry in proclaiming that 'extraordinary' and 'reprehensible' circumstances existed which justified the Coalition in adopting the extraordinary policy of deferring Supply until such time as the Government agreed to submit to an election. Despite the House of Representatives passing Appropriation Bills Nos 1 and 2, the Senate deferred them by a majority of one on three occasions. The Government would not agree to an election even though it only had a very limited time before appropriated funds would run out. The Prime Minister stood on the principle that a government which maintains the confidence of the House of Representatives, which alone can make or break a government, is entitled to continue to govern. This remained the case, he maintained, even though the Senate had denied the Government Supply. Time, and appropriated funds, began to run out in November of 1975. However, the Prime Minister was unable to satisfy Governor-General Sir John Kerr that there were any legal alternatives available to the Government to continue to function when appropriated funds had run out. The Prime Minister also chose not to advise an election to end the impasse. In these circumstances, the Governor-General, exercising his reserve powers, dismissed the Prime-Minister and appointed the Opposition Leader as Caretaker Prime Minister on condition that he would call an election. The election duly took place in the most rancorous of circumstances. The Governor-General has been criticised, then and since, for failing to give the Prime Minister some proper warning, or at least to discuss his concerns openly with him. The precise grounds relied upon by the Governor-General will be examined and discussed below. It suffices to note here that the power that was left in the hands of the Senate by the Constitution to deny a government Supply, even one which still enjoyed the confidence of

**17** See Chapter 2, Part III.1.

**18** See George Winterton, '1975: The Dismissal of the Whitlam Government' in George Winterton and H P Lee (eds), *Australian Constitutional Landmarks* (Cambridge University Press, 2003) ch 10.

the House of Representatives, had been exercised in a manner that resulted in the dismissal of a Prime Minister and the fall of a government.

This instance aside, however, the government of the Commonwealth is ordinarily carried on by the Prime Minister and Ministers of the Crown who maintain the confidence of the House of Representatives.

To a greater extent than is the case with the Commonwealth's legislative and judicial power, the text of the Constitution relating to executive power is sparse, and less than definitive. It cannot alone be relied on to provide a complete understanding of the Commonwealth Executive and its power. Reference must be made to several underlying constitutional fundamentals of which 'responsible government' is only the first. These others include parliamentary supremacy, the separation of powers, and federalism, as these doctrines have been adapted, with responsible government, to Australian conditions.[19] A complete understanding of the Commonwealth Executive and its power within a system of 'responsible government' thus requires, in addition to the text of the Constitution and the history of its drafting in Australia, an appreciation of the constitutional practice and history of the United Kingdom surveyed in Chapter 1 – including the constitutional conflicts of the seventeenth century, the Revolution Settlement of 1688, the evolution of Cabinet government in the eighteenth century and of representative 'responsible government', particularly following the *Reform Act 1832* (UK), and its subsequent evolution and application in Britain's colonies.[20] As George Winterton noted:

> While constitutional discourse should reflect present constitutional realities, one of these is that the Constitution was not inscribed upon a *tabula rasa*. It was born into a common law world ... An interpretation of Ch II which ignores British and Australian constitutional history by taking its words at face value is not 'postcolonial', but rather one which judges the constitutional architecture merely by its façade. Moreover, it is potentially dangerous, for it could lead to grossly exaggerated views of the Governor-General's independent powers.[21]

In short, Chapter II of the Constitution is in many respects merely formal. Its understatement of the substance of the power, and its actual location, is nevertheless sufficient to leave little doubt in the mind of those with an appreciation of the organic development of Anglo-Australian constitutional law and practice that the real power lies with Cabinet, the Prime Minister and responsible ministers being members of Parliament. Thus, although the actual language used by the framers of the Constitution might suggest otherwise, their clear expectation that responsible government would shape the practical functioning of the Constitution permits of confidence that their words were not to be taken literally – that the Governor-General would not substantively wield executive power. In

**19** See Chapter 2, Parts I.2–3 and II.1.
**20** See Chapter 1, Part I.2–3.
**21** George Winterton, 'The Relationship Between Commonwealth Legislative and Executive Power' (2004) 25 *Adelaide Law Review* 21, 34–5.

*Re Patterson; Ex parte Taylor*, Gleeson CJ summarised the system of government established by the Constitution in this way:

> There was to be a constitutional monarchy. There was to be a separation of legislative, executive and judicial powers. The executive power of the Commonwealth was to be vested in the Queen, and exercisable by her representative, the Governor-General. The Governor-General was to act upon the advice of a Federal Executive Council, chosen by the Governor-General and holding office during his or her pleasure. The Governor-General in Council was empowered to establish departments of State, and to appoint, from among the members of the Federal Executive Council, officers to administer such departments. They were to be the Queen's Ministers of State for the Commonwealth. A Minister of State was to be either a senator or a member of the House of Representatives, and thus answerable in and to Parliament for matters relating to the administration of government. Parliament was empowered to make provision as to the number of Ministers of State at any one time, and also to prescribe the offices such Ministers should hold. In the absence of such parliamentary prescription it was to be for the Governor-General to direct which offices should be held by Ministers. Parliament, however, was to control the size of the Ministry.
>
> For the framers of the Constitution to have descended into greater specificity would have imposed an unnecessary and inappropriate degree of inflexibility upon constitutional arrangements that need to be capable of development and adaptability. The deliberate lack of specificity is demonstrated by the absence of any reference to such prominent features of our system of democratic government as the office of Prime Minister, or the Cabinet.
>
> The concept of administration of departments of State, appearing in s 64, is not further defined. This is hardly surprising. The practices and conventions which promote efficient and effective government administration alter over time, and need to be able to respond to changes in circumstances.[22]

This chapter will examine the structure, institutions and offices of 'the Executive Government' of the Commonwealth which are provided for in Chapter II of the Constitution, while Chapter 7 will focus on the nature and ambit of 'the executive power of the Commonwealth'. These two concepts – 'the Executive Government' and 'executive power' – cannot be understood apart from each other in light of the practical and historical context in which the Australian Constitution came into being. An understanding of s 61 'executive power' is enhanced by an initial examination of the structure of 'the Executive Government'.

## II 'Executive power' and 'the Executive'

### 1 Modern definitions and their limitations

To a greater degree than the Commonwealth's legislative and judicial power, 'the executive power of the Commonwealth' is a concept which cannot be equated simply with 'executive power', although the latter may assist in understanding

**22** *Re Patterson; Ex parte Taylor* (2001) 207 CLR 391, 402.

the former. According to its modern connotation, executive power can be taken to refer to that power: to govern the political state pursuant to its laws; to execute its laws (as distinct from enacting those laws, or adjudicating legal disputes); to form and implement the policies by which it is to be governed; and to administer the state. The following is a useful modern definition:

> [T]he executive function is to administer the provisions of the law.... [G]enerally, ... the executive government carries out a collection of administrative functions including the operation of public service facilities, the expenditure of public funds, the formulation of administrative policies and guidelines, the exercise of discretionary powers and the performance of instrumental tasks to implement laws.[23]

Another commentator has 'broadly' defined 'the executive' as 'the authority within the State which administers the law, carries on the business of government and maintains order within and security from without the State'.[24]

While these may be useful for an initial understanding, they emphasise the functional aspects of the power without necessarily ascribing any substantive content to it. The second definition implies that defence, and the maintenance of the peace, may be inherently executive functions, thus adding some substantive content. But if that is so, could one therefore add 'the defence of the state from invasion and subversion and the maintenance of its peace' to the general definition? Does it include an even more general, though undefinable, discretionary power to take action in an emergency – natural disaster, rebellion, acts of terrorism and so on – in order to preserve the polity and to protect its people? Or, taking one further step, can one add whatever power necessarily inheres in the sovereignty of the nation state based on the imperatives placed upon the government of such a state – that is, an inherent executive 'nationhood' power? This progression, it may have been noticed, is towards increasingly nebulous conceptions of the power, progressively more difficult to define pursuant to legally discernible criteria and corresponding with an increasing reliance on subjective considerations and policy. The difficulties in attempting a definition based on a purely abstract conceptualisation become apparent.

While many, if not all, of these functions or powers are essential for the functioning of the modern state, the question arises: is it necessary to ascribe to them a label – 'executive' – if the important point is that they be exercised at all, pursuant to legal constraints, rather than that they be exercised by any particular branch of the government? It may be advisable to avoid confusing the nature or content of 'executive' power with the person(s) or institution(s) within the polity charged with their exercise. There is no general reason, for example, except expediency and efficiency, why the Governor-General (on advice from responsible Ministers) should have the power to conduct foreign relations and declare

**23** Kevin Booker, Arthur Glass and Robert Watt, *Federal Constitutional Law* (Butterworths, 2nd ed, 1990) 120.

**24** W Anstey Wynes, *Legislative, Executive and Judicial Powers in Australia* (Law Book Company, 4th ed, 1970) 364.

war and peace instead of, say, Parliament. The United States Constitution, for example, vests the legislature with the power to declare war.[25] That being so, would such a power then become 'legislative' because it was exercised by the legislature? However it is labelled, and irrespective of the body which exercises it, the power is the same; although there may be differences in the way it is exercised because of the different institutional context. And if it can be exercised by either the legislature or the government, the link between the nature of the power and the term used to describe it is broken.

Nomenclature nevertheless remains relevant. The separation of powers requires that some definitional clarity be given to the powers of each of the three branches of government in order to maintain and enforce the separation.[26] It is also important when a constitution expressly vests 'the executive power' of a particular polity in a particular person, office or institution. However, there is little to be gained in attempting to give substantive content to the notion of 'executive' power in the abstract by reference purely to the nature of the body exercising it. There is even less to be gained by speculating in the abstract as to which powers are inherently 'executive' in nature and thence proceed to determine that such powers must be exercised by the body which constitutes 'the executive' in any polity; that is, of course, unless one is speculating as to an ideal state of affairs.

That 'the executive', the government, exercises a particular power in any particular polity from time to time is purely a function of the constitution, laws, conventions and usages of that polity which pertain at the time the power is being exercised. Thus, in considering whether 'the defence of the realm' is an executive power, there is little point in conjuring up images of Edward III, that prodigy of medieval chivalry, at the head of his host; that is, unless the object of enquiry is the nature of executive power in fourteenth century England. The reason why the above-mentioned 'modern' definitions of executive power 'ring true' is not because they can be measured against a universally accepted standard of what constitutes such power. It is rather because their authors were adopting (and their readers were assuming) a particular point of reference: in this case, the organisation of government which pertains generally in Westminster-style jurisdictions and their analogues. It is based on certain assumptions: a distinction between governmental powers; and that legislative power and judicial power are sufficiently distinct concepts to enable one to speak separately of executive power. In any event, the power may be 'defined' in a purely functional way (executing laws, administration, 'maintaining the constitution' and so on) without ascribing any substantive content to it. For it is from the laws it is executing, and the specific constitutional grants of power which it exercises, that such substantive content is derived. Otherwise executive power remains, 'something

**25** United States Constitution (1787), art I, sec 8.
**26** See Peter Gerangelos, 'Interpretational Methodology in Separation of Powers Jurisprudence' (2005) 8 *Constitutional Law and Policy Review* 1.

of a mystery'[27] in relation to which commentators have noted the 'futility of attempting to define the ambit of … executive power by allusion to abstract notions of "executive power"'.[28] It is 'barren ground for an analytical approach', 'a trackless waste', in the words of David Gwynn Morgan.[29] Leslie Zines made the same point more prosaically:

> The principle that the executive government has no power at common law to levy a tax is not derived from contemplating the concept of executive power. It is because of English historical development, particularly the struggles of the 17th century. If the executive power in Britain and Australia includes the declaration of war, it is because the English Parliament was prepared to leave this power with the King, content with the control it had of the standing arm and the appropriation of money to conduct the war.[30]

In Britain, Australia, Canada, New Zealand and other monarchical polities in the Commonwealth, further clarity can be derived from the fact that the power is formally vested in the Queen. This is because reference can be made to the prerogative powers and capacities of the Crown recognised by the common law within a system of responsible government. These were inherited by Britain's constitutional progeny, and, as their complete independence developed, so did their governments gain those plenary prerogative powers relating to foreign affairs.[31] While the common law does provide a source of legally discernible criteria in this regard, clarity may be lacking in extreme and exceptional circumstances, especially where the very security of the polity is at stake.

In the case of Australia, the framers appear to have avoided spelling out the content of Commonwealth's executive power for two main reasons. First, their minds were elsewhere. 'One issue was dominant':[32] they were taxed by the particular problem of accommodating responsible government in a system of government which was federal in nature. Secondly, they could afford a certain degree of complacency, perhaps distraction, because they chose indeed to establish responsible government. As Michael Crommelin has pointed out in his detailed study of the Convention Debates on this issue, responsible government as it had developed in England was a matter of constitutional convention, and it was therefore 'unnecessary, inappropriate, perhaps even impossible' to provide a full account of it in the Constitution.[33] The framers thought it sufficient to prescribe the composition of the executive, while leaving the scope of the power to inference, and the relationship between the legislature and the executive to convention. For at no time 'was it seriously contested that the executive would

**27** Winterton, above n 21, 21.
**28** Winterton, above n 10, 70.
**29** David Gwynn Morgan, *The Separation of Powers in the Irish Constitution* (Round Hall Sweet and Maxwell, 1997) 272.
**30** Leslie Zines, 'The Inherent Executive Power of the Commonwealth' (2005) 16 *Public Law Review* 279, 279.
**31** See Geoffrey Lindell, *Responsible Government and the Australian Constitution – Conventions Transformed into Law?* (Federation Press, 2004).
**32** Michael Crommelin, 'The Executive' in Gregory Craven (ed), *The Convention Debates 1891–1898* (Legal Books, 1986) 127.
**33** Ibid.

comprise the Queen, a Governor-General, a Federal Executive Council, Ministers and Departments'.[34]

It is clear that the default position, one might even say the constitutional 'mindset' of the framers, was entirely British, at least when it came to executive power. This mindset was most apparent when Alfred Deakin discussed the office of Governor-General, and the appointment of the Governor-General by the Queen:

> To make it the object of ambition you must change its character altogether, and make it an office like that of the President of the United States ... At the present time we say that the Governor-General exercises no such authority. He exercises the power of the Sovereign of Great Britain, and no more than the people of Great Britain feel degraded and limited, because no one there can hope to aspire to be monarch of that country, do we feel degraded and limited, because we cannot aspire to be Governor-General. We are satisfied with all the other offices in the state being open to us, it being possible for the meanest, humblest and poorest to aspire to the highest office in the Commonwealth – that is, the premiership. We feel no regret through being debarred from this one ceremonial office. High though it may be, it is but ceremonial, and we feel no deprivation in any sense because it is closed to us.[35]

That being the case, it is possible to state that when the framers were contemplating executive power, while they understood it to be separate to the legislative and judicial power, they thought about it in the pragmatic and empirical way of British constitutionalism. As a consequence, apart from any statutory grant of power to the Crown, they expected the content of the power to be determined essentially by reference to the 'prerogative'. Andrew Inglis Clark, noting that the 'supreme depositary of executive authority in the Commonwealth is the King', observed: 'and he possesses and may exercise within the Commonwealth [through the Governor-General] all the prerogative rights and powers which are inherent in the British Crown and which may be exercised by him under the provisions of the Constitution of the Commonwealth ...'.[36] The Constitution, by establishing the Commonwealth as a government of the Queen, and making the executive power of the Commonwealth 'exercisable by the Governor-General', 'has introduced a portion of the common law of England which may not otherwise have found a place there'.[37] If the Constitution had provided for a government separated from the Crown, with, say, a President at its head, the content of the executive power would have been derived only, to use the words of Inglis Clark, from 'such executive powers and functions as the Constitution of the Commonwealth and the laws of the Parliament of the Commonwealth would have *expressly* conferred upon him'.[38] Beyond these sources – common

**34** Ibid.
**35** *Convention Debates, Sydney* (1891) 571. See also 564–5. Australians can be appointed to the office of Governor-General, the first Australian born Governor-General being Sir Isaac Isaacs who served in that office from 1931 until 1936.
**36** Andrew Inglis Clark, *Studies in Australian Constitutional Law* (Legal Books, 1901, reprinted 1997) 191.
**37** Ibid, 190.
**38** Ibid, 190–91 (emphasis added).

law, express statutory or constitutional provision – an inherent content to executive power does not seem to have been contemplated. The only concession may have been to such power as may be necessary in extreme situations, emergencies – for which the common law may have already made ample provision – and situations where the very existence of the polity was at stake. But in any event, these last may be recognised as 'prerogative' as John Locke had noted, as discussed in the next section.

## 2 A 'metaphysical' quality?

Even if precise constitutional provisions permit a certain level of definitional clarity, there is another aspect to executive power whose 'metaphysical' quality resists even the most rigorous techniques of positivist analysis. This is the case even with the common law as it pertains to the prerogative power of the Crown. Hence, the power is forever burdened with a certain lack of clarity at the edges. In *The Second Treatise of Government* (1690), John Locke gave eloquent expression to this when he acknowledged that 'it is impossible to foresee, and so by laws to provide for, all accidents and necessities, ... [and] therefore there is a latitude left to the executive power, to do many things ... which the laws do not prescribe'.[39] The power of which this latitude permits was famously called 'prerogative': 'to act according to discretion, for the public good, without the prescription of the law, and sometimes even against it'.[40] The exercise of such a power would (or should) arise only in very exceptional circumstances: emergencies threatening the welfare of the people (extreme situations of 'riot and pestilence', etc), the very existence of the state or its system of government (war, invasion, rebellion, etc), its ability to function as such, and so on. It could only ever be regarded as 'valid' (but if purely discretionary, by what standard?) when exercised unambiguously (by which criteria?) 'for the public good'. This 'prerogative' aspect to the power, permitting of some virtually unreviewable discretion in those who wield it, will continue to ensure the elusiveness of any precise definition, especially, but not exclusively, in exceptional circumstances which may require government action.

This is particularly well illustrated in the constitutional jurisprudence of the United States where the question is asked: Can a completely discretionary or prerogative power, at least in emergencies, be implied from the vesting clause in article II, section 1 of the Constitution – the clause which vests 'the executive power of the United States' in the President – together with the President's constitutionally prescribed oath to 'preserve, protect and defend the Constitution'?[41] The argument in support contrasts this simple language with the language used

**39** John Locke, *The Second Treatise of Government* (1690) in Peter Laslett (ed), *Two Treatises of Government* (Cambridge University Press, 1988) 375.
**40** Ibid.
**41** United States Constitution art II sec 1.

in the vesting of legislative power in article I, section 1 which uses the phrase '*all* legislative power herein granted',[42] implying that the Constitution provides exhaustively for legislative power on the one hand, but not, on the other, for executive power in relation to which this same phrase is not used. The existence of a prerogative element to executive power is supported by the constitutionally prescribed position of the President as 'commander-in-chief' of the armed forces (s 2), the leading executive of a sovereign nation, the official with principal responsibility for the maintenance of law and order (s 3).

The contrary argument ascribes 'perfection' to the Constitution. That is, its express grants of power provide completely and exhaustively for executive power in all possible circumstances, including emergencies – the only other source thereof being legislation enacted pursuant to the Constitution. This excludes the existence of any discretionary 'prerogative' power – of any implied inherent executive power even in emergencies. In support of this position, Hughes CJ, in *Home Building and Loan Association v Blaisdel*, stated: 'The Constitution was adopted in a period of grave emergency. Its [express] grants of power to the federal government ... were determined in the light of emergency and they are not altered by emergency'.[43]

The concurring opinion of Jackson J in *Youngstown Steel and Tube Company v Sawyer*[44] highlights the difficult nature of the issue and the reasons why the door can never be shut against an undefinable prerogative power even in the teeth of arguments maintaining the Constitution's 'perfection'. In that case, the Supreme Court held that the executive seizure of the steel mills in 1952 during the Korean War was invalid because it was not authorised by the Constitution or by statute. In the most nuanced reasoning in the case, Jackson J identified three relevant scenarios. First, if authorised by statute, the President's power in an emergency stood on the surest constitutional footing. Secondly, if the President acts contrary to the express or implied will of Congress, then 'his power is at its lowest ebb'[45] and the validity of the presidential action could be upheld by the Court 'only by disabling the Congress from acting upon the subject'.[46] The seizure of the steel mills was held to have fallen into this category. Thirdly, if neither authorised nor prohibited by statute, the President must then rely on any independent power provided for by the Constitution. This last category enters into the realm of uncertainty which plagues executive power, it being perceived as through a glass, darkly – validity 'is likely to depend on the imperative of events and contemporary imponderables rather than abstract theories of law'.[47] Jackson J was unable to provide for exhaustive criteria by which to make determinations arising under this third scenario. It remains a contested

**42** Emphasis added.
**43** 290 US 398, 425 (1934).
**44** 343 US 579 (1952).
**45** *Youngstown Steel and Tube Company v Sawyer* 343 US 579 (1952).
**46** Ibid, 637–8.
**47** Ibid, 637.

issue. Although the context of emergency powers provides the highest case giving rise to the 'mystery' of executive power in the United States and many other jurisdictions, including Australia,[48] the mystery is certainly not limited to these. Australian constitutional law has not been able to avoid this issue and, in the absence of legislative authorisation, whether one relies on the prerogative or an implied national executive power derived from s 61, the limits to such a power in an emergency remain very difficult to discern.

## 3 A moveable feast?

To add to the difficulty, it is not often appreciated that facile assumptions about the discrete nature of 'executive power' betray a modern mindset, or at least one which post-dates the early modern period of European history. For most of that history it was often more usual to speak of the power *of government*, 'of the sword', of 'the magistrate' or 'the prince', in terms which did not necessarily distinguish those powers and functions which in modern usage are designated as 'executive', 'legislative' and 'judicial'. In centralised, monarchical or oligarchic polities, the prince or ruling elite could, and did, exercise all such powers personally. Even in more democratic or republican forms of government, such as sixth-century-BC Athens or republican Rome, the fusion of these powers was not uncommon. The fact that in the United Kingdom, for example, Parliament, formally consisting of both Houses and the monarch, has traditionally been referred to as the 'High Court of Parliament', to which the Ministers of the Crown have been accountable, is suggestive of a fusion of legislative, executive and judicial powers consistent with the supremacy and sovereignty of Parliament. As noted by Quick and Garran:

> The term government is sometimes specially used to denote the Executive authority of a political State. Strictly speaking, however, it comprehends all the organic agencies engaged in the legislative, administrative, and judicial regulation of public affairs.[49]

The significance of Quick and Garran's statement goes beyond the recognition of a fusion of these three discrete powers under the term 'government', for it implies a recognition of an underlying unity of these powers which renders a mutually-exclusive definition of each virtually impossible. Their comment underscores one of the important conclusions reached by Maurice Vile:[50] that the denotation of the terms 'executive', 'legislative' and 'judicial' has not been uniform over time and, from the perspective of an overview of western political evolution, the variation in meaning has been internally interchangeable *amongst* those concepts. What may, in the present age, be designated as 'judicial' has at

**48** See H P Lee, *Emergency Powers* (Law Book Company, 1984); H P Lee, P J Hanks and V Morabito, *In the Name of National Security* (Law Book Company, 1995).
**49** John Quick and Robert Garran, *The Annotated Constitution of the Australian Commonwealth* (LexisNexis Butterworths, 1901) 699.
**50** M J C Vile, *Constitutionalism and the Separation of Powers* (Liberty Fund, 2nd ed, 1998).

one time been designated as 'executive', what was designated 'legislative' has been designated 'judicial', and so on. Vile's historical analysis amply illustrates the internal mutability of these concepts depending on the fundamental influence of dominant theories of law and sovereignty which underpin them. A fundamental reason for their mutability was that the current assumption that 'law could be *made* by human agency, that there was a real power to make law, to legislate' did not apply. Rather:

> [L]aw was a fixed unchanging pattern of divinely-inspired custom, which could be applied and interpreted by man, but not *changed* by him. In so far as men were concerned with 'legislation' they were in fact declaring the law, clarifying what the law really was, not creating it. Legislation was in fact part of the judicial procedure. … [T] he actions of the King in his Council making formal statements of law were seen as clarificatory acts. There could, therefore, be only one 'function' of government – the judicial function; all acts of government were in some way justified as aspects of the application and interpretation of the law.[51]

It therefore required a significant evolution in the theory of 'law' before there began to emerge a separate concept of 'executive power' in the modern sense, based in the division of royal power into *gubernaculum* (government) and *juridictio* (jurisdiction). When exercising the former, the King was legally unrestrained; whereas when exercising the latter, he had to comply with the law. Moreover, as Vile explained:

> [T]he desire to limit the monarch by subjecting him to a law which he did not himself make, provided the basis of the evolution of a 'legislative power' independent of the will of the King. As a corollary, there emerged the idea of an executive power in the King, by virtue of which he ensured that the law was put into effect.[52]

This development of the notion of 'positive law' made by human agents, although meant to be in conformity with the more generally-expressed universal and unchanging principles of a divine or 'natural' law, encouraged the development of discrete concepts of legislative and executive functions. This was illustrated in the writings of Marsilius of Padua in the fourteenth century, and was signalled by a return to classical notions found in Aristotle and Cicero (especially), thus providing a bridge forward to the discernibly 'modern' writings of Locke and Montesquieu.

On their view, the legislator performs the primary role of establishing the other institutions of the state, while the ruler exercises a secondary role of implementing or executing the law.[53] Even in the early modern period, the 'executive' function was not yet regarded as distinct from the function that would later be regarded as 'judicial'. This did not begin to occur until the eighteenth century. For, in the early modern world, the precise function of applying the law in courts of law, headed by the ruler, and adjudicating disputes based on interpreting

**51** Ibid, 26–7 (emphasis in original).
**52** Ibid, 29 (citations omitted).
**53** Ibid, 31.

positive law, was part of the executive function to execute and implement the law. Indeed, it would be more accurate to say that the executive function may have been regarded as being a part of the judicial. As Vile has pointed out, 'the modern notion of an executive power distinct from the machinery of law enforcement through the courts, could hardly be envisaged in an age when almost the only impact of government upon the ordinary citizens was through the courts and the law-enforcement officers'.[54]

It was not until the end of the Civil War in England in the mid seventeenth century that it became increasingly common to see distinctions being drawn between what moderns would recognise as 'executive' and 'judicial' functions. Declaring what the law is, and the power to determine individual points of law, was the role of 'the Judges of the Realme' – not of the King, who retains 'the sovereign power of government' and who is 'our only Supream Governour'; or of Parliament, whose function is 'only to make new laws'.[55] On the eve of the Restoration in 1660, the writings of George Lawson, which Vile regards as 'extremely important' in understanding the emergence of the modern tripartite division of the powers of government, witnessed to a broadening of the conceptions of the *execution* of the law to include, in addition to 'acts of Judgement, more strictly so called [ie, the hearing and decision of causes upon evidence], the infliction of penalties, the dispensations of judgement, suspension of execution, and pardons'.[56] Vile explained that according to Lawson, an effective state depended upon an '"executive power and a coactive force" that would ensure the obedience of the subject to laws and judgments made under them'. In his view:

> [I]n all government there must be a sword, which is an outward coactive strength and force, for Legislation, Judgement and Execution by the Sword, are the three essential acts of supreme Power civil in the administration of the State'.[57]

The 'sword', however, was not limited to the enforcement of law within the state, but was also that power, in the same hands, which defended the state from external enemies. As Lawson stated: 'One and same sword must protect from enemies without and unjust subjects within. For the sword of war and justice are but one sword'.[58]

## 4 Emergence of the separation of powers

It is not until the writings of Locke and Montesquieu, which are far more well-known and influential, that the notion of a separation of powers begins to emerge unambiguously in the modern sense. Here one can discern a clearer

**54** Ibid, 32.
**55** Ibid, 51–2.
**56** Ibid, 60–61.
**57** Ibid, 61.
**58** Ibid, 62.

conception of executive power as a power discrete from legislative power (making positive law) and judicial power (adjudication under law). On this view, executive power is principally concerned with executing the law and with its administration. While in *The Second Treatise of Government* the judicial power, as a separate power, is treated equivocally by Locke,[59] it is in Montesquieu's *De l'Esprit des Lois*, first published anonymously in 1748,[60] that one can first discern an unequivocally discrete description of 'judicial power' as separate from both 'executive' and 'legislative' power.[61] This modern understanding of the three powers was soon reflected in constitutional instruments – most famously in the Constitution of the United States, in which the separation of powers was legally entrenched for the first time, albeit with supplementary 'checks and balances' cutting across the demarcation. Thereafter, 'executive' power was increasingly limited to the execution of laws made by the legislature, to exercising constitutionally defined grants of power (as in the United States and Australia, exemplified in specific grants of power to the President and Governor-General respectively), and to exercising those 'prerogative' powers which the common law recognises as residing in the Crown in the United Kingdom, Australia, Canada, New Zealand and other Westminster-based monarchical constitutions. When this occurred, 'executive power' came to mean that power in the polity which undertakes the administration of the polity – a power residing principally in the government. On this view, government implementation of policy must be pursuant to the laws and constitutional provisions which it is executing and with which it must comply.

Thus, while some understanding can be gained by attempting an analysis of 'executive power' in the abstract, it is an analysis which achieves little on its own when considering the precise ambit of executive power in any particular polity. Resort must be had to a positivist analysis of the constitution and laws of the particular polity being examined, the political structure thereby established and its history. Without historical context, this point cannot be fully appreciated.

## III Parliamentary supremacy and the Executive

An examination of the institutional and structural basis of 'the Executive Government' in the Australian federal system is an essential prerequisite to the determination of the ambit of 'the executive power of the Commonwealth'. As one of the more complex issues in Australian constitutional jurisprudence, the resolution of this question presently constitutes a principal concern of constitutional lawyers and the High Court. Before examining issues of structure and ambit, it is necessary to highlight the continuingly relevant aspects of executive

**59** See Ibid, 65.
**60** The first English translation by Thomas Nugent was published in 1750. The standard edition of the work is J Brethe de la Gressay (ed), *De l'Esprit des Lois* (Belles Lettres, 1950).
**61** Vile, above n 50, ch 4.

power in Australia which derive from the Commonwealth's constitutional antecedents in the United Kingdom. As explained in Chapter 1, the constitutional conflicts of the seventeenth century, although many-faceted, brought to the fore the tension that had been simmering over the primacy of Acts of Parliament vis-à-vis the prerogative powers of the monarch.[62] While well-managed by the pragmatism and reasonableness of Elizabeth I, the tension could not be contained by the likes of Charles I and James II, influenced as they were by the more absolutist views of monarchy pursuant to continental (especially French) political theory and developments. The replacement of James II with Mary and William of Orange, effected by Parliament in a 'bloodless revolution' as a result of James's intemperate exercise of royal power, resulted in the Revolution Settlement of 1688. The Bill of Rights[63] was its constitutional centrepiece. That instrument – despite lingering difficulties for a time with Non-Jurors and Jacobites – eventually settled the vexed questions over which Crown, Parliament and the common lawyers had been fighting for nearly a century.

Thus, it became settled that the Crown could not suspend or dispense with any laws or their execution without the consent of Parliament. It could not levy taxation by reliance on royal prerogative alone, without a grant by Parliament. Petitioning the King was established as a right of the subject. The free election of members of Parliament was established, together with parliamentary privilege, especially the immunity from prosecution or impeachment with respect to any speeches or debates in Parliament. Parliaments, it was stated, 'ought to be held frequently'. The imposition of fines, penalties and forfeitures without conviction was declared illegal and void; and it was determined that such fines (or bail) as are imposed must not be excessive, and no 'cruell and unusuall Punishments' are to be inflicted.

The key principles embodied by the Bill of Rights have found modern expression in the Commonwealth Constitution. Thus, s 6 provides that a session of Parliament shall be held at least once within a twelve month period; and ss 81 and 83 provide that all moneys or revenues received by the government 'shall form one Consolidated Revenue Fund' which can only be appropriated for Commonwealth purposes 'under appropriation made by law'. In *A v Hayden*[64] and *White v Director of Military Prosecutions*[65] it was held that the executive cannot dispense with obedience to the law. Brennan J in *Hayden* referred to this incapacity of the executive as 'the cornerstone of a *parliamentary democracy*'.[66] Noting the use of the dispensing power by medieval kings as an aspect of their prerogatives, his Honour noted its demise in the Bill of Rights and subsequent legislation. He also quoted Griffith CJ that: 'If an act is unlawful – forbidden by law – a person who does it can claim no protection by saying that he acted

**62** See Chapter 1, Part I.2.
**63** *1 Will and Mary 2 c 2.*
**64** (1984) 156 CLR 532, 580–81.
**65** (2007) 231 CLR 570, 592.
**66** (1984) 156 CLR 532, 580 (emphasis added).

under the authority of the Crown'.[67] In *Davis v Commonwealth*,[68] it was further held that the executive cannot create a new offence; in *Vasiljkovic v Commonwealth*,[69] that it cannot, without statutory authorisation, order extradition from Australia; and in *Commonwealth v Colonial Combing, Spinning & Weaving Co Ltd* ('the *Wooltops* case'),[70] that it cannot impose taxation without statutory authorisation. That the Crown is bound by statute is, under present constitutional arrangements and generally speaking, axiomatic and incontrovertible. The extent to which legislation can regulate and control executive power derived directly from a constitutional grant of power is an issue which will be examined in more detail in the next chapter.[71]

Whether the Crown is bound by any particular statute is dependent on the construction of the statute, the (weak) presumption being that legislation expressed in general terms does not bind the Crown. As noted by Gleeson CJ and Gaudron J in *Commonwealth v Western Australia*,[72] the rationale for this is that general legislation is intended to regulate citizens and not the government in respect of which it may operate differently. In *Bropho v Western Australia*,[73] the High Court eased the previous requirement that an intention to bind the Crown had to be either stated expressly, or arise from the 'necessary implication', that the purpose of the legislation would be 'wholly frustrated unless the Crown were bound'.[74] In its place, a standard both flexible and light was applied which permitted the Court to take into account, in addition to the statute's terms, its 'subject matter and disclosed purpose and policy'. For example, in *Bropho* itself, it was stated that where the Crown is engaged in commercial activities, the presumption that a statute does not apply to the Crown will be at its weakest, 'represent[ing] little more than a starting point' to ascertain legislative intention.[75] It was emphasised that the issue was to be determined pursuant to principles of statutory construction – it was not a case involving any purported prerogative power of the Crown to override or dispense with the law as stated in an act of Parliament.[76] The joint judgment in *Bropho* did recognise the possibility of a qualified intention to bind the Crown; that is, an intention that it apply to the Crown but not the Sovereign herself, or to a Crown instrumentality but not its employees.[77] But this, too, remained a matter of statutory interpretation:

> For so long as 'the Crown' encompassed little more than the Sovereign, his or her direct representatives and the basic organs of government, there may well have been

**67** Ibid, citing *Clough v Leahy* (1904) 2 CLR 139, 155–6.
**68** (1988) 166 CLR 79, 112.
**69** (2006) 227 CLR 614, 634–5.
**70** (1922) 31 CLR 421.
**71** See Chapter 7, Part V.2.
**72** (1999) 196 CLR 392, 410.
**73** (1990) 171 CLR 1.
**74** *Bropho v Western Australia* (1990) 171 CLR 1, quoting *Province of Bombay v Municipal Corporation of Bombay* [1947] AC 68, 63.
**75** Ibid, 22.
**76** Ibid, 18–19.
**77** Ibid, 23–4.

> convincing reasons for an assumption that a legislative intent that general statutory provisions should bind the Crown and those who represent it would be either stated in express terms or made 'manifest from the very terms of the statute'. The basis of an assumption to that effect lay in a mixture of considerations: regard for the dignity and majesty of the Crown; concern to ensure that any proposed statutory derogation from the authority of the Crown was made plain in the legislative provisions submitted for the royal assent; and, the general proposition that, since laws are made by rulers for subjects, a general description of those bound by a statute is not to be read as including the Crown ... Whatever force such considerations may continue to have in relation to legislative provisions which would deprive the Crown 'of any part of [the] ancient prerogative, or of those rights which are ... essential to [the] regal capacity' ... they would seem to have little relevance, at least in this country, to the question whether a legislative provision worded in general terms should be read down so that it is inapplicable to the activities of any of the employees of the myriad of governmental commercial and industrial instrumentalities covered by the shield of the Crown.[78]

This passage was referred to with approval by the joint majority judgment in the more recent case of *ACCC v Baxter Healthcare Pty Ltd*.[79] The High Court was engaged with the issue of whether the relevant provisions of the *Trade Practices Act 1974* (Cth) – prohibiting misuse of market power and exclusive dealing by corporations – were applicable to non-government trading corporations which had entered into supply contracts with the State Purchasing Authorities of the States and Territories (these being part of the executive of the respective States and Territories) and where the government's conduct was not in the course of carrying on a business. Baxter Healthcare argued that when a corporation, in the course of carrying on its business, negotiates for, enters into or performs a contract with a State or Territory government not itself carrying on a business, the relevant provisions do not apply to the corporation. The argument was based on a notion of 'derivative immunity' which had previously been applied by the High Court.[80] Because the arguments relating to 'derivative immunity' 'had a flavour of assertion of executive prerogative', the above quotation from the joint judgment of *Bropho* was adopted with approval.[81] The majority insisted that:

> [a]lways, the ultimate questions must be whether the presumption against the Crown being bound has, in all the circumstances, been rebutted, and, if it has, *the extent to which* it was the legislative intent that that particular Act should bind the Crown and/or those covered by the prima facie immunity of the Crown.[82]

The relevant considerations became the terms of the statute, its subject matter, the nature of the mischief to be redressed, the general purpose and effect of the statute, and the nature of the activities of the executive government which

**78** Ibid, 18–19.
**79** (2007) 232 CLR 1, 26–7.
**80** *Bradken Consolidated Ltd v Broken Hill Proprietary Co Ltd* (1979) 145 CLR 107, decided before *Bropho*.
**81** *ACCC v Baxter Healthcare Pty Ltd* (2007) 232 CLR 1, 27.
**82** Ibid, quoting with approval the decision in *Bropho* (emphasis in original).

would be affected if the Crown were bound. In finding that the relevant provisions of the Act did apply to Baxter Healthcare, the joint reasoning stated:

> It is one thing to read the Act so as not to divest the Crown of legal rights. It is another thing altogether to read the Act as giving an executive government (as distinct from Parliament ...) including all its servants and agents, a freedom not enjoyed when the government itself is carrying on business, from any impact of laws enacted for the promotion of competition and fair trading in the public interest. And it is even more unlikely that that freedom extends to all persons dealing with that executive government.[83]

Thus it is clear that, subject to the Constitution, the executive power is subject to the legislative power and intention of Parliament as expressed in its enactments. This is a fundamental consequence of the reception of the principles of responsible government in Australia as they had evolved and they continue to evolve in the more precise context of Australian law and practice.

## IV Structure of the Executive

In the previous section, reference was made to those aspects of British constitutional principles which had found their way into the Commonwealth Constitution and to how certain understandings relating to the relationship between the Crown and Parliament had become manifest in Australian constitutional law. However, the federal nature of the new polity known as 'the Commonwealth' prevented a simple and unqualified translation of these principles into its constitutional arrangements. This certainly did tax the minds of the framers and it is not possible to understand the nature and ambit of 'the executive power of the Commonwealth' without examining it through the prism of the Convention Debates and the thoughts of the early commentators of the Constitution.

### 1 The Crown and the monarch

Executive power, at both Commonwealth and State levels, continues formally and legally to reside in the Queen and is exercised in virtually all respects by Her Majesty's representatives: the Governor-General in the Commonwealth, and the respective Governors in the States.

The Queen is the 'Queen of Australia and Her other Realms and Territories'.[84] The government is carried on in the Queen's name. Section 2 of the Commonwealth Constitution provides that the Governor-General is appointed by the Queen and 'shall be Her Majesty's representative in the Commonwealth'. Section 61 vests the Queen, not the Governor-General, with 'the executive power

**83** Ibid, 37.
**84** *Royal Style and Titles Act 1973* (Cth), s 2(1).

of the Commonwealth', albeit that the power is 'exercisable' by the Governor-General. Section 64 makes reference to 'the Queen's Ministers of State for the Commonwealth', being members of the Federal Executive Council which advises the Governor-General. It is as 'the Queen's representative' that the Governor-General is vested with 'the command in chief' of the armed forces pursuant to s 68 of the Constitution. The principal function of the Queen is to appoint (and, by implication, dismiss) the Governor-General and State governors – a power which is nevertheless exercised on the advice of Commonwealth or State ministers respectively.[85]

The Queen is also a constituent element of the 'Federal Parliament' which s 1 of the Constitution vests with 'the legislative power of the Commonwealth'. The assent of the Governor-General in the Queen's name is necessary before a bill becomes law.[86] The bill may also be 'reserved' by the Governor-General for 'the Queen's pleasure',[87] and the Queen may disallow 'any law' to which the Governor-General has given assent.[88] Both these latter powers are, however, essentially 'dead letter'.[89] Reserving a bill for the Queen's pleasure has not been exercised since the earliest days of federation, excepting in relation to those bills which were so desired to be reserved by the Australian government for sentimental reasons such as the *Flags Act 1953* (Cth) and the *Royal Style and Titles Act 1973* (Cth). Disallowance has never been exercised. At State level similar formal powers have not been exercised in the last century.[90] The Australian Constitutional Convention on three occasions recommended abolition – a recommendation which would have been achieved had the Constitution Alteration (Removal of Outmoded and Expended Provisions) Bill 1983 (which had been passed by the Senate) become law.[91]

The Constitution establishes the Queen as the formal Head of State of the Commonwealth.[92] The Preamble recites that 'the people' of the various Australian colonies 'have agreed to unite in one indissoluble Federal Commonwealth under the Crown of the United Kingdom' and 'under the Constitution hereby established'.[93] While the concept of 'the Head of State' may be regarded by some as a mere formality, to others it has more transcendent overtones. A range of

**85** It is noted that the appointment of the Governor-General by the monarch was on the advice of British Ministers until 1931. Since then, in light of the autonomy and new national status of the Dominions following the Imperial Conference in 1926 and the Balfour Declaration, this appointment has always been on the advice of Australian Ministers. See Winterton, above n 10, 19–20. At the State level, s 7(5) of the *Australia Act 1986* (Cth) expressly provides that the relevant State Premier shall advise the Queen as to the appointment of a Governor.
**86** Constitution, s 58.
**87** Ibid.
**88** Ibid, s 59.
**89** See Winterton, above n 10, 18–20.
**90** George Winterton, *Monarchy to Republic* (Oxford University Press, 1986) 29–30. See also H R Anderson, 'The Constitutional Framework' in S R Davis (ed), *The Government of the Australian States* (Longmans, 1960) 3, 6.
**91** *Convention Debates, Adelaide* (1983) 321.
**92** See Advisory Committee on Executive Government, Constitutional Commission, *Report of the Advisory Committee on Executive Government* (1987) ch 1.
**93** See Winterton, above n 10, 17.

views was summarised in the Report of the Advisory Committee on Executive Power of the Constitutional Commission of 1987. It was there observed that the role of a 'Head of State' includes: (a) representing, symbolising and acting for the nation as a whole in the execution of such defining acts as the declaration of war, the summoning of Parliament, the swearing in of a ministry and other circumstances where an individual enters into a relationship with the nation as a whole, such as in taking an oath of office;[94] (b) personifying the body politic; (c) acting as a focus of loyalty for the community; and (d) representing the nation on ceremonial occasions.[95] The Advisory Committee regarded the role of Head of State as both 'appropriate and desirable' and quoted the submission of Saul Encel that a 'large and complicated body which exercises authority over all of us, like the state, should have some kind of ... symbolic head, who has been appointed outside ... party politics and who retains a certain amount of continuity'.[96] In its final report, the Constitutional Commission recommended 'that a Head of State be maintained in our system of government, whether Monarchical or republican'.[97]

It is noted that while it is proper to refer to 'the Queen of Australia', there is no separate construct 'the Queen of New South Wales [or any other State]', although one may appropriately refer to 'the Crown in right of the Commonwealth', 'the Crown in right of New South Wales [or any other State]' and so on. While the Queen is 'the Queen of Australia', it remains the position that the succession to the Crown is determined pursuant to statutory rules (*Act of Settlement* and *Royal Marriages Act*) and common law which pertain to the succession to the Crown of the United Kingdom of Great Britain and Northern Ireland. Covering clause 2 of the *Commonwealth of Australia Constitution Act 1900* (UK) expressly provides that references to 'the Queen' 'shall extend to Her Majesty's heirs and successors in the sovereignty of the United Kingdom'. If these rules were to be altered by an Act of the United Kingdom Parliament, it is likely that these amendments would not apply automatically to Australia. As the High Court pointed out in *Sue v Hill*, s 1 of the *Australia Act 1986* (Cth) provides that no such Act 'shall extend, or be deemed to extend' to the Commonwealth, States or Territories as part of their 'law', and that Australian legislation would be necessary to give these legal effect.[98] This would mean that Australian laws relating to succession could differ to those applicable in Great Britain, and Australia and Britain 'could finish up with different monarchs'.[99] However, covering clause 2 of the *Commonwealth of Australia Constitution Act 1900* (UK) may prevent such Australian legislation taking effect if that section is interpreted literally to require that the sovereign of Australia must be the person who is the sovereign of Great Britain.

**94** See Paul Hasluck, *The Office of Governor-General* (Melbourne University Press, 1979) 6–7.
**95** Advisory Committee on Executive Government, above n 92, 2.
**96** Ibid.
**97** Constitutional Commission, *Final Report of the Constitutional Commission* (1988) vol 1, 314.
**98** *Sue v Hill* (1999) 199 CLR 462, 502.
**99** Leslie Zines, *The High Court and the Constitution* (The Federation Press, 5th ed, 2008) 435.

Zines, concurring with the reasoning of Kenneth Bailey, argued, to the contrary, that such an interpretation of s 2 is 'anachronistic', because it does not take into account the changed circumstances pertaining to Australian sovereignty (and indeed that of other former British Dominions) which followed from the *Statute of Westminster 1931* (Imp) and the *Australia Acts 1986* (UK and Cth). In 1900, the Crown was 'Imperial', one and indivisible, and it is 'difficult to understand why the British Parliament would see the need to provide Australia with a rule of succession separate from that operating throughout the Empire'.[100] In other words, prior to the *Statute of Westminster*, the law of succession operated as 'Imperial law' and assumed the existence of an 'Imperial Crown'. As a consequence:

> s 2 does not enact, but assumes, the existence of succession law operating in Australia. Section 2 refers us back to the law of succession. So far as the reference to the sovereignty of the United Kingdom is concerned, ... the section does not imply a reference to United Kingdom law as distinct from law operating in other dominions.[101]

On this view, the reasoning in *Sue v Hill* is, with respect, correct.[102] If that view were not accepted and there were changes to the constitution of the United Kingdom, this might lead to great confusion. The ultimate test would be the establishment of a republic in Britain because '[t]here would be no queen to which s 2 could refer and all Australian governmental institutions would either immediately or eventually cease to exist'.[103] Zines therefore concluded:

> Any doubts there may be should now be resolved in favour of Australian sovereignty and independence. It seems therefore that these matters – succession to the Throne and Royal Style and Titles – are within the inherent power of the Commonwealth, derived from its status as the central government of the nation, and that s 2 of the Constitution Act does not restrict that power.[104]

The Executive Government Advisory Committee of the Constitutional Commission adopted this view,[105] which view was also maintained by the Constitutional Commission in its Final Report. To reflect what it believed to be the current position of Australia as an independent nation, it recommended that in s 2 of the Constitution Act, and in the Note to the Schedule to the Constitution, the words 'the United Kingdom' and 'the United Kingdom and Ireland' be substituted respectively with 'Australia'.[106] Its rationale is illuminating:

**100** Ibid, 436.
**101** Ibid.
**102** Gleeson CJ, Gummow and Hayne JJ in *Sue v Hill* (1999) 199 CLR 462. 502.
**103** Zines, above n 99, 437.
**104** Ibid.
**105** Advisory Committee on Executive Government, above n 92. 'We take the view that the recital in the preamble to the Constitution only identifies and defines the monarch as it existed in 1901 and does not preclude the later description of the monarch by a different style and title': 7–8. See also Constitutional Commission, above n 97, 80–82. For an analysis of these issues and issues relating to the termination of constitutional links with the United Kingdom, see Zines, above n 99, 432–8, 417–32.
**106** Constitutional Commission, above n 97, 80.

> [T]he sovereignty of the United Kingdom in 1900 referred to the sovereignty of the entire empire of that country. There was in law and in fact no distinct Monarch of Australia, Canada, New Zealand, etc. There was just one and indivisible sovereign of all parts of the Queen's dominions. When the Queen, as distinct from the Governor-General or a Governor, acted in relation to either the United Kingdom or overseas possessions of the Crown she acted on the advice of ministers of the United Kingdom. ... That is no longer the case. The sovereignty of each of the countries that recognize Queen Elizabeth II as their Queen is separate and distinct from that of any other country. Whether in domestic or foreign affairs, the 'Crown of the United Kingdom' may pursue quite different policies from that of the Crown of Australia. The Queen's advisers are different in each case. The reference to the United Kingdom is therefore a source of confusion and does not reflect the position of the Crown today.[107]

The words of the preamble to the Constitution – proclaiming that the Commonwealth was established 'under the Crown of the United Kingdom' – suggest that the framers took it for granted that the Commonwealth would be a government of the Queen and that the Queen would be the Head of State. Such a view also appears in various places in the Convention Debates.[108] Even those with republican sympathies, such as Andrew Inglis Clark, did not register any objection.[109] Quick and Garran remarked as follows with respect to this reference to the Crown:

> [It] has been introduced rather out of an abundance of caution, than from any consideration that its omission might suggest doubt or from any present idea of actual necessity. ... Throughout the political campaign which preceded the election of the Federal Convention, not a solitary public figure seriously discussed the possibility, much less the probability, of separation.[110]

There is no suggestion that the framers contemplated otherwise than that executive power in both the Commonwealth and the States would continue to be vested in the Queen and exercised by her representatives. Quick and Garran remarked: '[the text of s 61] stereotypes the theory of the British Constitution that the Crown is the source and the fountain of Executive authority, and that every administrative act must be done by and in the name of the Crown'.[111] Thus, Harrison Moore was able to observe:

> The Crown does in fact pervade every part of our political system, and is the hardest worked of our legal institutions. The Crown establishes the Commonwealth, is a part of the Commonwealth Parliament, and is the depositary of the federal executive power. ... [T]he executive government of a colony proceeds in the King's name; the governor is merely the King's delegate to exercise so much of the royal power as has been committed to him.[112]

**107** Ibid, 79.
**108** See the various references to the Convention Debates in this regard made by Winterton: Winterton, above n 10, 3 nn 16–19. See also *Convention Debates, Adelaide* (1897) 613–20.
**109** See generally George Winterton, 'The Evolution of a Separate Australian Crown' (1993) 19 *Monash University Law Review* 1. On Inglis Clark, see Frank Neasey, 'Andrew Inglis Clark Senior and Australian Federation (1969) 15(2) *Australian Journal of Politics and History* 1, 1–3, 15.
**110** Quick and Garran, above n 49, 294–5.
**111** Ibid, 702.
**112** W Harrison Moore, *The Constitution of the Commonwealth of Australia* (Legal Books, 2nd ed, 1910) 85.

## 2 The Queen's representatives

When it comes to the actual exercise of executive power, the role of the Queen is in virtually all respects formal, the Queen's powers being exercised by the Governor-General and State Governors, themselves being merely formal repositories of the power in almost all respects.

The fact that a distinction needs to be drawn between the formal and actual exercise of power is a direct consequence of 'responsible government under the Crown', one of the 'four great constitutional principles'[113] embodied by the Australian Constitution, the others being representative government, federalism and the separation of powers. In essence, it requires that power be exercised by ministers, themselves members of Parliament, who are 'responsible' to Parliament (ultimately the electorate) and whose confidence is a prerequisite to their exercise of ministerial power.[114] The Queen does exercise the power to appoint the persons to be her representatives, but does so pursuant to the advice of the relevant ministers at Commonwealth or State level, that is, the Prime Minister or relevant Premier. In relation to executive powers provided for by the Constitution,[115] these are exercisable by the Queen's representative. Section 2 of the Constitution expressly provides for the office of 'Governor-General', the person holding that office to be 'appointed by the Queen'. As the Queen's representatives, the power exercised by the Governor-General and State Governors,[116] is exercised essentially in a formal manner and on advice of relevant Commonwealth or State Ministers, excepting the 'reserve powers'[117] which may be exercised in extraordinary circumstances without or contrary to advice. When referring to the establishment of the Federal Executive Council to advise the Governor-General (s 62), Quick and Garran noted:

> Whilst the Constitution, in sec. 61, recognizes the ancient principle of the Government of England that the Executive power is vested in the Crown, it adds as a graft to that principle the modern political institution, known as responsible government, which shortly expressed means that the discretionary powers of the Crown are exercised by the wearer of the Crown or by its Representative according to the advice of ministers, having the confidence of that branch of the legislature which immediately represents the people.[118]

However, as will be seen, tensions were created by the attempt to combine the principle of responsible government with the principle of federalism, without spelling out in precise detail how responsible government would work and how it would interact with the contrary imperatives arising from federalism, in particular the role of the Senate as a 'States' house'.

**113** Winterton, above n 10, 1.
**114** For more detail on 'responsible government' see Part V below.
**115** See Part VI below.
**116** With respect to State Governors, by s 7 of the *Australia Act 1986* (Cth).
**117** See *Sue v Hill* (1999) 199 CLR 462, 494, 499.
**118** Quick and Garran, above n 49, 702.

## 3 Ministers of the Crown, Executive Council and Cabinet

The actual exercise of executive power at both Commonwealth and State levels is undertaken by Ministers of State who are responsible to Parliament. Ministers are placed at the head of the Departments of State and hold particular portfolios: Prime Minister, Treasurer, Attorney-General, Minister for Foreign Affairs and so on. The principal Ministers – those in charge of the larger and more important Departments of State – form the Cabinet which constitutes the central core of government under the leadership of the Prime Minister. In political terms, it is the Prime Minister and Cabinet which directly exercises, and directs the exercise of, the executive power of the Commonwealth. However, the Cabinet is not mentioned in the Constitution. In the formal legal sense, executive power is wielded by the Governor-General advised by the Federal Executive Council. The following was noted by Quick and Garran, when referring to the establishment of the Federal Executive Council:

> The practical result is that the Executive power is placed in the hands of a Parliamentary Committee, called the Cabinet, and the real head of the Executive is not the Queen but the Chairman of the Cabinet, or in other words the Prime Minister. There is therefore a great and fundamental difference between the traditional ideal of the British Constitution, as embodied in sec. 61, giving full expression to the picture of Royal authority painted by Blackstone and by Hearn, and the modern practice of the Constitution as crystallised in the polite language of sec. 62, 'there shall be a Federal Executive Council to advise the Governor-General in the Government of the Commonwealth'.[119]

The Constitution provides in s 64 that the Governor-General 'may appoint officers to administer such departments of State of the Commonwealth as the Governor-General in Council may establish'. These hold office 'at the pleasure of the Governor-General'. When interpreted consistently with responsible government, this means that they hold office so long as they maintain the confidence of the House of Representatives: individually as holders of a particular portfolio and collectively as members of the government.[120] The requirements of responsible government are reinforced by the express requirement in s 64 that ministers may only hold office for three months unless they become a senator or member of the House of Representatives. Section 44 of the Constitution exempts Ministers of State from disqualification from being senators or members of the lower house for the reasons provided in s 44(iv); that is, for holding any 'office of profit under the Crown' or any Commonwealth pension. For, as a Minister of State performing duties in an office of the government, a person will be receiving remuneration and would, without s 44(iv), be otherwise disqualified from sitting in Parliament.

Section 4 of the *Ministers of State Act 1952* (Cth) currently limits the number of Ministers of State specifically designated as Parliamentary Secretaries to 12

**119** Ibid, 703.
**120** See Lindell, above n 31.

and the number of Ministers of State to 30. The latter are ordinarily appointed to administer a government department. In *Re Patterson; Ex parte Taylor*,[121] an issue arose as to whether the Governor-General, having appointed the Hon Phillip Ruddock as Minister of State to administer the Department of Immigration and Multicultural Affairs, could then appoint another member of Parliament (in this case a senator) to administer the same department as Parliamentary Secretary to Minister Ruddock. The matter came to court when a decision by the Parliamentary Secretary, exercising the statutory powers vested in 'the Minister' to determine visa applications under the *Migration Act 1958* (Cth), was challenged. It was held that the appointment of the Parliamentary Secretary in this capacity was not invalid and that s 64 allowed the appointment of two persons to administer the same department, thus resolving previous uncertainty on this point.[122] Gleeson CJ explained:

> It is for Parliament to determine the procedures by which those two persons will answer for the conduct of such administration. ... The characteristics of responsible government are not immutable. They are certainly capable of accommodating the arrangements made by the Governor-General in the present case.[123]

Section 64 of the Constitution provides that those officers appointed to administer the Departments of State shall be members of the Federal Executive Council. Section 62 provides that the Federal Executive Council is 'to advise the Governor-General in the government of the Commonwealth'. The State constitutions similarly provide for an 'Executive Council'. As stated by Dixon J in the *Communist Party* case: 'An order, proclamation or declaration of the Governor-General in Council is the formal legal act which gives effect to the advice tendered to the Crown by the Ministers of the Crown'.[124] The same applies to the Governor in Council in State executives. This was clearly stated by the various justices in *FAI Insurances Ltd v Winneke*[125] with respect to the Governor in Council in Victoria, a concept applicable by analogy to the Commonwealth. Wilson J stated:

> First, the Governor in Council is not a deliberative body. It is no more than a formal stage in the process whereby decisions of Ministers and the government are transformed into effective decisions. The Royal Instructions provide for a quorum of two members, the membership consisting theoretically of all Ministers past or present. The practice is that no more than two Ministers, both present members of the Government chosen on a roster basis, constitute a 'working' session of the Executive Council, and there is neither occasion nor opportunity for any discussion of the matters that require the decision of the Governor. The papers placed before the Governor convey

**121** (2001) 207 CLR 391.
**122** See the relevant discussion in the reasoning of Gummow and Hayne JJ at: *Re Patterson; Ex parte Taylor* (2001) 207 CLR 391, 458–9.
**123** Ibid, 403. Gummow and Hayne JJ reasoned along similar lines: see 462. Gaudron, Kirby and Callinan JJ all concurred: see 415, 498, 519.
**124** *Australian Communist Party v Commonwealth* (1951) 83 CLR 1, 179.
**125** (1982) 151 CLR 342.

> the recommendation of the responsible Minister, and those Ministers who constitute the Council on any particular occasion formally convey that 'advice' to the Governor.
>
> Second, it is contrary to convention and principle that the Governor should assume any personal responsibility for the decisions of the Governor in Council. For him to direct the Council, and therefore the government, would be contrary to the institution of responsible government and it would offend basic democratic principles. He is in fact no more than a rubber stamp, bound to give effect to the advice which is tendered to him. Although cl vi of the Royal Instructions empowers him to refuse to follow that advice in specified circumstances and thereupon to report the matter immediately to Her Majesty, that clause must now in the Solicitor-General's submission be regarded as a dead letter and any attempt by a Governor of an Australian State to exercise such an independent judgment would provoke a constitutional crisis.[126]

In the words of Aickin J:

> [The Governor in Council] is the body which gives the force of law to, and thus makes effective, decisions of the executive government, ie the Cabinet and individual Ministers. That is the body in which executive power is vested by the constitutional system although the mode of the carrying into effect of the decisions of executive government differs according to the circumstances. Some executive acts may be wholly performed by Ministers or delegated to heads of government departments or to statutory authorities and some may be a formal order of the Governor in Council. Under the present legislation the Governor in Council is the body which gives legal operation to a decision made by a particular Minister who is responsible for the administration of the relevant legislation.[127]

The practice which pertains is that only ministers are in fact appointed to the Council. Being appointed for an unlimited term, they cease to be members only upon resignation. In practice, it is only those members who are currently ministers who are summoned to attend Council meetings, such meetings being called by the Governor-General or the Council's Vice President who is a minister. A quorum consists of the Governor-General or the Vice President and two ministers, or three ministers in the absence of the Governor-General or Vice President.[128]

Meetings of the Executive Council are summoned only when there is business to transact, with regular meetings occurring during the Autumn and Budget sessions of Parliament. The meetings are formal in nature. A recommendation, or 'Minute', is presented to indicate that something which is required by the Constitution or statute to be done or made is so done or made. The Minute is signed by the responsible minister and is accompanied by an explanatory memorandum. Once approved, the Governor-General so marks and signs it. Other instruments, principally regulations, will need to be so executed before they can have legal effect. In the absence of the Governor-General at a meeting, Minutes are submitted subsequently to the Governor-General for signature.[129]

**126** *FAI Insurances Ltd v Winneke* (1982) 151 CLR 342, 396–7.
**127** Ibid, 382.
**128** See Peter Hanks, Frances Gordon and Graeme Hill, *Constitutional Law in Australia* (LexisNexis Butterworths, 3rd ed, 2012) 212.
**129** See Constitutional Commission, above n 97, 334. The recommendations of the Commission are set out at 332.

In light of the formal nature of the Executive Council's deliberations, an appreciation of how executive decisions are in fact made requires an understanding of the workings of Cabinet. There is no mention of 'the Cabinet' or 'the Prime Minister' in the Constitution. Nor are these offices or their equivalents mentioned in any State constitution, except that of Queensland which devotes Part 3, inter alia, to 'Cabinet and Ministers of State'. Section 42 declares, among other things, that the 'Cabinet is collectively responsible to the Parliament'. As Bagehot explained, the Cabinet is the very centre of government. It is the chief executive authority responsible for legislative policy.[130] It directs government policy and makes decisions about national issues and the resolution of national problems. It deliberates upon Bills presented to it by ministers from their particular departments, considering their merit and cost, and recommending to ministers whether the Bill should proceed to Parliament or amendments be made. Ministerial sub-committees may examine issues in more detail. While at the State level all Ministers of the Crown are members of Cabinet, at the Commonwealth level it is only those senior ministers or those holding the more significant portfolios (Treasury, Foreign Affairs, Defence, Finance, Attorney-General's, etc) who are in the Cabinet. It has been the practice (since 1956, and excepting the years of the Whitlam Labor Government, 1972–5) that the ministry is divided between the Cabinet and 'the outer ministry'.

While Cabinet has no formal legal status, it is one of those conventional emanations of the workings of responsible government which, having evolved from unprepossessing circumstances, has become central to the workings of government in the United Kingdom and Australia. As H E Renfree noted:

> The conventions supporting the Cabinet system appear to be deeply entrenched, both in Great Britain and Australia. ... There has been no controversy as to the existence of these pillars of responsible government [Prime Minister and Cabinet], and they seem to be likely to continue unchallenged unless and until there is a 'revolution' in our form of government. ... The British conventions as to the structure of the 'government', such as the existence and operation of Cabinet, a Prime Minister, other Ministers and a Leader of the Opposition have been accepted as applicable to Australia. So also is the system of Party Government with its related rules as to the person entitled to be appointed as Prime Minister, the persons entitled to be appointed as Ministers and the circumstances in which the Government will go out of office. The rules as to Ministerial responsibility have also been accepted as applying.[131]

The important conventions which apply to Cabinet relate to Cabinet secrecy and solidarity. These are incidental or ancillary aspects of responsible government. Secrecy is required to enhance full and frank discussion on the matters of high moment which come before it.[132] Cabinet records cannot be accessed for at least

**130** Walter Bagehot, *The English Constitution* (Fontana, 1963) 59–81.
**131** H E Renfree, *The Executive Power of the Commonwealth of Australia* (Legal Books, 1984) 61–3.
**132** See Tony Lupton, 'Cabinet Confidentiality and Parliamentary Scrutiny in the Information Age' (2012) 27 *Australasian Parliamentary Review* 151; D Busfield-Birch and R Hazell, 'Opening the Cabinet Door: Freedom of Information and Government Policy Making' [2011] *Public Law* 260.

20 years, since the 2010 amendments to the *Archive Act 1983* (Cth), down from 30 years previously. Cabinet solidarity requires that the decisions of the Cabinet be unanimous. This means that all members of Cabinet must publically support any final decision of Cabinet whether or not any individual member may have advocated a contrary position during actual deliberations. If a minister is unable to support the ultimate position, that minister must resign from Cabinet.[133] While the position of 'the Cabinet', despite its actual centrality, indeed primacy, in the government of the nation remains somewhat nebulous, it is perhaps a good thing that its workings are not prescribed by binding legal rules so that they be allowed to evolve as the political system evolves.[134] The Advisory Committee on Executive Government to the Constitutional Commission concluded thus:

> Nor do we consider that the Constitution should specifically provide for 'the cabinet'. This is because the cabinet is essentially an informal body; it is unsuited to formal statement in a constitution. Practices as to its composition and operation can and do change from one government to the next. It is even possible that some system other than the present one of a 'cabinet' might evolve. Again, much of this desirable flexibility could be lost if 'the cabinet' were written into the Constitution.[135]

In its Final Report the Constitutional Commission made no recommendation that provision be made for the Cabinet in the Constitution.[136] The need for adaptability to accommodate evolving political circumstances are common rationales for this view. Gaudron, Gummow and Hayne JJ stated in *Egan v Willis* that '[i]t should not be assumed that the characteristics of a system of responsible government are fixed'.[137] Similarly, in *Re Patterson; Ex parte Taylor*, Gleeson CJ stated: '[R]esponsible government is a concept based upon a combination of law, convention, and political practice. The characteristics of responsible government are not immutable'.[138] As Gummow and Hayne JJ pointed out: 'The content of the various principles and practices which together may be identified in Australia as comprising "responsible government" is a matter of continued debate between constitutional lawyers, political scientists and politicians themselves'.[139]

**133** For an important discussion of the conventions relating to Cabinet, see Lindell, above n 31, 4–7. See also J W Shaw, 'The Established Principles of Cabinet Government' (2001) 73 *The Australian Quarterly* 21.
**134** For more on Cabinet secrecy and solidarity, see Lindell, above n 31, 4–7; Winterton, above n 10, 81–5.
**135** Advisory Committee on Executive Government, above n 92, 15.
**136** Constitutional Commission, above n 97. The Commission's recommendations and reasons are contained in chapter 5 of the report.
**137** (1998) 195 CLR 424, 451.
**138** (2000) 207 CLR 391, 403.
**139** *Re Patterson; Ex parte Taylor* (2001) 207 CLR 391, 460. In relation to the evolving nature of Cabinet government, see Jenny Menzies and Pat Weller, 'Government in 2020' (2004) 1 *Public Administration Today* 10. In relation to Cabinet government generally, see: S Encel, *Cabinet Government in Australia* (Melbourne University Press, 1962); W Ivor Jennings, *Cabinet Government* (Cambridge University Press, 1937); Enid Campbell, 'Ministers, Public Servants and the Executive Branch' in Gareth Evans (ed), *Labor and the Constitution: 1972–1975* (Heineman Educational, 1977) 136; G Sawer, 'Cabinets, Councils and Ministers in Australia' [1956] *Public Law* 110.

While the Cabinet is the substantive fulcrum of the executive government, it is the Australian Public Service and Commonwealth statutory agencies which conduct the work of the Commonwealth Executive, the latter subject to the particular Act of Parliament which established them, with varying degrees of independence from the government. In relation to the Public Service, the Constitution does provide for Departments of State (s 64) and the 'Appointment of civil servants' (s 67), but the balance of matters is regulated by statutes such as the *Public Service Act 1999* (Cth). Generically, they may be referred to as 'the Commonwealth' or 'the Crown' or 'the Executive', although this may not necessarily be the case with statutory agencies depending on the terms of their governing statute and the extent to which they are endowed with 'the preferences, immunities and exceptions' enjoyed by the Crown.

# V Responsible government

## 1 Responsible government in the Constitution

The structure of the executive government of the Commonwealth is informed throughout by responsible government. Responsible government is fundamental to an understanding of the structure of the executive, as well as to an understanding of the 'executive power of the Commonwealth' which will be examined in the next chapter. Quick and Garran stated: '[F]or better or for worse, the system of Responsible Government as known to the British Constitution has been practically embedded in the Federal Constitution, in such a manner that it cannot be disturbed without an amendment to the instrument'.[140]

While it is both relevant and instructive to observe the evolution of responsible government in the United Kingdom, a simple transference of that principle into the Australian federal context without qualification is not possible. For one thing, the principles of responsible government in the United Kingdom exist as convention; albeit in that more elevated sense of those customary practices and expectations which have developed without a written constitution, which possess an ancient lineage and have arisen by way of organic evolution over many centuries. This is not quite the case in Australia. For one thing, the Commonwealth Constitution is a written instrument. Moreover, and very significantly, the polity it establishes is a federal one. It is also clear from the intentions of the framers, and the repeated affirmations of the High Court,[141] that the Commonwealth Constitution establishes by implication a system of responsible government. The text of the Constitution clearly permits this implication, especially

**140** Above n 49, 706–7.

**141** See especially *Lange v Australian Broadcasting Corporation* (1997) 189 CLR 520, 558, 561. Prior authorities are ample. In addition to *Sue v Hill* (1999) 199 CLR 462, 499 and *Re Patterson; Ex parte Taylor* (2001) 207 CLR 391, 416, 462–5, see the references in Geoffrey Lindell, 'Responsible Government' in P D Finn (ed), *Essays on Law and Government, Vol 1* (Law Book Co, 1995) 75, 85 n 42 and in Winterton, above n 10, 76 n 298.

ss 44(iv), 53, 57, 62, 63 and 64.[142] However, a confusion may arise because the written instrument gives expression only to some of the principles of responsible government, thus creating a dichotomy between what is clearly stated in the text, giving them a clear constitutional and legal status, and what is left unexpressed and sustained as part of the conventional rules of responsible government.

This is well-illustrated by s 64. The section gives explicit recognition to the convention which requires ministers to be members of Parliament by mandating that Commonwealth Ministers must become members of either House of the Parliament within a particular time frame. This aspect of responsible government, being clearly stated in the text, is therefore legally binding and judicially enforceable. However, the other critical aspect, that ministers must have and retain the confidence of Parliament in order to remain in office, is not mentioned. The latter aspect thus remains, prima facie at least, within the realm of convention and, accordingly, may not have the same legally binding character of the expressly stated requirement. This is not to deny, however, that that conventional aspect of responsible government may be used to interpret s 64 and other written provisions.

Geoffrey Lindell has suggested that 'the founders of the Constitution failed to go further than merely to establish the *machinery* by which the rules of responsible government could operate and develop'.[143] On this view, those aspects of the doctrine not expressly mentioned in the Constitution were recognised to the extent that they were able to assist in the interpretation of those express provisions, but were not regarded necessarily as legally enforceable. As Lindell put it, on a view which he has now qualified to an extent following the decision in *Lange v Australian Broadcasting Corporation*:[144]

> [T]he Constitution was deliberately structured to make it possible to permit compliance with the rule of responsible government without necessarily requiring such compliance. To the extent that those rules could operate consistently with the Constitution they operated according to their general tenor ie as rules of *convention* and not *law*.[145]

Such an approach is very suitable to a principle, or set of principles, which exist primarily as convention and whose status as convention provides the requisite degree of flexibility to enable them to develop and evolve over time in accordance with political realities. Moreover, it is an approach that is able to accommodate the fact that apart from the fundamental principles of responsible government – the Queen's representative must act on ministerial advice and the ministry must retain the confidence of the lower house – many of the principles remained somewhat uncertain.

**142** See Winterton, above n 10, 77–8.
**143** Lindell, above n 141, 80.
**144** (1997) 189 CLR 520. Lindell's revised view is discussed below.
**145** Lindell, above n 31, 2.

What can be stated with a degree of confidence, however, is that the Constitution established a 'parliamentary executive' as opposed to a 'presidential executive' as is the case, for example, in the United States. By establishing responsible government, the Constitution maintains the supremacy of Parliament over the executive – the legacy of the victory of Parliament over the Crown in the constitutional conflicts of the seventeenth century in England. Responsible government requires that the Queen or the Queen's representative (the Governor-General) must act on the 'advice' of ministers who are members of Parliament and who have the confidence of Parliament (or, more precisely, the more popularly elected house in a bicameral legislature) to whom they are 'responsible', collectively and individually; and of course ultimately to the electorate. '[T]he Crown acts on the advice of its Ministers and ... Ministers are responsible to the Parliament for the actions of the Crown'.[146] There are also incidental aspects which form part of its essential character, such as Cabinet solidarity and Cabinet secrecy.[147] The withdrawal of confidence will require the resignation of a minister from the government and, if the loss of confidence is directed to the prime minister or the ministry collectively, the government itself must fall. Under responsible government, the ambit of executive power is ultimately subject to legislative control. In Anglo-Australian constitutional practice, this is reflected in the fact that the prerogatives of the Crown – those powers recognised by the common law which may be exercised without legislative authorisation – are essentially a residue of powers which Parliament has deigned to leave to the Crown, and which it can always abnegate or regulate.[148] While these prerogative powers are exercisable on 'advice', there are some which may be exercised by the Queen or the Queen's representative without or contrary to advice and are referred to as the 'reserve' powers, discussed in more detail below.[149]

Beyond these core principles, there exist a 'penumbra of conventions and practices free to evolve with changing political patterns', a view in relation to which certain of the framers were quite explicit and which holds good today.[150] As to the desirability of maintaining the flexible, evolutionary character of responsible government, there is little controversy. The High Court has tended to regard it as a dynamic, evolving concept, as the *dicta* in *Egan v Willis*[151] and *Re Patterson; Ex parte Taylor*,[152] noted earlier, confirm.

The High Court has often acknowledged that responsible government is implied by the Constitution, and has often relied on it in constitutional interpretation.[153] In *Engineers*, it was referred to as 'pervading the instrument' and it was

**146** *New South Wales v Commonwealth* (1975) 135 CLR 337, 365.
**147** Lindell, above n 31, 5.
**148** For an excellent account of the operation of responsible government, see Lindell, Ibid, and further Lindell, above n 141. The seminal work of George Winterton should also be examined: Winterton, above n 10, 13–26, 71–84. See also Zines, above n 99, 339–40.
**149** For more on the operation of responsible government, see Lindell, above nn 31 and 141; Winterton, above n 10, 13–26, 71–84; and Zines, above n 99, 339–40.
**150** See especially Winterton, above n 10, 80.
**151** (1998) 195 CLR 424, 451.
**152** (2001) 207 CLR 391, 403.
**153** *New South Wales v Commonwealth* (1975) 135 CLR 337, 364–5; *Victorian Stevedoring & General Contracting Co Pty Ltd v Dignan* (1931) 46 CLR 73, 114; *New South Wales v Commonwealth* (the *Wheat* case) (1915) 20 CLR 54, 89.

said that it must be 'taken into account in determining the meaning of its language'.[154] It has also been referred to as 'the central feature of the Australian constitutional system'[155] and 'one of the central features of our polity'.[156] In the *Wooltops* case, Isaacs J referred to 'the impossibility of regarding the mere written words of the Constitution as affording the only test of validity'.[157] He continued:

> The doctrine of responsible government ... is invisibly but none the less inextricably and powerfully interwoven with the texture of the written word, and any interpretation of the document which disregarded the implication of the doctrine would be false and misleading.[158]

The imprint of responsible government demands a certain interconnectedness, if not partial fusion, of the legislative and executive branches. It also implies a hierarchy which places the legislature at the top. This must somehow be accommodated, at the Commonwealth level, with the separation of powers which demands branch separation and implies the equality of the branches. One issue created by this tension, for example, is whether the separation of executive and legislative power, coupled with express constitutional grants of power to the executive, permits, or indeed compels, the executive to possess a sphere of action beyond legislative control. This tension and its consequences will be considered in more detail in the next chapter. However, this is but one of the problems thrown up by Australia's dual British and American constitutional inheritance. For it is essentially the American inheritance – the separation of powers and federalism – from which spring the imperatives to limit the ambit of Commonwealth legislative power in its relationship to executive power, and to limit the ambit of the Commonwealth executive vis-à-vis that of the executives of the Australian States. This gives rise to a set of tensions between responsible government and federalism. Here, the other difficulty is identifying what each of these principles means beyond the core of the idea, and how they play out precisely in the sphere of government and politics, and especially how they may regulate the precise relationship between ministers, Parliament and the Governor-General.

## 2 The framers and responsible government

The framers were acutely conscious, as have been others then and since, of the difficulty of attempting to accommodate responsible government within the federal nature of the polity they were establishing.[159] This is one reason why they tended to avoid a more precise statement of that institution. Their reticence in this regard should not discount the fact that it was ultimately decided, after considerable debate, and despite some dissenting voices, that

**154** *Amalgamated Society of Engineers v Adelaide Steamship Co Ltd* (1920) 28 CLR 129, 146.
**155** *R v Kirby; Ex parte Boilermakers' Society of Australia* (1956) 94 CLR 254, 275.
**156** *Victorian Stevedoring & General Contracting Co Pty Ltd v Dignan* (1931) 46 CLR 73, 114.
**157** *Commonwealth v Colonial Combing, Spinning & Weaving Co Ltd* (1922) 31 CLR 421, 446.
**158** Ibid.
**159** Winterton, above n 10, 72.

responsible government should be established.[160] The framers were, however, reluctant to set out in the text the actual position as it pertained in Britain – that the Queen acted on the advice of her Ministers, who themselves held the confidence of the House of Commons – and adopted rather a form of words which *assumed* the invisible restraining hand of responsible government with adaptions permitted to accommodate federalism. Their reluctance to spell it out seems to have stemmed in part from provincial sensitivities to avoid giving the impression, especially to British lawyers, of a lack of constitutional refinement if they presumed to set out in a legal instrument what may well have been regarded as a constitutional truism, if not platitude.[161] Thus, while the powers of the Queen, exercisable by the Governor-General, as described in the text of the Constitution may appear fitting for an early seventeenth century monarch, the clear adoption of responsible government by the framers manifested a confidence on their part that no constitutional lawyer would read the text literally in this regard.

This explains the distinction drawn by Quick and Garran between 'the traditional ideal of the British Constitution, as embodied in sec 61, giving full expression to the picture of Royal authority painted by Blackstone' and 'the modern practice of the Constitution', by which 'polite' expression is given to the constitutional need for the Queen's representative to act on advice.[162] At the Sydney Convention in 1891, Henry Wrixon remarked:

> Therefore instead of seeking to limit the powers which the Sovereign may depute to the governor-general ... we have to take care to thoroughly establish responsible government, and, if we do that, the rest will take care of itself.[163]

Thus also Alfred Deakin at the same Convention:

> [I]f I can see established in Australia responsible government in the fullest acceptation of the term – a government in which the governor can take no action which is not countersigned by his responsible advisers, who must answer for their conduct to their parliament, and in which the governor-general, so far as his political status is concerned, has no authority whatever except to choose his advisers subject to the approval of parliament, I shall be satisfied.[164]

The wisdom of avoiding some more detailed exposition of responsible government, especially in light of the federal nature of the polity they were seeking to establish, is another question. Such exposition certainly had not been attempted before in any analogous constitutional instrument, being oft-regarded as either unnecessary or impossible.[165] There had been no explicit, express entrenchment of the principle in Canada or the Australian colonies. Nonetheless, certain

**160** Ibid 3–5, 71–85. See also Nicholas Aroney, *The Constitution of a Federal Commonwealth* (Cambridge University Press, 2009) 1–2, 6, 189–93, 198, 201–5, 210–16, 238–9, 339–40, 359–62; Crommelin, above n 32, esp 136–44.
**161** Winterton, above n 10, 3; with references to the Convention Debates at nn 16, 17.
**162** Quick and Garran, above n 49, 703.
**163** *Convention Debates, Sydney* (1891) 575.
**164** Ibid, 571. See also 2252–5.
**165** See, further, Winterton, above n 10, 72 nn 245–6.

provisions of the Commonwealth Constitution certainly manifest the influence of responsible government, such as ss 64, 81 and 83. Thus, it cannot be denied that the vesting of executive power in the Queen, exercisable by the Governor-General, was to be understood in a purely formal sense, actual power being wielded by responsible ministers in Cabinet advising the Governor-General, subject to conventions of collective ministerial responsibility, Cabinet solidarity and secrecy.

Adopting responsible government was one thing; how to reconcile it with the demands of federalism was another. There were two principal problems with doing this. The first was how to set out those principles which precisely regulated the interrelationship between the monarch's representative, Ministers of State, and Parliament. The framers 'resolved' this problem by avoidance – that is, by choosing not to codify the conventions of responsible government except beyond a skeleton few. The more pressing problem – the one which dominated the debates on this issue – was how to reconcile responsible government with a bicameral legislature in the form established. As indicated in Chapter 2, the Senate was established to represent 'the people of the States' and the House of Representatives to represent 'the people of the Commonwealth', each house thus, arguably, representing two separate 'peoples'.[166] If one were simply to examine representation by virtue of the Australian population – that is, in an absolute sense – it could be said that the Senate is the less popularly elected house; and yet, because it represents the people of the States on the basis of State equality as a condition of federation, it was given virtually equal power with the House of Representatives. Given that the Senate was conferred with the power to reject Appropriation Bills, was it the case that the government was 'responsible' – in the formal constitutional sense, as opposed to being merely accountable politically – to the Senate as well as the House of Representatives?

Clear resolutions to these problems are not easily discernible from the Convention Debates. In the view of some of the framers, it was simply not feasible, indeed it was impractical, to have a government responsible to two houses, especially when their respective political make-up may differ and thus result in different views on policy and the direction of government.[167] The precedents from Britain and the Australian colonies indicated a form of responsible government operating in non-federal polities, and which essentially required ministerial responsibility to the lower, or more democratically elected, house. As stated by Sir Richard Baker:

> The essence of federation is the existence of two houses, if not of actually co-equal power, at all events of approximately co-equal power. The essence of responsible government is the existence of one chamber of predominant power. Now, how are we to reconcile two irreconcilable propositions?[168]

**166** See Chapter 2, Part II.2–3.
**167** *Convention Debates, Sydney* (1897) 533; *Convention Debates, Melbourne* (1898) 2470; *Convention Debates, Adelaide* (1897) 52, and (1897) 499–500; *Convention Debates, Sydney* (1891) 58, and (1891) 424.
**168** *Convention Debates, Sydney* (1897) 784.

Others referred to this as a 'riddle'.[169] Others still joined Baker in concluding that it was a riddle with no solution and hence suggested, as did Griffith, Cockburn, Inglis Clark and Hackett, that it was best to abandon the specifically British model of responsible government.[170] While the *British* model of it may indeed have been abandoned, responsible government itself, however, was not abandoned but rather adapted to Australian conditions, with the aspiration that it would continue to adapt. For one thing, it had to be reconciled with the establishment of a strong Senate with almost equal powers to the House of Representatives. That the latter was desired, indeed required, was clear from the early deliberations resulting in what became known as 'the compromise of 1891' – the Senate was to have power to reject bills appropriating money for the ordinary services of government, though it could not amend such bills, nor were such bills permitted to originate in that house. This was eventually given formal expression in s 53. Moreover, the influence of Griffith in particular resulted in avoiding any clear statement in the Constitution that ministers were to be responsible to the lower house only, it being sufficient that they be members of Parliament.

It therefore cannot be denied that the framers were conscious of the power they were giving the Senate to deny Supply to the government, even if it continued to maintain the confidence of the House. However, it is not entirely clear whether the full constitutional implications of this and the extent to which this modified the form of responsible government as traditionally understood – that the government is 'responsible' only to the lower house – had been carefully considered. On the other hand, it was certainly understood by many that the Senate could, by denying Supply, bring down a government which otherwise maintained the confidence of the House, the inevitable result of the denial of Supply, even if not intended to be the immediate result.[171] Griffith noted that if the Senate 'insisted in withholding that confidence and refused to provide the necessary Supplies ... it is hard to see what alternative there would be to a change of Ministers'.[172] That the denial of Supply is the clearest expression of a lack of confidence in a government and the most decisive sanction of ministerial responsibility was well understood.[173] To this extent, the views of Griffith and others of like mind prevailed to ensure that the *British* model of responsible government was not adopted without modification.

That the Senate was given the capacity, if it wished, to make the government responsible to it cannot be denied. The events of 1975 certainly confirmed this view. But it is not clear in what sense 'responsible' was meant in these

**169** *Convention Debates, Melbourne* (1898) 2154.
**170** Winterton, above n 10, 200–10 n 40, esp 201 n 42; Quick and Garran, above n 49, 706; Crommelin, above n 32, 136–44; *Convention Debates, Sydney* (1891) 280, (1891) 466–77, 465–6; *Convention Debates, Adelaide* (1897) 28–30. See also J A La Nauze, *The Making of the Australian Constitution* (Melbourne University Press, 1972) 39–42.
**171** Winterton, above n 10, 6; *Convention Debates, Adelaide* (1897) 110–11, 295. See also Harrison Moore, above n 112, 144, 145.
**172** Samuel Griffith, *Notes on Australian Federation: Its Nature and Probable Effects* (1896) 19.
**173** Ibid, 18. See also *Convention Debates, Adelaide* (1897) 23; Robert Garran, *The Coming Commonwealth* (Angus and Robertson, 1897) 150.

circumstances: did the framers intend that the government be responsible to the Senate in the fullest sense of that term? That is, *money bills aside*, was it intended that the loss of confidence in the government by the Senate should equate to a loss of confidence by the House of Representatives, obliging it to advise a dissolution of the House or indeed a double dissolution if the requirements of s 57 had been met, or to resign? Moreover, in the situation of a rejection of Supply by the Senate, and a refusal by a government which retains the confidence of the House to advise a dissolution or resign, at which point may a Governor-General intervene to exercise the reserve powers to dismiss the government, and on what precise grounds? If a loss of confidence by the Senate is not to be equated with a loss of confidence by the House, then the 'mere' fact of its denial of Supply may not be the trigger for immediate constitutional consequences: resignation, advising dissolution, failing which, dismissal. It would rather be the case that the government may continue to govern so long as it has appropriated funds available to it. And only when such funds run out, or are about to run out, should the government advise a dissolution or resign – not because it has lost the confidence of the Senate per se, but rather because the withholding of Supply (of course, representing a loss of confidence) prevents it from governing, and spending money, without breaching the Constitution (ss 81 and 83); that is, because it would be acting illegally. On this view, if a government in such a case were to remain intransigent, the Governor-General may exercise a reserve power to dismiss on the latter ground – ie, the government not being able to access funds constitutionally – and not directly because the Senate per se lost confidence in the government. The difference here may be nice, but it remains important.

In short, a distinction is being drawn between two grounds of dismissal. The first is the denial of Supply by the Senate, ipso facto. The second ground is based not on the 'mere' denial of Supply, but on its consequence. That is, when appropriated funds run out, the government will no longer be able to govern legally, constitutionally. If, in the latter circumstances, a Prime Minister fails to resign or advise a dissolution, the Governor-General may dismiss that Prime Minister. The latter principle is arguably more consistent with the principles of responsible government as applied in their Australian context. That is, it does not deny that the confidence of the House is essential for the formation of government and its continuance in office. It does not deny the Senate the power to deny Supply. It does not deny a government which continues to enjoy the confidence of the House its right to govern, so long as it has existing appropriated funds available to it. And it does not prevent the Governor-General dismissing a government when such funds have run out and the government fails to resign or advise an election. Arguably, had the Governor-General in 1975 based his decision to dismiss on this latter ground exclusively, he may have found greater support for his actions.

However, it may be argued that while any other expression of no confidence by the Senate does not have constitutional consequences with respect to the continuation of the government in office, a denial of Supply, ultimately preventing the government from being able to access funds constitutionally, must inevitably result in the demise of the government. This would be so even if the government maintained the confidence of the House. Given the inevitability of its fall – and this being clearly understood by the framers – could it therefore be argued that the denial of Supply was the one method by which the Senate could hold the government responsible – the ultimate sanction – and that it was therefore to be regarded as the *particular* expression of a loss of confidence which triggered the constitutional imperatives of advising a dissolution, resignation, failing which, dismissal? The latter conclusion cannot be drawn with any certainty, at least if the views of those who opposed giving such power to the Senate are taken into consideration. McMillan, for example, insisted that matters must never come to such a head: it would be 'inviting a revolution in the country', one which would only be brought on by a 'lunatic'.[174] Harrison Moore considered it to be 'a contingency so remote as hardly to be within the range of practical politics'.[175]

What then is to be made of it? It is clear that not giving power to the Senate to reject any bill was a 'deal-breaker' as far as federation itself was concerned. This power, including over appropriation bills, was accepted both in 1891 and again in Adelaide in 1897.[176] That it could be used to force a government to an election had not seriously been contemplated until at least 1973–4.[177] Having said that, and despite certain views to the contrary, it is clear that the Senate does have that power to deny Supply and that this was intended by the framers. This was given expression in s 53, especially its fourth and fifth paragraphs.[178] This has also been acknowledged by the High Court.[179] Moreover, any deadlocks over Supply could still be resolved by the mechanism of s 57 which also applies to appropriation bills. This is subject of course to: successful navigation of the practicalities involved in the three month period required by the s 57 mechanism; and the imminence or otherwise of the government running out of existing appropriated funds, which may make resort to s 57 impracticable – as appears to have been the case in the constitutional crisis of 1975.[180] Therefore, while there is surely a degree of uncertainty as to the precise intentions, Winterton neatly summarised the position thus:

> At the end of the day, the founders envisaged a system of responsible government fundamentally similar to that of Britain, with the government chosen from the majority

**174** *Convention Debates, Adelaide* (1897) 220. See also *Convention Debates, Melbourne* (1898) 2165.
**175** Harrison Moore, above n 112, 154.
**176** *Convention Debates, Melbourne* (1898, 1997–8); La Nauze, above n 170, 39–42; Dennis Pearce, 'The Legislative Power of the Senate' in Leslie Zines (ed) *Commentaries on the Australian Constitution* (Butterworths, 1977) 119, 124–5.
**177** George Winterton, '1975: The Dismissal of the Whitlam Government', in George Winterton and H P Lee (eds), *Australian Constitutional Landmarks* (Cambridge University Press, 2003) 229, 245.
**178** See Winterton, above n 10, 6–7.
**179** *Victoria v Commonwealth* (1975) 134 CLR 81, 121, 143, 168, 185; *Attorney-General (NSW) v Trethowan* (1931) 44 CLR 394, 420.
**180** See John Kerr, *Matters for Judgment* (MacMillan, 1978) 326–7; Colin Howard and Cheryl Saunders, 'The Blocking of the Budget and Dismissal of the Government' in Gareth Evans (ed), *Labor and the Constitution 1972–1975* (Heinemann, 1977) 259, 264–5; R Eggleston, 'Comment' in ibid 297, 299–300.

> party in the House of Representatives, and responsible only to it. *In practice*, responsible government has operated in this way; there has been recognition from authoritative sources that the government needs to retain the confidence only of the House of Representatives, and that after a general election, the leader of the majority party (or parties) in the lower is entitled to be commissioned to form a government. … [T]he Constitution, in ss 53 and 57, itself hints at this.[181]

It is not clear that the framers finally decided upon the precise constitutional consequences of a denial of Supply by the Senate, although they clearly did grant the Senate the power to do so.

## 3 Responsible government: Old issues, modern problems

### Senate power and confidence in the government

How then is this to be reconciled with the events of 1975 which resulted in a 'constitutional crisis' and dismissal of Prime Minister Gough Whitlam by the Governor-General, Sir John Kerr?

To the extent that the events of 1975 can be treated as a precedent – how can they not? – the operation of responsible government as envisaged by the framers has been modified, at least to the extent that an opposition with a majority in the Senate, with Supply running out, may be willing to use its power to reject Supply to bring down the government and not merely to reject a particular spending measure. Even that possibility may have shifted the balance of power between the two houses post-1975, the Senate being able to act more assertively. As Winterton concluded:

> In sum, the implications of this aspect of the conflict between responsible government and the federal principle remain very much in a state of flux, leaving the relations between the two Houses, and the government and the Senate, dangerously uncertain.[182]

It is debatable whether the passage of time since 1983, when Winterton made this statement, warrants the removal of the adverb 'dangerously'. That the matter remains (at least) uncertain cannot be denied. It also remains unclear, in particular, whether responsible government requires that the government be responsible to the Senate in this very limited sense: it may not need the confidence of the Senate to form government, but it needs the confidence of the Senate as expressed by the continued provision of Supply in order to remain in government. Only when expressed by a denial of Supply will the Senate's lack of confidence have immediate constitutional consequences. On the other hand, is it not more correct to say that the principle of responsible government remains unaltered in its main feature, with the qualification under the Commonwealth Constitution that the Senate can bring down a government by denial of Supply on grounds *other than that it is the ultimate expression of lack of confidence*? In

**181** Winterton, above n 10, 7 (emphasis added).
**182** Ibid, 11.

other words, the government must eventually fall because it simply cannot continue to fund its operations when appropriated funds run out. Only when such a point is reached must it resign, advise an election, or face dismissal if it seeks to use funds in breach of the Constitution. In short, the government must resign, or face dismissal, not by the mere fact of the denial of Supply, but rather on the ground that it cannot continue to govern legally. Such a view seems the most consistent with responsible government and yet accommodating of the Senate's very considerable power.

**Legal status of responsible government**

If the framers avoided providing a detailed expression of the principles of responsible government in the Constitution, how then was it to be regarded? It seems that it was meant to operate as an underlying doctrine of the Constitution, operating '*according to its general tenor*, that is, in a *permissive* sense as resting only upon convention, except where expressly indicated to the contrary'.[183] However, the events of 1975 drew attention to a perceived clash of express constitutional provisions and convention – the Senate's power in s 53 to reject money bills and the principle of responsible government which permitted a ministry to remain in government if it retained the confidence of the lower house. '[I]t can be an uphill battle', as Winterton noted, 'to maintain that the unwritten principles of responsible government should prevail – as the events of 1975 demonstrated'.[184] Even though some at least have found partial expression in the Constitution, for example, as in s 62 which provides for Federal Executive Council to 'advise the Governor-General' and s 64 which requires that Ministers of State be members of Parliament, these provide only partial guidance.

This gave rise to some concern to ensure that responsible government's core principles, at least – that the Governor-General must act on ministerial advice, and that a ministry which enjoys the confidence of the House is entitled to govern – should be given some greater constitutional protection than their conventional status may allow. Winterton, for example, advanced the thesis that the clear entrenchment of responsible government ensured that at least some of its principles were legally entrenched and judicially enforceable.[185] What then is the precise legal status of responsible government in the Constitution?

The High Court has recognised that responsible government 'pervades' the Constitution and that this may have *legal* consequences even if the particular conventions of responsible government are not themselves legally enforceable as such. For example, responsible government has been used to assist in the interpretation of the Constitution in relation to the Commonwealth's capacity to enter into contracts without statutory authorisation,[186] the Parliament's ability

**183** Lindell, above n 31, 86 (emphasis in original).
**184** Ibid, 4.
**185** Winterton, above n 10, ch 7, ch 8 150–51.
**186** *Commonwealth v Colonial Combing, Spinning & Weaving Co Ltd* (1922) 31 CLR 421, 448–51; *New South Wales v Bardolph* (1934) 52 CLR 455, 509, 517–18. Although now see *Williams (No 1)* and *Williams (No 2)* discussed in the next chapter.

to delegate its legislative power to the executive,[187] and the Governor-General's power to dissolve the House of Representatives and to order a double dissolution pursuant to s 57.[188] Principles emanating from responsible government have also been used by the High Court to assist in the determination of the ambit of the general executive power of the Commonwealth in s 61 in its 'depth' aspect (determining the extent to which such power may be immune from legislative control) and its 'breadth' aspect (determining the subject matters over which it can be exercised to accommodate federal concerns). This is dealt with in detail in Chapter 7.

It is far less certain, however, whether reliance can be placed on responsible government beyond this. For example, when exercising executive power vested in the Governor-General by the Constitution, either in s 61 or in specific grants of power, to what extent can it be said that the Constitution *requires*, or *mandates*, that the Governor-General act only pursuant to ministerial advice, leaving aside for a moment the question of reserve powers? And if the Governor-General should fail to do so, would a court be able to intervene to enforce this requirement? Similar questions may be asked with respect to the appointment of a Prime Minister following an election. While s 64 permits of a 'reserve' power in the Governor-General to appoint Ministers of State who will form the government, it only expressly requires that such persons be, or become within three months, members of Parliament. Pursuant to the principles of responsible government, however, a Governor-General should seek to appoint as Prime Minister that person who is likely to command a majority in the House of Representatives and who enjoys its confidence. It would be fanciful to suggest that a Governor-General would breach this principle, and hence the issue of whether the High Court would enforce it is hardly likely to come up. For even if the result of an election was inconclusive, the Governor-General's choice would ultimately be tested on the floor of the House and not in a court of law. Nevertheless, in the event that such were to occur, assuming its justiciability, how would the Court regard such a fundamental principle when making a declaration as to the validity or otherwise of the Governor-General's action?

The principles upon which the above examples were based can be said to constitute fundamental, core aspects of responsible government, clearly recognised in 1900 and, the most likely, if such a view were to be accepted, to be regarded as entrenched and enforceable legal rules. In the view of Winterton,[189] if such core principles can be implied from the Constitution, then they should be judicially enforceable in the same way the High Court enforces other implied powers and prohibitions. Some support for this view may be garnered from Quick and Garran when they wrote, following their cataloguing of the express

**187** *Victorian Stevedoring & General Contracting Co Pty Ltd v Dignan* (1931) 46 CLR 73, 114; *R v Kirby; Ex parte Boilermakers' Society of Australia* [1957] AC 288, 314–15; *R v Anderson, Ex parte Ipec-Air Pty Ltd* (1965) 113 CLR 177, 206; *Radio Corporation Pty Ltd v Commonwealth* (1938) 59 CLR 170.
**188** *Western Australia v Commonwealth* (1975) 134 CLR 201, 278, 293.
**189** Winterton, above n 10, 124–5.

powers vested in the Governor-General, that these are 'powers and functions vested in the Governor-General by statute, to be exercised by him in accordance with the recognised principles of Responsible Government'.[190] Winterton also pressed this view in relation to the exercise of reserve powers, which, he argued, had to be exercised consistently with responsible government, at least in its core aspects. If they were not so exercised, the Governor-General would be acting beyond the ambit of his or her power.[191] This would occur, for example, if a Governor-General purported to dismiss a Prime Minister who retains the confidence of the House and who has not acted illegally or clearly breached the Constitution. The argument would be that in such circumstances the power to dismiss contained in s 64 has in fact been exceeded, exercised *ultra vires*.[192] Winterton also proposed that the powers conferred on the executive by the Constitution, like the powers conferred on the executive by legislation, had to be exercised in good faith, pursuant to the principles of natural justice, and without reliance on relevant considerations.[193]

Some commentators have suggested that these views were given a degree of comfort by decisions of the High Court,[194] culminating in its unanimous decision in *Lange*,[195] which gave recognition to an implied freedom of political communication, inferred from the system of representative government established by the Constitution. These cases gave rise to speculation that some of the principles of *responsible* government could be similarly implied because, in describing the type of representative government so established, the unanimous reasoning made reference to the 'system of responsible ministerial government',[196] with detailed reference being made to the particular provisions of the Constitution which gave some expression to this.[197] Lindell opined, for example, that it 'is difficult in principle to distinguish between the ability to draw implications from representative government and those from the particular kind of representative government known as responsible government'.[198] Accordingly, '*if* this is correct', he ventured tentatively, 'it would *seem* to follow that *some* rules of constitutional convention have now become *transformed* into rules of law so as to become constitutionally entrenched'.[199] Commenting on Lindell's arguments, Zines observed that if this was in fact the case, then those conventions of responsible government would be transformed into legal rules which 'are designed to ensure that the will of the people's representatives, and ultimately that of the

**190** Quick and Garran, above n 49, 390.
**191** Winterton, above n 10, 125–6.
**192** Ibid, 13–15, 80, 125–6.
**193** Ibid, 127–39.
**194** See Chapter 5, Part V, discussing *Nationwide News Pty Ltd v Wills* (1992) 177 CLR 1 and *Australian Capital Television Pty Ltd v Commonwealth* (1992) 177 CLR 106, in which the existence of a constitutional guarantee of freedom of political communication was recognised as a necessary implication from the constitutionally prescribed system of representative government.
**195** *Lange v Australian Broadcasting Corporation* (1997) 189 CLR 520.
**196** Ibid, 558.
**197** Ibid, 558–9.
**198** Lindell, above n 31, 3.
**199** Ibid (emphasis added).

people themselves, is made effective'.[200] These would include 'those rules that generally require the Governor-General to follow the advice of ministers and to choose ministers that have the confidence of the House of Representatives [without] deny[ing] the discretion given to the Governor-General in respect of 'reserve powers'.[201] If the reasoning of *Lange* was pursued further, that is, 'if representative government is constitutionally required', Zines opined that 'it could hardly exist if the powers granted to the Governor-General were exercised regardless of rules that have developed from British constitutional conventions'. He continued: 'It would seem to follow that they are, to that extent, legally enforceable'.[202]

It is emphasised that this does not *necessarily* accord with the intention of the framers, nor has there been any High Court decision directly stating that some or any of the conventions of responsible government are to be regarded as entrenched legal rules. Indeed, it is contrary to the position taken by Lindell himself in his earlier, pre-*Lange*, writings.[203] His present observations simply explore the consequences of *Lange* if those aspects of the reasoning mentioned above are to be pressed. However, there is by no means a consensus that the reasoning in *Lange* permits of such speculation.[204] It can be argued that the reasoning of the Court did not quite amount to the position that the Court would enforce the specific content of the conventions as a matter of law,[205] for the thrust of the Court's reasoning in *Lange* was focused on the text and structure of the Constitution rather than on the specific content of particular conventions.[206] At the core of these arguments is the problem of identifying the distinction between 'convention' and 'law'. As the literature on the topic has shown, the concept of 'convention' is very difficult to define precisely. Much will depend on the context in which it operates and the theoretical perspective of those who would seek to define it. The essential meaning of a *constitutional* convention is a non-judicially enforceable rule of conduct, or of political morality, which is generally regarded as binding by the key political and constitutional players to which it may apply. Such conventions have evolved from a combination of usage, precedent, pragmatism and notions of political morality. Their practical force lies in the political censure and sanctions that would result upon their breach. However, they are not fixed but instead evolve in tandem with political realities. This much can be said of the conventions of responsible government which evolved in Britain and which were adopted in Australia, adapted to its conditions. As with the concept of 'executive power',

**200** Zines, above n 99, 340.
**201** Ibid.
**202** Ibid, 340–41.
**203** Lindell, above n 141; Geoffrey Lindell, Book Review (1983) 6 *UNSW Law Journal* 261, 17.
**204** See Nicholas Aroney, 'On the distinction between law and convention' in Brian Galligan and Scott Brenton (eds), *Constitutional Conventions in Westminster Systems* (Cambridge University Press, forthcoming) 20–24.
**205** Ibid, 23.
**206** Ibid.

the legal status of responsible government can only best be understood in the particular constitutional context in which it is being considered. However 'convention' is defined,[207] it is clear that in the Australian context, the term is used in contradistinction to 'law' in the sense that while both guide conduct, it is only the latter that is judicially enforceable in the breach. While the legal enforceability of conventions is a *conceptual* possibility, an example of legal enforcement remains something of a 'holy grail'.[208] Indeed, the indications from *Egan v Willis*[209] suggest a preference on the part of the High Court to maintain the flexible nature of the principles of responsible government which they derive from their status as convention. This would mean that the resolution of questions relating to executive action based purely on the application of responsible government would have to be resolved politically and not judicially. This certainly echoes the views of Sir Robert Garran, that:

> We must not ... attempt to fix the present pattern of responsible government as a thing to be clung to for all time; we must allow scope for its development – for its being moulded to fit the political ideas of each successive generation. Responsible government, as we know it, is a new thing, and a changing thing; it depends largely upon the unwritten rules which are constantly varying, growing, developing, and the precise direction of whose development is impossible to forecast. To try to crystallize this fluid system into a hard and fast code of written law would spoil its chief merit; we must be careful to lay down only the essential principles of popular government. Leaving the details of form as elastic as possible. Some fundamental principles must be fixed by the Constitution (subject to a more or less difficult process of amendment); whilst the great mass of merely accidental, and not essential, characteristics of government may be left at large, to be controlled from time to time by the Parliament and the will of the people, as is the case to-day in Great Britain and in every self-governing British colony.[210]

Nonetheless, it remains possible that the reasoning in *Lange* may give rise to the proposition that at least the core elements of responsible government are legally entrenched (ie, acting on advice, ministerial responsibility, confidence). Lindell has explored further the consequences in a number of scenarios.[211] Whatever position is ultimately adopted, care must be taken to ensure that maximum flexibility is permitted for the development of the evolution of those conventions which are, for want of a better term, 'non-core', and whose contours remain uncertain. While legal rules may to a degree be adapted and change as their application to new circumstances is considered, it is nevertheless the case that legal rules will, ipso facto, be more rigid and less flexible than constitutional

**207** For a more detailed consideration, see Geoffrey Marshall, *Constitutional Conventions* (Clarendon Press, 1984); L J M Cooray, *Conventions, the Australian Constitution and the Future* (Legal Books, 1979); Nick Barber, 'Laws and Constitutional Conventions' (2009) 125 *Law Quarterly Review* 294; Joseph Jaconelli, 'Do Constitutional Conventions Bind?' (2005) 64 *Cambridge Law Journal* 149.
**208** Aroney, above n 204, 5.
**209** (1998) 195 CLR 424, 475 [100].
**210** Robert Garran, *The Coming Commonwealth* (Angus and Robertson, 1897) 149.
**211** Lindell, above n 31, 10–24.

conventions. At the very least, as Zines has noted, this should 'provide a warning against the courts going beyond the enforcement of reasonably clear rules basic to the system and attempting to make judicial pronouncements in situations better left to the political process'.[212] Whether even these basic rules will eventually become judicially reviewable, or simply left to political resolution, remains to be seen. To engage in detailed discussion of the consequences of judicial enforcement of each of these rules is beyond the scope of the present work. They give rise not only to complex issues relating to judicial review, but also to issues of justiciability,[213] and thus to considerable uncertainty. It suffices to observe that these issues await clarification by the High Court.[214] The point must also be made that many conventions are themselves uncertain in formulation, and subject to considerable disagreement.[215]

### Clarification of conventions

The Australian Constitutional Convention, during its 1985 Brisbane deliberations, sought to clarify the specific content of the conventions of responsible government.[216] These were discussed by the Advisory Committee on Executive Government of the Constitutional Commission[217] and some were adopted,[218] others modified.[219] Although the members of the Committee could not agree as to whether these should be embodied in the Constitution, in statute or in the resolutions of some authoritative body,[220] their articulation provides an informative guide as to how the conventions of responsible government may be interpreted and applied in various circumstances.[221] It is noted that many of these rules are simply applications of the core, essential principles – recognisable in 1900 when the Constitution was settled – relating to advice, ministerial responsibility, and parliamentary confidence.[222]

In relation to the general power of the Governor-General, the Committee was of the view that the Governor-General has a right to be consulted, to encourage and to warn when exercising his or her constitutional powers and responsibilities.

With respect to the appointment and dismissal of a government, the Committee considered that the conventions of responsible government require the following:

**212** Zines, above n 99, 341. See also Lindell, above n 31.
**213** For a more detailed examination, see Lindell, above n 31; Winterton, above n 10, 13–26, 71–84, ch 7.
**214** For discussion, see the references in the previous note, and Geoffrey Sawer, *Federation Under Strain* (Melbourne University Press, 1977) chs 8, 9.
**215** See, for example, Lindell's discussion of Cabinet solidarity and secrecy in Lindell, above n 31, 14–17.
**216** *Official Record of Debates of the Australian Constitutional Convention* (Brisbane, 1985) vol 1, 415–17.
**217** Advisory Committee on Executive Government, above n 92, 38–43.
**218** Ibid, practices H, I, J, K, Q and R.
**219** Ibid, practices B, C, D, E, F, L and M.
**220** Ibid, 38.
**221** This was set out in detail at Ibid 38–43.
**222** Ibid, 38–43. As the Committee's report explains, there was a lack of unanimity with respect to a number of these principles. This does not make their articulation less valuable for present purposes.

(a) When a government is defeated at a general election, the Governor-General should appoint as Prime Minister that person who, in his or her opinion, can form a ministry which has the confidence of the House of Representatives.

(b) If an alternate Prime Minister is clearly designated as a result of the election, the outgoing Prime Minister should resign as soon as the outcome of the general election is known.

(c) Where the outcome of the election is not clear, the incumbent Prime Minister may remain in office until such time as the House of Representatives meets to determine whether he or she enjoys its confidence. If a Prime Minister resigns, before doing so he or she may advise the Governor-General as to his or her successor. The Governor-General should follow that advice. If no advice is given, the Governor-General should consult whomever he or she wishes as to the person who may enjoy the confidence of the House to form a government and the Governor-General should appoint that person who in his opinion will enjoy such confidence.

(d) If a Prime Minister dies in office, the Governor-General should follow the advice of the next most senior minister in cabinet rank as to the person who should be appointed Prime Minister, being that person who can form a ministry which has the confidence of the House.

(e) Where the House of Representatives upholds a motion of no-confidence in the Prime Minister or government, there was a divergence in the Committee:

    (i) On one view, the Governor-General must act on the advice of the defeated Prime Minister, acting in good faith, to send for that person to form a ministry whom the Prime Minister believes enjoys the confidence of the House, or dissolving the House if so advised.

    (ii) The alternate view was that the ultimate decision should be the Governor-General's as to whether to dissolve the House or appoint another person; and he or she should dissolve the House only if he or she does not think that there is a person who will enjoy the confidence of the House to form a ministry. But in exercising this discretion, the advice of the defeated prime minister must at least be taken into account, although the Governor-General may consult whomever he or she wishes.

    However, if following the vote of no-confidence, the House itself names the person who enjoys its confidence, then the Governor-General must appoint that person as Prime Minister.

(f) While the death of a Prime Minister does not per se result in the termination of the commissions of other ministers, the resignation of a Prime Minister following defeat in a general election or in the House terminates the commission of all other ministers.

(g) If a Prime Minister following defeat at an election, or in a vote of no confidence in the House, fails to resign or to advise a dissolution of the House, the Governor-General shall dismiss the Prime Minister.

(h) If the Prime Minister persists in 'grossly unlawful or illegal conduct', including a serious breach of the Constitution, the Governor-General can dismiss the Prime Minister when the High Court has declared the matter to be justiciable, and has declared the matter to be unlawful, illegal or a breach of the Constitution. If the High Court declares the matter not to be justiciable, the Governor-General may still dismiss the Prime Minister if there is no alternative to prevent the Prime Minister engaging in such conduct. The Committee was of the view that in circumstances where the Senate blocks Supply, with the Prime Minister retaining the confidence of the House, the Governor-General may not dismiss him or her if he or she fails to resign or advise a dissolution on the ground that the government failed to secure Supply through the Senate. Rather, the grounds should be limited to those already indicated in this paragraph, viz, 'grossly unlawful or illegal conduct, including a serious breach of the Constitution'. That is, the rejection of Supply by the Senate is not enough *in itself* to constitute a ground of dismissal by the Governor-General absent these other factors.

With respect to the dissolution of Parliament, the Committee identified the following principles as being most consistent with responsible government:

(a) The Governor-General may dissolve the House only on the advice of the Prime Minister.

(b) If a Prime Minister has the confidence of the House when tendering such advice, the Governor-General shall act upon that advice.

(c) If a motion of no confidence against the government is pending, (say) within eight days, in the House of Representatives, the Governor-General shall not dissolve the House of Representatives or grant a double dissolution. The granting of a double dissolution shall be governed by the conditions which apply to the dissolution of the House, except that the conditions specified in s 57 of the Constitution must be satisfied.

(d) Following any general election, the Governor-General shall not dissolve the House until such time as it has had the opportunity to consider who shall be commissioned as Prime Minister. In advising a dissolution, and 'so far as is possible', the Prime Minister must be in a position to assure the Governor-General that the government has been granted sufficient funds by Parliament – or will be so granted before any dissolution – to enable the administration to carry on during the election period.

Various other miscellaneous principles were also suggested by the Committee. While these expert expressions of opinion are helpful and illustrative, it needs to be understood that it is very difficult to achieve consensus on these matters. As already indicated, these conclusions of the Advisory Committee were not identical to those of the Constitutional Convention. This may support the view that, at least beyond the most obvious breaches, it is very difficult in any event to achieve that degree of certainty needed to resolve without controversy the very difficult issues which may be thrown up in difficult circumstances such as those described.

### The reserve powers

In certain situations, the Governor-General is required to exercise his or her own independent judgment and discretion and not to follow advice. These include situations involving the dissolution of the House of Representatives or both Houses, as well as the dismissal of a Prime Minister and the government. The Governor-General's powers in such circumstances are referred to as 'reserve powers'. Most commonly, they are said to arise when the Governor-General is exercising the power to:

(a) appoint a Prime Minister (s 62);
(b) dismiss a Prime Minister (s 64, providing that Minister shall hold office at the Governor-General's pleasure);
(c) dissolve (or to refuse to dissolve) the House of Representatives (s 5); and,
(d) dissolve both Houses of Parliament (s 57).

The reserve powers constitute an *exception* – internally recognised by responsible government – to the principle that the Governor-General must act on ministerial advice. While uncertainty will always persist, there are certain circumstances where the application of the core principles of responsible government is straightforward. For example, few (if any) would deny constitutional propriety to the dismissal of a Prime Minister by the Governor-General if the former, having lost a vote of confidence in the House, refused to resign, or advise a replacement or a dissolution. Less susceptible to consensus is a situation, such as occurred in 1975, where a government that retains the confidence of the House is nevertheless denied Supply by the Senate. The express provisions of the Constitution itself provide little guidance as to how the reserve powers are to be exercised. The conventional practices of responsible government, such as they are, provide the major source of assistance in this regard. It is for this reason that the Constitutional Convention in 1985, and the Advisory Committee to the Constitutional Commission in 1987, attempted to provide the guidance discussed above. The paper presented as Appendix 6 to the Report of the Republic Advisory Committee (1993) constitutes a more recent precise exploration of the guiding principles relating specifically to the reserve powers.[223] It pointed out that:

> [b]ecause the reserve powers come into play in situations to which the system of constitutional conventions does not supply a ready solution, and because they involve the exercise of discretion by a head of state or representative who has no electoral mandate and generally plays no part in political decisions, their exercise tends to be both rare and controversial. The establishment of conventions, including those relating to the reserve powers, depends on the accumulation of precedents and on consensus developing as to whether a power is properly exercised in a particular cause. In the case

**223** The Republic Advisory Committee, *An Australian Republic: The Options* (1993) vol 2, appendix 6.

of at least some of the reserve powers, there are very few precedents and there is disagreement as to whether those precedents establish conventions or represent breaches thereof. There is also room for doubt as to whether the absence of any exercise of a power over a long period demonstrates that the power no longer exists. These factors often make it impossible to state with any confidence the extent of the independent discretion and the circumstances in which it arises. This is a disadvantage of the system of convention often cited as an argument for the codification of the reserve powers, although it can also be argued that the very uncertainty of the conventions governing the reserve powers makes codification a difficult exercise.[224]

## VI Conclusions

The executive power of the Commonwealth is vested in the Queen and exercised by the Governor-General, conventionally on the advice of Ministers of State who have the confidence of the House of Representatives. An understanding of the Executive under the Commonwealth Constitution thus requires an understanding of both the legal repositories of the power (the Queen, the Governor-General, the Federal Executive Council and responsible ministers) and the conventional rules of parliamentary responsible government which dictate how the executive power of the Commonwealth is to be exercised. While the framers of the Constitution accepted that executive power could be distinguished from legislative and judicial power, they expected it to be exercised in a manner that reflected the supremacy of the Parliament over the Executive.

The framers also intended to create a federation, which they believed must include a Senate in which the people of each Original State would be equally represented and which would exercise powers very nearly equal to those of the House of Representatives. While the Senate cannot initiate or amend money bills, the framers gave it the power to refuse to pass such bills, which amounted to a capacity to deny necessary funding to a government. This created a tension in the constitutional system because it was also anticipated that governments would ordinarily depend on the support of a majority in the House of Representatives, not the Senate. In 1975 the Senate used its power to deny Supply in circumstances which culminated in the exercise by the Governor-General of his reserve power to dismiss the Prime Minister. Since those events, much has been done to clarify the content of the conventions of responsible government and the conditions under which the reserve powers ought to be exercised, but disagreement still exists about certain important details.

**224** Ibid, 246.

# 7

# Executive power

*The executive power of the Commonwealth ... extends to the execution and maintenance of this Constitution, and of the laws of the Commonwealth.*[1]

## I Introduction

Section 61 of the Constitution declares that the 'executive power of the Commonwealth' is 'vested in the Queen' and that it 'extends to the execution and maintenance' of the 'Constitution' and the 'laws of the Commonwealth'. The executive power of the Commonwealth is thus composed of several elements. Its exact content and ambit is one of the most pressing and complex issues in Australian constitutional law.

By declaring that the executive power is vested in the Queen, the framers of the Constitution understood that, subject to the Constitution, this incorporated the various powers customarily exercised by British monarchs as recognised by the common law. Andrew Inglis Clark put it this way:

> [T]he supreme depositary of the executive authority in the Commonwealth is the King, and he possesses and may exercise within the Commonwealth all the prerogative rights and powers which are inherent in the ... Crown. ... [T]he Crown possesses prerogative rights and powers which have their source in the common law, and it is therefore evident that a portion of the common law attaches to the Constitution of the Commonwealth.[2]

William Harrison Moore further maintained, without apparent qualification, that:

> [w]here a power or duty committed to 'the Commonwealth' is of such a kind as is according to common law exerciseable by the Executive, the Commonwealth Executive is empowered to take such action as the common law allows.[3]

The executive power of the Commonwealth extends to the 'execution' of the Constitution. This reinforces the primacy of the Constitution as the ultimate

**1** Commonwealth Constitution, s 61.
**2** Andrew Inglis Clark, *Studies in Australian Constitutional Law* (Legal Books, [1901] 1997) 191–2. Inglis Clark wrote after the demise of Queen Victoria, and therefore referred to King Edward VII.
**3** W Harrison Moore, *The Constitution of the Commonwealth of Australia* (Legal Books, 2nd ed, 1910) 297.

source of Commonwealth governmental authority within the federation. That the power also extends to the execution of Commonwealth laws reflects the principle, noted in Chapter 2, that the Constitution accords a certain normative priority to the role of the Parliament in legislating and holding the Executive Government to account, a role that is fundamental to responsible government and important in establishing the rule of law.[4] This feature of the executive power also reflects the federal nature of the Constitution, for in this respect the power is limited to the execution of Commonwealth laws the subject matter of which is limited by ss 51 and 52 and 122.[5]

The 'maintenance' aspect of the executive power is more elusive and potentially problematic if its ambit is regarded as extending beyond the Crown's common law powers. This constitutes an issue of real difficulty and some controversy, particularly as a result of a developing jurisprudence which suggests that it includes a power to perform functions that can only be undertaken effectively by the Commonwealth as the *national* government.[6] The historically recognised prerogatives and powers of the Crown obtain a substantial measure of definition through the common law – resort to which is legitimate when interpreting British statutes – including constitutional statutes such as the *Commonwealth of Australia Constitution Act 1900*. However, a further source of difficulty is that the prerogatives and capacities of the Crown developed in the context of a unitary state. To what extent are these constrained by the federal principle that the Commonwealth is a government of enumerated and limited powers? As Michael Crommelin has observed, while in a federation it is necessary to distribute both legislative and executive power between the two levels of government, the contrast between the detail in Chapter I of the Constitution and Chapter II is 'stark', Chapter I providing a far more detailed account of the distribution of legislative power than does Chapter II relating to executive power:

> Chapter II is 'suggestive rather than expressive'[7] concerning the distribution of executive power. ... The dual sources of executive power, statute and prerogative, were recognised in the Conventions. But it is far from clear how they were reflected in the Commonwealth Constitution.[8]

The nature and ambit of the executive power of the Commonwealth thus depends on three important sources of law – the common law, the laws of the Commonwealth and the Constitution itself. However, the exact scope of the executive power, and the way in which these three sources of law interact, is not immediately discernible. Unlike the definition of legislative power in ss 51 and

**4** See Chapter 2, Part I, citing John Quick and Robert Randolph Garran, *The Annotated Constitution of the Australian Commonwealth* (Angus and Robertson, 1901) 385.
**5** See Chapter 3.
**6** *Pape v Commissioner of Taxation* (2009) 238 CLR 1; *Williams v Commonwealth (No 1)* (2012) 248 CLR 156, discussed in Part IV.1 below.
**7** W Harrison Moore, *The Constitution of the Commonwealth of Australia* (John Murray, 1902) 213.
**8** Michael Crommelin, 'The Executive' in G Craven (ed), *The Convention Debates 1891–1898* (Legal Books, 1986) 130–31 (footnotes omitted).

52, s 61 describes the metes and bounds of executive power in general terms. As was seen in Chapter 3, the methodologies of literalism and textualism have had a prevailing influence on the interpretation of the scope of Commonwealth legislative power. Given the limited assistance that can be drawn from the text of s 61, however, textualism and literalism are limited in their usefulness. As will be seen in this chapter, reliance has therefore had to be placed, to varying degrees, on alternative methodologies, such as originalism and structuralism, as well as to the historic content of the common law.[9] The text of the Constitution relating to executive power can only sensibly be interpreted by reference to the fundamental principles embodied in the instrument and intended by its framers, the most immediately relevant being responsible government and the supremacy of Parliament. Moreover, the interpretation of s 61 must accommodate the federal structure of the Constitution and, to a lesser degree, the separation of powers. In addition, there is an evolutionary aspect to the practical operation of s 61. This is consistent with the view, affirmed by the High Court in *Egan v Willis*, that the principles of responsible government are themselves evolving in accord with political realities as well as the development of Australia's legal independence from the United Kingdom.[10]

# II The metes and bounds of executive power

## 1 Executive power and the rule of law

The fundamental principle that the executive power of the Commonwealth is defined and limited by law was affirmed in *Commonwealth v Colonial Combing, Spinning & Weaving Co Ltd*.[11]At issue was the validity of contracts entered into by the Commonwealth during the First World War under which it was agreed that, in return for the Commonwealth giving consent to the manufacture and sale of particular goods by the company, the company would provide a share of its profits to the Commonwealth. The High Court held that entering such contracts was beyond the executive power of the Commonwealth.

Knox CJ and Gavan Duffy J regarded s 61 as strictly delimiting the executive power of the Commonwealth to the execution and maintenance of the Constitution and Commonwealth laws. They held that the contracts were not valid because they had not been authorised by the relevant legislation and were not in execution or maintenance of the Constitution. They recognised that s 64, in referring to the administration of Commonwealth government departments, authorised entry into contracts necessary for such administration, but the *Wooltops* contracts could not be justified on this basis.[12]

**9** For more on these methodologies, see Chapter 1, Part IV.2.
**10** *Egan v Willis* (1998) 195 CLR 424.
**11** *Wooltops* case (1922) 31 CLR 421.
**12** Ibid, 431–3.

Isaacs J adopted a wider view of what the Constitution authorises. While s 61 'marks the external boundaries' of Commonwealth executive power, he said, it leaves 'entirely untouched the definition of that power and its ascertainment in any given instance', it being essentially a 'starting-point, and the extent it marks out cannot be exceeded'.[13] Starke J stated similarly that s 61 'simply marks out the field of the executive power of the Commonwealth, and the validity of any particular act within that field must be determined by reference to the Constitution or the laws of the Commonwealth, or to the prerogative or inherent powers of the King',[14] a point with which Isaacs J agreed.[15] In his judgment, Isaacs J conceived of the Commonwealth and State Governments as operating in distinct spheres through the separate execution of the laws of their respective Parliaments.[16] However, this was also associated with his characteristic nationalism, evident in the joint judgment which he delivered in the *Engineers* case two years earlier.[17] Maintaining that 'the written words of the Constitution applied to s 61 form the only necessary solving test', Isaacs J added:

> [T]he domain of the Commonwealth executive power ... *is described but not defined* in sec 61 ... Executive action to execute or maintain the Constitution is clearly within the field of Commonwealth power, and no intrusion into the constitutional domain of the State. But the legal warrant for the particular step, if challenged by an individual affected, remains to be determined. In other words, the third declaration is a definite constitutional delimitation as between Commonwealth and States, but does not definitely determine the internal validity of executive action towards His Majesty's subjects.[18]

What made the contracts unlawful in Isaacs J's view was that they amounted to the imposition of taxation without legislative authorisation (as required by one of the most important principles established in the English Bill of Rights) that their subject matter (intrastate trade and manufacture) took them outside the 'prima facie' scope of the executive power of the Commonwealth, and that they could not be justified as falling within the prerogative capacity of the Crown to respond to the exigencies of the national war effort.[19]

A similar view of the executive power of the Commonwealth was expressed by Evatt J in *R v Hush; Ex parte Devanney*:

> [Section 61] only defines the general limits of the King's executive authority in respect of the Commonwealth and does not determine what the Executive may lawfully do upon any given occasion. Whatever powers or duties are conferred or imposed upon the King's executive government, by any section of the Constitution, or by such

**13** Ibid, 447–8.
**14** Ibid, 61.
**15** Ibid, 437–40
**16** Ibid, 440.
**17** Ibid, 438–9. See *Amalgamated Society of Engineers v Adelaide Steamship Co Ltd* (1920) 28 CLR 129 discussed in Chapter 3, Part III.1 and Chapter 4, Part III.2.
**18** Ibid, 440–41 (emphasis added).
**19** Ibid, 441–5.

> portion of the Royal prerogative as is applicable, may lawfully be exercised; but sec 61 *itself* gives no assistance in the ascertainment or definition of such powers and duties.[20]

More recent cases join the refrain. Mason CJ, Deane and Gaudron JJ in *Davis v Commonwealth* remarked that '[t]he scope of the executive power of the Commonwealth has often been discussed but never defined',[21] with Brennan J adding that it was 'not amenable to exhaustive definition'.[22] Similar views were expressed more recently in *R v Hughes*,[23] *Pape*[24] and *Williams (No 1)*,[25] although in the last two mentioned cases, the Court emphasised that the substantive content of Commonwealth executive power derived directly from s 61 and recognised the existence of an implied 'nationhood' power in which it inhered. This contrasts with the view of Evatt J, who did not regard s 61 as a direct source of the Commonwealth Executive's non-statutory powers, except to the extent that they incorporated the prerogative. The uncertainties to which the sparse constitutional text of s 61 has given rise indicate that it can only be used as a 'rough map suggesting the contours of federal executive power'.[26] As Isaacs J put it, the 'specific limits' of the power 'have to be determined *aliunde*'.[27]

## 2 Textual analysis: Execution and maintenance

In the *Communist Party* case,[28] Williams J proposed a threefold definition of the 'execution and maintenance' aspects of s 61. The 'execution' of the Constitution, he said, 'means the doing of something immediately prescribed or authorized by the Constitution'.[29] The 'maintenance' of the Constitution 'means the protection and safeguarding of something immediately prescribed or authorized by the Constitution'.[30] The 'execution and maintenance' of the laws of the Commonwealth 'must mean the doing and protection and safeguarding of something authorized by some law of the Commonwealth made under the Constitution'.[31] Williams J also affirmed that the power includes the prerogative powers of the Crown as appropriate to be exercised by a body politic of limited powers within a federation. It is convenient to deal with these each in turn.

**20** *R v Hush; Ex parte Devanney* (1932) 48 CLR 487, 511 (emphasis added). See also *Federal Commissioner of Taxation v Official Liquidator of E O Farley Ltd* (1940) 63 CLR 278, 321. H V Evatt was the author of the seminal *The King and His Dominion Governors* (Frank Cass Publishers, 2nd ed, 1967).
**21** (1988) 166 CLR 79, 92.
**22** Ibid, 107.
**23** (2000) 202 CLR 535, 555.
**24** *Pape v Commissioner of Taxation* (2009) 238 CLR 1, 64–5, 126–7.
**25** *Williams v Commonwealth (No 1)* (2012) 248 CLR 156, 197–209, 232.
**26** George Winterton, *Parliament, the Executive and the Governor-General: A Constitutional Analysis* (Melbourne University Press, 1983) 28.
**27** *Le Mesurier v Connor* (1929) 42 CLR 481, 514.
**28** *Australian Communist Party v Commonwealth* (1951) 83 CLR 1, discussed in Chapter 3, Part III.2.
**29** *Wooltops* (1922) 31 CLR 421, 423. This was adopted by Williams J in *Australian Communist Party v Commonwealth* (1951) 83 CLR 1 at 230.
**30** *Australian Communist Party v Commonwealth* (1951) 83 CLR 1, 230.
**31** Ibid.

First, executive action can and must be undertaken to meet the obligations imposed on the Commonwealth Government by the Constitution itself. Of foremost importance is the need to ensure that the essential institutions of the Commonwealth are adequately funded and resourced. The Constitution refers explicitly to several specific functions of the Governor-General including the summoning, dissolving and proroguing of Parliament, the determination of the time for holding of its sessions and the holding of joint sittings (ss 5, 57), the issue of writs for general elections for the House of Representatives (s 32) and transmission of messages to the Parliament recommending the appropriation of money (s 56). In addition, as the High Court pointed out in *Brown v West*, 'there is no doubt' that the Executive must facilitate the functioning of Parliament, by providing for its necessary funding and administrative support, subject to the appropriation of funds.[32] But, the Court observed, it is 'not self-evident' that the executive power extends to the provision of pecuniary allowances to individual members of Parliament, 'who may draw upon the benefit as they will'.[33]

By parity of reasoning, s 61 must likewise require the Executive to facilitate the exercise of the judicial power of the Commonwealth, not only by appointing federal judges (s 72) but also by providing for the payment of judicial salaries, the administration of justice, the functioning of the courts and the execution of their judgments and orders, subject to the necessary parliamentary appropriation of funds. The Constitution also provides for the appointment of Ministers of State and the establishment of Commonwealth government departments to be administered under their authority (ss 64, 69), and it requires the payment of certain salaries authorised or prescribed by the Constitution, such as those of the Governor-General and ministers (ss 3 and 66). It similarly provides for the collection and control of customs and excise duties (s 86), the payment of surplus revenues to the States (ss 87, 89, 93 and 94), and the command-in-chief of the armed forces and all that that entails (s 68).

Secondly, s 61 states that the Commonwealth's executive power also extends to the execution of Commonwealth laws. The phrase 'laws of the Commonwealth' refers only to laws, and includes subordinate legislation enacted under the authority of the Commonwealth Parliament. It does not include the common law.[34] When executing such laws, the Commonwealth must itself act according to the laws it is implementing.[35] As stated in *Brown v West*: 'A valid law of the Commonwealth may so limit or impose conditions on the exercise of the executive power that acts which would otherwise be supported by the executive power fall outside its scope'.[36]

**32** (1990) 169 CLR 195.
**33** Ibid.
**34** *Wooltops* case (1922) 31 CLR 421, 432; *Sankey v Whitlam* (1978) 142 CLR 1, 30, 31, 92, 104–5.
**35** A contrary view has been expressed in certain United States judicial pronouncements that the Executive has a broad discretion to choose whatever means it may think appropriate, even military force, if not forbidden to do so by legislation: see Winterton, above n 26, 31.
**36** (1990) 169 CLR 195, 202.

The maintenance aspect of the executive power is more elusive. Williams J interpreted it as 'the protection and safeguarding of something immediately prescribed or authorised' by the Constitution or Commonwealth laws.[37] Protecting Australia from invasion or subversion is plainly permitted, which power in any event would come within the prerogative powers relating to war, defence and foreign relations.[38] The Commonwealth is also required by s 119 to protect every State from invasion and, upon application by a State, from domestic violence. Absent State consent, however, the Commonwealth's power to address domestic violence is limited. It has been argued that, under the maintenance limb, the Commonwealth may protect its particular interests from domestic violence, such as the protection of the mail, interstate commerce, the right of an elector to vote in federal elections,[39] financial and trading corporations, banks and insurance companies, federal legislative, executive, judicial, administrative and military institutions, public authorities and statutory bodies.[40] In a statement apparently approved by Dixon J in *R v Sharkey*,[41] Quick and Garran remarked:

> If ... domestic violence within a State is of such a character as to interfere with the operation of the Federal Government, or with the rights and privileges of federal citizenship, the Federal Government may clearly, without a summons from the State, interfere to restore order. ... [T]he Executive Government [may] interfere to suppress by force a rebellion which cripples its powers.[42]

Beyond this, however, definitional clarity becomes elusive. Even in relation to matters of defence and national security, the precise field of permissible executive action, absent statute, remains cloudy. It is cloudier still when one considers 'emergency' situations which do not permit of a precise prior assessment of what action may be required of the Commonwealth. Thus, while the Commonwealth has power to take whatever action is necessary, in a military sense, to repel the enemy in war, the ambit of the ancillary measures necessary for national security is not clear.[43] Complications arise from unconventional circumstances such as those arising from, for example, terrorist activity.[44] To what extent can the government take action – including the use of coercion, forced detention and the destruction of property – in emergency situations that fall short of declared war or outright insurrection? The relevant question is probably not whether there is a 'war' or 'insurrection' per se, but whether there

**37** *Communist Party* case (1951) 83 CLR 1, 230.

**38** *Cadia Holdings Pty Ltd v New South Wales* (2010) 242 CLR 195, 210. See also Leslie Zines, 'The Inherent Executive Power of the Commonwealth' (2005) 16 *Public Law Review* 279, 286–90; H P Lee, *Emergency Powers* (Law Book Co, 1984) ch 3.

**39** Quick and Garran, above n 4, 964.

**40** Zines, above n 38, 289.

**41** (1949) 79 CLR 121, 151, also discussed in relation to the 'legislative' aspect of the implied 'nationhood' power in Chapter 3, Part IV.3.

**42** Quick and Garran, above n 4, 964.

**43** See George Winterton, 'The Relationship Between Commonwealth Legislative and Executive Power' (2004) 25 *Adelaide Law Review* 21, 26.

**44** Zines, above n 38, 302.

is an emergency which threatens the very existence of the Commonwealth, its Constitution and its system of government. Dixon J invoked these kinds of considerations in the *Communist Party* case when he referred to 'that power ... which forms part of a paramount authority to preserve both its own existence and the supremacy of its laws necessarily implied in the erection of a national government'.[45]

The maintenance aspect of the executive power thus raises numerous problems of interpretation. Writing in the late seventeenth century, though pertinent to a modern age, John Locke observed that it is in the very nature of the prerogative 'to act according to discretion, for the public good, without the prescription of the law, and sometimes even against it'. He also remarked that there is often 'a latitude left to the executive power, to do many things ... which the laws do not prescribe ... to act according to discretion, for the public good, without the prescription of the law, and sometimes even against it'.[46] When the safeguarding of the very polity itself is at stake, the degree of latitude permitted to a government will remain an abiding issue.[47] However, as Locke argued, unless definite legal limits are placed on the executive powers of the Crown, it may be questioned whether these powers will necessarily be exercised beneficially and appropriately. The problem posed especially by the maintenance limb is precisely how these limitations are to be identified. How far can the idea of an implied 'nationhood' executive power, said to be implicit in the maintenance limb, legitimately be extended? Do the definitions of the prerogative historically recognised by the common law provide sufficiently precise and effective guidance?

## 3 Historical context: Prerogatives, capacities and federal limitations

Had s 61 only referred to the 'execution' of the Constitution and of Commonwealth laws, as Sir Samuel Griffith's first draft of the Constitution proposed,[48] many of these latter uncertainties might have been avoided. The 'maintenance' aspect has added a somewhat vague and potentially expansive source of power unless interpreted consistently with the implications arising from the fundamental principles of the Constitution. When the 'maintenance' limb was added at the 1898 Convention, there was no elaboration of its precise meaning. All that can reliably be discerned from the debates was that the main source of the executive power, and the main determinants of its content, were to be Commonwealth laws, and, in their absence, the prerogatives and capacities of the Crown recognised by the common law, as applicable to the Commonwealth

**45** *Communist Party* case (1951) 83 CLR 1.
**46** John Locke, *Second Treatise of Government*, Ch XIV, sec 160.
**47** See Lee, above n 38; H P Lee, P J Hanks and V Morabito, *In the Name of National Security: the Legal Dimensions* (Law Book Company, 1995).
**48** See *Pape v Commissioner of Taxation* (2009) 238 CLR 1 at 56–8.

and qualified as necessary by the principles of responsible government and federalism.[49]

Understood in light of the constitutional understandings of the age, and the fact that the position of the Crown was retained, the surest conclusion which may be drawn is that the main source of the executive power, and the main determinants of its content, were to be Commonwealth laws, and, in their absence, the prerogatives and capacities of the Crown recognised by the common law applicable to the Commonwealth. From the time of British settlement, it was an established principle that the prerogatives of the Crown were, in principle, vested in each colonial Governor as the Queen's representative in the colony. The powers of the Governor were limited by the terms of his Commission, as well as by any statute operating within the colony by paramount force. After the establishment of responsible government in the Australian colonies in the 1850s, it was also expected that the Governor would exercise his powers on the advice of ministers responsible to the colonial Parliament. Upon federation, these fundamental assumptions were expected to apply to the Commonwealth, as to the States, subject to the Constitution.[50] The one important qualification was that, given the status of the Commonwealth within the British Empire, the powers exercisable by the Governor-General would not include the full ambit of the external affairs prerogatives, such as declaring war.

That the common law powers of the Crown were intended to inform the content of the Commonwealth's executive power is amply supported by the views expressed by leading delegates at the Conventions of the 1890s. Given their recognition of the existence of prerogatives residing in the colonies prior to federation, together with their intention to incorporate a moderated form of responsible government, it can only be concluded that they envisaged an exercise by the Commonwealth of executive power based on the historically recognised prerogatives and capacities of the Crown, these being powers which, by definition, did not require prior legislative authorisation. And, to the extent that these understandings were not spelt out, this does not necessarily indicate uncertainty in this regard. On the contrary, it may be said that some constitutional principles are so universally accepted, indeed almost to the point of being regarded as truisms, that silence, or at least a reticence to spell them out, bespeaks of their clear and unambiguous acceptance. As Crommelin has pointed out, because the framers thought it possible to accommodate responsible government to federalism, this allowed them the luxury of neglecting the executive.

> Justification lay in the fact that responsible government, derived from England, was attributable to convention rather than statute. It was therefore unnecessary, inappropriate, perhaps even impossible, to provide a full account of the executive branch in

**49** Winterton, above n 26; Crommelin, above n 8, 131–2.
**50** *Kielley v Carson* (1841–2) 4 Moo PC 63; 13 ER 225, cited in Quick and Garran, above n 4, 15.

> the Commonwealth Constitution. Suffice it to prescribe the composition of the executive. The scope of its power could then be left to inference … .[51]

Crommelin traversed the various exchanges by leading members of the Conventions and concluded as follows on the meaning attributable to the precursors of s 61:

> Agreement was thereby reached as to the object, namely, to ensure that the Constitution conferred upon the officers [appointed by the Governor-General to administer Departments of State, ie Ministers] all the prerogative powers appropriate to the Commonwealth … [and] the intention to confer substantial prerogative powers upon the Governor-General was clear.

Because the Commonwealth Executive would operate within a federal system, however, its sphere of operation necessarily had to be limited to its particular constitutional responsibilities. The Commonwealth Executive could not have the same unlimited breadth of powers as the British Government. As Williams J put it in the *Communist Party* case, '[t]he executive power of the Commonwealth at the date of the Constitution presumably included such of the then existing prerogative powers of the King … as were applicable to a body politic with limited powers'.[52]

At the Constitutional Convention in Sydney in 1891, Samuel Griffith stated unambiguously: '[A]ll the prerogatives of the Crown exist in the governor-general as far as they relate to Australia. I never entertained any doubt upon the subject at all.'[53] In response to this statement, Alfred Deakin expressed concern, however, that the Constitution should make clear that Commonwealth ministers would have the capacity to 'exercise all the prerogatives of the Crown which may be necessary in the interests of the Commonwealth'.[54] To meet this need, he invited Griffith to suggest an appropriate provision – an invitation which Griffith accepted. This resulted in the wording of what became s 64, which refers to the appointment of 'the Queen's Ministers of State for the Commonwealth' as officers charged with the responsibility of administering the various government departments that would be established. Importantly, however, neither Griffith, nor it seems anybody else, made specific reference to the clause that would become s 61 as the source of the Commonwealth's prerogative powers.[55] The failure of the framers to make clear reference to this clause as a source of the Commonwealth's prerogative powers is intriguing. But that the Constitution was intended to ensure that the prerogative was exercisable by the

**51** Crommelin, above n 8, 127.
**52** (1951) 83 CLR 1, 230.
**53** *Convention Debates, Sydney* (1891) 772.
**54** Ibid, 773.
**55** The clause read: 'The Executive power and authority of the Commonwealth is vested in the Queen and shall be exercised by the Governor-General as the Queen's Representative'. See *Convention Debates, Sydney* (1891) 955. Neither, does it seem, was the clause that became s 2 of the Constitution seen to be the source. That clause provided that the Governor-General was to be the Queen's representative with such powers and functions 'as the Queen may think fit to assign him'.

Governor-General and Ministers of State, as appropriate, cannot be denied. Crommelin has observed that the position of Griffith 'seems to have been that the conferral of appropriate prerogative powers upon the Governor-General would be a natural consequence of the establishment of the Commonwealth, rather than a result of any one provision of Chapter II of the Constitution'.[56]

In his later commentary on the Constitution, Inglis Clark placed greater emphasis on s 61. The vesting of the executive power of the Commonwealth 'in the Queen', he said:

> must be read *as a declaration of an existing fact, and not as an original grant of executive authority to her within the Commonwealth*, which could not be alleged to be made to her without the untenable presumption that she did not previously possess it, or without clear and positive predication which deprived the Crown of all executive authority within the Commonwealth under the common law and made the Constitution of the Commonwealth the sole source of the powers and functions to be possessed and exercised by the Crown or its representative [within the Commonwealth].[57]

Inglis Clark further denied that the inclusion of s 2 in the Constitution, which refers to 'such powers and functions of the Queen' that are assigned by Her Majesty to the Governor-General, contradicted this, for it is expressed to be 'subject to this Constitution'. Rather, he grounded the prerogatives exercisable by the Governor-General in the common law:[58]

> [T]he King possesses and may exercise within the Commonwealth all the prerogative rights and powers which are inherent in the British Crown, and which may be exercised by him under the provisions of the Constitution of the Commonwealth. ... When it is said that the Crown possesses, and may exercise within the Commonwealth, such prerogative rights and powers as are above mentioned, the statement is made in reference to the Commonwealth as a single territory over which the Parliament of the Commonwealth has legislative jurisdiction, and not in reference to the Commonwealth as composed of a number of separate States, in each of which a separate parliament possesses legislative authority and separate representative of the Crown is the organ of a concurrent executive authority within the limits of the States. ... In relation to the Commonwealth as a single territory, *the Crown possesses prerogative rights and powers which have their source in the common law, and it is therefore evident that a portion of the common law attaches to the Constitution of the Commonwealth.*[59]

As George Winterton has explained:

> Because the Constitution is a British statute operating in a common law environment, the vesting of the executive power in the Crown *automatically* ... brought to the Crown in right of the Commonwealth the common law or prerogative powers of the Crown.[60]

**56** Crommelin, above n 8, 134.
**57** Inglis Clark, above n 2, 64 (emphasis added).
**58** Ibid, 65.
**59** Ibid, 191–2 (emphasis added).
**60** Winterton, above n 26, 23–4 (emphasis added).

For, as Zines put it, '[t]he Commonwealth was born into a common law world where rules existed as to the powers and legal position of the Crown, which the Commonwealth inherited as a government of the Queen'.[61]

During the Convention Debates, the federal limitations that would apply to Commonwealth executive power were also considered. Clause 8 of Chapter II of the draft Constitution submitted to the 1891 Convention in Sydney is most pertinent. Noting that cl 1 then referred to the executive power 'and authority' of the Commonwealth as being vested in the Queen and made exercisable by the Governor-General, cl 8 provided:

> The Executive power and authority of the Commonwealth shall extend to all matters with respect to which the Legislative powers of the Parliament may be exercised, excepting only matters, being within the Legislative powers of a State, with respect to which the Parliament of that State for the time being exercises such powers.[62]

In debate on these clauses, Griffith indicated that the breadth of the Commonwealth's executive power was to be limited by reference to the Commonwealth's legislative power:

> These provisions introduce what we call responsible government – not necessarily party government, which is another division of responsible government, but a government responsible in name and form to the head of the state and in *substance to the parliament of the commonwealth. It is proposed that its executive authority shall be co-extensive with its legislative power. That follows as a matter of course.*[63]

However, the clause was later amended, on Griffith's motion, to read simply thus:

> The Executive power and authority of the Commonwealth shall extend to the execution of the provisions of this Constitution, and the Laws of the Commonwealth.[64]

Commenting on the change in wording, Griffith explained that it was not intended to detract from the substantive meaning of the original wording: '[i]t does not alter its intention', he said.[65] He also observed that instead of stipulating 'a negative limitation upon the powers of the executive', the revised clause gave 'a positive statement as to what they are to be'.[66]

There is some ambiguity in Griffith's meaning. One obvious interpretation is that by saying that executive power would be 'co-extensive' with legislative power Griffith meant that it would extend to any matter in respect of which the Commonwealth has power to make laws, whether the Parliament actually legislates or not. An alternative interpretation is that he was speaking somewhat loosely when referring to the powers being co-extensive, and that he actually meant that the executive power would *ordinarily* be limited to the execution of

**61** Zines, above n 38, 292.
**62** *Convention Debates, Sydney* (1891) 777.
**63** Ibid, 527 (emphasis added).
**64** Ibid, 955.
**65** Ibid, 777.
**66** Ibid, 777–8.

laws enacted by the Commonwealth Parliament. What is the better view? The question is complex for several reasons. One is that the executive power was clearly understood to include the prerogatives, which, by definition, do not depend on legislative authorisation. This consideration supports the view that, at least in relation to the prerogative, the first interpretation of Griffith's meaning is to be preferred. This seems to have been the understanding advanced by Edmund Barton, when he observed:

> Executive Acts of the Crown are primarily divided into two classes: those exercised by the prerogative ... and those which are ordinary Executive Acts, where it is prescribed that the Executive shall act in Council. These are the offsprings of Statutes. The others are Acts so far as they are not affected by Statutes. Now there is no necessity to make any alteration in this clause. The clause has been drafted in precisely the ordinary way – it was similarly drafted in 1891 – which is simply to express in a document of this character the depository of the Executive power in the kingdom or the Commonwealth. Moreover there is no necessity to add the words:
>
> With the advice of the Governor in Council,
>
> because in a constitution of this kind it is no more possible than it is under the English Constitution for the prerogative to be exercised as a personal act of the Crown.[67]

It was plainly contemplated that the prerogative would continue to reside in the government of the Commonwealth, and that the text of the Constitution had to be interpreted consistently with the principles of responsible government. This is reinforced by Barton's reference to fundamental tenets of responsible government, in particular 'Cabinet' government, in their practical – and not merely formal – manifestation to inform the operation of the Constitution:

> [I]t is understood that the Crown exercises the prerogative only upon ministerial advice, and it is exercised not personally by the Crown, but only with the advice of the Ministry or a Minister. ... The survival of the prerogative really means that where the prerogative act is to be exercised the Cabinet meets, and the Governor or the Queen cannot for a moment intrude. The Cabinet, of course, is not expressed in any Constitution, but it is one of the living powers which must exist in such a Constitution as this. The Cabinet meets and something is determined, or where the Act does not require the assistance of the Cabinet, the Minister determines to do it. In both these cases a formal resolution is passed by the Executive Council with the Governor as chairman, or, when he is not there, with the vice-president as chairman. That act is approved, and becomes the act of the Crown; indeed, that process is the same where the act is the exercise of the prerogative, or where it relates to one of those duties which is to be performed by the Governor or Queen in Council.[68]

However, there is a second complicating factor. This arises from the original text of the clause that became s 61 and Griffith's specific comments on it. As originally drafted, the clause stated that the executive power 'shall extend to all matters with respect to which the Legislative powers of the Parliament may

**67** *Convention Debates, Adelaide* (1897) 910.
**68** Ibid, 910–11.

be exercised, excepting only matters, being within the Legislative powers of a State, with respect to which the Parliament of that State for the time being exercises such powers'. As Griffith observed, the clause thus imposed 'a negative limitation upon the powers of the executive'.[69] Defining the relationship between Commonwealth and State power in this negative way suggested that the scope of the Commonwealth's executive power would be diminished by any exercise of State legislative power. This was reminiscent of the State reserved powers doctrine that both Griffith and Barton later embraced,[70] except that it turned on an exercise of legislative power by the States, not the bare existence of a sphere of State reserved powers. As a consequence, the original clause would have left it open to the Commonwealth to legislate, albeit only within its enumerated powers, to displace the effect of any State law (relying on the operation of s 109).[71] In other words, the effect would have been to enable the Commonwealth Parliament to legislate so as to bring a matter within the executive power of the Commonwealth. This context sheds a somewhat different light on Griffith's observation that the simplification of the language of s 61 to give 'a positive statement' of the executive power of the Commonwealth 'did not alter its intention'. It suggests that he may indeed have meant that Commonwealth executive power would be 'co-extensive' with its legislative power only in the context that it actually legislated to authorise executive action.

A wider view of the executive power – a view which Griffith is more likely to have shared – in its basics was later proposed by Alfred Deakin when, as Attorney-General of the new Commonwealth, he advised the Prime Minister that:

> The executive power of the Commonwealth unlike the legislative is derived directly and independently from its fountain head – the Crown. It may be contended that it has a higher and larger scope than that of the States (see sections 61 and 64) but it is not necessary to discuss such a claim here. *Its powers are at least coextensive with its legislative charter.*[72]

Writing soon thereafter in the oft-quoted so-called *Vondel* opinion of 1902, Deakin expressed the view that the drafters of the Constitution had eschewed an exhaustive definition in order to avoid the risk of 'undue, perhaps unintentional, limitation of the executive power'. He added: 'Had it been intended to limit the scope of the executive power to matters on which the Commonwealth Parliament had legislated, *nothing would have been easier than to say so*'.[73] He asserted as follows:

**69** *Convention Debates, Sydney* (1891) 777–8.
**70** See Chapter 3, Part III.1.
**71** See Chapter 4, Part II.
**72** Alfred Deakin, 'Position of Commonwealth and States in Relation to Treaties: Source and Extent of Commonwealth Executive Power and External Affairs Power: Nature of Adherence to Treaties: Channel of Communication Between States and Empire or Foreign Powers' in Patrick Brazil and Bevan Mitchell (eds), *Opinions of Attorneys-General of the Commonwealth of Australia, Volume 1: 1901–14* (Australian Government Publishing Service, 1981) 2, 3 (emphasis added).
**73** Alfred Deakin, 'Channel of Communication with Imperial Government: Position of Consuls: Executive Power of the Commonwealth' in Ibid, 130 (emphasis added). This was referred to with apparent approval by French CJ in *Pape* at 59.

> Executive power exists antecedently to, and independently of, legislation; and its *scope* must be, *at least*, equal to that of the legislative power – *exercised or unexercised*. … For the exercise of many executive powers no legislation is needed, and this is especially the case in the administration of external affairs.[74]

He also emphasised the following point:

> These words [of s 61] are advisedly declaratory, not enacting; they express the broad constitutional principle that the whole body of the prerogative, *so far as it is capable of exercise in relation to the affairs of the Commonwealth*, is exercisable by the Governor-General, and of course, exercisable, in accordance with the principles of responsible government, by and with the advice of Commonwealth Ministers.[75]

The emphasised words indicate an awareness of the limits to the power, presumably both in relation to its breadth within Australia, but also its reach vis-à-vis the British Government with respect to the external affairs of the Empire. However, Deakin rejected the proposition that executive power would not exist in the absence of legislation:

> Shorn of prerogative powers, the Commonwealth Executive would be a mere appendage to the Parliament – a board of subordinate officers exercising such powers as might be conferred upon it, but without independent authority of any kind. *Such a conception of the executive is wholly at variance, not only with every principle of English constitutional law, but with the clear and unmistakable provisions of the Constitution*. Responsible government, though far more clearly established there than in any of the State Constitutions, would then be much more restricted in authority, character, and domain than it is in the States under their less explicit charters … the vast fund of powers held by the Crown in trust for the people would disappear; and the Commonwealth, instead of inheriting the fullest development of constitutional rights and privileges, would find its new political organisation had dwindled from a national to a municipal body, for making and executing continental by-laws.[76]

According to Deakin, the federal structure of the Constitution placed a relevant limitation upon the executive power, but it did so by reference to the scope of the legislative powers of the Commonwealth, not the exercise of those powers in the form of legislation:

> It is impossible to resist the conclusion that the Commonwealth has executive power, independently of Commonwealth legislation, *with respect to every matter to which its legislative power extends*. It is not contended that the Commonwealth Government has power to administer State Acts which remain in force relating to matters within the concurrent power of the State Parliaments; nor that there are no executive acts requiring prior authority. What is clear is that *in all matters within the scope of the legislative power* of the Commonwealth, its executive possesses *all the powers of the Crown* properly exercisable within the Commonwealth. … As a general rule, wherever the

**74** Ibid, 130.
**75** Ibid (emphasis added).
**76** Ibid.

> executive power of the Commonwealth extends, that of the States is correspondingly reduced.[77]

Deakin also drew attention to Griffith's amendment to the original clause, emphasising Griffith's intention that the effect of the clause would remain the same. However, Deakin also acknowledged that the amendment avoided the 'negative limitation':

> The original clause, therefore, extended the executive power of the Commonwealth to all matters within the legislative power of the Parliament, with a negative limitation applying to the execution of State laws on matters within the concurrent power of the States. *The form was altered, to avoid even a negative limitation, but the intention remained the same.*[78]

Deakin did not quite explain how the intention might be the same (as he understood it) when the force and effect of the negative limitation had been removed. Nonetheless, this wider view of the executive power was asserted by other important figures, including Commonwealth Attorney-General Littleton Groom in 1907:

> [I]t must be taken to be settled law that the executive power of the Commonwealth is *coextensive with the whole range of its legislative powers, whether those powers are exercised or unexercised*: and further, that there is vested in the Governor-General under section 61 of the Constitution the whole undefined mass of executive powers which are necessarily implied in the creation of a new political entity, sovereign within its own sphere. These general propositions are of course subject to the limitation that where the matter is one which is governed by a State law which has not been displaced by a law of the Commonwealth, the State executive power under the State law still remains. ... It follows from this that the Government of the Commonwealth must have the power of regulating a matter of this kind, which is clearly within its legislative power, by mere executive act, *even in the absence of any legislation.*[79]

These understandings of the breadth and depth of Commonwealth executive power were repeated by Harrison Moore, when he stated:

> The power to execute and maintain the Constitution does not mean that the Executive Government may do all acts necessary to carry out any provision of the Constitution; it must be construed, like everything else in the Constitution, by reference to established principle of English law ... . ... But where a power or duty committed to 'the Commonwealth' *is of such a kind as is according to common law exerciseable by the Executive, the Commonwealth Executive is empowered to take such action as the common law allows.*[80]

**77** Ibid, 131–2 (emphasis added).
**78** Ibid, 132 (emphasis added).
**79** Alfred Deakin, 'Executive Power of Commonwealth – Whether Coextensive with Legislative Power: When is State Executive Power Displaced: Whether Commonwealth has Power by Executive Act to Permit Landing of Foreign Troops or Crews' in Brazil and Mitchell, above n 72, 360 (emphasis added). This was referred to with approval by Heydon J in *Williams (No 1)* (2012) 248 CLR 156 (at 312).
**80** Moore, above n 3, 297 (emphasis added).

## III The depth and breadth of executive power

In his important treatise, *Parliament, the Executive and the Governor-General*, Winterton argued that an analytical distinction needs to be drawn between the 'depth' and the 'breadth' of the executive power of the Commonwealth. The continuing usefulness of this approach according to its terms has been acknowledged in judicial *dicta* and by leading constitutional commentators.

Justice Heydon, for example, described it as 'not only neat but illuminating'.[81] On Winterton's analysis, the term 'breadth' refers to the federally demarcated sphere within which the Commonwealth may exercise its executive power. This is primarily determinable by reference to the subject matters in respect of which Commonwealth Parliament may legislate. The term 'depth' refers to the precise actions, activities or enterprises which may be undertaken by the Commonwealth within the sphere of its competence without statutory authorisation.[82] Questions of depth are primarily determined by reference to the common law prerogatives and capacities of the Crown. To be constitutionally valid, Commonwealth executive action must not exceed the depth and breadth dimensions of the power.

*Johnson v Kent*[83] provides a simple illustration of what Winterton considered to be 'the correct model for assessing the constitutionality of executive action'.[84] At issue was the proposed construction of a telecommunications tower on Crown land within the Australian Capital Territory pursuant to an executive decision made by the Governor-General in Council. In upholding its validity, the High Court first determined that the activity came within the breadth of permissible Commonwealth executive activity as determined by its power to make laws for the government of any Territory pursuant to s 122 of the Constitution. The depth element was determined by reference to the prerogative in the broad sense, although arguably it would have been more precise to have referred to the capacities of the Crown because the Commonwealth was simply seeking to develop its own land and thus to exercise capacities it has in common with ordinary persons. Barwick CJ stated:

> [W]hat the executive does upon and in respect of such lands will be done by virtue of the prerogative and not by virtue of proprietorship. There can be no objection ... to the Commonwealth, in the absence of any statutory provisions, establishing parks, gardens, sports grounds, tourist facilities and the like upon land it possesses in Canberra. ... Such a conclusion would cover the erection in the present circumstances of a restaurant and viewing facilities, assuming that there is no relevant statutory impairment of the prerogative.[85]

**81** *Williams (No 1)* (2012) 248 CLR 156, 312 [385] n 578; Cheryl Saunders, *The Constitution of Australia: A Contextual Analysis* (Hart, 2011), 177–81.
**82** Winterton, above n 26, chs 2, 3.
**83** (1975) 132 CLR 164.
**84** Winterton, above n 26, 34.
**85** *Johnson v Kent* (1975) 132 CLR 164, 170.

*Barton v Commonwealth*[86] provides another example. In that case the question was whether the Commonwealth had the constitutional authority to request the extradition of a fugitive in the absence of an extradition treaty with the relevant nation. The Solicitor-General, Sir Maurice Byers QC, adopted a depth/breadth approach. He argued that the requirement of breadth was satisfied by the Commonwealth's power with respect to 'external affairs' (s 51(xxix)) and that the requirement of depth was satisfied by the relevant prerogatives embedded in s 61. Because the subject matter came within the Commonwealth's legislative competence via the external affairs power, the breadth question was not particularly in issue. In relation to depth, the submission which rested on the existence of the relevant prerogative was accepted by the Court. Barwick CJ, Mason and Jacobs JJ (McTiernan and Menzies JJ not explicitly) held that the prerogative permitted a request by the Commonwealth to a foreign State to detain a person alleged to have committed an offence against the law of Australia, pending the making of a request for his extradition.

In order to determine the reach of the Commonwealth's executive power it is thus necessary to consider the scope of the prerogatives and capacities of the Crown for the purposes of depth, and the federal limitations placed on the Commonwealth – essentially by reference to its legislative competence – for the purposes of breadth. The prerogatives and capacities of the Crown are essentially a product of the common law, while the federal limitations derive from the Constitution itself. What complicates this picture is that the Commonwealth's executive power extends to the execution and maintenance of the Constitution and the laws of the Commonwealth. However, the exact scope of the maintenance limb, and the exact relationship between the executive power and Commonwealth laws enacted under ss 51 and 52, are matters of some complexity. Moreover, the High Court has held that, associated with the maintenance limb of s 61 and the incidental legislative power in s 51(xxxix), the character and status of the Commonwealth as a 'national' government gives rise to an implied executive power commonly known as the 'nationhood' power.

The two most obvious sources of the content of s 61 executive power, in its depth component, are the powers conferred by statute and those powers 'necessary or incidental to the execution and maintenance of a law of the Commonwealth'.[87] The other three which have been given recognition were listed by French CJ in *Williams (No 1)*: 'powers defined by reference to such of the prerogatives of the Crown as are properly attributable to the Commonwealth'; 'powers defined by the capacities of the Commonwealth common to legal persons'; and 'inherent authority derived from the character and status of the Commonwealth as the national government'.[88] Each will now be examined.

**86** (1974) 131 CLR 477.
**87** *Williams v Commonwealth (No 1)* (2012) 248 CLR 156, 184–5.
**88** Ibid, 184–5 nn 11–13.

## 1 The common law: Prerogatives and capacities

Writing in the late eighteenth century, William Blackstone defined the prerogative narrowly as 'those rights and capacities which the king enjoys alone, in contradistinction to others, and not ... those which he enjoys in common with any of his subjects'.[89] On this view, the 'prerogative' does not include those 'capacities' which the Crown shares with natural persons by virtue of legal personality, such as entering into a contract, creating a trust, registering a company, acquiring and disposing of property, suing and being sued, and so on. Around a century later, A V Dicey proposed a wider definition, arguing that the prerogative includes all of the non-statutory powers and capacities of the Executive that are recognised by the common law, whether unique to the Crown or shared with ordinary natural persons.[90] On either view, because the prerogative depends on the common law, it is subject to legislative regulation or abnegation.[91]

While arguments as to whether or not 'the prerogative' should include 'capacities' may seem to be merely definitional, the distinction is potentially important because '[d]ifferent principles and policies may be applicable to the two sets of powers'.[92] One very important difference is that while exercises of the prerogative (in the narrower sense) can be 'capable of interfering with what would otherwise be the legal rights and duties of others', the exercise of executive capacities cannot of themselves 'override legal rights and duties', and when exercising them the Executive must comply with the general rules of common law, equity and statute.[93] Given these subtleties, and to avoid confusion, this usage by which 'capacities' are distinguished from the 'prerogative' will be adopted herein unless otherwise stated.

Prior to his appointment as a justice of the High Court and his later political career, H V Evatt proposed an even more complex categorisation.[94] First, he suggested, there are the 'executive prerogatives' (in the broad sense) pursuant to which the Crown has the power to do various important acts of state, such as to execute treaties and conduct foreign relations, declare war, make peace, coin money, incorporate bodies by Royal charter, pardon offenders and confer honours. Under this category, Dr Evatt also located the executive 'capacities' enjoyed by the Crown as a juristic person. This category is of particular importance in the determination of depth. Secondly, there are the 'immunities and preferences' of the Crown. These include its entitlement to be paid in preference to other

**89** William Blackstone, *Commentaries on the Laws of England* (15th ed) vol I, 239, cited in *Victoria v Australian Building and Construction Employees' and Builders Labourers' Federation* (1982) 152 CLR 25, 70.
**90** Albert Venn Dicey, *Introduction to the Study of the Law of the Constitution* (Palgrave Macmillan, 10th ed, 1959) 424–5, cited in *Williams (No 1)* (2012) 248 CLR 156, 185, 343–4.
**91** *Attorney-General v De Keyser's Royal Hotel Ltd* [1920] AC 508. See also *Cadia Holdings Pty Ltd v New South Wales* (2010) 242 CLR 195, 205, 231; *Ruddock v Vadarlis* (2001) 110 FCR 491, 501–4, 539–40.
**92** Leslie Zines, *The High Court and the Constitution* (Federation Press, 5th ed, 2008) 345.
**93** Ibid, 346.
**94** H V Evatt, *The Royal Prerogative* (Law Book, 1987) 29–31, 50. (This was the published version of Evatt's doctoral thesis at The University of Sydney, submitted in 1924.)

creditors,[95] its immunity from the ordinary processes of the courts, its freedom from distress for rent,[96] from costs and discovery of documents. Thirdly, there are certain 'proprietary' rights of the Crown such as its entitlement to the royal metals, royal fish, treasure trove, escheat, ownership of the foreshore, the seabed and subsoil (and possibly even the sea, but within its territorial limits).[97]

In Evatt's analysis, which in its broad outline remains good today, the category to which a prerogative belongs may determine which polity in the federation inherits it. Thus, the proprietary prerogatives, originally inherited by the colonies, presently reside with the States unless transferred to the Commonwealth by the Constitution.[98] The preferences and immunities, as they inhere in 'the Crown', have been inherited by both the Commonwealth and the States. The executive prerogatives have been divided between the Commonwealth and the States, primarily according to the division of legislative powers between them – those inherited by the States being subject to Commonwealth legislation.[99] The Commonwealth may also exercise all of the relevant executive prerogatives extant in 1901, including today all those which pertain to foreign affairs, Australia having become a fully independent nation as a consequence of the collective effect of the Balfour Declaration (1926), *Statute of Westminster 1931* (UK), *Statute of Westminster Adoption Act 1942* (Cth) and *Australia Acts 1986* (UK) and (Cth).[100] The particular powers considered here include the prerogative relating to foreign affairs,[101] war,[102] peace,[103] entry into treaties,[104] extradition,[105] appointment of diplomats,[106] stationing and control of the armed forces,[107] and construction of facilities on its own land.[108]

**95** *Cadia Holdings Pty Ltd v New South Wales* (2010) 242 CLR 195, 210; *Commonwealth v Cigamatic Pty Ltd (in liq)* (1962) 108 CLR 372, 377; *Uther v Federal Commissioner of Taxation* (1947) 74 CLR 508, 514, 525–6, 531, 535; *Federal Commissioner of Taxation v Official Liquidator of E O Farley Ltd* (1940) 63 CLR 278, 286, 291, 294, 303–4; *In re KL Tractors Ltd (in Liquidation)* (1961) 106 CLR 318, 336; *Bank of New South Wales v Deputy Commissioner of Taxation* (1979) 28 ALR 43, 51, 54.
**96** Assumed in *Repatriation Commission v Kirkland* (1923) 32 CLR 1; *Federal Commissioner of Taxation v Official Liquidator of E O Farley Ltd* (1940) 63 CLR 278, 322.
**97** These were the particular immunities, preferences and proprietary rights recognised at the time Evatt was writing in 1924.
**98** See *Cadia Holdings Pty Ltd v New South Wales* (2010) 242 CLR 195.
**99** Winterton, above n 26, 49.
**100** See Chapter 1, Part IV.1. See, further, Leslie Zines, 'Commentary' in H V Evatt, above n 94, 29–31, 50; *Victoria v Commonwealth* (1996) 187 CLR 416, 476–80.
**101** *R v Burgess; Ex parte Henry* (1936) 55 CLR 608, 644, adopted in *Barton v Commonwealth* (1974) 131 CLR 477, 498; *New South Wales v Commonwealth* (1975) 135 CLR 337, 379, 381, 503; *Cadia Holdings Pty Ltd v New South Wales* (2010) 242 CLR 195, 210.
**102** *Farey v Burvett* (1916) 21 CLR 433, 452; *Johnston Fear & Kingham & Offset Printing Co Pty Ltd v Commonwealth* (1943) 67 CLR 314, 318, 325. See also *Burmah Oil Co (Burma Trading) Ltd v Lord Advocate* [1965] AC 75; *Attorney-General v De Keyser's Royal Hotel Ltd* [1920] AC 508.
**103** See the opinion of Sir Kenneth Bailey S-G examined by Zines, above n 100, C6. See also Leslie Zines 'The Growth of Australian Nationhood and Its Effect on the Powers of the Commonwealth' in Leslie Zines (ed) *Commentaries on the Australian Constitution* (1977) 1, 34.
**104** *Industrial Relations Act Case* (1996) 187 CLR 416, 476–80; *Koowarta v Bjelke-Petersen* (1982) 153 CLR 168, 193, 212, 213, 214, 223, 237–40, 249; *R v Burgess; Ex parte Henry* (1936) 55 CLR 608, 644, 683–4.
**105** *Barton v Commonwealth* (1974) 131 CLR 477.
**106** See M H Byers S-G 'Opinion on Governor-General's Instructions', 5 September 1975, para 4(F), 14, cited in Winterton, above n 26, 49 n 38. Winterton opined that the Queen's assignment to the Governor-General in 1954 of the power to appoint diplomats was 'probably unnecessary': at 242 n 38.
**107** *Marks v Commonwealth* (1964) 111 CLR 549, 564. See *Chandler v DPP* [1964] AC 763, 791, 796, 798, 800, 807, 814; *China Navigation Co, Ltd v Attorney-General* [1932] 2 KB 197, 214–15, 217, 227–8, 239.
**108** *Johnson v Kent* (1975) 132 CLR 164, 170.

One of the most important Commonwealth 'capacities' is the ability to enter into contracts.[109] Until very recently, it was a 'common assumption' that these capacities, subject to the general law, were capable of exercise by the Commonwealth within the sphere of Commonwealth legislative competence. This assumption has now had to be qualified following the decision of the High Court in *Williams (No 1)*[110] so that the capacity to contract and spend apart from specific statutory authorisation is limited to that class of contracts which relate, or are incidental, to the ordinary, well-recognised functions of government. Other important capacities which the Commonwealth enjoys by virtue of its status as a juristic person[111] are its ability to create trusts, transfer property, register companies, enter into partnerships and joint ventures, sue and be sued, and so on. *Williams (No 1)* may have implications for these capacities as well. Authoritative recognition has also been given to the Commonwealth's ability to conduct enquiries, commonly called Royal Commissions,[112] although different views have been expressed as to whether the establishment of a royal commission is an exercise of prerogative power or a capacity.[113] Whatever its classification, the ability to conduct inquiries does not include an inherent power to compel witnesses to attend or to compel the production of documents. For these, legislative authorisation is necessary.[114]

The Crown's proprietary prerogatives in relation to certain metals was acknowledged in *Cadia Holdings Pty Ltd v New South Wales* and the cases cited therein,[115] understood as *prerogatives* and not in the nature of 'capacities'.[116] It was held that, to the extent that these proprietary prerogatives were exercisable by the Crown's representatives in a particular colony, they remained exercisable by the executive of the relevant State,[117] although there was a suggestion in the case that the prerogative in mines of gold and silver belonged to the Commonwealth.[118]

Excepting emergencies such as war, invasion and other extreme events, the prerogative does not generally support the use of coercion. The courts have tended to avoid recognising a prerogative power which may interfere with the life, liberty or property of the subject.[119] Thus, the prerogative will not permit

**109** *Ansett Transport Industries (Operations) Pty Ltd v Commonwealth* (1977) 139 CLR 54, 61, 113. See also *Kidman v Commonwealth* [1926] ALR 1, 2. For a detailed examination of this capacity, see Nick Seddon, *Government Contracts* (Federation Press, 5th ed, 2013).

**110** (2012) 248 CLR 156.

**111** Zines, above n 92, 346.

**112** *Huddart, Parker & Co Pty Ltd v Moorehead* (1909) 8 CLR 330, 378; *Lockwood v Commonwealth* (1954) 90 CLR 177, 182, 186.

**113** See Nicholas Aroney, 'A power "singular and eccentrical": Royal commissions and executive power after *Williams*' (2014) 25 *Public Law Review* 101.

**114** *Clough v Leahy* (1904) 2 CLR 139, 153; *McGuiness v Attorney-General (Vic)* (1940) 63 CLR 73, 83, 91, 98–9, 106; *R v Collins; Ex parte ACTU-Solo Enterprises Pty Ltd* (1976) 8 ALR 691, 695; *Lloyd v Costigan* (1983) 48 ALR 241.

**115** (2010) 242 CLR 195, 206–9.

**116** Ibid, 223.

**117** Ibid, 210–11; 226.

**118** Ibid, 211 (citations omitted); see also 226.

**119** See *A v Hayden* (1984) 156 CLR 532.

the Executive 'to deprive a person of liberty' and there is 'no inherent power to deport, extradite or detain'.[120] During wartime, however, there appears to be a prerogative power to intern enemy aliens,[121] requisition ships,[122] and to destroy property to prevent it from entering enemy hands.[123] In relation to the requisition, damage or destruction of property, compensation is generally payable, at least if this does not occur while actually fighting the enemy ('battle damage').[124] On the other hand, the need for statutory authority to support extradition from Australia of fugitive offenders was affirmed in *Vasiljkovic v Commonwealth*.[125] Also of historic and continuing importance is the incapacity of the Executive Government to dispense with obedience to the law.[126]

In emergencies short of war or its imminence, the extent of the prerogative is 'remarkably abstruse' and uncertain.[127] The House of Lords postulated in *Burmah Oil Co Ltd v Lord Advocate* that the maintenance of public safety lies within prerogative power regardless of whether a state of war exists or is imminent.[128] In the words of Viscount Radcliffe, '[r]iot, pestilence and conflagration might well be other circumstances' which trigger the power.[129] More controversially, the English Court of Appeal appears to have held that there exists a general prerogative to maintain or keep the peace.[130] The risk is that such an amorphous concept may provide an overzealous Executive, or one tempted to an excess of zeal, well-intentioned or otherwise, with excessive unregulated power. Zines, for one, regretted this decision, expressing the hope that Australian courts would not follow it:

> The potential width of this new-found prerogative is worrying, requiring the making of broad evaluations by the judiciary. One writer has described the decision as like 'Pandora's box, from which a host of evils were loosed upon the world, and in which nothing remained but Hope'.[131]

The decision is indeed unlikely to be followed in Australia. It is strongly arguable that, rather than apply an existing prerogative to new circumstances, the Court of Appeal constructed a new prerogative power where none existed before – a course that Australian courts are not likely to follow.

While the prerogatives are recognised by the common law, there abides within them a certain quality which distinguishes them 'as being out of the ordinary

**120** *Ex parte Walsh and Johnson; In re Yates* (1925) 37 CLR 36; *Barton v Commonwealth* (1974) 131 CLR 477; *Re Bolton; Ex parte Beane* (1981) 162 CLR 514, 547.
**121** *R v Botrill; Ex parte Kuechenmeister* [1947] KB 41.
**122** *The Broadmayne* [1916] P 64. Zines noted that during the Falklands War in 1982, a United Kingdom Order in Council provided for the requisition of ships subject to compensation: Zines, above n 38, 287 n 59.
**123** *Burmah Oil Co (Burma Trading) Ltd v Lord Advocate* [1965] AC 75.
**124** Ibid.
**125** (2006) 227 CLR 614, 634–5.
**126** *A v Hayden* (1984) 156 CLR 532, 580–81; *White v Director of Military Prosecutions* (2007) 231 CLR 570, 592.
**127** Zines, above n 38, 287, quoting S De Smith and R Brazier, *Constitutional and Administrative Law* (Penguin, 7th ed, 1994) 566 n 13.
**128** [1965] AC 75.
**129** *Burmah Oil Co (Burma Trading) Ltd v Lord Advocate* [1965] AC 75, 114–15.
**130** *R v Home Secretary; Ex parte Northumbria Police Authority* [1989] 1 QB 26.
**131** Zines, above n 38, 287.

course of the common law'[132] without rendering them completely *sui generis*. This is a reflection of the particular historical antecedents of executive power, especially as it developed through the various disputes over the prerogative between Parliament and the Stuart Kings in seventeenth century England. As the issue was decided in favour of Parliament, the prerogative was rendered subject to legislation: a strange *prerogative* indeed if it depended on the consent and forbearance of the legislature, but a 'prerogative' nevertheless. Following the Revolution Settlement of 1688, those prerogative powers which were left in the hands of the Crown were those which Parliament permitted it to retain, shaped largely by contemporary assessments of governmental necessity and sometimes expediency, as well as the continuing influence of long usage and traditional conceptions of the powers properly belonging to princes. Foreign affairs, entering treaties, and declaring war and peace remain the classic examples. But even these prerogatives are subject to parliamentary statute.

As a consequence, one of the most important qualities of the prerogative is its residual character. It is 'the residue of discretionary power left at any moment in the hands of the Crown'.[133] It is not a dynamic area of the common law, with many aspects of the prerogative having become subject to atrophy; not necessarily a bad thing. Its second quality, a corollary of the first, is that no new prerogatives can be created. As Diplock LJ noted:

> It is 350 years and a civil war too late for the Queen's courts to broaden the prerogative. The limits within which the executive government may impose obligations or restraints on citizens ... without any statutory authority are now well settled and incapable of extension.[134]

Thirdly, the prerogative may be abrogated by statute. As Winterton put it, because the prerogative is subject to legislation, 'it can be seen as merely an interim measure of executive power until Parliament regulates the subject by legislation'.[135] Fourthly, the prerogative is generally subject to judicial review.[136] Fifthly, it cannot be used to permit a dispensation from the application of the law,[137] to create an offence[138] or to impose a tax.[139]

If an enactment abrogates or alters a particular prerogative, it is not the case that mere repeal of the Act will revive the prerogative. On the other hand, if a statute of the United Kingdom Parliament amends or removes a particular

**132** *Cadia Holdings Pty Ltd v New South Wales* (2010) 242 CLR 195, 226.
**133** *R v Secretary of State for the Home Department; Ex parte Fire Brigades Union* [1995] 2 AC 513, 573.
**134** *British Broadcasting Corporation v Johns* [1965] Ch 32, 79, quoted with approval by Black CJ in *Ruddock v Vadarlis* (2001) 110 FCR 491, 501.
**135** Winterton, above n 43, 35.
**136** *Council of Civil Service Unions v Minister for the Civil Service* [1985] AC 374; *Minister for the Arts, Heritage and Environment v Peko-Wallsend Ltd* (1987) 15 FCR 274; *R (Bancoult) v Secretary of State for Foreign and Commonwealth Affairs [No 2]* [2009] 1 AC 453.
**137** *Vestey v Inland Revenue Commissioners* [1980] AC 1148, 1195; *A v Hayden* (1984) 156 CLR 532, 580–82; *Ridgeway v The Queen* (1995) 184 CLR 19, 54.
**138** *Case of Proclamations* (1611) 77 ER 1352; *Davis v Commonwealth* (1988) 166 CLR 79, 112.
**139** *Bill of Rights 1688* art 4; *Bowles v Bank of England* [1913] 1 Ch 57, 84–5; *Wooltops* case (1922) 31 CLR 421, 433–4.

prerogative, that prerogative may survive in Australia despite its abolition in the United Kingdom.[140] However, rather than simply abrogate a prerogative, it is far more common for Parliament to *displace* the prerogative with legislation granting the government powers similar to those conferred by the prerogative or by providing a statutory method for accomplishing the objectives sought to be implemented by the prerogative. Such legislation supersedes the prerogative; and the Executive must exercise the powers conferred subject to the conditions in the statute, and cannot simply fall back on the prerogative.[141] The same applies to executive capacities, which are in any event subject to the general law.

A more difficult issue is whether a prerogative may be lost by desuetude – that is, by prolonged disuse.[142] Lord Simon of Glaisdale maintained that:

> The true doctrine ... is that a rule of the English common law, once clearly established, does not become extinct merely by disuse, and remains capable of recrudescence in *propitious* circumstances, *but not when it would be grossly anomalous and anachronistic*. ... If a rule of English common law cannot become as dead as the dodo, it can at least go into cataleptic trance. ... In such a state, the rule in question cannot ... be revived at the mere call of any passing litigant, but only if its appropriate moment has come again *to operate usefully and without gross anomaly*.[143]

Although it may be that the personal opinion of the judges becomes determinative of what constitutes 'propitious', or 'grossly anomalous and anachronistic circumstances', this moderate approach to the question is consistent with the reality that true desuetude is very rare. For, in any case, the vast expanse of modern legislation has overwhelmed many subject matters previously covered by the prerogative.[144] Moreover, whether or not desuetude has extinguished a prerogative, and if there is no analogous statutory power, there is nothing to prevent Parliament by statute vesting power in the Executive to meet the need, subjecting it to such conditions and controls as it deems appropriate.

Despite the subsidiary and residual character of the prerogative, it cannot be regarded as being totally ossified. Although no new prerogatives may be created, they can be developed, in the way of the common law, to apply to new circumstances.[145] The prerogative thus partakes of the evolutionary character of the common law, but only in an attenuated way: such development may not result in the creation of an entirely new species of the prerogative. Thus, for example, the war prerogative is applicable to modern and unconventional forms of warfare. But being a *prerogative* power, the role of the courts in its attenuated evolution must be very circumspect, allowing only its applicability to novel

**140** See Winterton, above n 26, 117.
**141** See Chapter 6, Part III where the particular requirements for the displacement of the prerogative by statute are discussed. The leading case remains *Attorney-General v De Keyser's Royal Hotel Ltd* [1920] AC 508, and see also *Burmah Oil Co Ltd v Lord Advocate* [1965] AC 75. For a detailed consideration of the ouster of the prerogative see Winterton, above n 43, 42–8 and Winterton, *Parliament, the Executive and the Governor-General*, above n 26, ch 6.
**142** Winterton, *Parliament, the Executive and the Governor-General*, above n 26, ch 6, 117.
**143** *M'Kendrick v Sinclair* (1972) SC 25 (HL) 60–61 (emphasis added).
**144** For a more detailed consideration, see Winterton, above n 26, 120–22.
**145** Ibid, 117–20.

circumstances where warranted, but not allowing for the creation of a new prerogative.

While the precise content of the prerogative may remain difficult to discern in certain circumstances, many prerogatives and executive capacities are well settled and of continuing modern relevance. As Winterton observed, 'the prerogative constitutes a substantial body of principles, rules and precedents, established over hundreds of years, the subject of considerable literature and heritage shared with comparable nations such as the United Kingdom, Canada and New Zealand'.[146] The common law provides a source of legally discernible criteria to determine the validity of executive action in circumstances where there is no relevant statute. Given the extraordinary nature of executive power, especially in emergencies relating to national security and the like, it may be reassuring that its source is a residue, that it is inherently subject to legislation and that its exercise may be but an interim measure pending legislation. Given these qualities of the prerogative, reliance upon it to determine the ambit of s 61 executive power is consistent with a Constitution which maintains the supremacy of Parliament and the Constitution and provides for a system of responsible government.

## 2 Governmental necessities: The implied 'nationhood' power

The recognition of an implied executive 'nationhood' power,[147] and its status as the ultimate determinant of the ambit of s 61, is the product of a more recent evolution in constitutional jurisprudence, crystalising in *Pape*.[148] Its development needs to be understood in relation to the Commonwealth's corresponding legislative power with respect to 'matters incidental to the execution of any power vested by [the] Constitution ... in the Government of the Commonwealth ... or in any department or officer of the Commonwealth' (s 51(xxxix)).

As seen in Chapter 3, the incidental legislative power was held in a line of cases to include 'every ancillary power that is necessary to the existence of the Government, and the proper exercise of the direct power it is intended to execute',[149] and to extend to laws protecting the Government and its departments and officers through laws responding to threats of physical attack and interference, as well as to the utterance of words intended to excite disaffection against Australia's governing institutions.[150] The associated idea that the Commonwealth possesses an implied nationhood power was developed in several important cases that followed. Two crucial cases concerned the interpretation of s 81 of the Constitution relating to the appropriation of funds from Consolidated

**146** Winterton, above n 43, 34–5.
**147** This term will be used as simple shorthand to refer to this implied nationhood power derived from s 61, although the High Court has not expressly adopted the use of this term.
**148** *Pape v Commissioner of Taxation* (2009) 238 CLR 1.
**149** *R v Kidman* (1915) 20 CLR 425, 440; *Ex parte Walsh and Johnson; In re Yates* (1925) 37 CLR 36, 94; *R v Hush; Ex parte Devanny* (1932) 48 CLR 487, 506.
**150** *Burns v Ransley* (1949) 79 CLR 101, 109–10, 111, 116.

Revenue 'for the purposes of the Commonwealth'. In the *Pharmaceutical Benefits* case,[151] at issue was the validity of legislation purporting to apply appropriated funds to subsidise prescribed medicines. At the heart of the case was whether the appropriation was 'for the purposes of the Commonwealth'. In the course of his judgment, Dixon J observed:

> Even upon the footing that the power of expenditure is limited to matters to which the Federal legislative power is to be addressed, it necessarily includes whatever is incidental to the existence of the Commonwealth as a state and to the exercise of the functions of a national government.[152]

In the *AAP* case,[153] the validity of the appropriation for the Australian Assistance Plan – a scheme for regional development and the provision of social welfare services – was impugned. There was no statutory authorisation for the Plan beyond the legislative appropriation. The court was evenly divided on this central question: McTiernan, Jacobs and Murphy JJ held the appropriation valid; Barwick CJ, Gibbs and Mason JJ dissented. The scheme was upheld because Stephen J denied that the States had standing to impugn an appropriation. Barwick CJ and Gibbs J, in accord with Dixon J's proposition above, adopted the majority position in *Pharmaceutical Benefits* that 'purposes of the Commonwealth' meant 'purposes in respect of which Parliament has power to make laws', including those incidental to the function of a national government.[154] This was not necessarily suggestive of some recognition of an *executive* nationhood power, however. It was rather a recognition of a general power to *legislate* with respect to matters appropriate to a national government.[155] At most, the *AAP* case recognised an executive power to engage in activities of a national character, and a legislative power to authorise them.[156] Exploration and research were given as examples.[157] However, Barwick CJ, Gibbs and Mason JJ were concerned to articulate limitations, especially to ensure that these powers did not extend beyond the sphere of Commonwealth legislative competence. Mason J joined Barwick CJ and Gibbs J even though he held that 'for the purposes of the Commonwealth' is determinable by Parliament. He differed to them on the basis that, while it was within executive power to administer an appropriation to undertake simple expenditure, this did not extend to permitting the Commonwealth to be involved in a scheme such as the Australian Assistance Plan. In an influential *dictum*, Mason J stated:

> There is to be deduced from the existence and character of the Commonwealth as a national government and from the presence of ss 51(xxxix) and 61 a capacity to engage

**151** *Attorney-General (Vic); Ex rel Dale v Commonwealth* (1945) 71 CLR 237.
**152** Ibid, 269.
**153** *Victoria v Commonwealth and Hayden* (1975) 134 CLR 338.
**154** Ibid, 363, 375.
**155** See Winterton, above n 26, 42.
**156** *Victoria v Commonwalth and Hayden* (1975) 134 CLR 338, 396–8, 412–13.
**157** Ibid, 362, 397, 413.

> in enterprises and activities *peculiarly adapted to the government of a nation* and which *cannot otherwise be carried on for the benefit of the nation.*[158]

The depth of this implied power thus seems to have been limited by reference to two important criteria relating both to the *unique* position of the national government to undertake the activity and the fact that the activity could only be undertaken efficaciously by the national government. With respect to the breadth of the power, Mason J stated:

> [I]n its scope it is not unlimited and ... its content does not reach beyond the area of responsibilities allocated to the Commonwealth by the Constitution, responsibilities which are ascertainable from the distribution of powers, *more particularly the distribution of legislative powers*, effected by the Constitution itself and the character and status of the Commonwealth as a national government.[159]

Jacobs J advocated a still wider view:

> The growth of national identity results in corresponding growth in the area of activities which have an Australian rather than a local flavour. Thus, the complexity and values of a modern national society result in the need for co-ordination and integration in ways and means of planning for that complexity and reflecting those values. Inquiries on a national scale are *necessary* and like-wise planning on a national scale *must* be carried out. Moreover, the complexity of society ... requires coordination of services designed to meet [its] needs. Research and exploration likewise have a national, rather than a local flavour.[160]

Although he adopted the most expansive view of the power, Jacobs J set a high threshold for its valid exercise, emphasising that national government action must be both necessary and uniquely efficacious. However, unlike Mason J who appeared to derive his test directly from s 61, he made reference to the prerogative as the basis of the power:

> The prerogative is now exercisable by the Queen through the Governor-General acting on the advice of the Executive Council on all matters which are the concern of Australia as a nation. Within the words 'maintenance of this Constitution' ... in s 61 lies the idea of Australia as a nation within itself and in its relationship with the external world.[161]

Whatever one is to make of these important differences in detail, three justices in the *APP* case certainly appeared to recognise an implied executive 'nationhood' power.

A year after the *AAP* case was decided, Geoffrey Sawer observed what he described as a 'preponderant drift' in the Court's jurisprudence towards the acknowledgment of 'an area of inherent authority derived partly from the Royal Prerogative, and probably even more from the necessities of a modern national

**158** Ibid, 397 (emphasis added) (hereafter referred to as 'Mason J's test').
**159** Ibid, 396 (emphasis added).
**160** Ibid, 412–13 (emphasis added).
**161** Ibid, 405–6.

government', sourced in s 61.[162] In *Davis v Commonwealth*, decided in 1988, this trend continued.[163] The Court there held that s 61 authorises the government to commemorate Australia's Bicentenary without apparent reliance on the prerogative but rather directly from s 61, pursuant to Mason J's test in the *AAP* case. As Mason CJ, Deane and Gaudron JJ put it, 'the commemoration of the Bicentenary is pre-eminently the business and the concern of the Commonwealth as the national government and as such falls fairly and squarely within the federal executive power'.[164] In the *APP* case, Mason J had concluded, without express reference to the prerogative, that scientific research and 'inquiries, investigation and advocacy in relation to matters affecting public health' were executive actions permitted by s 61.[165] In *Davis*, the other justices expressed similar views.[166] Although Brennan J referred, like Jacobs J, to the prerogative, he did not employ it in his reasoning, adopting the view of Jacobs J in the *AAP* case that the phrase 'imports the idea of Australia as a nation' and authorises the government to act for 'the protection and advancement of the Australian nation'.[167] Winterton proposed that the justices in *Davis* were suggesting that celebrating the nation was an *activity* that was authorised by s 61.[168] Zines, however, identified the issue as 'whether the purposes of a celebration of this kind came within the area of responsibilities of the Commonwealth'. On this latter view, the case was essentially concerned with the breadth of Commonwealth executive power, not its depth.[169] Celebrating the Bicentenary was considered a subject matter which was appropriate to the Commonwealth's status as a national government. It could therefore take such executive action as permissible to it in this regard. Thus, for Zines, the case did not hold that the Commonwealth can undertake any activity to celebrate the nation, but rather that it had power to incorporate a company for the purposes of celebrating the Bicentenary which came within the sphere (or breadth) of Commonwealth responsibility. The criterion of depth was satisfied because the incorporation of a company came within the Commonwealth's executive capacities.[170]

In *Ruddock v Vadarlis*, these propositions were taken a step further by a majority of the Full Federal Court, who unequivocally accepted the existence of an executive nationhood power, but rejected the prerogative as its basis and measure.[171] At issue was the legality of the government's action to avert from

**162** Geoffrey Sawer, 'The Executive Power of the Commonwealth and the Whitlam Government' (unpublished Octagon Lecture, University of Western Australia, 1976) 10. See Winterton, above n 43, 33.
**163** *Davis v Commonwealth* (1988) 166 CLR 79, 93, 103, 111, 119.
**164** Ibid, 94.
**165** *Victoria v Commonwealth and Hayden* (1975) 134 CLR 338, 397.
**166** *Davis v Commonwealth* (1988) 166 CLR 79, 104, 114, 119.
**167** Ibid, 110.
**168** Winterton, above n 43, 32.
**169** Zines, above n 38, 281.
**170** Ibid, 291.
**171** *Ruddock v Vadarlis* (2001) 110 FCR 491. French and Beaumont JJ, Black CJ dissenting. Black CJ based his conclusions exclusively on the prerogative and did not agree with the recognition of an executive nationhood power beyond the prerogative. See Simon Evans, 'The Rule of Law, Constitutionalism and the MV Tampa' (2002) 13 *Public Law Review* 94.

Australian territorial waters a Norwegian ship ('MV Tampa') which had taken on board some 400 persons seeking asylum in Australia, having rescued them from their own sinking vessel. The asylum seekers were detained and prevented from disembarking when the ship was boarded by Australian military personnel upon entering Australian waters. In determining whether the Commonwealth had executive power to undertake these actions, a majority of the court located within s 61 an inherent executive power to prevent the entry of non-citizens into Australia and to do such things as are necessary to effect such exclusions, including the use of coercion:

> The power to determine who may come into Australia is so central to its sovereignty that it is not to be supposed that the Government of the nation would lack under the power conferred upon it *directly* by the Constitution, the ability to prevent people not part of the Australian community, from entering.[172]

The power was said to enable the Commonwealth to prevent a person or vessel from proceeding into Australia as well as to compel a person or vessel to leave.[173] In the majority, French J's leading judgment proposed a novel account of the relationship between the prerogatives of the Crown and the executive powers of the Commonwealth:

> [T]he Executive power of the Commonwealth under s 61 cannot be treated as a species of the royal prerogative ... While the Executive power may derive some of its content by reference to the royal prerogative, it is a power conferred as part of a negotiated federal compact expressed in a written Constitution distributing powers between the three arms of government ...[174]

It is one thing to interpret s 61 as incorporating an implied nationhood power; it is quite another to determine its precise content. In certain respects, much of the implied power will overlap with the content of the more established executive prerogatives, especially those relating to foreign affairs and defence. But as the nationhood power is not determinable solely by reference to the legally discernible criteria of the common law, it is not at all clear how its outer bounds are to be determined even if the question is approached incrementally as cases come before the Court. That is not to say that the common law itself always provides clear answers. Rather, the point is that relying solely on 'national' and 'practical' considerations to determine the ambit of the maintenance component of s 61 is especially prone to subjective, policy-type considerations that are not ideally suited to judicial determination. Even if one were to adopt Mason J's test to define and confine the power, reasonable minds will differ as to what is peculiarly adapted to the government of a nation for its benefit. The result is likely to be a gradual expansion of Commonwealth power.

In his dissenting judgment in *Vadarlis*, Black CJ adopted a more orthodox depth/breadth analysis. He found that the Commonwealth's actions were not

**172** *Ruddock v Vadarlis* (2001) 110 FCR 491, 543 (emphasis added).
**173** Ibid, 544.
**174** Ibid, 540.

authorised by the relevant statute, the *Migration Act 1958* (Cth), and nor were they supported by the prerogative and non-prerogative powers incorporated in s 61.[175] Furthermore, his Honour refused to countenance the existence of any inherent executive power in s 61 independent of the prerogative. In relation to the detention of friendly 'aliens' in times of peace, he concluded that it was 'at best, doubtful that the asserted prerogative continues to exist at common law'.[176] Addressing the question whether 'some larger source of such a power' might be found in s 61, he responded:

> It would be a very strange circumstance if the at best doubtful and historically long-unused power to exclude or expel should emerge in a strong modern form from s 61 of the Constitution by virtue of general conceptions of 'the national interest'. This is all the more so when according to English constitutional theory new prerogative powers cannot be created.

Black CJ considered that the conclusion of the majority, authorising the coercive action undertaken by the Australian authorities against the MV Tampa and its asylum-seeking passengers, extended beyond executive powers recognised in earlier cases.[177]

In sharp contrast to the approach of Black CJ, French J, with whom Beaumont J agreed, not only expressly rejected the role of the prerogative as the measure of the ambit of the Commonwealth's non-statutory powers – he appeared also to downplay its continuing relevance:

> The Executive power of the Commonwealth under s 61 cannot be treated as a species of the royal prerogative. ... While the Executive power may derive some of its content by reference to the royal prerogative, it is a power conferred as part of a negotiated federal compact expressed in a written Constitution distributing powers between the three arms of government reflected in Chs I, II and III of the Constitution.[178]

The Constitution is undoubtedly the result of a negotiated federal compact, but it does not necessarily follow that the executive powers conferred upon the Commonwealth cannot be treated as a species of the prerogative, especially given that the executive powers exercised by the colonies were themselves understood in this way. However, French J concluded that the Commonwealth could validly undertake the action, which involved coercion, based on national sovereignty and the ability which inheres therein to prevent the entry of aliens, even 'friendly' ones.[179] Citing a *dictum* of Gummow J that '[i]n Australia ... one looks not to the content of the prerogative in Britain, but rather to s 61 of the Constitution, by which the executive power is vested', French J referred to the prerogative only as 'the common law *ancestor*' of the executive power in s 61.[180] He was

**175** Ibid, 495–501.
**176** Ibid, 500–01.
**177** Ibid, 501.
**178** Ibid, 540.
**179** Ibid, 543.
**180** Ibid, 539 (emphasis added).

thus able to conclude that the determination of who may come to Australia is 'so central' to its sovereignty that it was inconceivable that the national government lacked constitutional authority to prevent the entry of aliens into the community.[181]

Critics have drawn attention to the subjectivity inherent in such a conception of inherent executive power.[182] Reasonable minds are very likely to differ as to what may be permitted by such a power. Zines referred to French J's approach as 'highly subjective' and pointed out that it could just as easily be said that 'as the government action involves use of coercive force against unarmed people "it is not to be supposed" that the Constitution (or the common law) would provide such power in the absence of its conferral by Parliament'.[183] The majority nevertheless did find that such action was authorised by s 61.[184] If sole reliance is increasingly being placed on a 'nationhood' power, rather than the common law and its legally-discernible criteria, it will be increasingly difficult for the courts to skirt political controversy. Moreover, unlike the prerogative, which is a mere residue, the nationhood approach permits of an ever-pregnant executive power whose limits cannot easily be discerned.

These developments culminated in *Pape v Federal Commissioner of Taxation*.[185] The case concerned the validity of aspects of the Commonwealth's 'fiscal stimulus package', developed in response to the Global Financial Crisis of 2008. The supporting legislation provided that an individual tax payer whose income was below a certain threshold was entitled to a Tax Bonus in the form of a one-off cash payment. The issue was whether the legislation was a valid exercise of the incidental power in s 51(xxxix), that is, incidental to an exercise of s 61 executive power.

In determining this question, it was necessary first to determine whether there existed a relevant executive power to enliven s 51(xxxix). On the facts, it would have to be a power to provide a fiscal stimulus during a financial crisis by way of direct monetary payments. Staying close to the facts of the case, and eschewing any general definition of the power, French CJ maintained:

> The executive power of the Commonwealth conferred by s 61 of the Constitution extends to the power to expend public moneys for the purpose of avoiding or mitigating the large scale adverse effects of the circumstances affecting the national economy *disclosed on the facts of this case*, and which expenditure is on a scale and within a time-frame *peculiarly within the capacity of the national government*. ... The aspect of the power engaged in this case involves the expenditure of money to support a short-term national fiscal stimulus strategy calculated to offset the adverse effects of a global financial crisis on the national economy.[186]

**181** Ibid, 543.
**182** See Simon Evans, above n 171; Simon Evans, 'Developments – Australia – *Ruddock v Vadarlis* (The Tampa Litigation)' (2003) 1 *International Journal of Constitutional Law* 123; Ernst Wilheim 'MV Tampa: The Australian Response' (2003) 15 *International Journal of Refugee Law* 159.
**183** Zines, above n 38, 292.
**184** *Ruddock v Vadarlis* (2001) 110 FCR 491, 543.
**185** (2009) 238 CLR 1.
**186** *Pape* (2009) 238 CLR 1, 23–4 (emphasis added).

The basis for this more expansive view of s 61 his Honour explained thus:

> The collection of statutory and prerogative powers and non-prerogative capacities form part of, but do not complete, the executive power. They lie within the scope of s 61, which is informed by history and the common law relevant to the relationship between the Crown and the Parliament. That history and common law emerged from what might be called an organic evolution. Section 61 is an important element of a written constitution for the government of an independent nation. While history and the common law inform its content, it is not a locked display cabinet in a constitutional museum. It has to be capable of serving the proper purposes of a national government.[187]

In his positive expression of the power, his Honour tended to be conservative and did not venture beyond 'the aspect of the power engaged in this case'. He also avoided referring to a 'nationhood' power. He counselled restraint:

> Future questions about the application of the executive power to the control or regulation of conduct or activities under coercive laws, absent authority supplied by a statute made under some head of power other than s 51(xxxix) alone, are likely to be answered conservatively. They are likely to be answered bearing in mind the cautionary words of Dixon J in the *Communist Party Case*.[188]

These words of Dixon J have often been quoted as a warning of the dangers of an unbridled executive power. Dixon J stated:

> History and not only ancient history, shows that in countries where democratic institutions have been unconstitutionally superseded, it has been done not seldom by those holding the executive power. Forms of government may need protection from dangers likely to arise from within the institutions to be protected.[189]

While Gummow, Crennan and Bell JJ generally concurred, they gave expression to a nationhood power in more expansive terms:

> [T]he executive power of the Commonwealth enables the undertaking of action appropriate to the position of the Commonwealth as a polity created by the Constitution and having regard to the spheres of responsibility vested in it. ... [Section] 61 imports more than a species of what is identified as 'the prerogative' in constitutional theory.[190]

As such, the continuing relevance of the prerogatives and capacities incorporated in s 61 was maintained, but it was denied that they are the sole determinants of its ambit. Without undertaking an exhaustive definition, their Honours stated that 'the Executive Government is the arm of government capable of and empowered to respond to a crisis be it war, natural disaster or a financial crisis *on the scale here*'.[191] Although referring to the criteria in Mason J's test, they

**187** Ibid, 60.
**188** Ibid, 24.
**189** *Australian Communist Party v Commonwealth* (1951) 83 CLR 1, 187.
**190** *Pape* (2009) 238 CLR 1, 90.
**191** Ibid, 96.

concluded, more expansively than French CJ, that 'this case may be resolved without going beyond the notions of national emergency and the fiscal means of promptly responding to that situation'.[192] The 'present is an example of the engagement by the Executive Government in activities peculiarly adapted to the government of the country and which otherwise could not be carried on for the public benefit'.[193] They were able so to decide because they drew conclusions as to the scale of the 'global and financial crisis here'. 'It can hardly be doubted', their Honours opined, 'that the current financial and economic crisis concerns Australia as a nation'.[194]

Of course, the difficulty which immediately presents itself is the subjectivity of such a determination. The majority judgments were able to rely on the fact that it was not contested that the financial crisis was very exceptional in its (global) seriousness.[195] If this had been contested, on what basis would they have been able to decide on the exceptional nature of the crisis – that is, if in fact it was a 'crisis' at all, and if so, whether the Commonwealth alone could take efficacious action? The relevant constitutional fact – the sufficiency of the financial crisis to invoke a successful application of the implied national power – is a very difficult issue to submit for judicial determination. Indeed, even on the apparently agreed facts, the minority (Hayne, Heydon and Kiefel JJ) were not able to accept that the magnitude of the crisis warranted executive action pursuant to the implied nationhood power. Their reasons, which will be examined in more detail below, are telling.[196]

## 3 The evolution of executive power

The authoritative recognition of an executive 'nationhood' power has not rendered the executive prerogatives entirely obsolete. As is evident from a consideration of the large range of matters covered by the prerogative, it remains an essential, albeit diminished, measure of the ambit of executive power. Following *Pape*, the majority joint judgment in *Cadia Holdings Pty Ltd v New South Wales* stated that:

> [Section] 61 enables the Commonwealth to undertake executive action appropriate to its position under the Constitution and to that end includes the prerogative powers accorded the Crown by the common law. Dixon J spoke of common law prerogatives of the Crown in England ... as having been 'carried into the executive authority of the Commonwealth'.[197]

As Winterton noted, continuing resort to the common law 'implements the well-established principle ... that the common law is employed to interpret ambigu-

**192** Ibid, 98.
**193** Ibid, 99.
**194** Ibid, 96.
**195** Ibid, 69, 95, 96, 98.
**196** Ibid, 121.
**197** (2010) 242 CLR 195, 226.

ous provisions in written instruments, including constitutions and statutes'.[198] Zines explained the fundamental position of the common law within the Australian constitutional settlement when he noted that '[t]he Commonwealth was born into a common law world where rules existed as to the powers and legal position of the Crown, which the Commonwealth inherited as a government of the Queen'.[199] As a consequence, 'in so far as s 61 includes them, *they would exist apart from s 61*, and s 61 has not changed them'.[200] He was thus able to state: 'It follows that in respect of Crown prerogatives and capacities s 61 seems to make no difference'.[201] Thus, despite its ancient historical antecedents, or perhaps because of them, the prerogative cannot entirely be relegated to antiquarian interest.[202] Nor need it be regarded as a reminder of Australia's former provincial status. This is especially the case as it is Australian common law that is relevant, ultimately determinable by Australian courts, even though the decisions of the courts of the United Kingdom and analogous Commonwealth jurisdictions remain persuasive.

The recognition of an executive 'nationhood' power has not been without its critics, concerned about the unavoidable subjectivity involved, rendering it less suitable than the prerogatives and capacities for judicial determination and making it more prone to an aggrandisement of executive power. These concerns had emerged prior to *Pape*. Indeed, a view appeared to have prevailed among leading constitutional commentators that s 61 did not extend beyond those executive powers already recognised by the common law. This view, variously expressed by Campbell, Zines and Winterton, essentially maintained that s 61, *at most*, 'incorporates' these common law powers and its ambit is essentially determinable by them.[203] This was partly because they tended to downplay the significance of s 61 as a *source* of executive power. Typical of this view, Campbell queried whether s 61 is 'a grant of substantive power at all. ... It is unthinkable that it would be construed as empowering the Crown to do what was, under common law, forbidden unless authorised by statute'.[204] This approach also reflected the position taken by Harrison Moore in the early years of federation:

> In pursuance of its duty to maintain the Constitution and the law of the Commonwealth, the Executive may, without any further statutory authority, take whatever measures are ordinarily allowed to the Executive *by the common law* to protect every branch ... of the Federal Government in the performance of its duties.[205]

Zines was also of the view that the authorities, prior to *Pape*, did 'not support the proposition that s 61 confers "inherent" power beyond that which the Crown

**198** Winterton, above n 43, 35.
**199** Zines, above n 38, 292.
**200** Ibid (emphasis added). See also Winterton, above n 26, 48–49, 97; Zines, above n 103.
**201** Zines, above n 38, 280.
**202** *Pape* (2009) 238 CLR 1, 60.
**203** E Campbell, 'Parliament and the Executive' in Zines, above n 103, 88–9; Zines, above n 38, 280–82; Winterton, above n 26, 24–36.
**204** Campbell, above n 203, 89.
**205** Moore, above n 3, 297–8 (emphasis added).

possesses at common law' and he argued that the contrary reasoning of the *Vadarlis* majority, at least insofar as it permitted coercive action in the circumstances, 'should not be followed'.[206] He did not think it possible to understand executive power at a purely abstract conceptual level or to attribute inherent content to it.[207] 'The reason why making treaties and declaring war are executive powers', he wrote, 'is not because of any inherent meaning of the concept but because of events in English history and their effect on the common law'.[208] Moreover, since the 1688 settlement, the prerogative has not been sought to be expanded upon; hence the reference to it as a 'residue'.

An inherent 'nationhood' executive power which derives from an express constitutional provision, whether s 61 generally or the 'maintenance' component therein, will, unlike the prerogative, tend to be a developing and expanding power, *adding* depth and breadth to the power, and yet without necessarily providing legally discernible criteria by which it can be ascertained. Zines expressed concern about this when he opined that '[i]t is difficult to accept that the framers of the Constitution believed that the modern democratic constitution that they had designed conferred inherent coercive power on the Commonwealth government that was denied to the Imperial government'.[209]

The tendency to place greater reliance on the text of s 61 is a significant factor behind the recognition of the implied national power. Indeed, this suggests that textualism applied to s 61 opens the way to a more expansive interpretation of Commonwealth's executive power, just as the application of textualism to s 51 has enabled an expansive interpretation of the Commonwealth's legislative power.[210] On the other hand, if emphasis is placed on the fact that the Commonwealth is a government of the Queen, the common law prerogatives are then naturally attributed to it, so far as is relevant to its circumstances, and the depth, as well as the breadth, of the power is relatively confined. Section 61 is then seen as important for other reasons, the first and second limbs being the most significant. For example, it ensures that the Commonwealth's executive powers are exercisable by the Governor-General on the advice of Commonwealth Ministers, thus establishing in Australia the essential relationship between the Executive and Parliament at the heart of Westminster notions of responsible government and parliamentary supremacy.[211] Such a purpose for s 61 gives recognition to Australian nationhood, and is not the exclusive provenance of the nationhood view.

However, if an inherent executive power is located in s 61, its significance as the direct source of Commonwealth power is enhanced without necessarily

**206** Zines, above n 38, 281.
**207** Zines, above n 92, 359. See also Zines, above n 38, 279; Winterton, above n 26, 66–8.
**208** Zines, above n 92, 358.
**209** Ibid, 359.
**210** See Chapter 3, Part III.
**211** See Zines, above n 38, 282, where reference is made to other purposes served by s 61 and hence the need for such a provision in the Constitution.

assisting in the determination of the precise ambit of the power, especially if the demands of 'nationhood' are linked with a broad interpretation of what the 'maintenance of this Constitution' may require. Nevertheless, even when the common law view of s 61 was more in favour, the High Court did not unambiguously close the door on such a power. Perhaps this was because it was understood that the common law provided the limit in the absence of any relevant statutory provision: a not unreasonable proposition in light of the 'traditional conceptions' of the common law and constitutional convention in the context of which the Constitution was enacted.[212] Campbell observed that 'nowhere is this reliance on the *resourcefulness* of traditional conceptions to fill the vacancies in the text of the Constitution more marked' than in determining the role of the Executive and its relationship inter se with the legislature.[213] Section 61 in particular 'has to be read', she stated, 'subject to many of those traditional conceptions which the Constitution assumes'.[214] Yet the relevant *dicta* in the cases, especially in the *AAP* case, appear to have suggested more. While it was the case that, in the early years of federation and in light of Australia's legally dependent status within the British Empire, the prerogative relating to foreign affairs was very limited, this position rapidly changed as Australia's legal independence evolved. There is no doubt at present that the executive power of the Commonwealth is plenary in its external affairs dimensions, subject only to considerations relating to the federal distribution of powers and parliamentary supremacy. As Winterton put it, 'the subjects in respect of which Commonwealth executive power can be exercised are those on which it can legislate, including matters appropriate to a national government, which should be seen as falling within s 51 (xxxix) in domestic matters and s 51 (xxix) in foreign affairs'.[215]

In this respect, it can be said that the common law view itself accommodated, indeed facilitated, the development of Australian nationhood consistently with the Constitution without recourse to a separate, free-standing, nationhood power:

> [I]t had already been seen that the growth and attainment of independent nationhood was reflected in the 'transfer', in effect, of the exercise of prerogative powers from the Queen, acting on British advice, to the Governor-General, acting on Australian advice, with the result that judicial interpretation of the scope of the prerogative incorporated in s 61 has changed over the years.[216]

Nevertheless, the recognition of an implied executive nationhood power must now be taken into account to complement any power derived from common law.

**212** Campbell, above n 203, 88, citing *Communist Party* case (1951) 83 CLR 1, 193.
**213** Ibid (emphasis added).
**214** Ibid.
**215** Winterton, above n 43, 29.
**216** Winterton, above n 26, 40.

# IV The changing dimensions of executive power

## 1 The expanding breadth of executive power

The question of 'breadth' is concerned with the limitations placed on the scope of Commonwealth executive power by reference to the federal structure created by the Constitution. Unlike the detailed statement of the heads of Commonwealth legislative power expressly provided for in Chapter I of the Constitution, there is no such clear statement in Chapter II with respect to executive power. But in light of the establishment of responsible government, by which executive power is generally regarded as following legislative power, breadth has generally been determined by reference to the division, or distribution, of legislative powers and responsibilities between the Commonwealth and the States.

As the foregoing discussion suggests, the rise of the implied nationhood power has had implications for both the depth and the breadth of the executive power of the Commonwealth. The question is whether the exceptional nature of this power, and the exceptional circumstances in which it operates, provide sufficient basis for limiting the breadth of the power as appropriate within a federation. If it is indeed the case that the action in issue is *peculiarly* adapted to the government of a nation and can *only* be efficaciously exercised by the *national* government, it can be argued that the power does not undermine the distribution of powers between the Commonwealth and the States. The question, however, is whether this is indeed the case, for the implied power certainly involves a more liberal application of determinations of breadth based explicitly on the subject matters of Commonwealth legislative power.

How precisely breadth may be determined has become a very important question. Winterton was able to say that 'to fix the "breadth" of the executive power of the Commonwealth, that is the subject matters on which it can operate, the High Court has applied the principle that the contours of executive power generally follow those of the legislative power'.[217] He expressly referred to four influential statements by a majority of justices in the *AAP* case: Barwick CJ, Gibbs, Mason and Jacobs J.[218] While Winterton's formulation was consistent with these and other *dicta*, as will be seen, it is possible to perceive certain nuanced differences in some of them which may suggest a wider view of the breadth of the power. Winterton, however, avoided overly dogmatic statements and spoke of 'the contours of executive power *generally*',[219] but always with legislative competence as the referent. And his conception of breadth was comprehensive, taking into account both the Commonwealth's international position as well as its domestic status as the national government. On this view, the subject matters in respect of which Commonwealth executive power can be exercised

**217** Ibid, 30.
**218** Ibid, citing *AAP* case (1975) 134 CLR 338, 362, 396–7, 379, 405–6.
**219** Ibid (emphasis added).

are not limited to those expressly stated in the Constitution. Judicial reasoning had indicated that legislative power extended to matters appropriate to a national government and this could be accommodated, especially when reliance is placed on the incidental power, s 51(xxxix). In the *AAP* case, Mason J influentially suggested that the breadth of the executive power is 'ascertainable from the distribution of powers, more particularly the distribution of legislative powers, effected by the Constitution and the character and status of the Commonwealth as a national government'[220] and that it 'does not reach beyond *the area of responsibilities* allocated to the Commonwealth by the Constitution', determinable by the distribution of legislative powers.[221] For Mason J, the 'scope' of the power is not unlimited, for its 'content' cannot reach beyond 'the areas of responsibility' constitutionally allocated to the Commonwealth (breadth). But while breadth was particularly determined by 'the distribution of legislative powers', it was supplemented by what Mason J called 'the character and status of the Commonwealth as a national government'.[222] Barwick CJ and Gibbs J, however, were more cautious. Barwick CJ said that 'the executive *may* [if depth requirements are satisfied] only do that which has been or could be the subject of valid legislation'.[223] On this view, a precise subject matter of Commonwealth legislative competence would have to be identified and it would be necessary to define or characterise the subject matter of the executive action.[224] Gibbs J stated the position a little more liberally, but essentially in accord with Barwick CJ. He stated: '[the final clause of s 61] limit[s] the power of the Executive and … makes it clear that the Executive cannot act in respect of a matter which falls entirely outside the legislative competence of the Commonwealth.[225] Jacobs J, like Mason J, was more expansive. Referring to the fact that breadth is not limited by the *express* heads of legislative power, Jacobs J pointed to a very broad conception of national power, namely 'all matters which are the concern of Australia as a nation'.[226]

How expansive the executive power can become under these formulas, especially those of Mason and Jacobs JJ, depends not only on the concept of 'nationhood' but also on the existence of the implied *legislative* nationhood power. If the legislative power is limited to the range of powers over foreign affairs and domestic matters conferred by s 51, supported by the incidental power in s 51(xxxix), a more conservative determination of its breadth would result. But if the implied national legislative power is considered to extend beyond this, it not

**220** *AAP* case (1975) 134 CLR 338, 396.
**221** Ibid, 396–7 (emphasis added). For a critique, see Winterton, above n 43, 27–8.
**222** *AAP* case (1975) 134 CLR 338, 396.
**223** Ibid, 362.
**224** As will be seen, in *Williams (No 1)* (2012) 248 CLR 156, 192, French CJ referred to this inquiry as locating the capacity 'in a universe of hypothetical laws'. In a possible sign that the determination of breadth strictly pursuant to legislative subject matter may not long survive, at least in the determination of the ambit of the Commonwealth's *capacities*, he stated that this was 'not a means by which to judge its scope'.
**225** *AAP* case (1975) 134 CLR 338, 379.
**226** Ibid, 405–6.

only undermines the explicit division of legislative powers and responsibilities between the Commonwealth and States but may also have implications for the scope of the executive power. The abiding problem is that, once admitted, it is difficult to be precise about the breadth of the 'nationhood' power and to control its implications.

The problem is well-illustrated by *Pape*. French CJ recognised that the nationhood power in its depth dimension 'has to be capable of serving the proper purposes of a national government'.[227] In then considering the breadth dimension, he stated:

> [T]he exigencies of 'national government' cannot be invoked to set aside the distribution of powers between Commonwealth and States and between the three branches of government for which this *Constitution* provides. ... But to say that is to say no more than that there are *broadly defined* limits to the power which must be respected and applied case by case. As for this case, it is difficult to see how the payment of moneys to taxpayers, as a short-term measure to meet an urgent national economic problem, is in any way an interference with the constitutional distribution of powers.[228]

Here it seems that the breadth dimension is not determined by reference to the subject matters of Commonwealth legislative competence strictly conceived. Rather the limit is stated passively by reference to the *non-interference* with the constitutional distribution of powers, '*broadly defined*'. Whether this constitutes a real step beyond the *AAP* case or is merely a change of emphasis is not certain. However, it does seem to involve a subtle shift toward the view that the determinant of breadth is not whether the executive action comes within an identified subject matter of Commonwealth legislative power, but whether, *because of its unambiguously national character*, it does not *interfere* in a more general (though not precisely specified) way with *the distribution* of powers between Commonwealth and States. The further problem is that if a view is taken as to the unambiguously *national* character of Commonwealth government action, then it may almost automatically follow that it cannot be regarded as undermining the division of powers and responsibilities between the Commonwealth and the States, based on the criterion of *non-interference* with the division of powers and responsibilities, *broadly defined*. The danger here is that the executive power may become self-defining insofar as the breadth requirement is concerned. In the circumstances of the *Pape* case, for example, this would amount to a power, residing with the Executive itself, to determine whether there indeed was a crisis which defined the content of the power and warranted its exercise. In *Pape*, French CJ made reference to the agreed facts relating to the financial crisis, and the precise measures taken by the government, to make the point that these were '*rationally adjudged* as adapted to avoiding or mitigating the adverse effects of the global financial crisis affecting Australia as a whole'.[229] This would

**227** *Pape* (2009) 238 CLR 1, 60.
**228** Ibid, 65–6 (emphasis added).
**229** Ibid, 63–4 (emphasis added).

appear to permit the Commonwealth Executive some scope – how much is not clear – to determine the question whether the circumstances warrant the particular action, so long as its determination is a rational one as adjudged by the Court.[230]

In effect, the reasoning of Gummow, Crennan and Bell JJ in *Pape* was similar, although a precise and particular consideration of breadth is not readily discernible. Initially they appeared to consider that the particular 'spheres of responsibility' vested in the Commonwealth were relevant,[231] but they then seemed to affirm that if executive action satisfies Mason J's test – that it is action which is uniquely appropriate and necessary for the national government to perform to benefit the nation – then its exercise is constitutionally authorised because it is within the spheres of responsibility vested in it without disturbing the division of such responsibilities from a federal perspective.

To the extent (if at all) that this is so, it is a more expansive position than that of the Chief Justice and indeed of Mason J himself. Mason J was very concerned to emphasise that, whatever the depth component of any nationhood power, it was to be strictly limited by the subject matters of legislative competence, including incidentals. But by not emphasising the latter point sufficiently, the plurality judgment suggests that one does not need to ask precisely whether, as discrete questions, depth and breadth have been satisfied. If that is in fact the case, then Winterton's criticisms of the subjectivity of considerations based on 'nationhood' will carry through to questions of *both* breadth and depth. The lack of a clear distinction between these dimensions becomes apparent in their Honours' conclusions:

> [T]hat there is a global financial and economic crisis is not contested in this proceeding. It can hardly be doubted that the current financial and economic crisis concerns Australia as a nation. Determining that there is the need for an immediate fiscal stimulus to the national economy in the circumstances set out above is somewhat analogous to determining a state of emergency in circumstances of a natural disaster. The Executive Government is the arm of government capable of and empowered to respond to a crisis be it war, natural disaster or a financial crisis on the scale here. This power ... in [its] form today in Australia is a power to act on behalf of the federal polity.[232]

Their Honours proceeded to draw analogies with those powers which may arise in (non-financial) emergencies which may be exercised for the protection of the nation, and explained why these lay beyond the power of the States to remedy. 'The point is that only the Commonwealth has the resources to meet the emergency which is presented to it as a nation state by responding on the scale of the Bonus Act'.[233] If that was in fact the case, it would appear that breadth

**230** See the excellent discussion in Peter Hanks, Francis Gordon and Graeme Hill, *Constitutional Law in Australia* (LexisNexis, 3rd ed, 2012) 221.
**231** *Pape* (2009) 238 CLR 1, 83.
**232** Ibid, 89.
**233** Ibid, 91.

considerations are thereby met, ipso facto it would seem. There is no encroachment upon the areas of responsibility of the States.

Is the Court best placed to be the arbiter of this question? Upon which criteria is it making its assessment of the critical matters necessary for its determination – matters which reside more comfortably in the realm of economic analysis as opposed to legal adjudication? It is notable that their Honours did not make reference to, or attempt to extrapolate from, the relevant prerogatives that might have justified the action, such as those relating to insurrection, riot, pestilence and natural emergencies.[234] It is true that they explicitly denied that '*any* subject which the Executive regards as of national interest and concern' would have enlived the incidental legislative power in s 51(xxxix).[235] But this came after they had already determined that the need for an immediate fiscal stimulus to the national economy brought the matter 'within the executive power'.[236] The difficulty is that the initial determination of this key question seemed to depend on the government's own assessment that there was a national crisis, that it was the arm of government best adapted to respond to a crisis or emergency,[237] and that it had the requisite resources to deal with a crisis on such a scale.[238] It is difficult to avoid the conclusion that, at least in these very exceptional circumstances, the Executive is able to assert for itself a kind of self-defining power.

In their dissenting judgment, Hayne and Kiefel JJ made reference to the need to determine the question of breadth by reference to the division of responsibilities between the Commonwealth and the States with legislative power as the referent.[239] And yet, even in their judgment, there was a suggestion that, in certain circumstances, the breadth of the power might exceed the heads of power in s 51, namely: 'to the extent of matters going to the very survival of the polity and a class of matters like national symbols and celebrations, the executive power of the Commonwealth is not bounded by the express grants of legislative power'.[240] In other respects, however, their reasoning emphasised the limits of the Commonwealth's powers and denied that the mere assertion by the Executive, no matter how rational, of the existence of a crisis cannot be determinative of whether the Commonwealth in fact has the constitutional power to respond to it.[241]

Hayne and Kiefel JJ thus did not reject the existence of a nationhood power,[242] but they did express fundamental disquiet with the approach of the majority, particularly as it permitted a broad, inherent executive power, potentially self-defining in both its depth and its breadth.[243] That subjective policy

**234** See also *Burmah Oil Co Ltd v Lord Advocate* [1965] AC 75; Zines, above n 38, 287.
**235** *Pape* (2009) 238 CLR 1, 87 (emphasis added).
**236** Ibid, 89.
**237** Ibid.
**238** Ibid, 91.
**239** Ibid, 124.
**240** Ibid, 103.
**241** Ibid, 123.
**242** Ibid, 121, and using criteria along the lines suggested by Mason J's test: at 116–17.
**243** Ibid, 122–3.

considerations entered into its determination was apparent to them. Although it was undeniable that there was a very serious global financial crisis, even on objective grounds, they were not persuaded that arguments based on the existence of a 'crisis' or an 'emergency' would yield the requisite 'criteria of constitutional validity'. On their view, the argument added up to no more than the proposition '[t]here is a crisis; [and] if the Commonwealth cannot do this, who can?'[244] In their view, such an argument was circular and incapable of yielding legally-discernible criteria for its application:

> What that and similar forms of rhetorical question obscure is a conflation of distinct questions about ends and means ... because the legislative power to enact the Impugned Act is treated as depending upon the execution of a power, said to be implicitly vested by the *Constitution* in the Executive, to meet a national crisis (in this case a financial or economic crisis). But if that is the *end* to which the exercise of power is to be directed, it by no means follows that any and every *means* of achieving that end must be within power. To argue from the existence of an emergency to either a general proposition that the Executive may respond to the crisis in any way it sees fit, or to some more limited proposition that the Executive has power to make this particular response, is circular.[245]

In his dissenting judgment, Heydon J similarly insisted on the need for the Commonwealth to demonstrate that the requirements of Mason J's test were satisfied. Without affirming that the test was necessarily correct, he held that the Commonwealth had not shown that it alone could deal with the crisis and that State powers were insufficient. The Commonwealth, in other words, had failed to establish that there were no practical alternatives.[246] In reasoning in this way, Heydon J remained closest to the orthodox view of the breadth of the power, affirming unambiguously that it is limited in all circumstances by the ambit of Commonwealth legislative competence.[247] Because the creation of a right to receive, and a duty to pay, the stimulus bonuses fell outside the Commonwealth's constitutional spheres of responsibility based on its legislative competence, he concluded that it could not be authorised by s 61.[248] Thus, the executive action was invalid, irrespective of whether it met the depth requirement. On the question of an implied nationhood legislative power, Heydon J took a narrow approach, denying the existence of such a power beyond the express heads of legislative power plus the incidental power in s 51(xxxix),[249] a view in line with that approach preferred by Winterton. His Honour was thus able to keep quite distinct questions relating to breadth from those relating to depth. Such an approach ensures that Commonwealth executive power is limited and is less likely to encroach upon the powers of State Executives. It thus avoids the very expansive potential of the majority reasoning, especially that of the joint majority.

**244** Ibid, 122.
**245** Ibid, 122–3 (emphasis in original).
**246** Ibid, 178–80.
**247** Ibid, 198–9.
**248** Ibid.
**249** Ibid, 169–77.

## 2 The contracting depth of executive power

It is one of the ironies of the Court's jurisprudence in this area that, while the breadth of the executive power has undergone expansion, in two of its most recent judgments, the Court has initiated a remarkable contraction of the depth of the power, at least in relation to the capacity of the Commonwealth to enter contracts and spend money.

In *Williams (No 1)*,[250] the High Court modified the position which, it was assumed, had hitherto applied with respect to the Commonwealth Executive's capacity to enter into contracts and spend. The majority limited the depth of this capacity by permitting only an exempt class of Commonwealth contracts – those contracts which relate, or are incidental, to the ordinary, well-recognised functions of government – to be entered into without prior legislative authorisation. All other Commonwealth contracts would require legislative authorisation. This development was not easily foreseeable given that the capacity to contract and spend was well-established. Whereas it may have been thought that breadth would have been the main issue in this case, it was depth which received the greater attention.

The decision of *Pape* relating to s 81 and the 'nationhood' power was affirmed. The Court in *Williams (No 2)* refused the application by the Commonwealth to reopen *Williams (No 1)*.[251] The *Williams* cases thus affirmed:

(a) that s 81 is the source of a power to appropriate funds, but not to spend, in relation to which another head of power must be found; and
(b) s 61 is a source of inherent executive power based on 'nationhood' considerations, the ambit of its 'maintenance' component being no longer ultimately determinable by the prerogative alone.

*Williams (No 1)* concerned the validity of a Commonwealth agreement with Scripture Union Queensland, under which the Commonwealth paid Scripture Union for the provision of chaplaincy services in Queensland State schools as part of the Commonwealth's National School Chaplaincy Program (NSCP). A majority of French CJ, Gummow, Bell and Crennan JJ[252] held that the Funding Agreement and payments made pursuant to it exceeded the executive power of the Commonwealth and were accordingly invalid, not having been specifically authorised by any relevant statute.[253] It was held to be not sufficient for validity that the Commonwealth had simply been exercising one of its most commonly recognised capacities – to enter into contracts and spend – provided the expenditure was the subject of a valid appropriation for the purposes of s 81. The majority considered that unless the agreement could be shown to belong to a class of exempt contract – those contracts which relate, or are incidental, to

**250** *Williams v Commonwealth (No 1)* (2012) 248 CLR 156.
**251** *Williams v Commonwealth (No 2)* (2014) 309 ALR 41; 88 ALJR 701, 713–14.
**252** *Williams (No 1)* (2012) 248 CLR 156, 184–5, 233–5, 342.
**253** Ibid, 193–4, 224, 241–52, 341, 362.

the ordinary, well-recognised functions of government – specific statutory authorisation was required before the Commonwealth could validly enter into it.

Prior to this case, commentators generally believed that the Commonwealth had the same capacities as a natural person by virtue of its legal personality: the Commonwealth was an emanation of the Crown as a corporation sole and hence had juristic personality.[254] As Evatt J stated in *New South Wales v Bardolph*:

> No doubt the King had special powers, privileges, immunities and prerogatives. But he never seems to have been regarded as being less powerful to enter into contracts than one of his subjects.[255]

On this broad view, the Commonwealth, like a natural person, has a capacity to enter and execute contracts for essentially any purpose. In addition to the fundamental requirement that any expenditure by the Commonwealth must be validly appropriated, the only significant qualification on the Commonwealth's contracting and spending powers was that the subject matter of the contract must fall within the Commonwealth's legislative responsibilities. This reasonably settled view was given confident expression in the 1987 Report of the Advisory Committee to the Constitutional Commission when it was stated, with little controversy, that the ambit of s 61 'is confined to that conferred by the common law or "prerogative" powers of the Crown'.[256] The limits to the power existed, rather, in the breadth dimension: the 'High Court has clearly established, at least as a general principle, that Commonwealth executive power is confined to the topics of Commonwealth legislative power'.[257]

Accordingly, on the view which hitherto prevailed, if the subject matter of the Funding Agreement was within Commonwealth legislative competence, the Commonwealth could validly enter into such an agreement without statutory authorisation provided the relevant funds had been validly appropriated. As Zines put it: '[t]he legislative and executive powers were regarded as riding in tandem'.[258]

There were also two issues relating to government contracts which had arisen prior to *Williams (No 1)* which did not affect these general propositions about the capacities of the Crown in right of the Commonwealth. The first was whether restrictions ought to apply to those contracts which were not in the ordinary course of government administration, were of exceptional character, or involved

**254** See Zines, above n 92, 348–9; Zines, above n 38, 283; Geoffrey Lindell, 'The Changed Landscape of the Executive Power of the Commonwealth after the *Williams* Case' (2012) 39 *Monash University Law Review* 1, 14 n 58.

**255** (1934) 52 CLR 455, 475. See, further, William Maitland, 'The Crown as Corporation' in H A L Fisher (ed), *The Collected Papers of Frederic William Maitland* (1911) vol 3, 244; Ernst H Kantorowicz, *The King's Two Bodies: A Study in Mediaeval Political Theology* (1957).

**256** See Advisory Committee on Executive Government, *Report of the Advisory Committee on Executive Government* (1987) 55. The term 'prerogative' was used in the broad, Diceyan sense.

**257** Ibid, 52. Eg, *AAP Case* (1975) 134 CLR 338, 379.

**258** Zines, above n 92, 379.

the grant of money or proprietary rights. In light of the difficulties involved in determining what is in the ordinary course of government administration, and the uncertainty which thereby arises for parties seeking to enter into agreements with the Commonwealth, the view that these kinds of contracts should be distinguished did not prevail.[259] Zines queried whether it was an appropriate judicial function to distinguish what is 'normal' government business from that which is 'extraordinary'.

> What activities the government should engage in is the province of the executive. What is normal or not will depend partly on what policies and activities have in the past been pursued and for what length of the time. Why should this matter to the issue of whether parliamentary authorisation is needed?[260]

The second issue was whether the power of the Commonwealth to enter into contracts was to be limited by the federal distribution of powers. That it should not be so limited was a view espoused by Campbell and Winterton on the basis that rights and duties created by contract do not arise from the exercise of governmental powers.[261] This view did not gain judicial support, the above-mentioned position in the *AAP* case prevailing.

These two issues aside, it was the 'common assumption', as it came to be called, that became the focus of attention in *Williams (No 1)*. In its broader manifestation, it resembled the position taken by Campbell and Winterton in relation to Commonwealth contracting, namely that the Commonwealth's capacity to contract and spend is not limited by reference to the subject matters of the Commonwealth's legislative competence. No member of the Court accepted this proposition and it is unlikely that the proposition will prevail in the future. In its narrower manifestation the 'common assumption' seemed settled and uncontroversial: the Commonwealth had the capacity to contract and spend if the subject matter of the contract came within Commonwealth legislative competence so that, potentially, Parliament could legislate to authorise the contract. Prior to *Williams (No 1)* this narrower formulation seemed settled and uncontroversial. All parties, in both written and initial oral submissions, were agreed about it.[262] However, despite this consensus about the 'common assumption', the majority in *Williams (No 1)* took the highly unexpected course of rejecting it in both its broader and narrower manifestations. Given that the contracts in issue were not authorised by Commonwealth legislation, the majority held that entry into the contracts and the expenditure of the funding would be regarded as a valid exercise of executive power only if it was:

**259** Ibid, 349. This view has been criticised: see Enid Campbell, 'Commonwealth Contracts' (1970) 44 *Australian Law Journal* 14, 14–16.
**260** Zines, above n 92, 350.
**261** Campbell, above n 259, 14; Winterton, above n 26, 44–7.
**262** *Williams (No 1)* (2012) 248 CLR 156, 295.

(a) required for, or incidental to, the carrying out of the ordinary and well-recognised functions of government;[263] or
(b) authorised by the implied nationhood power.[264]

While these difficulties will now have to be navigated by the Commonwealth and those who contract with it, there remains the question: Why was the common assumption rejected? It was an assumption which was supported by the drafting history of s 61 – at least on what might be regarded as the more likely reading – as well as by the views of the early commentators, including Attorneys-General. It appears to have been an underlying assumption in a number of decisions of the High Court. In *HIH Claims Support Ltd v Insurance Australia Ltd*,[265] for example, the Commonwealth provided financial assistance to beneficiaries of insurance policies in circumstances where the insurer had become insolvent. In *Davis v Commonwealth*,[266] it was held that the Commonwealth could incorporate a company to celebrate the Bicentenary. In *Johnson v Kent*,[267] the Commonwealth was held to have validly exercised its executive power to construct a tower upon land which it owned. Although this was held to be an exercise of 'prerogative', it could perhaps be more precisely defined as an exercise of a capacity which the Commonwealth had as the proprietor of land. And in the early case of *Clough v Leahy*,[268] it was held that the Commonwealth, without further statutory authorisation, has the capacity to conduct an inquiry in the same way as a natural person, though it could not compel witnesses or the production of documents.[269] On the common assumption, it was never proposed that the exercise of such powers was unbounded. For one thing, the Parliament controlled the purse-strings by virtue of its power over appropriations, which remain a necessary pre-condition before the Commonwealth can embark on activities and transactions involving the expenditure of funds from Consolidated Revenue. Moreover, Parliament could always regulate the Executive's exercise of its capacities within the Commonwealth's legislative responsibilities by enacting suitable legislation. In addition, both houses of Parliament have the capacity to undertake inquiries into government expenditure and administration, thereby exercising supervisory control over them.

Part of the difficulty lies in the distinction between the prerogatives and capacities of the Crown. If the framers are taken to have affirmed that the common law powers of the Crown, generically understood, were incorporated into s 61, then it would follow that they expected both the capacities and the prerogatives

**263** Ibid, 179–80, 216–17; 233–4, 236–9; 353–5. The precise reasoning of the majority differs in a number of respects and the author is grateful for the assistance provided by Professor Geoffrey Lindell in discussion and in having been granted access to a draft of his published article, G Lindell, above n 254. On the ratio of the case, see Lindell's analysis at 13–14, 300.
**264** *Williams (No 1)* (2012) 284 CLR 156, 179–80, 216–17, 238, 348.
**265** (2011) 244 CLR 72, 78, 79.
**266** (1988) 166 CLR 79.
**267** (1975) 132 CLR 164.
**268** (1904) 2 CLR 139.
**269** Although see Aroney, above n 113, as to whether this was in fact regarded as an exercise of a capacity or was more appropriately to be regarded as an exercise of the prerogative (in the narrow sense).

of the Crown to be included, *both* sharing the principal characteristic of being exercisable absent legislation: a quality of the power which was not diminished by incorporation in s 61. Alternatively, it is not unlikely that the framers were influenced by Dicey's usage, in which the term 'prerogative' subsumes what are otherwise referred to as 'capacities'.[270] To the extent this is so, when the framers referred to the prerogative, they did so in its wider sense as embracing the capacities as well. Moreover, in Dicey's analysis, the most significant criterion by which the prerogative (in the wide sense) was to be identified was not whether these common law powers were unique to the Crown or exercisable in common with other legal persons, but rather, that they could be exercised by the Crown *without statutory authorisation*.

With this in mind, the common assumption may have been better formulated thus, adopting the words of Deakin in the *Vondel* opinion:

> What is clear is that *in all matters within the scope of the legislative power* of the Commonwealth, its executive possesses *all the powers of the Crown* properly exercisable within the Commonwealth.[271]

Notably, Deakin did not say that the Commonwealth Executive had a power, in the absence of legislation, to do what the Commonwealth legislature could authorise it to do by enacting legislation. For what it could do without legislation was determined by separate reference to the 'powers of the Crown' as incorporated in s 61. Thus, if the principal definitional discrimen was that those powers could be exercised without statutory authorisation, including the capacity to contract and spend, then it must necessarily share that quality. Persistence with this usage would reinforce Heydon J's dissenting reasoning in *Williams (No 1)* which accepted the correctness of the common assumption: one could not reject the manifestation of the common assumption as it applied to contracts without explaining how, in a legal sense, this could be reconciled with the common assumption writ large.

If the 'common assumption' was so settled, why did the majority in *Williams (No 1)* reject it? Several considerations were relevant.[272]

### Text, history and structure

The general textual and historical considerations relevant to determining the scope of the executive power were canvassed in Part II above. In the judgments of French CJ in the majority and Heydon J in dissent, historical considerations loomed especially large. On Heydon J's analysis, Griffith's explanation that the revised wording of the clause that became s 61 did not 'alter its intention' constituted evidence that the 'contemporary meaning' of the words

**270** Dicey's usage was adopted throughout Winterton's seminal text, above n 26. See also Winterton, above n 43.
**271** Alfred Deakin, above n 73, 129, 131–2 (emphasis added).
**272** The following discussion draws on Nicholas Aroney, 'The High Court on Constitutional Law – The 2012 Term: Explanatory Power and the Modalities of Constitutional Reasoning' (2013) 36 *University of New South Wales Law Journal* 863, 877–91.

'execution … of the laws of the Commonwealth' used in s 61 included all matters on which Commonwealth legislative power might be exercised, *even though it had not been exercised*, subject to the stated exception.[273] In response, French CJ drew attention to the exact wording of s 61, including its predecessors in the drafting stage. In his view, the amended clause 'did not, in terms or by any stretch of the textual analysis, describe an executive power to do *any act* dealing with the subject matter falling within a head of Commonwealth legislative power'.[274] This is likely the case. However, the more fundamental issue was not whether the Executive could do *any* act, but rather whether it could only undertake such action permitted it by the prerogative so long as it falls within legislative competence. An affirmative response to the latter question arguably has a stronger basis in the historical record of the drafting of s 61. French CJ also drew attention to aspects of the legislative history to which Heydon J did not refer, such as Edmund Barton's view that, apart from the prerogative, the executive power would include a category of activities in which the Executive would have to 'act in Council', which he described as the 'offspring of statutes',[275] and the view of Inglis Clark that that executive power is primarily a power to enforce the law, and only secondarily includes 'the discretionary power of the Crown within the Commonwealth'.[276]

Despite the importance of the textual and historical arguments, there was a sense in which the Court regarded them as insufficient to resolve the question before it. The text of s 61 does not address the question directly. The historical evidence, while capable of competing interpretation, may indicate that the framers did envisage the existence of non-statutory executive power residing in the Commonwealth based on the common law powers of the Crown, including both prerogatives and capacities. It was, nevertheless, necessary for the Court to consider other forms of argument. As a consequence, prominent in the majority judgments were structural arguments concerning the balance of power between the Commonwealth and the States, and the relationship between the Executive and the Parliament. As was noted in Chapter 3, French CJ opened his reasoning with the proposition that the central purpose of the Constitution was to establish 'a truly federal government', the 'essential and distinctive feature' of which would be 'the preservation of the separate existence and corporate life of each of the component States of the commonwealth' while at the same time securing the capacity of the Commonwealth to operate as a real 'government', whose laws would be enforced directly and effectively in each State.[277] These statements were concerned with the distribution of powers between the Commonwealth and the States, but the majority judgments drew attention to the

**273** *Williams (No 1)* (2012) 248 CLR 156, 197, citing *Convention Debates, Sydney* (1891) 777–8.
**274** *Williams (No 1)* (2012) 284 CLR 156, 197–8 (emphasis added).
**275** *Convention Debates, Adelaide* (1897) 910; *Williams (No 1)* (2012) 284 CLR 156, 198.
**276** Inglis Clark, above n 2, 38, 64, cited in *Williams (No 1)* (2012) 284 CLR 156, 199.
**277** *Williams (No 1)* (2012) 248 CLR 156, 178, citing Inglis Clark, *Studies in Australian Constitutional Law* (1901), 12–13.

way in which the Parliament plays an important role in the supervision and control of Commonwealth activities and the equally important role of the Senate, as representative of the peoples of the States, in this supervisory process.

In their majority judgments, Gummow and Bell JJ and Hayne J, as well as French CJ, placed emphasis on the role of the Senate as an essential element of the constitutional system of parliamentary supremacy over the Executive. Here the argument was that a broad executive capacity to enter contracts and spend money on any topic within Commonwealth legislative power but without specific statutory authorisation would mean that the only supervisory role of the Parliament would be to appropriate the necessary funds. However, the power of the Senate over appropriation laws is limited: it cannot initiate or amend them; it can only suggest amendments or refuse to pass them in their entirety (s 53). But if, in addition to appropriation, separate legislation authorising expenditure is required, then a fuller, co-ordinate role for the Senate is maintained, for the consent of the Senate is usually required for the passage of ordinary legislation.[278] As the Chief Justice put it:

> A Commonwealth Executive with a general power to deal with matters of Commonwealth legislative competence is in tension with the federal conception which informed the function of the Senate as a necessary organ of Commonwealth legislative power. It would undermine parliamentary control of the executive branch and weaken the role of the Senate.[279]

Another structural argument concerned the capacity of the Commonwealth to make grants to the States (s 96). Here the majority considered that if the Commonwealth were able to make grants to any person or body simply through the exercise of an inherent capacity to spend money, this would render s 96 otiose. For although s 96 has received an expansive interpretation by the Court enabling the Commonwealth to use it to shape State policy in fields lying outside of the Commonwealth's legislative competence, the majority pointed out that it operates only through the States' acceptance of funding on the terms and conditions proposed by the Commonwealth.[280] The weaker financial position of the States means that they may be pressured into accepting the Commonwealth's proposals in relation to matters falling outside the Commonwealth's legislative powers. However, the Commonwealth must still rely on their agreement. This gives the States at least some negotiating capacity. By contrast, when the Commonwealth uses the 'incidental' power in s 51(xxxix) to enact a law to support a scheme that involves the expenditure of money by the Executive under s 61, the law that has been enacted '*demands* obedience'.[281] As the majority pointed out, the coercive nature of the Commonwealth law therefore potentially triggers the application of the *Melbourne Corporation* principle to protect the constitutional

**278** That is, apart from joint sittings under s 57.
**279** *Williams (No 1)* (2012) 248 CLR 156, 205.
**280** Ibid, 234, 235–6, 267–8, 346–7, 373.
**281** Ibid, 276, [248] (emphasis in original).

integrity and autonomy of the States.[282] Interpreting the executive power narrowly is accordingly to be preferred, they concluded, because it coheres with these aspects of the federal design and interpretation of the Constitution. As Mason J had observed in the *AAP* case:

> [the] presence [of s 96] confirms what is otherwise deducible from the Constitution, that is, that the executive power is not unlimited and that there is a very large area of activity which lies outside the executive power of the Commonwealth but which may become the subject of conditions attached to grants under s 96.[283]

Against these structural arguments, Heydon J responded by highlighting the role that the Senate can still play in the legislative consideration of appropriations through its power to suggest amendments and, subject to the possibility of a double dissolution and joint sitting under s 57, refuse to pass an appropriation bill.[284] He could also emphasise the fact that far from being a provision that constrains the Commonwealth and protects the States, s 96 confers a power on the Commonwealth to exercise very substantial influence over State policy by offering necessary financial resources to the States on conditions which they may not be in a position to refuse.[285]

**Assumptions, precedents and doctrine**

Arguments from the structure of the Constitution can assist in the interpretation of ambiguous provisions, but they are not necessarily decisive. In *Williams (No 1)* it was also necessary for members of the Court to grapple with the relevant decided cases. Faced with a long-standing practice by the Commonwealth to assume the existence of a general capacity to contract and spend, and an array of cases in which statements had been made which seemed to support the 'common assumption' to this effect, the majority in *Williams* downplayed the force of the case-law by identifying precisely what had been said in the previous cases and limiting their authority to those reasons that were strictly necessary for the resolution of the exact issues before the Court. The essential point made by the majority was that in no previous decision had a clear majority of the Court unambiguously supported the unqualified proposition that the Commonwealth's power to contract and spend extends to matters about which the Commonwealth is empowered to legislate. Early decisions, such as *Wooltops*,[286] *Australian Shipping Board*[287] and *Colonial Ammunition*,[288] were referred to as

**282** See *Melbourne Corporation v Commonwealth* (1947) 74 CLR 31 and, in particular, *Austin v Commonwealth* (2003) 215 CLR 185, 220, 269, 298.

**283** *Victoria v Commonwealth and Hayden* (1975) 134 CLR 338, 398. See also *Attorney-General (Vic); Ex rel Dale v Commonwealth* (1945) 71 CLR 237, 266, 282. On Mason J's observations about the Commonwealth's power to spend, see *Victoria v Commonwealth and Hayden* (1975) 134 CLR 338, 395, discussed in Cheryl Saunders, 'The Development of the Commonwealth Spending Power' (1977–8) 11 *Melbourne University Law Review* 369, 374.

**284** *Williams (No 1)* (2012) 248 CLR 156, 316–17.

**285** Ibid, 347–8.

**286** *Commonwealth v Colonial Combing, Spinning & Weaving Co Ltd* (1922) 31 CLR 421.

**287** *Commonwealth v Australian Commonwealth Shipping Board* (1926) 39 CLR 1.

**288** *Commonwealth v Colonial Ammunition Co Ltd* (1924) 34 CLR 198.

instances where the power to engage in contractual relations without statutory authority had actually been denied,[289] and two other decisions could be cited as examples where the existence of legislation was considered to be an essential prerequisite to the exercise of executive power in the circumstances.[290]

Other important cases, however, provided support for the common assumption. In *New South Wales v Bardolph*,[291] for example, the High Court had held that a State Government could, without prior parliamentary appropriation, enter into a binding contract for the expenditure of money. The majority considered that this case could be limited to its specific facts, primarily because it was concerned with the States, which have 'unitary' constitutions, unlike the 'federal' nature of the Commonwealth.[292] Some of the judgments in the *Pharmaceutical Benefits* case[293] also posed problems. However, the majority sought to show that the opinions expressed in that case were diverse and were in any event specifically concerned with the interpretation of the words 'purposes of the Commonwealth' in s 81 rather than the meaning and scope of the executive power in s 61.[294] There were also the statements made by Barwick CJ, Gibbs, Mason and Jacobs JJ in the *AAP* case discussed above[295] which tended towards a wide view of the executive power. The majority characterised these statements as merely *obiter dicta* and interpreted them narrowly.[296]

In his dissenting judgment, Heydon J responded that the common assumption about the scope of the executive power was so widely acknowledged in the cases and learned commentary that it should be 'treated as law'.[297] Read as abstract statements of principle, the passages in the various cases and commentaries certainly seemed to speak for themselves, and his Honour reproduced them with little commentary or gloss in his judgment.[298] He also drew attention to several statements that were not addressed by the majority,[299] and in response to those statements that were cited by the majority to support their conclusions, Heydon J pointed out that these were 'obscure' and could be distinguished.[300] On his analysis, there were peculiarities in the facts of the apparently contrary cases which enabled them to be sufficiently distinguishable so as to make them not contrary to the 'common assumption' in its narrower formulation. In referring to so many statements in favour of the common assumption, including

**289** *Williams (No 1)* (2012) 248 CLR 156, 188, 207–8, 230; see also 257, 364, 369–70, 373–4.
**290** *Attorney-General (Vic) v Commonwealth* (1935) 52 CLR 533; *Australian Woollen Mills Pty Ltd v Commonwealth* (1954) 92 CLR 424, discussed in *Williams (No 1)* (2012) 284 CLR 156, 211, 236.
**291** (1934) 52 CLR 455.
**292** *Williams (No 1)* (2012) 248 CLR 156, 211–13, 345, 353–4; see also 224–5, 369.
**293** *Attorney-General (Vic); Ex rel Dale v Commonwealth* (1945) 71 CLR 237.
**294** *Williams (No 1)* (2012) 284 CLR 156, 246–7, 363, 370–71.
**295** *Victoria v Commonwealth and Hayden* (1975) 134 CLR 338.
**296** *Williams (No 1)* (2012) 284 CLR 156, 188, 229–30, 356–7; see also 247–8, 364.
**297** Ibid, 319.
**298** Ibid, 301–8, 308–12.
**299** Eg: *Attorney-General (Vic) v Commonwealth* (1935) 52 CLR 533, 567; *Barton v Commonwealth* (1974) 131 CLR 477, 498; *Ansett Transport Industries (Operations) Pty Ltd v Commonwealth* (1977) 139 CLR 54, 61, 113; *Western Australia v Ward* (2002) 213 CLR 1, 391; see *Williams (No 1)* (2012) 248 CLR 156, 301, 302, 307, 308.
**300** *Williams (No 1)* (2012) 284 CLR 156, 314.

sources not addressed by the majority, the explanatory power of Heydon J's reasoning gained significant ground. The principal weakness in the argument from the authorities, however, was that, as his Honour acknowledged, the statements were generally in the nature of *obiter*.[301] The case therefore had to turn on more than doctrine alone. For it was arguable that the 'commonness' of the common assumption explained why there had never been a conclusive, authoritative statement affirming it. The principle was such a fundamental constitutional principle that it did not need explicit affirmation.

### Critical reception of the decision

The decision in *Williams (No 1)* has received a mixed reception from commentators. On one hand, the case suggests the possibility of a remarkable shift in the High Court's approach to the federal nature of the Constitution, at least in relation to the ambit of the executive power. The 'common assumption' – that at the least the Commonwealth could contract and spend money within its areas of legislative competence without specific statutory warrant – certainly placed limits on the Commonwealth by reference to the federal distribution of legislative powers. But by insisting on the need for specific authorising legislation for contracting and spending, the decision in *Williams (No 1)* placed an even more exacting limitation on its powers. The Commonwealth was forced to enact general legislation to authorise its expenditure across a whole array of matters but, as was seen in Chapter 3, in *Williams (No 2)* this was struck down in its operation in respect of the funding of the Chaplaincy Program. As a consequence, the Commonwealth had to enter into negotiations with the States about the continuing operation and funding of the program through grants under s 96. In this last respect, *Williams (No 1)* does seem to have bolstered the position of the States in relation to the Commonwealth. However, the fact that the Senate very readily passed the remedial legislation suggests that while the decision certainly placed the Senate in a position to block such legislation, the realities of Australian politics meant that very little actual deliberation was undertaken into the merits of Commonwealth spending in such a wide array of matters.

In relation to the s 96 issues, it has been argued that any undermining of the States' negotiating position is more a result of vertical fiscal imbalance in the Commonwealth, facilitated by the High Court's interpretation of that section. That being the case, it has been asked whether a reformulation of the Commonwealth's contractual capacity should be considered a suitable remedy for this situation. Similarly, it has been argued that French CJ's concern that the maintenance of an expansive Commonwealth contracting power may diminish the powers of the States, 'seems to represent an attempt … impliedly [to] reserve state executive powers even though such a method of interpretation is not permissible with legislative powers'.[302] And in relation to the considerations

**301** Ibid, 301.
**302** Lindell, above n 254, 370.

relating to the Senate's power in reviewing Commonwealth contracting, it has been asked 'whether it is for the courts to remedy perceived deficiencies in the way the Parliament has been constituted'.[303]

Beyond these questions, an observer of the proceedings would have been struck by the shifting in the position of the parties after oral hearing had commenced when it emerged that the common assumption would come into question.[304] This '*great renversement des alliances*', as Heydon J put it,[305] left the Commonwealth with the unexpected imperative to defend the common assumption; yet, it would seem, without the benefit of clear submissions from the other parties. It has been suggested that as a result of these shifts – 'puzzling, sudden and unexpected'[306] – that the Commonwealth was not given proper opportunity to prepare argument in support of the common assumption. In this respect, Heydon J drew attention to the considerable support for the common assumption in academic commentary,[307] thus highlighting the significance of the change effected by the majority decision. Heydon J asked: 'Is the Common Assumption in truth so wrong as a matter of principle as distinct from authority that the authorities supporting it should be overruled?'[308] In his view it was not appropriate to address such a question in circumstances where the submissions relating to it 'betrayed signs of disorganisation'.[309] He continued:

> It is important that points of fundamental significance such as the one that this case belatedly raised be pondered by counsel for years – as they often are when appeals come to this court – or at least for months – as is usual when matters in the original jurisdiction are brought to the Full Court. Above all, they need to be considered calmly. Radical changes in the construction of the Constitution should not be made without better assistance than the unpredicted conspiracy of circumstances permitted counsel to provide in this case.[310]

His Honour further noted, perhaps complained, that attention focused 'on what Winterton called the "breadth" element in s 61, and distracted from the "depth" element'. 'No attention', Heydon J continued, 'was given to the "depth" element before the *renversement des alliances*, and very little after it'.[311]

Given the circumstances in which *Williams (No 1)* was decided, in *Williams (No 2)* the Commonwealth submitted that the issue should be reopened. However, these submissions were rejected. The majority in the second case observed that the Commonwealth's arguments nevertheless 'stopped well short'

**303** Ibid, 372.
**304** *Williams (No 1)* (2012) 284 CLR 156, 180.
**305** Ibid, 304.
**306** Lindell, above n 254, 7.
**307** *Williams (No 1)* (2012) 284 CLR 156, 301–13
**308** Ibid, 329.
**309** This was further hampered by the urgent litigation which came before the Court at the same time relating to the government's asylum seeker policy, 'The Malaysia Solution' (*Plaintiff M70/2011 v Minister for Immigration and Citizenship* (2011) 244 CLR 144) and which 'must have depleted the relevant resources of Commonwealth energy and distracted those who were to tap them': Ibid, 329.
**310** *Williams (No 1)* (2012) 284 CLR 156, 329–30.
**311** Ibid, 330–31.

of suggesting that the original decision was made 'in ignorance of any relevant legal argument or decision' or 'want of procedural fairness'. That there were 'deficiencies' in the way the original case was decided was rejected.[312]

Heydon J referred to the need for fundamental questions such as the one addressed in *Williams (No 1)* to be 'considered calmly' and 'pondered' upon over periods of time. Since the decision was brought down, academic commentators, reflecting upon the practical and technical implications of the decision, have drawn attention to further potential problems with the decision. One of these criticisms is that the exception the majority recognised concerning the ordinary and well-recognised functions of government may prove to be very difficult to apply in practice. It would appear that contracts which relate to the administration of departments under s 64 of the Constitution would pass the test.[313] Beyond this, however, the situation is very uncertain. Lindell has asked, for example, whether a contract to buy new submarines would need further and specific statutory authorisation.[314] Would such a contract be treated differently to a new contract to develop alternative and solar sources of energy?

> Would those examples and others require the Court to inquire into whether functions fulfilled by these contracts are truly governmental from those that are not and thus require judges to expose their own subjective values and views on the role of government – something they have tried to avoid in the past ... .[315]

As Campbell once remarked, albeit in a slightly different context:

> How is a court to adjudge whether a contract is made 'in the ordinary course of government administration'? Equally important, how can a party negotiating with the Crown be sure whether the proposed contract will be valid?[316]

That the majority treated the implied nationhood power as an exception to the rule in *Williams (No 1)* suggests that that aspect of the Court's expansionist jurisprudence concerning the Commonwealth's executive power will be allowed to continue uncontrolled by the requirement of statutory authorisation.

Another line of academic criticism has concerned the conceptual and practical problems which the majority regarded as undermining the common assumption. In *Williams (No 1)*, French CJ stated that there is a qualitative difference between legislative and executive power: the subject matters of Commonwealth legislative power are there for the purpose of determining the validity of Commonwealth laws, he said, and 'not to give content to the executive power'.[317] In his view, the common assumption called for the validity of executive action to be tested by reference to 'hypothetical laws'.[318] While the first part of the statement

**312** *Williams (No 2)* (2014) 309 ALR 41; 88 ALJR 701, 713–14, 718.
**313** *Williams (No 1)* (2012) 284 CLR 156, 193 and 217–18. See Lindell, above n 254, 25.
**314** Lindell, above n 254, 25–6.
**315** Ibid.
**316** Campbell, above n 259, 14–16, quoted in Lindell, above n 254, 20–21.
**317** (2012) 248 CLR 156, 187.
**318** Ibid, 192.

is unexceptionable, the second has not been without its critics. In the words of Lindell, it 'asserts what with respect needs to be substantiated'.[319] Despite the difficulties, it is a determination which can be made. This is particularly so because one fundamental consequence of responsible government must be that the legislative power leads the executive; that legislative and executive power coincide to the extent that it is possible for the legislature to make laws controlling executive power. In the final analysis, executive power must not be permitted to extend beyond the ability of the legislature to control it. Moreover, it is unavoidable that, in a system which adopts responsible government, resort must be had to considerations based on the ambit of federal legislative powers to determine the subject matters in relation to which executive action can be taken. In any event, the determination is manageable. Lindell, for example, has suggested that the inquiry can be undertaken:

> by concentrating on the activity undertaken by the Executive and the documentation it has used to describe that activity. The question would then be posed whether the Parliament could use its legislative powers to authorise the Executive to undertake that activity.[320]

The majority, however, suggested that the common assumption involved an unworkable formula because it required the Court to determine whether the Commonwealth had the legislative competence to provide statutory authorisation to enable it to legislate with respect to the subject matter of a contract. However, it has been pointed out that this did not appear to have caused previous courts and, indeed, the minority justices in the case, such a difficulty as to warrant the rejection of the formula. There appear to have been two limbs to the majority's objection: the first was that some of the Commonwealth's legislative powers – eg, marriage and divorce, bankruptcy and insolvency, taxation – do not lend themselves, easily or at all, to a determination of the ambit of related executive power.[321] Lindell, however, has responded by pointing to specific examples where such determinations can sensibly be made.[322] But Lindell's objection was more fundamental. The broader limb of the majority's objection, as articulated by French CJ, was this:

> [The application of the common assumption] invites the Court to determine whether there is an hypothetical law which could validly authorise or require contractual or spending activity by the Commonwealth. The location of the contractual capacity of the Commonwealth in a universe of hypothetical laws which would, if enacted, support its exercise, is not a means by which to judge its scope.[323]

Despite the criticisms advanced by the majority, the efficacy of the common assumption also received support from the judgments of Hayne and Kiefel JJ

**319** Lindell, above n 254, 22 n 104.
**320** Ibid, 22.
**321** *Williams (No 1)* (2012) 284 CLR 156, 192, 232.
**322** Lindell, above n 254, 22.
**323** *Williams (No 1)* (2012) 284 CLR 156, 192.

in the case. Accepting the correctness of the assumption for the sake of argument, although they found that the Funding Agreement could not have been authorised by a Commonwealth law, whether pursuant to s 51(xx), the corporations power, or s 51(xxiiiA) with respect to 'benefits to students', they at least showed that it could sensibly be applied to the circumstances of the case. In his dissenting judgment, on the other hand, Heydon J found the funding agreement to be valid because its subject matter came within s 51(xxiiiA). On this view, 'benefits to students' extended to the funding of services delivered by persons other than the Commonwealth itself, and was not limited to the supply of goods or services for which students would otherwise have to pay.[324] The chaplaincy and counselling services for which the agreement provided were of the relevant type.[325] Heydon J's reasoning thus went some way to counter the objection that the common assumption requires the Court to divine the content of hypothetical laws. It suggested that the common assumption and depth/breadth analysis may be capable of yielding sensible results consistent with what had hitherto been regarded as constitutional orthodoxy. At the least, the difficulties which may be involved in measuring executive action by reference to the Commonwealth's legislative powers may well prove no less demanding than the difficulties involved in identifying those governmental activities that are incidental to the carrying out of the ordinary functions of government. By emphasising the importance of the breadth element to s 61 executive power, it was able to accommodate federal concerns and thus differentiate the executive power which resides in the Commonwealth, as the polity created by the Constitution, from the power of the British Executive which operates in a unitary system.

He also made reference to earlier statements of the majority justices in previous cases suggestive of support for the common assumption. He quoted Gummow J's question in the argument in *Pape*:

> Why should not the newly created polity the Commonwealth of Australia have received all the executive capacities of the United Kingdom executive save in so far as it is necessary to give effect to the interests of the States under federal considerations?[326]

Whether such considerations will result in a re-evaluation by the Court of the position adopted, only time will tell. The clear indications from *Williams (No 2)* are that the position will stand.

### Fundamental grounds and wider consequences of the decision

The decision in *Williams (No 1)* represents a fundamental reconfiguration of the Court's treatment of the executive power of the Commonwealth in relation to the exercise of its common law 'capacities'. As such, the decision can be seen as

**324** Ibid, 328–9.
**325** It is not the point of this chapter to examine the interpretation of particular heads of legislative power. In any event, these are discussed in Lindell, above n 254, 9–13. Lindell prefers the interpretation of Heydon J in respect to s 51(xxiiiA).
**326** *Williams (No 1)* (2012) 284 CLR 156, 330.

the most recent in a line of cases in which the Court has gradually shifted from a conception of the executive power as grounded in the concept of the Crown as a juristic person to a conception of the executive power as one of three basic types of governmental power distributed among the three branches of government. Examined closely, the position adopted by the majority was not so much to reject outright the notion that the Commonwealth has legal personality but rather to reject the view that its capacities can simply be equated with the capacities of a natural person. French CJ stated that it is 'an error to treat the Commonwealth Executive as a separate juristic person'.[327] For him the executive power of the Commonwealth must be understood as 'that power exercised by the Commonwealth as a polity through the executive branch of its government'.[328] In other words, the relevant juristic personality is that of the Commonwealth, which includes its executive, legislative and judicial branches. In any examination of the capacities of the Executive, its relationship in particular to the legislative branch is a most relevant consideration. In the words of French CJ, '[t]he character of the Executive Government as a branch of the national polity is relevant to the relationship between the power of that branch and the powers and functions of the legislative branch … '.[329]

That the majority did not deny that the Executive branch nonetheless retains some capacities which it may have in common with natural persons seems to be clearly indicated by French CJ's unequivocal affirmation that the executive power 'extends to: ... powers defined by the capacities of the Commonwealth common to legal persons'.[330] The point, rather, is that these capacities cannot simply be *equated* with those of natural persons. The fundamental reason for this appears to be that when the government exercises a capacity that it shares with natural persons, the substantial effect and significance of the activity is qualitatively different. As Winterton observed, 'governmental action is inherently different from private action. Governmental action inevitably has a far greater impact on individual liberties, and this affects its character'.[331] Concerns about the regulative and coercive implications of government action have led to suggestions by commentators that executive capacities should be exercised only with statutory authorisation. However, these suggestions appear to have been limited to those precise circumstances where the action is not authorised by the prerogative (in the narrow sense) and where the liberty of the individual may be affected.[332] Moreover, difficulties may arise in determining the sufficiency of the similarity between action undertaken by government and the same action undertaken by private persons.[333] Prior to *Williams (No 1)*, these suggestions had not been adopted in any decision mandating an additional requirement that the

**327** Ibid, 184.
**328** Ibid.
**329** Ibid.
**330** Ibid, 184.
**331** Ibid, 193, 213–14, 352. See also Zines, above n 92, 357.
**332** Zines, above n 92, 357.
**333** Ibid, 355–7. See also Zines, above n 38, 284.

capacity be exercised only when authorised by legislation.[334] And in *Williams (No 1)* the requirement of legislative authorisation was not limited to coercive laws.

Supporting the wider view that Commonwealth contracting and spending must be authorised by legislation, the majority pointed out that the Commonwealth differs from the Crown in the United Kingdom in that it was created by the Constitution and was not like a natural person in that respect.[335] They noted that public money is different from private money in that it can only be used for governmental purposes.[336] They also observed that the regulatory oversight offered by the law of contract is designed to address dealings between individuals, not governments and individuals.[337] The most important drift in the majority reasoning was, however, away from an examination of the capacities of 'the Crown' – which may entail a treatment of the matter similar to that which would occur in the United Kingdom – towards a conceptualisation of the capacities of the Commonwealth as a polity or body politic which operates *through* the executive and other branches of its government. Contrary to the older conception of the king as a 'corporation sole', which supported the idea that the king, in his natural person, has all the natural capacities of an ordinary person in addition to the special prerogative that he enjoys as the Sovereign, the majority insisted that the Commonwealth Executive is not to be conceived as an ordinary natural person but as a kind of body politic in what might be called a more 'republican' conception of the Executive under the Australian Constitution. On this view, the relevant legal personality is that of the entire body politic of the Commonwealth, the governing powers of which are exercised by the three branches of government, of which the Executive is only one.[338]

How is this to be understood? Certainly it was well-established that the Commonwealth, as an emanation of the Crown, has legal personality as a corporation sole,[339] with the ability to exercise in its executive role the capacities which emanate therefrom without statutory authorisation. As Lindell has noted, the acknowledgment that the Commonwealth is a juristic person is 'necessary so as to give the Commonwealth the legal capacities it needed to exist and carry on its functions'.[340] So, while it may be the case that the source of the capacities is no longer to be determined by simple reference to the capacities of natural persons, is it being denied that the Commonwealth has juristic personality entirely? If not, what is the precise nature of this juristic personality of the Commonwealth? Is it to be determined solely from the text of s 61 or is it possible to draw

**334** Zines, above n 92, 355–7.
**335** *Williams (No 1)* (2012) 284 CLR 156, 237, 258–9, 368, 373–4.
**336** Ibid, 236, 352, 368–9.
**337** Ibid, 236.
**338** This passage draws on Aroney, above n 113, 110.
**339** Lindell, above n 254, 361.
**340** Ibid. Lindell explores this issue in more detail, including contrary views by certain commentators (at 361, n 58). It is clear, however, that judicial authority in the United Kingdom supports the view that the Crown is to be regarded as having juristic personality as a corporation sole.

conclusions from the establishment of the Commonwealth as a self-governing polity governed by three branches of government, one of which is the Executive? Alternatively, is it possible to reconceptualise what had hitherto been referred to as a capacity and to consider it instead as part of the prerogative? That is, if a capacity exercised by government is qualitatively different to the same capacity exercised by a private person, does it follow that such a capacity, when exercised by the Executive, is better conceived of as a prerogative in the narrow sense? If so, what then is to be made of the established proposition that the prerogative is not subject to the general law in the same way that the capacities are?[341] While *Williams (No 1)* was specifically concerned with Commonwealth contracts and spending, the majority reasoning does not identify a principle by which to limit the outcome to these particular activities of government. It remains an open question whether, in the future, the Court will require statutory authorisation for the exercise of other executive capacities. These potentially include the ability of the Commonwealth Executive to conduct inquiries such as through Royal Commissions,[342] and to incorporate and acquire shares in companies. How would the decision in *Davis*, for example, stand? Moreover, despite indications to the contrary in the majority reasoning,[343] can the reasoning be limited only to the capacities and not be extended to the prerogative? Lindell has pointed out that it was suggested in some of the judgments that the exercise of the nationhood power will not require additional legislative authorisation. If that is the case, the judgments fail to explain why the concerns about accountability do not apply to the exercise of that power:

> It would seem rather odd because, if correct, it would follow that the Tax Bonus payments in *Pape* could be upheld as an exercise of that power without the need for legislative approval when the same was not the case with the payment for the NSCP. The same might conceivably apply to the government guarantee of large deposits in the banks during the Global Financial Crisis, depending on whether such a guarantee could be justified by reference to the nationhood power … .[344]

There was no indication in *Williams (No 2)* that the Court was willing to expand upon these last-mentioned issues. Moreover, the submissions which the Commonwealth made were not regarded by the Court as going to the narrower basis of the 'common assumption', but rather seemed to be a refined restatement of the broad basis for the assumption. As the Court put it:

> [It was] no more than a repetition of what were referred to as the 'broad basis' submissions … in *Williams (No 1)*. … Notably absent from the list of … limitations proffered by the Commonwealth parties was any limitation by reference to the areas in which (in the sense of subjects for or about which) the Commonwealth may spend or contract.[345]

**341** See Aroney, above n 113, 112.
**342** Ibid.
**343** *Williams (No 1)* (2012) 284 CLR 156, 191, 342.
**344** Lindell, above n 254, 37.
**345** *Williams (No 2)* (2014) 309 ALR 41; 88 ALJR 701, 714.

That being the case, not much more can be said about the 'common assumption' in its narrower manifestation except that the Court did not repent its decision.

In *Williams (No 2)* the Court limited itself more precisely to the determination of the validity of the legislation which purported to authorise the chaplaincy funding agreement in particular, and not others referred to in the legislation, and therefore these issues were not addressed beyond what had already been stated in *Williams (No 1)*. The centrepiece of the new legislation was s 32B which provided that if the Commonwealth does not otherwise have power to make or administer an arrangement or grant, then the Commonwealth is, by this statute, granted that power, subject to compliance with other laws, where the arrangement or grant: a) is specified in the regulations to the Act; b) is included in a class of arrangements or grants specified in the regulations; or c) is for the purposes of a program specified in the regulations. The legislation also amended the regulations with immediate effect to specify a range of spending programs for the purposes of the new s 32B. Because these included the successor to the Chaplaincy Program successfully impugned in *Williams (No 1)*, in addition to a large number of other programs with the potential for the specification of other programs in the future, Mr Williams brought proceedings. The Court decided the case simply on the validity of the legislation as it applied to the Chaplaincy Program, holding that there was no relevant head of legislative power to authorise such arrangements and expenditure on the program. In particular, there was no relevant head of power under s 51(xxiiiA)[346] or s 51(xx).[347]

On the broader question of the validity of the mechanism provided for by s 32B – that is, the delegation of authority to the Executive to authorise expenditure across a range of programs specified, or specifiable in the future – the Court restrained its hand as it was not necessary to resolve the case before it. The power to enact s 32B derives from every head of legislative power that supports the making of the payments to which s 32B relates. That section should be read down to authorise the Commonwealth to make, vary or administer arrangements or grants only where it is within the legislative competence of Parliament to give it power. While the Commonwealth applied to reopen *Williams (No 1)* with respect to the rejection of the 'common assumption' and associated arguments, this was rejected by the Court.[348]

It remains, therefore, an open question whether the rationale underlying the majority reasoning in *Williams (No 1)* will be applied beyond what had hitherto been recognised as the capacity to contract and spend.

**346** Ibid, 710–11, 718–20.
**347** Ibid, 712, 718.
**348** Ibid, 713–14.

## 3 The key sources of Commonwealth executive power: Concluding summary

As can be seen from the foregoing, identifying the sources of Commonwealth executive power is complex and controversial. Nonetheless, the key sources of the executive power of the Commonwealth can be summarised in the following way. In the first place, there are three distinct sources in the Constitution itself. These include, first, the general power which derives from the third limb of s 61 relating to the 'execution and maintenance' of the Constitution and Commonwealth laws, and to which the executive power 'extends'. Secondly, the Constitution contains an array of specific grants of power contained in particular constitutional provisions, some of which are vested in the 'Governor-General' and others in 'the Governor-General in Council'.[349] These include the power of:

- issuing writs for House of Representatives elections (s 32) or by-elections (s 33);
- recommending to the Houses of Parliament the purposes of an appropriation in any appropriation bill (s 56);
- assenting to bills passed by Parliament in the Queen's name, reserving them for the Queen's assent, and returning them to the House in which they originated with recommendations (s 58);
- disallowing any Act of Parliament within a year of enactment (vested in the Queen only by s 59);
- appointment of civil servants (s 67);
- acting as commander-in-chief of the armed forces (s 68); and
- appointing justices of the High Court and federal courts (s 72).

Thirdly, there are those specific grants of power to the Governor-General that are regarded as 'reserve' powers. These may be exercised by the Governor-General without, or contrary to, the advice of responsible ministers, namely:

- the appointment of the Ministers of State to administer the government, ie, appointing the Prime Minister and thus the government (s 64);
- dissolving the House of Representatives (ss 5 and 28); and
- dissolving both Houses (s 57) and dismissing the Prime Minister and other ministers (s 64).

While these powers may be exercised without or contrary to advice, as explained in Chapter 6, they must be exercised consistently with the principles of responsible government. Most importantly, this requires that only a person who has the confidence of the House of Representatives (or is mostly likely to, subject to confidence being tested in the House) should be appointed Prime Minister and may only remain Prime Minister so long as that confidence is maintained.

In addition to the constitutional sources, executive power is also derived from Acts of Parliament. These may confer powers on the Governor-General (who must act on advice), on a relevant Minister of State, or on other statutory

**349** This difference is of no constitutional significance for present purposes, as, excepting for the reserve powers, responsible government requires that the Governor-General act on ministerial advice in all circumstances.

office-holders. Statutes remain the most straightforward source of executive power and clearly reflect that aspect of government power which involves the 'execution' of the laws of the Commonwealth.

Finally, there are several unspecified powers inferred from s 61. These derive principally from the fact that the Commonwealth is constituted as a 'government of the Queen' and that it is the government of an independent, sovereign, federal nation. As has been seen, the nature of these powers is an issue of some nicety, and indeed uncertainty. Part of the reason for this is that s 61, especially its 'execution and maintenance' limb, lacks definitional clarity and cannot be interpreted accurately solely by reference to the text. This broad category of executive power includes those powers of the Crown recognised by the common law (sometimes referred to generically as 'the prerogative') which are attributed to the Commonwealth. These in turn include 'prerogative' powers understood in the narrow sense, meaning those powers which belong uniquely to the government, such as declaring war and peace, conducting foreign affairs, entering treaties, conferring honours, pardoning offenders, and an array of undefined powers in times of grave emergency and where the very survival of the polity may be at stake. They also in principle include those 'capacities' of the Government that it shares with ordinary citizens by virtue of legal personality, such as entering into contracts, registering corporations, creating trusts, the acquisition and disposition of property, suing and being sued, and so on.[350] Lastly, the High Court has held that there is an inherent power implied from the fact that the Commonwealth is a government of a national, independent, federal polity, the content of which power is determined by reference to the imperatives that derive from nationhood.[351] This is sometimes referred to as an implied executive 'nationhood' power, in addition to the legislative aspect of the implied nationhood power discussed in Chapter 3.[352] Although this remains a rather elusive concept, the most important guiding criterion appears to be that it is that power which is peculiarly adapted to the government of a nation and which the national government alone is able to exercise for the benefit of the nation.[353]

## V The relationship between executive and legislative power

To what extent can Parliament regulate and control the exercise of Commonwealth executive power? Does the answer depend on the position taken with respect to the ambit of the power? Following *Pape* and *Williams*, these continue to remain pertinent questions. In a constitutional system which entrenches

**350** As a result of *Williams v Commonwealth (No 1)* (2012) 284 CLR 156, a qualification must now be made to the ambit of the Commonwealth's power to contract and spend as discussed in this chapter.
**351** This was first unambiguously accepted in *Pape v Commissioner of Taxation* (2009) 238 CLR 1.
**352** See Chapter 3, Part IV.3.
**353** *Victoria v Commonwealth and Hayden* (1975) 134 CLR 338, 397.

responsible government and parliamentary supremacy, it is easily assumed that Parliament is able to control, indeed abnegate, these powers by legislation. However, two aspects of the Australian constitutional system need to be addressed before such a conclusion can be stated with confidence. First, there is impliedly incorporated a legal separation of powers at Commonwealth level.[354] Secondly, executive power is provided for expressly in provisions of the Constitution: generally, in s 61, and in more specific grants of power to the Governor-General in other sections of the Constitution. Closer examination is therefore warranted.

At first sight, these considerations seem not to have resulted in much academic or judicial reticence in giving expression to the imperatives of responsible government and parliamentary supremacy over the executive.[355] Thus, Harrison Moore stated:

> The executive power is so closely allied to the legislative that it may be impossible to draw any other line than that which expediency and practical good sense command. ... [W]e are not encouraged to believe that the executive can make good an independent sphere of its own, free from legislative interference and control.[356]

An influential *dictum* of Jacobs J in the *AAP* case reads thus:

> The Parliament is sovereign over the Executive and whatever is within the competence of the Executive under s 61, including or as well as the exercise of the prerogative within the area of the prerogative attached to the Government of Australia, may be the subject of legislation of the Australian Parliament.[357]

It was stated emphatically in *Brown v West*: '*Whatever the scope of the executive power of the Commonwealth might otherwise be*, it is susceptible to control by statute'.[358] That would now include, one assumes, any inherent 'nationhood' power in s 61. This conforms with the position that the executive power runs only so far as the writ of Commonwealth legislative competence, whether that is by reference to express heads of power, the incidental legislative power in s 51(xxxix), or an implied legislative 'nationhood' power.[359]

However, some qualification cannot be avoided in a written constitution which provides expressly for the vesting of executive power and which also maintains a separation of powers. For if the Constitution expressly grants a power to the Governor-General, and if the separation of powers demands some separation of executive and legislative power, there is always some degree of impetus towards a sphere of executive power immune from parliamentary control. In this regard, different considerations apply when considering the general 'executive power of the Commonwealth' in s 61 and the specific grants of power to the Governor-General elsewhere in the Constitution.

**354** *R v Kirby; Ex parte Boilermakers' Society of Australia* (1956) 94 CLR 254, 275; *Attorney-General for Australia v R* [1957] AC 288, 315.
**355** See Zines, above n 92, 374.
**356** Moore, above n 3, 98.
**357** *AAP* case (1975) 134 CLR 338, 406.
**358** *Brown v West* (1990) 169 CLR 195, 202.
**359** Zines, above n 92, 359. See also *Davis v Commonwealth* (1988) 166 CLR 79.

## 1 Section 61 executive power

That component of s 61 which relates to the *execution* of Commonwealth laws must clearly be exercised in accordance with the provisions of the relevant statute that is being executed. Parliament also may direct and regulate the manner of implementation of Commonwealth laws. This remains straightforward.

The 'maintenance' component of the Constitution does not, as ever, yield such straightforward responses. Pursuant to the common law view, the Commonwealth's powers in this regard are inherently subject to parliamentary regulation and abnegation. This is one of the particular advantages of this view. However, as s 61 is now regarded as a direct source of inherent executive power, this position cannot be maintained in its simplicity. While there is no suggestion in *Pape* that Commonwealth executive power is wholly or partly immune from legislative control, the position taken by the Court therein nevertheless gave some (inadvertent) comfort to the contrary view – a view which has not been without its supporters. Jack Richardson, for example, had argued that s 61 confers upon the Governor-General a broad power to *maintain* the Constitution:

> [Section 61] cannot become a complete sacrificial victim to the legislative powers. The extension of the executive power to the maintenance of the Constitution is a power to maintain a law superior to any Act of the Commonwealth Parliament. It suggests, therefore, that *the executive power is partly inalienable and not within reach of the federal Parliament,* and that this should be so also in relation to laws of the Commonwealth. It must be remembered that Chapter II, and not Chapter I, is the principal source of executive authority, just as Chapter III, and not Chapter I, contains the sources of judicial power.[360]

Winterton, an exacting critic of such expansive notions of a power to 'maintain' the Constitution,[361] identified similar tendencies elsewhere. He noted the comments of Sir Maurice Byers, the Commonwealth Solicitor-General (1973–83), under interrogation by the Senate in 1975 and at a subsequent Senate committee enquiry, that the Parliament could not validly 'take away any power [which] the Constitution give[s] to the Executive' and that 'no function of the Executive may constitutionally be discharged by the Parliament'.[362] Thus, while the executive power to enter into treaties could be regulated by Parliament, no law could take it away directly or indirectly. A law which gave Parliament a power to veto treaty ratification was given as an example of an indirect removal.

The difficulty with this approach is that it appears to treat s 61 as if it were one of the specific grants of executive power found elsewhere in the Constitution. Because specific, they are more precisely defined and therefore clearly vested in the Governor-General and, at least to this extent, protected from being so divested by Parliament. But the same cannot be said of s 61 which provides

**360** J E Richardson, 'The Executive Power of the Commonwealth' in Zines (ed), above n 103, 50, 82 (emphasis added).
**361** Winterton, above n 26, 96–8.
**362** See Winterton, above n 43, 38–9.

for executive power generally. To use the same example, the power to enter into treaties is not an immutable executive power. It is simply part of the prerogative incorporated in s 61. It cannot be said to be an inherently executive power, unless of course an argument is made that, in any event, it comes within the implied nationhood power. Leaving the latter question aside, Winterton has warned:

> But to treat s 61 as analogous to provisions conferring specific executive powers requires an assumption that 'the executive power of the Commonwealth' conferred by s 61 has an ascertainable meaning, with a fixed minimum content, including for example, the power to conclude treaties.[363]

Because this is highly questionable in his view, it is not feasible to maintain a legal separation between legislative and executive power. This would mean that any prerogative power, including the power to enter into treaties, could indeed be regulated, even abrogated, by Parliament. Nevertheless, such a view cannot be stated with the same confidence under the prevailing nationhood view. And, it has to be conceded, even before this position was adopted, the elevation of s 61 as the source of the Commonwealth's prerogative powers (or at least as the basis of their incorporation) was suggestive of their *statutory* basis, albeit in the higher statute, the Constitution. This provided support to the view that they too were expressly vested powers similar to the other specific grants of power – hence the suggestion that Parliament could not abrogate, fetter or repeal that power; although it could, arguably, regulate it.[364]

If it is now the position, following *Pape*, that there is indeed an ascertainable inherent content to executive power in s 61 based on national imperatives, then the Byers arguments have greater traction. How much traction can only be ascertained once the Court has had the opportunity to clarify the matter further. However, all indications from the Court seem to suggest that there is little room to doubt that the principle of parliamentary supremacy over the Executive would trump any arguments favouring even some small sphere of immunity for s 61 executive power based on the separation of powers and the express vesting of power in the text. Albeit writing before *Pape*, Zines was able to state with some confidence that:

> it seems clear ... that basic British constitutional principles are applicable and these, generally speaking, ensure that, despite the terms of s 61, '[t]he Parliament is sovereign over the executive and whatever is within the competence of the executive under s 61 ... may be the subject of legislation by the Australian Parliament'.[365]

Winterton had reasoned similarly. Being contained in a British statute, he argued, the legislative and executive powers conferred by the Constitution should be interpreted 'in light of the British conceptions of those powers'. Noting, moreover,

**363** Ibid, 39.
**364** See Zines, above n 92, 363.
**365** Ibid, 360, quotation from the *AAP* case (1975) 134 CLR 338, 406.

the implied entrenchment of responsible government, he maintained that, as in Britain, the relationship between legislative and executive power ought to be one of parliamentary supremacy over the Executive.[366] This position is consistent with that stated by Jacobs J in the *AAP* case:

> It does not follow that any subject matter of the exercise of the prerogative which is properly exercisable through the Governor-General on the advice of the Executive Council cannot be the subject of legislation of the Parliament which may deny or limit or replace the prerogative by legislative provision. The same is true of any executive power expressly conferred by the Constitution ... .[367]

Be that as it may, there is sufficient uncertainty to warrant, at least out of an abundance of caution, some more careful consideration of this precise question.[368]

Assuming the position remains that there is complete legislative control over executive power in s 61, the sources of that power would of course be the express heads (plus incidents) of legislative power, and perhaps an implied legislative nationhood power. Thus to interpret the constitutional situation in a manner consistent with 'traditional conceptions' and the principles of responsible government suggests that legislative power must be understood as leading the executive power, and not vice versa.

At this point, it is necessary to express a note of caution on the interpretation of s 51(xxxix). This is in response to the nice argument that the section is strictly limited to laws *incidental* to the *execution* of power vested in the government, thus not extending simply to laws generally with respect to executive power.[369] Whatever the precise position, it has been argued that this ought not to result in an overly restrictive reading of s 51(xxxix); for the placitum needs to be read consistently with the principles of responsible government and parliamentary supremacy.[370] As Winterton noted, 'surely, regulation of the manner in which executive power is exercised, or the means by which executive action is implemented, is legislation on matters incidental to the execution of executive power'.[371] As was stated in the unanimous judgment of the High Court in *R v Hughes*:

> It is plain enough that s 51(xxxix) empowers the Parliament to legislate in aid of an exercise of the executive power. However, it would be another matter to conclude that this means that the Parliament may legislate in aid of any subject which the Executive Government regards as of national interest and concern.[372]

**366** Winterton, above n 26, 96.
**367** (1975) 134 CLR 338, 406.
**368** See *Final Report of the Constitutional Convention Vol 2* (AGPS: 1988) ch 4, and George Winterton, *We the People* (Oxford University Press, 1994).
**369** This was raised by Brennan J in *Davis v Commonwealth* (1988) 166 CLR 79 at 111–12. Zines noted that, if this proposition were to be accepted, it would not be 'incidental to the executive power to make contracts to prohibit or restrict such a power by legislation': Zines, above n 92, 361.
**370** See Zines, above n 92, 362.
**371** Winterton, above n 26, 95.
**372** (2000) 202 CLR 535, 555.

Thus, while it is likely that s 61 executive power will always remain subject to legislative control, this position may need refinement to the extent to which the notion of an inherent executive power therein based on national considerations becomes established, at least to the extent that this transforms s 61 into a provision containing powers that resemble the express grants of power to the Governor-General provided for elsewhere in the Constitution.[373]

## 2 Non-section 61 executive powers

The situation differs with respect to the specific grants of executive power.[374] As these powers are constitutionally vested in the Governor-General, albeit as their *formal* repository, Parliament cannot alter this formal position by removing these powers from the Governor-General and vesting them elsewhere. However, when interpreted consistently with responsible government and parliamentary supremacy, it is likely the case that Parliament may otherwise regulate the manner in which these powers are exercised. For example, while Parliament may not authorise a judicial commission to appoint federal judges under s 72, that power being expressly vested in the Governor-General in Council, it has been argued that it may make their appointment conditional upon the approval of a judicial commission.[375] Similarly, while the Parliament could not vest someone other than the Governor-General with the 'command in chief' of the armed forces under s 68, Parliament may regulate matters such as the recruitment, financing, discipline and deployment of the forces.[376] Arguably, this principle is applicable even to the reserve powers, which are, after all, specific grants of power. Thus Parliament could regulate the Governor-General's powers to dissolve the House of Representatives (s 28) or both houses (s 57, though consistently with the section) and the power to appoint and dismiss ministers (ss 62–64). Winterton has argued that Parliament might, for example, direct the Governor-General to act only on ministerial advice, and he has even suggested that it might impose limitations on the giving of that advice in certain circumstances, provided that the constitutional requirement that it is the Governor-General or Governor-General in Council who exercises the power as a matter of law.[377] Other commentators[378] have suggested that the Constitution does more than merely give expression to the formal repository of the power and that it grants the Governor-General a complete discretion as to how these powers should be exercised. In the words of Ryan, to attempt 'to limit in any way the discretions which are conferred

**373** As to whether 'the Governor-General', ie the government, must be the executor of Commonwealth legislation, see Winterton, above n 26, 101–10.
**374** See Chapter 6 for a detailed exposition.
**375** Winterton, above n 26, 100–01. See the concurring views of Zines: Zines, above n 92, 374.
**376** Winterton, above n 26, 101.
**377** Ibid, 100.
**378** This case was made most forcefully in Richardson, above n 360, at 72, and in Australian Constitutional Convention 1978, *Opinion Prepared for Standing Committee 'D' by Professor KW Ryan*, quoted in Zines, above n 92, 373. For more detail see Winterton, above n 26, 287 n 47.

in unfettered form on the Governor-General by the Constitution would … be unconstitutional'.[379] Adherents of this view would hold that Parliament cannot regulate the exercise of specifically conferred executive powers.

While the point therefore cannot be said to be certainly settled, this latter view certainly tends to contradict the proposition that constitutional provisions conferring powers on the Governor-General must be read in the light of certain constitutional fundamentals such as responsible government. The constitutional provisions which confer power upon the Governor-General, argued Winterton, 'cannot be interpreted literally, as if the Constitution were inscribed upon a *tabula rasa*. … [T]hey must be interpreted in conformity with parliamentary supremacy, with the result that Parliament can regulate their exercise by the Governor-General acting on ministerial advice'.[380] As the joint judgment in *Re Residential Tenancies Tribunal (NSW)* observed, 'it is of the very nature of executive power in a system of responsible government that it is susceptible of control by the exercise of legislative power by Parliament'.[381] It is indeed arguable that, excepting that the formal repository of the power cannot be altered, this position pertains also to the specific grants of power.

Such as analysis suggests that s 61 executive power is subject to legislative control and indeed abrogation. In relation to the other specific constitutional grants of power, the position would be that these powers can probably be regulated although they may not be abrogated, at least without a constitutional amendment.

## 3 Generic and specific executive power

There are also other possible consequences of *Pape* that need to be considered. Following that case, the Commonwealth's executive power, including the prerogative and 'nationhood', being now directly sourced in s 61, are to be regarded as based on specific provisions of the Constitution, thus having a 'statutory' basis, rather than common law. But is it therefore possible to continue to maintain the distinction being drawn between the generic executive powers in s 61 and the specific grants of executive power? This makes Zines' exploratory comment, posed before *Pape*, presently pertinent:

> Assuming that Parliament has no power to control functions conferred on the Governor-General by provisions such as ss 5, 32 or 72 … it would follow that powers derived from s 61 are in the same position. The Constitution gives them to the Governor-General, and what the Constitution gives the Parliament cannot take away.[382]

However, his rationale for distinguishing s 61 as a special case in order to negate this proposition, persuasive as it is, may now need qualification to account for

**379** See Zines, above n 92, 374.
**380** Winterton, above n 26, 99–100 n 47.
**381** (1997) 190 CLR 410, 441.
**382** See Zines, above n 92, 363.

the recognition of inherent power therein. Pre-*Pape*, the case could more easily be made that s 61 is a special case because its primary constitutional function is not to act as the font of Commonwealth executive power, such power rather residing in the Commonwealth as a government of the Queen. That is, s 61 in this precise regard was otiose because the common law powers of the Crown operated independently of it and those relevant to its position were simply inherited by the Commonwealth. As *dicta* of the High Court subtly indicated, they are 'within the operation of the section' but nevertheless, as Zines also noted, 'they are not related to particular powers of government, but operate for the benefit of the Commonwealth as a government of the Queen'.[383] Section 61 was thus important not as the direct source of executive power, but because it served other purposes: for example, establishing expressly, not by implication, that executive power was to be exercised by the Governor-General on the advice of Australian ministers, enabling reliance on s 51(xxxix) incidental legislative power to support the Executive and ensuring that litigation relating to executive power was a 'matter ... arising under this Constitution' for the purposes of s 76(i).[384]

Following *Pape*, it is not entirely clear whether the uniqueness of s 61 can be maintained. For it seems that s 61 itself has become the 'statutory' source of power, to be exercised by the Governor-General (on advice), which power is now also to be regarded as an inherent (albeit ill-defined) executive power based on the status of the government as an independent federal government and the imperatives upon it which thereby arise. If this power exists in s 61 independently of the common law, with an ascertainable meaning, must not the content of the power be treated in the same way as the specific grants of power in its relationship with Parliament: that is, it may be regulated, but cannot be abrogated? Thus, is it therefore necessary to distinguish the way this implied national power is to be treated from the way the common law powers are to be treated, the latter being subject to both regulation and abnegation by Parliament? This is an issue which may also need further clarification by the High Court.

## 4 The separation of executive and legislative power

An underlying theme in the above discussion is the precise impact of the separation of powers on the relationship between executive and legislative power. This is because the separation of powers adds weight to the view that, because the Constitution specifically vests power in the Executive, whether generally, as in s 61, or in specific grants of powers elsewhere, the legislature is limited in how it may regulate or control such power.

A constitutionally entrenched separation of powers doctrine is a fundamental aspect of the United States influence on the Commonwealth Constitution. The

**383** Ibid, 364.
**384** Ibid, 363.

High Court early established that, as in the US Constitution, the Commonwealth Constitution implements, by implication, a legal separation of powers.[385] This legal separation, prima facie, extends to the legislative and executive powers.[386] Yet, while the separation of powers implies a legal equality between the branches of government, in Australia it co-exists in an uneasy tension with responsible government, also implied in the Constitution, because the latter implies a hierarchy in which supremacy is attributed to Parliament. This is despite the fact that, in modern practice, the Executive usually controls Parliament through the party system and discipline.

This tension has been accommodated in Australia by the High Court's adoption of a rather pragmatic, functionalist approach to the separation of executive and legislative power, reserving a far more rigorous approach, even formalistic in part, to the separation of judicial power.[387] Of course, the rigour with which the High Court may enforce the latter separation is not compromised by the imperatives of responsible government, essentially applying to the relationship between the political branches, and indeed is supported by sound constitutional policy, namely the need to maintain the institutional and decisional independence of a judicial branch[388] which must decide intergovernmental disputes in a federation, as in the United States. But in the context of the separation of the political branches, both the implied hierarchical tendencies of responsible government, and indeed its tendency to fusion as opposed to separation, has meant that this more pragmatic, flexible approach makes good constitutional sense. There has in fact been no High Court decision which has invalidated legislation on the basis that it breached the separation between legislative and executive power. In *Victorian Stevedoring and General Contracting Co Pty Ltd v Dignan*, the High Court permitted a very wide delegation of legislative power to the Executive,[389] although it did not deny that the separation of powers was a relevant limiting factor.[390] Although this may indicate that the High Court has been willing to be guided by pragmatic, structural and historical factors in considering questions relating to the separation of powers,[391] *Dignan* itself was not concerned with the issue of legislative control of executive power. Nor has legislation been held invalid for vesting executive power in a body other than the Governor-General.[392]

**385** *New South Wales v Commonwealth* (1915) 20 CLR 54.
**386** *R v Kirby; Ex parte Boilermakers' Society of Australia* (1956) 94 CLR 254, 275; *Attorney-General for Australia v R* [1957] AC 288, 315.
**387** As in, for example, *R v Kirby; Ex parte Boilermakers' Society of Australia* (1956) 94 CLR 254, 275; *Attorney-General for Australia v R* [1957] AC 288, 315; *Re Wakim; Ex parte McNally* (1999) 198 CLR 511.
**388** For a detailed examination of this question, see Peter Gerangelos, *The Separation of Powers and Legislative Interference in Judicial Process* (Hart Publishing, 2009).
**389** (1931) 46 CLR 73.
**390** See *Giris Pty Ltd v Federal Commissioner of Taxation* (1969) 119 CLR 365, 379; *Victorian Stevedoring & General Contracting Co Pty Ltd v Dignan* (1931) 46 CLR 73, 101.
**391** See Peter Gerangelos, 'Interpretational Methodology in Separation of Powers Jurisprudence: the Formalist/Functionalist Debate' (2005) 8(1) *Constitutional Law and Policy Review* 1.
**392** See Winterton, above n 26, 101–10. Richardson has argued that s 61 does impose legal constraints in this respect: see Richardson, above n 360, 102–3.

However, this pragmatic approach does not ameliorate those concerns which arise when depth is added to s 61 beyond the prerogative and the capacities. A strong case can be made that a separation of legislative and executive power cannot be maintained because it is simply not possible, or at least it is highly questionable, whether it is possible to give an ascertainable meaning with a fixed minimum content to the 'executive power of the Commonwealth' in s 61 based on abstract, conceptual reasoning. If this is accepted, then any argument favouring some immunity from legislative control must sustain itself purely by reference to the text of the Constitution. Therefore, when it is held, even very cautiously – as it was by French CJ in *Pape* – that '[s 61] executive power extends ... to short-term fiscal measures to meet adverse economic conditions affecting the nation as a whole, where such measures are on their face peculiarly within the capacity and resources of the Commonwealth Government',[393] one is witnessing an attempt to give some minimum content to s 61 executive power without reliance on the legally discernible criteria provided by the common law. Irrespective of the philosophical objections, the fact that this is now regarded as possible significantly enhances the ability to apply the separation of powers to provide some immunity to such power, as incrementally defined, from legislative control.

It is not suggested, of course, that this was the majority's intention in *Pape*. There is no indication that the High Court would be willing to countenance such immunity. Indeed, all the indications are to the contrary. Moreover, the separation of powers has always tended to be discounted when it comes to legislative and executive power in favour of responsible government and parliamentary supremacy. As Winterton has stated: 'the alleged separation of these powers, which cannot be implemented feasibly, ... is simply too tenuous a ground on which to resist the implications of the fundamental constitutional concept of parliamentary supremacy'.[394]

However, if it *was* held that the separation of powers must apply to the separation of legislative and executive branches, it has been argued that this separation should be applied pursuant to a 'purposive functional approach'.[395] To be distinguished from 'formalism', this approach would – most appropriately in a system establishing responsible government – acknowledge the impossibility of keeping hermetically sealed these two branches of government from influence or interference by the other. Such interference by one branch would be permitted to the extent that it does not 'reach some unspecified level of intensity' whereby 'it undermine[s] another branch's performance of its essential function' and does not permit the accretion of excessive power to the interfering

**393** *Pape* (2009) 238 CLR 1, 69.
**394** Winterton, above n 26, 100.
**395** See Anthony Mason, 'A New Perspective on Separation of Powers' (1996) 82 *Canberra Bulletin of Public Administration* 1, 2. For a detailed examination of formalism and functionalism in Australian constitutional jurisprudence, see Gerangelos, above n 391. Winterton also advocated the adoption of such a position in the event that the separation of powers was to be applied to the separation of executive and legislative power: see Winterton, above n 43, 39–40.

branch. While there are difficulties in the consistent application of such an approach across all branches,[396] this would nevertheless appear to be the only sensible approach, under responsible government, with respect to the relationship between the Executive and the legislature. The courts would thus only invalidate legislation which posed a significant impediment to the exercise of those executive powers conferred on the Executive by the Constitution along the lines suggested in the United States Supreme Court cases of *Morrison v Olson*[397] and *Nixon v Administrator of General Services*.[398] The courts would also, indeed especially, be sensitive to legislation which aggrandises the power of the legislature in usurping or significantly encroaching on executive functions.[399] But translating this into predictable limits is difficult. Contrary to his own preferred position, Winterton, relying in relevant United States precedents, ventured that legislation which authorised the Parliament to ratify international treaties would almost certainly be invalid, as would legislation authorising Parliament or one of its committees to veto ratification:

> However, legislation which left the treaty-ratification power in the hands of the executive but sought to regulate its exercise – for example, by requiring the executive to take specified considerations into account or imposing procedural requirements, such as reporting to Parliament or a committee thereof or to the State or the Council of Australian Governments (COAG) – would probably be valid.[400]

Similar formulations may be ventured with respect to other executive powers in s 61 and to the specific grants of power. That is, while the constitutionally vested power cannot be abolished, or removed from the control of the Executive, its exercise may be regulated by legislation. The appointment of judges pursuant to s 72 illustrates the point well. While the Parliament could not remove that power from the Governor-General in Council and vest it in a judicial commission, it could require that the Governor-General in Council take into account the recommendations of such a commission.

In any event, there has been no decision of the High Court which has indicated that the executive power of the Commonwealth is not subject to legislative control. This was so in *Cadia Holdings*, important because it came after the decision in *Pape*. Of course, these include the treaty-making powers which were not in issue in that case. Even though *Pape* was expressly referred to, the Court did not venture to engage with potential separation of powers issues relating to legislative and executive power.[401] For the sake of clarity, and especially as the Court has now recognised the possibility of minimum inherent content to the

**396** Gerangelos, above n 391.
**397** 487 US 654, 691, 693 (1988): 'impede the President's ability to perform his constitutional duty' and 'unduly interfering with the role of the Executive Branch'.
**398** 433 US 425, 443 (1977).
**399** See especially the following cases: *Metropolitan Washington Airports Authority v Citizens for the Abatement of Aircraft Noise Inc* 501 US 252, 273–5, 277 (1991); *Mistretta v United States* 488 US 361, 382 (1989); *Morrison v Olson* 487 US 654, 680–83, 694–5 (1988).
**400** Winterton, above n 43, 40.
**401** (2010) 242 CLR 195, 226.

executive power in s 61, some clear judicial statement would be welcome. Nevertheless, it seems most unlikely that the Court would hold that, subject to the Constitution, there is a pocket of executive power immune from legislative regulation or control. 'I am inclined to agree', wrote Zines, 'with Professor Winterton that the powers granted to the Governor-General and s 51 (xxxix) should be interpreted in the light of the general principle of parliamentary supremacy'.[402]

## VI Conclusions

The analysis of the ambit of the general executive power of the Commonwealth undertaken in this chapter has had to contend with the limitations imposed by a sparse constitutional text. This has entailed an increased reliance on the Convention Debates and historical precedents, the prerogatives and capacities of the Crown, the federal nature of the polity, responsible government and parliamentary supremacy. These considerations have figured significantly in the deliberations of the High Court on this issue, and relative to the legislative and judicial powers, probably more significantly. A noteworthy aspect to the problem is the impossibility of deriving from a purely abstract conceptual analysis any inherent content to the notion of 'executive power'. Hence the need to rely on usage, history, current practice, as well as particular legal and constitutional prescription within a particular polity to determine its definition when the constitutional text is reticent. Traditionally, in Anglo-Australian constitutional law, the scope of executive power has been determined by reference to the non-statutory powers of the Crown, the 'prerogative' in the broad sense of the term, which Parliament has deigned to leave in its hands – a residue which, in any event, it can control and indeed abnegate. In short, in determining the content of executive power in Britain and its constitutional progeny, reference is made to the common law, statute, or express constitutional provision to determine its content – not to abstract conceptual analysis of what 'executive power' may entail. It is for this reason that the particular object of enquiry in this chapter has been the particular concept of 'the executive power *of the Commonwealth*'.

From an examination of the Convention Debates, it becomes apparent that while detailed attention was given to the structure of the Executive and its composition, the framers were more concerned with how to reconcile responsible government and federalism than they were with defining precisely the content and the ambit of the power. This was an understandable response to a complex issue; although from the perspective of clarity and certainty, it may be regarded as an opportunity lost. Recourse was simply had to the prerogatives of the Crown. But which of these were to be inherited by the Commonwealth the framers were unable to state with precision, especially as the Commonwealth was a government of limited powers due to federal constraints and its dependent

**402** Zines, above n 92, 374.

status within the British imperial system. Perhaps some attempt could have been made to give expression to these but, as Griffith confessed, '[a]t this moment I believe no one knows what they all are. No one could at once enumerate them all'.[403] Harrison Moore similarly noted the virtual silence of colonial constitutions on the subject which resulted in the limited guidance available to the framers.[404] These constitutions sought to ensure that the legislature could make full provision for the execution of laws, beyond which reliance was placed on the prerogative. The latter constituted a 'large measure of executive power', but there was little guidance to determine which precise prerogatives could or should reside in a provincial government. While it was evident from the Convention Debates that both statute and prerogative were to be regarded as the principle sources of executive power, it is not entirely clear how these were intended to be expressed in the Constitution.

As for the relationship between the executive and legislative branches, this was left to be governed by the conventional principles of responsible government 'which are not under continual direction of organic laws, but are freely organized as utility has suggested or may suggest within the ultimate bounds of law'.[405] Again, this did not easily convert into a clear statement in the Constitution as to how the two branches were to operate within the federal system. Federalism was a most significant aspect of the new Constitution and, given the complexities of reconciling it with responsible government and parliamentary supremacy along British lines, the exact lines of demarcation were not specified in the Constitution. Some have apportioned blame for the 1975 crisis to this omission.

This may explain the ambiguity apparent in the statements of Griffith in the course of the drafting history of what became s 61.[406] It is clear that Griffith intended to ensure a close connection between executive and legislative power – 'executive authority shall be co-extensive with … legislative power'. But in the process of amendment toward the shortened version of what became s 61, his comments taken alone may possibly bear the interpretation that he did not envisage the existence of s 61 executive power absent statutory authorisation. On that interpretation at least, it could be argued that he was not expressing a view that the breadth of non-statutory executive power was limited by the subject matters of Commonwealth legislative competence. Alternatively, in light of his clear acceptance of the prerogative, it is possible that he envisaged the existence of executive powers exercisable without prior legislative authorisation; although whatever these were, they could not extend beyond the sphere of Commonwealth legislative competence. His views need to be understood alongside the diverse views of Barton, Deakin, Inglis Clark and other leading participants.

**403** *Convention Debates, Sydney* (1891) 772.
**404** Moore, above n 3, 212.
**405** Ibid.
**406** See above n 63 and more generally Part III.

That there would be limitations on such a power was certainly not denied. The first clear limitation was in the sphere of external affairs due to the Commonwealth's position within the Empire – something that is clearly no longer the case – and the second was in the sphere of its reach vis-à-vis the States due to federalism. This latter limitation, the 'breadth' of the power, was assumed to be determinable by reference to the limitations on Commonwealth legislative subject matter as detailed amply in Chapter I of the Constitution. On the whole, this was the view which came to be accepted by the early constitutional commentators, including Inglis Clark and Harrison Moore, and which was manifested in the opinions of Deakin and Groom as Attorneys-General.

Despite some early uncertainties in the *Wooltops* case, this latter eventually became the position broadly assumed by constitutional commentators and, in all likelihood, by most members of the Court. That the Commonwealth could execute the laws of the Commonwealth and provisions of the Constitution there was little doubt. As for the non-statutory powers of the Commonwealth, the High Court recognised that a source of these remained the prerogative and capacities of the Crown. These have been accepted as being incorporated within s 61, although arguably, despite the silence of the framers on this precise question, more from the vesting of the executive power of the Commonwealth in the Queen than from the 'execution' and 'maintenance' limbs of that section. As Australia's independence was fully developed, these also included all the external affairs prerogatives. On one view, shared by many commentators and manifested in a number of *dicta* of the Court, the depth of the power was limited to the 'execution' component of the power and, in the 'maintenance' limb, by the common law prerogatives and capacities. The breadth of the power, reflecting federal limitations, was limited by the extent of the Commonwealth's legislative competence. This was thought to be manageable because the prerogative and capacities, being recognised by the common law and maintaining now their status as common law, were always subject to legislative regulation and abnegation, thus also ensuring parliamentary supremacy over the Executive in a system which maintains the principles of responsible government. On this view as well, the principle of responsible government would tend to trump any contrary pressure from the separation of powers that some element of Commonwealth executive power must remain immune from legislative control.

However, because the High Court has now given recognition to an implied executive 'nationhood' power as an element within the 'the executive power of the Commonwealth', it has become necessary to consider the 'executive power of the Commonwealth' as a construct from which some inherent content must be derived; in part, from conceptual analysis based on what the Commonwealth's 'nationhood' may entail. The High Court has attempted to do this by reference to the status of the Commonwealth as the government of an independent federal polity. This last development, as has been shown, is the product of the more recent jurisprudence of the High Court, building on prior dicta indicative of this potential development. In certain respects it is an innovation. The difficulty, however, with the concept remains the absence of legally discernible criteria by which to determine its content, although the common law will remain instructive, and hence its definition will have to contend with the spectres of subjectivity, and, as some commentators have suggested, assertion.[407] For reasonable minds will certainly differ, as both the *Vadarlis* and *Pape* cases have shown, as to whether only the national government can undertake efficacious action which is for the benefit of the nation in any particular situation. Nevertheless, this new conception of the power must now be accommodated as part of the 'executive power of the Commonwealth'. This has implications for a potential aggrandisement of Commonwealth executive power, but also provides some comfort to those who may maintain that s 61 power is at least partially immune from legislative regulation and control. While it is most unlikely, in light of its clear pronouncements in other contexts, that the High Court will countenance any such immunity, this may be something that may need some clarification in any future examination of the 'nationhood' power.

Another matter which may warrant further attention is the extent to which the depth/breadth analytical schema, which can certainly accommodate the addition to depth resulting from 'nationhood', may need to be reconsidered following the *Williams* cases. The hitherto 'common assumption', that the Commonwealth government has the capacity (depth) to enter into contracts and spend subject to federal constraints (breadth), has now been rejected. To what extent, it now has to be asked, does the Court's rationale for requiring statutory authorisation for all but an exempt class of contracts apply to limit other hitherto recognised capacities, or indeed even aspects of the prerogative? To the extent that this development extends along these lines, not only will it constitute a narrowing of depth, but it may also have consequences for the very concept of breadth and the methodology of its determination. This is particularly the case because aspects of the majority reasoning have cast doubt on the efficacy of relying on the enumerated heads of legislative subject matter to determine the breadth of executive power in the absence of actual legislation. At the time of writing, it is not possible to predict with any certainty how this particular issue will develop. It nevertheless will ensure that the issue of the ambit of the executive power of the Commonwealth will continue to constitute a major, if not the major, focus of attention in Australian constitutional law and policy.

**407** Eg, Winterton, above n 43, 27.

# 8

# The judicature

> *The judicial power of the Commonwealth shall be vested in a Federal Supreme Court, to be called the High Court of Australia, and in such other federal courts as the Parliament creates, and in such other courts as it invests with federal jurisdiction. The High Court shall consist of a Chief Justice, and so many other Justices, not less than two, as the Parliament prescribes.*[1]

## I Introduction

The previous chapters have covered the federal legislature and Executive. Chapter I of the Constitution vests the legislative power of the Commonwealth in the federal Parliament, to be constituted by the Queen and the two houses of Parliament.[2] Chapter II of the Constitution vests the executive power of the Commonwealth in the Queen, to be exercised by the Governor-General as the Queen's representative.[3] Chapter III of the Constitution vests the judicial power of the Commonwealth in three categories of courts: the High Court of Australia; other federal courts that the Parliament creates; and such other courts that it invests with federal jurisdiction, principally the courts of the constituent States.

The creation of the federal judicature by Chapter III of the Constitution was intended to give effect to two primary objectives. Firstly, from the 1840s there had been various suggestions, from the Colonial Office in the United Kingdom and the colonies, regarding the creation of a court of appeal for Australasia that would replace the Privy Council as the ultimate court of appeal from the superior courts of the colonies. When the delegates to the Constitutional Conventions met to discuss the terms of the proposed federal compact, the creation of a general court of appeal, and its relationship to the Privy Council, naturally fell for consideration. Secondly, the establishment of an effective federal system would not be complete without the creation of a judicial arm of government. As Alfred Deakin said at the 1890 Australasian Federation Conference preceding

**1** Commonwealth Constitution, s 71.
**2** See Chapter 2, Part II.
**3** See Chapter 6, Part IV.

the Constitutional Conventions of the 1890s, '[w]hat we shall require will be, not simply some Federal Court of Appeal to hear cases after they have been dealt with in the courts of the colony, but a Federal Judiciary, with Federal Courts in all the colonies'.[4] It was essential and vital that the federal tier of government possess each of the 'three great arms of state'.[5]

Consequently, Chapter III of the Constitution firstly deals broadly with the framework for appeals from lower federal and State courts, including the continuing role for the Privy Council and, secondly, creates the institutional structure of the judicial arm of government through which Commonwealth judicial power is exercised. Despite its sparse terms, its interpretation by the High Court has had significant implications for the way in which parliaments in Australia – both federal and State – design their governmental institutions and distribute governmental power across the arms of government. It has given rise to some of the most significant High Court cases over the last 15 years, and continues to provide fertile ground for constitutional innovation.

This chapter will introduce the architecture of the federal judicature, and will start by outlining the place of the Crown in the judicial structures created by Chapter III. Unlike the position of the federal legislature and Executive government, the Crown is not invested with Commonwealth judicial power.[6] However, prior to federation, appeals were taken from colonial courts to the Queen in Council, and s 74 contemplates appeals to the Queen in Council from the High Court in some cases. As will be seen, a continuing role for the Privy Council as an appellate court created considerable controversy during the drafting of the Constitution.

The jurisdiction given to the High Court to hear appeals from lower federal and State courts will then be considered. As with other parts of the Constitution, the US Constitution provided a useful blueprint for the drafting of Chapter III and, in many important respects, the terms of Article III of the US Constitution were transplanted to the Australian context. However, the framers of Chapter III departed from the American model in relation to the appellate jurisdiction of the High Court. To give effect to the long-standing objective of establishing a general court of appeal, the High Court was given appellate jurisdiction from federal and State courts. This was in contrast to the US provisions that limit the US Supreme Court to appeals from federal courts or in relation to federal issues determined in State courts.

This chapter will then outline the way in which the Constitution creates the federal judicial structure through which Commonwealth judicial power is exercised. The design of this federal structure marks a second point of departure from the American model. Largely for purposes of expediency and efficiency, Commonwealth judicial power can be exercised by State courts as well as

**4** *Australasian Federation Conference, Melbourne* (1890) 26.
**5** *Convention Debates, Sydney* (1891) 96.
**6** *Re Refugee Review Tribunal; Ex parte Aala* (2000) 204 CLR 82, 92.

federal courts. Under Article III of the US Constitution, the judicial power of the United States is vested only in federal courts. As will be seen in this chapter and the next, these two departures from the US model have had considerable impact upon the development of Chapter III principles.

The position of Territory courts will also be considered. As neither federal courts nor State courts, Territory courts have hovered somewhere in between these two constitutional markers. As will be seen, the High Court has struggled to navigate this difficult constitutional terrain. Finally, s 80 of the Constitution requires a particular judicial structure when Commonwealth judicial power is being exercised to determine criminal guilt when a federal offence has been tried on indictment. As will be explained, this deceptively simple provision has created enormous uncertainty in constitutional interpretation.

## II Appeals to the Privy Council

### 1 A continuing role for the Privy Council

When the delegation representing the federating colonies arrived in England in 1900 to negotiate the enactment of the Australian Constitution through the Imperial Parliament, the main point of controversy was the role to be played by the Privy Council in the judicial affairs of the new federal body politic and in the continuing judicial systems of the States. The controversy was not to be unexpected, as the continuation of Privy Council appeals had been a divisive issue during the Convention Debates.

The Judicial Committee of the Privy Council (that is, a committee of the Crown in Council) had been the ultimate court of appeal within the colonial judicial systems prior to federation. There had been attempts, prior to the federal Constitutional Conventions of the 1890s, to establish a general court of appeal for the Australian colonies. Some premature ideas of a substitute court of appeal had been mooted since the 1840s. However, it was not until the 1880s that such proposals received serious consideration by the colonial governments.[7] As J M Bennett observed, '[w]ith a growing mood of Australian nationalism and a sense of independence becoming pronounced from the 1880s it was increasingly questioned whether a new forum, possibly an Australasian Court of Appeal, might be established in this country'.[8] These attempts, however, were overtaken by the federal movement in the 1890s, and the creation of a general court of appeal became inextricably tied to the creation of a federal judicial system. Sir Henry Parkes, the then Premier of New South Wales, and driving force behind the federal movement, proposed a resolution at the commencement of the 1891 Sydney Convention for the creation of:

**7** See generally J M Bennett, *Keystone of the Federal Arch* (AGPS, 1980) 3–6.
**8** Ibid, 3.

> A Judiciary, consisting of a Federal Supreme Court, which shall constitute a High Court of Appeal for Australia.[9]

Parkes intended this Supreme Court to be the ultimate court of appeal in Australia. '[We] shall make a great mistake', Parkes insisted, 'if we allow any appeal to be made outside the shores of the new Australia'.[10]

This proposal to sever ties with the Privy Council gave rise to considerable debate and disagreement, with contributions by the delegates reflecting a wide range of concerns and interests, leading to a complex array of suggested judicial models.[11] Delegates in favour of severing ties, or at least limiting the opportunities for Privy Council appeals, pointed to broad objectives of nation-building, independence and autonomy, a preference for local judges familiar with local circumstances, and a more expedient resolution of legal disputes. Dissatisfaction with the quality of Privy Council decisions was also a concern expressed by some delegates.

By contrast, arguments in favour of preserving Privy Council appeals reflected a strong desire to retain ties with the 'mother country', to preserve the unity of the common law, and to protect imperial commercial and industrial interests. Concerns about the limited pool from which local judges might be drawn, and the lower quality of their judgments, were also expressed by those opposed to severing ties.

These different concerns and interests gave rise to a range of suggestions for the constitutional design of Australian judicial systems. There were those delegates who favoured the complete exclusion of the Privy Council from the constitutional framework. Other delegates wanted to retain the Privy Council at the apex of the State and federal judicial systems. There were also delegates who favoured the retention of appeals from State courts, and those who sought to preserve Privy Council appeals for constitutional cases or cases involving imperial interests. There were even delegates who questioned whether an Australian court of appeal was needed at all.

At the end of the 1891 Convention, the compromise reached to satisfy a majority of the delegates was to give the federal Parliament the power to require appeals to be taken from State courts to a new Australian court of appeal, with the judgment of the Australian court to be final and conclusive.[12] Thus, a majority of the delegates considered it prudent to leave it to the federal Parliament to make the political judgement about the design of Australian judicial systems, rather than locking in an arrangement in advance. This was with one important qualification. The draft clause also sought to preserve the Crown prerogative to grant leave to appeal to the Privy Council from any Australian court 'in any case

**9** John Williams, *The Australian Constitution: A Documentary History* (Melbourne University Press, 2005) 47.
**10** *Convention Debates, Sydney* (1891) 26.
**11** For a detailed discussion of these contributions, see James Stellios, *The Federal Judicature: Chapter III of the Constitution* (LexisNexis, 2010) 9–14.
**12** See the draft clause in Williams, above n 9, 451.

in which the public interests of the Commonwealth, or of any State, or of any other part of the Queen's Dominions, are concerned'.[13] This qualification had been inserted by Sir Samuel Griffith, the leader of the Convention, chair of the 1891 Drafting Committee and the delegate responsible for much of the drafting changes during the 1891 Constitutional Convention. Griffith's qualification was designed to reflect the prevailing Privy Council practice in relation to appeals from the Supreme Court of Canada.

The same concerns and interests were ventilated during the 1897–8 Constitutional Convention, with similar proposals put forward for the institutional design of Australian judicial systems.[14] There were, however, three notable developments. Firstly, the Chief Justices of Tasmania, New South Wales and Queensland (most notably, Sir Samuel Griffith, by then Chief Justice of the Queensland Supreme Court) weighed in on the debate in favour of preserving Privy Council appeals. These views communicated to the Convention delegates were supported by a Judge of the New Zealand Supreme Court, who stressed that 'British capital' had to be protected and that cessation of Privy Council appeals would have a 'prejudicial effect on the financial interests of [the] colonies'.[15] Secondly, Sir Joseph Chamberlain, the Colonial Secretary, urged the colonial Premiers to rethink the abolition of Privy Council appeals. His reasons provided to George Reid, the Premier of New South Wales, captured many of the concerns and interests already expressed in the Australian debates.[16] Thirdly, a flood of petitions from commercial and business groups was received by the Convention, expressed in broadly similar terms, urging the Convention delegates to retain Privy Council appeals. Chief among the concerns expressed was a desire to prevent serious prejudice to:

> the material interests of Australia by depriving the British capitalist of his right to appeal to his own courts in serious cases, and thus prevent the inflow of British capital, upon which the colonies largely depend for their development.[17]

This prompted a strong response from many of the delegates, with Josiah Symon, a delegate from South Australia and Chair of the Judiciary Committee, protesting in the following terms:

> We are not making a Constitution for the merchants and people of England; we are making a Constitution for the people of Australia, and we ought to bear that in mind.[18]

However, the weight of British capital was to influence the remainder of the debates and, by the end of the 1897–8 Convention, after further intense exchanges among the delegates, a new compromise – captured in clause 74 of the draft

**13** Ibid.
**14** See Stellios, above n 11, 15–27.
**15** Letter from Mr Justice Richmond, read by Sir Joseph Abbott, *Convention Debates, Adelaide* (1897) 970–71.
**16** Williams, above n 9, 719–20.
**17** *Convention Debates, Melbourne* (1898) 4.
**18** *Convention Debates, Melbourne* (1898) 2306.

Constitution – was reached. The first feature of that compromise was to preserve constitutional questions – other than those raising imperial interests – for the new Australian court of appeal, the High Court. Secondly, except where the constitutional qualification applied, unsuccessful litigants in a State court could choose to appeal to the High Court or the Privy Council. Thirdly, appeals could be taken from the High Court to the Privy Council if Her Majesty in Council granted special leave, but Parliament was given the power to limit 'the matters in which such leave may be asked'.[19]

Thus, at the conclusion of the Constitutional Conventions, the nation-building exercise engaged in by the delegates produced Australian judicial systems that retained the Crown in Council as a significant feature. Indeed, although some delegates considered their brief as being to lay the foundations for an independent nation, others did not. This tension is well captured in the exchange between Sir John Downer (South Australia) and Sir Joseph Carruthers (New South Wales) during the Adelaide session of the 1897–8 Convention. In the midst of intense discussion about the place of the Privy Council in the constitutional framework, Downer urged the delegates in the following terms:

> We have come to the conclusion that we may cease to be provincial, and form the foundation of a nation. We do not propose in any way to separate from the British Crown, but on the other hand we look to it with reverence. We consider ourselves the same people, but the very essence of the difference is that we think we can make laws which will suffice us; in other words, to put it colloquially, we think we can manage our own affairs.[20]

Carruthers replied:

> The hon member speaks of this as one of the essentials to our becoming a nation, but we are not becoming a nation. ... We are becoming a dependency; we are a dependency; we, are not an independent nation.[21]

The nation-building exercise, to the extent there was one, was to encounter further hurdles during the passage of the Constitution through the Imperial Parliament. Once the framers' draft had cleared the colonial referenda processes, the Constitution was forwarded to the Imperial Parliament for enactment. The Imperial government had monitored the drafting process and provided comments on the successive drafts. As mentioned earlier, Chamberlain, the Colonial Secretary, had communicated his opposition to a cessation of Privy Council appeals. How would the draft provision – clause 74 – be received?

As La Nauze[22] and Williams[23] record in illuminating detail, there was some disagreement within the Imperial bureaucracy concerning the response to the Australian proposal. The Colonial Office considered clause 74 to be misguided,

**19** Ibid, 2536.
**20** *Convention Debates, Adelaide* (1897) 975.
**21** Ibid, 979.
**22** See J A La Nauze, *The Making of the Australian Constitution* (Melbourne University Press, 1974) ch 16.
**23** See above, n 9, 1160–68.

but that this was a mistake for the colonies to make. On the other hand, the Law Officers of the Crown opposed the cessation of appeals. The Imperial government, acting through the Colonial Secretary, informed the Australian delegates and the colonial Premiers that abolition of Privy Council appeals would risk the flight of British capital, and that clause 74 should be reconsidered. Following continuing disagreement between Chamberlain and the colonial delegates, some in-fighting within the Australian delegation, and a campaign by some colonial judicial officers (including Sir Samuel Griffith) to undermine the clause, Chamberlain introduced the Bill (containing the Constitution) into the Imperial Parliament without clause 74. From that point it was inevitable that clause 74, as agreed to by voters at the colonial referenda, would be compromised. After further exchanges between Chamberlain and the delegates, consultation with the colonial governments, and drafting advice offered by Sir Samuel Griffith, s 74 was reduced to its final form and enacted along with the rest of the draft Constitution, by covering clause 9 of the *Australian Constitution Act 1901* (Imp). The final version of s 74 has three key features. First, '[n]o appeal shall be permitted to the Queen in Council from a decision of the High Court upon any question, howsoever arising, as to the limits inter se of the Constitutional powers of the Commonwealth and those of any State or States, or as to the limits inter se of the Constitutional powers of any two or more States, unless the High Court shall certify that the question is one which ought to be determined by Her Majesty in Council'. The High Court can give a s 74 certificate for 'any special reason'.

Secondly, '[e]xcept as provided in this section, this Constitution shall not impair any right which the Queen may be pleased to exercise by virtue of Her Royal prerogative to grant special leave of appeal from the High Court to Her Majesty in Council'. However, the Parliament was given the power to 'make laws limiting the matters in which such leave may be asked, but proposed laws containing any such limitation shall be reserved by the Governor-General for Her Majesty's pleasure'. Thirdly, the provision says nothing about appeals from State courts, even in constitutional cases involving inter se questions.

Thus, at federation, the High Court was not intended to take its place at the apex of the Australian judicial systems. The disruption to colonial (soon to be State) judicial structures would, initially at least, be minimal. Following federation, there would be two types of jurisdiction that State courts could exercise: State jurisdiction (that is, where the authority to decide the dispute did not derive from Commonwealth legislation) and federal jurisdiction (that is, where authority to decide the dispute came from Commonwealth legislation enacted under s 77(iii) of the Constitution). In relation to State jurisdiction, the appellate pathway to the Privy Council would be preserved. As for federal jurisdiction, to save the Commonwealth government the expense of setting up its own set of lower federal courts, it was contemplated that State courts would be heavily utilised for the exercise of federal jurisdiction.[24] The appellate pathway to

**24** See below at Part IV.6.

the Privy Council from these federal jurisdiction cases would, subject to Commonwealth legislation to be discussed below, also remain. This would include constitutional cases heard in State courts, even those raising inter se questions. Finally, even the decisions of the High Court would be subject to appeal to the Privy Council. In cases not involving inter se questions, appeals would be taken until Parliament, with the Queen's approval, decided to bring them to an end. As for cases involving inter se questions, there was the facility for the High Court to grant a s 74 certificate.

It can be seen from this final institutional design that the nation-building objectives of many of the Convention delegates were not fully realised. Indeed, the Privy Council remained in the dominant position at the apex of the Australian judicial systems. The High Court was envisaged by many during the 1891 Convention (as reflected in Parkes's opening resolution) to be the ultimate court of appeal, the judgments of which would be final and conclusive. However, through the course of the Convention process and the negotiations with the Imperial government, that vision of the High Court was considerably compromised.

It was not until 1986 that Parkes's vision of the High Court as the ultimate court of appeal was finally and fully realised and, as will now be explained, that vision of autonomy was achieved through multiple stages of development by a combination of High Court interpretation and political will at both the federal and State levels.

## 2 The emergence of Australian judicial autonomy

There were four threads connecting Australian judicial systems to the Privy Council and undermining the place of the High Court at the apex of the judicial systems: appeals to the Privy Council from State courts exercising federal jurisdiction; the s 74 certificate procedure for appeals to the Privy Council from the High Court in cases involving inter se questions; appeals to the Privy Council from the High Court in cases not involving inter se questions; and appeals to the Privy Council from State courts exercising State jurisdiction. The severing of those threads occurred in multiple stages and, as will be seen, the High Court has played a significant role in the development of Australian judicial autonomy.

### Appeals from State courts exercising federal jurisdiction

The first thread to be severed was appeals to the Privy Council from State courts exercising federal jurisdiction. To understand the way in which this occurred, a short overview is needed of the scheme created by Chapter III for the exercise of federal jurisdiction. A more detailed explanation will follow below. As will be explained, ss 75 and 76 set out the nine heads (or subject areas) of original federal jurisdiction. Section 75 confers jurisdiction on the High Court in all matters identified in its five paragraphs. Section 76 confers power on Parliament to confer additional federal jurisdiction in the four matters set out in s 76.

The 'autochthonous expedient' in s 77(iii) of the Constitution allows the Commonwealth Parliament to vest original federal jurisdiction (that is, federal authority to decide a case) in relation to the nine heads of federal jurisdiction in State courts. Importantly, s 77(ii) allows the federal Parliament to define 'the extent to which the jurisdiction of any federal court shall be exclusive of that which belongs to or is invested in the courts of the States'. Thus, the Commonwealth Parliament has the power to preserve areas of federal jurisdiction for the High Court or a lower federal court.

Nevertheless, when Parliament enacted the *Judiciary Act* in 1903, it decided to vest all heads of federal jurisdiction in State courts (s 39(2)), subject to some exceptions (s 38). Accordingly, State courts had federal jurisdiction to determine federal matters, including matters 'arising under [the] Constitution, or involving its interpretation' (s 76(i)). However, the High Court had overlapping original jurisdiction. In addition to the five heads in s 75, Parliament conferred additional original jurisdiction pursuant to s 76. Most notably, s 30(a) of the *Judiciary Act* vested the jurisdiction over matters 'arising under [the] Constitution, or involving its interpretation'. Consequently, both the High Court and State courts could hear matters of federal jurisdiction, and the heads of jurisdiction in each overlapped.

Because the High Court was not the final court of appeal for the Australian judicial systems, this presented potential problems for their seamless integration. A State court case decided in federal jurisdiction could be taken on appeal to the Privy Council, instead of the High Court, and, even if taken to the High Court, it could then be taken on appeal from the High Court to the Privy Council if special leave were given. Thus, it was clear that the High Court was not the final court of appeal in most cases in federal jurisdiction and, if a federal jurisdiction case was taken directly to the Privy Council, then the High Court was cut out of the equation altogether. While this was unpalatable for those who desired to see the High Court as the ultimate court of appeal, it was structurally sound in cases where the Privy Council was the final court of appeal. To that extent, the Privy Council would sit at the apex of the Australian judicial systems, and all courts would be bound to follow its decisions.

However, the system broke down in cases of inter se constitutional questions. In those cases, s 74 gave the High Court control of appeals from its decisions to the Privy Council through the certificate mechanism, but the High Court could be by-passed by an appeal from State courts directly to the Privy Council. As Henry Higgins had inquired during the Convention Debates: which court would have the final say?[25]

As has been noted in previous chapters, the first three appointees to the High Court in 1903 were closely involved in drafting the Constitution.[26] In

**25** *Convention Debates, Melbourne* (1898) 337.
**26** See, eg, Chapter 3, Part III.

particular, Griffith CJ had played a significant role in the drafting process during the 1891 Convention and, although not a delegate to the 1897–8 Convention, had played a pivotal role in advising Chamberlain, the Colonial Secretary, on the compromise over Privy Council appeals, and in drafting the terms of s 74 to reflect the arrangement acceptable to the Imperial government. Barton J had been the leader of the 1897–8 Convention and was a member of the delegation that negotiated the terms of the compromise reflected in s 74. Barton had pushed strongly for the cessation of Privy Council appeals. While Griffith initially favoured the cessation of Privy Council appeals, he appeared to lobby for retention of such appeals when he advised Chamberlain on the issue in 1900. Given that context, it is not surprising that the relationship between the High Court and the Privy Council on inter se questions was dealt with very early in the High Court's life.

When s 74 was being finalised in 1900, Griffith had advised Chamberlain that appeals from State courts to the Privy Council in matters of federal jurisdiction could be prevented by vesting jurisdiction in such cases exclusively in federal courts.[27] However, that solution could not be adopted because Parliament had decided to use State courts for the exercise of federal jurisdiction. Instead, the Commonwealth enacted s 39(2)(a) of the *Judiciary Act 1903* which provided:

> Every decision of the Supreme Court of a State, or any other Court of a State from which at the establishment of the Commonwealth an appeal lay to the Queen in Council, shall be final and conclusive except so far as an appeal may be brought to the High Court.

Section 39(2) vested federal jurisdiction in State courts and, thus, the intention of s 39(2)(a) was to require appeals from State courts, *when exercising federal jurisdiction*, to be taken to the High Court.

The relationship between the High Court and the Privy Council on inter se questions, and the effectiveness of s 39(2) to channel State court appeals in cases involving federal jurisdiction to the High Court, were issues that gave rise to early disagreements and tension between State courts, the High Court and the Privy Council. As explained in Chapter 4, these issues were agitated in a series of cases dealing with the power of State Parliaments to levy taxes on Commonwealth officers.[28] State courts and the Privy Council took the view that Commonwealth officers were subject to State laws, and vice versa. However, the High Court took the view that the Commonwealth and the States were separate sovereigns within the federal system, and that their respective laws could not bind each other's officers and agents. The Privy Council and State court view was based on English precedent relating to the constitutional position in Canada.[29] The High Court's view was based on doctrines developed by the US Supreme Court.[30]

**27** La Nauze, above n 22, 267, 304.
**28** See Chapter 4, Part III.1.
**29** *Bank of Toronto v Lambe* [1887] 12 App Cas 575.
**30** *McCulloch v Maryland* 17 US (4 Wheat) 316 (1819).

The Victorian Supreme Court was the first to consider the issue in *In re the Income Tax Acts (No 4)* ('*Wollaston's* case'),[31] deciding to follow the Privy Council decision from the Canadian constitutional context in *Bank of Toronto v Lambe*. The Tasmanian Supreme Court soon followed in *Pedder v D'Emden*,[32] but the High Court on appeal in *D'Emden v Pedder* disagreed, preferring the constitutional analogy to the United States Constitution and the decision of the US Supreme Court in *McCulloch v Maryland*. The Victorian Supreme Court was presented with the issue again in *In re the Income Tax Acts (No 4)* (*Deakin's and Lyne's* cases'),[33] and again chose to follow the decision of the Privy Council. On the choice between High Court and Privy Council authority, Madden CJ of the Victorian Supreme Court said:

> we have before us actual decisions of the Privy Council, which is at least a concurrent Court of ultimate appeal with the High Court, for our guidance in our decisions. ... The High Court is also a Court certainly of ulterior appeal, and it may be of ultimate appeal, as the Privy Council always is; and on this particular question it will be or will not be the Court of ultimate appeal according as it may seem fit to the High Court to give leave to appeal thereto, or to withhold such leave. But if the High Court takes a different view of this case from what we take, or of our reasons in *Wollaston's Case,* we will show it all the respect we are in duty bound to show it according as it may turn out to be the ultimate Court of Appeal, and its decision the final ascertainment of the law on the matter. That will depend on the relation of the one Court to the other.[34]

On appeal in *Deakin v Webb*, the High Court followed its previous decision and refused to grant a s 74 certificate to appeal to the Privy Council.[35] Griffith CJ, Barton and O'Connor JJ took the view that s 74 of the Constitution identified the High Court as 'the tribunal of ultimate appeal'[36] on inter se questions. Reflecting on the drafting process, Griffith CJ said:

> We know historically that that responsibility was only cast upon us after long consideration and negotiation. Various proposals were made, and the establishment of the Commonwealth very nearly fell through in consequence of the differences of opinion upon the point. The final solemn determination of the English Parliament, with the assent of Australia, was that that responsibility should be cast upon the High Court.[37]

With the High Court's view clear, both as to its status as the ultimate court of appeal on inter se questions and on the substantive constitutional issue, the Victorian government manufactured a case in the Victorian Supreme Court with the intention of having the issue appealed directly to the Privy Council.[38] Without

**31** (1902) 28 VLR 357.
**32** (1903) 2 TLR 146.
**33** *In re the Income Tax Acts (No 4)* (1904) 29 VLR 748.
**34** Ibid, 764.
**35** (1904) 1 CLR 585.
**36** Ibid, 622.
**37** Ibid, 622; see also 626–8, 630–31.
**38** See Anthony Blackshield, Michael Coper and John Goldring, 'Privy Council' in Anthony Blackshield, Michael Coper and George Williams (eds), *The Oxford Companion to the High Court of Australia* (Oxford University Press, 2001) 560.

the Commonwealth's knowledge of the proceedings, the Victorian Supreme Court in *In re the Income Tax Acts* (*Outtrim's* case)[39] applied the High Court's decision in *Deakin v Webb* and then granted leave to appeal to the Privy Council. On the operation of s 39(2)(a) of the *Judiciary Act*, which seemed to suggest that the appeal could only go to the High Court,[40] Hodges J of the Victorian Supreme Court said that nothing in the Constitution authorised Parliament 'to deprive the subject of the right of appeal' to the Privy Council and his Honour doubted that s 39(2)(a) operated to prevent an appeal.[41] On appeal, the Privy Council in *Webb v Outtrim*[42] rejected the High Court's view in *Deakin v Webb* and tended to agree with Hodges J that s 39(2)(a) was ineffective to prevent an appeal to the Privy Council.

Further litigation immediately followed, with State courts following the decision of the Privy Council in *Webb v Outtrim*. In *Baxter v Commissioners of Taxation (NSW)*[43] the High Court had another opportunity to consider the issues. Would it stand its ground or follow the decision of the Privy Council? In a joint judgment, Griffith CJ, Barton and O'Connor JJ reaffirmed the Court's decision in *D'Emden v Pedder* and strongly asserted its place at the apex of the Australian judicial system on inter se questions:

> In our opinion, the intention of the British legislature was to substitute for a distant Court, of uncertain composition, imperfectly acquainted with Australian conditions, unlikely to be assisted by counsel familiar with those conditions, and whose decisions would be rendered many months, perhaps years, after its judgment has been invoked, an Australian Court, immediately available, constant in its composition, well versed in Australian history and conditions, Australian in its sympathies, and whose judgments, rendered as the occasion arose, would form a working code for the guidance of the Commonwealth.[44]

Alluding to the Privy Council's decision in *Webb v Outtrim*, their Honours said that 'it would not, perhaps, have been extravagant to expect that the Judicial Committee would recognize the intention of the Imperial legislature to make the opinion of the High Court final in such matters. But that is their concern, not ours …'.[45] Isaacs and Higgins JJ, who also were active delegates during the Convention Debates, had been appointed to the High Court by the time it heard the appeal in *Baxter*. Isaacs J agreed with the joint judgment,[46] but Higgins J dissented, concluding that there was nothing in the Constitution that altered the ultimate authority of the Privy Council in inter se cases.[47] On the validity of s 39(2)(a) of the *Judiciary Act*, the joint judgment took the view that it operated

**39** [1905] VLR 463.
**40** Since the Victorian Supreme Court seemed to be exercising federal jurisdiction to determine a constitutional question.
**41** *In re the Income Tax Acts* [1905] VLR 463, 468.
**42** (1906) 4 CLR 356 (PC).
**43** (1907) 4 CLR 1087.
**44** Ibid, 1118.
**45** Ibid, 1117.
**46** Ibid, 1148.
**47** Ibid, 1176–7.

to deprive the Supreme Court of the power to grant leave to appeal, but left the Crown's prerogative to grant special leave untouched.[48] Isaacs J expressed no view on the issue, but Higgins J considered it to be invalid.

In refusing to grant a s 74 certificate to appeal to the Privy Council,[49] Griffith CJ suggested steps for the Commonwealth Parliament to take to remove this tension and possibility for conflict between the High Court and the Privy Council at the apex of the Australian judicial systems. If the Commonwealth were to give the High Court exclusive jurisdiction under s 77(ii) to hear inter se questions, there would be no opportunity for State Supreme Courts to hear such claims and, thus, no appeal would be possible to the Privy Council. This mechanism had been suggested by Griffith to Chamberlain in 1900 when advising on the wording of s 74. However, these provisions had not been enacted when the Commonwealth Parliament established the High Court in 1903.[50] With a clear indication forward from the High Court, Parliament inserted ss 38A and 40A into the *Judiciary Act*[51] to give the High Court exclusive jurisdiction and to require State court proceedings raising inter se questions to be transferred to the High Court.

Thus, by 1907, the *Judiciary Act* provisions operated so that matters determined in federal jurisdiction were required to go on appeal from State Supreme Courts to the High Court (s 39(2)(a)) and any State court cases involving inter se questions had to be transferred to the High Court which would have exclusive jurisdiction. A majority of the High Court upheld the validity of s 39(2)(a) in *Commonwealth v Limerick Steamship Co Ltd & Kidman*.[52] As for any tension with the view of the Privy Council in *Webb v Outtrim* (and that of Hodge J of the Victorian Supreme Court) doubting the constitutional validity of s 39(2)(a), the majority in *Kidman* considered that *Webb v Outtrim* had been decided by the Victorian Supreme Court in *State* jurisdiction and, thus, there was no occasion in that case to consider the validity of s 39(2)(a). Sections 38A and 40A were then upheld in *Pirrie v McFarlane*.[53]

### Appeals from the High Court to the Privy Council in inter se matters

The High Court essentially has neutralised the s 74 certificate procedure. It has only once 'taken the exceptional course'[54] of granting a s 74 certificate, and the provision was considered by six High Court judges, in the 1985 case of *Kirmani v Captain Cook Cruises Pty Ltd*,[55] to be 'the vestigial remnant of the hierarchical

**48** Ibid, 1139.
**49** *Flint v Webb* (1907) 4 CLR 1178.
**50** See La Nauze, above n 22, 268.
**51** Inserted by the *Judiciary Act 1907* (Cth), ss 2 and 5.
**52** (1924) 35 CLR 69.
**53** (1925) 36 CLR 170. They were later repealed by ss 7 and 9 of the *Judiciary Amendment Act 1976* (Cth).
**54** *Attorney-General (Cth) v Colonial Sugar Refining Co Ltd* (1913) 17 CLR 644, 645 (PC), discussed in Chapter 3, Part III.1.
**55** (1985) 159 CLR 461, 463, 465.

connexion which formerly existed between Australian courts exercising federal jurisdiction and the Privy Council'. As their Honours said:

> Although the jurisdiction to grant a certificate stands in the Constitution, such limited purpose as it had has long since been spent. The march of events and the legislative changes that have been effected – to say nothing of national sentiment – have made the jurisdiction obsolete. Indeed an exercise of the jurisdiction now would involve this Court in passing the responsibility for final decision to the Privy Council in that class of constitutional case which the Constitution marked out above all others as the class of case which should be reserved for the final decision of this Court ...

### Appeals from the High Court in non-inter se cases

Pursuant to its power in s 74 of the Constitution to 'make laws limiting the matters in which [special] leave may be asked' of Her Majesty in Council for an appeal from the High Court, the Commonwealth Parliament brought non-inter se appeals to an end in two stages. In 1968, the Commonwealth enacted the *Privy Council (Limitation of Appeals) Act 1968* (Cth) providing that special leave could only be sought where the High Court's decision was given on appeal from a State court exercising non-federal jurisdiction and that did not involve the application or interpretation of the Constitution or a Commonwealth law (s 3).[56] In 1975, the Commonwealth then enacted the *Privy Council (Appeals from the High Court) Act 1975* (Cth) to abolish Privy Council appeals from the High Court in relation to matters left unregulated by the 1968 Act. Both Acts were reserved for her Majesty's pleasure and the Queen's assent was provided.[57]

An obvious objection to these Acts was that they sought to *abolish* Privy Council appeals entirely, and not *limit* them as provided for in s 74. Quick and Garran had written in 1901 that the power given by s 74 was 'to limit, and not to abolish'.[58] 'It is conceived', they continued, 'that a law of the Federal Parliament, purporting to abolish the right of asking for leave in all matters whatever, would be outside the scope of the Constitution'.[59] The response to a challenge to the validity of the 1968 Act was easy enough – that Act did not abolish appeals 'in all matters whatever', and this argument was accepted by the Privy Council when the provision was challenged in *Kitano v Commonwealth*.[60] Of course, the same could not be said for the 1975 Act. When read with the 1968 Act, all appeals to the Privy Council, other than those through the s 74 certificate process, would be abolished. Nevertheless, the constitutional validity of the 1975 Act was upheld by the High Court in *Attorney-General of the Commonwealth v T & G Mutual Life Society Ltd*.[61]

**56** It also brought to an end appeals from lower federal courts and Territory Supreme Courts (s 4).
**57** The enactment of these two Acts was part of a bigger Commonwealth project to abolish all Australian appeals to the Privy Council: see Anne Twomey, *The Chameleon Crown* (2006) ch 11.
**58** John Quick and Robert Garran, *Annotated Constitution of the Australian Commonwealth* (2001) 763.
**59** Ibid.
**60** (1975) 132 CLR 231 (PC).
**61** (1978) 144 CLR 161.

Two reasons were advanced by the Court in support of reading the power in s 74 broadly to allow Parliament to abrogate all Privy Council appeals. The first was that s 74 required such a law to be reserved for Her Majesty's pleasure. That, it was thought, was a sufficient check on the exercise of power under s 74.[62] Secondly, a broad construction would lead to absurd outcomes. If Parliament were required to leave some matters for Privy Council appeal, it might cleverly circumvent that requirement by identifying 'matters which in practice would never be likely to arise' and preserve them for the Privy Council. Gibbs ACJ, Mason and Jacobs JJ noted that '[a] construction which would make the validity of a law depend upon the ingenuity of the legislature in this way would serve no constitutional purpose and cannot have been intended by the framers of the Constitution'.[63]

The Court's reasoning is strong on the first point, but is at its weakest on the second. Appealing to the intention of the framers in this particular context, even a putative one, is fraught with danger. As the discussion above highlights, the framers were deeply divided in their views on the continuation of Privy Council appeals and, in any event, their views were trumped by the Imperial government's desire to maintain appeals as much as possible. It seems that the decision was driven more by 'the ultimate goal that judgments of [the High Court] should be final',[64] and demonstrates clearly the important role played by the High Court in shaping the Australian judicial system.

### Appeals to the Privy Council from State courts exercising State jurisdiction

The most stubborn of the four strands were appeals from State courts exercising State jurisdiction. State governments resisted attempts to deny litigants the option of appealing from State courts to the Privy Council when the case involved State matters.[65] It was not until the passage of the *Australia Acts 1986* (Cth and UK) that such appeals were brought to an end. Because appeals from the High Court had ceased in 1975, the continuation of appeals from State courts 'saw a bizarre situation of dualism – and political conflict – at the apex of the Australian hierarchy of courts', a situation that gave rise to 'delicate problems of precedent and judicial comity'.[66] As former Chief Justice of the High Court, Sir Anthony Mason, has said, it was not until the enactment of the Australia Acts that 'the High Court was in a position authoritatively to declare the law for Australia, without being bound by Privy Council decisions'.[67] Thus, what Parkes had proposed in 1891 at the commencement of the Constitutional Conventions – an Australian court of appeal sitting at the apex of the Australian judicial systems,

**62** Ibid, 170.
**63** Ibid.
**64** Ibid, 169–70
**65** See Twomey, above n 57, ch 11.
**66** Blackshield, Coper and Goldring, above n 38, 560.
**67** Sir Anthony Mason, 'The Evolving Role and Function of the High Court' in Brian Opeskin and Fiona Wheeler (eds), *The Australian Federal Judicial System* (Melbourne University Press, 2000) 95, 101–2.

and Australian judicial autonomy – was not fully realised until this final strand of connection to the Privy Council was severed.

## III Appellate jurisdiction of the High Court

It was envisaged from the very beginning that the High Court would be a general court of appeal. Indeed, one of the main departures from the American model in Article III of the US Constitution is that the High Court is a court of appeal from lower federal courts and State courts, irrespective of whether State courts exercise federal or State judicial power. As will be seen in Chapter 9, this and other unique aspects of the Chapter III architecture have been considered by the High Court to be important when drawing implications from the text and structure of Chapter III.

Section 73 of the Constitution provides that the High Court 'shall have jurisdiction, with such exceptions and subject to such regulations as the Parliament prescribes, to hear and determine appeals from all judgments, decrees, orders, and sentences': (i) of the High Court when exercising original jurisdiction; (ii) of any lower federal court, court exercising federal jurisdiction, or State Supreme Court; and (iii) of the Inter-State Commission. There are four important features of s 73: the reference to the Inter-State Commission; the meaning of 'exceptions' and 'regulations'; the meaning of 'judgments, decrees, orders, and sentences'; and the reference to 'courts exercising federal jurisdiction' and the place of Territory courts (discussion of which is deferred until later in the chapter).

### 1 The Inter-State Commission

The Inter-State Commission is a creature of the Constitution. Section 101 provides that '[t]here shall be an Inter-State Commission, with such powers of adjudication and administration as the Parliament deems necessary for the execution and maintenance, within the Commonwealth, of the provisions of this Constitution relating to trade and commerce, and of all laws made thereunder'. On the face of the Constitution, the Inter-State Commission does not fall neatly into the tripartite arrangement of federal government institutions into the legislature, executive and judiciary. On the one hand, it has some features that are aligned with the judicial bodies referred to in s 71 that exercise the judicial power of the Commonwealth. Section 101 refers to the power of *adjudication* and, as noted, appeals from the Commission on questions of law go to the High Court under s 73(iii). Furthermore, the constitutional protections for commissioners, as set out in s 103 of the Constitution, are virtually identical to the protections for federal judges under s 72 of the Constitution.[68]

**68** The difference being that commissioners are to be appointed for seven years, whereas the tenure of judges was interpreted (initially) to mean life tenure. An amendment to the Constitution in 1977 set the retirement age for High Court judges at 70 and allows Parliament to set the retirement age for other federal court judges to a maximum of 70 years.

However, there are also features that are more akin to a body of executive character. The Commission's powers include those of *administration*, and it is intended to *execute and maintain* laws of trade and commerce. The *execution and maintenance* of federal laws is identified in s 61 as an executive function. The utility of the Commission was, presumably, its capacity to exercise a combination of judicial and executive powers.

The Commission was created by the *Inter-State Commission Act 1912* (Cth), and was invested with a range of judicial and non-judicial powers. It could hear and determine certain complaints as a court of record, and could grant relief including damages and injunctions. Importantly, it could exercise judicial review of the validity of State legislation and could impose penalties where its orders were not complied with. As will be explained in Chapter 9, these are core judicial powers. The conferral of these judicial powers on the Commission was challenged in *New South Wales v Commonwealth*.[69] The High Court held that Chapter III of the Constitution identified a clear scheme for the exercise of judicial power. The institutions that could exercise the judicial power of the Commonwealth were identified in s 71 and a negative implication arose from the text which prevented Commonwealth judicial power being exercised in any other way. According to Griffith CJ, the provisions in Chapter III 'are complete and exclusive, and there cannot be a third class of Courts which are neither federal Courts nor State Courts invested with federal jurisdiction'.[70] For Isaacs J, the three arms of government had been 'delimited with scrupulous care',[71] and consequently, the Commission had been invested unlawfully with judicial power. As a consequence, the Commission's utility – as a hybrid institution – was greatly reduced and it was abandoned in 1920. Further attempts to revive it in the 1970s were unsuccessful.[72]

## 2 'Exceptions' and 'regulations'

Section 73 allows Parliament to make 'exceptions' and 'regulations' to the appellate jurisdiction of the High Court. When the provision was drafted, some of the delegates expressed concern that the power of Parliament to control the appellate jurisdiction of the Court in this way, particularly by making 'exceptions', 'would allow too great an interference with the appellate jurisdiction'.[73] However, these concerns were rejected: Parliament should have the power 'to prevent an abuse of the judicial machinery'[74] and should be trusted not to 'degrade or improperly interfere with the administration of justice'.[75]

**69** (1915) 20 CLR 54.
**70** Ibid, 62.
**71** Ibid, 90.
**72** For a history of the Commission, see Michael Coper, 'The Second Coming of the Fourth Arm: The Role and Functions of the Inter-State Commission' (1989) 63 *Australian Law Journal* 731.
**73** *Convention Debates, Melbourne* (1898) 331.
**74** *Convention Debates, Melbourne* (1898) 1887.
**75** *Convention Debates, Melbourne* (1898) 1892. See the discussion in *Smith Kline & French Laboratories (Australia) Ltd v Commonwealth* (1991) 173 CLR 194, 208–11.

The precise scope of this power to regulate the appellate jurisdiction is unclear. Certainly, the power does not allow Parliament to '"eat up or destroy" the general regime specified in s 73 of the Constitution as to the appellate jurisdiction of the High Court'.[76] Furthermore, it is unlikely that it 'extend[s] to excluding altogether one of the heads specifically mentioned by s 73' – for example, appeals from the Inter-State Commission.[77]

By contrast, it would seem to be a permissible 'exception' for Parliament to prevent appeals from lower State courts exercising discrete matters of federal jurisdiction, at least where a specialist federal court has been created to hear such appeals. For example, in *Cockle v Isaksen*,[78] the High Court considered provisions of the *Conciliation and Arbitration Act 1904* (Cth) providing that the Commonwealth Industrial Court was to hear appeals from the judgments of lower State courts exercising federal jurisdiction in matters arising under that Act, and which prohibited appeals to the High Court from those lower State courts when exercising that federal jurisdiction. In holding the provisions to be valid, Dixon CJ, McTiernan and Kitto JJ commented on the meaning of the word 'exception':

> An exception assumes a general rule or proposition and specifies a particular case or description of case which would be subsumed under the rule or proposition but which, because it possesses special features or characteristics, is to be excluded from the application of the rule or proposition. It is not a conception that can be defined in the abstract with exactness or applied with precision; it must depend very much upon context.[79]

The exceptions considered in *Cockle* were 'defined by reference to the matter involved in the appeal' and, consequently, the exception did not 'eat up or destroy the general rule laid down by the Constitution that appeals shall lie to [the High] Court from judgments decrees and sentences of courts of a State exercising federal jurisdiction'.[80]

The appellate jurisdiction of the High Court is now regulated by special leave provisions. For example, s 35 of the *Judiciary Act* provides that special leave is required to appeal from State courts, whether exercising federal or State jurisdiction, and whether the case is criminal or civil. The statutory criteria, applied to determine whether special leave will be granted, include whether the case raises a question of law of 'public importance', whether the High Court is required to 'resolve differences of opinion between different courts' and 'whether the interests of the administration of justice ... require consideration by the High Court' (s 35A). Similar provisions regulate appeals from Territory courts (s 35AA of the

**76** *Sue v Hill* (1999) 199 CLR 462, 485, quoting from *Cockle v Isaksen* (1957) 99 CLR 155, 166.
**77** *Collins v Charles Marshall Pty Ltd* (1955) 92 CLR 529, 544.
**78** (1957) 99 CLR 155.
**79** Ibid, 165.
**80** Ibid. See also 172, 174, and 175–6. See also *Federated Engine-Drivers and Firemen's Association of Australasia v Colonial Sugar Refining Co Ltd* (1916) 22 CLR 103; *Watson v Federal Commissioner of Taxation* (1953) 87 CLR 353.

*Judiciary Act*), the Federal Court (s 33 of the *Federal Court of Australia Act 1976* (Cth)) and the Family Court (s 95 of the *Family Law Act 1975* (Cth)). These provisions were upheld as 'regulations' of the High Court's appellate jurisdiction in *Smith Kline & French Laboratories (Australia) Ltd v Commonwealth*.[81]

## 3 'Judgments, decrees, orders, and sentences'

The High Court has always taken the view that the expression 'judgments, decrees, orders and sentences' is 'confined to decisions made in the exercise of judicial power'.[82] However, the High Court initially took a very narrow view of what an exercise of judicial power involved in this context. As the Court said of this initial approach in *Swiss Aluminium Australia Ltd v Federal Commissioner of Taxation*:

> It is well settled that an order must finally determine the rights of parties before it will qualify as an order within the meaning of s 73 of the Constitution.[83]

This approach had particular implications in circumstances where a State legislative scheme allowed for questions to be reserved for, or referred to, a State Supreme Court from a lower court or tribunal. If the legislative scheme provided that the referring court or tribunal (and the parties) were bound to apply the answers provided to determine the rights of the parties in dispute, then the Supreme Court's answers would be considered to involve an exercise of judicial power and, consequently, would be capable of appeal to the High Court.[84] By contrast, where the answers were not directly determinative of the rights of the parties in this way, then the answers were considered to be advisory or consultative only. For example, in *Saffron v The Queen*,[85] the High Court considered State provisions that allowed for the referral of questions of law from a criminal trial court to the NSW Court of Criminal Appeal following the acquittal of an accused. Because the answers given would have had no impact on the rights of the acquitted person, the answers were considered by the High Court to be advisory in nature and, consequently, not subject to appeal to the High Court.

Recognising the rigidities that these principles imposed, and the consequences it had for the High Court 'as the final appellate court of the nation',[86] the High Court reformulated the operation of s 73 in *Mellifont v Attorney-General (Qld)*.[87] In *Mellifont*, the Court considered s 669A(2) of the *Criminal Code 1899* (Qld) that allowed the referral of questions of law by the Attorney-General to the

**81** (1991) 173 CLR 194.
**82** *Mobil Oil Australia Pty Ltd v Victoria* (2002) 211 CLR 1, 38.
**83** (1987) 163 CLR 421, 425.
**84** See, eg, *Smith v Mann* (1932) 47 CLR 426.
**85** (1953) 88 CLR 523. See also *Fisher v Fisher* (1986) 161 CLR 438; *Swiss Aluminium Australia Ltd v Federal Commissioner of Taxation* (1987) 163 CLR 421.
**86** *O'Toole v Charles David Pty Ltd* (1991) 171 CLR 232, 268; see also at 283–4.
**87** (1991) 173 CLR 289.

Court of Criminal Appeal in circumstances where an accused had been acquitted of a charge, or discharged following the Crown's withdrawal of the charge, as a result of a ruling by the trial judge on the referred legal question. Thus, the proceeding would no longer be on foot when the Court of Criminal Appeal provided answers to the referred questions. On the pre-*Mellifont* understanding of s 73, the answers would not be determinative of the rights of the parties and, consequently, no appeal was possible.

The High Court in *Mellifont* rejected this narrow approach. A majority of the Court (Mason CJ, Deane, Dawson, Gaudron and McHugh JJ) reiterated the core proposition underlying s 73 that 'the reference to judgments, decrees, orders and sentences relates to determinations made by the relevant courts in the exercise of judicial power'.[88] However, in an attempt to rework the analysis underlying the pre-*Mellifont* cases, the Court went on to consider whether the case-stated mechanism satisfied the requirements set out in *In re Judiciary and Navigation Acts*.[89] As will be explained in Chapter 9, the High Court in *In re Judiciary* held invalid certain Commonwealth provisions that allowed the Governor-General to refer a constitutional question to the High Court in the absence of a concrete legal dispute. From *In re Judiciary*, the majority in *Mellifont* extracted two propositions:

> One is the notion of an abstract question of law not involving the right or duty of any body or person; the second is the making of a declaration of law divorced or dissociated from any attempt to administer it.[90]

Neither concept is offended, the majority said, by a case stated procedure whilst a matter is pending – the answers to reserved questions 'are given as an integral part of the process of determining the rights and obligations of the parties which are at stake in the proceedings in which the questions are reserved'.[91] In such circumstances, the answers would be given in the exercise of judicial power 'because the seeking and the giving of the answers constitutes an important and influential, if not decisive, step in the judicial determination of the rights and liabilities in issue in the litigation'.[92]

However, in relation to the legislation before the Court, the answers would not operate in that way since they would not affect an acquittal or be determinative of any rights where a charge had been withdrawn. Nevertheless, the majority held that the referred questions and answers '*[arose] out of* the proceedings on the indictment and [were] a statutory extension of those proceedings'[93] so that:

> ... the decision on the reference was made with respect to a 'matter' which was the subject-matter of the legal proceedings at first instance and was not divorced from

**88** Ibid, 300.
**89** (1921) 29 CLR 257. See below at Chapter 9.
**90** *Mellifont* (1991) 173 CLR 289, 303.
**91** Ibid.
**92** Ibid.
**93** Ibid, 304 (emphasis in original).

> the ordinary administration of the law. The decision is therefore to be distinguished from the abstract declaration sought by the Executive Government in *In re Judiciary and Navigation Acts*. That opinion was academic, in response to an abstract question, and hypothetical in the sense that it was unrelated to any actual controversy between parties.[94]

The fact that the referral procedure was designed to correct an error of law at trial was the characteristic of the proceedings 'that stamp[ed] them as an exercise of judicial power' and was sufficient to trigger the appellate jurisdiction in s 73.[95]

Despite this more liberal approach, there must still be a connection between the answers and a legal dispute. As Gaudron, Gummow and Hayne JJ said about *Mellifont* in *Director of Public Prosecutions (SA) v B*, 'it was the relationship between the question reserved and the trial which was critical to the conclusion reached'.[96] In *Momcilovic v The Queen*,[97] the High Court considered the validity of provisions of the Victorian *Charter of Human Rights and Responsibilities Act 2006* (Vic). The Charter creates a dialogue model of human rights protection which provides, in part, that Victorian legislation is to be interpreted consistently with a range of human rights set out in the Act. Where the Supreme Court, when considering Victorian legislation, reaches the conclusion that a provision cannot be read consistently with human rights, it is authorised to make a declaration of incompatibility indicating that the provision is incompatible with human rights.

One of the questions before the High Court in *Momcilovic* was whether a declaration of incompatibility made by the Victorian Court of Appeal could be appealed to the High Court, it having been held by a majority of the Court to involve an exercise of non-judicial power. Because of the way in which the members of the Court resolved the other issues in the case, no clear answer was given to this question. However, French CJ (with Bell J agreeing on this point) considered that the High Court could not consider the validity of the declaration because, as an exercise of non-judicial power, it could not be appealed to the High Court.[98] This was despite the fact that the power to make the declaration was exercised in the course of a dispute involving an interpretation of the very legislation that became the subject of the declaration.[99]

**94** Ibid, 305.
**95** Ibid, 305. The conclusion followed irrespective of whether the Crown had an intention to present a fresh indictment in the case where the accused's charge had been withdrawn (at 306).
**96** (1998) 194 CLR 566, 576. See also *Re McBain; Ex parte Australian Catholic Bishops Conference* (2002) 209 CLR 372, 409 ('The decision of the Court of Criminal Appeal was held to involve the exercise of judicial power by that Court because the procedure was directed to correcting errors in a criminal trial.').
**97** (2011) 245 CLR 1.
**98** Ibid, 70.
**99** For an analysis and critique of French CJ's conclusion, see Will Bateman and James Stellios, 'Chapter III of the Constitution, Federal Jurisdiction and Dialogue Models of Human Rights' (2012) 36 *Melbourne University Law Review* 1, 33–6.

# IV The federal judicial system

## 1 Original federal jurisdiction

As has been seen, one of the objectives of the framers of the Constitution was to create an Australian court of appeal. The progressive achievement of that objective after federation and the jurisdiction of the High Court to hear appeals from lower courts were considered above. In addition to the creation of a court of appeal, the framers, from very early in the Convention Debates, contemplated the creation of a set of courts to exercise the *original* jurisdiction of the new federal tier of government.[100] Without a set of federal courts, the Constitution was thought to be 'imperfect'[101] and put in place a 'mutilated government'.[102] The judiciary provisions in the United States Constitution had three key features. First, the US Supreme Court had been created, and thus constitutionally entrenched, by the Constitution. Secondly, Congress was given the power to create a set of lower federal courts. Thirdly, the Constitution identified the subject areas of federal concern (ie, areas in relation to which federal jurisdiction might be exercised) that would attract the jurisdiction of a federal court when authorised to exercise the judicial power of the United States (in contrast to the judicial power of the American States). These key features appealed to Inglis Clark, who copied this architecture into the draft Constitution that he distributed to Convention delegates prior to the commencement of the 1891 Convention. Despite some changes to this core design during the 1891 Convention, these features were restored during the 1897–8 Convention and are given effect by the provisions of Chapter III.

A final feature of the federal judicature created by Chapter III for the exercise of federal jurisdiction was raised during the committee stage at the Adelaide session of the 1897–8 Convention. Walter James, a delegate for Western Australia, had raised concerns about the expense that the new federal government would be put to if required to create a set of lower federal courts in the early years of the new Commonwealth. Could State courts be required to exercise Commonwealth judicial power? This would mark a significant departure from the American model and the core features adopted by Inglis Clark in his 1891 draft. Convention delegates sought the advice of Sir Samuel Griffith, who had been appointed Chief Justice of Queensland. Griffith approved of this structural design and, thus, the 'autochthonous expedient' of investing State courts with federal jurisdiction was agreed to by the 1897–8 Convention.[103]

These key elements find their place in Chapter III. Section 71 provides that 'judicial power of the Commonwealth' is vested in 'the High Court of Australia',

**100** For more detail on the Convention Debates, see Stellios, above n 11, 52–5.
**101** *Convention Debates, Sydney* (1891) 96.
**102** Ibid, 253.
**103** See La Nauze, above n 22, 130–31. For the expression 'autochthonous expedient' see *R v Kirby; Ex parte Boilermakers' Society of Australia* (1956) 94 CLR 254, 268.

in lower 'federal courts' created by Parliament and 'in such other courts as it invests with federal jurisdiction'. Thus, s 71 assumes the existence of the High Court[104] as a receptacle of Commonwealth judicial power, and contemplates the creation of lower federal courts by Parliament and the facility of State courts for the exercise of Commonwealth judicial power.

The circumstances that might attract an exercise of Commonwealth judicial power were identified as 'matters' of *original* federal jurisdiction in ss 75 and 76 of the Constitution. Section 75 sets out five heads of original jurisdiction and confers that jurisdiction on the High Court, thereby constitutionally entrenching its exercise. Section 76 sets out four additional heads of federal jurisdiction, and empowers Parliament to vest the High Court with that jurisdiction. The content of these matters, considered to be appropriate for federal jurisdiction, were drawn by Inglis Clark from Article III of the US Constitution.[105] The more important of those paragraphs will be outlined below.

Section 77 of the Constitution completes the picture by empowering the federal Parliament to authorise lower federal courts (s 77(i)) and State courts (s 77(iii)) to exercise federal jurisdiction in relation to any of the 'matters' identified in ss 75 and 76. It should also be emphasised that Territory courts can exercise federal jurisdiction. Section 122 of the Constitution empowers Parliament to make laws 'for the government of any territory'. This section provides the source of legislative authority for the creation of Territory courts, whether those courts are created (directly) by the federal Parliament or (indirectly) by a legislative assembly created by Parliament for a Territory. Despite not being mentioned in s 77 of the Constitution, the High Court has accepted that Territory courts can exercise federal jurisdiction and, thus, are 'other courts' that can exercise Commonwealth judicial power.[106]

Of course, courts have to be authorised to exercise federal jurisdiction in relation to the matters identified in ss 75 and 76. As for the High Court, s 75 vests original federal jurisdiction in relation to the matters identified in that section. Additionally, under s 76 of the Constitution, Parliament has conferred jurisdiction on the High Court 'in all matters arising under the Constitution or involving its interpretation'[107] and 'in trials of indictable offences against the laws of the Commonwealth'.[108] Apart from a few discrete pockets of jurisdiction deriving

**104** Although its operation had to wait for enabling federal legislation enacted in 1903: *Judiciary Act 1903* (Cth).

**105** See Inglis Clark's memorandum reproduced in Williams, above n 9, 69.

**106** See *Blunden v Commonwealth* (2003) 218 CLR 330; *North Australian Aboriginal Legal Aid Service Inc v Bradley* (2004) 218 CLR 146; *John Pfeiffer Pty Ltd v Rogerson* (2000) 203 CLR 503.

**107** Jurisdiction in s 76(i) conferred on the High Court by s 30(a) of the *Judiciary Act 1903* (Cth).

**108** Conferred by s 30(c) of the *Judiciary Act 1903* (Cth). On one view, this is a subset of the jurisdiction in s 76(ii). However, on another view, it would constitute a matter under s 75(iii) of the Constitution ('a matter ... in which the Commonwealth, or a person suing or being sued on behalf of the Commonwealth, is a party'). The latter appears to be consistent with the decision, in *Momcilovic v The Queen* (2011) 245 CLR 1, that a criminal prosecution by the Crown in right of one State of a resident of another State is a matter '... between a State and a resident of another State' (s 75(iv)).

from s 76(ii) of the Constitution,[109] Parliament has not conferred other matters of jurisdiction in s 76 on the High Court.

The 'autochthonous expedient' of using State courts for the exercise of federal jurisdiction was utilised very early by the federal Parliament, rather than going to the expense of creating a full set of lower federal courts. Despite the subsequent creation of lower federal courts, Parliament continues to vest federal jurisdiction in State courts. Section 39(2) of the *Judiciary Act* vests matters of jurisdiction identified in ss 75 and 76, subject to exceptions listed in s 38 of the *Judiciary Act*. Additionally, federal criminal jurisdiction, conferred by s 68(2) of the *Judiciary Act*, is primarily[110] exercised by State courts.[111]

Until the 1970s, the Commonwealth Parliament had only created specialised industrial relations and bankruptcy courts. Since the mid-1970s, Parliament has progressively broadened the jurisdiction of lower federal courts. Currently, there are three lower federal courts: the Family Court with specialised family law related jurisdiction; the Federal Court with broad federal jurisdiction under ss 75(iii), (v) and 76(i), (ii) of the Constitution; and the Federal Circuit Court with more confined federal jurisdiction, largely arising under s 76(ii) of the Constitution.[112]

## 2 Central concepts

There are three core concepts that are central to an understanding of the way in which the federal judicial system operates: *federal jurisdiction*, *Commonwealth judicial power* and *'matter'*. The expression 'federal jurisdiction' refers to the 'authority to exercise the judicial power of the Commonwealth'.[113] In other words, it is 'the authority to adjudicate derived from the Commonwealth Constitution and laws'.[114] Thus, if a legal controversy or dispute falls within one of the heads of federal jurisdiction set out in ss 75 and 76, and the court hearing the dispute has been authorised by the Constitution or a federal law to determine a matter of that kind, then the court will be exercising federal jurisdiction.[115]

**109** See *Nauru (High Court Appeals) Act 1976* (Cth); *Commonwealth Electoral Act 1918* (Cth); *Judiciary Act 1903* (Cth), s 40(3).

**110** Parliament has more recently vested federal criminal jurisdiction in the Federal Court in relation to serious cartel offences: see *Federal Court of Australia Amendment (Criminal Jurisdiction) Act 2009* (Cth).

**111** There are other federal Acts that confer federal jurisdiction on State courts – see, eg, *Jurisdiction of Courts (Cross-vesting Act) 1987* (Cth), s 4.

**112** See also Australian Law Reform Commission, *The Judicial Power of the Commonwealth: A Review of the Judiciary Act 1903 and Related Legislation*, Report No 92 (2001) ch 4; Robert French, 'Federal Courts Created by Parliament' in Brian Opeskin and Fiona Wheeler (eds), *The Australian Federal Judicial System* (Melbourne University Press, 2000) ch 5; Leslie Zines, *Federal Jurisdiction in Australia* (Federation Press, 3rd ed, 2002) 108–15.

**113** *Ah Yick v Lehmert* (1905) 2 CLR 593, 603.

**114** *Baxter v Commissioners of Taxation (NSW)* (1907) 4 CLR 1087, 1142; see also *Minister for Immigration and Multicultural and Indigenous Affairs v B* (2004) 219 CLR 365, 377, 394.

**115** Any State jurisdiction that a State court may have had to resolve the dispute will have been removed by the operation of s 39(1) of the *Judiciary Act 1903* (Cth) or will be inconsistent with that provision and, thus, inoperative: see *Felton v Mulligan* (1971) 124 CLR 367; *MZXOT v Minister for Immigration and Citizenship* (2008) 233 CLR 601.

'Commonwealth judicial power' is the power to resolve a dispute arising in federal jurisdiction. The classic statement of what the concept involves was set out by Griffith CJ in *Huddart, Parker & Co Pty Ltd v Moorehead*:

> the words 'judicial power' as used in sec 71 of the Constitution mean the power which every sovereign authority must of necessity have to decide controversies between its subjects, or between itself and its subjects, whether the rights relate to life, liberty or property.[116]

As will be discussed further, the identification of whether a power or function is judicial can be a difficult process. However, Griffith CJ's indicium remains the core characteristic of judicial power: it is the sovereign power to determine a dispute about existing rights. 'Commonwealth' judicial power, then, is the sovereign power of the federal body politic to determine disputes that fall within the matters of federal jurisdiction identified in ss 75 and 76.

In addition to the concepts of federal jurisdiction and Commonwealth judicial power, the High Court has given considerable constitutional content to the word 'matter' that appears in ss 75 and 76. The content given to the expression operates at multiple levels. For example, the court has held that traditional standing requirements have been subsumed into the word 'matter'.[117] Furthermore, a dispute about rights and obligations which depend 'entirely on political sanctions'[118] will not present a 'matter' for determination. Nor is there a 'matter' where the parties do not have a dispute with each other.[119] Underlying these principles is an understanding of the word 'matter' that overlaps with the core characteristic of judicial power – that is, that there is no 'matter' unless the court is determining a dispute about existing rights. The overlap between the core characteristic of Commonwealth judicial power and the word 'matter' arises as a consequence of the High Court's decision in *In re Judiciary and Navigation Acts*.[120] The relationship between the meaning of Commonwealth judicial power and the requirement of a matter will be considered further in Chapter 9.

## 3 Heads of federal jurisdiction

As already indicated, the heads of federal jurisdiction are set out in ss 75 and 76 of the Constitution. Where a legal dispute falls within one of those heads, and a court – whether federal or State – has been authorised by the Constitution[121]

**116** (1909) 8 CLR 330, 357.
**117** See *Pape v Commissioner of Taxation* (2009) 238 CLR 1, 35; 68–9; 99; *Plaintiff S10/2011 v Minister for Immigration and Citizenship* (2012) 246 CLR 636, 659.
**118** *Re Ditford; Ex parte Deputy Commissioner of Taxation* (1988) 19 FCR 347, 370.
**119** See for example, *Re McBain; Ex parte Australian Catholic Bishops Conference* (2002) 209 CLR 372, where the High Court held that the federal Attorney-General had no interest in disturbing the decision of a Federal Court judge when the Attorney was not a party to the dispute before the Federal Court.
**120** (1921) 29 CLR 257.
**121** In the case of the High Court under s 75 of the Constitution.

or a federal law[122] to exercise federal jurisdiction in relation to that head, the dispute is determined by the court with an exercise of Commonwealth judicial power. When reviewing the operation of Chapter III in 2001, the Australian Law Reform Commission said that '[o]f the nine paragraphs, there are four that are central to the operation of the federal judicial system and in which the Commonwealth, as a polity, has an undoubted interest':[123] ss 75(iii), (v) and 76(i), (ii). This chapter will now focus on these four heads of jurisdiction.[124]

## 4 Sections 75(iii) and (v)

### Drafting history

The drafting history of ss 75(iii) and (v) shows that the provisions are inextricably linked. Section 75(iii), which identifies 'matters ... in which the Commonwealth, or a person suing or being sued on behalf of the Commonwealth, is a party', was a copy of one of the heads of federal jurisdiction in the US Constitution. Article III, s 2(1) provides that '[t]he judicial Power [of the United States] shall extend to Controversies to which the United States shall be a party'.

Section 75(v) has no analogue in Article III of the United States Constitution. Its inclusion in Chapter III resulted from a rather confused understanding of the classic US Supreme Court decision of *Marbury v Madison*.[125] As will be discussed later, the Court in *Marbury v Madison* held that the US Supreme Court did not have jurisdiction to issue mandamus to compel a federal executive officer (James Madison), the Secretary of State, to deliver a judicial commission to William Marbury. Marbury's nomination for office had been confirmed by the Senate, and the official seal of the United States had been affixed to the commission. All the constitutional and statutory requirements for appointment had been satisfied, other than the delivery of the commission. Despite finding an entitlement to delivery of the commission and that mandamus would ordinarily be an appropriate remedy, the US Supreme Court refused to grant relief because it had no jurisdiction to do so. Article III of the US Constitution set out the jurisdiction of the Supreme Court and divided it between *original* and *appellate* jurisdiction. Although it had jurisdiction to determine 'Controversies to which the United States shall be a party', Article III only gave the Supreme Court *appellate* jurisdiction in such controversies. Since Marbury's claim had been instituted in the Supreme Court's original jurisdiction, the Court lacked the jurisdiction to hear the claim.[126]

When drafting the judiciary clauses of the Constitution distributed to delegates prior to the 1891 Convention, Inglis Clark was well aware of this history.

**122** In the case of the High Court, pursuant to s 76 of the Constitution; in the case of a lower federal court, pursuant to s 77(i) of the Constitution; in the case of a State court, pursuant to s 77(iii) of the Constitution.
**123** Australian Law Reform Commission, above n 112, 90.
**124** See Stellios, above n 11, ch 7; Zines, above n 112, ch 1.
**125** 1 Cranch 137, 5 US 137 (1803).
**126** See James Stellios, 'Exploring the Purposes of Section 75(v) of the Constitution' (2011) 34 *University of New South Wales Law Journal* 70 for a detailed explanation of this point.

In order to ensure that the High Court would have the jurisdiction that was held in *Marbury v Madison* to be lacking in the US Supreme Court, Inglis Clark expressly included the forerunner of s 75(v) in the original jurisdiction of the High Court. Thus, to cure the perceived defect in the United States judicature provisions as exposed by the Supreme Court in *Marbury v Madison*, Inglis Clark intended that the High Court have original, as opposed to appellate, jurisdiction in such matters.

By the end of the drafting process over the two Conventions in 1891 and 1897–8, this understanding of the forerunner to s 75(v) was forgotten. The clause was struck out during the 1897–8 Convention because, in Inglis Clark's absence, no-one could remember why it had been inserted. With Inglis Clark's intercession, the provision was re-inserted, but the debate that followed displayed considerable uncertainty about its purpose. As has been explained in more detail elsewhere,[127] there were two other views – in addition to Inglis Clark's intention – expressed as to the reason for having s 75(v) as part of Chapter III. The first, advanced by Josiah Symon, was to ensure that 'officers of the Commonwealth' were protected from an exercise of State judicial power by State courts. By including s 75(v) as a head of original *federal* jurisdiction, Commonwealth officers would not be exposed to the uncertainties of State judicial power.[128]

The other theory for the operation of s 75(v) was put forward by Edmund Barton. This alternative view saw s 75(v) performing an accountability purpose. The original jurisdiction was to be given to the High Court to ensure that there was jurisdiction in which to hold officers of the Commonwealth accountable for their actions. As Barton said, s 75(v) would be included 'so that when a person wishes to obtain the performance of a clear statutory duty, or to restrain an officer of the Commonwealth from going beyond his duty, or to restrain him in the performance of some statutory duty from doing some wrong, he can obtain a writ of mandamus, a writ of prohibition, or a writ of injunction'.[129]

### The purpose of s 75(v)

In explaining the purpose of s 75(v), the High Court has seized upon Barton's accountability function. In *Bank of New South Wales v Commonwealth*,[130] Dixon J said that s 75(v) was included 'to make it constitutionally certain that there would be a jurisdiction capable of restraining officers of the Commonwealth from exceeding Federal power'. This view was endorsed by the Court in *Plaintiff S157/2002 v Commonwealth*,[131] with the joint judgment of five judges saying:

> The reservation to this Court by the Constitution of the jurisdiction in all matters in which the named constitutional writs or an injunction are sought against an officer of the Commonwealth is a means of assuring to all people affected that officers of the

**127** Ibid.
**128** *Convention Debates, Melbourne* (1898) 1875, 1881–4.
**129** Ibid, 1884.
**130** (1948) 76 CLR 1, 363.
**131** (2003) 211 CLR 476.

> Commonwealth obey the law and neither exceed nor neglect any jurisdiction which the law confers on them. The centrality, and protective purpose, of the jurisdiction of this Court in that regard places significant barriers in the way of legislative attempts (by privative clauses or otherwise) to impair judicial review of administrative action. Such jurisdiction exists to maintain the federal compact by ensuring that propounded laws are constitutionally valid and ministerial or other official action lawful and within jurisdiction. In any written constitution, where there are disputes over such matters, there must be an authoritative decision-maker. Under the Constitution of the Commonwealth the ultimate decision-maker in all matters where there is a contest, is this Court. The Court must be obedient to its constitutional function. In the end, pursuant to s 75 of the Constitution, this limits the powers of the Parliament or of the Executive to avoid, or confine, judicial review.[132]

This view of s 75(v) is now well established.[133] Contrastingly, there has been no mention of the alternative explanations of s 75(v), particularly the protection of federal officers from State judicial power.

### Operation of s 75(v)

Section 75(v) of the Constitution confers that head of jurisdiction on the High Court. Additionally, Parliament has conferred the jurisdiction on the Federal Court pursuant to s 77(i) of the Constitution,[134] and State courts have been denied that jurisdiction pursuant to s 77(ii).[135] The core operational dimensions of s 75(v) are reasonably clear. 'Officer of the Commonwealth' is a sufficiently broad expression to cover judicial as well as executive officers,[136] although State court judges are not 'officers of the Commonwealth' even when exercising federal jurisdiction.[137] A Commonwealth officer is likely to remain an 'officer of the Commonwealth' when performing functions under State or Territory legislation.[138]

One of the main issues of uncertainty in this respect is whether the expression 'officer of the Commonwealth' extends to cover a body corporate created or incorporated by the Commonwealth.[139] Another area of uncertainty is whether private actors exercising government powers would fall within the expression. The High Court had the opportunity to consider this second issue in *Plaintiff M61/2010E v Commonwealth*.[140] In that case, one of the questions that arose for

**132** Ibid, 513–14. See also 482–3.
**133** It has been repeated in *Bodruddaza v Minister for Immigration and Multicultural Affairs* (2007) 228 CLR 651, 668–9; *MZXOT v Minister for Immigration and Citizenship* (2008) 233 CLR 601, 614.
**134** *Judiciary Act 1903* (Cth), s 39B.
**135** *Judiciary Act 1903* (Cth), s 38(e).
**136** *R v Commonwealth Court of Conciliation and Arbitration; Ex parte Whybrow* (1910) 11 CLR 1; *R v Commonwealth Court of Conciliation and Arbitration; Ex parte Brisbane Tramways Co Ltd* (1914) 18 CLR 54.
**137** *R v Murray and Cormie; Ex parte the Commonwealth* (1916) 22 CLR 437.
**138** See *Re Cram; Ex parte NSW Colliery Proprietors' Association Ltd* (1987) 163 CLR 117; Graeme Hill, 'Reviewing Decisions by Commonwealth Bodies Made under State or Territory Legislation' (2006) 17 *Public Law Review* 112, 117.
**139** See the authorities referred to in *McGowan v Migration Agents Registration Authority* (2003) 129 FCR 118.
**140** (2010) 243 CLR 319.

the Court was whether a private contractor could be considered to be an officer of the Commonwealth when undertaking an inquiry and making recommendations for the purposes of informing a decision by the Minister for Immigration to allow an application for a protection visa under the *Migration Act 1958* (Cth). Because the Commonwealth and Minister were also named as parties, the Court otherwise had jurisdiction under both sections 75(iii) and (v). Consequently, the Court was not required to explore the reach of the expression 'officer of the Commonwealth'.

If an accountability understanding of s 75(v) were to be taken seriously, Commonwealth corporations and private actors exercising government powers may well be considered to fall within the expression 'officers of the Commonwealth'. On that view, the Commonwealth should not be permitted to contract out highly sensitive decision-making to avoid the supervisory jurisdiction of the courts. In other words, preventing 'colourable evasion'[141] by the Commonwealth of this accountability jurisdiction may well justify taking a broad view of the expression in these contexts.[142] This was certainly the view of Greenwood J of the Federal Court in *Broadbent v Medical Board of Queensland*,[143] where his Honour considered that a statutory corporation was in no different position under s 75(v) to a non-corporate body of people.

The remedies identified in s 75(v) are mandamus, prohibition and injunction. The first two have their origins as prerogative writs, but have been described in the context of s 75(v) as 'constitutional writs'.[144] Injunctive relief has its origins in equity, and it is unclear from the drafting history why it was included alongside the constitutional writs. When Inglis Clark initially drafted the clause, only the constitutional writs were included. However, after it had been struck out during the 1897–8 Convention, it was re-introduced by Barton with the addition of injunction. No explanation was given for the inclusion of the extra remedy.

The other important prerogative writs – *certiorari* and *habeas corpus* – are not mentioned in s 75(v). It should be remembered, however, that s 75(v) does not confer the *power* to issue the remedies mentioned: it creates a head of *jurisdiction*. Once s 75(v) is triggered – or any other head of jurisdiction for that matter – the High Court will have the power to issue whatever remedy is required to resolve the dispute. Thus, as the joint judgment said in *Plaintiff S157/2002 v Commonwealth*, 'it has long been accepted that certiorari may issue as ancillary to the constitutional writs of mandamus and prohibition', or may issue in exercise of the jurisdiction in s 75(iii) or s 76(i).[145]

**141** See *Bank of New South Wales v Commonwealth* (1948) 76 CLR 1, 367.
**142** See Peter Cane and Leighton McDonald, *Principles of Administrative Law: Legal Regulation of Governance* (Oxford University Press, 2nd ed, 2012) 47–9; Mark Aronson and Matthew Groves, *Judicial Review of Administrative Action* (Lawbook, 5th ed, 2013) 41–3.
**143** (2011) 195 FLR 438.
**144** *Bodruddaza v Minister for Immigration and Multicultural Affairs* (2007) 228 CLR 651, 666.
**145** (2003) 211 CLR 476, 507. See The Hon William Gummow AC, 'The Scope of Section 75(v) of the *Constitution*: Why Injunction but No Certiorari?' (2014) 42 *Federal Law Review* 241; Lisa Burton, 'Why These Three? The Significance of the Selection of Remedies in Section 75(v) of the Australian Constitution' (2014) 42 *Federal Law Review* 253.

Finally, the High Court has accepted that the constitutional writs operate by reference to the difficult concept of *jurisdictional error*.[146] Conduct or a decision by a Commonwealth officer will be affected by jurisdictional error if the officer has acted in excess of jurisdiction (ie, in excess of authority). In such circumstances, the Court can issue *prohibition* to prevent the officer from exceeding authority. Furthermore, there will be jurisdictional error when a Commonwealth officer fails to perform a duty, and *mandamus* can issue to require the officer to perform that duty. The concept of jurisdictional error is a difficult one, as is the task of distinguishing *jurisdictional* errors from *non-jurisdictional* errors.[147] The High Court has recognised as much in *Kirk v Industrial Court (NSW)*,[148] noting the 'functional' role played by such a concept 'to validate review when review is felt to be necessary': 'jurisdiction' is not 'a metaphysical absolute but simply expresses the gravity of the error'.[149]

It is apparent that the High Court has taken an expansive approach to determining what errors will constitute jurisdictional error.[150] The familiar administrative law grounds of review have all been held to give rise to jurisdictional error:[151] breach of procedural fairness or natural justice;[152] bad faith;[153] identifying the wrong issue or asking the wrong question;[154] relevant/irrelevant considerations; *Wednesbury* unreasonableness;[155] and, at least in relation to jurisdictional fact-finding, irrationality or illogicality.[156] Additionally, there will be jurisdictional error where a Commonwealth officer has failed to comply with a mandatory statutory requirement.[157]

## Privative clauses

The most contentious issue around s 75(v) has been the extent to which Parliament, by the use of a privative clause, can exclude or limit the jurisdiction of the High Court under that entrenched provision. The classic type of privative clause that has been used by Parliament, often referred to as a *Hickman*-style[158]

**146** See *Commissioner of Taxation v Futuris Corporation Ltd* (2008) 237 CLR 146, 161–2.
**147** For an excellent analysis, see Mark Aronson, 'Jurisdictional Error Without Tears' in Matthew Groves and H P Lee (eds) *Australian Administrative Law: Fundamentals, Principles and Doctrines* (Cambridge University Press, 2007) 330–44.
**148** (2010) 239 CLR 531.
**149** Ibid 570–71, quoting from Jaffe 'Judicial Review: Constitutional and Jurisdictional Fact' (1957) 70 *Harvard Law Review* 953, 963.
**150** For example, they are not limited to the grounds of review that may have been recognised at 1900: *Re Refugee Review Tribunal; Ex parte Aala* (2000) 204 CLR 82.
**151** For a detailed consideration of the grounds of review, see Cane and McDonald, above n 142, ch 5; Aronson and Groves, above n 142, chs 4–9.
**152** *Plaintiff S157/2002 v Commonwealth* (2003) 211 CLR 476.
**153** *Commissioner of Taxation v Futuris Corporation Ltd* (2008) 237 CLR 146.
**154** *Kirk v Industrial Court (NSW)* (2010) 239 CLR 531.
**155** *Minister for Immigration and Citizenship v SZIAI* (2009) 83 ALJR 1123; 259 ALR 429. For a recent reformulation (and possible broadening) of reasonableness as a ground of review, see *Minister for Immigration and Citizenship v Li* (2013) 249 CLR 332. See Leighton McDonald, 'Rethinking Unreasonableness Review' (2014) 25 *Public Law Review* 117.
**156** *Minister for Immigration and Citizenship v SZMDS* (2010) 240 CLR 611.
**157** *SAAP v Minister for Immigration and Multicultural and Indigenous Affairs* (2005) 228 CLR 294.
**158** Referring to the form of privative clause at issue in *R v Hickman; Ex parte Fox and Clinton* (1945) 70 CLR 598.

privative clause, provides that a decision-maker's decision 'shall not be challenged, appealed against, quashed or called into question, or be subject to prohibition, mandamus or injunction, in any court on any account whatever'.[159] If this provision is read literally, it would present a direct conflict with the investiture of jurisdiction in the High Court by s 75(v). However, the High Court has not read the clause literally, although it has offered two different accounts of how such clauses should be interpreted.

The first of those interpretations appeared to be put forward by Dixon J in *R v Hickman; Ex parte Fox and Clinton*.[160] His Honour considered that privative clauses, when included in a legislative scheme, sought to expand the jurisdiction of the decision-maker. Since the legislative scheme otherwise imposed limits on the scope of jurisdiction, the privative clause had to be reconciled with those limitations. The reconciliation was achieved in the following way:

> Such a clause is interpreted as meaning that no decision which is in fact given by the body concerned shall be invalidated on the ground that it has not conformed to the requirements governing its proceedings or the exercise of its authority or has not confined its acts within the limits laid down by the instrument giving it authority, provided always that its decision is a bona fide attempt to exercise its power, that it relates to the subject matter of the legislation, and that it is reasonably capable of reference to the power given to the body.[161]

Provided that the three *Hickman* provisos were satisfied, there would be no jurisdictional error for the purposes of s 75(v), and the decision would be valid. Thus, the privative clause was seen as operating to expand the jurisdiction of a Commonwealth officer by impliedly repealing any statutory limitations that otherwise would have applied. In subsequent cases a fourth proviso was emphasised by the High Court: a decision would give rise to jurisdictional error if there was non-compliance with 'imperative duties or inviolable limitations or restraints'.[162]

This view of *Hickman*-style privative clauses was, however, rejected by the High Court in *Plaintiff S157/2002 v Commonwealth*,[163] a case considering a privative clause in the *Migration Act 1958* (Cth), which was specifically included on the understanding explained above.[164] In a joint judgment, Gaudron, McHugh, Gummow, Kirby and Hayne JJ held that Dixon J's explanation of privative clauses had been misunderstood. Privative clauses could not be assumed in advance in all cases to expand the jurisdiction of a Commonwealth officer so that it was subject only to the *Hickman* provisos. Instead, the provisos represented the

**159** This common form of words was used in reg 17 of the *National Security (Coal Mining Industry Employment) Regulations 1941* (Cth), which was in issue in *R v Hickman; Ex parte Fox and Clinton* (1945) 70 CLR 598.

**160** (1945) 70 CLR 598.

**161** Ibid, 615.

**162** See, eg, *R v Metal Trades Employers' Association; Ex parte Amalgamated Engineering Union, Australian Section* (1951) 82 CLR 208, 248; *R v Coldham; Ex parte Australian Workers' Union* (1983) 153 CLR 415, 419.

**163** (2003) 211 CLR 476.

**164** See the Second Reading Speech at Australian House of Representatives, *Parliamentary Debates* (Hansard), 26 September 2001, 31559, 31561.

maximum extent to which the jurisdiction of the Commonwealth officer could be expanded. How far jurisdiction had been expanded was to be determined in the individual case according to the detail of the legislative provisions in question, including the privative clause.[165] Thus, the Court still engaged in a reconciliation exercise, but that exercise could not be undertaken by assuming in advance that the privative clause would trump all limitations and restrictions. However, although the privative clause was to be taken into account in the reconciliation process, the plurality read the provision in a way that denied it any effective operation. The clause in question, s 474 of the *Migration Act 1958*, defined a 'privative clause decision' as a 'decision of an administrative character made, proposed to be made, or required to be made … under this Act …'. The plurality considered that the word 'decision' referred to a decision unaffected by jurisdictional error. Thus, a decision affected by jurisdictional error – the claim in that case being a breach of procedural fairness – was not a decision covered by the privative clause. On that reading, the privative clause had no impact on the scope of the Commonwealth officer's jurisdiction.

By contrast to *Hickman*-style privative clauses, there are other clauses, now commonly referred to as 'no-invalidity clauses',[166] that seek directly to expand the jurisdiction of a decision-maker by deeming a decision to be valid despite non-compliance with statutory limitations or requirements. A clause of this nature included in the *Income Tax Assessment Act 1936* (Cth) was considered by the High Court in *Commissioner of Taxation v Futuris Corporation Ltd*.[167] The provision in that case, s 175 of the *Income Tax Assessment Act*, provided that '[t]he validity of any assessment shall not be affected by reason that any of the provisions of this Act have not been complied with'. Unlike the conclusion reached in *Plaintiff S157/2002*, the High Court held in *Futuris* that this style of clause was effective to expand the jurisdiction of the decision-maker. Gummow, Hayne, Heydon and Crennan JJ concluded that '[w]here s 175 applies, errors in the process of assessment do not go to jurisdiction and so do not attract the remedy of a constitutional writ under s 75(v) of the Constitution …'.[168]

Importantly, there are two qualifications to this position. First, the Court held that the no-invalidity clause could not insulate a decision affected by bad faith or 'conscious maladministration of the assessment process'.[169] Secondly, the taxation scheme has within it a detailed mechanism of appeals and reviews.[170] It is unclear to what extent this dimension of the scheme contributed to the Court's reasoning and whether the Court's conclusion could be applied to other legislative contexts without a system of appeals and reviews.[171]

**165** *Plaintiff S157/2002 v Commonwealth* (2003) 211 CLR 476, 502–4.
**166** See Leighton McDonald, 'The Entrenched Minimum Provision of Judicial Review and the Rule of Law' (2010) 21 *Public Law Review* 14.
**167** (2008) 237 CLR 146.
**168** *Commissioner of Taxation v Futuris Corporation Ltd* (2008) 237 CLR 146, 157.
**169** Ibid.
**170** See Part IVC of the *Taxation Administration Act 1953* (Cth).
**171** See McDonald, above n 166, 29.

### The relationship between ss 75(iii) and (v)

The relationship between ss 75(iii) and (v) has not been explored extensively by the High Court. The drafting history again demonstrates some confusion in this respect. Inglis Clark and, at least, Isaac Isaacs, considered that s 75(v) was a subset of s 75(iii), and was included by Inglis Clark in response to *Marbury v Madison* to ensure that the High Court had original jurisdiction to hear matters in s 75(v).[172] However, in the 1897–8 Convention, Barton expressed concern that, given the narrow US authority on the scope of the American equivalent of s 75(iii),[173] proceedings for relief identified in s 75(v) would not fall within s 75(iii) and, thus, there was a need for a separate head of jurisdiction. This uncertainty was recognised by Gaudron and Gummow JJ in *Re Refugee Review Tribunal; Ex parte Aala:*

> It appears that s 75(v) was included as a safeguard against the possibility that the provision in s 75(iii) respecting matters in which a person being sued on behalf of the Commonwealth is a party would be read down by reference to decisions construing Article III of the United States Constitution.[174]

Given this uncertainty, it is not surprising that the High Court has not grappled in detail with this connection. While it is clear that there is a significant degree of overlap, the two paragraphs are certainly not coterminous. Thus, a federal court judge is considered to be an 'officer of the Commonwealth' for the purposes of s 75(v), but any proceedings for mandamus, prohibition or injunction against a judicial officer would probably not involve a 'matter ... in which the Commonwealth, or a person ... being sued on behalf of the Commonwealth, is a party'.

### The operation of s 75(iii)

As for the operation of s 75(iii), there was no detailed consideration of it during the Convention Debates. Ironically, however, both Symon's and Barton's understandings of the operation of s 75(v) find reflection in the High Court's consideration of s 75(iii). This is most obvious from two important passages. The first is from Dixon J in *Bank of New South Wales v Commonwealth*,[175] where his Honour identified the connection between ss 75(iii) and (v):

> The purpose of s 75(iii) obviously was to ensure that the political organization called into existence under the name of the Commonwealth and armed with enumerated powers and authorities, limited by definition, fell in every way within a jurisdiction

**172** This was at a time when the forerunner of s 75(iii) had not been allocated to the original jurisdiction of the High Court. By the time Isaac Isaacs made his contributions to the debate, the forerunner of s 75(iii) had been allocated to the original jurisdiction of the Court. Accordingly, he took the view that there was no need for s 75(v) to be inserted. See Stellios, above n 126.

**173** At the time of the Australian Convention Debates, the US Supreme Court had taken the view that the United States equivalent of s 75(iii) was limited to actions that named the United States as a party on the record (see *Bank of New South Wales v Commonwealth* ('*Bank Nationalisation* case') (1948) 76 CLR 1, 366–7).

**174** (2000) 204 CLR 82, 92; citing *Ah Yick v Lehmert* (1905) 2 CLR 593, 608–9; *Bank of New South Wales v Commonwealth* ('*Bank Nationalisation*' case) (1948) 76 CLR 1, 363–8; *Deputy Commissioner of Taxation v Richard Walter Pty Ltd* (1995) 183 CLR 168, 178–9, 204, 221, 231–2. See also *Aala* (2000) 204 CLR 82, 138–9.

**175** *Bank Nationalisation* case (1948) 76 CLR 1.

> *in which it could be impleaded* and *which it could invoke*. Section 75(iii) cannot be read without s 75(v) which, it is apparent, was written into the instrument to make it constitutionally certain that there would be a jurisdiction capable of restraining officers of the Commonwealth from exceeding Federal power.
>
> ...
>
> At all events, the purpose of providing a jurisdiction which might be invoked by or against the Commonwealth could not, in modern times, be adequately attained and secured against colourable evasion, unless it was expressed so as to cover the enforcement of actionable rights and liabilities of officers and agencies in their official and governmental capacity, when in substance they formed part of or represented the Commonwealth.[176]

If we focus on the italicised words in this quotation, there is some correspondence with the language used in the drafting history of s 75(v). The first set of italicised words matches Barton's *accountability* justification for s 75(v), and the second is suggestive of Symon's justification of *protecting* the Commonwealth from State jurisdiction.

These two purposes of section 75(iii) were again emphasised by Barwick CJ in *Inglis v Commonwealth Trading Bank of Australia*,[177] where his Honour said:

> The fundamental purpose, as it seems to me, of including [s 75(iii)] ... was to ensure that the Commonwealth either in its form as established under the Constitution, or in any form with which it may lawfully clothe itself *should not be compelled to pursue its rights in the courts of the States*. ... If in reality the Commonwealth is before the Court in the litigation, no matter of form or of nomenclature can be allowed to deny the Court jurisdiction to hear and determine the *rights asserted by or against it*.[178]

As a consequence of these purposes, the High Court has taken a broad view of the jurisdiction in s 75(iii) and, in assessing whether a person or body is, in substance, 'the Commonwealth, or a person suing or being sued on behalf of the Commonwealth', the High Court has focused on the degrees to which the Commonwealth controls the person or body in the exercise of their functions.[179] A similar approach has also been taken to the meaning of 'State' in s 75(iv), despite the absence of the trailing words that appear in s 75(iii).[180]

## 5 Sections 76(i) and (ii)

Sections 76(i) and (ii) create federal jurisdiction, respectively, in matters 'arising under this Constitution, or involving its interpretation' and 'arising under any laws made by the Parliament'. These heads of jurisdiction are especially

**176** *Bank of New South Wales v Commonwealth* ('*Bank Nationalisation* case') (1948) 76 CLR 1, 363, 367 (emphasis added).
**177** (1969) 119 CLR 334.
**178** Ibid, 335–6 (emphasis added).
**179** See *Bank of New South Wales v Commonwealth* ('*Bank Nationalisation*' case) (1948) 76 CLR 1; *Inglis v Commonwealth Trading Bank of Australia* (1969) 119 CLR 334.
**180** See *Crouch v Commissioner for Railways (Qld)* (1985) 159 CLR 22; *State Bank of New South Wales v Commonwealth Savings Bank of Australia* (1986) 161 CLR 639.

important in enabling the High Court to play a key role in the interpretation of the Constitution and its application to Commonwealth legislation. The key words 'arising under' have been given a broad interpretation by the High Court. In the context of s 76(ii), there will be a matter 'arising under' a federal law 'if the right or duty in question in the matter owes its existence to Federal law or depends upon Federal law for its enforcement'. This will be the case 'whether or not the determination of the controversy involves the interpretation (or validity) of the law'.[181] This is an expansive view of when s 76(ii) will be triggered. For example, in *LNC Industries Limited v BMW (Australia) Limited*,[182] there was a contractual dispute where the subject matter of the contract was an import licence granted under Commonwealth regulations. The question was whether the NSW Supreme Court was exercising federal jurisdiction when resolving the contractual dispute, as an appeal to the Privy Council was precluded by s 39(2)(a) of the *Judiciary Act* if it were. In a joint judgment, Gibbs CJ, Mason, Wilson, Brennan, Deane and Dawson JJ held that the dispute involved a matter under s 76(ii), as the subject matter of the contract existed as a result of the federal law.[183] Accordingly, since the Supreme Court was exercising federal jurisdiction, an appeal could not be taken to the Privy Council.

The same approach applies to s 76(i): where the subject matter of a claim is a constitutional one, the matter will be heard in federal jurisdiction. In *British American Tobacco Australia Ltd v Western Australia*,[184] the appellants were tobacco wholesalers who had paid franchise fees under Western Australian legislation. New South Wales legislation in similar terms had been held invalid in breach of s 90 of the Constitution in *Ha v New South Wales*.[185] The appellants instituted proceedings in the Supreme Court of Western Australia for a declaration that the Western Australian provisions were invalid and for the recovery of the amounts already paid as money had and received. The recovery claim was held to give rise to a matter under s 76(i) 'because the asserted obligation to repay would not exist were it not for the operation of s 90 [of the Constitution] to invalidate the [Western Australian provisions]'.[186]

Of course, s 76(i) is worded differently to s 76(ii): it extends to matters 'arising under' the Constitution and '*involving its interpretation*' and, thus, its scope is broader. The High Court has adopted a similarly broad view of this second dimension of s 76(i). For example, a matter will arise under s 76(i) in cases where the interpretation of the Constitution is only one of the claims dealt with by a court, and even if the case is disposed of without determining the constitutional claim.[187] Furthermore, there will be a matter under s 76(i) in cases 'where it is

**181** *R v Commonwealth Court of Conciliation and Arbitration; Ex parte Barrett* (1945) 70 CLR 141, 154.
**182** (1983) 151 CLR 575.
**183** *LNC Industries Limited v BMW (Australia) Limited* (1983) 151 CLR 575, 581.
**184** (2003) 217 CLR 30.
**185** (1997) 189 CLR 465.
**186** (2003) 217 CLR 30, 52.
**187** *Attorney-General (NSW) v Commonwealth Savings Bank* (1986) 160 CLR 315.

contended that the interpretation of a provision of the Constitution is relevant to the determination of a question of statutory interpretation, this question being the only issue for determination in the cause'.[188] Section 76(i) will be triggered if the question of constitutional interpretation is 'essential or relevant' to the question of statutory interpretation.[189]

Section 76(i) is an obvious federal jurisdictional head for the exercise by a court of the power of judicial review to determine the constitutional validity of government action – whether legislative, executive or judicial. As noted in Chapter 1, this power of judicial review was first asserted by the US Supreme Court in the iconic case of *Marbury v Madison*,[190] and has been received into the Australian constitutional landscape as 'axiomatic'.[191]

However, as a head of jurisdiction, s 76(i) cannot be the constitutional source of *power* to exercise judicial review. This is even more so because s 76 contains heads of jurisdiction that can be conferred on the High Court by Parliament in its discretion. As it happens, Parliament has conferred this jurisdiction on the High Court by s 30(a) of the *Judiciary Act*, but there is nothing in the Constitution to require its conferral and, presumably, it could be withdrawn.

Although it is now a moot point, it has been argued that the function of judicial review finds no firm textual support within the Constitution.[192] Nevertheless, it is clear that the framers intended the courts in Australia to exercise judicial review,[193] and it seems to be accepted that the adoption of a written *federal* Constitution logically involves the performance of judicial review. As Dixon CJ, McTiernan, Fullagar and Kitto JJ said in *R v Kirby; Ex parte Boilermakers' Society of Australia*:

> In a federal form of government a part is necessarily assigned to the judicature which places it in a position unknown in a unitary system or under a flexible constitution where Parliament is supreme. A federal constitution must be rigid. The government it establishes must be one of defined powers; within those powers it must be paramount, but it must be incompetent to go beyond them. The conception of independent governments existing in the one area and exercising powers in different fields of action carefully defined by law could not be carried into practical effect unless the ultimate responsibility of deciding upon the limits of the respective powers of the governments were placed in the federal judicature.[194]

**188** Ibid, 327.
**189** Ibid.
**190** 1 Cranch 137; 5 US 137 (1803).
**191** *Australian Communist Party v Commonwealth* (1951) 83 CLR 1, 262. See Chapter 1, Part IV.2.
**192** See James Thomson, 'Constitutional Authority for Judicial Review: A Contribution from the Framers of the Australian Constitution' in Gregory Craven (ed), *The Convention Debates 1891–1898* (Legal Books, 1986) 173, 186–201; P H Lane, *The Australian Federal System* (Lawbook, 2nd ed, 1979) 1135–7.
**193** See, eg, Brian Galligan, 'Judicial Review in the Australian Federal System: Its Origin and Function' (1979) 10 *Federal Law Review* 367; Helen Irving, '*Its First and Highest Function*: The Framers' Vision of the High Court as Interpreter of the Constitution' in Peter Cane (ed) *Centenary Essays for the High Court of Australia* (LexisNexis Butterworths, 2004) 17.
**194** (1956) 94 CLR 254, 267–8. See also *Plaintiff S157/2002 v Commonwealth* (2003) 211 CLR 476, 514.

Section 76(i) jurisdiction has been conferred on the High Court,[195] the Federal Court of Australia[196] and State courts.[197] Section 76(ii) jurisdiction has been conferred on the Federal Court and State courts.[198] There are pockets of s 76(ii) jurisdiction conferred on the High Court;[199] however, the Court has been spared the workload that would follow a general grant of jurisdiction under s 76(ii).

## 6 Federal courts and State courts exercising federal jurisdiction

As mentioned, the Parliament has power to confer federal jurisdiction on lower federal courts (s 77(i)) and State courts (s 77(iii)). Parliament has exercised that power by investing lower federal courts (the Family Court of Australia, the Federal Court of Australia and the Federal Circuit Court of Australia)[200] and, as envisaged at federation, State courts with extensive federal jurisdiction.[201]

Federal courts can only exercise federal jurisdiction. Parliament cannot, alone or together with the Parliaments of the States, confer State jurisdiction on federal courts. Cooperative attempts by the Commonwealth and the States to confer State jurisdiction on federal courts, in an effort to alleviate jurisdictional complications that arise in a federal legal system, were invalidated by the High Court in *Re Wakim; Ex parte McNally*.[202] While s 77(iii) empowers the federal Parliament to confer federal jurisdiction on State courts, there is no constitutional mechanism for the federal or State Parliaments to confer, or consent to the conferral, of State jurisdiction on federal courts. In *Re Wakim*, the High Court held that the express provision for the conferral of federal jurisdiction on State courts gave rise to a negative implication that the reverse was not constitutionally permissible.

Unlike federal courts, State courts are not created by the Commonwealth Parliament. As Knox CJ, Rich and Dixon JJ said in *Le Mesurier v Connor*, 'the Courts of a State are the judicial organs of another Government'.[203] Consequently, there are limits to what Parliament can do with State courts and the jurisdiction that 'belongs to'[204] them. To the extent that Parliament seeks to vest federal jurisdiction in State courts pursuant to s 77(iii) to resolve a legal dispute, it has the power under s 77(ii) to displace any State jurisdiction that might otherwise have been exercised by State courts to determine that dispute. This power of displacement has been exercised by the Commonwealth Parliament in

**195** *Judiciary Act*, s 30(a).
**196** *Judiciary Act*, s 39B.
**197** *Judiciary Act*, s 39(2).
**198** Respectively, ss 39B and 39(2) of the *Judiciary Act*.
**199** See *Nauru (High Court Appeals) Act 1976* (Cth); *Commonwealth Electoral Act 1918* (Cth); *Judiciary Act 1903* (Cth), s 40(3).
**200** This federal jurisdiction is conferred by a plethora of federal Acts, including s 39B of the *Judiciary Act 1903* (Cth).
**201** Primarily by the *Judiciary Act 1903* (Cth), ss 39(2) and 68(2).
**202** (1999) 198 CLR 511.
**203** (1929) 42 CLR 481, 495.
**204** See Constitution, s 77(ii).

the following way. First, with the enactment of s 39(1) of the *Judiciary Act*, Parliament has ousted from State courts *State* jurisdiction in relation to legal disputes falling into the matters of federal jurisdiction exercised by the High Court. Secondly, with the enactment of s 39(2), Parliament has, with some exceptions, given State courts a broad grant of *federal* jurisdiction in relation to matters in ss 75 and 76 of the Constitution, thereby replacing the ousted *State* jurisdiction with *federal* jurisdiction.

This difficult point may be illuminated by an example. Where a resident of one State sues a resident of another for a breach of contract, a State court with appropriate State jurisdiction to resolve the claim could, in the absence of federal jurisdiction, do so with an exercise of State judicial power. However, such a claim falls into the head of federal jurisdiction under s 75(iv) of the Constitution, and Parliament has, by s 39(2) of the *Judiciary Act*, conferred federal jurisdiction on State courts to resolve federal matters under s 75(iv). When resolving that matter (ie, the legal claim by the resident of State A against the resident of State B), the State court in question will be exercising federal jurisdiction – State jurisdiction having been displaced by s 39(1) of the *Judiciary Act*.[205]

However, the Commonwealth Parliament cannot seek to displace State jurisdiction over a legal dispute, unless it is also in the process of 'defining the extent to which the jurisdiction of any federal court shall be exclusive of that which belongs to or is invested in the courts of the States'.[206] In other words, its power to oust State jurisdiction can only be exercised in the course of exercising its power under s 77(ii) to make a matter or matters of federal jurisdiction exclusive to a federal court. This is well demonstrated by the Court's decision in *Re Tracey; Ex parte Ryan*,[207] where the High Court considered the validity of provisions of the *Defence Force Discipline Act 1982* (Cth) which confer jurisdiction on military discipline tribunals ('service tribunals') to hear and determine a range of service offences set out or identified in the Act. These service tribunals are not federal courts and have not been considered by the High Court to be exercising Commonwealth judicial power.[208] The jurisdiction is disciplinary in nature and finds its source in the defence power in s 51(vi) of the Constitution; it is not judicial federal jurisdiction having its source in ss 75 and 76. The service offences, however, mirror civilian criminal offences which might otherwise be heard and determined by a State civilian criminal court under State criminal legislation. In order to avoid a member of the military being exposed to double punishment, the *Defence Force Discipline Act* provided that, where a person had been convicted of an offence under that Act, or where a service offence had been taken into account by the service tribunal, the person was not to be liable to be

**205** As has been explored, the purpose of s 39 'was to exclude appeals as of right to the Privy Council' in relation to 'the whole field of Federal jurisdiction': *Minister of State for the Army v Parbury Henty & Co Pty Ltd* (1945) 70 CLR 459, 505.
**206** Constitution, s 77(ii).
**207** (1989) 166 CLR 518.
**208** See Chapter 9.

tried by a civilian criminal court for a civilian criminal offence that was 'substantially the same offence' as the service offence. The Act further provided that a person acquitted or convicted of a service offence was deemed not to be liable to be tried by a civilian criminal court for a substantially similar civilian criminal offence. The High Court held that the Commonwealth Parliament could not oust State criminal jurisdiction in this way. As Brennan and Toohey JJ explained, the relevant Commonwealth provisions:

> purport to withdraw from the civil courts the jurisdiction otherwise vested in them to try a civil court offence. By these sub-sections, [those persons subject to service offences] are preserved from what was submitted by the Commonwealth to be double jeopardy. However that may be, provisions which purport to prohibit the exercise of the ordinary criminal jurisdiction vested in State courts by State law can find no support in the Constitution. State courts are an essential branch of the government of a State and the continuance of State Constitutions by s 106 of the Constitution precludes a law of the Commonwealth from prohibiting State courts from exercising their functions. It is a function of State courts to exercise jurisdiction in matters arising under State law.[209]

As a reminder, the jurisdiction conferred on the service tribunals was disciplinary in character, not judicial federal jurisdiction under ss 75 and 76, and the tribunals were not lower federal courts. Accordingly, Parliament could not use s 77(ii) to oust State jurisdiction.

When vesting federal jurisdiction in State courts pursuant to s 77(iii), Parliament can define the federal jurisdiction to be exercised and may 'extend or limit the jurisdiction of a State court in respect of persons, locality, amount or otherwise, as it may think proper'.[210] It may also prescribe how the court is to be constituted when exercising federal jurisdiction.[211] Parliament also can regulate the practice and procedure of a State court when exercising federal jurisdiction, including the rules of evidence that are to be applied.[212] However, State courts remain 'State courts': '[t]hey are created by State law; their existence depends upon State law; that law, primarily at least, determines the constitution of the Court itself, and the organizations through which its powers and jurisdictions are exercised'.[213] Consequently, as is often said, 'when the federal Parliament makes a law investing federal jurisdiction in a State court, the Parliament "must take the State court as it finds it"'.[214] As Gummow, Hayne and Crennan JJ summarised in *Forge v ASIC*, '[t]he provisions of Ch III do not give power to the federal Parliament to affect or alter the constitution or the organisation of State courts'.[215] For

**209** *Re Tracey; Ex parte Ryan* (1989) 166 CLR 518, 574–5. See also 547.
**210** *Peacock v Newtown Marrickville and General Co-operative Building Society (No 4) Ltd* (1943) 67 CLR 25, 39.
**211** See *Troy v Wrigglesworth* (1919) 26 CLR 305, where federal provisions required the Victorian Court of Petty Sessions to be constituted by a police magistrate. The court in that case had been improperly constituted by two justices of the peace.
**212** *Russell v Russell* (1976) 134 CLR 495.
**213** *Le Mesurier v Connor* (1929) 42 CLR 481, 495–6.
**214** See, eg, *Forge v Australian Securities and Investments Commission* (2006) 228 CLR 45, 75.
**215** Ibid.

example, in *Le Mesurier v Connor*, the High Court considered federal legislation which conferred federal bankruptcy jurisdiction on the Supreme Court of Western Australia. The federal legislation further authorised the appointment of a federal officer, as the Bankruptcy Registrar, to perform duties in relation to the exercise of bankruptcy jurisdiction by the State court. While the conferral of jurisdiction was valid under s 77(iii) of the Constitution, the provisions appointing the Bankruptcy Registrar sought to interfere with the constitution or organisation of the State Supreme Court through which the jurisdiction was exercised and, thus, were held invalid.

Differentiating between permissible provisions that invest federal jurisdiction and those which impermissibly interfere with the constitution or organisation of a court can sometimes be a difficult exercise. In *Russell v Russell*,[216] the High Court considered the validity of federal provisions which sought to regulate the way in which federal family law jurisdiction could be exercised by State courts. One of the provisions in question required State courts to exercise jurisdiction in closed courts; the other prohibited judges and counsel from robing. Two judges (Barwick CJ and Gibbs J) held both provisions invalid. Two other judges (Mason and Jacobs JJ) held both provisions to be valid. The fifth judge (Stephen J), with the deciding vote, considered that the requirement to close the doors of the court was invalid, but that the robing prohibition was valid.

Despite the very different constitutional positions of State courts and lower federal courts, the institutional features of each have converged considerably. The next chapter will consider the respective Chapter III limitations on State and federal Parliaments when conferring functions on their courts. For now, it is enough to note the rules about who can exercise federal jurisdiction in State and federal courts.

The High Court initially took a very restrictive view of what constitutes a State 'court' for the purposes of exercising federal jurisdiction conferred under s 77(iii) of the Constitution. In *Kotsis v Kotsis*[217] and *Knight v Knight*,[218] the Court held a State 'court' was composed of judicial officers, and only judicial officers could exercise federal jurisdiction. However, in *Commonwealth v Hospital Contribution Fund*,[219] the High Court rejected this earlier approach, instead preferring the dissenting view of Gibbs J in *Kotsis* that, when Chapter III 'spoke of investing State courts with federal jurisdiction, it meant to refer to State courts with the organization and structure provided by State law', including non-judicial officers.[220] In explaining the adoption of the new approach, Mason J referred to the 'great inconvenience to the States and their courts if the structure and composition of a State court for the exercise of federal jurisdiction is to

**216** (1976) 134 CLR 495.
**217** (1970) 122 CLR 69.
**218** (1971) 122 CLR 114.
**219** (1982) 150 CLR 49.
**220** *Kotsis v Kotsis* (1970) 122 CLR 69, 110.

differ from that selected by the State for the exercise of its similar non-federal jurisdiction'.[221] This, for Mason J, would 'constrain the States' freedom of action in the organization of their courts'.[222]

When the question of the composition of federal courts came before the High Court, the decision in *Commonwealth v Hospital Contribution Fund* made it very difficult to reach a different view for federal courts. In *Harris v Caladine*,[223] the Court held that non-judicial officers of federal courts could exercise the judicial power of the Commonwealth delegated to them provided that two conditions are satisfied:

> The first condition is that the delegation must not be to an extent where it can no longer properly be said that, as a practical as well as a theoretical matter, the judges constitute the court. This means that the judges must continue to bear the major responsibility for the exercise of judicial power at least in relation to the more important aspects of contested matters. The second condition is that the delegation must not be inconsistent with the obligation of a court to act judicially and that the decisions of the officers of the court in the exercise of their delegated jurisdiction, powers and functions must be subject to review or appeal by a judge or judges of the court. For present purposes it is sufficient for us to say that, if the exercise of delegated jurisdiction, powers and functions by a court officer is subject to review or appeal by a judge or judges of the court on questions of both fact and law, we consider that the delegation will be valid. Certainly if the review is by way of hearing de novo, the delegation will be valid.[224]

As will be seen in Chapter 9, there are many other ways in which the institutional features of federal and State courts have converged as a consequence of the inclusion of State courts in Chapter III of the Constitution as receptacles of Commonwealth judicial power and federal jurisdiction.

## V The expanding reach of federal jurisdiction

Despite the creation of Commonwealth judicial power, federal jurisdiction and a judicial system through which that power and jurisdiction are exercised, State jurisdiction and judicial power to be exercised by State courts retained a distinct existence from the federal judicial system created by Chapter III. However, as a result of High Court interpretation, there has been an expansion of the jurisdictional opportunities for the exercise of Commonwealth judicial power, by both federal and State courts, squeezing out the exercise of State jurisdiction and judicial power. One of the main reasons for that shifting jurisdiction has been the development of the concept of *accrued jurisdiction*.

**221** *Commonwealth v Hospital Contribution Fund* (1982) 150 CLR 49, 62.
**222** Ibid.
**223** (1991) 172 CLR 84.
**224** Ibid, 95.

## 1 Accrued jurisdiction

Federal jurisdiction is created and identified in ss 75 and 76 of the Constitution by reference to the word 'matter'. Parliament's power to vest additional federal jurisdiction in the High Court (s 76) and federal jurisdiction in lower federal courts (s 77(i)) and State courts (s 77(iii)) is conditioned by the existence of a 'matter'. In a series of cases in the early 1980s,[225] the High Court read the word 'matter' to refer to the underlying 'justiciable controversy, identifiable independently of the proceedings which are brought for its determination and encompassing all claims made within the scope of the controversy',[226] whether federal or State-based. Furthermore, the Court took a very liberal view of when federal and State claims form part of the same 'matter': if they are non-severable, in the sense that they arise from the same substratum of facts, then a court will hear the State claim in 'accrued' *federal* jurisdiction.[227]

Thus, where a federal claim and a State claim arise out of the same substratum of facts, the State claim falls to be decided within the same 'matter' of federal jurisdiction as the federal claim, and is determined with an exercise of Commonwealth judicial power. The expansion of these jurisdictional opportunities for an exercise of Commonwealth judicial power can be assessed through their impact, respectively, on federal courts and State courts.

## 2 Federal courts

The key High Court decisions in the early 1980s focused on the exercise by lower federal courts of jurisdiction over claims that otherwise would have been decided by a State court exercising State jurisdiction. In particular, the conferral of exclusive jurisdiction on the Federal Court by the *Trade Practices Act 1974* (Cth) in certain matters arising under that Act raised the question of whether the Federal Court could hear related State-based claims. For example, in *Philip Morris Inc v Adam P Brown Male Fashions Pty Ltd*,[228] the High Court considered whether the Federal Court could hear a claim for equitable relief for the common law tort of passing off along with the *Trade Practices Act* claims. A majority of the Court considered that it could within its accrued jurisdiction – the State claim fell within the 'matter' in relation to which the Federal Court had been given jurisdiction (that is, a matter arising under a law made by Parliament – s 76(ii)). In his influential judgment, Mason J said:

> [T]he framers ... looked to 'matters' in the broadest sense of the term as one which would catch up, as far as possible, the controversy which parties brought for

**225** *Philip Morris Inc v Adam P Brown Male Fashions Pty Ltd* (1981) 148 CLR 457; *Fencott v Muller* (1983) 152 CLR 570; *Stack v Coast Securities Pty Ltd (No 9)* (1983) 154 CLR 261.
**226** *Fencott v Muller* (1983) 152 CLR 570, 603.
**227** See, eg *Re Wakim; Ex parte McNally* (1999) 198 CLR 511, 585; *Fencott v Muller* (1983) 152 CLR 570, 607–8.
**228** (1981) 148 CLR 457.

> determination by a court. It is highly unlikely that they intended to embrace a narrow technical meaning which would result in undue fragmentation of a total controversy, leaving its resolution to decisions by both State courts and this Court or State courts and federal courts.[229]

The consequence of these principles is that State-based claims which otherwise would have been litigated in a State court exercising State jurisdiction and power, can be litigated in a federal court if the State-based claims and federal claims are non-severable. And, significantly, the High Court has adopted a liberal view of the connection needed for a State-based claim and a federal claim to be non-severable.[230]

### 3 State courts

As has been explained, the federal Parliament, with an exercise of power under s 77(iii), can confer federal jurisdiction on State courts in relation to any of the 'matters' identified in ss 75 and 76. With some exceptions, Parliament has conferred jurisdiction on State courts in relation to all matters of federal jurisdiction in ss 75 and 76.[231] The federal jurisdiction conferred to determine these 'matters' includes the authority to determine State-based claims that fall within the federal 'matter'. And, significantly, the High Court has held that State judicial power has not survived the vesting of State courts with federal jurisdiction in relation to matters set out in ss 75 and 76. The power in s 77(ii) of the Constitution to define 'the extent to which the jurisdiction of any federal court shall be exclusive of that which belongs to or is invested in the courts of the States' has been read by the Court to allow Parliament to strip State courts of State jurisdiction and invest them with federal jurisdiction under s 77(iii) to resolve the same matters.[232] Accordingly, the entire 'matter', comprising federal and State claims, is determined with an exercise of federal jurisdiction and judicial power. Thus, again, there is an expansion of the jurisdictional opportunities for the exercise of Commonwealth judicial power, displacing the exercise of State jurisdiction and judicial power.

## VI Territory courts

There is no express mention of Territory courts in Chapter III of the Constitution. Whether created directly by the Commonwealth Parliament or by a Territory

**229** Ibid, 512–13.
**230** These jurisdictional matters subsided whilst the federal/State cross-vesting schemes were fully operational. When first enacted, those schemes vested State jurisdiction in federal courts and vice versa. However, the invalidation of the conferral on federal courts of State jurisdiction in *Re Wakim; Ex parte McNally* (1999) 198 CLR 511 has given new life to the principles of accrued jurisdiction.
**231** *Judiciary Act*, s 39(2).
**232** *MZXOT v Minister for Immigration and Citizenship* (2008) 233 CLR 601; *Felton v Mulligan* (1971) 124 CLR 367.

legislative assembly (itself created by the federal Parliament), the source of power to create Territory courts is s 122 of the Constitution – not Chapter III. Because self-governing territories were not highest on the agenda during the Convention Debates, the place of Territory courts within the federal judicial system was not thought through and, consequently, has been left to be worked out by the High Court. The High Court has struggled to find a place for Territory courts within the federal judicial system created by Chapter III. As Menzies J said in *Spratt v Hermes*, the High Court's decisions dealing with the relationship between s 122 and Chapter III have 'not resulted in a coherent body of doctrine'.[233]

To locate the place of Territory courts, it is useful to start with the text of Chapter III. Section 71 provides for the vesting of Commonwealth judicial power in the High Court, 'such *other federal courts as the Parliament creates*, and in such *other courts as it invests with federal jurisdiction*'. Parliament's power to vest federal jurisdiction in lower courts refers to lower 'federal courts' (s 77(i)) and 'courts of a State' (s 77(iii)). Territory courts are clearly not State courts, and so the High Court was presented with three options in relation to Territory courts and Chapter III. Firstly, that Territory courts were completely separate from Chapter III. The consequence would be that Territory courts would be limited to Territory jurisdiction and judicial power and could not exercise federal jurisdiction or Commonwealth judicial power. Furthermore, in setting up Territory courts and vesting them with power and jurisdiction, the Commonwealth Parliament would not be subject to the limitations, to be discussed in the next chapter, deriving from Chapter III of the Constitution. Standing entirely outside Chapter III, there would be no guarantee that an appeal could go from a Territory court to the High Court under s 73.

Secondly, Territory courts could be considered to be 'federal courts' created by Parliament and, consequently, be fully integrated into Chapter III of the Constitution. The jurisdiction given to Territory courts would be federal jurisdiction, and the power to be exercised would be Commonwealth judicial power. Parliament would be entirely subject to the limitations deriving from Chapter III that are applicable to federal courts, and the judges of Territory courts would have to be appointed consistently with the requirements in s 72 of the Constitution. The judgments of Territory courts could be appealed to the High Court under s 73(ii) of the Constitution.

Thirdly, Territory courts could be considered to not be 'federal courts', but nonetheless capable of exercising federal jurisdiction and Commonwealth judicial power. Judges of Territory courts would not need to be appointed consistently with s 72, and Parliament would not be subject to the full range of Chapter III limitations that are applicable to federal courts. This third option would cleverly integrate Territory courts into Chapter III, but not to the same extent as federal courts. As for appeals to the High Court, s 73(ii) would only guarantee an appeal where a Territory court was exercising federal jurisdiction.

**233** (1965) 114 CLR 226, 265.

Faced with the complexities of integration, and in a context of territories consisting of external territories and internal territories with small political communities, the early High Court favoured the first option – excluding Territory courts from Chapter III entirely.[234] However, with the development of self-governing territories in the Northern Territory and the Australian Capital Territory, judicial support for the complete exclusion of Territory courts from Chapter III has progressively diminished.[235] Option two, however, was not favoured by the Court and so Territory courts are not federal courts.[236] So, what about option three?

The difficulty for the High Court with option three would be to try to find a textual basis for it. There is some flexibility in the way in which s 71 of the Constitution is worded: '*such other courts as it invests with federal jurisdiction*' is not limited to 'State' courts. However, the vesting of federal jurisdiction under s 77(iii) is limited to State courts. The solution for the High Court has been to see s 122 as capable of triggering federal jurisdiction. A law under s 122 is capable of giving rise to a 'matter' under s 76(ii) of the Constitution[237] and, thus, when a Territory court determines such a matter, it is exercising federal jurisdiction and Commonwealth judicial power.

Adoption of the third view, thus, partially integrates Territory courts into Chapter III. They are not federal courts but, like State courts, they can exercise federal jurisdiction.[238] They are not necessarily subject to the same Chapter III limitations that apply to federal courts,[239] but they are subject to the same Chapter III limitations, to be discussed in the next chapter, that apply to State courts because they are capable of exercising federal jurisdiction.[240] Unlike federal courts and State Supreme Courts, there is no guarantee that an appeal can be taken to the High Court. Like lower State courts, an appeal is only guaranteed when a Territory court is exercising federal jurisdiction. However, the High Court has accepted that Parliament can confer jurisdiction on the High Court to hear an appeal from a Territory court.[241] A number of questions remain about the place of Territory courts within Chapter III,[242] including the important question of whether there is any such thing as Territory jurisdiction when a Territory court is determining a 'matter'.[243]

**234** See, eg, *R v Bernasconi* (1915) 19 CLR 629, 635.
**235** For an extensive discussion, see Jennifer Clarke, Patrick Keyzer and James Stellios, *Hanks Australian Constitutional Law* (LexisNexis, 9th ed, 2013) 422–37.
**236** See *Re Governor, Goulburn Correctional Centre; Ex parte Eastman* (1999) 200 CLR 322.
**237** See, eg, *Northern Territory v GPAO* (1999) 196 CLR 553.
**238** *Blunden v Commonwealth* (2003) 218 CLR 330; *John Pfeiffer Pty Ltd v Rogerson* (2000) 203 CLR 503; *North Australian Aboriginal Legal Aid Service Inc v Bradley* (2004) 218 CLR 146.
**239** Although this would depend on how extensive the federal jurisdiction of Territory courts is seen to be.
**240** *North Australian Aboriginal Legal Aid Service Inc v Bradley* (2004) 218 CLR 146; *Attorney-General (NT) v Emmerson* (2014) 88 ALJR 522; 307 ALR 174.
**241** *Porter v The King; Ex parte Yee* (1926) 37 CLR 432.
**242** See Stellios, above n 11, 460–62.
**243** For the view that Territory courts exercise federal jurisdiction in all matters before them, see Zines, above n 112, 179; Mark Leeming, *Authority to Decide: The Law of Jurisdiction in Australia* (Federation Press, 2012) 24–5; Stephen McDonald, 'Territory Courts and Federal Jurisdiction' (2005) 33 *Federal Law Review* 57, 84. This does not mean that a Territory court cannot exercise Territory jurisdiction, but it cannot do so where it is determining a 'matter'.

# VII Section 80 jury trials

Section 80 provides that '[t]he trial on indictment of any offence against any law of the Commonwealth shall be by jury, and every such trial shall be held in the State where the offence was committed, and if the offence was not committed within any State the trial shall be held at such place or places as the Parliament prescribes'. Where a trial court is determining guilt in relation to a federal offence and imposing a penalty, it is exercising federal jurisdiction and Commonwealth judicial power. A dispute between the Crown and the accused as to whether a federal offence has been committed gives rise to a 'matter' of federal jurisdiction under s 76(ii) of the Constitution, and a trial court authorised to determine the dispute (ie, to adjudge and punish criminal guilt for the federal offence) is exercising Commonwealth judicial power.[244] When that trial is on indictment, then the requirements of s 80 must be complied with.

Section 80 is certainly one of the few provisions in the Constitution that *appears* to be 'rights'-protecting.[245] However, as Amelia Simpson and Mary Wood have recognised, it is not entirely clear what the framers sought to achieve by including s 80 in the Constitution,[246] and this uncertainty has created considerable difficulty for the Court when determining the operation of the section. This part of the chapter will outline the main controversies that have arisen in relation to s 80 and sketch the purposes that have been seen to inform its operation.[247]

## 1 The operation of s 80

The main s 80 cases generally fall into two categories: those that deal with the elements of s 80 that enliven its operation, and those that deal with the requirements of s 80 once it has been enlivened. As for the enlivening elements, the High Court has considered: what law is a 'law of the Commonwealth'; when an offence is tried 'on indictment'; and what constitutes an 'offence' for the purposes of s 80.

A 'law of the Commonwealth' is one 'made under the legislative powers of the Commonwealth'[248] and extends to State offences that are picked up and applied by Commonwealth provisions.[249] However, on current authority, it does not apply to a Territory offence, whether enacted by the Commonwealth Parliament or a legislative assembly created by Parliament.[250]

**244** *Chu Kheng Lim v Minister for Immigration, Local Government and Ethnic Affairs* (1992) 176 CLR 1, 27.
**245** See Chapter 5, Part I.
**246** Amelia Simpson and Mary Wood, '"A Puny Thing Indeed" – *Cheng v The Queen* and the Constitutional Right to Trial by Jury' (2001) 21 *Federal Law Review* 95.
**247** For more detail see Stellios, above n 11, ch 11.
**248** *Re Colina; Ex parte Torney* (1999) 200 CLR 386, 397.
**249** For example, *Commonwealth Places (Application of Laws) Act 1970* (Cth), s 4(1) which picks up State offences and applies them in Commonwealth places.
**250** *R v Bernasconi* (1915) 19 CLR 629.

One of the central s 80 controversies considered by the High Court is whether Parliament can choose for itself what offences are to be tried on indictment and, thus, avoid the operation of s 80 by simply requiring a summary procedure for the trial of an offence. In *R v Archdall and Roskruge; Ex parte Carrigan and Brown*,[251] the defendants had been convicted summarily by a police magistrate for an offence which could have been tried either on indictment or by summary conviction. It was argued before the High Court that the offences had been indictable as at 1900 and, thus, could not be prescribed by Parliament to be tried summarily. The Court dismissed the argument in the following terms: 'The suggestion that the Parliament, by reason of sec 80 of the Constitution, could not validly make the offence punishable summarily has no foundation and its rejection needs no exposition'.[252] With notable dissents,[253] this position has been maintained ever since.[254] Most recently, in *Cheng v The Queen*,[255] without deciding the correctness of this line of authority, a majority of the Court indicated that the *Archdall* view seemed to be the correct interpretation.[256]

Another main controversy has been whether Parliament can differentiate between, on the one hand, the elements of an offence – which are to be determined by a jury, and, on the other hand, aggravating factors going to penalty – which are to be determined by the trial judge. In *Kingswell v The Queen*, a majority of the Court held that Parliament could do so consistently with s 80.[257]

By contrast to these cases, the High Court has taken a more robust approach to the requirements of s 80 once it has been enlivened. The Court held in *Brown v The Queen*[258] that a jury trial cannot be waived. The mandatory language of s 80, the lack of supporting precedent or common law practice and the importance of the jury to the system of justice were reasons relied upon by a majority of the Court to reject the argument that a jury trial could be waived at the election of the accused.[259] Additionally, in *Cheatle v The Queen*,[260] the Court held that a jury's guilty verdict must be unanimous. The common law institution of jury trial as at 1900 was characterised by unanimity and, the Court held, there was no good reason to depart from that position.

However, the High Court has recognised that the common law institution should not be frozen as at 1900 and can be reformed to enhance its efficiency as an instrument of justice. Of course, there must be limits, and the Court has developed a framework for determining which aspects of the common law

**251** (1928) 41 CLR 128.
**252** Ibid, 136. See also 139–40.
**253** *R v Federal Court of Bankruptcy; Ex parte Lowenstein* (1938) 59 CLR 556, 581–3; *Kingswell v The Queen* (1985) 159 CLR 264, 319; *Re Colina; Ex parte Torney* (1999) 200 CLR 386, 422, 426–7.
**254** See, eg, *Kingswell v The Queen* (1985) 159 CLR 264.
**255** (2000) 203 CLR 248.
**256** Ibid, 268–9; 295–8.
**257** (1985) 159 CLR 264, 285; 276–7; Brennan J (at 292–4) and Deane J (at 308) dissenting.
**258** (1986) 160 CLR 171.
**259** Ibid, 194–7, 202–5, 208–17; Gibbs CJ (at 179) and Wilson J (at 190) dissenting.
**260** (1993) 177 CLR 541.

institution must be retained and which can be reformed. A distinction has been drawn between essential and inessential attributes, and reforms can be made to the jury system as long as they are not inconsistent with the essential functional attributes of a jury. The essential attributes that have been identified include representativeness, impartiality, randomness and measured group deliberation. In *Brownlee v The Queen*,[261] the Court considered jury provisions that allowed the reduction in the number of jurors from 12 to 10 during the course of the trial and permitted the jury members to separate at the end of each day during their deliberations. At common law, a jury consisted of 12 jurors and the jury members were sequestered during their deliberations. The High Court held that neither change in jury practice was incompatible with the essential functional attributes of a jury.[262]

## 2 The purpose of s 80

Given its guarantee of a trial by jury for an accused tried on indictment for a federal criminal offence, s 80 has been assumed by judges and commentators to be a constitutional limitation protective of rights.[263] The classic statement of this purpose was given by Dixon and Evatt JJ in *R v Federal Court of Bankruptcy; Ex parte Lowenstein*:

> The Commonwealth Constitution contains no guarantee against deprivation of life, liberty or property without due process of law, like the fifth and fourteenth amendments in the United States Constitution. To establish personal liberty by constitutional restrictions upon the exercise of governmental power was not a guiding purpose in framing the Australian instrument, which in this respect departs widely from its American model. It is true that checks against legislative encroachment on individual freedom are not completely absent from the Australian Constitution. There are two or three; and one of them, that contained in sec 80 relating to trial by jury, cannot be dismissed from consideration.[264]

But, if the purpose of s 80 is to protect a right or interest, what right or interest is protected? Perhaps it protects the accused from oppressive exercises of government power. However, the creation of an *independent* judiciary to exercise Commonwealth judicial power operates to protect individuals from excessive executive and legislative power. An Australian court can strike down legislation if Parliament has exceeded legislative power, and s 75(v) provides the jurisdiction for judicial control of excessive exercises of federal executive power. Perhaps,

**261** (2001) 207 CLR 278.
**262** The essential/inessential framework was subsequently applied to uphold supplementary jury provisions in *Ng v The Queen* (2003) 217 CLR 521 and *Fittock v The Queen* (2003) 217 CLR 508. Providing for additional or reserve jurors was not considered to be inconsistent with the functional attributes of a jury.
**263** See, eg, George Williams and David Hume, *Human Rights under the Australian Constitution* (Oxford University Press, 2nd ed, 2013) ch 9; Peter Bailey, *The Human Rights Enterprise in Australia and Internationally* (LexisNexis, 2009) 92–4; Hilary Charlesworth, 'Individual Rights and the Australian High Court' (1986) 4 *Law in Context* 52.
**264** (1938) 59 CLR 556, 580.

then, s 80 is primarily designed to protect against overzealous judges – that is, a protection for the accused against the exclusive exercise of judicial power by judges to determine guilt. This role for the jury might work in combination with the principle – to be discussed in the next chapter – that the adjudgement and punishment of criminal guilt requires an exclusive exercise of Commonwealth judicial power. On this understanding, the federal separation of judicial power principles ensure that individuals can only be adjudged guilty of, and punished for, an offence through an exercise of judicial power by a court and, when an accused is being tried on indictment, that adjudgement of criminal guilt can only be effected by a jury's determination. Although, as Dixon and Evatt JJ noted in *Lowenstein*, the framers of the Constitution were not primarily concerned with judicially enforceable protection for rights, s 80 might have been seen as an exception.

Alternatively, s 80 might protect the entitlements of the members of the community to be involved in an exercise of government power to determine guilt in circumstances where an accused is tried on indictment for a federal offence. On this understanding, a judge sitting alone can determine guilt when a federal offence is tried summarily. However, when a federal offence is tried on indictment, the democratic interests of the community are vindicated by the community's direct involvement in the determination of guilt. This democratic explanation for the s 80 guarantee might be refined further within the federal system created by the Constitution. Perhaps s 80 guarantees that the local State community, in which the offence is committed and from which the jury is drawn, should have the responsibility and entitlement for determining guilt when a federal offence is tried on indictment. This may not say very much about the types of offences that should be tried on indictment, but when Parliament chooses to have a jury trial through the indictment process, then the jury should be drawn from the local community in which the offence occurred. This federal democratic understanding of s 80 is consistent with the broader efforts of the framers to recognise and differentiate between the different federal communities: the national and the local.

To complicate matters further, s 80 need not be seen as protecting rights or interests at all. Perhaps it might just be seen as a structural provision that facilitates the exercise of Commonwealth judicial power within the new federal system created by the Constitution. Without the inclusion of s 80 in Chapter III, jury members – as lay persons – might not otherwise have been able to exercise Commonwealth judicial power to adjudge and punish criminal guilt. Section 71 specifies that judicial power is to be exercised by a court referred to in s 71 and, for federal courts, judicial power can only be exercised by judges appointed consistently with s 71 or non-judicial officers under their supervision. For State courts hearing federal offences, the federal Parliament cannot determine their structure. Section 80 then operates to prevent State Parliaments from adopting alternative forms of judicial mechanisms for the determination of guilt where federal offences are tried on indictment. And, of course, where Parliament decides that a federal offence should be tried on indictment, s 80 operates to tell us where the trial should take place.[265] This structural view says nothing about the interests or rights to be vindicated by the jury trial that is referred to in s 80. Those matters are left to the federal Parliament when deciding whether or not an offence should be tried on indictment. This structural view is consistent with the federal architecture of the Constitution and the framers' aversion to rights-protecting constitutionalism. Although the framers' views on the purpose of s 80 were unclear, the structural view is certainly consistent with the main thrust of the debates. Many of these ideas – particularly the rights-protecting views of s 80 – are hinted at in the s 80 cases, but a clearly defined understanding of the purpose of the section is yet to emerge from High Court case-law.

## VIII Conclusions

It is clear that the High Court has played a pivotal role in designing the federal architecture of Chapter III. The decisions of the Court minimised the role played by the Privy Council as an alternate court of appeal from Australian courts. It endorsed the Commonwealth Parliament's attempts to channel appeals in cases of federal jurisdiction from State courts to the High Court; it permitted the Commonwealth Parliament to terminate appeals to the Privy Council in non-inter se cases and adopted a blanket rule against granting s 74 certificates for appeals from the High Court to the Privy Council in inter se cases. Its decisions created the 'bizarre situation' of having two ultimate courts of appeal, making it unpalatable for the continuation of Privy Council appeals from State courts and precipitating the cessation of such appeals with the enactment of the *Australia Acts*. Thus, over the course of the twentieth century, the High Court's decisions facilitated the creation of an integrated judicial system in Australia with the High Court at its apex.

This growing integration has had considerable implications for the distinctiveness of State judicial systems. The erosion of the role of the Privy Council is an example – the Privy Council was intended to be an integral part of State judicial systems. Furthermore, the expansion of federal jurisdiction through juridical constructs like *accrued jurisdiction* has facilitated a subtle shift in judicial power and jurisdiction from the States to the Commonwealth. Disputes that would otherwise be determined with an exercise of State jurisdiction and judicial power are determined with an exercise of federal jurisdiction and judicial power if they form part of the same legal controversy as a claim that attracts federal jurisdiction. The converging or centralising consequences of this shift will be explored further in Chapter 9.

**265** For a detailed explanation of this structural account, see James Stellios, 'The Constitutional Jury: A "Bulwark of Liberty"?' (2005) 27 *Sydney Law Review* 113.

# 9

# Judicial power

> *[T]he separation of the judicial powers from other powers is affected by different considerations. The position and constitution of the judicature could not be considered accidental to the institution of federalism: for upon the judicature rested the ultimate responsibility for the maintenance and enforcement of the boundaries within which governmental power might be exercised and upon that the whole system was constructed.*[1]

## I Introduction

Chapter 8 introduced the architecture of the federal judicature set out in Chapter III of the Constitution. Central to the operation of the federal judicial system is s 71 of the Constitution which vests 'the judicial power of the Commonwealth' in the High Court, 'such other federal courts as the Parliament creates' and 'such other courts as it invests with federal jurisdiction'. This is in contrast to the investiture of federal legislative power by s 1 in the Commonwealth Parliament and the vesting of Commonwealth executive power by s 61 of the Constitution.

This plan for the distribution of governmental power – legislative, executive and judicial – across the three arms of the federal government – the legislature, the executive and the judiciary – has had an enormous impact on the design of federal government institutions and the allocation of power across government decision-makers. Of particular interest to this chapter is the separate identification of Commonwealth judicial power and its allocation to the courts referred to in s 71. From this allocation of power, the High Court has established two fundamental principles about the exercise of Commonwealth judicial power. The first is that only courts referred to in s 71 can exercise Commonwealth judicial power. The second is that courts exercising Commonwealth judicial power can only exercise judicial power and also non-judicial power that is incidental to the exercise of judicial power.

**1** *R v Kirby; Ex parte Boilermakers' Society of Australia* (1956) 94 CLR 254, 275–6.

This chapter will begin by exploring the understandings and assumptions of the framers about the separate allocation of judicial power in Chapter III of the Constitution. The writings of Montesquieu and others advocating a separation of powers to protect the liberty of the individual have had an enduring impact on western political thinking. However, there is little evidence of such an influence on the drafters of the Constitution. It will be seen that, while the framers did not have extensive discussions about a separation of powers, they did appreciate the constitutional tradition and central importance of an independent and impartial judiciary within the new federal system. The judiciary was to determine questions in federal jurisdiction, some of which, as was seen in Chapter 8, would involve claims between State governments, or between the Commonwealth and State governments. Other federal claims would involve litigation between residents of different States, or between the resident of one State and the government of another. And, of course, there would be litigation between the government and residents of the new federal body politic. The federal claims to be heard by courts in the course of this litigation would include constitutional claims, involving challenges to the validity of Commonwealth or State legislation. In performing all these functions, the independence and impartiality of the federal judiciary, particularly the High Court at the apex of the system, would have to be secured and protected. As Josiah Symon said during the 1897 Constitutional Convention, '[t]he Federal High Court is placed in a position to safeguard the liberties of the subject and the rights of the individual States against encroachment of the Legislature. It is placed in a position in which its independence must be absolutely assured'.[2] This was partly achieved by s 72 of the Constitution that sought to protect the tenure of federal court judges. But, as will be seen in this chapter, independence and impartiality are also protected by implications drawn by the High Court from the terms and structure of Chapter III.

This chapter will then turn to explain how the High Court has established the two separation of judicial power principles that limit the Commonwealth Parliament's power, and the range of rationales or justifications that have been put forward to support such implications. For the principles to operate effectively, there needs to be a reasonably clear conception of what Commonwealth 'judicial power' is. It will be necessary to explore the High Court's approach to demarcating judicial power from the other categories of power – legislative and executive – and to identify a framework for characterising power as judicial in nature. The chapter will then explain the ways in which these separation of judicial power principles have been applied to shape the design of government institutions and the distribution of powers across government decision-makers. The exceptions that exist to those principles and the developing area of 'due process' protections will also be outlined.

**2** *Convention Debates, Adelaide* (1897) 950.

Finally, it will be necessary to consider the Chapter III limitations that apply to State courts. Although the separation of judicial power principles only apply as limitations on the Commonwealth Parliament, the High Court has developed principles that control the way that State Parliaments deal with their judicial systems so as to protect the institutional integrity and essential characteristics of State courts. These principles, which have their origin in the High Court's decision in *Kable v Director of Public Prosecutions* (NSW),[3] have been developed in recognition of the uniquely integrated character of the federal judicature. As explained in Chapter 8, the framers of the Constitution decided that the High Court would operate as a general court of appeal from lower courts, and that the Commonwealth Parliament should be empowered to authorise State courts to exercise federal jurisdiction. As a result of this institutional integration, there are various implications for the power of State Parliaments to regulate the powers and functions of State courts and their judges.

# II Separation of judicial power

## 1 Political theories and the views of the framers

As noted in previous chapters, the separation of powers has a rich and long tradition in political theory.[4] In his classic work, *The Spirit of Laws*, published in 1748, the French philosopher Baron de Montesquieu wrote about the virtues of a separation of powers:

> When the legislative and executive powers are united in the same person, or in the same body of magistrates, there can be no liberty; because apprehensions may arise, lest the same monarch or senate should enact tyrannical laws, to execute them in a tyrannical manner.
>
> Again, there is no liberty, if the judiciary power be not separated from the legislative and executive. Were it joined with the legislative, the life and liberty of the subject would be exposed to arbitrary control; for the judge would be then the legislator. Were it joined to the executive power, the judge might behave with violence and oppression.[5]

These ideas were influential for William Blackstone. In his *Commentaries on the Laws of England* written in 1765, similar liberty-protecting values were to be promoted by a separation of courts and judicial power from the other arms of government:

> In this distinct and separate existence of the judicial power, in a peculiar body of men, nominated indeed, but not removeable at pleasure, by the crown, consists one preservation of the public liberty; which cannot subsist long in any state, unless the administration of common justice be in some degree separated both from the legislative and

**3** (1996) 189 CLR 51.
**4** See Chapter 1, Part II.2, Chapter 3, Part II.1 and Chapter 6, Part II.3–4.
**5** Charles de Secondat Montesquieu, *The Spirit of Laws* (Thomas Nugent trans, Hafner, 1949) XI.6.

> also from the executive power. Were it joined with the legislative, the life, liberty and property, of the subject would be in the hands of arbitrary judges, whose decisions would be then regulated only by their opinions, and not by any fundamental principles of law; which, though legislators may depart from, yet judges are bound to observe. Were it joined with the executive, this union might soon be an over-balance for the legislature.[6]

Montesquieu's ideas were also influential for James Madison and Alexander Hamilton, who endorsed the liberty-protecting objectives of a separation of powers when writing in support of a structural separation of legislative, executive and judicial power in the US Constitution.[7]

By contrast, when the framers of the Australian Constitution met in the Constitutional Conventions of 1891 and 1897–8, there was little discussion of these political theories of separating power. It seems reasonably clear from the historical work that has been done that the framers did not seek to incorporate Montesquieu's ideas into the Australian Constitution.[8] As was recognised by French CJ in *South Australia v Totani*, '[t]he historical record does not indicate that the members of the Convention expressly adverted to the broader concept of the separation of judicial power in their debates'.[9] The most that we can say confidently is that the framers intended to create an independent and impartial federal judiciary.[10] While there were statements which emphasised that the Constitution would create the three arms of government,[11] as John Finnis has observed, '[t]here is nothing in the debates … that must be taken to be a discussion, still less a commendation, of the Abstract doctrine of separation of powers'.[12] Geoffrey Sawer put the position in the following terms:

> There is no evidence that the Federal Fathers in general had the slightest desire to imitate the French theory of separation of powers, which was based upon a misrepresentation of English practice, nor the American theory which was based upon a misrepresentation of the French.[13]

By contrast, it is quite clear that the framers contemplated the creation of a strong and independent judiciary. As Blackstone's writing demonstrated, the independence of the judiciary had developed as an incident of British constitutional government, strengthened by the protection provided by the *Act of Settlement 1701* (UK) for judges' terms of appointment. As Robert Garran, Secretary to the Drafting Committee during the 1897–8 Convention, was later to say, 'for the independence of the judiciary under the Australian Constitution we

**6** William Blackstone, *Commentaries on the Laws of England* (Clarendon Press, 1765–69) vol 1, ch 7, 259.
**7** *Federalist Papers*, No's 47, 51 and 78 (1788).
**8** See Geoffrey Sawer, *Australian Federalism in the Courts* (Melbourne University Press, 1967) 152; J M Finnis, 'Separation of Powers in the Australian Constitution' (1968) 3 *Adelaide Law Review* 159; Fiona Wheeler, 'Original Intent and the Doctrine of Separation of Powers in Australia' (1996) 7 *Public Law Review* 96.
**9** (2010) 242 CLR 1, 44.
**10** James Stellios, *The Federal Judicature: Chapter III of the Constitution* (LexisNexis, 2010) 69–72.
**11** Ibid, 52–3.
**12** Finnis, above n 8, 171. See also Wheeler, above n 8, 103.
**13** Sawer, above n 8, 152.

need look no further than British tradition, backed up by the judges' security of tenure'.[14]

There are two broad objectives identifiable in the Convention Debates as to why judicial independence was thought to be so important. The first was the protection of the federal compact to be entered into by the Colonies. A strong current running through the debates was the desire for an independent judiciary to protect the States from the federal Parliament and to provide a 'calm judicial atmosphere' in which the States could resolve disputes amongst themselves, rather than 'fly[ing] to secession because they cannot get justice in any other way'.[15]

The second identifiable objective was for an independent judiciary to protect 'the liberties of the subject'.[16] It is not entirely clear what was assumed by the delegates when making these statements. It is possible that the liberties of the people were equated with the rights of the States.[17] It is also possible that it was assumed that an independent judiciary would continue, in the British constitutional tradition, to resolve disputes between individuals and between individuals and the government, thereby, as Blackstone had in mind, preserving the life, liberty and property of the individual.

The important point, however, is that the framers fully contemplated that the federal judicial system that would be created by the Constitution was to be an independent and impartial one. While a separation of powers may have been within the comprehension of some of the framers, the political theories of separated power did not appear to provide a blueprint for the drafting of the Constitution.

## 2 The establishment of the separation principles

The High Court has accepted the existence of two separation of judicial power principles: first, that Commonwealth judicial power can only be exercised by courts referred to in s 71 of the Constitution and, second, that courts exercising Commonwealth judicial power can only exercise judicial power or non-judicial power incidental to the exercise of Commonwealth judicial power.

The first principle is generally regarded to have been established by two key cases: *New South Wales v Commonwealth*[18] and *Waterside Workers' Federation of Australia v J W Alexander Ltd.*[19] The first case is considered in Chapter 5.[20] There, the Inter-State Commission, established by s 101 of the Constitution and given jurisdiction by the *Inter-State Commission Act 1912* (Cth), was considered to be

**14** Sir Robert Garran, *Prosper the Commonwealth* (Angus & Robertson, 1958) 194.
**15** *Convention Debates, Adelaide* (1897) 25.
**16** Ibid, 950.
**17** Jeffrey Goldsworthy, 'The Constitutional Protection of Rights in Australia', Gregory Craven (ed) *Australian Federation* (Melbourne University Press, 1992) 151, 158.
**18** (1915) 20 CLR 54.
**19** (1918) 25 CLR 434.
**20** See Chapter 5, Part III.3.

a non-judicial body that could not exercise judicial power. The Court held that Commonwealth judicial power could only be exercised by a court referred to in s 71 and, since the Inter-State Commission was not such a court, it could not be invested with judicial power.

In *Alexander*, the Court considered whether Parliament had validly constituted, and vested judicial powers of enforcement in, the Court of Conciliation and Arbitration. The Court was created to settle and prevent industrial disputes, and was given a range of judicial powers to enforce awards and impose penalties for non-compliance. The President of the Court was to be appointed 'from among the Justices of the High Court' for a term of seven years. It had been argued that, since the Court was a federal court created by Parliament, the appointment for a fixed period was in breach of the requirement in s 72 of the Constitution. For a majority of the Court, judicial powers had been invalidly conferred on a body that did not satisfy the s 72 requirement (as it then was) of life tenure. The principle is captured by Griffith CJ:

> It is impossible under the Constitution to confer such functions upon any body other than a Court, nor can the difficulty be avoided by designating a body, which is not in its essential character a Court, by that name, or by calling the functions by another name. In short, any attempt to vest any part of the judicial power of the Commonwealth in any body other than a Court is entirely ineffective.[21]

The second separation of judicial power principle was not accepted by a majority of the High Court until the decision in *R v Kirby; Ex parte Boilermakers' Society of Australia*.[22] It was raised, but avoided, in *In re Judiciary and Navigation Acts*.[23] It was firmly endorsed by Dixon J in *Victorian Stevedoring & General Contracting Co Pty Ltd v Dignan*,[24] but did not find favour with most of the Court in *R v Federal Court of Bankruptcy; Ex parte Lowenstein*.[25] In the latter case, at least three of the majority judges preferred a less severe limitation that prevented courts exercising Commonwealth judicial power from exercising non-judicial power if *inconsistent* or *incompatible* with an exercise of Commonwealth judicial power.[26]

As already noted, the Court in *Alexander* held that the conferral of judicial power on the Court of Conciliation and Arbitration was invalid. Importantly, the invalidity arose because the Court was not constituted according to s 72 of the Constitution so as to exercise the judicial power of the Commonwealth. No question arose for determination whether a combination of judicial and arbitral (ie, non-judicial) powers was consistent with Chapter III. Indeed, following *Alexander*, Parliament assumed that it was possible to vest courts with some non-judicial power and, in 1926, Parliament reconstituted the Court of Conciliation and Arbitration to consist of s 72 judges. It was conferred with judicial powers, but it also retained arbitration as its principal function.

**21** *Waterside Workers' Federation of Australia v J W Alexander Ltd* (1918) 25 CLR 434, 442.
**22** (1956) 94 CLR 254.
**23** (1921) 29 CLR 257.
**24** (1931) 46 CLR 73, 98.
**25** (1938) 59 CLR 556.
**26** Ibid, 567, 591.

In *Boilermakers'*, it was argued that Parliament could not confer judicial powers on a body that had, as its principal function, the arbitration of disputes (ie, the exercise of non-judicial power) and that Chapter III did not permit a combination of judicial and non-judicial power. A majority of the Court (Dixon CJ, McTiernan, Fullagar and Kitto JJ; Williams, Webb and Taylor JJ dissenting) agreed. Having affirmed the first separation of powers principle established in *Alexander*, the majority proceeded to establish the second:

> A number of considerations exist which point very definitely to the conclusion that the Constitution does not allow the use of courts established by or under Chap III for the discharge of functions which are not in themselves part of the judicial power and are not auxiliary or incidental thereto.[27]

Their Honours concluded that the Court of Conciliation and Arbitration 'remained a tribunal established and equipped primarily and predominantly for the work of industrial conciliation and arbitration'[28] and, as such, it could not exercise judicial power. Although their Honours sought to establish the second separation principle, the decision of the Court rests squarely on the *Alexander* principle. Once it was accepted that the Court of Conciliation and Arbitration was not a Chapter III court, then, in accordance with *Alexander*, it could not be conferred with judicial power.

Three judges dissented, instead favouring, as three of the judges did in *Lowenstein*, a less strict test that looked to the *inconsistency* or *incompatibility* of the non-judicial power with the exercise of Commonwealth judicial power.[29] The majority's view was upheld on appeal to the Privy Council in *Attorney-General (Cth) v The Queen*.[30] Doubts were subsequently expressed about the necessity and utility of this second principle;[31] however, it is 'now firmly entrenched, by precedent and by institutional practices and doctrines to which the precedents have given rise'.[32]

## 3 Rationales for the principles

On one view, the allocation of legislative, executive and judicial power across the three arms of government might be seen as 'a draftsman's neat arrangement, without any hint of further significance'.[33] This view would provide little foundation for rigid separation of judicial power principles. So, what justifies a departure from that view?

**27** (1956) 94 CLR 254, 271–2.
**28** Ibid, 286.
**29** Ibid, 313–14, 328–9. See also 341.
**30** (1957) 95 CLR 529 (PC).
**31** See, eg, *R v Joske; Ex parte Australian Building Construction Employees and Builders' Labourers' Federation* (1974) 130 CLR 87, 90, 102.
**32** Cheryl Saunders, 'The Separation of Powers', in Brian Opeskin and Fiona Wheeler (eds), *The Australian Federal Judicial System* (Melbourne University Press, 2000) 3, 13.
**33** Garran, above n 14, 194. See also Williams J in *Boilermakers'* (1956) 94 CLR 254, 301–2.

The two principles can readily be produced by using ordinary techniques of statutory interpretation. The express delineation of what powers can be exercised by which bodies in ss 1, 61 and 71 of the Constitution, along with the interpretive principle of *expressio unius est exclusio alterius*, can be seen as giving rise to the two principles. The text expressly identifies which arm of government should exercise which government power and a negative implication arises preventing other arms of government from exercising that power. However, given the significant limitations imposed on Parliament by the separation of judicial power principles – limitations that control the political choices made through the democratic processes of the legislature – one might expect to see reliance upon something more than a simple rule of construction.

The High Court has not spoken with a clear and consistent voice as to what that something else might be. There have been three main rationales put forward by the Court to support the separation of judicial power principles. The first is that the role of the federal judiciary is to protect the federal compact, and that courts can only perform that role properly if they have independence and impartiality. The separation of judicial power principles, it is said, are necessary to preserve that independence and impartiality. In relation to the *Alexander* side of the separation equation, the protection afforded by the appointment requirements in s 72 would be entirely frustrated if Parliament were free to vest judicial power in bodies other than courts. This is reflected in the judgment of Isaacs and Rich JJ in *Alexander* when considering the tenure requirement: 'sec 72 is one of the strongest guarantees in the Constitution for the security of the States. … It is plain that the independence of the tribunal would be seriously weakened if the Commonwealth Parliament could fix any less permanent tenure than for life, subject to proved misbehaviour or incapacity'.[34] Life tenure was needed to secure independence, and independence was needed to police the federal system.

Of course, this rationale is only partly effective, as s 72 has no application to the appointment of State court judges. Nevertheless, as will be seen later in this chapter, the High Court has imposed the requirements of impartiality and independence on State courts through the *Kable* line of cases, and has partly justified the imposition of those Chapter III limitations on the basis that State courts must be independent and impartial in order to police the federal compact.[35]

Federalism considerations have also supported the *Boilermakers'* side of the separation equation. In *Boilermakers'* itself, Dixon CJ, McTiernan, Fullagar and Kitto JJ said that the 'position and constitution of the judicature could not be considered accidental to the institution of federalism: for upon the judicature rested the ultimate responsibility for the maintenance and enforcement of the boundaries within which governmental power might be exercised and upon that the whole system was constructed'.[36] Thus, while the executive and the legislative power might commingle, judicial power had to be separated because its full

**34** *Waterside Workers' Federation of Australia v J W Alexander Ltd* (1918) 25 CLR 434, 469–70.
**35** See *Forge v Australian Securities and Investments Commission* (2006) 228 CLR 45, 73.
**36** *R v Kirby; Ex parte Boilermakers' Society of Australia* (1956) 94 CLR 254, 276.

separation helped to maintain the federal system. On appeal, the Privy Council put it in even clearer terms: '[I]n a federal system the absolute independence of the judiciary is the bulwark of the constitution against encroachment whether by the legislature or by the executive. To vest in the same body executive and judicial power is to remove a vital constitutional safeguard'.[37] This rationale has continued to be reflected in more recent decisions.[38]

A second rationale that can be found in the cases is one that focuses on the rights-protective effect that a separation of judicial power might have. This rationale has been advanced in different ways. On the one hand, resembling the views of Montesquieu, the allocation of powers to different arms of government is seen as dispersing the exercise of that power and, consequently, protecting against the concentration of power in one decision-maker.[39] On the other hand, there has been a recognition, in the Blackstonian tradition, that over the course of constitutional development in England, the judicial power, as exercised by an independent judiciary, has provided protection for life, liberty and property.[40] On this view, a separated judicial power is seen as providing protection for 'basic rights'.[41] These two forms of the argument are not clearly differentiated in the cases;[42] however, at the core of each is the idea of an independent judiciary exercising judicial power.[43]

A third rationale put forward to justify the separation of judicial power principles has been that they protect the independence of the courts to provide a check on the other arms of government.[44] As Brennan CJ, Dawson, Toohey, McHugh and Gummow JJ said in *Wilson*, 'the separation of functions is designed to provide checks and balances on the exercise of power by the respective organs of government in which the powers are reposed'.[45] Similarly, more recently, Hayne, Crennan, Kiefel and Bell JJ said in *TCL Air Conditioner (Zhongshan) Co Ltd v Judges of the Federal Court of Australia*: 'The doctrine of the separation of powers is directed to ensuring an independent and impartial judicial branch of government to enforce lawful limits on the exercise of public power'.[46]

Under each rationale, judicial independence and impartiality operate as the core functional attributes that are needed by the courts. Whether the courts are seen as protecting the federal compact, protecting liberty or operating as a check on the other arms of government, the judiciary is required to be independent

**37** *Attorney-General (Cth) v The Queen* (1957) 95 CLR 529, 540–41 (PC).
**38** *Forge v Australian Securities and Investments Commission* (2006) 228 CLR 45, 73; *Wilson v Minister for Aboriginal and Torres Strait Islander Affairs* (1996) 189 CLR 1, 11–13; *Polyukhovich v Commonwealth* (1991) 172 CLR 501, 648.
**39** *R v Davison* (1954) 90 CLR 353, 380–81.
**40** *Huddart, Parker & Co Pty Ltd v Moorehead* (1909) 8 CLR 330, 381–3; *R v Quinn; Ex parte Consolidated Foods Corp* (1977) 138 CLR 1, 11.
**41** *R v Quinn; Ex parte Consolidated Foods Corp* (1977) 138 CLR 1, 11; *Attorney-General (Cth) v Breckler* (1999) 197 CLR 83, 109.
**42** See, eg, *Wilson v Minister for Aboriginal and Torres Strait Islander Affairs* (1996) 189 CLR 1, 12.
**43** Ibid, 11.
**44** *Polyukhovich v Commonwealth* (1991) 172 CLR 501, 684–5.
**45** *Wilson v Minister for Aboriginal and Torres Strait Islander Affairs* (1996) 189 CLR 1, 11.
**46** (2013) 251 CLR 533, 574.

and impartial, and independence and impartiality are said to be advanced by a separation of judicial power.[47]

## III Commonwealth judicial power

For these separation of judicial power principles to work effectively, there needs to be a reasonably clear understanding of what the 'judicial power of the Commonwealth' means. Identifying the hallmarks of judicial power has been a very difficult task. This is, in part, because our understanding of government power has been informed by a British constitutional tradition which did not always recognise clear distinctions between judicial and non-judicial power. The High Court has on many occasions acknowledged the difficulties in identifying the parameters of the concept. As Gummow, Hayne and Bell JJ said recently in *Saraceni v Jones*, the High Court 'often has observed that it is not possible to frame a definition of "judicial power" which is at once exclusive and exhaustive'.[48]

Despite the undoubted difficulties, there is a reasonably clear framework that has emerged from the cases that allows an identification of government power as *judicial* in nature. As will be seen, the cases have identified a core defining characteristic: the determination of a dispute about pre-existing rights. The High Court has accepted a broad distinction between the *creation* of rights and the *determination* of a dispute about rights. Rights are *created* by the Parliament (often through decision-making by the executive arm of government pursuant to legislative authorisation). By contrast, a dispute about pre-existing rights is *determined* through an exercise of judicial power.

There are clear examples where an exercise of power involves an exercise of *judicial power* because there is a determination of a dispute about pre-existing rights. Indeed, these examples are considered to be *exclusively* judicial in nature so that, as a general rule, they cannot be exercised by other arms of government. The determination of whether legislative, executive and judicial decision-making is valid – whether constitutionally valid or otherwise within the scope of statutory authority – is a function that is exclusively judicial.[49] So too is the determination of common law claims based in tort or contract,[50] and of claims based in equity.[51] The determination of criminal guilt and the imposition of

**47** Independence and impartiality may also be advanced by a less stringent *incompatibility* or *inconsistency* test favoured by judges in *Lowenstein* and by the dissent in *Boilermakers'*. See, eg, Sir Anthony Mason, 'A New Perspective on Separation of Powers' (1996) 82 *Canberra Bulletin of Public Administration* 1, 5–6; Leslie Zines, *The High Court and the Constitution* (Federation Press, 2008) 299; Peter Gerangelos, 'Interpretational Methodology in Separation of Powers Jurisprudence: The Formalist/Functionalist Debate' (2005) 8 *Constitutional Law and Policy Review* 1; James Stellios, 'Reconceiving the Separation of Judicial Power' (2011) 22 *Public Law Review*113; Sarah Murray, *The Remaking of the Courts – Less-Adversarial Practice and the Constitutional Role of the Judiciary in Australia* (Federation Press, 2014).
**48** (2012) 246 CLR 251, 256.
**49** *Plaintiff S157/2002 v Commonwealth* (2003) 211 CLR 476, 514.
**50** *Brandy v Human Rights and Equal Opportunity Commission* (1995) 183 CLR 245, 258.
**51** *Attorney-General (Cth) v Breckler* (1999) 197 CLR 83, 109.

punishment have also been held to require an exclusive exercise of Commonwealth judicial power.[52] Whether this also means that the deprivation of a person's liberty requires an exclusive exercise of judicial power remains somewhat unclear from High Court jurisprudence.

There are exceptions to the general propositions that courts only determine disputes about pre-existing rights and that the determination of existing rights is exclusively a judicial function. There are some cases where a power will be judicial in character when exercised by a court even though it creates rights. This is primarily the case where there is a strong *historical* practice of courts exercising such powers. Additionally, there are times when a power looks like it has the core defining characteristic of judicial power, yet the power is not considered to be exclusively judicial. The enforcement of military discipline is an example that will be discussed briefly below. Finally, the High Court has recognised that some powers are neither inherently judicial nor inherently non-judicial in character, and may take on a judicial character if exercised by courts and a non-judicial character if exercised by a non-judicial body. These innominate powers and the operation of the chameleon principle present a number of difficulties which are beyond the scope of this chapter.[53]

## 1 The defining characteristic

The framers of the Constitution did not discuss in much detail their understandings of judicial power. Many of the leading framers suggested that the courts should be limited to the resolution of disputes between parties. On that understanding, judicial functions were to be limited to occasions when a legal dispute had arisen, and courts were to resist giving their opinion in the absence of such a dispute – the existence of a real dispute enhanced the quality of decision-making as courts would be able to see the consequence of their decisions. The need for an actual dispute was also emphasised when a majority of the framers rejected proposals for the High Court to be given power to provide an advisory opinion on the constitutional validity of federal legislation in advance of a dispute arising. The prevailing view was that such a function would not involve an exercise of judicial power, and its conferral on the judiciary would involve it unnecessarily in political controversy.[54]

These basic propositions about judicial power were accepted very early by the High Court. In a statement which is now regarded as classical, Griffith CJ in *Huddart, Parker & Co Pty Ltd v Moorehead*[55] described judicial power in the following way:

> I am of opinion that the words 'judicial power' as used in sec 71 of the Constitution mean the power which every sovereign authority must of necessity have to decide

**52** *Chu Kheng Lim v Minister for Immigration, Local Government and Ethnic Affairs* (1992) 176 CLR 1, 27.
**53** See Stellios, above n 10, 146–58.
**54** Ibid.
**55** (1909) 8 CLR 330.

> controversies between its subjects, or between itself and its subjects, whether the rights relate to life, liberty or property.[56]

Griffith CJ's statement identifies two key elements of judicial power. First, it is an exercise of *sovereign* power. Accordingly, it does not include the exercise of arbitral power pursuant to private agreement. Private arbitration does not involve an exercise of power by the *state* and, thus, cannot come within the concept of judicial power.[57] Secondly, and as anticipated by many of the framers, judicial power involves the resolution of a dispute about pre-existing rights.

The need for a dispute to exist before a court can exercise Commonwealth judicial power was emphasised in *Federated Saw Mill, Timber Yard and General Woodworkers Employés Association of Australasia v James Moore & Sons Pty Ltd*.[58] The Court of Conciliation and Arbitration had stated a case to the High Court identifying a series of questions to be answered. In providing answers to those questions, Griffith CJ[59] and O'Connor J[60] expressed concern that the Court was not exercising judicial power because the Court of Conciliation and Arbitration had not determined any of the underlying facts that gave rise to the dispute between the parties. Griffith CJ said that '[t]he questions submitted in the case are to a great extent of an abstract character' and that 'I entertain some doubts whether I am performing a judicial duty'.[61] O'Connor J expressed similar concerns: '[a]s yet no fact has been determined, nor is the inquiry as to the nature of the dispute closed'.[62] The other judges accepted that the giving of an opinion in the absence of a dispute would not involve an exercise of judicial power, but considered that there was an underlying dispute to be resolved.

Thus, as many of the framers anticipated, judicial power cannot be exercised in the absence of a clearly identified factual dispute, and this early principle has remained a central tenet of judicial power doctrine. As Isaacs J stated in *Australian Commonwealth Shipping Board v Federated Seamen's Union of Australasia*,[63] '[i]t is abundantly established by cases of the highest authority that a Court does not give judgments on hypothetical facts'.

A more recent example is *Bass v Permanent Trustee Co Ltd*,[64] where a single judge of the Federal Court had referred a series of questions to a Full Court of the Federal Court. It was held by the High Court on appeal from the Full Court's answers that the underlying facts had not been 'found or agreed' and were, thus, 'hypothetical'.[65] Consequently, the Full Court should not have provided those answers to the Federal Court judge at first instance. In reaching that conclusion,

**56** Ibid, 357.
**57** See below at 9.3.8.
**58** (1909) 8 CLR 465.
**59** Ibid, 484–6, 500–01.
**60** Ibid, 501.
**61** Ibid, 485, 500–1.
**62** Ibid, 501.
**63** (1925) 36 CLR 442, 451.
**64** (1999) 198 CLR 334.
**65** Ibid, 357.

the High Court emphasised that a judicial determination 'includes a conclusive or final decision based on a concrete and established or agreed situation which aims to quell a controversy'.[66]

## 2 The jurisdictional requirement of a 'matter'

The search for the meaning of judicial power is complicated somewhat by the High Court's decision in *In re Judiciary and Navigation Acts*.[67] During the Convention Debates, there were proposals for the insertion of a constitutional provision that would allow judicial proceedings to be instituted for an advisory opinion on the constitutional validity of legislation. There were also arguments that, in any event, the provisions of Chapter III, as finally enacted, were broad enough to allow proceedings to be instituted in the High Court for such advisory opinions. The prevailing view in response to these arguments was that the terms of Chapter III – the use of the word 'matter' to identify the heads of federal jurisdiction – would not allow such proceedings. The word 'matter', although broad, would be limited to 'such matters as can arise for judicial determination'.[68] Furthermore, a clear majority of drafters considered it undesirable for provisions to be inserted to allow for such an advisory opinion. The clear message from the debates was that the provision of advisory opinions on the constitutional validity of legislation in the absence of a dispute would not involve an exercise of judicial power.[69]

In 1910, the Commonwealth Parliament amended the *Judiciary Act 1903* (Cth) to insert Part XII. The new provisions created a procedure to allow the Governor-General to refer to the High Court questions of law as to the validity of Commonwealth legislation. Jurisdiction was conferred on the High Court to hear and determine the referred questions. The questions were to be heard by the Full Court, and State Attorneys-General would be given the opportunity to appear before the Court. The determination of the Court was to be final and conclusive and not subject to appeal. Pursuant to those provisions, the Governor-General referred to the Court the question of whether the *Navigation Act 1912* was valid. Having reached a view that Part XII was invalid, a majority of the Court refused to answer the question.

Given the Convention Debates and the tenor of prior cases like *Federated Saw Mill, Timber Yard, and General Woodworkers Employés Association of Australasia v James Moore & Sons Pty Ltd*, it seemed open to the Court to conclude that such an advisory opinion did not involve an exercise of Commonwealth judicial power, and that, consequently, it could not be conferred on the Court. That principle, however, had not yet been established by the High Court, and the Court in *In re Judiciary* avoided having to confront the question by concluding that the

**66** Ibid, 355.
**67** (1921) 29 CLR 257.
**68** *Convention Debates, Melbourne* (1898) 320.
**69** For a detailed discussion, see Stellios, above n 10, 72–9.

giving of an advisory opinion was a 'judicial function'.[70] Accordingly, the Court refrained from expressing an opinion on the second separation of judicial power principle later established in *Boilermakers'*.

Rather than assessing the provisions according to separation of judicial *power* principles, the High Court turned to the *jurisdiction* that could be given to the High Court. Although the constitutional question to be decided by the Court would have fallen within the words of s 76(i) ('arising under this Constitution, or involving its interpretation'), the Court focused on the word 'matter' in the introductory wording of s 76. The Commonwealth had argued that the word 'matter' meant a *legal proceeding*, and that Part XII had set up a new proceeding raising questions within s 76(i). The Court (Knox CJ, Gavan Duffy, Powers, Rich and Starke JJ; Higgins J dissenting) disagreed in the following terms:

> We do not accept this contention; we do not think that the word 'matter' in sec 76 means a legal proceeding, but rather the subject matter for determination in a legal proceeding. In our opinion there can be no matter within the meaning of the section unless there is some immediate right, duty or liability to be established by the determination of the Court. If the matter exists, the Legislature may no doubt prescribe the means by which the determination of the Court is to be obtained, and for that purpose may, we think, adopt any existing method of legal procedure or invent a new one. But it cannot authorize this Court to make a declaration of the law divorced from any attempt to administer that law.[71]

Their Honours continued with similar statements of principle: '... a matter ... must involve some right or privilege or protection given by law, or the prevention, redress or punishment of some act inhibited by law' and 'nothing in Ch III ... lend[s] colour to the view that Parliament can confer power or jurisdiction upon the High Court to determine abstract questions of law without the right or duty of any body or person being involved'.[72]

Thus, the Court could not be given *jurisdiction* to give an advisory opinion. Importantly, *jurisdiction* was said to be conditioned by the need for the establishment of an 'immediate right, duty or liability'. This 'matter' requirement appears to be the same as the requirement identified by Griffith CJ in *Huddart, Parker* that characterises Commonwealth judicial power – that is, the determination of a dispute about existing rights and obligations. Indeed, the Court's conclusion that no '*power* or *jurisdiction*' could be given to the High Court to determine abstract questions suggests that the requirements of 'matter' and 'judicial power' were being, perhaps inadvertently, synchronised. Although the High Court did not establish the second separation of judicial power principle until *Boilermakers'*, it would seem that the principle was effectively established in *In re Judiciary*, since the *judicial power* of the Commonwealth cannot be exercised without *federal jurisdiction* to do so.

**70** *In re Judiciary and Navigation Acts* (1921) 29 CLR 257, 264.
**71** Ibid, 265.
**72** Ibid, 266, 267.

As a consequence, the core characteristic of rights determination is sometimes pursued by the High Court through the separation of judicial power principles, and sometimes through the jurisdictional question of whether a 'matter' exists.[73] This has led to an unfortunate conflation of *power* and *jurisdiction*. The High Court and Privy Council were later to doubt the Court's assumption that the advisory opinion was a judicial function. In *Boilermakers'*, both the High Court[74] and the Privy Council[75] seemed to suggest that the advisory opinion power was better seen as non-judicial in nature. This would certainly have been a neater doctrinal solution, which would have avoided the bifurcated analysis of whether a function conferred on a court is *judicial* and whether there is *jurisdiction* to exercise such a power – both inquiries involving the same line of analysis.

## 3 Determining or creating rights

As indicated, the core requirement for the exercise of Commonwealth judicial power is that there be a determination of a dispute about existing rights. The High Court has accepted that judicial power can be differentiated from legislative and executive power on the basis that non-judicial power involves the *creation* of rights. Thus, Parliament enacts legal rules and, in many cases, those legal rules only become operational once an administrative decision-maker makes a determination pursuant to a statute. For example, whether an asylum seeker is entitled to enter into Australia depends upon whether that person satisfies the statutory test in the *Migration Act 1958* (Cth) for a protection visa, and that will depend upon the determination by the Minister for Immigration or a delegate as to whether the test is satisfied.

In terms of administrative decision-making that creates rights pursuant to legislative authority, the decision-maker is often described in the cases as having determined a *factum* upon which the legislation operates to create or alter rights for the future. The Minister for Immigration, for example, determines whether Australia has protection obligations in respect of the visa applicant under the *Convention Relating to the Status of Refugees* (the factum) and, if that factum is found, then the provisions of the *Migration Act* operate to confer rights of entry on the asylum seeker. Thus, High Court doctrine provides a bright-line rule: courts exercising judicial power *determine* a dispute about pre-existing rights, whereas administrative decision-makers determine facta upon which legislation operates to *create* rights.

The distinction between rights *determination* and rights *creation* may be demonstrated by contrasting two cases involving similar circumstances, decided contemporaneously by the High Court: *Re Cram; Ex parte Newcastle Wallsend Coal Co Pty Ltd*[76] and *Re Ranger Uranium Mines Pty Ltd; Ex parte Federated*

**73** See, eg, *Re McBain; Ex parte Australian Catholic Bishops Conference* (2002) 209 CLR 372, 409–10.
**74** (1956) 94 CLR 254, 274.
**75** (1957) 95 CLR 529, 541 (PC).
**76** (1987) 163 CLR 140.

*Miscellaneous Workers' Union of Australia*.[77] In *Re Cram*, an administrative tribunal – the Local Coal Authority – had been created by Commonwealth legislation to consider industrial relations disputes within the coal mining industry. A dispute was notified to the Authority involving the standing down of employees and non-payment of wages in breach of the existing industry award. The Authority determined that the employees had, in breach of the award, been stood down and refused payment of wages. In *Re Ranger*, the Conciliation and Arbitration Commission – a non-judicial body – had been notified of an industrial dispute arising from the dismissal of employees. The representatives of the employees sought an order from the Commission for the reinstatement of the employees. There were no provisions within the existing award for the reinstatement of the employees, so orders were sought for the variation of the award.

In *Re Cram*, the High Court held that a determination of the claim involved an exercise of judicial power: '... a claim for the enforcement of a provision in an award for the payment of wages to an employee is ... a claim for the enforcement of an existing legal right. Claims for the enforcement of existing legal rights necessarily invoke the exercise of judicial power'.[78] Thus, the Local Coal Authority could not make that determination as it was not a court referred to in s 71. By contrast, the Commission could make the reinstatement determination sought in *Re Ranger*. As the Court said: 'the dispute is properly to be viewed as a claim for the creation of an obligation on the part of the employer to reinstate the dismissed employee or employees. The creation of new rights and obligations is a function which is properly performed in the exercise of arbitral power'.[79]

## 4 Complicating principles

The rights *creation* versus rights *determination* distinction provides a conceptually neat framework for differentiating between judicial and non-judicial power. However, if applied too rigidly, the distinction may become unworkable, resulting in constraints on the federal Parliament when designing government institutions and allocating decision-making authority. This is particularly the case in a modern regulatory state where non-judicial bodies are increasingly entering fields that were occupied previously by judicial decision-makers. Nevertheless, as highlighted earlier, the main objective of the separation of judicial power principles is to secure the independence and impartiality of the judiciary, and deviations from a clear distinction between rights *determination* and *creation* must not threaten those core constitutional values.

The High Court has developed various rules and techniques that operate to soften the distinction. The first draws from *historical* exercises of power by the judiciary to allow a power to be characterised as judicial even though it lacks

**77** (1987) 163 CLR 656.
**78** (1987) 163 CLR 140, 148.
**79** (1987) 163 CLR 656, 664.

the core characteristic of rights-determination. Thus, even if a power given to a Court, once exercised, creates rights that were not in existence prior to the power being exercised, it may still be characterised as judicial in circumstances where, in the past, it has been given to a court. In *R v Davison*,[80] Kitto J explained the position in the following way:

> Where the action to be taken is of a kind which had come by 1900 to be so consistently regarded as peculiarly appropriate for judicial performance that it then occupied an acknowledged place in the structure of the judicial system, the conclusion, it seems to me, is inevitable that the power to take that action is within the concept of judicial power as the framers of the Constitution must be taken to have understood it.[81]

In *Davison*, the power in question was to make a sequestration order under the *Bankruptcy Act 1931* (Cth) on the application of a debtor. There would be no dispute between the debtor and another party, and there would be no determination of any pre-existing rights – the order giving rise to new rights and obligations, having their source in the *Bankruptcy Act*, to govern the debtor's relationship with his or her creditors. The court held that this power was nonetheless capable of being judicial in character because of historical exercises by courts.

Dixon CJ and McTiernan J gave further examples of powers lacking the core characteristic of judicial power, but nonetheless being characterised as judicial in the hands of a court on the basis of some historical practice or analogy. These examples included: the administration of assets or trusts by the Court of Chancery; orders relating to the maintenance and guardianship of infants; the consent to the marriage of a ward; the administration of enemy property; the declaration of legitimacy; the winding up of companies; and the granting of probate of a will or letters of administration.[82] For Dixon CJ and McTiernan J, these exercises of power lacked the core characteristic of determining a dispute about pre-existing rights. Yet, because of some historical practice or analogy, they could be considered judicial in nature if exercised by a court.[83]

Two more recent examples demonstrate the operation of this principle. In *Thomas v Mowbray*,[84] the High Court considered provisions of the *Criminal Code* (Cth) that conferred powers on federal courts to impose control orders on persons suspected of terrorism related intentions. Section 104.4 of the *Criminal Code* authorised the court to make a control order in relation to a person if the making of the order 'would substantially assist in preventing a terrorist act' or 'that the person has provided training to, or received training from, a listed terrorist organization' and 'the court is satisfied on the balance of probabilities that each of the obligations, prohibitions and restrictions to be imposed on the person by the order is reasonably necessary, and reasonably appropriate and adapted,

**80** (1954) 90 CLR 353.
**81** Ibid, 382.
**82** Ibid, 368.
**83** See also *Peacock v Newtown Marrickville & General Co-operative Building Society (No 4) Ltd* (1943) 67 CLR 25.
**84** (2007) 233 CLR 307.

for the purpose of protecting the public from a terrorist act'. Control orders, once imposed, operated to restrict a person's liberty in various ways.

On a conventional analysis, these control orders do not determine a dispute about pre-existing rights – they operate to impose obligations on the person subject to the order which did not exist prior to the order being made. In the language often used by the High Court, the court determined a factum upon which the *Criminal Code* operated to impose obligations for the future. How could this involve an exercise of Commonwealth judicial power? For Gleeson CJ[85] and Gummow and Crennan JJ,[86] the control order regime had historical analogies, namely: binding over powers to prevent a breach of the peace and powers of the Court of Chancery to grant a writ of *supplicavit* requiring a person's detention in custody when there were threats to life. Although the analogies were not exact, they were close enough to support the control order regime.

In *Saraceni v Jones*,[87] Gummow, Hayne and Bell JJ applied this approach in relation to the power to make an order under the *Corporations Act 2001* (Cth) for the mandatory examination of a person about the examinable affairs of the corporation. Again, the exercise of that power would not determine a dispute about rights – there was no judicial dispute to which the power was referable, and the order would operate to impose obligations on the person to be examined. In refusing special leave to appeal to the High Court, their Honours endorsed the observations of Kitto J in *Davison*. After noting that the relevant powers had historical antecedents in the *Companies Act 1862* (UK) (which, their Honours observed, became the model for the companies legislation of the Australian colonies), it was concluded that '[t]he making on application of a receiver of a mandatory examination order is an action of a kind which had come by 1900 to be so consistently regarded as peculiarly appropriate for judicial performance that it then occupied an acknowledged place in the structure of the judicial system'.[88]

The second complication to the rights creation versus rights determination framework is the acceptance by the High Court that some provisions – double functions provisions – operate to simultaneously create rights and obligations *and* vest jurisdiction in a court for their determination.[89] Although, on their face, these provisions look like they are conferring power on the court to create rights, they are taken to be a statutory creation of rights *and* the conferral of jurisdiction on the court to enforce the rights. As Dixon CJ, McTiernan, Williams, Webb, Fullagar, Kitto and Taylor JJ explained in *Hooper v Hooper*,[90] the preferable approach to drafting would be to have separate provisions creating rights and then conferring jurisdiction on a court to grant a remedy. However, their Honours continued, 'this is not invariably the simplest or easiest course to follow, and it is by no means uncommon for an Act to be drafted in such a way

**85** Ibid, 327–9.
**86** Ibid, 356–7, with Heydon and Callinan JJ agreeing in this respect.
**87** (2012) 246 CLR 251.
**88** Ibid, 256–7.
**89** See *Precision Data Holdings Ltd v Wills* (1991) 173 CLR 167, 191.
**90** (1955) 91 CLR 529, 535–6.

that the two things are done ... by providing that in certain specified circumstances a person may take proceedings in a particular court to obtain a specified remedy...'. By reading the provisions in this way, they 'fit ... into the pattern of Chapter III of the Constitution'.[91]

Dixon J had earlier given examples of such provisions in *R v Commonwealth Court of Conciliation and Arbitration; Ex parte Barrett*:[92] the power to order a patentee to grant compulsory licences; the power to declare that a patent had not been sufficiently exercised; the power to order the removal of a trademark from the register for non-use; the power to remove a master of a ship and appoint another; the power to deal with application and investment of compensation money; and the power to order the sale of an estate to pay estate duty.

A more recent example was accepted by the High Court in *Baker v The Queen*,[93] where the Court considered the validity of State provisions allowing a person serving an existing life sentence to apply to the NSW Supreme Court for the determination of a non-parole period. The exercise of judicial power – in a traditional sense – to determine rights and obligations had ended with the adjudgment and punishment of criminal guilt and the imposition of a life sentence. The exercise of the power to set a non-parole period would not, on its face, determine any rights. The court would be determining a factum upon which the legislation would operate to create new (or at least alter) rights and obligations. However, the High Court accepted that this was an example of a double function provision that simultaneously created rights and conferred jurisdiction on the court to determine rights.[94]

The double function technique presents difficulties, both in conceptual appeal and in the identification of potential limits. As to its conceptual appeal, it might be accepted that the double function drafting technique can operate where the statute confers power on a court to make an order on the satisfaction (or non-satisfaction) of a fixed rule (say, the non-use of a trademark). It can readily be accepted that the Parliament, for convenience, can combine the enactment of the statutory rule with the conferral of jurisdiction to determine whether it has been satisfied and, thus, has complied with the rights creation versus rights determination framework.

However, where the statute does not set out a fixed rule, but instead relies upon judicial discretion to determine whether the legal rule should operate, the court order would seem to be assisting in the creation of the legal rule. Many of the examples given by Dixon J in *Barrett* required the court to exercise discretion when exercising the relevant power. His Honour appeared to recognise the conceptual problem, but took the view that Parliament should not be limited in its use of this double function technique to laying down 'inflexible rules'. Of obvious concern to Dixon J was the potential disruption to the operation of

**91** *R v Commonwealth Court of Conciliation and Arbitration; Ex parte Barrett* (1945) 70 CLR 141, 167.
**92** Ibid.
**93** (2004) 223 CLR 513.
**94** Ibid, 529.

existing provisions drafted in the double function form. However, one wonders whether a preferable approach might have been to justify those powers within the historical analogy qualification.

The second difficulty that arises is how to contain this technique. For example, State Parliaments have enacted preventative detention measures which authorise courts to order the continuing detention of a person if he or she poses a threat to the community. High Court cases considering the constitutional validity of such schemes will be considered below. For present purposes, it is important to emphasise the character of such judicial orders: on a conventional analysis, they do not determine rights – they create rights and obligations for the future. The court is not involved in a determination of whether a person has breached criminal rules and, consequently, committed a criminal offence for which punishment may follow. The court order requires the continuing detention of a person (ie, creates an obligation) because of a threat posed by that person to the community.

Could this not be a double function provision that creates obligations (albeit with the assistance of judicial discretion) and, simultaneously, confers jurisdiction on the court to grant a remedy? In *Kable v Director of Public Prosecutions (NSW)*,[95] the Court appeared to characterise such a power as non-judicial in nature, implicitly (and, in the case of Gummow J, explicitly) recognising that the double function rationale could not support a characterisation of the power as judicial. However, in the subsequent decision of *Fardon v Attorney-General (Qld)*,[96] McHugh J appeared to accept that this kind of power could be described as a double function provision, identifying it as having the same 'jurisprudential character' as powers to make orders 'upon determining that a particular fact or status exists' as in 'cases of matrimonial causes, bankruptcy, probate and the winding up of companies'.[97] This view now appears to have been accepted by the High Court in *New South Wales v Kable*,[98] with at least Gageler J using the double function rationale to support his conclusion that the power was judicial in nature.[99]

## 5 Discretion and policy

Whatever may have been the case in the past, it is now generally accepted that courts, when exercising judicial power, can exercise discretion. Discretionary exercises of power are not the exclusive domain of executive decision-making. Furthermore, when exercising that discretion, it is not unusual for judicial decision-makers to apply policy considerations. Although Kitto J once

**95** (1996) 189 CLR 51.
**96** (2004) 223 CLR 575, 596–7.
**97** *Fardon v Attorney-General (Qld)* (2004) 223 CLR 575, 597.
**98** *New South Wales v Kable* (2013) 252 CLR 118 ('*Kable No. 2*').
**99** See James Stellios, '*Kable*, Preventative Detention and the Dilemmas of Chapter III' (2014) 88 *Australian Law Journal* 52.

proclaimed that '[t]he courts have nothing to do with policy',[100] his Honour 'spoke too broadly'.[101] As Gummow and Crennan JJ said in *Thomas v Mowbray*:

> Where legislation is designed to effect a policy, and the courts then are called upon to interpret and apply that law, inevitably consideration of that policy cannot be excluded from the curial interpretive process. No principle of the separation of the judicial power from that of the other branches of government should foreclose that activity, for it is apt to lead to the just determination of controversies by the courts.[102]

Provided the judicial discretion is not unconfined, and exercised according to sufficiently precise criteria, there is nothing controversial about the proposition that courts can exercise discretion and apply policy considerations consistently with separation of judicial power principles.

The dividing line between judicial and non-judicial criteria is a difficult one to draw. Indeed, there are some criteria which may be equally applied by courts and non-judicial decision-makers. Although there are limits to the criteria that can be applied by a court when exercising Commonwealth judicial power, the High Court has increasingly allowed Parliament considerable latitude when identifying the criteria to guide the exercise of judicial power.

The classic example of criteria found to be insufficiently judicial in nature was in *R v Spicer; Ex parte Australian Builders' Labourers' Federation*.[103] Provisions in the *Conciliation and Arbitration Act 1904* (Cth) had empowered the Commonwealth Industrial Court to disallow rules of registered industrial associations on certain grounds, including that they were contrary to law, were 'tyrannical', 'oppressive' or imposed unreasonable conditions on members. A majority of the Court held that the Commonwealth provisions were invalid. Although this power had 'a degree of resemblance to some other powers which have been given to courts in the past',[104] the statutory context indicated that the power was not judicial in nature. In particular, the vagueness and generality of the criteria to be applied, and the industrial policy objectives sought to be achieved, gave the power a distinctive administrative flavour. Also important to the conclusion was the fact that the Court was given the power to act on its own motion and that there were no provisions defining the jurisdiction of the court to exercise the power of disallowance.

Parliament redefined the legislative scheme to respond to the Court's decision. The amended provisions provided that a rule of an industrial organisation could not be contrary to law or impose conditions on members which were 'oppressive, unreasonable or unjust'. The Commonwealth Industrial Court was given jurisdiction to make an order that a rule contravened the statutory condition, and the jurisdiction was to be exercised on the application of a member of the industrial organisation in question. This reconfigured statutory scheme was

**100** *Australian Communist Party v Commonwealth* (1951) 83 CLR 1, 277.
**101** *Thomas v Mowbray* (2007) 233 CLR 307, 348.
**102** Ibid.
**103** (1957) 100 CLR 277.
**104** Ibid, 305.

held to be valid in *R v Commonwealth Industrial Court; Ex parte the Amalgamated Engineering Union, Australian Section*.[105] Although vague and general to some extent, the words 'oppressive, unreasonable or unjust' were considered to be capable of judicial application. Although there were other changes to the legislative scheme that helped to explain the different conclusion, the slight change in expression was seen as important.

Other cases demonstrate the latitude allowed to Parliament when defining judicial criteria. In *Cominos v Cominos*,[106] State courts were empowered by Parliament to make maintenance and property settlement orders under the *Matrimonial Causes Act 1959* (Cth) according to what the court considered to be 'proper' or necessary 'to do justice'. In *R v Joske; Ex parte Shop Distributive and Allied Employees' Association*,[107] the Court considered provisions of the *Conciliation and Arbitration Act 1904* (Cth) that empowered the Australian Industrial Court to rectify invalidity in the affairs of a registered organisation if the invalidity caused 'substantial injustice' to the organisation. In *Thomas v Mowbray*,[108] the Court considered provisions of the *Criminal Code* (Cth) which authorised a federal court to impose a control order on a person if the order would 'substantially assist in preventing a terrorist act' and the court was satisfied on the balance of probabilities that the order was 'reasonably necessary, and reasonably appropriate and adapted, for the purpose of protecting the public from a terrorist act'. The legislation considered in *Hogan v Hinch*[109] authorised the exercise of judicial discretion in the 'public interest'. In all these cases, the High Court held that the criteria were sufficiently legal in nature to be capable of judicial application. As Gummow and Crennan JJ concluded in *Thomas v Mowbray*, 'the case law shows acceptance of broadly expressed standards'.[110]

## 6 Merits review

It is well accepted that, consistently with separation of judicial power principles, a tribunal can be established by Parliament to remake primary administrative decisions. These merits review tribunals may look very much like courts and are characterised by processes that are familiarly judicial. The consistency of these merits review tribunals with separation of judicial power principles was accepted very early by the High Court. In *British Imperial Oil Co Ltd v Federal Commissioner of Taxation*,[111] the High Court invalidated a Board of Appeal established to review the tax assessment determinations of the Commissioner of Taxation. The Board of Appeal operated too much like a court, with power to determine whether the Commissioner's decision had been validly made.

**105** (1960) 103 CLR 368.
**106** (1972) 127 CLR 588.
**107** (1976) 135 CLR 194.
**108** (2007) 233 CLR 307.
**109** (2011) 243 CLR 506.
**110** *Thomas v Mowbray* (2007) 233 CLR 307, 345.
**111** (1925) 35 CLR 422.

A reconfigured legislative scheme, which limited the jurisdiction of the review body (renamed the Board of Review) was upheld by the High Court in *Federal Commissioner of Taxation v Munro*.[112] Rather than extending to a review of the lawfulness of the Commissioner's decision, the jurisdiction of the Board of Review was narrowed to the remaking of the primary decision. The Board was given the powers of the Commissioner, and its decisions were deemed to be those of the Commissioner.[113]

The High Court's decision in *Munro* opened the door for the creation of a range of federal merits review tribunals that stand in the shoes of the primary decision-maker. Modern examples of these tribunals include the Administrative Appeals Tribunal, the Refugee Review Tribunal, the Migration Review Tribunal and the Social Securities Appeals Tribunal. In each case, the review tribunal stands in the shoes of the primary decision-maker and remakes the decision, and such a jurisdiction is consistent with the separation of judicial power principles.

Indeed, a merits review function cannot be given to a court. For example, in *Queen Victoria Memorial Hospital v Thornton*,[114] provisions of the *Re-establishment and Employment Act 1945* (Cth) conferred a right on ex-servicemen to preference in employment opportunities. An employer deciding between two ex-servicemen had to consider a range of factors when making the employment decision. An unsuccessful applicant could apply to a State court for reconsideration of the employment decision. The court was required to take into account the same factors as considered by the employer, and make an order that was 'just and reasonable in the circumstances'. In a unanimous judgment, the High Court held that the court's order making an appointment was 'in substitution for the appointment made by an employer' and, thus, entirely administrative in nature.[115]

## 7 Regulatory tribunals

Like individual administrative decision-makers, administrative tribunals may also make primary decisions that have considerable impact on rights, by creating, altering or cancelling such rights. In fact, some of the judgments made by tribunals in the course of decision-making can sometimes look very much like the judgments that a court might make when faced with similar questions. Because of this similarity between tribunal and judicial decision-making, it can sometimes be very difficult to differentiate between an exercise of administrative power and an exercise of judicial power. A series of examples can assist in illuminating this difference.

**112** (1926) 38 CLR 153.
**113** The Privy Council agreed: *Shell Company of Australia v Federal Commissioner of Taxation* (1930) 44 CLR 530 (PC). See also *R v Hegarty; Ex parte City of Salisbury* (1981) 147 CLR 617.
**114** (1953) 87 CLR 144.
**115** *Queen Victoria Memorial Hospital v Thornton* (1953) 87 CLR 144, 150.

In *Rola Co (Australia) Pty Ltd v Commonwealth*,[116] federal regulations – the Women's Employment Regulations – established two administrative bodies for the regulation of the employment rights of women. The first of these bodies was the Women's Employment Board and the second was the Committee of Reference. Under the Regulations, an employer was required to apply to the Board for a decision as to whether certain categories of work were permitted to be undertaken by women and the applicable pay rates. Questions arising as to what women were employed to do the work specified in the Board's decision, and the nature of the work they were employed to do, could be referred to a Committee of Reference. On one view, the Committee was making a determination of the existing rights that had been created by the Board and, thus, exercising judicial power. On another view, both bodies were making determinations that provided the basis for the creation of the rights and duties conferred by the Regulations and, thus, exercising non-judicial power. A majority of the High Court favoured the latter view of the legislative scheme and, consequently, held the provisions creating and conferring functions on both bodies to be valid. The dissenting judges (Rich and Williams JJ) favoured the former view. As Rich J said, the Committee's function was:

> to determine, with respect to particular individuals or individuals of a particular class, a fact the determination of which decides whether they are entitled to legal rights which, if they have them at all, they possess because these rights have already been conferred upon them independently by another body.[117]

These difficult judgments also can be demonstrated by three cases involving broadly similar legislative schemes: *R v Trade Practices Tribunal; Ex parte Tasmanian Breweries Pty Ltd*;[118] *Precision Data Holdings Ltd v Wills*[119] and *Attorney-General (Cth) v Alinta Ltd*.[120] In *Tasmanian Breweries*, the *Trade Practices Act 1965* (Cth) had conferred power on the Trade Practices Tribunal to determine whether agreements were anti-competitive. An agreement contrary to the public interest became unenforceable and orders could be made restraining performance. In determining whether the agreement was contrary to the public interest, the Tribunal was to take account of a range of factors: the impact on competition; the interests of consumers, employers, proprietors, investors and small business; the promotion of new enterprises; the achievement of efficiencies; and the international competitiveness of Australian business. A majority of the High Court (McTiernan, Kitto, Windeyer, Owen and Walsh JJ; Menzies J dissenting) held that the Tribunal was exercising non-judicial power. The Tribunal was not tasked with determining whether there had been a breach of the agreement and requiring performance of its terms – a classic exercise of judicial power – it was making a determination which would have the consequence of

**116** (1944) 69 CLR 185.
**117** Ibid, 207. See also 216–17.
**118** (1970) 123 CLR 361.
**119** (1991) 173 CLR 167.
**120** (2008) 233 CLR 542.

altering the contractual rights and duties of the parties into the future. As Kitto J said:

> The determination [of whether the agreement was contrary to the public interest] ... constitutes the factum by reference to which the Act operates to alter the law in relation to the particular case. And an [enforcement] order ... restrains future conduct, not as being in breach of ascertained obligations, but as being in conformity with ascertained obligations or practices – not in order to ensure observance of them but to prevent observance of them, because it is considered that their observance would be against the public interest. The Act ... operates upon the order to give its provisions the force of law, and thus to alter the law for the future in relation to the particular case.[121]

A similar outcome resulted from a challenge to provisions of the Corporations Law in *Precision Data Holdings Ltd v Wills*.[122] The Corporations and Securities Panel was empowered to declare that a takeover had been 'unacceptable'. Such a declaration could be made if there had been 'unacceptable circumstances' surrounding the acquisition, and having regard to the public interest in maintaining 'an efficient competitive and informed market'. Whether there had been 'unacceptable circumstances' turned on: the sufficiency of the information provided to shareholders and directors to assess the takeover; and the reasonableness of the time allowed to consider the proposal. Once a declaration had been made that a takeover was 'unacceptable', the Panel could make a range of orders affecting the rights of shareholders: it could prohibit voting rights; prohibit the acquisition or disposal of shares; order the disposal of shares; and, ultimately, order the cancellation of the takeover agreement. As with *Tasmanian Breweries*, in a unanimous judgment, the High Court considered that the administrative tribunal was exercising non-judicial power – it was altering the contractual rights for the future, not determining a contractual dispute that had arisen under the agreement:

> [T]he object of the Panel's inquiry and determination is to create a new set of rights and obligations, that is, rights and obligations arising from such orders as the Panel may make in a particular case, being rights and obligations which did not exist antecedently and independently of the making of the orders.[123]

The High Court reached the same conclusion in *Attorney-General (Cth) v Alinta Ltd* when it heard a challenge to an amended takeovers scheme enacted in the *Corporations Act 2001* (Cth). One of the main changes to the legislative scheme was that the (newly named) Takeovers Panel could declare circumstances to be unacceptable where it formed the view that the circumstances gave rise to a contravention of offence provisions in the Act. Thus, in exercising what had been held to be a non-judicial power in *Precision Data*, the Panel could now form a view about pre-existing rights and obligations – that is, whether an offence had been committed. If that judgment were made by a court in the

**121** *R v Trade Practices Tribunal; Ex parte Tasmanian Breweries Pty Ltd* (1970) 123 CLR 361, 378.
**122** (1991) 173 CLR 167.
**123** Ibid, 190.

course of adjudging and punishing criminal guilt for that offence, the exercise of power would be indisputably judicial in character. Was the character of the function performed by the Panel transformed from non-judicial to judicial because it would form a view about that same question? The High Court held that the Panel's function remained non-judicial in character, despite this new statutory dimension. As Crennan and Kiefel JJ said in their joint judgment, '[a] non-judicial function ... does not cease to be so because the decision-maker forms an opinion as to existing legal rights and obligations'.[124]

These three cases also show that the criteria to be applied by a tribunal when exercising power will be significant in determining the character of the power exercised. In all three cases, the High Court considered that the criteria applied were insufficiently legal in nature. For example, whether the agreements in *Precision Data* were 'in the public interest', having regard to 'an efficient, competitive and informed market', required the application of ill-defined criteria requiring considerations of economic policy that were more appropriate for a non-judicial body.

There are many examples of cases where the High Court has applied the separation of judicial power principles to invalidate the conferral of judicial power on non-judicial bodies. In *New South Wales v Commonwealth*,[125] the High Court held invalid the conferral of judicial powers on the Inter-State Commission. The same result was reached in both *Alexander* and *Boilermakers'* where provisions conferring judicial powers on the Court of Conciliation and Arbitration (held not to be a Chapter III court) were held invalid. Two more recent examples are *Brandy v Human Rights and Equal Opportunity Commission*[126] and *Lane v Morrison*.[127]

In *Brandy*, the High Court considered provisions of the *Racial Discrimination Act 1975* (Cth) that authorised the Commission to hear complaints of unlawful discrimination. The Commission could hold an inquiry at which the complainant and the respondent presented their respective arguments and, if the claim were substantiated, the Commission was given the power to declare the conduct to be unlawful under the Act and to determine that the respondent pay compensation. While closely resembling a judicial process for the enforcement of statutory rights, the determination of the Commission was 'not binding or conclusive between any parties to the determination'. If the process ended there, the exercise of power would have been considered to be non-judicial in character because the declaration by the Commission had no impact on the rights and

**124** *Attorney-General (Cth) v Alinta Ltd* (2008) 233 CLR 542, 595. Their Honours drew support for this proposition from the earlier case of *Re Ranger Uranium Mines Pty Ltd; Ex parte Federated Miscellaneous Workers' Union of Australia* (1987) 163 CLR 656. See also *Visnic v Australian Securities and Investments Commission* (2007) 231 CLR 381 and *Albarran v Companies Auditors and Liquidators Disciplinary Board* (2007) 231 CLR 350 where the High Court upheld the power of professional standards bodies to impose disciplinary sanctions on professionals, even when the determination made required a view to be formed that offences had been committed.
**125** (1915) 20 CLR 54.
**126** (1995) 183 CLR 245.
**127** (2009) 239 CLR 230.

duties of the parties. As Mason CJ, Brennan and Toohey JJ said, the determination was confined to saying what the respondent 'should' do rather than what the respondent 'must' do.[128]

However, the legislative scheme required the Commission to lodge the determination in a Federal Court registry and, upon registration, it took effect as an order of the Federal Court. Although the respondent could apply to review the determination, if no application were made within the time permitted, the determination became enforceable as an order of the Court. Even if an application were made by the respondent, the Court had power to review the Commission's determination but could not take into account new evidence without leave. The High Court held that this extra layer to the legislative scheme transformed the power of the Commission from non-judicial to judicial. The determination of the Commission would, in circumstances where no review application was made, be automatically transformed into an enforceable judicial order. Even when a review application was made, the scope of the review to be undertaken was not sufficiently extensive – a full consideration of the facts and law need not have been undertaken by the Court, and there was reduced scope for new evidence. Thus, the Federal Court registration and enforcement provisions transformed the power given to the Commission from non-judicial to judicial.

In *Lane v Morrison*, the High Court considered amendments to the *Defence Force Discipline Act 1982* (Cth) which sought to create the Australian Military Court. Despite its title, the Military Court was not intended to be a lower federal court contemplated by Chapter III of the Constitution. Relying upon a long line of authority that military discipline, with its legislative source in the defence power in s 51(vi) of the Constitution, could be exercised by a military tribunal outside the Chapter III framework,[129] Parliament sought to confer this non-judicial power on a non-judicial body, albeit with the nomenclature of a 'court'. However, the High Court held that the justification for the long line of High Court authority supporting military tribunals was that they operated within the command structures of the military. The Australian Military Court had been established as an independent and impartial tribunal and, thus, operated outside the chain of command. Its independence from the military was, thus, its undoing. The jurisdiction exercised lost its historical support to be non-judicial in nature and, accordingly, the character of the power exercised was transformed from non-judicial to judicial. The plurality judgment of Hayne, Heydon, Crennan, Kiefel and Bell JJ explained the conclusion in the following way:

> That the [Australian Military Court] is to make binding and authoritative decisions on the issues identified without further intervention from within the chain of command

**128** *Brandy v Human Rights and Equal Opportunity Commission* (1995) 183 CLR 245, 257.
**129** See below at Chapter 9, Part IV.

is reason enough to conclude that it is to exercise the judicial power of the Commonwealth.[130]

The creation of the Australian Military Court was held to be invalid.

## 8 Sovereign authority

As early as 1905, the High Court recognised that a core feature of judicial power is that it involves an exercise of *sovereign* authority.[131] Thus, the exercise of arbitral power, by private agreement, does not attract a judicial character. This view was confirmed in *TCL Air Conditioner (Zhongshan) Co Ltd v Judges of the Federal Court of Australia*,[132] where the High Court held that international arbitration awards, made by an arbitrator to resolve a contractual dispute, could be recognised and enforced by Australian courts pursuant to federal legislation. The resolution of the contractual dispute by the arbitrator did not involve an exercise of sovereign power. The arbitration award set out rights and obligations that had their source in the private agreement of the parties. The federal legislation allowing for the recognition and enforcement of arbitration awards in Australian courts gave rise to statutory rights and obligations of recognition and enforcement.[133] It was then the proceedings for the recognition and enforcement of the awards that involved an exercise of federal judicial power.

*Attorney-General (Cth) v Breckler*[134] provides another interesting illustration of this proposition. The Superannuation Complaints Tribunal, a non-judicial federal body, was conferred with powers under the *Superannuation (Resolution of Complaints) Act 1993* (Cth) to review decisions made by trustees of private superannuation funds for the payment of superannuation benefits. The Tribunal could review a trustee's decision on the ground that it was 'unfair or unreasonable', and had the power to affirm or vary the decision, remit it to the trustee for further consideration, or set it aside and substitute a new decision. Where a new decision was substituted, it was taken to be the decision of the trustee. The Act required the trustee to comply with the Tribunal's determination.

Mr Breckler was a member of a superannuation fund. Upon his death, the trustees of the fund paid 17 per cent of the benefit to his surviving child, with the remainder going to his personal legal representative. A complaint was made to the Tribunal that the payment was 'unfair or unreasonable'. The terms of the trust agreement had been changed to recognise the dispute resolution process established by the Act, and required the trustees to comply with the Tribunal's determination. The Tribunal set aside the decision and substituted a payment of

**130** *Lane v Morrison* (2009) 239 CLR 230, 261. For a critique of the judgment, see Stellios, above n 10, 258–9; Henry Burmester, 'The Rise, Fall and Proposed Rebirth of the Australian Military Court' (2011) 39 *Federal Law Review* 195.
**131** See *Ah Yick v Lehmert* (1905) 2 CLR 593, 603. See also *Huddart, Parker & Co Pty Ltd v Moorehead* (1909) 8 CLR 330, 357.
**132** (2013) 251 CLR 533.
**133** Giving rise to a 'matter' under s 76(ii) of the Constitution.
**134** (1999) 197 CLR 83.

50 per cent of the benefit. The scheme was challenged on the basis that it conferred judicial power on a non-judicial body.

This scheme, operating at the interface of private and public decision-making, presented the High Court with an interesting challenge in its application of the separation of judicial power principles. If the Tribunal were tasked with determining whether the trustee had breached the trust agreement, then the conclusion would have followed that there was an impermissible conferral of judicial power. If the trustee had been a federal government decision-maker, then the Tribunal would have been undertaking a conventional exercise of merits review by standing in the shoes of the primary decision-maker. However, this scheme crossed the private/public divide. In deciding that the provisions were valid, the High Court considered that the trust agreement had contemplated that the rights and obligations under the trust would be determined by the Tribunal if a complaint were made. It followed, the Court concluded, that 'the determination by the Tribunal involved not the exercise of the *sovereign* power ... but the arbitration of a dispute using procedures and criteria adopted by the [trust agreement] ... for the resolution of certain disputes arising thereunder'.[135] Consequently, no judicial power had been conferred on the Tribunal.

## IV Exceptions to the separation principles

There are various exceptions to this general scheme for the distribution of government powers and jurisdiction. First, it is well accepted that military tribunals (ie, non-judicial bodies) can determine whether a member of the military has committed a disciplinary offence and impose a form of punishment as a consequence of that contravention. Service tribunals currently determine whether members of the military have contravened 'offences' under the *Defence Force Discipline Act 1982* (Cth). The source of power for the military justice system comes from the defence power in s 51(vi) of the Constitution, not Chapter III, and the High Court has accepted that disciplinary jurisdiction under s 51(vi) can be exercised without intruding into the federal civilian justice system created by Chapter III.[136] As Dixon J said in *R v Cox; Ex parte Smith*,[137] '[t]o ensure that discipline is just, tribunals acting judicially are essential to the organization of an army or navy or air force. But they do not form part of the judicial system administering the law of the land'.

The dividing line between the military justice system (sourced in s 51(vi)) and the federal civilian justice system (sourced in Chapter III) has been the subject of ongoing debate and uncertainty. Some judges have allowed Parliament considerable latitude to determine for itself whether conduct should be subject to military discipline.[138] Other judges have tried to minimise the extent to which

**135** Ibid, 110–11 (emphasis added).
**136** See, eg, *Re Tracey; Ex parte Ryan* (1989) 166 CLR 518.
**137** (1945) 71 CLR 1, 23.
**138** See, eg, *Re Tracey; Ex parte Ryan* (1989) 166 CLR 518, 545.

the military justice system overlaps with the civilian justice system.[139] The prevailing view appears to take a middle path of considering whether the exercise of disciplinary authority to enforce a military offence can, in the circumstances of the case, 'reasonably be regarded as substantially serving the purpose of maintaining or enforcing military discipline'.[140] While this approach appears to enjoy majority support, it has more recently been applied in a generous way. Thus, for example, in *White v Director of Military Prosecutions*,[141] the plaintiff, a Chief Petty Officer with the Navy, was charged with assault under s 33 of the *Defence Force Discipline Act 1982* and with acts of indecency under s 61 of the Act.[142] The alleged conduct giving rise to these disciplinary offences involved other Navy personnel, but did not occur on Commonwealth property and occurred whilst the officers were off duty. If proved, the alleged conduct would have given rise to offences under the *Crimes Act 1958* (Vic). A constitutional challenge to the jurisdiction of the service tribunal to hear and determine the disciplinary offences was rejected by the High Court.

A second exception to the separation principles is Parliament's authority to punish (including by way of imprisonment) a person for contempt of Parliament. In *R v Richards; Ex parte Fitzpatrick & Browne*,[143] the High Court upheld the imprisonment of two journalists for publishing articles making false allegations about a member of Parliament with the intention of intimidation. It was held that s 49 of the Constitution, setting out the powers and privileges of Parliament, authorised the commitment of a person for trial for contempt, and for the imposition of punishment by Parliament.

Thirdly, to the extent that the deprivation of liberty might be considered to be exclusively judicial in character, and to result only from the usual curial process of adjudgment and punishment of criminal guilt,[144] there are recognised exceptions. These exceptions include: the detention of aliens, even for an indefinite period;[145] arrest and detention in custody;[146] involuntary detention in cases of mental illness or infectious disease;[147] and perhaps executive detention of disloyal citizens in time of war.[148]

Finally, it has been accepted that federal court judges can exercise non-judicial powers in their personal capacity; that is, as *persona designata*. So that the underlying purpose of the separation of judicial power principles is not undermined, the use of judges in their personal capacity is subject to strict

**139** See, eg, Ibid, 585–6, 600.
**140** Ibid, 570.
**141** (2007) 231 CLR 570.
**142** Section 61 of the Act picks up provisions from the *Crimes Act 1900* (ACT) and applies them as military offences to be determined by military tribunals.
**143** (1955) 92 CLR 157.
**144** There is uncertainty about the continuing acceptance of this proposition. See Stellios, above n 10, 221–32.
**145** *Chu Kheng Lim v Minister for Immigration, Local Government and Ethnic Affairs* (1992) 176 CLR 1; *Al-Kateb v Godwin* (2004) 219 CLR 562.
**146** *Chu Kheng Lim v Minister for Immigration, Local Government and Ethnic Affairs* (1992) 176 CLR 1, 27.
**147** Ibid.
**148** *Re Woolley; Ex parte Applicants M276/2003* (2004) 225 CLR 1, 24–5.

conditions: first, the Commonwealth provisions conferring the function must be clear (either expressly or impliedly) that it is to be exercised by the judge as *persona designata*; secondly, the judge must consent to the exercise of power; and thirdly, the performance of the function must not be *incompatible* with the exercise of functions by the judge or his or her court.

As Brennan CJ, Deane, Dawson and Toohey JJ recognised in *Grollo v Palmer*,[149] 'the *incompatibility* condition may arise in a number of different ways'. The judge's time might be so occupied with the performance of non-judicial functions 'that the further performance of substantial judicial functions … is not practicable'.[150] Alternatively, the nature of the function, or the context of its performance, might affect perceptions of judicial integrity – whether those perceptions are directed at the court as an institution or the judge's capacity to perform judicial functions. Judicial integrity might be threatened, and thus *incompatibility* arises, if the function to be performed by the judge undermines judicial *independence* or *impartiality*.[151]

The cases have suggested that those requirements will not be satisfied in the following circumstances. First, if the function is 'an integral part of, or is closely connected with, the functions of the Legislature or the Executive Government', incompatibility will appear if the function is not 'required to be performed independently of any instruction, advice or wish of the Legislature of the Executive Government'.[152] Even where required to perform the function independently of instruction, incompatibility will still arise where the discretion to be exercised by the judge is 'to be exercised on political grounds – that is, on grounds that are not confined by factors expressly or impliedly prescribed by law'.[153]

In *Wilson v Minister for Aboriginal and Torres Strait Islander Affairs*,[154] a Federal Court judge had been appointed under a legislative scheme to prepare a report for a Commonwealth Minister prior to the making of a ministerial decision to protect Aboriginal sacred sites. The judge's report would have covered a range of matters including the extent of the area that should be covered by the decision, the restrictions that should be imposed and the extent to which the area was protected by State law. The High Court held that the appointment of the judge to act as a reporter failed the incompatibility test. The report by the judge would form the basis of an exercise of discretionary power by the Minister, placing the judge 'firmly in the echelons of administration, liable to removal by the Minister before the report is made and shorn of the usual judicial protections'.[155] Judicial *independence* was, thus compromised. Additionally, the

**149** (1995) 184 CLR 348, 365 (emphasis added).
**150** Ibid, 365.
**151** The cases described these requirements in terms of undermining public confidence in the judiciary. However, *public confidence*, as a constitutional test, has since fallen out of favour in other contexts. See below at Part VI.5.
**152** *Wilson v Minister for Aboriginal and Torres Strait Islander Affairs* (1996) 189 CLR 1, 17.
**153** Ibid.
**154** (1996) 189 CLR 1.
**155** Ibid, 18–19.

function of the reporter was akin to that of 'a ministerial adviser': to advise the Minister on matters that would affect the competing interests of Aboriginal and other proprietary and pecuniary interests. That, for the Court, was 'essentially a political function' or 'political in character'.[156]

By contrast, the High Court has held that federal court judges may issue law enforcement warrants on an *ex parte* basis. In *Grollo v Palmer*,[157] the High Court held that federal court judges, acting in their personal capacity, could issue telecommunications interception warrants under the *Telecommunications (Interception) Act 1979* (Cth). Law enforcement officers could apply, on an *ex parte* basis, for a warrant to intercept communications passing over a telecommunications system. The subject of the warrant was not informed of the application for, or the granting of, the warrant and, indeed, might never have known that his or her telecommunications system was, or had been, under surveillance.

Because this scheme involved judges authorising covert surveillance, McHugh J held that the function undermined public perceptions of independence and impartiality. For his Honour, 'public perception must be diminished when the judges of the Federal Court are involved in secret, ex parte administrative procedures, forming part of the criminal investigative process, that are carried out as a routine part of their daily lives'. However, his Honour was in dissent. Somewhat surprisingly, the majority held that the function could be conferred on federal court judges in their personal capacity. In fact, it was considered that it was:

> precisely because of the intrusive and clandestine nature of interception warrants and the necessity to use them in today's continuing battle against serious crime that some impartial authority, accustomed to the dispassionate assessment of evidence and sensitive to the common law's protection of privacy and property (both real and personal), be authorised to control the official interception of communications.[158]

Thus, it was the judges' independence, and their capacity to maintain that independence in the performance of their function, that preserved the public perception of the judiciary and, consequently, saved the provisions from invalidity.

Elizabeth Handsley has observed that *Wilson* and *Grollo* present contradictory images of judicial independence: in *Wilson*, it is easily undermined and needs protection from the other arms of government; in *Grollo* it is 'durable' and can be asserted confidently against the other arms of government.[159] Perhaps in recognition that many of our Chapter III principles are built upon the prudential protection of the judiciary from the other arms of government, more recent

**156** Ibid, 19. A third concern of the High Court was that the judge would provide an advisory opinion on questions of State law: a function 'quite alien to the exercise of the judicial power of the Commonwealth' (at 19–20).
**157** (1995) 184 CLR 348. A similar legislative scheme had been upheld earlier by the High Court in *Hilton v Wells* (1985) 157 CLR 57.
**158** *Grollo v Palmer* (1995) 184 CLR 348, 367.
**159** Elizabeth Handsley, 'Public Confidence in the Judiciary: A Red Herring for the Separation of Powers' (1998) 20 *Sydney Law Review* 183, 201.

comments in *Wainohu v New South Wales*[160] tend to suggest that the function in *Grollo* can only be justified on the basis of the judiciary's long historical involvement in the issuing of law enforcement warrants.[161]

## V Due process protections

There were attempts during the framing of the Constitution to include provisions resembling the due process and equal protection limitations in the United States Constitution.[162] Proposals to include a due process protection were rejected, and a proposed equal protection clause was watered down to prevent discrimination on the basis of State residence (in s 117 of the Constitution). Despite the rejection of these attempts, Chapter III of the Constitution has provided a basis for the protection of various aspects of the traditional judicial process, including equality of treatment, in the exercise of Commonwealth judicial power. A comprehensive analysis of this area is beyond the scope of this book;[163] however, the core features of that developing area of jurisprudence will now be outlined.

### 1 The constitutional basis

'Due process' is an expression borrowed from the United States constitutional context. As such, care must be taken with its use in Australian constitutional discourse.[164] High Court judges have cautioned that a broad 'due process' principle has not been accepted in Australia.[165] Nevertheless, it has been adopted by judges and commentators alike to describe the constitutional protection available for various aspects of the judicial process.[166] The precise basis for these limitations is yet to be clearly identified, but there are three suggested possibilities.

The first two suggested bases rely on an acceptance that the concept of 'judicial power' incorporates *procedural* dimensions. On that basis, a power that is exercised according to a process that lacks the requisite standards is not judicial in nature. Using the separation of judicial power principles, the argument might be presented in two ways. First, relying on the *Alexander* principle, a Commonwealth law that alters or removes the constitutionally required features of a judicial process constitutes a legislative usurpation of, or an impermissible

**160** (2011) 243 CLR 181.
**161** Ibid, 226.
**162** See the 5th and 14th Amendments to the United States Constitution.
**163** For more detailed analysis, see Peter Gerangelos, *The Separation of Powers and Legislative Interference in Judicial Process* (Hart, 2009); Stellios, above n 10, ch 6.
**164** See *International Finance Trust Co Ltd v New South Wales Crime Commission* (2009) 240 CLR 319, 353.
**165** See *Thomas v Mowbray* (2007) 233 CLR 307, 335; *International Finance Trust Co Ltd v New South Wales Crime Commission* (2009) 240 CLR 319, 353.
**166** See Fiona Wheeler, 'Due Process, Judicial Power and Chapter III in the New High Court' (2004) 32 *Federal Law Review* 205, 211.

interference with, judicial power. Alternatively, drawing from the *Boilermakers'* principle, such a law might confer a non-judicial power on a court. Either way, the provision is invalid.

It has long been accepted that *judicial power* is characterised by procedural dimensions. Classically, Mason, Murphy, Brennan and Deane JJ in *Fencott v Muller*[167] said that '[t]he unique and essential function of the judicial power is the quelling of … controversies by the ascertainment of the facts, by application of the law and by exercise, where appropriate, of judicial discretion'.[168] A legislative denial of the constitutionally protected process features of judicial power thus leads to an application of either *Alexander* or *Boilermakers'*.

A third basis for protecting the judicial process may be found in the constitutional meaning of the word 'court' in Chapter III. Commonwealth judicial power can only be given to 'courts' referred to in s 71, and the definition of 'court' may be seen as requiring certain procedural dimensions. It will be seen later in this chapter that the High Court has developed a similar line of reasoning in relation to State 'courts' exercising federal jurisdiction. Starting with the High Court's decision in *Kable v Director of Public Prosecutions (NSW)*,[169] the constitutional definition of State 'courts' has been seen as protecting their essential features from legislative interference by State Parliaments. It is unclear to what extent this reasoning might apply to identify the due process limitations that control the way in which the Commonwealth Parliament vests Commonwealth judicial power in courts. The High Court is yet to embrace an integration of the *Kable* line of cases and the Chapter III limitations that apply to the federal Parliament.[170] However, the two sets of cases seem to draw from similar underlying concerns to protect the judicial process, and there may be further scope for the High Court to converge these lines of authority.[171]

## 2 Features of the judicial process

As the Court in *Fencott v Muller* emphasised, the exercise of judicial power involves 'the quelling of … controversies by the ascertainment of facts, by application of the law and by exercise, where appropriate, of judicial discretion'. This is a useful starting point. Where Parliament itself seeks to exercise judicial power by determining the dispute about rights, finding the essential facts or removing, limiting or directing the exercise of discretion, arguments may be made that due process protections are being undermined. A clear example is a bill of attainder

**167** (1983) 152 CLR 570.

**168** *Fencott v Muller* (1983) 152 CLR 570, 608. See also *Bass v Permanent Trustee Co Ltd* (1999) 198 CLR 334, 359; *R v Trade Practices Tribunal; Ex parte Tasmanian Breweries Pty Ltd* (1970) 123 CLR 361, 374; *R v Federal Court of Bankruptcy; Ex parte Lowenstein* (1938) 59 CLR 556, 588, where Dixon and Evatt JJ highlighted impartiality as an essential feature of judicial power.

**169** (1996) 189 CLR 51.

**170** See *TCL Air Conditioner (Zhongshan) Co Ltd v Judges of the Federal Court of Australia* (2013) 251 CLR 533, 573.

**171** See Will Bateman, 'Procedural Due Process under the Australian Constitution' (2009) 31 *Sydney Law Review* 411.

(the imposition of the death penalty) or a bill of pains and penalties (the imposition of a lesser form of penalty), where the legislature itself determines that a person is guilty of an offence or imposes punishment on the basis of a legislative determination of wrongdoing. Such exercises of power are clear examples of legislative usurpations of judicial power and are, consequently, invalid.[172]

While the legislative determination of the ultimate facts in issue might present Chapter III problems, the regulation of the rules of evidence for the determination of those facts would not, generally speaking, breach Chapter III requirements. In *Nicholas v The Queen*,[173] the accused had been prosecuted for possession of narcotics in breach of the *Customs Act 1901* (Cth). The events leading up to the alleged contravention involved undercover law enforcement officers importing the narcotics into Australia for sale to the accused. However, the law enforcement officers were not authorised to do so and, thus, had themselves contravened the *Customs Act*. The trial judge hearing the accused's prosecution exercised a discretion to exclude the evidence obtained from the unlawful actions of the law enforcement officers, and ordered a permanent stay on proceedings. The Parliament then amended the *Crimes Act 1914* (Cth) to provide that, in determining whether evidence of unlawful conduct by law enforcement officers should be admitted, the trial judge was to disregard the unlawfulness of the behaviour. On the prosecutor's application, the trial judge then vacated the permanent stay on the accused's prosecution. A majority of the High Court held that the amendments to the *Crimes Act* operated as a rule of evidence and, consequently, did not breach due process limitations. As Gummow J observed, the amendments did not 'deem to exist, or to have been proved to the satisfaction of the tribunal of fact, any ultimate fact, being an element of the offences with which the accused is charged'; nor did they 'change the amount or degree of proof essential to convict him from that required when the alleged offences were committed'.[174] In short, the court was left free to determine, according to the usual criminal standard of proof, whether the offence had been committed and, in fact, now had additional evidence in order to perform that function.

Even the regulation of the onus and burdens of proof for the establishment of the facts in issue may be within legislative control. Much depends, however, on the detail of the provisions in question. In *Williams v Ah On*,[175] Isaacs J gave an example to highlight the distinction between a provision that regulates the onus of proof and one that impermissibly impairs the judicial function:

**172** See, eg, *Liyanage v The Queen* [1967] 1 AC 259; *Polyukhovich v Commonwealth* (1991) 172 CLR 501, 536, 612, 646, 686, 721. Cf *Haskins v Commonwealth* (2011) 244 CLR 22. Whether legislation is invalid if it retrospectively criminalises conduct after it has taken place is a somewhat undecided question. Although a majority of the High Court rejected such a challenge in *Polyukhovich*, the reasoning of Toohey J differed considerably from the other three majority judges (Mason CJ, Dawson and McHugh JJ): see Leslie Zines, 'A Judicially Created Bill of Rights' (1994) 16 *Sydney Law Review* 166, 172; Leslie Zines, *The High Court and the Constitution* (Federation Press, 5th ed, 2008) 293–5. See also *Nicholas v The Queen* (1998) 193 CLR 173, 221–2, 234.

**173** (1998) 193 CLR 173.

**174** Ibid, 236, 238.

**175** (1926) 39 CLR 95.

> It is one thing to say, for instance, in an Act of Parliament, that a man found in possession of stolen goods shall be conclusively deemed to have stolen them, and quite another to say that he shall be deemed to have stolen them unless he personally proves that he got them honestly.[176]

The first leaves no room for judicial inquiry into the facts that give rise to the offence; the second is a mere evidentiary provision, reversing the onus of proof, but leaving the judicial function of determining facts intact. Of course, the extent to which the judicial function is left intact may vary, and it may be that the change to the rules of evidence might be so extensive as to deny any independent judgment for the court or make it practically impossible for the reverse onus to be satisfied. However, as long as the legislation 'prescribes a reasonable approach to the assessment'[177] of the evidence in order to establish the ultimate facts in issue, then the provision is likely to survive constitutional scrutiny.

In *Magaming v The Queen*,[178] the High Court considered the constitutionality of Commonwealth provisions that gave prosecuting authorities a choice of prosecuting an offence in its simple form or with aggravating elements. Section 233A(1) of the *Migration Act 1958* (Cth) made it an offence for a people smuggler to organise the bringing of an unlawful non-citizen to Australia. Section 233C(1), the aggravated offence, criminalised the smuggling of at least five people. The simple form of the offence carried no mandatory minimum term of imprisonment; the aggravated offence had a mandatory five-year minimum imprisonment term.

The provisions were challenged on the basis that they breached Chapter III principles: the core claims essentially being (i) that Parliament had authorised the prosecutor to exercise judicial power by allowing a choice of which offence to prosecute; and (ii) that by attaching a mandatory minimum sentence to the aggravated offence, Parliament had usurped judicial power by removing the trial court's discretion to determine the sentence.

A majority of the Court rejected the Chapter III challenge. Their Honours held that '[l]egislative prescription of a mandatory minimum term of imprisonment ... is not, on that account alone inconsistent with Chapter III'.[179] As for the choice available to prosecutors, the Court concluded 'that it is for the prosecuting authorities (not the courts) to decide who will be prosecuted and for what offences'. Although the choice 'may well affect what punishment will be imposed', that does not entail 'that the prosecutor exercises judicial power in choosing to charge an aggravated form of offence rather than a simple form of that offence'.[180] In short, '[p]rosecutorial choice between the two charges is not an exercise of judicial power',[181] and that conclusion was not affected by the fact

**176** Ibid, 108.
**177** See Brennan CJ in *Nicholas v The Queen* (1998) 193 CLR 173, 190.
**178** (2013) 252 CLR 381.
**179** Ibid, 396.
**180** Ibid, 394.
**181** Ibid.

that one of the options was an aggravated version of the offence that carried a mandatory minimum penalty.[182]

As for other aspects of the judicial process that might receive constitutional protection, there seems to be broad agreement that a court exercising Commonwealth judicial power must accord *natural justice* to litigants.[183] Natural justice would require that a party be given the 'opportunity to present ... evidence and to challenge the evidence led' against that party;[184] however, recent indications are that the High Court will look closely to see whether 'practical injustice'[185] has resulted from a lack of opportunity to be heard. *Impartiality* and *independence* are also features of the judicial process that would attract protection. As Dixon and Evatt JJ said in *R v Federal Court of Bankruptcy; Ex parte Lowenstein*, '[a] long course of development produced a conception of the judicial process which placed the court in the position of a detached tribunal entertaining and determining civil and criminal pleas brought before it'.[186] Qualified support has also been given to the requirements of an 'open and public enquiry',[187] a fair trial[188] and equality before the law,[189] although many of these statements have appeared in dissenting judgments, so their contemplated scope of operation remains undeveloped.

As already mentioned, there may well be scope for the High Court to synchronise many of these protected process features for the exercise of Commonwealth judicial power with those recognised to be essential characteristics of State courts for the purposes of the *Kable* line of cases, to be discussed in the next section. As will be observed further below, this provides increased opportunities for federal standards to be incorporated as limitations on State Parliaments.

# VI Chapter III limitations and State courts

## 1 State courts and the federal judicature

In Chapter 8 it was seen that State courts are an important part of the federal judicial system. Rather than being forced to create a set of lower federal courts for the exercise of federal judicial power, it was considered sensible to allow the federal Parliament to use the existing State court systems for the exercise of

**182** Ibid.
**183** See, eg, *Leeth v Commonwealth* (1992) 174 CLR 455, 470; *TCL Air Conditioner (Zhongshan) Co Ltd v Judges of the Federal Court of Australia* (2013) 251 CLR 533, 553. See also Wheeler, above n 166, 211; Zines, above n 172, 273.
**184** *Bass v Permanent Trustee Co Ltd* (1999) 198 CLR 334, 359.
**185** *Assistant Commissioner Condon v Pompano Pty Ltd* (2013) 252 CLR 38, 100. These comments were made in the context of a *Kable* challenge to State legislation (see below at Part VI.5), but the requirements would equally apply to the due process context.
**186** (1938) 59 CLR 556, 588.
**187** See, eg, *TCL Air Conditioner (Zhongshan) Co Ltd v Judges of the Federal Court* (2013) 251 CLR 533, 553; *Re Nolan; Ex parte Young* (1991) 172 CLR 460, 496; *Grollo v Palmer* (1995) 184 CLR 348, 379, 394.
**188** See, eg, *Nicholas v The Queen* (1998) 193 CLR 173, 208–9; *Re Nolan; Ex parte Young* (1991) 172 CLR 460, 496.
**189** See, eg, *Leeth v Commonwealth* (1992) 174 CLR 455, 470, 487, 502–3.

federal jurisdiction. The Parliament elected to take that option with the enactment of the *Judiciary Act 1903* (Cth), whereby State courts were vested with fairly broad federal jurisdiction.[190] The provisions vesting that federal jurisdiction operated to deprive State courts of the corresponding State jurisdiction that they otherwise would have had, to resolve a dispute falling within the heads of invested federal jurisdiction. Thus, for example, where a State court is hearing a contract dispute between parties resident in different States, the dispute is determined with an exercise of federal jurisdiction – any State jurisdiction to resolve the dispute having been stripped out by s 39(1) of the *Judiciary Act*.[191]

The High Court has accepted that the federal Parliament has the exclusive power to decide what laws are applied in federal jurisdiction.[192] Accordingly, State laws that would otherwise be applied by a State court exercising State jurisdiction must be picked up and applied as 'surrogate' federal laws. This is primarily achieved by ss 68(1) and 79(1) of the *Judiciary Act*. An important consequence of these principles is that State laws cannot be picked up as 'surrogate' federal laws by State courts if they would be incompatible with the principle in *Boilermakers'*.

For example, in *Momcilovic v The Queen*,[193] the High Court considered whether s 36(2) of the *Charter of Human Rights and Responsibilities Act 2006* (Vic) could be picked up in federal jurisdiction. That provision authorises the Victorian Supreme Court to make a declaration of inconsistent interpretation when Victorian legislation cannot be interpreted consistently with human rights set out in that Act. A majority of the Court concluded that s 36(2) cannot be picked up because the making of a declaration involves neither judicial nor incidental non-judicial power. The dispute before the Court involved a matter between Victoria and a non-resident (ie, the prosecution of Ms Momcilovic who was resident in Queensland) triggering federal jurisdiction, and s 79(1) of the *Judiciary Act* could not be used to pick up the non-judicial power in s 36(2).[194]

In Chapter 8, it was explained that the High Court has allowed an expansive reach for federal jurisdiction into disputes that would otherwise have been determined with an exercise of State jurisdiction.[195] When combined with the rule that State laws can only be picked up and applied in federal jurisdiction by federal laws, the consequence has been that disputes once determinable with an exercise of State judicial power by State courts that are not subject to separation of judicial power principles, are now determined in federal jurisdiction subject to federal separation of judicial power limitations.

**190** *Judiciary Act 1903* (Cth), ss 38, 39 and 68.
**191** *Felton v Mulligan* (1971) 124 CLR 367; *MZXOT v Minister for Immigration and Citizenship* (2008) 233 CLR 601.
**192** See, eg, *Solomons v District Court of New South Wales* (2002) 211 CLR 119.
**193** (2011) 245 CLR 1.
**194** For the complications that arose on this point, see Will Bateman and James Stellios, 'Chapter III of the Constitution, Federal Jurisdiction and Dialogue Models of Human Rights' (2012) 26 *Melbourne University Law Review* 1.
**195** See Chapter 8, Part V.

## 2 Separation of judicial power at the State level

Although these principles affect the way in which State courts exercise their federal jurisdiction conferred by the Commonwealth Parliament, *State* Parliaments were, for a long time, considered to be free of Chapter III limitations in relation to their courts. The composition, constitution and organisation of, and State power and jurisdiction given to, State courts – indeed their continuing existence – were generally accepted to be matters for State Parliaments. The separation of judicial power principles that are applicable to the Commonwealth Parliament do not apply to State Parliaments, and State Constitutions do not entrench the position of State courts or a separation of judicial power.[196] This position was well captured by Mason J in *Commonwealth v Hospital Contribution Fund of Australia*, where his Honour said:

> Generally speaking, the Parliament of a State may in the exercise of its plenary legislative power alter the composition, structure, and organization of its Supreme Court for the purposes of the exercise of State jurisdiction. ... Chapter III of the Constitution contains no provision which restricts the legislative competence of the States in this respect. Nor does it make any discernible attempt to regulate the composition, structure or organization of the Supreme Courts as appropriate vehicles for the exercise of invested federal jurisdiction.[197]

However, the potential for Chapter III to impact on State legislative power emerged from the High Court's decision in *Commonwealth v Queensland*.[198] Queensland legislation had authorised the referral of questions of law from the Queensland Supreme Court to the Privy Council. The High Court held the provisions invalid because they were contrary to limitations 'clearly implicit in Ch III'.[199] The potential of this latent limitation was realised by the High Court's decision in *Kable v Director of Public Prosecutions (NSW)*.[200]

## 3 The decision in *Kable*

In *Kable*, the High Court held invalid NSW legislation that authorised the NSW Supreme Court to order the continuing detention of Gregory Wayne Kable. Kable had been convicted for the manslaughter of his wife. Nearing the end of his period of imprisonment, he had written threatening letters to members of his wife's family. His imminent release led to the enactment of the *Community Protection Act 1994* (NSW) that authorised his continuing detention if the Supreme Court was satisfied on reasonable grounds that he was more likely than not to commit a serious act of violence, and if the detention was appropriate to protect the community.

**196** See the cases collected by French CJ in *South Australia v Totani* (2010) 242 CLR 1, 45.
**197** *Commonwealth v Hospital Contribution Fund of Australia* (1982) 150 CLR 49, 61.
**198** (1975) 134 CLR 298.
**199** Ibid, 315.
**200** (1996) 189 CLR 51.

A majority of the Court (Toohey, Gaudron, McHugh and Gummow JJ) held that the provisions were invalid. The judgments of Gaudron, McHugh and Gummow JJ[201] established two principles which are now reasonably well accepted:[202] first, that Chapter III requires the continuing existence of State Supreme Courts, and perhaps other State courts; and, secondly, that Chapter III prevents State Parliaments from conferring powers and functions on State courts if they are incompatible with an exercise of federal judicial power.[203] There were strong dissents by Brennan CJ and Dawson J, preferring to maintain the conventional view that Chapter III did not impose limitations on State Parliaments.

What is the foundation for these limitations? The key majority judgments emphasised the 'integrated' nature of the federal judicature in Chapter III: s 77(iii) authorises Parliament to vest federal jurisdiction in State courts and appeals are guaranteed from State Supreme Courts to the High Court under s 73(ii).[204] This level of integration was seen as elevating the status of State courts – as Gaudron J put it, 'they have a role and existence which transcends their status as courts of the States'.[205]

In the subsequent case of *Forge v Australian Securities and Investments Commission*,[206] the High Court appeared to shift the conceptual foundation for the limitations away from this general Chapter III scheme to the meaning of State 'courts' as referred to in Chapter III.[207] Thus, the references to State courts – particularly State Supreme Courts in s 73(ii) – constitutionally protect their existence and their essential characteristics. Any exercise of State legislative power that undermines the existence or essential characteristics of State courts is invalid. As will be seen below, this textual grounding of the *Kable* limitations provides fertile ground for the further development of Chapter III limitations on State Parliaments. Despite this shift in *Forge*, the High Court often continues to apply *Kable* in terms initially set out in that case.[208]

## 4 An unstable principle?

The decision in *Kable* effected a significant shift in the constitutional arrangements of State governments. As such, it has been highly controversial, and there are a number of reasons for that controversy. First, only three of the majority

**201** Ibid, 102–8; 110–24; 131–43.
**202** The *Kable* principles were later attacked by Heydon J in *Public Service Association and Professional Officers' Association Amalgamated of NSW v Director of Public Employment* (2012) 250 CLR 343, 369–70.
**203** Toohey J reached a similar conclusion on this second proposition, although his Honour limited the limitation to circumstances where the State court is exercising federal jurisdiction ((1996) 189 CLR 51, 94).
**204** Subject to valid exceptions and regulations.
**205** (1996) 189 CLR 51, 103.
**206** (2006) 228 CLR 45.
**207** See Anna Dziedzic, '*Forge v Australian Securities and Investments Commission*: The *Kable* Principle and the Constitutional Validity of Acting Judges' (2007) 35 *Federal Law Review* 129.
**208** See, eg, *Assistant Commissioner Condon v Pompano Pty Ltd* (2013) 252 CLR 38. All members of the Court expressed the analysis in terms of the *Kable* incompatibility test and the *Forge* inquiry focusing on the essential characteristics of a court: 71, 88–90, 105, 106, 108. See also *Attorney-General (NT) v Emmerson* (2014) 307 ALR 174, where both formulations were again referred to: [40], [44].

judges saw the limitation operating when a State court is exercising State jurisdiction. Thus, there was no firm majority for the extended form of limitation that has been accepted since by the High Court.

Secondly, the limitations seemed to arise as implications from the constitutional scheme set out in Chapter III for the exercise of federal judicial power. While it might have been assumed at 1900 that State courts exercising federal jurisdiction would exercise their functions independently and impartially,[209] translating that assumption into a constitutionally entrenched standard is another matter. State courts were adopted as vehicles for the exercise of federal judicial power for reasons of expediency and convenience. Rather than being options available to the federal Parliament, *Kable* requires State Parliaments to retain State courts of a particular quality or character to give Parliament a real choice between creating its own courts and using State courts. Thus, rather than Chapter III presenting a scheme which offers a mere facility for the use of State courts according to the terms and conditions presented by the States, Chapter III now requires that facility to meet certain minimum constitutional standards that are acceptable for the exercise of federal jurisdiction. However, since federal jurisdiction may arise at any point in a proceeding, these constitutional standards are to apply not only for the exercise of federal jurisdiction, but for the exercise of State jurisdiction as well. Perhaps in response to criticisms directed to the interpretive method adopted to effect such a fundamental shift in constitutional understanding, the High Court appears to have shifted the constitutional foundation for the limitation to the words State 'courts' as they appear in Chapter III.

Thirdly, the imposition of constitutionally entrenched limitations on what State Parliaments can do with their courts has the effect of dampening innovative and experimental uses of State judiciaries and distorting the way in which State Parliaments design their governmental decision-making institutions.[210] As will be seen further below, new developments of *Kable* principles may in fact impact on the way in which State Parliaments confer powers on other State government entities. As such, miniature versions of the federal separation of judicial power principles are imposed on State Parliaments. This is particularly ironic given that a distinctive feature of the colonial (State) governments at 1900 was the absence of an entrenched separation of power. These concerns are reflected in the comments of Heydon J in *Public Service Association and Professional Officers' Association Amalgamated of NSW v Director of Public Employment*, shortly before his Honour's retirement:

> A federation is a system of government permitting diversity. It allows its component units to engage in their own legislative experiments. It leaves them free to do so untrammelled by what other units have done or desire to do. And it leaves them free to do so untrammelled by what the central legislature has done or desires to do, subject to a provision like s 109 of the Australian Constitution.

**209** See John Quick and Robert Garran, *The Annotated Constitution of the Australian Commonwealth* (Angus & Robertson, 1901) 804.

**210** See Gabrielle Appleby, 'The High Court and Kable: A Study in Federalism and Rights Protection' (2015) *Monash University Law Review* (forthcoming).

> In 1996, *Kable v Director of Public Prosecutions (NSW)* cut into that concept of the Australian federation by reducing the legislative freedom of the States. Statements in that case have been much debated in this Court over the last sixteen years. Some of them have been invoked successfully to strike down State legislation. ... No express language in the *Constitution* corresponds with the *Kable* statements. ... But those statements raise questions. Has the basis of the decision changed over time? Does the case lack a ratio decidendi? Are the *Kable* statements, being 'insusceptible of further definition in terms which necessarily dictate future outcomes', inconsistent with the rule of law because they are so uncertain that they make prediction impossible and give too much space within which the whims of the individual judge can take effect without constraint? ... [A harsh] critic might conclude that legal satire became obsolete when *Kable's* case referred to the need to keep State courts as fit receptacles for the exercise of the judicial power of the Commonwealth, untainted by powers repugnant to or incompatible with that exercise, as if those State courts were inferior institutions, uncouth, uncultured and coarse, needing always to be scrutinised to prevent pollution of the snow-white purity of federal jurisdiction.[211]

Following the decision in *Kable*, the High Court seemed to lose enthusiasm for a rigorous application of the limitation. In *Fardon v Attorney-General (Qld)*,[212] the High Court upheld the validity of sexual predator legislation which conferred power on the Queensland Supreme Court to order the continuing detention of a prisoner serving imprisonment for a serious sexual offence if the Court formed the view that there was an unacceptable risk that the person would commit a serious sexual assault and, thus, present a serious danger to the community. In upholding the validity of the provisions, the surviving judges from *Kable* (McHugh and Gummow JJ) were careful to distinguish the two legislative schemes in reaching the result. But, for McHugh J, a key member of the majority in *Kable*, the decision in *Kable* was seen as a rare case: '[t]he combination of circumstances which gave rise to the perception in *Kable* [that the three arms of government were acting in concert] is unlikely to be repeated'.[213]

With the retirement of McHugh J, the complexion of the Court changed; only Gummow J remained from the decision in *Kable*. *Kable* arguments challenging the power to appoint acting judges to the NSW Supreme Court were unsuccessful in *Forge v Australian Securities and Investments Commission*,[214] and claims for a denial of natural justice were rejected in *Gypsy Jokers Motorcycle Club Inc v Commissioner of Police*[215] and *K-Generation Pty Ltd v Liquor Licensing Court*.[216] The lack of success seemed to substantiate Kirby J's concerns that *Kable* had become 'a constitutional guard-dog that would bark but once'.[217]

**211** (2012) 250 CLR 343, 369–70 (footnotes omitted).
**212** (2004) 223 CLR 575.
**213** Ibid, 601.
**214** (2006) 228 CLR 45.
**215** (2008) 234 CLR 532.
**216** (2009) 237 CLR 501.
**217** *Baker v The Queen* (2004) 223 CLR 513, 535. Even at the lower court level, the *Kable* principle had only been applied once to that point to invalid State legislation: See *Re Criminal Proceeds Confiscation Act 2002 (Qld)* [2004] 1 Qd R 40.

However, in *International Finance Trust Co Ltd v New South Wales Crime Commission*[218] and *South Australia v Totani*,[219] the High Court struck down State legislation for conferring functions on State courts that were incompatible with an exercise of Commonwealth judicial power. The same result was narrowly avoided in *Momcilovic v The Queen*,[220] where three judges were prepared to invalidate s 36(2) of the *Charter of Human Rights and Responsibilities Act 2006* (Vic), which confers on the Victorian Supreme Court the power to make a declaration of inconsistent interpretation.[221] Additionally, as will be discussed below, the High Court applied *Kable* principles in new directions in *Kirk v Industrial Court of New South Wales*[222] and *Wainohu v New South Wales*.[223] Nevertheless, as the statement of Heydon J in *Public Service Association and Professional Officers' Association Amalgamated of NSW v Director of Public Employment* suggests, criticism of the Court's decision in *Kable* persists.

## 5 Incompatibility and the essential features of 'State courts'

The central inquiry to determine whether the *Kable* limitation is breached is whether there is *incompatibility* with the exercise of Commonwealth judicial power. In its reformulation in *Forge*, it is presented as a question about the *essential characteristics* of State 'courts'. What are the constitutional standards or characteristics that will result in invalidity?

In *Kable*, a range of ideas was expressed about the offending features of the legislative scheme. The standard common to all majority judgments was the requirement to maintain the court's *institutional integrity*. The legislation failed that requirement because of a combination of features. The legislation targeted Kable – indeed, it was his imminent release that resulted in the executive government taking action to enact the legislation. Despite the generality of language used in the Act, it was clear that the legislation was *ad hominem*. Although the order of the court would result in continuing detention, the proceedings were to be civil in nature, with the threshold legal standard to be the balance of probabilities. Furthermore, the rules of evidence were relaxed in various ways to allow the admission of evidence in the proceeding which may not have been otherwise admissible in criminal proceedings. Furthermore, the Supreme Court was not allowed a discretion. If the Court was satisfied of the requisite statutory test of risk of violence and need to protect the community, then a detention order was required to be made. When taken together, all the circumstances suggested to a majority of the High Court that the Supreme Court was being used as 'an instrument of executive government policy'.[224] In other words, its institutional independence had been undermined.

**218** (2009) 240 CLR 319.
**219** (2010) 242 CLR 1.
**220** (2011) 245 CLR 1.
**221** See above at Part VI.1 for a discussion of this case.
**222** (2010) 239 CLR 531.
**223** (2011) 243 CLR 181.
**224** *Kable v Director of Public Prosecutions (NSW)* (1996) 189 CLR 51, 124.

There were, however, other ideas expressed. For example, the majority judgments pointed to the significant departures from the traditional curial process and the impact on public confidence in the judiciary. The fact that *Kable* was being denied his liberty otherwise than through the usual curial method of adjudging and punishing criminal guilt was also identified as a problematic feature of the legislative scheme. These features led Gummow J in particular to conclude that the authority given to the Supreme Court was 'repugnant to the judicial process in a fundamental degree'.[225]

In *Fardon*, the *Dangerous Prisoners (Sexual Offenders) Act 2003* (Qld) authorised the Supreme Court of Queensland to order the continuing detention of a prisoner serving a sentence for committing a serious sexual offence. The drafters had responded to the judgments in *Kable* by restoring curial processes. The Court's assessment of whether the person posed a serious danger to the community was to be made on the basis of 'acceptable, cogent evidence' and to a high degree of probability. In making the assessment, the Court would be required to take account of psychiatric and medical reports and had the option of supervised release rather than continuing detention. Furthermore, the legislation was not *ad hominem* – it was to have general application to circumstances as they arose. Thus, attempts were made to distance the Court's decision-making process from the executive government's intention to have a person held in preventative detention. However, the nature of the inquiry and the impact on the detained person would remain the same as those present in the *Kable* scheme. The person would be denied their liberty, not following a traditional curial process of adjudging and punishing criminal guilt, but following an assessment of a person's future threat to the community.

A majority of the Court in *Fardon* held that the legislative scheme was valid.[226] In doing so, the Court refined the *Kable* standard to one of *institutional integrity*. The differences between the *Kable* and the *Fardon* legislative schemes were considered by a majority of the Court to be sufficient to avoid the conclusion in *Fardon* that the institutional integrity of the Supreme Court was being undermined. Many of the other standards identified in *Kable* were sidelined or rejected. For example, Gleeson CJ[227] and Gummow J (with Hayne J agreeing in this respect)[228] discounted the criterion of *public confidence*, and *repugnancy to the judicial process* was rejected by McHugh J as an appropriate constitutional test.[229] Since a person subject to the detention order would be denied their liberty otherwise than in accordance with the usual criminal process, it too was not seen as sufficient to result in invalidity.[230]

**225** Ibid, 132.
**226** Subsequent legislation authorising the executive to order a person's detention (including that of Fardon), despite a court having released the person from judicially ordered preventative detention, was held invalid by the Queensland Court of Appeal in *Attorney-General (Qld) v Lawrence* (2013) 306 ALR 281.
**227** *Fardon v Attorney-General (Qld)* (2004) 223 CLR 575, 593.
**228** Ibid, 617–18.
**229** Ibid. 600–1.
**230** Significantly, Gummow J indicated that his conclusion may have been different if the person subject to detention had not been identified as a person serving a sentence for an offence of the same character as the one giving rise to an order of detention under the Act (ibid, 619).

The Court elaborated on the criterion of *institutional integrity* in *Forge*[231] and, as already mentioned, identified it as an essential characteristic of a State 'court', thereby attracting constitutional protection. Although it was not possible for the Court to identify a 'single all-embracing statement of the defining characteristics of a court',[232] at the very least, institutional integrity includes *independence* and *impartiality*.[233] In *Forge*, a former Federal Court judge had been appointed as an acting judge of the NSW Supreme Court for four consecutive 12-month periods pursuant to s 37 of the *Supreme Court Act 1970* (NSW). In a challenge to the validity of the appointment, it was argued that the appointment of acting judges (without tenure protections) undermined the independence and impartiality of the Supreme Court. A majority of the High Court rejected the challenge, but comments were made by three of the majority judges (Gummow, Hayne and Crennan JJ) suggesting that acting judge appointments may, in some circumstances, undermine the Court's institutional integrity. For example, their Honours warned that the practice of appointing acting judges could not become so widespread that the Court was constituted 'predominantly or chiefly'[234] by acting judges. Additionally, the appointment of some persons might be more suspect than others. The appointment of a retired Federal Court judge or serving interstate judge for a limited period might be viewed with less suspicion than the appointment of a person in active practice. The latter 'may be thought by some to be concerned about prospects of future permanent appointment'.[235] Similar concerns might be held for the appointment of a judicial officer of a lower court. Much will depend on the circumstances of the case.[236]

The protected characteristics of independence and impartiality were put to the test in *Gypsy Jokers Motorcycle Club Inc v Commissioner of Police* and *K-Generation Pty Ltd v Liquor Licensing Court*. The legislation challenged in *Gypsy Jokers* authorised the Western Australian Supreme Court to review the decision of the Police Commissioner to order the removal of fortifications around premises suspected of being involved in criminal activity. The Commissioner could identify confidential information which was to be heard in closed court and was to be kept confidential from the other party. The legislation considered in *K-Generation* gave jurisdiction to the South Australian Licensing Court to review licensing decisions of the Liquor and Gambling Commissioner. There were similar provisions to those considered in *Gypsy Jokers* allowing the Police Commissioner to identify criminal intelligence which was to be heard in closed court and was to be kept from the other party. Neither set of provisions was considered by a majority of the High Court to undermine the respective

**231** *Forge v Australian Securities and Investments Commission* (2006) 228 CLR 45.
**232** Ibid, 76.
**233** See also *North Australian Aboriginal Legal Aid Service Inc v Bradley* (2004) 218 CLR 146.
**234** (2006) 228 CLR 45, 79.
**235** Ibid, 86.
**236** The remaining three majority judges (Gleeson CJ, Callinan and Heydon JJ) were less enthusiastic about the possibility of challenging acting judge appointments. Kirby J in dissent held that s 37 was invalid as the appointment practice had already resulted in a distortion of the independence of the Supreme Court.

State court's independence or impartiality. Of central importance in both cases was that the provisions were read by a majority to allow the relevant court to determine for itself whether the information in question was confidential or criminal intelligence as defined in the relevant Act. In other words, the courts were not forced to accept the executive's determination of what information had to be heard in closed court and kept from the other side. Furthermore, although the other party was likely to be denied access to the confidential information and criminal intelligence, the court would be able to test the evidence and place upon it appropriate weight when determining the issues before the court.

As mentioned earlier, Gummow J in *Kable* had held that the legislative provisions were 'repugnan[t] to the judicial process in a fundamental degree'. However, McHugh J in *Fardon* had commented that '[t]he pejorative phrase – "repugnancy to the judicial process" – is not the constitutional criterion' and that:

> [t]he bare fact that particular State legislation invests a State court with powers that are or jurisdiction that is repugnant to the traditional judicial process will seldom, if ever, compromise the institutional integrity of that court to the extent that it affects that court's capacity to exercise federal jurisdiction impartially and according to federal law.[237]

The test, however, reappeared in the judgments of three judges in *International Finance Trust Co Ltd v New South Wales Crime Commission*,[238] where a majority of the High Court reinvigorated the *Kable* principle by striking down s 10 of the *Criminal Assets Recovery Act 1990* (NSW). Subsection 10(2) of the Act authorised the NSW Supreme Court, on application of the NSW Crime Commission, to issue a restraining order against the assets of a person suspected of engaging in serious crime. The Court was required to make the order if the application by the Commission disclosed reasonable grounds for the suspicion. The application was heard *ex parte* and, as interpreted by a majority of the Court, the statutory provisions allowed no opportunity for the order to be set aside once made. For French CJ, the provisions undermined the Court's *institutional integrity* because it was left with no discretion to allow an opportunity for the affected party to be heard. The remaining three majority judges (Gummow and Bell JJ, and Heydon J) considered the provisions to be invalid because they were *repugnant to the judicial process in a fundamental degree*. For Gummow and Bell JJ, the Court was unable to test the affidavit evidence presented by the Commission in support of the application for an order. For Heydon J, there was repugnancy because the affected party was denied entirely an opportunity to be heard.[239]

The success in *International Finance Trust* was followed by the majority's decision in *South Australia v Totani*.[240] The South Australian Attorney-General

**237** (2004) 223 CLR 575, 600–01.
**238** (2009) 240 CLR 319.
**239** The dissenting judges (Hayne, Crennan and Kiefel JJ) took the view that the Supreme Court was empowered to set aside the restraining order and, thus, the Court retained its *institutional integrity*.
**240** (2010) 242 CLR 1.

was authorised by s 10(1) of the *Serious and Organised Crime (Control) Act 2008* (SA) to declare certain organisations. The declaration could be made where the Attorney-General was satisfied that members of the organisation were involved in criminal activity and the organisation was a risk to public safety and security. The Commissioner of Police could then apply to the South Australian Magistrates Court for a control order to be issued against a member of that declared organisation. The Court was required by s 14(1) of the Act to issue the control order if satisfied that the person was a member of that organisation. There was no role for the Court to consider the matters that formed the basis of the Attorney-General's declaration. Once issued, a control order prevented a person from associating with other members and from possessing dangerous items and prohibited weapons.

A majority of the High Court (with only Heydon J dissenting) held that s 10 undermined the Court's *independence* and, thus, its *institutional integrity*. There were various ideas expressed in support of that conclusion, some of which find their inspiration in federal separation of judicial power cases. For example, those subject to a control order would have their liberty affected on the basis of alleged criminal activity without the adjudgment and punishment of criminal guilt, and the Supreme Court would be denied the opportunity to look behind the declaration of the Attorney-General to test criminal culpability. Furthermore, the person subject to the control order need not have been involved in any of the criminal activities that formed the basis of the Attorney-General's declaration – it was sufficient that the person was a member of the organisation. And breach of a control order, or association with a person subject to a control order, constituted a criminal offence. Additionally, the Court was allowed no discretion in making an order. The role to be performed by the court was a long way from its traditional function in the administration of criminal justice of adjudging and punishing criminal guilt. Even the control order provisions in *Thomas*, which were supported by historical analogy, required the court, itself, to make an assessment of future risk based on the individual's past or future conduct. That was not the case with the control order provisions in *Totani*. In short, all of these factors suggested that the Magistrates Court was being used to rubber stamp the objectives of the executive. As Gummow J concluded, s 14(1) involved 'the conscription of the Magistrates Court to effectuate' the political function of the executive government.[241]

A challenge to a differently designed control order regime, this time in Queensland, was considered by the High Court in *Assistant Commissioner Condon v Pompano Pty Ltd*.[242] Section 10 of the *Criminal Organisation Act 2009* (Qld) confers a power on the Queensland Supreme Court to declare an organisation to be a 'criminal organisation' if satisfied that its members had been involved in serious criminal activity and that the organisation posed a risk to public safety.

**241** Ibid, 66.
**242** (2013) 252 CLR 38.

The Court can then, under s 18, make a control order against a member or associate of a criminal organisation. The application for a declaration, supported by affidavit evidence, is made by the Queensland Police Commissioner. The application and supporting affidavit had to set out the particulars of the allegations against the organisation and how the Commissioner would establish those allegations.

Central to the challenge in *Pompano*, s 63(1) of the Act provides that the Commissioner may apply to the Supreme Court for a declaration that certain information is 'criminal intelligence'; that is, information about criminal activities the disclosure of which would be prejudicial to investigations, would allow the discovery of an informant's identity, or would endanger life or safety. The application for a declaration of 'criminal intelligence' is considered in advance of the 'criminal organisation' declaration or control order proceedings, and must be considered on an *ex parte* basis, without the affected person being given notice. If information is declared to be 'criminal intelligence' by the Court, and if the criminal intelligence is relied upon in support of the application for a 'criminal organisation' declaration, then the Court must order a *closed* hearing when considering the criminal intelligence and exclude everyone from the hearing except law enforcement officers and necessary court staff. Thus, the criminal intelligence cannot be accessed by the persons affected by the control order or their legal representatives. It was argued that the determination of an issue in the absence of the affected party, and in circumstances where the affected party cannot access the adverse information, constituted such a departure from traditional procedural fairness principles that the institutional integrity of the Court was undermined.

Following the judgments of Gummow and Bell JJ and Heydon J in *International Finance Trust*, one might have expected part of the analysis to inquire whether the procedure adopted for criminal intelligence was repugnant to the judicial process in a fundamental degree. However, the Court in *Pompano* returned to an institutional integrity analysis, with a refined application of much of the reasoning in *Gypsy Jokers* and *K-Generation*. Indeed, the joint judgment of Hayne, Crennan, Kiefel and Bell JJ, echoing the comments of McHugh J in *Fardon*, indicated that novelty in the procedures adopted – ie, departures from traditional methods – was not the focus of the inquiry.[243] The question was whether the process would undermine the *institutional integrity* of the court and, importantly, institutional integrity was now said to direct attention 'to questions of independence, impartiality and *fairness*'.[244] Their Honours continued: 'Where, as here, a novel procedure is said to deny procedural fairness, attention must be directed to questions of fairness and impartiality'.[245]

Whether procedural fairness had been denied was to be assessed as an 'essentially practical' matter and not as 'an abstract concept' – the concern of

**243** Ibid, 94.
**244** Ibid, 103 (emphasis added).
**245** Ibid.

procedural fairness is to 'avoid practical injustice'.[246] Their Honours concluded that, when taken as a whole, the Supreme Court's procedure did not result in 'practical injustice'. That conclusion was reached for the following reasons. First, the fairness to a respondent was a matter taken into account by the Supreme Court when deciding whether to make a declaration that certain information was 'criminal intelligence'.[247] Secondly, although the provisions denied access to 'criminal intelligence', the respondent would have access to *what* the allegation was.[248] Thirdly, when determining an application for a 'criminal organisation' declaration, the Court would know that certain information could not be contested and, accordingly, would decide how much weight to give to that information.[249] Looking at the scheme as a whole, their Honours held that the Supreme Court retains its capacity to act fairly and impartially: the Act does not 'in any way alter the duty of the Supreme Court to assess the cogency and veracity of the evidence that is tendered in an application for a declaration of an organisation as a criminal organisation'.[250] Consequently, its institutional integrity was preserved.[251]

A *Kable* argument was narrowly unsuccessful in *Momcilovic v The Queen*.[252] It was argued that the power to make a declaration of inconsistent interpretation conferred on the Victorian Supreme Court by s 36(2) of the *Charter of Human Rights and Responsibilities Act 2006* (Vic) undermined the Court's institutional integrity. The argument was accepted by Gummow, Hayne and Heydon JJ, but rejected by the majority of French CJ, Crennan, Kiefel and Bell JJ. For the majority, the power was discretionary and could be exercised by the Supreme Court independently of any executive interference. Thus, its institutional integrity was left unimpaired.[253] A *Kable* challenge was also unsuccessful in *Attorney-General (NT) v Emmerson*,[254] where the High Court considered the validity of Northern Territory property forfeiture provisions that operate on a declaration made by the Supreme Court of the Northern Territory. Section 36A of the *Misuse of Drugs Act* (NT) authorises the Court, on an application of the Director of Public Prosecutions, to declare a person to be a 'drug trafficker' if the person had committed certain drug offences within a previous 10-year period. Once a declaration is made, s 94(1) of the *Criminal Property Forfeiture Act* (NT) operates to forfeit the person's property to the Territory. A claim that the provisions undermined the Supreme Court's institutional integrity was rejected by the Court. The High Court held that the function given to the Supreme Court was 'an unremarkable example of conferring jurisdiction on a court to determine a controversy between parties

**246** Ibid, 99.
**247** Ibid, 101.
**248** Ibid.
**249** Ibid, 102.
**250** Ibid, 103.
**251** The challenge was rejected by French CJ and Gageler J in separate judgments.
**252** (2011) 245 CLR 1.
**253** See Bateman and Stellios, above n 194.
**254** (2014) 307 ALR 174; (2014) 88 ALJR 522.

which, when determined, will engage stated statutory consequences'.[255] The function was to be 'exercised in accordance with standards characterising ordinary judicial processes'.[256] The fact that the process was initiated by an application by the Director of Public Prosecutions did not affect that conclusion. Nor did the fact that 'the determination of whether the statutory criteria are satisfied may readily be performed, because of the ease of proof of the criteria'.[257]

Thus, *institutional integrity* has emerged as the benchmark for assessing a *Kable* challenge. Conceptualised in the way it was in *Forge*, institutional integrity is a key defining characteristic of a State court, and given constitutional protection from State Parliaments. Although the Court has emphasised that the concept is 'not readily susceptible of definition in terms which will dictate future outcomes',[258] depending on the context, *Kable* is assessed by considering the impact of State legislation on the court's *independence*, *impartiality* and *fairness*.[259] Repugnancy to the traditional judicial process, as a separate test of validity, does not appear to enjoy majority support. However, as was evident from the judgment of French CJ in *International Finance Trust* and the joint judgment in *Pompano*, procedural deficiencies can now be assessed through the lens of the institutional integrity requirement of fairness.

## 6 The further evolution of *Kable*

As mentioned, the *Kable* limitation was given a firmer textual basis by the High Court in *Forge*, by anchoring it to the meaning of the words State 'court'. Thus, the functional characteristics of *institutional integrity*, *independence*, *impartiality* and *fairness* are required for State courts to exercise federal jurisdiction. In *Kirk v Industrial Court of New South Wales*,[260] the High Court took this conceptual foundation to a new level. The appellants in *Kirk* (a corporation and its director) had been convicted of certain offences under the *Occupational Health and Safety Act 1983* (NSW). The offences had been prosecuted in the Industrial Court of New South Wales. The appellants had applied to the NSW Supreme Court for prerogative relief (in the nature of certiorari) to quash the convictions, arguing that the Industrial Court had committed jurisdictional error. However, a privative clause in the State legislation sought to prevent such a review by providing that the decision of the Industrial Court was to be 'final and may not be appealed against, reviewed, quashed or called into question by any court or tribunal'.

**255** Ibid, [60]. Curiously, this is despite the fact that the determination provides a factum upon which the legislation creates rights, rather than determining a dispute about pre-existing rights. The answer to this puzzle may lie in a characterisation of the power as a double function provision: see at [102] (Gageler J) and the footnote reference to *Baker v The Queen* (2004) 223 CLR 513.

**256** Ibid, [58]. See also at [65]–[66].

**257** Ibid, [65], [66].

**258** *Assistant Commissioner Condon v Pompano Pty Ltd* (2013) 252 CLR 38, 89.

**259** It has also been suggested that, as a general rule, State courts are characterised by openness (*Hogan v Hinch* (2011) 243 CLR 506, 530; *Assistant Commissioner Condon v Pompano Pty Ltd* (2013) 252 CLR 38, 71); and that they provide reasons (*Wainohu v New South Wales* (2011) 243 CLR 181, 213–15).

**260** (2010) 239 CLR 531.

As was seen in Chapter 8, the High Court held in *Plaintiff S157/2002 v Commonwealth*[261] that such clauses in federal legislation cannot prevent the High Court from exercising its review jurisdiction under s 75(v) of the Constitution to correct jurisdictional errors. The privative clause was read so as not to apply to decisions affected by jurisdictional error. In *Kirk*, the High Court drew from the words 'Supreme Court' to achieve the same result for privative clauses in State legislation.

In reaching that conclusion, the High Court in *Kirk* relied upon the reasoning in *Forge* that 'State courts' have constitutionally entrenched characteristics that are beyond the control of State Parliaments. Their Honours held that, at 1900:

> [a] defining characteristic of State Supreme Courts is the power to confine inferior courts and tribunals within the limits of their authority to decide by granting relief in the nature of prohibition and mandamus and ... [certiorari], directed to inferior courts and tribunals on grounds of jurisdictional error.[262]

Thus, a State privative clause, which sought to remove the jurisdiction of the Supreme Court to correct jurisdictional errors, would be invalid as purporting to remove a defining characteristic of the Supreme Court. As occurred in *Plaintiff S157*, the High Court read down the State privative clause so as not to apply to decisions affected by jurisdictional error, thereby avoiding invalidity. While in *Forge* the Court constitutionalised certain *functional characteristics* of State Supreme Courts needed to exercise federal jurisdiction, in *Kirk*, the same analysis was used to constitutionalise a *function* that was characteristic of State Supreme Courts in 1900.

Further development of *Kable* was undertaken in *Wainohu v New South Wales*,[263] which considered the validity of provisions of the *Crimes (Criminal Organisations Control) Act 2009* (NSW) conferring power on a NSW Supreme Court judge to declare an organisation to be a criminal organisation. Importantly, the power was conferred on the judge acting in his or her personal capacity. Echoing the language of the provisions considered in *Totani* and *Pompano*, the declaration could be made where the judge was satisfied that the members of the organisation were involved in serious criminal activity and posed a risk to public safety. Once the declaration was made, an application could be made to the NSW Supreme Court for a control order placing special obligations on the person subject to the order. Crucial to the way in which the case was decided, s 13(2) of the Act provided that eligible judges were generally not required to provide reasons supporting their declarations.

In response to a *Kable* challenge to the control order scheme, the High Court focused on the power given to the judge to make a declaration in his or her personal capacity and, particularly, to the absence of an obligation to provide reasons in support of that declaration. As has been seen, the High Court has

**261** (2003) 211 CLR 476.
**262** (2010) 239 CLR 531, 566.
**263** (2011) 243 CLR 181.

accepted that the federal Parliament can confer non-judicial functions on federal court judges in their personal capacity (ie, the *persona designata* doctrine), provided that certain conditions are satisfied.[264] In *Wainohu*, the limitations applicable to the doctrine at the federal level were synchronised with the *Kable* principle and imposed on State legislative power. Thus, the NSW Act could not confer non-judicial powers on State court judges in their personal capacity if they would undermine the institutional integrity of the courts. A majority of the Court (French CJ and Kiefel J, and Gummow, Hayne, Crennan and Bell JJ; Heydon J dissenting) held s 13(2) of the Act to be invalid.

The plurality of Gummow, Hayne, Crennan and Bell JJ considered that the absence of an obligation to give reasons was fatal to validity. The legislative scheme utilised the 'confidence in impartial, reasoned and public decision-making of [the judges] in the daily performance of their offices as members of the Supreme Court to support inscrutable decision-making' under the Act.[265] In other words, the legislative scheme borrowed the reputation of the judiciary to support inscrutable government decision-making and, consequently, undermined the institutional integrity of the courts. For French CJ and Kiefel J, the provision of reasons is an essential characteristic of a court, and since the function of making the declaration by the judge was integral to the role of the Supreme Court in issuing a control order, the absence of a duty to give reasons would 'affect perceptions of the role of a judge of the Court, to the detriment of the Court'.[266]

The Court's decisions in *Kirk* and *Wainohu* demonstrate an increased willingness to develop the *Kable* principle. While the traditional *Kable* focus was to inquire whether certain powers or functions can be conferred by State Parliaments on their courts, *Kirk* and *Wainohu* look to see whether there are any limits on State Parliaments removing powers from courts or conferring them on persons outside the institution of the court.

## VII Conclusions

The High Court's interpretation of Chapter III has had considerable impact on the shape of the federal judicial system. The previous chapter showed how the High Court has expanded federal jurisdiction, squeezing out State jurisdiction. One consequence of this expansion was to marginalise the role of the Privy Council at the apex of State judicial systems. While the compromise reached during the constitutional drafting process preserved a distinctive place for the Privy Council as the ultimate court of appeal from State courts, as explained in Chapter 8, the High Court's expansion of federal jurisdiction eroded the opportunities to take cases on appeal from State courts to the Privy Council.

**264** See above at Part IV.
**265** (2011) 243 CLR 181, 230.
**266** Ibid, 219.

Another consequence of this expansion is that many disputes, ordinarily determined through an exercise of State jurisdiction, are now determined through the exercise of federal judicial power in both federal and State courts. As explained in this chapter, this has expanded the applicability of the federal separation of judicial power principles to these disputes. Consequently, while these disputes would otherwise have been resolved without the federal separation of judicial power constraints, their determination in federal jurisdiction – whether by a federal court or State court – is now subject to separation of judicial power disciplines.

The High Court has also converged – or centralised[267] – the judicial systems in Australia through the development of the *Kable* principles. While it was once thought that State Parliaments were not limited by entrenched separation of judicial power principles, the decision in *Kable* established a platform for the imposition of miniature versions of separation principles on State Parliament. As a miniature version of the *Boilermakers'* principle, State Parliaments cannot confer non-judicial powers on State courts if they are incompatible with an exercise of Commonwealth judicial power or inconsistent with the essential characteristics of State courts. If the State provisions undermine the institutional integrity of State courts, they will be invalid. Some judges have taken this further: State provisions will be invalid if they affect curial procedure in a way that is repugnant to the judicial process in a fundamental degree. Focusing on the independence, impartiality and fairness of a State court and its traditional judicial functions and curial processes brings the *Kable* limitation into close alignment with the 'due process' limitations applicable to the federal Parliament.

Furthermore, the development of *Kable* in *Kirk* and *Wainohu* establishes a platform for the imposition of a miniature version of the *Alexander* principle. Once it is accepted that functions can be characteristic of State courts at 1900, then taking those functions away from State courts (as was the case in *Kirk*), and giving them to another body or person, may risk constitutional trouble. Similarly, the borrowing of judicial reputation to effect the implementation of State executive policy may, as was the case in *Wainohu*, imperil provisions conferring functions on persons outside the judicial system.

**267** For more detail, see James Stellios, 'The Centralisation of Judicial Power within the Australian Federal System' (2014) 42 *Federal Law Review* 357.

# 10

# The States

> *The Constitution of each State of the Commonwealth shall, subject to this Constitution, continue as at the establishment of the Commonwealth, or as at the admission or establishment of the State, as the case may be, until altered in accordance with the Constitution of the State.*[1]

## I Introduction

On 1 January 1901, the colonies together formed 'a Federal Commonwealth under the name of the Commonwealth of Australia'[2] based upon the continuance of the colonies in a new political form.[3] Each constituent State maintained its colonial constitutional heritage – its Constitution and governmental structures – with the only qualifications to this being those in the Commonwealth Constitution necessitated by Australia's federal union. Therefore, rather than being 'subordinate',[4] the six States were accorded a hybrid 'original' and 'continuing' status.[5]

Previous chapters have shown how the colonies were integral to the formation of the Commonwealth,[6] how the States are integral to the representative character of the Commonwealth Parliament,[7] and how the distribution of legislative, executive and judicial power under the Commonwealth Constitution presupposes the prior existence of the colonies as the fundamental constituents of the federation.[8] Other vital aspects of the Constitution address the legal relationship between the Commonwealth and the States,[9] and even the limits on legislative power that are contained in the Constitution are shaped

**1** Commonwealth Constitution, s 106.
**2** *Commonwealth of Australia Constitution Act 1900* (UK), cl 3.
**3** John Quick and Robert Randolph Garran, *The Annotated Constitution of the Australian Commonwealth: Part 2* (Angus & Robertson, 1901) 927. See also Nicholas Aroney, *The Constitution of a Federal Commonwealth* (Cambridge University Press, 2009) 265–6.
**4** *Melbourne Corporation v Commonwealth* (1947) 74 CLR 31, 50.
**5** *Commonwealth of Australia Constitution Act 1900* (UK), preamble and cls 3, 6; Commonwealth Constitution, s 106.
**6** Chapter 1, Part II.
**7** Chapter 2, Part II.
**8** Chapters 3, 7 and 9.
**9** Chapter 4.

fundamentally by its character as the constitution of a federal commonwealth.[10] This chapter traces the Australian States' constitutional ancestry.[11] It explores what the 'continuing' constitutional status of the States and their constitutions means, including an analysis of the constitutional powers and limitations pursuant to which they function. The chapter also touches on the implications for the States of proposals for constitutional reform.

## II The continuing States

> The States existed as colonies prior to the passing of the Federal Constitution, and possessed their own charters of government, in the shape of the Constitutions granted to them by the Imperial Parliament. Those charters have been confirmed and continued by the Federal Constitution, not created thereby. Hence, though the powers reserved to the States are not wide, general and national, no badge of inferiority or subordination can be associated with those powers, or with the State institutions through which they are exercised.[12]

In *Williams v Commonwealth*,[13] French CJ opened his judgment with Andrew Inglis Clark's statement that central to the federation was the 'preservation of the separate existence and corporate life of each of the component States of the commonwealth'.[14] For while federation saw the official political and legal transformation of the colonies into 'States', the Commonwealth of Australia was based upon the pre-existence of them as self-governing colonies. With some qualifications for the exigencies of the federation, the Commonwealth of Australia saw the colonies' constitutions and legislative powers 'continue' 'as at the establishment of the Commonwealth'[15] in the form of the six 'Original States',[16] while simultaneously contemplating that new States could be 'admi[tted]or establish[ed]'.[17]

Recognising the status of the colonies prior to federation and their continuance post-1901, albeit as States, is vital for a fulsome appreciation of the constitutional implications of the creation of the Commonwealth of Australia. The preamble and covering clauses of the *Commonwealth of Australia Constitution Act 1900* (UK) plainly demonstrate that the federation is based upon the prior

**10** Chapter 5.
**11** A detailed consideration of the constitutional position of the Territories lies beyond the scope of this chapter: For a discussion of the constitutional position of the Territories, see generally: Gerard Carney, *The Constitutional Systems of the Australian States and Territories* (Cambridge University Press, 2006) 436; Jennifer Clarke, Patrick Keyzer and James Stellios, *Hanks Australian Constitutional Law: Materials and Commentary* (LexisNexis, 8th ed, 2009) ch 4.
**12** Quick and Garran, above n 3, 928. See also *Convention Debates, Sydney* (1891) 281.
**13** (2012) 86 ALJR 713, [1].
**14** Inglis Clark, *Studies in Australian Constitutional Law* (Charles F Maxwell, 1901) 12. See also Kiefel J's comment in *Williams v Commonwealth* that the 'relationship between the six separate "constitutional units" in Australia' is 'comprised of the six colonies that existed prior to federation': (2012) 86 ALJR 713, [578].
**15** Commonwealth Constitution, ss 106 and 107.
**16** See Commonwealth Constitution, s 7; *Commonwealth of Australia Constitution Act 1900* (UK), cl 6.
**17** Commonwealth Constitution, s 121.

existence of the colonies, and the text of the Constitution, particularly 'Ch V – The States' is built upon their founding and continuing status. The colonies were deliberately called 'States' and not merely 'provinces' to indicate their status as constituent self-governing political communities.[18]

At the time of the enactment of the *Commonwealth of Australia Constitution Act 1900* (UK) it was not clear whether the colony of Western Australia would agree to join the federation as an 'Original State'.[19] However, by the time the Imperial Act was Proclaimed, Western Australia had, as covering clause 3 contemplated, agreed to join New South Wales, Victoria, South Australia, Queensland and Tasmania to form the Commonwealth. As was explained in Chapter 1,[20] it was out of respect to the people of Western Australia that the colony was not included in the preamble because the requisite referendum, confirming that the colony would join the federation, was only concluded by the end of July. New Zealand, although referred to as a potential State in covering clause 6, decided not to join federation.[21]

As Original States, 'mean[ing] such States as are parts of the Commonwealth at its establishment',[22] the six former colonies were, by s 7 of the Commonwealth Constitution, assured the same number of senators and, by s 24, a guarantee of at least five seats in the House of Representatives, independently of their population. Their 'continuing' constitutional status was secured particularly by ss 106, 107 and 108.[23] Notably, any newly admitted States would also have this 'continuing' constitutional status extended to them.

Section 106 of the Commonwealth Constitution was inserted to ensure that the State Constitutions would continue in existence after federation (and that the States would continue to have an independent capacity to amend their own Constitutions, subject only to inconsistent provisions in the Commonwealth Constitution and validly enacted Commonwealth legislation (covering clause 5 and s 109)).[24] An overwhelming majority of the framers rejected the proposition that it would be appropriate for the Commonwealth Constitution to alter the substance of the State Constitutions as far as the internal affairs of the States were concerned. The colonies were self-governing political communities which already possessed substantial power to alter their own Constitutions.[25] Accordingly, as Quick and Garran observed, the allocation of powers within the federation:

**18** *Convention Debates, Sydney* (1891) 183, 373.
**19** *Commonwealth of Australia Constitution Act 1900* (UK) where the preamble omits any reference to Western Australia.
**20** Chapter 1, Part I.
**21** For more detail, see Nicholas Aroney, 'New Zealand, Australasia and Federation' (2010) 16 *Canterbury Law Review* 31.
**22** *Commonwealth of Australia Constitution Act 1900* (UK), cl 6.
**23** See, eg *Re Tracey; Ex parte Ryan* (1989) 166 CLR 518, 599; 575.
**24** Eg, Commonwealth Constitution, ss 52, 69, 107, 109. The State Constitutions have also been affected by the enactment of the *Australia Acts 1986* (Cth & UK).
**25** Aroney, above n 3, 250–66.

> left the States in the full possession and enjoyment of their original institutions and previously acquired powers, minus only this deduction and transfer [of powers to the Commonwealth]. Thus the States retain their Constitutions, their Parliaments, their Executive, and Judicial organizations, subject only to the loss of those powers which by the Federal Constitution are withdrawn from the scope and operation of the State Constitutions and brought within the sphere of the Federal Constitution.[26]

In *New South Wales v Commonwealth* (the *Seas and Submerged Lands* case), Stephen J explored this notion of the 'continuity of the Australian colonies'.[27] His Honour interpreted covering clauses 3 and 6 of the *Commonwealth of Australia Constitution Act* as having the consequence that the colonies were 'given the new title of States'. He continued:

> Sections 106 and 107 of the Constitution then give effect to the union of the colonies by providing for the continuance of their several constitutions and of the powers of their several colonial parliaments, other than those powers vested in federal Parliament or withdrawn from the State Parliaments.[28]

His Honour also cited Evatt J's opinion that:

> constitutionally speaking, the status of the States of Australia is equal to, or co-ordinate with, that of the Commonwealth itself. Sovereignty is not attributable to one authority more than to the others; it is divided between them in accordance with the demarcation of functions set out in the Commonwealth Constitution.[29]

This raises an important question: has s 106 effectively 'incorporated' the State constitutional documents into the Commonwealth Constitution in a way that has altered their independent imperial origins?[30] Differing judicial views have been expressed.[31] In *McGinty*, Brennan CJ observed:

> [S]ection [106] has a dual operation. Its first operation is to prescribe what the new elements of the Federal polity – the States – shall be. When the people of the Australian Colonies were united in the Commonwealth of Australia by the proclamation made pursuant to Covering Cl 3 and those Colonies became Original States of the Commonwealth by operation of Covering Cl 6, the Colonies – the old constitutional entities – acquired a new constitutional status. They became States, as the text of ss 107 and 108 shows, deriving their existence as States from the Commonwealth Constitution. Secondly, s 106 conferred on the respective States substantially the Constitutions of the antecedent Colonies. The same Constitutions as had been conferred on the Colonies prior to 1 January 1901 were continued as the Constitutions of the respective States thereafter, subject to such modifications as were effected by the *Commonwealth of Australia Constitution Act* 1900 (Imp) and the Commonwealth Constitution....

**26** Quick and Garran, above n 3, 929–30.
**27** (1975) 135 CLR 337, 447.
**28** Ibid. See also 372.
**29** Ibid, 447, citing *Broken Hill South Ltd v Commissioner of Taxation* (NSW) (1937) 56 CLR 337, 378.
**30** See, eg Quick and Garran, above n 3, 930; but cf 928.
**31** See, eg, Anne Twomey, 'One In, All In: The Simultaneous Implementation of a Republic at Commonwealth and State Levels' in Sarah Murray (ed), *Constitutional Perspectives on an Australian Republic: Essays in Honour of Professor George Winterton* (Federation Press, 2010) 20, 26ff.

> Although the States owe their existence to the Commonwealth Constitution and although their respective Constitutions in 1901 were conferred by operation of s 106 of the Commonwealth Constitution, the powers vested in the respective State legislatures were subject not only to the other provisions of the Constitution but also to the limitations which had been imposed on the powers of the antecedent colonial legislatures (s 107). The Australian Colonies did not retain their colonial status for the purposes of the constitutional law of the Commonwealth, but their general legislative and constituent powers then remained amenable to affection by laws enacted by the United Kingdom Parliament. That amenability to affection by Imperial legislation was removed only by the enactment of the *Australia Act* 1986.[32]

The reference by Brennan CJ to State Constitutions being 'conferred by operation of s 106 of the Commonwealth Constitution', could, if read in isolation, be taken to support Toohey J's view that the 'present source' of the State Constitutions' 'authority' is s 106.[33] Such a view is difficult to square, however, with the plain language of s 106, which refers to the States as 'continuing' rather than as deriving their authority from the Commonwealth Constitution. As Burt CJ explained in *Wilsmore*, 'the full legislative power of a State is continued by ss 106 and 107 of the [Commonwealth] Constitution, but the sources of that power remains as before'.[34] The Chief Justice also cited with approval the view that the State Constitutions were 'confirmed and continued by the Federal Constitution, not created thereby'.[35] This continuing imperial heritage would also seem consistent with the later enactment of the *Australia Acts 1986* (Cth & UK) based on prior State enactments pursuant to s 51(xxxviii) of the Commonwealth Constitution.[36] Further, on a more practical level, it is evidenced by State communications with the Queen occurring through State Governors on the advice of ministers responsible to their respective State Parliaments, rather than being directed through the Governor-General.[37]

Section 107 confirms that the powers of the State parliaments would continue, subject to those powers 'exclusively vested in the Parliament of the Commonwealth or withdrawn from the Parliament of the State'.[38] For instance, s 52 of the Commonwealth Constitution sets out the exclusive powers of the Commonwealth Parliament which are beyond the legislative powers of the States.[39] Further provisions such as ss 90, 92 and 117 impose additional limitations on

**32** *McGinty v Western Australia* (1996) 186 CLR 140, 171–2 (footnotes omitted).
**33** Ibid, 208. For further support for this view see: *Victoria v Commonwealth* (1971) 122 CLR 353, 371; *New South Wales v Commonwealth* (1975) 135 CLR 337, 372; *Bistricic v Rokov* (1971) 135 CLR 552, 566; *Western Australia v Wilsmore* (1981) 149 CLR 79, 86.
**34** *Western Australia v Wilsmore* (1981) 149 CLR 79.
**35** Quick and Garran, above n 3, 928.
**36** Eg, *Australia Acts (Request) Act 1985* (NSW).
**37** Aroney, above n 3, 264–5, 356–7. Anne Twomey, *The Chameleon Crown* (Federation Press, 2006) 235–6.
**38** Note that the absence of the words 'subject to this Constitution' in s 107 were not seen as significant when the States are limited by this phrase's inclusion in s 106: Deane J in *Theophanous v Herald & Weekly Times Ltd* (1994) 182 CLR 104, 165.
**39** See Chapter 4, Part II.2.

the States' legislative powers,[40] while s 109 renders inconsistent State legislation inoperative while an inconsistent Commonwealth Act remains in force.[41] State consultation and agreement (or that of a majority of State electors) is, however, required by several important provisions, including ss 123, 124 and 128.

The saving of prior colonial laws is guaranteed by s 108, which provides:

> Every law in force in a Colony which has become or becomes a State, and relating to any matter within the powers of the Parliament of the Commonwealth, shall, subject to this Constitution, continue in force in the State; and, until provision is made in that behalf by the Parliament of the Commonwealth, the Parliament of the State shall have such powers of alteration and of repeal in respect of any such law as the Parliament of the Colony had until the Colony became a State.[42]

Deane J in *Theophanous* noted that s 108's reference to State Parliaments' 'powers of alteration and of repeal' conferred no new powers on those parliaments.[43]

While not affecting all State departmental functions, s 69 of the Commonwealth Constitution allowed certain colonial government departments to be centralised after federation. However, all other State departments continued until altered as determined by the government of each State.

## III Role in the federation

> We should satisfy the mind of each of the colonies that we have no intention to cripple their powers, to invade their rights, to diminish their authority, except so far as it is absolutely necessary in view of the great end to be accomplished.[44]

Quick and Garran explained in their foundational constitutional work that the States 'are welded into the very structure and essence of the Commonwealth... they are inseparable from it and as enduring and indestructible as the Commonwealth itself'.[45] Even though the powers of the Commonwealth Parliament have through constitutional amendment and judicial interpretation expanded since federation, the High Court has consistently recognised (even in the context of rejecting the viability of a reserved powers doctrine)[46] that the States have a constitutional status which 'limit[s] the capacity of the Federal Parliament to legislate in a manner inconsistent with the constitutional role of the States'.[47] For example, the *Melbourne Corporation* doctrine,[48] as formulated and

**40** See Chapter 5, Parts I and III.
**41** See Chapter 4, Part II.
**42** See Chapter 4, Part II.2.
**43** *Theophanous v Herald & Weekly Times Ltd* (1994) 182 CLR 104, 165.
**44** *Convention Debates, Sydney* (1891) 24.
**45** Quick and Garran, above n 3, 336.
**46** See Chapter 3, Part III.1.
**47** *Austin v Commonwealth* (2003) 215 CLR 185, [17].
**48** *Melbourne Corporation v Commonwealth* (1947) 74 CLR 31.

developed by the High Court, is based upon the vital role played by the States in the federation.[49] As explained in Chapter 4, according to the doctrine's refashioning in *Austin*, the Commonwealth cannot act so as to interfere or impair the ability of the States to function as governments, noting that the Constitution necessitates that 'there will continue to be State governments separately organised'.[50] Further, in *Clarke*, Gummow, Heydon, Kiefel and Bell JJ identified as vital 'the capacity of [each] State to function in accordance with the constitutional conception of the Commonwealth and States as constituent entities of the federal structure'.[51] The continued functioning of the States as governments, at the very least, extends to their political[52] and executive functioning[53] as well as the preservation of their court structures.[54]

Despite the central role that the States would play within federation, Quick and Garran anticipated in 1901 that the powers of the States would lessen:

> In the early history of the Commonwealth the States will not seriously feel the deprivation of legislative power intended by the Constitution, but as Federal legislation becomes more active and extensive the powers contemplated by the Constitution will gradually be withdrawn from the States and absorbed by the Federal Parliament.[55]

This prediction has proved to be correct. As discussed in Chapter 3, since *Engineers*,[56] there has been a gradual expansion, and therefore centralisation, of Commonwealth powers. This has arisen from several inter-related reasons: expansive High Court interpretations of the Commonwealth Parliament's heads of legislative power (such as the corporations, external affairs and defence powers),[57] increasing vertical fiscal imbalance and an increase in Commonwealth power through constitutional amendments (eg, ss 51(xxiiiA), 51(xxvi) and 105A), and referrals of State legislative power to the Commonwealth Parliament under s 51(xxxvii) of the Commonwealth Constitution. This has meant that the States' practical role within the federation has become, to an extent, less significant. As Chapter 2 identified, party political more than jurisdictional considerations, have come to dominate the role and functions of the Senate. The increasing financial dependence of the States and expansion in Commonwealth power has also seen an increase in Commonwealth financial assistance grants to the States, under s 96, along with cooperative federalist action through forums

**49** See Chapter 4, Part III.3.
**50** *Austin v Commonwealth* (2003) 215 CLR 185, [115]. See also [281].
**51** *Clarke v Commissioner of Taxation* (2009) 240 CLR 272, [65]. See also [32]. Refer also to *Leeth v Commonwealth* (1992) 174 CLR 455, 485 (Deane and Toohey JJ referring to 'the implication of a more general principle protecting' the States' 'continued existence and political viability').
**52** *Australian Capital Television Pty Ltd v Commonwealth* (1992) 177 CLR 106, 242, 163–4.
**53** *Clarke v Commissioner of Taxation* (2009) 240 CLR 272, [33] (French CJ noting that a 'gubernatorial privileges tax', would, if imposed by the Commonwealth, interfere with 'the constitutional office of Governor... inconsistent[ly] with the status of the States as independent entities under the Constitution').
**54** See, eg, *Re Tracey; Ex parte Ryan* (1989) 166 CLR 518, 575: 'State courts are an essential branch of the government of a State and the continuance of State Constitutions by s 106 of the Constitution precludes a law of the Commonwealth from prohibiting State courts from exercising their functions'. See also 547, 599.
**55** Quick and Garran, above n 3, 933.
**56** *Amalgamated Society of Engineers v Adelaide Steamship Co Ltd* (1920) 28 CLR 129.
**57** See, eg, *New South Wales v Commonwealth* (2006) 229 CLR 1.

such as the Council of Australian Governments (COAG) and ongoing negotiations of intergovernmental agreements.

However, the role of the States has not been rendered constitutionally nugatory. As identified above, the High Court has consistently emphasised that the Commonwealth is unable to act in a way that would impair the ability of the States to function as governments.[58] Further, governmental cooperation is central to the operation of the federation (such as through ss 51(xxxvii) and 51(xxxviii) of the Commonwealth Constitution[59] and s 15(1) of the *Australia Acts 1986* (Cth & UK)).[60] Consequently the States are not constitutional 'also-rans'. While the Commonwealth may not, for political reasons, always want to use States as s 96 financial conduits, recent judicial authority suggests that there may be more limitations (such as s 51(xxxi)) on the use of the s 96 grants power than previously envisaged.[61] Additionally, *Pape*[62] and *Williams*[63] signify that the Commonwealth executive's ability to enter into intergovernmental agreements and contracts to spend money directly, without using s 96, might be more limited than was previously thought.[64] While these High Court decisions may also have implications for State executive power,[65] the judgments reveal a definite cautiousness as to the danger for the States of sweeping unconstrained direct exercises of Commonwealth executive power.[66]

# IV State Constitutions

## 1 History

The history of the State Constitutions is as varied as the colonies. As Chapter 1 explained,[67] the declaration of New South Wales as the first penal colony in Australia in 1786 was the beginning of numerous colonial and imperial Acts and imperial orders seeking to legitimise the regulation and governance of the Australian colonies. All colonies, other than Western Australia, were originally within New South Wales' territorial limits and colonial powers.

**58** *Austin v Commonwealth* (2003) 215 CLR 185; *Clarke v Commissioner of Taxation* (2009) 240 CLR 272. See also *Re Tracey; Ex parte Ryan* (1989) 166 CLR 518.
**59** The enactment of the *Australia Acts 1986* (Cth & UK) being an excellent example.
**60** See, eg, Andrew Lynch, 'Commonwealth Financial Powers – Taxation, Direct Spending and Grants – Scope and Limitations' (2011) 6(1/2) *Public Policy* 23. See also *Gould v Brown* (1998) 193 CLR 346, 477.
**61** *ICM Agriculture Pty Ltd v Commonwealth* (2009) 240 CLR 140. See also Anne Twomey, 'Future Directions in Federalism – Where Will the High Court Go?' (2011) 6(1/2) *Public Policy* 133, 148.
**62** *Pape v Commissioner of Taxation* (2009) 238 CLR 1.
**63** *Williams v Commonwealth* (2012) 86 ALJR 713.
**64** See Chapter 7, Part IV.2. See also Shipra Chordia, Andrew Lynch and George Williams, '*Williams v Commonwealth* – Commonwealth Executive Power and Australian Federalism' (2013) 37(1) *Melbourne University Law Review* 189, 218.
**65** Grant Donaldson, 'Aspects of State Executive Power' (2013) 36(2) *University of Western Australia Law Review* 145; Kathleen Foley, 'What is the Relevance of *Williams* and *Plaintiff M61* for the Exercise of State Executive Power?' (2013) 36(2) *University of Western Australia Law Review* 168.
**66** See further Chapter 7, Part IV.2.
**67** Chapter 1, Part II.1.

Gradually, the colonists' desire for self-government, under representative and responsible governmental principles, resulted in the reduction of the initially expansive powers of the colonial Governors. The colonies of Victoria and New South Wales were the first to have their autochthonous Constitutions,[68] scheduled to Imperial enactments, moving beyond the governance forms contemplated by the *Australian Constitutions Act 1842* (Imp) and the *Australian Constitutions Act (No 2) 1850* (Imp). These constitutional documents saw the introduction of bicameral colonial parliaments, which while not entirely representative,[69] had greater legislative powers (including constitutional amendment powers) although these were ultimately subject to the greater powers of the UK Parliament. The constitutions of these two States are now found in the *Constitution Act 1902* (NSW) and the *Constitution Act 1975* (Vic), respectively.

Although becoming an independent colony in 1825, Tasmania (or Van Diemen's Land as it was then called) did not obtain its own constitution and representative bicameral parliament until the end of convict transportation in the 1850s. When transportation ceased, the Legislative Council passed, pursuant to the *Australian Constitutions Act 1850 (No 2)* (Imp), a Constitution Act which subsequently received the royal assent[70] and which established a representative upper and lower house, designed to operate on the basis of the principle of responsible government. Even after the legislative consolidation of this constitution into the *Constitution Act 1934* (Tas), it is accepted that Tasmanian Parliament's legislative powers still derive from the *Australian Constitutions Act (No 2) 1850* (Imp).[71]

South Australia also attained, through the *Australian Constitutions Act 1850 (No 2)* (Imp), a bicameral parliament which subsequently enacted the *Constitution Act 1855–56* (SA), following an initial failed attempt to get royal assent for a more expansive constitution. The newly formed South Australian Parliament was comprised of elected and responsible parliamentary members. The State's constitution is now in the *Constitution Act 1934* (SA).

Uniquely, an 1859 Imperial Order in Council was responsible for the establishment of Queensland as a separate colony and for the establishment of its first dyadic or bicameral Parliament, mirroring that existing in New South Wales. This Queensland Parliament then enacted the *Constitution Act 1867* (Qld).[72] Significant constitutional changes, such as the abolition of the Queensland

**68** *Constitution Act 1855* (NSW) and *Constitution Act 1855* (Vic) were scheduled to the 18 and 19 Vict c 54 and 18 and 19 Vict c 55, respectively: see generally Anne Twomey, *The Constitution of New South Wales* (Federation Press, 2004), ch 1; Greg Taylor, *The Constitution of Victoria* (Federation Press, 2006) ch 2; R D Lumb, *The Constitutions of the Australian States* (University of Queensland Press, 1991); Carney, above n 11, ch 2.

**69** The New South Wales lower house was elected (albeit, with a restrictive franchise) while its upper house were appointed by the Governor.

**70** *Constitution Act 1856* (Tas).

**71** *Strachan v Graves* (1997) 141 FLR 283, 289 discussed in David Clark, *Principles of Australian Public Law* (LexisNexis, 3rd ed, 2010) 127.

**72** See s 13 of the *Australia Acts 1986* (Cth & UK).

Legislative Council, were consolidated into the *Constitution of Queensland Act 2001* (Qld).

Western Australia was the last colony to obtain its own Constitution. This was partly due to reservations about the colony's readiness for self-government, the late cessation of convict arrivals, various legal uncertainties and the implications of the colony governing such a large tract of land.[73] The Constitution Bill 1889, passed by the colony's Parliament, was eventually introduced (with minor modification) as a Schedule to an enabling Imperial Act, the *Western Australian Constitution Act 1890* (Imp). On this basis it followed most closely the New South Wales and Victorian constitutional enactment experience. The *Constitution Act Amendment Act 1889* (WA) was, in 1899, complemented by the *Constitution Act 1899* (WA), which among other things changed the composition of the legislature. These Acts have not been consolidated, leaving Western Australia with two working Constitution Acts.[74]

Several of the State Constitutions contain provisions or a preamble recognising the State's Aboriginal inhabitants as the 'first people' of that State.[75] For instance s 2 of the *Constitution Act 1902* (NSW) provides:

(1) Parliament, on behalf of the people of New South Wales, acknowledges and honours the Aboriginal people as the State's first people and nations.

(2) Parliament, on behalf of the people of New South Wales, recognises that Aboriginal people, as the traditional custodians and occupants of the land in New South Wales:

 (a) have a spiritual, social, cultural and economic relationship with their traditional lands and waters, and

 (b) have made and continue to make a unique and lasting contribution to the identity of the State.

(3) Nothing in this section creates any legal right or liability, or gives rise to or affects any civil cause of action or right to review an administrative action, or affects the interpretation of any Act or law in force in New South Wales.

Typically, this provision includes a 'no effect' clause (in this case, s 2(3)) which seeks to remove the legal force or effect of this recognition for any other Act or cause of action.[76]

Significantly, the scope of a State's Constitution travels further than the Constitution Acts alone.[77] Other 'constitutional' legislation addresses issues of vital

**73** See Carney, above n 11, 50–51; Sarah Murray and James Thomson, 'A Western Australian Constitution? Documents, Difficulties and Dramatis Personae' (2013) 36(2) *University of Western Australia Law Review* 1.

**74** For a discussion as to the reasons for this see: Sarah Murray and James Thomson, 'A Western Australian Constitution? Documents, Difficulties and Dramatis Personae' (2013) 36(2) *University of Western Australia Law Review* 1, 27–9. Note that the *Constitution Act 1889* (WA) was also amended by s 14 of the *Australia Acts 1986* (Cth & UK).

**75** *Constitution Act 1902* (NSW), s 2; *Constitution of Queensland Act 2001* (Qld), Preamble, s 3A; *Constitution Act 1975* (Vic), s 1A; *Constitution Act 1934* (SA), s 2.

**76** Megan Davis and Zrinka Lemezina, 'Indigenous Australians and the Preamble: Towards a More Inclusive Constitution or Entrenching Marginalisation?' (2010) 33 *University of New South Wales Law Journal* 239.

**77** George Winterton, 'Australian States: Cinderellas No Longer?' in George Winterton, *State Constitutional Landmarks* (Federation Press, 2006) 1, 2.

importance, such as laws dealing with the electoral system, the Parliament and the judicial system (especially the State Supreme Court). This suite of constitutional legislation is, subject to applicable valid and binding manner and form provisions,[78] able to be more readily amended than the Commonwealth Constitution. There are also British enactments such as the *Australia Acts 1986* (Cth & UK) that are fundamental to the Constitution of each State. The *Australia Acts 1986* was a significant constitutional step in terms of the States' legislative independence and powers. Prior to its enactment the States were still technically regarded as 'self-governing colonial dependencies',[79] ultimately subject to the legislative supremacy of the Imperial Parliament.[80] The *Australia Acts* removed the UK Parliament's legislative powers in relation to the States and, by s 3(1), ended the repugnancy restrictions to which State Parliaments had been subject by the *Colonial Laws Validity Act 1865* (UK).[81]

## 2 Government structure

The States, like the Commonwealth, each have a 'Parliament'.[82] The Parliaments structurally comprise one or two houses of parliament[83] along with the 'Queen'.[84] Members of the State lower houses (called the Legislative Assembly or House of Assembly) are typically elected for four-year (mostly fixed) terms,[85] except for Queensland's three-year terms.[86] The Legislative Councils' terms vary.[87] Eligibility to be elected as a State Parliamentarian is determined by electoral and parliamentary legislation, together with constitutional provisions,[88] as is the eligibility to vote.[89]

As discussed in Chapter 2, in *Roach*,[90] the High Court, by majority, held that ss 7 and 24 of the Commonwealth Constitution limit the Commonwealth

**78** See Part IV.4 below.
**79** Twomey, above n 37, 19.
**80** See, eg, *China Ocean Shipping Co v South Australia* (1979) 145 CLR 172, 184.
**81** *Sue v Hill* (1999) 199 CLR 462, [59].
**82** *Constitution Act 1902* (NSW), s 3; *Constitution Act 1867* (Qld), s 2A; *Constitution Act 1934* (Tas), s 10; *Constitution Act 1975* (Vic), s 15; *Constitution Act 1889* (WA), s 2(2). Cf *Constitution Act 1934* (SA), s 4.
**83** *Constitution Act Amendment Act 1922* (Qld): Carney, above n 11, 77.
**84** Note, however, the exceptions of Tasmania (which refers to the 'Governor' in s 10 of the *Constitution Act 1934* (Tas)) and South Australia (which refers to neither the Queen nor the Governor in its definition of Parliament in s 4 of the *Constitution Act 1934* (SA), however, royal assent is part of the process for the enactment of a law).
**85** *Constitution Act 1902* (NSW), ss 24B, 7A; *Constitution Act 1934* (Tas), ss 23, 41A; *Constitution Act 1975* (Vic), ss 8, 8A, 18(2)(a); *Constitution Acts Amendment Act 1899* (WA), s 21; *Electoral Act 1907* (WA), s 64; *Constitution Act 1934* (SA), ss 28 and 28A. See also Peter Congdon, 'In a Fix: Fixed-Term Parliaments in the Australian States' (2013) 41 *Federal Law Review* 265.
**86** *Constitution Act Amendment Act 1890* (Qld), s 2; *Constitution Act Amendment Act 1934* (Qld), s 4.
**87** *Constitution Act 1902* (NSW), s 22B; *Constitution Act 1934* (SA), s 14; *Constitution Act 1975* (Vic), s 28(2); *Constitution Acts Amendment Act 1899* (WA), s 8(2); *Constitution Act 1934* (Tas), s 19.
**88** *Constitution Act 1902* (NSW), ss 13, 13A; *Constitution Act 1975* (Vic), s 44; *Constitution Act 1934* (SA), ss 17, 31; *Electoral Act 1907* (WA), ss 76A, 76B; *Constitution Acts Amendment Act 1899* (WA), Div 3; *Constitution of Queensland Act 2001* (Qld), s 21; *Parliament of Queensland Act 2001* (Qld), s 64; *Constitution Act 1934* (Tas), s 14.
**89** *Parliamentary Electorates and Elections Act 1912* (NSW), Part 3B; *Electoral Act 1992* (Qld), s 64; *Constitution Act 1975* (Vic), ss 48, 18(2)(e); *Electoral Act 1985* (SA), s 29; *Electoral Act 1907* (WA), ss 17, 18; *Electoral Act 1992* (Qld), s 64; *Electoral Act 2004* (Tas), s 31.
**90** *Roach v Electoral Commissioner* (2007) 233 CLR 162.

Parliament's legislative powers to regulate the Commonwealth franchise in ways that are not consistent with a 'direct choice by the people'. On that basis, the decision invalidated an amendment to the *Commonwealth Electoral Act 1918* (Cth) which prevented an elector from voting in House of Representatives or Senate elections if they were serving a prison sentence for committing an offence against a Commonwealth, State or Territory law. This invalidation meant that the *Commonwealth Electoral Act 1918* (Cth) reverted to its prior incarnation of disenfranchising prisoners subject to a prison term of three years or more. Subsequently, the Western Australian Parliament amended the *Electoral Act 1907* (WA) to remove the 'blanket ban' on all prisoners voting so that only prison terms of greater than one year would exclude potential voters. During debate of the amending Western Australian Bill it was stated:

> The government has received and accepted legal advice that a blanket ban on all sentenced prisoners being prevented from voting in state elections is unconstitutional.[91]

This advice presumably relies upon s 73(2)(c) in the *Constitution Act 1889* (WA), which is protected by a manner and form provision, and refers to WA parliamentary members being 'directly chosen by the people'.[92]

The office of Governor in each State, as confirmed by s 7(1) of the *Australia Acts 1986* (Cth & UK), is the Queen's Representative.[93] If the Queen is not in Australia,[94] all the Queen's powers are exercisable only by the Governor (such as the power to assent to Bills, to summon or dissolve parliament), other than the power to appoint or terminate the appointment of the Governor.[95] Historically, the Governors directly exercised considerable legal power in the colonies; however, this was modified after the establishment of responsible and representative government. The office of Governor is regulated by Letters Patent as well as State constitutional provisions,[96] which in some States are entrenched by manner and form provisions.[97] The Governor is appointed by the Queen on the advice of the Premier, and generally acts only on ministerial advice.[98]

State Constitutions expressly refer to the Judiciary. Even so, the States are typically seen to lack the formal separation of judicial power from legislative

**91** Hansard, Western Australian Legislative Council (11 November 2008), 59b.

**92** See, also *Stephens v West Australian Newspapers Ltd* (1994) 182 CLR 211, *McGinty v Western Australia* (1996) 186 CLR 140 and *Muldowney v South Australia* (1996) 186 CLR 352, discussed in Chapter 2, Part II.3 and Chapter 5, Part V.2, concerning similar implications said to be derived from the Western Australian and South Australian Constitutions.

**93** See Chapter 6. The legal designation of the office of the 'Queen', along with the abandonment of the fiction of the indivisibility of the Crown, has led to differing views as to whether there is one Crown or multiple Crowns across Australia; however, the Queen is at least acting in different capacities when taking advice from responsible ministers for the Commonwealth and each of the Australian States: Anne Twomey, *The Australia Acts 1986 – Australia's Statutes of Independence* (Federation Press, 2010) 457–75. See also *Sue v Hill* (1999) 199 CLR 462, [165].

**94** *Australia Acts 1986* (Cth & UK), s 7(4).

**95** *Australia Acts 1986* (Cth & UK), s 7(3).

**96** See, eg, *Constitution Act 1902* (NSW), Part 2A.

**97** See, eg, *Constitution Act 1889* (WA), ss 50 and s 51 are protected by s 73(2)(e); *Constitution Act 1975* (Vic), Part 1 which is protected by s 18(2)(a); *Constitution Act 1867* (Qld), ss 11A, 11B, 2A(2), protected by s 53.

**98** See Chapter 6, Part IV.2. See, eg, *Constitution Act 1902* (NSW), s 35A.

and executive powers[99] that Chapter III entrenches for the High Court and federal courts. However, as detailed in Chapter 9, a degree of de facto separation in the States is guaranteed by Chapter III the Commonwealth Constitution and the role it contemplates for 'court[s] of a State'. Additionally, some commentators have argued that the double entrenchment of Supreme Court functions in some State constitutions[100] provides, at least, a degree of separation for the judiciary in those jurisdictions.[101]

## 3 Plenary legislative power

The State Constitutions confer powers on the State legislatures to make laws 'for the peace, order and good government'[102] or the 'peace, welfare and good government'[103] of the State, or in Victoria, to make laws 'in and for Victoria in all cases whatsoever'.[104] Australian Courts have held that there are no legal distinctions between these textual variants.[105] Unlike s 51 of the Commonwealth Constitution,[106] the State parliamentary conferrals are *not* followed by a list of subjects 'with respect to' which the State Parliaments can make laws.[107] Therefore, State legislative power is in principle 'ample and plenary',[108] although subject to any specific State and Commonwealth constitutional limitations that may apply.[109]

State Parliaments can amend their Constitutions, subject to any applicable valid and binding manner and form provisions. This amending power is contemplated by the reference in s 106 to alterations made 'in accordance with the Constitution of the State'. It was originally conferred by the particular British statutes and other instruments which first established the colonial Parliaments, and was confirmed by the *Colonial Laws Validity Act 1865* (UK), and more recently by the *Australia Acts 1986* (Cth & UK). The decision of the Privy Council in

**99** See, eg, *Building Construction Employees and Builders Labourers' Federation (NSW) v Minister for Industrial Relations* (1986) 7 NSWLR 372, 381, 401, 407, 408–9, 412, 419; *City of Collingwood v Victoria (No 2)* [1994] 1 VR 652, 663; *Kable v Director of Public Prosecutions (NSW)* (1996) 189 CLR 51, 67, 77–8, 93, 109, 118, 132.

**100** See, eg, *Constitution Act 1889* (WA), 73(6); *Constitution Act 1975* (Vic), s 18(2AA).

**101** Peter Johnston, 'Going it Alone – Republican States under a Monarchical Commonwealth' in Murray, above n 31, 82, 101; Cheryl Saunders, 'The Separation of Powers' in Brian Opeskin and Fiona Wheeler (eds), *The Australian Federal Judicial System* (Melbourne University Press, 2000) 18.

**102** *Constitution Act 1889* (WA), s 2(1).

**103** *Constitution Act 1902* (NSW), s 5; *Constitution Act 1867* (Qld), s 2 (which by *Constitution of Queensland Act 2001* (Qld), s 3, remains in force). The Tasmanian and South Australian equivalent is found in s 7 of the *Australian Constitutions Act (No 2) 1850* (Imp) to which the *Constitution Act 1934* (Tas) (preamble – 'peace, welfare and good government') and *Constitution Act 1934* (SA), s 5, refer.

**104** *Constitution Act 1975* (Vic), s 16.

**105** *Union Steamship Co of Australia Pty Ltd v King* (1988) 166 CLR 1, 9; *Mobil Oil Australia Pty Ltd v Victoria* (2002) 211 CLR 1, [46].

**106** Which refers to the power to make laws 'for the peace, order and good government of the Commonwealth'.

**107** Cf Commonwealth Constitution, ss 51, 52.

**108** See eg, *Union Steamship Co of Australia Pty Ltd v King* (1988) 166 CLR 1, 9–10, referring to *R v Burah* (1878) 3 App Cas 889; *Hodge v The Queen* (1883) 9 App Cas 117; *Powell v Apollo Candle Co* (1885) 10 App Cas 282; *Riel v The Queen* (1885) 10 App Cas 675. See also *McCawley v The King* [1920] AC 691, 712.

**109** Such as those which apply from the Commonwealth Constitution and the *Australia Acts 1986* (Cth & UK). See Part IV.4 below.

*McCawley's* case is the classic judicial exegesis of the typically flexible nature of the State Constitutions.[110] This case concerned the validity of the *Industrial Arbitration Act 1916* (Qld) which was said to alter the *Constitution Act 1867* (Qld) in allowing Supreme Court judges to be appointed from the Court of Industrial Arbitration, for which appointees had seven-year terms. This contradicted provisions of the *Constitution Act 1867* (Qld) which granted Supreme Court judges life tenure. The case was first brought in the Queensland Supreme Court and was appealed to the High Court, and ultimately to the Privy Council.

The majority and minority judgments in the High Court differed in relation to the general constitutional theory by which the relevant provisions should be interpreted. In their majority judgments, Griffith CJ and Barton J leaned towards treating the *Constitution Act* as a kind of fundamental law that would place constraints on the powers of the Parliament. Although they could not deny that the *Constitution Act* was in the nature of an ordinary statute of the Parliament and therefore subject to its ordinary legislative powers, they associated the protections of judicial tenure contained in the Act with the British instruments from which they were derived, and proposed that such provisions could only be amended explicitly and directly. On the other hand, in their minority judgments, Isaacs and Higgins JJ preferred to regard the colonial legislatures as having been granted 'plenary powers of legislation as large, and of the same nature, as those of [the Imperial] Parliament itself'.[111]

When the matter was taken to the Judicial Committee of the Privy Council, the High Court was overruled,[112] their Lordships unequivocally finding that the Queensland Parliament possessed 'full power' to amend the Constitution of Queensland simply by legislating inconsistently with it.[113] In finding the legislation valid, Lord Birkenhead LC declared: '[i]t is of the greatest importance to notice that where the Constitution is uncontrolled the consequences of its freedom admit of no qualification whatever'.[114] The Lord Chancellor continued:

> It was not the policy of the Imperial Legislature, at any relevant period, to shackle or control in the manner suggested the legislative powers of the nascent Australian Legislatures. Consistently with the genius of the British people, what was given was given completely, and unequivocally, in the belief, fully justified by the event, that these young communities would successfully work out their own constitutional salvation ... The Legislature of Queensland is the master of its own household, except in so far as its powers have in special cases been restricted.[115]

**110** *McCawley v The King* [1920] AC 691. See Nicholas Aroney, 'Politics, Law and the Constitution in McCawley's Case' (2006) 30 *Melbourne University Law Review* 605.
**111** *McCawley v The King* (1918) 26 CLR 9, 64–5, citing *R v Burah* (1873) 3 App Cas 889, 904–5.
**112** *McCawley v The King* [1920] AC 691.
**113** Ibid, 701, 714.
**114** Ibid, 704. Cf, for example, *McCawley v The King* (1918) 26 CLR 9, 21 (discussed in detail in Aroney, above n 110, 636 ff).
**115** *McCawley v The King* [1920] AC 691, 706. Cf this with the position if the State Constitutions were to be re-introduced via popular referendum as 'fundamental laws': Nicholas Aroney, 'Popular Ratification of the State Constitutions' in Paul Kildea, Andrew Lynch and George Williams (eds), *Tomorrow's Federation – Reforming Australian Government* (Federation Press, 2012) 210.

The decision of the Privy Council in *McCawley* thus affirmed the plenary legislative powers of the State Parliaments and the flexibility of the State Constitutions in emphatic terms. Although a majority of the High Court had disagreed, the view of the Privy Council prevailed, not least because it cohered with the general approach to interpreting grants of legislative power that would be adopted by a differently constituted High Court in the landmark *Engineers* case in 1920.[116]

## 4 Restrictions on legislative power

As explored in earlier chapters, there are restrictions on State Parliaments deriving from the Commonwealth Constitution[117] as well as the *Australia Acts 1986* (Cth and UK).[118] State constitutions can also limit the kinds of laws that State Parliaments can enact, through limitations on the legislative amendment powers of the upper house,[119] or by manner and form provisions which are found to be valid and binding.[120] This section will discuss these forms of limitation and conclude by exploring the degree to which a federal or State based implied freedom of political communication is relevant to the States. But before turning to those issues, it is convenient to consider whether there are any substantive limits on State legislative power that might be derived from the terms in which their legislative powers are conferred.

### Substantive limits?

In *Union Steamship*,[121] the High Court probed the important constitutional question of whether 'peace, order [or welfare] and good government' could operate as a substantive constraint on the kinds of laws a State Parliament could enact. In other words, did the Courts have the constitutional power to invalidate State legislation on the basis of it not being conducive to 'peace, order [or welfare] and good government'? In rejecting the comments of some members of the New South Wales Court of Appeal in the *BLF* case,[122] the unanimous judgment of the Hight Court held that these were not 'words of limitation' because:

> [t]hey did not confer on the courts of a colony, just as they do not confer on the courts of a State, jurisdiction to strike down legislation on the ground that, in the opinion of a court, the legislation does not promote or secure the peace, order and good government of the colony.[123]

**116** *Amalgamated Society of Engineers v Adelaide Steamship Co Ltd* (1920) 28 CLR 129.
**117** Eg, Chapter III, ss 92, 109.
**118** Eg, ss 6 and 9.
**119** See, eg, *Constitution Act 1934* (Tas), s 42; *Constitution Acts Amendment Act 1899* (WA), s 46.
**120** See discussion in Part IV.4.
**121** *Union Steamship Co of Australia Pty Ltd v King* (1988) 166 CLR 1.
**122** *Building Construction Employees and Builders Labourers' Federation (NSW) v Minister for Industrial Relations* (1986) 7 NSWLR 372, 384, 421. Cf 413; 406 (the example cited here, at 402, related to Parliament dictating that 'all blue-eyed babies should be murdered').
**123** *Union Steamship Co of Australia Pty Ltd v King* (1988) 166 CLR 1, 10. See also *Kable v Director of Public Prosecutions (NSW)* (1996) 189 CLR 51, 75–6 (where Dawson J held that such a principle would run counter to the notion of parliamentary sovereignty: 'a doctrine as deeply rooted as any in the common law').

Having said this, the Court left open the question whether there were some limits derived from 'rights deeply rooted in our democratic system of government and the common law'.[124]

In *Durham Holdings*,[125] the Court had to determine whether the NSW Parliament has legislative power to acquire land without just compensation and whether such legislation would infringe some 'deeply rooted' right to that effect. The joint judgment indicated that such an implication would go beyond the terms of s 2(2) of the *Australia Acts 1986* (Cth and UK) and would 'involve modification of the arrangements which comprise the Constitutions of the States within the meaning of s 106 of the Constitution, and by which the State legislatures are erected and maintained, and exercise their powers'.[126] More recently, in *Totani*, French CJ observed of this enigmatic issue that:

> [w]hatever the answer to th[is] unexplored question, it is self-evidently beyond the power of the courts to maintain unimpaired common law freedoms which the Commonwealth Parliament or a State Parliament, acting within its constitutional powers, has, by clear statutory language, abrogated, restricted or qualified.[127]

It therefore seems unlikely that judicial support for a 'deeply rooted rights' limitation will revive sufficiently to allow judicial invalidation of State legislation on this ground alone.[128] As Kirby J explained in *Durham Holdings*, judicial review should tend to focus upon 'the observance of parliamentary procedures and the conformity of the resulting law with the State and federal Constitutions' and not rely upon a 'judge's own notions of fundamental rights, apart from those constitutionally established'.[129]

### Extra-territoriality

While State Parliaments have extra-territorial legislative power, they are limited in terms of their ability to make laws of extra-territorial effect without some connection to the State concerned.[130] The conferral of powers to make laws for the 'peace, order [or welfare], and good government' *of each State* have been interpreted as words which, while not proscribing extra-territorial laws altogether, impose a degree of territorial limitation. This means that a State law which applies beyond the boundaries of the State is likely to be read down (where this is possible), unless there is a relevant connection between the State and the extra-territorial subject of the law.

**124** *Union Steamship Co of Australia Pty Ltd v King* (1988) 166 CLR 1, 10; a notion rejected by Lord Reid in *Pickin v British Railways Board* [1974] AC 765, 782.
**125** *Durham Holdings Pty Ltd v New South Wales* (2001) 205 CLR 399.
**126** Ibid, [13]. Kirby J agreed in a separate judgment (at [63]), but see [74]–[75] as to implications deriving from the Commonwealth Constitution's reference to 'laws of a State'; see further George Winterton, 'Justice Kirby's Coda in Durham' (2002) 13 *Public Law Review* 165.
**127** *South Australia v Totani* (2010) 242 CLR 1, [31].
**128** Cf Crennan and Kiefel JJ's equivocal suggestion in *Momcilovic* that there might be a place for the 'rule of law' as a limit on State and federal legislatures: *Momcilovic v The Queen* (2011) 245 CLR 1, [562]–[563].
**129** *Durham Holdings Pty Ltd v New South Wales* (2001) 205 CLR 399, [61].
**130** Although see comments of Gibbs J in *Pearce v Florenca* (prior to the *Australia Acts 1986* (Cth and UK)) as to whether the State Parliaments have the ability to remove this constitutional limitation: (1976) 135 CLR 507, 515.

The ability of State Parliaments to make laws with extra-territorial operation was further elaborated in the *Australia Acts 1986* (Cth & UK). Section 2(1) of the Acts provide:

> It is hereby declared and enacted that the legislative powers of the Parliament of each State include full power to make laws for the peace, order and good government of that State that have extra-territorial operation.

Additionally, s 2(2) states:

> It is hereby further declared and enacted that the legislative powers of the Parliament of each State include all legislative powers that the Parliament of the United Kingdom might have exercised before the commencement of this Act for the peace, order and good government of that State but nothing in this subsection confers on a State any capacity that the State did not have immediately before the commencement of this Act to engage in relations with countries outside Australia.[131]

Section 2(2) thus confirms that State Parliaments are in the possession of all of the legislative powers which were previously the province of the United Kingdom Parliament, subject to the Commonwealth Constitution (as s 5 of the *Australia Acts 1986* (Cth & UK) provides).

In cases like *Commissioner of Stamp Duties (NSW) v Millar*[132] and *Welker v Hewett*[133] the High Court held that the subject matter of the legislation in question had too remote a connection with the enacting State for it to be constitutionally valid. In *Millar*, the New South Wales law sought to apply death duty to any shareholder, wherever located, who died while the owner of shares in a company that carried on certain categories of business within New South Wales. In *Welker*, a road levy extended to the director of any company whose vehicles were driven on New South Wales roads.

In *Broken Hill South Ltd v Commissioner of Taxation (NSW)*,[134] the High Court confirmed the validity of a New South Wales taxing Act which levied tax on income 'derived or deemed to be derived directly or indirectly from any source in the State' and included 'interest upon money secured by the mortgage of any property in the State'. In a much quoted passage, Dixon J stated:

> The important question remains whether the attempt to include in the income liable to tax interest on money secured by the mortgage of any property in New South Wales exceeds the territorial limitations upon the legislative power. The power to make laws for the peace, order and good government of a State does not enable the State Parliament to impose by reference to some act, matter or thing occurring outside the State a liability upon a person unconnected with the State whether by domicil, residence or otherwise. But it is within the competence of the State legislature to make any fact, circumstance, occurrence or thing in or connected with the territory the occasion of

**131** For debate as to whether s 2 expands or confirms State extra-territorial power see Christopher Gilbert, 'Extraterritorial State Laws and the Australia Acts' (1987) 17 *Federal Law Review* 25, 35; Mark Moshinsky, 'State Extraterritorial Legislation and the Australia Acts 1986' (1987) 61 *Australian Law Journal* 779; Twomey, above n 93, 213.
**132** (1932) 48 CLR 618.
**133** (1969) 120 CLR 503.
**134** (1937) 56 CLR 337.

> the imposition upon any person concerned therein of a liability to taxation or of any other liability. It is also within the competence of the legislature to base the imposition of liability on no more than the relation of the person to the territory. The relation may consist in presence within the territory, residence, domicil, carrying on business there, or even remoter connections. *If a connection exists, it is for the legislature to decide how far it should go in the exercise of its powers ... it is of no importance upon the question of validity that the liability imposed is, or may be, altogether disproportionate to the territorial connection* or that it includes many cases that cannot have been foreseen.
>
> In the present case no relation between the territory and the person, as distinguished from the transaction to which he is a party, is made the occasion of the tax. The thing in respect of which the taxpayer is made liable is the interest on money borrowed or otherwise owing. The imposition of the liability is based upon the fact that a security exists under the law of New South Wales over property in New South Wales for the repayment of the money. In my opinion this connection is sufficient. The interest grows out of the debt. If the creditor chooses to avail himself of rights in property conferred by the law of New South Wales in respect of land or chattels under the authority of the legislature, the law of New South Wales can impose upon him any liability which is relevant to the purpose of his doing so; and the purpose of his doing so is to secure repayment of the moneys.[135]

This classic extra-territorial connection test was applied by Gibbs J in *Pearce v Florenca*.[136] That decision concerned the Western Australian Parliament's ability to make laws regulating fishing off the State's coast. Gibbs J held that the test should be 'liberally applied' and that it was clearly met in *Pearce* when all that was required by that test was 'any real connection – even just a remote or general connection – between the subject matter of the legislation and the State'.[137]

*Union Steamship* confirmed that the Australian States have clear extra-territorial legislative competence, as did their colonial predecessors.[138] However, the Court agreed with Gibbs J's approach in *Pearce v Florenca* that there remained a 'territorial limitation', even after the *Australia Acts*, 'however slight that limitation may be'.[139] In *Union Steamship*, the question was whether the *Workers' Compensation Act 1926* (NSW) extended to an employee solely because they were rendered deaf while working on a ship registered in New South Wales. The Court held that there was a sufficient connection between the State and the enacted law.

While its extent is unclear, there is some suggestion that State Parliaments may be subject to implied territorial limits deriving from the Commonwealth Constitution's federal structure[140] which, absent an equivalent provision to

**135** *Broken Hill South Ltd v Commissioner of Taxation (NSW)* (1937) 56 CLR 337, 375 (emphasis added).
**136** (1976) 135 CLR 507.
**137** *Pearce v Florenca* (1976) 135 CLR 507, 518.
**138** *Union Steamship Co of Australia Pty Ltd v King* (1988) 166 CLR 1, 12.
**139** Ibid, 14.
**140** Twomey notes that s 2 of the *Australia Acts 1986* is constrained by the Commonwealth Constitution (see s 5 of the *Australia Acts*): Twomey, above n 93, 213.

s 109,[141] limits a State legislature's ability to pass laws which impair the operation of another State.[142] How this principle might interact with earlier case law is uncertain. However, it is clear that this federal structural limitation would not extend to all State laws having implications for another State. As Gleeson CJ explained in *Mobil Oil Australia Pty Ltd*:

> There is nothing either uncommon, or antithetical to the federal structure, about legislation of one State that has legal consequences for persons or conduct in another State or Territory. ... The idea that all transactions and relationships giving rise to legal consequences can be located 'in' one particular State or Territory is unrealistic.[143]

It should also be noted that the uncertainty surrounding State offshore legislative competence following the offshore boundary determination in *New South Wales v Commonwealth*[144] was addressed by the Offshore Constitutional Settlement. This included among other legislation, the *Coastal Waters (State Powers) Act 1980* (Cth) enacted pursuant to s 51(xxxviii) of the Commonwealth Constitution.[145] The *Coastal Waters (State Powers) Act 1980* (Cth) confirmed State legislative power to make laws (with some more generous legislative powers for mining, shipping facilities and fisheries) within the territorial sea boundary stretching outwards three nautical miles from a State's coast.[146] Section 5 provides:

> The legislative powers exercisable from time to time under the constitution of each State extend to the making of:
> (a) all such laws of the State as could be made by virtue of those powers if the coastal waters of the State, as extending from time to time, were within the limits of the State, including laws applying in or in relation to the sea-bed and subsoil beneath, and the airspace above, the coastal waters of the State;
> (b) laws of the State having effect in or in relation to waters within the adjacent area in respect of the State but beyond the outer limits of the coastal waters of the State, including laws applying in or in relation to the sea-bed and subsoil beneath, and the airspace above, the first-mentioned waters, being laws with respect to:
> (i) subterranean mining from land within the limits of the State; or
> (ii) ports, harbours and other shipping facilities, including installations, and dredging and other works, relating thereto, and other coastal works; and

**141** Commonwealth Constitution.
**142** *Union Steamship Co of Australia Pty Ltd v King* (1988) 166 CLR 1, 14; *Durham Holdings Pty Ltd v New South Wales* (2001) 205 CLR 399, [14]; *Mobil Oil Australia Pty Ltd v Victoria* (2002) 211 CLR 1, [15]-[16]; [47]; [131], [133], [138]-[141], [177]; *BHP Billiton v Shultz* (2004) 221 CLR 440, [200]. See further Carney, above n 11, ch 7.
**143** *Mobil Oil Australia Pty Ltd v Victoria* (2002) 211 CLR 1, [16].
**144** (1975) 135 CLR 337.
**145** See *Port Macdonnell Professional Fishermen's Association Inc v South Australia* (1989) 168 CLR 340.
**146** See further: Michael White, *Australian Offshore Laws* (Federation Press, 2009). This also closed off doubts relating to State Parliaments' offshore legislative powers following *Robinson v Western Australian Museum* (1977) 138 CLR 283.

(c) laws of the State with respect to fisheries in Australian waters beyond the outer limits of the coastal waters of the State, being laws applying to or in relation to those fisheries only to the extent to which those fisheries are, under an arrangement to which the Commonwealth and the State are parties, to be managed in accordance with the laws of the State.

## Manner and form provisions

Manner and form provisions are restrictive procedures which seek to make it procedurally more difficult for a Parliament to enact amending or repealing legislation.[147] 'Manner' provisions (procedures such as referendums and/or special legislative majorities) and 'form' provisions (which require express language to amend or repeal legislation, thus preventing implied legislative amendment or repeal) can be found in Constitution Acts[148] and in other pieces of legislation.[149] If manner and form provisions are valid and binding they can limit the ability of a Parliament to enact legislation inconsistently with the terms of the manner and form provision.[150] The imposition of such limits is constitutionally unproblematic when imposed by a superior legislature, such as the Imperial Parliament. The quandary presented by such provisions is why a prior Parliament should have the legal ability to compel a subsequent Parliament to follow a more onerous legislative procedure in order to amend or repeal a statute.[151]

The constitutional position of the Commonwealth and the States is different in relation to this question.[152] As noted in Chapter 3, while the capacity of the Commonwealth Parliament to adopt legally effective manner and form provisions is doubtful, the capacity of the State Parliaments to do so has been upheld in several decisions of the High Court. The most important constitutional basis for the effectiveness of manner and form provisions at a State level lies in provisions of the *Colonial Laws Validity Act* and the *Australia Acts*, both of which operate (or once operated) with paramount force within each State. Section 5 of the *Colonial Laws Validity Act* provided:

> Every colonial legislature shall have, and be deemed at all times to have had, full power within its jurisdiction to establish courts of judicature, and to abolish and reconstitute the same, and to alter the constitution thereof, and to make provision for the administration of justice therein; and every representative legislature shall, in respect to the colony under its jurisdiction, have, and be deemed at all times to have had, full power to make laws respecting the constitution, powers, and procedure of such

**147** See generally, Carney, above n 11, ch 6; Anne Twomey, 'Manner and Form' (Gilbert + Tobin Constitutional Law Conference, Sydney, 18 February 2005, <http://www.gtcentre.unsw.edu.au/sites/gtcentre.unsw.edu.au/files/mdocs/5_AnneTwomey.pdf>. See also discussion in relation to the Commonwealth Parliament in Chapter 3, Part II.1.

**148** Eg, *Constitution Act 1889* (WA), ss 73(1), (2); *Constitution Act 1902* (NSW), ss 7A, 7B; *Constitution Act 1975* (Vic), s 18.

**149** See, eg, *Western Australian Future Fund Act 2012* (WA), s 10.

**150** But see *Australia Acts 1986* (Cth & UK), s 14.

**151** *Attorney-General (WA) v Marquet* (2003) 217 CLR 545, [63]. See also H L A Hart, *The Concept of Law* (1994, 2nd ed) 149–50.

**152** See Chapter 3, Part II.1.

> legislature; provided that such laws shall have been passed in such manner and form as may from time to time be required by any Act of Parliament, letters patent, Order in Council, or colonial law for the time being in force in the said colony.

It was subsequently replaced by s 6 of the *Australia Acts*, which provides:

> a law made after the commencement of this Act by the Parliament of a State respecting the constitution, powers or procedure of the Parliament of the State shall be of no force or effect unless it is made in such manner and form as may from time to time be required by a law made by that Parliament, whether made before or after the commencement of this Act.

The basic reason for the effectiveness of manner and form provisions at a State level was expressed by Lord Birkenhead LC in *McCawley*, when he stated, '[t]he Legislature of Queensland is master of its own household, *except in so far as its powers have in special cases been restricted*'.[153] Manner and form requirements imposed by State Parliaments have been held to be legally effective due to the particular terms in which legislative power has been conferred by these provisions of the *Colonial Laws Validity Act* and *Australia Acts*.

In *Trethowan*, Dixon J concluded that the principles of parliamentary sovereignty did not resolve whether a manner and form provision applied to a Bill which sought to repeal the New South Wales Legislative Council. He stated:

> Sec. 7A of the *Constitution Act* assumes to require the approval of the majority of the electors as a condition which must be fulfilled before either a Bill for the abolition of the Legislative Council, or a Bill for the repeal of the provisions of sec. 7A which prescribe this requirement, may be presented for the royal assent or become a valid law. ... Thus the case depends upon the question whether the Bill for the repeal of sec. 7A may be presented for the royal assent and become a valid law without compliance with the condition which that section itself prescribes requiring that a Bill for its repeal shall first be approved by a majority of the electors. This question must be answered upon a consideration of the true meaning and effect of the written instruments from which the Parliament of New South Wales derives its legislative power. It is not to be determined by the direct application of the doctrine of parliamentary sovereignty, which gives to the Imperial Parliament its supremacy over the law. It is the law, derived mediately or immediately from the Imperial Parliament, which gives to the Legislature of New South Wales its powers, and it is that law which determines the extent of those powers and the conditions which govern their exercise.[154]

The effectiveness of manner and form provisions also depends upon their being sufficiently entrenched. For example, s 78 of the *Constitution of Queensland Act 2001* (Qld) provides that a referendum is necessary to 'en[d] the system of local government in Queensland'. So long as s 78 exists, the referendum requirement will apply. However, this could be side-stepped if the Queensland Parliament were to repeal or amend s 78 and then proceed to abolish local government.[155] To avoid this, the manner and form provision must itself be protected

**153** *McCawley v The King* [1920] AC 691, 714 (emphasis added).
**154** *Attorney-General (NSW) v Trethowan* (1931) 44 CLR 394, 425.
**155** Also see *Constitution Act 1934* (Tas), s 41A.

against repeal or amendment, and to avoid an infinite regress of manner and form requirements, the provision must be reflexive. This is referred to as 'double entrenchment'.[156] Such entrenchment is, for example, found in s 53 of the *Constitution Act 1867* (Qld), which expressly extends its application to itself. It provides:

> (1) A Bill that expressly or impliedly provides for the abolition of or alteration in the office of Governor or that expressly or impliedly in any way affects any of the following sections of this Act namely –
>
> sections 1, 2, 2A, 11A, 11B; and
>
> this section 53
>
> shall not be presented for assent by or in the name of the Queen unless it has first been approved by the electors in accordance with this section and a Bill so assented to consequent upon its presentation in contravention of this subsection shall be of no effect as an Act.

The validity of another manner and form provision, this time a Western Australian law, was considered by the High Court in *Attorney-General (WA) v Marquet*. The case concerned the validity and binding nature of an absolute majority requirement in s 13 of the *Electoral Districts Act 1947* (WA). Gleeson CJ, Gummow, Hayne and Heydon JJ explained that:

> Discussion of the application of manner and form provisions has provoked much debate about the theoretical underpinnings for their operation. Thus, to ask whether a Parliament has power to bind its successors by enacting a manner and form provision has, in the past, led into debates cast in the language of sovereignty or into philosophical debates about whether a generally expressed power includes power to relinquish part of it.[157]

Their Honours considered that the legislative powers of the Australian States are subject to Imperial or Commonwealth laws that require compliance with prior manner and form provisions.[158] The ability of State Parliaments themselves to enact manner and form provisions, and also to be bound by them, was confirmed by s 5 of the *Colonial Laws Validity Act* and later by s 6 of the *Australia Acts*. The majority observed:

> It is of particular importance to recognise that the *Australia Act* stands as a form of law to which the Parliament of Western Australia is relevantly subordinate. To the extent to which s 6 applies, the powers of the Parliament of Western Australia to legislate are confined. What has been seen as the conundrum of whether a body given general power to legislate can give up part of that power need not be resolved. By federal law, effect must be given to some manner and form provisions found in State legislation.[159]

**156** See, eg, *Constitution Act 1889* (WA), s 73(2); *Constitution Act 1902* (NSW), ss 7A, 7B.
**157** *Attorney-General (WA) v Marquet* (2003) 217 CLR 545, [63].
**158** Ibid, [65].
**159** Ibid, [68].

There are two primary issues which need to be addressed to determine whether a later Parliament is subject to the dictates of a prior manner and form provision.[160] The provision must be validly enacted, and it must be relevantly binding.

**Validity**

The validity of a manner and form provision is a multi-faceted inquiry. There are several matters to be considered. First, a manner and form provision might be invalid if it was not itself validly created. Invalid creation might arise because a manner and form provision did not itself comply with a relevant, prior, valid and binding manner and form provision. Second, there is limited judicial support for the view that constitutional manner and form provisions[161] need to comply (at the time of their introduction) with their own procedures for such provisions to be validly created. Gummow J in *McGinty* indicated that the only way to avoid this was for a constitutional manner and form provision to have been inserted by paramount force.[162] There is undoubted constitutional logic in Gummow J's approach.[163] However, in spite of being the subject of legislative prescription in some jurisdictions,[164] it has not been favoured by a majority of the High Court.[165]

Third, a provision might also be invalid if it amounts to a 'substantive restraint' on legislative power.[166] A substantive restraint differs from a manner and form provision in restraining parliaments from legislating, rather than just making the enactment of legislation more procedurally onerous. To the extent that a purported manner and form provision effectively prevents a parliament from legislating, it will be invalid. Typical examples of substantive restraints are extra-parliamentary requirements, such as requiring the consent of a company or other private entity to pass a law.[167] Referendums, although extra-parliamentary, by virtue of their democratic basis and involvement of the electorate, do not typically amount to a substantive restraint.[168] However, a very high special majority requirement either at a referendum or for a Bill to pass through Parliament may amount to a substantive restraint if the approval threshold means that obtaining the approval is a practical impossibility. The threshold at which a

**160** Note that the question of justiciability of a manner and form provision can also arise. But see *Constitution Act 1889* (WA), s 73(6).

**161** *McGinty v Western Australia* (1996) 186 CLR 140, 297.

**162** See eg, *Constitution Act 1889* (WA), s 73(1), which was attached as a Schedule to the *Western Australian Constitution Act 1890* (UK).

**163** Note also comment by Kirby J in *Attorney-General (WA) v Marquet* (2003) 217 CLR 545, [216] as to the 'constitutional legitimacy' of legislative 'restrictions' as inevitably needing to find 'their source in the approval of the electors of Australia'.

**164** For example, Twomey, above n 147, 10 refers to the *Australian Capital Territory (Self-Government) Act 1988* (Cth), s 26.

**165** *Attorney-General (WA) v Marquet* (2003) 217 CLR 545. Note also the broader view is supported by *McCawley v The King* (1920) 28 CLR 106.

**166** See generally, Carney, above n 11, 175ff.

**167** *Commonwealth Aluminium Corporation Ltd v Attorney-General (Qld)* [1976] Qd R 231; *West Lakes Ltd v South Australia* (1980) 25 SASR 389.

**168** *West Lakes Ltd v South Australia* (1980) 25 SASR 389, 397.

special majority transforms from a manner and form provision to a substantive restraint is not a bright line. Much will depend on the nature of the legislation which contains the provision. King CJ asserted in the *West Lakes* decision that more fundamental or 'constitutional' legislation could justify a higher majority because of the importance of the law being protected. His Honour explained:

> A question might arise as to whether a particular statutory provision is truly a manner and form provision, which must be observed . . . as a condition of the validity of the Act, or whether it is a limitation or restraint of substance, which would not invalidate legislation inconsistent with the limitation or restraint. . . . There must be a point at which a special majority provision would appear as an attempt to deprive the parliament of powers rather than as a measure to prescribe the manner or form of their exercise. This point might be reached more quickly where the legislative topic which is the subject of the requirement is not a fundamental constitutional provision. When one looks at extraparliamentary requirements, the difficulty of treating them as relating to manner and form becomes greater.[169]

If a protecting provision contains multiple procedures, some characterised as manner and form provisions and some characterised as substantive restraints, it may be that the offending substantive restraints can be severed from the relevant provision, rather than making the provision invalid in its entirety.

### Bindingness

Assuming that a manner and form provision is valid, it is then necessary to determine whether the provision will be binding on a subsequent enactment of the same Parliament. The High Court has proclaimed that 'at the very least in the field in which s 6 [of the *Australia Act*] operates',[170] it is probably the only source to render a manner and form provision binding on a later State Parliament. If s 6 applies, its terms require that the later law is of 'no force or effect'. As set out above, s 6 of the *Australia Acts 1986* (Cth & UK) requires the later 'law'[171] (the law seeking to amend or repeal the protected statutory provision) to be characterised as a law 'respecting the constitution, powers or procedures of the Parliament of the State'.

In *Marquet*, the High Court considered that the 'constitution...of the Parliament of the State' is not limited to the Parliament's 'nature and composition' and that:

> s 6 is not to be read as confined to laws which abolish a House, or altogether take away the 'representative' character of a State Parliament or one of its Houses. At least to some extent the 'constitution' of the Parliament extends to features which go to give it, and its Houses, a representative character. Thus, s 6 may be engaged in cases in which the legislation deals with matters that are encompassed by the general description 'representative' and go to give that word its application in the particular case. So, for example, an upper House whose members are elected in a single State-wide electorate

**169** Ibid, 396–7.
**170** *Attorney-General (WA) v Marquet* (2003) 217 CLR 545, [80].
**171** 'Law' rather than a 'Bill'.

> by proportional representation is differently constituted from an upper House whose members are separately elected in single member provinces by first past the post voting. Each may properly be described as a 'representative' chamber, but the parliament would be differently constituted if one form of election to the upper House were to be adopted in place of the other. Not every matter which touches the election of members of a Parliament is a matter affecting the Parliament's constitution.[172]

The scope of 'powers or procedure of the Parliament of the State' is less clear. One question presented is whether the fact that the later Act is affecting a manner and form provision means that the later Act can be characterised as respecting the 'powers or procedure' of Parliament.[173] As has been noted by some commentators,[174] the implications of such a broad application of the 'powers or procedure' category, make this approach unlikely. It would mean that the impact on a prior manner and form provision was sufficient for a law to come within s 6 of the *Australia Acts*, independently of the essential content of the subsequent law.[175] On this approach one would assume that all manner and form provisions would be rendered binding. The further question is whether the express, as opposed to the implied, repeal of a manner and form provision should change the characterisation of the later Act in terms of its character for the purpose of s 6.[176]

This scope of s 6 can have implications for a range of issues, including whether a later law seeking to abolish the State judiciary by standard procedures might be prevented from doing so by a pre-existing manner and form provision.[177] One question becomes whether such an amendment would restrict curial review of the 'powers or procedure' of parliaments and therefore result in the later amending law falling within the terms of s 6 of the *Australia Acts* and hence being bound by the manner and form provision.

Consider also the extra-constitutional manner and form provision in the *Western Australian Future Fund Act 2012* (WA). This Act is designed to ensure that the benefits of the mining boom are accumulated for the future and ss 6, 7, 8, and 9 relate to the crediting and application of the Future Fund set up under the Act. Section 10(2) of the Act provides:

> A Bill to repeal or amend section 6, 7, 8 or 9 or this section must not be presented for assent by or in the name of the Queen during the accumulation period unless the second and third readings of the Bill have been passed with the concurrence of an absolute majority of the whole number of the members for the time being of the Legislative Council and Legislative Assembly respectively.

**172** *Attorney-General (WA) v Marquet* (2003) 217 CLR 545, [76]–[77].

**173** See, eg, *Commonwealth Aluminium Corporation Ltd v Attorney-General (Qld)* [1976] Qd R 231, 248 (Hoare J, dissenting, who saw the implied repeal of an earlier manner and form provision as sufficient for the 'constitution, powers or procedures' requirement to be satisfied).

**174** For example, Twomey, above n 147, 6–7; Suri Ratnapala, *Australian Constitutional Law: Foundations and Theory* (Oxford University Press, 2nd ed, 2007) 342.

**175** Ratnapala, above n 174, 342.

**176** Compare Jeffrey Goldsworthy, 'Manner and Form in the Australian States' (1987) 16 *Melbourne University Law Review* 403 and Carney, above n 11, 165–6 with Twomey, above n 147, 6–7. See also *Constitution Act 1975* (Vic), s 10(1BA).

**177** See, eg, *Constitution Act 1975* (Vic), ss 18(1B), 18(2AA), 18(2A); *Constitution Act 1889* (WA), s 73(6).

For s 10(2) to bind a later Parliament (and hence require a repealing or amending Bill to be passed by an absolute majority of the Legislative Council and Legislative Assembly), the repealing or amending law would need to come within the 'constitution, powers or procedures of the Parliament of the State'. It is likely that such a later law would not, other than by characterising that later law as expressly or impliedly repealing s 10(2).[178] This probably means that s 10(2) is unlikely to be rendered binding by s 6 of the *Australia Acts*.

Does this mean that s 10(2), or another manner and form provision falling outside s 6, cannot be made binding on any other basis? The High Court in *Marquet* did not entirely derail the possibility of other grounds, although their comments did render their application increasingly unlikely. The prime sources outside of s 6 of the *Australia Acts* are s 106 of the Commonwealth Constitution, the *Ranasinghe* principle and the reconstitution of the legislature.[179] Importantly, s 106 and the *Ranasinghe* principle are confined to manner and form provisions contained within legislation of a constitutional character (and hence would not apply to manner and form provisions such as s 10(2) of the *Western Australian Future Fund Act 2012* (WA)).

Section 106, as noted, provides that:

> The Constitution of each State of the Commonwealth shall, subject to this Constitution, continue as at the establishment of the Commonwealth, or as at the admission or establishment of the State, as the case may be, until altered in accordance with the Constitution of the State.

The argument that has been proposed is that the words 'until altered in accordance with the Constitution of the State' give State constitutional manner and form provisions some 'higher' source to render them binding.[180] The text of s 106 makes this reading of its final phrase difficult to accept,[181] and as the majority in *Marquet* intimated, s 106 is ultimately subject to the *Australia Acts* in any event.[182]

The *Ranasinghe* principle derives from *Bribery Commissioner v Ranasinghe*,[183] where Lord Pearce observed that 'a legislature has no power to ignore the conditions of law-making that are imposed by the instrument which itself regulates its power to make law'.[184] While it has received some judicial support,[185] this *dictum* has been criticised in terms of its application to the constitutional position of the Australian States.[186] As Kirby J noted in *Marquet*, in the absence of another source of validity, a State:

**178** See Antonio Buti and Ben Wyatt, 'Entrenchment of the Future Fund Bill: A Matter of Manner and Form' (2012) 39(11) *Brief* 10, 13.
**179** See more generally Goldsworthy, above n 182, 403.
**180** *Wilsmore v Western Australia* [1981] 51 FLR 348, 354.
**181** See eg, Goldsworthy, above n 176, 426–7.
**182** *Attorney-General (WA) v Marquet* (2003) 217 CLR 545, [80]. See also *McGinty v Western Australia* (1996) 186 CLR 140, 296–7.
**183** [1965] AC 172.
**184** *Bribery Commissioner v Ranasinghe* [1965] AC 172, 197.
**185** *Victoria v Commonwealth and Hayden* (1975) 134 CLR 338, 163–4.
**186** *McGinty v Western Australia* (1996) 186 CLR 140, 297.

> legislature enjoys full power to repeal the purported conditions or limitations on its law-making. Once it does so, it is not bound by those conditions or limitations. It is free to ignore them. They do not then control its 'power to make laws'.[187]

State Parliaments arguably have the ability to reconstitute themselves,[188] by the 'continuing constituent power'[189] in s 2(2) of the *Australia Acts*. This could include the institution of a referendum requirement or the abolition or addition of a House of Parliament. The usefulness of this method is somewhat compromised, however, by the fact that manner and form provisions in many States[190] regulate the ability to reconstitute the Parliament in the first place.[191] Hence, if those procedures are valid and binding, and are not followed, the Parliament will not have been validly reconstituted.

Additional paramount sources may also apply in some jurisdictions. For example s 73(1) of the *Constitution Act 1889* (WA) was scheduled to the *Western Australian Constitution Act 1890* (UK)[192] and can therefore be rendered binding by virtue of s 5 of that Imperial Act[193] which operates as a 'higher' source binding the Western Australian Parliament.[194]

As noted above, for a manner and form provision to be effective it must also be entrenched such that the manner and form procedure cannot itself be removed through ordinary procedures, leaving the protected provision susceptible to amendment.[195]

## 5 Implied freedom of political communication

While the implied freedom of political communication is discussed in detail in Chapter 5, it is worth touching on the relevance of the constitutional implication to the States. The implied freedom is based on the importance of maintaining voters' abilities to discuss political matters freely so that informed choices can be made at the ballot box, consistent with the constitutionally prescribed system of representative and responsible government required by the Commonwealth Constitution.

**187** *Attorney-General (WA) v Marquet* (2003) 217 CLR 545, [215].
**188** See, eg, *Attorney-General (NSW) v Trethowan* (1931) 44 CLR 394, 429–30.
**189** Goldsworthy, above n 176, 412.
**190** See eg, *Constitution Act 1902* (NSW), ss 7A and 7B.
**191** See, eg, Carney, above n 11, 187; Goldsworthy, above n 176, 412.
**192** As compared with s 73(2) of the *Constitution Act 1889* (WA), which was only inserted into the *Constitution Act 1889* (WA) in 1978.
**193** Section 5 provides that 'It shall be lawful for the legislature for the time being of Western Australia to make laws altering or repealing any of the provisions of the scheduled Bill in the same manner as any other laws for the good government of that colony, *subject, however, to the conditions imposed by the scheduled Bill on the alteration of the provisions thereof in certain particulars until and unless those conditions are repealed or altered by the authority of that legislature*' (emphasis added).
**194** *Attorney-General (WA) v Marquet* (2003) 217 CLR 545, [65].
**195** See for example, *Constitution Act 1889* (WA), s 73; *Constitution Act 1975* (Vic), s 18; *Constitution Act 1902* (NSW), ss 7A and 7B. Cf *Constitution Act 1934* (Tas), s 41A and *Constitution of Queensland Act 2001* (Qld), s 78.

It has been held that the State Parliaments[196] are bound by the implication from the Commonwealth Constitution.[197] In *Coleman v Power*, McHugh J concluded that the nature of the Commonwealth Constitution, and the fact that ss 106 and 107 are 'subject to this Constitution', means that State legislative powers are restricted to the extent necessary to preserve the implied freedom of political communication required for the political functioning of the Commonwealth.[198] Whether State legislation contravenes the federal implication will depend on the nature of the law and whether it can be said to impede the 'freedom of communication imposed by ss 7, 24, 64 or 128 of the [Commonwealth] Constitution'.[199] For example, in *Lange v Australian Broadcasting Corporation* the Court noted that:

> Section 128, by directly involving electors in the States and in certain Territories in the process for amendment of the Constitution, necessarily implies a limitation on legislative and executive power to deny the electors access to information that might be relevant to the vote they cast in a referendum to amend the Constitution.[200]

Further, the implied freedom of political communication does not only protect political communications concerning federal matters. Although sourced from the Commonwealth Constitution, the implied freedom can have constitutional implications for federal and State laws which impair the ability to communicate about State political matters. The unresolved question is the degree to which the State political matters need to be linked with the federal political sphere to be protected by the implied freedom. In *Australian Capital Television Pty Ltd v Commonwealth*, Mason J seemed to assume that that no specific federal connection needed to be established because of the intertwined nature of the Australian political landscape.[201] His Honour said:

> The concept of freedom to communicate with respect to public affairs and political discussion does not lend itself to subdivision. Public affairs and political discussion are indivisible and cannot be subdivided into compartments that correspond with, or relate to, the various tiers of government in Australia. Unlike the legislative powers of the Commonwealth Parliament, there are no limits to the range of matters that may be relevant to debate in the Commonwealth Parliament or to its workings. The consequence is that the implied freedom of communication extends to all matters of public affairs and political discussion, notwithstanding that a particular matter at a given time might appear to have a primary or immediate connexion with the affairs of a

**196** *Lange v Australian Broadcasting Corporation* (1997) 189 CLR 520, 567.
**197** See, for example, *Coleman v Power* (2004) 220 CLR 1 where a majority of the High Court found that s 7(1)(d) of the *Vagrants, Gaming and Other Offences Act 1931* (Qld) had to be narrowly construed or have words severed so as to avoid infringing the implied freedom of political communication.
**198** *Coleman v Power* (2004) 220 CLR 1, 49. See also *Levy v Victoria* (1997) 189 CLR 579, 622. This can be compared with the inability of using the Commonwealth Constitution to require equality of voting power between Western Australian electorates for State elections (*McGinty v Western Australia* (1996) 186 CLR 140) when this did not impact on the operation of the key federal constitutional provisions of ss 7, 24 and 128. (For a further example of where the federal implication did not extend to provisions in the *Electoral Act 1985* (SA) regulating upper house elections: see *Muldowney v South Australia* (1996) 186 CLR 352.)
**199** *Lange v Australian Broadcasting Corporation* (1997) 189 CLR 520, 567
**200** (1997) 189 CLR 520, 561.
**201** (1992) 177 CLR 106, 142.

> State, a local authority or a Territory and little or no connexion with Commonwealth affairs. Furthermore, there is a continuing inter-relationship between the various tiers of government. To take one example, the Parliament provides funding for the State governments, Territory governments and local governing bodies and enterprises. That continuing inter-relationship makes it inevitable that matters of local concern have the potential to become matters of national concern.[202]

Similarly in *Nationwide News Pty Ltd v Wills*, Deane and Toohey JJ stated:

> Under the Australian federal system, however, it is unrealistic to see the three levels of government Commonwealth, State and local – as isolated from one another or as operating otherwise than in an overall national context ...
>
> Clearly enough, the relationship and interaction between the different levels of government are such that an implication of freedom of communication about matters relating to the government of the Commonwealth would be unrealistically confined if it applied only to communications in relation to Commonwealth governmental institutions. Accordingly, there is obviously much to be said for the view that the Constitution's implication of freedom of discussion extends to all political matters, including matters relating to other levels of government within the national system which exists under the Constitution.[203]

While Mason CJ, Toohey and Gaudron JJ in *Stephens v West Australian Newspapers Ltd*,[204] seemed to assume that 'all political discussion' (including State-focused communication) could come within the freedom, Brennan J seemed more circumspect, asserting that:

> the performance by members of the Western Australian Parliament of their official functions is irrelevant to the government of the Commonwealth and is unaffected by the implication.[205]

Following *Lange v Australian Broadcasting Corporation*,[206] where the definitive two-stage test was unanimously set down by the Court, it seemed that some federal political connection may in fact be necessary. Their Honours suggested that the freedom sourced in the Commonwealth Constitution could only extend to protect communications about State political matters from legislative interference if there was the requisite link with the representative governmental requirements of Commonwealth constitutional provisions such as ss 7, 24 and 128.[207] Their Honours, however, underscored the high level of State, Territory and Commonwealth political integration in Australia, implicitly suggesting that establishing the necessary federal political connection is not going to

**202** Ibid.
**203** (1992) 177 CLR 1, 75–6.
**204** (1994) 182 CLR 211, 232.
**205** *Stephens v West Australian Newspapers Ltd* (1994) 182 CLR 211, 235.
**206** (1997) 189 CLR 520. See also *Australian Broadcasting Corporation v Lenah Game Meats Pty Ltd* (2001) 208 CLR 199, 281.
**207** (1997) 189 CLR 520, 571–2. See also *Muldowney v South Australia* (1996) 186 CLR 352, 365; *Levy v Victoria* (1997) 189 CLR 579, 595.

be onerous.[208] The ease of establishing this connection was also confirmed in *Hogan v Hinch* where French CJ explained that:

> [t]he limit propounded, despite its logical attraction, is not of great practical assistance. There is today significant interaction between the different levels of government in Australia. The use of cooperative executive and legislative arrangements between Commonwealth and State and Territory governments through the Council of Australian Governments, Ministerial Councils and otherwise, makes it difficult to identify subjects not capable or potentially capable of discussion as matters which are or should be or could be of concern to the national government.[209]

The majority in *Unions New South Wales*, while not definitively resolving the Commonwealth connection point, confirmed the intermingled nature of governmental matters in Australia such that it becomes 'difficult to identify subjects not capable of discussion as matters which do or could potentially concern a federal governmental or political matter'.[210]

An implied freedom of political communication can also arguably be drawn at a State constitutional level, at the very least in Western Australia.[211] In the High Court case of *Stephens*[212] Brennan J held that:

> Section 73(2)(c) [of the *Constitution Act 1889* (WA)], inserted by amendment in 1978...entrenches in the *Constitution Act* the requirement that the Legislative Council and the Legislative Assembly be composed of members chosen directly by the people. This requirement is drawn in terms similar to those found in ss. 7 and 24 of the Commonwealth Constitution from which the implication that effects a constitutional freedom to discuss government, governmental institutions and political matters is substantially derived. By parity of reasoning, a similar implication can be drawn from the *Constitution Act* with respect to the system of government of Western Australia therein prescribed.[213]

Carney notes that the key to the basis of this constitutional implication is that s 73(2)(c) in the *Constitution Act 1889* (WA) is a protected constitutional provision.[214] He asserts that '[w]hile a constitutional implication might still be derived from unentrenched provisions, it is of limited value given its susceptibility to abrogation by subsequent inconsistent enactment'.[215] In other words,

**208** Often the relevant federal connection has been conceded: See, eg *Coleman v Power* (2004) 220 CLR 1, 23–4.
**209** (2011) 243 CLR 506, [48]. And see [49]. See also *Attorney-General (SA) v Corporation of the City of Adelaide* (2013) 87 ALJR 289, 312.
**210** *Unions New South Wales v New South Wales* (2013) 88 ALJR 227, [22], [155].
**211** In relation to the implied freedom being drawn from the *Constitution Act 1934* (SA) see: *Muldowney v South Australia* (1996) 186 CLR 352. For discussion of a possible implication from the *Constitution Act 1902* (NSW) see Anne Twomey, 'The Application of the Implied Freedom of Political Communication to State Electoral Funding Laws' (2012) 35(3) *University of New South Wales Law Journal* 625, 639–42. The Court in *Unions New South Wales v New South Wales* (2013) 88 ALJR 227 did not need to decide whether an implication derived from the *Constitution Act 1902* (NSW).
**212** *Stephens v West Australian Newspapers Ltd* (1994) 182 CLR 211.
**213** Ibid, 236. Note also 232.
**214** See submissions in *Muldowney v South Australia* (1996) 186 CLR 352, 354 as to entrenchment of 'representative government or democracy' in the *Constitution Act 1934* (SA).
**215** Comparing *Constitution of Queensland Act 2001* (Qld), s 10 with the entrenchment of s 26 of the *Constitution Act 1902* (NSW); Carney, above n 11, 132–3.

a later law can override a constitutional provision's guarantee of representative government, if that guarantee is not protected from later express or implied repeal.

# V States and constitutional change

## 1 New States

While not yet used, s 121 of the Commonwealth Constitution allows for new States to be admitted to the Commonwealth, and s 124 contemplates new States being formed out of the territory of another State. The most likely new State to become part of the Commonwealth of Australia, via s 121, is the Northern Territory. While the Northern Territory's attempted conversion to Statehood failed at a referendum in 1998, it has recently again been on the Territory's constitutional agenda and is likely to re-emerge in light of the constitutional disadvantages that apply to territories (eg, pursuant to ss 92, 122, 128 of the Commonwealth Constitution).[216]

## 2 Amendments to the Commonwealth Constitution

Amendments to the Commonwealth Constitution are notoriously rare because of the difficulty of achieving s 128's demands of approval by a majority of electors in a majority of States and a majority of electors overall (and sometimes also a majority in the State affected by a particular reform). That said, proposed amendments such as the recognition of local government[217] and the recognition of Aboriginal and Torres Strait Islanders in the Commonwealth Constitution[218] may have implications for the States. For example, Commonwealth funding of States could be adjusted if constitutional amendments contemplate local governments receiving funds directly. Further, proposals to recognise Indigenous Peoples have contemplated inserting a new s 116A into the Commonwealth Constitution which would impose a constitutional prohibition against racial discrimination by the States.

Other proposals which have been raised include amending s 128 itself to allow State Parliaments to be involved in the initiation of reform proposals.[219] This is currently the exclusive province of the Commonwealth Parliament and

**216** See Anne Twomey, 'A Constitution for a New State: Dilemmas for the Northern Territory' (2007) 18(3) *Public Law Review* 200; George Williams, 'The Path to Statehood: The Northern Territory as Australia's Seventh State' (2012) 2 *Northern Territory Law Journal* 145.

**217** Nicola McGarrity and George Williams, 'Recognition of Local Government in the Commonwealth Constitution' (2010) 21 *Public Law Review* 164; Anne Twomey, 'Always the Bridesmaid – Constitutional Recognition of Local Government' (2012) 38(2) *Monash University Law Review* 142.

**218** See, eg, Anne Twomey, 'The Preamble and Indigenous Recognition' (2011) 15(2) *Australian Indigenous Law Review* 4.

**219** Different models for State initiation have been proposed: see Sarah Murray, 'State Initiation of Section 128 Referenda' in Paul Kildea, Andrew Lynch and George Williams (eds), *Tomorrow's Federation: Reforming Australian Government* (Federation Press, 2012) 332.

means that s 128 proposals tend to be focused on federal interests. Of course, the essential difficulty in bringing about this reform of the constitutional amendment mechanism is convincing the Commonwealth Parliament to propose such an amendment when it is likely to disrupt the Commonwealth's current monopoly on amendment proposals.

If Australia were to become a Republic, this would present a number of thorny constitutional issues for the States. The complexity is brought about by the inter-relationship of the State and Federal vice-regal representatives and how these textual reflections in the State Constitutions, the Commonwealth Constitution and the *Australia Acts* might be republicanised. For example, would it be constitutionally possible to have a Republic at the federal level while retaining monarchical structures at a State level?[220] What constitutional amendments would be necessary to the State and Commonwealth Constitutions to bring about a Republic, and what constitutional procedures would need to be followed? Is s 128 of the Commonwealth Constitution sufficient to bring about such a wide-scale reform? While a number of these issues arose with the unsuccessful attempt in 1999 to convert Australia to a Republic,[221] these constitutional debates are likely to arise again if republican reform is attempted again in the future.

## VI Conclusions

The framers of the Commonwealth Constitution understood the States to be the presuppositions of the federation and that, as a consequence, it was not their role to try to intervene in the constitutional affairs of the constituent States. This did not mean, however, that no thought was given to the State Constitutions as fundamental constituting documents. Samuel Griffith had hoped that the State Constitutions would eventually be popularly ratified in line with the 'American theory' of popular sovereignty.[222] While the Commonwealth of Australia and the Australian States have now secured an almost complete constitutional independence from the British authorities, popular ratification of the State Constitutions has failed to eventuate. The State Constitutions still derive their legally binding force ultimately from Imperial foundations and they continue to be subject to the legislative authority of the State Parliaments.[223]

If a State Constitution was to be popularly ratified, what would be the result? At the least, by engaging the public through the act of ratification, the legitimacy

**220** While a detailed consideration of these constitutional issues lies beyond the scope of this chapter, refer to: Murray, above n 31, particularly Janine Pritchard, 'Monarchical States under a Republican Commonwealth', 106–23.
**221** Many were side-stepped or avoided by requiring the States to independently decide to convert to a republican form: Anne Twomey, 'One In, All In – The Simultaneous Implementation of a Republic at Commonwealth and State Levels' in Ibid, 20–40.
**222** *Convention Debates, Sydney* (1891) 490. For more detail, see Aroney, above n 115.
**223** Aroney, above n 115, 213.

of a State's constitutional architecture would be enhanced, albeit without necessarily having great substantive and interpretative impact. More fundamentally, popular ratification could transform the whole basis of the State's manner and form provisions, by converting the State Constitution into a kind of 'superior' law that binds the State Parliament. This potential consequence may, however, also make popular ratification more difficult to achieve at a State political level because it could wrest control of Constitutions from the State governments.

There is even a possibility that ratification by the populace could influence the High Court's interpretation of the Commonwealth Constitution. Popular ratification of the State Constitutions would reconfigure the founding logic of the federation: it would mean that the State Constitutions, and not only the Commonwealth Constitution, were popularly approved; indeed, it would mean that the State Constitutions had received that approval more recently than the Commonwealth. If, even more radically, the State Constitutions were to assert certain subject matters as having been reserved to the States, this would give the High Court explicit textual grounds for reading the scope of Commonwealth powers in the light of the continuing powers of the States. Though a significant act indeed, this would have potential to allow a reconception of the State–Commonwealth balance of power through a refashioning of the State constitutional relationship with the Commonwealth Constitution. Popular ratification could therefore have significant constitutional consequences for the post-*Engineers* interpretations of the Commonwealth Constitution, noting that the *Engineers* decision transformed the High Court's jurisprudence to focus on the Commonwealth Constitution as sourcing its operative force from the Imperial Parliament and its political legitimacy from the Australian people.

Over 20 years ago, George Winterton referred to the State Constitutions as constitutional 'Cinderellas'.[224] While Winterton later considered this moniker to be no longer applicable, it is the case that State constitutional matters tend to receive less of the constitutional spotlight. This chapter has illustrated, however, that a proper understanding of the Commonwealth Constitution, and the basis on which it was formed, requires a familiarity with the State constitutional landscape. This is because the formation of the Commonwealth of Australia depended on the constitutional heritage of the colonies to form the federal union. The Commonwealth Constitution can only therefore be properly comprehended alongside an appreciation of the Constitutions of the States. The relevance of each State Constitution is therefore 'continuing', as s 106 of the Commonwealth Constitution contemplates.

**224** Winterton, above n 77, 1, fn 1.

# Index